Topic Tackler CD-ROM

The Topic Tackler CD is included FREE with each new copy of the text.

This software is a complete tutorial focusing on those concepts in financial accounting that give students the most trouble. Help is provided for 2 key topics in every chapter using a step-by-step sequence of video clips, PowerPoint® slides, interactive exercises, and self-test quizzes. Help screens are provided that show the solution and explain why an answer is correct.

Concepts appearing in the text that receive additional treatment in Topic Tackler are marked by this unique icon in the margin.

Video Clips provide an engaging introduction to each concept and an enlightening, real-world perspective from a variety of professionals who rely on accounting for important business activities as well as accounting experts.

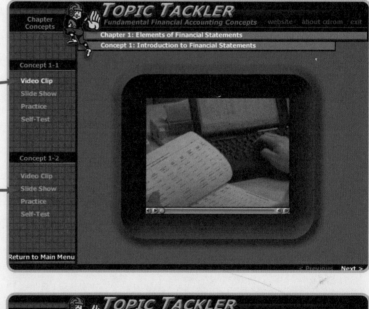

Slide Shows presented in PowerPoint offer step-by-step coverage of challenging topics, providing a great resource for review. Some feature animations and/or audio.

The **Practice** element includes a mixture of drag-and-drop and fill-in-the-blank exercises that reinforce chapter concepts by providing immediate feedback and explanation.

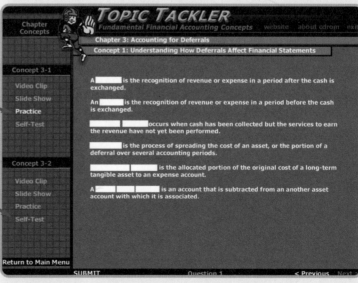

With **Self-Test**, students have an ideal vehicle for quizzing themselves on their comprehension of the material.

Fourth Edition

Fundamental Financial
ACCOUNTING
Concepts

Thomas P. Edmonds
University of Alabama–Birmingham

Frances M. McNair
Mississippi State University

Edward E. Milam
Mississippi State University

Philip R. Olds
Virginia Commonwealth University

Cindy D. Edmonds
Contributing Author
University of Alabama-Birmingham

Nancy W. Schneider
Contributing Author
Lynchburg College

McGraw-Hill
Irwin

Boston   Burr Ridge, IL   Dubuque, IA   Madison, WI   New York   San Francisco   St. Louis
Bangkok   Bogotá   Caracas   Kuala Lumpur   Lisbon   London   Madrid   Mexico City
Milan   Montreal   New Delhi   Santiago   Seoul   Singapore   Sydney   Taipei   Toronto

McGraw-Hill

*A Division of The **McGraw·Hill** Companies*

FUNDAMENTAL FINANCIAL ACCOUNTING CONCEPTS

Published by McGraw-Hill/Irwin, a business unit of The McGraw-Hill Companies, Inc. 1221 Avenue of the Americas, New York, NY, 10020. Copyright © 2003, 2000, 1998, 1996 by The McGraw-Hill Companies, Inc. All rights reserved. No part of this publication may be reproduced or distributed in any form or by any means, or stored in a database or retrieval system, without the prior written consent of The McGraw-Hill Companies, Inc., including, but not limited to, in any network or other electronic storage or transmission, or broadcast for distance learning.

Some ancillaries, including electronic and print components, may not be available to customers outside the United States.

This book is printed on acid-free paper.

domestic   3 4 5 6 7 8 9 0 KGP/KGP 0 9 8 7 6 5 4 3
international   2 3 4 5 6 7 8 9 0 KGP/KGP 0 9 8 7 6 5 4 3

ISBN   0-07-247296-0

Publisher: *Brent Gordon*
Sponsoring editor: *Melody Marcus*
Managing developmental editor: *Gail Korosa*
Marketing manager: *Richard Kolasa*
Senior project manager: *Kimberly D. Hooker*
Production supervisor: *Debra Sylvester*
Senior producer, Media technology: *David Barrick*
Freelance design coordinator: *Laura J. Entringer*
Supplement producer: *Becky Szura*
Photo research coordinator: *Jeremy Cheshareck*
Photo researcher: *Connie Gardner*
Cover design: *Ellen Pettengell Design*
Interior design: *Ellen Pettengell Design*
Typeface: *10/12 Times Roman*
Compositor: *GAC Indianapolis*
Printer: *Quebecor World Kingsport*

Library of Congress Cataloging-in-Publication Data

Fundamental financial accounting concepts / Thomas P. Edmonds ... [et. al.] — 4th ed.
    p. cm.
    A variety of multi-media instructional aids, including a web site, are available to supplement the text.
    Includes index.
    ISBN 0-07-247296-0 (alk. paper)—ISBN 0-07-119457-6 (international : alk. paper)
    1. Accounting. I. Edmonds, Thomas P.
HF5635.F95 2003
657—dc21   2002016638

INTERNATIONAL EDITION   ISBN 0-07-119457-6

www.mhhe.com

This book is dedicated to our students whose questions have so frequently caused us to reevaluate our method of presentation that they have, in fact, become major contributors to the development of this text.

Thomas P. Edmonds, Ph.D.

Dr. Edmonds holds the Friends and Alumni Professorship in the Department of Accounting at the University of Alabama at Birmingham (UAB). He has been actively involved in teaching accounting principles throughout his academic career. Dr. Edmonds has **coordinated the accounting principles courses at the University of Houston and UAB.** He currently teaches introductory accounting in mass sections that frequently include more than 180 students. Dr. Edmonds has received five prestigious teaching awards including the UAB President's Excellence in Teaching Award and the distinguished Ellen Gregg Ingalls Award for excellence in classroom teaching. He has written a number of articles for many publications including *Issues in Accounting;* the *Journal of Accounting Education; Advances in Accounting Education; Accounting Education: A Journal of Theory, Practice and Research;* the *Accounting Review; Advances in Accounting;* the *Journal of Accountancy; Management Accounting;* the *Journal of Commercial Bank Lending;* the *Banker's Magazine;* and the *Journal of Accounting, Auditing, and Finance.* He has published four textbooks, five practice problems (including two computerized problems), and a variety of supplemental materials including study guides, working papers, and solutions manuals. Dr. Edmonds's writing is influenced by a wide range of business experience. He was a successful entrepreneur, worked as a management accountant for Refrigerated Transport, a trucking company, and worked in the not-for-profit sector as a commercial lending officer for the Federal Home Loan Bank. In addition, he has acted as a consultant to major corporations including First City Bank of Houston, AmSouth Bank in Birmingham, Texaco, and Cortland Chemicals. Dr. Edmonds began his academic training at Young Harris Community College in Young Harris, Georgia. He received a B.B.A. degree with a major in finance from Georgia State University in Atlanta, Georgia. He obtained an M.B.A. degree with a concentration in finance from St. Mary's University in San Antonio, Texas. His Ph.D. degree with a major in accounting was awarded by Georgia State University. Dr. Edmonds's work experience and academic training have enabled him to bring a unique user perspective to this textbook.

Frances M. McNair, Ph.D., CPA

Dr. McNair holds the KPMG Peat Marwick Professorship in Accounting at Mississippi State University (MSU). She has been involved in teaching principles of accounting for the past 12 years and currently serves as the **coordinator for the principles of accounting courses at MSU.** She joined the MSU faculty in 1987 after receiving her Ph.D. from the University of Mississippi. The author of various articles that have appeared in the *Journal of Accountancy, Management Accounting, Business and Professional Ethics Journal, The Practical Accountant, Taxes,* and other publications, she also coauthored the book *The Tax Practitioner* with Dr. Denzil Causey. Dr. McNair is currently serving on committees of the American Taxation Association, the American Accounting Association, and the Institute of Management Accountants as well as numerous School of Accountancy and MSU committees.

Edward E. Milam, Ph.D., CPA

Dr. Milam is Professor of Accounting at Mississippi State University (MSU). He has been the recipient of several prestigious awards including the Federation of Schools of Accountancy Outstanding Educator Award, the Mississippi Society of Certified Public Accountants' Educator of the Year Award, the Outstanding Teacher in the School of Accountancy at the University of Mississippi, and the Outstanding Graduate Teacher of the Year in the College of Business and Industry at MSU. Prior to joining the faculty at MSU, Dr. Milam served on the accounting faculty at the University of Mississippi. He was chair of the accounting department when the School of Accountancy was established. He became the first dean of the School of Accountancy, and during his tenure the School of Accountancy became one of the first 20 schools in the nation to receive separate accounting accreditation. Dr. Milam also has been instrumental in helping MSU obtain separate accounting accreditation. In addition, Dr. Milam has been heavily involved in the design, development, and implementation of a graduate program in taxation at MSU. He has served as President of the Federation of Schools of Accountancy, on the Standards Committee of American Assembly of Collegiate Schools of Business (business and accounting accrediting association), as Treasurer/Secretary of the American Taxation Association (ATA), on the board of directors of the Mississippi Tax Institute, and on various committees of the American Tax Association, FSA, American Institute of Certified Public Accountants, American Accounting Association, and the Mississippi Society of Certified Public Accountants. He has authored numerous articles that have appeared in publications including *Journal of Accountancy, Taxes, Management Accounting, Financial Executive, Estate Planning, Trusts and Estates,* the *CPA Journal,* and others. He also coauthored seven books.

Philip R. Olds, Ph.D., CPA

Professor Olds is Associate Professor of Accounting at Virginia Commonwealth University (VCU). He serves as the **coordinator of the introduction to accounting courses at VCU.** Professor Olds received his A.S. degree from Brunswick Junior College in Brunswick, Georgia (now Costal Georgia Community College). He received a B.B.A. in Accounting from Georgia Southern College (now Georgia Southern University) and his M.P.A. and Ph.D. degrees are from Georgia State University. After graduating from Georgia Southern, he worked as an auditor with the U.S. Department of Labor in Atlanta, Georgia. A CPA in Virginia, Professor Olds has published articles in various professional journals and presented papers at national and regional conferences. He also served as the faculty adviser to the VCU chapter of Beta Alpha Psi for five years. In 1989, he was recognized with an Outstanding Faculty Vice-President Award by the national Beta Alpha Psi organization.

The fourth edition of *Fundamental Financial Accounting Concepts* continues to be a conceptually based, user-oriented book that stresses meaningful learning over rote memorization. More specifically, the text focuses on the relationships between business events and financial statements. **The primary objective is to develop students who can explain how any given business event will affect the income statement, balance sheet, and the statement of cash flows.** Did the event cause assets to increase, decrease, or stay the same? Similarly, what was its effect on liabilities, equity, revenue, expense, gains, losses, net income, and dividends? Furthermore, how did the event affect cash flows? These are the *big picture* relationships that both accounting majors and general business students need to understand to function effectively in the business world. This edition of the text contains several significant changes that promote these goals and objectives. These changes include:

1. The horizontal financial statements model (discussed in the following section of the preface) is introduced earlier and is emphasized to a greater degree in the first three chapters of the text. It is now easier for those who want to use the model early in the course to do so. Problem materials related to the statements model are more abundant in the earlier chapters. However, those who desire to introduce events and statements through the accounting equation are still able to do so. A liberal supply of exercises and problems that focus on the accounting equation are available.

2. The matching concept is introduced in Chapter 2 and is referred to throughout the text. As an example, we have replaced the percent of receivables method of estimating bad debts expense with the percent of sales method.

3. An expanded discussion of the closing concept has been added in Chapters 1, 2, and 3.

4. Efforts to focus on key concepts have persisted. Specifically, in Chapter 8 we have moved some of the more advanced topics such as accounting for investment securities to an appendix.

5. The effort to isolate concepts and introduce them in a stepwise fashion has been expanded. For example, in Chapter 5, we have separated the discussion of purchases discounts from the discussion of sales discounts. Similarly, the discussion of purchases returns and allowances has been separated from that of sales returns and allowances.

6. The use of real-world terminology has been expanded throughout the text. The term *contributed capital* has been replaced with the term *common stock;* the term *distributions* has been replaced with *dividends,* and *owners' equity* has been replaced with *stockholders' equity.* Generic dates such as 20X1 have been replaced with realistic dates such as 2001.

7. Updates related to the latest FASB pronouncements have been included. For example, the text material relating to accounting for intangible assets has been revised to comply with FASB Statement Numbers 141 and 142.

8. The end-of-chapter materials have been expanded to include a mirror image "B" set of exercises in each chapter.

9. Beyond the text itself, we have made a special effort to expand the test bank. In addition, the number of accuracy checkers has been expanded to ensure exceptionally high quality.

10. Active learning has been enhanced through the insertion of an in-chapter brief exercise titled Check Yourself that enables students to apply the materials that they are reading. An example of the Check Yourself exercises is shown on the following page. In addition, a self-study review problem section has been added at the end of each chapter.

Check Yourself 1-3

Mahoney, Inc., was started when it issued common stock to its owners for $300,000. During its first year of operation Mahoney received $523,000 in cash for providing services to customers. Mahoney paid $233,000 cash to employees and cash advertising costs of $102,000. Other cash operating expenses amounted to $124,000. Finally, Mahoney paid a $25,000 cash dividend to its stockholders. What amount of net income would Mahoney report on its earnings statement for the year?

Answer Mahoney would report net income of $64,000 ($523,000 revenue − $233,000 salary expense − $102,000 advertising expense − $124,000 other operating expenses). The cash received from issuing stock is not revenue because it did not result from earnings activities. In other words, the business did not work (perform services) for this money. Likewise, the cash dividends are not expenses because they were not paid for the purpose of generating revenue. Instead, cash dividends (which decrease cash) represent a transfer of wealth to the owners.

Some of the popular features of the last edition that have been retained are discussed in the following section of the preface.

▌Innovative Features

A Horizontal Financial Statements Model Is the Primary Teaching Platform

A horizontal financial statements model replaces the accounting equation as the predominant teaching platform. The model enables students to visualize the simultaneous effects of a single business event on the income statement, balance sheet, and statement of cash flows by arranging the statements horizontally across a single line of text in the following manner:

Assets = Liabilities + Stockholders' Equity	Revenue − Expense = Net Income	Cash Flow

One of the more powerful explanatory features of the horizontal statements model stems from the fact that **individual** events are recorded directly in financial statements. Traditionally, a series of events is recorded in accounts, and summative information is presented in the statements. Accordingly, students do not observe the **effects of individual events on financial statements.** The horizontal statements model remedies this condition by requiring students to record statement effects transaction by transaction. For example, Event No. 1 in Exhibit 1 (see following page) demonstrates that the recognition of revenue on account affects the balance sheet and income statement but not the statement of cash flows. These effects are *visibly* isolated from the effects of other events. Accordingly, students can see how a particular event affects the financial statements. The horizontal statements model also provides an effective means for comparing the effects of one transaction with the effects of another transaction. By comparing Event No. 1 with Event No. 2 in Exhibit 1, students can see how the recognition of cash revenue differs from the recognition of revenue on account. Similarly, a comparison of Events No. 3 and 4 highlights differences between the effects of cash dividends versus stock dividends. Note that students also are required to identify cash flows as being financing activities (FA), investing activities (IA), or operating activities (OA) by placing the appropriate letters in the cash statement column.

The horizontal model also can be used to demonstrate how alternative accounting procedures affect financial statements. For example, the recognition of unrealized gains on investment securities affects financial statements differently, depending on whether the securities are classified as (1) held to maturity, (2) trading, or (3) available for sale. Exhibit 2 demonstrates how

Exhibit 1 *Financial Statements Model*

	Balance Sheet									Income Statement						Cash Statement
	Assets		=	Liabilities		+	Stockholders' Equity			Rev.	−	Exp.	=	Net Inc.		Cash Flow
Event No.	Cash	+ Acct. Rec.	=	Acct. Pay	+	Common Stock	+	Ret. Earn.								
1	NA	+ 500	=	NA	+	NA	+	500		500	−	NA	=	500		NA
2	500	+ NA	=	NA	+	NA	+	500		500	−	NA	=	500		500 OA
3	(800)	+ NA	=	NA	+	NA	+	(800)		NA	−	NA	=	NA		(800) FA
4	NA	+ NA	=	NA	+	800	+	(800)		NA	−	NA	=	NA		NA

Exhibit 2 *Horizontal Statements Models*

	Balance Sheet							Income Statement						Cash Statement
	Assets		Stockholders' Equity											
Type	Investment Securities	=	Liab.	+	Retained Earnings	+	Unreal. Gain	Rev./ Gain	−	Exp./ Loss	=	Net Inc.		Cash Flow
Held	NA		NA	=	NA	+	NA	NA	−	NA	=	NA		NA
Trading	700		NA	=	700	+	NA	700	−	NA	=	700		NA
Available	700		NA	=	NA	+	700	NA	−	NA	=	NA		NA

the recognition of a $700 unrealized gain affects financial statements under each of the three alternative accounting treatments.

A Separate Section of Innovative End-of-Chapter Materials Encourages Students to Analyze, Think, Communicate

An innovative activities section entitled Analyze, Think, Communicate (ATC) has been added to the end-of-chapter materials. This section is composed of business applications cases, writing assignments, group exercises, Excel spreadsheet applications, ethics cases, and Internet assignments and are indicated by logos shown below. These activities let you decide the appropriate level of emphasis between a user- versus a preparer-oriented approach to accounting education. Furthermore, the material in this section permits you to stress computer applications to the extent you deem appropriate. Although the text is not designed to teach spreadsheet technicalities, Excel problems and exercises do include instructional tips that facilitate the students' ability to use spreadsheets. Spreadsheet problems were created by Linda Bell of William Jewell College.

By focusing on the materials in the ATC section, you can place heavy emphasis on a user orientation or on computer technology. Indeed, you can even teach the course without debits and credits if you are inclined to do so. However, the text includes a healthy supply of problems that require the use of debits and credits, journal entries, T-accounts, and other technical recording procedures. Accordingly, you can emphasize the preparer approach by selectively choosing the end-of-chapter materials that contain traditional requirements. The ATC section of the end-of-chapter materials permits you to emphasize those areas that you consider to be most important for your particular academic environment. An example of an ATC case from Chapter 2 follows; and an example of an ATC Excel assignment from Chapter 5 is shown.

Writing

Group

Technology

Ethics

Internet

ATC 2-3   REAL-WORLD CASE *Unusual Types of Liabilities*

In the liabilities section of its 2000 balance sheet, First Union Corporation reported "noninterest-bearing deposits" of almost $30 billion. First Union is a very large banking company. In the liabilities section of its 2000 balance sheet, Newmont Mining Corporation reported "reclamation and remediation liabilities" of more than $160 million. Newmont Mining is involved in gold mining and refining activities. In the accrued liabilities reported on its 2000 balance sheet, Phillips Petroleum Company included $702 million for "accrued dismantlement, removal, and environmental costs."

Required

a. For each of the preceding liabilities, write a brief explanation of what you believe the nature of the liability to be and how the company will pay it off. To develop your answers, think about the nature of the industry in which each of the companies operates.

b. Of the three liabilities described, which do you think poses the most risk for the company? In other words, for which liability are actual costs most likely to exceed the liability reported on the balance sheet? Uncertainty creates risk.

ATC 5-10   SPREADSHEET ANALYSIS *mastering Excel*

At the end of 2004, the following information is available for Short and Wise Companies:

Required

a. Set up the spreadsheet shown here. Complete the income statements by using Excel formulas.

b. Prepare a common size income statement for each company by completing the % Sales columns.

c. One company is a high-end retailer, and the other operates a discount store. Which is the discounter? Support your selection by referring to the common size statements.

d. Compute the return on assets and return on equity for each company.

e. Which company is more profitable from the stockholders' perspective?

f. Assume that a shortage of goods from suppliers is causing cost of goods sold to increase 10 percent for each company. Change the respective cost of goods sold balances in the Actual income statement column for each company. Note the new calculated amounts on the income statement and in the ratios. Which company's profits and returns are more sensitive to inventory price hikes?

Spreadsheet Tip

(1) Cell C3 (% Sales) can be copied down the income statement if the formula in cell C3 designates Sales (cell B3) as a fixed number. Designate a number as fixed by positioning $ signs within the cell address. Notice that the formula for C3 is =B3/$B$3.

Financial Statement Effects Are Demonstrated Over Multiple Accounting Cycles

The text also employs the use of a **vertical statements model,** which presents the statements in an upright pattern from the top to the bottom of the page. The income statement is presented first, the balance sheet directly after the income statement; and the statement of cash flows directly after the balance sheet. Financial data for a sequence of accounting cycles are displayed in adjacent columns. An example of a vertical statements model from Chapter 9 follows.

Exhibit 9–5 *Financial Statements under Double-Declining-Balance Depreciation*

DRYDEN ENTERPRISES
Financial Statements

	2001	2002	2003	2004	2005
Income Statements					
Rent Revenue	$15,000	$ 9,000	$ 5,000	$ 3,000	$ 0
Depreciation Expense	(12,000)	(6,000)	(2,000)	0	0
Operating Income	3,000	3,000	3,000	3,000	0
Gain	0	0	0	0	500
Net Income	$ 3,000	$ 3,000	$ 3,000	$ 3,000	$ 500
Balance Sheets					
Assets					
Cash	$16,000	$25,000	$30,000	$33,000	$37,500
Van	24,000	24,000	24,000	24,000	0
Accumulated Depreciation	(12,000)	(18,000)	(20,000)	(20,000)	0
Total Assets	$28,000	$31,000	$34,000	$37,000	$37,500
Stockholders' Equity					
Common Stock	$25,000	$25,000	$25,000	$25,000	$25,000
Retained Earnings	3,000	6,000	9,000	12,000	12,500
Total Stockholders' Equity	$28,000	$31,000	$34,000	$37,000	$37,500
Statements of Cash Flows					
Operating Activities					
Inflow from Customers	$15,000	$ 9,000	$ 5,000	$ 3,000	$ 0
Investing Activities					
Outflow to Purchase Van	(24,000)				
Inflow from Sale of Van					4,500
Financing Activities					
Inflow from Stock Issue	25,000				
Net Change in Cash	16,000	9,000	5,000	3,000	4,500
Beginning Cash Balance	0	16,000	25,000	30,000	33,000
Ending Cash Balance	$16,000	$25,000	$30,000	$33,000	$37,500

you ~~....nt in this are~~ ~~.~~ ~~....priate sectio~~ ~~.~~ ~~....overage.~~

The vertical statements model enables the instructor to link related events **over multiple accounting cycles.** A student can see how expense recognition is spread over an asset's useful life. Furthermore, since a full set of statements is presented on a single page, the student can visually contrast expense recognition with cash flow. Similarly, the vertical statements model enables a student to observe the multi-cycle effects of accumulating depreciation or amortizing a bond discount. An important difference between a vertical statements model and the traditional comparative financial statements is that the vertical statements model is presented in a simplified form on a single page of paper. Students cannot comprehend the linkage between financial statements as easily when the statements and/or accounting periods are shown on separate pages.

The statements models are presented for instructional purposes. They are very helpful in understanding how accounting events affect financial statements. Accordingly, statements models are used extensively in this text. Notice, however, that the models are not intended to represent the formal presentation formats that appear in annual reports. For example, although a full set of four financial statements is normally presented in published financial statements, the horizontal model shows only a partial set of statements. Similarly, the vertical instructional model may vary in form and content, depending on the learning task. Since the statements are presented in aggregate, the description of dates (i.e., "as of" versus "for the period ended") cannot be used to distinguish periodic from cumulative data. When using this text, keep in mind that statement models are intended to facilitate learning tasks. They do not conform to the detailed requirements of formal reporting practices.

Effects of Cash Flows Are Shown Throughout the Entire Text

Coverage of the statement of cash flows begins in the first chapter and continues throughout the text. Students can be taught to prepare a statement of cash flows in the first chapter of an introductory accounting text by having them analyze the Cash account. When the Cash account is used as the data source, preparing a statement of cash flows is simply a matter of learning how to classify events as operating, investing, or financing activities. This approach provides a logical learning environment that facilitates an understanding of the essential differences between cash flow and accrual-based income. More complicated topics such as the indirect method and a T-account approach for the conversion of accruals to cash are covered in a separate chapter at the end of the text.

Accounting Concepts Are Introduced in a Logical Stepwise Fashion

Students are confused when too many new concepts are introduced simultaneously. Most books overwhelm students by introducing cash, accrual, and deferral events in the first chapter. This text introduces these components in a logical stepwise manner. Cash transactions are discussed in Chapter 1. Accruals are introduced in Chapter 2, and deferrals are covered in Chapter 3. Nontechnical terminology (i.e., increase/decrease) is used to discuss the effects of events on the elements of financial statements in the first three chapters of the text. Recording procedures including debits and credits are demonstrated in Chapter 4. Accordingly, technical details are delayed until students have grasped the *big picture* relationships associated with articulating financial statements.

An Appropriate Balance Between Theory and Practice Is Maintained

A conceptual foundation enables students to think instead of memorize. Students who understand concepts are better able to communicate ideas and are more effective at solving unstructured problems. Accordingly, **this text addresses the issues raised by the accounting**

education change movement. It is important to note, however, that the call for change in accounting education is not a call for the abandonment of technical competence. Instead, the enhancement of communication and thinking skills must accompany technical proficiency. Practicing accountants continue to book transactions, and real-world communication requires nonaccountants to possess an adequate technical vocabulary. Although the coverage of recording procedures has been significantly curtailed, it has not been eliminated. We continue to cover the basic components of double-entry bookkeeping including debits and credits, journal entries, T-accounts, and trial balances. Accordingly, **it is not necessary to change your intermediate accounting course if you adopt this book.** Indeed, users of previous editions have consistently reported that their students are better prepared for intermediate accounting than they were under the traditional approach. This edition of the text continues to maintain the delicate balance between enhanced relevance and technical competence.

Business Transactions Are Classified Into Four Logical Categories

Instead of attempting to memorize transactions, students learn to identify events as belonging to one of four conceptual categories. More specifically, students learn to classify transactions as being (1) asset sources, (2) asset uses, (3) asset exchanges, or (4) claims exchanges. This classification approach encourages students to think about the effects of events rather than to memorize recording procedures.

A Consistent Point of Reference Is Provided

Do you ever wonder why good students sometimes have so much trouble grasping the simplest concepts? For example, why do so many students have difficulty distinguishing the effects of an owner investment from those of a business investment? A participant in a recent introductory accounting workshop provided the answer that enabled us to avoid a common pitfall that needlessly confuses so many students. Normally, accounting events are described from the perspective of the business entity. For example, we say that the business borrowed money, purchased assets, earned revenue, or incurred expenses. For some unknown reason, however, we usually shift the point of reference when we speak of equity transactions. We say that the owners contributed capital, provided cash, or invested assets in the business. From the perspective of the business, these are capital acquisitions, not owner investments. To understand how this *reference shift* affects the entry-level accounting student, try it on a different type of transaction. Suppose that we say, "A customer purchased services from the business." What kind of transaction is this? It is a revenue transaction, of course. How about "a supplier provides services to the business?" This is just a more confusing way of saying the business incurred an expense. Likewise, an owner investment is just a more confusing way of saying the business acquired assets from the owner. Your students will certainly appreciate the fact that this text uses the business entity as a consistent point of reference in the description of all accounting events. We steadfastly use the terminology "the business acquired cash from the issue of stock" rather than saying "the owner invested in the business" when describing equity events.

Content That Is Manageable and Relevant

Accounting is a dynamic discipline. It changes to reflect new and emerging business practices. As academicians, we are certainly obligated to keep current and to introduce our students to the latest developments. As teachers, however, we must also recognize the limited ability of our students to meaningfully process an ever increasing supply of information. **Remember that information overload equals memorization.** Although we have found it necessary to add new material, we determined that eliminating the older, less relevant subject matter is equally important. The first editions of our text made real progress toward the elimination of alternative recording procedures, meaningless details, and subject matter that is too advanced for introductory accounting students. Like its predecessors, the new edition contains only 12 chapters.

Stimulating Student Interest

A good textbook must be more than pedagogically sound. It must be designed in a manner that motivates student interest. Toward this end, we have included several features that highlight real-world applications. Each chapter of the revised text opens with a scenario entitled **The Curious Accountant.** Each scenario poses a question regarding a real-world accounting issue. The question is answered in a separate box a few pages after the question. Pictures that stimulate interest are included. An example of the Curious Accountant feature follows. The new edition contains other real-world features such as actual financial statements, footnote quotations, and management analyses drawn from the **annual reports of well-known companies.** Most chapters now contain a box that discusses interesting **international accounting issues.** In addition, most chapters include colorful graphs that provide summary facts about financial reporting. The data source for these graphs is the AICPA's source book *Accounting Trends and Techniques.* Finally, the end-of-chapter material includes real-world cases requiring the use of the **World Wide Web.**

Financial ratios introduced throughout the book are logically related to the chapter material. For example, accounts receivable turnover is introduced in the chapter that covers bad debts, and the times interest earned ratio is discussed in the bonds chapter. Industry data are shown to provide students with a basis for establishing a sense of normalcy regarding business practice. The 2001 annual report for Dell Computer Corporation is included in Appendix B, and the "Analyze, Think, Communicate" section that relates directly to the annual report is in the end-of-chapter material.

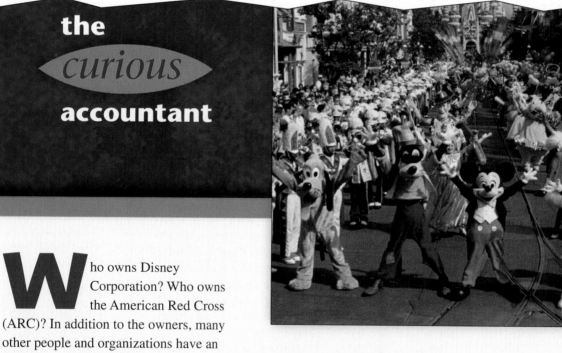

the *curious* accountant

Who owns Disney Corporation? Who owns the American Red Cross (ARC)? In addition to the owners, many other people and organizations have an interest in the operations of Disney and the ARC. The parties that are interested in operations of an organization are called *stakeholders.* Among others, they include lenders, employees, suppliers, customers, benefactors, research institutions, hospitals, doctors, patients, lawyers, bankers, financial analysts, and government agencies such as the Internal Revenue Service and the Securities and Exchange Commission. Organizations communicate information to stakeholders through documents called *financial reports.* How do you think the financial reports of Disney might differ from those of the ARC?

answers to the *curious* accountant

Anyone who owns "stock" in Disney owns a part of the company. Disney has many owners. In contrast, nobody actually owns the American Red Cross (ARC). The ARC has a board of directors that is responsible for overseeing its operations, but the board is not its owner.

Ultimately, the purpose of a business entity is to increase the wealth of its owners. To this end, it "spends money to make money." The expense that Disney incurs for advertising is a cost incurred in the hope that it will generate revenues when its movie tickets are sold. The financial statements of a business show, among other things, whether and how the company made a profit during the current year.

The ARC is a "not-for-profit" entity. It operates to provide services to society at large, not to make a profit. It cannot increase the wealth of its owners because it has no owners. When the ARC spends money to help flood victims, it does not spend this money in the expectation that it will generate "revenues." The revenues of the ARC come from contributors who wish to support efforts related to disaster assistance. Because the ARC does not spend money to make money, it has no reason to prepare an *income statement* like that of Disney.

Not-for-profit entities do prepare financial statements that are similar in appearance to those of commercial enterprises. The financial statements of not-for-profit entities are called the *statement of financial position,* the *statement of activities,* and the *cash flow statement.*

focus on International Issues

Is There Global GAAP?

This chapter introduces the fact that financial reporting is a measurement and communication discipline based on a set of rules referred to as *generally accepted accounting principles.* Business students must be aware that the accounting rules that are the primary focus of this course are based on the GAAP of the United States. Not all economies throughout the world use the same accounting rules. Although there are many similarities among the GAAP used in different countries, there also are major differences. There have been attempts to create

international accounting standards, but individual countries have retained the authority to establish their own GAAP. Simply put, each country has its own GAAP; there is no single "global GAAP." Throughout this book, text examples of how financial reporting in other countries differ from those in the United States are presented.

Accounting rules differ among countries due to a variety of factors, including the economic and legal environments that exist in each country and how the GAAP in that country is established. Generally accepted accounting principles in the United States are primarily established by the Financial Accounting Standards Board (FASB). The FASB is a nongovernment rule-making body that was established by the accounting profession. In some countries, Germany and Japan, for example, the GAAP is established by government bodies. Thus, the establishment of GAAP in these countries is more like the way federal laws and regulations are established in the United States.

Furthermore, in the United States there is very little connection between GAAP established by the FASB and tax accounting regulations established by Congress and the Internal Revenue Service (IRS). As discussed in Chapter 8, in some countries there is a close connection between tax accounting rules and GAAP.

▌Supplemental Materials

The text is supported by a complete package of supplements. The author team has been heavily involved with the development of these materials. Accordingly, you can rest assured that the supplements match the text. The package includes the following items.

■ For Instructors

Instructor's Manual: Prepared by Thomas P. Edmonds and Nancy Schneider (ISBN 0-07-247319-3)

The text is suitable to new teaching approaches such as group dynamics and active pedagogy. The Instructors' Guide provides step-by-step, explicit instructions as to how the text can be used to implement these alternative teaching methodologies. Guidance is also provided for instructors who choose to use the traditional lecture method. The guide includes lesson plans and demonstration problems with student work papers, as well as solutions for them.

Solutions Manual: Prepared by Frances M. McNair, Edward E. Milam, and Philip R. Olds (ISBN 0-07-247303-7)

The Solutions Manual has been prepared by the authors and contains complete answers to all questions, exercises, problems, and cases. The manual has been tested using a variety of quality control procedures to ensure accuracy. It was proofed and checked for accuracy by two independent error checkers: Janice Kelly of St. Louis Community College, Forest Park, and Kimberly Temme of Maryville University. Although the author team retains the responsibility for any errors that may occur, we express our appreciation for the individuals who have exhibited a zero tolerance attitude that is required to maintain the highest standards of excellence.

Solutions Transparencies: Prepared by Frances M. McNair, Edward E. Milam, and Philip R. Olds (ISBN 0-07-247297-9)

Transparencies are prepared in easy-to-read 14-point bold type. They are mirror images of the answers provided in the solutions manual and are consistent with the forms contained in the working papers. This ensures congruence between your in-class presentations and the follow-up exposure that students attain when they view the solutions manual or use the working papers.

Test Bank: Prepared by Bill Reynolds (St. Louis Community College at Florissant Valley) (ISBN 0-07-247302-9)

The Test Bank has been significantly revised and expanded. It includes true/false, multiple-choice, and short discussion questions as well as open-ended problems. The testing material is coded by learning objective and level of difficulty.

Computest

A computerized version of the test bank for more efficient use is available in a Windows platform on the Instructor Presentation CD-ROM.

Presentation Manager CD-ROM (ISBN 0-07-247317-7)

This integrated CD allows instructors to customize their own classroom presentations. It contains key supplements such as PowerPoint slides, Test Bank, Instructor's Manual, Solutions Manual, and Videos. The Presentation Manager makes it easy for instructors to create multimedia presentations.

Financial Accounting Video Library
(ISBN 0-07-237616-3)

These short videos developed by Dallas County Community College provide the impetus for lively classroom discussion. The focus is on the preparation, analysis, and use of accounting information for business decision making.

Web Page (http://www.mhhe.com/edmonds2003)

Our Web page was created for both students and instructors. It includes the Online Learning Center that follows the text chapter by chapter. Students will find learning objectives and their explanations, key terms, Excel templates, check figures, Internet exercises, PowerPoint slides, and self-assessment quizzes. A secured Instructor Center includes text updates, sample syllabi, downloadable supplements, and much more.

■ For Students

Topic Tackler CD-ROM: Prepared by Linda J. Schain

A key new feature of this edition is our Topic Tackler CD *free* with the purchase of a new text. This software is a complete student tutorial focusing on those areas in the financial accounting course that give students the most trouble. It offers video clips, PowerPoint slide shows, interactive exercises, and self-test quizzes. The key concepts are indicated in the text by a Topic Tackler logo that tells students they can refer to the CD for additional instruction.

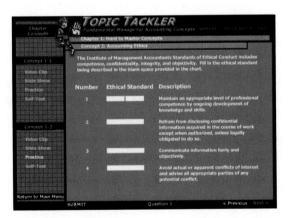

Study Guide: Prepared by Philip R. Olds
(ISBN 0-07-247304-5)

Each chapter of the Study Guide includes a review and an explanation of the chapter's learning objectives, as well as multiple-choice problems and short exercises. Unique to this Study Guide is a series of articulation problems that require students to indicate how accounting events affect (i.e., increase, decrease, have no effect on) the elements of financial statements. They not only reinforce the student's understanding of how events affect statements but also help them to understand how the income statement, balance sheet, and statement of cash flows interrelate. The guide contains approximately 270 pages and includes appropriate working papers and a complete set of solutions.

General Ledger Applications Software: Prepared by Jack Terry of ComSource Associates, Inc.

This *free* software allows students to solve selected end-of-chapter assignments that call for journal entries and are available on the text Website. These assignments are indicated by the following logo.

Excel Templates: Prepared by Jack Terry of ComSource Associates, Inc.

This *free* software is provided for selected problems in the text and is shown by an Excel logo. The templates gradually become more complex, requiring students to build a variety of formulas. "What-if" questions are added to show the power of spreadsheets, and a simple tutorial is included. These templates are available on the text Website. The selected problems are identified with the following logo.

Working Papers: Prepared by Frances M. McNair and Edward E. Milam (ISBN 0-07-247305-3)

The working papers provide forms that are useful in the completion of both exercises and problems. Working papers for the exercises provide headings and prerecorded example transactions that enable students to get started quickly and to work in an efficient manner. The forms provided for the problems can be used with either series A or B problems.

Check Figures

These are available for selected exercises and problems on the text Website.

NetTutor

NetTutor is a live, online tutor that guides students through their accounting problems step by step. It allows students to communicate with live tutors in a variety of ways: through a live tutor center, a Q&A center, and an archive center. NetTutor is *free* with all new texts.

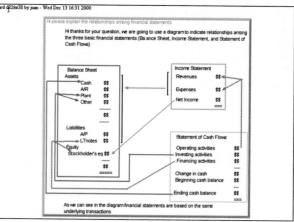

PowerWeb

Keeping your accounting course timely can be a job in itself, and McGraw-Hill now does it for you. PowerWeb is a site from which you can access all of the latest news and developments pertinent to your course without all the clutter and dead links of a typical online search. Students can visit PowerWeb to take a self-grading quiz or check a daily news feed analyzed by an expert in financial accounting. This is *free* with the purchase of a new text.

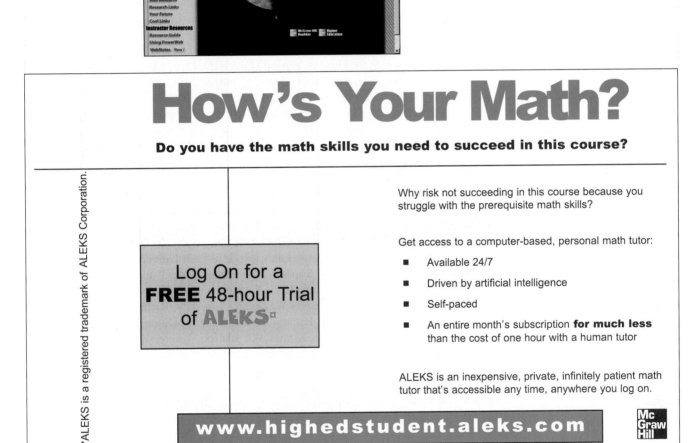

■ Acknowledgments

We are indebted to many individuals who have contributed to the development of this textbook. Our sincere appreciation is extended to

Sheila Ammons
   Austin Community College
Ronald Colley
   State University of West Georgia
Ruth Epps
   Virginia Commonwealth University
Diane Glowacki
   Tarrant County College
Kenneth Hiltebeitel
   Villanova

Alan Mayer-Sommer
   Georgetown University
Kathy Perdue
   DeVry Institute of Technology at Decatur
Michael Riordan
   James Madison University
Kim Shaughnessy
   James Madison University
John Shaver
   Louisiana Tech University

Lewis Shaw
Suffolk University
Jill Smith
Idaho State University

Tim Stephens
DeVry Institute of Technology at Addison

The text underwent an extensive review process that included a diverse group of instructors located at schools across the country. The comments and suggestions of the reviewers and seminar participants have significantly influenced the writing of the text. Our efforts to establish a meaningful but manageable level of content was greatly influenced not only by their suggestions regarding what to include but also by their opinions regarding what to leave out. Our grateful appreciation is extended to those who reviewed previous editions: Charles Richard Aldridge, Western Kentucky University; Debra Barbeau, Southern Illinois University–Carbondale; Beryl Barkman, University of Massachusetts–Dartmouth; Jim Bates, Mountain Empire Community College; Linda Bell, William Jewell College; Wilbur Berry, Jacksonville State University; Nancy Bledsoe, Millsaps College; Cendy Boyd, Northeast Louisiana State; Arthur Boyett, Francis Marion University; Cassie Bradley, Troy State University; Gregory Bushong, Wright State University; Judith Cadle, Tarleton State University; James Cahsell, Miami University; Scott Cairns, Shippensburg College; Eric Carlsen, Kean University; Frederic J. Carlson, LeTourneau University; Joan Carroll, SUNY-College at Oswego; Alan Cherry, Loyola Marymount University; William Cress, University of Wisconsin–La Cross; Walter Doehring, Genesee Community College; George Dow, Valencia Community College; Melanie Earls, Mississippi State University; M. J. Edwards, Adirondack Community College; Ralph Fritzsch, Midwestern State University; Lou Fowler, Missouri Western State College; Mary Anne Gaffney, Temple University; David Ganz, University of Missouri–Saint Louis; Michael Garner, Salisbury State University; William T. Geary, College of William and Mary; Frank Gersich, Gustavus Adolphus College; Claudia Gilbertson, North Hennepin Community College; Lorraine Glasscock, University of North Alabama; Larry Hagler, East Carolina University; Penny Hanes, Virginia Tech University; Leon Hanouille, Syracuse University; Phillip Harsha, Southwest Missouri State University; Charles Hart, Copiah-Lincoln Community College; Inez Heal, Youngstown State University; Nitham Hindi, Shippensburg College; Karen Hull, Kansas Wesleyan University; Richard Hulme, California State Polytechnic University–Pomona; Pamela Jones, Mississippi State University; Khondkar Karim, Monmouth University; Nathan Kranowski, Radford University; Helen LaFrancois, University of Massachusetts–Dartmouth; Robert Landry, Massasoit Community College; William Lathen, Boise State University; David Law, Youngstown State University; William Link, University of Missouri–Saint Louis; Larry Logan, University of Massachusetts–Dartmouth; Catherine Lumbattis, Southern Illinois University–Carbondale; Joseph Marcheggiani, Butler University; Herb Martin, Hope College; Nancy Meade, Radford University; George Minmier, University of Memphis; Cheryl Mitchem, Virginia State University; Lu Montondon, Southwest Texas State University; Tim Nygaard, Madisonville Community College; Brian O'Doherty, East Carolina University; Joseph Onyeocha, South Carolina State University; Lawrence Ozzello, University of Wisconsin–Eau Claire; Eileen Peacock, Oakland University; Thomas Phillips, Jr., Louisiana Tech University; Cathy Pitts, Highline Community College; Mary Raven, Mount Mary College; Jane Reimers, Florida State University; Ken Ruby, Idaho State University; Nancy Schneider, Lynchburg College; Jeffrey Schwartz, Montgomery College; Suzanne Sevalstad, University of Nevada–Las Vegas; Jill Smith, Idaho State University; Paul E. Solomon; John Sperry, Virginia Commonwealth University; Paul Steinbart, Saint Louis University–Saint Louis; Mary Stevens, University of Texas–El Paso; Leonard Stokes, Siena College; Janice Swanson, Southern Oregon University; James Swayze, University of Nevada, Las Vegas; Maurice Tassin, Louisiana Tech University; Kim Temme, Maryville University; Bor-Yi Tsay, University of Alabama–Birmingham; Suneel Udpa, St. Mary's College of California; Beth Vogel, Mount Mary College; J.D. Weinhold, Concordia College; Judith Welch, University of Central Florida; Sterling Wetzel, Oklahoma State University; Thomas Whitacre, University of South Carolina; Macil C. Wilkie, Jr., Grambling State University; Stephen Willits, Bucknell University; Marie Winks, Lynchburg College; Kenneth Winter, University of Wisconsin–La Cross.

Special thanks to the talented people who prepared the supplements. These take a great deal of time and effort to write and we appreciate their efforts. Bill Reynolds of St. Louis Community college at Florissant Valley prepared the Test Bank. Leonard Stokes of Siena College prepared the Internet Quizzes. Larry Bergin of Winona State University prepared the PowerPoint slides. We also thank our accuracy checkers who proofed the text and supplements. They include Janice Kelly of St. Louis Community College—Forest Park, Kim Temme of Maryville University, Beth Woods, Kristine Palmer of Longwood College, and Alice Sineath of Forsyth Community College. We also sincerely thank Linda Schain of Hofstra University who did a great job developing the elements of Topic Tackler.

We are deeply indebted to our sponsoring editor, Melody Marcus. Her direction and guidance have added clarity and quality to the text. We especially appreciate the efforts of our developmental editor, Gail Korosa. Gail has coordinated the exchange of ideas among our class testers, reviewers, copy editor, and error checkers; she has done far more than simply pass along ideas. She has contributed numerous original suggestions that have enhanced the quality of the text. Our editors have certainly facilitated our efforts to prepare a book that will facilitate a meaningful understanding of accounting. Even so, their contributions are to no avail unless the text reaches its intended audience. We are most grateful to Rick Kolasa and Melissa Larmon, and the sales staff for providing the informative advertising that has so accurately communicated the unique features of the concepts approach to accounting educators. Many others at McGraw-Hill/Irwin at a moment's notice redirected their attention to focus their efforts on the development of this text. We extend our sincere appreciation to Kimberly Hooker, Ed Przyzycki, Dave Barrick, Debra Sylvester, Laurie Entringer, Jeremy Cheshareck, and Becky Szura. We deeply appreciate the long hours that you committed to the formation of a high-quality text.

Thomas P. Edmonds
Frances M. McNair
Edward E. Milam
Philip R. Olds

Brief Contents

Contents

Chapter 3   Accounting for Deferrals   102

Chapter 4   The Recording Process   148

Chapter 5   Accounting for Merchandising Business   214

Chapter 6 Internal Control and Accounting for Cash 264

Chapter 7 Accounting for Accruals—Advanced Topics: *Receivables and Payables* 310

Chapter 8 Asset Valuation *Accounting for Inventories*   360

Chapter 9 Long-Term Operational Assets   410

Chapter 10 Accounting for Long-Term Debt 462

Chapter 11 Accounting for Equity Transactions 518

Chapter 12 Statement of Cash Flows 566

Fundamental Financial
ACCOUNTING
Concepts

Elements of Financial Statements

After completing this chapter, you should be able to:

1 Explain the role of accounting in society.

2 Distinguish between financial and managerial accounting.

3 Explain the need for measurement rules (generally accepted accounting principles [GAAP]).

4 Identify, describe, and prepare the four basic financial statements.

5 Identify the major elements of financial statements.

6 Describe the relationships expressed in the accounting equation.

7 Record business events in a financial statements model.

8 Classify business events as asset source, use, or exchange transactions.

9 Record business events in general ledger accounts.

10 Identify the steps in the accounting cycle including the closing process.

11 Calculate and explain the meaning of the price-earnings ratio.

12 Identify the major components of real-world annual reports and some of the technical terms used in them.

the *curious* accountant

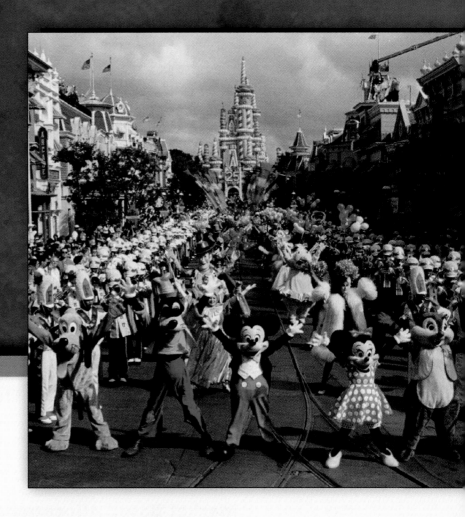

Who owns Disney Corporation? Who owns the American Red Cross (ARC)? In addition to the owners, many other people and organizations have an interest in the operations of Disney and the ARC. The parties that are interested in operations of an organization are called *stakeholders*. Among others, they include lenders, employees, suppliers, customers, benefactors, research institutions, hospitals, doctors, patients, lawyers, bankers, financial analysts, and government agencies such as the Internal Revenue Service and the Securities and Exchange Commission. Organizations communicate information to stakeholders through documents called *financial reports*. How do you think the financial reports of Disney might differ from those of the ARC?

Why should you study accounting? You should study accounting because it can help you succeed in business. In fact, your chances of success are pretty dismal if you are ignorant about accounting. Think about trying to play a game such as football or monopoly when you do not know how to keep score. Accounting is how you keep score in business. Make no mistake about it: Business is highly competitive, and if you do not know the rules of the game, you will be severely disadvantaged.

*   ***Accounting** is information. Instead of making or selling goods, accountants provide information services to their clients. More specifically, they provide information that helps their clients make better decisions. Do not underestimate the importance of reliable information. If you had reliable information regarding the winner of next year's Superbowl, think of the money you could make. Likewise, reliable information about a company's earnings potential could make you a wealthy Wall Street investor.*

*Who uses accounting information? The parties that use accounting information are frequently called **stakeholders.** Information stakeholders (**users**) can have either a direct or an indirect interest in the organizations that issue accounting reports. Stakeholders that have a direct interest include owners, managers, creditors, suppliers, and employees. These individuals are directly affected by what happens to the business. For example, owners and employees of a business prosper when the business makes money. Likewise, they suffer when the business incurs losses. Stakeholders that have an indirect interest in the reporting companies include financial analysts, brokers, attorneys, government regulators, and news reporters. These individuals use information in financial reports to advise and influence their clients. For example, financial analysts frequently advise clients to buy or sell stock of companies that they do not personally own.*

As this discussion implies, accounting is a dynamic discipline. It affects a wide range of individuals and organizations. Accounting is so important that it has been called the language of business. *Indeed, accounting affects not only individual businesses but also society as a whole.*

▊Role of Accounting in Society

LO1 Explain the role of accounting in society.

How much should society emphasize producing food versus developing a cure for cancer? Should we devote more time and energy to making computers or cars? Should you invest your money in IBM or General Motors? Accounting provides information that is useful in answering such resource allocation questions.

Market-Based Allocations

Suppose you want to start a business. You probably have heard the phrase "you have to have money to make money." In fact, you will need more than just money to operate a business. You are likely to need a variety of resources such as equipment, land, materials, employees, and so on. If you do not have the resources you need, how can you get them? In the United States, you would compete for the resources in open markets.

A **market** is a group of people or organizations that come together for the purpose of exchanging things of value. The market for business resources includes three distinct participants: consumers, conversion agents, and resource owners. *Consumers* are resource users. Frequently, however, resources are not in a form that consumers desire. For example, nature provides trees but consumers want furniture. *Conversion agents* (businesses) exist for the purpose of transforming resources (e.g., trees) into products (e.g., furniture) that satisfy consumer preferences. *Resource owners* control the distribution of resources to the conversion agents.

Resource owners expect to be rewarded for the resources they provide conversion agents. Conversion agents (businesses) are able to deliver the rewards that resource owners demand by engaging in a transforming process that adds value to the resources. The outputs (goods and services) created from the inputs (resources) are *more valuable* because they are more useful to consumers after transformation. For example, a house is more valuable than the materials and labor used in its construction. Labor or materials alone will not provide shelter. By transforming the labor and materials into a house, the conversion agent produces an output (house) that is more valuable than the sum of the inputs (labor and materials). For example, a house that cost $220,000 to build could have a market value of $250,000.

The added value created in the transformation process is commonly called **profit, income,** or **earnings.** It is defined as the difference between the cost of a product or service and the selling price of that product or service. For example, the house described earlier has a cost of $220,000 and a market value of $250,000, thereby producing earnings or profit of $30,000 ($250,000 − $220,000 = $30,000). Conversion agents who successfully satisfy consumer preferences in an efficient manner (at a low cost) are rewarded with high earnings. Since these earnings are shared with resource owners, conversion agents who exhibit high earnings potential are more likely to obtain resources. We now return to our original question. If you want to start a business, how do you get the resources you need? To get resources, you must go to the open markets and convince resource owners that you can produce sustainable above average earnings.

In summary, open markets are composed of resource owners, conversion agents, and consumers. The resource owners and conversion agents provide the *supply* of goods and services that respond to consumer demand. Consumers motivate resource providers and conversion agents to satisfy their demands by paying prices that result in high profits. As a result, resources are allocated according to consumer demand. Exhibit 1–1 illustrates the market trilogy involved in resource allocation. The following section of the text discusses specific types of resources that businesses commonly use to satisfy consumer demand.

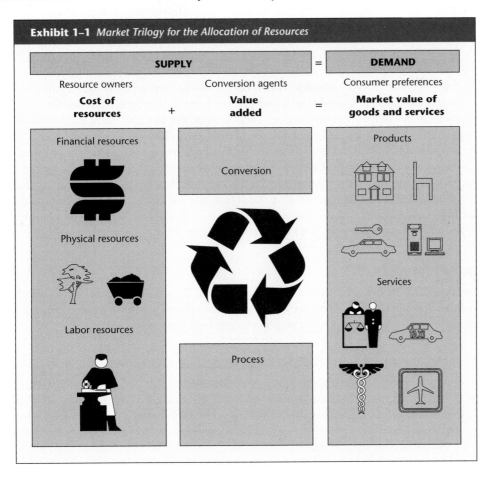

Exhibit 1–1 *Market Trilogy for the Allocation of Resources*

Financial Resources

As previously suggested, conversion agents need **financial resources** (money) to establish and operate their businesses. The *investors* and *creditors* are two primary types of financial resource providers. **Investors** accept ownership interests in a business. As such, they share in the distribution of income. If the business prospers, they are rewarded handsomely. If it fails, they risk losing the resources they invested in the business. Investors allocate their resources to businesses according to the investors' assessment of the likelihood of profitability versus the risk of failure. **Creditors** lend financial resources to businesses. Instead of receiving ownership interests in a business, creditors expect businesses to return the borrowed resources at some future date.

In the event of a business failure, any resources (assets) that remain in the business are returned to the resource providers (creditors and investors). The process of dividing the assets and returning them to the resource providers is called a business **liquidation.** Creditors normally receive first priority in business liquidations. In other words, assets are distributed to creditors first. After creditor claims have been satisfied, the remaining assets are distributed to the investors (owners). To illustrate, suppose that a business acquired $100 in cash from investors and $200 in cash from creditors. Now assume that the business loses $75 and returns the remaining $225 ($300 − $75) to the resource providers. The creditors receive $200, whereas the owners receive only $25. If the business lost $120, only $180 ($300 − $120) is available to return to the creditors. Nothing is returned to the investors. Accordingly, creditors as well as investors can lose resources when businesses fail. Even so, creditors are in a more secure position than owners because they are first in line to receive resources in case of a business liquidation. Because of their more secure position, creditors normally do not share in profitability. Instead, they receive a fixed fee, known as **interest.** Creditors prefer to provide financial resources to businesses (conversion agents) that have high earnings potential because these companies have lower risk of business failure and liquidation. In practice, companies with lower risk are able to obtain lower interest rates because creditors are more confident that such companies will be able to satisfy their obligations.

Physical Resources

In their most primitive form, **physical resources** are natural resources. However, the conversion process can include several stages that involve numerous independent businesses. One conversion agent's output becomes another agent's input. For example, most furniture makers do not own timberlands. Instead, they buy wood from sawmills to make their products. Likewise, sawmills might buy cut trees from the timberlands' owner. Accordingly, physical resources are composed of natural resources that could be at different stages of transformation. Owners of physical resources want to transfer their resources to businesses that are profitable because these businesses are more likely to be able to pay for the resources entrusted to them. Accordingly, physical as well as financial resources are allocated on the basis of a business's ability to add value (produce income) in the conversion process.

Labor Resources

Labor resources include intellectual as well as physical labor. Like other resource providers, workers seek relationships with businesses (conversion agents) with high income potential because these businesses are in a better position to pay high wages.

Accounting Provides Information

In summary, conversion agents (businesses) that effectively satisfy consumer demand are rewarded with high profits. Resource owners (financial, physical, and labor) are more willing to supply resources to businesses with high earnings potential because profitable businesses are in a better position to pay competitive prices for the resources. How do the resource owners identify the conversion agents with high profit potential? This is where accounting enters the picture. *Accounting* provides information that is useful in evaluating a conversion agent's profit potential and relative risk. Accordingly, accounting provides information that is useful in deciding how resources will be assigned to conversion agents.

Types of Accounting Information

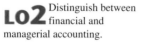
LO2 Distinguish between financial and managerial accounting.

Accounting information that is designed to satisfy the needs of external resource providers is called **financial accounting.** Since resource providers are viewed as entities that are separate from the business, they are frequently called *external users* of accounting information. Another branch of accounting, known as **managerial accounting,** provides information that is useful in operating a business. Since managers and employees are responsible for operating the business, they are commonly called *internal users* of accounting information. The information needs of both user groups frequently overlap. For example, both external and internal users are interested in the amount of income a business earns. However, managerial accounting information is usually more detailed than financial information. Whereas an investor is interested in knowing whether Wendy's or Burger King produces more income relative to risk, a regional manager of Wendy's is interested in knowing which of the restaurants under her control produces the highest amount of earnings. Indeed, a manager is interested in many nonfinancial measures, such as the number of employees needed to operate a restaurant, the number of parking spaces needed, the times at which customer demand is high versus low, and the measures of cleanliness and customer satisfaction.

Nonbusiness Resource Allocations

The economy of the United States is not *purely* market based. Many factors other than profitability affect the allocation of resources. For example, governments make allocations for national defense, the redistribution of wealth, or the protection of the environment. Foundations, religious groups, the Peace Corps, and other benevolent organizations allocate resources on the basis of humanitarian concerns. Similarly, groups are formed to support art, music, dance, and theater. These organizations also add value through a transformation process. For example, like a profit-oriented restaurant, a nonprofit soup kitchen adds value by transforming raw meats and vegetables into a form more desirable for human consumption. It is not the *existence* but the *treatment* of added value that differs between profit and not-for-profit organizations. The consumers who eat at a soup kitchen are unable to pay its operating costs, much less a charge for the added value they receive. Accordingly, the motive for delivering the resources and added value is humanitarian rather than profit based. Organizations that are not motivated by profit are called **not-for-profit entities** (also called *nonprofit* or *nonbusiness entities*).

The absence of a profit motive by no means negates the need for accounting. Accounting information can be useful in measuring the goods and services provided by a not-for-profit organization, its efficiency and effectiveness in producing goods and providing services, and its ability to continue to produce goods and provide services. This information is useful to a host of stakeholders, including taxpayers, contributors, lenders, suppliers, employees, managers, financial analysts, attorneys, and beneficiaries. As depicted in Exhibit 1–2, accounting serves

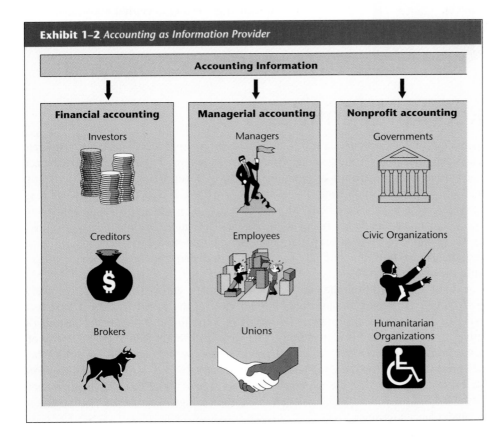

Exhibit 1–2 *Accounting as Information Provider*

Accounting Information

Financial accounting	**Managerial accounting**	**Nonprofit accounting**
Investors	Managers	Governments
Creditors	Employees	Civic Organizations
Brokers	Unions	Humanitarian Organizations

the information needs of a variety of business and nonbusiness user groups. The exhibit shows three distinct areas of accounting. In practice, these areas frequently overlap. Certainly, managers of not-for-profit organizations as well as those of business entities use managerial accounting information.

Measurement Rules

LO3 Explain the need for measurement rules (GAAP).

To facilitate communication, accountants establish rules that businesspeople can use to ensure that they are talking about the same thing. Suppose that a store sells a compact disk player in December to a customer who agrees to pay for it in January. Should the storeowner recognize the sale in December or in January? Recognition when the sale occurred in December is an *accrual accounting* rule. A *cash accounting* rule requires recognition when cash is collected in January. Whether the storeowner uses the accrual or the cash rule is not important as long as

a third rule is established that requires the owner to disclose which method he uses. Accordingly, rule making does not preclude diversity in financial reporting. Even when different reporting rules are used, clear communication can be accomplished through full and fair disclosure.

Certainly, communication would be easier if only one measurement method were used to report each type of business activity. Unfortunately, world economies have not yet evolved to the point at which it is possible to attain uniformity in financial reporting. Indeed, significant diversity continues to exist even in highly sophisticated countries such as the United States. A well-educated businessperson must be able to understand and interpret accounting information that has been prepared using a variety of measurement rules. The rules of measurement for accounting used in the United States are called **generally accepted accounting principles (GAAP).** This textbook introduces you to these principles so that you will be able to understand business activity as it is presented in accounting reports.

Reporting Entities

We begin our study of accounting by discussing the reports that accountants use to summarize business activities. First, you must understand that accounting reports summarize the activities of particular organizations or individuals known as **reporting entities.** Each entity is treated as a separate reporting unit. For example, a business is a reporting entity that is separate from its owners and its creditors. More specifically, a business, the person who owns the business, and a bank that loans money to the business are three separate reporting entities. In this case, accountants prepare a separate set of reports to describe the economic activities of each of the three entities. Accordingly, the first step in understanding accounting reports is to identify the reporting entity.

Our study is directed from the perspective of a business entity. This perspective likely requires you to make a mental adjustment in your view of the world. You are accustomed to thinking from a customer perspective. For example, you think that—from the customer perspective—a sales discount is a great thing. The view is different from the perspective of the business granting the discount. A sales discount means that the item did not sell at the expected price. To move the item, the business had to settle for less money than it expected to make. From this perspective, the sales discount is not a good thing. To understand accounting, it will be helpful for you to retrain yourself to interpret things from the perspective of a business rather than a consumer.

In a recent business transaction, land was exchanged for cash. Did the amount of cash increase or decrease?

Answer The answer depends on the reporting entity to which the question pertains. One entity sold land. The other entity bought land. For the entity that sold land, cash increased. For the entity that bought land, cash decreased.

Financial Statements

Business entities communicate information to the public through a process known as *financial reporting.* The central feature of external financial reporting is a set of **financial statements.** Accordingly, financial statements constitute the principal means of communicating economic information to individuals and institutions outside the reporting enterprise. The four general-purpose financial statements are the (1) income statement, (2) statement of changes in equity, (3) balance sheet, and (4) statement of cash flows.

LO4 Identify, describe, and prepare the four basic financial statements.

The statements can have other names. For example, the income statement can be called a *statement of operations* or an *earnings statement.* The frequency of use of these terms is shown in Exhibit 1–3. Similarly, alternative names exist for the other statements. The balance sheet is also known as a *statement of financial position.* The statement of changes in equity can also be called a *capital statement* or *statement of stockholders' equity.* Since the **Financial Accounting Standards Board** (FASB)[1] has specifically called for using the title *statement of cash flows,* title diversity virtually does not exist for this statement.

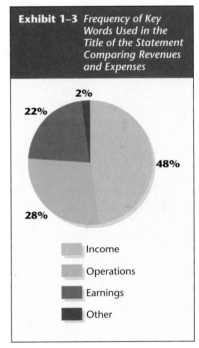

Exhibit 1–3 *Frequency of Key Words Used in the Title of the Statement Comparing Revenues and Expenses*

- Income
- Operations
- Earnings
- Other

Data Source: AICPA, *Accounting Trends and Techniques,* 2000.

Elements of Financial Statements

The items reported in financial statements are organized into classes or categories known as **elements.** The FASB has identified 10 elements of financial statements. Eight of these elements are discussed in this chapter: assets, liabilities, equity, common stock, revenue, expenses, distributions, and net income. The other two elements, gains and losses, are discussed in a later chapter. In practice, many different titles are used to identify the elements of financial statements. For example, *net income, net earnings,* and *net profit* are used interchangeably to describe the same element. Similarly, *common stock* can be called *contributed capital, owner's capital,* and *partners' equity.* Furthermore, *distributions, withdrawals,* and *dividends* all describe the transfer of assets from a business to its owners. Think of accounting as a language. Be prepared for the fact that different terms can be used to describe the same business event.

LO5 Identify the major elements of financial statements.

The elements represent broad classifications as opposed to specific items. In other words, cash, equipment, buildings, and land are particular economic resources and should not be identified as elements. Rather, they represent specific items or subclassifications of the element known as *assets.* The subclassifications of the elements are frequently called **accounts.** The accounts appear in the financial statements under the broader classifications that have been identified as elements. For example, the balance sheet contains the element assets, which includes accounts that describe specific items such as cash, inventory, equipment, and land.

How many accounts does a business use? The number depends on a company's information-gathering objectives. Companies create and use the number of accounts that are necessary to store the information that they need to make decisions. Some managers want very detailed

[1]The Financial Accounting Standards Board is a privately funded organization with the primary authority for establishing accounting standards in the United States. The FASB consists of seven full-time members appointed by the supporting organization, the Financial Accounting Foundation (FAF). The FAF membership is intended to represent the broad spectrum of individuals and institutions that have an interest in accounting and financial reporting. FAF members include representatives of the accounting profession, industry, financial institutions, the government, and the investing public.

information; others want highly summarized data. Accordingly, the number of accounts used in an accounting system varies from company to company.

Elements of the Accounting Equation

LO6 Describe the relationships expressed in the accounting equation.

The resources that a business uses to produce earnings are called **assets.** Examples of assets include land, buildings, equipment, materials, and supplies. To comply with generally accepted accounting principles, assets may be recognized in financial statements only when they result from historical events. For example, if a business owns a truck that was purchased in a past transaction, the truck is an asset of the business. However, a truck that a business *plans* to purchase in the future is not considered an asset of that business, no matter how certain the future purchase might be.

The assets of a business belong to the resource providers who are said to have **claims** on the assets. An expression of the relationship between the assets and the claims on those assets is known as the **accounting equation:**

$$\text{Assets} = \text{Claims}$$

Since the creditors have first claim on the assets, the *owners* are said to have a **residual interest.** This means that in the case of a business liquidation, the owners receive the assets that are left after the debts to creditors have been paid. The following expression of the accounting equation recognizes the relationship among the assets, creditors' claims (called **liabilities**), and owners' claims (called **equity**).

$$\text{Assets} = \overset{\text{Claims}}{\overline{\text{Liabilities} + \text{Equity}}}$$

Liabilities can also be viewed as *obligations of the enterprise.* When the obligations are settled in the future, the business probably will have to relinquish some of its assets (e.g., pay off its debts with cash), provide services to its creditors (e.g., work off its debts), or accept other obligations (e.g., trade short-term debt for long-term debt).

Algebraically, the amount of total assets minus total liabilities equals the *equity.* Since equity equals the net difference between the assets and the liabilities, it is also called **net assets.** Accordingly, *equity, net assets,* and *residual interest* are synonyms for the ownership interest in the business. To illustrate, assume that Hagan Company has assets of $500, liabilities of $200, and equity of $300. These amounts appear in the accounting equation as follows:

$$\text{Assets} = \overset{\text{Claims}}{\overline{\text{Liabilities} + \text{Equity}}}$$
$$\$500 = \$200 + \$300$$

Given the equality expressed in the accounting equation, the equity (net assets or residual interest) can be computed as follows:

$$\text{Assets} - \text{Liabilities} = \text{Equity}$$
$$\$500 - \$200 = \$300$$

Asset Sources

The claims side of the accounting equation (liabilities plus equity) can be viewed as a list of the sources of assets. For example, when a bank loans assets (e.g., money) to a business, it establishes a claim for the return of those assets at some future date. In other words, the bank has a claim on the assets because it provided them to the business. As a result, in some circumstances, liabilities can be viewed as sources of assets.

Equity can also be viewed as a source of assets. In fact, equity is composed of two distinct sources of assets. First, a business might acquire assets from its owners. To acknowledge the receipt of assets from owners, businesses frequently issue certificates known as **common**

stock. Expanding this terminology, the owners of the business are often called **stockholders,** and the ownership interest in the business is called **stockholders' equity.** Second, a business might obtain assets through its earnings activities (the business acquires assets by working for them). Assets that have been earned by the business can be either distributed to the owners or kept in the business. Accordingly, the portion of assets that have been provided by earnings activities is appropriately named **retained earnings.** An accounting equation that depicts the three sources of assets (liabilities, common stock, and retained earnings) follows:

$$\text{Assets} = \frac{\text{Sources or Claims}}{\text{Liabilities} + \text{Common Stock} + \text{Retained Earnings}}$$

The combination of common stock and retained earnings is called stockholders' equity. Accordingly, the accounting equation also can be written as follows:

$$\text{Assets} = \text{Liabilities} + \frac{\text{Stockholders' Equity}}{\text{Common Stock} + \text{Retained Earnings}}$$

Introduction to Financial Statements

LO4 Identify, describe, and prepare the four basic financial statements.

Recall that accountants communicate information through four financial statements: a balance sheet, an income statement, a statement of cash flows, and a statement of changes in stockholders' equity. The following section of the text provides a brief explanation of the balance sheet, income statement, and statement of cash flows. A discussion of the statement of changes in equity is in a later section of the chapter.

Balance Sheet

The *balance sheet* draws its name from the *accounting equation*; it lists the assets of a business and corresponding claims on those assets. Specifically, the assets must balance with (be equal to) the sources of those assets. Balance sheets are normally divided into two sections. The first section lists the company's assets, and the second section shows the sources of those assets (liabilities and stockholders' equity).

Check Yourself 1–2

Try to create a balance sheet that describes your personal financial condition. List your assets first and then your liabilities. Determine the amount of your equity by subtracting your liabilities from your assets.

Answer Answers for this exercise will vary depending on each student's particular assets and liabilities. Some common types of personal assets include automobiles, computers, stereos, TVs, phones, CD players, and clothes. Common types of liabilities include car loans, mortgages, and credit card debt. The difference between the assets and the liabilities is the equity.

Income Statement

Businesses use assets to generate increased quantities of other assets. The **income statement** measures the difference between the asset increases and the asset decreases associated with operating a business.[2] Asset increases resulting from the operating activities are called **revenues.** Asset decreases incurred to generate revenues are called *expenses.* If revenues are greater than expenses, the difference between these two elements is called **net income.** If expenses exceed the revenues, the difference is referred to as a **net loss.** Accordingly, net income indicates that a company has succeeded in earning more assets than it used. A net loss shows

---

[2]This description of the income statement is expanded in subsequent chapters as additional relationships among the elements of the financial statement are introduced.

that a business used more assets than it earned. Note that assets transferred from a business to its owners are called **dividends.** Cash dividends paid to stockholders are not expenses because the asset decrease (cash) is not incurred to generate revenue. Accordingly dividends are not shown on the income statement.

Check Yourself 1–3

Mahoney, Inc., was started when it issued common stock to its owners for $300,000. During its first year of operation Mahoney received $523,000 in cash for providing services to customers. Mahoney paid $233,000 cash to employees and cash advertising costs of $102,000. Other cash operating expenses amounted to $124,000. Finally, Mahoney paid a $25,000 cash dividend to its stockholders. What amount of net income would Mahoney report on its earnings statement for the year?

Answer Mahoney would report net income of $64,000 ($523,000 revenue − $233,000 salary expense − $102,000 advertising expense − $124,000 other operating expenses). The cash received from issuing stock is not revenue because it did not result from earnings activities. In other words, the business did not work (perform services) for this money. Likewise, the cash dividends are not expenses because they were not paid for the purpose of generating revenue. Instead, cash dividends (which decrease cash) represent a transfer of wealth to the owners.

Statement of Cash Flows

The **statement of cash flows** explains how a company obtained and used *cash* during the accounting period (usually one year). The sources of cash are called *cash inflows,* and the uses are known as *cash outflows.* The statement classifies cash receipts (inflows) and payments (outflows) into three categories: financing activities, investing activities, and operating activities.

Businesses normally start with an idea. For example, suppose that you notice a shortage of apartment rental space and decide to build an apartment complex. Implementing the idea usually requires cash. In this case, you would need cash to build the apartments. The efforts to acquire cash to start a business are called **financing activities.** Specifically, financing activities include obtaining cash from (cash inflows) or paying to (cash outflows) owners, including dividends. Also, borrowing cash from (cash inflows) or repaying principal to (cash outflows) creditors is shown in the financing activities section. Note, however, that interest paid to creditors is considered to be an expense and is included in the operating activities section of the statement of cash flows.

Once you obtained cash from financing activities, you would invest it in the productive assets that will be used to operate the business. The cash paid for (cash outflows) productive assets or the cash received from (cash inflows) the sale of productive assets is shown in the **investing activities** section of the statement of cash flows. **Productive assets** are sometimes called *long-term assets* because they are normally used for more than one accounting period. For example, cash outflows to purchase land or cash inflows from selling a building are reported in the investing activities section of the statement of cash flows. In contrast, cash spent to purchase supplies goes in the operating activities section because the supplies represent short-term assets that are generally used within a single accounting period.

Once the productive assets have been acquired and put into place, you would begin to operate the business. The cash received from revenue (cash inflows) and the cash paid for expenses (cash outflows) are reported in the **operating activities** section of the statement of cash flows.

The primary cash inflows and outflows associated with each type of business activity are shown in Exhibit 1–4. The exhibit and the preceding discussion are limited to the business events discussed in this chapter. As subsequent chapters introduce new events, their effects on the statement of cash flows will be added to the exhibit.

Exhibit 1–4 *Statement of Cash Flows Classification Scheme*

Cash Flows from Operating Activities
Cash receipts (inflows) from revenue (including interest)
Cash payments (outflows) for expenses (including interest)

Cash Flows from Investing Activities
Cash receipts (inflows) from the sale of long-term assets
Cash payments (outflows) for the purchase of long-term assets

Cash Flows from Financing Activities
Cash receipts (inflows) from borrowed funds
Cash receipts (inflows) from the issue of common stock
Cash payments (outflows) to repay borrowed funds
Cash payments (outflows) for dividends

Check Yourself 1-4

Classify each of the following cash flows as an operating, investing, or financing activity.

1. Cash acquired from owners.
2. Cash borrowed from creditors.
3. Cash paid to purchase land.
4. Cash earned as revenue.
5. Cash paid for salary expenses.
6. Cash paid for dividends.
7. Cash paid for interest.

Answer (1) financing activity; (2) financing activity; (3) investing activity; (4) operating activity; (5) operating activity; (6) financing activity; (7) operating activity.

Horizontal Statements Model

LO7 Record business events in a financial statements model.

The **horizontal statements model** is so named because it arranges financial statement information horizontally across a single page of paper. It presents the balance sheet first, followed by the income statement, and then the statement of cash flows. An example of a financial statements model follows. Note that the elements have been divided into subclassifications known as *accounts*. For example, the *element assets* has been divided into *two accounts* (Cash and Land). Recall that the number of accounts a company uses depends on the nature of its business and the level of detail that management needs to operate the business. For example, Sears would have a Cost of Goods Sold account, but GEICO Insurance would not. This is so because Sears sells goods (merchandise), but GEICO does not.

Balance Sheet			Income Statement		Statement of Cash Flows
Assets	= Liab. +	Stockholders' Equity			
Cash + Land	= N. Pay +	C. Stk. + Ret. Ear.	Rev. − Exp. = Net Inc.		Flows

The statements have been color coded for easy identification. The background of the *balance sheet* is in red, of the *income statement* is in blue, and of the *statement of cash flows* is in green.

▮ Rustic Camp Sites Illustration: Events for 2004

An **accounting event** is an economic occurrence that causes changes in an enterprise's assets, liabilities, and/or equity. Events can be internal actions, such as using raw materials or equipment to produce goods or services. Events also can relate to external actions, such as an exchange of goods or services with another company. A **transaction** is a particular type of event that involves the transfer of something of value between two entities. Examples of transactions include acquiring assets from owners, borrowing funds from creditors, and purchasing or selling goods and services. The following section of the text explains how several different types of accounting events affect a company's financial statements.

Asset Source Transactions

Businesses obtain assets from three primary sources: they acquire assets from owners, they borrow them from creditors, and they earn them through their operations. Asset source transactions increase total assets and total claims.

Event 1 Rustic Camp Sites (RCS) is formed on January 1, 2004, when it acquires $120,000 cash from the issue of common stock.

When RCS issued stock, it received cash and gave the investors stock certificates as receipts. Since this transaction provided $120,000 of assets (cash) to the enterprise, it is an **asset source transaction.** It increases the business's assets (Cash account) and its stockholders' equity (Common Stock account). Notice that the business did not work (perform earnings activities) for this money, but acquired the money by issuing stock. Since the business did not work for the money, this transaction does not affect the income statement. The cash inflow resulted from a financing activity (acquisition from owners). In the Statement of Cash Flows column, activity classifications are identified with a simple two-letter designation: cash flow from operating activities with OA; investing activities with IA; and financing activities with FA. The designation "NA" indicates that an account is not affected by an event. These effects are shown in the following financial statements model.

Balance Sheet										Income Statement					Statement of Cash Flows
Assets			=	Liab.	+	Stockholders' Equity									
Cash	+	Land	=	N. Pay	+	C. Stk.	+	Ret. Ear.		Rev.	−	Exp.	=	Net Inc.	
120,000	+	NA	=	NA	+	120,000	+	NA		NA	−	NA	=	NA	120,000 FA

Notice that this single transaction is recorded in the balance sheet twice, once as an asset (Cash) and a second time as the source of that asset (Common Stock). All subsequent transactions will be recorded at least twice in the balance sheet accounts. The **double-entry bookkeeping** system derives its name from this practice.

Event 2 RCS acquires an additional $400,000 of assets by borrowing cash from creditors.

This transaction would also be classified as an asset source transaction. It acts to increase assets (Cash) and liability claims (Notes Payable). The account title Notes Payable derives its name from the fact that the borrower is normally required to issue a promissory note to the creditors (e.g., a bank). A promissory note, among other things, describes the amount of interest that will be charged and the length of time for which the money will be borrowed. Since the event did not result from operating the business (performing work), the income statement is not affected. The event provided a cash inflow from financing activities. These effects on the financial statements follow.

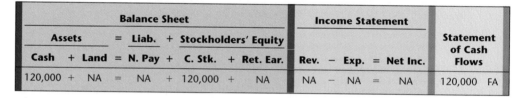

Balance Sheet									Income Statement					Statement of Cash Flows
Assets			=	Liab.	+	Stockholders' Equity								
Cash	+	Land	=	N. Pay	+	C. Stk.	+	Ret. Ear.	Rev.	−	Exp.	=	Net Inc.	
400,000	+	NA	=	400,000	+	NA	+		NA	−	NA	=	NA	400,000 FA

Asset Exchange Transactions

Businesses frequently trade one asset for another asset. In this case, the amount of one asset decreases and the amount of another asset increases. Total assets are unaffected by asset exchange transactions. The following event introduces asset exchange transactions.

Event 3 RCS pays $500,000 cash to purchase land.

This asset exchange transaction reduces the asset account Cash and increases the asset account Land. The amount of total assets is not affected. An asset exchange transaction simply registers the change in the composition of assets. In this case, the company traded cash for land. Accordingly, the amount of cash decreased by $500,000, and the amount of land increased by the same amount. The income statement is not affected because the business did not engage in earnings activities. However, the statement of cash flows shows a $500,000 cash outflow from investing activities. Notice that we have followed the convention of using parentheses to designate decreases in account balances and cash outflows.

Balance Sheet						Income Statement			Statement of Cash Flows
Assets		= Liab.	+ Stockholders' Equity						
Cash	+ Land	= N. Pay	+ C. Stk.	+		Rev.	− Exp.	= Net Inc.	
(500,000)	+ 500,000 =	NA	+ NA	+		NA	− NA =	NA	(500,000) IA

If the market value of the land at the end of the accounting period were $525,000. it would still be shown on the financial statements at $500,000. A concept known as **historical cost** requires assets to be shown in financial statements at the actual prices paid for them regardless of changes in their market values.

Another Asset Source Transaction

Event 4 RCS obtains $85,000 cash by leasing campsites to customers.

An *increase in assets* obtained from earnings activities (providing customers with goods and services) is called *revenue*. Accordingly, revenue transactions also can be viewed as *asset source transactions*. In this case, the asset account, Cash, increases. This increase is balanced by an increase in the retained earnings section of stockholders' equity (revenue increases the amount of earnings that can be retained in the business). The income statement is affected because the increase in assets resulted from earnings activities. The statement of cash flows shows an $85,000 inflow from operating activities. The effects of this transaction on the financial statements follow:

Balance Sheet						Income Statement			Statement of Cash Flows
Assets		= Liab.	+ Stockholders' Equity						
Cash	+ Land	= N. Pay	+ C. Stk.	+ Ret. Ear.		Rev.	− Exp.	= Net Inc.	
85,000	+ NA =	NA	+ NA	+ 85,000		85,000	− NA =	85,000	85,000 OA

Asset Use Transactions

Businesses use assets for a variety of purposes. For example, they can use assets to pay off liabilities. Similarly, businesses can transfer assets to the owners. Businesses also can use assets to generate earnings. All asset use transactions result in decreases in the total amount of assets and the total amount of claims on assets (liabilities or stockholders' equity).

Event 5 RCS paid $50,000 cash for operating expenses such as salaries, rent, and interest. (Separate accounts could be established for each type of expense. However, RCS's management team does not desire to have this level of detail. Remember, the number of accounts that a business uses depends on the level of information that is needed to make decisions.)

Normally, a business consumes some of its assets in the process of trying to obtain other assets. The assets acquired by operating activities are called *revenues;* the assets used in generating the revenues are called *expenses.* Since the owners bear the ultimate risk and reap the rewards of operating the business, revenues increase stockholders' equity (**retained earnings**), and expenses decrease retained earnings. In this case, the asset account, Cash, decreases. This decrease is balanced by a decrease in the retained earnings section of stockholders' equity (expenses decrease the amount of earnings that can be retained in the business). Since the assets were used in generating earnings, the income statement reflects an increase in expenses and a decrease in net income. The statement of cash flows shows a cash outflow from operating activities. The effect of this asset use transaction on the financial statements is as follows:

Balance Sheet									Income Statement			Statement of Cash Flows
Assets			=	Liab.	+	Stockholders' Equity						
Cash	+	Land	=	N. Pay	+	C. Stk.	+	Ret. Ear.	Rev.	− Exp.	= Net Inc.	
(50,000)	+	NA	=	NA	+	NA	+	(50,000)	NA	− 50,000	= (50,000)	(50,000) OA

The minus sign in front of the Expenses column does not mean that expenses decreased. Indeed, in this case, expenses increased by $50,000. Instead, the minus sign indicates that expenses are subtracted from revenues to determine the amount of net income.

Event 6 RCS pays a $4,000 cash dividend to its owners.

The enterprise's *net assets* have increased by $35,000 (that is, $85,000 revenue − $50,000 expense) as a result of its earnings activities. Since the risks and rewards of operating a business rest with its owners, the owners are entitled to the assets that are generated through earnings activities. The enterprise can choose to keep the additional assets in the business or transfer them to the owners. If the business chooses to transfer some or all of the earned assets to the owners, the transfer is frequently called a *dividend*. Since assets distributed to owners are not used for generating revenue, the income statement is not affected. In other words, *dividends are wealth transfers, not expenses*. The cash outflow appears in the financing activities section of the statement of cash flows. The effect on the financial statements is as follows:

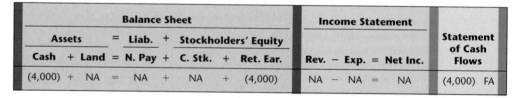

Balance Sheet									Income Statement			Statement of Cash Flows
Assets			=	Liab.	+	Stockholders' Equity						
Cash	+	Land	=	N. Pay	+	C. Stk.	+	Ret. Ear.	Rev.	− Exp.	= Net Inc.	
(4,000)	+	NA	=	NA	+	NA	+	(4,000)	NA	− NA	= NA	(4,000) FA

A dividend and an expense have the same effect on the accounting equation. Both cause a decrease in assets and a corresponding decrease in stockholders' equity (retained earnings). The difference between expenses and dividends results from the reason for the decline in assets. An *expense* is recognized when assets decline because of a firm's efforts to earn revenue. A *dividend* occurs when assets decline because of transfers of wealth from the business to its owners. In summary, expenses are incurred to produce revenue, and dividends are wealth transfers made to satisfy the owners.

Types of Transactions

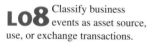
LO8 Classify business events as asset source, use, or exchange transactions.

The transactions just described have been classified into one of three categories: (1) asset source transactions, (2) asset exchange transactions, and (3) asset use transactions. A fourth category, claims exchange transactions, will be introduced in a later chapter. As previously indicated, *asset source transactions result in an increase in the total amount of assets and an increase in the total amount of claims.* In its first year of operation, RCS received assets from three sources. First, it acquired assets from owners (Event 1). Next, RCS borrowed assets (Event 2). Finally, it obtained assets through earnings activities (Event 4). *Asset exchange transactions result in a decrease in one asset account and an increase in another asset account. The total amount of assets is not affected by asset exchange transactions.* RCS experienced one asset exchange transaction when it used cash to purchase land (Event 3). *Asset use transactions cause the amount of total assets and total claims to decrease.* RCS used assets to pay expenses (Event 5) and to pay dividends (Event 6). As you proceed through this text, we encourage you to practice classifying transactions into one of the four categories. Businesses engage in thousands of transactions every day. It is far more effective to learn how to classify the transactions into meaningful categories than it is to attempt to memorize the effects of thousands of transactions.

Summary of Transactions

The horizontal statements model is presented for instructional purposes. It is very helpful in understanding how accounting events affect financial statements. Accordingly, this book extensively uses **statements models.** However, note that the models do *not* represent presentation formats that appear in accounting practice. For example, although a full set of four financial statements is normally presented in published financial statements, the horizontal model shows only a partial set of statements.

LO9 Record events in ledger accounts.

To facilitate your review of the Rustic Camp Sites' illustration, the six business events that the company experienced during 2004 are summarized here.

1. RCS acquired $120,000 cash from the owners.
2. RCS borrowed $400,000 cash.
3. RCS paid cash to purchase $500,000 worth of land.
4. RCS earned $85,000 of cash revenue.
5. RCS paid $50,000 for cash expenses.
6. RCS paid a $4,000 cash dividend to the owners.

In practice, accountants record transactions in accounts. The full collection of accounts is called the **general ledger.** The information in the ledger accounts is used to prepare the financial statements. The general ledger accounts that contain the transaction data for RCS's 2004 accounting period are shown in Exhibit 1–5. The accounts have been organized under the accounting equation. To promote communication, we follow this practice throughout the text. Because of space limitations the revenue, expense, and dividend accounts are shown in the Retained Earnings column. The titles of these accounts are shown immediately to the right of the monetary amounts that appear in the Retained Earnings column.

Exhibit 1–5 *General Ledger Accounts Organized under the Accounting Equation*

	Assets			= Liabilities +	Stockholders' Equity			
Event No.	Cash	+	Land	= Notes Payable +	Common Stock	+ Retained Earnings		Other Account Titles
Beg. Bal.	0		0	0	0	0		
1	120,000				120,000			
2	400,000			400,000				
3	(500,000)		500,000					
4	85,000					85,000		Revenue
5	(50,000)					(50,000)		Expense
6	(4,000)					(4,000)		Dividend
	51,000	+	500,000	= 400,000	+ 120,000	+ 31,000		

As indicated earlier, accounting information is normally presented to external users in four general-purpose financial statements. The data in the general ledger are color coded to facilitate your understanding of the source of information used to prepare financial statements. The numbers in *green* are used in the *statement of cash flows.* The numbers in *red* are used to prepare the *balance sheet.* Finally, the numbers in *blue* are used to prepare the *income statement.* The numbers appearing in the statement of changes in stockholders' equity have not been color coded because they appear in more than one statement. The next section explains how the information in the table is used to prepare financial statements.

Elements Presented in Financial Statements

LO4 Identify, describe, and prepare the four basic financial statements.

The *income statement, statement of changes in stockholders' equity (or statement of retained earnings),* and *statement of cash flows* provide unique perspectives on the performance of the enterprise *during some span of time,* which is called the *accounting period.* The *balance sheet* provides information about the financial condition of the enterprise *at some particular point in time.*

Income Statement

Exhibit 1–6

RUSTIC CAMP SITES
Income Statement
For the Year Ended December 31, 2004

Revenue *(asset increases)*	$85,000
Operating Expenses *(asset decreases)*	(50,000)
Net Income *(change in net assets)*	$35,000

The income statement for RCS is shown in Exhibit 1–6. Observe the phrase, *For the Year Ended December 31, 2004,* in the heading of the income statement. Income is measured over a span of time called the **accounting period.** The customary length of the accounting period is one year, but it is not required. Indeed, income can be measured weekly, monthly, quarterly, semiannually, or over any other time period that the users deem appropriate in relation to their needs for information.

Statement of Changes in Stockholders' Equity

Exhibit 1–7

RUSTIC CAMP SITES
Statement of Changes in Stockholders' Equity
For the Year Ended December 31, 2004

Beginning Common Stock	$ 0	
Plus: Common Stock Issued	120,000	
Ending Common Stock		$120,000
Beginning Retained Earnings	0	
Plus: Net Income	35,000	
Less: Dividends	(4,000)	
Ending Retained Earnings		31,000
Total Stockholders' Equity		$151,000

The **statement of changes in stockholders' equity** is used to explain the effects of transactions on stockholders' equity during the accounting period. It includes the beginning and ending balances for the amount of common stock and reflects any new stock issued during the accounting period. It also shows the portion of the net earnings that are retained in the business. The statement of changes in stockholders' equity for RCS is shown in Exhibit 1–7. This statement is also dated with the phrase, *For the Year Ended December 31, 2004,* because it describes what happened to stockholders' equity over that span of time.

Balance Sheet

Exhibit 1–8

RUSTIC CAMP SITES
Balance Sheet
As of December 31, 2004

Assets		
Cash	$ 51,000	
Land	500,000	
Total Assets		$551,000
Liabilities		
Notes Payable		$400,000
Stockholders' Equity		
Common Stock	$120,000	
Retained Earnings	31,000	
Total Stockholders' Equity		151,000
Total Liabilities and Stockholders' Equity		$551,000

The statement that lists the assets and the corresponding claims on those assets is called the **balance sheet.** The balance sheet for RCS is shown in Exhibit 1–8. The total claims (liabilities plus stockholders' equity) equal the total assets. Note also the order of the assets in the balance sheet. Cash appears first, followed by the Land account. Assets are displayed in the balance sheet according to their level of **liquidity;** that is, assets are listed in order of how rapidly they can be converted to cash. Finally, note that the balance sheet is dated with the phrase, *As of December 31, 2004,* which indicates that it describes the company's financial condition at that particular point in time.

Statement of Cash Flows

The statement of cash flows for Rustic Camp Sites appears in Exhibit 1–9. The statement of cash flows explains the change between the beginning and ending cash balances during the accounting period. In this case, the amount of cash increased by $51,000 during the period. The beginning balance in the Cash account was zero; adding the $51,000 increase results in a $51,000 ending balance. The $51,000 ending balance equals the amount of cash shown on the December 31 year-end balance sheet. The statement of cash flows is dated with the phrase, *For the Year Ended December 31, 2004*, because it describes what happened to cash over that span of time.

Exhibit 1–9

RUSTIC CAMP SITES
Statement of Cash Flows
For the Year Ended December 31, 2004

Cash Flows from Operating Activities		
Cash Receipts from Revenue	$ 85,000	
Cash Payments for Expenses	(50,000)	
Net Cash Flow from Operating Activities		$ 35,000
Cash Flows from Investing Activities		
Cash Payments to Purchase Land		(500,000)
Cash Flows from Financing Activities		
Cash Receipts from Borrowed Funds	400,000	
Cash Receipts from Issue of Common Stock	120,000	
Cash Payments for Dividends	(4,000)	
Net Cash Flow from Financing Activities		516,000
Net Increase in Cash		51,000
Plus Beginning Cash Balance		0
Ending Cash Balance		$ 51,000

Closing Process

Accounting is a cyclical activity. This means that the recognition of business activities is divided into time periods called *cycles* that follow one after the other. The process continues for as long as the accounting entity exists. The information for balance sheet items (assets, liabilities, common stock, and retained earnings) is cumulative. Accordingly, last period's ending balances become next period's beginning balances. Since RCS had $551,000 of assets at the end of 2004, it begins the 2005 cycle with $551,000 of assets. Because of their continuing nature, the balance sheet accounts are sometimes called **permanent accounts.**

LO10 Identify the steps in the accounting cycle including the closing process.

In contrast, revenue, expense, and dividend accounts are **temporary accounts** that are used to collect information about a single cycle (one accounting period only). Because of their temporary nature, these accounts are referred to as **nominal accounts.** After the amounts in the nominal accounts (revenues, expenses, and dividends) are used to prepare the financial statements, the account balances are then transferred to the retained earnings account. The process of removing the balances from the revenue, expense, and dividend accounts is called **closing the accounts,** or **closing.** Since the balances in the nominal accounts are removed at the end of each accounting period, these accounts always have a zero balance at the beginning of each accounting period. In contrast, the Retained Earnings account is a summary account that contains cumulative data regarding revenues, expenses, and dividends that have existed from the company's inception. Accordingly, the 2004 ending balance in the Retained Earnings account becomes the 2005 beginning balance for that account.

■ Rustic Camp Sites: Events for Second Cycle

To demonstrate the cyclical nature of the accounting process, assume that RCS experienced the following events during the company's second accounting period. In this case, the second cycle is the 2005 calendar year. Assume that all transactions involve the payment or receipt of cash.

1. RCS acquired $20,000 cash by issuing common stock.
2. RCS provided services to customers and received $96,000.
3. RCS paid $12,000 for salaries expenses.
4. RCS paid a $5,000 cash dividend to the owners.
5. RCS paid the bank $70,000 to reduce its note payable liability.
6. RCS paid $40,000 for other operating expenses.

Anyone who owns "stock" in Disney owns a part of the company. Disney has many owners. In contrast, nobody actually owns the American Red Cross (ARC). The ARC has a board of directors that is responsible for overseeing its operations, but the board is not its owner.

Ultimately, the purpose of a business entity is to increase the wealth of its owners. To this end, it "spends money to make money." The expense that Disney incurs for advertising is a cost incurred in the hope that it will generate revenues when its movie tickets are sold. The financial statements of a business show, among other things, whether and how the company made a profit during the current year.

The ARC is a "not-for-profit" entity. It operates to provide services to society at large, not to make a profit. It cannot increase the wealth of its owners because it has no owners. When the ARC spends money to help flood victims, it does not spend this money in the expectation that it will generate "revenues." The revenues of the ARC come from contributors who wish to support efforts related to disaster assistance. Because the ARC does not spend money to make money, it has no reason to prepare an *income statement* like that of Disney.

Not-for-profit entities do prepare financial statements that are similar in appearance to those of commercial enterprises. The financial statements of not-for-profit entities are called the *statement of financial position,* the *statement of activities,* and the *cash flow statement.*

The effects of these events are shown in the general ledger accounts in Exhibit 1–10. The transaction data are color coded with *balance sheet items* shown in *red, income statement items* in *blue,* and *cash flow statement items* in *green.* The names of the nominal accounts also are shown to the right of the monetary amounts that appear in the Retained Earnings column.

Exhibit 1–10 *General Ledger Accounts for RCS*

Event No.	Assets			= Liabilities +	Stockholders' Equity		Other Account Titles
	Cash	+ Land	=	Notes Payable	+ Common Stock	+ Retained Earnings	
Beg. Bal.	51,000	500,000		400,000	120,000	31,000	
1	20,000				20,000		
2	96,000					96,000	Revenue
3	(12,000)					(12,000)	Salary Exp.
4	(5,000)					(5,000)	Dividend
5	(70,000)			(70,000)			
6	(40,000)					(40,000)	Other Operating Exp.
	40,000	+ 500,000	=	330,000	+ 140,000	+ 70,000	

■ Financial Statements for 2005

The 2005 income statement for RCS is shown in Exhibit 1–11. Notice that the amounts of revenue and expense shown on the income statement apply only to 2005. Remember that revenue and expense items that pertain to 2004 have been transferred to the Retained Earnings account through the closing process. Accordingly, the beginning balances in these accounts were zero. In contrast, the amounts in the balance sheet accounts contain cumulative information. For example, the ending Cash balance (i.e., $40,000) was determined by adding the current period changes (that is, 2005 data) to the beginning Cash balance.

The 2005 statement of changes in stockholders' equity is shown in Exhibit 1–12. This period's net income of $44,000 and the $5,000 dividend were combined with the $31,000 beginning

Exhibit 1–11

RUSTIC CAMP SITES
Income Statement
For the Year Ended December 31, 2005

Revenue *(asset increase)*	$96,000
Salary Expense *(asset decrease)*	(12,000)
Other Operating Expenses *(asset decrease)*	(40,000)
Net Income *(change in net assets)*	$44,000

Retained Earnings account balance resulting in an ending Retained Earnings balance of $70,000. Total stockholders' equity at the end of the period amounted to $210,000 ($140,000 common stock + $70,000 retained earnings).

The 2005 balance sheet is shown in Exhibit 1–13. This balance sheet shows that the company has $540,000 of assets of which $330,000 was borrowed from creditors, $140,000 was acquired from owners, and $70,000 was earned and retained in the business.

The 2005 statement of cash flows is shown in Exhibit 1–14. The operating activities section shows that $96,000 cash was received from revenue and $52,000 was paid for expenses. The net result was a $44,000 ($96,000 − $52,000) net cash inflow from operating activities. There were no investing activities. The financing activities section describes a $70,000 cash outflow to reduce debt, a $20,000 inflow from the issue of stock, and a $5,000 cash outflow for dividends paid to the owners. Accordingly, net cash outflow for financing activities amounted to $55,000 decrease [($70,000) + $20,000 + ($5,000)]. As a result, the net change in cash during 2005 was a decrease of $11,000 [$44,000 + ($55,000)]. The beginning cash balance of $51,000 minus the 2005 net decrease of $11,000 explains the ending cash balance of $40,000.

Stages of an Accounting Cycle

The complete accounting cycle contains several stages. To this point we have identified three distinct stages. Specifically, accounting data are recorded in accounts, the data are then used to make financial statements, and finally the nominal accounts are closed. After these three stages have been completed, a new cycle begins. Additional stages will be introduced as the text progresses. The three stages of the accounting cycle discussed to this point are depicted in the following illustration.

Record transactions

Close nominal accounts

Prepare statements

Exhibit 1–12

RUSTIC CAMP SITES
Statement of Changes in Stockholders' Equity
For the Year Ended December 31, 2005

Beginning Common Stock	$120,000	
Plus: Common Stock Issued	20,000	
Ending Common Stock		$140,000
Beginning Retained Earnings	31,000	
Plus: Net Income	44,000	
Less: Dividends	(5,000)	
Ending Retained Earnings		70,000
Total Stockholders' Equity		$210,000

Exhibit 1–13

RUSTIC CAMP SITES
Balance Sheet
As of December 31, 2005

Assets		
Cash	$ 40,000	
Land	500,000	
Total Assets		$540,000
Liabilities		
Notes Payable		$330,000
Stockholders' Equity		
Common Stock	$140,000	
Retained Earnings	70,000	
Total Stockholders' Equity		210,000
Total Liabilities and Stockholders' Equity		$540,000

Exhibit 1–14

RUSTIC CAMP SITES
Statement of Cash Flows
For the Year Ended December 31, 2005

Cash Flows from Operating Activities		
Cash Receipts from Revenue	$ 96,000	
Cash Payments for Expenses	(52,000)	
Net Cash Flow from Operating Activities		$ 44,000
Cash Flows from Investing Activities		0
Cash Flows from Financing Activities		
Cash Paid to Reduce Debt	(70,000)	
Cash Receipts from Stock Issue	20,000	
Cash Payments for Dividends	(5,000)	
Net Cash Flow from Financing Activities		(55,000)
Net Decrease in Cash		(11,000)
Plus Beginning Cash Balance		51,000
Ending Cash Balance		$ 40,000

Vertical Statements Model

As its name implies, the **vertical statements model** arranges a full set of financial statement information on a single page, with account titles arranged in a vertical pattern from the top to the bottom of the page. The income statement is presented first, and the statement of changes in stockholders' equity follows it. The balance sheet is presented directly below the statement of changes in stockholders' equity. Finally, the statement of cash flows is shown directly below the balance sheet. The 2004 and 2005 financial statements for Rustic Camp Sites are illustrated in the vertical statements model in Exhibit 1–15.

Exhibit 1–15 *Vertical Statements Model*

RUSTIC CAMP SITES
Financial Statements

For the Years	2004	2005
Income Statements		
Revenue	$ 85,000	$ 96,000
Expense	(50,000)	(52,000)
Net Income	$ 35,000	$ 44,000
Statements of Changes in Equity		
Beginning Common Stock	$ 0	$120,000
Plus: Stock Issue	120,000	20,000
Ending Common Stock	120,000	140,000
Beginning Retained Earnings	0	31,000
Plus: Net Income	35,000	44,000
Less: Dividends	(4,000)	(5,000)
Ending Retained Earnings	31,000	70,000
Total Stockholders' Equity	$151,000	$210,000
Balance Sheets		
Assets		
Cash	$ 51,000	$ 40,000
Land	500,000	500,000
Total Assets	$551,000	$540,000
Liabilities		
Notes Payable	$400,000	$330,000
Stockholders' Equity		
Common Stock	120,000	140,000
Retained Earnings	31,000	70,000
Total Stockholders' Equity	151,000	210,000
Total Liabilities and Stockholders' Equity	$551,000	$540,000
Statements of Cash Flows		
Cash Flows from Operating Activities		
Cash Receipts from Revenue	$ 85,000	$ 96,000
Cash Payments for Expenses	(50,000)	(52,000)
Net Cash Flows from Operating Activities	35,000	44,000
Cash Flows from Investing Activities		
Cash Payments to purchase Land	(500,000)	0
Cash Flows from Financing Activities		
Cash Receipts (Payments) for Borrowed Funds	400,000	(70,000)
Cash Receipts from Issue of Common Stock	120,000	20,000
Cash Payments for Dividends	(4,000)	(5,000)
Net Cash Flows from Financing Activities	516,000	(55,000)
Net Change in Cash	51,000	(11,000)
Plus Beginning Cash Balance	0	51,000
Ending Cash Balance	$ 51,000	$ 40,000

The vertical statements model enables you to visualize several important interrelationships among the financial statements over the two accounting cycles. Notice that the amount of net income is transferred to the statement of changes in stockholders' equity where it becomes part of the computation of the amount of ending retained earnings. The ending retained earnings is then shown on the balance sheet. By tracing these relationships, you can see how net income increases retained earnings. Also observe that last year's ending balances become this year's beginning balances. For example, the 2004 ending balance in the Retained Earnings account ($31,000) becomes the beginning balance for 2005. Finally, notice that the ending cash balance on the balance sheet is validated by the computations shown in the statement of cash flows. Specifically, the net change in cash is added to the beginning cash balance to produce the ending cash balance.

▌ Assessment of the Price of a Share of Stock

When you buy a share of stock, what do you really get? The stock certificate you receive is evidence of your right to share in the earnings of the company that issued the stock. The more the company earns, the more your wealth increases. This fact is evidenced by the willingness of investors to pay higher prices for companies with higher earnings potential. Indeed, the **price-earnings ratio,** frequently called the *P/E ratio,* is the most commonly reported measure of a company's value.

LO11 Calculate and explain the meaning of the price-earnings ratio.

Price-Earnings Ratio

The P/E ratio is computed by dividing the per share market price of the stock by the earnings per share (EPS).[3] To illustrate, assume that Western Company's stock is selling at $54 per share and that it produces earnings of $3 per share. In this case, Western's stock is selling at a P/E ratio of 18 ($54 investment ÷ $3 EPS). What does a P/E ratio of 18 mean? If Western continues to earn $3 per share of stock and pays all earnings out in the form of cash dividends, it would require 18 years for an investor to recover the price paid to obtain the stock. For comparison, assume that the Eastern Company's stock sells for $48 per share while its earnings per share are $4. This yields a P/E ratio of 12 ($48 investment ÷ $4 EPS). Under these circumstances, investors buying Eastern Company stock would get their money back 6 years more quickly (18 − 12) than investors who bought Western Company stock.

Why would investors buy a stock with a P/E ratio of 18 (Western Company) when they could buy one with a P/E ratio of 12 (Eastern Company)? If Western Company's earnings grow faster than Eastern's earnings, the higher P/E ratio could be justified. For example, suppose that Western Company's earnings double to $6 per share while Eastern's hold at $4 per share. Now the P/E ratio of Western drops to 9 ($54 investment ÷ $6 EPS) while Eastern's P/E ratio holds at 12 ($48 investment ÷ $4 EPS). This explains why high-growth companies sell for higher P/E multiples than do low-growth companies.

Measurement of Growth Through Percentage Analysis

An analysis of the 2002 and 2003 income statements of Cammeron, Inc., shows that earnings increased by $4.2 million. Comparable data for Diller Enterprises indicate earnings growth of $2.9 million. Does this mean that Cammeron is a better-managed company than Diller? The answer is not necessarily. It could mean that Cammeron is simply a larger company than Diller. Investors frequently use percentage analysis to compare companies of differing sizes on a level playing field. To illustrate, consider the following actual earnings data for the two companies:

---

[3]The amount of earnings per share is provided in the company's annual report. In its simplest form, it is computed by dividing the company's net income (net earnings) by the number of shares of outstanding common stock.

	2002*	2003*	Growth†
Cammeron	$42.4	$46.6	$4.2
Diller	9.9	12.8	2.9

*Earnings data shown in millions.
†Growth calculated by subtracting 2002 earnings from 2003 earnings.

The growth in earnings between 2002 and 2003 for the two companies can be measured in terms of a percentage by the following formula:

$$\frac{\text{Alternative year earnings} - \text{Base year earnings}}{\text{Base year earnings}} = \text{Percentage growth rate}$$

Cammeron, Inc.:

$$\frac{\$46.6 - \$42.4}{\$42.4} = 9.9\%$$

Diller Enterprises:

$$\frac{\$12.8 - \$9.9}{\$9.9} = 29.3\%$$

This analysis shows that although Cammeron is a larger company, Diller is growing much more rapidly. If this trend continues, Diller will eventually become a larger company with higher earnings than Cammeron. For this reason, investors value fast-growing companies. Indeed, the P/E ratios of real-world companies are highly correlated with their growth rates. This fact is demonstrated in the data reported in Exhibit 1–16. The data in this exhibit are based on the closing stock prices for July 10, 2001.

focus on International Issues

Is There Global GAAP?

This chapter introduces the fact that financial reporting is a measurement and communication discipline based on a set of rules referred to as *generally accepted accounting principles.* Business students must be aware that the accounting rules that are the primary focus of this course are based on the GAAP of the United States. Not all economies throughout the world use the same accounting rules. Although there are many similarities among the GAAP used in different countries, there also are major differences. There have been attempts to create

international accounting standards, but individual countries have retained the authority to establish their own GAAP. Simply put, each country has its own GAAP; there is no single "global GAAP." Throughout this book, text examples of how financial reporting in other countries differ from those in the United States are presented.

Accounting rules differ among countries due to a variety of factors, including the economic and legal environments that exist in each country and how the GAAP in that country is established. Generally accepted accounting principles in the United States are primarily established by the Financial Accounting Standards Board (FASB). The FASB is a nongovernment rule-making body that was established by the accounting profession. In some countries, Germany and Japan, for example, the GAAP is established by government bodies. Thus, the establishment of GAAP in these countries is more like the way federal laws and regulations are established in the United States.

Furthermore, in the United States there is very little connection between GAAP established by the FASB and tax accounting regulations established by Congress and the Internal Revenue Service (IRS). As discussed in Chapter 8, in some countries there is a close connection between tax accounting rules and GAAP.

Exhibit 1–16 *Real-World Price/Earnings Ratios and Growth Rates*		
	Price/Earnings Ratio	Average Annual Revenue Growth, 1998–2000
High-growth companies		
Oracle	39	20.9%
Dell	32	37.4
Medium-growth companies		
DuPont	24	7.1
Minnesota Mining & Manufacturing (3M)	24	5.4
Low-growth companies		
Burlington Northern Santa Fe	13	0.8
CSX Corp	14	(6.8)

Real-World Financial Reports

Organizations exist in many different forms. As previously indicated, two major classifications include *business* and *not-for-profit* entities. Business entities can be further subdivided into three categories: service, merchandising, and manufacturing. As the name implies, **service organizations** provide services to consumers. Service providers include doctors, attorneys, accountants, dry cleaners, and maids. **Merchandising businesses** are sometimes called *retail* or *wholesale companies;* they sell goods that other entities make. **Manufacturing companies** make the goods that they sell to their customers. Some businesses include combinations of these three categories. For example, an automotive repair shop might change oil (service function), sell parts such as oil filters (retail function), and rebuild engines or other parts (manufacturing function).

The nature of the reporting **entity** affects the form and content of the information contained in the entity's financial statements. For example, not-for-profit entities prepare statements of revenues, expenditures, and changes in fund equity while business entities produce income statements. Similarly, income statements of retail companies show an expense item called *cost of goods sold,* but service companies that do not sell goods have no such item in their income statements. Accordingly, you should expect some degree of diversity when viewing real-world financial statements.

LO12 Identify the major components of real-world annual reports and some of the technical terms used in them.

Annual Report for Dell Computer Corporation

Organizations normally provide information, including financial statements, to *stakeholders* yearly in a document known as an **annual report.** Appendix B to this text contains the annual

report for Dell Computer Corporation. This report contains the company's financial statements (see pages 27–30 of the report). Immediately following the statements are footnotes that provide more detailed information about the items described in the statements (see pages 31–48). In addition to financial statements, the annual report contains the *auditor's report,* discussed in Chapter 2. Annual reports also include written commentary that describes management's assessment of significant events that affected the company during the reporting period. This section of an annual report, called *management's discussion and analysis* (MD&A), is explained in Chapter 4.

Dell's annual report is the Form 10K that it submits to the U.S. Securities and Exchange Commission (SEC). The SEC is discussed in more detail in Chapter 4. Dell is famous for keeping its business expenses low. Traditionally, most large companies have distributed elaborate annual reports with many color photographs. However, these reports are very expensive to produce and distribute. Increasingly, companies are issuing more modest annual reports, or, like Dell, are simply distributing their 10K to shareholders and other interested parties.

Special Terms in Real-World Reports

The financial statements of real-world companies contain numerous items relating to advanced topics that are not covered in introductory accounting textbooks, especially the first chapter of an introductory accounting textbook. Do not let this discourage you from browsing through real-world annual reports. Indeed, your learning will significantly improve if you look at many annual reports and attempt to identify all the items that your current knowledge permits. As your academic knowledge grows, most likely you will experience a corresponding increase in interest in real-world financial reports and the business practices they describe. We encourage you to look up annual reports in your local library or ask your employer for a copy of your company's report. The Internet provides another excellent source for obtaining annual reports. Most companies provide links on their home page that lead to their annual reports. Look for links that are titled "about the company" or "investor relations" or other logical phrases that will lead to the company's financial reports. The best way to learn accounting is to become involved. Look at accounting information, and ask questions about things you do not understand. Accounting is the language of business. Learning the language will serve you well in almost any area of business that you pursue.

a look back

This chapter discussed the role of accounting in society and business. Accounting's role is to provide information that facilitates the ability to operate and evaluate organizational performance. Accounting is a measurement discipline. To facilitate communication, it is necessary to attain agreement on the rules of measurement. *Generally accepted accounting principles (GAAP)* constitute the set of rules used by the accounting profession in the United States to promote consistency in financial reporting. GAAP is a work in progress that will continue to evolve.

The chapter has described and discussed eight elements of financial statements: *assets, liabilities, equity, common stock (contributed capital), revenue, expenses, dividends,* and *net income.* The elements represent broad classifications of information that appear on financial statements. Four basic financial statements appear in public reports: the *balance sheet,* the *income statement,* the *statement of changes in stockholders' equity,* and the *statement of cash flows.* The chapter discussed the form and content of each statement as well as the interrelationships among the statements.

This chapter introduced a *horizontal financial statements model* as a tool to facilitate your understanding of how business events affect a set of financial statements. This model will be used throughout the text. Accordingly, you should carefully study this model before proceeding to Chapter 2.

To keep matters simple and to focus attention on the interrelationships among financial statements, this chapter considered only cash events. Obviously, many real-world events do not involve an immediate cash exchange. An example of a noncash event is a customer's use of telephone service throughout the month without paying for it until the end of the month. As mentioned briefly in this chapter, events such as this are called *accruals*. Understanding the effects that accrual events have on the financial statements is the subject of Chapter 2.

a look
forward

SELF-STUDY REVIEW PROBLEM

During 2006 Rustic Camp Sites experienced the following transactions.
1. RCS acquired $32,000 cash by issuing common stock.
2. RCS received $116,000 cash for providing services to customers.
3. RCS paid $13,000 cash for salaries expenses.
4. RCS paid a $9,000 cash dividend to the owners.
5. RCS sold land that had cost $100,000 for $100,000 cash.
6. RCS paid $47,000 cash for other operating expenses.

Required

a. Record the transaction data in a horizontal financial statements model like the following one. In the Cash Flow column, classify the cash flows as operating activities (OA), investing activities (IA), or financing activities (FA). The beginning balances have been recorded as an example. They are the ending balances shown on RCS's December 31, 2005, financial statements illustrated in the chapter.

	Balance Sheet									Income Statement					Statement of Cash Flows
	Assets			=	Liab.	+	Stockholders' Equity								
Event No.	Cash	+	Land	=	N. Pay	+	C. Stk.	+	Ret. Ear.	Rev.	−	Exp.	=	Net Inc.	
Bal.	40,000	+	500,000	=	330,000	+	140,000	+	70,000	NA	−	NA	=	NA	NA

b. Explain why there are no beginning balances in the Income Statement columns.
c. What amount of net income will RCS report on the 2006 income statement?
d. What amount of total assets will RCS report on the December 31, 2006, balance sheet?
e. What amount of retained earnings will RCS report on the December 31, 2006, balance sheet?
f. What amount of net cash flow from operating activities will RCS report on the 2006 statement of cash flows?
g. Assume that RCS has 20,000 shares of common stock outstanding that is selling at a market price of $33.60 per share. Determine the company's P/E ratio. Based on the information shown in Exhibit 1–16, indicate whether investors believe RCS has a high-, medium-, or low-earnings growth potential.

Answer
a.

	Balance Sheet									Income Statement					Statement of Cash Flows	
Event No.	Assets			=	Liab.	+	Stockholders' Equity									
	Cash	+	Land	=	N. Pay	+	C. Stk.	+	Ret. Ear.	Rev.	−	Exp.	=	Net Inc.		
Bal.	40,000	+	500,000	=	330,000	+	140,000	+	70,000	NA	−	NA	=	NA	NA	
1	32,000	+	NA	=	NA	+	32,000	+	NA	NA	−	NA	=	NA	32,000	FA
2	116,000	+	NA	=	NA	+	NA	+	116,000	116,000	−	NA	=	116,000	116,000	OA
3	(13,000)	+	NA	=	NA	+	NA	+	(13,000)	NA	−	13,000	=	(13,000)	(13,000)	OA
4	(9,000)	+	NA	=	NA	+	NA	+	(9,000)	NA	−	NA	=	NA	(9,000)	FA
5	100,000	+	(100,000)	=	NA	+	NA	+	NA	NA	−	NA	=	NA	100,000	IA
6	(47,000)	+	NA	=	NA	+	NA	+	(47,000)	NA	−	47,000	=	(47,000)	(47,000)	OA
Totals	219,000	+	400,000	=	330,000	+	172,000	+	117,000	116,000	−	60,000	=	56,000	179,000	NC*

*The letters NC on the last line of the column designate the net change in cash flow.

b. The revenue and expense accounts are temporary accounts used to capture data for a single accounting period. They are closed (amounts removed from the accounts) at the end of the accounting period and therefore always have zero balances at the beginning of the accounting cycle.

c. RCS will report net income of $56,000 on the 2006 income statement. Compute this amount by subtracting the expenses from the revenue ($116,000 Revenue − $13,000 Salaries expenses − $47,000 Other operating expense).

d. RCS will report total assets of $619,000 on the December 31, 2006, balance sheet. Compute total assets by adding the cash amount to the land amount ($219,000 Cash + $400,000 Land).

e. RCS will report retained earnings of $117,000 on the December 31, 2006 balance sheet. Compute this amount using the following formula: Beginning retained earnings + Net income − Dividends = Ending retained earnings. In this case, $70,000 + $56,000 − $9,000 = $117,000.

f. Net cash flow from operating activities is the difference between the amount of cash collected from revenue and the amount of cash spent for expenses. In this case, $116,000 cash inflow from revenue − $13,000 cash outflow for salaries expenses − $47,000 cash outflow for other operating expenses = $56,000 net cash inflow from operating activities.

g. Earnings per share = Net earnings ÷ Number of shares outstanding = $56,000 ÷ 20,000 shares = $2.80 per share. Price/Earning ratio = Market price per share ÷ Earnings per share = $33.60 ÷ $2.80 = 12 times. Based on the information in Exhibit 1–16, a P/E ratio of 12 indicates that investors see RCS as a company with medium earnings growth potential.

KEY TERMS

Account *9*
Accounting *3*
Accounting equation *10*
Accounting event *13*
Accounting period *18*
Annual report *25*
Asset *10*
Asset source transaction *14*
Balance sheet *18*
Claims *10*
Closing the accounts *19*
Common stock *10*
Creditor *5*
Dividend *12*
Double-entry bookkeeping *14*
Earnings *4*
Elements *9*
Entity *25*
Equity *10*

Financial accounting *6*
Financial Accounting
  Standards Board
  (FASB) *9*
Financial resources *5*
Financial statements *9*
Financing activities *12*
General ledger *17*
Generally accepted accounting
  principles (GAAP) *8*
Horizontal statements
  model *13*
Income *4*
Income statement *11*
Interest *6*
Investing activities *12*
Investors *5*
Labor resources *6*
Liabilities *10*

Liquidation *5*
Liquidity *18*
Managerial accounting *6*
Manufacturing companies *25*
Market *4*
Merchandising
  businesses *25*
Net assets *10*
Net income *11*
Net loss *11*
Nominal accounts *19*
Not-for-profit entities *7*
Operating activities *12*
Permanent accounts *19*
Physical resources *6*
Price-earnings ratio *23*
Productive assets *12*
Profit *4*
Reporting entities *8*

Residual interest *10*
Retained earnings *11, 15*
Revenue *11*
Service organizations *25*
Stakeholders *4*
Statement of cash flows *12*
Statement of changes in
  stockholders' equity *18*
Statements model *17*
Stockholders *11*
Stockholders' equity *11*
Temporary accounts *19*
Transaction *13*
Users *4*
Vertical statements
  model *21*

QUESTIONS

1. Explain the term *stakeholder.* Distinguish between stakeholders with a direct versus an indirect interest in the companies that issue accounting reports.

2. Why is accounting called the *language of business?*

3. What is the primary mechanism used to allocate resources in the United States?

4. In a business context, what does the term *market* mean?

5. What market trilogy components are involved in the process of transforming resources into finished products?

6. Give an example of a financial resource, a physical resource, and a labor resource.

7. What type of income or profit does an investor expect to receive in exchange for providing financial resources to a business? What type of income does a creditor expect from providing financial resources to an organization or business?

8. How do financial and managerial accounting differ?

9. Describe a not-for-profit or nonprofit enterprise. What is the motivation for this type of entity?
10. What are the U.S. rules of accounting information measurement called?
11. How does establishing GAAP in the United States differ from establishing accounting principles in Japan and Germany?
12. What body has the primary responsibility for establishing GAAP in the United States?
13. Distinguish between elements of financial statements and accounts.
14. What is the most basic form of the accounting equation?
15. What role do assets play in business profitability?
16. To whom do the assets of a business belong?
17. What is the nature of creditors' claims on assets?
18. What does *residual interest* mean? Identify two other terms that describe the residual interest.
19. What term describes creditors' claims on the assets of a business?
20. What is the accounting equation? Describe each of its three components.
21. Who ultimately bears the risk and collects the rewards associated with operating a business?
22. What does a *double-entry bookkeeping system* mean?
23. Identify the four types of accounting transactions. Provide an example of each type of transaction, and explain how it affects the accounting equation.
24. How does acquiring capital from owners affect the accounting equation?
25. What is the difference between assets that are acquired by issuing common stock and those that are acquired using retained earnings?
26. How does earning revenue affect the accounting equation?
27. Which accounts are closed at the end of an accounting period?
28. What are the three primary sources of assets?
29. What is the source of retained earnings?
30. How does distributing assets (paying dividends) to owners affect the accounting equation?
31. What are the similarities and differences between dividends and expenses?
32. What four general-purpose financial statements do business enterprises use?
33. Which of the general-purpose financial statements provides information about the enterprise at a specific designated date?
34. Explain why revenue, expense, and dividend accounts have zero balances at the beginning of each accounting period.
35. What causes a net loss?
36. What three categories of cash receipts and cash payments do businesses report on the statement of cash flows? Explain the types of cash flows reported in each category.
37. How are asset accounts usually arranged in the balance sheet?
38. What is the difference between a permanent account and a nominal account?
39. What type of information does a business typically include in its annual report?
40. Identify and discuss the three stages of an accounting cycle that this chapter introduced.

EXERCISES—SERIES A

EXERCISE 1–1A *Identifying Financial Statements*

L.O. 1, 2, 4

Accounting reports prepared for public use normally include four financial statements.

Required
Provide the names of the four financial statements and alternative names for any statements that have them.

EXERCISE 1–2A *Understanding Markets*

L.O. 1, 2

Free economies use open markets to allocate resources.

Required
Identify the three participants in a free business market. Write a brief memo explaining how these participants interact to ensure that goods and services are distributed in a manner that satisfies consumers.

EXERCISE 1–3A *Components of the Accounting Equation*

L.O. 6

Required
The following three requirements are independent of each other.

a. Wilson Auto Parts has assets of $6,200 and net assets of $1,200. What is the amount of liabilities? What is the amount of claims?

b. Clarke Juices, Inc., has liabilities of $1,200 and equity of $4,400. What is the amount of assets? What is the amount of net assets?

c. Ted's Tennis Shop has assets of $56,700 and liabilities of $32,300. What is the amount of its equity? What is the amount of its net assets?

L.O. 1   EXERCISE 1–4A *Distributions in a Business Liquidation*

Assume that McNeal Company acquires $400 cash from creditors and $600 cash from investors (stockholders). The company then has an operating loss of $500 cash and goes out of business.

Required
a. Define the term *business liquidation.*
b. What amount of cash will McNeal's creditors receive?
c. What amount of cash will McNeal's investors (stockholders) receive?

L.O. 6   EXERCISE 1–5A *Effect of Events on the Accounting Equation*

Solar Enterprises experienced the following events during 2006.
1. Acquired cash from the issue of common stock.
2. Provided services to clients for cash.
3. Paid operating expenses with cash.
4. Borrowed cash.
5. Purchased land with cash.
6. Paid a cash dividend to the stockholders.

Required
Explain how each of these events affect the accounting equation by writing the letter I for increase, the letter D for decrease, and NA for no effect under each of the components of the accounting equation. The first event is shown as an example.

| | | | | Stockholders' Equity | |
Event Number	Assets	= Liabilities +	Common Stock +	Retained Earnings
1	I	NA	I	NA

L.O. 7   EXERCISE 1–6A *Effect of Events on a Horizontal Financial Statements Model*

Greer Consulting Services experienced the following events during 2006.
1. Acquired cash by issuing common stock.
2. Collected cash for providing tutoring services to clients.
3. Paid cash for operating expenses.
4. Borrowed cash from a local government small business foundation.
5. Purchased land for cash.
6. Paid a cash dividend to the stockholders.

Required
Use a horizontal statements model to show how each event affects the balance sheet, income statement, and statement of cash flows. Indicate whether the event increases (I), decreases (D), or does not affect (NA) each element of the financial statements. Also, in the Cash Flows column, classify the cash flows as operating activities (OA), investing activities (IA), or financing activities (FA). The first transaction is shown as an example.

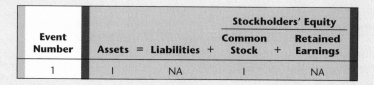

Event No.	Balance Sheet								Income Statement						Statement of Cash Flows
	Cash	+	Land	=	N. Pay	+	C. Stock.	+	Ret. Ear.	Rev.	−	Exp.	=	Net Inc.	
1.	I	+	NA	=	NA	+	I	+	NA	NA	−	NA	=	NA	I FA

EXERCISE 1–7A *Effects of Issuing Stock*   **L.O. 6, 9**

Chia Company was started in 2009 when it acquired $12,000 cash by issuing common stock. The cash acquisition was the only event that affected the business in 2009.

Required

Write an accounting equation, and record the effects of the stock issue under the appropriate general ledger account headings.

EXERCISE 1–8A *Effects of Borrowing*   **L.O. 6, 9**

Northern Rockies Company was started in 2007 when it issued a note to borrow $7,200 cash.

Required

Write an accounting equation, and record the effects of the borrowing transaction under the appropriate general ledger account headings.

EXERCISE 1–9A *Effects of Revenue, Expense, and Dividend Events*   **L.O. 4, 5, 6, 9**

Kwon Company was started on January 1, 2005. During 2005, the company experienced the following three accounting events: (1) earned cash revenues of $9,500, (2) paid cash expenses of $5,800, and (3) paid a $700 cash dividend to its stockholders. These were the only events that affected the company during 2005.

Required

a. Write an accounting equation, and record the effects of each accounting event under the appropriate general ledger account headings.
b. Prepare an income statement for the 2005 accounting period and a balance sheet at the end of 2005 for Kwon Company.
c. What is the name of the practice of transferring the balances from the revenue, expense, and dividend accounts to the Retained Earnings account at the end of an accounting period?

EXERCISE 1–10A *Record Events in the Horizontal Statements Model*   **L.O. 7, 9**

Maulder Mechanics was started in 2001. During 2001, the company (1) acquired $7,000 cash from the issue of common stock, (2) earned cash revenue of $14,000, (3) paid cash expenses of $6,800, and (4) paid a $1,000 cash dividend to the stockholders.

Required

a. Record these four events in a horizontal statements model. Also, in the Cash Flows column, classify the cash flows as operating activities (OA), investing activities (IA), or financing activities (FA). The first event is shown as an example.

Event No.		Balance Sheet						Income Statement				Statement of Cash Flows
	Cash	=	N. Pay	+	C. Stock.	+	Ret. Ear.	Rev.	− Exp.	=	Net Inc.	
1.	7,000	=	NA	+	7,000	+	NA	NA	− NA	=	NA	7,000 FA

b. What does the income statement tell you about the assets of this business?

EXERCISE 1–11A *Classifying Items for the Statement of Cash Flows*   **L.O. 5**

Required

Indicate how each of the following would be classified on the statement of cash flows as operating activities (OA), investing activities (IA), financing activities (FA), or not applicable (NA).
a. Paid $2,000 cash for salary expense.
b. Borrowed $5,000 cash from First State Bank.
c. Received $25,000 cash from the issue of common stock.
d. Purchased land for $6,000 cash.
e. Performed services for $12,000 cash.
f. Paid $2,400 cash for utilities expense.
g. Sold land for $4,000 cash.
h. Paid a cash dividend of $1,000 to the stockholders.
i. Hired an accountant to keep the books.
j. Paid $2,000 cash on the loan from First State Bank.

L.O. 4, 9 **EXERCISE 1–12A** *Effect of Transactions on General Ledger Accounts*

At the beginning of 2001, Sani Service Company's accounting records had the following general ledger accounts and balances.

Sani Service Company Accounting Equation							
Event	Assets		=	Liabilities	+	Stockholders' Equity		Acct. Titles for RE
	Cash	Land		Notes Payable		Common Stock	Retained Earnings	
Balance 1/1/2001	25,000	50,000		35,000		30,000	10,000	

Sani completed the following transactions during 2001:
1. Purchased land for $10,000 cash.
2. Acquired $15,000 cash from the issue of common stock.
3. Received $55,000 cash for providing services to customers.
4. Paid cash operating expenses of $38,000.
5. Paid $20,000 cash to creditors.
6. Paid a $3,000 cash dividend to the stockholders.

Required
a. Record the transactions in the appropriate general ledger accounts. Record the amounts of revenue, expense, and dividends in the Retained Earnings column. Provide the appropriate titles for these accounts in the last column of the table.
b. Determine the amount of net income for the 2001 period.
c. What is the amount of total assets at the end of 2001? What is the amount of net assets at the end of 2001?

L.O. 4, 6, 9 **EXERCISE 1–13A** *Preparing Financial Statements*

Kerry Company experienced the following events during 2002.
1. Acquired $25,000 cash from the issue of common stock.
2. Paid $9,000 cash to purchase land.
3. Borrowed $5,000 cash.
4. Provided services for $12,000 cash.
5. Paid $500 cash for rent expense.
6. Paid $7,000 cash for other operating expenses.
7. Paid a $2,000 cash dividend to the stockholders.

Required
a. The January 1, 2002, general ledger account balances are shown in the following accounting equation. Record the seven events in the appropriate general ledger accounts. Record the amounts of revenue, expense, and dividends in the Retained Earnings column. Provide the appropriate titles for these accounts in the last column of the table. The first event is shown as an example.

Kerry Company Accounting Equation							
Event	Assets		=	Liabilities	+	Stockholders' Equity		Acct. Titles for RE
	Cash	Land		Notes Payable		Common Stock	Retained Earnings	
Balance 1/1/2002	2,000	16,000		0		10,000	8,000	
1.	25,000					25,000		

b. Prepare an income statement, statement of changes in equity, year-end balance sheet, and statement of cash flows for the 2002 accounting period.

c. What are the balances in the revenue, expense, and dividend accounts on January 1, 2003?

EXERCISE 1–14A *Effect of Events on a Horizontal Statements Model*   **L.O. 5, 7**

Tax Time, Inc., was started on January 1, 2004. The company experienced the following events during its first year of operation.

1. Acquired $30,000 cash from the issue of common stock.
2. Paid $9,000 cash to purchase land.
3. Received $28,000 cash for providing tax services to customers.
4. Paid $9,500 cash for salary expenses.
5. Acquired $5,000 cash from the issue of additional common stock.
6. Borrowed $10,000 cash from the bank.
7. Purchased additional land for $5,000 cash.
8. Paid $6,000 cash for other operating expenses.
9. Paid a $2,800 cash dividend to the stockholders.

Required

a. Record these events in a horizontal statements model. Also, in the Cash Flows column, classify the cash flows as operating activities (OA), investing activities (IA), or financing activities (FA). The first event is shown as an example.

Event No.	Balance Sheet											Income Statement						Statement of Cash Flows	
	Cash	+	Land	=	N. Pay	+	C. Stock.	+	Ret. Ear.			Rev.	−	Exp.	=	Net Inc.			
1.	30,000	+	NA	=	NA	+	30,000	+	NA			NA	−	NA	=	NA		30,000	FA

b. What is the net income earned in 2004?
c. What is the amount of total assets at the end of 2004?
d. What is the net cash flow from operating activities for 2004?
e. What is the net cash flow from investing activities for 2004?
f. What is the net cash flow from financing activities for 2004?
g. What is the cash balance at the end of 2004?

EXERCISE 1–15A *Titles and Accounts Appearing on Financial Statements*   **L.O. 4, 5**

Annual reports normally include an income statement, a statement of changes in stockholders' equity, a balance sheet, and a statement of cash flows.

Required

Identify the financial statements on which each of the following titles or accounts would appear. If a title or an account appears on more than one statement, list all statements that would include it.

a. Common Stock
b. Land
c. Ending Cash Balance
d. Beginning Cash Balance
e. Notes Payable
f. Retained Earnings
g. Revenue
h. Dividends
i. Financing Activities
j. Salary Expense

EXERCISE 1–16A *Closing the Accounts*   **L.O. 3, 4**

The following information was drawn from the accounting records of Pearson Company as of December 31, 2007, before the nominal accounts had been closed. The Cash balance was $3,000, and Notes Payable amounted to $2,500. The company had revenues of $4,000 and expenses of $2,500. The company's Land account had a $5,000 balance. Dividends amounted to $500. There was $1,000 of common stock issued.

Required
a. Identify which accounts would be classified as permanent and which accounts would be classified as nominal (temporary).
b. Assuming that Pearson's beginning balance (as of January 1, 2007) in the Retained Earnings account was $3,500, determine its balance after the nominal accounts were closed at the end of 2007.
c. What amount of net income would Pearson Company report on its 2007 income statement?
d. Explain why the amount of net income differs from the amount of the ending Retained Earnings balance.
e. What are the balances in the revenue, expense, and dividend accounts on January 1, 2008?

L.O. 10 **EXERCISE 1–17A** *Closing Accounts and the Accounting Cycle*

Required
a. Identify which of the following accounts are temporary (will be closed to Retained Earnings at the end of the year) and which are permanent.
  1. Cash
  2. Salaries Expense
  3. Notes Payable
  4. Utilities Expense
  5. Service Revenue
  6. Dividends
  7. Common Stock
  8. Land
  9. Interest Revenue
  10. Retained Earnings
b. List and explain the three stages of the accounting cycle. Which stage must be first? Which stage is last?

L.O. 8 **EXERCISE 1–18A** *Classifying Events as Asset Source, Use, or Exchange*

Jacobs Company experienced the following events during its first year of operations.
  1. Acquired $6,000 cash from the issue of common stock.
  2. Borrowed $8,000 cash from First Bank.
  3. Paid $3,000 cash to purchase land.
  4. Received $4,500 cash for providing boarding services.
  5. Acquired an additional $2,000 cash from the issue of common stock.
  6. Purchased additional land for $3,500 cash.
  7. Paid $2,200 cash for salary expenses.
  8. Signed a contract to provide additional services in the future.
  9. Paid $1,000 cash for rent expense.
  10. Paid a $1,000 cash dividend to the stockholders.

Required
Classify each event as an asset source, use, or exchange transaction or as not applicable (NA).

L.O. 7, 8, 9 **EXERCISE 1–19A** *Types of Transactions and the Horizontal Statements Model*

Better Sports experienced the following events during its first year of operations, 2008.
  1. Acquired cash by issuing common stock.
  2. Provided services and collected cash.
  3. Borrowed cash from a bank.
  4. Paid cash for operating expenses.
  5. Purchased land with cash.
  6. Paid a cash dividend to the stockholders.

Required
a. Indicate whether each event is an asset source, use, or exchange transaction.
b. Use a horizontal statements model to show how each event affects the balance sheet, income statement, and statement of cash flows. Indicate whether the event increases (I), decreases (D), or does not

affect (NA) each element of the financial statements. Also, in the Cash column, classify the cash flows as operating activities (OA), investing activities (IA), or financing activities (FA). The first transaction is shown as an example.

Event No.	Balance Sheet								Income Statement			Statement of Cash Flows	
	Cash	+	Land	=	N. Pay	+	C. Stock.	+	Ret. Ear.	Rev.	−	Exp.	=	Net Inc.		
1.	I	+	NA	=	NA	+	I	+	NA	NA	−	NA	=	NA	I	FA

EXERCISE 1–20A *Relating Accounting Events to Entities*   L.O. 5, 8

Dundee Company was started in 2004 when it acquired $80,000 cash by issuing common stock to Don Sinclair.

Required
a. Was this event an asset source, use, or exchange transaction for Dundee Company?
b. Was this event an asset source, use, or exchange transaction for Don Sinclair?
c. Was the cash flow an operating, investing, or financing activity on Dundee Company's 2004 statement of cash flows?
d. Was the cash flow an operating, investing, or financing activity on Don Sinclair's 2004 statement of cash flows?

EXERCISE 1–21A *Missing Information in the Accounting Equation*   L.O. 6

Required
Calculate the missing amounts in the following table:

Company	Assets	=	Liabilities	+	Stockholders' Equity		
					Common Stock	+	Retained Earnings
A	$?		$48,000		$52,000		$36,000
B	90,000		?		25,000		40,000
C	87,000		15,000		?		37,000
D	102,000		29,000		42,000		?

EXERCISE 1–22A *Missing Information in the Accounting Equation*   L.O. 6

As of December 31, 2002, Betts Company had total assets of $156,000, total liabilities of $85,600, and common stock of $48,400. During 2003 Betts earned $22,000 of cash revenue, paid $12,500 for cash expenses, and paid a $500 cash dividend to the stockholders.

Required
a. Determine the amount of retained earnings as of December 31, 2002.
b. Determine the amount of net income earned in 2003.
c. Determine the amount of retained earnings as of December 31, 2003.

EXERCISE 1–23A *Missing Information for Determining Net Income*   L.O. 5, 6

The December 31, 2006, balance sheet for Trebing Company showed total stockholders' equity of $62,500. Total stockholders' equity increased by $53,400 between December 31, 2006, and December 31, 2007. During 2007 Trebing Company acquired $11,000 cash from the issue of common stock. Trebing Company paid an $8,000 cash dividend to the stockholders during 2007.

Required
Determine the amount of net income or loss Trebing reported on its 2007 income statement. (*Hint:* Remember that stock issues, net income, and dividends all change total stockholders' equity.)

L.O. 11 **EXERCISE 1–24A** *Price-Earnings Ratio*

The following information is available for two companies.

	Henry Company	Pager Company
Earnings per share	$ 1.05	$ 4.50
Market price per share	38.50	108.00

Required
a. Compute the price-earnings ratio for each company.
b. Explain why one company would have a higher price-earnings ratio than the other.

PROBLEMS—SERIES A

L.O. 7 **PROBLEM 1–25A** *Recording the Effect of Events in a Horizontal Statements Model*

Lighthouse Services experienced the following transactions during 2006.
1. Acquired cash by issuing common stock.
2. Borrowed cash from the local bank.
3. Received cash for performing services.
4. Paid cash expenses.
5. Purchased land for cash.
6. Paid cash to reduce the principal balance of the bank loan.
7. Paid a cash dividend to the stockholders.

Required
Use a horizontal statements model to show how each event affects the balance sheet, income statement, and statement of cash flows. Indicate whether the event increases (I), decreases (D), or does not affect (NA) each element of the financial statements. Also, in the Cash Flows column, classify the cash flows as operating activities (OA), investing activities (IA), or financing activities (FA). The first transaction is shown as an example.

Event No.	Balance Sheet													Income Statement						Statement of Cash Flows	
	Cash	+	Land	=	N. Pay	+	C. Stock.	+	Ret. Ear.					Rev.	–	Exp.	=	Net Inc.			
1.	I	+	NA	=	NA	+	I	+	NA					NA	–	NA	=	NA		I	FA

L.O. 5, 7 **PROBLEM 1–26A** *Recording Events in a Horizontal Statements Model*

Marx Company was started on January 1, 2003, and experienced the following events during its first year of operation.
1. Acquired $24,000 cash from the issue of common stock.
2. Borrowed $16,000 cash from State Bank.
3. Earned cash revenues of $36,000 for performing services.
4. Paid cash expenses of $25,000.
5. Paid a $4,000 cash dividend to the stockholders.
6. Acquired an additional $20,000 cash from the issue of common stock.
7. Paid $5,000 cash to reduce the principal balance of the bank note.
8. Paid $53,000 cash to purchase land.

Required
a. Record the preceding transactions in the horizontal statements model. Also, in the Cash Flows column, classify the cash flows as operating activities (OA), investing activities (IA), or financing activities (FA). The first event is shown as an example.

Event No.	Balance Sheet													Income Statement						Statement of Cash Flows	
	Cash	+	Land	=	N. Pay	+	C. Stock.	+	Ret. Ear.					Rev.	–	Exp.	=	Net Inc.			
1.	24,000	+	NA	=	NA	+	24,000	+	NA					NA	–	NA	=	NA		24,000	FA

b. Determine the amount of total assets that Marx would report on the December 31, 2003, balance sheet.

c. Identify the sources of the assets that Marx would report on the December 31, 2003, balance sheet. Determine the amount of each of these sources.

d. Determine the net income that Marx would report on the 2003 income statement. Explain why dividends do not appear on the income statement.

e. Determine the net cash flows from operating activities, financing activities, and investing activities that Marx would report on the 2003 statement of cash flows.

PROBLEM 1–27A *Preparing Financial Statements for Two Complete Accounting Cycles*

L.O. 4, 5, 6, 9

Reynolds Consulting experienced the following transactions for 2006, its first year of operations, and 2007. *Assume that all transactions involve the receipt or payment of cash.*

Transactions for 2006

1. Acquired $25,000 by issuing common stock.
2. Received $72,000 for providing services to customers.
3. Borrowed $16,000 from creditors.
4. Paid expenses amounting to $50,000.
5. Purchased land for $44,000.

Transactions for 2007

1. Acquired an additional $24,000 from the issue of common stock.
2. Received $94,000 for providing services.
3. Paid $10,000 to creditors to reduce debt principal.
4. Paid expenses amounting to $71,500.
5. Paid a $6,000 dividend to the stockholders.

Required

a. Write an accounting equation, and record the effects of each accounting event under the appropriate headings for each year. Record the amounts of revenue, expense, and dividends in the Retained Earnings column. Provide appropriate titles for these accounts in the last column of the table.

b. Prepare an income statement, statement of changes in stockholders' equity, year-end balance sheet, and statement of cash flows for each year. Use the vertical format when you prepare the financial statements.

c. Examine the balance sheets for the two years. How did assets change from 2006 to 2007?

d. Determine the percentage growth in net earnings from 2006 to 2007. Based on the data shown in Exhibit 1–16, is this a high-, medium-, or low-growth company?

PROBLEM 1–28A *Interrelationships among Financial Statements*

L.O. 4, 5

Chase Enterprises started the 2002 accounting period with $30,000 of assets (all cash), $18,000 of liabilities, and $4,000 of common stock. During the year, Chase earned cash revenues of $36,000, paid cash expenses of $23,000, and paid a cash dividend to stockholders of $2,000. Chase also acquired $10,000 of additional cash from the sale of common stock and paid $6,000 cash to reduce the liability owed to a bank.

Required

Prepare an income statement, statement of changes in stockholders' equity, period-end balance sheet, and statement of cash flows for the 2002 accounting period. (*Hint:* Determine the amount of beginning retained earnings before considering the effects of the current period events. It also might help to record all events under an accounting equation before preparing the statements.)

PROBLEM 1–29A *Relating Titles and Accounts to Financial Statements*

L.O. 5

Required

Identify the financial statements on which each of the following items (titles, date descriptions, and accounts) appears by placing a check mark in the appropriate column. If an item appears on more than one statement, place a check mark in every applicable column.

Item	Income Statement	Statement of Changes in Stockholders' Equity	Balance Sheet	Statement of Cash Flows
Ending cash balance				
Salary expense				
Consulting revenue				
Dividends				
Financing activities				
Ending common stock				
Interest expense				
As of (date)				
Land				
Beginning cash balance				
Notes payable				
Beginning common stock				
Service revenue				
Utility expense				
Cash from stock issue				
Operating activities				
For the period ended (date)				
Net income				
Investing activities				
Net loss				

L.O. 4, 5, 7, 10   **PROBLEM 1–30A** *Closing the Accounts*

The following accounts and account balances were taken from the records of Green View Company. Except as otherwise indicated, all balances are as of December 31, 2004, before the closing entries had been recorded.

Cash Received from Common Stock Issued during 2004	$ 3,500
Cash	7,800
Revenue	7,400
Salary Expense	2,900
Cash Flow from Operating Activities	2,500
Notes Payable	2,000
Utility Expense	600
Dividends	1,200
Cash Flow from Financing Activities	2,300
Rent Expense	1,400
Land	20,200
Retained Earnings, January 1, 2004	14,700
Common Stock, December 31, 2004	10,000

Required

a. Prepare the income statement Green View would include in its 2004 annual report.

b. Identify the accounts that should be closed to the Retained Earnings account.

c. Determine the Retained Earnings account balance at December 31, 2004. Identify the reasons for the difference between net income and the ending balance in Retained Earnings.

d. What are the balances in the revenue, expense, and dividend accounts on January 1, 2005? Explain.

PROBLEM 1–31A *Missing Information in Financial Statements*

L.O. 4, 5

Required

Fill in the blank (as indicated by the alphabetic letters in parentheses) in the following financial statements. Assume the company started operations January 1, 2001, and that all transactions involve cash.

	For the Years		
	2001	**2002**	**2003**
Income Statements			
Revenue	$ 700	$ 1,300	$ 2,000
Expense	(a)	(700)	(1,300)
Net Income	$ 200	$ (m)	$ 700
Statement of Changes in Stockholders' Equity			
Beginning Common Stock	$ 0	$ (n)	$ 6,000
Plus: Common Stock Issued	5,000	1,000	2,000
Ending Common Stock	5,000	6,000	(t)
Beginning Retained Earnings	0	100	200
Plus: Net Income (loss)	(b)	(o)	700
Less: Dividends	(c)	(500)	(300)
Ending Retained Earnings	100	(p)	600
Total Stockholders' Equity	$ (d)	$ 6,200	$ 8,600
Balance Sheets			
Assets			
Cash	$ (e)	$ (q)	$ (u)
Land	0	(r)	8,000
Total Assets	$ (f)	$11,200	$10,600
Liabilities	$ (g)	$ 5,000	$ 2,000
Stockholders' Equity			
Common Stock	(h)	(s)	8,000
Retained Earnings	(i)	200	600
Total Stockholders' Equity	(j)	6,200	8,600
Total Liabilities and Stockholders' Equity	$8,100	$11,200	$10,600
Statements of Cash Flows			
Cash Flows from Operating Activities			
Cash Receipts from Revenue	$ (k)	$ 1,300	$ (v)
Cash Payments for Expenses	(l)	(700)	(w)
Net Cash Flows from Operating Activities	200	600	700
Cash Flows from Investing Activities			
Cash Payments for Land	0	(8,000)	0
Cash Flows from Financing Activities			
Cash Receipts from Loan	3,000	3,000	0
Cash Payments to Reduce Debt	0	(1,000)	(x)
Cash Receipts from Stock Issue	5,000	1,000	(y)
Cash Payments for Dividends	(100)	(500)	(z)
Net Cash Flows from Financing Activities	7,900	2,500	(1,300)
Net Change in Cash	8,100	(4,900)	(600)
Plus: Beginning Cash Balance	0	8,100	3,200
Ending Cash Balance	$8,100	$ 3,200	$ 2,600

PROBLEM 1–32A *Classifying Events as Asset Source, Use, or Exchange*

L.O. 8

The following unrelated events are typical of those experienced by business entities.

1. Acquire cash by issuing common stock.
2. Pay monthly rent on an office building.
3. Purchase land with cash.
4. Borrow cash from a bank.
5. Purchase equipment with cash.
6. Hire a new office manager.

7. Provide services for cash.
8. Acquire land by accepting a liability (financing the purchase).
9. Pay a cash dividend to stockholders.
10. Pay cash for operating expenses.
11. Pay an office manager's salary with cash.
12. Receive cash for services that have been performed.
13. Discuss plans for a new office building with an architect.
14. Repay part of a bank loan.
15. Pay cash to purchase a new office building.

Required

Identify each of the events as an asset source, use, or exchange transaction. If an event would not be recorded under generally accepted accounting principles, identify it as *not applicable* (NA). Also indicate for each event whether total assets would increase, decrease, or remain unchanged. Organize your answer according to the following table. The first event is shown in the table as an example.

Event No.	Type of Event	Effect on Total Assets
1	Asset source	Increase

L.O. 11   **PROBLEM 1–33A** *Price-Earnings Relationships*

Earnings per share and market price per share data for Advantage, Inc., and Hi-Lite, Inc., follow.

Advantage, Inc.	2000	2001	2002
Earnings per share	$ 4.22	$ 4.13	$ 4.18
Market price per share	50.64	45.43	45.98

Hi-Lite, Inc.	2000	2001	2002
Earnings per share	$ 3.27	$ 4.19	$ 5.81
Market price per share	98.10	129.89	220.78

Required

a. Calculate the annual growth rate in the earnings per share of each company from 2000 to 2001 and from 2001 to 2002.
b. Calculate the price-earnings ratio for each company for all three years.
c. Explain what the price-earnings ratio means.
d. Why would the price-earnings ratios of the two companies be different?

EXERCISES—SERIES B

L.O. 5   **EXERCISE 1–1B** *Identifying Elements of Financial Statements*

Financial statements are subdivided into categories known as *elements*. This chapter identifies eight financial statement elements.

Required

a. Provide the names of the eight elements and alternative names for any elements that have them.
b. Identify the financial statement(s) on which each element appears.

L.O. 1, 2   **EXERCISE 1–2B** *Identifying Resources*

Resource owners provide three types of resources to conversion agents that transform the resources into products or services that satisfy consumer demands.

Required

Identify the three types of resources. Write a brief memo explaining how resource owners select the particular conversion agents to which they will provide resources.

L.O. 6   **EXERCISE 1–3B** *Components of the Accounting Equation*

Required

The following three requirements are independent of each other.

a. Jackson Camping Supplies has assets of $8,500 and net assets of $3,200. What is the amount of liabilities? What is the amount of claims?

b. Betty's Snow Cones has liabilities of $2,400 and equity of $4,400. What is the amount of its assets? What is the amount of its net assets?

c. Petrello Company has assets of $98,300 and liabilities of $56,200. What is the amount of its equity? What is the amount of its residual interest?

EXERCISE 1–4B *Distributions in a Business Liquidation*

L.O. 1

Assume that Clark Company acquires $800 cash from creditors and $900 cash from investors. The company then has operating losses of $600 cash and goes out of business.

Required
a. Explain the primary differences between investors and creditors.
b. What amount of cash will Clark's creditors receive?
c. What amount of cash will Clark's investors (stockholders) receive?

EXERCISE 1–5B *Effect of Events on the Accounting Equation*

L.O. 6

Olive Enterprises experienced the following events during 2007.
1. Acquired cash from the issue of common stock.
2. Paid cash to reduce the principal on a bank note.
3. Sold land for cash at an amount equal to its cost.
4. Provided services to clients for cash.
5. Paid utilities expenses with cash.
6. Paid a cash dividend to the stockholders.

Required
Explain how each of the events would affect the accounting equation by writing the letter I for increase, the letter D for decrease, and NA for no effect under each of the components of the accounting equation. The first event is shown as an example.

Event Number	Assets	=	Liabilities	+	Stockholders' Equity Common Stock	+	Stockholders' Equity Retained Earnings
1	I		NA		I		NA

EXERCISE 1–6B *Effect of Events on a Horizontal Financial Statements Model*

L.O. 7, 9

Lourens Auto Repair, Inc., experienced the following events during 2007.
1. Purchased land for cash.
2. Issued common stock for cash.
3. Collected cash for providing auto repair services to customers.
4. Paid a cash dividend to the stockholders.
5. Paid cash for operating expenses.
6. Paid cash to reduce the principal balance on a liability.

Required
Use a horizontal statements model to show how each event affects the balance sheet, income statement, and statement of cash flows. Indicate whether the event increases (I), decreases (D), or does not affect (NA) each element of the financial statements. Also, in the Cash Flows column, classify the cash flows as operating activities (OA), investing activities (IA), or financing activities (FA). The first transaction is shown as an example.

Event No.	Balance Sheet Cash	+	Land	=	N. Pay	+	C. Stock.	+	Ret. Ear.	Income Statement Rev.	–	Exp.	=	Net Inc.	Statement of Cash Flows	
1.	D	+	I	=	NA	+	NA	+	NA	NA	–	NA	=	NA	D	IA

EXERCISE 1–7B *Effects of Issuing Stock*

L.O. 4, 5, 6

Lambena Company was started in 2002 when it acquired $24,000 cash by issuing common stock. The cash acquisition was the only event that affected the business in 2002.

Required

Which financial statements would be affected by this event?

L.O. 4, 5, 6   EXERCISE 1–8B *Effects of Borrowing*

Southern Pacific Company was started in 2003 when it borrowed $19,500 from National Bank.

Required

Which financial statements would be affected by this event?

L.O. 4, 5, 6, 9   EXERCISE 1–9B *Effects of Revenue, Expense, and Dividend Events*

Kim Company was started on January 1, 2004. During 2004, the company completed three accounting events: (1) earned cash revenues of $12,500, (2) paid cash expenses of $8,600, and (3) paid a $1,000 cash dividend to the owner. These were the only events that affected the company during 2004.

Required

a. Write an accounting equation, and record the effects of each accounting event under the appropriate general ledger account headings.

b. Prepare an income statement for the 2004 accounting period and a balance sheet at the end of 2004 for Kim Company.

c. What are the balances in the revenue, expense, and dividend accounts on January 1, 2005?

L.O. 7, 9   EXERCISE 1–10B *Record Events in the Horizontal Statements Model*

Eaton Boat Repairs was started in 2002. During 2002, the company (1) acquired $9,000 cash from the issue of common stock, (2) earned cash revenue of $22,000, (3) paid cash expenses of $12,800, and (4) paid an $800 cash dividend to the stockholders.

Required

a. Record these four events in a horizontal statements model. Also, in the Cash Flows column, classify the cash flows as operating activities (OA), investing activities (IA), or financing activities (FA). The first event is shown as an example.

Event No.	Balance Sheet							Income Statement					Statement of Cash Flows
	Cash	=	N. Pay	+	C. Stock.	+	Ret. Ear.	Rev.	−	Exp.	=	Net Inc.	
1.	9,000	=	NA	+	9,000	+	NA	NA	−	NA	=	NA	9,000 FA

b. Why is the net income different from the net increase in cash for this business?

L.O. 5   EXERCISE 1–11B *Classifying Items for the Statement of Cash Flows*

Required

Indicate how each of the following would be classified on the statement of cash flows as operating activities (OA), investing activities (IA), financing activities (FA), or not applicable (NA).

a. Borrowed $8,000 cash from First State Bank.

b. Paid $5,000 cash for salary expense.

c. Signed a contract to provide services in the future.

d. Performed services for $25,000 cash.

e. Paid $9,000 cash to purchase land.

f. Paid $1,500 cash for utilities expense.

g. Sold land for $5,000 cash.

h. Paid $4,000 cash on the principal of a bank loan.

i. Paid a $2,000 cash dividend to the stockholders.

j. Received $30,000 cash from the issue of common stock.

L.O. 6, 9   EXERCISE 1–12B *Effect of Transactions on General Ledger Accounts*

At the beginning of 2001, Pete's Pest Control's accounting records had the following general ledger accounts and balances.

	Pete's Pest Control Accounting Equation							
Event	Assets		=	Liabilities	+	Stockholders' Equity		Acct. Titles for RE
	Cash	Land		Notes Payable		Common Stock	Retained Earnings	
Balance 1/1/2001	15,000	20,000		15,000		7,000	13,000	

Pete's completed the following transactions during 2001.
1. Purchased land for $5,000 cash.
2. Acquired $25,000 cash from the issue of common stock.
3. Received $65,000 cash for providing services to customers.
4. Paid cash operating expenses of $42,000.
5. Borrowed $10,000 cash from creditors.
6. Paid a $2,500 cash dividend to the stockholders.

Required
a. Record the transactions in the appropriate general ledger accounts. Record the amounts of revenue, expense, and dividends in the Retained Earnings column. Provide the appropriate titles for these accounts in the last column of the table.
b. Determine the net cash flow from financing activities.
c. What are the balances in the Retained Earnings, Revenue, Expense, and Dividend accounts as of January 1, 2002?

EXERCISE 1–13B *Preparing Financial Statements*

L.O. 4, 6, 9

J & A, Inc., experienced the following events during 2004.
1. Acquired $55,000 cash from the issue of common stock.
2. Paid $15,000 cash to purchase land.
3. Borrowed $5,000 cash.
4. Provided services for $21,000 cash.
5. Paid $1,500 cash for utilities expense.
6. Paid $11,000 cash for other operating expenses.
7. Paid a $2,000 cash dividend to the stockholders.

Required
a. The January 1, 2004, general ledger account balances are shown in the following accounting equation. Record the seven events in the appropriate general ledger accounts. Record the amounts of revenue, expense, and dividends in the Retained Earnings column. Provide the appropriate titles for these accounts in the last column of the table. The first event is shown as an example.

	J & A, Inc. Accounting Equation							
Event	Assets		=	Liabilities	+	Stockholders' Equity		Acct. Titles for RE
	Cash	Land		Notes Payable		Common Stock	Retained Earnings	
Balance 1/1/2004	12,000	20,000		0		15,000	17,000	
1.	55,000					55,000		

b. Prepare an income statement, statement of changes in stockholders' equity, year-end balance sheet, and statement of cash flows for the 2004 accounting period.
c. What are the balances in the revenue, expense, and dividend accounts on January 1, 2005?

EXERCISE 1–14B *Effect of Events on a Horizontal Statements Model*

L.O. 5, 7, 9

Joyce Higgins started Computer Software Services on January 1, 2006. The company experienced the following events during its first year of operation.

1. Acquired $20,000 cash by issuing common stock.
2. Paid $5,000 cash to purchase land.
3. Received $32,000 cash for providing computer consulting services to customers.
4. Paid $12,500 cash for salary expenses.
5. Acquired additional $4,000 cash from the issue of additional common stock.
6. Borrowed $15,000 cash from the bank.
7. Purchased additional land for $15,000 cash.
8. Paid $14,000 cash for other operating expenses.
9. Paid a $2,500 cash dividend to the stockholders.

Required

a. Record these events in a horizontal statements model. Also, in the Cash Flows column, classify the cash flows as operating activities (OA), investing activities (IA), or financing activities (FA). The first event is shown as an example.

Event No.	Balance Sheet											Income Statement					Statement of Cash Flows	
	Cash	+	Land	=	N. Pay	+	C. Stock.	+	Ret. Ear.			Rev.	−	Exp.	=	Net Inc.		
1.	20,000	+	NA	=	NA	+	20,000	+	NA			NA	−	NA	=	NA	20,000	FA

b. What is the net income earned in 2006?
c. What is the amount of total assets at the end of 2006?
d. What is the net cash flow from operating activities for 2006?
e. What is the net cash flow from investing activities for 2006?
f. What is the net cash flow from financing activities for 2006?
g. What is the cash balance at the end of 2006?

L.O. 4, 5   EXERCISE 1–15B *Titles and Accounts Appearing on Financial Statements*

Annual reports normally include an income statement, statement of changes in equity, balance sheet, and statement of cash flows.

Required

Identify the financial statements on which each of the following titles or accounts would appear. If a title or an account appears on more than one statement, list all statements that would include it.
a. Retained Earnings
b. Revenue
c. Common Stock
d. Financing Activities
e. Salaries Expense
f. Land
g. Ending Cash Balance
h. Beginning Cash Balance
i. Notes Payable
j. Dividends

L.O. 3, 4   EXERCISE 1–16B *Closing the Accounts*

The following information was drawn from the accounting records of Fulmer Company as of December 31, 2005, before the nominal accounts had been closed. The company's cash balance was $2,500, and its land account had a $6,500 balance. Notes payable amounted to $3,000. The balance in the Common Stock account was $1,500. The company had revenues of $5,500 and expenses of $2,000, and dividends amounted to $900.

Required

a. Identify the accounts that would be closed to Retained Earnings at the end of the accounting period.
b. Assuming that Fulmer's beginning balance (as of January 1, 2005) in the Retained Earnings account was $1,900, determine its balance after the nominal accounts were closed at the end of 2005.
c. What amount of net income would Fulmer Company report on its 2005 income statement?
d. Explain why the amount of net income differs from the amount of the ending Retained Earnings balance.
e. What are the balances in the revenue, expense, and dividend accounts on January 1, 2006?

EXERCISE 1–17B *Closing Accounts and the Accounting Cycle*

L.O. 10

Required

a. Identify which of the following accounts are temporary (will be closed to Retained Earnings at the end of the year) and which are permanent.
   1. Common Stock
   2. Notes Payable
   3. Cash
   4. Service Revenue
   5. Dividends
   6. Land
   7. Salaries Expense
   8. Retained Earnings
   9. Utilities Expense
   10. Interest Revenue

b. Bill bragged that he had five years of accounting experience. Jane disagreed, responding, "No. You have had one year of accounting experience five times." Explain what Jane meant. (*Hint:* Refer to the accounting cycle.)

EXERCISE 1–18B *Classifying Events as Asset Source, Use, or Exchange*

L.O. 8

Hill Company experienced the following events during its first year of operations.
1. Acquired $8,000 cash from the issue of common stock.
2. Paid $3,500 cash for salary expenses.
3. Borrowed $10,000 cash from New South Bank.
4. Paid $6,000 cash to purchase land.
5. Provided boarding services for $6,500 cash.
6. Acquired an additional $1,000 cash from the issue of common stock.
7. Paid $1,200 cash for utilities expense.
8. Paid a $1,500 cash dividend to the stockholders.
9. Provided additional services for $3,000 cash.
10. Purchased additional land for $2,500 cash.

Required

Classify each event as an asset source, use, or exchange transaction.

EXERCISE 1–19B *Types of Transactions and the Horizontal Statements Model*

L.O. 7, 8, 9

Computer Parts experienced the following events during its first year of operations, 2007.
1. Acquired cash by issuing common stock.
2. Purchased land with cash.
3. Borrowed cash from a bank.
4. Signed a contract to provide services in the future.
5. Paid a cash dividend to the stockholders.
6. Paid cash for operating expenses.

Required

a. Indicate whether each event is an asset source, use, or exchange transaction.

b. Use a horizontal statements model to show how each event affects the balance sheet, income statement, and statement of cash flows. Indicate whether the event increases (I), decreases (D), or does not affect (NA) each element of the financial statements. Also, in the Cash column, classify the cash flows as operating activities (OA), investing activities (IA), or financing activities (FA). The first transaction is shown as an example.

Event No.	Balance Sheet													Income Statement						Statement of Cash Flows	
	Cash	+	Land	=	N. Pay	+	C. Stock.	+	Ret. Ear.					Rev.	–	Exp.	=	Net Inc.			
1.	I	+	NA	=	NA	+	I	+	NA					NA	–	NA	=	NA			I FA

EXERCISE 1–20B *Relating Accounting Events to Entities*

L.O. 8

Jackling Company sold land for $50,000 cash to Power Company in 2004.

Required

a. Was this event an asset source, use, or exchange transaction for Jackling Company?

b. Was this event an asset source, use, or exchange transaction for Power Company?

c. Was the cash flow an operating, investing, or financing activity on Jackling Company's 2004 statement of cash flows?

d. Was the cash flow an operating, investing, or financing activity on Power Company's 2004 statement of cash flows?

L.O. 6   **EXERCISE 1–21B** *Missing Information in the Accounting Equation*

Required

Calculate the missing amounts in the following table.

					Stockholders' Equity		
Company	Assets	=	Liabilities	+	Common Stock	+	Retained Earnings
A	$?		$25,000		$48,000		$25,000
B	50,000		?		15,000		30,000
C	75,000		20,000		?		42,000
D	125,000		45,000		75,000		?

L.O. 6   **EXERCISE 1–22B** *Missing Information in the Accounting Equation*

As of December 31, 2004, Stone Company had total assets of $132,000, retained earnings of $74,300, and common stock of $45,000. During 2005 Stone earned $42,000 of cash revenue, paid $21,500 for cash expenses, and paid a $600 cash dividend to the stockholders. Stone also paid $5,000 to reduce its debt during 2005.

Required

a. Determine the amount of liabilities at December 31, 2004.

b. Determine the amount of net income earned in 2005.

c. Determine the amount of total assets as of December 31, 2005.

d. Determine the amount of total liabilities as of December 31, 2005.

L.O. 5, 6   **EXERCISE 1–23B** *Missing Information for Determining Revenue*

Total stockholders' equity of Zullo Company increased by $46,500 between December 31, 2005, and December 31, 2006. During 2006 Zullo acquired $15,000 cash from the issue of common stock. The company paid a $5,000 cash dividend to the stockholders during 2006. Total expenses during 2006 amounted to $22,000.

Required

Determine the amount of revenue that Zullo reported on its 2006 income statement. (*Hint:* Remember that stock issues, net income, and dividends all change total stockholders' equity.)

L.O. 11   **EXERCISE 1–24B** *Price-Earnings Ratio*

The following information is available for two companies:

	ARC Company	Pager Company
Earnings per share	$ 0.85	$ 2.25
Market price per share	46.50	75.40

Required

a. Compute the price-earnings ratio for each company.

b. Which company would you expect to have the higher earnings growth potential?

PROBLEMS—SERIES B

L.O. 9   **PROBLEM 1–25B** *Recording the Effect of Events in a Horizontal Statements Model*

Belzio Company was started in 2001. It had existing balances in various permanent accounts at the start of 2006. The company experienced the following transactions during 2006.

1. Paid a cash dividend to the stockholders.
2. Acquired cash by issuing additional common stock.
3. Signed a contract to perform services in the future.
4. Performed services for cash.
5. Paid cash expenses.
6. Sold land for cash at an amount equal to its cost.
7. Borrowed cash from a bank.

Required

Use a horizontal statements model to show how each event affects the balance sheet, income statement, and statement of cash flows. Indicate whether the event increases (I), decreases (D), or does not affect (NA) each element of the financial statements. Also, in the Cash Flows column, classify the cash flows as operating activities (OA), investing activities (IA), or financing activities (FA). The first transaction is shown as an example.

Event No.	Balance Sheet											Income Statement					Statement of Cash Flows
	Cash	+	Land	=	N. Pay	+	C. Stock.	+	Ret. Ear.			Rev.	−	Exp.	=	Net Inc.	
1.	D	+	NA	=	NA	+	NA	+	D			NA	−	NA	=	NA	D FA

PROBLEM 1–26B *Recording Events in a Horizontal Statements Model*

L.O. 5, 7, 9

Foreman Company was started January 1, 2003, and experienced the following events during its first year of operation.

1. Acquired $32,000 cash from the issue of common stock.
2. Borrowed $20,000 cash from National Bank.
3. Earned cash revenues of $42,000 for performing services.
4. Paid cash expenses of $28,000.
5. Paid a $6,000 cash dividend to the stockholders.
6. Acquired an additional $10,000 cash from the issue of common stock.
7. Paid $15,000 cash to reduce the principal balance of the bank note.
8. Paid $45,000 cash to purchase land.

Required

a. Record the preceding transactions in the horizontal statements model. Also, in the Cash Flows column, classify the cash flows as operating activities (OA), investing activities (IA), or financing activities (FA). The first event is shown as an example.

Event No.	Balance Sheet											Income Statement					Statement of Cash Flows
	Cash	+	Land	=	N. Pay	+	C. Stock.	+	Ret. Ear.			Rev.	−	Exp.	=	Net Inc.	
1.	32,000	+	NA	=	NA	+	32,000	+	NA			NA	−	NA	=	NA	32,000 FA

b. Determine the amount of total assets that Foreman would report on the December 31, 2003, balance sheet.

c. Identify the sources of the assets that Foreman would report on the December 31, 2003, balance sheet. Determine the amount of each of these sources.

d. Determine the net income that Foreman would report on the 2003 income statement. Explain why dividends do not appear on the income statement.

e. Determine the net cash flows from operating activities, investing activities, and financing activities that Foreman would report on the 2003 statement of cash flows.

PROBLEM 1–27B *Preparing Financial Statements for Two Complete Accounting Cycles*

L.O. 4, 5, 6, 9

Jim's Janitorial Services experienced the following transactions for 2001, the first year of operations, and 2002. *Assume that all transactions involve the receipt or payment of cash.*

Transactions for 2001

1. Acquired $60,000 by issuing common stock.
2. Received $100,000 for providing services to customers.

3. Borrowed $25,000 cash from creditors.
4. Paid expenses amounting to $70,000.
5. Purchased land for $40,000 cash.

Transactions for 2002

1. Acquired an additional $20,000 from the issue of common stock.
2. Received $120,000 for providing services in 2002.
3. Paid $10,000 to creditors.
4. Paid expenses amounting to $80,000.
5. Paid a $15,000 dividend to the stockholders.

Required

a. Write an accounting equation, and record the effects of each accounting event under the appropriate headings for each year. Record the amounts of revenue, expense, and dividends in the Retained Earnings column. Provide appropriate titles for these accounts in the last column of the table.
b. Prepare an income statement, statement of changes in stockholders' equity, year-end balance sheet, and statement of cash flows for each year. Use the vertical format when you prepare the financial statements.
c. Compare the information provided by the income statement with the information provided by the statement of cash flows. Point out similarities and differences.
d. Determine the percentage growth in earnings from 2001 to 2002. Based on the data shown in Exhibit 1–16, is this a high-, medium-, or low-growth company?

L.O. 4, 5   **PROBLEM 1–28B** *Interrelationships among Financial Statements*

Best Electronics started the accounting period with $10,000 of assets, $2,200 of liabilities, and $4,550 of retained earnings. During the period, the Retained Earnings account increased by $3,565. The bookkeeper reported that Best paid cash expenses of $5,010 and paid a $625 cash dividend to stockholders, but she could not find a record of the amount of cash that Best received for performing services. Best also paid $1,000 cash to reduce the liability owed to a bank, and the business acquired $2,000 of additional cash from the issue of common stock.

Required

Prepare an income statement, statement of changes in stockholders' equity, year-end balance sheet, and statement of cash flows for the accounting period. (*Hint:* Determine the beginning balance in the common stock account before considering the effects of the current period events. It also might help to record all events under an accounting equation before preparing the statements.)

L.O. 5   **PROBLEM 1–29B** *Relating Titles and Accounts to Financial Statements*

A random list of various financial statements components follows: (1) Retained Earnings account ending balance, (2) revenues, (3) Common Stock account beginning balance, (4) Common Stock account ending balance, (5) assets, (6) expenses, (7) operating activities, (8) dividends, (9) Retained Earnings beginning balance, (10) investing activities, (11) common stock issued during the period, (12) liabilities, and (13) financing activities.

Required

Set up a table with the following headings. Identify the financial statements on which each of the preceding components appears by placing the reference number for the component in the appropriate column. If an item appears on more than one statement, place the reference number in every applicable column. The first component is shown as an example.

Income Statement	Statement of Changes in Stockholders' Equity	Balance Sheet	Statement of Cash Flows
	1	1	

L.O. 3, 4, 5, 6   **PROBLEM 1–30B** *Closing the Accounts*

The following accounts and account balances were taken from the records of Peaks View Company. Except as otherwise indicated, all balances are as of December 31, 2005, before the closing entries had been recorded.

Consulting Revenue	$14,500
Cash	28,500
Cash Received from Common Stock Issued during 2005	4,500
Travel Expense	1,100
Dividends	3,000
Cash Flow from Investing Activities	3,400
Rent Expense	1,800
Payment to Reduce Debt Principal	8,000
Retained Earnings, January 1, 2005	19,000
Salary Expense	6,900
Cash Flow from Operating Activities	1,500
Common Stock, December 31, 2005	10,000
Other Operating Expenses	2,200

Required

a. Identify the accounts that should be closed to the Retained Earnings account.

b. Prepare the income statement that Peaks View would include in its 2005 annual report.

c. Determine the Retained Earnings account balance at December 31, 2005. Explain how the company could pay cash dividends in excess of the amount of net income earned in 2005.

d. Name the stages of the accounting cycle in the order in which they normally occur.

PROBLEM 1–31B *Missing Information in Financial Statements*   **L.O. 4, 5**

Required

Fill in the blanks (indicated by the alphabetic letters in parentheses) in the following financial statements. Assume the company started operations January 1, 2001 and all transactions involve cash.

	For the Years		
	2001	**2002**	**2003**
Income Statements			
Revenue	$ 400	$ 500	$ 800
Expense	(250)	(l)	(425)
Net Income	$ (a)	$ 100	$ 375
Statement of Changes in Stockholders' Equity			
Beginning Common Stock	$ 0	$ (m)	$ 9,100
Plus: Common Stock Issued	(b)	1,100	310
Ending Common Stock	8,000	9,100	(s)
Beginning Retained Earnings	0	25	75
Plus: Net Income (loss)	(c)	100	375
Less: Dividends	(d)	(50)	(150)
Ending Retained Earnings	25	(n)	300
Total Stockholders' Equity	$ (e)	$ 9,175	$ (t)
Balance Sheets			
Assets			
Cash	$ (f)	$ (o)	$ (u)
Land	0	(p)	2,500
Total Assets	$11,000	$11,650	$10,550
Liabilities	$ (g)	$ (q)	$ 840
Equity			
Common Stock	(h)	(r)	9,410
Retained Earnings	(i)	75	300
Total Stockholders' Equity	8,025	9,175	9,710
Total Liabilities and Stockholders' Equity	$11,000	$11,650	$10,550

continued

Statements of Cash Flows						
Cash Flows from Operating Activities						
Cash Receipts from Revenue	$	(j)	$	500	$	(v)
Cash Payments for Expenses		(k)		(400)		(w)
Net Cash Flows from Operating Activities		150		100		375
Cash Flows from Investing Activities						
Cash Payments for Land		0		(5,000)		0
Cash Receipt from Sale of Land		0		0		2,500
Net Cash Flows from Investing Activities		0		(5,000)		2,500
Cash Flows from Financing Activities						
Cash Receipts from Borrowed Funds		2,975		0		0
Cash Payments to Reduce Debt		0		(500)		(x)
Cash Receipts from Stock Issue		8,000		1,100		(y)
Cash Payments for Dividends		(125)		(50)		(z)
Net Cash Flows from Financing Activities		10,850		550		(1,475)
Net Change in Cash		11,000		(4,350)		1,400
Plus: Beginning Cash Balance		0		11,000		6,650
Ending Cash Balance		$11,000		$ 6,650		$8,050

L.O. 8   PROBLEM 1–32B *Classifying Events as Asset Source, Use, or Exchange*

The following unrelated events are typical of those experienced by business entities:
1. Acquire cash by issuing common stock.
2. Borrow cash from the local bank.
3. Paid office supplies expense.
4. Make plans to purchase office equipment.
5. Trade a used car for a computer with the same value.
6. Paid other operating supplies expense.
7. Agree to represent a client in an IRS audit and to receive payment when the audit is complete.
8. Receive cash from customers for services rendered.
9. Pay employee salaries with cash.
10. Pay back a bank loan with cash.
11. Pay interest to a bank with cash.
12. Transfer cash from a checking account to a money market account.
13. Sell land for cash at its original cost.
14. Paid a cash dividend to stockholders.
15. Learn that a financial analyst determined the company's price-earnings ratio to be 26.

Required

Identify each of the events as an asset source, asset use, or asset exchange transaction. If an event would not be recorded under generally accepted accounting principles, identify it as *not applicable* (NA). Also indicate for each event whether total assets would increase, decrease, or remain unchanged. Organize your answer according to the following table. The first event is shown in the table as an example.

Event No.	Type of Event	Effect on Total Assets
1	Asset source	Increase

L.O. 11   PROBLEM 1–33B *Price-Earnings Relationships*

Beta One, Inc., is a pharmaceutical company heavily involved in research leading to the development of genealogy-based medicines. While the company has several promising research studies in progress, it has brought only two viable products to market during the last decade. Earnings per share and market price per share data for the latest three years of operation follow.

Beta One, Inc.	2003	2004	2005
Earnings per share	$ 1.22	$ 1.19	$ 1.20
Market price per share	85.40	84.49	87.60

Required

a. Calculate the company's annual growth rate in earnings per share from 2003 to 2004 and from 2004 to 2005.

b. Based on the data shown in Exhibit 1–16, identify the company as a high-, medium-, or low-growth company.

c. Calculate the company's price-earnings ratio for all three years.

d. Based on the data shown in Exhibit 1–16, classify the price-earnings ratio as high, medium, or low.

e. Explain the size of the price-earnings ratio.

ANALYZE, THINK, COMMUNICATE

BUSINESS APPLICATIONS CASE *Dell's Annual Report*   ATC 1–1

Use the Dell Computer Corporation financial statements in Appendix B to answer the following questions.

a. What was Dell's net income for 2001?

b. How does net income for 2001 compare to net income for 2000?

c. What was Dell's accounting equation for 2001?

d. Determine which of the following had the largest percentage increase from 2000 to 2001: net revenue, cost of revenue, or total operating expenses.

GROUP ASSIGNMENT *Missing Information*   ATC 1–2

The following selected financial information is available for H&R Block. Amounts are in millions of dollars.

Income Statements	1999	1998	1997	1996
Revenue	$ (661)	$1,307	$ (a)	$ 894
Cost and Expenses	(a)	(a)	(1,859)	(769)
Income from Continuing Operations	(b)	174	71	(a)
Unusual Items	–0–	218	(b)	(b)
Net Income	$ 7	$ (b)	$ 47	$ 177

Balance Sheets	1999	1998	1997	1996
Assets				
Cash and Marketable Securities	$ 249	$1,247	$ (c)	$ 419
Other Assets	1,661	(c)	1,226	(c)
Total Assets	1,910	$2,904	$(d)	$1,418
Liabilities	$(c)	$ (d)	$907	$ (d)
Stockholders' Equity				
Common Stock	422	356	(e)	313
Retained Earnings	(d)	(e)	684	(e)
Total Stockholders' Equity	1,062	1,342	(f)	1,040
Total Liabilities and Stockholders' Equity	$1,910	$ (f)	$1,906	$1,418

Required

a. Divide the class into groups of four or five students each. Organize the groups into four sections. Assign Task 1 to the first section of groups, Task 2 to the second section, Task 3 to the third section, and Task 4 to the fourth section.

Group Tasks

(1) Fill in the missing information for 1996.

(2) Fill in the missing information for 1997.

(3) Fill in the missing information for 1998.

(4) Fill in the missing information for 1999.

b. Each section should select two representatives. One representative is to put the financial statements assigned to that section on the board, underlining the missing amounts. The second representative is to explain to the class how the missing amounts were determined.

c. Each section should list events that could have caused the unusual item category on the income statement.

ATC 1–3   REAL-WORLD CASE *Deciding Which Company Is the Best Investment*

Following are the net earnings of four large companies for the fiscal years from 1997 to 2000. Note that these amounts are in thousands of dollars.

		Net Earnings in $000			
Company	**Industry**	**2000**	**1999**	**1998**	**1997**
Autozone	Automobile parts retailer	$267,590	$244,783	$227,903	$195,008
H&R Block	Tax preparation service	251,895	215,366	392,130	47,755
Intuit	Software development	305,661	386,564	6,182	68,308
Kohl's	Department store chain	258,142	192,266	141,273	102,478

Required

Based on this information alone, decide which of the companies you think would present the best investment opportunity for the future and which would be the worst. Write a brief memorandum supporting your choices, and show any computations that you used to reach your conclusions. As part of your analysis, compute the annual growth rates for each company's earnings. To do this, compute by what percentage each company's earnings increased or decreased from the year before. You will not be able to compute a growth rate for 1997 since the earnings for 1996 are not given. Perform whatever additional analysis you think is useful.

ATC 1–4   BUSINESS APPLICATIONS CASE *Use of Real-World Numbers for Forecasting*

The following information was drawn from the annual report of Machine Import Company (MIC):

	For the Years	
	2001	**2002**
Income Statements		
Revenue	$600,000	$690,000
Operating Expenses	480,000	552,000
Income from Continuing Operations	120,000	138,000
Extraordinary Item—Lottery Win		62,000
Net Income	$120,000	$200,000
Balance Sheets		
Assets	$880,000	$880,000
Liabilities	$200,000	$ 0
Stockholders' Equity		
Common Stock	380,000	380,000
Retained Earnings	300,000	500,000
Total Liabilities and Stockholders' Equity	$880,000	$880,000

Required

a. Compute the percentage of growth in net income from 2001 to 2002. Can stockholders expect a similar increase between 2002 and 2003?

b. Assuming that MIC collected $200,000 cash from earnings (i.e., net income), explain how this money was spent in 2002.

c. Assuming that MIC experiences the same percentage of growth from 2002 to 2003 as it did from 2001 to 2002, determine the amount of income from continuing operations that the owners can expect to see on the 2003 income statement.

d. During 2003, MIC experienced a $40,000 loss due to storm damage (note that this would be shown as an extraordinary loss on the income statement). Liabilities and common stock were unchanged from 2002 to 2003. Use the information that you computed in Part *c* plus the additional information provided in the previous two sentences to prepare an income statement and balance sheet as of December 31, 2003.

WRITING ASSIGNMENT *Elements of Financial Statements Defined*

Bob and his sister Marsha both attend the state university. As a reward for their successful completion of the past year (Bob had a 3.2 GPA in business, and Marsha had a 3.7 GPA in art), their father gave each of them 100 shares of The Walt Disney Company stock. They have just received their first annual report. Marsha does not understand what the information means and has asked Bob to explain it to her. Bob is currently taking an accounting course, and she knows he will understand the financial statements.

Required

Assume that you are Bob. Write Marsha a memo explaining the following financial statement items to her. In your explanation, describe each of the two financial statements and explain the financial information each contains. Also define each of the elements listed for each financial statement and explain what it means.

Balance Sheet
Assets
Liabilities
Stockholders' Equity
Income Statement
Revenue
Expense
Net Income

ETHICAL DILEMMA *Loyalty Versus the Bottom Line*

Assume that Jones has been working for you for five years. He has had an excellent work history and has received generous pay raises in response. The raises have been so generous that Jones is quite overpaid for the job he is required to perform. Unfortunately, he is not qualified to take on other, more responsible jobs available within the company. A recent job applicant is willing to accept a salary $5,000 per year less than the amount currently being paid to Jones. The applicant is well qualified to take over Jones's duties and has a very positive attitude. The following financial statements were reported by your company at the close of its most recent accounting period.

Required

a. Reconstruct the financial statements, assuming that Jones was replaced at the beginning of the most recent accounting period. Both Jones and his replacement are paid in cash. No other changes are to be considered.

b. Discuss the short- and long-term ramifications of replacing Jones. There are no right answers. However, assume that you are required to make a decision. Use your judgment and common sense to support your choice.

Financial Statements		
Income Statement		
Revenue		$57,000
Expense		(45,000)
Net Income		$12,000
Statement of Changes in Stockholders' Equity		
Beginning Common Stock	$20,000	
Plus: Stock issued	5,000	
Ending Common Stock		$25,000
Beginning Retained Earnings	50,000	
Net Income	12,000	
Dividends	(2,000)	
Ending Retained Earnings		60,000
Total Stockholders' Equity		$85,000
		continued

Balance Sheet	
Assets	
Cash	$85,000
Equity	
Common Stock	$25,000
Retained Earnings	60,000
Total Stockholders' Equity	$85,000

Statement of Cash Flows		
Operating Activities		
Inflow from Customers	$57,000	
Outflow for Expenses	(45,000)	
Net Inflow from Operations		$12,000
Investing Activities		0
Financing Activities		
Inflow from Stock Issue	5,000	
Outflow for Dividends	(2,000)	
Net Inflow from Financing Activities		3,000
Net Change in Cash		15,000
Plus: Beginning Cash Balance		70,000
Ending Cash Balance		$85,000

ATC 1–7 SPREADSHEET ASSIGNMENT *Using Excel*

The financial statements for Simple Company are reported here using an Excel spreadsheet.

Required

Recreate the financial statements using your own Excel spreadsheet.

a. For each number with an arrow by it, enter a formula in that particular cell address to solve for the number shown. (Do not enter the arrow.)

b. When complete, print the spreadsheet with formulas rather than absolute numbers.

Spreadsheet Tips

(1) Widen a column by positioning the cursor on the vertical line between two column headings until a crosshair appears. Either double click to automatically widen or click and drag the crosshair to the desired width.

(2) Negative numbers can be parenthesized by choosing Format and then Cells. Under Category, choose Custom and under Type, choose the first option containing parentheses.

(3) The SUM function is one way to add a series of numbers. For example, the formula for net income in cell B6 is =SUM(B4:B5).

(4) Single and double lines can be drawn using the Borders icon.

(5) Print a spreadsheet on one page by choosing File, Page Setup, and Fit to 1.

(6) Print without gridlines by choosing File, Page Setup, and Sheet and uncheck Gridlines. Another option is to choose Tools and Options and uncheck Gridlines.

(7) Print formulas by choosing Tools, Options, and Formulas.

SPREADSHEET ASSIGNMENT *Mastering Excel*   ATC 1–8

Required

a. Enter the following headings for the horizontal statements model onto a blank spreadsheet.

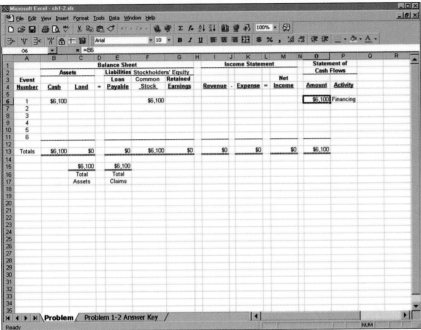

b. Under the appropriate headings, record the effects of each of the following accounting events for the first month of operations. The first event has been recorded as an example.

(1) Acquired $6,100 from the issue of common stock.

(2) Paid $4,400 to purchase land.

(3) Borrowed $3,000 cash.

(4) Provided services to customers and received $700 in cash.

(5) Paid $300 for expenses.

(6) Paid a $100 dividend to the stockholders.

(*Note:* The amounts on the statement of cash flows can be referenced to the Cash account on the balance sheet. In other words, recording the cash amounts twice is not necessary. Instead enter formulas in the Statement of Cash Flows column equating those cell addresses to the respective cell in the Cash column. Notice that the formula in cell O6 (statement of cash flows) is set equal to cell B6 (cash on the balance sheet). Once the formula is completed for cell O6, it can be easily copied to cells O7 through O11.)

c. Using formulas, sum each of the quantitative columns to arrive at the end-of-month amounts reported on the financial statements.

Spreadsheet Tips

(1) Center the heading *Balance Sheet* across columns by entering the entire heading in cell B1. Position the cursor on B1 until a fat cross appears. Click and drag the cursor across B1 through G1. Click on the Merge and Center icon (it is highlighted in the screen in the computer display).

(2) Enter arithmetic signs as headings by placing an apostrophe in front of the sign. For example, to enter the equals sign in cell D4, enter ' =.

(3) Copy cells by positioning the cursor in the bottom right corner of the cell to copy from (such as cell O6) until a thin cross appears. Click and drag the cursor down through the desired locations to copy to (through cell O11).

(4) To enter the dollar sign, choose Format, Cells, and Currency.

Accounting for Accruals

Learning Objectives

After completing this chapter, you should be able to:

1 Explain the concept of accrual versus cash accounting.

2 Identify business events that involve accruals.

3 Record events under an accounting equation.

4 Prepare simple financial statements for a business that engages in cash and accrual transactions.

5 Explain how accrual transactions (as well as cash transactions introduced in Chapter 1) affect the financial statements of a business.

6 Define *revenue* and *expense* in terms of their relationships to assets and liabilities.

7 Explain the effects of end-of-period adjustments related to accruals.

8 Describe the auditor's role in financial reporting.

9 Develop an appreciation of the importance of a code of ethics.

10 Classify accounting events into one of four categories, including
  a. asset source transactions.
  b. asset use transactions.
  c. asset exchange transactions.
  d. claims exchange transactions.

the *curious* accountant

Suppose a company located in St. Louis, Missouri, needs to ship goods to a customer located 868 miles away in Philadelphia, Pennsylvania. The company agrees to pay the CSX Corporation $1,500 to deliver the goods by rail. When should CSX report that it has earned revenue? More specifically, should the revenue be recognized before, during, or after the delivery of the goods?

All of the transactions presented in Chapter 1 had direct cash consequences. For example, revenue was recorded at the time cash was collected, and expenses were recorded at the time cash was paid. Such exact coincidence seldom occurs in business practice. Indeed, a "buy-now, pay-later" philosophy is predominant in all major industrialized economies. Customers frequently purchase services in one accounting period and pay for them in a different period. **Accrual accounting** *recognizes the effects of revenue and expense events in the period in which they occur regardless of when cash is exchanged. Suppose a business provides services in 2001 but collects cash for those services in 2002. Under accrual accounting, the business recognizes the revenue in 2001.*

Accrual accounting clearly distinguishes between the recognition of accounting events and the realization of cash receipts or payments. **Recognition** *means recording an event in the financial records.* **Realization** *usually refers to the collection or payment of cash. Revenues or expenses can be recognized (recorded) before or after cash is realized (collected or paid).*

Accrual accounting uses both accruals and deferrals. The term **accrual** *applies to earnings events that are recognized before cash is exchanged. For example, revenue may be recognized in 2001 although the associated cash is collected in 2002. The term* deferral *applies to earnings events that are recognized after cash has been exchanged. To illustrate, assume that supplies are purchased with cash in 2001 but are used in 2002. The supplies expense would be recognized in 2002 even though cash was paid in 2001. This chapter introduces the most common types of accruals. Deferrals will be explained in Chapter 3.*

Accrual Accounting Illustrated

Beth Conner started a consulting practice called Conner Consultants that specializes in the development and delivery of quality training programs. The business began operation on January 1, 2001. Since the training programs take place on the client's premises, Conner's clients provide office space and secretarial support. As a result, she is able to avoid many operating expenses. However, Conner does incur salary expenses for one instructor who is a part-time employee. During 2001, Conner experienced the following business events.

Effect of Events on Financial Statements

This section of the text describes seven events that Conner Consultants experienced during its first year of operation (2001). The effects of each event will be shown in a horizontal statements model.

Event 1 **The business was started when it acquired $5,000 cash by issuing common stock.**

The $5,000 stock issue is an **asset source transaction.** It increases the business's assets (cash) and its equity (common stock). Because the event did not result from operating the business, the transaction did not affect the income statement. The cash inflow is classified as a financing activity (acquisition from owners). These effects are shown in the following financial statements model:

Assets	=	Liab.	+	C. Stk.	+	Ret. Ear.	Rev.	–	Exp.	=	Net Inc.	Cash Flow	
5,000	=	NA	+	5,000	+	NA	NA	–	NA	=	NA	5,000	FA

Event 2 **During 2001 Conner Consultants provided $84,000 of consulting services to its clients. The work has been performed and bills have been sent to the clients, but Conner has not yet collected any cash. This type of transaction is frequently referred to as *providing services on account.***

Accrual accounting requires recognizing $84,000 of assets and the corresponding revenue in the 2001 accounting period (the period in which the work was done). The fact that cash has not been *collected* does not affect the amount of assets and revenue to be *recognized*. The specific asset that increases is called **accounts receivable.** As its name suggests, the receivables account represents amounts of future cash receipts that are due from customers (amounts that are expected to be collected in the future). The revenue recognition transaction is an *asset source transaction*. Its effect on the financial statements follows:

Assets		=	.Liab.	+	Stockholders' Equity								
Cash	+	Acc. Rec.	=	Liab.	+	C. Stk.	+	Ret. Ear.	Rev.	–	Exp.	=	Net Inc.	Cash Flow
NA	+	84,000	=	NA	+	NA	+	84,000	84,000	–	NA	=	84,000	NA

The event affects the income statement but not the statement of cash flows. Accrual accounting recognizes revenue in the period that it is earned (when the work is done) regardless of when cash is collected.

Event 3 **Conner collected $60,000 cash from customers in partial settlement of its accounts receivable.**

The conversion of $60,000 of accounts receivable to cash is an **asset exchange transaction.** The amount in the Cash account increases, and the amount in the Accounts Receivable account decreases. The amount of total assets is unchanged. The effect of the $60,000 collection of receivables on the financial statements is as follows:

Assets		=	Liab.	+	Stockholders' Equity					Rev.	–	Exp.	=	Net Inc.	Cash Flow
Cash	+ Acc. Rec.	=	Liab.	+	C. Stk.	+	Ret. Ear.			Rev.	–	Exp.	=	Net Inc.	Cash Flow
60,000 +	(60,000)	=	NA	+	NA	+	NA			NA	–	NA	=	NA	60,000 OA

Observe carefully that collecting the cash did not affect the income statement. The full $84,000 of revenue was recognized at the time that the work was done. Revenue would be double counted if it were recognized again when the cash is collected. The statement of cash flows reflects a cash inflow from operating activities.

Event 4 The instructor earned a salary of $16,000. No cash has yet been paid to the employee.

This event illustrates the common circumstance of recognizing expenses before paying cash. In this case, the $16,000 of salary expenses is offset by an increase in a liability account called *Salaries Payable*. As its name suggests, the **Salaries Payable** account represents amounts of future cash payments owed to the employee. The effect of the expense recognition on the financial statements follows:

Assets		=	Liab.	+	Stockholders' Equity					Rev.	–	Exp.	=	Net Inc.	Cash Flow
Cash +	Acc. Rec.	=	Sal. Pay.	+	C. Stk.	+	Ret. Ear.			Rev.	–	Exp.	=	Net Inc.	Cash Flow
NA +	NA	=	16,000	+	NA	+	(16,000)			NA	–	16,000	=	(16,000)	NA

This event is a **claims exchange transaction.** The claims of creditors (liabilities) increase, and the claims of owners (retained earnings) decrease by $16,000. Total claims remain unchanged. The expense is recognized on the income statement although cash has not been paid.

Be careful not to confuse liabilities with expenses. Although liabilities are sometimes affected when expenses are recognized, they are not the same thing as expenses. Expenses are economic sacrifices incurred in an effort to produce revenue. More specifically, expenses are decreases in assets or increases in liabilities that result from earnings activities. Expenses always reduce equity. In contrast, liabilities are obligations. They can arise from acquiring assets as well as recognizing expenses. For example, if a business borrows money from a bank, it recognizes a liability (an obligation to repay the bank). In this case, assets and liabilities both increase. Expenses are not affected. In summary, expenses are economic sacrifices that reduce equity; liabilities are obligations. Expenses are reported on the income statement; liabilities are reported on the balance sheet.

Event 5 Conner paid $10,000 to the instructor in partial settlement of salaries payable.

Cash payments to creditors are **asset use transactions.** When Conner pays the instructor, the asset account Cash and the liability account Salaries Payable both decrease by $10,000. The effect of this transaction on the financial statements follows:

Assets		=	Liab.	+	Stockholders' Equity					Rev.	–	Exp.	=	Net Inc.	Cash Flow
Cash	+ Acc. Rec.	=	Sal. Pay.	+	C. Stk.	+	Ret. Ear.			Rev.	–	Exp.	=	Net Inc.	Cash Flow
(10,000) +	NA	=	(10,000)	+	NA	+	NA			NA	–	NA	=	NA	(10,000) OA

The actual cash payment did not involve recognizing an expense. The expense was recognized in full at the time the employee did the work. Double counting would occur if it were recognized again when the cash payment is made. The statement of cash flows would reflect a cash outflow from operating activities.

Event 6 Conner paid $2,000 cash for advertising costs.

Cash payments for expenses are *asset use transactions*. Both the asset account Cash and the equity account Retained Earnings decrease by $2,000. Recognizing the expense decreases net income on the income statement. Since the expense was paid with cash, the statement of cash flows would reflect a cash outflow from operating activities. These effects on the financial statements follow:

Assets		=	Liab.	+	Stockholders' Equity						
Cash	+ Acc. Rec.	= Sal. Pay.	+	C. Stk.	+ Ret. Ear.	Rev.	– Exp.	= Net Inc.	Cash Flow
(2,000) +	NA	= NA	+	NA	+ (2,000)	NA	– 2,000	= (2,000)	(2,000) OA

Event 7 Conner signed contracts for $42,000 of consulting services to be performed in 2002.

The contracts for $42,000 of consulting services to be performed in 2002 are not recognized in the 2001 financial statements. Assets increase as the result of work that has actually been accomplished, *not* work that is expected to be accomplished. Since no work has been performed with respect to these contracts, assets have not increased and revenue has not been earned. More specifically, revenue is not recognized before the work is accomplished no matter how certain the likelihood of the future performance may be. As indicated, this event does not affect any of the financial statements.

Assets		=	Liab.	+	Stockholders' Equity						
Cash	+ Acc. Rec.	= Sal. Pay.	+	C. Stk.	+ Ret. Ear.	Rev.	– Exp.	= Net Inc.	Cash Flow
NA +	NA	= NA	+	NA	+ NA	NA	– NA	= NA	NA

Check Yourself 2–1

During 2004, Anwar Company earned $345,000 of revenue on account and collected $320,000 cash from accounts receivable. Expenses amounted to $300,000 and were paid with cash. Anwar paid a $12,000 cash dividend. Determine the amount of net income Anwar should report on the 2004 income statement and the amount of cash flow from operating activities Anwar should report on the 2004 statement of cash flows.

Answer Net income equals revenue minus expenses ($345,000 − $300,000 = $45,000). The cash flow from operating activities equals the amount of revenue collected in cash (collection of accounts receivable) minus the cash paid for expenses ($320,000 − $300,000 = $20,000). Dividend payments are classified as financing activities and do not affect either the determination of net income or cash flow from operating activities.

Summary of Transactions

LO3 Record events under an accounting equation.

Event 1 The business acquired $5,000 cash by issuing common stock.
Event 2 Conner provided $84,000 of consulting services on account.
Event 3 Conner collected $60,000 cash from customers in partial settlement of its accounts receivable.
Event 4 Conner recognized $16,000 of salary expense on account.
Event 5 Conner paid $10,000 to the part-time employee in partial settlement of the salary payable.
Event 6 Conner paid $2,000 cash for advertising costs.
Event 7 Conner signed contracts for $42,000 of consulting services to be performed in 2002.

The general ledger accounts used to record the transaction data for Conner Consultants' 2001 accounting period are shown in Exhibit 2–1. Event 7 is not shown in the illustration because it does not affect the balances in any of the ledger accounts. The data in the accounts are used to prepare the financial statements. Because of space limitations, the revenue and expense accounts are shown in the Retained Earnings column. The titles of these accounts are shown immediately to the right of the monetary amounts. The amounts have been color coded to facilitate tracing the data to the financial statements. Data in red appear on the balance sheet; data in blue on the income statement; and data in green on the statement of cash flows.

Exhibit 2-1 *Transaction Data Recorded in Accounts*

| | Assets | | = | Liabilities | + | Stockholders' Equity | | | |
| | Cash | + | Accounts Receivable = | Salaries Payable + | | Common Stock + | Retained Earnings | | Other Account Titles |
Event No.									
Beg. Bal.	0		0	0		0	0		
1	5,000					5,000			
2			84,000				84,000		Consulting Revenue
3	60,000		(60,000)						
4				16,000			(16,000)		Salary Expense
5	(10,000)			(10,000)					
6	(2,000)						(2,000)		Advertising Expense
End Bal.	53,000	+	24,000 =	6,000	+	5,000 +	66,000		

2001 Financial Statements

Conner Consultants' financial statements for the 2001 accounting period are shown in a vertical statements model in Exhibit 2–2.

Income Statement

The income statement explains the changes in stockholders' equity from all sources other than transactions with the owners of an enterprise. As such, it represents the change in net assets resulting from operating the business. In the case of Conner Consultants, the amount of net income ($66,000) represents the net economic benefit of owning the business. In other words, the wealth of the business increased as a result of performing consulting activities. Net income increases owner claims on business assets and thereby enhances the wealth of the owners.

Recognizing salaries expense in the Conner illustration expands the definition of expenses used in Chapter 1. In that chapter, expenses were defined as economic sacrifices resulting in asset decreases. In the Conner illustration, the recognition of salaries expense coincided with an increase in liabilities (salaries payable). So expenses actually can be defined as decreases in assets *or* increases in liabilities resulting from operating activities undertaken to generate revenue. Similarly, revenue recognition can coincide with decreases in liabilities. For example, a person could work off a debt rather than pay cash to the creditor, which would decrease the liability and increase revenue. As a result, the definition of **revenue** can be expanded as follows: an increase in assets *or* a decrease in liabilities resulting from the operating activities of a business enterprise.

Statement of Changes in Stockholders' Equity

The statement of changes in stockholders' equity reports the effects on equity of issuing common stock, earning net income, and paying dividends to stockholders. It identifies the ways in which an entity's equity increased and decreased as a result of transactions with owners and operating the business. In the Conner case, the statement shows that equity increased when the business acquired $5,000 cash by issuing common stock. The statement also indicates that equity increased by $66,000 as a result of earning income and that none of the $66,000 of net earnings was distributed to owners (no dividends were paid), so the amount of ending equity is $71,000 ($5,000 + $66,000).

Balance Sheet

The balance sheet provides information about an entity's assets, liabilities, and stockholders' equity at a particular time. It reports the economic resources (assets) that the enterprise has available for its operating activities. In addition, it displays the claims on those resources. Conner Consultants had two assets at the end of the 2001 accounting period: cash of $53,000

LO4 Prepare simple financial statements for a business that engages in cash and accrual transactions.

LO5 Explain how accrual transactions (as well as cash transactions introduced in Chapter 1) affect the financial statements of a business.

LO6 Define *revenue* and *expense* in terms of their relationships to assets and liabilities.

Exhibit 2–2 *Vertical Statements Model*		
CONNER CONSULTANTS **Financial Statements** **For the 2001 Accounting Period[1]**		
Income Statement		
Consulting Revenue		$84,000
Salary Expense		(16,000)
Advertising Expense		(2,000)
Net Income		$66,000
Statement of Changes in Stockholders' Equity		
Beginning Common Stock	$ 0	
Plus: Common Stock Issued	5,000	
Ending Common Stock		$ 5,000
Beginning Retained Earnings	0	
Plus: Net Income	66,000	
Less: Dividends	0	
Ending Retained Earnings		66,000
Total Stockholders' Equity		$71,000
Balance Sheet		
Assets		
Cash	$53,000	
Accounts Receivable	24,000	
Total Assets		$77,000
Liabilities		
Salaries Payable		$ 6,000
Stockholders' Equity		
Common Stock	$ 5,000	
Retained Earnings	66,000	
Total Stockholders' Equity		71,000
Total Liabilities and Stockholders' Equity		$77,000
Statement of Cash Flows		
Cash Flows from Operating Activities		
Cash Receipts from Customers	$60,000	
Cash Payments for Salary Expense	(10,000)	
Cash Payments for Advertising Expenses	(2,000)	
Net Cash Flow from Operating Activities		$48,000
Net Cash Flow from Investing Activities		0
Net Cash Flow from Financing Activities		
Cash Receipt from Issuing Common Stock		5,000
Net Change in Cash		53,000
Plus Beginning Cash Balance		0
Ending Cash Balance		$53,000

[1]As previously indicated, the vertical model format does not distinguish individual statement date characteristics ("as of" versus "for the year ended"). This practice is used through the text whenever the four financial statements are presented simultaneously. In real-world annual reports, financial statements are normally presented separately with appropriate descriptions of the date to indicate whether the statement applies to the entire accounting period or a specific point in time.

and accounts receivable of $24,000. These assets are listed on the balance sheet according to their respective levels of liquidity. Of the total $77,000 of assets, creditors have a $6,000 claim, leaving a $71,000 claim that represents owner interests.

Statement of Cash Flows

The statement of cash flows explains the change in cash from one accounting period to the next. It can be prepared by analyzing the Cash account. Since Conner Consultants was established in the 2001 accounting period, its beginning cash balance was zero. By the end of the accounting period, the balance increased to $53,000. The statement of cash flows explains this

The accrual concept requires a company to recognize revenue when it is "earned" rather than when it collects cash. In some business operations, it is not always easy to know precisely when the revenue is earned. CSX Corporation, a very large transportation company, recognizes revenue "proportionately as shipments move from origin to destination."

This means that if CSX agrees to ship goods 868 miles for $1,500, it recognizes approximately $1.73 of revenue for every mile the goods are moved. If you are thinking that this must require a very sophisticated computer system, you are correct!

Notice that the "recognize-as-you-go" practice does not violate the rule that revenue cannot be recognized before it is earned. CSX cannot recognize the entire $1,500 until the point of destination has been reached. However, the company can recognize the revenue in proportion to the amount of the trip that is completed. If one-half of the trip is completed, one-half of the revenue can be recognized.

increase. Specifically, the Cash account balance increased by $60,000 from consulting activities (operating the business). Furthermore, $12,000 was paid for expenses. As a result, Conner experienced a net cash inflow from operating activities of $48,000. Also, the business acquired $5,000 cash by issuing common stock. This combination of activities explains the $53,000 (or $48,000 + $5,000) increase in cash during the 2001 accounting period.

Closing the Accounts

Recall from Chapter 1 that the balances in the nominal accounts (revenues, expenses, and dividends) are transferred out of those accounts at the end of each accounting period through a process known as *closing the accounts*. Exhibit 2–3 shows the general ledger accounts for Conner Consultants after the revenue and expense accounts have been closed to Retained Earnings. In this case, there were three **closing entries,** which transferred the balances of the nominal accounts to the Retained Earnings account at the end of the accounting period. These entries are labeled Cl.1, Cl.2, and Cl.3 to facilitate your review. The first entry (Cl.1) transferred the balance in the Consulting Revenue account to the Retained Earnings account. The second (Cl.2) and third (Cl.3) closing entries transferred the balances in the expense accounts

Exhibit 2–3 *General Ledger Accounts for Conner Consultants*

Assets		=	Liabilities		+	Stockholders' Equity	
Cash			**Salaries Payable**			**Common Stock**	
[1]	5,000		[4]	16,000		[1]	5,000
[3]	60,000		[5]	(10,000)			
[5]	(10,000)					**Retained Earnings**	
[6]	(2,000)		Bal.	6,000		Cl.1	84,000
Bal.	53,000					Cl.2	(16,000)
						Cl.3	(2,000)
Accounts Receivable						Bal.	66,000
[2]	84,000						
[3]	(60,000)					**Consulting Revenue**	
Bal.	24,000					[2]	84,000
						Cl.1	(84,000)
						Bal.	0
						Salary Expense	
						[4]	(16,000)
						Cl.2	16,000
						Bal.	0
						Advertising Expense	
						[6]	(2,000)
						Cl.3	2,000
						Bal.	0

to the Retained Earnings account. As a result of the closing entries, the balances for these revenue and expense accounts will be zero at the beginning of the 2002 accounting period. The balances from these accounts are now summarized in Retained Earnings. The Retained Earnings account reflects the cumulative effect of revenues, expenses, and dividends since the company's inception.

Matching Concept

Businesses must make economic sacrifices (incur expenses) to produce economic benefits (earn revenues). A business is successful to the extent that the benefits exceed the sacrifices. Accrual accounting seeks to measure the success (profitability) of a business enterprise by matching the expenses (sacrifices) with the revenues (benefits) that they produce. The income statement reports the result of the matching process.

In the case of Conner Consultants, the instructor's salary expense can be matched easily with the revenue that the teaching activity generated. However, the advertising expense presents a more challenging matching issue. The advertising cost can generate revenue in future accounting periods as well as the present period. For example, a prospective customer could save an advertising brochure for several years. At some future date when the customer needs training services, he might retrieve the brochure and call Conner to perform those services. In cases such as these, where the relationship between the expense and the corresponding revenue is vague, common practice is to match the expense with the period in which it is incurred. With respect to Conner's advertising cost, the entire $2,000 is matched with (recognized in) the 2001 accounting period even though some of that cost might generate revenue in future accounting periods. Expenses that are matched with the period in which they were incurred are frequently called **period costs**.

LO2 Identify business events that involve accruals.

▌Second Accounting Cycle

Assume that the following accounting events apply to the operations of Conner Consultants during 2002:

Event 1 Conner Consultants acquired $25,000 cash by issuing common stock.
Event 2 During the period, $96,000 of revenue was recognized on account.
Event 3 Conner collected $102,000 of cash from accounts receivable.
Event 4 Conner accrued $22,000 of salary expense.
Event 5 Cash paid toward the settlement of salaries payable was $20,000.
Event 6 Conner paid a $10,000 cash dividend to stockholders.

These events are conceptually identical to transactions that have been discussed previously. The effects of these events on the general ledger accounts are shown in Exhibit 2–4. If you are having difficulty understanding these effects, review the previous material.

Event 7 On March 1, 2002, Conner invested $60,000 in a certificate of deposit (CD).

LO5 Explain how accrual transactions (as well as cash transactions introduced in Chapter 1) affect the financial statements of a business.

The purchase of the certificate of deposit is an asset exchange transaction. It represents an **investment** made by Conner. The event decreases the asset account Cash and increases the asset account Certificate of Deposit. Total assets remain unchanged. The income statement is not affected. The statement of cash flows shows an outflow from investing activities. The effects of this transaction on the financial statements are shown here.

Assets		= Liab. +	Stockholders' Equity						
Cash	+ CD	= Liab. +	C. Stk. +	Ret. Ear.	Rev. −	Exp. =	Net Inc.	Cash Flow	
(60,000)	+ 60,000	= NA +	NA +	NA	NA −	NA =	NA	(60,000)	IA

Adjusting the Accounts

Event 8 **On December 31, 2002, Conner adjusted the books to recognize interest revenue earned on the certificate of deposit. The certificate had a 6 percent annual rate of interest and a one-year term to maturity. Interest is due in cash on the maturity date (February 28, 2003).**

When Conner invested in (purchased) the certificate of deposit, the company, in fact, loaned the bank money. In exchange for the privilege of using Conner's money, the bank agreed to return the money (principal) and an additional 6 percent of the principal amount (interest) to Conner one year from the date that it borrowed the funds. In other words, in exchange for receiving $60,000 on March 1, 2002, the bank agreed to pay Conner $63,600 (or $60,000 + [0.06 × $60,000]) on February 28, 2003. Conner will receive $3,600 (0.06 × $60,000) per year as compensation for letting the bank use its cash.

It is important to recognize that interest is earned continually even though the full amount of cash is not collected until the maturity date. In other words, the amount of interest due increases proportionally as time passes. Without using sophisticated computer equipment, recording (recognizing) interest continually is impossible.

As a practical matter, many businesses let interest accrue without recognition until it is time to prepare financial statements. The accounts are then *adjusted* to reflect the amount of interest due as of the date of the financial statements. For example, when Conner purchased the certificate of deposit (CD) on March 1, 2002, it recorded the asset exchange immediately (see Event 7). However, it would not recognize the interest earned on the certificate until the date of the financial statements, December 31, 2002. At that time, Conner would make an entry to recognize all of the interest that had been earned during the previous 10 months (March 1 through December 31). This entry is called an **adjusting entry** because it updates (adjusts) the account balances prior to preparing financial statements.

The amount of interest is computed by multiplying the face value (purchase price) of the CD by the annual interest rate and by the length of time for which the certificate has been outstanding.

Principal × Annual interest rate × Time outstanding = Interest revenue

$60,000 × 0.06 × (10/12) = $3,000

The effects of the adjusting entry on the financial statements follow.

Assets			= Liab. +	Stockholders' Equity					
Cash +	CD +	Int. Rec. =	Liab. +	C. Stk. +	Ret. Ear.	Rev. −	Exp. =	Net Inc.	Cash Flow
NA +	NA +	3,000 =	NA +	NA +	3,000	3,000 −	NA =	3,000	NA

The interest is treated as revenue in 2002 although the cash will not be collected until 2003. This practice is consistent with the **matching concept**. Interest revenue is recognized in (matched with) the period in which it is earned regardless of when the associated cash is collected. The adjusting entry is an asset source transaction. The asset account Interest Receivable increases, and the stockholders' equity account Retained Earnings increases. The income statement reflects an increase in revenue and net income. The statement of cash flows is not affected because cash will not be collected until the maturity date (February 28, 2003).

Mei Company purchased a $36,000 certificate of deposit (CD) from State Bank on October 1, 2004. The CD had a 5 percent annual interest rate and a two-year term to maturity. The interest is to be collected in cash on the maturity date. Determine the amount of interest revenue Mei would report on the 2004 income statement and the amount of cash flow from operating activities Mei would report on the 2004 statement of cash flows.

Answer Mei would report interest revenue of $450 on the 2004 income statement (see the following calculation). There would be no cash flow from operating activities to report on the 2004 statement of cash flows because Mei will not collect any cash for the interest until the CD matures on September 30, 2006. (Mei *would* report a $36,000 cash outflow in 2004 for the CD purchase as an investing activity, not an operating activity.)

$$\text{Principal} \times \text{Annual interest rate} \times \text{Time outstanding} = \text{Interest revenue}$$
$$\$36,000 \times 0.05 \times (3/12) = \$450$$

Because the interest rate is 5 percent *per year,* the denominator for the *time outstanding* is 12 months although the note has a 24-month term. Mei will earn 5 percent interest each year, a total of 10 percent for the full 24-month term.

Summary of Transactions

LO3 Record events under an accounting equation.

Event 1 Conner Consultants acquired $25,000 cash by issuing common stock.
Event 2 During the period, Conner recognized $96,000 of revenue on account.
Event 3 Conner collected $102,000 of cash from accounts receivable.
Event 4 Accrued salary expenses amounted to $22,000.
Event 5 Cash paid toward the settlement of salaries payable was $20,000.
Event 6 Conner paid a $10,000 cash dividend to stockholders.
Event 7 On March 1, 2002, Conner invested $60,000 in a certificate of deposit (CD).
Event 8 On December 31, 2002, Conner adjusted the books to recognize interest revenue earned on the certificate of deposit. The certificate had a 6 percent annual rate of interest and a one-year term to maturity. Interest is due in cash on the maturity date (February 28, 2003).

The general ledger accounts used to record the transaction data for Conner Consultants' 2002 accounting period are shown in Exhibit 2–4. The data in the accounts are used to prepare the financial statements. Because of space limitations, the revenue and expense accounts are shown in the Retained Earnings column. The titles of these accounts are shown immediately

Exhibit 2–4 *Transaction Data Recorded in Accounts*

Event No.		Assets			=	Liabilities +	Stockholders' Equity		
	Cash	+ Accounts Receivable	+ Interest Receivable	+ Certificate Of Deposit	=	Salaries Payable	+ Common Stock	+ Retained Earnings	Other Account Titles
Beg. Bal.	53,000	24,000	0	0		6,000	5,000	66,000	
1	25,000						25,000		
2		96,000						96,000	Consulting Revenue
3	102,000	(102,000)							
4						22,000		(22,000)	Salary Expense
5	(20,000)					(20,000)			
6	(10,000)							(10,000)	Dividends
7	(60,000)			60,000					
8			3,000					3,000	Interest Revenue
End Bal.	90,000 +	18,000 +	3,000 +	60,000	=	8,000 +	30,000 +	133,000	

to the right of the monetary amounts. The amounts have been color coded to facilitate tracing the data to the financial statements. Data in red appear on the balance sheet; data in blue on the income statement; and data in green on the statement of cash flows.

2002 Financial Statements

The ledger account balances shown in Exhibit 2–4 are used to prepare the financial statements shown in Exhibit 2–5. The relationships among the statements are discussed in the following section of the chapter.

LO4 Prepare simple financial statements for a business that engages in cash and accrual transactions.

Exhibit 2–5 *Vertical Statements Model*

HAYNES CONSULTANTS
Financial Statements
For the 2002 Accounting Period

Income Statements

Consulting Revenue	$ 96,000	
Interest Revenue	3,000	
Total Revenue		$ 99,000
Salary Expense		(22,000)
Net Income		$ 77,000

Statement of Changes in Stockholders' Equity

Beginning Common Stock	$ 5,000	
Plus: Common Stock Issued	25,000	
Ending Common Stock		$30,000
Beginning Retained Earnings	66,000	
Plus: Net Income	77,000	
Less: Dividends	(10,000)	
Ending Retained Earnings		133,000
Total Stockholders' Equity		$163,000

Balance Sheet

Assets		
Cash	$ 90,000	
Accounts Receivable	18,000	
Interest Receivable	3,000	
Certificate of Deposit	60,000	
Total Assets		$171,000
Liabilities		
Salaries Payable		$ 8,000
Stockholders' Equity		
Common Stock	$ 30,000	
Retained Earnings	133,000	
Total Stockholders' Equity		163,000
Total Liabilities and Stockholders' Equity		$171,000

Statement of Cash Flows

Cash Flows from Operating Activities		
Cash Receipts from Revenue	$102,000	
Cash Payments for Salaries Expense	(20,000)	
Net Cash Flow from Operating Activities		$ 82,000
Cash Flows from Investing Activities		
Cash Payment to Purchase CD		(60,000)
Cash Flows from Financing Activities		
Cash Receipt from Common Stock Issue	25,000	
Cash Payment for Dividends	(10,000)	
Net Cash Flow from Financing Activities		15,000
Net Change in Cash		37,000
Plus: Beginning Cash Balance		53,000
Ending Cash Balance		$ 90,000

Income Statement

Note that the amount of net income ($77,000) is not a cash-equivalent figure. The cash flow from operating activities is $82,000, as shown in the statement of cash flows. Although $96,000 of consulting revenue was recognized, $102,000 of cash was collected from customers because some of the revenue recognized in 2001 was actually collected in 2002. Also, the income statement reports recognition of $3,000 of interest revenue. None of this revenue was collected during 2002. Accordingly, the total amount of cash collected from revenue transactions was $102,000. Finally, although the amount of salary expense recognized was $22,000, the amount paid was only $20,000. Accordingly, the net cash inflow from operating activities was $82,000 ($102,000 − $20,000). In contrast, the income statement displays the amount of net income recognized ($96,000 + $3,000 − $22,000 = $77,000).

Statement of Changes in Stockholders' Equity

The beginning balances for the Common Stock and Retained Earnings accounts equal last year's ending balances. The $25,000 stock issue is added to the $5,000 beginning Common Stock balance to determine the $30,000 ending balance. Of the $77,000 of net income, $10,000 was distributed to the stockholders. Accordingly, Retained Earnings increases by $67,000 ($77,000 net income − $10,000 dividend) from a beginning balance of $66,000 to an ending balance of $133,000. The ending balance in total stockholders' equity amounts to $163,000 ($30,000 common stock + $133,000 retained earnings).

Balance Sheet

Although two additional asset accounts appear in the 2002 balance sheet, all assets continue to be listed according to their respective levels of liquidity. Total assets amount to $171,000, which equals the claims of $171,000. The claims are divided into the claim associated with creditors (salaries payable) of $8,000 and the stockholders' claim of $163,000.

Statement of Cash Flows

The $82,000 net cash inflow from operating activities is discussed in the section pertaining to the income statement. In addition to this amount, an analysis of the Cash account discloses a $60,000 cash outflow from purchasing the certificate of deposit. Furthermore, an additional $25,000 cash inflow resulted from issuing common stock, and, finally, a $10,000 cash outflow occurred in the form of a dividend paid to the stockholders. Accordingly, the net change in cash was a $37,000 increase ($82,000 − $60,000 + $15,000). This increase can be verified by comparing the Cash balance at the beginning of the period ($53,000) with the Cash balance at the end of the period ($90,000). The difference is a $37,000 increase.

LO7 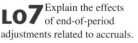 Explain the effects of end-of-period adjustments related to accruals.

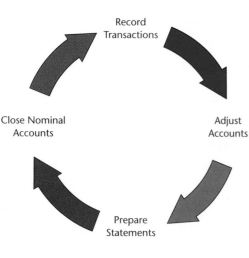

Accounting Cycle

The adjusting process described earlier applies to many different types of accounting events. Many of these events will be discussed in subsequent chapters. At this point you should recognize that adjusting the accounts is an integral part of the **accounting cycle.** So far, we have discussed four stages of the accounting cycle: (1) recording transactions, (2) adjusting the accounts, (3) preparing financial statements, and (4) closing the accounts. Stage 1 occurs throughout the accounting period. Stages 2, 3, and 4 normally occur at the end of the accounting period. Other stages will be added in the following chapters of the text.

■ Accounting for Notes Payable

LO5 Explain how accrual transactions (as well as cash transactions introduced in Chapter 1) affect the financial statements of a business.

This section of the text describes how borrowing funds from a bank affects a company's financial statements. Conner most likely engaged in numerous transactions during its 2003 and 2004 accounting periods, but we limit our discussion to the transactions associated with borrowing activities. The specific transactions discussed are shown in the following statements model.

	Assets	=	Liabilities			+	Stockholders' Equity								
Date	Cash	=	Note Pay.	+	Int. Pay.	+	C. Stk.	+	Ret. Ear.	Rev.	–	Exp.	=	Net Inc.	Cash Flow
09/01/03	90,000	=	90,000	+	NA	+	NA	+	NA	NA	–	NA	=	NA	90,000 FA
12/31/03	NA	=	NA	+	2,700	+	NA	+	(2,700)	NA	–	2,700	=	(2,700)	NA
08/31/04	NA	=	NA	+	5,400	+	NA	+	(5,400)	NA	–	5,400	=	(5,400)	NA
08/31/04	(8,100)	=	NA	+	(8,100)	+	NA	+	NA	NA	–	NA	=	NA	(8,100) OA
08/31/04	(90,000)	=	(90,000)	+	NA	+	NA	+	NA	NA	–	NA	=	NA	(90,000) FA

The transaction on September 1, 2003, shows that Conner borrowed money by issuing a $90,000 note to a local bank. This is an asset source transaction. The asset account Cash increases by $90,000, and the liability account Note Payable increases by the same amount. The account title **Note Payable** is used because the bank normally requires the borrower to sign a note that describes the loan terms. Typical items included in the note are the rate of interest, the term to maturity, and any collateral that is pledged to secure the loan. The borrower issues (gives) the note to the bank and receives money from the bank. The borrower is the **issuer of a note,** and the bank is called the *creditor* or *lender.* Borrowing funds is a financing activity that is reported on the statement of cash flows. The income statement is not affected by the borrowing activity.

The note had a 9 percent annual rate of interest and a one-year term. An *adjusting entry* is necessary to recognize the interest that accrued from September 1 through December 31. In this case four months of interest accrued by the closing date, December 31, 2003. The accrued interest is $2,700 ($90,000 × 0.09 × [4/12]). The entry to record the accrued interest reflects a claims exchange. The liability account Interest Payable increases, and the equity account Retained Earnings decreases. The income statement reflects interest expense although no cash was paid in 2003.

Three events recorded in the statements model are dated August 31, 2004 (the maturity date). The first entry records the $5,400 of interest that accrued in 2004 between January 1 and August 31 ($90,000 × 0.09 × [8/12]). This entry parallels the adjusting entry made on December 31, 2003. It is used to reflect the balance of the accrued interest on the note.

The second entry on August 31, 2004, reflects the cash paid for interest. This is an asset use transaction that reduces the Cash and Retained Earnings accounts by $8,100 ($90,000 × 0.09 × [12/12]). In other words, the entire amount of interest (four months accrued in 2003 and eight months accrued in 2004) is paid on August 31, 2004. There is no effect on the income statement because the interest expense was recognized previously. The statement of cash flows shows the cash outflow resulting from operating activities.

The final entry dated August 31, 2004, reflects the repayment of principal. This is an asset use transaction. The Cash account and the Notes Payable account decrease by $90,000. The income statement is not affected because repaying a loan is not an earnings activity. The statement of cash flows shows a $90,000 cash outflow from financing activities. Note carefully that the interest payment is classified as an operating activity while the principal repayment is treated as a financing activity.

Because this section discussed only a limited selection of transactions that occurred in 2003 and 2004, a full set of financial statements is not presented for these accounting periods.

Trent, Incorporated, borrowed $120,000 by issuing a note to the National Bank on November 1, 2004. The note had a 12 percent annual interest rate and a one-year term to maturity. Determine the amount of interest expense and the cash flow from operating activities Trent would report on the 2004 and 2005 financial statements.

Answer The amount of interest expense Trent would recognize each year is computed as follows:

	Principal ×	Annual interest rate ×	Time outstanding	= Interest expense
2004	$120,000 ×	0.12	× (2/12)	= $ 2,400
2005	$120,000 ×	0.12	× (10/12)	= $12,000

Because Trent will pay the total amount of interest ($120,000 × 0.12 × 12/12 = $14,400) on the maturity date (October 31, 2005), there is no cash flow from operating activities to report in 2004 and a $14,400 cash outflow from operating activities in 2005.

Check
Yourself
2–3

Under the accrual system, accountants recognize revenue after the work has been done but before the cash is collected. Investors are more aggressive than accountants with respect to income recognition. They recognize income even before the work is done. This explains why stock (ownership) of some companies sells for more than stock of other companies. Investors buy stock because they want to participate in the profit (net income) that the company earns. Accordingly, investors are willing to pay more for a company whose future earnings potential is significantly greater than average. For example, since Microsoft operates in an industry with significant growth potential, its stock may sell for 40 times earnings while Exxon's is selling for only 10 times earnings. This means if Microsoft and Exxon were earning $1 per share of stock, Microsoft's stock would be selling for $40 while Exxon's stock would be selling for $10. In other words, investors are basing their purchases on the companies' potential to earn future profits rather than their past earnings history as depicted in the companies' financial statements. Does this mean that financial statements are not useful in making investment decisions? This answer is no. Past earnings provide insight into the future. In other words, a company that has a history of earnings that grow at a rate of 30 percent per year is more likely to continue to experience rapid growth than a company with a 10 percent historical growth rate. Accordingly, financial statements that are based on accrual accounting can provide insight into the future even though they are historically based.

■ Role of the Independent Auditor

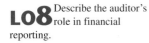

LO8 Describe the auditor's role in financial reporting.

The four basic financial statements presented in annual reports are the income statement, statement of changes in equity, balance sheet, and statement of cash flows. As previously indicated, these statements are prepared in accordance with certain rules, called *generally accepted accounting principles,* or simply *GAAP.* Thus, when General Electric publishes its financial statements, it is saying not only "here are our financial statements," but more specifically, "here are our financial statements prepared according to GAAP." As discussed throughout this course, the application of GAAP requires considerable judgment and calls for some interpretation, estimation, and assumption making. How can users of financial statements be sure that a company really did follow GAAP and whether it exercised reasonable judgment and good faith in the application of GAAP to its financial reporting practices? Users rely on **audits** conducted by certified public accountants (CPAs).

The following sections will discuss in detail the overall roles and responsibilities the independent auditor assumes. Briefly, the independent auditor performs several functions:

1. Conducts a financial audit, which is a detailed examination of a company's financial statements and documents.
2. Assumes both legal and professional responsibilities to the public, not to the company paying the auditor.
3. Guarantees that financial statements are materially correct rather than absolutely correct.
4. Presents conclusions in an audit report, which includes an opinion resulting from the audit. When necessary, the auditor issues a disclaimer.
5. Maintains professional confidentiality with clients. However, this does not exempt the auditor from legal obligations such as testifying in court.

The Financial Audit

What is an audit? First, you must realize that there are several different types of audits. The type most relevant to this course is called a **financial audit,** which is a detailed examination of a company's financial statements and the documents that support the information presented in those statements. The audit includes a verification process that tests the reliability of the underlying accounting system used to produce the financial reports. A financial audit is conducted by a CPA who is known as the **independent auditor.**

Understanding the role of an independent auditor is almost as important as understanding what a financial audit is. Normally, the term *independent auditor* designates a *firm of* **certified public accountants.** CPAs are licensed by state governments to provide accounting services to the public. CPAs who perform financial audits are paid by the companies that they audit. However, CPAs are not employees of those companies. In fact, neither the CPAs nor their immediate family members may own stock or have any other type of investment in the companies they audit. Furthermore, the payment of CPAs is not to be based on the outcome of the audit. The CPAs are to be as independent of the companies they audit as is reasonably possible.

Although the independent auditors are chosen by, paid by, and can be fired by the company that they are auditing, the auditors have a primary responsibility to *the public.* In fact, auditors have a legal responsibility to those members of the public who have a financial interest in the company being audited. If investors in a company lose money, they sometimes sue the independent auditors in an attempt to recover their losses. This is more likely to occur if the loss was due to something dramatic, such as the company's filing for bankruptcy. The lawsuit will be successful only if it can be shown that the auditors failed in their professional responsibilities when conducting the audit. The fact that a company declares bankruptcy does not imply that the auditors can be sued successfully. In reality, auditors are not sued very often, given the number of audits they perform.

Auditors' professional responsibility is to ensure that the company properly reports its financial situation, whether good or bad. Auditors get into trouble when a company has a problem that is not properly reported and the auditors do not detect the improper reporting practice. For example, a company might overstate the amount of its net income. If the auditors allow the incorrect amount to be reported and the size of the error is

Exhibit 2–6 *No Rubber Stamp for Accountants*

An accounting degree is, indeed, "the one degree with 360 degrees of possibilities." And personalities within the profession are as diverse as the range of job opportunities available to the accounting graduate. There is no rubber stamp for today's accountants. Consider the experiences of the following individuals.

Jerry Gibbons is a partner in the accounting firm Gibbons & Dees. Jerry teaches a course in the fundamentals of sports accounting in several Asian countries. As an adjunct professor for the United States Sports Academy, Jerry had the opportunity to meet with the Olympic committees when he taught in Hong Kong, Singapore, Kuala Lumpur, and Bangkok. Although it was his second Asian assignment, Gibbons says he was again overwhelmed with the friendliness and generosity of the Asian people.

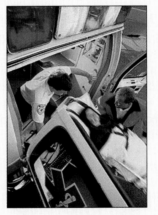

Danny Martin was recently promoted to manager at Wilson, Price, Barranco & Billingsley, a regional firm of certified public accountants. Danny worked his way through college as a paramedic and has just never gotten over the thrill of flying down the highway in an ambulance. "That's my stress management," says the father of two, who still works two weekends a month as a paramedic for Haynes Ambulance. His adventures with CPR, heart defibrillation, and drug therapy take him a world away from his job in the Business Services Department of his firm.

Sister Rose Marie of Divine Love left public accounting to enter the cloistered life at Our Lady of the Angels Monastery. She now helps the bookkeepers at Eternal Word Television Network (EWTN), a 24-hour-a-day network that has more than 160 employees and broadcasts into Europe, Moscow, the Middle East, Africa, and all the Americas. Sister Rose Marie took a vow of poverty when she entered the Order of Poor Clares of Perpetual Adoration (P.C.P.A.), which may be why one auditor at EWTN, she says, asked her if the initials after her name stood for "poor CPA."

material, the auditors create a problem for which they may suffer legal consequences.

Although the information in this chapter focuses on the audit function, CPAs provide many services across a wide spectrum of jobs. Reading the information in Exhibit 2–6 will give you a better understanding of the diversity of job opportunities that await graduates with degrees in accounting.

Materiality and Financial Audits

Now things get a bit fuzzy. What is a **material error?** An error, or other reporting problem, is considered *material* if knowing about the problem would affect the decisions of an *average* *prudent investor.* Thus, the concept of materiality is very subjective. However, it means that the auditors are not guaranteeing that the financial statements are absolutely correct—only that they are *materially* correct. If General Motors inadvertently overstated its sales by $1 million, would this be material? In 2000, GM had approximately $185 billion of sales! A $1 million error in computing sales at GM is like a $1 error in computing the pay of a person who makes $185,000 per year—not material at all!

A financial audit is not concerned with absolute precision, and it is not primarily looking for fraud on the part of the company's employees. Even so, auditors are responsible for providing *reasonable assurance* that their audits will detect material misstatements (fraud). Also, auditors are responsible for ensuring that internal control procedures (explained in Chapter 6) are in place to help prevent fraud. If fraud is widespread in a company, normal audit procedures should detect it.

Accounting majors take at least one and often two or more courses in auditing to understand how to conduct an audit to detect material accounting problems. Obviously, there is not enough time in this course to explain auditing techniques, but at least be aware that auditors do not review how the company accounted for every transaction. Along with other methods, auditors use statistical sampling to systematically review company records.

Types Of Audit Opinions

Once an audit is complete, the auditors present their conclusions in an audit report, which includes an *audit opinion.* There are three basic types of audit opinions, with variations.

An **unqualified opinion,** despite its negative-sounding name, is the best that auditors can give. It means that the auditor believes the financial statements are in compliance with GAAP without qualification, reservation, or exception.

The most negative report that an auditor can issue is an **adverse opinion.** This means that something(s) in the financial statements is (are) not in compliance with GAAP and the auditors

focus on International Issues

Is Historical Cost Used in Other Countries?

Accounting rules in the United States require the use of the **historical cost** to record most accounting transactions. Thus, if Coca-Cola Company purchased land in Atlanta for $10,000 in 1920, that land, if still owned, will be on the company's 2020 balance sheet at $10,000 even if it is worth

$5,000,000 by then. Not everyone in the United States thinks this is the best way to report accounting numbers, but U.S. GAAP requires the use of historical costs.

The accounting rules of most countries around the world also use the historical cost as the primary means of measuring and reporting costs; however, there are exceptions. The major exceptions occur in economies that have experienced high inflation. In the hypothetical Coca-Cola example, a time frame of 100 years was used to make the change in the value of the land look dramatic. In short time spans, land prices in the United States do not change so radically, so most accountants are comfortable with using historical costs. In some South American countries, prices have risen much faster than those in the United States. For example, while the annual rate of inflation in the United States typically ranges from 2 to 6 percent, in Brazil it has seldom been below 20 percent and in some years has exceeded 1,000 percent. Not surprisingly, the GAAP in Brazil does not use historical costs as the primary way of reporting financial information.

In some countries, such as the Netherlands, companies use historical costs as their primary way of measuring costs but may report the value of some assets, such as land and buildings, at the amount it would cost to replace them "today" rather than at their historical costs. Accounting is a discipline created to serve the needs of financial statement users. It is logical that accounting rules reflect the unique needs of users in different countries.

think these things would be material to the average prudent investor. The auditor's report explains the unacceptable accounting practice(s) that resulted in the adverse opinions being issued. Adverse opinions are very rare. To avoid receiving an adverse opinion, a company usually corrects the accounting issue that concerns the auditors.

A **qualified opinion** falls between an unqualified and an adverse opinion. A qualified opinion means that for the most part, the company's financial statements are in compliance with GAAP, but the auditors have reservations about something in the statements or have some other reason not to give a fully unqualified opinion. At least an entire chapter could be written about reasons to issue qualified opinions, but typically they result from the auditors' need to bring special attention to some accounting attribute in the financial statements. A qualified opinion usually does not imply a serious accounting problem, but users should read the auditors' report and draw their own conclusions about the relevance of the issues involved. The auditors' report explains why a qualified opinion is being issued.

If an auditor is unable to perform the audit procedures necessary to determine whether the statements are prepared in accordance with GAAP, the auditor cannot issue an opinion on the financial statements. Instead, the auditor issues a **disclaimer of audit opinion.** A disclaimer is neither negative nor positive; it simply means that the auditor is unable to obtain enough information to confirm compliance or noncompliance with GAAP.

It is very important to understand that the ultimate responsibility for the financial statements rests with the executives of the reporting company. Just like auditors, managers can be sued by investors who believe that they lost money due to improper financial reporting. This is one reason nonaccounting businesspeople should understand accounting fundamentals.

Confidentiality

The code of ethics for CPAs forbids auditors from **voluntarily disclosing** information that they have acquired as a result of their accountant-client relationships. However, accountants may be required to testify in a court of law. In general, federal law does not recognize an accountant-client privilege as it does with attorneys and clergy. Even so, federal courts have taken exception to this position, especially as it applies to tax cases. State law varies with respect to its treatment of accountant-client privilege. Furthermore, if auditors terminate a client relationship because of ethical or legal disagreements and they are subsequently contacted by a successor accountant, they may be required to inform the successor of the reasons that led to the termination. In addition, the particular circumstances surrounding the case must be considered when assessing the appropriateness of making such a disclosure. Given the legal diversity, with respect to the issue of accountant-client confidentiality, it is wise to seek legal counsel prior to making any disclosures of information obtained in an accountant-client relationship.

To illustrate, assume that Joe Smith, CPA, discovers that his client Jane Doe is misrepresenting information shown in her financial statements. Smith tries to convince Doe to reform her practices, but she refuses to cease and desist. Smith is required by the code of ethics to terminate his relationship with Doe. However, Smith is not permitted to disclose Doe's dishonest reporting practices unless he is called on to provide testimony in a legal hearing or is responding to an inquiry by Doe's successor accountant.

With respect to the discovery of significant fraud, the auditor is required to inform management at one level above the position of the employee who is engaged in the fraud and to notify the board of directors of the company. Suppose that Joe Smith, CPA, discovers that Jane Doe, employee of Western Company, is embezzling money from Western. Smith is required to inform Doe's supervisor and to notify Western's board of directors. However, Smith is restricted from speaking publicly about the fraud.

▌Importance of Ethics

The accountant's role in society cannot be performed without the establishment of trust and credibility. An audit opinion is worthless if the auditor is not trustworthy. Similarly, tax and consulting advice is useless if it comes from an incompetent person. In view of the high ethical standards required by the profession, "a certified public accountant assumes an obligation

LO9 Develop an appreciation of the importance of a code of ethics.

of self-discipline above and beyond requirements of laws and regulations."[2] Indeed, the **American Institute of Certified Public Accountants** requires its members to conduct themselves in accordance with its provisions, the **Code of Professional Conduct.** Section I of the code includes six articles that are summarized in Exhibit 2–7. The importance of ethical conduct is universally recognized across a broad spectrum of accounting organizations. The Institute of Management Accountants requires its members to follow a set of Standards of Ethical Conduct. Likewise, the membership of the Institute of Internal Auditors is required to subscribe to the organization's Code of Ethics.

Exhibit 2–7 *Articles of AICPA Code of Professional Conduct*

Article I Responsibilities

In carrying out their responsibilities as professionals, members should exercise sensitive professional and moral judgments in all their activities.

Article II The Public Interest

Members should accept the obligation to act in a way that will serve the public interest, honor the public trust, and demonstrate commitment to professionalism.

Article III Integrity

To maintain and broaden public confidence, members should perform all professional responsibilities with the highest sense of integrity.

Article IV Objectivity and Independence

A member should maintain objectivity and be free of conflicts of interest in discharging professional responsibilities. A member in public practice should be independent in fact and appearance when providing auditing and other attestation services.

Article V Due Care

A member should observe the profession's technical and ethical standards, strive continually to improve competence and the quality of services, and discharge professional responsibility to the best of the member's ability.

Article VI Scope and Nature of Services

A member in public practice should observe the principles of the Code of Professional Conduct in determining the scope and nature of services to be provided.

Common Features of Ethical Misconduct

People who become involved in unethical or criminal behavior usually do so unexpectedly. They start with small indiscretions that evolve gradually into more serious violations of trust. Accordingly, awareness constitutes a key ingredient for the avoidance of unethical or illegal conduct. In an effort to increase awareness, Donald Cressey studied hundreds of criminal cases to identify the primary factors that lead to trust violations.[3] Cressey found that three factors were common to all cases:

The existence of a nonsharable problem.
The presence of an opportunity.
The capacity for rationalization.

As the term implies, a *nonsharable problem* is one that must be kept secret. However, note that individuals have different ideas about what they think must be kept to themselves. Consider two responses to the problem of an imminent business failure. One person may feel so ashamed that he or she cannot discuss the problem with anyone. Another person in the same situation may want to talk to anyone, even a stranger, in the hope of getting help. Cressey's findings suggest that the person who is inclined toward secrecy is more likely to accept an unethical or illegal solution. In other words, secrecy increases vulnerability.

Accountants establish policies and procedures that are designed to reduce the opportunities for fraud. These policies and procedures are commonly called **internal controls.** Specific

---

[2]American Institute of Certified Public Accountants, Inc. (AICPA), *Code of Professional Conduct* (New York: AICPA, 1992).

[3]D. R. Cressey, *Other People's Money* (Montclair, NJ: Paterson Smith, 1973).

internal control procedures are tailored to meet the individual needs of particular businesses. For example, a bank may use vaults, but a university has little use for this type of equipment. Chapter 6 has a more detailed discussion of internal control procedures. At this point, simply recognize the fact that accountants are very aware of the need to reduce the opportunity for unethical and criminal activities.

Few individuals like to think of themselves as evil, so they develop rationalizations that enable the justification of their misconduct. Cressey found a significant number of embezzlers who contended that they were only "borrowing the money," even after being convicted and sentenced to jail. Some of the more common rationalizations include peer pressure, loyalty to unscrupulous superiors, family needs, revenge, and personal vices such as drug addiction, gambling, and promiscuity. To avoid involvement in ethical misconduct, accountants must develop a strong sense of personal responsibility. They cannot allow themselves to blame other people or unfair circumstances for their problems. They must learn to hold themselves personally accountable for their actions.

Ethical misconduct is a serious offense in the accounting profession. Accountants must realize that in this arena, their careers are vulnerable to a single mistake. If you are caught in white-collar crime, you normally lose the opportunity to hold a white-collar job. Second chances are rarely granted; it is extremely important that you learn how to recognize and avoid the common features of ethical misconduct. To help you prepare for the real-world situations you are likely to encounter, we include an ethical dilemma in the end-of-chapter materials. When working with these dilemmas, try to identify the (1) secret, (2) opportunity, and (3) rationalization associated with the particular ethical situation under consideration.

a look
back

LO10 Classify accounting events into one of four categories.

Chapters 1 and 2 introduced four types of transactions. It is helpful to identify transactions by type. Although businesses engage in an infinite number of different transactions, all transactions can be classified into one of four types. By learning to identify transactions by type, you can learn how to incorporate unfamiliar events within the bounds of a conceptual framework. The four types of transactions follow:

1. *Asset source transactions:* An asset account increases, and a corresponding claims account increases.
2. *Asset use transactions:* An asset account decreases, and a corresponding claims account decreases.
3. *Asset exchange transactions:* One asset account increases, and another asset account decreases.
4. *Claims exchange transactions:* One claims account increases, and another claims account decreases.

Also, the definitions of revenue and expense have been expanded. The complete definitions of these two elements are as follows:

LO6 Define *revenue* and *expense* in terms of their relationships to assets and liabilities.

1. **Revenue:** Revenue is the *economic benefit* associated with operating the business. Its recognition is triggered by an increase in assets or a decrease in liabilities that results from the normal operating activities of the business.
2. **Expense:** An expense is an *economic sacrifice* that is incurred in the process of generating revenue. Its recognition is triggered by a decrease in assets or an increase in liabilities that results from an effort to produce revenue.

Finally, this chapter introduced the *accrual accounting* concept. The application of this concept causes significant differences in the amount of revenues and expenses reported on the income statement and the amount of cash flow from operating activities on the statement of cash flows. These differences become readily apparent when relevant events are recorded in a horizontal financial statements model. To illustrate, review the following transactions and the corresponding statements model. To facilitate your understanding, set up a statements model on a piece of paper and try to record the effects of each event before you look at the explanation provided.

List of Events

1. Provided $600 of services on account.
2. Collected $400 cash from accounts receivable.
3. Accrued $350 of salary expense.
4. Paid $225 cash in partial settlement of salaries payable.

Event No.	Balance Sheet										Income Statement					Statement of Cash Flows	
	Cash	+	Acc. Rec.	=	S. Pay.	+	Ret. Earn.		Rev.	−	Exp.	=	Net Inc.			
1	NA	+	600	=	NA	+	600		600	−	NA	=	600		NA	
2	400	+	(400)	=	NA	+	NA		NA	−	NA	=	NA		400	OA
3	NA	+	NA	=	350	+	(350)		NA	−	350	=	(350)		NA	
4	(225)	+	0	=	(225)	+	NA		NA	−	NA	=	NA		(225)	OA
Totals	175	+	200	=	125	+	250		600	−	350	=	250		175	NC

Notice that the amount of net income ($250) is different from the amount of cash flow from operating activities ($175). A review of the entries in the statements model should make the reasons for this difference clear. Although $600 of revenue is recognized, only $400 of cash was collected. The remaining $200 is expected to be collected in the future and is currently shown on the balance sheet as Accounts Receivable. Also, although $350 of salary expense is recognized, only $225 was paid in cash. The remaining $125 is expected to be paid in the future. This obligation is shown as Salaries Payable on the balance sheet. You should study these relationships carefully to develop a clear understanding of how accrual accounting affects financial reporting.

a look forward

Chapter 3 continues the examination of the accrual accounting system. In addition to accruals, the accrual system also involves deferrals. *Deferrals* result when a company receives or pays cash before it recognizes the related revenue or expense. A magazine subscription is an example of a deferral event because magazine companies receive the cash before they provide magazines to their customers. The cash is collected in advance, but the revenue is not recognized until the magazines are delivered. Chapter 3 also reinforces what you have learned about asset source, use, and exchange transactions and claims exchange transactions. Also, you will be given the opportunity to broaden your understanding of how business events affect financial statements.

SELF-STUDY REVIEW PROBLEM

Walberg Company experienced the following accounting events during 2003.

1. Started operations in January 2003 when it acquired $22,000 cash by issuing common stock.
2. During the 2003 period, recognized $246,000 of revenue on account.
3. Collected $222,000 cash from accounts receivable.
4. Paid operating expenses of $205,000 in cash.
5. Paid a $14,000 cash dividend to stockholders.
6. On April 1, 2003, borrowed $18,000 by issuing a note to National Bank.
7. On December 31, 2003, adjusted the accounting records to recognize interest expense incurred on the note it had issued to National bank. The note had a 10 percent annual interest rate and a one-year term to maturity. Interest is due in cash on the maturity date (March 31, 2004).

Walberg Company experienced the following accounting events during 2004.

1. Accrued the remaining interest expense on the note payable through March 31, 2004.
2. Paid cash for the amount of interest payable as of March 31, 2004.
3. Paid cash to repay the principal due on the note payable as of March 31, 2004.
4. Recognized $259,000 of revenue on account.
5. Collected $262,000 cash from accounts receivable.
6. Paid operating expenses of $211,000 in cash.
7. Paid a $24,000 cash dividend to stockholders.

Required

a. Record the events in a financial statements model like the following one. The first event is recorded as an example.

Event No.	Assets		=	Liabilities		+	Stockholders' Equity		Rev.	–	Exp.	=	Net Inc.	Cash Flow
	Cash	+ Acc. Rec.	=	Note Pay. + Int. Pay.		+	C. Stk. +	Ret. Ear.						
1	22,000 +	NA	=	NA +	NA	+	22,000 +	NA	NA –		NA =		NA	22,000 FA

b. What amount of interest expense would Walberg report on the 2003 and 2004 income statements?
c. What amount of cash outflow for interest would Walberg report in the operating activities sections of the 2003 and 2004 statements of cash flows?
d. What are the 2004 opening balances for the revenue and expense accounts?
e. What amount of total assets would Walberg report on the 2003 balance sheet?
f. What claims on assets would Walberg report on the 2003 balance sheet?
g. Explain what caused the cash balance to change between December 31, 2003, and December 31, 2004.

Solution to Requirement a

The financial statements model follows.

Event No.	Assets		=	Liabilities		+	Stockholders' Equity		Rev.	–	Exp.	=	Net Inc.	Cash Flow
	Cash	+ Acc. Rec.	=	Note Pay. +	Int. Pay.	+	C. Stk. +	Ret. Ear.						
1	22,000 +	NA	=	NA +	NA	+	22,000 +	NA	NA –		NA =		NA	22,000 FA
2	NA +	246,000	=	NA +	NA	+	NA +	246,000	246,000 –		NA =		246,000	NA
3	222,000 +	(222,000)	=	NA +	NA	+	NA +	NA	NA –		NA =		NA	222,000 OA
4	(205,000) +	NA	=	NA +	NA	+	NA +	(205,000)	NA –		205,000 =		(205,000)	(205,000) OA
5	(14,000) +	NA	=	NA +	NA	+	NA +	(14,000)	NA –		NA =		NA	(14,000) FA
6	18,000 +	NA	=	18,000 +	NA	+	NA +	NA	NA –		NA =		NA	18,000 FA
7*	NA +	NA	=	NA +	1,350	+	NA +	(1,350)	NA –		1,350 =		(1,350)	NA
Totals	43,000 +	24,000	=	18,000 +	1,350	+	22,000 +	25,650	246,000 –		206,350 =		39,650	43,000 NC
	Asset, Liability, and Equity Account Balances Carry Forward								Rev. & Exp. Accts. Are Closed					
Bal.	43,000 +	24,000	=	18,000 +	1,350	+	22,000 +	25,650	NA –		NA =		NA	NA
1†	NA +	NA	=	NA +	450	+	NA +	(450)	NA –		450 =		(450)	NA
2	(1,800) +	NA	=	NA +	(1,800)	+	NA +	NA	NA –		NA =		NA	(1,800) OA
3	(18,000) +	NA	=	(18,000) +	NA	+	NA +	NA	NA –		NA =		NA	(18,000) FA
4	NA +	259,000	=	NA +	NA	+	NA +	259,000	259,000 –		NA =		259,000	NA
5	262,000 +	(262,000)	=	NA +	NA	+	NA +	NA	NA –		NA =		NA	262,000 OA
6	(211,000) +	NA	=	NA +	NA	+	NA +	(211,000)	NA –		211,000 =		(211,000)	(211,000) OA
7	(24,000) +	NA	=	NA +	NA	+	NA +	(24,000)	NA –		NA =		NA	(24,000) FA
Totals	50,200 +	21,000	=	0 +	0	+	22,000 +	49,200	259,000 –		211,450 =		47,550	7,200 NC

*Accrued interest expense for 2003 = $18,000 × .10 × 9/12 = $1,350.
†Accrued interest expense for 2004 = $18,000 × .10 × 3/12 = $450.

Solution to Requirements b–g

b. Walberg would report interest expense on the 2003 and 2004 income statements of $1,350 and $450, respectively.
c. Walberg made no cash interest payments in 2003. All cash for interest was paid in 2004. Walberg would report zero cash outflow for interest on the 2003 statement of cash flows and $1,800 cash outflow for interest on the 2004 statement.
d. Because all revenue and expense accounts are closed at the end of each accounting period, the beginning balances for revenue and expense accounts are always zero.

e. The total asset balance on the 2003 balance sheet would be $67,000 (Cash $43,000 + Accounts Receivable $24,000).

f. Creditors have a $19,350 (Note Payable $18,000 + Interest Payable $1,350) claim. Owners (investors) have a $47,650 (Common Stock $22,000 + Retained Earnings $25,650) claim on the assets. Total claims of $67,000 ($19,350 + $47,650) are equal to total assets.

g. The net cash inflow from operating activities was $49,200 ($262,000 revenue − $1,800 interest expense − $211,000 operating expense). There were no investing activities. The net cash outflow from financing activities was $42,000 ($18,000 debt payment + $24,000 dividends). The net change in cash was a $7,200 cash inflow ($49,200 from operating activities − $42,000 used by financing activities).

KEY TERMS

Accounting cycle 68
Accounts receivable 58
Accrual 57
Accrual accounting 57
Adjusting entry 65
Adverse opinion 72
American Institute of Certified
   Public Accountants' Code
   of Professional Conduct 74
Asset exchange
   transaction 58

Asset source
   transaction 58
Asset use transaction 59
Audit 70
Certified Public Accountant
   (CPA) 71
Claims exchange
   transaction 59
Closing entries 63
Code of professional
   conduct 74

Disclaimer of audit
   opinion 73
Expense 75
Financial audit 70
Historical cost 72
Independent auditor 71
Internal controls 74
Investment 64
Issuer of a note 69
Matching concept 65
Material error 71

Note payable 69
Period costs 64
Qualified opinion 73
Realization 57
Recognition 57
Revenue 75
Salaries payable 59
Unqualified opinion 72
Voluntarily disclosing 73

QUESTIONS

1. What does accrual accounting attempt to accomplish?
2. Define *recognition*. How is it independent of collecting or paying cash?
3. What does the term *asset source transaction* mean?
4. What effect does the issue of Common Stock have on the accounting equation?
5. How does the recognition of revenue on account (accounts receivable) affect the income statement compared to its effect on the statement of cash flows?
6. Give an example of an asset source transaction. What is the effect of this transaction on the accounting equation?
7. When is revenue recognized under accrual accounting?
8. Give an example of an asset exchange transaction. What is the effect of this transaction on the accounting equation?
9. What effect does expense recognition have on the accounting equation?
10. What does the term *claims exchange transaction* mean?
11. What type of transaction is a cash payment to creditors? How does this type of transaction affect the accounting equation?
12. When are expenses recognized under accrual accounting?
13. Why may net cash flow from operating activities on the cash flow statement be different from the amount of net income reported on the income statement?
14. What is the relationship between the income statement and changes in assets and liabilities?
15. What does the term *net assets* mean?
16. How does net income affect the stockholders' claims on the business's assets?
17. What does the term *expense* mean?
18. What does the term *revenue* mean?
19. What is the purpose of the statement of changes in stockholders' equity?
20. What is the main purpose of the balance sheet?
21. Why is the balance sheet dated *as of* a specific date when the income statement, statement of changes in stockholders' equity, and statement of cash flows are dated with the phrase *for the period ended?*
22. In what order are assets listed on the balance sheet?
23. What does the statement of cash flows explain?
24. When is interest earned on an investment recognized?
25. What does the term *adjusting entry* mean? Give an example.

26. What type of entry is the entry to record accrued interest revenue? How does it affect the accounting equation?
27. What type of entry is the entry to record accrued interest expense? How does it affect the accounting equation?
28. Is land purchased in 1920 reported on a current balance sheet at its current value? If not, at what value is it shown?
29. What is the historical cost concept of accounting measurement?
30. Do all countries use historical cost for accounting measurement? Why or why not?
31. What types of accounts are closed at the end of the accounting period? Why is it necessary to close these accounts?
32. Give several examples of period costs.
33. Give an example of a cost that can be directly matched with the revenue produced by an accounting firm from preparing a tax return.
34. List and describe the four stages of the accounting cycle discussed in Chapter 2.
35. What is a financial audit? Who is qualified to perform it?
36. What is an independent auditor? Why must auditors be independent?
37. What makes an error in the financial statements material?
38. What three basic types of auditors' opinions can be issued on audited financial statements? Describe each.
39. What are the implications of an unqualified audit opinion?
40. When might an auditor issue a disclaimer on financial statements?
41. In what circumstances can an auditor disclose confidential information about a client without the client's permission?
42. What are the six articles of ethical conduct set out under section I of the AICPA's Code of Professional Conduct?
43. What is the purpose of internal controls in an organization?

EXERCISES—SERIES A

Where applicable in all exercises, round computations to the nearest dollar.

EXERCISE 2–1A Effect of Earning Revenue on Account on the Financial Statements

L.O. 1, 3, 5

W. Harder started a computer training center in 2004. The only accounting event in 2004 was the recognition of $7,500 of service revenue earned on account.

Required
Use the following horizontal statements model to show how this event affects the balance sheet, income statement, and statement of cash flows. Indicate whether the event increases (I), decreases (D), or does not affect (NA) each element of the financial statements. Also, in the Cash Flows column, designate the classification of any cash flows using the letters OA for operating activities, IA for investing activities, and FA for financing activities.

Balance Sheet					Income Statement			Statement of Cash Flows
Cash	+ Acct. Rec.	= Com. Stk.	+ Ret. Ear.		Rev.	– Exp.	= Net. Inc.	

EXERCISE 2–2A Effect of Collecting Accounts Receivable on the Accounting Equation and Financial Statements

L.O. 1, 3, 5

Gayoso Company earned $4,500 of service revenue on account during 2008. The company collected $3,000 cash from accounts receivable during 2008.

Required
Based on this information alone, determine the following. (*Hint:* Record the events in general ledger accounts under an accounting equation before satisfying the requirements.)
a. The balance of the accounts receivable that Gayoso would report on the December 31, 2008 balance sheet.
b. The amount of net income that Gayoso would report on the 2008 income statement.

c. The amount of net cash flow from operating activities that Gayoso would report on the 2008 statement of cash flows.

d. The amount of retained earnings that Gayoso would report on the 2008 balance sheet.

e. Why are the answers to Requirements *b* and *c* different?

L.O. 1, 5, 7   **EXERCISE 2–3A** *Effects of Recognizing Accrued Interest on Financial Statements*

Gail Rogers started Rogers Company on January 1, 2005. The company experienced the following events during its first year of operation.
1. Earned $400 of cash revenue for performing services.
2. Borrowed $1,500 cash from the bank.
3. Adjusted the accounting records to recognize accrued interest expense on the bank note. The note, issued on September 1, 2005, had a one-year term and an 8 percent annual interest rate.

Required
a. What is the amount of interest expense in 2005?
b. What amount of cash was paid for interest in 2005?
c. Use a horizontal statements model to show how each event affects the balance sheet, income statement, and statement of cash flows. Indicate whether the event increases (I), decreases (D), or does not affect (NA) each element of the financial statements. Also, in the Cash Flows column, designate the cash flows as operating activities (OA), investing activities (IA), or financing activities (FA). The first transaction has been recorded as an example.

Event No.	Balance Sheet										Income Statement					Statement of Cash Flows
	Cash	=	Note Pay.	+	Int. Pay.	+	Com. Stk.	+	Ret. Earn.		Rev.	–	Exp.	=	Net Inc.	
1	I	=	NA	+	NA	+	NA	+	I		I	–	NA	=	I	I OA

L.O. 2, 3, 5   **EXERCISE 2–4A** *Net Income Versus Changes in Cash*

In the period 2004, Abbot Inc., billed its customers $75,000 for services performed. The company subsequently collected $68,000 of the amount billed. Abbot incurred $59,000 of other operating expenses but paid cash for only $50,000 of that amount. Abbot acquired $20,000 cash from the issue of common stock. The company invested $15,000 cash in the purchase of land.

Required
Use the preceding information to answer the following questions. (*Hint:* Identify the six events described in the paragraph and record them in general ledger accounts under an accounting equation before attempting to answer the questions.)
a. What amount of revenue will Abbot report on the 2004 income statement?
b. What amount of cash flow from revenue will Abbot report on the statement of cash flows?
c. What is the net income for the period?
d. What is the net cash flow from operating activities for the period?
e. Why is the amount of net income different from the net cash flow from operating activities for the period?
f. What is the amount of net cash flow from investing activities?
g. What is the amount of net cash flow from financing activities?
h. What amounts of total assets, liabilities, and equity will Abbot report on the year-end balance sheet?

L.O. 1, 5, 7   **EXERCISE 2–5A** *Effect of Accounts Receivable and Accounts Payable Transactions on Financial Statements*

The following events apply to Jones and Reed, a public accounting firm, for the 2004 accounting period.
1. Performed $85,000 of services for clients on account.
2. Performed $25,000 of services for cash.
3. Incurred $32,000 of other operating expenses on account.
4. Paid $15,000 cash to an employee for salary.
5. Collected $73,000 cash from accounts receivable.
6. Paid $28,000 cash on accounts payable.
7. Paid a $5,000 cash dividend to the stockholders.
8. Accrued salaries of $1,250 at the end of 2004.

Required

a. Show the effects of the events on the financial statements using a horizontal statements model like the following one. In the Cash Flow column, use OA to designate operating activity, IA for investment activity, FA for financing activity, and NC for net change in cash. Use NA to indicate the element is not affected by the event. The first event is recorded as an example.

Event No.	Assets		=	Liabilities		+	Equity					Cash Flow
	Cash	+ Acc. Rec.	=	Acct. Pay.	+ Sal. Pay.	+	Ret. Earn.	Rev.	− Exp.	= Net Inc.		
1	NA	+ 85,000	=	NA	+ NA	+	85,000	85,000	− NA	= 85,000		NA

b. What is the amount of total assets at the end of 2004?
c. What is the balance of accounts receivable at the end of 2004?
d. What is the balance of accounts payable at the end of 2004?
e. What is the difference between accounts receivable and accounts payable?
f. What is net income for 2004?
g. What is the amount of net cash flow from operating activities for 2004?

EXERCISE 2–6A *Effect of Accruals on the Financial Statements*

L.O. 3, 4, 5

John Carroll, Inc., experienced the following events in 2003.
1. Received $10,000 cash from the issue of common stock.
2. Performed services on account for $35,000.
3. Paid the utility expense of $700.
4. Collected $26,000 of the accounts receivable.
5. Recorded $12,000 of accrued salaries at the end of the year.
6. Paid a $2,000 cash dividend to the shareholders.

Required

a. Record the events in general ledger accounts under an accounting equation. In the last column of the table, provide appropriate account titles for the Retained Earnings amounts. The first transaction has been recorded as an example.

JOHN CARROLL, INC. General Ledger Accounts							
Event	Assets		=	Liabilities	+	Stockholders' Equity		Acct. Titles for RE
	Cash	Accounts Receivable		Salaries Payable		Common Stock	Retained Earnings	
1.	10,000					10,000		

b. Prepare the income statement, statement of changes in stockholders' equity, balance sheet, and statement of cash flows for the 2003 accounting period.
c. Why is the amount of net income different from the amount of net cash flow from operating activities?

EXERCISE 2–7A *Recognizing Accrued Interest Revenue*

L.O. 1, 5, 7

N&J Company invested $80,000 in a certificate of deposit on May 1, 2006. The certificate had a 6 percent annual rate of interest and a one-year term to maturity.

Required

a. What amount of interest revenue will N&J recognize for the year ending December 31, 2006?
b. Show how the December 31, 2006, adjusting entry to recognize the accrued interest revenue affects the accounting equation.
c. What amount of cash will N&J collect for interest revenue in 2006?
d. What is the amount of interest receivable as of December 31, 2006?
e. What amount of cash will N&J collect for interest revenue in 2007, assuming it does not renew the CD?
f. What amount of interest revenue will N&J recognize in 2007, assuming it does not renew the CD?
g. What is the amount of interest receivable as of December 31, 2007, assuming it does not renew the CD?

L.O. 1, 5, 7   EXERCISE 2–8A *Recognizing Accrued Interest Expense*

Carroll Corporation borrowed $80,000 from the bank on November 1, 2003. The note had a 7.5 percent annual rate of interest and matured on April 30, 2004. Interest and principal were paid in cash on the maturity date.

Required
a. What amount of interest expense was paid in cash in 2003?
b. What amount of interest expense was reported on the 2003 income statement?
c. What amount of total liabilities was reported on the December 31, 2003, balance sheet?
d. What total amount of cash was paid to the bank on April 30, 2004, for principal and interest?
e. What amount of interest expense was reported on the 2004 income statement?

L.O. 10   EXERCISE 2–9A *Identifying Source, Use, and Exchange Transactions*

Required
Indicate whether each of the following transactions is an asset source (AS), asset use (AU), asset exchange (AE), or claims exchange (CE) transaction.
a. Collected cash from accounts receivable.
b. Invested cash in a certificate of deposit.
c. Purchased land with cash.
d. Acquired cash from the issue of stock.
e. Paid a cash dividend to the stockholders.
f. Paid cash on accounts payable.
g. Incurred other operating expenses on account.
h. Paid cash for rent expense.
i. Performed services for cash.
j. Performed services for clients on account.

L.O. 10   EXERCISE 2–10A *Identifying Asset Source, Use, and Exchange Transactions*

Required
a. Name an asset source transaction that will *not* affect the statement of cash flows.
b. Name an asset source transaction that will affect the income statement.
c. Name an asset use transaction that will *not* affect the income statement.
d. Name an asset exchange transaction that will affect the statement of cash flows.
e. Name an asset source transaction that will *not* affect the income statement.

L.O. 2, 3, 5, 7   EXERCISE 2–11A *Effect of Transactions on the Balance Sheet*

Sun Corp. was formed on January 1, 2001. The business acquired $85,000 cash from the issue of common stock. The business performed $250,000 of services on account and collected $200,000 of the amount due. Other operating expenses incurred on account amounted to $215,000. By the end of 2001, $190,000 of that amount had been paid with cash. The business paid $30,000 cash to purchase land. Sun borrowed $25,000 cash from the bank. On December 31, 2001, there was $1,250 of accrued interest expense.

Required
Using the preceding information, answer the following questions. (*Hint:* Identify the eight events described in the preceding paragraph and record them in general ledger accounts under an accounting equation before answering the questions.)
a. What is the cash balance at the end of 2001?
b. What is the balance of accounts receivable at the end of 2001?
c. What is the amount of total assets at the end of 2001?
d. What is the amount of total liabilities at the end of 2001?
e. What is the amount of common stock at the end of 2001?
f. What is the amount of retained earnings at the end of 2001?

L.O. 1, 2, 5   EXERCISE 2–12A *Effects of Revenue and Expense Recognition on the Income Statement and Statement of Cash Flows*

The following transactions pertain to the operations of Clark & Co., CPAs.
1. Acquired $100,000 cash from the issue of common stock.
2. Performed accounting services and billed clients $80,000.

3. Paid a $10,000 cash dividend to the stockholders.
4. Collected $75,000 cash from accounts receivable.
5. Paid $55,000 cash for other operating expenses.
6. Performed accounting services for $6,000 cash.

Required

a. Identify which of these transactions result in revenue and expense recognition for Clark & Co., CPAs.
b. Based on your response to part *a*, determine the amount of net income Clark will report on its income statement.
c. Identify which of the preceding transactions affect(s) cash flow from operating activities.
d. Based on your response to part *c*, determine the amount of net cash flow from operating activities Clark will report on the statement of cash flows.

EXERCISE 2-13A *Complete Accounting Cycle*   L.O. 3, 5, 7

The following information is available for Zig Co. for the year 2001:
1. Acquired $65,000 cash from the issue of common stock.
2. Performed $175,000 of services on account.
3. Incurred other operating expenses on account in the amount of $105,000.
4. Purchased land for $25,000 cash.
5. Collected $95,000 cash from accounts receivable.
6. Paid $50,000 cash on accounts payable.
7. Performed services for $15,000 cash.
8. Paid $5,000 cash for salaries expense.
9. Paid a $10,000 cash dividend to the stockholders.
10. Borrowed $20,000 cash from State Bank.

Information for Adjusting Entry
11. Accrued interest expense at the end of the accounting period was $900.

Required

a. Explain how each of the transactions affects the elements of the accounting equation by placing a + for *increase,* − for *decrease,* and NA for *not affected* under each of the elements. Also record the dollar amount of the effect of each event on the accounting equation. In the last column of the table, provide appropriate account titles for Retained Earnings accounts. The first event is recorded as an example.

Event No.	Assets	=	Liabilities	+	Stockholders' Equity Common Stock	+	Retained Earnings	Acct. Title for RE
1	+65,000		NA		+65,000		NA	

b. What is the amount of net income for 2001?
c. What is the amount of total assets at the end of 2001?
d. What is the amount of total liabilities at the end of 2001?

EXERCISE 2-14A *Classifying Events on the Statement of Cash Flows*   L.O. 4, 5

The following transactions pertain to the operations of Smoltz Company for 2002:
1. Acquired $18,000 cash from the issue of common stock.
2. Provided $25,000 of services on account.
3. Incurred $15,000 of other operating expenses on account.
4. Collected $20,000 cash from accounts receivable.
5. Paid a $2,000 cash dividend to the stockholders.
6. Paid $10,000 cash on accounts payable.
7. Performed services for $4,000 cash.
8. Paid $600 cash for rent expense.

Required

a. Classify the cash flows from these transactions as operating activities (OA), investing activities (IA), or financing activities (FA). Use NA for transactions that do not affect the statement of cash flows.
b. Prepare a statement of cash flows. (There is no beginning cash balance.)

L.O. 4, 5, 6 **EXERCISE 2–15A** *Evaluating Cash Management*

The data in the following table apply to DeChow, Incorporated.

	2003	2004
Accounts receivable	$ 24,600,000	$ 27,060,000
Sales	332,700,000	382,606,000
Accounts payable	15,800,000	18,644,000
Operating expenses	257,300,000	285,603,000

Required

a. What is the percentage growth in the Accounts Receivable, Sales, Accounts Payable, and Operating Expenses accounts from 2003 to 2004?

b. Companies must incur interest expense to obtain cash. To minimize interest expense, companies attempt to collect cash from receivables as quickly as possible and to delay the payment of cash to settle payables as long as possible. Based on your answers to Requirement *a*, comment on DeChow's cash management.

L.O. 4 **EXERCISE 2–16A** *Relation of Elements to Financial Statements*

Required

Identify whether each of the following items would appear on the income statement (IS), statement of changes in stockholders' equity (SE), balance sheet (BS), or statement of cash flows (CF). Some items may appear on more than one statement; if so, identify all applicable statements. If an item would not appear on any financial statement, label it NA.

a. Note Payable

b. Notes Receivable

c. Accounts Receivable

d. Retained Earnings

e. Interest Receivable

f. Utilities Payable

g. Auditor's Opinion

h. Land

i. Interest Revenue

j. Dividends

k. Salaries Expense

l. Net Income

m. Interest Payable

n. Ending Cash Balance

o. Cash Flow from Investing Activities

L.O. 7 **EXERCISE 2–17A** *Matching Concept*

Companies make sacrifices known as *expenses* to obtain benefits called *revenues*. The accurate measurement of net income requires that expenses be matched with revenues. In some circumstances matching a particular expense directly with revenue is difficult or impossible. In these circumstances, the expense is matched with the period in which it is incurred.

Required

a. Identify an expense that could be matched directly with revenue.

b. Identify a period expense that would be difficult to match with revenue. Explain why.

L.O. 5, 7 **EXERCISE 2–18A** *Closing Entries*

Required

Which of the following accounts are closed at the end of the accounting period?

a. Cash

b. Accounts Receivable

c. Service Revenue

d. Advertising Expense

e. Accounts Payable

f. Certificate of Deposit

g. Notes Payable
h. Interest Expense
i. Interest Payable
j. Dividends
k. Retained Earnings
l. Utilities Expense

PROBLEM 2–19A *Effect of Events on the Financial Statements*

L.O. 3, 5

E_x

A-1 Auto experienced the following transactions during 2004.
1. Provided services to customers and billed them $8,600.
2. Borrowed $8,000 from the bank on September 1, 2004. The note had a 9 percent annual interest rate and a one-year term to maturity.
3. Paid $1,700 of salary expense.
4. Provided services to customers and collected $3,200 cash.
5. Incurred $3,900 of other operating expenses on account.
6. Collected $7,500 of the accounts receivable.
7. Paid $3,400 of the accounts payable.
8. Recognized the accrued interest on the note payable at December 31, 2004.

Required
a. Show the effects of the transactions on the financial statements using a horizontal statements model like the following one. In the Cash Flows column, use the letters OA for operating activity, IA for investing activity, FA for financing activity, and NC for net change in cash. Use NA to indicate not affected by the transaction. The first one is recorded as an example.

	Balance Sheet							Income Statement			Statement of Cash Flows
	Assets		=	Liab.			+ Stk. Equity				
Event No.	Cash +	Accts. Rec.	= Accts. Pay.	Note Pay.	Int. Pay. +		Ret. Earn.	Rev. –	Exp. =	Net Inc.	
1.	NA +	8,600	= NA	NA	NA		8,600	8,600 –	NA =	8,600	NA

b. What is the ending balance of Retained Earnings? What is the amount of net income? Why are these amounts the same in this problem? Is the balance in Retained Earnings likely to be the same as the amount of net income at the end of 2005? Explain your answer.

PROBLEM 2–20A *Effect of Events on the Accounting Equation*

L.O. 3

Required
Explain how each of the following independent accounting events would affect the accounting equation by writing the letter I for increase, the letter D for decrease, and NA for no effect under the appropriate columns. The effects of the first event are shown for you.

Letter of Event	Assets =	Liabilities +	Common Stock +	Retained Earnings
a	I	NA	I	NA

a. Acquired cash from the issue of common stock.
b. Paid cash for salary expense.
c. Performed services for clients on account.
d. Incurred operating expenses on account.
e. Collected cash from accounts receivable.
f. Paid a cash dividend to the stockholders.
g. Performed services for cash.
h. Paid cash to creditors on account.
i. Bought equipment by issuing a note payable.

j. Paid monthly rent expense.

k. Accrued interest expense on a note payable.

l. Repaid note payable and interest with cash.

L.O. 3, 5   **PROBLEM 2–21A** *Effect of Accrued Interest on Financial Statements*

Marshall Co. borrowed $12,000 from the local bank on May 1, 2008, when the company was started. The note had a 10 percent annual interest rate and a one-year term to maturity. Marshall Co. recognized $28,000 of revenue on account in 2008 and $34,000 of revenue on account in 2009. Cash collections from accounts receivable were $22,000 in 2008 and $32,000 in 2009. Marshall Co. paid $15,000 of salaries expense in 2008 and $18,000 of salaries expense in 2009. (*Hint:* Record the events in general ledger accounts under an accounting equation before answering the questions.)

Required

Based on the preceding information, answer the following questions.

a. What amount of net cash flow from operating activities would Marshall report on the 2008 cash flow statement?

b. What amount of interest expense would Marshall report on the 2008 income statement?

c. What amount of total liabilities would Marshall report on the December 31, 2008, balance sheet?

d. What amount of retained earnings would Marshall report on the December 31, 2008, balance sheet?

e. What amount of cash flow from financing activities would Marshall report on the 2008 statement of cash flows?

f. What amount of interest expense would Marshall report on the 2009 income statement?

g. What amount of cash flows from operating activities would Marshall report on the 2009 cash flow statement?

h. What amount of total assets would Marshall report on the December 31, 2009, balance sheet?

i. What amount of cash flow from investing activities would Marshall report on the 2009 cash flow statement?

j. If Marshall Co. paid a $700 dividend during 2009, what retained earnings balance would it report on the December 31, 2009, balance sheet?

L.O. 3, 4   **PROBLEM 2–22A** *Two Complete Accounting Cycles*

The following accounting events apply to Tri-State Company.

Accounting Events for 2003

1. The company started when it acquired $40,000 cash from the issue of common stock.

2. Recognized $97,000 of revenue on account during the period for services performed.

3. Collected $75,000 cash from accounts receivable.

4. Paid an $8,000 cash dividend.

5. Paid $32,000 cash for salaries expense.

6. Paid $21,000 cash for other operating expenses.

7. Invested $24,000 in a certificate of deposit with an 18-month term.

Information for Adjusting Entries (Books are closed on December 31)

8. Accrued salaries expense of $3,000.

9. Recorded accrued interest on the certificate of deposit. The certificate was purchased on June 30, 2003, and had a 5 percent annual rate of interest.

Accounting Events for 2004

1. Made cash payment of $3,000 for salaries payable.

2. Borrowed $40,000 from a local bank.

3. Received an additional $6,000 cash from the issue of common stock.

4. Recognized $120,000 of revenue on account during 2004 for services performed.

5. Collected $112,000 of cash on accounts receivable during the period.

6. Purchased land for the company that cost $50,000 cash. A few months later, the land was appraised at $60,000.

7. Paid a $12,000 cash dividend to the stockholders of the company.

8. Received the principal amount plus the interest earned on the certificate of deposit. (See Event No. 7 in year 2003 for details regarding the original investment.)

9. Paid cash of $40,000 for salaries expense.

10. Paid $33,000 cash for other operating expenses.

Information for Adjusting Entries

11. Accrued salaries expense of $7,000.
12. Recorded accrued interest expense on the bank note (see Event No. 2 in 2004). The note was issued to the bank on June 1, 2004. It had a 12 percent annual rate of interest and a two-year term to maturity.

Required
a. Record the effect of each of the events in general ledger accounts under an accounting equation for the 2003 and 2004 fiscal years. In the last column of the table, provide appropriate account title for Retained Earning accounts.
b. Prepare an income statement, statement of changes in stockholders' equity, balance sheet, and statement of cash flows for the 2003 and 2004 calendar years.

PROBLEM 2–23A *Identifying and Arranging Elements on Financial Statements*

L.O. 4

The following information was drawn from the records of Simmons & Associates at December 31, 2003:

Consulting Revenue	$60,000	Notes Payable	$24,000
Land	52,000	Salaries Payable	6,500
Dividends	8,000	Salary Expense	36,000
Cash Flow from Fin. Activities	33,000	Common Stock Issued	17,000
Interest Revenue	3,000	Beginning Common Stock	19,000
Ending Retained Earnings	56,500	Accounts Receivable	31,000
Cash	42,000	Cash Flow from Inv. Activities	(50,000)
Interest Payable	2,000	Cash Flow from Oper. Activities	40,000
Interest Expense	6,000		

Required
Use the preceding information to construct an income statement, statement of changes in stockholders' equity, balance sheet, and statement of cash flows. (Show only totals for each activity on the statement of cash flows).

PROBLEM 2–24A *Classifying Events as Source, Use, or Exchange and Effect of Events on Financial Statements—Horizontal Statements Model*

L.O. 5, 10

The following transactions pertain to L&N Advisory Services for 2002:
1. Business started when it acquired $50,000 cash from the issue of common stock.
2. Paid $25,000 cash to purchase land.
3. Paid $3,600 cash for rent expense.
4. Performed services for clients and billed them $15,200. Expected to collect cash at a later date (the revenue was earned on account).
5. Incurred $9,600 of other operating expenses on account (expected to make cash payment at a later date).
6. Received an $800 bill for utilities. The amount due was payable within 30 days.
7. Paid $4,400 cash on the account payable created in Event No. 5.
8. Acquired an additional $7,000 cash from the issue of common stock.
9. Paid $5,200 cash on the balance of the account payable created in Event No. 5.
10. Performed additional services for $4,500 cash.
11. Paid an $1,800 cash dividend to the stockholders.
12. Collected $8,600 cash from accounts receivable.

Required
a. Classify each of L&N's transactions as asset source (AS), asset use (AU), asset exchange (AE), or claims exchange (CE).
b. Show the effects of the events on the financial statements using a horizontal statements model like the following one. In the Cash Flow column, use the initials OA for operating activity, IA for investing activity, FA for financing activity, and NC for net change in cash. Use NA to indicate accounts not affected by the transaction. The first one is recorded as an example.

Event No.	Assets					=	Liab.	+	Stk. Equity						Rev.	–	Exp.	=	Net Inc.	Cash Flow	
	Cash	+	Acct. Rec.	+	Land	=	Acct. Pay.	+	Com. Stock	+	Ret. Earn.				Rev.	–	Exp.	=	Net Inc.	Cash Flow	
1	50,000	+	NA	+	NA	=	NA	+	50,000	+	NA				NA	–	NA	=	NA	50,000	FA

c. What is the amount of net income for 2002?

d. What is the amount of net cash flow from operating activities for 2002?

L.O. 3, 4, 5   **PROBLEM 2–25A** *Missing Information in Financial Statements*

Lake Properties had the following assets at the beginning of the accounting period (January 1, 2006): Cash—$21,000, Accounts Receivable—$33,000, Certificate of Deposit—$16,000, and Land—$62,000. The beginning balances in the liability accounts were Accounts Payable—$27,000 and Notes Payable—$20,000. A $51,000 balance was in Common Stock at the beginning of the accounting period. During the accounting period, service revenue earned on account was $44,000. The ending balance in the Accounts Receivable account was $31,000. Operating expenses incurred on account amounted to $29,000. There was $33,000 paid on accounts payable. In addition, there was $1,200 of accrued interest revenue and $1,700 of accrued interest expense as of the end of the accounting period (December 31, 2006). Finally, a $2,500 cash dividend was paid to the stockholders. (*Hint:* Record the events in general ledger accounts under an accounting equation before satisfying the requirements.)

Required

a. Determine the amount of cash collected from accounts receivable.

b. Prepare a balance sheet as of January 1, 2006.

c. Prepare an income statement, statement of changes in stockholders' equity, balance sheet, and statement of cash flows for the 2006 accounting period.

d. Determine the interest rate earned on the certificate of deposit.

e. Determine the interest rate paid on the note payable.

EXERCISES—SERIES B

Where applicable in all exercises, round computations to the nearest dollar.

L.O. 1, 3, 5   **EXERCISE 2–1B** *Effect of Accrued Salaries on the Financial Statements*

F. Aquillno recorded $7,500 of accrued salaries expense at the end of 2006.

Required

Use the following horizontal statements model to show how this event affects the balance sheet, income statement, and statement of cash flows. Indicate whether the event increases (I), decreases (D), or does not affect (NA) each element of the financial statements. Also, in the Cash Flows column, designate the classification of any cash flows using the letters OA for operating activities, IA for investing activities, and FA for financing activities.

Balance Sheet				Income Statement			Statement of Cash Flows
Cash = S. Pay + Com. Stk. + Ret. Ear.				Rev. − Exp. = Net Inc.			

L.O. 1, 3, 5   **EXERCISE 2–2B** *Effect of Collecting Accounts Receivable on the Accounting Equation and Financial Statements*

McNeil Company earned $13,000 of revenue on account during 2008. The company collected $7,000 cash from accounts receivable during 2008.

Required

Based on this information alone, determine the following. (*Hint:* It may be helpful to record the events in general ledger accounts under an accounting equation before satisfying the requirements.)

a. The balance of accounts receivable that McNeil would report on the December 31, 2008 balance sheet.

b. The amount of net income that McNeil would report on the 2008 income statement.

c. The amount of net cash flow from operating activities that McNeil would report on the 2008 statement of cash flows.

d. The amount of retained earnings that McNeil would report on the December 31, 2008, balance sheet.

e. Why are the answers to Requirements *b* and *c* different?

L.O. 1, 5, 7   **EXERCISE 2–3B** *Effects of Recognizing Accrued Interest on Financial Statements*

Bill Parker started Parker Company on January 1, 2007. The company experienced the following events during its first year of operation.

1. Earned $6,200 of cash revenue.
2. Borrowed $4,000 cash from the bank.
3. Adjusted the accounting records to recognize accrued interest expense on the bank note. The note, issued on September 1, 2007, had a one-year term and a 10 percent annual interest rate.

Required
a. What is the amount of interest payable at December 31, 2007?
b. What is the amount of interest expense in 2007?
c. What is the amount of interest paid in 2007?
d. Use a horizontal statements model to show how each event affects the balance sheet, income statement, and statement of cash flows. Indicate whether the event increases (I) decreases (D), or does not affect (NA) each element of the financial statements. Also, in the Cash Flows column, designate the cash flows as operating activities (OA), investing activities (IA), or financing activities (FA). The first transaction has been recorded as an example.

Event No.		Balance Sheet					Income Statement			Statement of Cash Flows
	Cash	=	Notes Pay.	+	Int. Pay.	+ Com. Stk.	+ Ret. Earn.	Rev. − Exp. = Net Inc.		
1	I	=	NA	+	NA	+ NA	+ I	I − NA = I		I OA

EXERCISE 2–4B *Net Income Versus Changes in Cash*   **L.O. 2, 3, 5**

In the period 2003, Best Company billed its customers $100,000 for services performed. The company subsequently collected $73,000 of the amount billed. Best incurred $69,000 of operating expenses but paid cash for only $62,000 of that amount. Best acquired $30,000 cash from the issue of common stock. The company invested $40,000 cash in the purchase of land.

Required
Use the preceding information to answer the following questions. (*Hint:* It may be helpful to identify the six events described in the paragraph and to record them in general ledger accounts under an accounting equation before answering the questions.)
a. What amount of revenue will Best report on the 2003 income statement?
b. What is the net income for the period?
c. What amount of cash flow from revenue will Best report on the statement of cash flows?
d. What is the net cash flow from operating activities for the period?
e. Why is the amount of net income different from the net cash flow from operating activities for the period?
f. What is the amount of net cash flow from investing activities?
g. What is the amount of net cash flow from financing activities?
h. What amount of total equity will Best report on the year-end balance sheet?

EXERCISE 2–5B *Effect of Accounts Receivable and Accounts Payable Transactions on*   **L.O. 1, 5, 7**
                  Financial Statements

The following events apply to Poole and Pierce, a public accounting firm, for the 2005 accounting period.
1. Performed $65,000 of services for clients on account.
2. Performed $40,000 of services for cash.
3. Incurred $35,000 of other operating expenses on account.
4. Paid $10,000 cash to an employee for salary.
5. Collected $47,000 cash from accounts receivable.
6. Paid $12,000 cash on accounts payable.
7. Paid an $8,000 cash dividend to the stockholders.
8. Accrued salaries of $2,000 at the end of 2005.

Required
a. Show the effects of the events on the financial statements using a horizontal statements model like the following one. In the Cash Flow column, use OA to designate operating activity, IA for investment activity, FA for financing activity, and NC for net change in cash. Use NA to indicate the element is not affected by the event. The first event is recorded as an example.

Event No.	Assets		=	Liabilities			+	Stk. Equity						
	Cash	+ Acct. Rec.	=	Acct. Pay.	+	Sal. Pay.	+	Ret. Earn.	Rev.	− Exp.	= Net Inc.		Cash Flow	
1	NA	+ 65,000	=	NA	+	NA	+	65,000	65,000	− NA	= 65,000		NA	

b. What is the amount of total assets at the end of 2005?
c. What is the balance of accounts receivable at the end of 2005?
d. What is the balance of accounts payable at the end of 2005?
e. What is the difference between accounts receivable and accounts payable?
f. What is net income for 2005?
g. What is the amount of net cash flow from operating activities for 2005?

L.O. 3, 4, 5   EXERCISE 2–6B *Effect of Accruals on the Financial Statements*

Market, Inc., experienced the following events in 2005, its first year of operations.
1. Received $15,000 cash from the issue of common stock.
2. Performed services on account for $42,000.
3. Paid the utility expense of $800.
4. Collected $32,000 of the accounts receivable.
5. Recorded $5,000 of accrued salaries at the end of the year.
6. Paid a $1,000 cash dividend to the stockholders.

Required
a. Record these events in general ledger accounts under an accounting equation. In the last column of the table, provide appropriate account titles for the Retained Earnings amounts. The first transaction has been recorded as an example.

	MARKET, INC. General Ledger Accounts							
Event	Assets		=	Liabilities	+	Stockholders' Equity		Acct. Titles for RE
	Cash	Accounts Receivable		Salaries Payable		Common Stock	Retained Earnings	
1.	15,000					15,000		

b. Prepare the income statement, statement of changes in stockholders' equity, balance sheet, and statement of cash flows for the 2005 accounting period.
c. Why is the ending cash balance the same as the net change in cash on the statement of cash flows?

L.O. 1, 5, 7   EXERCISE 2–7B *Recognizing Accrued Interest Revenue*

Pine Company invested $80,000 in a certificate of deposit on August 1, 2006. The certificate had a 6 percent annual rate of interest and a one-year term to maturity.

Required
a. What amount of interest income will Pine recognize for the year ending December 31, 2006?
b. Show how the December 31, 2006, adjusting entry to recognize the accrued interest revenue affects the accounting equation.
c. What amount of cash will Pine collect for interest revenue in 2006?
d. What is the amount of interest receivable as of December 31, 2006?
e. What amount of cash will Pine collect for interest revenue in 2007, assuming it does not renew the CD?
f. What amount of interest revenue will Pine recognize in 2007, assuming it does not renew the CD?
g. What is the amount of interest receivable as of December 31, 2007, assuming it does not renew the CD?

L.O. 1, 5, 7   EXERCISE 2–8B *Recognizing Accrued Interest Expense*

Seahawk Corporation borrowed $40,000 from the bank on October 1, 2004. The note had a 9 percent annual rate of interest and matured on March 31, 2005. Interest and principal were paid in cash on the maturity date.

Required
a. What amount of interest expense was paid in cash in 2004?

b. What amount of interest expense was recognized on the 2004 income statement?
c. What amount of total liabilities was reported on the December 31, 2004 balance sheet?
d. What total amount of cash was paid to the bank on March 31, 2005, for principal and interest?
e. What amount of interest expense was reported on the 2005 income statement?

EXERCISE 2–9B *Identifying Source, Use, and Exchange Transactions*

L.O. 10

Required
Indicate whether each of the following transactions is an asset source (AS), asset use (AU), asset exchange (AE), or claims exchange (CE) transaction.
a. Performed services for clients on account.
b. Paid cash for salary expense.
c. Acquired cash from the issue of common stock.
d. Incurred other operating expenses on account.
e. Performed services for cash.
f. Paid cash on accounts payable.
g. Collected cash from accounts receivable.
h. Paid a cash dividend to the stockholders.
i. Borrowed cash from the bank.
j. Purchased land with cash.

EXERCISE 2–10B *Identifying Asset Source, Use, and Exchange Transactions*

L.O. 10

Required
a. Name an asset use transaction that will affect the income statement.
b. Name an asset use transaction that will *not* affect the income statement.
c. Name an asset exchange transaction that will *not* affect the statement of cash flows.
d. Name an asset exchange transaction that will affect the statement of cash flows.
e. Name an asset source transaction that will *not* affect the income statement.

EXERCISE 2–11B *Effect of Transactions on the Balance Sheet*

L.O. 2, 3, 5, 7

Putnam Corp. was formed on January 1, 2003. The business acquired $105,000 cash from the issue of common stock. The business performed $300,000 of services on account and collected $250,000 of the amount due. Operating expenses incurred on account amounted to $185,000. By the end of 2003, $120,000 of that amount had been paid with cash. The business paid $20,000 cash to purchase land. The business borrowed $50,000 cash from the bank. On December 31, 2003, there was $750 of accrued interest expense.

Required
Using the preceding information, answer the following questions. (*Hint:* Identify the eight events described in the preceding paragraph and record them in general ledger accounts under an accounting equation before answering the questions.)
a. What is the cash balance at the end of 2003?
b. What is the balance of accounts receivable at the end of 2003?
c. What is the amount of total assets at the end of 2003?
d. What is the amount of total liabilities at the end of 2003?
e. What is the amount of common stock at the end of 2003?
f. What is the amount of net income for 2003?

EXERCISE 2–12B *Effects of Revenue and Expense Recognition on the Income Statement and Statement of Cash Flows*

L.O. 1, 2, 5

The following transactions pertain to the operations of Phillips & Co., CPAs.
1. Acquired $100,000 cash from the issue of common stock.
2. Performed accounting services and billed clients $130,000.
3. Paid $5,000 cash dividend to the stockholders.
4. Collected $80,000 cash from accounts receivable.
5. Paid $65,000 cash for operating expenses.
6. Performed accounting services for $5,000 cash.

Required
a. Which of these transactions resulted in revenue and expense recognition for Phillips & Co., CPAs?
b. Based on your response to Requirement *a,* determine the amount of net income that Phillips will report on the income statement.
c. Determine the net cash flow from operating activities for each of the preceding transactions.

L.O. 3, 5, 7 **EXERCISE 2–13B** *Complete Accounting Cycle*

The following information is available for Wilson Co. for the year 2004. The business had the following transactions:

1. Performed $150,000 of services on account.
2. Acquired $60,000 cash from the issue of common stock.
3. Purchased land for $20,000 cash.
4. Incurred other operating expenses on account in the amount of $80,000.
5. Performed services for $18,000 cash.
6. Paid $50,000 cash on accounts payable.
7. Collected $90,000 cash from accounts receivable.
8. Paid $20,000 cash dividend to the stockholders.
9. Paid $9,000 cash for salaries.
10. Borrowed $30,000 cash from State Bank.

Information for Adjusting Entry

11. Accrued interest expense at the end of the accounting period was $1,200.

Required

a. Explain how each of the transactions affects the elements of the accounting equation by placing a + for *increase,* − for *decrease,* and NA for *not affected* under each of the elements. Also record the dollar amount of the effect of each event on the accounting equation. In the last column of the table, provide appropriate account titles for Retained Earnings amounts. The first event is recorded as an example.

Event No.	Assets	=	Liabilities	+	Stockholders' Equity			Acct. Titles for RE
					Common Stock	+	Retained Earnings	
1	+150,000		NA		NA		+150,000	Service Revenue

b. What is the amount of net income for 2004?
c. What is the amount of total assets at the end of 2004?
d. What is the amount of total liabilities at the end of 2004?

L.O. 4, 5 **EXERCISE 2–14B** *Classifying Events on the Statement of Cash Flows*

The following transactions pertain to the operations of Harrison Company for 2006:
1. Acquired $20,000 cash from the issue of common stock.
2. Provided $80,000 of services on account.
3. Paid $20,000 cash on accounts payable.
4. Performed services for $5,000 cash.
5. Collected $65,000 cash from accounts receivable.
6. Incurred $42,000 of operating expenses on account.
7. Paid $1,800 cash for expenses.
8. Paid a $5,000 cash dividend to the stockholders.

Required

a. Classify the cash flows from each of these transactions as operating activities (OA), investing activities (IA), or financing activities (FA). Use NA for transactions that do not affect the statement of cash flows.
b. Prepare a statement of cash flows. (This is the first year of operations.)

L.O. 4, 5, 6 **EXERCISE 2–15B** *Evaluating Cash Management*

The data in the following table apply to Watts, Incorporated.

	2005	2006
Accounts receivable	$ 11,605,000	$ 14,736,000
Sales	232,100,000	245,600,000
Accounts payable	5,872,000	4,527,000
Operating expenses	146,800,000	150,900,000

Required

a. The accounts receivable balance is what percent of sales in 2005 and 2006?

b. The accounts payable balance is what percent of operating expenses in 2005 and 2006?

c. Companies must incur interest expense to obtain cash. To minimize interest expense, companies attempt to collect cash from receivables as quickly as possible and to delay the payment of cash to settle payables as long as possible. Based on your answers to Requirements *a* and *b*, comment on Watts' cash management.

EXERCISE 2–16B *Relation of Elements to Financial Statements*

L.O. 4

Required

Identify whether each of the following items would appear on the income statement (IS), statement of changes in stockholders' equity (SE), balance sheet (BS), or statement of cash flows (CF). Some items may appear on more than one statement; if so, identify all applicable statements. If an item would not appear on any financial statement, label it NA.

a. Accounts Receivable

b. Accounts Payable

c. Interest Payable

d. Dividends

e. Beginning Cash Balance

f. Ending Retained Earnings

g. Interest Expense

h. Ending Cash Balance

i. Salaries Expense

j. Net Income

k. Utilities Expense

l. Interest Revenue

m. Cash Flow from Operating Activities

n. Service Revenue

o. Auditor's Opinion

EXERCISE 2–17B *Matching Concept*

L.O. 7

Companies make sacrifices known as *expenses* to obtain benefits called *revenues*. The accurate measurement of net income requires that expenses be matched with revenues. In some circumstances matching a particular expense directly with revenue is difficult or impossible. In these circumstances, the expense is matched with the period in which it is incurred.

Required

Distinguish the following items that could be matched directly with revenues from the items that would be classified as period expenses.

a. Sales commissions paid to employees.

b. Advertising expense.

c. Interest expense.

d. The cost of land that has been sold.

EXERCISE 2–18B *Closing Entries*

L.O. 5, 7

Required

Which of the following accounts are closed at the end of the accounting period?

a. Land

b. Interest Revenue

c. Interest Receivable

d. Rent Expense

e. Notes Payable

f. Interest Payable

g. Retained Earnings

h. Cash

i. Dividends

j. Accounts Receivable

k. Common Stock

l. Advertising Expense

Where applicable in all problems, round computations to the nearest dollar.

L.O. 3, 4, 5   PROBLEM 2–19B *Effect of Events on the Financial Statements*

Expert Services experienced the following transactions during 2003.
1. Provided services to customers and received $5,000 cash.
2. Paid $1,000 cash for other operating expenses.
3. Borrowed $15,000 from the bank on March 1, 2003. The note had an 8 percent annual interest rate and a one-year term to maturity.
4. Provided services to customers and billed them $20,000.
5. Incurred $6,000 of other operating expenses on account.
6. Collected $12,000 of accounts receivable.
7. Paid $3,100 of the amount due on accounts payable.
8. Recognized the accrued interest on the note payable at December 31, 2003.

Required
a. Show the effects of the transactions on the financial statements using a horizontal statements model like the following one. In the Cash Flows column, use the letters OA for operating activity, IA for investing activity, FA for financing activity, and NC for net change in cash. Use NA to indicate accounts not affected by the transaction. The first one is recorded as an example.

Event No.	Balance Sheet								Income Statement				Statement of Cash Flows
	Assets		=	Liab.			+	Stk. Equity					
	Cash	+ Accts. Rec.	= Accts. Pay.	Note Pay.	Int. Pay.	+	Ret. Earn.	Rev.	– Exp.	= Net Inc.		
1.	5,000 +	NA	= NA	NA	NA	+	5,000	5,000 –	NA	= 5,000	5,000	OA

b. What is the ending balance of retained earnings? What is the amount of net income? Why are these amounts the same in this problem? Give an example of a transaction that would cause these amounts to be different.

L.O. 3   PROBLEM 2–20B *Effect of Events on the Accounting Equation*

Required
Explain how each of the following independent accounting events would affect the accounting equation by writing the letter I for increase, the letter D for decrease, and NA for no effect under the appropriate columns. The effects of the first event are shown for you.

Letter of Event	Assets	=	Liabilities	+	Common Stock	+	Retained Earnings
a	I				I		

a. Received cash from the issue of common stock.
b. Paid cash for interest expense accrued in a previous period.
c. Purchased land with cash.
d. Repaid borrowed funds with cash.
e. Collected cash from accounts receivable.
f. Paid cash for salaries.
g. Recognized service revenue on account.
h. Received utility bill; cash payment will be made in the future.
i. Borrowed cash from creditors.
j. Paid a cash dividend to the stockholders.
k. Accrued interest expense on note payable at the end of the accounting period.

L.O. 3, 5   PROBLEM 2–21B *Effect of Accrued Interest on Financial Statements*

Diamond Enterprises borrowed $18,000 from a local bank on July 1, 2006, when the company was started. The note had a 10 percent annual interest rate and a one-year term to maturity. Diamond Enterprises recognized $42,500 of revenue on account in 2006 and $45,000 of revenue on account in 2007. Cash collections of accounts receivable were $36,000 in 2006 and $35,000 in 2007. Diamond paid $24,000 of other operating expenses in 2006 and $28,000 of other operating expenses in 2007.

Required
Based on this information, answer the following questions. (*Hint:* Record the events in the general ledger accounts under an accounting equation before answering the questions.)
a. What amount of interest expense would Diamond report on the 2006 income statement?
b. What amount of net cash flow from operating activities would Diamond report on the 2006 statement of cash flows?
c. What amount of total liabilities would Diamond report on the December 31, 2006, balance sheet?
d. What amount of retained earnings would Diamond report on the December 31, 2006, balance sheet?
e. What amount of net cash flow from financing activities would Diamond report on the 2006 statement of cash flows?
f. What amount of interest expense would Diamond report on the 2007 income statement?
g. What amount of net cash flow from operating activities would Diamond report on the 2007 statement of cash flows?
h. What amount of total assets would Diamond report on the December 31, 2007, balance sheet?
i. What amount of net cash flow from investing activities would Diamond report on the 2007 statement of cash flows?
j. If Diamond Enterprises paid a $1,500 dividend during 2007, what retained earnings balance would it report on the December 31, 2007, balance sheet?

PROBLEM 2–22B *Two Complete Accounting Cycles*   L.O. 3, 4

The following accounting events apply to Maples Machine Co.

Accounting Events for 2007

1. Business started when it acquired $80,000 cash from the issue of common stock.
2. Recognized $190,000 of service revenue on account.
3. Collected $166,000 cash from accounts receivable.
4. Paid the stockholders a $10,000 cash dividend.
5. Paid $92,000 cash for salaries expense.
6. Invested $48,000 cash in a 12–month certificate of deposit.

Information for December 31, 2007 End-of-Year Adjusting Entries

7. Accrued salary expense of $6,000.
8. Recorded accrued interest on the certificate of deposit. The CD was purchased on July 1, 2007, and had a 10 percent annual rate of interest.

Accounting Events for 2008

1. Paid cash for salaries payable of $6,000.
2. Received an additional $60,000 cash from the issue of common stock.
3. Earned service revenue on account of $210,000 for the year.
4. Received cash collections of accounts receivable of $224,000.
5. Paid a $30,000 cash dividend.
6. Paid $70,000 cash for salaries expense.
7. Purchased for $280,000 cash a plot of land on May 31, 2008. The value of the land rose to $300,000 by December 31.
8. Borrowed on June 1, 2008, $84,000 cash on a two-year, 8 percent note issued to State Bank.
9. Received cash for the principal and interest due on the certificate of deposit of $52,800 when it matured on June 30, 2008.

Information for Adjusting Entries

10. Accrued salary expenses of $10,000.
11. Recorded accrued interest expense on the bank note (see Event No. 8 in 2008).

Required
a. Record the effect of each of the events in general ledger accounts under an accounting equation for the 2007 and 2008 fiscal years. In the last column of the table, provide appropriate account titles for Retained Earnings amounts.

b. Prepare an income statement, statement of changes in stockholders' equity, balance sheet, and statement of cash flows for the 2007 and 2008 calendar years.

L.O. 4   PROBLEM 2–23B *Identifying and Arranging Elements on Financial Statements*

The following information was drawn from the records of Vickers & Associates at December 31, 2004:

Land	$97,500	Common Stock Issued	$10,000
Salaries Payable	17,000	Salary Expense	22,500
Interest Expense	1,375	Beginning Common Stock	12,000
Accounts Receivable	20,600	Ending Retained Earnings	60,500
Notes Payable	35,000	Cash Flow from Inv. Activities	(7,700)
Cash Flow from Oper. Activities	30,800	Interest Payable	300
Cash	16,700	Interest Revenue	375
Service Revenue	51,000	Dividends	2,000
Cash Flow from Fin. Activities	(8,400)		

Required

Use the preceding information to construct an income statement, statement of changes in stockholders' equity, balance sheet, and statement of cash flows. (Show only totals for each activity on the statement of cash flows).

L.O. 5, 10   PROBLEM 2–24B *Classifying Events as Source, Use, or Exchange and Effect of Events on Financial Statements—Horizontal Statements Model*

The following transactions pertain to Bunyard Financial Services for 2002.
1. Business started when it acquired $10,000 cash from the issue of common stock.
2. Paid $1,200 cash for rent expense.
3. Performed services for clients and billed them $8,000. Expected to collect cash at a later date (the revenue was earned on account).
4. Incurred $1,750 of other operating expenses on account (expected to make cash payment at a later date).
5. Paid $1,400 cash on the account payable created in Event No. 4.
6. Acquired $1,500 cash from the issue of additional common stock.
7. Paid $350 cash on the balance of the account payable created in Event No. 4.
8. Performed additional services for $3,500 cash.
9. Paid a $500 cash dividend to the stockholders.
10. Collected $7,250 cash from accounts receivable.

Required
a. Classify each of Bunyard's transactions as asset source (AS), asset use (AU), asset exchange (AE), or claims exchange (CE).
b. Show the effects of the events on the financial statements using a horizontal statements model like the following one. In the Cash Flow column, use the initials OA for operating activity, IA for investing activity, FA for financing activity, and NC for net change in cash flow.

Use NA to indicate accounts not affected by the transaction. The first one has been recorded as an example.

Event No.	Cash	+	Acc. Rec.	=	Acc. Pay.	+	Common Stock	+	Ret. Earn.	Rev.	−	Exp.	=	Net Inc.	Cash Flow	
	Assets			=	**Liab.**	+	**Stockholders' Equity**									
1	10,000	+	NA	=	NA	+	10,000	+	NA	NA	−	NA	=	NA	10,000	FA

c. What is the amount of net income for 2002?
d. What is the amount of net cash flow from operating activities for 2002?

L.O. 3, 4, 5   PROBLEM 2–25B *Missing Information in Financial Statements*

Dudley Properties had the following assets at the beginning of the accounting period (January 1, 2007): Cash—$1,600, Accounts Receivable—$2,400, Certificate of Deposit—$5,000, and Land—$20,000. The beginning balances in the liability accounts were Accounts Payable—$1,000, and Notes Payable—

$8,000. A $5,400 balance was in the Common Stock account at the beginning of the accounting period. During the accounting period, $3,600 of service revenue was earned on account. The ending balance in the Accounts Receivable account was $3,800. Operating expenses incurred on account amounted to $2,100. There was $2,600 paid on accounts payable. In addition, there was $400 of accrued interest revenue and $700 of accrued interest expense as of the end of the accounting period (December 31, 2007). Finally, an $800 cash dividend was paid to the stockholders. (*Hint:* Record the events in general ledger accounts under an accounting equation before satisfying the requirements.)

Required
a. Determine the amount of cash collected from accounts receivable.
b. Prepare a balance sheet as of January 1, 2007.
c. Prepare an income statement, statement of changes in stockholders' equity, balance sheet, and statement of cash flows for December 31, 2007.
d. Determine the interest rate earned on the certificate of deposit.
e. Determine the interest rate charged on the note payable.

ANALYZE, THINK, COMMUNICATE

BUSINESS APPLICATIONS CASE *Dell's Annual Report*

ATC 2–1

Required
Using the Dell Computer Corporation financial statements in Appendix B, answer the following questions:
a. Who are the independent auditors for Dell?
b. What type of opinion did the independent auditors issue on Dell's financial statements?
c. On what date does it appear that the independent auditors completed the audit work related to Dell's 2001 financial statements?
d. Does the auditors' report give any information about how the audit was conducted? If so, what does it suggest was done?
e. Does the auditors' report tell the reader that the audit was concerned with materiality rather than absolute accuracy in the financial statements? Explain.

GROUP ASSIGNMENT *Missing Information*

ATC 2–2

Tricom, Inc., is a company composed of KFC, Pizza Hut, and Taco Bell. The following information, taken from the annual report, is available for the years 2000, 1999, and 1998.

	2000	1999	1998
Revenue	$7,093,000	$7,822,000	$8,479,000
Operating Expenses	6,233,000	6,582,000	7,451,000
Interest Expense	176,000	202,000	272,000

Required
a. Divide the class into groups of four or five students. Organize the groups into three sections. Assign each section of groups the financial data for one of the preceding accounting periods.

Group Tasks

(1) Determine the amount of net income for the year assigned.
(2) How does the result in Requirement *a* affect the retained earnings of the company?
(3) If the average interest rate is 7 percent, what is the average amount of debt for the year?
(4) Have representatives from each section put the income statement for their respective year on the board.

Class Discussion

b. Have the class discuss the trend in revenue and net income. The company has new leadership teams and new management processes that will make Tricom a company "that stands for growth." If this is true, what actual results would you expect to see from the company in 2001?

ATC 2–3　REAL-WORLD CASE　*Unusual Types of Liabilities*

In the liabilities section of its 2000 balance sheet, First Union Corporation reported "noninterest-bearing deposits" of almost $30 billion. First Union is a very large banking company. In the liabilities section of its 2000 balance sheet, Newmont Mining Corporation reported "reclamation and remediation liabilities" of more than $160 million. Newmont Mining is involved in gold mining and refining activities. In the accrued liabilities reported on its 2000 balance sheet, Phillips Petroleum Company included $702 million for "accrued dismantlement, removal, and environmental costs."

Required

a. For each of the preceding liabilities, write a brief explanation of what you believe the nature of the liability to be and how the company will pay it off. To develop your answers, think about the nature of the industry in which each of the companies operates.

b. Of the three liabilities described, which do you think poses the most risk for the company? In other words, for which liability are actual costs most likely to exceed the liability reported on the balance sheet? Uncertainty creates risk.

ATC 2–4　BUSINESS APPLICATIONS CASE　*Decisions about Materiality*

The accounting firm of Espey & Davis, CPAs, recently completed the audits of three separate companies. During these audits, the following events were discovered, and Espey & Davis is trying to decide if each event is material. If an item is material, the CPA firm will insist that the company modify the financial statements.

1. In 2003, Foxx Company reported service revenues of $1,000,000 and net earnings of $80,000. Because of an accounting error, the company recorded $6,000 as revenue in 2003 for services that will not be performed until early 2004.

2. Guzza Company plans to report a cash balance of $70,000. Because of an accounting error, this amount is $5,000 too high. Guzza also plans to report total assets of $4,000,000 and net earnings of $415,000.

3. Jeter Company's 2003 balance sheet shows a cash balance of $200,000 and total assets of $9,000,000. For 2003, the company had a net income of $750,000. These balances are all correct, but they would have been $5,000 higher if the president of the company had not claimed business travel expenses that were, in fact, the cost of personal vacations for him and his family. He charged the costs of these trips on the company's credit card. The president of Jeter Company owns 25 percent of the business.

Required

Write a memorandum to the partners of Espey & Davis, explaining whether each of these events is material.

ATC 2–5　BUSINESS APPLICATIONS CASE　*Limitations of Audit Opinion*

The statement of financial position (balance sheet) of Trident Company reports assets of $4,500,000. Jan Lewis advises you that a major accounting firm has audited the statements and attested that they were prepared in accordance with generally accepted accounting principles. She tells you that she can buy the total owner's interest in the business for only $2,750,000 and is seriously considering the opportunity. She says that the auditor's unqualified opinion validates the $4,500,000 value of the assets. Lewis believes she would be foolish to pass up the opportunity to purchase the assets at a price of only $2,750,000.

Required

a. What part of the accounting equation is Lewis failing to consider?

b. Comment on Lewis's misconceptions regarding the auditor's role in providing information that is useful in making investment decisions.

WRITING ASSIGNMENT　*Definition of Elements of Financial Statements*

ATC 2–6

Putting "yum" on people's faces around the world is the mission of Tricom, Inc., a new company that resulted from a spin-off from PepsiCo. The company is composed of KFC, Pizza Hut, and Taco Bell. A spin-off occurs when a company separates its operations into two or more distinct companies. In this case, the Tricom restaurants were operated as part of PepsiCo prior to the spin-off, which was financed by having Tricom borrow $4.55 billion. These funds were used to pay PepsiCo for the value of the fast-food restaurants. Tricom's net income for 1997 was $308 million.

Required

a. If Tricom's debt remains constant at $4.55 billion for 1998, how much interest will Tricom incur in 1998, assuming that the average interest rate is 7 percent?

b. Does this amount of debt seem excessive compared with the amount of net income? Explain.

c. Assume that you are the president of the company. Write a memo to the shareholders explaining how Tricom, Inc., could have negative equity. You will need to make your own assumptions. Also offer some explanation of how Tricom may be able to meet its interest payments.

ETHICAL DILEMMA *Now It Is Your Turn to Cover for Me*

ATC 2–7

Johnny Travera and Tim Sanders were unusual friends. Travera came from a background of poverty while Sanders had an extremely affluent family. Indeed, the two would have never known each other except for an unusual set of events. Sanders' parents bought him a new car for his 16th birthday. Not being used to the new vehicle, Sanders misjudged a curve and wrecked the car. Travera happened to see the accident and helped Sanders get out of the vehicle. Sanders was unhurt but extremely distraught. He told Travera that his parents would never trust him again. When the police arrived, Travera told them that he had seen a child run in front of Sanders' car and that Sanders had swerved off the road to save the child's life. Upon hearing the story, Sanders' parents considered him a hero. The insurance company bought a new car, and Sanders made a friend for life.

Sanders went to college and became a CPA in his father's accounting firm. Travera worked for several restaurants and finally managed to start one of his own. The restaurant became successful, and Travera turned the accounting work over to Sanders. Having no formal education, Travera had little knowledge of technical business practices.

At the beginning of 2006, Travera's balance sheet included cash of $10,000, other assets amounting to $380,000, liabilities of $80,000, and common stock of $25,000. Sanders provided Travera with accounting services for several years and was reasonably certain as to the accuracy of these figures. Since Sanders always advised Travera on financial matters, Sanders was aware that during 2006 Travera had paid cash to purchase $50,000 of restaurant equipment. Also, Travera had been able to repay $15,000 cash on a note payable that evidenced the restaurant's liability to a bank. Finally, Travera had received a $20,000 cash dividend from the restaurant. Travera made no contributions to the business during 2006. Even so, the records that Travera provided Sanders for 2006 indicated that the restaurant earned $200,000 in cash revenues and incurred $175,000 in cash expenses. The ending balance in the Cash account was $12,000.

After analyzing the data, Sanders became convinced that Travera was not reporting accurate information to him for the determination of net income. He confronted Travera with the issue, and Travera admitted that he was not reporting all sales information. He said he did not report some of the cash sales because he did not feel the income tax system was fair and he did not want to pay any more taxes than he had to pay. He defended himself by saying, "I'm only doing what everybody else does. Your dad's biggest client, Billy Abbott, has been skimming a million a year off his chain of restaurants. He's been doing it for the last five years. I know; I used to work for him. Even so, you and your dad give him an unqualified audit opinion every year. So why won't you do the same thing for me? I'm supposed to be your friend, and you keep telling me you think this Abbott guy is a real jerk." Indeed, Travera became so indignant that he told Sanders, "Either you sign my tax return, or I find a new accountant and a new friend to boot. I've always stood up for you, and this is the thanks I get."

Required

a. Based on the information provided in the case, determine the amount of Travera's unreported income. (*Hint:* The beginning balances were correct, but the entries for the current year transactions were recorded incorrectly. It may be helpful to use an accounting equation with the beginning balances provided in the case, and record the current period's transactions under the equation. Assume that the ending cash balance is an accurate measure of cash on hand at the end of the accounting period. The amount of unrecorded cash equals the amount of unrecorded income.)

b. Explain how Travera's failure to report cash revenue will affect the elements of financial statements by indicating whether each element will be overstated, understated, or not affected by the reporting omission. The elements to consider are assets, liabilities, common stock, retained earnings, revenue, expenses, net income, and dividends.

c. Explain how Sanders' audit firm could be honest and still have provided an unqualified opinion on Abbott's financial statements. What is the auditor's responsibility for the detection and reporting of fraud?

d. If you were Sanders, would you sign Travera's tax return as Travera presented it to you?

e. Assume that you are Sanders, that you refuse to sign Travera's tax return, and that some other CPA without knowledge of Travera's deceitful reporting practice signs his tax return. Would you report Travera to the Internal Revenue Service?

f. Suppose that you are Sanders and that you investigate Travera's charges regarding Abbott. You find that Abbott is in fact underreporting income to the extent that Travera accused him of so doing. Would you report Abbott to the Internal Revenue Service?

ATC 2–8   SPREADSHEET ASSIGNMENT   *Using Excel*

Required

a. Refer to Problem 2–23A. Use an Excel spreadsheet to construct the required financial statements. To complete Requirement *b,* use formulas where normal arithmetic calculations are made within the financial statements (in particular the statement of changes in stockholders' equity).

b. It is interesting to speculate about what would happen if certain operating results change for better or worse. After completing Requirement *a,* change certain account balances for each of the following independent operating adjustments. After each adjustment, notice how the financial statements would differ if the change in operations were to occur. After noting the effect of each adjustment, return the data to the original amounts in Problem 2–23A and then go to the next operating adjustment.

In the following table, note the new amounts on the financial statements for the various operating changes listed.

Original	1	2	3	4	5
Net Income					
Total Assets					
Total Liabilities					
Total Stockholders' Equity					
Total Liabilities & Stockholders' Equity					

Independent Operating Adjustments

1. Revenue and the related Accounts Receivable increased $10,000.
2. Revenue and the related Accounts Receivable decreased $10,000.
3. Salary Expense and the related Salaries Payable decreased $4,000.
4. Salary Expense and the related Salaries Payable increased $4,000.
5. Dividends paid decreased $500 and cash changed accordingly.

ATC 2–9   SPREADSHEET ASSIGNMENT   *Mastering Excel*

Refer to Problem 2–24A. Complete Requirements *b, c,* and *d* using an Excel spreadsheet. Refer to Chapter 1 problem ATC 1-9 for ideas on how to structure the spreadsheet.

Accounting for Deferrals

After completing this chapter, you should be able to:

1 Provide a more complete explanation of the accrual accounting system.

2 Identify business events that involve deferrals.

3 Record under an accounting equation.

4 Prepare financial statements that include cash, accrual, and deferral events.

5 Explain how deferral events affect the financial statements.

6 Explain the effects of end-of-period adjustments related to deferrals.

7 Distinguish between a cost that is an asset and a cost that is an expense.

8 Distinguish gains and losses from revenues and expenses.

9 Analyze financial statements and make meaningful comparisons between companies using a debt-to-assets ratio, a return-on-assets ratio, and a return-on-equity ratio.

10 Record deferral events in a financial statements model.

the *curious* accountant

I f a person wishes to subscribe to *Reader's Digest* for one year (12 issues), the subscriber must pay for the magazines before they are actually published. Suppose Paige Long sends $12 to the Reader's Digest Association in September 2003 for a one-year subscription; she will receive her first issue in October. How should Reader's Digest account for the receipt of this cash? How would this event be reported on Reader's Digest's December 31, 2003, financial statements?

In Chapter 2, we defined accruals *as the recognition of revenue and expense before the receipt or payment of cash. In this chapter, you will learn that accrual accounting is, in fact, a much broader concept that includes not only accruals but also deferrals and allocations. A deferral involves the recognition of revenue or expense at some time after cash has been collected or paid. For example, a business may collect cash in 2001 for services performed in 2002. In this case, revenue is recognized in 2002 even though the cash was collected in 2001. In summary, when recognition comes before cash flow, it is called an accrual. When recognition comes after cash flow, it is called a deferral.*

When deferred amounts are spread over several accounting periods, the process of assigning a portion of the total amount to each accounting period is called an allocation. To illustrate, assume that an attorney received a retainer fee of $30,000 from a client at the beginning of 2001. In exchange for the cash receipt, the attorney agreed to act as a trustee for the client's children for the years 2001, 2002, and 2003. From the perspective of accrual accounting, the cash receipt obligates the attorney to work for the three-year period. Because of this future obligation, a liability is established in 2001 when the cash is collected. The recognition of revenue is deferred until the attorney's obligation (liability) to work is satisfied. If the work were spread evenly over the three-year period, it would be reasonable to allocate the $30,000 evenly so that $10,000 of revenue was recognized during each of the three accounting periods.

LO1 Provide a more complete explanation of the accrual accounting system.

LO2 Identify business events that involve deferrals.

▮Accounting for Deferrals Illustrated

Stephen Peck is a brilliant young advertising executive employed by Westberry Corporation. Peck's ad campaigns were credited with a virtual doubling of Westberry's sales over a three-year period. Peck always wanted to start his own advertising agency so he could be the boss. He believed that his recent success with Westberry gave him the level of credibility necessary to attract a respectable client base. He informed his employer of his plans and tendered his resignation. Westberry was stunned. The company's executives encouraged Peck to reconsider his decision and offered a generous raise. Peck was grateful but refused the offer. In despera-

tion, Westberry negotiated the following deal. Peck was free to start his own company. Indeed, Westberry agreed to become Peck's first client, paying him $72,000 in advance to develop ad campaigns for the company. Peck's company, Marketing Magic, Inc. (MMI), began operations on January 1, 2004. The company experienced the following accounting events during its first year of operation.

Event 1   *MMI acquired $1,000 cash from the issue of common stock.*

The stock issue is an asset source transaction. Its impact on the financial statements was discussed in previous chapters. If you have difficulty understanding the effects of this event, see Chapters 1 and 2. The impact of the stock issue on the financial statements follows:

Assets				=	Liab.	+	Stockholders' Equity			Rev.	_	Exp.	=	Net Inc.	Cash Flow
Cash	+ Off. Equip.	_	Acc. Dep.	=	Unear. Rev.	+	C. Stk.	+	Ret. Ear.						
1,000	+ NA	_	NA	=	NA	+	1,000	+	NA	NA	_ NA	=	NA		1,000 FA

The statements model contains several accounts that have not been discussed previously. A full description of these accounts will be presented as additional accounting events are introduced.

Event 2   *MMI obtained a $72,000 cash receipt as an advance from Westberry for services to be performed between March 1, 2004, and February 28, 2005.*

On January 1, 2004, Marketing Magic received $72,000 cash. In exchange, Marketing Magic agreed to provide advertising development services for a one-year period between March 1, 2004, and February 28, 2005. Revenue could not be recognized on January 1, 2004, because services had not been performed (no work had been done). Even though the cash had been realized, the revenue recognition had to be *deferred* until the performance of services had been accomplished. The amount of the deferred revenue represents a liability to Marketing Magic because the company is *obligated* to perform services in the future. The descriptive title **unearned revenue** is used as the name of the liability reported in Marketing Magic's accounting records. The cash receipt is an *asset source* transaction. The asset, Cash, increases; and the liability account, Unearned Revenue, increases by the same amount, $72,000. The income statement is not affected when the cash is collected because no work has been performed. The revenue will be shown on the income statement after the service has been rendered. The statement of cash flows shows a $72,000 cash inflow from operating activities. The effects of this transaction on the financial statements are shown here:

Assets				=	Liab.	+	Stockholders' Equity			Rev.	_	Exp.	=	Net Inc.	Cash Flow
Cash	+ Off. Equip.	_	Acc. Dep.	=	Unear. Rev.	+	C. Stk.	+	Ret. Ear.						
72,000	+ NA	_	NA	=	72,000	+	NA	+	NA	NA	_ NA	=	NA		72,000 OA

Event 3   *MMI obtained contracts to provide $58,000 of marketing services in 2005.*

Notice that even though $58,000 of contracts was signed for services to be performed in 2005, no cash was exchanged with regard to these contracts. Accordingly, there is no historical activity to record in the financial statements. The contracts will be reported later when cash is received or when service is performed. Since no service has been performed and no cash has been exchanged, there is no realization or recognition to report in the financial statements.

Assets				=	Liab.	+	Stockholders' Equity		Rev.	–	Exp.	=	Net Inc.	Cash Flow
Cash	+ Off. Equip.	–	Acc. Dep.	=	Unear. Rev.	+ C. Stk.	+ Ret. Ear.							
NA	+ NA	–	NA	=	NA	+ NA	+ NA		NA	– NA	=		NA	NA

Event 4   *MMI paid $12,000 cash to purchase office equipment.*

The purchase of the equipment is an *asset exchange* transaction. The asset, Cash, decreases; and the asset, Office Equipment, increases. Total assets are unchanged. The income statement is not affected. An expense will be recognized later when the equipment has been used. The statement of cash flows shows a $12,000 outflow for investing activities. The effects of this transaction on the financial statements are shown here:

Assets				=	Liab.	+	Stockholders' Equity		Rev.	–	Exp.	=	Net Inc.	Cash Flow
Cash	+ Off. Equip.	–	Acc. Dep.	=	Unear. Rev.	+ C. Stk.	+ Ret. Ear.							
(12,000)	+ 12,000	–	NA	=	NA	+ NA	+ NA		NA	– NA	=		NA	(12,000) IA

Event 5   *MMI adjusted its accounts to recognize the revenue earned in 2004.*

Marketing Magic must recognize the amount of revenue earned on the Westberry contract during the 2004 accounting period. Marketing Magic began earning revenue on the Westberry contract on March 1, 2004. Assuming that the work is distributed evenly throughout the contract period, the earnings process is continuous. Recording revenue as it is earned (continuously) is impractical, if not impossible. A more reasonable approach is simply to adjust the accounting records at the end of the accounting period by the amount of revenue earned for the entire accounting period. For example, the $72,000 of unearned revenue can be divided by 12 to determine the amount of revenue to recognize on a monthly basis ($72,000 ÷ 12 = $6,000). Since 10 months of service were performed in 2004, $60,000 (or 10 × $6,000) of revenue could be recognized in a single year-end adjustment. This adjustment is made by removing $60,000 from the Unearned Revenue account and placing it into the Revenue account. This entry represents a *claims exchange* with the liability account, Unearned Revenue, decreasing and the equity increasing (recognizing the revenue will cause net income to increase and ultimately a corresponding increase in retained earnings). Total claims remain unchanged. It is the decrease in the liability account that triggers the recognition of the revenue. As the company satisfies its obligation to perform services, the creditor's claim on the firm's assets decreases and the owner's claim increases. Recall that *revenue* is defined as an increase in assets or a *decrease* in liabilities. The effect of the revenue recognition on the financial statements follows:

LO6 Explain the effects of end-of-period adjustments related to deferrals.

Assets				=	Liab.	+	Stockholders' Equity		Rev.	–	Exp.	=	Net Inc.	Cash Flow
Cash	+ Off. Equip.	–	Acc. Dep.	=	Unear. Rev.	+ C. Stk.	+ Ret. Ear.							
NA	+ NA	–	NA	=	(60,000)	+ NA	+ 60,000		60,000	– NA	=		60,000	NA

Event 6   *MMI adjusted its accounts to recognize an expense to reflect the portion of the computer equipment that was used during the 2004 accounting period. The equipment was purchased on January 1, 2004. It has an expected useful life of four years and a $2,000 salvage value.*

LO6 Explain the effects of end-of-period adjustments related to deferrals.

To assess the net economic benefit associated with running the business, it is necessary to determine how much of the computer equipment MMI sacrificed (used) in the process of earning the revenue. Assuming that the equipment is used evenly over its four-year life, it is logical to allocate an equal amount as expense for each year that the equipment is operated. Recall that the equipment cost $12,000 and has an estimated salvage value of $2,000. Since the $2,000 salvage value represents the portion of the cost that is expected to be recovered at the end of its useful life, only $10,000 worth of the equipment is ultimately expected to be used. Accordingly, the amount of expense to be recognized in the 2004 accounting period is $2,500 (that is, [$12,000 − $2,000] ÷ 4). This allocation plan is commonly referred to as the **straight-line method.** As this discussion implies, the formula for determining a straight-line allocation is *cost minus salvage, divided by the number of years of useful life.* The recognition of the use of a long-term, tangible asset is commonly called **depreciation expense.** *Long term* is usually defined as a period longer than the typical accounting cycle (longer than one year). The recognition of depreciation expense constitutes an *asset use* transaction. The use of the asset (decrease) triggers the expense recognition. Recall that an *expense* is defined as a *decrease* in assets or an increase in liabilities. The effects of the expense recognition on the financial statements follow.

Assets			=	Liab.	+ Stockholders' Equity		Rev.	−	Exp.	=	Net Inc.	Cash Flow
Cash	+ Off. Equip.	− Acc. Dep.	= Unear. Rev.	+ C. Stk.	+ Ret. Ear.							
NA	+ NA	− 2,500	= NA	+ NA	+ (2,500)		NA	− 2,500	=	(2,500)		NA

Note that the asset account, Office Equipment, was not directly decreased. Rather, a **contra asset account** called **Accumulated Depreciation** was used to reflect the reduction. This is the generally accepted approach for reporting the effects of depreciation. The Accumulated Depreciation account is subtracted from the original cost of the asset to determine the **book value** (carrying value) of the asset. Both the historical cost of the asset and the Accumulated Depreciation account are shown in the financial statements. This treatment is shown in the financial statements in Exhibit 3–1.

Event 7   *MMI paid a $50,000 cash dividend to the stockholders.*

As discussed in Chapters 1 and 2, the dividend represents an *asset use* transaction. Its effect on the financial statements is shown here:

Assets			=	Liab.	+ Stockholders' Equity		Rev.	−	Exp.	=	Net Inc.	Cash Flow
Cash	+ Off. Equip.	− Acc. Dep.	= Unear. Rev.	+ C. Stk.	+ Ret. Ear.							
(50,000)	+ NA	− NA	= NA	+ NA	+ (50,000)		NA	− NA	=	NA		(50,000) FA

Summary of Events and Ledger Accounts

Marketing Magic experienced seven business events during its 2004 accounting period. These events are summarized here.

1. Acquired $1,000 cash from the issue of common stock.
2. Obtained a $72,000 cash receipt as an advance from Westberry for services to be performed between March 1, 2004, and February 28, 2005.
3. Obtained contracts to provide $58,000 of marketing services in 2005.
4. Paid $12,000 cash to purchase office equipment.
5. Adjusted its accounts to recognize the revenue earned in 2004.
6. Adjusted its accounts to recognize an expense to reflect the portion of the computer equipment purchased on January 1, 2004, and used during the 2004 accounting period. It has an expected useful life of four years and a $2,000 salvage value.
7. Paid a $50,000 cash dividend to the stockholders.

The accounting events have been recorded in the following ledger accounts. The information in these accounts has been used to prepare the financial statements shown in Exhibit 3–1.

Assets				=	Liabilities		+	Stockholders' Equity		
Cash		**Office Equipment**			**Unearned Revenue**			**Common Stock**		**Retained Earnings**
(1)	1,000	(4)	12,000		(2)	72,000		(1)	1,000	0
(2)	72,000				(5)	(60,000)				
(4)	(12,000)	**Accumulated Depreciation**								
(7)	(50,000)				Bal	12,000				**Revenue**
Bal	11,000	(6)	(2,500)							(5) 60,000
										Depreciation Expense
										(6) (2,500)
										Dividends
										(7) (50,000)

Exhibit 3–1 *Vertical Statements Model*

MARKETING MAGIC
Financial Statements
for the 2004 Accounting Period

Income Statement

Service Revenue	$60,000
Depreciation Expense	(2,500)
Net Income	$57,500

Statement of Changes in Stockholders' Equity

Beginning Common Stock	$ 0	
Plus: Issue of Stock	1,000	
Ending Common Stock		$ 1,000
Beginning Retained Earnings	0	
Plus: Net Income	57,500	
Less: Dividends	(50,000)	
Ending Retained Earnings		7,500
Total Stockholders' Equity		$ 8,500

Balance Sheet

Assets		
Cash		$11,000
Office Equipment	$12,000	
Less: Accumulated Depreciation	(2,500)	9,500
Total Assets		$20,500
Liabilities		
Unearned Revenue		$12,000
Stockholders' Equity		
Common Stock	$ 1,000	
Retained Earnings	7,500	
Total Stockholders' Equity		8,500
Total Liabilities and Stockholders' Equity		$20,500

Statement of Cash Flows

Cash Flows from Operating Activities		
Cash Receipt from Receivables		$72,000
Cash Flows from Investing Activities		
Cash Payment for Computer Equipment		(12,000)
Cash Flows from Financing Activities		
Cash Receipt from Issue of Stock	$ 1,000	
Cash Payment for Dividends	(50,000)	
Net Cash Outflow from Financing Activities		(49,000)
Net Increase in Cash		11,000
Plus: Beginning Cash Balance		0
Ending Cash Balance		$11,000

LO4 Prepare financial statements that include cash, accrual, and deferral events.

The 2004 Financial Statements

Exhibit 3–1 contains the financial statements for Marketing Magic for the 2004 accounting period. You should be familiar with most of the components of the financial statements by this point. However, it is important to trace the effects of all transactions to the financial statements. Pay particular attention to the fact that deferrals as well as accruals cause differences between the amount of reported net income and the amount of cash flow from operations.

The income statement displays the allocations for revenue recognition $60,000 and depreciation expense ($2,500), thereby showing a reported net income of $57,500. In contrast, the operating activities section of the statement of cash flows shows the $72,000 of cash received from the Westberry contract. Note that the $12,000 cash paid for office equipment is shown in the investing activities section rather than the operating activities section. This treatment applies to the purchase or sale of any long-term asset.

Another item that should be scrutinized is the treatment of the Accumulated Depreciation account. Note that the full amount of the original cost is shown in the Office Equipment account. The amount of the accumulated depreciation is subtracted from this amount to arrive at the carrying value (book value) of the asset ($12,000 − $2,500 = $9,500). It is the carrying value ($9,500) that is added to the other assets to arrive at the amount of total assets appearing on the balance sheet.

Check Yourself 3–1

Sanderson & Associates received a $24,000 cash advance as a retainer to provide legal services to a client. The contract called for Sanderson to render services during a one-year period beginning October 1, 2006. Based on this information alone, determine the cash flow from operating activities Sanderson would report on the 2006 and 2007 statements of cash flows. Also determine the amount of revenue Sanderson would report on the 2006 and 2007 income statements.

Answer Since Sanderson collected all of the cash in 2006, the 2006 statement of cash flows would report a $24,000 cash inflow from operating activities. The 2007 statement of cash flows would report zero cash flow from operating activities. Revenue is recognized in the period in which it is earned. In this case revenue is earned at the rate of $2,000 per month ($24,000 ÷ 12 months = $2,000 per month). Sanderson rendered services for three months in 2006 and nine months in 2007. Sanderson would report $6,000 (3 months × $2,000) of revenue on the 2006 income statement and $18,000 (9 months × $2,000) of revenue on the 2007 income statement.

Key Accounting Concepts

You may have noticed that the depreciation expense represented the part of the asset that was used during the period from January 1 through December 31, 2004. Conversely, the revenue was recognized from a starting point on March 1, 2004. Accordingly, it could be argued that the computer was used for purposes other than generating the revenue related to the Westberry contract. In other words, revenues and expenses do not perfectly match. As discussed in Chapter 2, many expenses are not directly related to particular revenues and are therefore matched with the period in which they are incurred. However, it does not make sense to recognize all of the cost of the equipment in the period in which it was purchased. Since the equipment will be used to produce revenue over a four-year period, it is logical to spread its cost over the four-year useful life. The process of spreading the cost over several accounting periods is frequently called a **systematic allocation.**

As the preceding discussion suggests, the **matching concept** is accomplished on three levels. First, possible costs are matched directly with the revenues they generate (expenses are recognized in the same period as the related revenue). Common examples include cost of land that has been sold and sales commissions. Second, the cost of items with short or undeterminable useful lives is matched with the period in which they are incurred (expenses are recognized in the period in which they are incurred). Examples of period expenses include advertising, rent, and utilities. Finally, the costs of long-term assets with definable useful lives are systematically allocated over the assets' useful lives (expenses are spread over the periods in which the assets are used). Depreciation is an example of an expense that is recognized through the systematic allocation of cost.

Because the Reader's Digest Association receives cash from customers before actually providing any magazines to them, the company has not earned any revenue when it receives the cash. Thus, Reader's Digest has a liability, which is called *unearned revenue*. If Reader's Digest closed its books on December 31, then $3 of Paige Long's subscription would be recognized as revenue in 2003. The remaining $9 would appear on Reader's Digest's balance sheet as a liability.

Reader's Digest actually ends its accounting year on June 30, each year. Exhibit 3–2 is a copy of the June 30, 2000, balance sheet for Reader's Digest. Notice the liability for unearned revenue amounting to $289.4 million—this liability represented about 23 percent of Reader's Digest's total liabilities!

Will Reader's Digest need cash to pay off these subscription liabilities? Not exactly. The liabilities will not be paid off with cash. Instead, they will be satisfied by providing magazines to the subscribers. However, Reader's Digest will need cash to pay for the production and distribution of the magazines supplied to the customers. Even so, the amount of cash required to provide magazines will probably differ significantly from the amount of unearned revenues. In most cases, subscription fees do not cover the cost of producing and distributing magazines. Publishers collect significant advertising revenues that enable them to provide magazines to customers at prices well below the cost of publication. Accordingly, the amount of unearned revenue is not likely to represent the amount of cash needed to cover the cost of satisfying the company's obligation to produce and distribute magazines. Although the association between unearned revenues and the cost of providing magazines to customers is not direct, a knowledgeable financial analyst can use the information to make estimates regarding future cash flows and revenue recognition.

Exhibit 3–2 *Excerpt from the Reader's Digest 2000 Annual Report*

THE READER'S DIGEST ASSOCIATION, INC., AND SUBSIDIARIES
Consolidated Balance Sheets (in millions)

	June 30, 2000	June 30, 1999
Assets		
Current Assets		
Cash and Cash Equivalents	$ 49.7	$ 413.4
Receivables, Net	285.3	319.9
Inventories, Net	120.3	94.9
Prepaid and Deferred Promotion Costs	115.5	109.0
Prepaid Expenses and Other Current Assets	201.7	193.5
Total Current Assets	772.5	1,130.7
Marketable Securities	173.5	20.9
Property, Plant and Equipment, Net	152.4	148.4
Intangible Assets, Net	438.8	68.5
Other Noncurrent Assets	221.6	248.0
Total Assets	$1,758.8	$1,616.5
Liabilities and Stockholders' Equity		
Current Liabilities		
Loans and Notes Payable	$ 89.4	$ 0.4
Accounts Payable	146.4	130.7
Accrued Expenses	309.6	352.2
Income Taxes Payable	38.7	56.0
Unearned Revenue	289.4	336.5
Other Current Liabilities	30.9	16.5
Total Current Liabilities	904.4	892.3
Postretirement and Postemployment Benefits Other than Pensions	142.3	146.9
Other Noncurrent Liabilities	207.8	195.8
Total Liabilities	1,254.5	1,235.0
Stockholders' Equity		
Capital Stock	28.9	24.8
Paid-In Capital	223.1	146.2
Retained Earnings	1,106.6	955.4
Accumulated Other Comprehensive Income (Loss)	31.0	(56.6)
Treasury Stock, at Cost	(885.3)	(688.3)
Total Stockholders' Equity	504.3	381.5
Total Liabilities and Stockholders' Equity	$1,758.8	$1,616.5

The treatment of depreciation also highlights the fact that financial reports contain information from approximate, rather than exact, measures. Notice that the amounts of both the asset's salvage value and its expected useful life are estimated amounts. Accordingly, the amounts of depreciation expense, net income, and retained earnings constitute estimated, rather than exact, amounts. Estimates and other slight imperfections are to be expected. Indeed, the **concept of materiality** recognizes practical limitations in financial reporting matters. Proper treatment is required for material items only. As previously indicated, an omission or misstatement of accounting information is considered material if the decision of a reasonable person would have been influenced by the omission or misstatement. Generally accepted accounting principles do not apply to items that would not affect the decisions of a reasonable person (immaterial items).

▌Second Accounting Cycle

LO2 Identify business events that involve deferrals.

Stephen Peck moved the offices of Marketing Magic to a new location on January 1, 2005. Westberry continued to be a client but decided to pay for services as rendered rather than in advance. Marketing Magic consummated the following transactions during the 2005 accounting period.

1. Acquired an additional $5,000 cash from the issue of more common stock.
2. Paid $400 cash for supplies.
3. Paid $1,200 cash for an insurance policy that covered the company for one year, beginning February 1, 2005.
4. Recognized revenue for services provided on account in the amount of $108,000.
5. Collected $89,000 of the receivables due from customers.
6. Recognized accrued operating expenses, other than supplies and insurance, charged on account in the amount of $32,000.
7. Paid suppliers $28,000 of the amount due on the accounts payable.
8. Paid a $70,000 cash dividend to stockholders.
9. Purchased land that cost $3,000 cash.

Adjusting Entries

10. Recognized the remainder of the unearned revenue. All services had been provided by February 28, 2005, as per the original contract.
11. Recognized depreciation expense.
12. Recognized supplies expense; $150 of supplies was on hand at the close of business on December 31, 2005.
13. Recognized 11 months of insurance expense.

Exhibit 3–3 is a summary of the effects of the transactions on the accounting equation. The effects are referenced by the transaction number in parentheses to the left of the transaction amount. The beginning balances were carried forward from the last period's ending balances. Many of the transactions were introduced in previous sections of this book. Those transactions that are new are discussed in the following section of the text.

Effect of 2005 Transactions on the Accounting Equation and the Financial Statements

LO3 Record under an accounting equation.

LO7 Distinguish between a cost that is an asset and a cost that is an expense.

LO5 Explain how deferral events affect financial statements.

LO6 Explain the effects of end-of-period adjustments related to deferrals.

Transaction 2 is a deferral. The cost of the supplies is first placed in an asset account (*asset exchange* transaction). The conversion of the asset to an expense is deferred until the supplies are used in the process of earning revenue. It is helpful at this point to draw a clear distinction between *cost* and *expense*. A *cost* can be either an asset or an expense. If the item acquired has already been used in the process of earning revenue, its cost represents an *expense*. If the item will be used in the future to generate revenue, its cost represents an *asset*. The cost is held in the asset account (the expense recognition is deferred) until the item is used to produce revenue. When the revenue is generated, the asset is converted to an expense to match revenues with their related expenses. Exhibit 3–4 demonstrates the relationship between a cost and an expense.

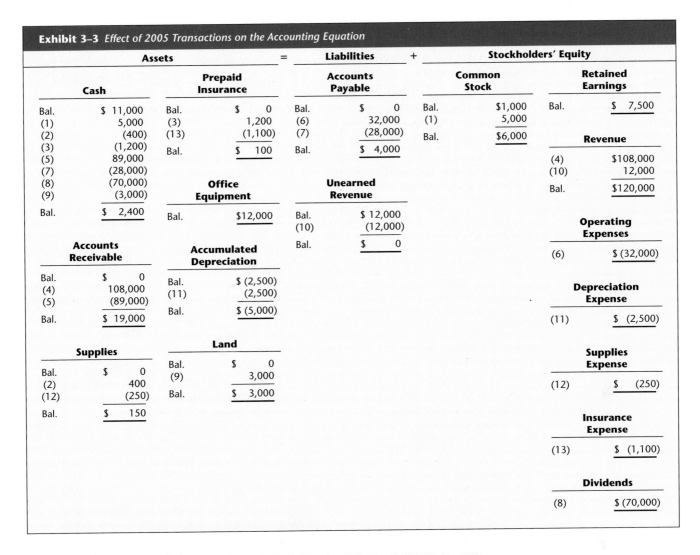

Exhibit 3-3 *Effect of 2005 Transactions on the Accounting Equation*

	Assets		=	Liabilities		+	Stockholders' Equity	

Cash

Bal.	$ 11,000
(1)	5,000
(2)	(400)
(3)	(1,200)
(5)	89,000
(7)	(28,000)
(8)	(70,000)
(9)	(3,000)
Bal.	$ 2,400

Accounts Receivable

Bal.	$ 0
(4)	108,000
(5)	(89,000)
Bal.	$ 19,000

Supplies

Bal.	$ 0
(2)	400
(12)	(250)
Bal.	$ 150

Prepaid Insurance

Bal.	$ 0
(3)	1,200
(13)	(1,100)
Bal.	$ 100

Office Equipment

Bal.	$12,000

Accumulated Depreciation

Bal.	$ (2,500)
(11)	(2,500)
Bal.	$ (5,000)

Land

Bal.	$ 0
(9)	3,000
Bal.	$ 3,000

Accounts Payable

Bal.	$ 0
(6)	32,000
(7)	(28,000)
Bal.	$ 4,000

Unearned Revenue

Bal.	$ 12,000
(10)	(12,000)
Bal.	$ 0

Common Stock

Bal.	$1,000
(1)	5,000
Bal.	$6,000

Retained Earnings

Bal.	$ 7,500

Revenue

(4)	$108,000
(10)	12,000
Bal.	$120,000

Operating Expenses

(6)	$ (32,000)

Depreciation Expense

(11)	$ (2,500)

Supplies Expense

(12)	$ (250)

Insurance Expense

(13)	$ (1,100)

Dividends

(8)	$ (70,000)

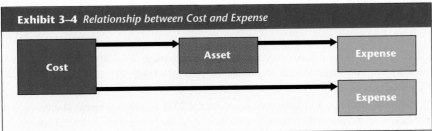

Exhibit 3-4 *Relationship between Cost and Expense*

Cost → Asset → Expense

Cost → Expense

It is impractical to recognize supplies expense as the supplies are being used. For example, it is too tedious to record an expense every time a pencil, a piece of paper, or an envelope is used. Instead, normal practice is to recognize the total amount of supplies used during the entire accounting period in a single adjusting entry at the end of the accounting period. The amount of supplies used is determined by subtracting the amount of supplies on hand at the end of the period from the amount of supplies that were available for use. Since Marketing Magic had no supplies at the beginning of the period, the only supplies available for use were the $400 of supplies purchased during 2005. Transaction 12 states that $150 of supplies was on hand at the end of the accounting period. In practice, this amount is determined by counting the supplies on hand at the end of the period. Based on the information provided in the case, $250 of supplies must have been used during the period (that is, $400 − $150). This explains the year-end adjusting entry (Transaction 12) that removes the amount of the used supplies from the asset account and transfers it into the Supplies Expense account. Recall that an *expense* is defined as a decrease in assets or an increase in liabilities. In this case, the decrease in the asset, Supplies, triggers the expense recognition. The $150 of supplies on hand at the end of the accounting period is shown as an asset on the balance sheet. The parentheses surrounding the amounts in the expense and dividend accounts indicate that the business events acted to decrease the Retained Earnings equity account. Although events 6, 8, 11, 12, and 13 increase the amount of an expense or dividends account, they acted to decrease stockholders' equity.

Note that the deferral causes a difference between the amount of expense recognized and the amount of cash flow. Although $400 of cash is paid for supplies, only $250 of this is recognized as an expense. The remaining $150 is deferred as an asset. The $400 appears as an outflow under the operating activities section of the statement of cash flows, the $250 is reported as supplies expense on the income statement, and the $150 is displayed as an asset (supplies) on the balance sheet. Verify these effects by reviewing the financial statements shown in Exhibit 3–5.

Transaction 3 is also a deferral. The $1,200 cost of the insurance must be allocated between an asset account and an expense account. Since the insurance policy provided coverage for one year, the cost of coverage per month is $100 ($1,200 ÷ 12). By the end of the accounting period, 11 months of the coverage have been used and one month of coverage is available for use in 2006. Accordingly, $1,100 ($100 × 11) should be charged to expense, and the remaining $100 represents an asset. Since the insurance is paid for in advance of its use, the title *Prepaid Insurance* is an appropriate descriptor of the asset account.

As a practical matter, the full cost of the insurance is placed in the Prepaid Insurance account at the time of the purchase (see Transaction 3 in Exhibit 3–3). An adjusting entry is made at the end of the accounting period to recognize the amount of the insurance that has been used. The adjustment (Transaction 13) moves the amount of used insurance from the asset account to the expense account. Be aware that other recording schemes are possible. For example, some sophisticated computer programs can allocate costs between asset and expense accounts on a continuous basis. Regardless of the recording method, the ultimate impact on the financial statements is the same.

The deferral for the insurance cost causes a difference between the amount of insurance expense and the cash flow. The $1,200 cash cost is shown in the cash flow from operating activities section of the statement of cash flows. The used portion of the cost is shown as an $1,100 expense on the income statement, and the remaining $100 is deferred as an asset, Prepaid Insurance, on the balance sheet. Verify this allocation and the effects of the remaining transactions by reviewing the financial statements in Exhibit 3–5.

Check Yourself 3–2

Rujoub, Inc., paid $18,000 cash for one year of insurance coverage that began on November 1, 2005. Based on this information alone, determine the cash flow from operating activities that Rujoub would report on the 2005 and 2006 statements of cash flows. Also determine the amount of insurance expense Rujoub would report on the 2005 income statement and the amount of prepaid insurance (an asset) that Rujoub would report on the December 31, 2005, balance sheet.

Answer Since Rujoub paid all of the cash in 2005, the 2005 statement of cash flows would report an $18,000 cash outflow from operating activities. The 2006 statement of cash flows would report zero cash flow from operating activities. The expense would be recognized in the periods in which the insurance is used. In this case, insurance expense is recognized at the rate of $1,500 per month ($18,000 ÷ 12 months). Rujoub used two months of insurance coverage in 2005 and therefore would report $3,000 (2 months × $1,500) of insurance expense on the 2005 income statement. Rujoub would report a $15,000 (10 months × $1,500) asset, prepaid insurance, on the December 31, 2005, balance sheet. The $15,000 of prepaid insurance would be recognized as insurance expense in 2006 when the insurance coverage is used.

Exhibit 3–5 *Vertical Statements Model*

MARKETING MAGIC
Financial Statements
For the 2005 Accounting Period

Income Statement

Service Revenue		$120,000
Operating Expenses	$32,000	
Depreciation Expense	2,500	
Supplies Expense	250	
Insurance Expense	1,100	
Total Expenses		(35,850)
Net Income		$ 84,150

Statement of Changes in Stockholders' Equity

Beginning Common Stock	$ 1,000	
Plus: Issue of Stock	5,000	
Ending Common Stock		$ 6,000
Beginning Retained Earnings	7,500	
Plus: Net Income	84,150	
Less: Dividends	(70,000)	
Ending Retained Earnings		21,650
Total Stockholders' Equity		$ 27,650

Balance Sheet

Assets		
Cash		$ 2,400
Accounts Receivable		19,000
Supplies		150
Prepaid Insurance		100
Office Equipment	$12,000	
Less: Accumulated Depreciation	(5,000)	7,000
Land		3,000
Total Assets		$ 31,650
Liabilities		
Accounts Payable		$ 4,000
Stockholders' Equity		
Common Stock	$ 6,000	
Retained Earnings	21,650	
Total Stockholders' Equity		27,650
Total Liabilities and Stockholders' Equity		$ 31,650

Statement of Cash Flows

Cash Flows from Operating Activities		
Cash Receipt from Receivables		$ 89,000
Cash Payment for Supplies	$ (400)	
Cash Payment for Insurance	(1,200)	
Cash Payment for Operating Expenses	(28,000)	
Total Cash Outflows from Operations		(29,600)
Net Cash Flow from Operating Activities		59,400
Cash Flows from Investing Activities		
Cash Outflow to Purchase Land		(3,000)
Cash Flows from Financing Activities		
Cash Receipt from Issue of Stock	5,000	
Cash Payment for Dividends	(70,000)	
Net Cash Outflow from Financing Activities		(65,000)
Net Decrease in Cash		(8,600)
Plus Beginning Cash Balance		11,000
Ending Cash Balance		$ 2,400

Third Accounting Cycle

Marketing Magic consummated the following transactions during the 2006 accounting period.

1. Acquired an additional $1,000 cash from the issue of common stock.
2. Sold the land that it owned for $2,500 cash.
3. Purchased $400 of supplies with cash.
4. Borrowed $20,000 from a local bank on February 1, 2006. The bank note carried a 9 percent annual rate of interest and a one-year term.
5. Paid $1,200 cash to renew the insurance policy for a one-year term beginning February 1, 2006.
6. Recognized revenue for services provided on account in the amount of $167,000.
7. Collected $129,000 of the receivables due from customers.
8. Recognized accrued operating expenses, other than supplies and insurance. These operating expenses were charged on account in the amount of $62,000.
9. Paid suppliers $65,000 of the amount due on the accounts payable.
10. Received advance payment of $18,000 cash from a customer. Marketing Magic agreed to provide marketing services to the customer for a one-year period beginning December 1, 2006.
11. Paid an $80,000 cash dividend to stockholders.

Adjusting Entries

12. Recognized one month of the unearned revenue.
13. Recognized depreciation expense.
14. Recognized supplies expense; $200 of supplies was on hand at the close of business on December 31, 2006.
15. Recognized 12 months of insurance expense.
16. Recognized the accrued interest on the bank note.

The effects of the 2006 accounting events are shown in Exhibit 3–6 on the following page.

Effect of 2006 Transactions on the Accounting Equation and the Financial Statements

Transaction 1 demonstrates the fact that ownership interest may be shared by two or more individuals. Indeed, literally millions of individuals and institutions hold ownership interests in major corporations, such as General Motors, Sears, and International Business Machines (IBM). The treatment of the $1,000 cash acquired from the issue of common stock is no different from the effects of other acquisitions shown previously. The acquisition is an *asset source* transaction that is recorded by an increase in the asset account, Cash, and a corresponding increase in the stockholders' equity account, Common Stock.

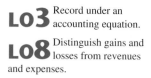

The sale of the land resulted in the recognition of a $500 loss. Since the asset was carried on the books at $3,000 and was sold for $2,500, total assets decreased by $500. This decrease in assets is called a loss. **Losses** are similar to expenses in that they are defined as decreases in assets or increases in liabilities. Losses differ from expenses in that losses result from **peripheral (incidental) transactions,** rather than ordinary operating activities. In this case, Marketing Magic is not in the business of selling land. The sale is incidental to its normal operating activities. Accordingly, the decrease in assets is labeled a *loss* rather than an *expense*. **Gains** are similar to revenues in that they are defined as increases in assets or decreases in liabilities. However, gains differ from revenues in that gains result from peripheral rather than ordinary operating activities.

The sale of the land results in an increase in the Cash account. Furthermore, it is necessary to remove the amount in the Land account from the records and to recognize the loss as a reduction in stockholders' equity. Recording the effects requires a $2,500 increase to the Cash account, a $3,000 decrease to the Land account, and a $500 reduction in Retained Earnings. These effects are shown in Exhibit 3–6, labeled as Transaction 2. The $500 loss is shown on

Cynthia J. Koch

20 Winesap Road Reelsville, Indiana 46171
Telephone: (765)672-4052
E-mail: ckoch@ccrtc.com

OBJECTIVE: To apply the skills acquired through training and experience for the betterment of myself and my employer.

EDUCATION

Associate of Applied Science in Office Administration
Ivy Tech State College—Terre Haute, Indiana
Anticipated graduation date   2005

CERTIFICATIONS

- Microsoft Word   2004
- Non-credit major: Business and Industry   2003-2004
- Participation in Student Leadership Academy   2003-2004

SUMMARY OF SKILLS AND EXPERIENCE

- Familiar with standard office procedures
- Proficient in following detailed instructions
- Demonstrated ability for problem solving
- Excellent verbal skills
- More than 20 years of working with the public

EMPLOYMENT EXPERIENCE

Operator--Mallory/North American Capacitor Corporation   1999-2003
Greencastle, Indiana
- Proven ability to learn and follow specific procedures
- Adept at working with diverse groups
- Assisted in training of new employees
- Maintained production and scrap records

Temporary Worker—Indiana Temporaries   1999-1999
Greencastle, Indiana
- Successful in adjusting to numerous working situations
- Followed directions as given

Cashier—McClure Oil Corporation   1995-1999
Greencastle, Indiana
- Responsible for accurate cash handling
- Instructed new employees on proper procedures
- Responsible for milk and grocery orders
- Experienced in handling customer complaints

REFERENCES AVAILABLE UPON REQUEST

Cynthia J. Koch
20 Winesap Road
Reelsville, Indiana 46171
Telephone: (765)672-4052
ckoch@ccrtc.com

References:

Citifinancial
104 North Fifth Street
Greencastle, IN 46135
(765) 653-5154
Mr. Tim Williams, Manager

Mallory/North American Capacitor Corporation
1107 Indianapolis Road
Greencastle, In 46135
(765) 653-3151
Carol Butler, Human Resources Director

Mallory/North American Capacitor Corporation
1107 Indianapolis Road
Greencastle, In 46135
(765) 653-3151
Joseph Hein, Supervisor

Exhibit 3–6 *Effect of 2006 Transactions on the Accounting Equation*

| Assets | = | Liabilities | + | Equity |

Cash | **Prepaid Insurance** | **Accounts Payable** | **Common Stock** | **Retained Earnings**

Cash		Prepaid Insurance		Accounts Payable		Common Stock		Retained Earnings
Bal.	$ 2,400	Bal.	$ 100	Bal.	$ 4,000	Bal.	$6,000	Bal. $ 21,650
(1)	1,000	(5)	1,200	(8)	62,000	(1)	1,000	
(2)	2,500	(15)	(1,200)	(9)	(65,000)	Bal.	$7,000	**Service**
(3)	(400)	Bal.	$ 100	Bal.	$ 1,000			(6) $167,000
(4)	20,000							(12) 1,500
(5)	(1,200)	**Office Equipment**		**Unearned Revenue**				Bal. $168,500
(7)	129,000							
(9)	(65,000)	Bal.	$12,000	Bal.	$ 0			**Operating Expense**
(10)	18,000			(10)	18,000			
(11)	(80,000)	**Accumulated Depreciation**		(12)	(1,500)			(8) $ (62,000)
Bal.	$ 26,300			Bal.	$ 16,500			
		Bal.	$ (5,000)					**Depreciation Expenses**
Accounts Receivable		(13)	(2,500)	**Interest Payable**				
		Bal.	$ (7,500)					(13) $ (2,500)
Bal.	$ 19,000			(16)	$ 1,650			
(6)	167,000	**Land**						**Supplies Expense**
(7)	(129,000)			**Notes Payable**				
Bal.	$ 57,000	Bal.	$ 3,000					(14) $ (350)
		(2)	(3,000)	(4)	$ 20,000			
Supplies		Bal.	$ 0					**Insurance Expense**
Bal.	$ 150							(15) $ (1,200)
(3)	400							
(14)	(350)							**Interest Expense**
Bal.	$ 200							(16) $ (1,650)
								Loss on Sale of Land
								(2) $ (500)
								Dividends
								(11) $ (80,000)

the income statement as a separate line item after **income from operations,** which is determined by subtracting expenses from revenues. However, the loss does not measure the cash flow consequences of the sale. Recall that the land was sold for $2,500 cash. This amount is shown as a source (cash inflow) of funds under the investing activities section of the statement of cash flows. Cash flow from operations is not affected by the sale. Remember, the loss was associated with a *peripheral activity* rather than an ordinary operating activity. Verify these effects by reviewing the financial statements in Exhibit 3–7 on pages 116.

The amount of supplies expense is determined by the same approach that was used in 2005 except that there is a beginning balance in the Supplies account in this case. Since the Supplies account has a beginning balance of $150 and $400 of supplies is purchased during the period, $550 of supplies is available to be used. Given that $200 of supplies was on hand at December 31, 2006, then $350 of supplies must have been used during the accounting period. Accordingly, the year-end adjusting entry (Transaction 14) removes $350 from the asset account, Supplies, and places it in the Supplies Expense account. Note that the amount of supplies expense

LO6 Explain the effects of end-of-period adjustments related to deferrals.

Exhibit 3–7 *Vertical Statements Model*

MARKETING MAGIC
Financial Statements
For the 2006 Accounting Period

Income Statement

Service Revenue		$168,500
Operating Expenses	$ 62,000	
Depreciation Expense	2,500	
Supplies Expense	350	
Insurance Expense	1,200	
Interest Expense	1,650	
Total Expenses		(67,700)
Net Operating Income		100,800
Less: Loss on Sale of Land		(500)
Net Income		$100,300

Statement of Changes in Stockholders' Equity

Beginning Common Stock	$ 6,000	
Plus: Issue of Stock	1,000	
Ending Common Stock		$ 7,000
Beginning Retained Earnings	21,650	
Plus: Net Income	100,300	
Less: Dividends	(80,000)	
Ending Retained Earnings		41,950
Total Stockholders' Equity		$ 48,950

Balance Sheet

Assets		
Cash		$ 26,300
Accounts Receivable		57,000
Supplies		200
Prepaid Insurance		100
Office Equipment	$ 12,000	
Less Accumulated Depreciation	(7,500)	4,500
Total Assets		$ 88,100
Liabilities		
Accounts Payable	$ 1,000	
Unearned Revenue	16,500	
Interest Payable	1,650	
Notes Payable	20,000	
Total Liabilities		$ 39,150
Stockholders' Equity		
Common Stock	7,000	
Retained Earnings	41,950	
Total Stockholders' Equity		48,950
Total Liabilities and Stockholders' Equity		$ 88,100

Statement of Cash Flows

Cash Flows from Operating Activities		
Cash Receipt from Receivables	$129,000	
Cash Receipt from Advance Collections	18,000	
Cash Payment for Supplies	(400)	
Cash Payment for Insurance	(1,200)	
Cash Payment for Operating Expenses	(65,000)	
Net Cash Flow from Operating Activities		$ 80,400
Cash Flows from Investing Activities		
Cash Receipt from Sale of Land		2,500
Cash Flows from Financing Activities		
Cash Receipt from Bank Loan	20,000	
Cash Receipt from Issue of Stock	1,000	
Cash Payment for Dividends	(80,000)	
Net Cash Outflow from Financing Activities		(59,000)
Net Increase in Cash		23,900
Plus Beginning Cash Balance		2,400
Ending Cash Balance		$ 26,300

does not correspond to the amount of cash spent. The operating activities section of the statement of cash flows displays the $400 cash outflow made to purchase supplies. Note that the beginning balances in the revenue, expense, and dividend accounts are assumed to be zero because the prior year balances were closed (transferred) to the Retained Earnings account.

The Prepaid Insurance account increased as a result of $1,200 of insurance purchased on February 1, 2006 (Transaction 5). Given the $100 beginning balance in the Prepaid Insurance account, $1,300 of insurance is available to use over a 13-month period. Since 12 months of insurance were used in 2006, the year-end adjusting entry removes $1,200 from the Prepaid Insurance account and places it in the Insurance Expense account (Transaction 15).

The borrowed funds from the bank loan (Transaction 4) require the accrual of interest expense. The amount of interest is determined by multiplying the principal by the rate by the time ($20,000 × 0.09 × [11 ÷ 12] = $1,650). The accrued interest represents a liability to Marketing Magic as of December 31, 2006. The increase in liabilities requires the recognition of interest expense as depicted in Transaction 16 in Exhibit 3–6.

The advance payment described in Transaction 10 is a deferral. The cash receipt is first recorded as a liability, called *unearned revenue*. Assuming that the work associated with the contract is spread evenly over the one-year period, the monthly allocation for revenue recognition is $1,500 ($18,000 ÷ 12). Since one month of service has been provided by the close of business on December 31, 2006, the year-end adjusting entry (Transaction 12) removes $1,500 from the liability account and places it in the revenue account. Note that this treatment is consistent with the definition of revenue as being a decrease in liabilities. The deferral causes a difference between the amount of revenue recognized on the income statement (that is, $1,500 is included in the $168,500 of revenue reported on the income statement) and the amount of cash receipt shown in the operating activities section of the statement of cash flows ($18,000). Trace the effect of these transactions to the financial statements.

The other transactions for 2006 should be familiar to you. However, a positive reinforcement experience can be gained by tracing the results of each transaction to the related financial statements. Accordingly, you are encouraged to fully review all the effects of the transactions in Exhibit 3–6 and the financial statements in Exhibit 3–7.

On January 1, 2002, Lambert Company paid $28,000 cash to purchase office furniture. The furniture has a $3,000 salvage value and a five-year useful life. Explain how Lambert would report this asset purchase on the 2002 statement of cash flows. Also, determine the amount of depreciation expense and accumulated depreciation Lambert would report in the *2004* financial statements.

Answer Lambert would report a $28,000 cash outflow in the investing activities section of the 2002 statement of cash flows. During 2004 and every other year of the asset's useful life, Lambert would report $5,000 ([$28,000 − $3,000] ÷ 5) of depreciation expense on the income statement. The accumulated depreciation would increase by $5,000 each year of the asset's useful life. As of December 31, 2004, Lambert would report accumulated depreciation on the balance sheet of $15,000 (3 years × $5,000 per year).

Check Yourself 3–3

■ Analysis of Financial Statements to Assess Managerial Performance

Assessment of the Effective Use of Assets

Suppose you are told that a company earned net income of $1,000,000. Does this mean that the company's performance has been good or bad? If the company is General Motors, the answer is probably poor performance. If it is Al Bundy's shoe store, $1,000,000 indicates outstanding performance. Clearly, the evaluation of performance requires reference to the size of the investment required to produce the income. The relationship between the level of income and the size of the investment can be expressed in a single figure known as the **return on assets ratio,** which is defined as follows:

LO9 Analyze financial statements and make meaningful comparisons between companies using a debt-to-assets ratio, a return-on-assets ratio, and a return-on-equity ratio.

$$\frac{\text{Net income}^1}{\text{Total assets}}$$

This ratio provides a common unit of measure that enables comparisons between different-size companies. To illustrate the importance of comparing ratios rather than absolute dollar values, consider the following comparison between Ford Motor Company and Chrysler Corporation. Both Ford and Chrysler had positive net incomes in 1997. Ford's earnings for that year were $6.9 billion, and Chrysler's were $2.8 billion, making Ford's earnings more than double those of Chrysler. However, the return on asset ratios for the two companies reveal that Chrysler produced higher earnings relative to the amount of assets invested. Ford's ratio was 2.5 percent while Chrysler's was 4.6 percent. This analysis suggests that even though Chrysler generated a lower amount of income expressed in total dollars, the company did a better job of managing its assets. Accordingly, different companies cannot be compared fairly on the basis of absolute dollar values.

Although the preceding example demonstrates the usefulness of a particular relationship (income relative to assets), other ratios that also enhance the capacity to analyze financial statements could be computed. Two of these ratios are discussed in the following paragraphs.

Assessment of the Risk of Debt

Borrowing money can be a risky business. To illustrate, assume that two companies have the following financial structures:

	Assets	=	Liabilities	+	Stockholders' Equity
Eastern Company	100	=	20	+	80
Western Company	100	=	80	+	20

Which company has the greater financial risk? To answer, look at the financial structures that will exist if each company incurs a $30 loss.

	Assets	=	Liabilities	+	Stockholders' Equity
Eastern Company	70	=	20	+	50
Western Company	70	=	80	+	(10)

Clearly, Western Company is at greater risk. Notice that Eastern Company would survive a $30 loss that reduced assets and stockholders' equity. After such a loss, Eastern Company would still have a $50 balance in stockholders' equity and would still have more than enough assets ($70) to cover the creditor's $20 claim. In contrast, a $30 loss would throw Western Company into bankruptcy. The company would have a $10 deficit (negative) balance in stockholders' equity. Furthermore, the remaining balance in assets ($70) would be insufficient to cover the creditor's $80 claim on assets.

The level of risk can be measured in part through the computation of a **debt to assets ratio.** The ratio is as follows:

$$\frac{\text{Total debt}}{\text{Total assets}}$$

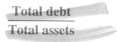

For example, Eastern Company has a 20 percent debt to assets ratio ($20 ÷ $100) while Western Company has an 80 percent debt to assets ratio ($80 ÷ $100). Why would the owners of Western Company be willing to accept greater risk? To answer this question, assume that both companies produce $12 of revenue and that they are required to pay 10 percent interest on the money they have borrowed. Income statements for the two companies appear as follows:[2]

---

[1]The use of net income in this ratio does not consider the effects of debt financing and income taxation. The application of these topics to the return on assets is discussed in Chapter 10.

[2]This illustration does not consider the effect of income taxes on debt financing. This subject is covered in Chapter 10.

	Eastern Company	Western Company
Revenue	$12	$12
Interest Expense	2	8
Net Income	$10	$ 4

At first glance, it appears that the owners of Eastern Company are still better off because that company produced higher net income. However, a closer look discloses that, in fact, the owners of Western Company are better off. Remember that the owners of Eastern Company had to put $80 of their own money into the business in order to get the $10 of income. Accordingly, the return on their invested funds is 12.5 percent ($10 ÷ $80). In contrast, the owners of Western Company were required to invest only $20 to obtain $4 of net income. Their

focus on International Issues

Why Not Have One Global GAAP?

Although no two countries have exactly the same accounting rules, there are many similarities in the various accounting systems used around the world. Furthermore, geographic, political, and social forces tend to promote similar views within selected sets of countries. For example, the GAAP of the United Kingdom is more likely to match the GAAP of New Zealand than the GAAP of Brazil. This has led some to try to group countries based on the similarity of their respective accounting rules.

One accounting research study* concluded that the world's accounting systems can be divided into four groups: (1) British Commonwealth model, (2) Latin American model, (3) Continental European model, and (4) U.S. model.

According to this study, countries with accounting rules similar to (but not exactly the same as) GAAP in the United States include Canada, Japan, Mexico, Panama, and the Philippines.

If there already exist similarities among the GAAP of different countries, why not have only one set of accounting rules for all countries? There are many reasons that one set of rules, and one rule-making body, does not exist for the entire world, but consider two easy examples. First, different countries have different political structures (e.g., democracy versus communism). What are the chances that a country with strong government controls would allow its accounting rules to be established by a nongovernment body such as the Financial Accounting Standards Board? Second, different countries have different economic structures. In the United States, most industries, even those related to national defense, are privately owned. In some countries, major industries are owned by the government while smaller industries are privately owned. In a few countries, almost all resources are owned by the government. It is impossible to have one set of rules that would work well in such diverse settings.

Even though each country establishes its own GAAP, there is an international "rule-suggesting" body for accounting. The

International Accounting Standards Committee (IASC) has more than 100 member countries participating in its activities. The IASC tries to improve the uniformity of accounting practices around the world by recommending the appropriate accounting treatment for various business events. However, the IASC has no enforcement power, so its pronouncements are simply recommendations, not requirements.

*R. D. Nair and W. G. Frank, "The Impact of Disclosure and Measurement Practices on International Accounting Classifications," *The Accounting Review,* July 1980.

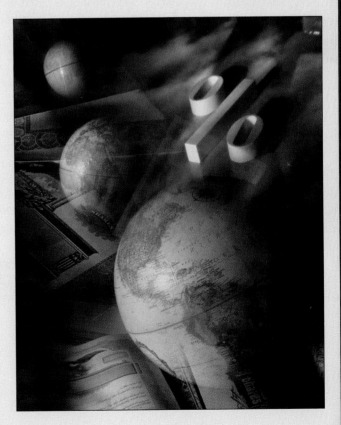

return on invested funds amounts to 20 percent ($4 ÷ $20). In different terms, an $80 investment would buy four companies like Western Company or one like Eastern Company. Four companies like Western Company would produce $16 of net income ($4 income per company × 4 companies). This compares favorably to $10 of net income produced by Eastern Company. Clearly, Western Company is the more profitable investment. The relationship between the amount of net income and the stockholders' equity is called the **return on equity ratio.** As suggested, the return on equity ratio is:

$$\frac{\text{Net income}}{\text{Stockholders' equity}}$$

In business, the practice of using borrowed money to increase the return on stockholders' investment is called **financial leverage.** Financial leverage explains why companies are willing to accept the risk of debt. Companies borrow money to make money. If a company can borrow money at 10 percent and invest it at 12 percent, the owners will be better off by 2 percent of the amount borrowed. A business that does not use borrowed funds may be missing an opportunity to increase its return on equity.

Real-World Data

Exhibit 3–8 shows the debt to assets, return on assets, and return on equity ratios for six real-world companies in two different industries. These ratios are for 2000.

Notice that Cigna's 2000 return on assets ratio was 1.0 percent and Aflac's was 1.9 percent. Taken in isolation, neither ratio seems very good; banks often pay more than 1.9 percent interest on deposits in savings accounts. However, the *return on equity* ratios for Cigna and Aflac show a different picture; Cigna's was 18.2 percent and Aflac's was 14.6 percent—much better than banks pay depositors. Also note in Exhibit 3–8 that while Cigna's return on assets ratio was lower than Aflac's, its return on equity ratio was higher than Aflac's (18.2 percent versus 14.6 percent). How did this happen? Compare their debt to assets ratios. Cigna financed 94 percent of its assets with debt compared to 87 percent for Aflac. Because it is more highly leveraged, Cigna's return on assets ratio translated into a higher return on equity ratio than Aflac's.

Given that leveraged companies produce higher returns, why does every company not leverage itself to the maximum? Remember the downside. These data are drawn for economic periods in which prosperity and growth prevailed. In hard economic times, highly leveraged companies are likely to produce lower rather than higher returns. Increased risk usually accompanies increased returns.

Finally, in Exhibit 3–8, compare the debt to assets ratios for companies in the oil industry to the same ratios for companies in the insurance industry. There are distinct differences *between* industries, but there are considerable similarities *within* each industry. The debt to assets ratio is significantly higher for the insurance industry than for the oil industry. However, within each industry,

Exhibit 3–8 Three Ratios (in Percentages) for Six Real-World Companies				
Industry	**Company**	**Debt to Assets**	**Return on Assets**	**Return on Equity**
Insurance	Aflac	87	1.9	14.6
	John Hancock	94	1.0	15.5
	Cigna	94	1.0	18.2
Oil	Chevron	52	12.6	26.0
	Exxon	53	11.9	25.0
	Texaco	55	25.5	56.7

the ratios tend to be clustered fairly close together. Distinct differences between industries accompanied by similarities within industries are common features of business practice. Thus, when you compare accounting information for different companies, you must consider the industries in which those companies operate.

Scope of Coverage

Throughout this text, new ratios directly related to the topics being covered in each chapter are introduced. Even so, only a few of the many ratios available to users of financial statements are introduced. A more extensive examination of ratios and other topics related to financial statement analysis is part of most introductory finance courses. Many business programs include an entire course that focuses solely on financial statement analysis. These courses develop students' capacity to make judgments regarding the ratio results that signal "good" or "bad" performance. However, the development of such judgment requires an understanding of how accounting policies and procedures can affect financial ratios. The ratios introduced in this text are designed to enhance your understanding of accounting and thereby give you the foundation that you will need to further your comprehension of business practice as you are introduced to more advanced topics in subsequent courses.

This chapter introduced the practice of deferring revenue and expense recognition. More specifically, *deferrals* involve the recognition of revenue or expense at some time *after* cash has been collected or paid. Deferrals cause significant differences in the amount of revenue and expenses reported on the income statement and the amount of cash flow from operating activities. These differences become readily apparent when relevant events are recorded in a horizontal financial statements model. To illustrate, review the following transactions and the corresponding statements model that follows them. To facilitate your understanding, draw a statements model on a piece of paper and try to record the effects of each event before you look at the explanation provided in the text.

a look

back

LO10 Record deferral events in a financial statements model.

List of Events

1. Received an advanced payment of $1,200 cash for services to be performed in the future.
2. Provided $800 of the services agreed on in Event 1.
3. Paid $900 in advance for a one-year contract to rent office space.
4. Used eight months (that is, $600) of the office space leased in Event 3.

Event No.	Balance Sheet								Income Statement					Statement of Cash Flows	
	Assets			=	Liab.	+	Stockholders' Equity		Rev.	−	Exp.	=	Net Inc.		
	Cash	+	P. Rent	=	U. Rev.	+	Ret. Earn.								
1	1,200	+	NA	=	1,200	+	NA		NA	−	NA	=	NA	1,200	OA
2	NA	+	NA	=	(800)	+	800		800	−	NA	=	800	NA	
3	(900)	+	900	=	NA	+	NA		NA	−	NA	=	NA	(900)	OA
4	NA	+	(600)	=	NA	+	(600)		NA	−	600	=	(600)	NA	
Totals	300	+	300	=	400	+	200		800	−	600	=	200	300	NC

Note that the amount of net income ($200) is different from the amount of cash flow from operating activities $300. A review of the entries in the statements model should make the reasons for this difference clear. Although $1,200 of cash was collected, only $800 of revenue was recognized. The remaining $400 will be recognized in the future when the work is done. The $400 obligation to perform the work in the future is currently shown on the balance sheet as unearned revenue. Also, although $900 cash was paid for rent, only $600 of rent expense was recognized. The remaining $300 is shown on the balance sheet as an asset called *prepaid rent*. In general, costs are **capitalized** (recorded) in asset accounts when cash is paid. Expense recognition is deferred until the time that the assets (capitalized costs) are used to produce revenue. This practice is applied to many costs, including those incurred for supplies, insurance, equipment, and buildings. Study these relationships carefully to develop a clear understanding of how deferrals affect financial reporting.

a look

forward

To this point, we have used plus and minus signs to record the effects of business events on financial statements. In the real world, so many transactions occur that recording them with simple mathematical notations is impractical. In practice, accountants frequently maintain records under a system of rules known as a *double-entry bookkeeping*. Chapter 4 introduces you to the basic components of this bookkeeping system. You will learn how to record business events using a debit/credit format. You will be introduced to ledgers, journals, and trial balances. When you finish Chapter 4, you will have a clear understanding of how accountants maintain records of business activity.

SELF-STUDY REVIEW PROBLEM

Gifford Company experienced the following accounting events during 2005.

1. *Started operations on January 1 when it acquired $20,000 cash by issuing common stock.*
2. *On January 1 paid $15,000 cash to purchase computer equipment.*
3. *On March 1 collected $36,000 cash as an advance for services to be performed in the future.*
4. *Paid cash operating expenses of $17,000.*
5. *Paid a $2,700 cash dividend to the stockholders.*
6. *On December 31, 2005, adjusted the books to recognize the revenue earned by providing services related to the advance described in Event 3. The contract required Gifford to provide services for a one-year period starting March 1.*
7. *On December 31, 2005, Gifford adjusted the books to recognize depreciation expense on the computer equipment. The equipment has a three-year useful life and a $3,000 salvage value.*

Gifford Company experienced the following accounting events during 2006.

1. *Recognized $38,000 of cash revenue.*
2. *Paid cash operating expenses of $21,000.*
3. *Paid a $5,000 cash dividend to the stockholders.*
4. *On December 31, 2005, adjusted the books to recognize the remaining revenue earned by providing services related to the advance described in Event 3 of 2005.*
5. *On December 31, 2005, Gifford adjusted the books to recognize depreciation expense on the computer equipment purchased in Event 2 of 2005. The equipment has a three-year useful life and a $3,000 salvage value.*

Required
a. Record the events in a financial statements model like the following one. The first event is recorded as an example.

Event No.	Assets			=	Liab.	+	Stockholders' Equity		Rev. − Exp. = Net Inc.	Cash Flow
	Cash +	Comp. Equip. −	Acc. Dep.	=	Unear. Rev. +		C. Stk. +	Ret. Ear.		
1	20,000 +	NA	− NA	=	NA	+	20,000 +	NA	NA − NA = NA	20,000 FA

b. What amount of depreciation expense would Gifford report on the 2005 and 2006 income statements?
c. What amount of cash flow for depreciation would Gifford report on the 2006 statement of cash flows?
d. What amount of unearned revenue would Gifford report on the 2005 and 2006 year-end balance sheets?
e. What are the 2006 opening balances for the revenue and expense accounts?
f. What amount of total assets would Gifford report on the December 31, 2005, balance sheet?
g. What claims on the assets would Gifford report on the December 31, 2006, balance sheet?

Solution to Requirement a

The financial statements model follows.

Event No.	Cash	+ Comp. Equip.	− Acc. Dep.	= Unear. Rev.	+ C. Stk.	+ Ret. Ear.	Rev.	− Exp.	= Net Inc.	Cash Flow	
		Assets		= Liab. +	Stockholders' Equity		Rev. − Exp. = Net Inc.			Cash Flow	
1	20,000 +	NA	− NA	= NA	+ 20,000 +	NA	NA −	NA =	NA	20,000	FA
2	(15,000) +	15,000	− NA	= NA	+ NA +	NA	NA −	NA =	NA	(15,000)	IA
3	36,000 +	NA	− NA	= 36,000	+ NA +	NA	NA −	NA =	NA	36,000	OA
4	(17,000) +	NA	− NA	= NA	+ NA +	(17,000)	NA −	17,000 =	(17,000)	(17,000)	OA
5	(2,700) +	NA	− NA	= NA	+ NA +	(2,700)	NA −	NA =	NA	(2,700)	FA
6*	NA +	NA	− NA	= (30,000)	+ NA +	30,000	30,000 −	NA =	30,000	NA	
7†	NA +	NA	− 4,000	= NA	+ NA +	(4,000)	NA −	4,000 =	(4,000)	NA	
Bal.	21,300 +	15,000	− 4,000	= 6,000	+ 20,000 +	6,300	30,000 −	21,000 =	9,000	21,300	NC
	Asset, Liability, and Equity Account Balances Carry Forward						Rev. & Exp. Accts. Are Closed				
Bal.	21,300 +	15,000	− 4,000	= 6,000	+ 20,000 +	6,300	NA −	NA =	NA	NA	
1	38,000 +	NA	− NA	= NA	+ NA +	38,000	38,000 −	NA =	38,000	38,000	OA
2	(21,000) +	NA	− NA	= NA	+ NA +	(21,000)	NA −	21,000 =	(21,000)	(21,000)	OA
3	(5,000) +	NA	− NA	= NA	+ NA +	(5,000)	NA −	NA =	NA	(5,000)	FA
4*	NA +	NA	− NA	= (6,000)	+ NA +	6,000	6,000 −	NA =	6,000	NA	
5†	NA +	NA	− 4,000	= NA	+ NA +	(4,000)	NA −	4,000 =	(4,000)	NA	
Bal.	33,300 +	15,000	− 8,000	= 0	+ 20,000 +	20,300	44,000 −	25,000 =	19,000	12,000	NC

*Revenue is earned at the rate of $3,000 ($36,000 ÷ 12 months) per month. Revenue recognized in 2005 is $30,000 ($3,000 × 10 months). Revenue recognized in 2006 is $6,000 ($3,000 × 2 months).
†Depreciation expense is $4,000 ([$15,000 − $3,000] ÷ 3 years) per year.

Solutions to Requirements b–g

b. Gifford would report depreciation expense in 2005 of $4,000 ([$15,000 − $3,000] ÷ 3 years). This same amount would be recognized in 2005, 2006, and 2007.

c. There is no cash flow for depreciation in 2006 or any other year. The total cash outflow from purchasing the computer equipment ($15,000) would be reported as a cash outflow from investing activities in the year in which the equipment was purchased.

d. The December 31, 2005, balance sheet will report $6,000 of unearned revenue, which is the amount of the cash advance less the amount of revenue recognized in 2005 ($36,000 − $30,000). The December 31, 2006, balance is zero.

e. Since revenue and expense accounts are closed at the end of each accounting period, the beginning balances in these accounts are always zero.

f. Assets on the December 31, 2005, balance sheet consist of Gifford's cash at year end and the book value (cost − accumulated depreciation) of the computer equipment. Specifically, the amount of total assets is $32,300 ($21,300 + [$15,000 − $4,000]).

g. Since all unearned revenue would be recognized before the financial statements were prepared at the end of 2006, there would be no liabilities on the 2006 balance sheet. Common Stock and Retained Earnings would be the only claims as of December 31, 2006, for a claims total of $40,300 ($20,000 + $20,300).

KEY TERMS

Accumulated depreciation *106*
Allocation *103*
Book value *106*
Capitalized *122*
Concept of materiality *110*
Contra asset account *106*

Debt to assets ratio *118*
Deferral *103*
Depreciation expense *106*
Financial leverage *120*
Gains *114*

Income from operations *115*
Losses *114*
Matching concept *108*
Peripheral (incidental) transactions *114*

Return on assets ratio *117*
Return on equity ratio *120*
Straight-line method *106*
Systematic allocation *108*
Unearned revenue *104*

QUESTIONS

1. What role do assets play in business profitability?
2. What does the term *deferral* mean?
3. If cash is collected in advance of performing services, when is the associated revenue recognized?
4. What does the term *salvage value* mean?
5. What is the effect on the claims side of the accounting equation when cash is collected in advance of performing services?
6. What does the term *unearned revenue* mean?
7. How is straight-line depreciation computed?
8. Define the term *depreciation expense.* On what type of asset is depreciation recognized?
9. Define the term *contra asset account.* What is an example?
10. How is the book value of an asset determined?
11. If a piece of equipment originally cost $12,000, has an estimated salvage value of $1,000, and has accumulated depreciation of $10,000, what is the book value of the equipment?
12. What does the term *financial leverage* mean?
13. In which section of the statement of cash flows is cash paid for office equipment reported?
14. What is the difference between a cost and an expense?
15. When does a cost become an expense? Do all costs become expenses?
16. How and when is the cost of the *supplies used* recognized in an accounting period?
17. Give an example of an asset whose cost is systematically allocated over several accounting periods.
18. List the three ways in which expenses are matched with the revenues they produce.
19. Define *losses.* How do losses differ from expenses?
20. Define *gains.* How do gains differ from revenues?
21. How is income from operations computed?
22. What does the term *peripheral activity* mean?
23. Assume that Company A has revenues of $45,000, operating expenses of $36,000, and a gain from the sale of land of $12,500. What is the amount of income from operations? What is the amount of net income?
24. Explain the *concept of materiality.*
25. What are several factors that prevent the establishment of a global GAAP?
26. How is the return on assets ratio computed? How is this measure useful in comparing two companies?
27. How is the debt to assets ratio computed? What does this ratio measure?
28. How can financial leverage increase the return on equity ratio?

EXERCISES—SERIES A

L.O. 1   **EXERCISE 3–1A** *Transactions That Affect the Elements of Financial Statements*

Required
Give an example of a transaction that will do the following:
a. Increase an asset and increase equity (asset source event).
b. Increase a liability and decrease equity (claims exchange event).
c. Decrease an asset and decrease equity (asset use event).
d. Decrease an asset and decrease a liability (asset use event).
e. Decrease a liability and increase equity (claims exchange event).
f. Increase an asset and decrease another asset (asset exchange event).
g. Increase an asset and increase a liability (asset source event).

L.O. 2   **EXERCISE 3–2A** *Identifying Deferral and Accrual Events*

Required
Identify each of the following events as accruals, deferrals, or neither.
a. Provided services on account.
b. Recognized interest on a note payable before cash is paid.
c. Paid one year's rent in advance.
d. Purchased a computer with a three-year life.
e. Incurred other operating expenses on account.
f. Paid cash for utilities expense.

g. Collected $1,200 in advance for services to be performed over the next six months.
h. Paid cash to purchase supplies to be used over the next several months.
i. Recorded expense for salaries owed to employees at the end of the accounting period.
j. Issued common stock for cash.

EXERCISE 3–3A *Effect of Deferrals on the Accounting Equation*

L.O. 6

Required

For each of the following independent cases, show the effect on the accounting equation of both the deferral and the related December 31, 2001, adjustment.
a. Global Shipping paid $24,000 for a 12-month lease on warehouse space on August 1, 2001.
b. Unistar Services purchased a new computer system for $22,000 on January 1, 2001. The computer system has an estimated useful life of three years and a $1,000 salvage value.
c. Tommy Holliman, J.D., accepted a $30,000 advance from his client on October 1, 2001, for services to be performed over the next six months.

EXERCISE 3–4A *Identifying Transaction Type and Effect on the Financial Statements*

L.O. 3, 10

Required

Identify whether each of the following transactions is an asset source (AS), asset use (AU), asset exchange (AE), or claims exchange (CE). Also show the effects of the events on the financial statements using the horizontal statements model. Indicate whether the event increases (I), decreases (D), or does not affect (NA) each element of the financial statements. In the Cash Flows column, designate the cash flows as operating activities (OA), investing activities (IA), or financing activities (FA). The first two transactions have been recorded as examples.

Event No.	Type of Event	Assets	=	Liabilities	+	Common Stock	+	Retained Earnings	Rev.	−	Exp.	=	Net Inc	Cash Flows
a	AS	I		I		NA		NA	NA		NA		NA	I OA
b	AU	D		D		NA		NA	NA		NA		NA	D OA

a. Received cash advance for services to be provided in the future.
b. Paid cash on accounts payable.
c. Acquired cash from the issue of common stock.
d. Purchased office equipment for cash.
e. Incurred other operating expenses on account.
f. Paid cash to purchase office supplies to be used in the future.
g. Performed services on account.
h. Paid cash advance for rent on office space.
i. Adjusted books to reflect the amount of prepaid rent expired during the period.
j. Paid cash for operating expenses.
k. Performed services for cash.
l. Paid a cash dividend to the stockholders.
m. Recorded accrued salaries.
n. Purchased a building with cash *and* issued a note payable.
o. Collected cash from accounts receivable.
p. Recorded depreciation expense on office equipment.
q. Paid cash for salaries accrued at the end of a prior period.

EXERCISE 3–5A *Effect of Prepaid Rent on the Accounting Equation and Financial Statements*

L.O. 3, 4, 5, 7

The following events apply to 2007, the first year of operations of Management Consulting Services:
1. Acquired $12,000 cash from the issue of common stock.
2. Paid $9,000 cash in advance for one-year rental contract for office space.
3. Provided services for $18,000 cash.
4. Adjusted the records to recognize the use of the office space. The one-year contract started on February 1, 2007. The adjustment was made as of December 31, 2007.

Required

a. Write an accounting equation and record the effects of each accounting event under the appropriate general ledger account headings.
b. Prepare an income statement and statement of cash flows for the 2007 accounting period.
c. Explain the difference between the amount of net income and amount of net cash flow from operating activities.

L.O. 5, 6, 7, 10   **EXERCISE 3–6A** *Effect of Supplies on the Financial Statements*

Quick Printing, Inc., started the 2005 accounting period with $5,000 cash, $2,000 of common stock, and $3,000 of retained earnings. Quick Printing was affected by the following accounting events during 2005:

1. Purchased $7,200 of paper and other supplies on account.
2. Earned and collected $15,000 of cash revenue.
3. Paid $5,000 cash on accounts payable.
4. Adjusted the records to reflect the use of supplies. A physical count indicated that $1,400 of supplies was still on hand on December 31, 2005.

Required

a. Show the effects of the events on the financial statements using a horizontal statements model like the following one. In the Cash Flows column, use OA to designate operating activity, IA for investing activity, FA for financing activity, and NC for net change in cash. Use NA to indicate accounts not affected by the event. The beginning balances are entered in the following example.

Event No.	Assets		=	Liab.	+	Stockholders' Equity		Rev.	−	Exp.	=	Net Inc.	Cash Flows
	Cash	Supplies		Acct. Pay.		C. Stock	Ret. Earn.						
Beg. Bal.	5,000	0	=	0	+	2,000	3,000	0	−	0	=	0	0

b. Explain the difference between the amount of net income and amount of net cash flow from operating activities.

L.O. 3, 5, 6, 7   **EXERCISE 3–7A** *Effect of Depreciation on the Accounting Equation and Financial Statements*

The following events apply to Tasty Pizza for the 2008 fiscal year:

1. Started the company when it acquired $12,000 cash from the issue of common stock.
2. Purchased a new pizza oven that cost $11,000 cash.
3. Earned $8,000 in cash revenue.
4. Paid $2,000 for cash operating expenses.
5. Adjusted the records to reflect the use of the pizza oven. The oven, purchased on January 1, 2008, has an expected useful life of five years and an estimated salvage value of $1,000. Use straight-line depreciation. The adjusting entry was made as of December 31, 2008.

Required

a. Write an accounting equation and record the effects of each accounting event under the appropriate general ledger account headings.
b. What amount of depreciation expense would Tasty Pizza report on the 2009 income statement?
c. What amount of accumulated depreciation would Tasty Pizza report on the December 31, 2009, balance sheet?
d. Would the cash flow from operating activities be affected by depreciation in 2009?

L.O. 5, 6, 10   **EXERCISE 3–8A** *Effect of Unearned Revenue on Financial Statements*

Kim Vanderbilt started a personal financial planning business when she accepted $72,000 cash as advance payment for managing the financial assets of a large estate. Vanderbilt agreed to manage the estate for a one-year period, beginning March 1, 2003.

Required

a. Show the effects of the advance payment and revenue recognition on the 2003 financial statements using a horizontal statements model like the following one. In the Cash Flows column, use OA to designate operating activity, IA for investing activity, FA for financing activity, and NC for net change in cash. Use NA if the account is not affected.

	Assets	=	Liab.	+	Stockholders' Equity		Rev.	−	Exp.	=	Net Inc.		Cash Flows
Event No.	Cash		Unearn. Rev.		Ret. Earn.								

b. How much revenue would Kim recognize on the 2004 income statement?

c. What is the amount of cash flow from operating activities in 2004?

EXERCISE 3–9A *Effect of Gains and Losses on the Accounting Equation and*   **L.O. 8**
                 Financial Statements

On January 1, 2002, IBC purchased a parcel of land for $6,000 cash. At the time of purchase, the company planned to use the land for future expansion. In 2004, IBC Enterprises changed its plans and sold the land.

Required

a. Assume that the land was sold for $5,500 in 2004.
   (1) Show the effect of the sale on the accounting equation.
   (2) What amount would IBC report on the income statement related to the sale of the land?
   (3) What amount would IBC report on the statement of cash flows related to the sale of the land?

b. Assume that the land was sold for $7,000 in 2004.
   (1) Show the effect of the sale on the accounting equation.
   (2) What amount would IBC report on the income statement related to the sale of the land?
   (3) What amount would IBC report on the statement of cash flows related to the sale of the land?

EXERCISE 3–10A *Effect of Accounting Events on the Income Statement and Statement of*   **L.O. 5, 6**
                  Cash Flows

Required

Explain how each of the following events and the related adjusting entry will affect the amount of *net income* and the amount of *cash flow from operating activities* reported on the year-end financial statements. Identify the direction of change (increase, decrease, or no effect) and the amount of the change. Organize your answers according to the following table. The first event is recorded as an example. If an event does not have a related adjusting entry, record only the effects of the event.

	Net Income		Cash Flows from Operating Activities	
Event No.	Direction of Change	Amount of Change	Direction of Change	Amount of Change
a	Increase	$12,000	Increase	$10,000

a. Earned $12,000 of revenue on account. Collected $10,000 cash from accounts receivable.

b. Paid $3,600 cash on November 1 to purchase a one-year insurance policy.

c. Accrued salaries amounting to $6,000.

d. Paid $20,000 cash to purchase equipment. The equipment, purchased on January 1, had an estimated salvage value of $4,000 and an expected useful life of four years.

e. Purchased $1,600 of supplies on account. Paid $1,200 cash on accounts payable. The ending balance in the Supplies account, after adjustment, was $200.

f. Provided services for $5,400 cash.

g. Paid cash for other operating expenses of $2,000.

h. Collected $2,400 in advance for services to be performed in the future. The contract called for services to start on April 1 and to continue for one year.

i. Acquired $24,000 cash from the issue of common stock.

j. Sold land that cost $7,000 for $9,000 cash.

EXERCISE 3–11A *Effect of Accruals and Deferrals on Financial Statements: the Horizontal*   **L.O. 10**
                  Statements Model

R. Ross, Attorney at Law, experienced the following transactions in 2002, the first year of operations:

1. Accepted $15,000 on April 1, 2002, as a retainer for services to be performed evenly over the next 12 months.
2. Purchased $900 of office supplies on account.
3. Performed legal services for cash of $35,300.
4. Paid cash for salaries expenses of $21,400.
5. Paid a cash dividend to the stockholders of $4,000.
6. Paid $700 of the amount due on accounts payable.
7. Determined that at the end of the accounting period, $75 of office supplies remained on hand.
8. On December 31, 2002, recognized the revenue that had been earned for services performed in accordance with Transaction 1.

Required

Show the effects of the events on the financial statements using a horizontal statements model like the following one. In the Cash Flow column, use the initials OA to designate operating activity, IA for investing activity, FA for financing activity, and NC for net change in cash. Use NA to indicate accounts not affected by the event. The first event has been recorded as an example.

| Event No. | Assets | | | = | Liabilities | | | + | Equity | Rev. | – | Exp. | = | Net Inc. | Cash Flow |
	Cash	+	Supp.	=	Acct. Pay.	+	Unearn. Rev.	+	Ret. Earn.						
1	15,000	+	NA	=	NA	+	15,000	+	NA	NA	–	NA	=	NA	15,000 OA

L.O. 7   EXERCISE 3–12A *Distinguishing Between an Expense and a Cost*

Mike Kosko tells you that the accountants where he works are real hair splitters. For example, they make a big issue over the difference between a cost and an expense. He says the two terms mean the same thing to him.

Required

a. Explain to Mike the difference between a cost and an expense from an accountant's perspective.
b. Explain whether each of the following events produces an asset or an expense.
   (1) Purchased equipment for cash.
   (2) Purchased supplies on account.
   (3) Used supplies to produce revenue.
   (4) Purchased equipment on account.
   (5) Recognized accrued interest.

L.O. 7   EXERCISE 3–13A *Matching Concept*

Required

Place a check mark in the appropriate cell of the following table to indicate whether each of the following costs would be expensed through (1) direct matching, (2) period matching, or (3) systematic allocation.

Cost	Matched Directly With Revenue	Matched With the Period Incurred	Systematically Allocated
Rent			
Office equipment			
Land that has been sold			
Utilities			
Sales commissions			
Furniture			
Advertising			

L.O. 5, 6   EXERCISE 3–14A *Effect of an Error on Financial Statements*

On March 1, 2007, Stotzy Corporation paid $7,200 to purchase a 24-month insurance policy. Assume that Stotzy records the purchase as an asset and that the books are closed on December 31.

Required

a. Provide the adjusting entry to record the 2007 insurance expense.

b. Assume that Stotzy Corporation failed to record the adjusting entry to reflect the expiration of insurance. How would the error affect the company's 2007 income statement and balance sheet?

EXERCISE 3–15A *Revenue and Expense Recognition*

Required
a. Describe a revenue recognition event that results in a decrease in liabilities.
b. Describe a revenue recognition event that results in an increase in assets.
c. Describe an expense recognition event that results in an increase in liabilities.
d. Describe an expense recognition event that results in a decrease in assets.

EXERCISE 3–16A *Unearned Revenue Defined as a Liability*

Jacob Huron received $600 in advance for tutoring fees when he agreed to help Kev Saia with his introductory accounting course. Upon receiving the cash, Jacob mentioned that he would have to record the transaction as a liability on his books. Saia asked, "Why a liability? You don't owe me any money, do you?"

Required
Respond to Saia's question regarding Huron's liability.

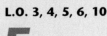

PROBLEMS—SERIES A

PROBLEM 3–17A *Recording Events in a Horizontal Statements Model*

The following events pertain to Midwest Company:
1. Acquired $8,000 cash from the issue of common stock.
2. Provided services for $2,000 cash.
3. Provided $10,000 of services on account.
4. Collected $7,500 cash from the account receivable created in Event 3.
5. Paid $800 cash to purchase supplies.
6. Had $150 of supplies on hand at the end of the accounting period.
7. Received $3,000 cash in advance for services to be performed in the future.
8. Performed $500 of the services agreed to in Event 7.
9. Paid $3,200 for salaries expense.
10. Incurred $1,200 of other operating expenses on account.
11. Paid $1,000 cash on the account payable created in Event 10.
12. Paid an $800 cash dividend to the stockholders.

Required
Show the effects of the events on the financial statements using a horizontal statements model like the following one. In the Cash Flows column, use the letters OA to designate operating activity, IA for investing activity, FA for financing activity, and NC for net change in cash. Use NA to indicate accounts not affected by the event. The first event is recorded as an example.

	Assets			=	Liabilities		+	Stockholders' Equity			Rev.	–	Exp.	=	Net Inc.		Cash Flows
Event No.	Cash	+ Acc. Rec.	+ Supp.	=	Acc. Pay.	+ Unearn. Rev.	+	Com. Stk.	+ Ret. Earn.								
1	8,000	+ NA	+ NA	=	NA	+ NA	+	8,000	+ NA		NA	–	NA	=	NA		8,000 FA

PROBLEM 3–18A *Effect of Deferrals on Financial Statements: Three Separate Single-Cycle Examples*

E_x

Required
a. On March 1, 2005, Wax Made was formed when it received $50,000 cash from the issue of common stock. On May 1, 2005, the company paid $48,000 cash in advance to rent office space for the coming year. The office space was used as a place to consult with clients. The consulting activity generated $65,000 of cash revenue during 2005. Based on this information alone, record the events in the general ledger accounts under the accounting equation. Determine the amount of net income and cash flows from operating activities for 2005.

b. On January 1, 2001, the accounting firm of Copeland & Associates was formed. On April 1, 2001, the company received a retainer fee (was paid in advance) of $21,000 for services to be performed monthly during the coming year. Assuming that this was the only transaction completed in 2001, prepare an income statement, statement of changes in stockholders' equity, balance sheet, and statement of cash flows for 2001.

c. Fashion Cents was started when it received $35,000 cash from the issue of common stock on January 1, 2003. The cash received by the company was immediately used to purchase a $35,000 asset that had a $5,000 salvage value and an expected useful life of five years. The company earned $10,000 of cash revenue during 2003. Show the effects of these transactions on the financial statements using the horizontal statements model.

L.O. 3, 6   **PROBLEM 3–19A** *Effect of Adjusting Entries on the Accounting Equation*

Required

Each of the following independent events requires a year-end adjusting entry. Show how each event and its related adjusting entry affects the accounting equation. Assume a December 31 closing date. The first event is recorded as an example.

	Total Assets					Stockholders' Equity		
Event/ Adjustment	Asset 1	+	Asset 2	=	Liabilities	+	Common Stock	+	Retained Earnings
a	−18,000		+18,000		NA		NA		NA
Adj.	NA		+450		NA		NA		+450

a. Invested $18,000 cash in a certificate of deposit that paid 5 percent annual interest. The certificate was acquired on July 1 and had a one-year term to maturity.

b. Paid $4,200 cash in advance on September 30 for a one-year insurance policy.

c. Purchased $2,000 of supplies on account. At year's end, $200 of supplies remained on hand.

d. Paid $9,000 cash in advance on March 1 for a one-year lease on office space.

e. Borrowed $10,000 by issuing a one-year note with 12 percent annual interest to National Bank on April 1.

f. Paid $19,000 cash to purchase a delivery van on January 1. The van was expected to have a three-year life and a $4,000 salvage value. Depreciation is computed on a straight-line basis.

g. Received a $6,000 cash advance for a contract to provide services in the future. The contract required a one-year commitment starting August 1.

L.O. 1, 3, 4   **PROBLEM 3–20A** *Events for Two Complete Accounting Cycles*

Nevada Drilling Company was formed on January 1, 2002.

Events Affecting the 2002 Accounting Period

1. Acquired cash of $40,000 from the issue of common stock.
2. Purchased office equipment that cost $17,000 cash.
3. Purchased land that cost $8,000 cash.
4. Paid $600 cash for supplies.
5. Recognized revenue on account of $16,000.
6. Paid $7,200 cash for other operating expenses.
7. Collected $10,000 cash from accounts receivable.

Information for Adjusting Entries

8. Incurred accrued salaries of $4,100 on December 31, 2002.
9. Had $100 of supplies on hand at the end of the accounting period.
10. Used the straight-line method to depreciate the equipment acquired in Event 2. Purchased on January 1, it had an expected useful life of five years and a $1,000 salvage value,

Events Affecting the 2003 Accounting Period

1. Acquired an additional $6,000 cash from the issue of common stock.
2. Paid $4,100 cash to settle the salaries payable obligation.
3. Paid $2,100 cash in advance for a lease on office facilities.
4. Sold the land that cost $8,000 for $7,500 cash.
5. Received $4,800 cash in advance for services to be performed in the future.

6. Purchased $1,000 of supplies on account during the year.
7. Provided services on account of $12,000.
8. Collected $13,000 cash from accounts receivable.
9. Paid a cash dividend of $1,000 to the stockholders.

Information for Adjusting Entries

10. The advance payment for rental of the office facilities (see Event 3) was made on May 1 for a one-year lease term.
11. The cash advance for services to be provided in the future was collected on August 1 (see Event 5). The one-year contract started August 1.
12. Had $120 of supplies on hand at the end of the period.
13. Recorded depreciation on the office equipment for 2003.
14. Incurred accrued salaries of $4,000 at the end of the accounting period.

Required

a. Identify each event affecting the 2002 and 2003 accounting periods as asset source (AS), asset use (AU), asset exchange (AE), or claims exchange (CE). Record the effects of each event under the appropriate general ledger account headings of the accounting equation.
b. Prepare an income statement, statement of changes in stockholders' equity, balance sheet, and statement of cash flows for 2002 and 2003.

PROBLEM 3–21A *Effect of Events on Financial Statements*   L.O. 3, 5

Topez Company had the following balances in its accounting records as of December 31, 2001:

Assets		Claims	
Cash	$ 70,000	Accounts Payable	$ 44,000
Accounts Receivable	41,000	Common Stock	80,000
Land	40,000	Retained Earnings	27,000
Totals	$151,000		$151,000

The following accounting events apply to Topez's 2002 fiscal year:

Jan.	1	Acquired an additional $10,000 cash from the issue of common stock.
	1	Purchased a delivery van that cost $18,000 and that had a $3,000 salvage value and a three-year useful life.
Mar.	1	Borrowed $8,000 by issuing a note that had a 12 percent annual interest rate and a one-year term.
May	1	Paid $3,900 cash in advance for a one-year lease for office space.
June	1	Paid a $1,000 cash dividend to the stockholders.
July	1	Purchased land that cost $16,000 cash.
Aug.	1	Made a cash payment on accounts payable of $7,000.
Sep.	1	Received $5,600 cash in advance as a retainer for services to be performed monthly during the next eight months.
Sept. 30		Sold land for $17,000 cash that had originally cost $20,000.
Oct.	1	Purchased $1,500 of supplies on account.
Nov.	1	Purchased a one-year $10,000 certificate of deposit that paid a 6 percent annual rate of interest.
Dec. 31		Earned $45,000 of service revenue on account during the year.
	31	Received $47,000 cash collections from accounts receivable.
	31	Incurred $6,000 other operating expenses on account during the year.
	31	Incurred accrued salaries expense of $2,000.
	31	Had $100 of supplies on hand at the end of the period.

Required

Based on the preceding information, answer the following questions. All questions pertain to the 2002 financial statements. (*Hint:* Record the events in general ledger accounts under an accounting equation before answering the questions.)

a. What additional five transactions during the year need adjusting entries at the end of the year?
b. What amount of interest expense would Topez report on the income statement?
c. What amount of net cash flow from operating activities would Topez report on the statement of cash flows?

d. What amount of rent expense would Topez report in the income statement?

e. What amount of total liabilities would Topez report on the balance sheet?

f. What amount of supplies expense would Topez report on the income statement?

g. What amount of unearned revenue would Topez report on the balance sheet?

h. What amount of net cash flow from investing activities would Topez report on the statement of cash flows?

i. What amount of interest payable would Topez report on the balance sheet?

j. What amount of total expenses would Topez report on the income statement?

k. What amount of retained earnings would Topez report on the balance sheet?

l. What total amount of all revenues would Topez report on the income statement?

m. What amount of cash flows from financing activities would Topez report on the statement of cash flows?

n. What is the amount of the loss on sale of land Topez would report on the income statement?

o. What amount of net income would Topez report on the income statement?

L.O. 4   PROBLEM 3–22A *Identifying and Arranging Elements on Financial Statements*

The following accounts and balances were drawn from the records of Highpoint Company at December 31, 2005:

Cash	$30,000	Cash Flow from Operating Act.	$15,000
Land	12,000	Beginning Retained Earnings	12,000
Insurance Expense	1,500	Beginning Common Stock	6,500
Dividends	2,500	Service Revenue	50,000
Prepaid Insurance	6,000	Cash Flow from Financing Act.	5,500
Accounts Payable	3,000	Issue Common Stock	28,000
Supplies	150	Accumulated Depreciation	11,500
Supplies Expense	850	Cash Flow from Investing Act.	(20,000)
Depreciation Expense	2,000	Operating Expenses	10,000
Accounts Receivable	18,000	Office Equipment	28,000

Required

Use the accounts and balances from Highpoint Company to construct an income statement, statement of changes in stockholders' equity, balance sheet, and statement of cash flows (show only totals for each activity on the statement of cash flows).

L.O. 4   PROBLEM 3–23A *Relationship of Accounts to Financial Statements*

Required

Identify whether each of the following items would appear on the income statement (IS), statement of changes in stockholders' equity (SE), balance sheet (BS), or statement of cash flows (CF). Some items may appear on more than one statement; if so, identify all applicable statements. If an item would not appear on any financial statement, label it NA.

a. Total Assets

b. Consulting Revenue

c. Depreciation Expense

d. Supplies Expense

e. Salaries Payable

f. Notes Payable

g. Ending Common Stock

h. Interest Payable

i. Office Equipment

j. Interest Revenue

k. Land

l. Operating Expenses

m. Total Liabilities

n. Debt to Equity Ratio

o. Salaries Expense

p. Net Income

q. Service Revenue

r. Cash Flow from Operating Activities

s. Return on Assets Ratio

t. Interest Receivable

u. Salary Expense

v. Notes Receivable

w. Unearned Revenue

x. Cash Flow from Investing Activities

y. Insurance Expense

z. Ending Retained Earnings

aa. Accumulated Depreciation

bb. Supplies

cc. Beginning Retained Earnings

dd. Certificate of Deposit

ee. Cash Flow from Financing Activities

ff. Accounts Receivable

gg. Prepaid Insurance

hh. Cash

ii. Interest Expense

jj. Accounts Payable

kk. Beginning Common Stock

ll. Dividends

PROBLEM 3–24A *Missing Information in Financial Statements*

L.O. 3, 4

The following data are relevant to the revenue and expense accounts of Cornell Corporation during 2004. The Accounts Receivable balance was $45,000 on January 1, 2004. Consulting services provided to customers on account during the year were $128,000. The receivables balance on December 31, 2004, amounted to $28,000. Cornell received $21,000 in advance payment for training services to be performed over a 24-month period beginning March 1, 2004. Furthermore, Cornell purchased a $30,000 certificate of deposit on September 1, 2004. The certificate paid 15 percent interest, which was payable in cash on August 31 of each year. During 2004, Cornell recorded depreciation expense of $18,000. Salaries earned by employees during 2004 were $25,000. The Salaries Payable account increased by $3,500 during the year. Other operating expenses paid in cash during 2004 amounted to $70,000. No other revenue or expense transactions occurred during 2004.

Required

a. Prepare an income statement, assuming that Cornell uses the accrual basis of accounting.

b. Determine the net cash flows from operating activities for 2004.

PROBLEM 3–25A *Using Accounting Information*

L.O. 1, 9

Louise Mayes is trying to decide whether to start a small business or put her capital into a savings account. To help her make a decision, two of her friends shared their investing experiences with her. Donna Everhart had started a small business three years ago. As of the end of the most recent year of operations, Everhart's business had total assets of $185,000 and net income of $11,220. The second friend, Analisa Harrison, had deposited $20,000 in a bank savings account that paid $900 in interest during the last year.

Required

a. Assume you are an investment counselor. Show Mayes how the return on assets ratio shows whether Everhart's or Harrison's investment is producing a higher return.

b. Using your personal judgment, identify any other factors that Mayes should consider before she decides whether to start her own business or deposit her money in a savings account. Recommend to Mayes which alternative you think she should accept.

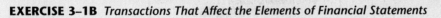

EXERCISES—SERIES B

EXERCISE 3–1B *Transactions That Affect the Elements of Financial Statements*

L.O. 1

Required

Give an example of a transaction that will

a. Increase an asset and decrease another asset (asset exchange event).

b. Increase an asset and increase a liability (asset source event).

c. Decrease an asset and decrease a liability (asset use event).

d. Decrease an asset and decrease equity (asset use event).

e. Increase a liability and decrease equity (claims exchange event).

f. Increase an asset and increase equity (asset source event).

g. Decrease a liability and increase equity (claims exchange event).

EXERCISE 3–2B *Identifying Deferral and Accrual Events*

L.O. 2

Required

Identify each of the following events as accruals, deferrals, or neither.

a. Paid cash for utilities expense.

b. Collected $2,400 in advance for services to be performed over the next 12 months.

c. Incurred other operating expenses on account.

d. Recorded expense for salaries owed to employees at the end of the accounting period.

e. Paid a cash dividend to the stockholders.

f. Paid cash to purchase supplies to be used over the next several months.

g. Purchased a delivery van with a five-year life.

h. Provided services on account.

i. Recognized interest income on a certificate of deposit before receiving the cash.

j. Paid one year's rent in advance.

L.O. 6   **EXERCISE 3–3B** *Effect of Deferrals on the Accounting Equation*

Required

For each of the following independent cases, show the effects on the accounting equation of both the deferral and the related December 31, 2001, adjustment.

a. Andy Shipp, owner of Shipp Business Services, purchased a new computer system for $12,400 on January 1, 2001. The computer system has an estimated useful life of four years and a $1,400 salvage value.

b. Ray's Wholesale paid $15,000 for a 12-month lease on warehouse space on October 1, 2001.

c. Amanda Sherman, J.D., accepted a $50,000 advance from a client on November 1, 2001. The services are to be performed over the next eight months.

L.O. 3, 10   **EXERCISE 3–4B** *Identifying Transaction Type and Effect on the Financial Statements*

Required

Identify whether each of the following transactions is an asset source (AS), asset use (AU), asset exchange (AE), or claims exchange (CE). Also show the effects of the events on the financial statements using the horizontal statements model. Indicate whether the event increases (I), decreases (D), or does not affect (NA) each element of the financial statements. In the Cash Flows column, designate the cash flows as operating activities (OA), investing activities (IA), or financing activities (FA). The first two transactions have been recorded as examples.

Event No.	Type of Event	Assets	=	Liabilities	+	Common Stock	+	Retained Earnings	Rev.	−	Exp.	=	Net Inc.	Cash Flows
						Stockholders' Equity								
a	AE	DI		NA		NA		NA	NA		NA		NA	D IA
b	AS	I		NA		I		NA	NA		NA		NA	I FA

a. Purchased land for cash.

b. Acquired cash from the issue of common stock.

c. Paid cash on accounts payable.

d. Received cash advance for services to be provided in the future.

e. Collected cash from accounts receivable.

f. Paid cash for operating expenses.

g. Recorded accrued salaries.

h. Paid cash to purchase office equipment.

i. Performed services on account.

j. Paid cash advance for rent on office space.

k. Recorded depreciation expense on office equipment.

l. Performed services for cash.

m. Purchased a building with cash *and* issued a note payable.

n. Paid cash for salaries accrued at the end of a prior period.

o. Paid a cash dividend to the stockholders.

p. Adjusted books to reflect the amount of prepaid rent expired during the period.

q. Incurred operating expenses on account.

L.O. 3, 4, 5, 7   **EXERCISE 3–5B** *Effect of Prepaid Rent on the Accounting Equation and Financial Statements*

The following events apply to 2007, the first year of operations of Belview Services:

1. Acquired $25,000 cash from the issue of common stock.

2. Paid $18,000 cash in advance for one-year rental contract for office space.

3. Provided services for $28,000 cash.

4. Adjusted the records to recognize the use of the office space. The one-year contract started on April 1, 2007. The adjustment was made as of December 31, 2007.

Required

a. Write an accounting equation and record the effects of each accounting event under the appropriate general ledger account headings.

b. Prepare a balance sheet at the end of the accounting period ending 2007.

c. What amount of rent expense will Belview report on the 2007 income statement?

d. What amount of net cash flow from operating activities will Belview report on the 2007 statement of cash flows?

EXERCISE 3–6B *Effect of Supplies on the Financial Statements*   **L.O. 5, 6, 7, 10**

A&I Express started the 2003 accounting period with $2,000 cash, $1,200 of common stock, and $800 of retained earnings. A&I was affected by the following accounting events during 2003:
1. Purchased $2,400 of copier toner and other supplies on account.
2. Earned and collected $10,800 of cash revenue.
3. Paid $1,800 cash on accounts payable.
4. Adjusted the records to reflect the use of supplies. A physical count indicated that $200 of supplies was still on hand on December 31, 2003.

Required
a. Show the effects of the events on the financial statements using a horizontal statements model like the following one. In the Cash Flows column, use OA to designate operating activity, IA for investing activity, FA for financing activity, and NC for net change in cash. Use NA to indicate accounts not affected by the event. The beginning balances are entered in the following example.

	Assets		= Liab.	+	Stk. Equity		Rev.	− Exp.	= Net Inc.	Cash Flows
Event No.	Cash	Supplies	Acct. Pay.		C. Stock	Ret. Earn.				
Beg. Bal.	2,000	0	0		1,200	800	0	0	0	0

b. Explain the difference between the amount of net income and amount of net cash flow from operating activities.

EXERCISE 3–7B *Effect of Depreciation on the Accounting Equation and Financial Statements*   **L.O. 3, 4, 5, 6, 7**

The following events apply to Papa's Deli Delight for the 2006 fiscal year:
1. Started the company when it acquired $30,000 cash by issuing common stock.
2. Purchased a new stove that cost $22,000 cash.
3. Earned $21,000 in cash revenue.
4. Paid $4,000 of cash for salaries expense.
5. Adjusted the records to reflect the use of the stove. Purchased on January 1, 2006, the stove has an expected useful life of four years and an estimated salvage value of $1,000. Use straight-line depreciation. The adjusting entry was made as of December 31, 2006.

Required
a. Write an accounting equation and record the effects of each accounting event under the appropriate general ledger account headings.
b. Prepare a balance sheet as of 2006 and a statement of cash flows for the 2006 accounting period.
c. What is the net income for 2006?
d. What is the amount of depreciation expense Papa's would report on the 2007 income statement?
e. What amount of accumulated depreciation would Papa's report on the December 31, 2007, balance sheet?
f. Would the cash flow from operating activities be affected by depreciation in 2007?

EXERCISE 3–8B *Effect of Unearned Revenue on Financial Statements*   **L.O. 5, 6, 10**

Robby Holder started a personal financial planning business when he accepted $30,000 cash as advance payment for managing the financial assets of a large estate. Robby agreed to manage the estate for a twelve-month period, beginning April 1, 2003.

Required
a. Show the effects of the advance payment and revenue recognition on the 2003 financial statements using a horizontal statements model like the following one. In the Cash Flows column, use OA to designate operating activity, IA for investing activity, FA for financing activity, and NC for net change in cash. Use NA if the account is not affected.

	Assets	=	Liab.	+ Stk. Equity		Rev.	− Exp.	= Net Inc.	Cash Flows
Event No.	Cash		Unearn. Rev.	Ret. Earn.					

b. How much revenue would Holder recognize on the 2004 income statement?

c. What is the amount of cash flow from operating activities in 2004?

L.O. 8   **EXERCISE 3–9B** *Effect of Gains and Losses on the Accounting Equation and Financial Statements*

On January 1, 2002, Mega Enterprises purchased a parcel of land for $16,000 cash. At the time of purchase, the company planned to use the land for a warehouse site. In 2004, Mega Enterprises changed its plans and sold the land.

Required

a. Assume that the land was sold for $15,000 in 2004.

   (1) Show the effect of the sale on the accounting equation.

   (2) What amount would Mega report on the 2004 income statement related to the sale of the land?

   (3) What amount would Mega report on the 2004 statement of cash flows related to the sale of the land?

b. Assume that the land was sold for $18,000 in 2004.

   (1) Show the effect of the sale on the accounting equation.

   (2) What amount would Mega report on the 2004 income statement related to the sale of the land?

   (3) What amount would Mega report on the 2004 statement of cash flows related to the sale of the land?

L.O. 5, 6   **EXERCISE 3–10B** *Effect of Accounting Events on the Income Statement and Statement of Cash Flows*

Required

Explain how each of the following events and the related adjusting entry will affect the amount of *net income* and the amount of *cash flow from operating activities* reported on the year-end financial statements. Identify the direction of change (increase, decrease, or no effect) and the amount of the change. Organize your answers according to the following table. The first event is recorded as an example. If an event does not have a related adjusting entry, record only the effects of the event.

	Net Income		Cash Flows from Operating Activities	
Event No.	Direction of Change	Amount of Change	Direction of Change	Amount of Change
a	Decrease	$1,000	Decrease	$6,000

a. Paid $6,000 cash on November 1 to purchase a one-year insurance policy.

b. Purchased $1,000 of supplies on account. Paid $700 cash on accounts payable. The ending balance in the Supplies account, after adjustment, was $100.

c. Paid $36,000 cash to purchase machinery on January 1. It had an estimated salvage value of $6,000 and an expected useful life of four years.

d. Provided services for $8,000 cash.

e. Collected $1,800 in advance for services to be performed in the future. The contract called for services to start on May 1 and to continue for one year.

f. Accrued salaries amounting to $3,200.

g. Sold land that cost $2,000 for $4,500 cash.

h. Acquired $20,000 cash from the issue of common stock.

i. Earned $8,000 of revenue on account. Collected $5,000 cash from accounts receivable.

j. Paid cash operating expenses of $3,000.

L.O. 10   **EXERCISE 3–11B** *Effect of Accruals and Deferrals on Financial Statements: Horizontal Statements Model*

Moody Attorney at Law experienced the following transactions in 2001, the first year of operations:

1. Accepted $24,000 on April 1, 2001, as a retainer for services to be performed evenly over the next 12 months.

2. Performed legal services for cash of $29,000.

3. Purchased $1,400 of office supplies on account.
4. Paid $1,000 of the amount due on accounts payable.
5. Paid a cash dividend to the stockholders of $5,000.
6. Paid cash for operating expenses of $16,200.
7. Determined that at the end of the accounting period $150 of office supplies remained on hand.
8. On December 31, 2001, recognized the revenue that had been earned for services performed in accordance with Transaction 1.

Required

Show the effects of the events on the financial statements using a horizontal statements model like the following one. In the Cash Flows column, use the initials OA to designate operating activity, IA for investing activity, FA for financing activity, and NC for net change in cash. Use NA to indicate accounts not affected by the event. The first event has been recorded as an example.

| Event No. | Assets | | | = | Liabilities | | | + | Stk. Equity | Rev. | – | Exp. | = | Net Inc. | Cash Flow |
	Cash	+	Supplies	=	Acct. Pay.	+	Unearn. Rev.		Ret. Earn.						
1	24,000	+	NA	=	NA	+	24,000	+		NA	–	NA	=	NA	24,000 OA

EXERCISE 3–12B *Asset Versus Expense*   L.O. 7

A cost can be either an asset or an expense.

Required
a. Distinguish between a cost that is an asset and a cost that is an expense.
b. List three costs that are assets.
c. List three costs that are expenses.

EXERCISE 3–13B *Matching Concept*   L.O. 7

Required
Place a check mark in the appropriate cell of the following table to indicate whether each of the following costs would be expensed through (1) direct matching, (2) period matching, or (3) systematic allocation.

Cost	Matched Directly With Revenue	Matched With the Period Incurred	Systematically Allocated
Delivery van			
Office manager's salary			
Office supplies			
Insurance			
Office building			
Loss on the sale of a warehouse			
Sales commissions			

EXERCISE 3–14B *Effect of an Error on Financial Statements*   L.O. 5, 6

On May 1, 2007, Black Corporation paid $9,000 cash in advance for a one-year lease on an office building. Assume that Black records the prepaid rent and that the books are closed on December 31.

Required
a. Provide the adjusting entry to record the 2007 rent expense.
b. Assume that Black Corporation failed to record the adjusting entry to reflect using the office building. How would the error affect the company's 2007 income statement and balance sheet?

EXERCISE 3–15B *Revenue and Expense Recognition*   L.O. 1

Required
a. Describe a revenue recognition event that results in an increase in assets.
b. Describe a revenue recognition event that results in a decrease in liabilities.
c. Describe an expense recognition event that results in an increase in liabilities.
d. Describe an expense recognition event that results in a decrease in assets.

L.O. 1, 5   EXERCISE 3–16B *Unearned Revenue Defined as a Liability*

Janie, an accounting major, and Bill, a marketing major, are watching a *Matlock* rerun on late-night TV. Of course, there is a murder and the suspect wants to hire Matlock as the defense attorney. Matlock will take the case but requires an advance payment of $100,000. Bill remarks that Matlock has earned a cool $100,000 without lifting a finger. Janie tells Bill that Matlock has not earned anything but has a $100,000 liability. Bill asks "How can that be?"

Required
Assume you are Janie. Explain to Bill why Matlock has a liability and when Matlock would actually earn the $100,000.

PROBLEMS—SERIES B

L.O. 10   PROBLEM 3–17B *Recording Events in a Horizontal Statements Model*

The following events pertain to Ice Land:
1. Acquired $8,000 cash from the issue of common stock.
2. Provided $9,000 of services on account.
3. Provided services for $3,000 cash.
4. Received $2,500 cash in advance for services to be performed in the future.
5. Collected $5,600 cash from the account receivable created in Event 2.
6. Paid $1,100 for cash expenses.
7. Performed $1,400 of the services agreed to in Event 4.
8. Incurred $2,800 of expenses on account.
9. Paid $2,400 cash in advance for one-year contract to rent office space.
10. Paid $2,200 cash on the account payable created in Event 8.
11. Paid a $1,500 cash dividend to the stockholders.
12. Recognized rent expense for nine months' use of office space acquired in Event 9.

Required
Show the effects of the events on the financial statements using a horizontal statements model like the following one. In the Cash Flows column, use the letters OA to designate operating activity, IA for investing activity, FA for financing activity, and NC for net change in cash. Use NA to indicate accounts not affected by the event. The first event is recorded as an example.

Event No.	Assets			=	Liabilities		+	Stockholders' Equity		Rev. − Exp. = Net Inc.	Cash Flows
	Cash +	Acc. Rec. +	Prep. Rent =		Acc. Pay. +	Unearn. Rev. +		Common Stock +	Ret. Earn.		
1	8,000 +	NA +	NA =		NA +	NA +		8,000 +	NA	NA − NA = NA	8,000 FA

L.O. 3, 4, 5, 6, 10   PROBLEM 3–18B *Effect of Deferrals on Financial Statements: Three Separate Single-Cycle Examples*

Required
a. On February 1, 2006, Oliver Company was formed when it acquired $10,000 cash from the issue of common stock. On June 1, 2006, the company paid $2,400 cash in advance to rent office space for the coming year. The office space was used as a place to consult with clients. The consulting activity generated $5,200 of cash revenue during 2006. Based on this information alone, record the events in general ledger accounts under the accounting equation. Determine the amount of net income and cash flows from operating activities for 2006.
b. On August 1, 2005, the consulting firm of Cooper & Associates was formed. On September 1, 2005, the company received a $12,000 retainer (was paid in advance) for monthly services to be performed over a one-year period. Assuming that this was the only transaction completed in 2005, prepare an income statement, statement of changes in stockholders' equity, balance sheet, and statement of cash flows for 2005.
c. Eagle Company was started when it acquired $10,000 cash from the issue of common stock on January 1, 2004. The company immediately used the cash received to purchase a $10,000 machine that

had a $2,000 salvage value and an expected useful life of four years. The machine was used to produce $5,200 of cash revenue during the accounting period. Show the effects of these transactions on the financial statements using the horizontal statements model.

PROBLEM 3–19B *Effect of Adjusting Entries on the Accounting Equation* **L.O. 3, 6**

Required

Each of the following independent events requires a year-end adjusting entry. Show how each event and its related adjusting entry affects the accounting equation. Assume a December 31 closing date. The first event is recorded as an example.

Event/	Total Assets					Stockholders' Equity		
Adjustment	Asset 1	+	Asset 2	=	Liabilities	+	Common Stock	+ Retained Earnings
a	−3,600		+3,600		NA		NA	NA
Adj.	NA		−900		NA		NA	−900

a. Paid $3,600 cash in advance on October 1 for a one-year insurance policy.

b. Borrowed $20,000 by issuing a one-year note with 9 percent annual interest to National Bank on April 1.

c. Paid $19,000 cash to purchase a delivery van on January 1. The van was expected to have a four-year life and a $4,000 salvage value. Depreciation is computed on a straight-line basis.

d. Received an $1,800 cash advance for a contract to provide services in the future. The contract required a one-year commitment, starting April 1.

e. Purchased $800 of supplies on account. At year's end, $140 of supplies remained on hand.

f. Invested $8,000 cash in a certificate of deposit that paid 6 percent annual interest. The certificate was acquired on May 1 and had a one-year term to maturity.

g. Paid $7,200 cash in advance on August 1 for a one-year lease on office space.

PROBLEM 3–20B *Events for Two Complete Accounting Cycles* **L.O. 1, 3, 4**

Great Plains Company was formed on January 1, 2005.

Events Affecting the 2005 Accounting Period

1. Acquired $25,000 cash from the issue of common stock.
2. Purchased communication equipment that cost $6,000 cash.
3. Purchased land that cost $12,000 cash.
4. Paid $500 cash for supplies.
5. Recognized revenue on account of $9,000.
6. Paid $2,400 cash for other operating expenses.
7. Collected $7,000 cash from accounts receivable.

Information for Adjusting Entries

8. Incurred accrued salaries of $3,200 on December 31, 2005.
9. Had $100 of supplies on hand at the end of the accounting period.
10. Used the straight-line method to depreciate the equipment acquired in Event 2. Purchased on January 1, the equipment had an expected useful life of four years and a $2,000 salvage value.

Events Affecting the 2006 Accounting Period

1. Acquired $12,000 cash from the issue of common stock.
2. Paid $3,200 cash to settle the salaries payable obligation.
3. Paid $6,000 cash in advance for a lease on computer equipment.
4. Sold the land that cost $12,000 for $18,000 cash.
5. Received $8,400 cash in advance for services to be performed in the future.
6. Purchased $2,000 of supplies on account during the year.
7. Provided services on account of $11,000.
8. Collected $9,000 cash from accounts receivable.
9. Paid a cash dividend of $2,000 to the stockholders.

Information for Adjusting Entries

10. The advance payment for rental of the computer equipment (see Event 3) was made on February 1 for a one-year term.

11. The cash advance for services to be provided in the future was collected on October 1 (see Event 5). The one-year contract started on October 1.
12. Had $200 of supplies remaining on hand at the end of the period.
13. Recorded depreciation on the computer equipment for 2006.
14. Incurred accrued salaries of $6,000 at the end of the accounting period.

Required

a. Identify each event affecting the 2005 and 2006 accounting periods as an asset source (AS), asset use (AU), asset exchange (AE), or claims exchange (CE). Record the effects of each event under the appropriate general ledger account headings of the accounting equation.
b. Prepare an income statement, statement of changes in stockholders' equity, balance sheet, and statement of cash flows for 2005 and 2006.

L.O. 3, 5   PROBLEM 3–21B *Effect of Events on Financial Statements*

Juan Company had the following balances in its accounting records as of December 31, 2003:

Assets		Claims	
Cash	$23,000	Accounts Payable	$ 5,000
Accounts Receivable	7,000	Common Stock	24,000
Land	42,000	Retained Earnings	43,000
Total	$72,000	Total	$72,000

The following accounting events apply to Juan Company's 2004 fiscal year:

Jan.	1	Acquired $12,000 cash from the issue of common stock.
	1	Purchased a truck that cost $22,000 and had a $2,000 salvage value and a four-year useful life.
Feb.	1	Borrowed $10,000 by issuing a note that had a 9 percent annual interest rate and a one-year term.
	1	Paid $3,000 cash in advance for a one-year lease for office space.
Mar.	1	Paid a $1,000 cash dividend to the stockholders.
April	1	Purchased land that cost $28,000 cash.
May	1	Made a cash payment on accounts payable of $2,000.
July	1	Received $5,400 cash in advance as a retainer for services to be performed monthly over the coming year.
Sept.	1	Sold land for $60,000 cash that had originally cost $42,000.
Oct.	1	Purchased $3,000 of supplies on account.
Nov.	1	Purchased a one-year $50,000 certificate of deposit that paid a 6 percent annual rate of interest.
Dec.	31	Earned $35,000 of service revenue on account during the year.
	31	Received cash collections from accounts receivable amounting to $40,000.
	31	Incurred other operating expenses on account during the year that amounted to $6,000.
	31	Incurred accrued salaries expense of $4,800.
	31	Had $50 of supplies on hand at the end of the period.

Required

Based on the preceding information, answer the following questions. All questions pertain to the 2004 financial statements. (*Hint:* Enter items in general ledger accounts under the accounting equation before answering the questions.)

a. Based on the preceding transactions, identify five additional adjustments and describe them.
b. What amount of interest expense would Juan report on the income statement?
c. What amount of net cash flow from operating activities would Juan report on the statement of cash flows?
d. What amount of rent expense would Juan report in the income statement?
e. What amount of total liabilities would Juan report on the balance sheet?
f. What amount of supplies expense would Juan report on the income statement?
g. What amount of unearned revenue would Juan report on the balance sheet?
h. What amount of net cash flow from investing activities would Juan report on the statement of cash flows?
i. What amount of interest payable would Juan report on the balance sheet?

j. What amount of total expenses would Juan report on the income statement?

k. What amount of retained earnings would Juan report on the balance sheet?

l. What total amount of all revenues would Juan report on the income statement?

m. What amount of cash flows from financing activities would Juan report on the statement of cash flows?

n. What is the amount of the gain on sale of land Juan would report on the income statement?

o. What amount of net income would Juan report on the income statement?

PROBLEM 3–22B *Preparing Financial Statements*

L.O. 4

The following accounts and balances were drawn from the records of Johnson Company:

Supplies	$ 300	Beginning Retained Earnings	$14,500
Cash Flow from Investing Act.	(7,800)	Cash Flow from Financing Act.	−0−
Prepaid Insurance	600	Depreciation Expense	1,500
Service Revenue	45,450	Dividends	6,000
Operating Expenses	35,000	Cash	9,000
Supplies Expense	750	Accounts Receivable	7,000
Insurance Expense	1,800	Office Equipment	16,000
Beginning Common Stock	24,000	Accumulated Depreciation	8,000
Cash Flow from Operating Act.	10,450	Land	36,000
Common Stock Issued	6,000	Accounts Payable	16,000

Required

Use the accounts and balances from Johnson Company to construct an income statement, statement of changes in stockholders' equity, balance sheet, and statement of cash flows.

PROBLEM 3–23B *Relationship of Accounts to Financial Statements*

L.O. 4

Required

Identify whether each of the following items would appear on the income statement (IS), statement of changes in stockholders' equity (SE), balance sheet (BS), or statement of cash flows (CF). If some items appear on more than one statement, identify all applicable statements. If an item will not appear on any financial statement, label it NA.

a. Depreciation Expense

b. Interest Receivable

c. Certificate of Deposit

d. Unearned Revenue

e. Service Revenue

f. Cash Flow from Investing Activities

g. Consulting Revenue

h. Interest Expense

i. Ending Common Stock

j. Total Liabilities

k. Debt to Assets Ratio

l. Cash Flow from Operating Activities

m. Operating Expenses

n. Supplies Expense

o. Beginning Retained Earnings

p. Beginning Common Stock

q. Prepaid Insurance

r. Salary Expense

s. Accumulated Depreciation

t. Cash

u. Supplies

v. Cash Flow from Financing Activities

w. Interest Revenue

x. Ending Retained Earnings

y. Net Income

z. Dividends

aa. Office Equipment

bb. Debt to Equity Ratio

cc. Land

dd. Interest Payable

ee. Salaries Expense

ff. Notes Receivable

gg. Accounts Payable

hh. Total Assets

ii. Salaries Payable

jj. Insurance Expense

kk. Notes Payable

ll. Accounts Receivable

PROBLEM 3–24B *Missing Information in Financial Statements*

L.O. 3, 4

Deluxe Technology started the 2002 accounting period with $6,500 cash, accounts receivable of $8,000, prepaid rent of $4,500, supplies of $150, computers that cost $35,000, accumulated depreciation on computers of $7,000, accounts payable of $10,000, and common stock of $15,000. During 2002, Deluxe recognized $93,000 of revenue on account and collected $84,000 of cash from accounts receivable. It paid $5,000 cash for rent in advance and reported $6,000 of rent expense on the income statement. Deluxe paid $1,000 cash for supplies, and the income statement reported supplies expense of $1,100.

Depreciation expense reported on the income statement amounted to $3,500. It incurred $38,600 of operating expenses on account and paid $34,000 cash toward the settlement of accounts payable. The company acquired capital of $10,000 cash from the issue of common stock. A $700 cash dividend was paid. (*Hint:* Record the events under the general ledger accounts of an accounting equation before satisfying the requirements.)

Required
a. Determine the balance in the Retained Earnings account at the beginning of the accounting period.
b. Prepare an income statement, statement of changes in stockholders' equity, balance sheet, and statement of cash flows as of the end of the accounting period.

L.O. 1   **PROBLEM 3–25B** *Using Accounting Information*

Marty Fairchild told his friend that he was very angry with his father. He had asked his father for a sports car, and his father had replied that he did not have the cash. Fairchild said that he knew his father was not telling the truth because he had seen a copy of his father's business records, which included a balance sheet that showed a Retained Earnings account of $650,000. He said that anybody with $650,000 had enough cash to buy his son a car.

Required
Explain why Fairchild's assessment of his father's cash position may be invalid. What financial statements and which items on those statements would enable him to make a more accurate assessment of his father's cash position?

ANALYZE, THINK, COMMUNICATE

ATC 3–1   **BUSINESS APPLICATIONS CASE** *Dell's Annual Report*

Required
Using the Dell Computer Corporation financial statements in Appendix B, answer the following questions:
a. What was Dell's debt to assets ratio for 2001?
b. What was Dell's return on assets ratio for 2001?
c. What was Dell's return on equity ratio for 2001?
d. Why was Dell's 2001 return on equity ratio greater than its 2001 return on assets ratio?

ATC 3–2   **GROUP ASSIGNMENT** *Missing Information*

Little Theater Group is a local performing arts group that sponsors various theater productions. The company sells season tickets for the regular performances. It also sells tickets to individual performances called *door sales*. The season tickets are sold in June, July, and August for the season that runs from September through April of each year. The season tickets package contains tickets to eight performances, one per month. The first year of operations was 2003. All revenue not from season ticket sales is from door sales. The following selected information was taken from the financial records for December 31, 2003, 2004, and 2005, at the company's year end:

	2003	2004	2005
Revenue (per income statement)	$450,000	$575,000	$625,000
Unearned Revenue (per balance sheet)	127,000	249,000	275,000
Operating Expense	231,000	326,000	428,000

Required
a. Divide the class into groups consisting of four or five students. Organize the groups into three sections. Assign the groups in each section the financial data for one of the preceding accounting periods.

Group Tasks

1. Determine the total amount of season ticket sales for the year assigned.
2. Determine the total amount of season door sales for the year assigned.
3. Compute the net income for the year assigned.
4. Have a representative of each section put its income statement on the board.

Class Discussion

b. Compare the income statements for 2003, 2004, and 2005. Discuss the revenue trend; that is, are door sales increasing more than season ticket sales? What is the company's growth pattern?

REAL-WORLD CASE *Different Numbers for Different Industries*   ATC 3–3

The following are the debt to assets, return on assets, and return on equity ratios for four companies from two different industries. The range of interest rates each company was paying on its short-term debt is provided. Each of these public companies is a leader in its particular industry, and the data are for the fiscal years ending in 2000. *All numbers are percentages.*

	Debt to Assets	Return on Assets	Return on Equity	Approximate Average Short-term Interest Rates
Banking Industry				
SunTrust Bank	92	1.3	15.7	5.9
Wells Fargo & Co.	90	1.5	15.2	6.2
Home Construction Industry				
Pulte Corporation	57	6.5	15.1	6.9
Ryland Group	67	6.0	18.1	7.3

Required

a. Based only on the debt to assets ratios, the banking companies appear to have the most financial risk. Generally, lower interest rates are usually charged for companies that have lower financial risk. Given this, explain why the banking companies can borrow money at lower interest rates than the construction companies.

b. Explain why Ryland's return on equity is higher than Pulte's even though its return on assets ratio is lower.

BUSINESS APPLICATIONS CASE *Using Ratio Analysis to Assess Financial Risk*   ATC 3–4

The following information was drawn from the balance sheets of two companies:

Company	Assets	=	Liabilities	+	Stockholders' Equity
Men's Clothier	215,000		58,000		157,000
Women's Fashions	675,000		256,500		418,500

Required

a. Compute the debt to assets ratio to measure the level of financial risk of both companies.

b. Compare the two ratios computed in part *a* to determine whether Men's Clothier or Women's Fashions has the higher level of financial risk.

BUSINESS APPLICATIONS CASE *Using Ratio Analysis to Make Comparisons between*   ATC 3–5
Companies

At the end of 2007, the following information is available for El Greco Pizza and Athenian Pizza.

Statement Data	El Greco Pizza	Athenian Pizza
Total Assets	$127,000	$753,000
Total Liabilities	93,000	452,000
Stockholders' Equity	34,000	301,000
Net Income	8,000	45,000

Required

a. For each company, compute the debt to assets ratio and the return on equity ratio.

b. Determine what percentage of each company's assets was financed by the owners.

c. Which company had a higher level of financial risk?

d. Based on profitability alone, which company performed better?

e. Do the preceding ratios support the concept of financial leverage? Explain.

ATC 3–6   WRITING ASSIGNMENT *Effect of Land Sale on Return on Assets*

Toyo Company is holding land that cost $900,000 for future use. However, plans have changed and the company may not need the land in the foreseeable future. The president is concerned about the return on assets. Current net income is $425,000 and total assets are $3,500,000.

Required

a. Write a memo to the company president explaining the effect of disposing of the land, assuming that it has a current value of $1,500,000.
b. Write a memo to the company president explaining the effect of disposing of the land, assuming that it has a current value of $600,000.

ATC 3–7   ETHICAL DILEMMA *What Is a Little Deceit Among Friends?*

Glenn's Cleaning Services Company is experiencing cash flow problems and needs a loan. Glenn has a friend who is willing to lend him the money he needs provided she can be convinced that he will be able to repay the debt. Glenn has assured his friend that his business is viable, but his friend has asked to see the company's financial statements. Glenn's accountant produced the following financial statements:

Income Statement		Balance Sheet	
Service Revenue	$ 38,000	Assets	$ 85,000
Operating Expenses	(70,000)	Liabilities	$ 35,000
Net Loss	$(32,000)	Stockholders' Equity	
		Common Stock	82,000
		Retained Earnings	(32,000)
		Total Liabilities and	
		Stockholders' Equity	$ 85,000

Glenn made the following adjustments to these statements before showing them to his friend. He recorded $82,000 of revenue on account from Barrymore Manufacturing Company for a contract to clean its headquarters office building that was still being negotiated for the next month. Barrymore had scheduled a meeting to sign a contract the following week, so he was sure that he would get the job. Barrymore was a reputable company, and Glenn was confident that he could ultimately collect the $82,000. Also, he subtracted $30,000 of accrued salaries expense and the corresponding liability. He reasoned that since he had not paid the employees, he had not incurred any expense.

Required

a. Reconstruct the income statement and balance sheet as they would appear after Glenn's adjustments. Comment on the accuracy of the adjusted financial statements.
b. Comment on the ethical implications of Glenn's actions. Before you answer, consider the following scenario. Suppose you are Glenn and the $30,000 you owe your employees is due next week. If you are unable to pay them, they will quit and the business will go bankrupt. You are sure you will be able to repay your friend when your employees perform the $82,000 of services for Barrymore and you collect the cash. However, your friend is risk averse and is not likely to make the loan based on the financial statements your accountant prepared. Would you make the changes that Glenn made to get the loan and thereby save your company? Defend your position with a rational explanation.

ATC 3–8   SPREADSHEET ASSIGNMENT *Using Excel*

Set up the following spreadsheet for Hubbard Company to calculate financial ratios based on given financial information.

Steps to Prepare Spreadsheet

1. Enter the information in Column A.
2. Enter the headings in rows 1 and 2.
3. In row 3, enter the numbers for the Original Amounts.
4. In Column B, beginning with row 8, formulate the ratios based on the Original Amounts. Format the ratios as percentages.
5. The following independent transactions apply to Hubbard Corporation.
   a. Acquired $10,000 cash from the issue of common stock.
   b. Borrowed $10,000 cash.
   c. Earned $5,000 revenue and received cash.

```
X Microsoft Excel - ch3-1.xls                                                    _ |□| X|
S] File  Edit  View  Insert  Format  Tools  Data  Window  Help                   _ |8| X|

D  🖻 🖫 🖨 🖪 ᵂ  🗶 🖻 🛍 ᵈ  🕁 ᵛ 🕁 ᵛ  🝾 🌑  Σ ƒⁿ ᴬ↓ ᶻ↓  🏦 🦉 🐓  100% ▾ 🔁
🖙 ψ ⋽ᶜ  🕂 🔒 🕂 🕮  Arial              ▾ 10 ▾  B  I  U  ▤ ▥ ▦ ▦  $ %  ,  ‰ ‰ ⋵ ⋵  ▭ ▾ 🞧 ▾ A ▾
      B5        ▾        = =B3+B4
        A            B   C   D    E    F        G   H        I    J    K    L    M    N    O    P
                  Total      Total      Stockholders'    Net
 1
 2                Assets  =  Liabilities  +  Equity          Income
 3  Original Amounts  100,000   40,000        60,000          20,000
 4  Transaction     10,000       0          10,000              0
 5  Revised Amounts  110,000    40,000        70,000          20,000
 6
 7      Ratios     Original    Revised
 8  Debt to Assets   40.00%   36.36%
 9  Debt to Equity   66.67%   57.14%
10  Return on Assets  20.00%   18.18%
11  Return on Equity  33.33%   28.57%
12
13
...
35
K ◄ ► N \ Problem /  Problem 3-1 Answer Key  / Sheet 2 / Sheet2 / Shee ◄          ►|
Ready                                                                        NUM
```

    d. Accrued $3,000 of expenses.

    e. Incurred and paid $3,000 of expenses.

Required

a. In row 4, enter the effect of Transaction *a* on both the accounting equation and net income.

b. Formulate the revised amounts in row 5 for each heading after considering the effect of Transaction *a* on the original amounts.

c. Design formulas for the ratios in Column D based on the Revised Amounts.

d. Enter the ratios for the Original and Revised Transaction *a* amounts in the following table.

		Ratios for Various Transactions				
Ratios	**Original**	*a*	*b*	*c*	*d*	*e*
Debt to Assets						
Equity to Assets						
Return on Assets						
Return on Equity						

e. Delete the effect of Transaction *a* in row 4. Enter the effect of Transaction *b* in row 4. Notice that Excel automatically recalculates the Revised Amounts and Ratios on your spreadsheet as the result of the changed data.

f. Continue to delete transactions in row 4 as completed and enter the effect of each subsequent transaction *c* through *e* one at a time. Enter the ratios for each independent transaction in the preceding table.

Spreadsheet Tip

1. Format percentages by choosing Format, Cells, and Percentage.

SPREADSHEET ASSIGNMENT *Mastering Excel*   ATC 3–9

a. Refer to Problem 3–22A. Using an Excel spreadsheet, prepare the financial statements as indicated. To complete Requirement *b* here, use formulas where normal arithmetic calculations are made in the financial statements.

b. It is interesting to speculate what would happen if certain operating results change for better or worse. After completing Requirement *a,* change certain account balances for each of the following independent operating adjustments. After each adjustment, note how the financial statements would differ if the change in operations were to occur. After the effect of each adjustment is noted, return the data to the original amounts in Problem 3–22A, and then go to the next operating adjustment.

In the following table, record the new amounts on the financial statements for the various operating changes listed.

	Original	1	2	3	4	5
Net Income						
Total Assets						
Total Liabilities						
Total Stockholders' Equity						
Total Liabilities & Stockholders' Equity						

Independent Operating Adjustments

1. Service Revenue increased $7,500. Assume that all services are provided on account.
2. Insurance Expense decreased $500. The related Prepaid Insurance account changed accordingly.
3. Supplies Expense decreased $100. The related Supplies account changed accordingly.
4. Depreciation Expense increased $300. The related Accumulated Depreciation account changed accordingly.
5. Dividends paid decreased $1,000 and the Cash account changed accordingly.

The Recording Process

Learning Objectives

After completing this chapter, you should be able to:

1 Explain the fundamental concepts associated with double-entry accounting systems.

2 Describe business events using debit/credit terminology.

3 Record transactions in T-accounts.

4 Identify the events that need adjusting entries and record them.

5 State the need for and record closing entries.

6 Prepare and interpret a trial balance.

7 Record transactions using the general journal format.

8 Describe the components of an annual report, including the management, discussion, and analysis (MD&A) section and the footnotes to financial statements.

9 Describe the role of the Securities and Exchange Commission (SEC) in financial reporting.

the *curious* accountant

As previously indicated, most companies prepare financial statements at least once a year. The year for which accounting records are maintained is called the company's **fiscal year.** This book usually assumes that the fiscal year is the same as a calendar year; that is, it ends on December 31. In practice, many companies have fiscal years that do not end on December 31. For example, Polo Ralph Lauren, a company that produces clothing, has a fiscal year that ends around March 31. The Limited, a company that sells clothing, has a fiscal year that ends on January 31. Why do you think these companies choose these dates to end their fiscal years?

The task of accounting for business activity becomes more complex as the size of the business increases. Double-entry accounting systems provide the structure necessary to maintain the records for complex as well as simple business organizations. This chapter discusses the fundamental concepts associated with double-entry accounting systems.

*A simplified accounting form known as a **T-account** is a good starting point for learning the recording procedures used in double-entry accounting systems. The account title is placed at the top of the horizontal bar of the T, and increases and decreases are placed on either side of the vertical bar. This account form omits the detailed information concerning a transaction and thereby permits observers to focus their attention on the accounting concepts. As a result, the T-account form is frequently used in the classroom, in textbooks, and in business discussions. However, it does not appear in the formal records of a business. It should be viewed simply as a convenient format that enhances communication.*

▌Debit/Credit Terminology

The left side of the T-account is referred to as the **debit** side, and the right side is called the **credit** side. It is common practice to abbreviate the terms *debit* and *credit* with the initials Dr. and Cr., respectively. Furthermore, it is customary to say that an account has been *debited* when an amount is placed on the left side of the account and *credited* when an amount is entered on the right side. For any given account, the difference between the debit and credit amounts is known as the **account balance.** An account can have either a debit or a credit balance.

The **double-entry accounting** system is designed so that total debits always equal total credits. Accordingly, the recording of each transaction can be checked for accuracy by verifying that the debits and credits are equal. Furthermore, the entire list of accounts can be checked by verifying that the total of all debit balances is equal to the total of all credit balances. However, this system cannot ensure complete accuracy. For example, although it may have been appropriate to make a debit entry, the accountant may select the wrong account when recording the debit. As a result, the debits and credits will be equal, but the records will be inaccurate. Although the system is not perfect, it has proved very effective in eliminating or reducing incomplete entries, transposed or incorrect amounts, and inaccurate entries to accounts.

The double-entry accounting system has two fundamental equality requirements: (1) The equality of the basic accounting equation (assets = claims) must be maintained and (2) total debits must equal total credits. A recording scheme that maintains these two equalities simultaneously is discussed now.

Suppose that a company borrows $1,000 from a bank. In accordance with the first equality requirement, assets and liabilities increase, thereby maintaining the equality of the accounting equation. If the increase in assets is recorded as a debit, the second equality rule (debits = credits) requires that the corresponding increase in liabilities be recorded as a credit. Therefore, the financing activity is recorded as a debit to Cash and a credit to Notes Payable. Similarly, increases in all asset accounts are recorded as debits, and increases in liability and equity accounts are recorded as credits. Extending the logic requires that decreases in asset accounts be recorded as credits and decreases in liability and equity accounts be recorded as debits. Accordingly, the repayment of the $1,000 debt is recorded with a debit to Notes Payable and a credit to Cash.

Other recording schemes could be devised to satisfy the two equality requirements. Such schemes could function with equal effectiveness. Accordingly, the establishment of the recording scheme is somewhat arbitrary. However, once established, the scheme must be followed by everyone if there is to be effective communication. It is useful to draw a parallel between the requirements of the recording process and those of a simpler system, such as a traffic light. It makes no difference whether *red* is defined as *go* or *stop;* what is important is that the users of the system agree on the definition. Similarly, the users of the double-entry accounting system must agree on the recording rules. In summary, these rules are as follow:

1. Debits increase assets and decrease liabilities and equity.
2. Credits increase liabilities and equity and decrease assets.

The rules for debits and credits are shown in T-account form here.

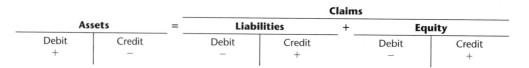

	Assets		=		Claims				
					Liabilities		+	Equity	
Debit +		Credit −		Debit −		Credit +		Debit −	Credit +

▌Collins Consultants Case

The rules for debits and credits will be demonstrated by recording the accounting events that affect a small business, Collins Consultants. Assume that Raymond Collins started his consulting practice on January 1, 2003. The accounting equation reflects zero assets and zero claims at the inception of the practice. The case utilizes the following format: Business events are introduced. The impact of each event is described in debit/credit terminology and then is visually demonstrated in T-account format. The effects of each event on the balance sheet, income statement, and statement of cash flows are shown in a horizontal statements model. The events are numbered, and the event number is used as a recording reference. Recall that accounting events can be divided into four categories. The transactions used in the Collins Consultants case are organized according to the following categories:

1. Asset source transactions
2. Asset exchange transactions
3. Asset use transactions
4. Claims exchange transactions

Asset Source Transactions

A business may obtain assets from three primary sources: (1) acquired from the owners, (2) borrowed from creditors, or (3) produced through operating activities. The debit/credit recording scheme is identical for all three source transactions. They all result in an increase to an asset account, which is recorded with a debit entry, and a corresponding increase in a claims account, which is recorded with a credit entry.

Event 1 Owners Provide Assets
Collins Consultants was established on January 1, 2003, when it acquired $15,000 cash from Collins.

This accounting event acts to increase assets and equity. The increase in assets (Cash) is recorded as a debit, and the increase in equity (Common Stock) as a credit. In T-account form, this transaction appears as follows:

Assets		=	Liabilities	+	Equity	
Cash					**Common Stock**	
Debit	Credit				Debit	Credit
+						+
(1) 15,000						15,000 (1)

The entry affects the elements of the financial statements as indicated:

Assets	=	Liab.	+	Equity	Rev.	−	Exp.	=	Net Inc.	Cash Flow
15,000	=	NA	+	15,000	NA	−	NA	=	NA	15,000 FA

Event 2 Creditor Provides Assets
On February 1, Collins Consultants borrowed $10,000 from National Bank.

Collins issued a note to the bank that obligated the company to pay 12 percent annual interest. The note carried a one-year term to maturity. Interest and principal were payable in cash at the maturity date. Since the party borrowing the money *issues* the note, that party is called the *issuer of a note,* as previously indicated. In this case, Collins Consultants is the issuer. From Collins's perspective, issuing the note in exchange for cash acts to increase assets and liabilities. The increase in assets (Cash) is recorded as a debit, and the increase in liabilities (Notes Payable) is recorded as a credit. After the transaction has been recorded, the T-accounts appear as follows:

Assets		=	Liabilities		+	Equity
Cash			**Notes Payable**			
Debit	Credit		Debit	Credit		
+				+		
(2) 10,000				10,000 (2)		

Because of space limitations, only the accounts affected by the particular event being analyzed are shown. Since Event 2 affects Cash and Notes Payable, these are the only two accounts shown. Collins's records still contain the Common Stock account created in Event 1, even though that account is not shown here. Furthermore, only the effects of the particular event being discussed are shown in the accounts. For example, even though the first transaction affected the Cash account, only the effects of the second transaction are shown in the T-account for Cash. The effects of each event are labeled with the event number shown in parentheses, in this case (2). This practice is continued throughout the chapter. Cumulative data for all accounts are shown later in this chapter.

The entry affects the elements of the financial statements as indicated:

Assets	=	Liab.	+	Equity	Rev.	–	Exp.	=	Net Inc.	Cash Flow
10,000	=	10,000	+	NA	NA	–	NA	=	NA	10,000 FA

Event 3 Creditor Provides Assets
On February 17, Collins Consultants purchased $850 of office supplies on account (agreed to pay for the supplies at a later date) from Morris Supply Company.

Purchasing the supplies on account acts to increase assets and liabilities. The increase in assets (Supplies) is recorded as a debit, and the increase in liabilities (Accounts Payable) is recorded as a credit. After the transaction is recorded, the T-accounts appear as follows:

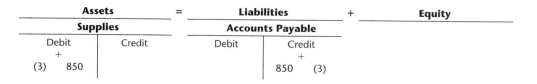

The entry affects the elements of the financial statements as indicated:

Assets	=	Liab.	+	Equity	Rev.	–	Exp.	=	Net Inc.	Cash Flow
850	=	850	+	NA	NA	–	NA	=	NA	NA

Event 4 Creditor Provides Assets
On February 28, Collins Consultants agreed to review the internal control structure of Kendall Food Stores. Kendall paid Collins $5,000 in advance for the services to be performed.

Although Collins Consultants is not required to pay Kendall Food Stores any cash, the firm is obligated to provide services to the food store. As a result, a liability will be converted to revenue. The liability is called *unearned revenue*. Recording the event acts to increase assets and liabilities. The increase in assets (Cash) is recorded as a debit, and the increase in liabilities (Unearned Revenue) is recorded as a credit. After the transaction is recorded, the T-accounts appear as follows:

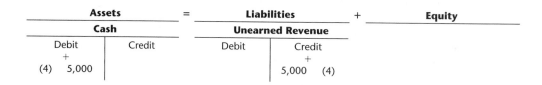

The entry affects the elements of the financial statements as indicated:

Assets	=	Liab.	+	Equity	Rev.	–	Exp.	=	Net Inc.	Cash Flow
5,000	=	5,000	+	NA	NA	+	NA	=	NA	5,000 OA

Event 5 Creditor Provides Assets

On March 1, Collins Consultants received $18,000 as a result of signing a contract that required Collins to provide advice to Harwood Corporation over the coming year.

The event acts to increase assets and liabilities. The increase in assets (Cash) is recorded as a debit, and the increase in liabilities (Unearned Revenue) is recorded as a credit. After the transaction is recorded, the T-accounts appear as follows:

Assets		=	Liabilities		+	Equity
Cash			**Unearned Revenue**			
Debit	Credit		Debit	Credit		
+				+		
(5) 18,000				18,000 (5)		

The entry affects the elements of the financial statements as indicated in the following statements model:

Assets	=	Liab.	+	Equity	Rev.	–	Exp.	=	Net Inc.	Cash Flow
18,000	=	18,000	+	NA	NA	–	NA	=	NA	18,000 OA

Event 6 Operating Activity Provides Assets

On April 10, Collins Consultants provided services on account (agreed to receive payment at a future date) to Rex Company.

Collins sent Rex a bill for the amount of $2,000. Recognition of the revenue acts to increase assets and equity. The increase in assets (Accounts Receivable) is recorded as a debit, and the increase in equity (Consulting Revenue) is recorded as a credit. After the transaction is recorded, the T-accounts appear as follows:

Assets		=	Liabilities	+	Equity	
Accounts Receivable					**Consulting Revenue**	
Debit	Credit				Debit	Credit
+						+
(6) 2,000						2,000 (6)

The entry affects the elements of the financial statements as indicated:

Assets	=	Liab.	+	Equity	Rev.	–	Exp.	=	Net Inc.	Cash Flow
2,000	=	NA	+	2,000	2,000	–	NA	=	2,000	NA

Event 7 Operating Activity Provides Assets

On April 29, Collins completed a two-week training seminar for which his company was paid $8,400 in cash.

Recognizing the revenue acts to increase assets and equity. The increase in assets (Cash) is recorded as a debit, and the increase in equity (Consulting Revenue) is recorded as a credit. After the transaction has been recorded, the T-accounts would appear as follows:

Assets	=	Liabilities	+	Equity

Cash				Consulting Revenue	
Debit	Credit			Debit	Credit
+					+
(7) 8,400					8,400 (7)

The entry affects the elements of the financial statements as indicated:

Assets	=	Liab.	+	Equity	Rev.	–	Exp.	=	Net Inc.	Cash Flow
8,400	=	NA	+	8,400	8,400	–	NA	=	8,400	8,400 OA

Summary of Asset Source Transactions

To facilitate your understanding of the application of the rules of debits and credits, it is helpful to emphasize that each of the preceding transactions supplied assets to the business. In each case, an asset and a corresponding claims account increased. Since debits are used to increase assets and credits are used to increase equities, each transaction resulted in a debit to an asset account and an offsetting credit to a liability or equity account. Other transactions that provide assets to a business are recorded similarly.

What are the three sources of assets? Which accounts are debited and credited when a business acquires an asset?

Answer The three sources of assets are creditors, investors, and earnings. When a company acquires an asset, the asset account is debited and the source account is credited. For example, if a company earns revenue on account, the receivables account is debited and the revenue account is credited.

Asset Exchange Transactions

Certain transactions involve an exchange of one asset for another asset. Because the decline in one asset account is offset by an increase in another asset account, the amount of total assets is unchanged by asset exchange transactions. Such transactions are recorded by crediting the account for the asset that decreased (the asset given) and debiting the account for the asset that increased (the asset obtained). In T-account form, the effects on the accounting equation appear as follows:

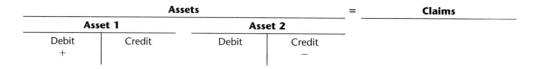

Assets				=	Claims
Asset 1		Asset 2			
Debit	Credit	Debit	Credit		
+			–		

Event 8 Exchange Cash for Note Receivable
On May 1, Collins Consultants loaned Reston Company $6,000. Reston issued a one-year note to Collins and agreed to pay a 9 percent annual rate of interest.

From Collins's perspective, the loan represents an investment in Reston. Recognizing the loan (investment) acts to increase one asset account and decrease another. The increase in assets (Notes Receivable) is recorded as a debit, and the decrease in assets (Cash) is recorded as a credit. After the transaction is recorded, the T-accounts appear as follows:

Assets		=	Claims

Notes Receivable

Debit	Credit
+	
(8) 6,000	

Cash

Debit	Credit
	−
	6,000 (8)

The entry would affect the elements of the financial statements as indicated:

Assets			= Liab.	+ Equity	Rev.	− Exp.	= Net Inc.	Cash Flow
Cash	+	**Note Rec.**						
(6,000)	+	6,000	= NA	+ NA	NA	− NA	= NA	(6,000) IA

Event 9 Exchange Cash for Office Equipment
On June 30, Collins paid cash to purchase $42,000 of office equipment for his business.

The equipment was expected to have a five-year useful life and a $2,000 salvage value. The purchase of equipment acts to increase one asset account and decrease another. The increase in assets (Office Equipment) is recorded as a debit, and the decrease in assets (Cash) is recorded as a credit. After the transaction is recorded, the T-accounts appear as follows:

Assets		=	Claims

Office Equipment

Debit	Credit
+	
(9) 42,000	

Cash

Debit	Credit
	−
	42,000 (9)

The entry affects the elements of the financial statements as indicated:

Assets			= Liab.	+ Equity	Rev.	− Exp.	= Net Inc.	Cash Flow
Cash	+	**Office Equip.**						
(42,000)	+	42,000	= NA	+ NA	NA	− NA	= NA	(42,000) IA

Event 10 Exchange Cash for Prepaid Rent
On July 31, Collins entered into a contract with the owner of a building to rent office space.

Collins paid $3,600 cash in advance for rent for the coming year. The advance payment for rent acts to increase one asset account and to decrease another. The increase in assets (Prepaid Rent) is recorded as a debit, and the decrease in assets (Cash) is recorded as a credit. After the transaction is recorded, the T-accounts appear as follows:

Assets		=	Claims

Prepaid Rent

Debit	Credit
+	
(10) 3,600	

Cash

Debit	Credit
	−
	3,600 (10)

The entry affects the elements of the financial statements as indicated:

Assets			= Liab.	+ Equity	Rev.	− Exp.	= Net Inc.	Cash Flow
Cash	+	**Pr Pd Rent**						
(3,600)	+	3,600	= NA	+ NA	NA	− NA	= NA	(3,600) OA

Event 11   Exchange Receivable for Cash
On August 8, Collins Consultants collected a $1,200 partial payment on the receivable from Rex Company (see Event 6).

The collection acts to increase one asset account and to decrease another. The increase in assets (Cash) is recorded as a debit, and the decrease in assets (Accounts Receivable) is recorded as a credit. After the transaction is recorded, the T-accounts appear as follows:

Assets				=	Claims
Cash		**Accounts Receivable**			
Debit	Credit	Debit	Credit		
+			−		
(11) 1,200			1,200 (11)		

The entry affects the elements of the financial statements as indicated:

Assets			=	Liab.	+	Equity	Rev.	−	Exp.	=	Net Inc.	Cash Flow
Cash	+	Acct. Rec.										
1,200	+	(1,200)	=	NA	+	NA	NA	−	NA	=	NA	1,200 OA

Summary of Asset Exchange Transactions

Events 8–11 represent exchanges of assets. In each case, one asset account is increased and another is decreased. The increase in the asset account is recorded with a debit entry, and the decrease in the other asset account is recorded with a credit entry. The amounts of total assets and total claims are unaffected by these transactions.

Asset Use Transactions

There are three primary purposes for the use of assets. First, a company may use assets in the process of producing revenue. Recall that assets used to produce revenue are called *expenses.* Second, assets may be used to pay off liabilities. Third, a business may want to transfer some of the assets generated by its operating activities to the owners. Assets used for this purpose are called *dividends.* The debit/credit recording scheme for all three asset use transactions results in a credit to an asset account and a debit to a claims account. Both assets and claims decrease.

Event 12   Assets Used to Produce Revenue (Expenses)
On September 4, Collins Consultants paid $2,400 for salaries of employees who worked part-time for the company.

Recognizing the expense acts to decrease assets and equity. The decrease in assets (Cash) is recorded as a credit, and the decrease in equity (Salaries Expense) is recorded as a debit. After the transaction is recorded, the T-accounts appear as follows:

Assets		=	Liabilities	+	Equity	
Cash					**Salaries Expense**	
Debit	Credit				Debit	Credit
	−				+ Expense	
	2,400 (12)				− Equity	
					(12) 2,400	

Observe carefully that the debit entry has a dual effect on the equity elements. If Collins were to pay additional salaries, this amount would be added (debited) to the Salaries Expense account. Accordingly, debit entries act to increase expense accounts. However, expenses act to decrease equity. As a result, debits to expense accounts are considered additions to the ultimate reduction in equity. In summary, debits act to increase expenses, and expenses act to reduce equity.

The entry affects the elements of the financial statements as indicated:

Assets	=	Liab.	+	Equity	Rev.	–	Exp.	=	Net Inc.	Cash Flow
(2,400)	=	NA	+	(2,400)	NA	–	2,400	=	(2,400)	(2,400) OA

Event 13 Assets Transferred to Owners (Dividends)
On September 20, Collins Consultants paid a $1,500 cash dividend to its owner.

Recognizing the dividend acts to decrease assets and equity. The decrease in assets (Cash) is recorded as a credit, and the decrease in equity (Dividends) is recorded as a debit. After the transaction is recorded, the T-accounts appear as follows:

Assets	=	Liabilities	+	Equity
Cash				**Dividends**

Debit	Credit		Debit	Credit
	–		+ Div.	
	1,500 (13)		– Equity	
			(13) 1,500	

The debit entry can be viewed as an increase (+) in the dividends account or a decrease (−) in equity. The traditional practice is to view the debit as an increase in the dividends account. Accordingly, it is said that debit entries increase the dividends account. The total balance in the dividends account then acts to reduce equity (Retained Earnings).

The entry affects the elements of the financial statements as indicated:

Assets	=	Liab.	+	Equity	Rev.	–	Exp.	=	Net Inc.	Cash Flow
(1,500)	=	NA	+	(1,500)	NA	–	NA	=	NA	(1,500) FA

Event 14 Assets Used to Pay Liabilities
On October 10, Collins Consultants paid the $850 owed to Morris Supply Company (see Event 3).

Recognizing the cash payment acts to decrease assets and liabilities. The decrease in assets (Cash) is recorded as a credit, and the decrease in liabilities (Accounts Payable) is recorded as a debit. After the transaction is recorded, the T-accounts appear as follows:

Assets	=	Liabilities	+	Equity
Cash		**Accounts Payable**		

Debit	Credit	Debit	Credit	
	–	–		
	850 (14)	(14) 850		

The entry affects the elements of the financial statements as indicated:

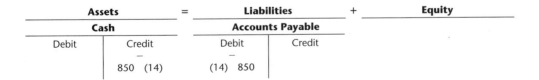

Assets	=	Liab.	+	Equity	Rev.	–	Exp.	=	Net Inc.	Cash Flow
(850)	=	(850)	+	NA	NA	–	NA	=	NA	(850) OA

Summary of Asset Use Transactions

Each of these transactions acted to reduce assets and either liabilities or equity. Debit entries increased expense and dividends accounts. The total balances in these accounts then acted to reduce equity. Each entry for asset use transactions required a debit to a liability or an equity account and a credit to an asset account.

Claims Exchange Transactions

Certain transactions involve an exchange of one claims account for another claims account. The amount of total claims is unaffected by these transactions because the decrease in one account is offset by an increase in another account. Such transactions are recorded by debiting one claims account and crediting the other.

Event 15 Recognition of Revenue (Unearned to Earned)
On November 15, Collins completed the work for the review of the internal control structure of Kendall Food Stores (see Event 4).

Kendall accepted Collins's report and expressed satisfaction with the services performed. The original contract price was $5,000. Recognition of the revenue acts to decrease liabilities and to increase equity. The decrease in liabilities (Unearned Revenue) is recorded as a debit, and the increase in equity (Consulting Revenue) is recorded as a credit. After the transaction is recorded, the T-accounts appear as follows:

Assets	=	Liabilities	+	Equity
		Unearned Revenue		**Consulting Revenue**
		Debit	Credit	Debit	Credit
		−			+
		(15) 5,000			5,000 (15)

The entry affects the elements of the financial statements as indicated:

Assets	=	Liab.	+	Equity	Rev.	−	Exp.	=	Net Inc.	Cash Flow
NA	=	(5,000)	+	5,000	5,000	−	NA	=	5,000	NA

Event 16 Recognition of Expense
On December 18, Collins Consultants received a $900 bill from Creative Ads for advertisements placed in regional magazines.

Collins plans to pay the bill later. The event acts to increase liabilities and to decrease equity. The increase in liabilities (Accounts Payable) is recorded as a credit, and the decrease in equity (Advertising Expense) is recorded as a debit. After the transaction is recorded, the T-accounts appear as follows:

Assets	=	Liabilities	+	Equity
		Accounts Payable		**Advertising Expense**
		Debit	Credit	Debit	Credit
			+	+ Expense	
			900 (16)	− Equity	
				(16) 900	

The entry affects the elements of the financial statements as indicated:

Assets	=	Liab.	+	Equity	Rev.	−	Exp.	=	Net Inc.	Cash Flow
NA	=	900	+	(900)	NA	−	900	=	(900)	NA

Summary of Claims Exchange Transactions

The two preceding transactions reflect exchanges on the claims side of the accounting equation. In each case, one claims account was debited, and another claims account was credited. Total claims and total assets were unaffected by the transactions.

Adjustments for Accruals

Assume that the preceding 16 events described represent all accounting events that affected Collins Consultants during 2003. As previously indicated, accrual accounting requires the recognition of revenues and expenses in the period in which they are earned or incurred, regardless of when cash changes hands. Collins's accounts were affected by three accruals during 2003. Since Collins has both notes receivable and notes payable that require accruals for interest, it is necessary to recognize interest revenue and interest expense in the adjusting process. Also, there is an unrecorded transaction for accrued salaries that is discussed in this section of the text.

LO4 Identify the events that need adjusting entries and record them.

Asset/Revenue Adjustments

When Collins Consultants loaned Reston Company $6,000, Reston agreed to pay Collins interest for the privilege of using the money. The interest is expressed as a percentage of the amount borrowed for a designated time. Accordingly, as time passes, the amount of interest due increases. The accrual acts to increase assets and revenue on Collins's books. Thus, the adjustment made to reflect the accrual of revenue is called an **asset/revenue adjustment.**

Adjustment 1 **Accrual of Interest Revenue**
Collins Consultants loaned Reston the $6,000 on May 1 at an annual interest rate of 9 percent (see Event 8).

As a result, Collins earned $360 ([$6,000 × 0.09] × [8/12]) in interest revenue during 2003. The required adjusting entry acts to increase assets and equity. The increase in assets (Interest Receivable) is recorded as a debit, and the increase in equity (Interest Revenue) is recorded as a credit. After the transaction has been recorded, the T-accounts would appear as follows:

Assets		=	Liabilities	+	Equity	
Interest Receivable					**Interest Revenue**	
Debit	Credit				Debit	Credit
+						+
(A1) 360						360 (A1)

Note that the transaction is labeled (A1). This notation is used to represent the first adjusting entry. The second adjusting entry is labeled (A2). Subsequent entries follow this referencing scheme.

The adjustment affects the elements of the financial statements as indicated:

Assets	=	Liab.	+	Equity	Rev.	−	Exp.	=	Net Inc.	Cash Flow
360	=	NA	+	360	360	−	NA	=	360	NA

Liability/Expense Adjustments

When Collins Consultants borrowed funds from National Bank, Collins agreed to pay the bank interest. As with interest revenue, interest expense increases with the length of time for which the money is borrowed. The increase in interest expense is offset by a corresponding increase in liabilities. Accordingly, the adjustments made to reflect the accrual of expenses are called **liability/expense adjustments.**

Adjustment 2 **Accrual of Interest Expense**
On February 1, Collins Consultants borrowed $10,000 from National Bank at a 12 percent annual interest rate (see Event 2).

Interest expense on the note for the 2003 accounting period amounts to $1,100 ([$10,000 $\times$ 0.12] $\times$ [11/12]). The required adjusting entry acts to increase liabilities and to decrease equity. The increase in liabilities (Interest Payable) is recorded as a credit, and the decrease in equity (Interest Expense) is recorded as a debit. After the transaction is recorded, the T-accounts appear as follows:

Assets	=	Liabilities	+	Equity
		Interest Payable		**Interest Expense**
		Debit | Credit		Debit | Credit
		| +		+ Expense |
		| 1,100 (A2)		− Equity |
				(A2) 1,100 |

The adjustment affects the elements of the financial statements as indicated:

Assets	=	Liab.	+	Equity	Rev.	−	Exp.	=	Net Inc.	Cash Flow
NA	=	1,100	+	(1,100)	NA	−	1,100	=	(1,100)	NA

Adjustment 3 **Accrual of Salary Expense**
Another common liability/expense adjustment involves accrued but unpaid salaries.

Note that the last time Collins Consultants paid salaries was on September 4 (see Event 12). Assume that Collins owes $800 to part-time employees for work they performed during 2003. Collins agreed to pay these salaries in 2004 when the projects on which the employees worked will be completed. The required adjusting entry acts to increase liabilities and to decrease equity. The increase in liabilities (Salaries Payable) is recorded as a credit, and the decrease in equity (Salaries Expense) is recorded as a debit. After the transaction is recorded, the T-accounts appear as follows:

Assets	=	Liabilities	+	Equity
		Salaries Payable		**Salaries Expense**
		Debit | Credit		Debit | Credit
		| +		+ Expense |
		| 800 (A3)		− Equity |
				(A3) 800 |

The adjustment affects the elements of the financial statements as indicated:

Assets	=	Liab.	+	Equity	Rev.	−	Exp.	=	Net Inc.	Cash Flow
NA	=	800	+	(800)	NA	−	800	=	(800)	NA

Adjustments for Deferrals

As indicated in Chapter 3, deferrals involve revenue and expense recognition that succeeds (comes after) the cash realizations. During 2003, Collins Consultants was affected by four deferrals. Cash was paid for office equipment, prepaid rent, and supplies, but no expenses were recognized to reflect the use of these resources during the accounting periods. Also, cash was collected for services provided, but revenue was not recognized. Each of these four deferrals requires adjustments on Collins's books to reflect the appropriate recognition of revenue and expenses for the 2003 fiscal year.

Asset/Expense Adjustments

When Collins acquired the equipment, rent, and supplies, their costs were placed in asset accounts. At the end of the accounting period, the portion of the costs that represents used resources must be removed from the asset accounts and placed into expense accounts. Since the entry involves an asset account and an expense account, it is referred to as an **asset/expense adjustment.** Three asset/expense adjustments are shown next.

Adjustment 4 Equipment Used to Produce Revenue (Depreciation Expense)
Since the office equipment was purchased on June 30, it was used for one-half of the year (see Event 9).

Accordingly, the depreciation expense amounts to $4,000 ([$42,000 − $2,000] ÷ 5 = $8,000 ÷ 2 = $4,000). The adjusting entry necessary to record depreciation acts to decrease assets and equity. The decrease in assets (office equipment) is recorded as a credit to the contra asset account Accumulated Depreciation; and the decrease in equity (Depreciation Expense) is recorded as a debit. After the transaction is recorded, the T-accounts appear as follows:

Assets	=	Liabilities	+	Equity	
Accumulated Depreciation				**Depreciation Expense**	
Debit	Credit			Debit	Credit
	+ Acc. Depr.			+ Expense	
	− Assets			− Equity	
	4,000 (A4)			(A4) 4,000	

The plus sign in the Accumulated Depreciation account indicates that the balance in this account increases when additional amounts of depreciation are credited to the account. Accordingly, credit entries act to increase accumulated depreciation. However, increases in the Accumulated Depreciation account act to reduce total assets. Since the Accumulated Depreciation account has a balance that is opposite the normal asset balances, it is called a **contra account.**

The adjustment affects the elements of the financial statements as indicated:

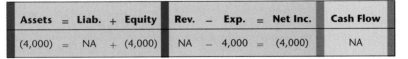

Assets	=	Liab.	+	Equity	Rev.	−	Exp.	=	Net Inc.	Cash Flow
(4,000)	=	NA	+	(4,000)	NA	−	4,000	=	(4,000)	NA

Adjustment 5 Office Space Used to Produce Revenue (Rent Expense)
On July 31, Collins paid $3,600 in advance for a one-year lease of office space (see Event 10).

The monthly rate of $300 ($3,600 ÷ 12 months) is multiplied by the five months for which the office was *used* during 2003 to determine the amount of rent expense ($300 × 5 = $1,500). Recognition of the rent expense acts to decrease assets and equity. The decrease in assets (Prepaid Rent) is recorded as a credit, and the decrease in equity (Rent Expense) is recorded as a debit. After the transaction is recorded, the T-accounts appear as follows:

Assets	=	Liabilities	+	Equity	
Prepaid Rent				**Rent Expense**	
Debit	Credit			Debit	Credit
	−			+ Expense	
	1,500 (A5)			− Equity	
				(A5) 1,500	

The adjustment affects the elements of the financial statements as indicated:

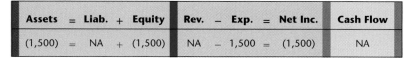

Assets	=	Liab.	+	Equity	Rev.	−	Exp.	=	Net Inc.	Cash Flow
(1,500)	=	NA	+	(1,500)	NA	−	1,500	=	(1,500)	NA

Adjustment 6 Supplies Used to Produce Revenue (Supplies Expense)
Assume that a physical count indicates that $125 worth of supplies is on hand at the end of the accounting period (see Event 3).

Accordingly, $725 ($850 − $125) of supplies must have been used during the period. The recognition of the supplies expense acts to decrease assets and equity. The decrease in assets (Supplies) is recorded as a credit and the decrease in equity (Supplies Expense) is recorded as a debit. After the transaction is recorded, the T-accounts appear as follows:

Assets	=	Liabilities	+	Equity
Supplies				**Supplies Expense**

Debit	Credit			Debit	Credit
	−			+ Expense	
	725 (A6)			− Equity	
				(A6) 725	

The adjustment affects the elements of the financial statements as indicated:

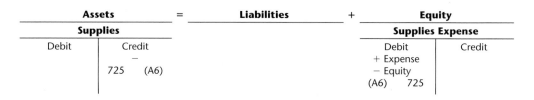

Assets	=	Liab.	+	Equity	Rev.	−	Exp.	=	Net Inc.	Cash Flow
(725)	=	NA	+	(725)	NA	−	725	=	(725)	NA

Liability/Revenue Adjustments

When the cash was received from Harwood Corporation in Event 5, Collins recorded the receipt as a liability to reflect the obligation to provide services over the one-year contract period. By the end of the accounting period, Collins would have provided some of the services that it had obligated itself to perform. Accordingly, an amount of revenue representing the services provided must be recognized by transferring that amount from the liability to the revenue account. Since the entry involves a liability and a revenue account, it is referred to as a **liability/revenue adjustment.**

Adjustment 7 Recognition of Revenue (Unearned to Earned)
On March 1, Collins Consultants received $18,000 as a result of signing a contract that required Collins to provide services to Harwood Corporation for a one-year period (see Event 5).

By December 31, 2003, Collins would have provided Harwood services for 10 months. Accordingly, $15,000 ($18,000 ÷ 12 = $1,500 × 10 = $15,000) of the obligation would have been satisfied during 2003. This amount must be removed from the Unearned Revenue (liability) account and placed into the Consulting Revenue account. The recognition of the revenue acts to decrease liabilities and to increase equity. The decrease in liabilities (Unearned Revenue) is recorded as a debit, and the increase in equity (Consulting Revenue) is recorded as a credit. After the transaction is recorded, the T-accounts appear as follows:

Assets	=	Liabilities	+	Equity
		Unearned Revenue		**Consulting Revenue**

Debit	Credit			Debit	Credit
Debit	Credit			Debit	Credit
	−				+
(A7) 15,000					15,000 (A7)

The adjustment affects the elements of the financial statements as indicated in the following statements model:

Assets	=	Liab.	+	Equity	Rev.	−	Exp.	=	Net Inc.	Cash Flow
NA	=	(15,000)	+	15,000	15,000	−	NA	=	15,000	NA

Can an asset exchange transaction be an adjusting entry?

Answer No. Adjusting entries always involve revenue or expense accounts. Since an asset exchange transaction involves only asset accounts, it cannot be an adjusting entry.

Check Yourself 4–2

Overview of Debit/Credit Relationships

A review of the transactions presented in this chapter reveals the relationships shown in Panel A, Exhibit 4–1. These relationships are also depicted in T-account form in Panel B. Debit/credit terminology is essential to the communication of accounting information. Practice using the termi-

LO2 Describe business events using debit/credit terminology.

Exhibit 4–1 *Debit/Credit Relationships*

Panel A

Account	Debits	Credits
Assets	Increase	Decrease
Contra Assets	Decrease	Increase
Liabilities	Decrease	Increase
Equity	Decrease	Increase
Common Stock	Decrease	Increase
Revenue	Decrease	Increase
Expenses	Increase	Decrease
Dividends	Increase	Decrease

Panel B

Assets		=	Liabilities		+	Equity	
Debit	Credit		Debit	Credit		Debit	Credit
+	−		−	+		−	+

Contra Assets	
Debit	Credit
+ Assets	− Assets
− Contra	+ Contra

Common Stock	
Debit	Credit
−	+

Revenue	
Debit	Credit
−	+

Expense	
Debit	Credit
− Equity	+ Equity
+ Exp.	− Exp.

Dividends	
Debit	Credit
− Equity	+ Equity
+ Div.	− Div.

nology until it becomes a natural part of your vocabulary. It is very important for you to establish a solid foundation early so you can easily incorporate new concepts into your base of knowledge.

▌Summary of T-Accounts

LO3 Record transactions in T-accounts.

Exhibit 4–2 is a summary of the accounts affected by the preceding transactions. It is important to verify that the application of the recording scheme has resulted in the satisfaction of the two equality requirements. In recording each transaction, debits were always equal to credits. Furthermore, each transaction was recorded in accordance with the requirement that total assets equal total claims. As a result, the total of all asset balances amounted to $48,635, which is equal to the total amount of all balances in the liability and equity accounts. Note that the balance of an account is located on the plus (increase) side of that account. As a result, asset, dividend, and expense accounts are said to carry *debit balances;* liability, equity, and revenue accounts are said to carry *credit balances.*

▌The Ledger

LO1 Explain the fundamental concepts associated with double-entry accounting systems.

A collection of accounts as in Exhibit 4–2 is commonly referred to as a **ledger.** In manual systems, a ledger may be a book containing pages that represent accounts. Transaction information is recorded on the books by hand. In more sophisticated systems, a set of magnetic tapes may constitute the ledger. Input of transaction information to this type of ledger may be provided by electronic keyboards or scanners. Ledger accounts are generally assigned a name and a number that are descriptive of certain classifications of data. The accounts are frequently listed in the ledger according to the sequence of their numbers. A list of the various accounts and their corresponding account numbers, which are contained in the ledger, is called a **chart of accounts.** Since it contains all accounts, the ledger is the primary information source for the financial statements.

▌The General Journal

LO1 Explain the fundamental concepts associated with double-entry accounting systems.

As business activity expands, it becomes increasingly difficult to enter transaction data directly into ledger accounts. For example, think about the number of entries that would be required to record a single day's cash transactions for a large grocery store. If customers were required to wait for the cashier to make a formal entry to ledger accounts for every food item sold, lines would become so long that shopping would be discouraged and the store would lose business. To simplify the record-keeping process, transaction data are usually recorded by nonaccounting personnel on general-purpose business documents before the data are transferred to the accounting department. For example, a salesclerk may record data about a sales transaction on a cash register tape. The tape then becomes a **source document** that the accountant uses to enter the transaction data into the accounting system. Other examples of source documents include invoices, time cards, check stubs, and cash receipts.

Ledger accounts contain information about a particular part of a transaction. For example, a debit in the ledger account for Cash indicates that cash increased. However, it does not identify the cause of the increase, nor does it explain when the increase occurred in relation to the timing of other transactions. To maintain a *complete chronological record* (a record arranged in order of time) of all business transactions, accountants initially record the data from source documents in a **journal.** In other words, *information is recorded in journals before it is entered in the ledger accounts.* Accordingly, journals are frequently referred to as the **books of original entry.**

A single company may use several different journals to maintain a chronological record of accounting events. Most transactions are recorded in a **general journal.** However, **special journals** could be used to record repetitive transactions that occur frequently. For example, a journal could be specially designed to record only transactions involving sales on account. A different journal could be used to record receipts of cash. Special journals are frequently

Exhibit 4–2 *Ledger Accounts*

Assets	=	Liabilities	+	Equity

Assets

Cash

(1)	15,000	6,000	(8)
(2)	10,000	42,000	(9)
(4)	5,000	3,600	(10)
(5)	18,000	2,400	(12)
(7)	8,400	1,500	(13)
(11)	1,200	850	(14)
Bal.	1,250		

Accounts Receivable

(6)	2,000	1,200	(11)
Bal.	800		

Supplies

(3)	850	725	(A6)
Bal.	125		

Prepaid Rent

(10)	3,600	1,500	(A5)
Bal.	2,100		

Notes Receivable

(8)	6,000	
Bal.	6,000	

Interest Receivable

(A1)	360	
Bal.	360	

Office Equipment

(9)	42,000	
Bal.	42,000	

Accumulated Depreciation

		4,000	(A4)
		4,000	Bal.

Liabilities

Accounts Payable

(14)	850	850	(3)
		900	(16)
		900	Bal.

Unearned Revenue

(15)	5,000	5,000	(4)
(A7)	15,000	18,000	(5)
		3,000	Bal.

Notes Payable

	10,000	(2)
	10,000	Bal.

Interest Payable

	1,100	(A2)
	1,100	Bal.

Salaries Payable

	800	(A3)
	800	Bal.

Equity

Common Stock

	15,000	(1)
	15,000	Bal.

Consulting Revenue

	2,000	(6)
	8,400	(7)
	5,000	(15)
	15,000	(A7)
	30,400	Bal.

Interest Revenue

	360	(A1)
	360	Bal.

Salaries Expense

(12)	2,400	
(A3)	800	
Bal.	3,200	

Advertising Expense

(16)	900	
Bal.	900	

Interest Expense

(A2)	1,100	
Bal.	1,100	

Depreciation Expense

(A4)	4,000	
Bal.	4,000	

Rent Expense

(A5)	1,500	
Bal.	1,500	

Supplies Expense

(A6)	725	
Bal.	725	

Dividends

(13)	1,500	
Bal.	1,500	

Total Assets	=	Total Liabilities	+	Total Equity
		15,800		32,835
		Total Claims		
48,635		48,635		

Do all accounting systems require the use of debits and credits? The answer is a definite no. Indeed, many small businesses use a single-entry system. A checkbook constitutes a sufficient accounting system for many business owners. Deposits represent revenues, and payments constitute expenses. Many excellent automated accounting systems do not require data entry through a debit/credit recording scheme. Quick Books is a good example of this type of system. Data are entered into the Quick Books software program through a user-friendly computer interface that does not require knowledge of debit/credit terminology. Even so, the Quick Books program produces traditional financial reports such as an income statement, balance sheet, and statement of cash flows. How is this possible? Before you become too ingrained in the debit/credit system, recall that throughout the first three chapters of this text, we maintained accounting records without using debits and credits. Financial reports can be produced in many ways without using a double-entry system. Having recognized this point, we also note the fact that the vast majority of medium- to large-size companies use the double-entry system. Indeed, debit/credit terminology is a part of common culture. Most people have an understanding of what is happening when a business tells them that their account is being debited or credited. Accordingly, it is important for you to embrace the double-entry system as well as other financial reporting systems.

named to be consistent with the types of transactions recorded in them. The journal used to record purchases on account may be called a *purchases journal*. Likewise, cash payments may be recorded in a *cash payments journal*.

After complete transaction data have been recorded in a journal, portions of the data are summarized and transferred to the ledger accounts. For example, the total amount of many cash transactions that were recorded individually in a cash receipts journal may be posted as a single debit to the Cash account in the general ledger. The process of transferring information from journals to ledgers is called **posting.** After the information has been posted to the ledger accounts, the respective debit and credit balances of the accounts are determined and tested for equality. Finally, the ledger account balances are used to prepare financial statements. Accordingly, the recording process is composed of five steps: (1) preparing and analyzing source documents, (2) journalizing the transaction data selected from the analysis of the source documents, (3) posting the transaction data from the journals to ledger accounts, (4) determining balances of the ledger accounts and testing the equality of debits and credits, and (5) using the ledger account balances to prepare financial statements.

An increasing number of companies are using computer technology to facilitate the process of recording transaction data and preparing financial statements. Although the computer can accomplish the required work at incredible speed with unparalleled accuracy, it follows the same basic five-step sequence that is used in manual systems. Accordingly, the analysis of a simple manual accounting system can provide significant insight into the more complex operation of computer-based systems. In recognition of this point, the following section demonstrates the recording procedures used in a simple manual accounting system.

LO7 Record transactions using the general journal format.

The illustration uses a general journal. While *special journals* can facilitate the recording process, their use is not required. As in the case described later, all transactions can be recorded in the *general journal*. At a minimum, the general journal provides space for the date, account titles, and amount of each transaction. Exhibit 4–3 shows the typical format used in a general journal; it contains entries for all transactions discussed thus far for Collins Con-

Exhibit 4–3 *General Journal*

Date		Account Titles	Debit	Credit
Jan.	1	Cash	15,000	
		Common Stock		15,000
Feb.	1	Cash	10,000	
		Notes Payable		10,000
	17	Supplies	850	
		Accounts Payable		850
	28	Cash	5,000	
		Unearned Revenue		5,000
Mar.	1	Cash	18,000	
		Unearned Revenue		18,000
April	10	Accounts Receivable	2,000	
		Consulting Revenue		2,000
	29	Cash	8,400	
		Consulting Revenue		8,400
May	1	Notes Receivable	6,000	
		Cash		6,000
June	30	Office Equipment	42,000	
		Cash		42,000
July	31	Prepaid Rent	3,600	
		Cash		3,600
Aug.	8	Cash	1,200	
		Accounts Receivable		1,200
Sept.	4	Salaries Expense	2,400	
		Cash		2,400
	20	Dividends	1,500	
		Cash		1,500
Oct.	10	Accounts Payable	850	
		Cash		850
Nov.	15	Unearned Revenue	5,000	
		Consulting Revenue		5,000
Dec.	18	Advertising Expense	900	
		Accounts Payable		900
		Adjusting Entries		
Dec.	31	Interest Receivable	360	
		Interest Revenue		360
	31	Interest Expense	1,100	
		Interest Payable		1,100
	31	Salaries Expense	800	
		Salaries Payable		800
	31	Depreciation Expense	4,000	
		Accumulated Depreciation		4,000
	31	Rent Expense	1,500	
		Prepaid Rent		1,500
	31	Supplies Expense	725	
		Supplies		725
	31	Unearned Revenue	15,000	
		Consulting Revenue		15,000

sultants. The date of the transaction is recorded in the first column. The account to be debited is written first at the extreme left edge of the column provided for the account titles. The account to be credited is indented and placed on the line directly below the account to be debited. The money amount of the transaction is recorded in the Debit and Credit columns on the same lines with their respective account titles.

Financial Statements

The general ledger contains the information necessary to prepare the financial statements for Collins Consultants. The income statement, statement of changes in equity, balance sheet, and statement of cash flows are shown in Exhibits 4–4, 4–5, 4–6, and 4–7.

Exhibit 4–4

COLLINS CONSULTANTS
Income Statement
For the Year Ended December 31, 2003

Revenue		
Consulting Revenue	$30,400	
Interest Revenue	360	
Total Revenue		$30,760
Less Expenses		
Salaries Expense	3,200	
Advertising Expense	900	
Interest Expense	1,100	
Depreciation Expense	4,000	
Rent Expense	1,500	
Supplies Expense	725	
Total Expenses		(11,425)
Net Income		$19,335

Exhibit 4–5

COLLINS CONSULTANTS
Statement of Changes in Equity
For the Year Ended December 31, 2003

Beginning Common Stock	$ 0	
Plus: Stock Issued	15,000	
Ending Common Stock		$15,000
Beginning Retained Earnings	0	
Plus: Net Income	19,335	
Less: Dividends	(1,500)	
Ending Retained Earnings		17,835
Total Equity		$32,835

Exhibit 4–6

COLLINS CONSULTANTS
Balance Sheet
As of December 31, 2003

Assets			
Cash		$ 1,250	
Accounts Receivable		800	
Supplies		125	
Prepaid Rent		2,100	
Notes Receivable		6,000	
Interest Receivable		360	
Office Equipment	$42,000		
Less: Accumulated Depreciation	(4,000)	38,000	
Total Assets			$48,635
Liabilities			
Accounts Payable		$ 900	
Unearned Revenue		3,000	
Notes Payable		10,000	
Interest Payable		1,100	
Salaries Payable		800	
Total Liabilities			$15,800
Equity			
Common Stock		15,000	
Retained Earnings		17,835	
Total Equity			32,835
Total Liabilities and Equity			$48,635

Exhibit 4–7

COLLINS CONSULTANTS
Statement of Cash Flows
For the Year Ended December 31, 2003

Cash Flow from Operating Activities		
Inflow from Customers*	$32,600	
Outflow for Rent	(3,600)	
Outflow for Salaries	(2,400)	
Outflow for Supplies	(850)	
Net Cash Inflow from Operations		$25,750
Cash Flow from Investing Activities		
Outflow for Loan	(6,000)	
Outflow to Purchase Equipment	(42,000)	
Net Cash Outflow from Investing		(48,000)
Cash Flow from Financing Activities		
Inflow from Issue of Stock	15,000	
Inflow from Borrowing	10,000	
Outflow for Dividends	(1,500)	
Net Cash Inflow from Financing		23,500
Net Change in Cash		1,250
Plus: Beginning Cash Balance		0
Ending Cash Balance		$ 1,250

*The sum of cash inflows from Events 4, 5, 7, and 11.

Closing Entries

Exhibit 4–8 shows the **closing entries** for Collins Consultants in general journal form. After the closing entries are posted to the ledger accounts, the revenue, expense, and dividends accounts have zero balances. The closing process clears the nominal accounts of all 2003 information and therefore readies them for use during the 2004 fiscal year.

LO5 State the need for and record closing entries.

Suppose that all companies close their books on December 31 of each year. Under these circumstances, the demand for financial reporting services would cluster around one specific time period. Accountants, printers, lawyers, government agencies, and others who work with the production and distribution of annual reports would be caught in a year-end bottleneck that

Exhibit 4–8 *Closing Entries*

Date	Account Titles	Debit	Credit
	Closing Entries		
Dec. 31	Consulting Revenue	30,400	
	Interest Revenue	360	
	Retained Earnings		30,760
31	Retained Earnings	11,425	
	Salaries Expense		3,200
	Advertising Expense		900
	Interest Expense		1,100
	Depreciation Expense		4,000
	Rent Expense		1,500
	Supplies Expense		725
31	Retained Earnings	1,500	
	Dividends		1,500

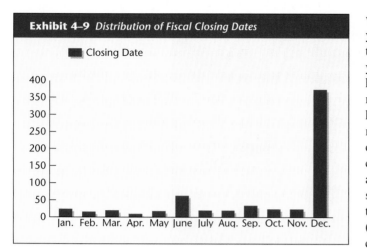

Exhibit 4–9 *Distribution of Fiscal Closing Dates*

■ Closing Date

(bar chart, vertical axis 0 to 400 in increments of 50; horizontal axis Jan. Feb. Mar. Apr. May June July Aug. Sep. Oct. Nov. Dec.)

would overburden their resources. Furthermore, after the year-end rush was over, there would be very little work to keep employees busy during the other parts of the year. In an effort to smooth the workload, companies have been encouraged to adopt a natural business year. A natural business year ends when the activities of an entity have reached the lowest point in an annual cycle. In many instances, the natural business year ends on December 31. However, as we indicated in the Curious Accountant, many companies have business cycles that end at times other than December 31. Indeed, Exhibit 4–9 shows that almost one-half of the companies sampled in the American Institute of Certified Public Accountants' (AICPA) *Accounting Trends and Techniques* survey closed their books in months other than December.

■ Trial Balance

LO6 Prepare and interpret a trial balance.

As previously indicated, the double-entry system permits a check on the accuracy of the recording and posting practices through a test of the equality of debits and credits. This test is commonly referred to as a **trial balance.** A trial balance is a list of ledger account titles and their respective balances. The debit and credit balances are arranged in separate columns. Each column is totaled, and the two totals are compared for the verification of equality. A failure to attain this equality signals an error in the recording process. Even if the debits balance with the credits, caution must still be taken regarding the level of assurance assigned to the "balance." For example, the trial balance does not reveal errors such as the failure to record an important transaction, misclassifications such as recording debits or credits to the wrong accounts, or counterbalancing errors such as overstating both debit and credit amounts of an entry. It follows then that the attainment of equal debits and credits in the trial balance should be viewed as evidence, as opposed to proof, of accuracy in journalizing and posting transactions.

A trial balance should be prepared whenever the accountant feels that it would be useful to test the equality of debits and credits. Some companies prepare a trial balance daily; others may prepare one monthly or quarterly. Again, the needs of the company should dictate the accounting policy, and a trial balance should be prepared whenever it is beneficial to do so. Exhibit 4–10 is a trial balance of the accounts of Collins Consultants after the closing entries have been posted to the ledger.

Exhibit 4–10 *Trial Balance*

Account Titles	Debit	Credit
Cash	$ 1,250	
Accounts Receivable	800	
Supplies	125	
Prepaid Rent	2,100	
Notes Receivable	6,000	
Interest Receivable	360	
Office Equipment	42,000	
Accumulated Depreciation		$ 4,000
Accounts Payable		900
Unearned Revenue		3,000
Notes Payable		10,000
Interest Payable		1,100
Salaries Payable		800
Common Stock		15,000
Retained Earnings		17,835
Totals	$52,635	$52,635

Check Yourself 4-3

Describe an error that would not cause a trial balance to be out of balance.

Answer Many potential errors would not cause a trial balance to be out of balance, such as debiting or crediting the wrong account. For example, if revenue earned on account were recorded with a debit to Cash instead of Accounts Receivable, total assets would be correct and the totals in the trial balance would equal each other even though the balances in the Cash and Accounts Receivable accounts would be incorrect. Recording the same incorrect amount in both the debit and credit part of an entry also would not cause a trial balance to be out of balance. For example, if $20 of revenue earned on account were recorded as a $200 debit to Accounts Receivable and a $200 credit to Consulting Revenue, the totals in the trial balance would equal each other although Accounts Receivable and Consulting Revenue amounts would be incorrect.

Part 1

The process of closing the books and going through a year-end audit is time consuming for a business. Also, it is time spent that does not produce revenue. Thus, companies whose business is highly seasonal often choose "slow" periods to end their fiscal year. The Limited does heavy business during the Christmas season, so it might find December 31 an inconvenient time to close its books. Toward the end of January, business activity is slow, and inventory levels are at their low points. This is a good time to count the inventory and to assess the financial condition of the company. For these reasons, The Limited has chosen to close its books to end its fiscal year at the end of January.

Now that you know why a business like The Limited might choose to end its fiscal year at the end of January, can you think of a reason why Polo Ralph Lauren closes its books at the end of March?

▮ Components of an Annual Report

Published annual reports, also called _financial reports,_ usually are printed in color on high-quality paper and contain lots of photographs, which is why accountants sometimes refer to them as the company's "glossies." Although this book focuses on financial statements, you should understand that accounting information involves much more than just the financial statements. Annual reports are often 40 or more pages long. The financial statements themselves require only four to six of these pages, so what are all those other pages for?

LO8 Describe the components of an annual report, including the management, discussion, and analysis (MD&A) section and the footnotes to financial statements.

For the purposes of this course, the annual report of a large company can be divided into the following four major sections: (1) financial statements, (2) footnotes to the financial statements, (3) management's discussion and analysis, and (4) auditors' report. Previous chapters introduced the financial statements and the auditors' report, but the bulk of the annual report actually consists of footnotes and management's discussion and analysis.

Footnotes to the Financial Statements

Footnotes to the financial statements help explain the information contained in the financial statements themselves. The need for this additional information will become clearer in

Part 2

Polo Ralph Lauren sells most of its clothes through retailers. Therefore, it must ship goods weeks before they will eventually be sold by stores such as The Limited. The end of March probably is a relatively slow time of year for Polo Ralph Lauren.

The Christmas season has passed and most of the spring clothing probably has been shipped to retailers by the end of March, so this is a good time of year for clothing manufacturers to close their books. Tommy Hilfiger also closes its fiscal year at the end of March.

future chapters, but for now, keep in mind that companies have to make estimates when performing accounting calculations. They also often have the option of accounting for a given transaction in different ways. Generally accepted accounting principles (GAAP) allow considerable flexibility. Footnotes explain some of the estimates that were made as well as which of the options available under GAAP were used. It would be foolish, and even dangerous, for a user to try to understand a company's financial statements without reading the footnotes. To emphasize this point, financial statements often have a statement at the bottom of the pages, such as "the accompanying footnotes are an integral part of these financial statements."

Management's Discussion and Analysis

Management's discussion and analysis (MD&A) is usually located at the beginning of the annual report. MD&A is the section of the annual report that management uses to explain

focus on International Issues

Is There a Global GAAP Leader?

Chapter 3 discussed some reasons that there is no single set of global GAAP. Nevertheless, one may wonder if there are certain countries that tend to take the lead in the establishment of GAAP. Although no single country has led in

the overall development of accounting rule making, a few countries have led in some specific areas of accounting development.

For example, the double-entry bookkeeping system explained in this chapter began in Italy. This system was first formally publicized in the late 1400s by an Italian monk, Luca Pacioli. Pacioli did not actually develop the double-entry system; he published an explanation of the system as he had observed it in use by Italian merchants of his day. The use of the terms *debit* and *credit* results from the Italian origins of the bookkeeping system. Today, this system is used throughout the world.

As another example, consider that the public accounting profession as we know it in the United States and many other countries originated in the United Kingdom. The idea of an independent auditing professional (the CPA in the United States) came to the United States from the United Kingdom around the turn of the twentieth century. Not all countries have the strong nongovernment accounting profession that exists in the United Kingdom and United States, but those that do can trace their roots back to the United Kingdom. No doubt, this is the reason why four of the "Big 5" accounting firms in the world originated, at least in part, in the United Kingdom. The remaining firm originated entirely in the United States.

many different aspects of the company's past performance and future plans. For example, MD&A typically discusses this year's sales compared to those of the past year and explains reasons for the changes. If the company is planning significant acquisitions of assets or other businesses, this information should be included in MD&A. Likewise, plans to dispose of part of the existing business should be discussed. Some events included in MD&A might also be discussed in the footnotes.

Role of the Independent Auditor Revisited

The auditors' report is explained in Chapter 2. A well-educated businessperson should be aware that the auditor has a different role and responsibility for different parts of the annual report. Auditors have great responsibility for the financial statements and the footnotes to those statements. From an auditor's point of view, the footnotes are a part of the financial statements, which means that information in the footnotes is audited in the same manner as information in the balance sheet.

Auditors' responsibility for information in MD&A is less than that for the financial statements and footnotes, but they do have some responsibility for this section of the annual report. Auditors *review* the MD&A section to be sure it does not contain comments that conflict with information in the financial statements. For example, if the current year's net income is down from last year's, management cannot say in MD&A that "earnings continue to grow."

However, MD&A often contains expressions of opinion not found in the financial statements or footnotes. If current earnings are down relative to last year's earnings, management could say, "We *believe* the decline to be temporary and expect substantial growth in the coming year." Management's opinion cannot be verified, or audited, in the same way as the balance in the Cash account can be.

The Securities and Exchange Commission

A final note about published financial reports is in order. Much of the preceding discussion relates more to large- and medium-size companies than to small companies, even though many small companies are audited. (*Small* is obviously a subjective term.) The annual reports of large companies are often different from those of small companies because large companies are more likely to be registered with the **Securities and Exchange Commission,** usually referred to as the **SEC.** SEC companies, as they are often called, have to follow the reporting rules of the SEC as well as GAAP. These rules require some additional disclosures not required by GAAP. For example, SEC rules require that annual reports include an MD&A section. GAAP rules do not, so non-SEC companies usually do not include MD&A, although they could if management wanted.

LO9 Describe the role of the Securities and Exchange Commission in financial reporting.

The SEC is a government organization whose responsibilities include overseeing the accounting rules to be followed by SEC companies. Although in theory the SEC could "overrule" GAAP that are established by the private accounting profession, this has very seldom occurred. More often, the SEC requires companies registered with it to give information in addition to GAAP. All companies whose stock trades on public stock exchanges, and some that do not, are required to register with the SEC. The SEC has no jurisdiction over non-SEC companies.

SEC companies must file a good deal of information directly with the SEC. There are many different reports, and each is referred to by a different form number, but the most common are 10-Ks and 10-Qs. The *10-K* is a company's annual report. Recall that Dell Computer Corporation's 10-K is included in Appendix B. The major differences between the 10-K filed with the SEC and the glossies are the absence of pictures in the 10-Ks and the fact that the 10-Ks often contain more detailed information than is included in the glossies. The *10-Q*s are quarterly reports. They normally contain less detail than the 10-Ks.

Most of the reports filed with the SEC are available electronically through the SEC's EDGAR database. EDGAR is an acronym for Electronic Data Gathering, Analysis, and

Retrieval system, and it is accessible through the World Wide Web on the Internet. Instructions for using EDGAR are in Appendix A.

a look back

This chapter introduced the *double-entry accounting* system, which has been in existence since at least the 1400s, and is used by most companies that have formal bookkeeping systems. You should be familiar with the following components of the double-entry system.

1. Business events can be described succinctly using debit/credit terminology. *Debits* are used to record increases in asset accounts and decreases in liability and equity accounts. *Credits* are used to record decreases in asset accounts and increases in liability and equity accounts.
2. *T-accounts* are frequently used to communicate information. The account title is placed at the top of the horizontal bar of the T, and increases and decreases are placed on either side of the vertical bar. Debits are recorded on the left side and credits are recorded on the right side of a T-account.
3. To maintain a complete chronological record of all business events, accountants initially record data into journals. The *general journal* recording format is used not only for data entry but also to communicate information in a succinct manner. Each journal entry contains at least one debit and one credit. The entry is recorded in at least two lines with the debit recorded on the top line and the credit on the bottom line. The credit is indented to distinguish it from the debit. The general journal format is illustrated here:

Debit	xxx	
Credit		xxx

4. Information is posted (transferred) from the journals to *ledger* accounts. The ledger accounts provide a means to summarize information for presentation in the financial statements.
5. *Trial balances* are used to check the accuracy of the recording process. Ledger accounts with their associated debit and credit balances are listed in the trial balance. The debit and credit amounts are totaled and compared. An equal amount of debits and credits provides evidence that transactions have been recorded correctly, although errors may still exist. A failure to attain a balance between debits and credits is proof that errors exist.

It is important to remember that the double-entry system is just another way to organize accounting data. No matter how we organize the data, the objective is to convert it into information that is useful for making decisions. Most decisions that are based on accounting data use information obtained from companies' financial statements. Therefore, whether data are organized using the horizontal model, a manual debit/credit system, or a computerized system, it is important that business managers understand how business events affect financial statements and the related ratios.

a look forward

If you think back on the types of businesses discussed in Chapters 1 through 4, you will realize that they are service enterprises. None of them sold a physical product. Obviously, in the real world, many businesses do sell products. The early chapters of this course used service businesses to keep matters relatively simple. Chapter 5 introduces some special accounting issues associated with companies that purchase and sell products. A word of caution is in order. If you do not understand Chapter 5, you cannot possibly understand Chapter 8, so give Chapter 5 careful attention.

SELF-STUDY REVIEW PROBLEM

The following events apply to the first year of operations for Mestro Financial Services Company:
1. Acquired $28,000 cash by issuing common stock on January 1, 2003.

2. Purchased $1,100 of supplies on account.
3. Paid $12,000 cash in advance for a one-year lease on office space.
4. Earned $23,000 of consulting revenue on account.
5. Incurred $16,000 of general operating expenses on account.
6. Collected $20,000 cash from receivables.
7. Paid $13,000 cash on accounts payable.
8. Paid a $1,000 cash dividend to the stockholders.

Information for Adjusting Entries

9. There was $200 of supplies on hand at the end of the accounting period.
10. The one-year lease on the office space was effective beginning on October 1, 2003.
11. There was $1,200 of accrued salaries at the end of 2003.

Required

a. Record the preceding events in ledger T-accounts.
b. Prepare an adjusted trial balance.
c. Prepare an income statement, statement of changes in stockholders' equity, balance sheet, and statement of cash flows.
d. Prepare the appropriate closing entries in general journal format.

Solution to Requirement a

MESTRO FINANCIAL SERVICES COMPANY
T-Accounts, 2003

Assets				=	Liabilities				+	Equity	

Cash

1.	28,000	3.	12,000
6.	20,000	7.	13,000
		8.	1,000
Bal.	22,000		

Accounts Payable

7.	13,000	2.	1,100
		5.	16,000
		Bal.	4,100

Common Stock

		1.	28,000
		Bal.	28,000

Accounts Receivable

4.	23,000	6.	20,000
Bal.	3,000		

Salaries Payable

		11.	1,200
		Bal.	1,200

Consulting Revenue

		4.	23,000

Supplies

2.	1,100	9.	900
Bal.	200		

General Operating Expenses

5.	16,000	

Salaries Expense

11.	1,200	

Prepaid Rent

3.	12,000	10.	3,000
Bal.	9,000		

Supplies Expense

9.	900	

Rent Expense

10.	3,000	

Dividends

8.	1,000	

Solution to Requirement b

MESTRO FINANCIAL SERVICES COMPANY Adjusted Trial Balance December 31, 2003		
Account Titles	**Debit**	**Credit**
Cash	$22,000	
Accounts Receivable	3,000	
Supplies	200	
Prepaid Rent	9,000	
Accounts Payable		$ 4,100
Salaries Payable		1,200
Common Stock		28,000
Dividends	1,000	
Consulting Revenue		23,000
General Operating Expenses	16,000	
Salaries Expense	1,200	
Supplies Expense	900	
Rent Expense	3,000	
Totals	$56,300	$56,300

Solution to Requirement c

MESTRO FINANCIAL SERVICES COMPANY Financial Statements For 2003		
Income Statement		
Consulting Revenue		$23,000
Expenses		
General Operating Expenses	$16,000	
Salaries Expense	1,200	
Supplies Expense	900	
Rent Expense	3,000	
Total Expenses		(21,100)
Net Income		$ 1,900
Statement of Changes in Stockholders' Equity		
Beginning Common Stock	$ 0	
Plus: Common Stock Issued	28,000	
Ending Common Stock		$28,000
Beginning Retained Earnings	0	
Plus: Net Income	1,900	
Less: Dividends	(1,000)	
Ending Retained Earnings		900
Total Stockholders' Equity		$28,900
Balance Sheet		
Assets		
Cash	$22,000	
Accounts Receivable	3,000	
Supplies	200	
Prepaid Rent	9,000	
Total Assets		$34,200
Liabilities		
Accounts Payable	$ 4,100	
Salaries Payable	1,200	
Total Liabilities		$ 5,300
Stockholders' Equity		
Common Stock	28,000	
Retained Earnings	900	
Total Stockholders' Equity		28,900
Total Liabilities and Stockholders' Equity		$34,200

Statement of Cash Flows		
Cash Flows from Operating Activities		
Inflow from Customers	$20,000	
Outflow for Expenses	(25,000)	
Net Cash Flow from Operating Activities		$(5,000)
Cash Flows from Investing Activities		0
Cash Flows from Financing Activities		
Inflow from Issue of Common Stock	28,000	
Outflow for Dividends	(1,000)	
Net Cash Flow from Financing Activities		27,000
Net Change in Cash		22,000
Plus: Beginning Cash Balance		0
Ending Cash Balance		$22,000

Solution to Requirement d

Date	Account Titles	Debit	Credit
	Closing Entries		
Dec. 31	Consulting Revenue	23,000	
	Retained Earnings		23,000
Dec. 31	Retained Earnings	21,100	
	General Operating Expenses		16,000
	Salaries Expense		1,200
	Supplies Expense		900
	Rent Expense		3,000
Dec. 31	Retained Earnings	1,000	
	Dividends		1,000

KEY TERMS

Account balance *150*
Asset/expense adjustment *161*
Asset/revenue adjustment *159*
Books of original entry *164*
Chart of accounts *164*
Closing entries *169*
Contra account *161*
Credit *150*

Debit *150*
Double-entry accounting *150*
Fiscal year *149*
Footnotes to the financial statements *171*
General journal *164*
Journal *164*

Ledger *164*
Liability/expense adjustment *160*
Liability/revenue adjustment *162*
Management's Discussion and Analysis (MD&A) *172*

Posting *166*
Securities and Exchange Commission (SEC) *173*
Source document *164*
Special journals *164*
T-account *149*
Trial balance *170*

QUESTIONS

1. What are the two fundamental equality requirements of the double-entry accounting system?
2. Define *debit* and *credit*. How are assets, liabilities, stockholders' equity, retained earnings, revenues, expenses, and dividends affected (increased or decreased) by debits and by credits?
3. How is the balance of an account determined?
4. What are the three primary sources of business assets?
5. What are the three primary ways a business may use assets?
6. Why is an adjusting entry necessary to record depreciation expense? What accounts are affected? How are the account balances affected?
7. What is an asset/revenue adjustment? Give an example.
8. What is a liability/expense adjustment? Give an example.

9. Explain and give two examples of an asset/expense adjustment. What accounts are affected in your examples? Are the accounts debited or credited? Do the account balances increase or decrease?

10. Explain and give an example of a liability/revenue adjustment. What accounts are debited or credited in your example? Do the account balances increase or decrease?

11. How does a debit to an expense account ultimately affect retained earnings? Stockholders' equity?

12. What accounts normally have debit balances? What accounts normally have credit balances?

13. What is the primary source of information for preparing the financial statements?

14. What is the purpose of a journal?

15. What is the difference between the *general journal* and special journals?

16. What is a ledger? What is its function in the accounting system?

17. What are the five steps in the recording process?

18. What is the purpose of closing entries?

19. At a minimum, what information is recorded in the general journal?

20. What is the purpose of a trial balance?

21. When should a trial balance be prepared?

22. What does the term *posting* mean?

23. Where did the terms *debit* and *credit* originate?

24. What country is responsible for the accounting profession's having "independent accounting professionals"?

25. What type of information is found in the footnotes to the financial statements?

26. What type of information is found in the MD&A section of the annual report?

27. What is the Securities and Exchange Commission? What are its responsibilities concerning a company's financial statements? What types of companies are under the SEC's jurisdiction?

EXERCISES—SERIES A

L.O. 1, 2   **EXERCISE 4–1A** *Debit/Credit Rules*

Debbie, Josh, and Deshonda, three accounting students, were discussing the rules of debits and credits. Debbie says that debits increase account balances and credits decrease account balances. Josh says that Debbie is wrong, that credits increase account balances and debits decrease account balances. Deshonda interrupts and declares that they are both correct.

Required

Explain what Deshonda meant and give examples of transactions where debits increase account balances, credits decrease account balances, credits increase account balances, and debits decrease account balances.

L.O. 2   **EXERCISE 4–2A** *Matching Debit and Credit Terminology with Accounts*

Required

Complete the following table by indicating whether a debit or credit is used to increase or decrease the balance of the following accounts. The appropriate debit/credit terminology has been identified for the first account as an example.

Account Titles	Used to Increase This Account	Used to Decrease This Account
Cash	Debit	Credit
Notes Payable		
Common Stock		
Equipment		
Other Operating Expense		
Accumulated Depreciation		
Dividends		
Service Revenue		
Retained Earnings		
Rent Expense		

L.O. 2   **EXERCISE 4–3A** *Matching Debit and Credit Terminology with Account Titles*

Required

Indicate whether each of the following accounts normally has a debit balance or a credit balance.

a. Cash
b. Common Stock
c. Depreciation Expense
d. Accumulated Depreciation
e. Notes Payable

f. Unearned Revenue
g. Service Revenue
h. Dividends
i. Land
j. Prepaid Rent

EXERCISE 4–4A *Identifying Increases and Decreases in T-Accounts*

L.O. 1, 2, 4

Required

For each of the following T-accounts, indicate the side of the account that should be used to record an increase or decrease in the accounting element.

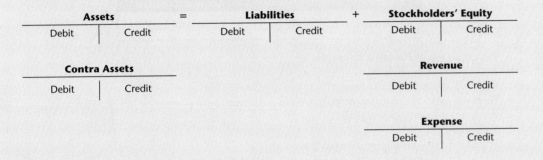

EXERCISE 4–5A *Applying Debit/Credit Terminology to Accounting Events*

L.O. 1, 2

Required

In parallel columns, list the accounts that would be debited and credited for each of the following unrelated transactions:
a. Acquired cash from the issue of common stock.
b. Provided services for cash.
c. Paid cash for salaries expense.
d. Borrowed cash from a local bank.
e. Incurred other operating expense on account.
f. Purchased land for cash.
g. Provided services on account.
h. Recorded accrued interest expense at the end of the accounting period.

EXERCISE 4–6A *T-Accounts and the Accounting Equation*

L.O. 2, 3

Required

Record each of the following Chandler Co. events in T-accounts and then explain how the event affects the accounting equation.
a. Received $10,000 cash by issuing common stock.
b. Purchased supplies for $500 on account.
c. Purchased land for $20,000, paying $5,000 cash and issuing a note payable for the balance.
d. Performed services on account for $4,000.

EXERCISE 4–7A *Recording Transactions in T-Accounts*

L.O. 3

The following events apply to Magnum Parcel Co. for 2002.
1. Received cash of $24,000 from the issue of common stock.
2. Purchased a delivery van for $15,000 cash. The delivery van has a salvage value of $3,000 and a three-year useful life.
3. Performed $65,000 of services on account.
4. Paid $24,000 cash for salaries expense.
5. Incurred $5,000 of other operating expenses on account.
6. Collected $47,000 of accounts receivable.
7. Performed $6,200 of services for cash.
8. Paid $3,400 of the accounts payable.
9. Paid a $3,000 dividend to the stockholders.
10. Recorded depreciation expense for the year on the delivery van.

Required

a. Record these events in the appropriate T-accounts and determine the ending balance in each account.
b. Determine the amount of total assets at the end of 2002.
c. Determine the amount of net income for 2002.

L.O. 2   **EXERCISE 4–8A** *Debit/Credit Terminology*

Required

For each of the following independent events, identify the account that would be debited and the account that would be credited. The accounts for the first event are identified as an example.

Event	Account Debited	Account Credited
a	Cash	Common Stock

a. Received cash by issuing common stock.
b. Provided services on account.
c. Paid cash for operating expenses.
d. Received cash for services to be performed in the future.
e. Recognized depreciation expense.
f. Paid salaries payable.
g. Repaid principal balance on note payable.
h. Recognized revenue for services completed; collected the cash in Event *d*.
i. Paid accounts payable.
j. Received cash in payment of accounts receivable.
k. Purchased office equipment with cash.
l. Recognized accrued interest expense.
m. Recognized accrued interest revenue.
n. Paid cash dividends to the stockholders.
o. Purchased supplies on account.

L.O. 1, 2   **EXERCISE 4–9A** *Identifying Transaction Type, Its Effect on the Accounting Equation, and Whether the Effect Is Recorded with a Debit or Credit*

Required

Identify whether each of the following transactions is an asset source (AS), asset use (AU), asset exchange (AE), or claims exchange (CE). Also explain how each event affects the accounting equation by placing a + for *increase,* − for *decrease,* and NA for *not affected* under each of the components of the accounting equation. Finally, indicate whether the effect requires a debit or credit entry. The first event is recorded as an example.

Event	Type of Event	Assets	=	Liabilities	+	Common Stock	+	Retained Earnings
a	AS	+ Debit		NA		NA		+ Credit

a. Provided services on account.
b. Purchased land by issuing a note.
c. Paid interest payable.
d. Borrowed cash by issuing a note.
e. Received cash in payment of accounts receivable.
f. Repaid principal balance on note payable.
g. Paid cash in advance for one-year's rent.
h. Received cash for services to be performed in the future.
i. Recognized accrued interest expense.
j. Incurred other operating expense on account.
k. Paid salaries payable.
l. Recognized revenue for services completed; cash collected previously.
m. Recognized accrued interest revenue.
n. Paid a cash dividend to the stockholders.
o. Recognized depreciation expense on the equipment.

EXERCISE 4–10A *Recording Events in the General Journal*   L.O. 7

Required

Record each of the following transactions in general journal form.

a. Received $5,000 cash for services to be performed at a later date.

b. Purchased supplies for $900 cash.

c. Performed $16,000 of services on account.

d. Purchased equipment that cost $36,000 by paying $8,000 cash and issuing a $28,000 note for the balance.

e. Charged $1,700 repairs made on equipment on account.

f. Sold land that cost $18,000 for $21,500.

g. Collected $12,200 cash on accounts receivable.

h. Paid $800 on accounts payable.

i. Paid $5,400 cash in advance for an insurance policy on the equipment.

j. Recorded accrued interest expense of $1,800.

k. Recorded $6,000 depreciation expense on the equipment.

l. Recorded the adjusting entry to recognize $4,800 of insurance expense.

EXERCISE 4–11A *Preparing a Trial Balance*   L.O. 6

Required

On December 31, 2005, Huang Company had the following account balances in its general ledger. Use this information to prepare a trial balance.

Cash	$30,000
Service Revenue	63,000
Dividends	5,000
Depreciation Expense	4,500
Prepaid Insurance	5,400
Land	12,500
Rent Expense	18,000
Accounts Payable	4,000
Common Stock	15,000
Salaries Expense	11,000
Office Supplies	1,800
Advertising Expense	1,500
Retained Earnings, 1–1–05	11,200
Unearned Revenue	22,000
Office Equipment	25,000
Accounts Receivable	8,500
Accumulated Depreciation	8,000

EXERCISE 4–12A *Preparing Closing Entries*   L.O. 5, 7

The following financial information was taken from the books of Refresh Day Spa.

Account Balances as of December 31, 2008	
Accounts Receivable	$28,000
Accounts Payable	7,500
Advertising Expense	2,500
Accumulated Depreciation	12,500
Cash	18,300
Certificate of Deposit	22,000
Common Stock	20,000
Depreciation Expense	4,800
Dividends	2,000
Equipment	30,000
Interest Receivable	400
Interest Revenue	1,800
Notes Payable	10,000
Prepaid Rent	3,200
Rent Expense	9,600
Retained Earnings	6,800
Salaries Expense	26,000
Salaries Payable	5,000
Service Revenue	85,500
Supplies	400
Supplies Expense	1,900

Required

a. Prepare the necessary closing entries at December 31, 2008, for Refresh Day Spa.

b. What is the balance in the Retained Earnings account after the closing entries are posted?

L.O. 3, 6   **EXERCISE 4–13A** *Recording Events in T-Accounts and Preparing a Trial Balance*

The following events apply to Custom Computer Services.

1. Received $20,000 cash from the issue of common stock.
2. Earned $20,000 of revenue on account.
3. Incurred $12,500 of operating expenses on account.
4. Borrowed $16,000 from First Bank.
5. Paid $4,000 cash to purchase office equipment.
6. Collected $18,000 of cash from accounts receivable.
7. Received an $8,200 cash advance for services to be provided in the future.
8. Purchased $800 of supplies on account.
9. Made an $8,000 payment on accounts payable.
10. Paid a $1,000 cash dividend to the stockholders.
11. Recognized $600 of supplies expense.
12. Recognized $4,000 of revenue for services provided to the customer in Event 7.
13. Recorded accrued interest expense of $1,500.
14. Recognized $1,200 of depreciation expense.

Required

a. Record the events in T-accounts and determine the ending account balances.

b. Test the equality of the debit and credit balances of the T-accounts by preparing a trial balance.

L.O. 6   **EXERCISE 4–14A** *Determining the Effect of Errors on the Trial Balance*

Required

Explain how each of the following posting errors affects a trial balance. State whether the trial balance will be out of balance because of the posting error, and indicate which side of the trial balance will have a higher amount after each independent entry is posted. If the posting error does not affect the equality of debits and credits shown in the trial balance, state that the error will not cause an inequality and explain why.

a. The collection of $800 of accounts receivable was posted to Accounts Receivable twice.

b. An $1,800 credit to Accounts Payable was posted as a credit to Cash.

c. A $900 credit to Notes Payable was not posted.

d. A $400 debit to Cash was posted as a $4,000 debit.

e. A $1,500 debit to Prepaid Rent was debited to Rent Expense.

L.O. 3, 5, 7   **EXERCISE 4–15A** *Recording Events in the General Journal, Posting to T-Accounts, and Preparing Closing Entries*

At the beginning of 2005, Advanced Lawn Care had the following balances in its accounts:

Account	Balance
Cash	$15,000
Accounts Receivable	9,500
Accounts Payable	6,200
Common Stock	12,000
Retained Earnings	6,300

The following events apply to Advanced for 2005.

1. Provided $80,000 of services on account.
2. Incurred $5,600 of other operating expenses on account.
3. Collected $82,000 of accounts receivable.
4. Paid $42,000 cash for salaries expense.
5. Paid $6,500 cash as a partial payment on accounts payable.
6. Paid a $5,000 cash dividend to the stockholders.

Required

a. Record these events in a general journal.

b. Open T-accounts, and post the beginning balances and the preceding transactions to the appropriate accounts. Determine the balance of each account.

c. Record the beginning balances and the events in a horizontal statements model such as the following one:

Assets			= Liab.	+	Stockholders' Equity		Rev.	−	Exp.	=	Net Inc.	Cash Flow
Cash	+	Accts. Rec.	= Accts. Pay.	+	Common Stock	+ Ret. Earn.							

d. Record the closing entries in the general journal and post them to the T-accounts. What is the amount of net income for the year?

e. What is the amount of *change* in retained earnings for the year? Is the change in retained earnings different from the amount of net income? If so, why?

EXERCISE 4–16A *Recording Receivables and Identifying Their Effect on Financial Statements*   L.O. 3, 5

Hubbard Company performed services on account for $45,000 in 2006 its first year of operations. Hubbard collected $32,000 cash from accounts receivable during 2006 and the remaining $13,000 in cash during 2007.

Required

a. Record the 2006 transactions in T-accounts.

b. Record the 2006 transactions in a horizontal statements model like the following one:

Assets			= Liab.	+	Stk. Equity	Rev.	−	Exp.	=	Net Inc.	Cash Flow
Cash	+	Accts. Rec.	= NA	+	Ret. Earn.						

c. Determine the amount of revenue Hubbard would report on the 2006 income statement.

d. Determine the amount of cash flow from operating activities Hubbard would report on the 2006 statement of cash flows.

e. Open a T-account for Retained Earnings, and close the 2006 Service Revenue account to the Retained Earnings account.

f. Record the 2007 cash collection in the appropriate T-accounts.

g. Record the 2007 transaction in a horizontal statements model like the one shown in Requirement *b.*

h. Assuming no other transactions occur in 2007, determine the amount of net income and the net cash flow from operating activities for 2007.

EXERCISE 4–17A *Recording Supplies and Identifying Their Effect on Financial Statements*   L.O. 3–6

Maria Cortez started and operated a small family consulting firm in 2005. The firm was affected by two events: (1) Cortez provided $12,000 of services on account, and (2) she purchased $2,000 of supplies on account. There were $400 of supplies on hand as of December 31, 2005.

Required

a. Open T-accounts and record the two transactions in the accounts.

b. Record the required year-end adjusting entry to reflect the use of supplies.

c. Record the above transactions in a horizontal statements model like the following one.

Assets		= Liab.	+	Stk. Equity	Rev.	−	Exp.	=	Net Inc.	Cash Flow
Accts. Rec.	Supp.	Accts. Pay.		Ret. Earn.						

d. Explain why the amount of net income and the net cash flow from operating activities differ.

e. Record and post the required closing entries, and prepare an after-closing trial balance.

EXERCISE 4–18A *Recording Prepaids and Identifying Their Effect on Financial Statements*   L.O. 4, 7

Utah Mining began operations by issuing common stock for $70,000. The company paid $54,000 cash in advance for a one-year contract to lease machinery for the business. The lease agreement was signed on March 1, 2005, and was effective immediately. Utah Mining earned $75,000 of cash revenue in 2005.

Required

a. Record the March 1 cash payment in general journal format.
b. Record in general journal format the asset/expense adjustment required as of December 31, 2005.
c. Record all 2005 events in a horizontal statements model like the following one:

Assets			=	Liab.	+	Stk. Equity	Rev.	–	Exp.	=	Net Inc.	Cash Flow
Cash	+	PrPd. Rent				Ret. Earn.						

d. What amount of net income would Utah Mining report on the 2005 income statement? What is the amount of net cash flow from operating activities for 2005?
e. Determine the amount of prepaid rent Utah Mining would report on the December 31, 2005, balance sheet.

L.O. 4, 7   **EXERCISE 4–19A** *Recording Accrued Salaries and Identifying Their Effect on Financial Statements*

On December 31, 2008, Big Ben Company had accrued salaries of $6,500.

Required

a. Record in general journal format the expense/liability adjustment required as of December 31, 2008.
b. Determine the amount of net income Big Ben would report on the 2008 income statement, assuming that Big Ben earns $12,000 of cash revenue. What is the amount of net cash flow from operating activities for 2008?
c. What amount of Salaries Payable liability would Big Ben report on the December 31, 2008, balance sheet?

L.O. 3, 4   **EXERCISE 4–20A** *Recording Depreciation and Identifying Its Effect on Financial Statements*

On January 1, 2007, Swan bought a computer for $28,000 cash. The computer had a useful life of four years and a salvage value of $4,000.

Required

a. Record in T-accounts Swan's purchase of the computer.
b. Record in T-accounts the asset/expense adjustment required on December 31, 2007.
c. Determine the book value of the computer Swan would report on the December 31, 2007, balance sheet.
d. Determine the amount of net income Swan would report on the 2007 income statement, assuming that Swan earned $12,000 of cash revenue in 2007.
e. What is the amount of net cash flow from operating activities for 2007?
f. What amount of depreciation expense would Swan report on the 2008 income statement?
g. Determine the book value of the computer Swan would report on the December 31, 2008, balance sheet.

L.O. 3, 4   **EXERCISE 4–21A** *Recording a Note Payable and Identifying Its Effect on Financial Statements*

On May 1, 2003, Brody Company borrowed $80,000 from First Bank. The note had a 9 percent annual interest rate and a one-year term to maturity.

Required

a. Identify the transaction type (asset source, use, or exchange or claims exchange), and record in T-accounts the entries for the financing event on May 1, 2003.
b. Identify the transaction type, and record in T-accounts the liability/expense adjustment as of December 31, 2003.
c. Determine the amount of net income on the 2003 income statement, assuming Brody Company earned $25,000 of cash revenue.
d. What is the amount of net cash flow from operating activities for 2003?
e. Determine the total liabilities on the December 31, 2003, balance sheet.
f. Record (1) the 2004 accrual of interest and (2) the cash payment of principal and interest on May 1, 2004.
g. Are the May 1, 2004, transactions asset source, asset use, asset exchange, or claims exchange transactions?

EXERCISE 4–22A *Recording Unearned Revenue and Identifying Its Effect on Financial*   **L.O. 3, 4**
                                 Statements

Shaw received a $72,000 cash advance payment on March 1, 2005, for legal services to be performed in the future. Services were to be provided for a one-year term beginning March 1, 2005.

Required
a. Record the March 1 cash receipt in T-accounts.
b. Record in T-accounts the liability/revenue adjustment required as of December 31, 2005.
c. Record the preceding transaction and related adjustment in a horizontal statements model like the following one:

Assets	=	Liab.	+	Stk. Equity	Rev.	−	Exp.	=	Net Inc.	Cash Flow

d. Determine the amount of net income on the 2005 income statement. What is the amount of net cash flow from operating activities for 2005?
e. What amount of Unearned Revenue liability would Shaw report on the December 31, 2005, balance sheet?

EXERCISE 4–23A *Using a T-Account to Determine Cash Flow From Operating Activities*   **L.O. 3**

Baird, Inc., began the accounting period with a $57,000 debit balance in its Accounts Receivable account. During the accounting period, Baird earned revenue on account of $126,000. The ending accounts receivable balance was $49,000.

Required
Based on this information alone, determine the amount of cash inflow from operating activities during the accounting period. (*Hint:* Use a T-account for Accounts Receivable. Enter the debits and credits for the given events, and solve for the missing amount.)

EXERCISE 4–24A *Using a T-Account to Determine Cash Flow From Operating Activities*   **L.O. 3**

Bell Company began the accounting period with a $20,000 credit balance in its Accounts Payable account. During the accounting period, Bell incurred expenses on account of $75,000. The ending Accounts Payable balance was $22,000.

Required
Based on this information, determine the amount of cash outflow for expenses during the accounting period. (*Hint:* Use a T-account for Accounts Payable. Enter the debits and credits for the given events, and solve for the missing amount.)

PROBLEMS—SERIES A

PROBLEM 4–25A *Identifying Debit and Credit Balances*   **L.O. 2**

Required
Indicate whether each of the following accounts normally has a debit or credit balance.
a. Supplies Expense
b. Prepaid Rent
c. Accumulated Depreciation
d. Equipment
e. Interest Payable
f. Service Revenue
g. Supplies
h. Accounts Payable
i. Depreciation Expense
j. Unearned Revenue
k. Loss on Sale of Equipment
l. Gain on Sale of Land
m. Truck
n. Operating Expense
o. Dividends
p. Interest Receivable
q. Land
r. Notes Payable
s. Salaries Expense
t. Certificate of Deposit
u. Interest Revenue
v. Rent Expense
w. Common Stock
x. Cash
y. Salaries Payable
z. Accounts Receivable
aa. Insurance Expense
bb. Prepaid Insurance
cc. Retained Earnings

L.O. 1, 2   PROBLEM 4–26A *Transaction Type and Debit/Credit Terminology*

The following events apply to Huff Enterprises.
1. Acquired $20,000 cash from the issue of common stock.
2. Paid salaries to employees, $3,000 cash.
3. Collected $18,400 cash for services to be performed in the future.
4. Paid cash for utilities, $600.
5. Recognized $18,000 of revenue on account.
6. Purchased equipment costing $100,000 by paying cash of $20,000 and borrowing the balance from Third National Bank by issuing a four-year note.
7. Paid a $3,000 cash dividend to the stockholders.
8. Purchased $1,500 of supplies on account.
9. Received $12,000 cash for services rendered.
10. Paid cash to rent office space for the next 12 months, $13,200.
11. Made a $10,000 principal payment on the bank note.
12. Paid cash of $10,000 for other operating expenses.
13. Paid creditor on account payable, $1,500.
14. Paid cash to purchase office furniture, $2,000.
15. Recognized $20,000 of depreciation expense.
16. Recognized $8,800 of rent expense that had been paid in cash in a prior transaction (see Event 10).
17. Recognized $12,200 of revenue for services performed for which cash had been previously collected (see Event 3).
18. Recognized $4,000 of accrued interest expense.

Required
Identify each event as asset source (AS), asset use (AU), asset exchange (AE), or claims exchange (CE). Also identify the account to be debited and the account to be credited when the transaction is recorded. The first event is recorded as an example.

Event No.	Type of Event	Account Debited	Account Credited
1	AS	Cash	Common Stock

L.O. 4, 7   PROBLEM 4–27A *Recording Adjusting Entries in General Journal Format*

Required
Each of the following independent events requires a year-end adjusting entry. Record each event and the related adjusting entry in general journal format. The first event is recorded as an example. Assume a December 31 closing date.

Date	Account Titles	Debit	Credit
Oct. 1	Prepaid Rent	3,500	
	Cash		3,500
Dec. 31	Rent Expense	875	
	Prepaid Rent		875

a. Paid $3,500 cash in advance on October 1 for a one-year lease on office space.
b. Borrowed $60,000 cash by issuing a note to Third National Bank on April 1. The note had a one-year term and a 7 percent annual rate of interest.
c. Paid $31,000 cash to purchase equipment on October 1. The equipment was expected to have a five-year useful life and a $5,000 salvage value. Depreciation is computed on a straight-line basis.
d. Invested $12,500 cash in a certificate of deposit that paid 4 percent interest annually. The certificate was acquired on April 1 and had a one-year term to maturity.
e. Purchased $2,400 of supplies on account on June 15. At year end, $250 of supplies remained on hand.
f. Received an $8,100 cash advance on July 1 for a contract to provide services for one year.
g. Paid $2,400 cash in advance on March 1 for a one-year insurance policy.

PROBLEM 4–28A *One Complete Accounting Cycle*

L.O. 3, 7

The following events apply to Travel Company's first year of operations:
1. Acquired $12,500 cash from the issue of common stock on January 1, 2005.
2. Purchased $500 of supplies on account.
3. Paid $3,400 cash in advance for a one-year lease on office space.
4. Earned $16,000 of revenue on account.
5. Incurred $10,200 of other operating expenses on account.
6. Collected $14,500 cash from accounts receivable.
7. Paid $8,000 cash on accounts payable.
8. Paid a $1,200 cash dividend to the stockholders.

Information for Adjusting Entries
9. There was $110 of supplies on hand at the end of the accounting period.
10. The lease on the office space covered a one-year period beginning October 1.
11. There was $1,400 of accrued salaries at the end of the period.

Required
a. Record these transactions in general journal form.
b. Post the transaction data from the journal to ledger T-accounts.
c. Prepare a trial balance.
d. Prepare an income statement, statement of changes in stockholders' equity, a balance sheet, and a statement of cash flows.
e. Close the nominal accounts (Revenue, Expense, and Dividends) to Retained Earnings.
f. Post the closing entries to the T-accounts, and prepare an after-closing trial balance.

PROBLEM 4–29A *Two Complete Accounting Cycles*

L.O. 3–7

Northeast Welding experienced the following events during 2001.
1. Started operations by acquiring $20,000 of cash from the issue of common stock.
2. Paid $3,000 cash in advance for rent during the period from February 1, 2001, to February 1, 2002.
3. Received $2,400 cash in advance for services to be performed evenly over the period from September 1, 2001, to September 1, 2002.
4. Performed services for customers on account for $38,500.
5. Incurred operating expenses on account of $17,000.
6. Collected $32,500 cash from accounts receivable.
7. Paid $12,000 cash for salaries expense.
8. Paid $14,500 cash as a partial payment on accounts payable.

Adjusting Entries
9. Made the adjusting entry for the expired rent. (See Event 2.)
10. Recognized revenue for services performed in accordance with Event 3.
11. Recorded $1,600 of accrued salaries at the end of 2001.

Events for 2002
1. Paid $1,600 cash for the salaries accrued at the end of the previous year.
2. Performed services for cash, $20,100.
3. Borrowed $15,000 cash from the local bank by issuing a note.
4. Paid $12,500 cash to purchase land.
5. Paid $3,600 cash in advance for rent during the period from February 1, 2002, to February 1, 2003.
6. Performed services for customers on account for $64,000.
7. Incurred operating expenses on account of $35,200.
8. Collected $42,500 cash from accounts receivable.
9. Paid $32,000 cash as a partial payment on accounts payable.
10. Paid $28,000 cash for salaries expense.
11. Paid a $5,000 cash dividend to the stockholders.

Adjusting Entries
12. Recognized revenue for services performed in accordance with Event 3 in 2001.
13. Made the adjusting entry for the expired rent. (*Hint:* Part of the rent was paid in 2001.)
14. Recorded accrued interest. The note was issued on March 1, 2002, for a one-year term and had an interest rate of 9 percent (see Event 3).

Required

a. Record the events and adjusting entries for 2001 in general journal form.

b. Post the events to T-accounts.

c. Prepare a trial balance.

d. Prepare an income statement, statement of changes in stockholders' equity, balance sheet, and statement of cash flows for 2001.

e. Record the entries to close the nominal accounts to Retained Earnings in the general journal and post to the T-accounts.

f. Prepare an after-closing trial balance for December 31, 2001.

g. Repeat Requirements *a* through *f* for 2002.

L.O. 2, 7   PROBLEM 4–30A *Identifying Accounting Events From Journal Entries*

Required

The following information is from the records of Bennett's Design Group. Write a brief description of the accounting event represented in each of the general journal entries.

Date		Account Titles	Debit	Credit
Jan.	1	Cash	12,500	
		Common Stock		12,500
Feb.	15	Cash	13,000	
		Unearned Revenue		13,000
Mar.	10	Supplies	1,550	
		Accounts Payable		1,550
Apr.	1	Office Equipment	17,000	
		Cash		4,000
		Note Payable		13,000
May	1	Prepaid Rent	10,200	
		Cash		10,200
	20	Accounts Receivable	18,400	
		Commission Revenue		18,400
June	15	Salaries Expense	6,100	
		Cash		6,100
Aug.	28	Cash	9,300	
		Commission Revenue		9,300
	30	Dividends	3,000	
		Cash		3,000
Sept.	19	Cash	16,000	
		Accounts Receivable		16,000
Oct.	31	Property Tax Expense	3,000	
		Cash		3,000
Dec.	31	Depreciation Expense	2,700	
		Accumulated Depreciation		2,700
	31	Supplies Expense	2,025	
		Supplies		2,025
	31	Rent Expense	6,400	
		Prepaid Rent		6,400
	31	Unearned Revenue	8,500	
		Commission Revenue		8,500

L.O. 3–6   PROBLEM 4–31A *Recording Events in Statements Model and T-Accounts and Preparing a Trial Balance*

The following accounting events apply to Chen Enterprises for the year 2002:

Asset Source Transactions

1. Began operations when the business acquired $10,000 cash from the issue of common stock.
2. Purchased $3,250 of equipment on account.
3. Performed services and collected cash of $600.
4. Collected $3,000 of cash in advance for services to be provided over the next 12 months.
5. Provided $6,500 of services on account.
6. Purchased supplies of $650 on account.

Asset Exchange Transactions

7. Purchased $5,000 of equipment for cash.
8. Collected $5,500 of cash from accounts receivable.
9. Loaned $500 to Ted Marples, who issued a 12-month, 9 percent note.
10. Purchased $400 of supplies with cash.
11. Purchased a $2,400 certificate of deposit that had a six-month term and paid 5 percent annual interest.

Asset Use Transactions

12. Paid $2,500 cash for salaries of employees.
13. Paid a cash dividend of $1,500 to the stockholders.
14. Paid for the equipment that had been purchased on account (see Event 2).
15. Paid $650 for supplies that had been purchased on account.

Claims Exchange Transactions

16. Placed an advertisement in the local newspaper for $125 and agreed to pay for the ad later.
17. Incurred utilities expense of $100 on account.

Adjusting Entries

18. Recognized $2,100 of revenue for performing services. The collection of cash for these services occurred in a prior transaction. (See Event 4.)
19. Recorded $40 of interest revenue that had accrued on the note receivable from Marples (see Event 9).
20. Recorded $45 of interest revenue that had accrued on the certificate of deposit (see Event 11).
21. Recorded $450 of accrued salary expense at the end of 2002.
22. Recognized $750 of depreciation on the equipment (see Events 2 and 7).
23. Recorded supplies expense. Had $75 of supplies on hand at the end of the accounting period.

Required

a. Use a horizontal statements model to show how each event affects the balance sheet, income statement, and statement of cash flows. Indicate whether the event increases (+), decreases (−), or does not affect (NA) each element of the financial statements. Also, in the Cash Flow column, use the letters OA to designate operating activity, IA for investing activity, and FA for financing activity. The first event is recorded as an example.

Assets	=	Liab.	+	Stk. Equity	Rev.	−	Exp.	=	Net Inc.	Cash Flow
+		NA		+	NA		NA		NA	+ FA

b. Record each of the preceding transactions in T-accounts and determine the balance of each account.
c. Prepare a before-closing trial balance.

PROBLEM 4–32A *Effect of Journal Entries on Financial Statements* L.O. 1, 7

Entry No.	Account Titles	Debit	Credit
1	Cash	xxx	
	Common Stock		xxx
2	Accounts Receivable	xxx	
	Commission Revenue		xxx
3	Salaries Expense	xxx	
	Cash		xxx
4	Cash	xxx	
	Commission Revenue		xxx
5	Dividends	xxx	
	Cash		xxx

(cont'd)

Entry No.	Account Titles	Debit	Credit
6	Cash	xxx	
	Unearned Revenue		xxx
7	Supplies	xxx	
	Accounts Payable		xxx
8	Office Equipment	xxx	
	Cash		xxx
	Note Payable		xxx
9	Prepaid Rent	xxx	
	Cash		xxx
10	Cash	xxx	
	Accounts Receivable		xxx
11	Property Tax Expense	xxx	
	Cash		xxx
12	Depreciation Expense	xxx	
	Accumulated Depreciation		xxx
13	Supplies Expense	xxx	
	Supplies		xxx
14	Rent Expense	xxx	
	Prepaid Rent		xxx
15	Unearned Revenue	xxx	
	Commission Revenue		xxx

Required

The preceding 15 different accounting events are presented in general journal format. Use a horizontal statements model to show how each event affects the balance sheet, income statement, and statement of cash flows. Indicate whether the event increases (+), decreases (−), or does not affect (NA) each element of the financial statements. Also, in the Cash Flow column, use the letters OA to designate operating activity, IA for investing activity, and FA for financing activity. The first event is recorded as an example.

Assets	=	Liab.	+	Stk. Equity	Rev.	−	Exp.	=	Net Inc.	Cash Flow	
+		NA		+	NA		NA		NA	+	FA

L.O. 6   PROBLEM 4–33A *Effect of Errors on the Trial Balance*

Required

Consider each of the following errors independently (assume that each is the only error that has occurred). Complete the following table. The first error is recorded as an example.

Error	Is the Trial Balance Out of Balance?	By What Amount?	Which Is Larger, Total Debits or Credits?
a	yes	90	debit

a. A credit of $430 to Accounts Payable was recorded as $340.

b. A credit of $620 to Accounts Receivable was not recorded.

c. A debit of $700 to Rent Expense was recorded as a debit of $700 to Salaries Expense.

d. An entry requiring a debit of $325 to Cash and a credit of $325 to Accounts Receivable was not posted to the ledger accounts.

e. A credit of $2,000 to Prepaid Insurance was recorded as a debit of $2,000 to Prepaid Insurance.

f. A debit of $200 to Cash was recorded as a credit of $200 to Cash.

PROBLEM 4–34A *Effect of Errors on the Trial Balance*   L.O. 6

The following trial balance was prepared from the ledger accounts of Forbes, Inc.:

FORBES, INC. Trial Balance May 31, 2006		
Account Title	Debit	Credit
Cash	$ 1,100	
Accounts Receivable	1,770	
Supplies	420	
Prepaid Insurance	2,400	
Office Equipment	10,000	
Accounts Payable		$ 1,500
Notes Payable		1,000
Common Stock		1,800
Retained Earnings		4,000
Dividends	400	
Service Revenue		19,600
Rent Expense	3,600	
Salaries Expense	9,000	
Operating Expense	2,500	
Totals	$31,190	$27,900

The accountant for Forbes, Inc., made the following errors during May 2006.
1. The cash purchase of a $2,110 typewriter was recorded as a $2,200 debit to Office Equipment and a $2,110 credit to Cash.
2. An $800 purchase of supplies on account was properly recorded as a debit to the Supplies account but was incorrectly recorded as a credit to the Cash account.
3. The company provided services valued at $7,500 to a customer. The accountant recorded the transaction in the proper accounts but in the incorrect amount of $17,500.
4. A $500 cash receipt for a payment on an account receivable was not recorded.
5. A $300 cash payment of an account payable was not recorded.
6. The May utility bill, which amounted to $600 on account, was not recorded.

Required
a. Identify the errors that would cause a difference in the total amounts of debits and credits that would appear in a trial balance. Indicate whether the Debit or Credit column would be larger as a result of the error.
b. Indicate whether each of the preceding errors would overstate, understate, or have no effect on the amount of total assets, liabilities, and equity. Your answer should take the following form:

Event No.	Assets	=	Liabilities	+	Stockholders' Equity
1	Overstate		No effect		No effect

c. Prepare a corrected trial balance.

PROBLEM 4–35A *Comprehensive Problem: Single Cycle*

The following transactions pertain to Atwood Corporation for 2003.

L.O. 3–7

Jan. 1   Began operations when the business acquired $60,000 cash from the issue of common stock.
Mar. 1   Paid rent for office space for two years, $19,200 cash.
Apr. 1   Borrowed $40,000 cash from First National Bank. The note issued had a 10 percent annual rate of interest and matured in one year.
  14   Purchased $600 of supplies on account.
June 1   Paid $30,000 cash for a computer system. The computer system had a five-year useful life and no salvage value.
  30   Received $36,000 cash in advance for services to be provided over the next year.
July 5   Paid $400 of the accounts payable from April 14.

Aug. 1   Billed a customer $6,600 for services provided during July.

       8   Completed a job and received $4,000 cash for services rendered.

Sept. 1   Paid employee salaries of $24,000 cash.

       9   Received $5,000 cash from accounts receivable.

Oct. 5   Billed customers $18,400 for services rendered on account.

Nov. 2   Paid an $800 cash dividend to the stockholders.

Dec. 31   Adjusted records to recognize the services provided on the contract of June 30.

     31   Recorded the accrued interest on the note to First National Bank. (See April 1.)

     31   Recorded depreciation on the computer system used in the business. (See June 1.)

     31   Recorded $1,800 of accrued salaries as of December 31.

     31   Recorded the rent expense for the year. (See March 1.)

     31   Physically counted supplies; $50 was on hand at the end of the period.

Required

a. Record the preceding transactions in the general journal.

b. Post the transactions to T-accounts and calculate the account balances.

c. Prepare a trial balance.

d. Prepare the income statement, statement of changes in stockholders' equity, balance sheet, and statement of cash flows.

e. Prepare the closing entries at December 31.

f. Prepare a trial balance after the closing entries are posted.

L.O. 3–7   **PROBLEM 4–36A** *Comprehensive Problem: Two Cycles*

This is a two-cycle problem. The second cycle is in Problem 4–36B. The first cycle *can* be completed without referring to the second cycle.

Sam and Barb organized a rental shop that began operations on April 1, 2007. Hawkins Rentals consummated the following transactions during the first month of operation.

April 1   Acquired $40,000 to establish the company, $20,000 from the issue of common stock and $20,000 from issuing a bank note. The note had a five-year term and a 9 percent annual interest rate. Interest was payable in cash on March 31 of each year.

      1   Paid $3,600 in advance rent for a one-year lease on office space.

      1   Paid $30,000 to purchase wedding décor. The décor was expected to have a useful life of five years and a salvage value of $3,000.

      6   Purchased supplies for $220 cash.

      9   Received $500 cash as an advance payment from Donna Oreen to reserve wedding décor to be used in May.

     10   Recorded rentals to customers. Cash receipts were $850, and invoices for rentals on account were $1,200.

     15   Paid $960 cash for employee salaries.

     16   Collected $450 from accounts receivable.

     23   Received monthly utility bills amounting to $233. The bills will be paid during May.

     25   Paid advertising expense for advertisements run during April, $240.

     30   Recorded rentals to customers. Cash receipts were $1,150 and invoices for rentals on account were $1,600.

     30   Paid $960 cash for employee salaries.

Information for April 30 Adjusting Entries

1. Counted the supplies inventory. Had $80 of supplies on hand.

2. Make adjustments for interest expense, rent expense, and depreciation expense.

Required

a. Record the transactions for April in general journal format.

b. Open a general ledger, using T-accounts, and post the general journal entries to the ledger.

c. Prepare an unadjusted trial balance.

d. Record and post the appropriate adjusting entries.

e. Prepare an adjusted trial balance.

f. Prepare an income statement, statement of changes in stockholders' equity, balance sheet, and statement of cash flows.

g. Record and post the closing entries.

h. Prepare an after-closing trial balance.

EXERCISE 4–1B *Debit/Credit Terminology*   L.O. 1, 2

Two introductory accounting students were arguing about how to record a transaction involving an exchange of cash for land. Trisha stated that the transaction should have a debit to Land and a credit to Cash; Tony argued that the reverse (debit to Cash and credit to Land) represented the appropriate treatment.

Required
Which student was correct? Defend your position.

EXERCISE 4–2B *Matching Debit and Credit Terminology with Accounting Elements*   L.O. 2

Required
Complete the following table by indicating whether a debit or credit is used to increase or decrease the balance of accounts belonging to each category of accounting element. The appropriate debit/credit terminology has been identified for the first category (assets) as an example.

Category of Element	Used to Increase This Element	Used to Decrease This Element
Assets	Debit	Credit
Contra Asset		
Liabilities		
Common Stock		
Retained Earnings		
Revenue		
Expense		
Dividends		

EXERCISE 4–3B *Matching Debit and Credit Terminology with Account Titles*   L.O. 1, 2

Required
Indicate whether each of the following accounts normally has a debit balance or a credit balance.

a. Land
b. Dividends
c. Accounts Payable
d. Unearned Revenue
e. Consulting Revenue
f. Salaries Expense
g. Accumulated Depreciation
h. Cash
i. Prepaid Insurance
j. Common Stock

EXERCISE 4–4B *Identifying Increases and Decreases in T-Accounts*   L.O. 1, 2, 4

Required
For each of the following T-accounts, indicate the side of the account that should be used to record an increase or decrease in the account balance.

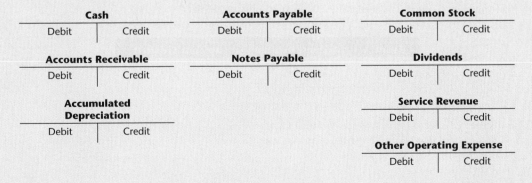

EXERCISE 4–5B *Applying Debit/Credit Terminology to Accounting Events*   L.O. 2

Required
In parallel columns, list the accounts that would be debited and credited for each of the following unrelated transactions:

a. Provided services on account.
b. Paid cash for operating expense.
c. Acquired cash from the issue of common stock.
d. Purchased supplies on account.
e. Purchased equipment for cash.
f. Paid a cash dividend to the stockholders.
g. Provided services for cash.
h. Recognized accrued salaries at the end of the period.

L.O. 2, 3   EXERCISE 4–6B *T-Accounts and the Accounting Equation*

Required

Record each of the following Brown Co. events in T-accounts, and then explain how the event affects the accounting equation.
a. Borrowed $5,000 cash by issuing a note to a bank.
b. Purchased supplies for $250 cash.
c. Purchased land for $10,000. The company paid $3,000 cash and issued a note for the balance.
d. Performed services for $800 cash.

L.O. 3   EXERCISE 4–7B *Recording Transactions in T-Accounts*

The following events apply to Palmer Company for 2005.
1. Received cash of $48,000 from the issue of common stock.
2. Purchased for $25,000 cash a delivery van that has a salvage value of $5,000 and a four-year useful life.
3. Performed $85,000 of services on account.
4. Incurred $8,000 of other operating expenses on account.
5. Paid $34,000 cash for salaries expense.
6. Collected $65,000 of accounts receivable.
7. Paid a $5,000 dividend to the stockholders.
8. Performed $9,200 of services for cash.
9. Paid $4,400 of the accounts payable.
10. Recorded depreciation expense for the year on the delivery van.

Required

a. Record the preceding transactions in the appropriate T-accounts and determine the ending balance in each account.
b. Determine the amount of total assets at the end of 2005.
c. Determine the amount of net income for 2005.

L.O. 2   EXERCISE 4–8B *Debit/Credit Terminology*

Required

For each of the following independent events, identify the account that would be debited and the account that would be credited. The accounts for the first event are identified as an example.

Event	Account Debited	Account Credited
a	Cash	Notes Payable

a. Borrowed cash by issuing a note.
b. Received cash for services to be performed in the future.
c. Recognized depreciation expense.
d. Paid salaries payable.
e. Provided services on account.
f. Repaid principal balance on note payable.
g. Paid cash for operating expenses.
h. Purchased supplies on account.
i. Recognized accrued interest expense.
j. Recognized revenue for services completed. Cash had been collected in Event *b*.
k. Paid accounts payable.

l. Purchased office equipment with cash.
m. Received cash in payment of accounts receivable.
n. Recognized accrued interest revenue.
o. Paid a cash dividend to the stockholders.

EXERCISE 4–9B *Identification of the Type of Transaction, Its Effect on the Accounting*   **L.O. 1, 2**
Equation, and Whether the Effect Is Recorded with a Debit or Credit

Required
Identify whether each of the following transactions is an asset source (AS), asset use (AU), asset exchange (AE), or claims exchange (CE). Also explain how each event affects the accounting equation by placing a + for *increase,* − for *decrease,* and NA for *not affected* under each of the components of the accounting equation. Finally, indicate whether the effect requires a debit or credit entry. The first event is recorded as an example.

| | | | | | | Stockholders' Equity | | |
| | Type of | | | | | Common | | Retained |
Event	Event	Assets	=	Liabilities	+	Stock	+	Earnings
a	AE	+ Debit − Credit		NA		NA		NA

a. Purchased office equipment with cash.
b. Provided services for cash.
c. Repaid principal balance on note payable.
d. Purchased supplies on account.
e. Paid accounts payable.
f. Acquired cash from the issue of common stock.
g. Received cash in payment of accounts receivable.
h. Paid cash in advance for one year of rent.
i. Paid salaries payable.
j. Received cash for services to be performed in the future.
k. Recognized accrued interest expense.
l. Paid a cash dividend to the stockholders.
m. Recognized revenue for services completed for which cash had been collected previously.
n. Recognized depreciation expense on the equipment.
o. Recognized accrued interest revenue.

EXERCISE 4–10B *Recording Events in the General Journal*   **L.O. 7**

Required
Record each of the following transactions in general journal form.
a. Performed $19,000 of services on account.
b. Purchased equipment that cost $24,000 by paying $4,000 cash and issuing a $20,000 note for the balance.
c. Purchased supplies for $530 cash.
d. Received $3,000 cash for services to be performed at a later date.
e. Collected $8,400 cash on accounts receivable.
f. Had repairs made on equipment; the $1,700 for repairs was charged on account.
g. Sold land that cost $10,000 for $13,400.
h. Paid $2,300 cash in advance for an insurance policy on the equipment.
i. Paid $1,200 on accounts payable.
j. Recorded the adjusting entry to recognize $800 of insurance expense.
k. Recorded $6,200 depreciation expense on the equipment.
l. Recorded accrued interest expense of $800.

EXERCISE 4–11B *Preparing a Trial Balance*   **L.O. 6**

Required
On December 31, 2006, Blue Company had the following account balances in its general ledger. Use this information to prepare a trial balance.

Land	$ 80,000
Unearned Revenue	52,000
Dividends	20,000
Depreciation Expense	6,000
Prepaid Rent	19,200
Cash	28,800
Salaries Expense	50,000
Accounts Payable	12,000
Common Stock	80,000
Operating Expense	50,000
Office Supplies	10,000
Advertising Expense	4,000
Retained Earnings, 1–1–06	18,000
Service Revenue	184,000
Office Equipment	64,000
Accounts Receivable	26,000
Accumulated Depreciation	12,000

L.O. 5, 7   EXERCISE 4–12B *Preparing Closing Entries*

The following financial information was taken from the books of Get In Shape Health Club, a small spa and health club.

Account Balances as of December 31, 2008	
Accounts Receivable	$ 6,150
Accounts Payable	5,500
Accrued Salaries Payable	2,150
Accumulated Depreciation	7,800
Cash	20,725
Certificate of Deposit	5,650
Depreciation Expense	3,150
Dividends	1,750
Equipment	12,500
Interest Expense	1,150
Interest Payable	250
Operating Expense	31,550
Prepaid Rent	600
Rent Expense	4,200
Retained Earnings 1, 1, 2008	32,650
Salaries Expense	11,200
Service Revenue	48,400
Supplies	400
Supplies Expense	4,240
Common Stock	6,515

Required

a. Prepare the necessary closing entries at December 31, 2008, for Get In Shape Health Club.

b. What is the balance in the Retained Earnings account after the closing entries are posted?

L.O. 3, 6   EXERCISE 4–13B *Recording Events in T-Accounts and Preparing a Trial Balance*

The following events apply to Cellular Services, Inc.

1. Acquired $80,000 cash from the issue of common stock.
2. Borrowed $64,000 from State Bank.
3. Earned $56,000 of revenue on account.
4. Incurred $30,400 of operating expenses on account.
5. Collected $52,800 cash from accounts receivable.
6. Made a $27,200 payment on accounts payable.
7. Paid a $4,000 cash dividend to the stockholders.
8. Paid $16,000 cash to purchase office equipment.
9. Received a $14,200 cash advance for services to be provided in the future.
10. Purchased $3,200 of supplies on account.
11. Recorded accrued interest expense of $4,160.
12. Recognized $3,200 of depreciation expense.
13. Recognized $4,800 of revenue for services provided to the customer in Event 9.
14. Recognized $2,400 of supplies expense.

Required
a. Record the events in T-accounts and determine the ending account balances.
b. Test the equality of the debit and credit balances of the T-accounts by preparing a trial balance.

EXERCISE 4–14B *Determining the Effect of Errors on the Trial Balance*   L.O. 6

Required
Explain how each of the following posting errors affects a trial balance. State whether the trial balance will be out of balance because of the posting error, and indicate which side of the trial balance will have a higher amount after each independent entry is posted. If the posting error does not affect the equality of debits and credits shown in the trial balance, state that the error will not cause an inequality and explain why.
a. A $400 debit to Rent Expense was posted twice.
b. A $1,200 credit to Accounts Payable was not posted.
c. A $400 credit to Notes Payable was credited to Revenue.
d. A $200 debit to Cash was posted as a $2,000 debit.
e. A $520 debit to Office Supplies was debited to Office Equipment.

EXERCISE 4–15B *Recording Events in the General Journal, Posting to T-Accounts, and*   L.O. 3, 5, 7
                    Preparing Closing Entries

At the beginning of 2006, Tony's Burgers had the following balances in its accounts:

Account	Balance
Cash	$13,000
Accounts Receivable	9,500
Accounts Payable	3,600
Common Stock	9,900
Retained Earnings	9,000

The following events apply to Tony's Burgers for 2006.
1. Provided $118,000 of services on account.
2. Incurred $11,980 of operating expenses on account.
3. Collected $124,000 of accounts receivable.
4. Paid $71,000 cash for salaries expense.
5. Paid $13,600 cash as a partial payment on accounts payable.
6. Paid an $11,000 cash dividend to the stockholders.

Required
a. Record these transactions in a general journal.
b. Open T-accounts, and post the beginning balances and the preceding transactions to the appropriate accounts.
c. Record the beginning balances and the transactions in a horizontal statements model such as the following one:

Assets		=	Liab.	+	Stockholders' Equity		Rev.	–	Exp.	=	Net Inc.	Cash Flow
Cash	+	Accts. Rec.	=	Accts. Pay.	+	Common Stock	+	Ret. Earn.				

d. Record the closing entries in the general journal and post them to the T-accounts. What is the amount of net income for the year?
e. What is the amount of *change* in retained earnings for the year? Is the change in retained earnings different from the amount of net income? If so, why?

EXERCISE 4–16B *Recording Receivables and Identifying Their Effect on Financial Statements*   L.O. 3, 5

Chambers Company performed services on account for $40,000 in 2006. Chambers collected $25,000 cash from accounts receivable during 2006, and the remaining $15,000 was collected in cash during 2007.

Required

a. Record the 2006 transactions in T-accounts.

b. Record the 2006 transactions in a horizontal statements model like the following one:

Assets		= Liab. +	Stk. Equity	Rev. –	Exp. =	Net Inc.	Cash Flow
Cash +	Accts. Rec. =	NA +	Ret. Earn.				

c. Determine the amount of revenue Chambers would report on the 2006 income statement.

d. Determine the amount of cash flow from operating activities Chambers would report on the 2006 statement of cash flows.

e. Open a T-account for Retained Earnings, and close the 2006 Revenue account to the Retained Earnings account.

f. Record the 2007 cash collection in the appropriate T-accounts.

g. Record the 2007 transaction in a horizontal statements model like the one shown in Requirement *b*.

h. Assuming no other transactions occur in 2007, determine the amount of net income and the net cash flow from operating activities for 2007.

L.O. 3-6   EXERCISE 4–17B *Recording Supplies and Identifying Their Effect on Financial Statements*

Jackie Harrison started and operated a small family architectural firm in 2007. The firm was affected by two events: (1) Harrison provided $25,000 of services on account, and (2) she purchased $6,000 of supplies on account. There were $500 of supplies on hand as of December 31, 2007.

Required

a. Open T-accounts and record the two transactions in the accounts.

b. Record the required year-end adjusting entry to reflect the use of supplies.

c. Record the preceding transactions in a horizontal statements model like the following one.

Assets		= Liab. +	Stk. Equity	Rev. –	Exp. =	Net Inc.	Cash Flow
Accts. Rec.	Supp.	Accts. Pay.	Ret. Earn.				

d. Explain why the amount of net income and the net cash flow from operating activities differ.

e. Record and post the required closing entries, and prepare an after-closing trial balance.

L.O. 4, 7   EXERCISE 4–18B *Recording Prepaids and Identifying Their Effect on Financial Statements*

The California Company began operations when it issued common stock for $50,000 cash. It paid $48,000 cash in advance for a one-year contract to lease delivery equipment for the business. It signed the lease agreement on March 1, 2007, which was effective immediately. California Company earned $60,000 of cash revenue in 2007.

Required

a. Record the March 1 cash payment in general journal format.

b. Record in general journal format the asset/expense adjustment required as of December 31, 2007.

c. Record all events in a horizontal statements model like the following one:

Assets		= Liab. +	Stk. Equity	Rev. –	Exp. =	Net Inc.	Cash Flow
Cash +	PrPd. Rent		Ret. Earn.				

d. What amount of net income will California Company report on the 2007 income statement? What is the amount of net cash flow from operating activities for 2007?

e. Determine the amount of prepaid rent California Company would report on the December 31, 2007, balance sheet.

L.O. 4, 7   EXERCISE 4–19B *Recording Accrued Salaries and Identifying Their Effect on Financial Statements*

On December 31, 2008, CD Company had accrued salaries of $9,600.

Required

a. Record in general journal format the expense/liability adjustment required as of December 31, 2008.

b. Determine the amount of net income CD would report on the 2008 income statement, assuming that CD earns $12,000 of cash revenue. What is the amount of net cash flow from operating activities for 2008?

c. What amount of Salaries Payable liability would CD report on the December 31, 2008, balance sheet?

EXERCISE 4–20B *Recording Depreciation and Identifying Its Effect on Financial Statements*   **L.O. 3, 4**

On January 1, 2007, Barco bought a computer for $40,000 cash. The computer had a useful life of three years and a salvage value of $7,000.

Required

a. Record in T-accounts Barco's purchase of the computer.

b. Record in T-accounts the asset/expense adjustment required on December 31, 2007.

c. Determine the book value of the computer Barco would report on the December 31, 2007, balance sheet.

d. Determine the amount of net income Barco would report on the 2007 income statement, assuming that Barco earned $14,000 of cash revenue in 2007.

e. What is the amount of net cash flow from operating activities for 2007?

f. What amount of depreciation expense would Barco report on the 2008 income statement?

g. Determine the book value of the computer Barco would report on the December 31, 2008, balance sheet.

EXERCISE 4–21B *Recording a Note Payable and Identifying Its Effect on Financial Statements*   **L.O. 3, 4**

On April 1, 2007, King Company borrowed $60,000 from First Boston Bank. The note had a 10 percent annual interest rate and a one-year term to maturity.

Required

a. Identify the transaction type (asset source, use, or exchange or claims exchange), and record in T-accounts the entries for the financing event on April 1, 2007.

b. Identify the transaction type, and record in T-accounts the liability/expense adjustment as of December 31, 2007.

c. Determine the amount of net income on the 2007 income statement, assuming King Company earned $10,000 of cash revenue.

d. What is the amount of net cash flow from operating activities for 2007?

e. Determine the total liabilities on the December 31, 2007, balance sheet.

f. Record (1) the 2008 accrual of interest and (2) the cash payment of principal and interest on April 1, 2008.

g. Are the April 1, 2008, transactions asset source, asset use, asset exchange, or claims exchange transactions?

EXERCISE 4–22B *Recording Unearned Revenue and Identifying Its Effect on Financial Statements*   **L.O. 3, 4**

Jamison received a $60,000 cash advance payment on June 1, 2005, for consulting services to be performed in the future. Services were to be provided for a one-year term beginning June 1, 2005.

Required

a. Record the June 1 cash receipt in T-accounts.

b. Record in T-accounts the liability/revenue adjustment required as of December 31, 2005.

c. Record the preceding transaction and related adjustment in a horizontal statements model like the following one:

Assets	=	Liab.	+	Stk. Equity	Rev.	–	Exp.	=	Net Inc.	Cash Flow

d. Determine the amount of net income on the 2005 income statement. What is the amount of net cash flow from operating activities for 2005?

e. What amount of liability would Jamison report on the 2005 balance sheet?

L.O. 3   EXERCISE 4–23B *Using a T-Account to Determine Cash Flow From Operating Activities*

MRX began the accounting period with a $58,000 debit balance in its Accounts Receivable account. During the accounting period, MRX earned revenue on account of $126,000. The ending accounts receivable balance was $54,000.

Required

Based on this information alone, determine the amount of cash inflow from operating activities during the accounting period. (*Hint:* Use a T-account for Accounts Receivable. Enter the debits and credits for the given events, and solve for the missing amount.)

L.O. 3   EXERCISE 4–24B *Using a T-Account to Determine Cash Flow From Operating Activities*

Scooba Company began the accounting period with a $40,000 credit balance in its Accounts Payable account. During the accounting period, Scooba incurred expenses on account of $95,000. The ending Accounts Payable balance was $28,000.

Required

Based on this information, determine the amount of cash outflow for expenses during the accounting period. (*Hint:* Use a T-account for Accounts Payable. Enter the debits and credits for the given events, and solve for the missing amount.)

PROBLEMS—SERIES B

L.O. 2   PROBLEM 4–25B *Identifying Debit and Credit Balances*

Required

Tell whether each of the following accounts normally has a debit or credit balance.

a. Common Stock	**p.** Depreciation Expense
b. Retained Earnings	**q.** Service Revenue
c. Certificate of Deposit	**r.** Notes Payable
d. Interest Expense	**s.** Notes Receivable
e. Accounts Receivable	**t.** Supplies
f. Interest Revenue	**u.** Utilities Payable
g. Insurance Expense	**v.** Consulting Revenue
h. Interest Payable	**w.** Interest Receivable
i. Cash	**x.** Supplies Expense
j. Dividends	**y.** Salaries Expense
k. Unearned Revenue	**z.** Equipment
l. Operating Expense	**aa.** Salaries Payable
m. Accumulated Depreciation	**bb.** Land
n. Accounts Payable	**cc.** Prepaid Insurance
o. Office Equipment	

L.O. 1, 2   PROBLEM 4–26B *Transaction Type and Debit/Credit Terminology*

The following events apply to Tank Enterprises.
1. Acquired $25,000 cash from the issue of common stock.
2. Paid salaries to employees, $1,750 cash.
3. Collected $8,100 cash for services to be performed in the future.
4. Paid cash for utilities, $402.
5. Recognized $22,500 of revenue on account.
6. Purchased equipment costing $15,000 by paying cash of $3,000 and borrowing the balance from First National Bank by issuing a four-year note.
7. Paid a $1,250 cash dividend to the stockholders.
8. Purchased $1,600 of supplies on account.
9. Received $6,250 cash for services rendered.
10. Paid cash to rent office space for the next 12 months, $6,000.
11. Made a $3,750 principal payment on the bank note.
12. Paid cash of $8,750 for other operating expenses.
13. Paid creditor on account payable, $876.

14. Paid cash to purchase office furniture, $5,000.
15. Recognized $3,750 of depreciation expense.
16. Recognized $1,500 of rent expense. Cash had been paid in a prior transaction (see Event 10).
17. Recognized $2,500 of revenue for services performed. Cash had been previously collected (see Event 3).
18. Recognized $376 of accrued interest expense.

Required
Identify each event as asset source (AS), asset use (AU), asset exchange (AE), or claims exchange (CE). Also identify the account that is to be debited and the account that is to be credited when the transaction is recorded. The first event is recorded as an example.

Event No.	Type of Event	Account Debited	Account Credited
1	AS	Cash	Common Stock

PROBLEM 4–27B *Recording Adjusting Entries in General Journal Format*   L.O. 4, 7

Required
Each of the following independent events requires a year-end adjusting entry. Record each event and the related adjusting entry in general journal format. The first event is recorded as an example. Assume a December 31 closing date.

Event No.	Date	Account Titles	Debit	Credit
a	Sept. 1	Prepaid Rent	15,000	
		Cash		15,000
a	Dec. 31	Rent Expense	5,000	
		Prepaid Rent		5,000

a. Paid $15,000 cash in advance on September 1 for a one-year lease on office space.
b. Borrowed $22,500 cash by issuing a note to Bay City National Bank on October 1. The note had a one-year term and an 8 percent annual rate of interest.
c. Paid $9,700 cash to purchase equipment on September 1. The equipment was expected to have a five-year useful life and a $2,500 salvage value. Depreciation is computed on a straight-line basis.
d. Invested $11,000 cash in a certificate of deposit that paid 6 percent interest annually. The certificate was acquired on June 1 and had a one-year term to maturity.
e. Purchased $2,000 of supplies on account on April 15. At year-end, $300 of supplies remained on hand.
f. Received a $3,600 cash advance on July 1 for a contract to provide services for one year.
g. Paid $5,100 cash in advance on February 1 for a one-year insurance policy.

PROBLEM 4–28B *One Complete Accounting Cycle*   L.O. 3–7

The following events apply to Copeland Company's first year of operations:
1. Acquired $20,000 cash from issuing common stock on January 1, 2006.
2. Purchased $600 of supplies on account.
3. Paid $12,000 cash in advance for a one-year lease on office space.
4. Earned $11,500 of revenue on account.
5. Incurred $8,970 of other operating expenses on account.
6. Collected $5,900 cash from accounts receivable.
7. Paid $6,500 cash on accounts payable.
8. Paid a $700 cash dividend to the stockholders.

Information for Adjusting Entries
9. There was $100 of supplies on hand at the end of the accounting period.
10. The lease on the office space covered a one-year period beginning September 1, 2006.
11. There was $2,200 of accrued salaries at the end of the period.

Required
a. Record these transactions in general journal form.
b. Post the transaction data from the journal to ledger T-accounts.

    c. Prepare a trial balance.

    d. Prepare an income statement, statement of changes in stockholders' equity, a balance sheet, and a statement of cash flows.

    e. Close the nominal accounts (Revenue, Expense, and Dividends) to Retained Earnings.

    f. Post the closing entries to the T-accounts, and prepare an after-closing trial balance.

L.O. 3–7   **PROBLEM 4–29B** *Two Complete Accounting Cycles*

Bricker Enterprises experienced the following events for 2006, the first year of operation.

1. Began operations by acquiring $13,000 cash from the issue of common stock.
2. Paid $4,000 cash in advance for rent. The payment was for the period April 1, 2006, to March 31, 2007.
3. Performed services for customers on account for $27,000.
4. Incurred operating expenses on account of $13,500.
5. Collected $25,150 cash from accounts receivable.
6. Paid $8,500 cash for salary expense.
7. Paid $11,500 cash as a partial payment on accounts payable.

Adjusting Entries

8. Made the adjusting entry for the expired rent. (See Event 2.)
9. Recorded $900 of accrued salaries at the end of 2006.

Events for 2007

1. Paid $900 cash for the salaries accrued at the end of the prior accounting period.
2. Performed services for cash of $8,500.
3. Borrowed $6,000 from the local bank by issuing a note.
4. Paid $4,500 cash in advance for rent. The payment was for one year beginning April 1, 2007.
5. Performed services for customers on account for $42,000.
6. Incurred operating expense on account of $19,250.
7. Collected $40,500 cash from accounts receivable.
8. Paid $20,000 cash as a partial payment on accounts payable.
9. Paid $14,000 cash for salary expense.
10. Paid a $6,000 cash dividend to the owners.

Adjusting Entries

11. Made the adjusting entry for the expired rent. (*Hint:* Part of the rent was paid in 2006.)
12. Recorded accrued interest. The note was issued on September 1, 2007, for a one-year term and had an interest rate of 9 percent. (See Event 3.)

Required

a. Record the events and adjusting entries for 2006 in general journal form.

b. Post the events to T-accounts.

c. Prepare a trial balance.

d. Prepare an income statement, statement of changes in stockholders' equity, balance sheet, and statement of cash flows for 2006.

e. Record the entries to close the nominal accounts to Retained Earnings in the general journal and post to the T-accounts.

f. Prepare an after-closing trial balance for December 31, 2006.

g. Repeat requirements *a* through *f* for 2007.

L.O. 2, 7   **PROBLEM 4–30B** *Identifying Accounting Events from Journal Entries*

Required

The following information is from the records of attorney Steve Ray. Write a brief description of the accounting event represented in each of the general journal entries.

Date	Account Titles	Debit	Credit
Jan. 1	Cash	20,000	
	Common Stock		20,000
Feb. 10	Cash	4,000	
	Unearned Revenue		4,000

(cont'd)

Date		Account Titles	Debit	Credit
Mar.	5	Supplies	2,000	
		Cash		2,000
Apr.	10	Office Equipment	12,000	
		Cash		2,000
		Note Payable		10,000
Apr.	30	Prepaid Rent	800	
		Cash		800
May	1	Accounts Receivable	24,000	
		Fees Revenue		24,000
June	1	Salaries Expense	2,000	
		Cash		2,000
Aug.	5	Accounts Receivable	12,000	
		Fees Revenue		12,000
	10	Dividends	1,000	
		Cash		1,000
Sept.	10	Cash	4,400	
		Accounts Receivable		4,400
Oct.	1	Property Tax Expense	3,000	
		Cash		3,000
Dec.	31	Depreciation Expense	1,000	
		Accumulated Depreciation		1,000
	31	Supplies Expense	800	
		Supplies		800
	31	Rent Expense	4,400	
		Prepaid Rent		4,400
	31	Unearned Revenue	6,240	
		Fees Revenue		6,240

PROBLEM 4–31B *Recording Events in Statements Model and T-Accounts and Preparing a*   **L.O. 3–6**
Trial Balance

The following accounting events apply to Mickey's Diner for the year 2007.

Asset Source Transactions
1. Began operations by acquiring $40,000 of cash from the issue of common stock.
2. Purchased $14,000 of equipment on account.
3. Performed services and collected cash of $2,000.
4. Collected $12,000 of cash in advance for services to be provided over the next 12 months.
5. Provided $24,000 of services on account.
6. Purchased supplies of $3,000 on account.

Asset Exchange Transactions
7. Purchased $8,000 of equipment for cash.
8. Collected $14,000 of cash from accounts receivable.
9. Loaned $4,800 to Jose, who issued a 12-month, 7 percent note.
10. Purchased $1,260 of supplies with cash.
11. Purchased a $9,600 certificate of deposit. The CD had a six-month term and paid 4 percent annual interest.

Asset Use Transactions
12. Paid $8,000 cash for salaries of employees.
13. Paid a cash dividend of $4,000 to the stockholders.
14. Paid for the equipment that had been purchased on account (see Event 2).
15. Paid off $1,260 of the accounts payable with cash.

Claims Exchange Transactions

16. Placed an advertisement in the local newspaper for $1,600 to be billed.
17. Incurred utility expense of $1,200 on account.

Adjusting Entries

18. Recognized $8,800 of revenue for performing services. The collection of cash for these services occurred in a prior transaction. (See Event 4.)
19. Recorded $200 of interest revenue that had accrued on the note receivable from Jose. (See Event 9.)
20. Recorded $336 of interest revenue that had accrued on the certificate of deposit. (See Event 11.)
21. Recorded $3,000 of accrued salary expense at the end of 2007.
22. Recognized $2,800 of depreciation on the equipment. (See Events 2 and 7.)
23. Recorded supplies expense. Had $1,200 of supplies on hand at the end of the accounting period.

Required

a. Use a horizontal statements model to show how each event affects the balance sheet, income statement, and statement of cash flows. Indicate whether the event increases (+), decreases (−), or does not affect (NA) each element of the financial statements. Also, in the Cash Flow column, use the letters OA to designate operating activity, IA for investing activity, and FA for financing activity. The first event is recorded as an example.

Assets	=	Liab.	+	Stk. Equity	Rev.	−	Exp.	=	Net Inc.	Cash Flow
+		NA		+	NA		NA		NA	+ FA

b. Record each of the preceding events in T-accounts.
c. Prepare a before-closing trial balance.

L.O. 1, 7   **PROBLEM 4–32B** *Effect of Journal Entries on Financial Statements*

Entry No.	Account Titles	Debit	Credit
1	Cash	xxx	
	Common Stock		xxx
2	Office Equipment	xxx	
	Cash		xxx
	Note Payable		xxx
3	Prepaid Rent	xxx	
	Cash		xxx
4	Dividends	xxx	
	Cash		xxx
5	Utility Expense	xxx	
	Cash		xxx
6	Accounts Receivable	xxx	
	Service Revenue		xxx
7	Salaries Expense	xxx	
	Cash		xxx
8	Cash	xxx	
	Service Revenue		xxx
9	Cash	xxx	
	Unearned Revenue		xxx
10	Supplies	xxx	
	Accounts Payable		xxx
11	Depreciation Expense	xxx	
	Accumulated Depreciation		xxx

(cont'd)

Entry No.	Account Titles	Debit	Credit
12	Cash	xxx	
	Accounts Receivable		xxx
13	Rent Expense	xxx	
	Prepaid Rent		xxx
14	Supplies Expense	xxx	
	Supplies		xxx
15	Unearned Revenue	xxx	
	Service Revenue		xxx

Required

The preceding 15 different accounting events are presented in general journal format. Use a horizontal statements model to show how each event affects the balance sheet, income statement, and statement of cash flows. Indicate whether the event increases (+), decreases (−), or does not affect (NA) each element of the financial statements. Also, in the Cash Flow column, use the letters OA to designate operating activity, IA for investing activity, and FA for financing activity. The first event is recorded as an example.

Assets	=	Liab.	+	Stk. Equity	Rev.	−	Exp.	=	Net Inc.	Cash Flow
+		NA		+	NA		NA		NA	+ FA

PROBLEM 4–33B *Effect of Errors on the Trial Balance* L.O. 6

Required

Consider each of the following errors independently (assume that each is the only error that has occurred). Complete the following table. The first error is recorded as an example.

Error	Is the Trial Balance Out of Balance?	By What Amount?	Which Is Larger, Total Debits or Credits?
a	no	NA	NA

a. A debit of $800 to Supplies Expense was recorded as a debit of $800 to Rent Expense.
b. A credit of $500 to Consulting Revenue was not recorded.
c. A credit of $360 to Accounts Payable was recorded as $680.
d. A debit of $3,000 to Cash was recorded as a credit of $3,000 to Cash.
e. An entry requiring a debit to Cash of $850 and a credit to Accounts Receivable of $850 was not posted to the ledger accounts.
f. A debit of $4,200 to Prepaid Rent was recorded as a credit of $4,200 to Prepaid Rent.

PROBLEM 4–34B *Effect of Errors on the Trial Balance* L.O. 6

The following trial balance was prepared from the ledger accounts of Kona Company.

When the trial balance failed to balance, the accountant reviewed the records and discovered the following errors:

1. The company received $470 as payment for services rendered. The credit to Service Revenue was recorded correctly, but the debit to Cash was recorded as $740.
2. A $430 receipt of cash that was received as a payment on accounts receivable was not recorded.
3. A $450 purchase of supplies on account was properly recorded as a debit to the Supplies account. However, the credit to Accounts Payable was not recorded.

KONA COMPANY
Trial Balance
April 30, 2006

Account Title	Debit	Credit
Cash	$ 7,150	
Accounts Receivable	40,000	
Supplies	2,400	
Prepaid Insurance	3,200	
Equipment	56,800	
Accounts Payable		$ 8,950
Notes Payable		32,000
Common Stock		96,000
Retained Earnings		56,720
Dividends	6,000	
Service Revenue		40,000
Rent Expense	7,200	
Salaries Expense	26,400	
Operating Expense	65,240	
Totals	$214,390	$233,670

4. Equipment valued at $10,000 was contributed to the business in exchange for common stock. The entry to record the transaction was recorded as a $10,000 credit to both the Equipment account and the Common Stock account.

5. A $200 rent payment was properly recorded as a credit to Cash. However, the Salaries Expense account was incorrectly debited for $200.

Required

Based on this information, prepare a corrected trial balance for Kona Company.

L.O. 3-7   **PROBLEM 4–35B** *Comprehensive Problem: Single Cycle*

The following transactions pertain to Moon Walk Company for 2008.

Jan. 30	Established the business when it acquired $75,000 cash from the issue of common stock.
Feb. 1	Paid rent for office space for two years, $24,000 cash.
Mar. 1	Borrowed $20,000 cash from National Bank. The note issued had a 9 percent annual rate of interest and matured in one year.
Apr. 10	Purchased $5,300 of supplies on account.
June 1	Paid $27,000 cash for a computer system which had a three-year useful life and no salvage value.
July 1	Received $50,000 cash in advance for services to be provided over the next year.
20	Paid $1,800 of the accounts payable from April 10.
Aug. 15	Billed a customer $32,000 for services provided during July.
Sept. 15	Completed a job and received $19,000 cash for services rendered.
Oct. 1	Paid employee salaries of $20,000 cash.
15	Received $25,000 cash from accounts receivable.
Nov. 16	Billed customers $37,000 for services rendered on account.
Dec. 1	Paid a dividend of $6,000 cash to the stockholders.
31	Adjusted records to recognize the services provided on contract of July 1.
31	Recorded the accrued interest on the note to National Bank. (See March 1.)
31	Recorded depreciation on the computer system used in the business. (See June 1.)
31	Recorded $4,500 of accrued salaries as of December 31.
31	Recorded the rent expense for the year. (See February 1.)
31	Physically counted supplies; $480 was on hand at the end of the period.

Required

a. Record the preceding transactions in the general journal.
b. Post the transactions to T-accounts and calculate the account balances.
c. Prepare a trial balance.
d. Prepare the income statement, statement of changes in stockholders' equity, balance sheet, and statement of cash flows.
e. Prepare the closing entries at December 31.
f. Prepare a trial balance after the closing entries are posted.

PROBLEM 4–36B *Comprehensive Problem: Two Cycles*   **L.O. 3–7**

This problem extends Problem 4–36A involving Hawkins Rentals and *should not* be attempted until that problem has been completed. The transactions consummated by Hawkins Rentals during May 2007 (the company's second month of operation) consisted of the following:

May	1	Recorded rentals of wedding décor to customers. Cash receipts were $420, and invoices for rentals on account were $1,200.
	2	Purchased supplies on account that cost $300.
	7	Collected $2,500 cash from customer accounts receivable.
	8	Donna Oreen rented the wedding décor that had been paid for in advance (see April 9 in Problem 4–36A).
	10	Paid the utility company for the monthly utility bills that had been received in the previous month, $233.
	15	Paid $2,100 cash for employee salaries.
	15	Purchased a one-year insurance policy that cost $1,200.
	16	Paid $300 on the account payable that was established when supplies were purchased on May 2.
	20	Paid a $300 cash dividend to the stockholders.
	27	Received monthly utility bills amounting to $310. The bills would be paid during the month of June.
	31	Recorded rentals of wedding décor to customers. Cash receipts were $625, and invoices for rentals on account were $1,100.
	31	Paid $2,100 cash for employee salaries.
	31	Counted the supplies inventory. Had $40 of supplies on hand.

Required

a. Open a general ledger with T-accounts, using the ending account balances computed in Problem 4–36A.

b. Record the preceding transactions directly into the T-accounts.

c. Record the adjusting entries directly into the T-accounts. (*Note:* Refer to Problem 4–36A to obtain all the information needed to prepare the adjusting entries.)

d. Prepare an income statement, statement of changes in stockholders' equity, balance sheet, and statement of cash flows.

e. Record the closing entries directly into the T-accounts.

f. Answer the following questions.

   (1) Why is the amount in the May 31, 2007, Retained Earnings account not equal to the amount of net income or loss for the month of May?

   (2) Why is the amount of Accumulated Depreciation on the May 31, 2007, balance sheet not equal to the amount of depreciation expense for the month of May?

ANALYZE, THINK, COMMUNICATE

BUSINESS APPLICATIONS CASE *Dell Annual Report*   **ATC 4–1**

Required

Using the Dell Computer Corporation financial statements in Appendix B, answer the following questions:

a. On February 2, 2001, Dell had a balance of $839 million in Retained Earnings. On January 28, 2000, the balance in Retained Earnings was $1,260 million. Explain the change in Retained Earnings during 2001.

b. What is the nature of Dell's business; that is, what does it produce and sell?

c. Could Requirement *b* be answered by examining only Dell's income statement, balance sheet, and statement of cash flows?

d. Does the Other account in the Stockholders' Equity section of the 2001 balance sheet have a debit or credit balance?

ATC 4-2   GROUP ASSIGNMENT *Financial Statement Analysis*

The account balances for Mabry Company were as follows:

	January 1		
	2002	2003	2004
Cash	$12,000	$ 5,800	$29,400
Accounts Receivable	6,000	10,000	6,000
Equipment	25,000	25,000	25,000
Accumulated Depreciation	(12,000)	(13,200)	(14,400)
Prepaid Rent	0	1,000	1,400
Accounts Payable	4,000	3,000	7,000
Notes Payable	12,000*	0	0
Interest Payable	300	0	0
Salaries Payable	0	0	2,100
Common Stock	10,000	10,000	10,000
Retained Earnings	4,700	15,600	28,300

*Funds were originally borrowed on October 1, 2001, with an interest rate of 10 percent.

Mabry Company experienced the following events for the accounting periods 2002, 2003, and 2004.

2002

1. Performed services for $36,000 on account.
2. Paid rent of $6,000 for the period March 1, 2002, to March 1, 2003.
3. Incurred operating expense of $18,000 on account.
4. Collected $32,000 of accounts receivable.
5. Paid $19,000 of accounts payable.
6. Paid note and interest due on October 1.
7. Recorded expired rent.
8. Recorded depreciation expense of $1,200.

2003

1. Performed services on account of $48,000.
2. Paid rent of $8,400 for the period March 1, 2003, to March 1, 2004, and recorded the expired rent for the period January 1, 2003, to March 1, 2003.
3. Incurred operating expenses of $24,000 on account.
4. Collected $52,000 of accounts receivable.
5. Paid $20,000 of accounts payable.
6. Recorded expired rent.
7. Recorded accrued salaries of $2,100.
8. Recorded depreciation expense of $1,200.

2004

1. Paid accrued salaries.
2. Performed services on account of $56,000.
3. Paid rent of $9,000 for the period March 1, 2004, to March 1, 2005, and recorded the expired rent for the period January 1, 2004, to March 1, 2004.
4. Incurred operating expenses of $32,000 on account.
5. Collected $55,000 of accounts receivable.
6. Paid $33,000 of accounts payable.
7. Sold equipment for $2,000; the equipment had a cost of $5,000 and accumulated depreciation of $4,000.
8. Recorded expired rent.
9. Recorded depreciation expense of $1,000.

Required

a. Divide the class into groups of four or five students. Organize the groups into three sections. Assign each section of groups the financial data for one of the preceding accounting periods.

Group Task

Prepare an income statement, balance sheet, and statement of cash flows. It may be helpful to open T-accounts and post transactions to these accounts before attempting to prepare the statements.

Class Discussion

b. Review the cash flows associated with the collection of receivables and the payment of payables. Comment on the company's collection and payment strategy.

c. Explain why depreciation decreased in 2004.

d. Did net income increase or decrease between 2002 and 2003? What were the primary causes?

e. Did net income increase or decrease between 2003 and 2004? What were the primary causes?

REAL-WORLD CASE *Date Used to Prepare the Numbers*   ATC 4–3

Consider the following brief descriptions of four companies, listed alphabetically, from different industries. Dekalb Genetics Corporation is a North American company that develops new varieties of seeds, such as corn, and sells them to farmers. KB Homes builds residential homes in seven western states and in France and Mexico. It claims to be the largest homebuilder west of the Mississippi River. Toys R Us, Inc., is the well-known international retailer of toys. Vail Resorts, Inc., operates several ski resorts in Colorado, including Vail Mountain, the largest in the United States, and Breckenridge Mountain.

This chapter explained that companies often choose to close their books when business usually is slow. Each of these companies ends its fiscal year on a different date. The closing dates, listed chronologically, are as follows:

January 31
July 31
August 31
November 30

Required

a. Try to determine which fiscal year end matches which company. Write a brief explanation of the reason for your decisions.

b. Because many companies deliberately choose to prepare their financial statements at a slow time of year, try to identify problems this may present for someone trying to analyze the balance sheet for Toys R Us. Write a brief explanation of the issues you identify.

BUSINESS APPLICATIONS CASE *Components of Financial Statements*   ATC 4–4

A stockbroker handed Dr. Nguyen a set of financial statements for a company the broker described as a "sure bet" for a major increase in stock price. The broker assured Nguyen that the company was a legitimate business. As proof, she stated that the company was listed with the Securities and Exchange Commission. After looking over the financial statements, Nguyen wanted additional information. He has an Internet connection and can access SEC files. Assume that Nguyen obtains a 10-K annual report through the EDGAR database.

Required

Identify three major sections of information that are likely to be contained in the 10-K annual report. Describe the content of each section, and explain the independent auditors' role as it relates to each section.

BUSINESS APPLICATIONS CASE *Components of Financial Statements*   ATC 4–5

Beth Hughes just finished reading the annual report of Muncy Company. Hughes is enthusiastic about the possibility of investing in the company. In the management's discussion and analysis section of the report, Muncy's new president, Bill Karn, stated that he was committed to an annual growth rate of 25 percent over the next five years. Hughes tells you that the company's financial statements received an unqualified audit opinion from a respected firm of CPAs. Based on the audit report, Hughes concluded that the auditors agree with Karn's forecast of a five-year, 25 percent growth rate. She tells you, "These accountants are usually very conservative. If they forecast 25 percent growth, actual growth is likely to be close to 35 percent. I'm not going to miss an opportunity like this. I am buying the stock."

Required

Comment on Hughes's understanding of the relationship between the auditors' report and management's discussion and analysis in a company's annual report.

ATC 4–6 WRITING ASSIGNMENT *Fiscal Closing Date*

Assume you are the auditor for Metro Auto Sales. Metro currently has a December 31 year end as of which you perform the audit. You would like for Metro to change the year end to another time (almost any time except December 31).

Required

Write a memo to the owners of Metro Auto Sales and propose a new year end. In the memo explain why it would be reasonable or better to have a different year end and specify what the year end would be. Also give reasons that the change would be beneficial from your perspective.

ATC 4–7 ETHICAL DILEMMA *Choice of Brothers: Ethics, Risk, and Accounting Numbers in a Medieval Setting*

In the late 1400s, a wealthy land owner named Caster was trying to decide which of his twin sons, Rogan or Argon, to designate as the first heir to the family fortune. He decided to set up each son with a small farm consisting of 300 sheep and 20 acres of land. Each twin would be allowed to manage his property as he deemed appropriate. After a designated period, Caster would call his sons before him to account for their actions. The heir to the family fortune would be chosen on the basis of which son had produced a larger increase in wealth during the test period.

On the appointed day of reckoning, Argon boasted that he had 714 sheep under his control while Rogan had only 330. Furthermore, Argon stated that he had increased his land holdings to 27 acres. The seven-acre increase resulted from two transactions: first, on the day the contest started, Argon used 20 sheep to buy 10 additional acres; and second, he sold three of these acres for a total of 9 sheep on the day of reckoning. Also, Argon's flock had produced 75 newborn sheep during the period of accounting. He had been able to give his friends 50 sheep in return for the help that they had given him in building a fence, thereby increasing not only his own wealth but the wealth of his neighbors as well. Argon boasted that the fence was strong and would keep his herd safe from predatory creatures for five years (assume the fence had been used for one year during the contest period). Rogan countered that Argon was holding 400 sheep that belonged to another herder. Argon had borrowed these sheep on the day that the contest had started. Furthermore, Argon had agreed to return 424 sheep to the herder. The 24 additional sheep represented consideration for the use of the herder's flock. Argon had agreed to return the sheep immediately after the day of reckoning.

During the test period, Rogan's flock had produced 37 newborn sheep, but 2 sheep had gotten sick and died during the accounting period. Rogan had also lost 5 sheep to predatory creatures. He had no fence, and some of his sheep strayed from the herd, thereby exposing themselves to danger. Knowing that he was falling behind, Rogan had taken a wife in order to boost his productivity. His wife owned 170 sheep on the day they were married; her sheep had produced 16 newborn sheep since the date of her marriage to Rogan. Argon had not included the wife's sheep in his count of Rogan's herd. If his wife's sheep had been counted, Rogan's herd would contain 516 instead of 330 sheep suggested by Argon's count.

Argon charged that seven of Rogan's sheep were sick with symptoms similar to those exhibited by the two sheep that were now dead. Rogan interjected that he should not be held accountable for acts of nature such as illness. Furthermore, he contended that by isolating the sick sheep from the remainder of the herd, he had demonstrated prudent management practices that supported his case to be designated first heir.

Required

a. Prepare an income statement, balance sheet, statement of sheep flow (cash flow) for each twin, using contemporary (2002) accounting standards. Note that you have to decide whether to include the sheep owned by Rogan's wife when making his financial statements (what is the accounting entity?). (*Hint:* Use the number of sheep rather than the number of dollars as the common unit of measure.)

b. Refer to the statements you prepared in Requirement *a* to answer the following questions:
   (1) Which twin has more owner's equity at the end of the accounting period?
   (2) Which twin produced the higher net income during the accounting period?
   (3) Which son should be designated heir based on conventional accounting and reporting standards?

c. What is the difference in the value of the land of the twins if the land is valued at market value (that is, three sheep per acre) rather than historical cost (that is, two sheep per acre)?

d. Did Argon's decision to borrow sheep increase his profitability? Support your answer with appropriate financial data.

e. Was Argon's decision to build a fence financially prudent? Support your answer with appropriate financial data.

f. Assuming that the loan resulted in a financial benefit to Argon, identify some reasons that the shepherd who owned the sheep may have been willing to loan them to Argon.

g. Which twin is likely to take risks to improve profitability? What would be the financial condition of each twin if one-half of the sheep in both flocks died as a result of illness? How should such risk factors be reported in financial statements?

h. Should Rogan's decision to "marry for sheep" be considered from an ethical perspective, or should the decision be made solely on the basis of the bottom-line net income figure?

i. Prepare a report that recommends which twin should be designated heir to the family business. Include a set of financial statements that supports your recommendation. Since this is a managerial report that will not be distributed to the public, you are not bound by generally accepted accounting principles.

EDGAR DATABASE *Investigating Nike's 10-K report*

ATC 4–8

As explained in this chapter, many companies must file financial reports with the SEC. Many of these reports are available electronically through the EDGAR database. EDGAR is an acronym for Electronic Data Gathering, Analysis, and Retrieval system, and it is accessible through the World Wide Web on the Internet. Instructions for using EDGAR are in Appendix A.

Using the most current 10-K available on EDGAR, answer the following questions about Nike Company.

a. In what year did Nike begin operations?

b. Other than athletic shoes and clothing, what business does Nike operate?

c. How many employees does Nike have?

d. Describe, in dollar amounts, Nike's accounting equation at the end of the most recent year.

e. Has Nike's performance been improving or deteriorating over the past three years? Explain your answer.

SPREADSHEET ASSIGNMENT *Use of Excel*

ATC 4–9

Adams Company started operations on January 1, 2002. Six months later on June 30, 2002, the company decided to prepare financial statements. The company's accountant decided to problem solve for the adjusting journal entries and the final adjusted account balances by using an electronic spreadsheet. Once the spreadsheet is complete, she will record the adjusting entries in the general journal and post to the ledger. The accountant has started the following spreadsheet but wants you to finish it for her.

Required

a. On a blank spreadsheet, enter the following trial balance in Columns A through C. Also enter the headings for Columns E through I.

	Trial Balance			Adjusting Journal Entries		Adjusted Trial Balance	
Account Titles	Debit	Credit		Debit	Credit	Debit	Credit
Cash	1500						
Certificate of Deposit	10000						
Accounts Receivable	12000						
Supplies	1500						
Prepaid Rent	12000						
Office Equipment	9000						
Accounts Payable		2500					
Unearned Revenue		5000	(1)	3000			2000
Common Stock		20000					
Retained Earnings		0					
Service Revenue		35000			(1)	3000	
Salaries Expense	12000						
Operating Expense	4500						
Totals	62500	62500		3000	3000	0	2000

(cell reference: I10 = =C10-E10+G10)

b. Each of the following events requires an adjusting journal entry. Instead of recording entries in general journal format, record the adjusting entries in the Debit and Credit columns under the heading Adjusting Journal Entries. Entry (1) has already been recorded as an example. Be sure to number your adjusting entries on the spreadsheet. It will be necessary to insert new accounts for the adjustments. Recall that the accounting period is for six months.

   (1) Received a $5,000 cash advance on April 1 for a contract to provide five months of service.
   (2) Had accrued salaries on June 30 amounting to $1,500.
   (3) On January 1 invested in a one-year, $10,000 certificate of deposit that had a 5 percent interest rate.
   (4) On January 1 paid $12,000 in advance for a one-year lease on office space.
   (5) Received in the mail a utility bill dated June 30 for $150.
   (6) Purchased $1,500 of supplies on January 1. As of June 30, $700 of supplies remained on hand.
   (7) Paid $9,000 for office equipment on January 1. The equipment was expected to have a four-year useful life and a $1,000 salvage value. Depreciation is computed on a straight-line basis.

c. Develop formulas to sum both the Debit and Credit columns under the Adjusting Journal Entries heading.

d. Develop formulas to derive the adjusted balances for the adjusted trial balance. For example, the formula for the ending balance of Unearned Revenue is =C10-E10+G10. In other words, a credit balance minus debit entries plus credit entries equals the ending balance. Once an ending balance is formulated for one credit account, that formula can be copied to all other credit accounts; the same is true for debit accounts. Once an ending balance is formulated for a debit account, that formula can be copied to all other debit accounts.

e. Develop formulas to sum both the Debit and Credit columns under the Adjusted Trial Balance heading.

Spreadsheet Tips

1. Rows and columns can be inserted by positioning the mouse on the immediate row or column after the desired position. Click on the *right* mouse button. With the *left* mouse button, choose Insert and then either Entire Column or Entire Row. Use the same method to delete columns or rows.

2. Enter the sequential numbering of the adjusting entries as labels rather than values by positioning an apostrophe in front of each entry. The first adjusting entry should be labeled '(1).

SPREADSHEET ASSIGNMENT *Mastery of Excel*   ATC 4–10

At the end of the accounting period, Adams Company's general ledger contained the following adjusted balances.

	A	B	C	D	E	F	G	H	I	J	K	L	M	N	O
		Adjusted Trial Balance			Closing Entries			Ending Trial Balance							
2	Account Titles	Debit	Credit		Debit		Credit	Debit	Credit						
3	Cash	1500													
4	Certificate of Deposit	10000													
5	Interest Receivable	250													
6	Accounts Receivable	12000													
7	Supplies	700													
8	Prepaid Rent	6000													
9	Office Equipment	9000													
10	Accumulated Depreciation		1000												
11	Accounts Payable		2650												
12	Salaries Payable		1500												
13	Unearned Revenue		2000												
14	Common Stock		20000												
15	Retained Earnings		0												
16	Service Revenue		38000												
17	Interest Revenue		250												
18	Salaries Expense	13500													
19	Rent Expense	6000													
20	Utilities Expense	150													
21	Supplies Expense	800													
22	Depreciation Expense	1000													
23	Operating Expense	4500													
24															
25	Totals	65400	65400												

Required

a. Set up the preceding spreadsheet format. (The spreadsheet tips for ATC 4–9 also apply for this problem.)

b. Record the closing entries in the Closing Entries column of the spreadsheet.

c. Compute the Ending Trial Balance amounts.

Chapter

5

Accounting for Merchandising Business

Learning Objectives

After completing this chapter, you should be able to:

1 Distinguish between service and merchandising businesses.

2 Distinguish between product costs and selling and administrative costs.

3 Show how product costs affect financial statements.

4 Compare and contrast the perpetual and periodic inventory systems.

5 Name and explain the primary features of the perpetual inventory system.

6 Explain the meaning of terms used to describe transportation costs, cash discounts, and returns or allowances.

7 Compare and contrast single- and multistep income statements.

8 Name the primary features of the periodic inventory system.

9 Show how lost, damaged, or stolen inventory affects financial statements.

10 Use common size financial statements to evaluate managerial performance.

11 Use ratio analysis to evaluate managerial performance.

12 Discuss the cost of financing inventory.

the *curious* accountant

Leila recently purchased a book for $25 from her local Borders bookstore. The next day she learned that Rachael had bought the same book from Amazon.com for only $20. Leila questioned how Amazon.com could sell the book for so much less than Borders, given the low markup that retail book sellers enjoy. Rachael suggested that although both booksellers purchase their books from the same publishers at about the same price, Amazon.com can charge lower prices because it does not have to operate expensive "bricks and mortar" stores, thus lowering its operating costs. Leila disagrees. She thinks the cost of operating huge distribution centers and Internet server centers would offset any cost savings Amazon.com enjoys from not owning retail bookstores. Use the companies' income statements that are presented in Exhibit 5–1 to settle this disagreement.

Previous illustrations and problems assumed that businesses generated revenue by providing services to their customers. Another large form of business activity generates revenue by selling goods to customers. Companies that sell goods normally accumulate a supply of those goods that is used for delivery when sales are made. This supply is called **inventory.**

Inventory includes goods that are in the process of being made (i.e., unfinished goods) as well as goods that are finished and ready for sale. For example, unprocessed lumber, partially assembled tables, and finished goods stored in a warehouse would all be included in the inventory of a furniture manufacturer. The term inventory *also describes stockpiles of goods that are used indirectly in the process of selling merchandise or providing services, such as supplies, stamps, stationery, cleaning materials, and so on.*

At this point, it is helpful to note that many businesses concentrate on the resale of finished goods. These businesses buy merchandise from a supplier and resell that merchandise to their customers. When the merchandise is resold, it is essentially in the same condition as it was when *it was purchased from the supplier. Finished goods held for resale are commonly called **merchandise inventory**. Companies that buy and sell merchandise inventory are called **merchandising businesses**. Merchandising businesses include **retail companies** (companies that sell goods to the final consumer) and **wholesale companies** (companies that sell to other businesses). Businesses that concentrate on the resale of goods include Sears Roebuck and Co., JC Penney, Sam's Clubs, and National Tire Wholesale (NTW).*

■ Product Costs Versus Selling and Administrative Costs

LO1 Distinguish between service and merchandising businesses.

LO2 Distinguish between product costs and selling and administrative costs.

Inventory costs are capitalized in (accumulated in) the Merchandise Inventory account and shown as an asset on the balance sheet. Any cost incurred to acquire goods or to make them ready for sale should be accumulated in the Inventory account. Examples of inventory costs incurred by merchandising companies include the price of goods purchased, transportation or packaging costs associated with obtaining merchandise, storage costs, and transit insurance. Note that all of these costs are associated with products. As a result, inventory costs are frequently referred to as **product costs.** Costs that cannot be directly traced to products are usually classified as **selling and administrative costs.** Typical examples of selling and administrative costs include advertising, administrative salaries, insurance, and interest. Since selling and administrative costs are usually recognized as expenses *in the period* in which they are incurred, they are sometimes called **period costs.** Product costs are expensed when the inventory is sold regardless of when it was purchased. In other words, product costs are matched directly with sales revenue, but selling and administrative costs are matched with the period in which they are incurred.

■ Allocation of Inventory Cost Between Asset and Expense Accounts

LO3 Show how product costs affect financial statements.

The total inventory cost for any given accounting period is determined by adding the cost of inventory on hand at the beginning of the period to the cost of inventory purchased during the period. The total cost (beginning inventory plus purchases) is called the **cost of goods available for sale.** The cost of goods available for sale is allocated between an asset account called *Merchandise Inventory* and an expense account called *Cost of Goods Sold.* The cost of the items that have not been sold (merchandise inventory) is shown as an asset on the balance sheet, and the cost of the items sold (**cost of goods sold**) is expensed on the income statement. The difference between the sales revenue and the cost of goods sold is called the **gross margin** or *gross profit.* The selling and administrative expenses (period costs) are subtracted from the gross margin to obtain the net income.

Exhibit 5–1 contains income statements drawn from the annual reports of Amazon.com, Inc., and Borders Group, Inc. For each company, review the most current income statement and determine the amount of gross margin. You should find a gross profit of $655,777 for Amazon.com and a gross margin of $916.7 for Borders.

■ Perpetual Inventory System

LO5 Name and explain the primary features of the perpetual inventory system.

Most modern companies maintain their inventory records under the perpetual inventory system. The **perpetual inventory system** derives its name from the fact that the balance in the Inventory account is adjusted perpetually (continuously). Each time merchandise is purchased, the Inventory account is increased; each time it is sold, the Inventory account is decreased. The following illustration demonstrates the basic features of the perpetual inventory system.

June Gardener was appropriately named. She loved plants, and they grew for her as they did for no one else. At the encouragement of her friends, Gardener decided to start a small

Exhibit 5–1

AMAZON.COM, INC.
Consolidated Statements of Operations
(dollars in thousands)

	Years Ended December 31,		
	2000	1999	1998
Net sales	$ 2,761,983	$1,639,839	$ 609,819
Cost of sales	2,106,206	1,349,194	476,155
Gross profit	655,777	290,645	133,664
Operating expenses			
Marketing and fulfillment	594,489	413,150	132,654
Technology and content	269,326	159,722	46,424
General and administrative	108,962	70,144	15,618
Stock-based compensation	24,797	30,618	1,889
Amortization of goodwill and other intangibles	321,772	214,694	42,599
Impairment-related and other	200,311	8,072	3,535
Total operating expenses	1,519,657	896,400	242,719
Loss from operations	(863,880)	(605,755)	(109,055)
Interest income	40,821	45,451	14,053
Interest expense	(130,921)	(84,566)	(26,639)
Other income (expense), net	(10,058)	1,671	—
Non-cash gains and losses, net	(142,639)	—	—
Net interest expense and other	(242,797)	(37,444)	(12,586)
Loss before equity in losses of equity-method investees, net	(1,106,677)	(643,199)	(121,641)
Equity in losses of equity-method investees, net	(304,596)	(76,769)	(2,905)
Net loss	$(1,411,273)	$ (719,968)	$(124,546)

BORDERS GROUP, INC.
Consolidated Statements of Operations
(dollars in millions)

	Fiscal Year Ended		
	January 28, 2001	January 23, 2000	January 24, 1999
Sales	$3,271.2	$2,968.4	$2,595.0
Cost of merchandise sold (includes occupancy)	2,354.5	2,127.6	1,859.4
Gross margin	916.7	840.8	735.6
Selling, general and administrative expenses	736.2	659.2	557.6
Pre-opening expense	6.4	7.8	7.8
Asset impairments and other writedowns	36.2	—	—
Goodwill amortization	2.8	2.8	2.9
Operating income	135.1	171.0	167.3
Interest expense	13.1	16.6	16.2
Income from continuing operations before income tax	122.0	154.4	151.1
Income tax provision	48.2	60.4	59.0
Income from continuing operations	73.8	94.0	92.1
Discontinued operations (Note 3)			
Loss from operations of All Wound Up, net of income tax credits of $7.0 and $2.4	10.8	3.7	—
Loss on disposition of All Wound Up, net of deferred income tax credit of $8.9	19.4	—	—
Net income	$ 43.6	$ 90.3	$ 92.1

he income statement data show that Amazon.com had higher operating expenses than Borders although it does not have to operate traditional stores. As explained later in this chapter, the *gross margin percentage* indicates to some degree how much a company is charging in relation to what it pays to purchase the goods it is selling (its cost of goods sold). The *return on sales ratio* reveals how much profit, as a percentage of sales, a company is making after *all* of its expenses have been taken into account. For the year 2000, the gross margin for Borders was 28.0 percent and for Amazon.com was 23.7 percent, indicating that, on average, Amazon.com really does charge less for its books. The return on sales for Borders was 2.3 percent and for Amazon.com was −40.1 percent, suggesting that Borders is the one with the lower operating costs. In fact, Amazon.com's operating expenses were more than double those of Borders. Excluding costs of goods sold, the operating expenses at Borders were 25.8 percent of sales and at Amazon.com were 63.8 percent.

retail plant store. She started June's Plant Shop (JPS) on January 1, 2001. During the first year of operation, the company experienced the following business events.

1. Acquired $15,000 cash through the issue of common stock.
2. Made a $14,000 cash purchase of inventory.
3. Sold inventory that cost $8,000 for $12,000 cash.
4. Made a $1,000 cash payment for selling expenses.

Effect of Events on Financial Statements

The effect of each of these events on the financial statements is discussed here.

Event 1 *JPS acquired $15,000 cash from the issue of common stock.*

This event is an asset source transaction. The $15,000 acquisition of cash acts to increase assets (Cash) and equity (Common Stock). The income statement is not affected. The statement of cash flows shows an $11,000 cash inflow from financing activities. These effects follow.

Cash	+	Inventory	=	C. Stk.	+	Ret. Earn.	Rev.	−	Exp.	=	Net Inc.	Cash Flow
15,000	+	NA	=	15,000	+	NA	NA	−	NA	=	NA	15,000 FA

Event 2 *JPS paid $14,000 cash to purchase inventory.*

The Merchandise Inventory account is increased when goods are purchased. Since cash is used to purchase the goods, the purchase constitutes an asset exchange. The asset account, Cash, decreases and the asset account, Merchandise Inventory, increases; the total amount of assets is unchanged. The income statement is not affected by this event. Product costs are expensed when the goods are sold, not when they are purchased. However, the $10,000 cash outflow is shown in the operating activities section of the statement of cash flows. These effects follow.

Cash	+	Inventory	=	C. Stk.	+	Ret. Earn.	Rev.	−	Exp.	=	Net Inc.	Cash Flow
(14,000)	+	14,000	=	NA	+	NA	NA	−	NA	=	NA	(14,000) OA

Event 3a *JPS recognized $12,000 of cash revenue on the sale of inventory that cost $8,000.*

This event is composed of two transactions. The *first transaction* is an asset source transaction (cash is acquired by generating sales revenue). As with other revenue transactions, *sales transactions* act to increase assets (Cash) and equity (Retained Earnings). The sales revenue acts to increase net income on the income statement. Also, the $12,000 cash inflow from the sale is shown in the operating activities section of the statement of cash flows. These effects are shown here.

Cash	+	Inventory	=	C. Stk.	+	Ret. Earn.	Rev.	−	Exp.	=	Net Inc.	Cash Flow
12,000	+	NA	=	NA	+	12,000	12,000	−	NA	=	12,000	12,000 OA

Event 3b *JPS recognized $8,000 of cost of goods sold.*

The second transaction associated with the sale of inventory is an asset use transaction. An expense (Cost of Goods Sold) is recognized because the asset, inventory, was used to produce the sales revenue. Accordingly, $8,000 of cost must be transferred from the asset account, Merchandise Inventory, to the expense account, Cost of Goods Sold. The effect on the balance sheet is to reduce assets (Inventory) and equity (Retained Earnings). On the income statement, the expense, cost of goods sold, will act to reduce net income. This event does not affect the statement of cash flows. The case outflow occurred when the goods were bought, not when they were sold. These effects follow.

Cash	+	Inventory	=	C. Stk.	+	Ret. Earn.	Rev.	−	Exp.	=	Net Inc.	Cash Flow
NA	+	(8,000)	=	NA	+	(8,000)	NA	−	8,000	=	(8,000)	NA

Event 4 *JPS paid $1,000 cash for selling expenses.*

This event is an asset use transaction. The payment acts to decrease assets (Cash) and equity (Retained Earnings). The increase in selling expenses decreases net income. The $1,000 cash outflow is shown in the operating activities section of the statement of cash flows. These effects are shown here:

Cash	+	Inventory	=	C. Stk.	+	Ret. Earn.	Rev.	−	Exp.	=	Net Inc.	Cash Flow
(1,000)	+	NA	=	NA	+	(1,000)	NA	−	1,000	=	(1,000)	(1,000) OA

Ledger T-Accounts

Exhibit 5–2 shows the ledger T-accounts containing the transaction data for the 2001 accounting period. Recall that the company experiences the following four accounting events.

1. Acquired $15,000 cash through the issue of common stock.
2. Made a $14,000 cash purchase of inventory.
3a. Recognized $12,000 cash revenue from sales.
3b. Recognized $8,000 of cost of goods sold.
4. Made a $1,000 cash payment for selling expenses.

The ledger accounts contain the event numbers shown in parentheses for easy reference. The closing entry, which is designated by *cl,* is necessary to transfer the balances in the revenue and expense accounts to the Retained Earnings account. The closing entry is a claims exchange transaction, with some equity accounts decreasing while others increase. The amount of total equity is not affected by the closing entry.

Phambroom Company began 2006 with $35,600 in its Inventory account. During the year, it purchased inventory costing $356,800 and sold inventory that had cost $360,000 for $520,000. Based on this information alone, determine (1) the inventory balance as of December 31, 2006, and (2) the amount of gross margin Phambroom would report on its 2006 income statement.

Answer

1. Beginning inventory + Purchases = Goods available − Ending inventory = Cost of goods sold

   $35,600 + $356,800 = $392,400 − Ending inventory = $360,000

   Ending inventory = $32,400

2. Sales revenue − Cost of goods sold = Gross margin

   $520,000 − $360,000 = $160,000

Check Yourself 5–1

Exhibit 5–2 *General Ledger*

Cash							=	Liabilities			+	Common Stock		
(1)	15,000	14,000	(2)						0	Bal.			15,000	(1)
(3a)	12,000	1,000	(4)										15,000	Bal.
Bal.	12,000													

Merchandise Inventory

					Retained Earnings		
(2)	14,000	8,000	(3b)			3,000	(cl.)
Bal.	6,000					3,000	Bal.

Sales Revenue

(cl.)	12,000	12,000	(3a)
		0	Bal.

Cost of Goods Sold

(3b)	8,000	8,000	(cl.)
Bal.	0		

Selling Expenses

(4)	1,000	1,000	(cl.)
Bal.	0		

Exhibit 5–3 *Financial Statements*

Income Statement		Balance Sheet			Statement of Cash Flows		
Sales Revenue	$12,000	Assets			Operating Activities		
Cost of Goods Sold	(8,000)	Cash	$12,000		Inflow from Customers	$ 12,000	
Gross Margin	4,000	Merchandise Inventory	6,000		Outflow for Inventory	(14,000)	
Less: Operating Exp.		Total Assets		$18,000	Outflow for Selling & Admin.	(1,000)	
Selling and Admin. Exp.	(1,000)				Net Cash Outflow from Operations		$ (3,000)
Net Income	$ 3,000	Liabilities		0			
					Investing Activities		0
		Stockholders' Equity					
		Common Stock	$15,000		Financing Activities		
		Retained Earnings	3,000		Inflow from Stock Issue		15,000
		Total Stockholders' Equity		$18,000	Net Change in Cash		12,000
		Total Liab. and Stk. Equity		$18,000	Plus Beginning Cash Balance		0
					Ending Cash Balance		$ 12,000

The ledger account balances are used to prepare the financial statements shown in Exhibit 5–3. To confirm your understanding of the statement preparation, trace the ledger account balances to the financial statements.

LO6 Explain the meaning of terms used to describe transportation costs, cash discounts, and returns or allowances.

■ Other Events Affecting Inventory Purchases

Three other accounting events frequently affect inventory purchases: (1) incurring transportation costs, (2) returning inventory or accepting purchase allowances, and (3) receiving cash discounts. The effects of these events are demonstrated by analyzing JPS's operating activities during its second accounting cycle. The closing balances for the 2001 fiscal year became the opening balances for the 2002 calendar year. Accordingly, the beginning balances are: Cash, $12,000; Inventory, $6,000; Common Stock, $15,000; and Retained Earnings, $3,000.

Effect of Events on Financial Statements

JPS experienced the following events during its 2002 accounting period.

Event 1 *JPS purchased $8,000 of merchandise inventory on account.*

The effect of the purchase on the balance sheet is to increase assets (Inventory) and liabilities (Accounts Payable). The income statement is not affected by this event. Revenue and expense recognition occurs at the point of sale rather than at the time of purchase. Since the goods were purchased on account, cash flow was not affected. These effects on the financial statements are as follows.

Cash	+	Accts. Rec.	+	Inv.	=	Accts. Pay.	+	Note Pay.	+	C. Stk.	+	Ret. Earn.	Rev.	−	Exp.	=	Net Inc.	Cash Flow
NA	+	NA	+	8,000	=	8,000	+	NA	+	NA	+	NA	NA	−	NA	=	NA	NA

Event 2 *JPS paid $300 cash for freight cost required to obtain goods purchased in Event 1.*

The party responsible for transportation costs is designated by the terms **FOB shipping point** and **FOB destination.** An easy way to interpret the terms is to note that the seller's responsibility ends at the point designated in the terms. If goods are shipped FOB shipping point, the seller's responsibility ends at the point of shipment and the buyer must pay the freight costs. On the other hand, if goods are shipped FOB destination, the seller retains ownership until the goods reach the destination point and is therefore responsible for the transportation costs. The following table summarizes the parties responsible for freight costs.

Transportation Terms	FOB Shipping Point	FOB Destination
Responsible party	Buyer	Seller

The cost of freight on goods purchased under terms FOB shipping point is called **transportation-in** or **freight-in.** Since transportation costs are a necessary part of obtaining inventory, they are added to the Inventory account. Assuming that the goods purchased in Event 1 were delivered under terms FOB shipping point, the buyer (JPS) is responsible for the freight. Accordingly, the freight costs act to increase the balance in the Inventory account and decrease the balance of the Cash account. The income statement is not affected by this transaction. Since the freight costs are included in the Inventory account, they will be expensed as part of *costs of goods sold* when the inventory is sold to customers, not when it is delivered to JPS. However, the cash paid for freight at the time of delivery is shown as an outflow in the operating activities section of the statement of cash flows. The effects of *transportation-in* costs on the financial statements follow.

Cash	+	Accts. Rec.	+	Inv.	=	Accts. Pay.	+	Note Pay.	+	C. Stk.	+	Ret. Earn.	Rev.	−	Exp.	=	Net Inc.	Cash Flow
(300)	+	NA	+	300	=	NA	+	NA	+	NA	+	NA	NA	−	NA	=	NA	(300) OA

Event 3 *JPS returned $1,000 of goods purchased in Event 1.*

"Satisfaction or your money back" is a guarantee frequently offered in today's economy. Goods may be returned because the buyer becomes dissatisfied with a product's size, color, design, and so on. Recall that the Inventory account is increased when goods are purchased. The reverse applies when goods are returned. In the case of JPS, the $1,000 purchase return acts to decrease assets (Inventory) and liabilities (Accounts Payable). The income statement and the statement of cash flows are not affected. These effects on the financial statements follow.

Cash	+	Accts. Rec.	+	Inv.	=	Accts. Pay.	+	Note Pay.	+	C. Stk.	+	Ret. Earn.	Rev.	−	Exp.	=	Net Inc.	Cash Flow
NA	+	NA	+	(1,000)	=	(1,000)	+	NA	+	NA	+	NA	NA	−	NA	=	NA	NA

It is sometimes advantageous to appease the dissatisfactions of the buyer by negotiating a reduction in the selling price of certain goods instead of accepting their return. Such reductions, referred to as **allowances,** are frequently granted to buyers who receive defective goods or goods that are of a lower quality than the customer ordered. Purchase allowances affect the financial statements exactly the same as purchase returns do.

Event 4 *JPS received a cash discount on goods purchased in Event 1.*

Assume that the goods described in Event 1 were purchased under terms 2/10, n/30. The terms **2/10, n/30** mean that the seller will give the purchaser a 2 percent discount on the account payable if the purchaser pays cash for the merchandise within 10 days from the date of purchase. The amount not paid within the first 10 days is due at the end of 30 days from the date of purchase. **Cash discounts** are extended to encourage prompt payment. Assuming that JPS pays for the goods within the discount period, the company will receive a $140 purchase discount (original cost of $8,000 − purchase return of $1,000 = $7,000 balance due × 0.02 discount = $140). The discount acts to reduce the cost of the inventory and thereby lowers the amount due on the account payable. Accordingly, the **purchase discount** reduces the asset account, *Inventory,* and the liability account, *Accounts Payable.* Recall that product costs are expensed when inventory is sold. Therefore, the income statement will be affected when goods are sold, not when the discount is acquired. Accordingly, this transaction does not affect the income statement. Although the purchase discount will affect future cash flows, it has no immediate impact. As a result, the discount event does not affect the statement of cash flows. The effects of the purchase discount on the financial statements are shown here.

Cash	+	Accts. Rec.	+	Inv.	=	Accts. Pay.	+	Note Pay.	+	C. Stk.	+	Ret. Earn.	Rev.	−	Exp.	=	Net Inc.	Cash Flow
NA	+	NA	+	(140)	=	(140)	+	NA	+	NA	+	NA	NA	−	NA	=	NA	NA

Event 5 *JPS paid remaining balance of $6,860 due on account payable.*

The effect of the payment on the balance sheet is to reduce assets (Cash) and liabilities (Accounts Payable), but the event does not affect the income statement. However, the $6,860 ($8,000 original cost − $1,000 purchase return − $140 cash discount) cash outflow is shown in the operating activities section of the statement of cash flows. The effects on the financial statements follow.

Cash	+	Accts. Rec.	+	Inv.	=	Accts. Pay.	+	Note Pay.	+	C. Stk.	+	Ret. Earn.	Rev.	−	Exp.	=	Net Inc.	Cash Flow
(6,860)	+	NA	+	NA	=	(6,860)	+	NA	+	NA	+	NA	NA	−	NA	=	NA	(6,860) OA

Event 6 *JPS borrowed $5,000 from State Bank.*

JPS issued an interest-bearing note with a six-month term and a 10 percent annual interest rate. The borrowing event increased assets (Cash) and liabilities (Note Payable). The income statement is not affected. The $5,000 inflow is classified as a financing activity on the statement of cash flows. These effects follow.

Cash	+	Accts. Rec.	+	Inv.	=	Accts. Pay.	+	Note Pay.	+	C. Stk.	+	Ret. Earn.	Rev.	−	Exp.	=	Net Inc.	Cash Flow
5,000	+	NA	+	NA	=	NA	+	5,000	+	NA	+	NA	NA	−	NA	=	NA	5,000 FA

Event 7a *JPS recognized $24,750 of cash revenue on the sale of merchandise that cost $11,500.*

The sale increases assets (Cash) and equity (Retained Earnings). The revenue recognition causes the net income to increase. Also, the $24,750 cash inflow from the sale is shown in the operating activities section of the statement of cash flows. These effects follow.

Cash	+	Accts. Rec.	+	Inv.	=	Accts. Pay.	+	Note Pay.	+	C. Stk.	+	Ret. Earn.	Rev.	−	Exp.	=	Net Inc.	Cash Flow
24,750	+	NA	+	NA	=	NA	+	NA	+	NA	+	24,750	24,750	−	NA	=	24,750	24,750 OA

Event 7b *JPS recognized $11,500 of cost of goods sold.*

Recall that when goods are sold, the product cost—*including a proportionate share of transportation-in and adjustments for purchase returns and allowances*—is taken out of the Merchandise Inventory account and placed into the Cost of Goods Sold expense account. Accordingly, the recognition of the cost of goods sold decreases assets (Inventory) and equity (Retained Earnings). The expense recognition for cost of goods sold causes the net income to decrease. Cash flow is not affected. These effects are shown here.

Cash	+	Accts. Rec.	+	Inv.	=	Accts. Pay.	+	Note Pay.	+	C. Stk.	+	Ret. Earn.	Rev.	−	Exp.	=	Net Inc.	Cash Flow
NA	+	NA	+	(11,500)	=	NA	+	NA	+	NA	+	(11,500)	NA	−	11,500	=	(11,500)	NA

Event 8 *JPS incurred $450 of freight costs on goods delivered to customers.*

Assume that the merchandise sold in Event 7 was delivered under terms FOB destination. The freight cost of $450 was paid in cash. Recall that FOB destination means that the seller is responsible for the merchandise until it reaches its destination. Accordingly, JPS is responsible for the freight costs in this case. If the seller is responsible for the freight costs, the cost is considered to be an operating expense that is shown on the income statement after the computation of gross margin. This treatment is logical because the cost of freight on goods delivered to customers is incurred *after* the goods are sold and, therefore, cannot be considered as part of the costs of obtaining goods or making them ready for sale. The freight cost for goods delivered to customers under terms of FOB destination is called **transportation-out** or **freight-out.** When paid in cash, transportation-out is an expense that reduces assets (Cash) and equity (Retained Earnings). The event increases operating expenses and thereby reduces net income. The $450 cash outflow is shown in the operating activities section of the statement of cash flows. These effects follow.

Cash	+	Accts. Rec.	+	Inv.	=	Accts. Pay.	+	Note Pay.	+	C. Stk.	+	Ret. Earn.	Rev.	−	Exp.	=	Net Inc.	Cash Flow
(450)	+	NA	+	NA	=	NA	+	NA	+	NA	+	(450)	NA	−	450	=	(450)	(450) OA

Event 9 *JPS purchased $14,000 of merchandise inventory under credit terms 2/10, n/30.*

The goods were shipped under freight terms FOB destination. The party responsible for the freight costs paid freight costs of $400 in cash. *Since the freight terms are FOB destination, the seller is responsible, and JPS's accounts are not affected.* Accordingly, Merchandise Inventory and Accounts Payable will increase by $14,000. Net income and cash flow are not affected. These effects are shown here.

Cash	+	Accts. Rec.	+	Inv.	=	Accts. Pay.	+	Note Pay.	+	C. Stk.	+	Ret. Earn.		Rev.	−	Exp.	=	Net Inc.		Cash Flow
NA	+	NA	+	14,000	=	14,000	+	NA	+	NA	+	NA		NA	−	NA	=	NA		NA

Event 10 *JPS paid interest on funds borrowed in Event 6.*

Assume that the six-month term on the note issued in Event 6 has expired. JPS must determine the amount of interest expense and pay this amount to the bank. Recall that the face value was $5,000, the term six months, and the interest rate 10 percent per year. Accordingly, the amount of interest expense is $250 ($5,000 × 0.10 × 6/12). Since the term has expired, the interest is payable in cash. The payment reduces assets (Cash) and equity (Retained Earnings). The recognition of interest expense causes a corresponding decrease in net income. The cash outflow is shown in the operating activities section of the statement of cash flows. These effects follow.

Cash	+	Accts. Rec.	+	Inv.	=	Accts. Pay.	+	Note Pay.	+	C. Stk.	+	Ret. Earn.		Rev.	−	Exp.	=	Net Inc.		Cash Flow
(250)	+	NA	+	NA	=	NA	+	NA	+	NA	+	(250)		NA	−	250	=	(250)		(250) OA

Event 11 *JPS repaid the principal on funds borrowed in Event 6.*

The repayment of the principal requires a $5,000 cash disbursement. This disbursement reduces assets (Cash) and liabilities (Note Payable). The repayment does not affect the income statement. The $5,000 cash outflow is shown in the financing activities section of the statement of cash flows. These effects are shown here.

Cash	+	Accts. Rec.	+	Inv.	=	Accts. Pay.	+	Note Pay.	+	C. Stk.	+	Ret. Earn.		Rev.	−	Exp.	=	Net Inc.		Cash Flow
(5,000)	+	NA	+	NA	=	NA	+	(5,000)	+	NA	+	NA		NA	−	NA	=	NA		(5,000) FA

Event 12a *JPS recognized $16,800 of revenue on account on the sale of merchandise that cost $8,660.*

Assume that the freight terms were FOB shipping point and that the party responsible paid freight costs of $275 in cash. The effect of the revenue recognition on the balance sheet is to increase assets (Accounts Receivable) and equity (Retained Earnings). The event increases revenue and net income. Since the sale was made on account, cash flow is not affected. These effects are as follows.

Cash	+	Accts. Rec.	+	Inv.	=	Accts. Pay.	+	Note Pay.	+	C. Stk.	+	Ret. Earn.		Rev.	−	Exp.	=	Net Inc.		Cash Flow
NA	+	16,800	+	NA	=	NA	+	NA	+	NA	+	16,800		16,800	−	NA	=	16,800		NA

Event 12b *JPS recognized $8,660 of cost of goods sold.*

To recognize the expense associated with the goods sold, $8,660 must be transferred from the Merchandise Inventory account to the Cost of Goods Sold account. The effect of the expense recognition on the balance sheet is to decrease assets (Inventory) and equity (Retained Earnings). The expense, cost of goods sold, increases and net income decreases. Cash flow is not affected. *Since the goods were delivered FOB shipping point, the buyer is responsible for the freight costs and JPS's accounts are not affected.* These effects are shown here.

Cash	+	Accts. Rec.	+	Inv.	=	Accts. Pay.	+	Note Pay.	+	C. Stk.	+	Ret. Earn.		Rev.	−	Exp.	=	Net Inc.		Cash Flow
NA	+	NA	+	(8,660)	=	NA	+	NA	+	NA	+	(8,660)		NA	−	8,660	=	(8,660)		NA

Event 13 *JPS made a $7,000 cash payment in partial settlement of the account payable generated in Event 9.*

Assume that the payment was made after the discount period had expired. Accordingly, JPS will not obtain a purchase discount from the supplier. The effect of the event on the balance sheet is to decrease assets (Cash) and liabilities (Accounts Payable). The income statement is not affected. The $7,000 cash outflow is included in the operating activities section of the statement of cash flows. These effects follow.

Cash	+	Accts. Rec.	+	Inv.	=	Accts. Pay.	+	Note Pay.	+	C. Stk.	+	Ret. Earn.		Rev.	−	Exp.	=	Net Inc.		Cash Flow
(7,000)	+	NA	+	NA	=	(7,000)	+	NA	+	NA	+	NA		NA	−	NA	=	NA		(7,000) OA

Event 14 *JPS paid cash for selling and administrative expenses amounting to $8,000.*

The effect of the event on the balance sheet is to decrease assets (Cash) and equity (Retained Earnings). The recognition of the selling and administrative expenses decreases net income. The $8,000 cash outflow is shown in the operating activities section of the statement of cash flows. These effects are as follows.

Cash	+	Accts. Rec.	+	Inv.	=	Accts. Pay.	+	Note Pay.	+	C. Stk.	+	Ret. Earn.		Rev.	−	Exp.	=	Net Inc.		Cash Flow
(8,000)	+	NA	+	NA	=	NA	+	NA	+	NA	+	(8,000)		NA	−	8,000	=	(8,000)		(8,000) OA

General Ledger Accounts

Exhibit 5–4 shows the ledger T-accounts that reflect the accounting events just described. A summary of these events is provided here for your convenience. To confirm your understanding of the accounting process, trace the event data to the ledger account balances. The ledger account balances are used to prepare the 2002 financial statements, which are shown in Exhibit 5–5. It is insightful to trace the ledger account balances to the financial statements.

Event 1   Purchased $8,000 of inventory on account.
Event 2   Paid $300 cash for transportation-in cost required to obtain goods purchased in Event 1.
Event 3   Returned $1,000 of goods purchased in Event 1.
Event 4   Received cash discount on goods purchased in Event 1.
Event 5   Paid remaining balance of $6,860 due on the account payable associated with Event 1.
Event 6   Borrowed $5,000 from State Bank.
Event 7a Recognized $24,750 of sales revenue.
Event 7b Recognized $11,500 of cost of goods sold.
Event 8   Incurred $450 of transportation-out cost on goods delivered to customers.
Event 9   Purchased $14,000 of inventory under credit terms 2/10, n/30.
Event 10 Paid interest on funds borrowed in Event 6.
Event 11 Repaid principal on funds borrowed in Event 6.
Event 12a Recognized $16,800 of sales revenue on account.
Event 12b Recognized $8,660 of cost of goods sold.
Event 13 Made a $7,000 cash payment in partial settlement of the account payable generated in Event 9.
Event 14 Paid cash for selling and administrative expenses amounting to $8,000.

Financial Statements

Carefully observe the format of the income statement shown in Exhibit 5–5. It provides more information than a simple comparison of revenues and expenses. It matches particular

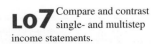

LO7 Compare and contrast single- and multistep income statements.

Exhibit 5-4 *Ledger Accounts*

Assets			=	Liabilities			+	Stockholders' Equity		

Assets

Cash

Bal.	12,000	300	(2)
(6)	5,000	6,860	(5)
(7a)	24,750	450	(8)
		250	(10)
		5,000	(11)
		7,000	(13)
		8,000	(14)
Bal.	13,890		

Accounts Receivable

(12a)	16,800	
Bal.	16,800	

Merchandise Inventory

Bal.	6,000	1,000	(3)
(1)	8,000	140	(4)
(2)	300	11,500	(7b)
(9)	14,000	8,660	(12b)
Bal.	7,000		

Liabilities

Accounts Payable

(3)	1,000	8,000	(1)
(4)	140	14,000	(9)
(5)	6,860		
(13)	7,000		
		7,000	Bal.

Note Payable

(11)	5,000	5,000	(6)
		0	Bal.

Stockholders' Equity

Common Stock

	15,000	Bal.

Retained Earnings

	3,000	Bal.
	12,690	(cl)
	15,690	Bal.

Sales Revenue

(cl)	41,550	24,750	(7a)
		16,800	(12a)
		0	Bal.

Cost of Goods Sold

(7b)	11,500	20,160	(cl)
(12b)	8,660		
Bal.	0		

Transportation-out

(8)	450	450	(cl)
Bal.	0		

Selling and Admin. Expenses

(14)	8,000	8,000	(cl)
Bal.	0		

Interest Expense

(10)	250	250	(cl)
Bal.	0		

Total Assets	=	**Total Liabilities**	+ **Total Stockholders' Equity**
$37,690		$7,000	$30,690

expenses with particular revenues. More specifically, the computation of gross margin provides information about the relationship between the cost of goods sold and the selling price. This information facilitates comparisons between companies or between stores within the same company. Such comparisons permit investors and managers to assess the competitiveness of pricing strategies, to evaluate the effectiveness of management, and to anticipate the likelihood of continued performance. The income statement in Exhibit 5–5 also distinguishes regular operating activities from peripheral nonoperating activities. The separation of operating from nonoperating activities promotes financial statement analysis. Analysts are able to distinguish recurring operating activities from items such as gains and losses, discontinued operating activities, and extraordinary items that are not likely to be repeated. Income statements that show these additional relationships are called **multistep income statements.** This title distinguishes them from the **single-step income statements** that display a single comparison of total revenues and total expenses. Exhibit 5–6 indicates that whereas most companies use a multistep format, many use the single-step approach.

Exhibit 5–5 *Financial Statements*

Income Statement			Balance Sheet			Statement of Cash Flows	
Sales	$41,550		Assets			Operating Activities	
Cost of Goods Sold	(20,160)		Cash	$13,890		Inflow from Customers	$24,750
Gross Margin	21,390		Accounts Rec.	16,800		Outflow for Inventory	(14,160)
Less: Operating Exp.			Merchandise Inv.	7,000		Outflow for Trans.-out	(450)
Sell. And Admin. Exp.	(8,000)		Total Assets	$37,690		Outflow for S&A Exp.	(8,000)
Transportation-out	(450)					Outflow for Interest	(250)
Operating Income	12,940		Liabilities			Net Cash Inflow from Oper.	1,890
Non-operating Items			Accounts Payable	$ 7,000			
Interest Expense	(250)					Investing Activities	0
Net Income	$12,690		Stockholders' Equity				
			Common Stock	15,000		Financing Activities	
			Retained Earnings	15,690		Inflow from Note Pay.	5,000
			Total Equity	30,690		Outflow to Repay Debt	(5,000)
			Total Liab. and Equity	$37,690		Net Cash Flow from Fin.	0
						Net Change in Cash	1,890
						Beginning Cash Bal.	12,000
						Ending Cash Bal.	$13,890

Note carefully that interest is classified as a nonoperating item on a *multistep income statement*. This treatment is inconsistent with the way interest is reported on the statement of cash flows. Recall that interest is reported as an operating activity on the *statement of cash flows*. When the Financial Accounting Standards Board (FASB) ruled on the classification of interest, there was considerable disagreement among accountants as to where it should be shown. Traditionally, interest had been shown as a nonoperating item. However, the FASB chose to depart from traditional practice by requiring that interest be reported as an operating item on the statement of cash flows. Unfortunately, the new requirement was not extended to the income statement. As a result, interest can be reported inconsistently as a nonoperating item on a multistep income statement and as an operating item on the statement of cash flows.

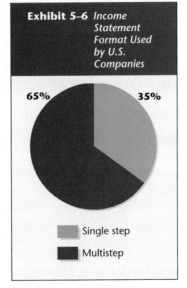

Exhibit 5–6 *Income Statement Format Used by U.S. Companies*

65%   35%

■ Single step
■ Multistep

Data Source: AICPA, *Accounting Trends and Techniques,* 2000.

■ Events Affecting Sales

Returns, allowances, and cash discounts also affect sales. To illustrate, assume JPS engages in the following events during January of 2003.

1. Sells merchandise for $8,500 under terms 1/10, net/30.
2. Recognizes cost of goods sold amounting to $4,800.
3. Accepts $500 of returned merchandise.
4. The cost of the returned merchandise referenced in Event 3 amounted to $300.
5. Grants a sales discount on the remaining account receivable when it is collected within the 30-day discount period. The amount of the discount is $80 ([$8,500 − $500] × 0.01).
6. Recognizes the cash collection of the remaining receivables balance ($8,500 sale − $500 return − $80 discount = $7,920).

The effects of these transactions on the financial statements follow.

Event No.	Cash	+	Accts. Rec.	+	Inv.	=	Accts. Pay.	+	Note Pay.	+	C. Stk.	+	Ret. Earn.		Rev.	−	Exp.	=	Net Inc.		Cash Flow
Bal.	13,890	+	16,800	+	7,000	=	7,000	+	0	+	15,000	+	15,690		NA	−	NA	=	NA		NA
1		+	8,500	+		=		+		+		+	8,500		8,500	−		=	8,500		NA
2		+		+	(4,800)	=		+		+		+	(4,800)			−	4,800	=	(4,800)		NA
3		+	(500)	+		=		+		+		+	(500)		(500)	−		=	(500)		NA
4		+		+	300	=		+		+		+	300			−	(300)	=	300		NA
5		+	(80)	+		=		+		+		+	(80)		(80)	−		=	(80)		NA
6	7,920	+	(7,920)	+		=		+		+		+				−		=			7,920 OA
Bal.	21,810	+	16,800	+	2,500	=	7,000	+	0	+	15,000	+	19,110		7,920	−	4,500	=	3,420		7,920 NC

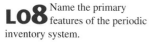

Check Yourself 5–2

Choi Company purchased $24,000 of inventory on account with payment terms of 2/10, n/30 and freight terms FOB shipping point. Freight costs were $1,200. Choi paid $18,000 of the accounts payable within the 10-day discount period and the remaining $6,000 within 30 days. Choi sold all of the inventory for $32,000. Based on this information, determine the amount of gross margin Choi would report on the income statement.

Answer The cost of the inventory is determined as follows:

List price	$24,000
Less: Purchase discount ($18,000 × .02)	(360)
Plus Transportation-in	1,200
Total cost	$24,840

The gross margin is $7,160 the sales price less cost of goods sold ($32,000 − $24,840).

■ Periodic Inventory System

LO8 Name the primary features of the periodic inventory system.

Under certain conditions, it is impractical to record inventory transactions as they occur. For example, consider the operations of a fast-food restaurant. If records were maintained perpetually, it would be necessary to transfer costs from the Inventory account to the Cost of Goods Sold account each time a hamburger, order of fries, soft drink, or any other food item was sold. Obviously, recording each item at the point of sale would be impractical without the availability of sophisticated computer equipment. The **periodic inventory system** offers a practical approach to recording inventory transactions in a low-technology, high-turnover environment.

Under the periodic method, the cost of goods sold is determined at the end of the period rather than at the point of sale. Indeed, the Inventory account is *not* affected by purchases or sales of inventory. When goods are purchased, the cost is recorded in a Purchases account, and no entry is made to reduce inventory when goods are sold. Purchase returns and allowances, purchase discounts, and transportation-in are recorded in separate accounts. The amount of cost of goods sold is determined by subtracting the amount of ending inventory from the total cost of goods available for sale. The amount of ending inventory is determined by making a year-end physical count. Goods that are not in stock at the end of the period are assumed to have been sold. This is the same logic used in earlier chapters to determine the amount of supplies used during an accounting period.

It is important to note that the perpetual and periodic inventory systems represent alternative procedures for recording the same information. The amounts of cost of goods sold and ending inventory reported in the financial statements will be the same regardless of which method is applied. For comparative purposes, Exhibit 5–7 shows the general journal entries used under the periodic inventory method to record the accounting events for JPS for the 2002 accounting

Exhibit 5–7 *General Journal Entries*

Event No.	Account Title	Debit	Credit
1	Purchases	8,000	
	Accounts Payable		8,000
2	Transportation-in	300	
	Cash		300
3	Accounts payable	1,000	
	Purchase Returns and Allowances		1,000
4	Accounts payable	140	
	Purchase Discounts		140
5	Accounts Payable	6,860	
	Cash		6,860
6	Cash	5,000	
	Note Payable		5,000
7	Cash	24,750	
	Sales Revenue		24,750
8	Transportation-out	450	
	Cash		450
9	Purchases	14,000	
	Accounts Payable		14,000
10	Interest Expense	250	
	Cash		250
11	Note Payable	5,000	
	Cash		5,000
12	Accounts Receivable	16,800	
	Sales Revenue		16,800
13	Accounts Payable	7,000	
	Cash		7,000
14	Selling and Administrative Expenses	8,000	
	Cash		8,000
ADJ	Cost of Goods Sold	20,160	
	Inventory	1,000	
	Purchase Returns and Allowances	1,000	
	Purchase Discounts	140	
	Purchases		22,000
	Transportation-in		300
CL	Sales Revenue	41,550	
	Cost of Goods Sold		20,160
	Transportation-out		450
	Selling and Administrative Expenses		8,000
	Interest Expense		250
	Retained Earnings		12,690

period. Observe carefully that the amount of cost of goods sold is recorded in an adjusting entry. This entry transfers the various product costs to the Cost of Goods Sold account and adjusts the Inventory account to reflect the amount of inventory on hand at the end of the accounting period. As its name implies, accountants using the *periodic inventory system* record changes in the balance of the Inventory and Cost of Goods Sold accounts at the end of the accounting period.

Schedule of Cost of Goods Sold

Since under the periodic system the cost of goods sold is not determined at the point of sale, it must be computed at the end of the period. The following logic is used to make the computation.

Exhibit 5–8 *Schedule of Cost of Goods Sold*

Beginning Inventory	$ 6,000
Purchases	22,000
Purchase Returns and Allowances	(1,000)
Purchase Discounts	(140)
Transportation-in	300
Cost of Goods Available for Sale	27,160
Ending Inventory	(7,000)
Cost of Goods Sold	$20,160

First, calculate the cost of goods available for sale. This computation includes the amount of beginning inventory, plus the cost of all purchases, less any purchase returns and allowances, less purchase discounts, plus the cost of transportation-in. The result represents the total cost of all merchandise inventory that *could* have been sold to customers (the *cost of goods available for sale*). The next step is to subtract the amount of inventory that is on hand at the end of the accounting period from the cost of goods available for sale. The result is the amount of *cost of goods sold.*

Exhibit 5–8 is the computation of cost of goods sold for JPS's 2002 accounting period. The **schedule of cost of goods sold** is used for internal reporting purposes and is not shown in the formal financial statements made available to the public. The amount of cost of goods sold is reported as a single line item on the income statement in exactly the same manner as demonstrated for the perpetual inventory. Indeed, the financial statements in Exhibit 5–5 will be the same regardless of whether JPS used the perpetual or periodic system to account for inventory transactions.

▌Lost, Damaged, or Stolen Inventory

LO9 Show how lost, damaged, or stolen inventory affects financial statements.

Although the *perpetual inventory system* is designed to capture information as it occurs, some events are not detectable at the time of occurrence. For example, when a shoplifter steals merchandise, the loss cannot be recorded until it is discovered, which usually occurs sometime after the theft occurred. Also, customers or employees may not report damage to merchandise when it happened. Finally, merchandise may be lost or misplaced. Again, the loss cannot be recorded until it is discovered. Discovery of lost, damaged, or stolen merchandise is normally accomplished by taking a physical count of the merchandise on hand at the end of the accounting period and comparing that amount with the book balance in the Inventory account.

When a discrepancy between the book balance and the physical count of inventory is discovered, an adjusting entry is needed to correct the book balance. If goods have been lost, damaged, or stolen, the book balance will be higher than the actual amount of inventory on hand. In this case, the adjusting entry acts to reduce assets and equity. More specifically, the Inventory account is reduced, and an expense for the amount of the lost, damaged, or stolen inventory is recognized.

Adjustment for Lost, Damaged, or Stolen Inventory

To illustrate, assume that Midwest Merchandising Company uses the perpetual inventory system. Furthermore, assume that the end-of-period physical count reveals $23,500 of merchandise on hand while the Inventory account contains a $24,000 balance. The effect of the inventory write-down on the financial statements is shown here. The event acts to decrease assets (Inventory) and equity (Retained Earnings). The write-down increases expenses and thereby decreases net income. Cash flow is not affected.

Assets	=	Liab.	+	Equity	Rev.	−	Exp.	=	Net Inc.	Cash Flow
(500)	=	NA	+	(500)	NA	−	500	=	(500)	NA

The following entry is used to record the transaction in the general journal:

Account Title	Debit	Credit
Inventory Loss (Cost of Goods Sold)	500	
Inventory		500

Theoretically, the inventory loss is an operating expense. However, such losses are normally immaterial in amount and are treated as additions to the amount of cost of goods sold for external reporting purposes. In a *periodic inventory system,* lost, damaged, or stolen merchandise is included in the cost of goods sold as part of the computational process. Since lost, damaged, or stolen merchandise would not be included in the year-end physical count, these goods are assumed to have been sold when the cost of goods sold is computed by subtracting ending inventory from cost of goods available for sale. From a managerial perspective, this is a major disadvantage of the periodic system. Since the periodic system does not separate the cost of lost, damaged, or stolen merchandise from the cost of goods sold, the amount of the inventory loss is unknown. Without knowing the amount of the inventory loss, management cannot make informed decisions regarding the cost/benefit trade-offs of various security systems.

Advantages and Disadvantages of the Periodic System Versus the Perpetual System

The chief advantage of the periodic method is recording efficiency. Recording inventory transactions occasionally (periodically) requires less work than recording them on a continuous basis (perpetually). The impracticality of a fast-food restaurant's use of a perpetual inventory system would be even greater for a typical grocery store. Think of the number of transactions the grocery would have to record every business day under a perpetual system. The recording

LO4 Compare and contrast the perpetual and periodic inventory systems.

advantage of the periodic system must be weighed against the control advantage inherent in the perpetual system. Since the perpetual system increases and decreases the Inventory account balance when purchases and sales are made, the book balance of inventory should agree with the amount of inventory in stock at any given time. Accordingly, the amount of lost, damaged, destroyed, or stolen inventory can be determined by checking the book balance against a physical count of inventory. Also, the availability of immediate feedback facilitates reorder decisions and profitability assessments.

Fortunately, the advent of computer technology has eliminated most of the practical constraints associated with recording inventory transactions on a continual basis. Electronic scanners can capture accounting information rapidly and efficiently. Computer programs that access the data captured by the scanners can update the accounting records instantaneously. As a result, the use of the perpetual inventory system has increased rapidly in recent years. Continued growth in the application of the perpetual system can be expected as technology advances. Accordingly, this book concentrates on the perpetual inventory system.

■ Financial Analysis for Merchandising Companies

Merchandising companies are in a very competitive business. A consulting enterprise may shelter itself from competition by hiring personnel whose expertise cannot be duplicated. A manufacturing company may hold a patent to a product that gives the company exclusive rights to produce it. Merchandising companies, however, usually sell products that are available for sale by other companies. Merchandise sold at Wal-Mart usually is sold at Kmart as well, and many customers shop where the prices are lowest. Because of the competitive nature of their business, merchandising companies watch their *margins* very carefully. One such margin is the *gross margin,* introduced earlier in the chapter. The gross margin is also called *gross profit.*

"Closed for Inventory Count" is a sign you frequently see on retail stores sometime during the month of January. As indicated in the chapter, companies using the periodic inventory method do not record inventory transactions at the time of sale. Accordingly, the amount of inventory on hand is unknown at any point in time. Even if companies use a perpetual inventory system, the amount of inventory on hand may be unknown because of lost, damaged, or stolen goods. The only way to determine the amount of inventory on hand is to count it. Why count it in January? Christmas shoppers and many after-Christmas sales shoppers are satiated by mid-January, leaving the stores low on both merchandise and customers. Accordingly, stores have less merchandise to count and "lost sales" are minimized during January. Companies that do not depend on seasonal sales (e.g., plumbing supplies wholesale business) may choose to count inventory at some other time during the year. Indeed, counting inventory is not a revenue-generating activity. It is a necessary evil that should be conducted when it least disrupts operations.

Common Size Financial Statements

LO10 Use common size financial statements to evaluate managerial performance.

Chapter 3 introduced ratios as a meaningful way to compare accounting information for a large company to that of a small company. It was shown that raw accounting numbers alone can be misleading. Suppose that Smith Company has a 10 percent return on assets while Jones Company is able to return only 8 percent on its invested assets. Furthermore, assume that Smith Company has $1,000,000 of assets while Jones Company has $2,000,000. Under these circumstances, Smith Company would report less income ($1,000,000 × 0.10 = $100,000) than Jones Company ($2,000,000 × 0.08 = $160,000) even though Smith Company was doing a better job of investing its assets. Similar problems can arise when a company tries to compare its financial statements from the current period to those of prior periods. How good is a $1,000,000 increase in net income? Certainly not as good if the company is Intel as it would be if the company were a small local computer store. To facilitate comparisons between companies or between periods, ratios can be used to prepare financial statements on a percentage basis. These are called **common size financial statements.** The discussion in this chapter focuses on *common size income statements.*

To prepare a common size income statement, each account balance on the statement, or at least those of interest, are converted to a percentage of sales. In most cases companies base common size income statements on **net sales** which is sales minus sales returns and allowances and sales discounts. In these cases, net sales become the base figure representing the 100% mark. Next, the cost of goods sold is divided by sales to determine the cost of goods sold percentage, and so on down the income statement, with each item being converted to a percentage by dividing it by net sales. Exhibit 5–9 demonstrates a common size income statement using data from the 2002 income statement shown in Exhibit 5–5 for JPS.

Gross Margin Percentage

Perhaps the most important percentage on the common size income statement is that for gross margin. Users of accounting information often compute this ratio even when common size statements are not prepared. It is often called the **gross margin percentage** and is defined as

Exhibit 5–9

JUNE'S PLANT SHOP
Common Size Income Statement*
For the Year Ended 2002

Net Sales	$41,550	100.00%
Cost of Goods Sold	(20,160)	(48.52)
Gross Margin	21,390	51.48
Less: Operating Expenses		
Selling and Administrative Expenses	(8,000)	(19.25)
Transportation-out	(450)	(1.08)
Operating Income	12,940	31.14
Nonoperating Items		
Interest Expense	(250)	(.60)
Net Income	$12,690	30.54%

*Percentages do not add exactly because they have been rounded.

$$\frac{\text{Gross margin}}{\text{Net sales}}$$

The gross margin percentage can indicate a lot about a retailer. For example, it provides some indication as to a company's pricing strategy. Companies with low margins have a small spread between their cost and their sales price. In other words, they price their merchandise low in relation to its cost. For example, assume that two stores purchase the same type of inventory item for resale. Suppose that the item costs $100. Store A sells the item for $130 while Store B charges $140. The gross margin percentage for Store A is 23.1 percent ($30 ÷ $130) and for Store B is 28.6 percent ($40 ÷ $140). Accordingly, lower margins suggest lower sales prices.

LO11 Use ratio analysis to evaluate managerial performance.

Real-World Data

Exhibit 5–10 shows the 2000 gross margin percentages and return on sales ratios for six companies. Three of these companies—Kmart, Wal-Mart, and Neiman Marcus—sell a variety of consumer goods; the other three companies sell office products.

Note that the retailers of consumer goods have a wide range of gross margin percentages. As expected, the upscale retailer, Neiman Marcus, has a much higher profit margin than the discount retailers. The profit margins also show that Kmart appears to be charging lower prices than its competitor, Wal-Mart.

However, it is possible that Kmart's lower profit margin is attributable to higher acquisition costs. In other words, Kmart could be paying more to obtain its inventory. This condition would also lead to a lower spread, assuming that the two stores sold inventory for the same prices. Due to its size, Wal-Mart is usually able to obtain favorable pricing through quantity discounts (price reductions given when a customer buys large quantities of goods). In 2000, Wal-Mart had sales of about $191 billion while Kmart's sales were much lower, at $37 billion. Given the competitive nature of the merchandising business, lower prices should translate to higher sales. Indeed, Wal-Mart has experienced phenomenal growth in sales during the past two decades.

In contrast to the stores selling consumer goods, Exhibit 5–10 reveals that the gross margin percentages for three leading merchandisers of office products are almost equal, although Office Depot's gross margin was slightly higher than that of its competitors.

The following sales data are from the records of two retail sales companies. All amounts are in thousands.

	Company A	Company B
Sales	$21,234	$43,465
Cost of goods sold	14,864	34,772
Gross margin	$ 6,370	$ 8,693

One company is an upscale department store, and the other is a discount sales store. Which company is the upscale department store?

Answer The gross margin percentage for Company A is approximately 30 percent ($6,370 ÷ $21,234). The gross margin percentage for Company B is approximately 20 percent ($8,693 ÷ $43,465). These percentages suggest that Company A is selling goods with a higher markup than Company B, which implies that Company A is the upscale department store.

Check Yourself 5–3

Exhibit 5–10		
Industry/Company	**Gross Margin %**	**Return on Sales**
Department stores		
Kmart	19.9%	(0.7%)
Wal-Mart	21.5	3.3
Neiman Marcus	34.7	4.7
Office supplies		
Office Depot	26.7	0.4
Office Max	24.3	(2.6%)
Staples	24.1	0.6

Return on Sales

Low prices motivate high sales, but there is a limit as to how low a company can go. The gross profit percentage must be high enough to cover the cost of other expenses that are necessary to operate the stores. Employees must be paid. A retailer must also pay for utilities, rent, office equipment, furnishings, taxes, and a variety of other operating activities that consume resources. If Staples sells its goods at lower prices, this means that the company will have less money to pay for other expenses. Does this mean that Staples will also have relatively lower profits? Another ratio from the common size income statement that can help answer this question is the **net income percentage.** The net income percentage (sometimes called **return on sales**) is determined as follows:

$$\frac{\text{Net income}}{\text{Net sales}}$$

Recall from Chapter 1 that if a company has unusual items, using *income from continuing operations* to compute ratios may be more appropriate than using net income.

Although Office Depot had a higher gross margin percentage than Staples in 2000 (26.7 percent versus 24.1 percent), Staples had a slightly higher return on sales than Office Depot (0.6 percent versus 0.4 percent). Accordingly, the data suggest that although Office Depot is selling its products at a higher price than Staples, it is also spending more to operate its business. This analysis suggests that one way Staples is able to sell for less is by exercising better control over its operating expenses.

Use of Common Size Financial Statements

The previous discussion focused on the use of common size income data to make comparisons among companies. Investors, creditors, and managers also find it useful to compare a particular company's performance over different periods. To illustrate, assume that June's Plant Shop decides to relocate its store to an upscale shopping mall with a wealthier customer base. June realizes that she will have to pay more for rent but believes that she will be able to cover the higher cost by selling her merchandise at higher prices. June changes location on January 1, 2003. Exhibit 5–11 shows common size income statements for 2002 and 2003. Comparisons between these two income statements can provide insight as to whether June's strategy was successful.

Exhibit 5–11				
JUNE'S PLANT SHOP **Common Size Income Statements***				
	2002		**2003**	
Net Sales	$41,550	100%	$49,860	100%
Cost of Goods Sold	(20,160)	49	(19,944)	(40)
Gross Margin	21,390	51	29,916	60
Less: Operating Expenses				
Selling and Administrative Expenses	(8,000)	(19)	(12,465)	(25)
Transportation-out	(450)	(1)	(500)	(1)
Operating Income	12,940	31	16,951	34
Nonoperating Items				
Interest Expense	(250)	(1)	(400)	(1)
Net Income	$12,690	30%	$16,551	33%

An analysis of the common size statements suggests that June's strategy did indeed increase the profitability of her business. By increasing prices, June was able to increase the absolute dollar value of sales by $8,310 ($49,860 − $41,550). Notice that operating expenses increased as expected. They now constitute 25 percent of sales instead of 19 percent. Although this constitutes a 6 percent increase in operating expenses, it is more than offset by the increase in the gross margin rate. Gross profit percentage in 2003 was 9 percent higher than in 2002 (60 − 51), which verifies the fact that June was able to raise her prices. Transportation cost remained relatively stable. Interest costs were higher, implying that it was necessary to borrow more funds to support the higher operating expenses. However, neither transportation nor interest costs changed drastically enough to affect the measurement in percentage terms. The overall impact of the new strategy is apparent in the net income percentage, which increased from 30 to 33 percent. Accordingly, profitability increased as expected.

Merchandise Inventory Financed

Suppose a store purchases inventory in October to sell during the Christmas season. Assume sales are made on account so that cash from the sale is collected in January or February of the next year. Since the cash from the sale is collected three or four months after the goods were purchased, how will the company get the money to pay for the inventory? One answer is to borrow the money. The company could pay for the merchandise in October with money borrowed from a bank. The bank could be repaid when the cash collections from sales come in during January and February.

LO12 Dicuss the cost of financing inventory.

The obvious drawback to obtaining a loan to pay for inventory is that it incurs interest expense on the borrowed funds. However, other alternative sources of financing inventory would also be expensive. If the owner's money is used, then these funds cannot be invested elsewhere. For example, the owner's money could be deposited in an interest-earning savings account. The loss of interest earned is called an **opportunity cost;** it is effectively a financing cost that is just as real as the interest expense. Net income falls regardless of whether a business incurs expenses or loses revenue.

A third alternative is to purchase the inventory on account. However, when purchases are made on account, the seller usually charges the buyer an interest fee. This charge may be "hidden" in the form of higher prices. So while interest costs are lower, the cost of goods sold is higher. As indicated earlier in this chapter, many companies recognize financing costs by offering buyers the opportunity to receive cash discounts by paying for purchases within a short time immediately following the sale. In summary, any way you look at it, merchandisers incur significant inventory-financing costs.

There is no way to eliminate the cost of financing inventory, but accounting information can help companies minimize this cost. As much as possible, businesses should reduce the time for which goods stay in inventory before being sold. Ratios that facilitate the management of inventory turnover are explained in Chapter 8. Companies should also try to shorten the time it takes to get customers to pay for the goods they purchase. This relates to managing accounts receivable turnover, which is explained in Chapter 7. Later chapters discuss efforts to control inventory costs; this chapter provided a clear explanation of the need for such control.

This chapter introduced accounting for *merchandising companies,* which earn a profit by selling inventory at a price that is higher than the cost of goods. Merchandising companies include retail companies (companies that sell goods to the final consumer) and *wholesale companies* (companies that sell to other merchandising companies). The term for the products sold by merchandising companies is *inventory.* The costs to purchase the inventory, to receive it, and to make inventory ready for sale are known as *product costs,* which are first accumulated in an inventory account (balance sheet asset account) and then recognized as cost of goods sold (income statement expense account) in the period in which goods are sold. The purchase and sale of inventory can be recognized when goods are bought and sold (perpetual system) or at the end of the accounting period (periodic system).

a look
back

Accounting for inventory includes the treatment of cash discounts, transportation costs, and returns and allowances. The cost of inventory is the list price less any *cash discount* offered by the seller. The cost of freight paid to acquire inventory (*transportation-in*) is considered to be a product cost. The cost of freight paid to deliver inventory to customers (*transportation-out*) is a selling expense. *Sales returns and allowances and sales discounts* are subtracted from sales revenue to determine the amount of *net sales* shown on the income statement. Purchase returns and allowances act to reduce product cost. Theoretically, the cost of lost, damaged, or stolen inventory is an operating expense. However, these costs are usually immaterial in amount and are frequently reported as part of cost of goods sold on the income statement.

Some companies show product costs separately from general, selling, and administrative costs on the income statement. Cost of goods sold is subtracted from sales revenue to determine the *gross margin.* General, selling, and administrative expenses are subtracted from gross margin to determine the amount of income from operations. This format is called a *multistep income statement.* Other companies report income under a *single-step format.* In this case, the cost of goods sold is listed along with general, selling, and administrative items in a single expense category that is subtracted in total from revenue to determine income from operations.

Merchandising businesses operate in a highly competitive environment. They must manage their operations closely to remain profitable. Managers of merchandising businesses frequently use *common size financial statements* (statements presented on a percentage basis) and ratio analysis to monitor their operations. Percentages (common size financial statements) permit comparisons among companies of different size. Although a $1 million increase in sales may be good for a small company and bad for a large company, a 10 percent increase represents an increment that is common to any size company. The two most common ratios used by merchandising companies are the *gross margin percentage* (gross margin ÷ net sales) and the *net income percentage* (net income ÷ net sales). Interpreting these ratios requires an understanding of industry practice. For example, a discount store such as Wal-Mart would be expected to have a much lower gross margin percentage than an upscale store such as Neiman Marcus.

Managers should be aware of the financing cost associated with carrying inventory. By investing funds in inventory, a firm loses the opportunity to invest them in interest-bearing assets. Accordingly, the financing cost of inventory is frequently called an *opportunity cost.* To minimize financing costs, a company should minimize the amount of inventory it carries, the length of time it holds the inventory, and the time it requires to collect accounts receivable.

a look forward

To this point, the text has covered the basic accounting cycle for service and merchandising businesses. The remainder of the book takes a closer look at specific accounting issues. For example, Chapter 6 examines internal control and accounting for cash. In Chapter 6 you will learn the accounting practices and procedures that companies use to protect their cash and other assets. You will learn to account for petty cash (small disbursements of cash) and to accomplish a bank reconciliation. Furthermore, you will learn to classify assets as being short or long term in nature. Finally, you will learn to use a ratio to assess the liquidity (the ability to satisfy short-term obligations) of a business.

SELF-STUDY REVIEW PROBLEM

Academy Sales Company (ASC) started the 2004 accounting period with the balances given in the following financial statements model. During 2004 ASC experienced the following business events.

1. Purchased $16,000 of merchandise inventory on account, terms 2/10, n/30.
2. The goods that were purchased in Event 1 were delivered FOB shipping point. Freight costs of $600 were paid in cash by the responsible party.
3. Returned $500 of goods purchased in Event 1.

4a. Recorded the cash discount on the goods purchased in Event 1.

4b. Paid the balance due on the account payable within the discount period.

5a. Recognized $21,000 of cash revenue from the sale of merchandise.

5b. Recognized $15,000 of cost of goods sold.

6. The merchandise in Event 5a was sold to customers FOB destination. Freight costs of $950 were paid in cash by the responsible party.

7. Paid cash of $4,000 for selling and administrative expenses.

Required

a. Record these transactions in a financial statements model like the following one.

Event No.	Cash	+	Inv.	=	Accts. Pay.	+	C. Stk.	+	Ret. Earn.	Rev.	–	Exp.	=	Net Inc.	Cash Flow
Bal.	25,000	+	3,000	=	0	+	18,000	+	10,000	NA	–	NA	=	NA	NA

b. Calculate the gross margin percentage. Based on ASC's gross margin percentage and the information shown in Exhibit 5–10, classify ASC as an upscale department store, a retail discount store, or an office supplies store.

Solution to Requirement a

Event No.	Cash	+	Inv.	=	Accts. Pay.	+	C. Stk.	+	Ret. Earn.	Rev.	–	Exp.	=	Net Inc.	Cash Flow
Bal.	25,000	+	3,000	=	0	+	18,000	+	10,000	NA	–	NA	=	NA	NA
1		+	16,000	=	16,000	+		+			–		=		
2	(600)	+	600	=		+		+			–		=		(600) OA
3		+	(500)	=	(500)	+		+			–		=		
4a		+	(310)	=	(310)	+		+			–		=		
4b	(15,190)	+		=	(15,190)	+		+			–		=		(15,190) OA
5a	21,000	+		=		+		+	21,000	21,000	–		=	21,000	21,000 OA
5b		+	(15,000)	=		+		+	(15,000)		–	15,000	=	(15,000)	
6	(950)	+		=		+		+	(950)		–	950	=	(950)	(950) OA
7	(4,000)	+		=		+		+	(4,000)		–	4,000	=	(4,000)	(4,000) OA
Bal.	25,260	+	3,790	=	0	+	18,000	+	11,050	21,000	–	19,950	=	1,050	260 NC

Solution to Requirement b

Gross margin equals sales minus cost of goods sold. In this case, the gross margin is $6,000 ($21,000 – $15,000). The gross margin percentage is computed by dividing gross margin by sales. In this case, the gross margin percentage is 28.6 percent ($6,000 ÷ $21,000). Since this percentage is closest to the percentage shown for the upscale department store, Neiman Marcus, the data suggest ASC is also an upscale store.

KEY TERMS

allowance *222*

cash discount *222*

common size financial statements *232*

cost of goods available for sale *216*

cost of goods sold *216*

FOB (free on board) destination *221*

FOB (free on board) shipping point *221*

gross margin *216*

gross margin percentage *232*

inventory *215*

merchandise inventory *216*

merchandising businesses *216*

multistep income statement *226*

net income percentage *234*

net sales *232*

opportunity cost *235*

period costs *216*

periodic inventory system *228*

perpetual inventory system *216*

product cost *216*

purchase discount *222*

retail companies *216*

return on sales *234*

schedule of cost of goods sold *230*

selling and administrative costs *216*

single-step income statement *226*

transportation-in (freight-in) *221*

transportation-out (freight-out) *223*

2/10, n/30 *222*

wholesale companies *216*

1. Define *inventory.* What items might be included in inventory?
2. Define *merchandise inventory.* Distinguish between inventory and merchandise inventory. What types of costs are included in the Merchandise Inventory account?
3. What is the difference between a product cost and a selling and administrative costs?
4. How is the cost of goods available for sale determined?
5. What portion of cost of goods available for sale is shown on the balance sheet? What portion is shown on the income statement?
6. When are period costs expensed? When are product costs expensed?
7. If PetCo had net sales of $600,000, goods available for sale of $450,000, and cost of goods sold of $375,000, what is its gross margin? What amount of inventory will be shown on its balance sheet?
8. Explain the difference between a perpetual inventory system and a periodic inventory system. Discuss the advantages of each. Must a physical inventory be taken with both systems? Why or why not?
9. What are the effects of the following types of transactions on the accounting equation? Also identify the financial statements that are affected. (Assume that the perpetual inventory system is used.)
   a. Acquisition of cash from the issue of common stock.
   b. Contribution of inventory by an owner of a company.
   c. Purchase of inventory with cash by a company.
   d. Sale of inventory for cash.
10. Northern Merchandising Company sold inventory that cost $12,000 for $20,000 cash. How does this event affect the accounting equation? What financial statements and accounts are affected? (Assume that the perpetual inventory system is used.)
11. If goods are shipped FOB shipping point, which party (buyer or seller) is responsible for the shipping costs?
12. Define *transportation-in.* Is it a product or a period cost?
13. Quality Cellular Co. paid $80 for freight on merchandise that it had purchased for resale to customers (transportation-in) and paid $135 for freight on merchandise delivered to customers (transportation-out). What account is debited for the $80 payment? What account is debited for the $135 payment?
14. Why would a seller grant an allowance to a buyer of the seller's merchandise?
15. Dyer Department Store purchased goods with the terms 2/10, n/30. What do these terms mean?
16. Eastern Discount Stores incurred a $5,000 cash cost. How does the accounting treatment of this cost differ if the cash were paid for inventory versus commissions to sales personnel?
17. What is the purpose of giving a cash discount to charge customers?
18. Define *transportation-out.* Is it a product cost or a period cost for the seller?
19. Explain the difference between purchase returns and sales returns. How do purchase returns affect the financial statements of both buyer and seller? How do sales returns affect the financial statements of both buyer and seller?
20. How is net sales determined?
21. What is the difference between a multistep income statement and a single-step income statement?
22. What is the purpose of preparing a schedule of cost of goods sold?
23. Why does the periodic inventory system impose a major disadvantage for management in accounting for lost, stolen, or damaged goods?
24. What is the advantage of using common size statements to present financial information for several accounting periods?
25. What information is provided by the return on sales ratio?

When the instructions for *any* exercise or problem call for the preparation of an income statement, use the *multistep format* unless otherwise indicated.

L.O. 1, 3, 5, 7   EXERCISE 5–1A *Comparing a Merchandising Company with a Service Company*

The following information is available for two different types of businesses for the accounting period. Darwin Consulting is a service business that provides consulting services to small businesses. University Book Mart is a merchandising business that sells books to college students.

Data for Darwin Consulting

1. Borrowed $10,000 from the bank to start the business.
2. Provided $12,000 of services to customers and collected $12,000 cash.
3. Paid salary expense of $7,200.

Data for University Book Mart

1. Borrowed $10,000 from the bank to start the business.
2. Purchased $8,250 of inventory for cash.
3. Inventory costing $6,500 was sold for $12,000 cash.
4. Paid $700 cash for operating expenses.

Required

a. Prepare an income statement, balance sheet, and statement of cash flows for each of the companies.
b. What is different about the income statements of the two businesses?
c. What is different about the balance sheets of the two businesses?
d. How are the statements of cash flow different for the two businesses?

EXERCISE 5–2A *Effect of Inventory Transactions on Journals, Ledgers, and Financial Statements: Perpetual System*   **L.O. 3, 5**

Hope Jackson started a small merchandising business in 2006. The business experienced the following events during its first year of operation. Assume that Jackson uses the perpetual inventory system.

1. Acquired $25,000 cash from the issue of common stock.
2. Purchased inventory for $22,000 cash.
3. Sold inventory costing $17,000 for $24,000 cash.

Required

a. Record the events in general journal format.
b. Post the entries to T-accounts.
c. Prepare an income statement for 2006 (use the multistep format).
d. What is the amount of total assets at the end of the period?

EXERCISE 5–3A *Effect of Inventory Transactions on the Income Statement and Statement of Cash Flows: Perpetual System*   **L.O. 3, 5**

During 2007, Stonebrook Merchandising Company purchased $50,000 of inventory on account. The company sold inventory on account that cost $36,000 for $56,000. Cash payments on accounts payable were $30,000. There was $40,000 cash collected from accounts receivable. Stonebrook also paid $8,000 cash for operating expenses. Assume that Stonebrook started the accounting period with $48,000 in cash and common stock.

Required

a. Identify the events described in the preceding paragraph and record them in a horizontal statements model like the following one:

Assets			=	Liab.	+	Stockholders' Equity			Rev.	–	Exp.	=	Net Inc.	Cash Flow
Cash	+ Accts. Rec.	+ Inv.	= A. Pay.			C. Stk.	+	Ret. Earn.						
48,000 +	NA	+ NA	= NA		+	48,000	+	NA	NA	–	NA	=	NA	NA

b. What is the balance of accounts receivable at the end of 2007?
c. What is the balance of accounts payable at the end of 2007?
d. What are the amounts of gross margin and net income for 2007?
e. Determine the amount of net cash flow from operating activities.
f. Explain any differences between net income and net cash flow from operating activities.

EXERCISE 5–4A *Recording Inventory Transactions in the General Journal and Posting Entries to T-Accounts: Perpetual System*   **L.O. 5**

Mary's Beauty Supply experienced the following events during 2006:

1. Acquired $10,000 cash from the issue of common stock.
2. Purchased inventory for $7,000 cash.
3. Sold inventory costing $5,200 for $7,800 cash.
4. Paid $600 for advertising expense.

Required

a. Record the general journal entries for the preceding transactions.
b. Post each of the entries to T-accounts.
c. Prepare a trial balance to prove the equality of debits and credits.

L.O. 6   EXERCISE 5–5A *Determining Which Party Is Responsible for Freight Cost*

Required

Determine which party, buyer or seller, is responsible for freight charges in each of the following situations:

a. Sold merchandise, freight terms, FOB shipping point.
b. Sold merchandise, freight terms, FOB destination.
c. Purchased merchandise, freight terms, FOB shipping point.
d. Purchased merchandise, freight terms, FOB destination.

L.O. 3   EXERCISE 5–6A *Effect of Purchase Returns and Allowances and Freight Costs on the Journal, Ledger, and Financial Statements: Perpetual System*

The trial balance for The Gift Shop as of January 1, 2003 was as follows:

Account Titles	Debit	Credit
Cash	$ 8,000	
Inventory	3,000	
Common Stock		$10,000
Retained Earnings		1,000
Total	$11,000	$11,000

The following events affected the company during the 2003 accounting period:

1. Purchased merchandise on account that cost $5,500.
2. Purchased goods FOB shipping point with freight cost of $250 cash.
3. Returned $800 of damaged merchandise for credit on account.
4. Agreed to keep other damaged merchandise for which the company received a $350 allowance.
5. Sold merchandise that cost $4,000 for $7,750 cash.
6. Delivered merchandise to customers under terms FOB destination with freight costs amounting to $200 cash.
7. Paid $4,000 on the merchandise purchased in Event 1.

Required

a. Record the transactions in general journal format.
b. Open general ledger T-accounts with the appropriate beginning balances, and post the journal entries to the T-accounts.
c. Prepare an income statement and statement of cash flows for 2003.
d. Explain why a difference does or does not exist between net income and net cash flow from operating activities.

L.O. 2, 5   EXERCISE 5–7A *Accounting for Product Costs: Perpetual Inventory System*

Which of the following would be debited to the Inventory account for a merchandising business using the perpetual inventory system?

Required

a. Purchase of inventory.
b. Allowance received for damaged inventory.
c. Transportation-out.
d. Purchase discount.
e. Transportation-in.
f. Purchase of a new computer to be used by the business.

L.O. 2, 3, 5   EXERCISE 5–8A *Effect of Product Cost and Period Cost: Horizontal Statements Model*

Turner Co. experienced the following events for the 2003 accounting period:

1. Acquired $2,500 cash from the issue of common stock.
2. Purchased $14,000 of inventory on account.
3. Received goods purchased in Event 2 FOB shipping point. Freight cost of $150 paid in cash.
4. Returned $600 of goods purchased in Event 2 because of poor quality.
5. Sold inventory on account that cost $8,250 for $14,350.
6. Paid freight cost on the goods sold in Event 5 of $60. The goods were shipped FOB destination. Cash was paid for the freight cost.
7. Collected $11,750 cash from accounts receivable.
8. Paid $10,000 cash on accounts payable.
9. Paid $275 for advertising expense.
10. Paid $500 cash for insurance expense.

Required

a. Which of these transactions result in period (selling and administrative) costs? Which result in product costs? If neither, label the transaction NA.
b. Record each event in a horizontal statements model like the following one. The first event is recorded as an example.

Assets				=	Liab.	+	Stockholders' Equity				Rev.	–	Exp.	=	Net Inc.	Cash Flow
Cash	+	Accts. Rec.	+ Inv.	=	A. Pay.	+	C. Stk.	+	Ret. Earn.							
2,500	+	NA	+ NA	=	NA	+	2,500	+	NA		NA	–	NA	=	NA	2,500 FA

EXERCISE 5–9A *Cash Discounts and Purchase Returns*

L.O. 6

On March 6, 2004, Rue's Imports purchased $12,400 of merchandise from The Glass Exchange, terms 2/10, n/45. On March 10, Rue returned $2,400 of the merchandise to The Glass Exchange for credit. Rue paid cash for the merchandise on March 15, 2004.

Required

a. What is the amount of the check that Rue must write to The Glass Exchange on March 15?
b. Prepare the journal entries for these transactions.
c. How much must Rue pay for the merchandise purchased if the payment is not made until March 20, 2004?
d. Why would The Glass Exchange sell merchandise with the terms 2/10, n/45?

EXERCISE 5–10A *Effect of Sales Returns and Allowances and Freight Costs on the Journal, Ledger, and Financial Statements: Perpetual System*

L.O. 3, 5, 6

Upton Company began the 2002 accounting period with $13,000 cash, $70,000 inventory, $40,000 common stock, and $43,000 retained earnings. During the 2002 accounting period, Upton experienced the following events:

1. Sold merchandise costing $60,400 for $90,800 on account to Jones' General Store.
2. Delivered the goods to Jones under terms FOB destination. Freight costs were $2,600 cash.
3. Received returned damaged goods from Jones. The goods cost Upton $5,600 and were sold to Jones for $8,800.
4. Granted Jones a $3,400 allowance for other damaged goods that Jones agreed to keep.
5. Collected partial payment of $56,000 cash from accounts receivable.

Required

a. Record the transactions in general journal format.
b. Open general ledger T-accounts with the appropriate beginning balances and post the journal entries to the T-accounts.
c. Prepare an income statement, balance sheet, and statement of cash flows.
d. Why would Upton grant the $3,400 allowance to Jones? Who benefits more?

EXERCISE 5–11A *Effect of Cash Discounts on the Journal, Ledger, and Financial Statements: Perpetual System*

L.O. 3, 5, 6

Stone Sales was started in 2005. The company experienced the following accounting events during its first year of operation:

1. Started business when it acquired $60,000 cash from the issue of common stock.
2. Purchased merchandise costing $36,000 on account, terms 2/10, n/30.
3. Paid off the account payable within the discount period.
4. Sold inventory on account that cost $20,000 for $30,000. Credit terms were 1/20, n/30.
5. Collected cash from the account receivable within the discount period.
6. Paid $7,600 cash for operating expenses.

Required
a. Record the transactions in general journal format.
b. Open general ledger T-accounts, and post the journal entries to the T-accounts.
c. Record the events in a horizontal statements model like the following one.

Assets			=	Liab.	+	Stockholders' Equity			Rev.	–	Exp.	=	Net Inc.	Cash Flow
Cash	+	Accts. Rec.	+ Inv. =	A. Pay.	+	C. Stk.	+	Ret. Earn.						

d. What is the amount of gross margin for the period? What is the net income for the period?
e. Why would Stone sell merchandise with the terms 1/20, n/30?
f. What do the terms 2/10, n/30 in event 2 mean to Stone?

L.O. 3, 5, 6   EXERCISE 5–12A *Effect of Inventory Transactions on the Financial Statements:*
Comprehensive Exercise With Sales and Purchase Returns and Discounts

Retail Sales Company had the following balances in its accounts on January 1, 2004:

Cash	$15,000
Merchandise Inventory	10,000
Common Stock	20,000
Retained Earnings	5,000

Retail experienced the following events during 2004:
1. Purchased merchandise inventory on account for $30,000, terms 1/10, n/30.
2. Paid freight of $500 on the merchandise purchased.
3. Sold merchandise inventory that cost $17,000 for $26,000 on account, terms 2/10, n/45.
4. Returned $1,000 of damaged merchandise purchased in Event 1.
5. Agreed to keep other merchandise that was slightly damaged and was granted an allowance of $200.
6. Received return of $4,000 of merchandise that had a cost of $2,400 from customer in Event 3.
7. Collected the balance of accounts receivable within the discount period.
8. Paid for one-half of the merchandise in Event 1 within the discount period.
9. Paid $3,200 cash for selling and administrative expenses.
10. Paid the balance of accounts payable (not within the discount period).

Required
a. Record each of these events in general journal format.
b. Open general ledger T-accounts. Post the beginning balances and the events to the accounts.
c. Prepare a trial balance.
d. Prepare an income statement, balance sheet (assume closing entries have been made), and a statement of cash flows.

L.O. 3, 5, 9   EXERCISE 5–13A *Effect of Inventory Losses: Perpetual System*

Burk Merchandising experienced the following events during 2002, its first year of operation:
1. Started the business when it acquired $80,000 cash from the issue of common stock.
2. Paid $56,000 cash to purchase inventory.
3. Sold inventory costing $43,000 for $68,400 cash.
4. Physically counted inventory showing $11,600 inventory was on hand at the end of the accounting period.

Required
a. Open appropriate ledger T-accounts, and record the events in the accounts.
b. Prepare an income statement and balance sheet for 2002.
c. Explain how differences between the book balance and the physical count of inventory could arise. Why is being able to determine whether differences exist useful to management?

EXERCISE 5–14A *Determining the Effect of Inventory Transactions on the Horizontal
Statements Model: Perpetual System*

L.O. 3, 5

Lobo Sales Company experienced the following events:
1. Purchased merchandise inventory for cash.
2. Purchased merchandise inventory on account.
3. Sold merchandise inventory for cash. Label the revenue recognition 3a and the expense recognition 3b.
4. Sold merchandise inventory on account. Label the revenue recognition 4a and the expense recognition 4b.
5. Returned merchandise purchased on account.
6. Paid cash for selling and administrative expenses.
7. Paid cash on accounts payable within the discount period.
8. Paid cash for transportation-in.
9. Collected cash from accounts receivable.
10. Paid cash for transportation-out.

Required
Identify each event as asset source (AS), asset use (AU), asset exchange (AE), or claims exchange (CE).
Also explain how each event affects the financial statements by placing a + for increase, − for decrease,
or NA for not affected under each of the components in the following statements model. Assume the use
of the perpetual inventory system. The first event is recorded as an example.

Event No.	Event Type	Assets	=	Liab.	+	Stk. Equity	Rev.	−	Exp.	=	Net Inc.	Cash Flow
1	AE	+ −	=	NA	+	NA	NA	−	NA	=	NA	− OA

EXERCISE 5–15A *Effect of Inventory Transactions on the Income Statement and Balance
Sheet: Periodic System*

L.O. 8

Bob Ott is the owner of The Sports Store. At the beginning of the year, Ott had $1,050 in inventory. During the year, Ott purchased inventory that cost $5,250. At the end of the year, inventory on hand amounted to $2,200.

Required
Calculate the following:
a. Cost of goods available for sale during the year.
b. Cost of goods sold for the year.
c. Inventory amount The Sports Store would report on its year-end balance sheet.

EXERCISE 5–16A *Single-Step and Multistep Income Statements*

L.O. 7

The following information was taken from the accounts of Quick Foods, a delicatessen. The accounts are
listed in alphabetical order, and each has a normal balance.

Accounts Payable	$150
Accounts Receivable	175
Accumulated Depreciation	50
Advertising Expense	100
Cash	205
Common Stock	100
Cost of Goods Sold	225
Interest Expense	35
Merchandise Inventory	75
Prepaid Rent	20
Retained Earnings	255
Sales Revenue	400
Salaries Expense	65
Supplies Expense	28

Required
First, prepare an income statement using the single-step approach. Then prepare another income statement using the multistep approach.

L.O. 8   **EXERCISE 5–17A** *Determining Cost of Goods Sold: Periodic System*

Valley Retailers uses the periodic inventory system to account for its inventory transactions. The following account titles and balances were drawn from Valley's records: beginning balance in inventory, $24,900; purchases, $306,400; purchase returns and allowances, $9,600; sales, $680,000; sales returns and allowances, $6,370; freight-in, $2,160; and operating expenses, $51,400. A physical count indicated that $29,300 of merchandise was on hand at the end of the accounting period.

Required
a. Prepare a schedule of cost of goods sold.
b. Prepare a multistep income statement.

L.O. 8   **EXERCISE 5–18A** *Basic Transactions: Periodic System, Single Cycle*

The following events apply to Joy Gift Shop for 2007.
1. Acquired $33,500 cash from the issue of common stock.
2. Issued common stock to Kayla Taylor, one of the owners, in exchange for gift merchandise worth $2,500 Taylor had acquired prior to opening the shop.
3. Purchased $43,500 of inventory on account.
4. Paid $2,750 for advertising expense.
5. Sold inventory for $77,500.
6. Paid $8,000 in salary to a part-time salesperson.
7. Paid $35,000 on accounts payable (see Event 3).
8. Physically counted inventory, which indicated that $7,000 of inventory was on hand at the end of the accounting period.

Required
a. Record each of these events in general journal form. Joy Gift Shop uses the periodic system.
b. Post each of the events to ledger T-accounts.
c. Prepare an income statement, statement of changes in stockholders' equity, balance sheet, and statement of cash flows for 2007.
d. Prepare the necessary closing entries at the end of 2007, and post them to the appropriate T-accounts.
e. Prepare an after-closing trial balance.
f. Discuss an advantage of using the periodic system instead of the perpetual system.
g. Why is the common stock balance on the statement of changes in stockholders' equity different from the common stock issued in the cash flow from financing activities section of the cash flow statement?

L.O. 3, 5, 12   **EXERCISE 5–19A** *Determining Cost of Financing Inventory*

On January 1, 2008, Al Smith started a small sailboat merchandising business that he named Al's Sails. The company experienced the following events during the first year of operation:
1. Started the business when Smith borrowed $25,000 from his parents. He issued them a one-year note dated January 1, 2008. The note had a 7 percent annual rate of interest.
2. Paid $20,000 cash to purchase inventory.
3. Sold a sailboat that cost $9,000 for $17,000 on account.
4. Collected $7,000 cash from accounts receivable.
5. Paid $2,500 for operating expenses.
6. Recognized accrued interest on the note payable on December 31.

Required
a. Record the events in general journal format, using the perpetual system.
b. Open general ledger T-accounts, and post the journal entries to the T-accounts.
c. Prepare an income statement, balance sheet, and statement of cash flows. (Assume that year-end closing entries have been made.)
d. "Since Al sold inventory for $17,000, he will be able to repay more than half of the $25,000 loan from his parents when it comes due on January 1, 2009." Do you agree with this statement? Why or why not?

L.O. 6, 12   **EXERCISE 5–20A** *Financing Inventory and Cash Discounts*

Kay Haynes came to you for advice. She has just purchased a large amount of inventory with the terms 2/10, n/60. The amount of the invoice is $260,000. She is currently short on cash but has good credit. She can borrow the money at the appropriate time to take advantage of the discount. The annual interest rate is 7% if she decides to borrow the money. Haynes is sure she will have the necessary cash by the due date of the invoice (but not by the discount date).

Required
a. For how long would Haynes need to borrow the money to take advantage of the discount?
b. How much money would Haynes need to borrow?
c. Write a memo to Haynes outlining the most cost-effective strategy for her to follow. Include in your memo the amount of savings from the alternative you suggest.

PROBLEMS—SERIES A

PROBLEM 5–21A *Basic Transactions for Three Accounting Cycles: Perpetual System*   L.O. 3, 5

Mackey Company was started in 2007 when it acquired $20,000 from the issue of common stock. The following data summarize the company's first three years' operating activities. Assume that all transactions were cash transactions.

	2007	2008	2009
Purchases of Inventory	$ 9,800	$12,000	$18,500
Sales	14,100	17,500	26,000
Cost of Goods Sold	7,150	9,500	15,000
Selling and Administrative Expenses	4,600	6,200	7,400

Required
Prepare an income statement and balance sheet for each fiscal year. (*Hint:* Record the transaction data for each accounting period in T-accounts before preparing the statements for that year.)

PROBLEM 5–22A *Identifying Product and Period Costs*   L.O. 2

Required
Indicate whether each of the following costs is a product cost or a period cost:
a. Cleaning supplies for the office.
b. Freight on goods purchased for resale.
c. Salary of the marketing director.
d. Freight on goods sold to customer with terms FOB destination.
e. Utilities expense incurred for office building.
f. Depreciation on office equipment.
g. Insurance on vans used to deliver goods to customers.
h. Salaries of sales supervisors.
i. Monthly maintenance expense for a copier.
j. Goods purchased for resale.

PROBLEM 5–23A *Identifying Freight Cost*   L.O. 2, 6

Required
For each of the following events, determine the amount of freight paid by Rick's Garage. Also indicate whether the freight is classified as a product or period cost.
a. Purchased inventory with freight costs of $550, FOB destination.
b. Sold merchandise to a customer. Freight costs were $200, FOB shipping point.
c. Purchased additional merchandise with costs of $190, FOB shipping point.
d. Shipped merchandise to customers with freight costs of $100, FOB destination.

PROBLEM 5–24A *Effect of Purchase Returns and Allowances and Purchase Discounts on the Financial Statements: Perpetual System*   L.O. 3, 5, 6

The following events were completed by Doss Heater Company in September 2009:

Sept. 1   Acquired $30,000 cash from the issue of common stock.
      1   Purchased $18,000 of merchandise on account with terms 2/10, n/30.
      5   Paid $800 cash for freight to obtain merchandise purchased on September 1.

8   Sold merchandise that cost $4,500 to customers for $8,800 on account.
8   Returned $900 of defective merchandise from the September 1 purchase to the supplier.
10 Paid cash for one-half of the balance due on the merchandise purchased on September 1.
15 Received cash from customers of September 8 sale in settlement of the account balances.
30 Paid the balance due on the merchandise purchased on September 1.
30 Paid $1,720 cash for selling expenses.

Required

a. Record each event in a statements model like the following one. The first event is recorded as an example.

Assets					=	Liab.	+	Stockholders' Equity			Rev.	−	Exp.	=	Net Inc.	Cash Flow
Cash	+	Accts. Rec.	+	Inv.	=	A. Pay.	+	C. Stk.	+	Ret. Earn.						
30,000	+	NA	+	NA	=	NA	+	30,000	+	NA	NA	−	NA	=	NA	30,000 FA

b. Record each of these transactions in general journal form.
c. Post each of the transactions to general ledger T-accounts.
d. Prepare an income statement for the month ending September 30.
e. Prepare a statement of cash flows for the month ending September 30.
f. Explain why there is a difference between net income and cash flow from operating activities.

L.O. 3, 5, 9   PROBLEM 5–25A *Comprehensive Cycle Problem: Perpetual System*

At the beginning of 2005, the W. Coyle Company had the following balances in its accounts:

Cash	$ 4,300
Inventory	9,000
Common Stock	10,000
Retained Earnings	3,300

During 2005, the company experienced the following events.
1. Purchased inventory that cost $2,200 on account from Blue Company under terms 1/10, n/30. The merchandise was delivered FOB shipping point. Freight costs of $110 were paid in cash.
2. Returned $200 of the inventory that it had purchased because the inventory was damaged in transit. The freight company agreed to pay the return freight cost.
3. Paid the amount due on its account payable to Blue Company within the cash discount period.
4. Sold inventory that had cost $3,000 for $5,500 on account, under terms 2/10, n/45.
5. Received returned merchandise from a customer. The merchandise originally cost $400 and was sold to the customer for $710 cash. The customer was paid $710 cash for the returned merchandise.
6. Delivered goods FOB destination. Freight costs of $60 were paid in cash.
7. Collected the amount due on the account receivable within the discount period.
8. Took a physical count indicating that $7,970 of inventory was on hand at the end of the accounting period.

Required

a. Identify each of these events as asset source (AS), asset use (AU), asset exchange (AE), or claims exchange (CE). Also explain how each event would affect the financial statements by placing a + for increase, − for decrease, or NA for not affected under each of the components in the following statements model. Assume that the perpetual inventory method is used. When an event has more than one part, use letters to distinguish the effects of each part. The first event is recorded as an example.

Event No.	Event Type	Assets	=	Liab.	+	Stk. Equity	Rev.	−	Exp.	=	Net Inc.	Cash Flow
1a	AS	+	=	+	+	NA	NA	−	NA	=	NA	NA
1b	AE	+ −	=	NA	+	NA	NA	−	NA	=	NA	− OA

b. Record the events in general journal format.
c. Open ledger T-accounts, and post the beginning balances and the events to the accounts.

d. Prepare an income statement, a statement of changes in stockholders' equity, a balance sheet, and a statement of cash flows.

e. Record and post the closing entries, and prepare an after-closing trial balance.

PROBLEM 5–26A *Preparing a Schedule of Cost of Goods Sold and Multistep and Single-Step Income Statements: Periodic System*   **L.O. 7, 8**

The following account titles and balances were taken from the adjusted trial balance of Pittman Sales Co. at December 31, 2004. The company uses the periodic inventory method.

Account Title	Balance
Advertising Expense	$12,800
Depreciation Expense	3,000
Income Taxes	10,700
Interest Expense	5,000
Merchandise Inventory, January 1	18,000
Merchandise Inventory, December 31	20,100
Miscellaneous Expense	800
Purchases	130,000
Purchase Returns and Allowances	2,700
Rent Expense	14,000
Salaries Expense	53,000
Sales	290,000
Sales Discounts	13,500
Sales Returns and Allowances	8,000
Transportation-in	5,500
Transportation-out	10,800

Required

a. Prepare a schedule to determine the amount of cost of goods sold.

b. Prepare a multistep income statement.

c. Prepare a single-step income statement.

PROBLEM 5–27A *Comprehensive Cycle Problem: Periodic System*   **L.O. 8**

The following trial balance pertains to Horner Home Products as of January 1, 2005:

Account Title	Debit	Credit
Cash	$14,000	
Accounts Receivable	9,000	
Merchandise Inventory	60,000	
Accounts Payable		$ 5,000
Notes Payable		20,000
Common Stock		50,000
Retained Earnings		8,000
Total	$83,000	$83,000

The following events occurred in 2005. Assume that Horner Home Products uses the periodic inventory system.

1. Purchased land for $8,000 cash and a building for $45,000 by paying $5,000 cash and issuing a 20-year note with an annual interest rate of 8 percent. The building has a 40-year estimated life with no salvage value.
2. Purchased merchandise on account for $23,000, terms 2/10, n/30.
3. The merchandise purchased was shipped FOB shipping point for $230 cash.
4. Returned $2,000 of defective merchandise purchased in Event 2.
5. Sold merchandise for $27,000 cash.
6. Sold merchandise on account for $50,000, terms 1/20, n/30.
7. Paid cash within the discount period on accounts payable due on merchandise purchased in Event 2.
8. Paid $1,200 cash for selling expenses.
9. Collected part of the balance due from accounts receivable. Collections were made after the discount period on $12,000 of the receivables. Collections were made during the discount period on $35,000 of the receivables.

10. Paid cash to the bank for one full year's interest on the note issued in Event 1.
11. Paid $2,000 on the principal of the note issued in Event 1.
12. Recorded one full year's depreciation on the building purchased in Event 1.
13. Performed a physical count indicating that $30,000 of inventory was on hand at the end of the accounting period.

Required

a. Record these transactions in a general journal.
b. Post the transactions to ledger T-accounts.
c. Prepare an income statement, a statement of changes in stockholders' equity, a balance sheet, and a statement of cash flows for 2005.

L.O. 10   **PROBLEM 5–28A** *Using Common Size Income Statements to Make Comparisons*

The following income statements were drawn from the annual reports of Marcy Company:

	2001*	2002*
Net Sales	$302,900	$370,500
Cost of Goods Sold	(217,400)	(264,700)
Gross Margin	85,500	105,800
Less: Operating Expense		
Selling and Administrative Expenses	(40,800)	(58,210)
Net Income	$ 44,700	$ 47,590

*All dollar amounts are reported in thousands.

The president's message in the company's annual report stated that the company had implemented a strategy to increase market share by spending more on advertising. The president indicated that prices held steady and sales grew as expected. Write a memo indicating whether you agree with the president's statements. How has the strategy affected profitability? Support your answer by measuring growth in sales and selling expenses. Also prepare common size income statements and make appropriate references to the differences between 2001 and 2002.

EXERCISES—SERIES B

When the instructions for *any* exercise or problem call for the preparation of an income statement, use the *multistep format* unless otherwise indicated.

L.O. 1, 2, 3, 5   **EXERCISE 5–1B** *Comparing a Merchandising Company with a Service Company*

The following information is available for two different types of businesses for the accounting period. Davis CPAs is a service business that provides accounting services to small businesses. Campus Dive Shop is a merchandising business that sells diving gear to college students.

Data for Davis CPAs
1. Borrowed $20,000 from the bank to start the business.
2. Provided $15,000 of services to customers and collected $15,000 cash.
3. Paid salary expense of $10,000.

Data for Campus Dive Shop
1. Borrowed $20,000 from the bank to start the business.
2. Purchased $12,500 inventory for cash.
3. Inventory costing $8,200 was sold for $15,000 cash.
4. Paid $1,800 cash for operating expenses.

Required

a. Prepare an income statement, balance sheet, and statement of cash flows for each of the companies.
b. Which of the two businesses would have product costs? Why?
c. Why does Davis CPAs not compute gross margin on its income statement?
d. Compare the assets of both companies. What assets do they have in common? What assets are different? Why?

EXERCISE 5–2B *Effect of Inventory Transactions on Journals, Ledgers, and Financial*   **L.O. 3, 5**
                  Statements: Perpetual System

Don Jones started a small merchandising business in 2005. The business experienced the following events during its first year of operation. Assume that Jones uses the perpetual inventory system.
1. Acquired $20,000 cash from the issue of common stock.
2. Purchased inventory for $15,000 cash.
3. Sold inventory costing $10,000 for $16,000 cash.

Required
a. Record the events in general journal format.
b. Post the entries to T-accounts.
c. Prepare an income statement for 2005 (use the multistep format).
d. What is the amount of net cash flow from operating activities for 2005?

EXERCISE 5–3B *Effect of Inventory Transactions on the Income Statement and Statement of*   **L.O. 3, 5**
                  Cash Flows: Perpetual System

During 2005, Bond Merchandising Company purchased $30,000 of inventory on account. Bond sold inventory on account that cost $25,000 for $35,000. Cash payments on accounts payable were $20,000. There was $22,000 cash collected from accounts receivable. Bond also paid $7,000 cash for operating expenses. Assume that Bond started the accounting period with $28,000 in cash and common stock.

Required
a. Identify the events described in the preceding paragraph and record them in a horizontal statements model like the following one:

Assets				=	Liab.	+	Stockholders' Equity			Rev.	–	Exp.	=	Net Inc.	Cash Flow
Cash	+	Accts. Rec.	+ Inv.	=	A. Pay.	+	C. Stk.	+	Ret. Earn.						
28,000	+	NA	+ NA	=	NA	+	28,000	+	NA	NA	–	NA	=	NA	NA

b. What is the balance of accounts receivable at the end of 2005?
c. What is the balance of accounts payable at the end of 2005?
d. What are the amounts of gross margin and net income for 2005?
e. Determine the amount of net cash flow from operating activities.
f. Explain why net income and retained earnings are the same for Bond. Normally would these amounts be the same? Why or why not?

EXERCISE 5–4B *Recording Inventory Transactions in the General Journal and Posting Entries*   **L.O. 5**
                  to T-Accounts: Perpetual System

Clark's Clothing Center experienced the following events during 2004:
1. Acquired $7,000 cash from the issue of common stock.
2. Purchased inventory for $4,000 cash.
3. Sold inventory costing $3,000 for $4,500 cash.
4. Paid $400 for advertising expense.

Required
a. Record the general journal entries for the preceding transactions.
b. Post each of the entries to T-accounts.
c. Prepare a trial balance to prove the equality of debits and credits..

EXERCISE 5–5B *Understanding the Freight Terms FOB Shipping Point and FOB*   **L.O. 6**
                  Destination

Required
For each of the following events, indicate whether the freight terms are FOB Destination or FOB Shipping Point.
a. Sold merchandise and paid the freight costs.
b. Purchased merchandise and paid the freight costs.
c. Sold merchandise and the buyer paid the freight costs.
d. Purchased merchandise and the seller paid the freight costs.

L.O. 3, 5 **EXERCISE 5–6B** *Effect of Purchase Returns and Allowances and Freight Costs on the Journal, Ledger, and Financial Statements: Perpetual System*

The trial balance for Vanity Gift Shop as of January 1, 2005 follows:

Account Titles	Debit	Credit
Cash	$32,000	
Inventory	12,000	
Common Stock		$40,000
Retained Earnings		4,000
Total	$44,000	$44,000

The following events affected the company during the 2005 accounting period:
1. Purchased merchandise on account that cost $22,000.
2. Purchased goods FOB shipping point with freight cost of $1,000 cash.
3. Returned $3,200 of damaged merchandise for credit on account.
4. Agreed to keep other damaged merchandise for which the company received a $1,400 allowance.
5. Sold merchandise that cost $16,000 for $31,000 cash.
6. Delivered merchandise to customers under terms FOB destination with freight costs amounting to $800 cash.
7. Paid $15,000 on the merchandise purchased in Event 1.

Required
a. Record the events in general journal format.
b. Open general ledger T-accounts with the appropriate beginning balances, and post the journal entries to the T-accounts.
c. Prepare an income statement, balance sheet, and statement of cash flows. (Assume that closing entries have been made.)
d. Explain why a difference does or does not exist between net income and net cash flow from operating activities.

L.O. 2, 5 **EXERCISE 5–7B** *Accounting for Product Costs: Perpetual Inventory System*

Which of the following would be debited to the Inventory account for a merchandising business using the perpetual inventory system?

Required
a. Purchase of inventory.
b. Allowance received for damaged inventory.
c. Transportation-in.
d. Cash discount given on goods sold.
e. Transportation-out.
f. Purchase of office supplies.

L.O. 2, 3, 5 **EXERCISE 5–8B** *Effect of Product Cost and Period Cost: Horizontal Statements Model*

Action Nature Goods experienced the following events for the 2004 accounting period:
1. Acquired $10,000 cash from the issue of common stock.
2. Purchased $56,000 of inventory on account.
3. Received goods purchased in Event 2 FOB shipping point; freight cost of $600 paid in cash.
4. Sold inventory on account that cost $33,000 for $57,400.
5. Paid freight cost on the goods sold in Event 5 of $420. The goods were shipped FOB destination. Cash was paid for the freight cost.
6. Customer in Event 4 returned $2,000 worth of goods that had a cost of $1,400.
7. Collected $47,000 cash from accounts receivable.
8. Paid $40,000 cash on accounts payable.
9. Paid $1,100 for advertising expense.
10. Paid $2,000 cash for insurance expense.

Required
a. Which of these events result in period (selling and administrative) costs? Which result in product costs? If neither, label the transaction NA.

b. Record each event in a horizontal statements model like the following one. The first event is recorded as an example.

Assets			=	Liab.	+	Stockholders' Equity			Rev.	–	Exp.	=	Net Inc.	Cash Flow
Cash	+	Accts. Rec.	+ Inv. =	A. Pay.	+	C. Stk.	+	Ret. Earn.						
10,000 +	NA	+ NA =	NA	+	10,000	+	NA		NA	–	NA	=	NA	10,000 FA

EXERCISE 5–9B Cash Discounts and Purchase Returns

L.O. 6

On April 6, 2003, Wang Exotics purchased $3,100 of merchandise from Exchange Emporium, terms 2/10, n/45. On April 5, Wang returned $600 of the merchandise to the Exchange Emporium for credit. Wang paid cash for the merchandise on April 15, 2003.

Required

a. What is the amount that Wang must pay the Exchange Emporium on April 15?
b. Prepare the journal entries for these events.
c. How much must Wang pay for the merchandise purchased if the payment is not made until April 20, 2003?
d. Why would Wang want to pay for the merchandise by April 15?

EXERCISE 5–10B Effect of Sales Returns and Allowances and Freight Costs on the Journal, Ledger, and Financial Statements: Perpetual System

L.O. 3, 5, 6

Smart Company began the 2004 accounting period with $7,000 cash, $38,000 inventory, $25,000 common stock, and $20,000 retained earnings. During 2004, Smart experienced the following events:

1. Sold merchandise costing $32,000 for $50,000 on account to Mitchell's Furniture Store.
2. Delivered the goods to Mitchell under terms FOB destination. Freight costs were $500 cash.
3. Received returned damaged goods from Mitchell. The goods cost Smart $3,000 and were sold to Mitchell for $4,000.
4. Granted Mitchell a $2,000 allowance for other damaged goods that Mitchell agreed to keep.
5. Collected partial payment of $30,000 cash from accounts receivable.

Required

a. Record the events in general journal format.
b. Open general ledger T-accounts with the appropriate beginning balances and post the journal entries to the T-accounts.
c. Prepare an income statement, balance sheet, and statement of cash flows.
d. Why would Mitchell agree to keep the damaged goods? Who benefits more?

EXERCISE 5–11B Effect of Cash Discounts on the Journal, Ledger, and Financial Statements: Perpetual System

L.O. 5, 6

Nelson Sand & Gravel was started in 2006 and experienced the following accounting events during its first year of operation:

1. Started business when it acquired $15,000 cash from the issue of common stock.
2. Purchased merchandise costing $9,000 on account, terms 2/10, n/30.
3. Paid off the account payable within the discount period.
4. Sold inventory on account that cost $5,000 for $7,500. Credit terms were 1/20, n/30.
5. Collected cash from the account receivable within the discount period.
6. Paid $1,900 cash for operating expenses.

Required

a. Record the transactions in general journal format.
b. Open general ledger T-accounts, and post the journal entries to the T-accounts.
c. Record the events in a horizontal statements model like the following one.

Assets			=	Liab.	+	Stockholders' Equity			Rev.	–	Exp.	=	Net Inc.	Cash Flow
Cash	+	Accts. Rec.	+ Inv. =	A. Pay.	+	C. Stk.	+	Ret. Earn.						

d. What is the amount of gross margin for the period? What is the net income for the period?

e. Why would Nelson sell merchandise with the terms 1/20, n/30?

f. What do the terms 2/10, n/30 mean to Nelson?

L.O. 3, 5, 6   **EXERCISE 5–12B** *Effect of Inventory Transactions on the Financial Statements: Comprehensive Exercise With Sales and Purchase Returns and Discounts*

Macomb Merchandise Company had the following balances in its accounts on January 1, 2006:

Cash	$20,000
Merchandise Inventory	15,000
Common Stock	25,000
Retained Earnings	10,000

Macomb experienced the following events during 2006:

1. Purchased merchandise inventory on account for $45,000, terms 2/10, n/30.
2. Paid freight of $600 on the merchandise purchased.
3. Sold merchandise inventory that cost $23,000 for $42,000 on account, terms 1/10, n/45.
4. Returned $1,500 of damaged merchandise purchased in Event 1.
5. Agreed to keep other merchandise that was slightly damaged and was granted an allowance of $500.
6. The customer in Event 3 returned $6,000 of merchandise that had a cost of $3,400.
7. Collected the balance of accounts receivable within the discount period.
8. Paid for one-half of the merchandise in Event 1 within the discount period.
9. Paid $4,300 cash for selling and administrative expenses.
10. Paid the balance of accounts payable (not within the discount period).

Required

a. Record each of these events in general journal format.

b. Open general ledger T-accounts. Post the beginning balances and the events to the accounts.

c. Prepare a trial balance.

d. Prepare an income statement, balance sheet (assume closing entries have been made), and a statement of cash flows.

L.O. 3, 5, 9   **EXERCISE 5–13B** *Effect of Inventory Losses: Perpetual System*

Carroll Traders experienced the following events during 2005, its first year of operation:

1. Started the business when it acquired $20,000 cash from the issue of common stock.
2. Paid $14,000 cash to purchase inventory.
3. Sold inventory costing $10,750 for $17,100 cash.
4. Physically counted inventory; had inventory of $2,900 on hand at the end of the accounting period.

Required

a. Open appropriate ledger T-accounts, and record the events in the accounts.

b. Prepare an income statement and balance sheet.

c. If all purchases and sales of merchandise are reflected as increases or decreases to the merchandise inventory account, why is it necessary for management to even bother to take a physical count of goods on hand (ending inventory) at the end of the year?

L.O. 3, 5   **EXERCISE 5–14B** *Determining the Effect of Inventory Transactions on the Accounting Equation: Perpetual System*

Marshall Company experienced the following events:

1. Purchased merchandise inventory on account.
2. Purchased merchandise inventory for cash.
3. Sold merchandise inventory on account. Label the revenue recognition 3a and the expense recognition 3b.
4. Returned merchandise purchased on account.
5. Sold merchandise inventory for cash. Label the revenue recognition 5a and the expense recognition 5b.
6. Paid cash on accounts payable within the discount period.
7. Paid cash for selling and administrative expenses.
8. Collected cash from accounts receivable. Label 8a as discount and 8b for cash received.
9. Paid cash for transportation-out.
10. Paid cash for transportation-in.

Required

Identify each event as asset source (AS), asset use (AU), asset exchange (AE), or claims exchange (CE). Also explain how each event affects the financial statements by placing a + for increase, − for decrease, or NA for not affected under each of the components in the following statements model. Assume the company uses the perpetual inventory system. The first event is recorded as an example.

Event No.	Event Type	Assets	=	Liab.	+	Stk. Equity	Rev.	−	Exp.	=	Net Inc.	Cash Flow
1	AS	+	=	+	+	NA	NA	−	NA	=	NA	NA

EXERCISE 5–15B *Effect of Inventory Transactions on the Income Statement and Balance Sheet: Periodic System* **L.O. 8**

Nat Briscoe owns Nat's Sporting Goods. At the beginning of the year, Nat's had $4,200 in inventory. During the year, Nat's purchased inventory that cost $21,000. At the end of the year, inventory on hand amounted to $8,800.

Required

Calculate the following:

a. Cost of goods available for sale during the year.
b. Cost of goods sold for the year.
c. Amount of inventory Nat's would report on the year-end balance sheet.

EXERCISE 5–16B *Single-Step and Multistep Income Statements* **L.O. 7**

The following information was taken from the accounts of Neighborhood Market, a small grocery store. The accounts are listed in alphabetical order, and all have normal balances.

Accounts Payable	$ 600
Accounts Receivable	700
Accumulated Depreciation	200
Advertising Expense	400
Cash	820
Common Stock	400
Cost of Goods Sold	900
Interest Expense	140
Merchandise Inventory	300
Prepaid Rent	80
Retained Earnings	1,020
Sales Revenue	1,600
Salaries Expense	260
Supplies Expense	110

Required

First, prepare an income statement using the single-step approach. Then prepare another income statement using the multistep approach.

EXERCISE 5–17B *Determining Cost of Goods Sold: Periodic System* **L.O. 8**

Hill Antiques uses the periodic inventory system to account for its inventory transactions. The following account titles and balances were drawn from Hill's records: beginning balance in inventory, $12,000; purchases, $150,000; purchase returns and allowances, $5,000; sales, $400,000; sales returns and allowances, $3,000; freight-in, $1,000; and operating expenses, $26,000. A physical count indicated that $15,000 of merchandise was on hand at the end of the accounting period.

Required

a. Prepare a schedule of cost of goods sold.
b. Prepare a multistep income statement.

EXERCISE 5–18B *Basic Transactions: Periodic System, Single Cycle* **L.O. 8**

The following transactions apply to Kay's Specialties Shop for 2005.

1. Acquired $70,000 cash from the issue of common stock.
2. Acquired $8,000 of gift merchandise from Kay Pierce, the owner, who had acquired the merchandise prior to opening the shop. Issued common stock to Kay in exchange for the merchandise.
3. Purchased $90,000 of inventory on account.
4. Paid $6,000 for radio ads.
5. Sold inventory for $160,000 cash.
6. Paid $20,000 in salary to a part-time salesperson.
7. Paid $75,000 on accounts payable (see Event 3).
8. Physically counted inventory, which indicated that $20,000 of inventory was on hand at the end of the accounting period.

Required
a. Record each of these transactions in general journal form using the periodic method.
b. Post each of the transactions to ledger T-accounts.
c. Prepare an income statement, statement of changes in stockholders' equity, balance sheet, and statement of cash flows for 2005.
d. Prepare the necessary closing entries at the end of 2005, and post them to the appropriate T-accounts.
e. Prepare an after-closing trial balance.
f. Give an example of a business that may want to use the periodic system. Given an example of a business that may use the perpetual system.
g. Give some examples of assets other than cash that are commonly contributed to a business in exchange for stock.

L.O. 3, 5, 12   EXERCISE 5–19B *Determining Cost of Financing Inventory*

On January 1, 2006, Jay Woo started a small home appliance merchandising business that he named J's Appliances. J's uses the perpetual system. The company experienced the following events during the first year of operation:
1. Started the business when Jay borrowed $100,000 by issuing a one-year note dated January 1, 2006. The note had a 7 percent annual rate of interest.
2. Paid $80,000 cash to purchase inventory.
3. Sold appliances that cost $36,000 for $68,000 on account.
4. Collected $28,000 cash from accounts receivable.
5. Paid $10,000 for operating expenses.
6. Recognized accrued interest on the note payable on December 31.

Required
a. Record the transactions in general journal format.
b. Open general ledger T-accounts, and post the journal entries to the T-accounts.
c. Prepare an income statement, balance sheet, and statement of cash flows. (Assume that year-end closing entries have been made.)

L.O. 6, 12   EXERCISE 5–20B *Financing Inventory and Cash Discounts*

Larry Braun came to you for advice. He has just purchased a large amount of inventory with the terms 1/10, n/45. The amount of the invoice is $65,000. He is currently short on cash but has good credit and so can borrow the money at the appropriate time to take advantage of the discount. The annual interest rate is 7 percent if he decides to borrow the money. Braun is sure he will have the necessary cash by the due date of the invoice (but not by the discount date).

Required
a. For how long would Braun need to borrow the money to take advantage of the discount?
b. How much money would Braun need to borrow?
c. What action would you recommend Braun take? Explain.

PROBLEMS—SERIES B

L.O. 3, 5   PROBLEM 5–21B *Basic Transactions for Three Accounting Cycles: Perpetual System*

Flower Company was started in 2002 when it acquired $80,000 cash from the issue of common stock. The following data summarize the company's first three years' operating activities. Assume that all transactions were cash transactions.

	2002	2003	2004
Purchases of Inventory	$60,000	$90,000	$130,000
Sales	102,000	146,000	220,000
Cost of Goods Sold	54,000	78,000	140,000
Selling and Administrative Expenses	40,000	52,000	72,000

Required

Prepare an income statement and balance sheet for each fiscal year. (*Hint:* Record the transaction data for each accounting period in T-accounts before preparing the statements for that year.)

PROBLEM 5–22B *Identifying Product and Period Costs*

L.O. 2

Required

Indicate whether each of the following costs is a product cost or a period (selling and administrative) cost.

a. Transportation-in.
b. Insurance on the office building.
c. Office supplies.
d. Costs incurred to improve the quality of goods available for sale.
e. Goods purchased for resale.
f. Salaries of salespersons.
g. Advertising costs.
h. Transportation-out.
i. Interest on a note payable.
j. Salary of the company president.

PROBLEM 5–23B *Identifying Freight Costs*

L.O. 2, 6

Required

For each of the following events, determine the amount of freight paid by The Book Shop. Also indicate whether the freight cost would be classified as a product or period (selling and administrative) cost.

a. Purchased additional merchandise with freight costs of $300. The merchandise was shipped FOB shipping point.
b. Shipped merchandise to customers, freight terms FOB shipping point. The freight costs were $100.
c. Purchased inventory with freight costs of $1,000. The goods were shipped FOB destination.
d. Sold merchandise to a customer. Freight costs were $500. The goods were shipped FOB destination.

PROBLEM 5–24B *Effect of Purchase Returns and Allowances and Purchase Discounts on the Financial Statements: Perpetual System*

L.O. 3, 5, 6

The following transactions were completed by The Jewel Shop in May 2008.

May 1 Acquired $100,000 cash from the issue of common stock.
   1 Purchased $60,000 of merchandise on account with terms 2/10, n/30.
   2 Paid $1,200 cash for freight to obtain merchandise purchased on May 1.
   4 Sold merchandise that cost $44,000 for $74,000 to customers on account.
   4 Returned $5,000 of defective merchandise from the May 1 purchase for credit on account.
   10 Paid cash for one-half of the balance due on the merchandise purchased on May 1.
   13 Received cash from customers of May 4 sale in settlement of the account balance.
   31 Paid the balance due on the merchandise purchased on May 1.
   31 Paid selling expenses of $7,800.

Required

a. Record each event in a horizontal statements model like the following one. The first event is recorded as an example.

Assets			=	Liab.	+	Stockholders' Equity			Rev.	–	Exp.	=	Net Inc.	Cash Flow
Cash	+	Accts. Rec.	+ Inv. =	A. Pay.	+	C. Stk.	+	Ret. Earn.						
100,000	+	NA	+ NA =	NA	+	100,000	+	NA	NA	–	NA	=	NA	100,000 FA

b. Record each of the transactions in general journal form.

c. Post each of the transactions to general ledger T-accounts.

d. Prepare an income statement for the month ending May 31.

e. Prepare a statement of cash flows for the month ending May 31.

f. Explain why there is a difference between net income and cash flow from operating activities.

L.O. 3, 5, 9   PROBLEM 5–25B *Comprehensive Cycle Problem: Perpetual System*

At the beginning of 2006, M & M Enterprises had the following balances in its accounts:

Cash	$8,400
Inventory	2,000
Common Stock	8,000
Retained Earnings	2,400

During 2006, M & M Enterprises experienced the following events:

1. Purchased inventory costing $5,600 on account from Smoot Company under terms 2/10, n/30. The merchandise was delivered FOB shipping point. Freight costs of $500 were paid in cash.

2. Returned $400 of the inventory that it had purchased because the inventory was damaged in transit. The freight company agreed to pay the return freight cost.

3. Paid the amount due on its account payable to Smoot Company within the cash discount period.

4. Sold inventory that had cost $6,000 for $9,000. The sale was on account under terms 2/10, n/45.

5. Received returned merchandise from a customer. The merchandise had originally cost $520 and had been sold to the customer for $840 cash. The customer was paid $840 cash for the returned merchandise.

6. Delivered goods FOB destination. Freight costs of $600 were paid in cash.

7. Collected the amount due on accounts receivable within the discount period.

8. Took a physical count indicating that $1,800 of inventory was on hand at the end of the accounting period.

Required

a. Identify each of these events as asset source (AS), asset use (AU), asset exchange (AE), or claims exchange (CE). Also explain how each event affects the financial statements by placing a + for increase, − for decrease, or NA for not affected under each of the components in the following statements model. Assume that the perpetual inventory method is used. When an event has more than one part, use letters to distinguish the effects of each part. The first event is recorded as an example.

Event No.	Event Type	Assets	=	Liab.	+	Stk. Equity	Rev.	−	Exp.	=	Net Inc.	Cash Flow
1a	AS	+	=	+	+	NA	NA	−	NA	=	NA	NA
1b	AE	+ −	=	NA	+	NA	NA	−	NA	=	NA	− OA

b. Record the events in general journal format.

c. Open ledger T-accounts and post the beginning balances and the events to the accounts.

d. Prepare an income statement, statement of changes in stockholders' equity, balance sheet, and statement of cash flows.

e. Record and post the closing entries, and prepare an after-closing trial balance.

L.O. 7, 8   PROBLEM 5–26B *Preparing Schedule of Cost of Goods Sold and Multistep and Single-Step Income Statements: Periodic System*

The following account titles and balances were taken from the adjusted trial balance of Martin Farm Co. for 2006. The company uses the periodic inventory system.

Account Title	Balance
Sales Returns and Allowances	$ 2,250
Income Taxes	3,700
Miscellaneous Expense	400
Transportation-out	600
Sales	69,750
Advertising Expense	2,750
Salaries Expense	7,900
Transportation-in	1,725
Purchases	40,000
Interest Expense	360
Merchandise Inventory, January 1	5,075
Sales Discounts	405
Rent Expense	5,000
Merchandise Inventory, December 31	4,050
Purchase Returns and Allowances	1,450
Depreciation Expense	710

Required
a. Prepare a schedule to determine the amount of cost of goods sold.
b. Prepare a multistep income statement.
c. Prepare a single-step income statement.

PROBLEM 5–27B *Comprehensive Cycle Problem: Periodic System*

L.O. 8

The following trial balance pertains to John's Jungle as of January 1, 2008:

Account Title	Debit	Credit
Cash	$26,000	
Accounts Receivable	4,000	
Merchandise Inventory	50,000	
Accounts Payable		$ 4,000
Notes Payable		6,000
Common Stock		37,000
Retained Earnings		33,000
Totals	$80,000	$80,000

The following events occurred in 2008. Assume that John's uses the periodic inventory method.
1. Purchased land for $20,000 cash and a building for $90,000 by paying $10,000 cash and issuing a 20-year note with an annual interest rate of 8 percent. The building has a 40-year estimated life with no residual value.
2. Purchased merchandise on account for $126,000, terms 1/10, n/45.
3. Paid freight of $1,000 cash on merchandise shipped FOB shipping point.
4. Returned $3,600 of defective merchandise purchased in Event 2.
5. Sold merchandise for $86,000 cash.
6. Sold merchandise on account for $120,000, terms 2/10, n/30.
7. Paid cash within the discount period on accounts payable due on merchandise purchased in Event 2.
8. Paid $11,600 cash for selling expenses.
9. Collected part of the balance due from accounts receivable. Collections were made after the discount period on $60,000 of the receivables. Collections were made during the discount period on $50,000 of the receivables.
10. Paid cash to the bank for one full year's interest on the note issued in Event 1.
11. Paid $10,000 on the principal of the note issued in Event 1.
12. Recorded one full year's depreciation on the building purchased in Event 1.
13. A physical count indicated that $27,600 of inventory was on hand at the end of the accounting period.

Required

a. Record these transactions in a general journal.

b. Post the transactions to ledger T-accounts.

c. Prepare an income statement, statement of changes in stockholders' equity, balance sheet, and statement of cash flows for 2008.

L.O. 10 **PROBLEM 5–28B** *Using Common Size Income Statements to Make Comparisons*

The following income statements were drawn from the annual reports of Madison Company:

	2002*	2003*
Net Sales	$74,507	$80,000
Cost of Goods Sold	(28,317)	(34,400)
Gross Margin	46,190	45,600
Less: Operating Expenses		
Selling and Administrative Expenses	(43,210)	(40,800)
Net Income	$ 2,980	$ 4,800

*All figures are reported in thousands of dollars.

Required

The president's message in the company's annual report stated that the company increased profitability by decreasing prices and controlling operating expenses. Write a memorandum indicating whether you agree with the president's statement. Support your answer by preparing common size income statements and making appropriate references to the differences between 2002 and 2003.

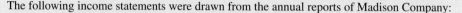

ANALYZE, THINK, COMMUNICATE

ATC 5–1 **BUSINESS APPLICATIONS CASE** *Dell's Annual Report*

Required

Using the Dell Computer Corporation financial statements in Appendix B, answer the following questions:

a. What is Dell's gross profit percentage for 2000 and 2001?

b. What was Dell's return on sales for 2000 and 2001?

c. Dell's gross profit percentage was lower for 2001 than for 2000. Ignoring taxes, how much higher would its 2001 net income have been if the gross profit percentage for 2001 had been the same as for 2000?

ATC 5–2 **GROUP EXERCISE** *Multistep Income Statement*

The following quarterly information is given for Reebok for the year ended 2000 (amounts shown are in thousands).

	First Quarter	Second Quarter	Third Quarter	Fourth Quarter
Net Sales	$1,481,605	$2,260,388	$2,891,237	$774,674
Gross Margin	561,247	855,353	1,107,323	295,970
Net Income	52,279	21,138	43,321	36,645

Required

a. Divide the class into groups and organize the groups into four sections. Assign each section financial information for one of the quarters.

(1) Each group should compute the cost of goods sold and operating expenses for the specific quarter assigned to its section and prepare a multistep income statement for the quarter.

(2) Each group should compute the gross margin percentage and cost of goods sold percentage for its specific quarter.

(3) Have a representative of each group put that quarter's sales, cost of goods sold percentage, and gross margin percentage on the board.

Class Discussion

b. Have the class discuss the change in each of these items from quarter to quarter and explain why the change might have occurred. Which was the best quarter and why?

REAL-WORLD CASE *Identifying Companies Based on Financial Statement Information*   ATC 5–3

Presented here is selected information from the 2000 fiscal-year 10-K reports of four companies. The four companies, in alphabetical order, are Caterpillar, Inc., a manufacturer of heavy machinery; Dollar Tree Corporation, a company that owns discount stores; Novell, Inc., a company that develops software for networks; and Tiffany & Company, a company that operates high-end jewelry and department stores. The data for the companies, presented in the order of the amount of their sales in millions of dollars, follow:

	A	B	C	D
Sales	$20,175	$1,688.1	$1,668.1	$1,161.7
Cost of goods sold	14,497	1,063.4	719.6	327.4
Net earnings	1,053	120.2	190.6	49.5
Inventory	2,692	258.7	651.7	2.6
Accounts receivable	2,608	0.0	107.0	196.7
Total assets	28,464	746.9	1,568.3	1,712.3

Required
Based on these financial data and your knowledge and assumptions about the nature of the businesses that the companies operate, determine which data relate to which companies. Write a memorandum explaining your decisions. Include a discussion of which ratios you used in your analysis, and show the computations of these ratios in your memorandum.

BUSINESS APPLICATIONS CASE *Using Ratios to Make Comparisons*   ATC 5–4

The following income statements were drawn from the annual reports of Richard Company and Jennifer Company.

	Richard	Jennifer
Net Sales	$32,600	$86,200
Cost of Goods Sold	17,930	64,650
Gross Margin	14,670	21,550
Less: Selling and Admin. Expenses	13,040	18,960
Net Income	$ 1,630	$ 2,590

*All figures are reported in thousands of dollars

Required
a. One of the companies is a high-end retailer that operates in exclusive shopping malls. The other operates discount stores located in low-cost stand-alone buildings. Identify the high-end retailer and the discounter. Support your answer with appropriate ratios.

b. If Richard and Jennifer have equity of $16,200 and $20,400, respectively, which company is the more profitable?

BUSINESS APPLICATIONS CASE *Using Common Size Statements and Ratios to Make Comparisons*   ATC 5–5

At the end of 2003, the following information is available for Karen and Patrick companies:

	Karen	Patrick
Sales	$1,000,000	$1,000,000
Cost of Goods Sold	650,000	550,000
Operating Expenses	250,000	375,000
Total Assets	1,200,000	1,200,000
Owners' Equity	450,000	300,000

Required

a. Prepare common size income statements for each company.

b. Compute the return on assets and return on equity for each company.

c. Which company is more profitable from the stockholders' perspective?

d. One company is a high-end retailer, and the other operates a discount store. Which is the discounter? Support your selection by referring to appropriate ratios.

ATC 5–6   WRITTEN ASSIGNMENT, CRITICAL THINKING *Effect of Sales Returns on Financial Statements*

Bell Farm and Garden Equipment reported the following sales information for 2005:

Net sales of equipment	$2,450,567
Other income	6,786
Cost of goods sold	1,425,990
Selling, general, and administrative expense	325,965
Depreciation and amortization	3,987
Net operating income	$ 701,411

Selected information from the balance sheet as of December 31, 2005 follows:

Cash and Marketable Securities	$113,545
Inventory	248,600
Accounts Receivable	82,462
Property, Plant, and Equipment—net	335,890
Other Assets	5,410
Total Assets	$785,907

Assume that a major customer returned a large order to Bell on December 31, 2005. The amount of the sale had been $146,800 with a cost of sales of $94,623. The return was recorded in the books on January 1, 2006. The company president does not want to correct the books. He argues that it makes no difference as to whether the return is recorded in 2005 or 2006. Either way, the return has been duly recognized.

Required

a. Assume that you are the CFO for Bell Farm and Garden Equipment Co. Write a memo to the president explaining how omitting the entry on December 31, 2005, could cause the financial statements to be misleading to investors and creditors. Explain how omitting the return from the customer would affect net income and the balance sheet.

b. Why might the president want to record the return on January 1, 2006, instead of December 31, 2005?

c. Would the failure to record the customer return violate the AICPA Code of Professional Conduct? (See Exhibit 2–7 in Chapter 2.)

d. If the president of the company refuses to correct the financial statements, what action should you take?

ATC 5–7   ETHICAL DILEMMA *Wait Until I Get Mine*

Ada Fontanez is the president of a large company that owns a chain of athletic shoe stores. The company was in dire financial condition when she was hired three years ago. In an effort to motivate Fontanez, the board of directors included a bonus plan as part of her compensation package. According to her employment contract, on January 15 of each year, Fontanez is paid a cash bonus equal to 5 percent of the amount of net income reported on the preceding December 31 income statement. Fontanez was sufficiently motivated. Through her leadership, the company prospered. Her efforts were recognized throughout the industry, and she received numerous lucrative offers to leave the company. One offer was so enticing that she decided to change jobs. Her decision was made in late December 2005. However, she decided to resign effective February 1, 2006, to ensure the receipt of her January bonus. On December 31, 2005, the chief accountant, Walter Smith, advised Fontanez that the company had a sizable quantity of damaged inventory. A warehouse fire had resulted in smoke and water damage to approximately $600,000 of inventory. The warehouse was not insured, and the accountant recommended that the loss be recognized immediately. After examining the inventory, Fontanez argued that it could be sold as *damaged goods* to customers at reduced prices. Accordingly, she refused to allow the write-off the accountant recommended. She stated that so long as she is president, the inventory stays on the books at cost. She told the accountant that he could take up the matter with the new president in February.

Required

a. How would an immediate write-off of the damaged inventory affect the December 31, 2005, income statement, balance sheet, and statement of cash flows?

b. How would the write-off affect Fontanez's bonus?

c. If the new president is given the same bonus plan, how will Fontanez's refusal to recognize the loss affect his or her bonus?

d. Assuming that the damaged inventory is truly worthless, comment on the ethical implications of Fontanez's refusal to recognize the loss in the 2005 accounting period.

e. Assume that the damaged inventory is truly worthless and that you are Smith. How would you react to Fontanez's refusal to recognize the loss?

EDGAR DATABASE *Analyzing Alcoa's Profit Margins*

ATC 5–8

Instructions for using EDGAR are in Appendix A. Using the most current 10-K annual report available on EDGAR, answer the following questions about Alcoa, Inc.

Required

a. What was Alcoa's gross margin percentage for the most current year?

b. What was Alcoa's gross margin percentage for the previous year? Has it changed significantly?

c. What was Alcoa's return on sales percentage for the most current year?

d. What percentage of Alcoa's total sales for the most current year was from operations in the United States?

e. Comment on the appropriateness of comparing Alcoa's gross margin with that of Ford Motor Company. If Ford has a higher/lower margin, does that mean that Ford is a better managed company?

SPREADSHEET ANALYSIS *Using Excel*

ATC 5–9

The following accounts, balances, and other financial information are drawn from the records of Vong Company for the year 2004:

Net Sales Revenue	$18,800	Beginning Common Stock	$ 9,000
Unearned Revenue	2,600	Land	8,000
Accounts Receivable	6,000	Certificate of Deposit	10,000
Cost of Goods Sold	6,000	Interest Revenue	100
Inventory	5,000	Interest Receivable	100
Accounts Payable	5,800	Dividends	1,500
Notes Payable	6,000	Beginning Retained Earnings	8,500
Interest Expense	550	Cash from Stock Issued	3,000
Accrued Interest Payable	550	Cash	7,200
Supplies	50	Gain on Sale of Land	1,050
Supplies Expense	750	Loss on Sale of Property	50
Office Equipment	3,500	Salaries Expense	1,400
Depreciation Expense	500	Accrued Salaries Payable	400
Accumulated Depreciation	1,000	Rent Expense	1,100
Transportation-out Expense	500	Prepaid Rent	100
Miscellaneous Operating Expense	4,500		

The Cash account revealed the following cash flows:

Received cash from advances from customers	$ 2,600
Purchased office equipment	(3,500)
Received cash from issuing stock	3,000
Collected cash from accounts receivable	3,800
Purchased land	(8,000)
Received cash from borrowing funds	6,000
Paid cash for rent	(1,200)
Sold land	10,000
Paid cash for dividends	(1,500)
Paid cash for operating expenses	(1,000)
Purchased certificate of deposit	(10,000)

Required

Build an Excel spreadsheet to construct a multistep income statement, statement of changes in stockholders' equity, balance sheet, and statement of cash flows for the year 2004.

ATC 5–10   SPREADSHEET ANALYSIS *Mastering Excel*

At the end of 2004, the following information is available for Short and Wise Companies:

	Short			Wise	
	Actual	% Sales		Actual	% Sales
Sales	1,500,000	100.00%		1,500,000	
Cost of Goods Sold	1,050,000			900,000	
Gross Margin					
Operating Expenses	375,000			450,000	
Net Income					
	Actual	Return		Actual	Return
Total Assets	1,800,000			1,800,000	
Stockholders' Equity	540,000			540,000	

(C3 = =B3/$B$3)

Required

a. Set up the spreadsheet shown here. Complete the income statements by using Excel formulas.

b. Prepare a common size income statement for each company by completing the % Sales columns.

c. One company is a high-end retailer, and the other operates a discount store. Which is the discounter? Support your selection by referring to the common size statements.

d. Compute the return on assets and return on equity for each company.

e. Which company is more profitable from the stockholders' perspective?

f. Assume that a shortage of goods from suppliers is causing cost of goods sold to increase 10 percent for each company. Change the respective cost of goods sold balances in the Actual income statement column for each company. Note the new calculated amounts on the income statement and in the ratios. Which company's profits and returns are more sensitive to inventory price hikes?

Spreadsheet Tip

(1) Cell C3 (% Sales) can be copied down the income statement if the formula in cell C3 designates Sales (cell B3) as a fixed number. Designate a number as fixed by positioning $ signs within the cell address. Notice that the formula for C3 is =B3/$B$3.

Chapter

6

Internal Control and Accounting for Cash

Learning Objectives

After completing this chapter, you should be able to:

1 Explain the types and purposes of internal controls.

2 Identify the key elements of a strong system of internal control.

3 Identify special internal controls for computer systems.

4 Identify special internal controls for cash.

5 Prepare a bank reconciliation.

6 Explain the use of a petty cash fund.

7 Prepare a classified balance sheet.

8 Identify the length of an operating cycle.

9 Use the current ratio to assess the level of liquidity.

Rent-Way, Inc., is the second largest operator of rental-purchase stores in the United States. As of the end of 2000, it operated more than 1,100 stores in 42 states. On October 30, 2000, Rent-Way announced that its expenses had been incorrectly understated by more than $25 million. By June 2001, this estimate had been raised to more than $125 million. Prior to being restated, Rent-Way's earnings for 1999 were only $14.6 million. The day before the announcement of the accounting problems, the company's stock had been trading at $23.44 per share. After the announcement, it fell to as low as $2.31 per share, and by June 2001, it was trading at around $9 per share. As a result of these accounting irregularities, several management members were fired or asked to resign. How could such a large understatement of expenses go undetected for so long, and how was it ultimately discovered?

The successful operation of a business enterprise requires control. How can upper management of a major retailer such as Wal-Mart know that all its stores will open at a certain time? How can the president of General Motors rest assured that the numbers in the company's financial reports accurately reflect the company's operating activities? How can the owner of a small restaurant be confident that the wait staff is not giving food to friends and relatives? The answer to each of these questions is by exercising effective control over the enterprise. The policies and procedures used to provide reasonable assurance *that the objectives of an enterprise will be accomplished are called **internal controls**.[1]*

Internal controls can be divided into two categories: accounting and administrative. ***Accounting controls*** *are composed of procedures designed to safeguard the assets and ensure*

[1]*AICPA Professional Standards,* vol. 1, sec. 320, par. 6 (June 1, 1989).

that the accounting records contain reliable information. **Administrative controls** *concern the evaluation of performance and the assessment of the degree of compliance with company policies and public laws.*

▮Key Features of Internal Control Systems

The mechanics of internal control systems vary from company to company. However, most systems include a common set of general policies and procedures that have proved effective in accounting practice. The more prevalent features of a strong system of internal control are now discussed.

Separation of Duties

There should be a clear **separation of duties.** The likelihood of fraud or theft is reduced if it becomes necessary to collude with others to accomplish an offense. For example, a person selling seats to a movie may be tempted to pocket some of the money received from customers who enter the theater. This temptation is reduced if the person staffing the box office is required to issue tickets that a different employee then collects as people come into the theater. The ticket stubs collected by a different employee could be compared with the cash receipts, and any cash shortages would become apparent. Furthermore, friends and relatives of the ticket agent would be precluded from entering the theater without paying. Theft or unauthorized entry would require collusion between the ticket agent and the usher who collects the tickets. Both individuals would have to be dishonest enough to agree to steal from the theater's owner, yet trustworthy enough to convince each other that they could keep the embezzlement secret. Clearly, the opportunity for crime is less than it would be if a single individual were permitted to sell the tickets and allow access to the theater.

Whenever possible, the functions of *authorization, recording,* and *custody* should be exercised by separate individuals. For example, one person should authorize the purchase of inventory, a second person should keep the inventory records, and a third person should manage the warehouse in which the goods are stored. With this design, each person acts as a check on the other two. If the purchasing agent agreed to permit a supplier to deliver fewer goods than were ordered, the accountant would notice that the quantities on the purchase order were larger than the quantities shown on the receiving report prepared by the warehouse supervisor. Accordingly, the likelihood of errors and embezzlement is minimized when duties are separated.

Quality of Employees

Employees should be competent. A business is only as good as the people who run it. Cheap labor is not a bargain if the quality of output is so inferior as to require rework. A job done once at a cost of $6 per performance is less expensive than one that has to be done twice at a cost of $4 per performance. Employees should be adequately trained to perform a variety of tasks. The ability of employees to substitute for one another prevents disruptions that occur when coworkers are absent due to illnesses, vacations, or other commitments. The capacity to rotate jobs also relieves boredom and increases respect for the contributions of other employees. Every business should strive to maximize the productivity of each and every employee. Ongoing training programs represent an essential ingredient in a strong system of internal control.

Bonded Employees

The adage "the best defense is a good offense" is especially true when it comes to hiring employees. The best way to ensure honesty is to hire employees with *high personal integrity.*

Employers should screen job applicants through interviews, background checks, and recommendations that prior employers or educators provided. Even the best screening programs may fail to identify character weaknesses. Indeed, many frauds are perpetrated by employees who have had long records of exemplary service prior to the commission of crime. In other words, some employees with impeccable records at the time of employment can change after they have been hired. Accordingly, employees in positions of trust should be bonded. A **fidelity bond** is insurance that the company buys to protect itself from loss due to employee dishonesty. Before a firm bonds an employee, the bonding company runs a check on the employee. This check is another review of the employee in addition to the verification performed by the hiring firm. Furthermore, the insurance company covers losses that the firm incurs when it proves that such losses occurred due to the illegal actions of a bonded employee.

Periods of Absence

Employees should be required to take extended vacations and should be periodically rotated. An employee may be able to cover up illegal or unscrupulous activities while being present in the work environment. However, such activities are likely to be discovered in the employee's absence. Consider the case of a collection agent for a city's parking meter division. If the same agent always covers the same area, there is no basis for comparing that employee's collection pattern with patterns of other individuals. However, if the routes are altered, or if someone else covers the route while the regular agent is on vacation, improprieties may be discovered when the replacement agent reports different levels of cash receipts. For example, an embezzlement was discovered when a meter reader who had covered the same route for several years with no vacation became sick. When the substitute reported more money each day than the regular reader usually reported, management checked past records. It found that the sick meter reader had been understating the cash receipts and pocketing the difference between the actual and reported collections. If management had required vacations or rotated the routes, the embezzlement would have been discovered much earlier.

Procedures Manual

There should be proper procedures for processing transactions. The procedures for processing transactions should be carefully designed to promote accuracy and to affect reasonable control. For example, a clerk should be instructed to prepare a check only after receiving a copy of the invoice and notification from the receiving department that the goods involved in the payment have arrived in acceptable condition. Furthermore, the check signer should not sign the check unless it is accompanied by adequate supporting documents. In this way, the check signer ensures that the clerk has followed the proper procedures in preparing the check. These and other appropriate accounting procedures should be established in a **procedures manual**. The manual should be constantly updated, and periodic reviews should be conducted to ensure that employees are following the procedures outlined in the manual.

Authority and Responsibility

Clear lines of authority and responsibility should be established. Motivation is maximized when individuals are given authority to act on their own judgment. Reasonable caution is exercised when employees are held accountable for their actions. Individuals often disagree on which course of action is most likely to lead to the accomplishment of the objectives of an organization. Businesses operate more effectively if clear lines of authority are established before disputes arise. Accordingly, businesses should prepare a manual that establishes a definitive *chain of command*. The authority manual should provide guidance for both specific and general authorizations. **Specific authorizations** outline the limitations that apply to different levels of management. For example, a production supervisor may be able to authorize overtime, and the plant manager may authorize the acquisition of production equipment. These authorizations apply to specific positions within the organization. In contrast, **general authority** applies across different levels of management. It includes making decisions

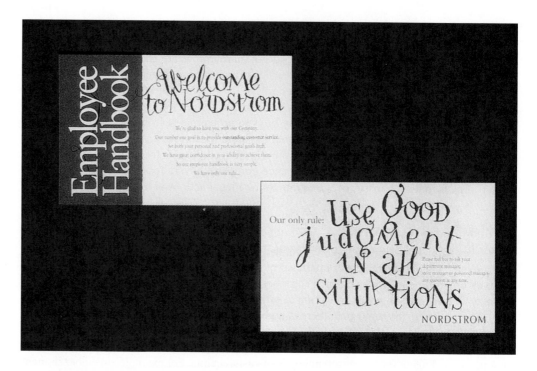

regarding items such as credit limits for customers, the class (coach or first class) of employees' flights on business trips, the price ranges for purchases, and the names of vendors from which goods and services may be acquired.

Prenumbered Documents

You have probably seen signs in stores that offer rewards to customers for reporting clerks who do not provide sales receipts. The signs read something like this: "If you fail to receive a valid sales receipt, your purchase is free." Without a record of sales transactions, management has no means of knowing how much money should be in the cash register. Accordingly, clerks could sell merchandise and keep the proceeds for themselves. Likewise, if management does not control the supply of unused sales receipts, clerks could give customers receipts but fail to report the fact that a receipt had been used. Again, management would be left in the dark, and the clerk could steal the proceeds from the unrecorded sales transaction. However, if clerks are required to use a supply of prenumbered sales receipts, the number of sales transactions can be determined by identifying the number of missing receipts. Accordingly, the use of *prenumbered documents* can diminish the likelihood of embezzlement.

Prenumbered forms should be used for all important documents such as purchase orders, receiving reports, invoices, and checks. The forms should be as simple and easy to use as possible to reduce errors. Also, the documents should allow for a signature by authorized personnel. For example, credit sales slips should be signed by the customer making the purchase. These procedures leave no doubt as to who made the purchase. Thus, the likelihood of unauthorized transactions is reduced.

Physical Control

There should be adequate physical control over assets. While most people would not think of leaving cash lying around, they are frequently more careless with respect to other valuable assets. Employees walk away with billions of dollars of business assets each year. To limit losses, inventory should be kept in a storeroom and not released without proper authorization. Serial numbers on equipment should be recorded along with the name of the individual to whom the equipment was assigned. Unannounced physical counts should be conducted to ensure that the equipment remains in the business. Certificates of deposit and marketable securities should be kept in fireproof vaults. Access to these vaults should be limited to authorized personnel.

These procedures protect the documents from fire and limit access to only those individuals who have the appropriate security clearance to handle the documents.

In addition to safeguarding assets, there should be physical control over the accounting records. The accounting journals, ledgers, and supporting documents should be kept in a fire-proof safe. Only personnel responsible for recording transactions into the journals should have access to them. With limited access, there is less chance that someone will change the records to hide fraud or embezzlement.

Performance Evaluations

There should be independent verification of performance because few people can evaluate their own performance objectively. Independent verification is essential. For example, someone other than the person who has control over the inventory should take a physical count of inventory. This count should be compared with the accounting records. Discrepancies could alert management to the fact that inventory is being lost, stolen, or damaged. Internal and external audits serve as independent verification of performance. These auditors should appraise the effectiveness of the internal control system as well as verify the accuracy of the accounting records. In addition, the external auditors attest to the application of generally accepted accounting principles in the reporting process.

A system of internal controls is designed to prevent errors and fraud. However, no system is perfect or foolproof. Internal controls can be circumvented by collusion among employees. Two or more employees working together can hide embezzlement by covering for each other. For example, if an embezzler goes on vacation, illegal activity will not be reported by a replacement who is in collusion with the embezzler. No system can prevent all fraud. However, a good system of internal controls minimizes illegal or unethical activities by reducing temptation and increasing the likelihood of early detection.

Check Yourself 6–1

What are nine features of an internal control system?

Answer The nine features follow.
1. Separating duties so that fraud or theft requires collusion.
2. Hiring and training competent employees.
3. Bonding employees to recover losses through insurance.
4. Requiring employees to be absent from their jobs so that their replacements can discover errors or fraudulent activity that might have occurred.
5. Establishing proper procedures for processing transactions.
6. Establishing clear lines of authority and responsibility.
7. Using prenumbered documents.
8. Implementing physical controls such as locking cash in a safe.
9. Conducting performance evaluations through independent internal and external audits.

Internal Control in Computer Systems

LO3 Identify special internal controls for computer systems.

The basic internal control features discussed earlier apply to both manual and computer systems. The use of computers does not negate the need to hire competent employees with high personal integrity. Persons in positions of trust should still be bonded. The segregation and rotation of duties remain important, and the physical control of assets continues as a high priority. Indeed, computers often require special environmental features such as climate control and sophisticated electric circuitry. Accordingly, the use of computers provides an added dimension that increases the need for internal controls rather than reduces its importance. Some of the additional control requirements follow:

1. Computers do not think independently. They are neutral to the size of numbers. They would treat a $1,000,000 sales order in exactly the same manner as a $100 sales order. Accordingly, *tests of reasonableness* must be built into the operating programs. For example, programs could be designed to require a coded access number prior to initiating delivery orders for

Some difference of opinion exists among the people involved about whether Rent-Way's problems are the result of legitimately pushing the boundaries of GAAP or truly improper accounting, according to *The Wall Street Journal* (June 8, 2001, pp. C-1 and C-14). The courts may ultimately settle these differences. However, some persons involved say the underreporting of expenses was not noticed because it was accomplished in a series of relatively small transactions. No single understatement was enough to raise suspicion, but cumulatively they were very material. The problems were noticed when the person allegedly responsible for them took a vacation, and his replacement noticed unusually high inventory levels and began investigating. In a press release filed with the SEC on December 12, 2000, William Morgenstern, chairman and CEO of the company, said, "I am outraged that a handful of senior personnel betrayed the trust that was shown in them. . . ." No matter how sophisticated a company's system of internal controls may be, it can never completely eliminate the need to rely on the honesty of employees.

For more information about this company's accounting problems, use EDGAR to download its 8-K reports that were filed with the SEC on October 31, 2000, and December 12, 2000. Appendix A provides instructions for using EDGAR.

Source: *The Wall Street Journal,* June 8, 2000, C-1 and C-14.

sales transactions in excess of $10,000 to motivate human scrutiny of major sales transactions. Similar controls should be incorporated to ensure that human logic remains an active component of business operations.

2. Significant technical expertise may be required to design and run the programs that operate an automated accounting system. Accordingly, the computer programmers may be more knowledgeable than the auditors who are assigned the task of monitoring the programmers' performance. Background checks and fidelity bonding for the programmers may be important under these circumstances.

3. Documentary evidence may be diminished in computer-based accounting systems. Information is usually stored on magnetic disks and therefore is unobservable to the human eye. These data can be easily destroyed or manipulated without the traditional traces that facilitate detection. To test the system, auditors may be required to **audit around the computer,** an expression used to describe a procedure in which the auditor provides input that is expected to result in a designated output. The system is tested by comparing the actual output with the expected output. If actual output is consistent with expectations, the procedure provides evidence of accurate processing. Differences signal the need for further investigation. For example, instead of analyzing a computer program to determine whether it was designed to compute payroll tax correctly, the auditor could input the gross salary of a test case and analyze the tax figures generated by the program to see if it is operating appropriately.

4. It may be more difficult to control access to sensitive data in automated accounting systems. Hackers have the ability to gain unauthorized access to highly sophisticated computer systems. Large quantities of data can be transferred across phone lines, thereby permitting thieves to commit their crimes without leaving the security of their own work environment. Care must be taken to control access to the system. Passwords and other screening devices should be employed to reduce the risk of unauthorized access to computer programs and data files.

5. It is important to maintain proper documentation regarding the development and operation of the computer programs used in the business. Without proper documentation, the operation of the system becomes dependent on the knowledge base of a particular programmer. If the programmer becomes ill or otherwise incapacitated, the operating system becomes dysfunctional as well. Many small businesses find the use of standard commercial programs to be a cost-effective alternative to writing their own programs. You do not have to build a car to obtain the benefits of automotive transportation; you simply buy, lease, or rent an automobile. Likewise, you do not have to write a computer program to obtain the benefits of an automated accounting system. Many existing commercial programs meet the needs of most small businesses. These programs provide proper documentation and technical support at affordable prices.

6. Finally, it is critically important to safeguard the programs and databases. Programs and databases are easily destroyed or sabotaged. Backup files should be maintained in a fire-proof vault in a separate location to minimize the danger associated with lost or damaged programs and data files.

Accounting for Cash

Cash is broadly defined for financial statement purposes. Generally, **cash** includes currency and other items that are payable *on demand,* such as checks, money orders, bank drafts, and certain savings accounts. Savings accounts that require substantial penalties for early withdrawal should be classified as *investments* rather than as cash. Furthermore, post-dated checks or IOUs represent *receivables* and should not be accounted for as cash. In practice, most companies use captions that highlight the fact that items other than currency are included in the cash classification. Exhibit 6–1 includes a list of the most frequently used balance sheet titles that include the word *cash.*

The amount of cash on hand must be closely monitored to ensure the viability and profitability of the business. There must be enough cash available to pay employees, suppliers, and creditors as amounts become due. When a company fails to pay legal debts, the creditors can force the business into bankruptcy. While the availability of cash is critical, management should avoid the accumulation of excess idle cash. The failure to invest excess cash in earning assets adversely affects profitability. Cash inflows and outflows must be properly managed to prevent a shortage or surplus of cash.

LO4 Identify special internal controls for cash.

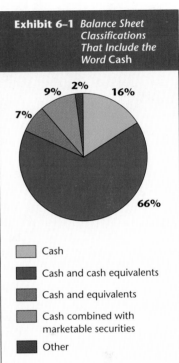

Exhibit 6–1 *Balance Sheet Classifications That Include the Word* **Cash**

- Cash
- Cash and cash equivalents
- Cash and equivalents
- Cash combined with marketable securities
- Other

Data Source: AICPA, *Accounting Trends and Techniques,* 1998.

Controlling Cash

Cash more than any other asset requires strict adherence to internal control procedures. It has universal appeal. Relatively small amounts of high-denomination currency can be used to represent significant amounts of value. Furthermore, specific identification as to who owns currency is difficult to prove. In most cases, possession equates to ownership. Because of these qualities, cash is highly susceptible to theft and must be kept under close scrutiny. Cash is most susceptible to embezzlement at the points of receipt and disbursement. The following procedures should be employed to reduce the likelihood of theft.

Cash Receipts

A record of all cash receipts should be prepared immediately. If cash receipts are recorded in a timely and accurate manner, missing amounts of money can be detected by comparing the actual balances of cash with the book balances. Customers should be given written copies of the receipts that evidence payment. This practice results in a control on the receipts clerk by the customer. A customer usually reviews the receipt to ensure that she or he has been given credit for the amount paid and calls any errors to the clerk's attention.

Cash receipts should be deposited in a bank or other financial institution on a timely basis. Cash collected late in the day should be deposited in a night depository. Every effort should be made to minimize the amount of cash on hand. Large amounts of cash not only place the business at risk of loss from theft but also place the employees in danger of being harmed by criminals who attempt to rob the company.

Cash Payments

To effectively control cash, a company should make all disbursements by check, thereby providing a record of cash payments. All checks should be prenumbered and kept under lock. When checks are prenumbered, lost or stolen checks are easily identifiable by comparing the

The Cost of Protecting Cash

Could you afford to buy a safe like the one shown here? The vault is only one of many expensive security devices used by banks to safeguard cash. By using checking accounts, companies are able to avoid many of the costs associated with keeping cash safe. In addition to providing physical control, checking accounts enable companies to maintain a written audit trail regarding cash receipts and payments. Indeed, checking accounts represent the most widely used internal control device in modern society. It is difficult to imagine a business operating without the use of checking accounts.

supply of unwritten and canceled checks with the list of prenumbered checks. If checks are kept locked and under the care of a responsible person, then there is less opportunity for unauthorized disbursements.

The duties of approving disbursements, signing checks, and recording transactions should be separated. If one person is authorized to approve, sign, and record checks, it is easy for that person to falsify supporting documents, write a check, and record it in the records. By separating these three duties, the check signer reviews the documentation provided by the approving agent before signing the check. Likewise, the recording clerk reviews the work of both the approval agent and the signer when information is input to the accounting records. Again, collusion is required to circumvent the system of controls created by the separation of these duties.

Supporting documents with authorized approval signatures should be required when checks are presented to the check signer. Supporting documents prove an actual need for payment. Before the payment is approved, invoice amounts should be checked and the payee verified as being a legitimate vendor. Thus, the authorized approval signature acts as a check on the documents submitted by the payables clerk. Both the supporting documents and an authorized approval help deter the payables clerk from creating fake documents with the disbursement being made to a friend or fictitious business. Also, the approver serves as a check on the accuracy of the work of the payables clerk.

Supporting documents should be marked *Paid* when the check is signed. If the documents are not indelibly marked, they could be retrieved from the file and resubmitted for a second payment. A payables clerk could work with the payee to share in any extra cash paid out by submitting the same supporting invoices for a second payment.

All spoiled and voided checks should be defaced and retained. An employee may claim that a certain check was written for an incorrect amount and therefore thrown away. Unless there is physical proof of the existence of the check, the firm has no way of knowing whether the clerk is telling the truth or he or she stole the check. To prevent this uncertainty, all spoiled and voided checks should be kept.

Checking Account Documents

The previous section clearly established the need for businesses and individuals to use checking accounts. The following are the four main types of forms associated with a bank checking account:

Signature Card

A bank **signature card** contains the bank account number and the signatures of the people authorized to write checks on the account. The form is retained in the bank's files. If a bank employee is unfamiliar with the signature on a check that is presented to the bank for payment, she or he can refer to the signature card to verify the signature for that particular account.

Deposit Ticket

Each deposit of cash or checks is accompanied by a **deposit ticket,** which normally contains the account number and the name of the account. The depositor fills in the amount of currency, coins, and checks deposited. The total of all currency, coins, and checks deposited is noted on the deposit ticket.

Bank Check

A written check involves three parties: (1) the person or business writing the check (the *payer*), (2) the bank on which the check is drawn, and (3) the person or business to whom the check is made payable (the *payee*). **Checks** are often multicopy, prenumbered forms, with the name of the business issuing them preprinted on the face. A remittance notice is usually attached to the check. This portion of the check gives the payer space in which to establish a record that identifies why the check is being written (e.g., what invoices are being paid), the amount being disbursed, and the date of payment. When signed by the person whose signature is on the signature card, the check authorizes the bank to transfer the face amount of the check from the payer's account to the payee.

Bank Statement

Periodically, the bank sends the depositor a **bank statement.** It is important to note that the bank statement is presented from the bank's point of view. Since the bank is obligated to pay back the money that customers have deposited in their accounts, a checking account is a liability to the bank. Accordingly, the checking account carries a credit balance on the bank's books. **Bank statement debit memos** describe transactions that reduce the balance of the bank's liability (the customer's account). **Bank statement credit memos** describe activities that increase the bank's liability (the customer's account balance). To avoid confusion, remember that the checking account is an asset (cash) to the depositor. Accordingly, a *debit memo* listed in the bank statement requires a *credit entry* to the Cash account on the depositor's books.

The information contained in the bank statement normally includes (a) the balance of the account at the beginning of the period, (b) additions created by customer deposits made during the period, (c) other additions described in credit memos (e.g., earned interest), (d) subtractions made for the payment of checks drawn on the account during the period, (e) other subtractions described in debit memos (e.g., service charges), (f) a running balance of the account, and (g) the balance of the account at the end of the period. Examples of these items are referenced with the letters in parentheses in the example of a bank statement in Exhibit 6–2. Normally, the canceled checks or copies of them are enclosed with the bank statement.

Reconciling the Bank Statement

Usually the balance shown on the bank statement differs from the balance shown in the Cash account on the depositor's books. The difference is normally attributable to timing. For example, a depositor deducts the amount of a check from the account immediately after writing the check. However, the bank has no knowledge of the check until the payee presents it for payment, which may occur several weeks or even months after the check is written. Similarly, there may be a delay between the time a bank adjusts a depositor's account and the time the

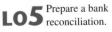

LO5 Prepare a bank reconciliation.

Exhibit 6–2

FIRST $ TATE BANK
of Frisco County

2121 Westbury Drive • Harrison, Nevada • 54269 - 0001

Green Shades Resorts, Inc
1439 Lazy Lane
Harrison, Nevada 54275 - 0023

Account Number
53-9872-3

Checking Account Summary	On This Date	Your Balance Was	Deposits Added	No. Deposits	Checks Paid	No. Checks
	8/31/2003	(a) 4,779.86	3,571.72	5	4,537.22	22
	Other Debits	Resulting in a Balance of			On This Date	Enclosures
	297.91	(g) 3,516.45			9/30/2003	29

Checks and Debits		Deposits and Credits		Date	Balance
(d) 15.82	24.85	(b) 600.25		9/3	(f) 5,339.44
249.08	497.00			9/5	4,593.36
42.53	124.61			9/7	4,426.22
79.87	859.38			9/8	3,486.97
685.00	742.59	711.43		9/9	2,770.81
25.75	38.98			9/12	2,706.08
36.45	59.91			9/14	2,609.72
	(e) 8.40 DM	(c) 940.00 CM		9/15	3,541.32
61.40		689.47		9/18	4,169.39
289.51 NS				9/19	3,879.88
71.59	82.00			9/21	3,726.29
312.87				9/24	3,413.42
25.00		630.57		9/27	4,018.99
227.00				9/28	3,791.99
95.06	180.48			9/30	3,516.45

LEGEND – NS Nonsufficient Funds • DM Debit Memo • CM Credit Memo

FIRST STATE BANK OF FRISCO COUNTY

customer becomes aware that the adjustment was made. For example, a customer may not be aware that the bank deposited interest in or subtracted service charges from his or her account until the customer receives and reads the bank statement. Accordingly, the bank statement may reflect a balance larger or smaller than the balance recorded in the depositor's books. The following items cause the balance on the bank statement to be larger than the balance shown in the depositor's cash account:

1. Outstanding checks. These are disbursements that have been properly recorded as cash deductions on the payer's books. However, the amounts have not been deducted from the payer's bank account because the checks have not yet been presented by the payee to the bank for payment; that is, the checks have not "cleared" the bank.
2. Deposits made by the bank. These are additions to the depositor's account made directly by the bank. They may be the result of collections made by the bank on behalf of the depositor or of interest paid to the depositor by the bank.

Alternatively, the balance reported on the bank statement may be less than the balance recorded in the depositor's books. This may be due to the following causes:

1. **Service charges.** These are fees charged by the bank for services performed or as a penalty for the depositor's failing to maintain a specified minimum cash balance throughout the period.

2. Deductions for **non-sufficient-funds (NSF) checks.** These are checks that were deposited. However, when the checks were submitted for payment to the bank on which they were drawn, the accounts did not have enough funds to cover the amount of the checks. When such checks are returned, they must be deducted from the depositor's bank account.
3. **Deposits in transit.** These are deposits that have been recorded by the depositor in the accounting records but have not yet been recorded by the bank.

Additionally, there may be differences between the bank statement's cash balance and the depositor's cash balance due to errors by either the bank or the depositor. For example, the bank may pay a check written by a customer named *Turpen* from the account of a customer named *Turpin*. In this case, both the Turpen and Turpin bank statements would be incorrect. All errors should be corrected immediately.

Determining True Cash Balance

A schedule is preapproved to reconcile the differences between the cash balance shown on the bank statement and the cash balance recorded in the depositor's accounting records. This schedule is called a **bank reconciliation statement.** It begins with the cash balance reported by the bank as of the statement date (the **unadjusted bank balance**). The schedule then lists the adjustments necessary to determine the amount of cash that the depositor actually has as of the date of the bank statement. The actual cash balance is called the **true cash balance.** The true cash balance is determined a second time by making adjustments to the **unadjusted book balance.** The bank statement is reconciled when the true cash balance determined from the perspective of the unadjusted *bank* balance agrees with the true cash balance determined from the perspective of the unadjusted *book* balance. The procedures necessary to arrive at the *true cash balance* from the two different perspectives are outlined here.

Adjustments to the Bank Balance

Step 1 in determining the true balance from the perspective of the bank statement is to compare the deposit tickets with deposits shown in the depositor's records. Any deposits recorded in the depositor's books but not yet recorded by the bank are, as noted, deposits in transit. Since deposits are frequently made in the night depository or on the day following the receipt of cash, this is a frequent occurrence. Deposits in transit have not been recorded by the bank, and therefore they are added to the unadjusted bank balance to arrive at the true cash balance.

Step 2 is to sort the checks returned with the bank statement into numerical sequence. These checks are then compared with checks listed in the depositor's cash records, and the amounts are verified. After verification of all the checks returned with the bank statement, there may be some checks that were issued by the depositor but not presented to the bank for payment. These **outstanding checks** must be deducted from the unadjusted bank balance to determine the true cash balance. Some banks do not return paid checks. In this case outstanding checks are identified by comparing the company's check register with the check numbers listed on the bank statement. A **certified check** is a check guaranteed by a bank to be a check drawn on an account having sufficient funds. Whereas a regular check is deducted from the customer's account when it is presented for payment, a certified check is deducted from the customer's account when the bank certifies that the check is good. Accordingly, all certified checks have been deducted by the bank in the determination of the unadjusted bank balance, whether they have cleared the bank or remain outstanding as of the date of the bank statement. For this reason, it is not necessary to deduct *outstanding certified checks* from the unadjusted bank balance to determine the true balance of cash.

Adjustments to the Book Balance

The unadjusted book balance must be adjusted to reflect the credit and debit memos shown in the bank statement. Credit memo items such as earned interest are added to the unadjusted book balance, and debit memo items such as service charges are subtracted from it. Non-sufficient-funds checks must be subtracted from the unadjusted book balance to determine the true cash balance.

Correction of Errors

Errors can affect the determination of the true cash balance from the perspective of either the bank statement or the depositor's books. If an error is found on the bank statement, the bank should be notified immediately, and the adjustment is made to the unadjusted bank balance to determine the true cash balance. In contrast, errors made by the depositor require adjustments to the book balance to arrive at the true cash balance.

Illustrating the Reconciliation Statement

The following example illustrates the process of preparing the bank reconciliation statement for Green Shades Resorts, Inc. (GSRI). Recall that Exhibit 6–2 is the bank statement for GSRI. Exhibit 6–3 represents the completed bank reconciliation statement. The items included in the reconciliation statement are now described.

Adjustments to Bank Balance

As of September 30, 2003, the bank statement shows an unadjusted balance of $3,516.45. Assume that a review of the bank statement discloses two adjustments that must be added to this amount. First, assume that a review of the deposit tickets indicated that there was $724.11 of deposits in transit. Second, assume that an examination of the returned checks disclosed that a $25 check written by Green Valley Resorts had been deducted from GSRI's bank account. Since the bank erroneously deducted this amount from GSRI's account, the amount must be added back to the unadjusted bank balance to arrive at the true balance.

Finally, assume that the returned checks included in the bank statement were sorted and compared to the cash records and that three checks were outstanding. Since these checks have not yet been deducted from GSRI's bank account, the unadjusted bank balance must be reduced. Exhibit 6–3 assumes that the amount of the outstanding checks was $235.25. After this deduction is made, the true cash balance is $4,030.31.

Exhibit 6–3

GREEN SHADES RESORTS, INC.
Bank Reconciliation Statement
September 30, 2003

Unadjusted Bank Balance, September 30, 2003	$3,516.45
Add: Deposits in Transit	724.11
Bank Error: Check drawn on Green Valley Resorts Charged to GSRI	25.00
Less: Outstanding Checks	

Check No.	Date	Amount
639	Sept. 18	$ 13.75
646	Sept. 20	29.00
672	Sept. 27	192.50

Total	(235.25)
True Cash Balance, Sept 30, 2003	$4,030.31
Unadjusted Book Balance, September 30, 2003	$3,361.22
Add: Receivable Collected by Bank	940.00
Error Made by Accountant (Check no. 633 recorded as $63.45 instead of $36.45)	27.00
Less: Bank Service Charges	(8.40)
NSF Check	(289.51)
True Cash Balance, September 30, 2003	$4,030.31

Adjustments to Book Balance

As indicated in Exhibit 6–3, GSRI's unadjusted book balance as of September 30, 2003, amounted to $3,361.22. This balance does not accurately reflect GSRI's true cash balance because of four unrecorded accounting events: (1) The bank collected a $940 account receivable for GSRI, (2) GSRI's accountant made a $27 recording error, (3) the bank charged GSRI an $8.40 service fee, and (4) GSRI accepted a $289.51 check from a customer who did not have sufficient funds to cover the check. Each event requires an adjustment to GSRI's accounting records. The adjustments and their effects on the financial statements are now explained.

Adjustment 1 *Recording the $940 receivables collection increases Cash and reduces Accounts Receivables.*

The event is an asset exchange transaction. The effect of the collection on GSRI's financial statements follows.

Assets			=	Liab.	+	Equity	Rev.	–	Exp.	=	Net Inc.	Cash Flow
Cash	+	Acct. Rec.										
940	+	(940)	=	NA	+	NA	NA	–	NA	=	NA	940 OA

Adjustment 2 *Assume that the $27 recording error occurred because GSRI's accountant made a transposition error when recording check no. 633.*

The check was written to pay utilities expense in the amount of $36.45 but was recorded as a $63.45 disbursement. Since cash payments are overstated by $27.00 ($63.45 − $36.45), this amount must be added back to GSRI's cash balance and deducted from the Utilities Expense account. Since the deduction causes the Utilities Expense account to decline, the net income increases. The effects on the financial statements are shown next.

Assets	=	Liab.	+	Equity	Rev.	–	Exp.	=	Net Inc.	Cash Flow
27	=	NA	+	27	NA	–	(27)	=	27	27 OA

Adjustment 3 *The $8.40 service charge is a typical expense item that reduces assets, equity, income, and cash flow.*

The effects are shown here.

Assets	=	Liab.	+	Equity	Rev.	–	Exp.	=	Net Inc.	Cash Flow
(8.40)	=	NA	+	(8.40)	NA	–	8.40	=	(8.40)	(8.40) OA

Adjustment 4 *The $289.51 NSF check reduces GSRI's cash balance.*

GSRI increased its Cash account when it originally accepted the customer's check. Now GSRI must reduce its Cash account because there is not enough money in the customer's bank account to pay the check. GSRI will try to collect the money directly from the customer. In the meantime, it will show the amount due as an account receivable. Accordingly, the adjusting entry required to record the NSF check is an asset exchange transaction. The Cash account decreases, and the Accounts Receivable account increases. The effect on GSRI's financial statements is as follows.

Assets			=	Liab.	+	Equity	Rev.	–	Exp.	=	Net Inc.	Cash Flow
Cash	+	Acct. Rec.										
(289.51)	+	289.51	=	NA	+	NA	NA	–	NA	=	NA	(289.51) OA

Determination of the True Cash Balance

Two of the adjustments increase the unadjusted cash balance. The other two adjustments decrease the unadjusted balance. After the adjustments have been recorded, the Cash account reflects the true cash balance of $4,030.31 ($3,361.22 unadjusted cash balance + $940.00 receivable collection + $27.00 recording error − $8.40 service charge − $289.51 NSF check). Since the true balance determined from the perspective of the bank account agrees with the true balance determined from the perspective of GSRI's books, the bank statement has been successfully reconciled with the accounting records.

Cash Balance Updated

The journal entries required for the four adjustments described are as follows:

Account Title	Debit	Credit
Cash	940.00	
Accounts Receivable		940.00
To record the account receivable collected by the bank		
Cash	27.00	
Utilities Expense		27.00
To correct error on recording check no. 633		
Bank Service Charge Expense	8.40	
Cash		8.40
To record service charge expense		
Accounts Receivable	289.51	
Cash		289.51
To establish receivable due from customer who wrote the bad check		

Cash Short and Over

Sometime errors are made when employees are collecting cash or making change to customers. If these errors occur, the amount of money in the cash register will not agree with the amount of cash receipts recorded on the cash register tape. For example, suppose that when a customer paid for $17.95 of merchandise with a $20 bill, the sales clerk returned $3.05 in change instead of the correct amount of $2.05. If, at the end of the day, the cash register tape shows total receipts of $487.50, the cash drawer contains only $486.50. The actual cash balance is less than the expected cash balance by $1. Any shortage of cash or excess of cash is recorded in a special account named **Cash Short and Over.** In this example, the shortage is recorded in the following journal entry:

Account Title	Debit	Credit
Cash	486.50	
Cash Short and Over	1.00	
Sales		487.50

A debit to the Cash Short and Over account indicates a cash shortage that represents an expense. An overage of cash is considered revenue and is recorded by crediting the Cash Short and Over account. As with other expense and revenue items, the balance of the Cash Short and Over account is closed to the Retained Earnings account at the end of the accounting period.

The following information was drawn from Reliance Company's October bank statement. The unadjusted bank balance on October 31 was $2,300. The statement showed that the bank had collected a $200 account receivable for Reliance. The statement also included $20 of bank service charges for October and a $100 check payable to Reliance that was returned NSF. A comparison of the bank statement with company accounting records indicates that there was a $500 deposit in transit and $1,800 of checks outstanding at the end of the month. Based on this information, determine the true cash balance on October 31.

Answer Since the unadjusted book balance is not given, start with the unadjusted bank balance to determine the true cash balance. The collection of the receivable, the bank service charges, and the NSF check are already recognized in the unadjusted bank balance, so these items are not used to determine the true cash balance. Determine the true cash balance by adding the deposit in transit to and subtracting the outstanding checks from the unadjusted bank balance. The true cash balance is $1,000 ($2,300 unadjusted bank balance + $500 deposit in transit − $1,800 outstanding checks).

Check
Yourself
6–2

Using Petty Cash Funds

Although it is best to make all disbursements by check, it may be more practical and convenient to make certain small payments in cash. Payments for postage, delivery charges, taxi fares, employees' supper money, and other small items are frequently made with cash. To allow for these small payments and still keep effective control over cash disbursements, a company may establish a **petty cash fund.** The fund is established for some specified dollar amount, such as $300, and is controlled by one employee, called the *petty cash custodian.*

LO6 Explain the use of a petty cash fund.

Petty cash funds are usually maintained on an **imprest basis,** which means that the cash disbursed is replenished on a periodic basis. The fund is created by drawing a check on the regular checking account, cashing it, and giving the currency to a petty cash custodian. The custodian normally keeps the cash under lock and key. In other words, the establishment of a petty cash fund merely transfers cash from a bank account to a safety box inside the company offices. As such, the event is an asset exchange. The Cash account decreases, and the Petty Cash account increases. The effect on the financial statements and the journal entry required to record the event are as follows.

Assets		= Liab.	+ Equity	Rev.	− Exp.	= Net Inc.	Cash Flow
Cash	+ Petty Cash						
(300)	+ 300	= NA	+ NA	NA	− NA	= NA	NA

Account Title	Debit	Credit
Petty Cash	300.00	
Cash		300.00

The amount of the petty cash fund depends on what it is used for, how often it is used, and how often it is replenished. It should be large enough to handle disbursements for a reasonable time, such as a week or a month.

When money is disbursed from the petty cash fund, the custodian should fill out a petty cash **voucher,** such as the one in Exhibit 6–4. Any supporting documents, such as an invoice, restaurant bill, or parking fee receipt, should be attached to the petty cash voucher. The person who receives the cash should always sign the voucher as evidence of the receipt. At any time, the total of the amounts recorded on the petty cash vouchers plus the remaining coin and currency should equal the balance of the petty cash ledger account. *There is no journal entry made in the accounting records when petty cash funds are disbursed.* The effect on the financial

Exhibit 6–4

Petty cash voucher no. _____

To: _____   Date _____ , 20____

Explanation: Account No. _____   Amount _____

Approved by _____   Received by _____

statements is recorded at the time when the petty cash fund is replenished (when additional cash is put into the petty cash safety box).

When the amount of cash in the petty cash fund is relatively low, the fund should be replenished. To accomplish the replenishment, the petty cash vouchers are totaled, the amount of any cash short or over is determined, and a check is issued to the bank to obtain the currency needed to return the fund to its full balance. For example, suppose the petty cash fund is replenished when the total amount of petty cash vouchers equals $216. The vouchers can be classified according to different types of expenses or listed in total as miscellaneous expense. Assuming that the Miscellaneous Expense account is used in this example, the journal entries to record the replenishment of the funds are as follows:

Account Title	Debit	Credit
Miscellaneous Expense	216.00	
Petty Cash		216.00
To record expenses paid from the petty cash fund		
Petty Cash	216.00	
Cash		216.00
To replenish the petty cash fund		

Note that the effect of the entries could have been recorded in a more efficient manner. Since the debit to the Petty Cash account is offset by the credit, a single entry debiting Miscellaneous Expense and crediting Cash would have the same effect on the accounts. Indeed, the entry more frequently used in practice to record the replenishment of petty cash appears as follows:

Account Title	Debit	Credit
Miscellaneous Expense	216.00	
Cash		216.00

The replenishment affects the financial statements in the same manner as any other cash expense. It acts to reduce assets, equity, income, and cash flow. The effects are shown here.

Assets	=	Liab.	+	Equity	Rev.	−	Exp.	=	Net Inc.	Cash Flow
(216)	=	NA	+	(216)	NA	−	216	=	(216)	(216) OA

If the vouchers and their amounts are separated as postage, $66; delivery charges, $78.40; taxi fares, $28; and supper money, $43.60, the journal entry to replenish the fund could be recorded as follows:

Account Title	Debit	Credit
Postage Expense	66.00	
Delivery Expense	78.40	
Taxi Fares Expense	28.00	
Employee Meal Expense	43.60	
Cash		216.00

Once the vouchers are checked, the fund replenished, and the journal entry recorded, the vouchers should be indelibly marked *Paid* so that they cannot be reused.

Sometimes, cash shortages and overages are discovered when a physical count is taken of the money in the petty cash fund. Suppose that a physical count reveals $212.30 in petty cash vouchers and only $87 in cash. Assuming a normal petty cash balance of $300, the journal entries necessary to record the replenishment are as follows:

Account Title	Debit	Credit
Miscellaneous Expense	212.30	
Cash Short and Over	.70	
Petty Cash		213.00
To record expenses paid from the petty cash fund		
Petty Cash	213.00	
Cash		213.00
To replenish the petty cash fund		

If a cash shortage or overage does not occur frequently and it is an insignificant amount, the shortage or overage may be included in miscellaneous expense.

Cornerstone Corporation established a $400 petty cash fund that was replenished when it contained $30 of currency and coins and $378 of receipts for miscellaneous expenses. Based on this information, determine the amount of cash short or over to be recognized. Explain how the shortage or overage would be reported in the financial statements. Also determine the amount of petty cash expenses that were recognized when the fund was replenished.

Answer The fund contained $408 of currency and receipts ($30 currency + $378 of receipts), resulting in a cash overage of $8 ($408 − $400). The overage would be reported as miscellaneous revenue on the income statement. The amount of petty cash expenses recognized would equal the amount of the expense receipts, which is $378.

Check Yourself 6–3

▌Assessment of the Level of Liquidity

Current Versus Noncurrent

Assets have been defined as items that have probable future economic benefits to a business, and *liabilities* as the creditors' claim on some of those assets. However, not all assets and liabilities are the same; a significant distinguishing feature relates to their liquidity. The more quickly an asset is converted to cash, the more *liquid* it is. This is important because companies usually pay their bills with cash. Land and buildings are valuable assets, but they cannot be used to pay this month's electric bill.

Why not keep all assets in cash or liquid investments? Because investments in liquid assets usually do not earn as much money as investments in other assets. Thus, a company must try

LO7 Prepare a classified balance sheet.

to maintain a proper balance between liquid assets (so it can pay its bills) and nonliquid assets (so it can earn a good return).

This distinction is so important that accountants organize items on the balance sheet according to liquidity. There are two major classes of assets: *current* and *noncurrent*. Current items are also referred to as *short term* and noncurrent items as *long term*. A **current (short-term) asset** is one that will be converted to cash or consumed within one year or an operating cycle, whichever is longer. For example, accounts receivable are usually expected to be collected (converted to cash) within one year. Therefore, they are classified as current.

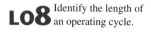

LO8 Identify the length of an operating cycle.

An **operating cycle** is defined as the average time it takes a business to convert cash to inventory, inventory to accounts receivable, and accounts receivable back to cash. Graphically, it can be shown as follows:

Operating cycles for most businesses are less than one year, but they can be longer. Consider the time it takes a construction company to build and sell a house—this time could easily exceed one year. Ratios that help measure the length of a company's operating cycle are introduced in Chapters 7 and 8. However, unless there is strong evidence to the contrary, assume that operating cycles are less than one year. Accordingly, the one-year rule usually prevails with respect to the classification of current assets.

Based on the definition of *current* as explained here, the typical current assets section of a balance sheet includes the following items:

> Current Assets
>   Cash
>   Marketable Securities
>   Accounts Receivable
>   Short-Term Notes Receivable
>   Interest Receivable
>   Inventory
>   Supplies
>   Prepaids

Given the definition of current assets, it seems logical that a **current (short-term) liability** would be one that must be repaid within one year or an operating cycle whichever is longer. This is almost always correct. However, this definition places some surprising accounts in the category of current liabilities. If a company issues bonds[2] that are to be repaid in 20 years, the bonds are included in long-term liabilities (until they have been outstanding for 19 years). After 19 years, the 20-year bonds become due within one year and are classified as a current liability on the balance sheet.

There is an exception to the general rule for determining which liabilities should be listed as short term. If a business does not plan to use any of its current assets to repay a debt, that debt is listed as long term even if it is due within one year. How can debt be repaid without using current assets? Assume that the 20-year bonds referred to are now due within the next year.

---

[2]*Bonds* are certificates issued to creditors that evidence a company's obligation to pay interest and return of principal on borrowed funds. They are normally issued to the general public in exchange for the receipt of borrowed money. Bonds usually carry long terms to maturity, with 20 years being typical. Chapter 10 of this book is devoted almost exclusively to the accounting treatment of bonds. More detailed information is provided there. At this point, all that is necessary for your comprehension of the subject matter under discussion is to know that bonds represent a form of long-term debt. Companies that issue bonds receive cash that they are obligated to repay at a future date. In the interim, they pay interest to the creditors for the privilege of using the borrowed funds.

The company may plan to issue new 20-year bonds (long-term debt) and use the proceeds from those bonds to repay the old bonds. In this case, the currently maturing debt is classified as long term. This situation is referred to as *refinancing short-term debt on a long-term basis*.

Liabilities typically found in the current section of a balance sheet include the following:

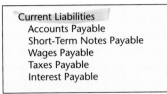

Current Liabilities
    Accounts Payable
    Short-Term Notes Payable
    Wages Payable
    Taxes Payable
    Interest Payable

Balance sheets that distinguish between current and noncurrent items are called **classified balance sheets.** To enhance the usefulness of accounting information, most real-world balance sheets are classified. However, there is no requirement to present information in this fashion. Exhibit 6–5 is an example of a classified balance sheet.

Liquidity Versus Solvency

Liquidity, as explained, deals with the ability to generate short-term cash flows. **Solvency** is the ability to repay liabilities in the long run. Liquidity and solvency are both important to the

Exhibit 6–5

LIMBAUGH COMPANY
Classified Balance Sheet
As of December 31, 2006

Assets

Current Assets		
Cash	$ 20,000	
Accounts Receivable	35,000	
Inventory	230,000	
Prepaid Rent	3,600	
Total Current Assets		$288,600
Property, Plant, and Equipment		
Office Equipment	$ 80,000	
Less: Accumulated Depreciation	(25,000)	55,000
Building	340,000	
Less: Accumulated Depreciation	(40,000)	300,000
Land	120,000	
Total Property, Plant, and Equipment		475,000
Total Assets		$763,600

Liabilities and Stockholders' Equity

Current Liabilities		
Accounts Payable	$ 32,000	
Notes Payable	120,000	
Salaries Payable	32,000	
Unearned Revenue	9,800	
Total Current Liabilities		$193,800
Long-Term Liabilities		
Note Payable		100,000
Total Liabilities		293,800
Stockholders' Equity		
Common Stock	200,000	
Retained Earnings	269,800	469,800
Total Liabilities and Stockholders' Equity		$763,600

survival of a business, but one may be more important to a particular user than the other. If a bank is considering loaning a company money that must be repaid in six months, obviously the bank is concerned more with the company's liquidity. An investor thinking of purchasing the company's 20-year bonds is interested in the company's solvency as well as its liquidity because a company that cannot pay its bills in the short term will not be around to repay the bonds 20 years from now.

Current Ratio

LO9 Use the current ratio to assess the level of liquidity.

Financial statement users calculate several ratios in the process of making the comparisons needed to evaluate a company's liquidity and solvency. The debt to assets ratio introduced in Chapter 3 is one tool used to examine solvency. The primary ratio used to evaluate liquidity is the **current ratio,** defined as

$$\frac{\text{Current assets}}{\text{Current liabilities}}$$

Since current assets normally exceed current liabilities, this ratio usually produces a result larger than 100 percent. Many individuals find large percentages difficult to interpret. Accordingly, the current ratio is frequently expressed as a decimal rather than as a percentage. For example, a company with $250 in current assets and $100 in current liabilities has a current ratio of 2.5 to 1 ($250 ÷ $100 = $2.50 in current assets for every $1 in current liabilities). This is, of course, the same as saying that current assets are 250 percent of current liabilities. However, as stated earlier, traditional practice tends to favor the decimal expression. Accordingly, this book uses that format when making reference to the current ratio.

Real-World Data

The current ratio is one of the most commonly used ratios to analyze accounting information. Current ratios can be too high, suggesting that the company has more assets available to pay current liabilities than are needed. This result would suggest that earnings could probably be improved by converting some of the short-term assets to longer-term investments that yield a higher return. Indeed, given the desire for profit maximization, you are likely to find more real-world companies with ratios that are too low than companies with those that are too high.

Exhibit 6–6 presents the 2000 current ratios and debt to assets ratios expressed in decimal format for six real-world companies from three different industries.

Which of these companies is exposed to the highest level of financial risk? Perhaps, the answer is Kroger because it has the highest debt to assets ratio. Notice that the electric utilities have higher debt to assets ratios and lower current ratios than those of the companies in the building supplies business. Does this mean that electric utilities are riskier investments? Not necessarily; since the companies are in different industries, one must be careful when comparing ratios. Utilities companies traditionally have high debt to asset ratios, so those of Duke Energy and Reliant Energy are not unusual. Remember that financial leverage can increase

Exhibit 6–6			
Industry	**Company**	**Current Ratio**	**Debt to Assets Ratio**
Electric utilities	Duke Energy	0.96	0.80
	Reliant Energy	0.62	0.80
Grocery stores	Kroger	0.97	0.83
	Safeway	0.85	0.66
Building supplies	Home Depot	1.77	0.30
	Lowe's	1.43	0.52

profitability if the return on invested funds exceeds the cost of interest, so high debt levels can be productive if a company operates in a relatively stable industry.

Finally, note that the debt to assets ratios for the companies tend to be "grouped by industry," with Kroger being an exception. Current ratios do vary somewhat among different industries, but they probably do not vary as much as the debt to asset ratios. Why? Because all companies, regardless of how they finance their total assets, must keep sufficient current assets on hand to repay current liabilities.

The policies and procedures used to provide reasonable assurance that the objectives of an enterprise will be accomplished are called *internal controls,* which can be subdivided into two categories: accounting controls and administrative controls. *Accounting controls* are composed of procedures designed to safeguard the assets and ensure that the accounting records contain reliable information. *Administrative controls* are designed to evaluate performance and the degree of compliance with company policies and public laws. While the mechanics of internal control systems vary from company to company, the more prevalent features include the following:

a look
back

1. *Separation of duties.* Whenever possible, the functions of authorization, recording, and custody should be exercised by different individuals.
2. *Quality of employees.* Employees should be qualified to competently perform the duties that are assigned to them. The enterprise must establish hiring practices to screen out unqualified candidates. Furthermore, procedures should be established to ensure that employees receive the appropriate training necessary to maintain competence.

focus on International Issues

Why Are These Balance Sheets Backward?

Many of the differences in accounting rules used around the world would be difficult to detect by merely comparing financial statements from companies in different countries. For example, if a balance sheet for a U.S. company and one for a U.K. company both report an asset called *land,* it might not be clear whether the reported amounts were computed by using the same measurement rules or different measurement rules. Did both companies use historical cost as a basis for measurement? Perhaps not, but this would be difficult to determine by merely comparing balance sheets from two countries.

However, one difference between financial reporting in the United Kingdom and the United States that is very obvious is the arrangement of assets on the balance sheet. In this chapter, we explain that U.S. GAAP require current assets to be shown first and noncurrent assets second; the same is true of liabilities. In the United Kingdom, noncurrent assets appear first, followed by current assets; however, liabilities are shown in the same order as in the United States. In other countries (e.g., France), both assets and liabilities are shown with noncurrent items first. The accounting rules of some countries require that equity be shown before liabilities; this is the opposite of the U.S. GAAP.

Therefore, to someone who learned accounting in the United States, the balance sheets of companies from some countries may appear "backward" or "upside down."

No matter in what order the assets, liabilities, and equity accounts are arranged on a company's balance sheet, one accounting concept is true throughout the free world:

Assets = Liabilities + Equity

3. *Bonded employees.* Employees in sensitive positions should be covered by a fidelity bond that provides insurance to reimburse losses that are due to illegal actions committed by employees.

4. *Periods of absence.* Employees should be required to take extended absences from their jobs so that they are not always present to hide unscrupulous or illegal activities.

5. *Procedures manual.* To promote compliance, the procedures for processing transactions should be clearly described in a manual.

6. *Authority and responsibility.* To motivate employees and promote effective control, clear lines of authority and responsibility should be established.

7. *Prenumbered documents.* Numbered documents minimize the likelihood of missing or duplicate documents. Accordingly, prenumbered forms should be used for all important documents such as purchase orders, receiving reports, invoices, and checks.

8. *Physical control.* Locks, fences, security personnel, and other physical devices should be employed to safeguard assets.

9. *Performance evaluation.* Because few people can evaluate their own performance objectively, independent performance evaluations should be performed. Substandard performance will likely persist unless employees are encouraged to take corrective action.

10. *Internal control in computer systems.* The basic internal control features discussed are applicable to computer systems as well as manual systems.

Because cash is so important to businesses and because some persons find it tempting to steal, much of the discussion of internal controls in this chapter related specifically to cash controls. Special procedures should be employed to control the receipts and payments of cash. One of the most common control devices is the use of *checking accounts.*

Bank statements should be compared with internal accounting records through a procedure known as a *bank reconciliation.* One common way to accomplish a reconciliation is to determine the true cash balance based on both bank and book records. Typical items shown on a bank reconciliation include the following:

Unadjusted Bank Balance	xxx	Unadjusted Book Balance	xxx
Add		Add	
Deposits in Transit	xxx	Interest Revenue	xxx
		Collection of Receivables	xxx
Subtract		Subtract	
Outstanding Checks	xxx	Bank Service Charges	xxx
		NSF Checks	xxx
True Cash Balance	xxx	True Cash Balance	xxx

Attaining equality between the two true cash balances provides evidence of accuracy in the accounting for cash transactions.

Another commonly used internal control device for the protection of cash is a *petty cash* fund. Normally, an employee who is designated as the petty cash custodian is entrusted with a small amount of cash. The custodian reimburses employees for small expenditures made on behalf of the organization and collects receipts from the employees at the time of the reimbursement. At any point in time, the receipts plus the remaining cash should equal the amount of funds entrusted to the custodian. Journal entries to recognize the expenses incurred are made at the time the fund is replenished.

Finally, the chapter discussed the assessment of organizational *liquidity.* The *current ratio* is determined by dividing current assets by current liabilities. The higher the ratio, the more liquid the organization.

a look forward

The material in Chapters 6 through 11 is organized primarily in the order of the arrangement of a classified balance sheet, which was discussed in this chapter. This chapter presented several issues related to accounting for cash; Chapter 7 addresses issues related to accounting for accounts receivable, and so on, until Chapter 11, which addresses issues related to accounting for equity. Stockholders' equity is the final section of a classified balance sheet.

The following information pertains to Terry's Pest Control Company (TPCC) for July:

1. The unadjusted bank balance at July 31 was $870.
2. The bank statement included the following items:
   a. A $60 credit memo for interest earned by TPCC.
   b. A $200 NSF check made payable to TPCC.
   c. A $110 debit memo for bank service charges.
3. The unadjusted book balance at July 31 was $1,400.
4. A comparison of the bank statement with company accounting records disclosed the following:
   a. A $400 deposit in transit at July 31.
   b. Outstanding checks totaling $120 at the end of the month.

Required

a. Prepare a bank reconciliation statement.
b. Prepare in general journal format the entries necessary to adjust TPCC's cash account to its true balance.

Solution to Requirement a

TERRY'S PEST CONTROL COMPANY Bank Reconciliation July 31	
Unadjusted bank balance	$ 870
Add: Deposits in transit	400
Less: Outstanding checks	(120)
True cash balance	$1,150
Unadjusted book balance	$1,400
Add: Interest revenue	60
Less: NSF check	(200)
Less: Bank service charges	(110)
True cash balance	$1,150

Solution to Requirement b

	General Journal		
Ref.	Account Title	Debit	Credit
1.	Cash	60	
	Interest Revenue		60
2.	Accounts Receivable	200	
	Cash		200
3.	Service Charge Expense	110	
	Cash		110

QUESTIONS

1. What are the policies and procedures called that are used to provide reasonable assurance that the objectives of an enterprise will be accomplished?
2. What is the difference between accounting controls and administrative controls?
3. What are several features of a strong internal control system?
4. What is meant by *separation of duties*? Give an illustration.
5. What are the attributes of a high-quality employee?
6. What is a fidelity bond? Explain its purpose.
7. Why is it important that every employee periodically take a leave of absence or vacation?
8. What are the purpose and importance of a procedures manual?
9. What is the difference between specific and general authorizations?
10. Why should documents (checks, invoices, receipts) be prenumbered?
11. What procedures are important in the physical control of assets and accounting records?
12. What is the purpose of independent verification of performance?
13. What are the six control requirements for computer systems discussed in this chapter? Explain each.
14. What items are considered cash?
15. Why is cash more susceptible to theft or embezzlement than other assets?
16. Giving written copies of receipts to customers can help prevent what type of illegal acts?
17. What procedures can help to protect cash receipts?
18. What procedures can help protect cash disbursements?
19. What effect does a debit memo in a bank statement have on the Cash account? What effect does a credit memo in a bank statement have on the Cash account?
20. What information is normally included in a bank statement?
21. Why might a bank statement reflect a balance that is larger than the balance recorded in the depositor's books? What could cause the bank balance to be smaller than the book balance?
22. What is the purpose of a bank reconciliation?
23. What is an outstanding check?
24. What is a deposit in transit?
25. What is a certified check?
26. How is an NSF check accounted for in the accounting records?
27. What is the purpose of the Cash Short and Over account?
28. What is the purpose of a petty cash fund?
29. What types of expenditures are usually made from a petty cash fund?
30. What is the difference between a current asset and a noncurrent asset?
31. What are some common current assets?
32. What does the term *operating cycle* mean?
33. What are some common current liabilities?
34. What is a classified balance sheet?
35. What is the difference between the liquidity and the solvency of a business?
36. How does the arrangement of assets and liabilities on financial statements differ for the United States, the United Kingdom, and France?
37. The higher the current ratio, the better the company's financial condition. Do you agree or disagree with this statement? Explain.
38. Does a high (80 to 95 percent) debt to assets ratio mean that a business is in financial difficulty? What types of businesses traditionally operate with high debt to assets ratios?

EXERCISES—SERIES A

L.O. 2   **EXERCISE 6–1A** *Features of a Strong Internal Control System*

Required
List and describe nine features of a strong internal control system described in this chapter.

EXERCISE 6–2A *Internal Controls for a Computer System*

Required

Basic internal control features apply to computer systems, but additional controls are necessary. List and explain the six control requirements for computers discussed in this chapter.

EXERCISE 6–3A *Features of Internal Control Procedures for Cash*

Required

List and discuss effective internal control procedures that apply to cash.

EXERCISE 6–4A *Internal Control Procedures*

Dick Haney is opening a new business that will sell sporting goods. It will initially be a small operation, and he is concerned about the security of his assets. He will not be able to be at the business all of the time and will have to rely on his employees and internal control procedures to ensure that transactions are properly accounted for and assets are safeguarded. He will have a store manager and two other employees who will be sales personnel and stock personnel and who will also perform any other duties necessary. Dick will be in the business on a regular basis. He has come to you for advice.

Required

Write a memo to Dick outlining the procedures that he should implement to ensure that his store assets are protected and that the financial transactions are properly recorded.

EXERCISE 6–5A *Internal Controls to Prevent Theft*

Rhonda Cox worked as the parts manager for State Line Automobiles, a local automobile dealership. Rhonda was very dedicated and never missed a day of work. Since State Line was a small operation, she was the only employee in the parts department. Her duties consisted of ordering parts for stock and as needed for repairs, receiving the parts and checking them in, distributing them as needed to the shop or to customers for purchase, and keeping track of and taking the year-end inventory of parts. State Line decided to expand and needed to secure additional financing. The local bank agreed to a loan contingent on an audit of the dealership. One requirement of the audit was to oversee the inventory count of both automobiles and parts on hand. Rhonda was clearly nervous, explaining that she had just inventoried all parts in the parts department and supplied the auditors with a detailed list. The inventory showed parts on hand worth $225,000. This seemed a little excessive, and the accountants decided they needed to verify at least a substantial part of the inventory. When the auditors began their counts, a pattern began to develop. Each type of part seemed to be one or two items short when the actual count was taken. This raised more concern. Although Rhonda assured the auditors the parts were just misplaced, the auditors continued the count. After completing the count of parts on hand, the auditors could document only $155,000 of actual parts. Suddenly, Rhonda quit her job and moved to another state.

Required

a. What do you suppose caused the discrepancy between the actual count and the count that Rhonda had supplied?

b. What procedures could be put into place to prevent this type of problem?

EXERCISE 6–6A *Treatment of NSF Check*

The bank statement of Best Supplies included a $125 NSF check that one of Best's customers had written to pay for supplies purchased.

Required

a. Show the effects of recognizing the NSF check on the financial statements by recording the appropriate amounts in a horizontal statements model like the following one.

Assets		= Liab. +	Equity	Rev.	–	Exp.	=	Net Inc.	Cash Flow
Cash	+ Accts. Rec.								

b. Is the recognition of the NSF check on Best's books an asset source, use, or exchange transaction?

c. Suppose the customer redeems the check by giving Best $150 cash in exchange for the bad check. The additional $25 paid a service fee charged by Best. Show the effects on the financial statements in the horizontal statements model in Requirement *a*.

d. Is the receipt of cash referred to in Requirement *c* an asset source, use, or exchange transaction?

L.O. 5 **EXERCISE 6–7A** *Adjustments to the Balance per Books*

Required

Identify which of the following items are added to or subtracted from the unadjusted *book balance* to arrive at the true cash balance. Distinguish the additions from the subtractions by placing a + beside the items that are added to the unadjusted book balance and a − beside those that are subtracted from it. The first item is recorded as an example.

Reconciling Items	Book Balance Adjusted?	Added or Subtracted?
Charge for checks	Yes	—
NSF check from customer		
ATM fee		
Outstanding checks		
Interest revenue earned on the account		
Deposits in transit		
Service charge		
Automatic debit for utility bill		

L.O. 5 **EXERCISE 6–8A** *Adjustments to the Balance per Bank*

Required

Identify which of the following items are added to or subtracted from the unadjusted *bank balance* to arrive at the true cash balance. Distinguish the additions from the subtractions by placing a + beside the items that are added to the unadjusted bank balance and a − beside those that are subtracted from it. The first item is recorded as an example.

Reconciling Items	Bank Balance Adjusted?	Added or Subtracted?
NSF check from customer	No	NA
Interest revenue		
Bank service charge		
Outstanding checks		
Deposits in transit		
Debit memo		
Credit memo		
ATM fee		
Petty cash voucher		

L.O. 5 **EXERCISE 6–9A** *Adjusting the Cash Account*

As of May 31, 2004, the bank statement showed an ending balance of $14,625. The unadjusted Cash account balance was $14,330. The following information is available:

1. Deposit in transit, $1,590.
2. Credit memo in bank statement for interest earned in May, $20.
3. Outstanding check, $1,873.
4. Debit memo for service charge, $8.

Required

a. Determine the true cash balance by preparing a bank reconciliation as of May 31, 2004, using the preceding information.

b. Record in general journal format the adjusting entries necessary to correct the unadjusted book balance.

L.O. 5 **EXERCISE 6–10A** *Determining the True Cash Balance, Starting with the Unadjusted Bank Balance*

The following information is available for Hill Company for the month of August:

1. The unadjusted balance per the bank statement on August 31 was $75,925.
2. Deposits in transit on August 31 were $2,600.
3. A debit memo was included with the bank statement for a service charge of $20.
4. A $4,925 check written in August had not been paid by the bank.
5. The bank statement included a $1,000 credit memo for the collection of a note. The principal of the note was $950, and the interest collected was $50.

Required
Determine the true cash balance as of August 31. (*Hint:* It is not necessary to use all of the preceding items to determine the true balance.)

EXERCISE 6–11A *Determining the True Cash Balance, Starting with the Unadjusted Book Balance*

L.O. 5

Peery Company had an unadjusted cash balance of $5,600 as of April 30. The company's bank statement, also dated April 30, included a $75 NSF check written by one of Peery's customers. There were $625 in outstanding checks and $250 in deposits in transit as of April 30. According to the bank statement, service charges were $50, and the bank collected a $500 note receivable for Peery. The bank statement also showed $15 of interest revenue earned by Peery.

Required
Determine the true cash balance as of April 30. (*Hint:* It is not necessary to use all of the preceding items to determine the true balance.)

EXERCISE 6–12A *Effect of Establishing a Petty Cash Account*

L.O. 6

Belcher Transfer Company established a $200 petty cash fund on January 1, 2003.

Required
a. Is the establishment of the petty cash fund an asset source, use, or exchange transaction?
b. Record the establishment of the petty cash fund in a horizontal statements model like the following one:

Assets		= Liab. + Equity	Rev. − Exp. = Net Inc.	Cash Flow
Cash +	Petty Cash			

c. Record the establishment of the fund in general journal format.

EXERCISE 6–13A *Effect of Petty Cash Events on the Financial Statements*

L.O. 6

Xterra, Inc., established a petty cash fund of $300 on January 2. On January 31, the fund contained cash of $52.50 and vouchers for the following cash payments:

Postage	$65.00
Office supplies	80.75
Printing expense	10.50
Entertainment expense	88.25

The four distinct accounting events affecting the petty cash fund for the period were (1) establishment of the fund, (2) reimbursements made to employees, (3) recognition of expenses, and (4) replenishment of the fund.

Required
a. Record each of the four events in a horizontal statements model like the following one. In the Cash Flow column, indicate whether the item is an operating activity (OA), investing activity (IA), or a financing activity (FA). Use NA to indicate that an account was not affected by the event.

Assets		= Liab. + Equity	Rev. − Exp. = Net Inc.	Cash Flow
Cash +	Petty Cash			

b. Record the events in general journal format.

L.O. 6   EXERCISE 6–14A *Determining the Amount of Petty Cash Expense*

Consider the following events:
1. A petty cash fund of $150 was established on April 1, 2006.
2. Employees were reimbursed when they presented petty cash vouchers to the petty cash custodian.
3. On April 30, 2006, the petty cash fund contained vouchers totaling $125.20 plus $26.80 of currency.

Required
Answer the following questions:
a. How did the establishment of the petty cash fund affect (increase, decrease, or have no effect on) total assets?
b. What is the amount of total petty cash expenses to be recognized during April?
c. When are petty cash expenses recognized (at the time of establishment, reimbursement, or replenishment)?

L.O. 7   EXERCISE 6–15A *Preparing a Classified Balance Sheet*

Required
Use the following information to prepare a classified balance sheet for Borg Co. at the end of 2003.

Office Equipment	$26,500
Accounts Receivable	42,500
Accounts Payable	11,000
Cash	15,260
Common Stock	40,000
Long-Term Notes Payable	23,000
Merchandise Inventory	32,000
Retained Earnings	45,460
Prepaid Insurance	3,200

L.O. 8   EXERCISE 6–16A *Operating Cycle*

Portland Co. sells gifts and novelty items mostly on account. It takes an average of 90 days to sell its inventory and an average of 35 days to collect the accounts receivable.

Required
a. Draw a diagram of the operating cycle for Portland Co.
b. Compute the length of the operating cycle based on the information given.

PROBLEMS—SERIES A

L.O. 1, 2, 4   PROBLEM 6–17A *Using Internal Control to Restrict Illegal or Unethical Behavior*

Required
For each of the following fraudulent acts, describe one or more internal control procedures that could have prevented (or helped prevent) the problems.
a. Paula Wissel, the administrative assistant in charge of payroll, created a fictional employee, wrote weekly checks to the fictional employee, and then personally cashed the checks for her own benefit.
b. Larry Kent, the receiving manager of Southern Lumber, created a fictitious supplier named F&M Building Supply. F&M regularly billed Southern Lumber for supplies purchased. Kent had printed shipping slips and billing invoices with the name of the fictitious company and opened a post office box as the mailing address. Kent simply prepared a receiving report and submitted it for payment to the accounts payable department. The accounts payable clerk then paid the invoice when it was received because Kent acknowledged receipt of the supplies.
c. Holly Baker works at a local hobby shop and usually operates the cash register. She has developed a way to give discounts to her friends. When they come by, she rings a lower price or does not charge the friend for some of the material purchased. At first, Baker thought she would get caught, but no one seemed to notice. Indeed, she has become so sure that there is no way for the owner to find out that she has started taking home some supplies for her own personal use.

L.O. 5   PROBLEM 6–18A *Preparing a Bank Reconciliation*

Kevin Long owns a construction business, Long Builders Inc. The following cash information is available for the month of October, 2001.

As of October 31, the bank statement shows a balance of $8,000. The October 31 unadjusted balance in the Cash account of Long Builders Inc. is $8,580. A review of the bank statement revealed the following information:

1. A deposit of $2,000 on October 31, 2001, does not appear on the October 31 bank statement.
2. A debit memo for $50 was included in the bank statement for the purchase of a new supply of checks.
3. When checks written during the month were compared with those paid by the bank, three checks amounting to $1,200 were found to be outstanding.
4. It was discovered that a check to pay for equipment was correctly written and paid by the bank for $3,030 but was recorded on the books as $3,300.

Required
a. Prepare a bank reconciliation at the end of October showing the true cash balance.
b. Prepare any necessary journal entries to adjust the books to the true cash balance.

PROBLEM 6–19A *Missing Information in a Bank Reconciliation*

L.O. 5

The following data apply to Barkley Flying Service for April 2007:
1. Balance per the bank on April 30, $10,000.
2. Deposits in transit not recorded by the bank, $1,000.
3. Bank error; check written by Barkley Office Supply was drawn on Barkley Flying Service's account, $800.
4. The following checks written and recorded by Barkley Flying Service were not included in the bank statement:

2012	$ 220
2052	380
2055	1,700

5. Note collected by the bank, $450.
6. Service charge for collection of note, $15.
7. The bookkeeper recorded a check written for $548 to pay for April's repair expense as $845 in the cash disbursements journal.
8. Bank service charge in addition to the note collection fee, $40.
9. NSF checks returned by the bank, $250.

Required
Determine the amount of the unadjusted cash balance per Barkley Flying Service's books.

PROBLEM 6–20A *Adjustments to the Cash Account Based on the Bank Reconciliation*

L.O. 5

Required
Determine whether the following items in Home Imports' bank reconciliation require adjusting or correcting entries on Home Imports' books. When an entry is required, record it in general journal format.
a. Home Imports wrote an $880 certified check that was still outstanding as of the closing date of the bank statement.
b. The bank collected $8,000 of Home Imports' accounts receivable. Home Imports had instructed its customers to send their payments directly to the bank.
c. The bank mistakenly gave Imports, Inc., credit for a $500 deposit made by Home Imports.
d. Deposits in transit were $4,550.
e. Home Imports' bank statement contained a $375 NSF check. Home Imports had received the check from a customer and had included it in one of its bank deposits.
f. The bank statement indicated that Home Imports earned $75 of interest revenue.
g. Home Imports' accountant mistakenly recorded a $156 check that was written to purchase supplies as $651.
h. Bank service charges for the month were $40.
i. The bank reconciliation disclosed the fact that $1,000 had been stolen from Home Imports' business.
j. Outstanding checks amounted to $1,500.

PROBLEM 6–21A *Bank Reconciliation and Adjustments to the Cash Account*

L.O. 5

The following information is available for Oceanside Hotel for October 2005:

Bank Statement
STATE BANK
Bolta Vista, NV 10001

Oceanside Hotel 10 Main Street Bolta Vista, NV 10001	Account number 12-4567 October 31, 2005

Beginning balance 9/30/2005	$ 8,831
Total deposits and other credits	29,075
Total checks and other debits	23,906
Ending balance 10/31/2005	14,000

Checks and Debits		Deposits and Credits		
Check No.	Amount	Date		Amount
2350	$3,761	October	1	$1,102
2351	1,643	October	10	6,498
2352	8,000	October	15	4,929
2354	2,894	October	21	6,174
2355	1,401	October	26	5,963
2357	6,187	October	30	2,084
DM	20	CM		2,325

The following is a list of checks and deposits recorded on the books of the Oceanside Hotel for October 2005:

Date		Check No.	Amount of Check	Date		Amount of Deposit
October	2	2351	$1,643	October	8	$6,498
October	4	2352	8,000	October	14	4,929
October	10	2353	1,500	October	21	6,174
October	10	2354	2,894	October	26	5,963
October	15	2355	1,401	October	29	2,084
October	20	2356	745	October	30	3,550
October	22	2357	6,187			

Other Information
1. Check no. 2350 was outstanding from September.
2. Credit memo was for collection of notes receivable.
3. All checks were paid at the correct amount.
4. Debit memo was for printed checks.
5. The September 30 bank reconciliation showed a deposit in transit of $1,102.
6. The unadjusted Cash account balance at October 31 was $13,000.

Required
a. Prepare the bank reconciliation for Oceanside Hotel at the end of October.
b. Record in general journal form any necessary entries to the Cash account to adjust it to the true cash balance.

L.O. 5   PROBLEM 6–22A *Effect of Adjustments to Cash on the Accounting Equation*

After reconciling its bank account, Putt Equipment Company made the following adjusting entries:

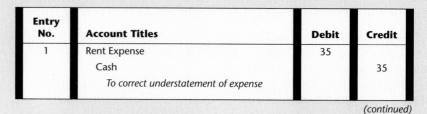

Entry No.	Account Titles	Debit	Credit
1	Rent Expense	35	
	Cash		35
	To correct understatement of expense		

Entry No.	Account Titles	Debit	Credit
2	Service Charge Expense	15	
	Cash		15
	To record bank service charge		
3	Cash	175	
	Accounts Receivable		175
	To record bank collection		
4	Cash	40	
	Interest Revenue		40
	To record interest revenue		
5	Accounts Receivable, K. Wilson	250	
	Cash		250
	To record NSF check from Wilson		

Required

Identify the event depicted in each journal entry as asset source (AS), asset use (AU), asset exchange (AE), or claims exchange (CE). Also explain how each entry affects the accounting equation by placing a + for increase, − for decrease, or NA for not affected under the following components of the accounting equation. The first event is recorded as an example.

Event No.	Type of Event	Assets	=	Liabilities	+	Common Stock	−	Retained Earnings
1	AU	−		NA		NA		−

PROBLEM 6–23A *Bank Reconciliation and Internal Control*   L.O. 2, 4, 5

Following is a bank reconciliation for Pete's Sandwich Shop for May 31, 2006:

	Cash Account	Bank Statement
Balance as of 5/31/06	$25,000	$22,000
Deposit in transit		4,250
Outstanding checks		(465)
Note collected by bank	1,815	
Bank service charge	(30)	
Automatic payment on loan	(1,000)	
Adjusted cash balance as of 5/31/06	$25,785	$25,785

Because of limited funds, Pete's employed only one accountant who was responsible for receiving cash, recording receipts and disbursements, preparing deposits, and preparing the bank reconciliation. The accountant left the company on June 8, 2006, after preparing the preceding statement. His replacement compared the checks returned with the bank statement to the cash disbursements journal and found the total of outstanding checks to be $5,000.

Required

a. Prepare a corrected bank reconciliation statement.
b. What is the total amount of cash missing, and how was the difference between the "true cash" per the bank and the "true cash" per the books hidden on the reconciliation prepared by the former employee?
c. What could Pete's do to avoid cash theft in the future?

PROBLEM 6–24A *Petty Cash Fund*   L.O. 6

The following data pertain to the petty cash fund of Crain Company:
1. The petty cash fund was created on an imprest basis at $100 on March 1.

2. On March 31, a physical count of the fund disclosed $8 in currency and coins, vouchers authorizing meal allowances totaling $42, vouchers authorizing purchase of postage stamps of $32, and vouchers for payment of delivery charges of $20.

Required

a. Prepare all general journal entries necessary to (1) establish the fund, (2) reimburse employees, and (3) replenish the fund as of March 31. (*Hint:* Journal entries may not be required for all three events.)

b. Explain how the Cash Short and Over account required in this case affects the income statement.

c. Identify the event depicted in each journal entry recorded in Requirement *a* as asset source (AS), asset use (AU), asset exchange (AE), or claims exchange (CE).

d. Record the effects on the financial statements of the events in Requirement *a* using a horizontal statements model like the following one. In the Cash Flow column, indicate whether the item is an operating activity (OA), investing activity (IA), or financing activity (FA). Use NA to indicate that an account was not affected by the event.

Assets			=	Liab.	+	S. Equity	Rev.	−	Exp.	=	Net Inc.	Cash Flow
Cash	+	Petty Cash										

L.O. 7   **PROBLEM 6–25A** *Classified Balance Sheet and Multistep Income Statement*

Required

Use the following information to prepare a classified balance sheet and a multistep income statement for Nixon Enterprises for the year end of December 31, 2005.

Accounts Receivable	$ 4,000
Common Stock	41,000
Salaries Expense	118,000
Interest Expense	12,200
Cash	3,600
Accounts Payable	1,000
Retained Earnings	42,000
Accumulated Depreciation	4,800
Unearned Revenue	9,600
Land	50,000
Salaries Payable	1,800
Cost of Goods Sold	174,000
Supplies	500
Note Receivable (long term)	6,000
Inventory	9,000
Office Equipment	58,000
Gain on Sale of Equipment	6,400
Interest Receivable (short term)	240
Operating Expenses	19,000
Sales Revenue	340,000
Prepaid Rent	9,600
Interest Payable (short term)	740
Interest Revenue	420
Notes Payable (long term)	40,000

EXERCISES—SERIES B

L.O. 1   **EXERCISE 6–1B** *Internal Control Procedures*

Required

a. Name and describe the two categories of internal controls.

b. What is the purpose of internal controls?

EXERCISE 6–2B *Internal Controls for Computer Systems*

L.O. 3

Required

a. Why are special internal control procedures needed for computer systems?

b. What does the term *audit around the computer* mean?

EXERCISE 6–3B *Internal Control for Cash*

L.O. 4

Required

a. Why are special controls needed for cash?

b. What is included in the definition of *cash*?

EXERCISE 6–4B *Internal Control Procedures to Prevent Embezzlement*

L.O. 1, 2

Bell Gates was in charge of the returns department at The Software Company. She was responsible for evaluating returned merchandise. She sent merchandise that was reusable back to the warehouse, where it was restocked in the supply of inventory. Gates was also responsible for taking the merchandise that she determined to be defective to the city dump for disposal. She had agreed to buy a friend a tax planning program at a discount through her contacts at work. That is when the idea came to her. She could simply classify one of the reusable returns as defective and bring it home instead of taking it to the dump. She did so and made a quick $150. She was happy, and her friend was ecstatic; he was able to buy a $400 software package for only $150. He told his friends about the deal, and soon Gates had a regular set of customers. She was caught when a retail store owner complained to the marketing manager that his pricing strategy was being undercut by The Software Company's direct sales to the public. The marketing manager was suspicious because The Software Company had no direct marketing program. When the outside sales were ultimately traced back to Gates, the company discovered that it had lost over $10,000 in sales revenue because of her criminal activity.

Required

Identify an internal control procedure that could have prevented the company's losses. Explain how the procedure would have stopped the embezzlement.

EXERCISE 6–5B *Internal Control Procedures to Prevent Deception*

L.O. 1, 2

Emergency Care Medical Centers (ECMC) hired a new physician, Ken Major, who was an immediate success. Everyone loved his bedside manner; he could charm the most cantankerous patient. Indeed, he was a master salesman as well as an expert physician. Unfortunately, Major misdiagnosed a case that resulted in serious consequences to the patient. The patient filed suit against ECMC. In preparation for the defense, ECMC's attorneys discovered that Major was indeed an exceptional salesman. He had worked for several years as district marketing manager for a pharmaceutical company. In fact, he was not a physician at all! He had changed professions without going to medical school. He had lied on his application form. His knowledge of medical terminology had enabled him to fool everyone. ECMC was found negligent and lost a $3 million lawsuit.

Required

Identify the relevant internal control procedures that could have prevented the company's losses. Explain how these procedures would have prevented Major's deception.

EXERCISE 6–6B *Treatment of NSF Check*

L.O. 5

Clark Stationery's bank statement contained a $300 NSF check that one of its customers had written to pay for supplies purchased.

Required

a. Show the effects of recognizing the NSF check on the financial statements by recording the appropriate amounts in a horizontal statements model like the following one:

Assets		=	Liab.	+	S. Equity	Rev.	−	Exp.	=	Net Inc.	Cash Flow
Cash	+ Accts. Rec.										

b. Is the recognition of the NSF check on Clark's books an asset source, use, or exchange transaction?

c. Suppose the customer redeems the check by giving Clark $320 cash in exchange for the bad check. The additional $20 paid a service fee charged by Clark. Show the effects on the financial statements in the horizontal statements model in Requirement *a*.

d. Is the receipt of cash referenced in Requirement *c* an asset source, use, or exchange transaction?

L.O. 5 **EXERCISE 6–7B** *Adjustments to the Balance per Books*

Required

Identify which of the following items are added to or subtracted from the unadjusted *book balance* to arrive at the true cash balance. Distinguish the additions from the subtractions by placing a + beside the items that are added to the unadjusted book balance and a − beside those that are subtracted from it. The first item is recorded as an example.

Reconciling Items	Book Balance Adjusted?	Added or Subtracted?
Interest revenue	Yes	+
Deposits in transit		
Debit memo		
Service charge		
Charge for checks		
NSF check from customer		
Note receivable collected by the bank		
Outstanding checks		
Credit memo		

L.O. 5 **EXERCISE 6–8B** *Adjustments to the Balance per Bank*

Required

Identify which of the following items are added to or subtracted from the unadjusted *bank balance* to arrive at the true cash balance. Distinguish the additions from the subtractions by placing a + beside the items that are added to the unadjusted bank balance and a − beside those that are subtracted from it. The first item is recorded as an example.

Reconciling Items	Book Balance Adjusted?	Added or Subtracted?
Deposits in transit	Yes	+
Debit memo		
Credit memo		
Certified checks		
Petty cash voucher		
NSF check from customer		
Interest revenue		
Bank service charge		
Outstanding checks		

L.O. 5 **EXERCISE 6–9B** *Adjusting the Cash Account*

As of June 30, 2006, the bank statement showed an ending balance of $13,879.85. The unadjusted Cash account balance was $13,483.75. The following information is available:

1. Deposit in transit, $1,476.30.

2. Credit memo in bank statement for interest earned in June, $35.

3. Outstanding check, $1,843.74.

4. Debit memo for service charge, $6.34.

Required

a. Determine the true cash balance by preparing a bank reconciliation as of June 30, 2006, using the preceding information.

b. Record in general journal format the adjusting entries necessary to correct the unadjusted book balance.

EXERCISE 6–10B *Determining the True Cash Balance, Starting with the Unadjusted*   **L.O. 5**
                    Bank Balance

The following information is available for Babin Company for the month of June:
1. The unadjusted balance per the bank statement on June 30 was $68,714.35.
2. Deposits in transit on June 30 were $1,464.95.
3. A debit memo was included with the bank statement for a service charge of $25.38.
4. A $4,745.66 check written in June had not been paid by the bank.
5. The bank statement included a $944 credit memo for the collection of a note. The principal of the note was $859, and the interest collected amounted to $85.

Required
Determine the true cash balance as of June 30. (*Hint:* It is not necessary to use all of the preceding items to determine the true balance.)

EXERCISE 6–11B *Determining the True Cash Balance, Starting with the Unadjusted*   **L.O. 5**
                    Book Balance

Kinard Company had an unadjusted cash balance of $6,450 as of May 31. The company's bank statement, also dated May 31, included a $38 NSF check written by one of Kinard's customers. There were $548.60 in outstanding checks and $143.74 in deposits in transit as of May 31. According to the bank statement, service charges were $30, and the bank collected a $450 note receivable for Kinard. The bank statement also showed $18 of interest revenue earned by Kinard.

Required
Determine the true cash balance as of May 31. (*Hint:* It is not necessary to use all of the preceding items to determine the true balance.)

EXERCISE 6–12B *Effect of Establishing a Petty Cash Account*   **L.O. 6**

Cole Company established a $300 petty cash fund on January 1, 2003.

Required
a. Is the establishment of the petty cash fund an asset source, use, or exchange transaction?
b. Record the establishment of the petty cash fund in a horizontal statements model like the following one:

Assets		= Liab. +	S. Equity	Rev.	−	Exp.	=	Net Inc.	Cash Flow
Cash	+ Petty Cash								

c. Record the establishment of the fund in general journal format.

EXERCISE 6–13B *Effect of Petty Cash Events on the Financial Statements*   **L.O. 6**

Family Vision Center established a petty cash fund of $100 on January 2. On January 31, the fund contained cash of $16.75 and vouchers for the following cash payments:

Postage	$34.68
Office supplies	18.43
Printing expense	7.40
Transportation expense	23.92

The four distinct accounting events affecting the petty cash fund for the period were (1) establishment of the fund, (2) reimbursements made to employees, (3) recognition of expenses, and (4) replenishment of the fund.

Required
a. Record each of the four events in a horizontal statements model like the following one. In the Cash Flow column, indicate whether the item is an operating activity (OA), investing activity (IA), or a financing activity (FA). Use NA to indicate that an account was not affected by the event.

Assets		= Liab.	+	S. Equity	Rev.	−	Exp.	=	Net Inc.	Cash Flow
Cash	+ Petty Cash									

b. Record the events in general journal format.

L.O. 6   **EXERCISE 6–14B** *Determining the Amount of Petty Cash Expense*

Consider the following events:
1. A petty cash fund of $220 was established on April 1, 2008.
2. Employees were reimbursed when they presented petty cash vouchers to the petty cash custodian.
3. On April 30, 2008, the petty cash fund contained vouchers totaling $184.93 plus $28.84 of currency.

Required
Answer the following questions:
a. How did the establishment of the petty cash fund affect (increase, decrease, or have no effect on) total assets?
b. What is the amount of total petty cash expenses to be recognized during April?
c. When are petty cash expenses recognized (at the time of establishment, reimbursement, or replenishment)?

L.O. 7   **EXERCISE 6–15B** *Preparing a Classified Balance Sheet*

Required
Use the following information to prepare a classified balance sheet for Coleman Co. at the end of 2003.

Accounts Receivable	$12,150
Accounts Payable	5,500
Cash	10,992
Common Stock	12,000
Land	12,500
Long-Term Notes Payable	11,500
Merchandise Inventory	16,000
Retained Earnings	22,642

L.O. 8   **EXERCISE 6–16B** *Operating Cycle*

O'Conner Co. sells fine silk articles mostly on account. O'Conner Co. takes an average of 80 days to sell its inventory and an average of 42 days to collect the accounts receivable.

Required
a. Draw a diagram of the operating cycle for O'Conner Co.
b. Compute the length of the operating cycle based on the information given.

PROBLEMS—SERIES B

L.O. 1, 3, 4   **PROBLEM 6–17B** *Using Internal Control to Restrict Illegal or Unethical Behavior*

Required
For each of the following fraudulent acts, describe one or more internal control procedures that could have prevented (or helped prevent) the problems.
a. Everyone in the office has noticed what a dedicated employee Jennifer Reidel is. She never misses work, not even for a vacation. Reidel is in charge of the petty cash fund. She transfers funds from the company's bank account to the petty cash account on an as-needed basis. During a surprise audit, the petty cash fund was found to contain fictitious receipts. Over a three-year period, Reidel had used more than $4,000 of petty cash to pay for personal expenses.
b. Bill Bruton was hired as the vice president of the manufacturing division of a corporation. His impressive resume listed a master's degree in business administration from a large state university and numerous collegiate awards and activities, when in fact Bruton had only a high school diploma. In a

short time, the company was in poor financial condition because of his inadequate knowledge and bad decisions.

c. Havolene Manufacturing has good internal control over its manufacturing materials inventory. However, office supplies are kept on open shelves in the employee break room. The office supervisor has noticed that he is having to order paper, tape, staplers, and pens on an increasingly frequent basis.

PROBLEM 6–18B *Preparing a Bank Reconciliation*   L.O. 5

Bob Carson owns a card shop, We Trade. The following cash information is available for the month of August, 2006.

As of August 31, the bank statement shows a balance of $17,000. The August 31 unadjusted balance in the Cash account of We Trade is $16,000. A review of the bank statement revealed the following information:

1. A deposit of $2,260 on August 31, 2006, does not appear on the August bank statement.
2. It was discovered that a check to pay for baseball cards was correctly written and paid by the bank for $4,040 but was recorded on the books as $4,400.
3. When checks written during the month were compared with those paid by the bank, three checks amounting to $3,000 were found to be outstanding.
4. A debit memo for $100 was included in the bank statement for the purchase of a new supply of checks.

Required
a. Prepare a bank reconciliation at the end of August showing the true cash balance.
b. Prepare any necessary journal entries to adjust the books to the true cash balance.

PROBLEM 6–19B *Missing Information in a Bank Reconciliation*   L.O. 5

The following data apply to Best Auto Supply, Inc., for May 2007.
1. Balance per the bank on May 31, $8,000.
2. Deposits in transit not recorded by the bank, $975.
3. Bank error; check written by Allen Auto Supply was drawn on Best Auto Supply's account, $650.
4. The following checks written and recorded by Best Auto Supply were not included in the bank statement:

3013	$ 385
3054	735
3056	1,900

5. Note collected by the bank, $500.
6. Service charge for collection of note, $10.
7. The bookkeeper recorded a check written for $188 to pay for the May utilities expense as $888 in the cash disbursements journal.
8. Bank service charge in addition to the note collection fee, $25.
9. Customer checks returned by the bank as NSF, $125.

Required
Determine the amount of the unadjusted cash balance per Best Auto Supply's books.

PROBLEM 6–20B *Adjustments to the Cash Account Based on the Bank Reconciliation*   L.O. 5

Required
Determine whether the following items included in Curtis Company's bank reconciliation will require adjusting or correcting entries on Curtis' books. When an entry is required, record it in general journal format.
a. An $877 deposit was recorded by the bank as $778.
b. Four checks totaling $450 written during the month of January were not included with the January bank statement.
c. A $54 check written to Office Max for office supplies was recorded in the general journal as $45.
d. The bank statement indicated that the bank had collected a $330 note for Curtis.
e. Curtis recorded $500 of receipts on January 31, 2006, which was deposited in the night depository of the bank. These deposits were not included in the bank statement.

f. Service charges of $22 for the month of January were listed on the bank statement.

g. The bank charged a $297 check drawn on Cave Restaurant to Curtis' account. The check was included in Curtis' bank statement.

h. A check of $31 was returned to the bank because of insufficient funds and was noted on the bank statement. Curtis received the check from a customer and thought that it was good when it was deposited into the account.

L.O. 5   PROBLEM 6–21B *Bank Reconciliation and Adjustments to the Cash Account*

The following information is available for Cooters Garage for March 2002:

BANK STATEMENT
HAZARD STATE BANK
215 MAIN STREET
HAZARD, GA 30321

Cooters Garage	Account number
629 Main Street	62-00062
Hazard, GA 30321	March 31, 2002

Beginning balance 3/1/2002	$15,000.00
Total deposits and other credits	7,000.00
Total checks and other debits	6,000.00
Ending balance 3/31/2002	16,000.00

Checks and Debits		Deposits and Credits	
Check No.	Amount	Date	Amount
1462	$ 1,163.00	March 1	$ 1,000.00
1463	62.00	March 2	1,340.00
1464	1,235.00	March 6	210.00
1465	750.00	March 12	1,940.00
1466	1,111.00	March 17	855.00
1467	964.00	March 22	1,480.00
DM	15.00	CM	175.00
1468	700.00		

The following is a list of checks and deposits recorded on the books of Cooters Garage for March 2002:

Date	Check No.	Amount of Check	Date	Amount of Deposit
March 1	1463	$ 62.00	March 1	$1,340.00
March 5	1464	1,235.00	March 5	210.00
March 6	1465	750.00		
March 9	1466	1,111.00	March 10	1,940.00
March 10	1467	964.00		
March 14	1468	70.00	March 16	855.00
March 19	1469	1,500.00	March 19	1,480.00
March 28	1470	102.00	March 29	2,000.00

Other Information

1. Check no. 1462 was outstanding from February.
2. A credit memo for collection of accounts receivable was included in the bank statement.
3. All checks were paid at the correct amount.
4. The bank statement included a debit memo for service charges.
5. The February 28 bank reconciliation showed a deposit in transit of $1,000.
6. Check no. 1468 was for the purchase of equipment.
7. The unadjusted Cash account balance at March 31 was $16,868.

Required

a. Prepare the bank reconciliation for Cooters Garage at the end of March.

b. Record in general journal form any necessary entries to the Cash account to adjust it to the true cash balance.

PROBLEM 6–22B *Effect of Adjustments to Cash on the Accounting Equation*   **L.O. 5**

After reconciling its bank account, Monroe Company made the following adjusting entries:

Entry No.	Account Title	Debit	Credit
1	Cash	845	
	Accounts Receivable		845
	To record bank collection		
2	Cash	44	
	Interest Revenue		44
	To record interest revenue		
3	Service Charge Expense	35	
	Cash		35
	To record bank service charge		
4	Accounts Receivable, D. Beat	174	
	Cash		174
	To record NSF check from Beat		
5	Cash	20	
	Supplies Expense		20
	To correct overstatement of expense		

Required

Identify the event depicted in each journal entry as asset source (AS), asset use (AU), asset exchange (AE), or claims exchange (CE). Also explain how each entry affects the accounting equation by placing a + for increase, − for decrease, or NA for not affected under the following components of the accounting equation. The first event is recorded as an example.

Event No.	Type of Event	Assets	=	Liabilities	+	Stockholders' Equity Common Stock	+	Retained Earnings
1	AE	+ −		NA		NA		NA

PROBLEM 6–23B *Bank Reconciliation and Internal Control*   **L.O. 2, 4, 5**

Following is a bank reconciliation for Park Company for June 30, 2005:

	Cash Account	Bank Statement
Balance as of 6/30/05	$1,618	$3,000
Deposit in transit		600
Outstanding checks		(1,507)
Note collected by bank	2,000	
Bank service charge	(25)	
NSF check	(1,500)	
Adjusted cash balance as of 6/30/05	$2,093	$2,093

When reviewing the bank reconciliation, Park's auditor was unable to locate any reference to the NSF check on the bank statement. Furthermore, the clerk who reconciles the bank account and records the adjusting entries could not find the actual NSF check that should have been included in the bank statement. Finally, there was no specific reference in the accounts receivable subsidiary account identifying a party who had written a bad check.

Required

a. Prepare the adjusting entry that the clerk would have made to record the NSF check.

b. Assume that the clerk who prepares the bank reconciliation and records the adjusting entries also makes bank deposits. Explain how the clerk could use a fictitious NSF check to hide the theft of cash.

c. How could Park Company avoid the theft of cash that is concealed by the use of fictitious NSF checks?

L.O. 6   **PROBLEM 6–24B** *Petty Cash Fund*

Hayes Co. established a petty cash fund by issuing a check for $250 and appointing Bob Potts as petty cash custodian. Potts had vouchers for the following petty cash payments during the month:

Stamps	$14.00
Miscellaneous items	25.00
Employee supper money	75.00
Taxi fare	80.00
Window-washing service	22.00

There was $32 of currency in the petty cash box at the time it was replenished.

Required

a. Prepare all general journal entries necessary to (1) establish the fund, (2) reimburse employees, (3) recognize expenses, and (4) replenish the fund. (*Hint:* Journal entries may not be required for all the events.)

b. Explain how the Cash Short and Over account required in this case will affect the income statement.

c. Identify the event depicted in each journal entry recorded in Requirement *a* as asset source (AS), asset use (AU), asset exchange (AE), or claims exchange (CE).

d. Record the effects of the events in Requirement *a* on the financial statements using a horizontal statements model like the following one. In the Cash Flow column, indicate whether the item is an operating activity (OA), investing activity (IA), or financing activity (FA). Use NA to indicate that an account was not affected by the event.

Assets		= Liab. + S. Equity	Rev. − Exp. = Net Inc.	Cash Flow
Cash + Petty Cash				

L.O. 7   **PROBLEM 6–25B** *Classified Balance Sheet and Multistep Income Statement*

Required

Use the following information to prepare a classified balance sheet as of December 31, 2004, and a multistep income statement for the year ending December 31, 2004.

Accounts Receivable	$ 6,000
Common Stock	68,000
Salaries Expense	154,000
Interest Expense	5,000
Cash	20,000
Accounts Payable	1,800
Retained Earnings 12/31	76,000
Accumulated Depreciation	10,000
Unearned Revenue	16,000
Land	90,000
Salaries Payable	3,400
Cost of Goods Sold	175,000
Supplies	900
Note Receivable (long term)	10,000
Inventory	16,000
Office Equipment	52,000
Gain on Sale of Equipment	10,000
Interest Receivable (short term)	400
Operating Expenses	34,000
Sales Revenue	400,000
Prepaid Rent	8,000
Interest Payable (short term)	1,200
Notes Payable (long term)	26,900
Interest Revenue	800

ANALYZE, THINK, **COMMUNICATE**

BUSINESS APPLICATIONS CASE *Dell's Annual Report*

ATC 6–1

Required

Using the Dell Computer Corporation financial statements in Appendix B, answer the following questions:

a. What is Dell's current ratio as of February 2, 2001?
b. Which of Dell's current assets had the largest balance at February 2, 2001?
c. What percentage of Dell's total assets consisted of current assets?
d. Does Dell have any restrictions placed on it by its creditors? (*Hint:* See page 36 of the company's 10-K report.)

GROUP ASSIGNMENT *Analyzing Financial Statements*

ATC 6–2

The following selected information was taken from the annual reports of three companies: Southwest Airlines, Pier 1 Imports, and Wendy's. Amounts are given in thousands of dollars.

	Company 1	Company 2	Company 3
Accounts Receivable	$ 76,530	$ 4,128	$ 66,755
Accounts Payable	160,891	105,541	107,157
Other Current Liabilities	707,622	4,845	105,457
Allowance for Depreciation	1,375,631	138,179	537,910
Cash	623,343	32,280	234,262
Property, Plant, and Equipment	4,811,324	355,015	1,803,410
Inventories	0	220,013	35,633
Retained Earnings	1,632,115	118,721	839,215
Common Stock	376,903	204,327	345,019
Other Current Assets	108,543	29,057	44,904
Other Long-Term Assets	4,051	67,954	294,626
Long-Term Liabilities	1,370,629	136,834	544,832

Required

a. Organize the class into three sections and divide each section into three groups of three to five students. Assign Company 1 to groups in section 1, Company 2 to groups in section 2, and Company 3 to groups in section 3.

Group Tasks

1. Identify the company that is represented by the financial data assigned to your group.
2. Prepare a classified balance sheet for the company assigned to your group.
3. Select a representative from a group in each section and put the balance sheet on the board.

Class Discussion

b. Discuss the balance sheets of each company and the rationale for matching the financial information with the company.

REAL-WORLD CASE *Whose Numbers Are They Anyway?*

ATC 6–3

The following excerpt, sometimes referred to as *management's statement of responsibility,* was taken from JC Penney's 10-K report for the fiscal year ended January 27, 2001. The authors have italicized and numbered selected portions of the excerpt.

Company Statement on Financial Information (partial)

  [1] *The Company is responsible for the information presented in this Annual Report.* The consolidated financial statements have been prepared in accordance with accounting principles generally accepted in the United States of America and present fairly, in all material respects, the Company's results of operations, financial position and cash flows. Certain amounts included in the consolidated financial statements are estimated based on currently available information and judgment as to the outcome of future conditions and circumstances. . . .

  The Company's system of internal controls is supported by written policies and procedures and supplemented by a staff of internal auditors. **[2]** *This system is designed to provide reasonable assurance, at* *suitable costs,* that assets are safeguarded and that transactions are executed in accordance with appropriate authorization and are recorded and reported properly. The system is continually reviewed, evaluated, and where appropriate, modified to accommodate current conditions. Emphasis is placed on the careful **[3]** *selection,* **[4]** *training and development of professional managers.*

An organizational alignment that is premised upon appropriate **[5]** *delegation of authority* and **[6]** *division of responsibility* is fundamental to this system. **[7]** *Communication programs are aimed at assuring that established policies and procedures are disseminated and understood* throughout the company.

The consolidated financial statements have been audited by independent auditors whose report appears below. This audit was conducted in accordance with auditing standards generally accepted in the United States of America, which include the consideration of the Company's internal controls to the extent necessary to form an independent opinion on the consolidated financial statements prepared by management.

The Audit Committee of the Board of Directors is composed solely of directors who are not officers or employees of the Company. . . .

Required

Assume that a colleague, who has never taken an accounting course, asks you to explain JC Penney's "company statement on financial information." Write a memorandum that explains each of the numbered portions of the material. When appropriate, include examples to explain these concepts of internal control to your colleague.

ATC 6–4   BUSINESS APPLICATIONS CASE *Using the Current Ratio*

	Code-Breakers	Cipher-Tec
Current assets	$40,000	$70,000
Current liabilities	25,000	55,000

Required

a. Compute the current ratio for each company.
b. Which company has the greater likelihood of being able to pay its bills?
c. Assuming that both companies have the same amount of total assets, speculate as to which company would produce the higher return on assets ratio.

ATC 6–5   BUSINESS APPLICATIONS CASE *Using Current Ratios to Make Comparisons*

The following accounting information pertains to Stillman and Tsay companies at the end of 2006:

Account Title	Stillman	Tsay
Cash	$ 15,000	$ 25,000
Wages Payable	20,000	25,000
Merchandise Inventory	30,000	55,000
Building	80,000	80,000
Accounts Receivable	35,000	30,000
Long-term Notes Payable	90,000	120,000
Land	45,000	50,000
Accounts Payable	40,000	45,000
Sales Revenue	220,000	270,000
Expenses	190,000	245,000

Required

a. Identify the current assets and current liabilities, and compute the current ratio for each company.
b. Assuming that all assets and liabilities are listed here, compute the debt to assets ratio for each company.
c. Determine which company has the greater financial risk in both the short term and the long term.

ATC 6–6   WRITING ASSIGNMENT *Internal Control Procedures*

Alison Marsh was a trusted employee of Small City State Bank. She was involved in everything. She worked as a teller, she accounted for the cash at the other teller windows, and she recorded many of the transactions in the accounting records. She was so loyal that she never would take a day off, even when she was really too sick to work. She routinely worked late to see that all the day's work was posted into the accounting records. She would never take even a day's vacation because they might need her at the bank. Tick and Tack, CPAs were hired to perform an audit, the first complete audit that had been done in several years. Marsh seemed somewhat upset by the upcoming audit. She said that everything had been properly accounted for and that the audit was a needless expense. When Tick and Tack examined some of the bank's internal control procedures, it discovered problems. In fact, as the audit progressed, it became apparent that a large amount of cash was missing. Numerous adjustments had been made to customer accounts with credit memorandums, and many of the transactions had been posted several days late. In addition, there were numerous cash payments for "office expenses." When the audit was complete, it was determined that more than $200,000 of funds was missing or improperly accounted for. All fingers pointed to Marsh. The bank's president, who was a close friend of Marsh, was bewildered. How could this type of thing happen at this bank?

Required
Prepare a written memo to the bank president, outlining the procedures that should be followed to prevent this type of problem in the future.

ETHICAL DILEMMA *See No Evil, Hear No Evil, Report No Evil*   ATC 6–7

Cindy Putman recently started her first job as an accounting clerk with the Wheeler Company. When reconciling Wheeler's bank statement, Putman discovered that the bank had given the company a $42,245 credit for a deposit made in the amount of $24,245. As a result, the bank account was overstated by $18,000. Putman brought the error to the attention of Ed Wheeler, who told her to reconcile the two accounts by subtracting the amount of the error from the unadjusted bank balance. Wheeler told Putman, "Don't bother informing the bank. They'll find the mistake soon enough." Three months later, Putman was still having to include the bank error in the bank reconciliation. She was convinced that the bank would not find the mistake and asked Wheeler what to do. He told Putman that it was not her job to correct bank mistakes. He told her to adjust the company books by making a debit to Cash and a credit to Retained Earnings. He said "We can always reverse the entry if the bank discovers the mistake." Putman was uneasy about this solution. Wheeler told her that his years of business experience had taught him to *go with the flow.* He said, "Sometimes you win, sometimes you lose. I'm sure that we have made mistakes that were to our disadvantage, and no one ever told us about them. We just got a good break. Keep quiet and share in the good fortune." At the end of the month, Putman discovered a $500 cash bonus included in her paycheck. She had been working hard, and she rationalized that she deserved the bonus. She told herself that it had nothing to do with the treatment of the bank error. Anyway, she thought that Wheeler was probably right. The bank would eventually find the mistake, she could reverse the adjusting entry, and everything would be set straight.

Two years later, a tax auditor for the Internal Revenue Service (IRS) discovered the adjusting entry that debited Cash and credited Retained Earnings for $18,000. The IRS agent charged Wheeler Company with income tax evasion. Being unable to identify the source of the increase in cash, the agent concluded that the company was attempting to hide revenue by making direct credits to Retained Earnings. Wheeler denied any knowledge of the entry. He told the agent that Putman rarely brought anything to his attention. He said that Putman was the independent sort who had probably made an honest mistake. He pointed out that at the time the entry was made, Putman had little experience.

Later in a private conversation, Wheeler told Putman to plead ignorance and that they both would get off the hook. He said that if she did not keep quiet, they would go down together. He reminded her of the $500 bonus. Wheeler told Putman that accepting payment to defraud the IRS constituted a crime that would land her in jail. Putman was shocked that Wheeler would not tell the truth. She had expected some loyalty from him, and it was clear that she was not going to get it.

Required
Answer the following questions:
a. Explain how the direct credit to retained earnings understated net income.
b. What course of action would you advise Putman to take?
c. Why was Putman foolish to expect loyalty from Wheeler?
d. Suppose Putman had credited Miscellaneous Revenue instead of Retained Earnings and the company had paid income taxes on the $18,000. Under these circumstances, the bank error would never have been discovered. Is it OK to hide the error from the bank if it is reported on the tax return?

ATC 6–8   EDGAR DATABASE *Analyzing Pep Boys' Liquidity*

Required

Using the most current 10-K available on EDGAR, answer the following questions about Pep Boys, Manny, Moe & Jack, for the most recent year reported. Type in *Pep Boys* as the company name when you search EDGAR. Instructions for using EDGAR are in Appendix A.

a. What is Pep Boys' current ratio?

b. Which of Pep Boys' current assets had the largest balance?

c. What percentage of Pep Boys' total assets consisted of current assets?

d. Did Pep Boys have any "currently maturing" long-term debt included in current liabilities on its balance sheet?

e. If Pep Boys were a company that manufactured auto parts rather than a retailer of auto parts, how do you think its balance sheet would be different?

ATC 6–9   SPREADSHEET ASSIGNMENT *Using Excel*

At the end of 2005, the following accounting information is available for Bainbridge and Crist Companies.

Classified Balance Sheet	Bainbridge	Crist	Multistep Income Statement	Bainbridge	Crist
Assets					
			Sales	500,000	575,000
Current Assets			Cost of Goods Sold	170,000	200,000
Cash	18,000	22,500	Gross Margin	330,000	375,000
Accounts Receivable	19,000	19,500	Operating Expenses	285,000	345,000
Inventory	14,000	18,000	Net Income	45,000	30,000
Total Current Assets	51,000	60,000			
Property, Plant and Equipment			**RATIOS**		
Land	52,500	50,000	Current Ratio	1.46	0.85
Building	135,000	120,000	Debt to Total Assets	46.12%	82.83%
Total Property, Plant and Equipment	187,500	170,000	Equity to Total Assets	53.88%	17.17%
			Gross Margin Percentage	66.00%	65.22%
Total Assets	238,500	230,000	Return on Sales	9.00%	5.22%
			Return on Assets	18.87%	13.04%
Liabilities			Return on Equity	35.02%	75.95%
Current Liabilities					
Accounts Payable	20,000	52,500			
Wages Payable	15,000	18,000			
Total Current Liabilities	35,000	70,500			
Long-Term Liabilities					
Notes Payable	75,000	120,000			
Total Liabilities	110,000	190,500			
Equity					
Common Stock	30,000	9,500			
Retained Earnings	98,500	30,000			
Total Equity	128,500	39,500			
Total Liabilities and Equity	238,500	230,000			

Required

a. Set up the preceding spreadsheet. Complete the balance sheet and income statement. Use Excel formulas for rows that "total" on the balance sheet and for gross margin and net income on the income statement.

b. Calculate the designated ratios using Excel formulas.

c. Which company is more likely to be able to pay its current liabilities?

d. Which company carries a greater financial risk?

e. Which company is more profitable from the stockholders' perspective?

f. Based on profitability alone, which company performed better?

g. Assume that sales increased 10 percent and that the additional sales were made on account. Adjust the balance sheet and income statement for the effects. Notice that Retained Earnings will also need to be adjusted to keep the balance sheet in balance. What is the resultant effect on the ratios?

h. Return the financial statements to the original data. Assume that operating expenses increased 10 percent and that the additional expenses were acquired on credit. Adjust the financial statements for the effects. Notice that Retained Earnings must be adjusted to keep in balance. What is the resultant effect on the ratios?

SPREADSHEET ANALYSIS *Mastering Excel*

ATC 6–10

Refer to Problem 6–25B.

Required

Complete the classified balance sheet and multistep income statement on an Excel spreadsheet.

Accounting for Accruals—Advanced Topics
Receivables and Payables

After completing this chapter, you should be able to:

1 Explain the importance of offering credit terms to customers.

2 Explain how the allowance method of accounting for bad debts affects financial statements.

3 Show how the direct write-off method of accounting for bad debts affects financial statements.

4 Explain how accounting for credit card sales affects financial statements.

5 Explain how accounting for warranty obligations affects financial statements.

6 Show how discount notes and related interest charges affect financial statements.

7 Explain the effects of the cost of financing credit sales.

the *curious* accountant

Suppose that Walgreen Drug Stores orders goods from Johnson & Johnson, Inc. Assume that Walgreen offers to pay for the goods on the day it receives them from Johnson & Johnson (a cash purchase) or 60 days later (a purchase on account). Assume that Johnson & Johnson is absolutely sure Walgreen will pay its account when due. Why should Johnson & Johnson care whether it makes the sale to Walgreen for cash or on account?

Many people are impulse buyers. A particular mix of environmental setting and emotional condition sparks an immediate urge to purchase. If people are forced to wait, because of a lack of funds, the mix of environment and emotion shifts and the desire to buy may dissipate. In recognition of this phenomenon, merchants offer credit terms that permit the customer to "buy now and pay later." By offering credit, businesses are able to increase their sales. The offsetting disadvantage of this strategy occurs when some customers are unable or unwilling to pay their bills. However, the widespread availability of credit attests to the fact that the advantages of increased sales generally outweigh the disadvantages arising from the associated bad debts.

*When a company permits one of its customers to buy now and pay later, the expected future receipt is called an **account receivable.** Typically, amounts due from accounts receivable are relatively small, and the terms to maturity are short. Collection on most accounts receivable occurs within 30 days. When a longer credit term is necessary or when the amount of the receivable is large, a note evidencing a credit agreement between the parties involved is usually exchanged. The note specifies the maturity date, rate of interest, and other credit terms. Receivables evidenced by such notes are called **notes receivable.** Accounts and notes receivable are shown as assets on the balance sheet. For every receivable listed on one company's books,* *there is a corresponding obligation listed on another company's books. In other words, if one company expects to collect, another company expects to pay. Current obligations to make future economic sacrifices such as cash payments are frequently called **payables**. Accounts and notes payable[1] are shown as liabilities on the balance sheet.*

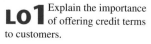

LO1 Explain the importance of offering credit terms to customers.

Receivables and payables represent future expected cash receipts or payments. However, most companies do not expect to receive the full face value of their receivables because they know that some of their customers will be unable or unwilling to pay the amounts due. Companies recognize this fact by reporting receivables at face value less an allowance for accounts whose collection is doubtful. The **net realizable value** (amount actually expected to be collected) is the amount included in the computation of total assets. In contrast, payables are normally carried at face value because companies operate under the **going concern assumption.** Since companies believe that they will continue to operate (they are going concerns), they assume they will be responsible for paying the full balance of their obligations. Accordingly, it is customary to carry receivables at net realizable value and payables at face value on the balance sheet.

The practice of reporting the net realizable value of receivables in the financial statements is commonly called the **allowance method of accounting for bad debts.** The following section demonstrates the application of the allowance method for Allen's Tutoring Services.

■ Accounting Events Affecting the 2001 Period

LO2 Explain how the allowance method of accounting for bad debts affects financial statements.

Allen's Tutoring Services was started as a part-time venture by an individual named Mark Allen. Allen is a bright, young college student who started the tutoring service during his sophomore year. Three accounting events that affected Allen's Tutoring Services during its first year of operation follow. As you read, try to anticipate the effect of each event on the financial statements. Then check the accuracy of your expectation by looking at the statements model following the transaction. You will learn more rapidly if you think about the possible effects of each transaction *before* you read the results. To facilitate your analysis of the illustration, the transaction data are referenced by the event number.

Event 1 Revenue Recognition
Allen's Tutoring Services recognized $14,000 of service revenue earrned on account during 2001.

By this point, you should be familiar with this type of event. It is an asset source transaction. Allen's Tutoring Services obtains assets (Accounts Receivable) by providing services to its customers. Accordingly, both assets and equity (Retained Earnings) increase. The event increases revenue and net income. Cash flow is not affected. These effects are shown in the following horizontal statements model:

Event No.	Assets	=	Liab.	+	Equity	Rev.	–	Exp.	=	Net Inc.	Cash Flow
1	14,000	=	NA	+	14,000	14,000	–	NA	=	14,000	NA

Event 2 Collection of Receivables
Allen's Tutoring Services collected $12,500 cash from accounts receivable in 2001.

[1]Notes payable can be classified as short term or long term, depending on the time to maturity. Short-term notes mature within one year or the operating cycle, whichever is longer. Notes with longer maturities are classified as long-term notes. This chapter focuses on accounting for short-term notes; accounting for long-term notes is discussed in Chapter 10.

This event is an asset exchange transaction. One asset, Cash, increases; and another asset, Accounts Receivable, decreases. The total amount of assets is unchanged. Net income is not affected because the revenue was recognized in the previous transaction. The cash inflow is shown in the operating activities section of the statement of cash flows.

Event No.	Assets			=	Liab.	+	Equity	Rev.	−	Exp.	=	Net Inc.	Cash Flow
	Cash	+	Accts. Rec.										
2	12,500	+	(12,500)	=	NA	+	NA	NA	−	NA	=	NA	12,500 OA

Event 3 Recognizing Bad Debts Expense
Allen's Tutoring Services recognized bad debts expense for accounts expected to be uncollectible in the future.

The ending balance in the receivable account is $1,500 ($14,000 of revenue on account − $12,500 of collections). Although Allen's Tutoring Services hopes to collect the full $1,500 in 2002, the company is not likely to do so because some of its customers may not pay the amounts due. Accordingly, the $1,500 receivables balance does not represent the amount of cash that is truly expected to be collected. Allen's Tutoring Services is reasonably certain that some of its customers will not pay, but the actual amount of uncollectible accounts cannot be known until the future period when the customers default (refuse to pay). Even so, the company can make a reasonable *estimate* of the amount of receivables that will be uncollectible.

Suppose that Allen's Tutoring Services believes that $75 of the receivables is uncollectible. To improve accuracy, the company can recognize the anticipated future write-down of receivables in the current accounting period. Specifically, the company records a year-end adjusting entry that recognizes **bad debts expense,** thereby reducing the book value of total assets and equity (Retained Earnings). Like any other expense recognition transaction, the adjusting entry for bad debts expense reduces the amount of reported net income. The statement of cash flows is not affected. The effects of the recognition of bad debts expense are shown in the following horizontal statements model:

Event No.	Assets	=	Liab.	+	Equity	Rev.	−	Exp.	=	Net Inc.	Cash Flow
3	(75)	=	NA	+	(75)	NA	−	75	=	(75)	NA

The amount of receivables that are expected to be uncollectible ($75) is accumulated in a contra asset account called **Allowance for Doubtful Accounts.** The difference between the amount in accounts receivable and the contra allowance account is called the *net realizable value of receivables.* In this case, the net realizable value of receivables is:

Accounts Receivable	$1,500
Less: Allowance for Doubtful Accounts	(75)
Net Realizable Value of Receivables	$1,425

The *net realizable value* of receivables represents the amount of receivables the company believes it will actually collect. Most companies disclose the amount of the allowance account as well as the net realizable value of receivables in their balance sheets. However, a significant number of companies show only the net balance. Some typical alternative balance sheet captions that could be used to report accounts receivable for Allen's Tutoring Services are shown on the following page:

ohnson & Johnson would definitely prefer to make the sale to Walgreen in cash rather than on account. Even though it may be certain to collect its accounts receivable from Walgreen, the sooner Johnson & Johnson gets its cash, the sooner the cash can be reinvested.

The interest cost related to a small account receivable of $50 that takes 60 days to collect may seem immaterial; at 6.5 percent, the lost interest amounts to less than $1. However, when one considers that Johnson & Johnson had approximately $4.5

billion of accounts receivable on December 31, 2000, the cost of financing receivables for a real-world company becomes apparent. At 6.5 percent, the cost of waiting 60 days to collect $4.5 billion of cash is $48 million ($4.5 billion × 0.065 × [60 ÷ 365]). For one full year, the cost to Johnson & Johnson would be more than $290 million ($4.5 billion × 0.065). In 2000 it took Johnson & Johnson approximately 55 days to collect its accounts receivable, and the weighted-average interest rate on its debt was approximately 6.4 percent.

Alternative 1	
Accounts Receivable	$1,500
Less Allowance for Doubtful Accounts	(75)
Total	$1,425
Alternative 2	
Trade Accounts Receivable, Less Allowance of $75	$1,425
Alternative 3	
Receivables, Less Allowance for Losses of $75	$1,425
Alternative 4	
Accounts and Notes Receivable, net	$1,425
Alternative 5	
Accounts Receivable	$1,425

As the different captions indicate, companies use a variety of terms and formats in reporting the amount of receivables in the balance sheet. Exhibit 7–1 provides insight regarding the most frequently used captions.

Exhibit 7–1 *Real-World Reporting Practices: Most Frequently Used Titles Related to the Reporting of Accounts Receivable*

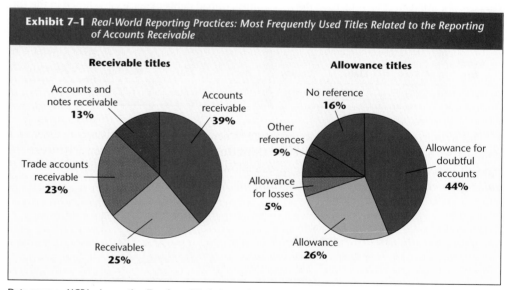

Data source: AICPA, *Accounting Trends and Techniques,* 2000.

Ledger T-Accounts

Exhibit 7–2 shows ledger T-accounts for the business events experienced by Allen's Tutoring Services. The exhibit includes the entry used to close the revenue and expense accounts at the end of the 2001 accounting period. The closing entry is a claims exchange transaction, with some equity accounts decreasing while others increase. The amount of total equity is not

Exhibit 7–2 *General Ledger*

Assets	=	Liabilities	+	Equity

Cash

(2)	12,500			0	Bal.
Bal.	12,500				

Liabilities

	0	Bal.

Retained Earnings

		13,925	(cl)
		13,925	Bal.

Accounts Receivable

(1)	14,000	12,500	(2)
Bal.	1,500		

Service Revenue

(cl)	14,000	14,000	(1)
		0	Bal.

Allowance for Doubtful Accounts

		75	(3)
		75	Bal.

Bad Debts Expense

(3)	75	75	(cl)
Bal.	0		

affected by the closing entry. Also, the income statement and the statement of cash flows are not affected by the closing entry. The ledger account balances are used to prepare the financial statements shown in Exhibit 7–3. To confirm your understanding of the accounting treatment for bad debts, trace the transactions to the ledger accounts and the account balances to the financial statements. The relevant accounting events are summarized here for your convenience:

1. Earned $14,000 of revenue on account.
2. Collected $12,500 cash from accounts receivable.
3. Adjusted the accounts to reflect management's estimate that bad debts expense[2] would be $75.
4. Closed the revenue and expense accounts. The letters *cl* are used as a posting reference for the closing entries.

Exhibit 7–3 *Financial Statements for 2001*

Income Statement		Balance Sheet			Statement of Cash Flows	
Service Revenue	$14,000	Assets			**Operating Activities**	
Bad Debts Exp.	(75)	Cash		$12,500	Inflow from Customers	$12,500
Net Income	$13,925	Accounts Receivable	$1,500		**Investing Activities**	0
		Less: Allowance	(75)			
		Net Realizable Value		1,425	**Financing Activities**	0
		Total Assets		$13,925	Net Change in Cash	12,500
					Plus: Beginning Cash	
					Balance	0
		Stockholders' Equity				
		Retained Earnings		$13,925	Ending Cash Balance	$12,500

Financial Statements

The practice of estimating bad debts improves the accuracy of the 2001 financial statements in two important ways. First, the net realizable value of accounts receivable is shown on the balance sheet. This presentation lets the statement users see not only the gross amount of receivables but also the amount that Allen's Tutoring Services actually expects to collect ($1,500 − $75 = $1,425). Furthermore, the amount of bad debts expense (that is, $75) is shown in the 2001

---

[2]The term *bad debts* may be misleading. In fact, it is the receivables that turn bad rather than some debt of the company. Even so, it is standard business practice to refer to bad receivables as *bad debts*. We believe that it is important to use real-world terminology, but we caution our readers to be aware of the misleading nature of the term *bad debts expense*.

income statement along with the revenue that was recognized when receivables were recorded. Since the associated revenues and expenses are shown on the same income statement, the allowance method improves matching and provides a better measure of managerial performance. As you continue to review the statements in Exhibit 7–3, observe carefully that the amount of cash flow from operations ($12,500) is different from the amount of net income ($13,925) because only cash collections are reported in the statement of cash flows, whereas the income statement includes revenues earned on account less the estimated amount of bad debts expense.

Check Yourself 7-1

Pamlico, Inc., began operations on January 1, 2006. During 2006, it earned $400,000 of revenue on account. The company collected $370,000 of accounts receivable. At the end of the year, Pamlico estimates bad debts expense will be 1 percent of sales. Based on this information alone, what is the net realizable value of accounts receivable as of December 31, 2006?

Answer Accounts receivable at year end are $30,000 ($400,000 sales on account − $370,000 collection of receivables). The amount in the allowance for doubtful accounts would be $4,000 ($400,000 credit sales × 0.01). The net realizable value of accounts receivable is therefore $26,000 ($30,000 − $4,000).

Estimation of Bad Debts Expense

In the case of Allen's Tutoring, we simply provided the estimated amount of bad debts expense. How do real-world accountants make such estimates? Most accountants start by reviewing their company's credit history. They ask how much of the company's credit sales (sales on account) could not be collected in the past? A convenient way to express the answer to this question is to state the estimated amount of bad debts expense as a percentage of credit sales. To illustrate, assume that in the previous accounting period, Tannon Company was unable to collect $10,000 of $1,000,000 sales on account. Accordingly, Tannon's bad debts expense amounted to 1 percent of the credit sales ($10,000 ÷ $1,000,000).

Before the historical percentage is applied to the current sales on account, it is normally adjusted for new circumstances that are anticipated to be experienced in the future. For example, the percentage could be lowered if the company plans to apply more rigorous approval standards to new credit applicants. Alternatively, the percentage may be increased if economic forecasts signal a downturn in the economy that would make future defaults more likely. To illustrate, assume that Tannon Company decides to relax its credit standards to expand sales in a recessionary economy. Specifically, the company decides to increase the estimated bad debts percentage from 1 to 1.5 percent of credit sales. Assuming current sales on account of $1,200,000, the estimated bad debts expense is $18,000 ($1,200,000 × 0.015).

Determining the estimated bad debts percentage of credit sales may be particularly difficult when a company is in its first year of operation because it has no credit history on which to base the estimate. In this case, it is necessary to consult with trade associations or business associates (other people in the same industry who do have experience) to develop a reasonable estimate of the expected losses.

■ Accounting Events Affecting the 2002 Period

LO2 Explain how the allowance method of accounting for bad debts affects financial statements.

Now we discuss eight accounting events that occurred during the 2002 accounting cycle. As in the previous section, you should anticipate the effect of each event on the financial statements prior to reviewing the appropriate statements model. An accounting textbook should not be merely read; it should be worked. Read the book with pencil in hand. Anticipate the results, trace the transactions, and verify the numbers. You will learn more by *doing* accounting than by *reading* about it. So do the accounting as you read the text.

Event 1 Write-Off of an Uncollectible Account Receivable
Allen Tutoring Services wrote off an uncollectible account receivable.

Since the impact of recognizing bad debts was shown in the 2001 financial statements, the actual *write-off of uncollectible accounts* does not affect the balance sheet. When a specific account is determined to be uncollectible, the balance of the account is removed from the Receivables account and from the Allowance for Bad Debts account. Accordingly, the event constitutes an asset exchange transaction. Total assets, liabilities, and equity are the same immediately after the write-off in 2002. Likewise, the income statement and the statement of cash flows are not affected by a write-off of an uncollectible account. To illustrate, assume that one of Allen's Tutoring Services' customers refuses to pay a $70 receivable balance. Allen's Tutoring Services has tried in every way to collect the amount due and has determined that regardless of further efforts, the funds are not collectible now or in the future. Accordingly, Allen's has decided to write off the account. The effect on the financial statements is shown in the following horizontal statements model.

Event	Assets			=	Liab.	+	Equity	Rev.	−	Exp.	=	Net Inc.	Cash Flow
No.	Acct. Rec.	−	Allow.										
1	(70)	−	(70)	=	NA	+	NA	NA	−	NA	=	NA	NA

As indicated, the write-off is an asset exchange transaction. The decrease in Accounts Receivable is offset by a reduction in the balance of the Allowance account. Note that while the balances in Accounts Receivable and the Allowance accounts decrease, the net realizable value of receivables—and therefore total assets—remains unchanged.

	Before Write-Off	After Write-Off
Accounts Receivable	$1,500	$1,430
Allowance for Doubtful Accounts	(75)	(5)
Net Realizable Value	$1,425	$1,425

Event 2 Investment in Note Receivable
Allen Tutoring Services invested in a note receivable.

After taking an accounting course, Mark Allen becomes concerned about the growing balance in his company's Cash account. He realizes that he could improve his company's profitability by investing some of the idle cash. Accordingly, on May 1, 2002, Allen's Tutoring Service loans $12,000 cash to another student who is starting a business of her own. The borrower issues a 9 percent interest-bearing note to Allen's. The note carries a one-year term. The loan represents an investment by Allen's Tutoring Services. One asset account, Cash, decreases; another asset account, Notes Receivable, increases. Total assets are unchanged. The income statement is unaffected by the event. The cash outflow is shown in the investing activities section of the statement of cash flows. These effects are reflected in the following statements model:

Event	Assets			=	Liab.	+	Equity	Rev.	−	Exp.	=	Net Inc.	Cash Flow
No.	Cash	+	Note Rec.										
2	(12,000)	+	12,000	=	NA	+	NA	NA	−	NA	=	NA	(12,000) IA

Event 3 Revenue Recognition
Allen's Tutoring Services provided $10,000 of tutoring services on account during the 2002 accounting period.

Assets (Accounts Receivable) and equity (Revenue) increase. The recognition of revenue acts to increase net income. Cash flow is not affected. The effects on the financial statements are shown here.

Event No.	Assets	=	Liab.	+	Equity	Rev.	−	Exp.	=	Net Inc.	Cash Flow
3	10,000	=	NA	+	10,000	10,000	−	NA	=	10,000	NA

Event 4   Collection of Accounts Receivable
Allen's Tutoring Services collected $8,430 cash from accounts receivable.

The balance in the Cash account increases, and the balance in the Receivables account decreases. Total assets are unaffected. Net income is not affected because revenue was recognized previously. The cash inflow is shown in the operating activities section of the statement of cash flows.

Event No.	Assets			=	Liab.	+	Equity	Rev.	−	Exp.	=	Net Inc.	Cash Flow
	Cash	+	Accts. Rec.										
4	8,430	+	(8,430)	=	NA	+	NA	NA	−	NA	=	NA	8,430 OA

Event 5   Recovery of Bad Debt: Reestablishment of Receivable
Allen's Tutoring Services recovered a bad debt that was previously written off.

Occasionally, a company receives payment from a customer whose account was previously written off. When this occurs, the customer's account should be reestablished and the collection should be recorded in ordinary fashion. This practice reflects a complete record of activity that may be useful in the event the customer requests additional credit at some future date or in case the company is asked to provide a credit history of the customer to a credit bureau, bank, or some other interested party. To illustrate, assume that Allen's Tutoring Services receives a $10 cash payment from a customer whose account had previously been written off. The first step is to reestablish the Receivable and Allowance accounts that were written off. The effect is simply the reverse of a write-off. Accounts Receivable increases, and the Allowance account increases. Since the Allowance is a contra asset account, the increase in this account offsets the increase in the Receivables account, and total assets are unchanged. Net income and cash flow are unaffected. These effects are shown here:

Event No.	Assets			=	Liab.	+	Equity	Rev.	−	Exp.	=	Net Inc.	Cash Flow
	Acct. Rec.	−	Allow.										
5	10	−	10	=	NA	+	NA	NA	−	NA	=	NA	NA

Event 6   Recovery of Bad Debt: Collection of Receivable
Allen's Tutoring Services collected the reestablished receivable.

The collection of $10 is treated as any other collection of a receivable account. The Cash account increases, and the Receivables account decreases.

Event No.	Assets			=	Liab.	+	Equity	Rev.	−	Exp.	=	Net Inc.	Cash Flow
	Cash	+	Accts. Rec.										
6	10	+	(10)	=	NA	+	NA	NA	−	NA	=	NA	10 OA

Event 7   Adjustment for Recognition of Bad Debts Expense
Allen's Tutoring Services recognized bad debts expense for 2002.

Assume that Allen's estimates bad debts expense to be 1.35 percent of credit sales. In this case, the amount of bad debts expense to recognize would be $135 ($10,000 × 0.0135). The recognition of the $135 bad debts expense acts to decrease assets (net realizable value of receivables) and equity (Retained Earnings). The recognition of the expense acts to decrease the amount of net income. The statement of cash flows is not affected. The effects on the financial statements follows.

Event No.	Assets			=	Liab.	+	Equity	Rev.	–	Exp.	=	Net Inc.	Cash Flow
	Accts. Rec.	–	Allow.										
7	NA	–	135	=	NA	+	(135)	NA	–	135	=	(135)	NA

Event 8 Recognition of Interest Revenue
Allen's Tutoring Services recognized interest revenue on the note receivable.

Recall that on May 1, 2002, Allen's Tutoring Services invested $12,000 in a note receivable with a one-year term and a 9 percent annual rate of interest. By December 31, 2002, the note will have earned $720 ($12,000 × 0.09 × [8 ÷ 12]). The recognition of the earned interest increases assets (Interest Receivable) and equity (Retained Earnings). The recognition of revenue increases net income. Cash flow is not affected. The effects on the financial statements are shown here.

Event No.	Assets	=	Liab.	+	Equity	Rev.	–	Exp.	=	Net Inc.	Cash Flow
8	720	=	NA	+	720	720	–	NA	=	720	NA

Ledger T-Accounts

Exhibit 7–4 shows ledger T-accounts for the 2002 business events experienced by Allen's Tutoring Services. The exhibit includes the entry used to close the revenue and expense accounts at the end of the 2002 accounting period. The ledger account balances are used to prepare the financial statements shown in Exhibit 7–5. The relevant accounting events are summarized for your convenience.

1. Wrote off a $70 uncollectible account receivable.
2. Invested $12,000 in a note receivable.
3. Earned $10,000 of tutoring service revenue on account.
4. Collected $8,430 cash from accounts receivable.
5. Reestablished a $10 account receivable that had previously been written off.
6. Collected $10 from the reestablished receivable.
7. Adjusted accounts to recognize $135 of estimated bad debts expense.
8. Adjusted accounts to recognize $720 of accrued interest revenue.
9. Closed the revenue and expense accounts. The letters *cl* are used as a posting reference for the closing entries.

Analysis of Financial Statements

Exhibit 7–5 shows the relevant financial statements. Observe carefully that the amount of bad debts expense ($135) is different from the ending balance of the Allowance account ($150). Recall that the Allowance account had a $15 balance just prior to the time that the 2002 adjusting entry for bad debts expense was made. This balance existed because the estimate for uncollectible accounts in 2001 was overstated. In 2001, Allen's Tutoring Services estimated that there would be $75 of uncollectible accounts when, in fact, only $70 of accounts was written off and $10 of those accounts was recovered, resulting in a net loss of

Exhibit 7–4 *General Ledger*

Assets	=	Liabilities	+	Equity

Cash

Bal.	12,500	12,000	(2)
(4)	8,430		
(6)	10		
Bal.	8,940		

Accounts Receivable

Bal.	1,500	70	(1)
(3)	10,000	8,430	(4)
(5)	10	10	(6)
Bal.	3,000		

Allowance for Doubtful Accounts

(1)	70	75	Bal.
		10	(5)
		135	(7)
		150	Bal.

Notes Receivable

(2)	12,000

Interest Receivable

(8)	720

Liabilities

	0	Bal.

Retained Earnings

	13,925	Bal.
	10,585	(cl)
	24,510	Bal.

Service Revenue

(cl)	10,000	10,000	(3)
		0	Bal.

Interest Revenue

(cl)	720	720	(8)
		0	Bal.

Bad Debts Expense

(7)	135	135	(cl)
Bal.	0		

Exhibit 7–5 *Financial Statements for 2002*

Income Statement		Balance Sheet			Statement of Cash Flows	
Service Revenue	$10,000	Assets			**Operating Activities**	
Bad Debts Exp.	(135)	Cash		$ 8,940	Inflow from Customers	$ 8,440
Operating Income	9,865	Accounts Receivable	$3,000		**Investing Activities**	
Interest Revenue	720	Less: Allowance	(150)		Outflow for the Note Rec.	(12,000)
Net Income	$10,585	Net Realizable Value		2,850	**Financing Activities**	0
		Note Receivable		12,000	Net Change in Cash	(3,560)
		Interest Receivable		720	Plus: Beginning Cash	
		Total Assets		$24,510	Balance	12,500
		Stockholders' Equity			Ending Cash Balance	$ 8,940
		Retained Earnings		$24,510		

uncollectible accounts of only $60. Accordingly, the expense for 2001 was overstated by $15. However, if no estimate had been made, the amount of bad debts expense would have been understated by $60. Remember that bad debts expense is an estimated amount. In some accounting periods the amount may be overstated; in others it may be understated. Although the allowance method does not result in perfection, it does improve the accuracy of the financial statements. Since there were no dividends, ending retained earnings are computed as last year's retained earnings plus this year's net income (that is, $13,925 + $10,585 = $24,510). Once again, the cash flow from operations ($8,440) is different from the amount of net income ($10,585) because the statement of cash flows does not include the effects of revenues earned on account or the recognition of bad debts expense.

Maher Company had beginning balances in Accounts Receivable and Allowance for Doubtful Accounts of $24,200 and $2,000, respectively. During the accounting period Maher earned $230,000 of revenue on account and collected $232,500 of cash from receivables. The company also wrote off $1,950 of uncollectible accounts during the period. Maher estimates bad debts expense will be 1 percent of credit sales. Based on this information, what is the net realizable value of receivables at the end of the period?

Answer The balance in the Accounts Receivable account is $19,750 ($24,200 + $230,000 − $232,500 − $1,950). The amount of bad debts expense for the period is $2,300 ($230,000 × 0.01). The balance in the Allowance for Doubtful Accounts is $2,350 ($2,000 − $1,950 + $2,300). The net realizable value of receivables is therefore $17,400 ($19,750 − $2,350).

Check Yourself 7–2

▌Recognition of Bad Debts Under the Direct Write-Off Method

If the amount of uncollectible accounts is immaterial, bad debts expense can be recognized when accounts are determined to be uncollectible. This method is called the **direct write-off method** of accounting for bad debts. Since the direct write-off method does not make an allowance for uncollectible accounts, it overstates the net realizable value of receivables on the balance sheet. Therefore, the method does not comply with generally accepted accounting principles. However, if the amount of uncollectible accounts is insignificant, the overstatement is tolerated as a fair trade-off for the recording convenience offered by the direct write-off method. This is an example of the application of the materiality concept. The reporting of immaterial items does not have to conform to GAAP.

No estimates, allowance account, or adjusting entries are needed under the direct write-off method. Simply record the bad debts as they occur. Sales or services on account are recognized in the customary fashion in the period in which goods or services are provided. Bad debts expense is then recognized in the period in which a particular account is determined to be uncollectible. To illustrate, assume that the following events apply to Dr. Price's optical services company.

LO3 Show how the direct write-off method of accounting for bad debts affects financial statements.

Event 1 Recognition of Revenue on Account
During 2001, the company provides $50,000 of services on account.

The effects of this event on the financial statements are shown here.

Event No.	Assets	=	Liab.	+	Equity	Rev.	−	Exp.	=	Net Inc.	Cash Flow
1	50,000	=	NA	+	50,000	50,000	−	NA	=	50,000	NA

The following entry is used to record the transaction in the general journal:

Account Title	Debit	Credit
Accounts Receivable	50,000	
Service Revenue		50,000

Event 2 Recognition of Bad Debts Expense
Assume that Price determines in 2002 that one of his customers who owes $200 for services delivered in 2001 is unable to pay the amount due.

The write-off of the account results in the recognition of bad debts expense in 2002, even though the associated revenue was recognized in 2001. In other words, the expense is recognized in the year in which an account is determined to be uncollectible. Accuracy is compromised because revenues are not matched with related expenses. As indicated earlier, such inaccuracies are tolerated only to the extent that they are deemed to be immaterial. The effect of the write-off of the uncollectible account on the financial statements follows.

Event No.	Assets	=	Liab.	+	Equity	Rev.	−	Exp.	=	Net Inc.	Cash Flow
2	(200)	=	NA	+	(200)	NA	−	200	=	(200)	NA

The only entry required to recognize bad debts is made in 2002. This entry is shown here in general journal format.

Account Title	Debit	Credit
Bad Debts Expense	200	
Accounts Receivable		200

Accounting for Credit Card Sales

LO4 Explain how accounting for credit card sales affects financial statements.

The effective management of credit is an involved task that can be very expensive in terms of time and money. Not only will a company incur bad debts expense but also it must incur considerable clerical costs. Creditworthiness must be established for each customer, and detailed records of each transaction must be maintained. Many businesses have chosen to pass these costs on to financial institutions that service the merchant's credit sales for a fee that typically ranges between 2 and 8 percent of gross sales.

The financial institution (credit card company) provides the customer a plastic card that permits the cardholder to charge purchases at various retail outlets. When a sale is made, the seller records the transactions on an invoice the customer signs. The invoice is forwarded to the credit card company, which immediately pays the merchant. The service charge is deducted from the gross amount of the invoice, and the merchant is paid the net balance (gross invoice less credit card discount) in cash. The credit card company collects the amount of the gross sales directly from the customer. Therefore, the merchant is able to avoid the risk of bad debts as well as the cost of maintaining credit records. To illustrate, assume that the following events apply to Joan Wilson's consulting practice.

Event 1 Recognition of Revenue and Expense on Credit Card Sales
Wilson accepts a credit card as payment for $1,000 of services rendered to one of her customers.

Assume that the credit card company charges a 5 percent fee for handling the credit ($1,000 $\times$ 0.05 = $50). Income increases by the amount of revenue ($1,000) and decreases by the amount of the credit card expense ($50). Accordingly, net income increases by $950. The event increases assets (Accounts Receivable due from the credit card company) and equity (Retained Earnings) by $950. Cash flow is not affected. The effect of the event on the financial statements is as follows:

Event No.	Assets	=	Liab.	+	Equity	Rev.	−	Exp.	=	Net Inc.	Cash Flow
1	950	=	NA	+	950	1,000	−	50	=	950	NA

The following entry is used to record the transaction in the general journal:

Account Title	Debit	Credit
Accounts Receivable—Credit Card Company	950	
Credit Card Expense	50	
Service Revenue		1,000

Event 2 Collection of Credit Card Receivable
The collection of the receivable due from the credit card company is treated as any other collection of a receivable.

When Wilson collects the net amount of $950 ($1,000 − $50) from the credit card company, one asset account (Cash) increases and another asset account (Accounts Receivable) decreases. Total assets are not affected. The income statement is not affected by the transaction. There is a $950 cash inflow shown in the operating activities section of the statement of cash flows. The effect of the collection on the financial statement elements is shown here.

Event No.	Assets			=	Liab.	+	Equity	Rev.	−	Exp.	=	Net Inc.	Cash Flow
	Cash	+	Accts. Rec.										
2	950	+	(950)	=	NA	+	NA	NA	−	NA	=	NA	950 OA

The following entry is used to record the transaction in the general journal.

Account Title	Debit	Credit
Cash	950	
Accounts Receivable		950

▌Warranty Obligations

Global competition has forced most companies to guarantee customer satisfaction. A promise to correct a deficiency or dissatisfaction in quality, quantity, or performance is called a **warranty.**

LO5 Explain how accounting for warranty obligations affects financial statements.

Warranties take many forms. Usually, they provide a guaranty that extends over some specified period after the point of sale. Within this period, the seller promises to replace or repair defective products without charge. Many companies promise satisfaction or "your money back." Some even offer double or triple money-back guarantees. Although the obligations stemming from warranties may be uncertain as to amount, timing, or customer, they usually represent legal liabilities that must be recognized in the accounts.

To demonstrate the accounting treatment for warranty obligations, assume that Perfect Picture Frame (PPF) Company had cash of $2,000, inventory of $6,000, common stock of $5,000, and retained earnings of $3,000 on January 1, 2005. The 2005 accounting period is affected by three accounting events: (1) sale of merchandise, (2) recognition of warranty obligations to customers who purchased the merchandise, and (3) settlement of a warranty claim made by a customer.

Event 1 Sale of Merchandise
PPF sold merchandise that cost $4,000 for $7,000 cash.

In the statements model shown here, the sale is referenced with the notation 1a and the cost of the sale as 1b. The recognition of sales revenue increases assets and equity. Net income also increases. The statement of cash flows includes a $7,000 cash inflow in the operating activities section. The recognition of expense (cost of goods sold) decreases assets and equity. Net income also decreases. Cash flow is not affected by the expense recognition. The effects on the financial statements are indicated here.

Event No.	Assets			=	Liab.	+	Equity	Rev.	–	Exp.	=	Net Inc.	Cash Flow
	Cash	+	Inventory										
1a	7,000	+	NA	=	NA	+	7,000	7,000	–	NA	=	7,000	7,000 OA
1a	NA	+	(4,000)	=	NA	+	(4,000)	NA	–	4,000	=	(4,000)	NA

Event 2 Recognition of Warranty Expense
PPF guaranteed the merchandise sold in event 1 to be free from defects for a one-year period following the date of sale.

Although the exact amount of future warranty claims is unknown, PPF must inform financial statement users of the obligation that the company has incurred. Accordingly, it is necessary for PPF to estimate the amount of the liability and to include that estimate in the current period's financial statements. Assume that the warranty obligation is estimated to be $100. Recognizing this obligation increases liabilities (Warranties Payable) and reduces equity (Retained Earnings). The recognition of the warranty expense reduces net income. The statement of cash flows is not affected by the recognition of the obligation and corresponding expense. The effects on the financial statements are shown here:

Event No.	Assets	=	Liab.	+	Equity	Rev.	–	Exp.	=	Net Inc.	Cash Flow
2	NA	=	100	+	(100)	NA	–	100	=	(100)	NA

Event 3 Settlement of Warranty Obligation
PPF paid $40 cash to repair defective merchandise returned by customers.

Note carefully that the payment for the repair is not an expense. The expense was recognized in the period in which the sale was made (when the Warranties Payable account was created). Accordingly, rather than being an expense, the cash payment reduces the Warranties Payable account. Therefore, the payment reduces the asset (Cash) and liabilities (Warranties Payable). The income statement is not affected by the repairs payment. However, there is a $40 cash outflow shown in the operating activities section of the statement of cash flows.

Event No.	Assets	=	Liab.	+	Equity	Rev.	−	Exp.	=	Net Inc.	Cash Flow
3	(40)	=	(40)	+	NA	NA	−	NA	=	NA	(40) OA

Ledger T-Accounts and Financial Statements

Exhibit 7–6 presents ledger T-accounts for the business events experienced by PPF. The exhibit includes the entry used to close the revenue and expense accounts at the end of the 2005 accounting period. The ledger account balances are used to prepare the financial statements shown in Exhibit 7–7. The relevant accounting events are summarized here for your convenience.

Transactions for 2005

1. Sold merchandise that cost $4,000 for $7,000 cash.
2. Recognized a $100 warranty obligation and the corresponding expense.
3. Paid $40 to satisfy a warranty claim.
4. Closed the revenue and expense accounts. The letters *cl* are used as a posting reference for the closing entries.

Exhibit 7–6 *General Ledger*

Assets		=	Liabilities		+	Equity	

Cash

Bal.	2,000	40	(3)
(1a)	7,000		
Bal.	8,960		

Warranties Payable

| (3) | 40 | 100 | (2) |
| | | 60 | Bal. |

Common Stock

| | | 5,000 | Bal. |

Inventory

| Bal. | 6,000 | 4,000 | (1b) |
| Bal. | 2,000 | | |

Retained Earnings

		3,000	Bal.
		2,900	(cl)
		5,900	Bal.

Sales Revenue

| (cl) | 7,000 | 7,000 | (1a) |
| | | 0 | Bal. |

Cost of Goods Sold

| (1b) | 4,000 | 4,000 | (cl) |
| Bal. | 0 | | |

Warranty Expense

| (2) | 100 | 100 | (cl) |
| Bal. | 0 | | |

Exhibit 7–7 *Financial Statements for 2005*

Income Statement		Balance Sheet		Statement of Cash Flows	
Sales Revenue	$7,000	Assets		**Operating Activities**	
Cost of Goods Sold	(4,000)	Cash	$ 8,960	Inflow from Customers	$7,000
		Inventory	2,000	Outflow for Warranty	(40)
Gross Margin	3,000				
Warranties Exp.	(100)	Total Assets	$10,960	Net Inflow from Oper.	6,960
Net Income	$2,900	Liabilities		**Investing Activities**	0
		Warranties Payable	$ 60	**Financing Activities**	0
		Stockholders' Equity			
		Common Stock	5,000	Net Change in Cash	6,960
		Retained Earnings	5,900	Plus: Beginning Cash Balance	2,000
		Total Liab. and Stockholders' Equity	$10,960	Ending Cash Balance	$8,960

M ost electrical appliances come with a manufacturer's warranty that obligates the manufacturer to pay for defects that occur during some designated period of time after the point of sale. Why would Circuit City issue warranties that obligate it to pay for defects that occur after the manufacturer's warranty has expired? Warranties are in fact insurance policies that generate profits. Indeed, the Circuit City Group reported that the gross dollar sales from extended warranty programs were 5.1 percent of its total sales in fiscal year 2001. Even more important, Circuit City notes that gross profit margins on products sold with extended warranties are higher than the gross profit margins on products sold without extended warranties. It should be noted that warranties produce revenues for manufacturers as well as retailers. The only difference is that the revenues generated from manufacturer's warranties are embedded in the sales price. Indeed, products with longer, more comprehensive warranties usually sell at higher prices than products with shorter, less extensive warranties.

■ Accounting for Discount Notes

LO6 Show how discount notes and related interest charges affect financial statements.

Up to this point, all notes payable have been assumed to be **interest-bearing notes.** At maturity, the amount due is the *face value* of the note *plus accrued interest.* In contrast, **discount notes** have the interest included in the face value of the note. Accordingly, a $5,000 face value discount note is repaid with a $5,000 cash payment at maturity. This payment includes principal and accrued interest. To illustrate, assume that the following four events apply to Beacon Management Services.

Event 1 Borrowing by Issuing a Discount Note
Beacon Management Services was started by issuing a $10,000 face value discount note to State Bank on March 1, 2001.

The note carried a 9 percent *discount rate* and a one-year term to maturity. As with interest-bearing notes, the **issuer of the note** gives the promissory note in exchange for the receipt of cash. The first step in accounting for the discount note is to divide the face amount between the discount and the principal (amount borrowed). The discount is computed by multiplying the face value of the note by the interest rate by the time period. In this case, the discount is $900 ($10,000 × 0.09). The amount borrowed is determined by subtracting the discount from the face value of the note ($10,000 − $900 = $9,100). Accordingly, in this case the **principal** (the amount of cash borrowed) is $9,100, and the **discount** (the amount of interest to be incurred over the term of the loan) is $900. In summary, *on the issue date,* assets and total liabilities increase by the amount borrowed (the $9,100 principal). The *income statement* is not affected by the borrowing transaction on the issue date. There is a $9,100 cash inflow shown in the financing activities section of the *statement of cash flows.* These effects are shown here.

Event No.	Assets	=	Liab.	+	Equity	Rev.	−	Exp.	=	Net Inc.	Cash Flow
1	9,100	=	9,100	+	NA	NA	−	NA	=	NA	9,100 FA

For internal record-keeping purposes, the amount of the discount is normally contained in a separate account titled **Discount on Notes Payable.** This account is a **contra liability account.** It is subtracted from the Notes Payable account to determine the carrying value of the liability. The *carrying value,* also known as the *book value,* gets its name from the fact that it is the amount at which the liability is shown (carried) on the books. In this case, Beacon's ledger contains the Notes Payable account with a $10,000 credit balance and the Discount on Notes Payable account with a $900 debit balance. The carrying value is computed as follows:

Notes Payable	$10,000
Discount on Notes Payable	(900)
Carrying value of liability	$ 9,100

Event 2 Recognition of Operating Expenses
Beacon incurred $8,000 of cash operating expenses.

The payment for these expenses reduces assets and equity. The effect of the event on the income statement is to increase expenses and decrease net income. The cash outflow is shown in the operating activities section of the statement of cash flows. These effects are shown here.

Event No.	Assets	=	Liab.	+	Equity	Rev.	−	Exp.	=	Net Inc.	Cash Flow
2	(8,000)	=	NA	+	(8,000)	NA	−	8,000	=	(8,000)	(8,000) OA

Event 3 Recognition of Revenue
Beacon recognized $12,000 of cash revenue.

The recognition of the revenue increases assets and equity. The amount of net income increases. The cash inflow is shown in the operating activities section of the statement of cash flows. These effects follow.

Event No.	Assets	=	Liab.	+	Equity	Rev.	−	Exp.	=	Net Inc.	Cash Flow
3	12,000	=	NA	+	12,000	12,000	−	NA	=	12,000	12,000 OA

Event 4 Adjustment for Accrued Interest
Beacon recognized accrued interest expense.

On December 31, 2001, Beacon is required to adjust the accounting records to reflect the accrual of 10 months of interest for the 2001 accounting period. Interest expense accrues at the rate of $75 per month ($900 discount ÷ 12). Accordingly, $750 ($75 × 10) of interest is accrued as of December 31. The reduction in equity caused by the recognition of the interest expense is balanced by an increase in liabilities. The increase in liabilities is accomplished by reducing the contra liability account, *Discount on Notes Payable.* Recall that the carrying value of the liability was $9,100 (that is, $10,000 face value less $900 discount) on the day the note was issued. The entry to record the accrued interest expense removes $750 from the discount account, leaving a $150 balance ($900 − $750) remaining after the adjusting entry is posted. The practice of converting the discount to interest expense over a designated period is referred to as the **amortization** of the discount. After 10 months of amortization, the carrying value of the liability shown on the December 31, 2001, balance sheet in Exhibit 7–9 is $9,850 ($10,000 face value − the $150 discount). The effect of the interest recognition on the income statement is to increase expenses and decrease net income by $750. The statement of cash flows is not affected by the accrual. Cash is paid for the interest at the maturity date. The effects of the adjusting entry for accrued interest expense are shown here.

Event No.	Assets	=	Liab.	+	Equity	Rev.	–	Exp.	=	Net Inc.	Cash Flow
4	NA	=	750	+	(750)	NA	–	750	=	(750)	NA

Ledger T-Accounts and Financial Statements

Exhibit 7–8 shows ledger T-accounts for the business events experienced by Beacon Management Services. The exhibit includes the entry used to close the revenue and expense accounts at the end of the 2001 accounting period. The ledger account balances are used to prepare the financial statements shown in Exhibit 7–9. The relevant accounting events are summarized here for your convenience.

1. Issued a $10,000 face value discount note with a 9 percent discount rate.
2. Paid $8,000 cash for operating expenses.
3. Earned $12,000 cash revenue.
4. Recognized $750 of accrued interest expense.
5. Closed the revenue and expense accounts. The letters *cl* are used as a posting reference for the closing entries.

Exhibit 7–8 *General Ledger*

Assets	=	Liabilities	+	Equity

Cash

(1)	9,100	8,000	(2)
(3)	12,000		
Bal.	13,100		

Notes Payable

	10,000	(1)
	10,000	Bal.

Discount on Notes Payable

(1)	900	750	(4)
Bal.	150		

Retained Earnings

	3,250	(cl)
	3,250	Bal.

Service Revenue

(cl)	12,000	12,000	(3)
		0	Bal.

Operating Expenses

(2)	8,000	8,000	(cl)
Bal.	0		

Interest Expense

(4)	750	750	(cl)
Bal.	0		

Exhibit 7–9 *Financial Statements for 2001*

Income Statement		Balance Sheet			Statement of Cash Flows	
Service Revenue	$12,000	Assets			**Operating Activities**	
Operating Exp.	(8,000)	Cash		$13,100	Inflow from Customers	$12,000
					Outflow for Expenses	(8,000)
Operating Income	4,000				Net Inflow from Oper.	4,000
Interest Exp.	(750)	Liabilities			**Investing Activities**	0
Net Income	$ 3,250	Notes Payable	$10,000		**Financing Activities**	
		Less: Disc. on Notes Pay.	(150)		Inflow from Creditors	9,100
		Total Liabilities		$ 9,850	Net Change in Cash	13,100
		Stockholders' Equity			Plus: Beginning Cash Balance	0
		Retained Earnings		3,250		
		Total Liab. and Stockholders' Equity		$13,100	Ending Cash Balance	$13,100

Accounting Events Affecting the 2002 Period

This section introduces four accounting events that apply to Beacon's 2002 accounting cycle.

LO6 Show how discount notes and related interest charges affect financial statements.

Event 1 Accrual of Interest for 2002
Beacon recognized 2 months of accrued interest.

Since the note carried a one-year term, two months of interest have to be accrued at the maturity date on February 28, 2002. Since interest expense accrues at the rate of $75 per month ($900 discount ÷ 12), there is $150 ($75 × 2) of interest expense accrued in 2002. The recognition of the interest increases liabilities (reduces the discount account to zero) and decreases equity. The effect of the recognition on the income statement is to increase expenses and decrease net income by $150. The statement of cash flows is not affected by the transaction. These effects are shown here.

Event No.	Assets	=	Liab.	+	Equity	Rev.	−	Exp.	=	Net Inc.	Cash Flow
1	NA	=	150	+	(150)	NA	−	150	=	(150)	NA

Event 2 Payment of Face Value
Beacon repaid face value on the discount note payable.

The face value ($10,000) of the note is due on the maturity date. The repayment of the note is an asset use transaction causing assets and liabilities to decrease. The income statement is not affected by the event. The $10,000 cash payment includes $900 for interest and $9,100 for principal. Accordingly, there is a $900 outflow shown in the operating activities section and a $9,100 outflow shown in the financing activities section of the statement of cash flows. These effects are shown here.

Event No.	Assets	=	Liab.	+	Equity	Rev.	−	Exp.	=	Net Inc.	Cash Flow
2	(10,000)	=	(10,000)	+	NA	NA	−	NA	=	NA	(900) OA
											(9,100) FA

Event 3 Revenue Recognition
Beacon recognized $13,000 of cash revenue.

Assets and equity increase as a result of the recognition. Net income also increases. The cash inflow is shown in the operating activities section of the statement of cash flows. These effects are shown here.

Event No.	Assets	=	Liab.	+	Equity	Rev.	−	Exp.	=	Net Inc.	Cash Flow
3	13,000	=	NA	+	13,000	13,000	−	NA	=	13,000	13,000 OA

Event 4 Recognition of Operating Expenses
Beacon incurred $8,500 of cash operating expenses.

This event causes assets and equity to decrease. Net income also decreases. The cash outflow is shown in the operating activities section of the statement of cash flows. These effects follow.

Event No.	Assets	=	Liab.	+	Equity	Rev.	–	Exp.	=	Net Inc.	Cash Flow
4	(8,500)	=	NA	+	(8,500)	NA	–	8,500	=	(8,500)	(8,500) OA

Ledger T-Accounts and Financial Statements

Exhibits 7–10 and 7–11 present the relevant ledger T-accounts and financial statements, respectively. Notice in Exhibit 7–11 that the balance in liabilities is zero because both interest and principal have been paid, leaving Beacon with no obligations as of the 2002 fiscal closing date. Retained earnings includes the total of net income for 2001 and 2002. This result occurs because all income was retained in the business since no dividends were made to owners during 2001 and 2002.

Exhibit 7–10 General Ledger

Assets				=	Liabilities			+	Equity		

Cash

Bal.	13,100	10,000	(2)
(3)	13,000	8,500	(4)
Bal.	7,600		

Notes Payable

(2)	10,000	10,000	Bal.
		0	Bal.

Discount on Notes Payable

Bal.	150	150	(1)
Bal.	0		

Retained Earnings

		3,250	Bal.
		4,350	(CL)
		7,600	Bal.

Service Revenue

(CL)	13,000	13,000	(3)
		0	Bal.

Operating Expense

(4)	8,500	8,500	(CL)
Bal.	0		

Interest Expense

(1)	150	150	(CL)
Bal.	0		

Exhibit 7–11 Financial Statements for 2002

Income Statement

Service Revenue	$13,000
Operating Expenses	(8,500)
Operating Income	4,500
Interest Exp.	(150)
Net Income	$ 4,350

Balance Sheet

Assets	
Cash	$7,600
Liabilities	$ 0
Stockholders' Equity	
Retained Earnings	7,600
Total Liab. & Stockholders' Equity	$7,600

Statement of Cash Flows

Operating Activities	
Inflow from Customers	$13,000
Outflow for Expenses	(8,500)
Outflow for Interest	(900)
Net Inflow from Oper.	3,600
Investing Activities	0
Financing Activities	
Outflow to Creditors	(9,100)
Net Change in Cash	(5,500)
Plus: Beginning Cash Balance	13,100
Ending Cash Balance	$ 7,600

Real-World Credit Costs

Costs of Managing Accounts Receivable

Why do companies sell goods on credit or *on account?* Why not simply require all customers to pay cash for the goods and services they receive? There are two good reasons that a business might allow customers to buy now and pay later. First, as explained earlier, experience has shown that people will buy more goods if credit sales are available. Second, if a business sells goods to other companies, it may be necessary for the selling company to give the buying company time to generate the cash needed to pay for the goods purchased.

To illustrate, assume that Mattel sells toys to Toys R Us. If the goods are delivered (sold) to Toys R Us on September 1, they may not be resold to retail customers until October or November. If Mattel gives Toys R Us 60 days to pay for the goods, Toys R Us can use the money it receives from selling the goods to its customers to pay Mattel. For many small companies that do not have cash available to pay up front, buying on credit is the only way to obtain the inventory that they need. If a manufacturer or wholesaler wants to sell to these customers, *sales on account* are the only means possible.

Costs of Making Credit Sales

Although the policy of allowing customers to buy goods on account may generate more sales, and more gross profit, it is not without additional costs. One such cost is obvious. Some customers may never pay their bills. Bad debts constitute a major cost of extending credit. Other costs are more subtle. As mentioned earlier, there is the cost of keeping the records related to accounts receivable. These costs can be significant. Large companies have entire departments devoted to managing their accounts receivable. For these companies, it may cost literally millions of dollars to buy the equipment and pay the staff necessary to operate their accounts receivable departments. Finally, there is an implicit interest charge associated with the extension of credit. When a customer is allowed to delay payment, the creditor loses the opportunity to use the amount due. Indeed, many real-world companies sell their receivables for less than the full amount due in order to obtain cash. The difference between the face value of the receivables and the amount of cash collected from the sale of the receivables is equivalent to the discount interest.

LO7 Explain the effects of the cost of financing credit sales.

Exhibits 7–12 and 7–13 are excerpts from the annual report of Tyco International Ltd. These excerpts provide insight as to the costs of credit incurred by real-world companies. First, note that the 2000 balance sheet shows a $442.1 million balance in the company's Allowance for Doubtful Accounts. Bad debts of more that $442.1 million certainly constitute a significant cost of credit. In addition, footnote 5 (Exhibit 7–13) indicates that the company has an agreement to sell some of its accounts receivable. The receivables are sold at a discount. The amount of the discount for the 2000 accounting period was $25.7 million. Since the new receivables will be sold at a discount, the interest will be a continuing expense incurred by the company. It is interesting to note that while the discount is, in fact, an interest cost, the footnote indicates that Tyco has chosen to include this cost in the selling, general, and administrative expense category on the income statement. Real-world reporting includes a great deal of diversity with respect to the classification of amounts. Reading the footnotes should expand your appreciation for diversity as well as your understanding of the costs of credit.

Average Number of Days to Collect Accounts Receivable

The longer it takes a company to collect accounts receivable, the higher the cost to the company. As explained earlier, when a company extends credit, it loses the opportunity to invest funds elsewhere, and the longer the funds are not available, the greater the lost income. Also, experience has shown that the older an account receivable becomes, the less likely it is to be

Exhibit 7–12		

TYCO INTERNATIONAL LTD.
Consolidated Balance Sheets
At September 30
(in millions, except share data)

Consolidated Balance Sheets

	September 30	
	2000	**1999**
Current Assets		
Cash and Cash Equivalents	$ 1,264.8	$ 1,762.0
Receivables, less Allowance for Doubtful Accounts of $442.1 in 2000 and $329.8 in 1999	5,630.4	4,582.3
Contracts in Progress	357.3	536.6
Inventories	3,845.1	2,849.1
Deferred Income Taxes	683.3	694.3
Prepaid Expenses and Other Current Assets	1,034.8	721.2
Total Current Assets	12,815.7	11,145.5
Construction in Progress—Tycom Global Network	111.1	—
Property, Plant and Equipment, Net	8,218.4	7,322.4
Goodwill and Other Intangible Assets, Net	16,332.6	12.158.9
Long-Term Investments	1,653.7	269.7
Deferred Income Taxes	532.5	668.8
Other Assets	740.3	779.0
Total Assets	$40,404.3	$32,344.3
Current Liabilities		
Loans Payable and Current Maturities of Long-Term Debt	$ 1,537.2	$ 1,012.8
Accounts Payable	3,291.9	2,530.8
Accrued Expenses and Other Current Liabilities	4,038.2	3,545.7
Contracts in Progress—Billings in Excess of Costs	835.0	977.9
Deferred Revenue	265.7	258.8
Income Taxes	1,650.3	798.0
Deferred Income Taxes	60.6	1.0
Total Current Liabilities	11,678.9	9,125.0
Long-Term Debt	9,461.8	9,109.4
Other Long-Term Liabilities	1,095.3	1,236.4
Deferred Income Taxes	791.6	504.2
Total Liabilities	23,027.6	19,975.0
Commitments and Contingencies		
Minority Interest	343.5	—
Shareholders' Equity		
Preference Shares, $1 Par Value, 125,000,000 Shares Authorized, None Issued	—	—
Common Shares, $0.20 Par Value, 2,500,000,000 Shares Authorized; 1,684,511,070 Shares Outstanding in 2000 and 1,690,175,338 Shares Outstanding in 1999, Net of 31,551,310 Shares Owned by Subsidiaries in 2000 and 11,432,678 Shares Owned by Subsidiaries in 1999	336.9	338.0
Capital in Excess		
Share Premium	5,233.3	4,881.5
Contributed Surplus, Net of Deferred Compensation of $59.4 in 2000 and $30.7 in 1999	2,786.3	3,607.6
Accumulated Earnings	8,427.6	3,992.3
Accumulated Other Comprehensive Income (Loss)	249.1	(450.1)
Total Shareholders' Equity	17,033.2	12,369.3
Total Liabilities and Shareholders' Equity	$40,404.3	$32,344.3

collected. Finally, taking longer to collect an account typically means that more money is spent on salaries, equipment, and supplies used in the process of trying to collect it. Accordingly, businesses are very interested in knowing the time it takes to collect their receivables. They want to know if they are taking more or less time to collect receivables than they took in

> **Exhibit 7–13** *Partial Footnote 5: Sale of Accounts Receivable*
>
> The Company has an agreement under which several of its operating subsidiaries sell a defined pool of trade accounts receivable to a limited purpose subsidiary of the Company. . . . The proceeds from the sales were used to reduce borrowings under TIG's commercial paper program and are reported as operating cash flows in the Consolidated Statements of Cash Flows. The proceeds of sale are less than the face amount of accounts receivable sold by an amount that approximates the cost that the limited purpose subsidiary would incur if it were to issue commercial paper backed by these accounts receivable. The discount from the face amount is accounted for as a loss on the sale of receivables and has been included in the selling, general and administrative expenses in the Consolidated Statement of Operations. Such discount aggregated $25.7 million, $15.7 million, and $17.3 million, or 6.6 percent, 5.6 percent and 5.8 percent of the weighted-average balance of the receivables outstanding, during Fiscal 2000, Fiscal 1999 and Fiscal 1998, respectively. The operating subsidiaries retain collection and administrative responsibilities for the participating interests in the defined pool.

past periods, or how their collection period compares to the collection periods of their competitors. Ratio analysis can help managers convert absolute dollar values to common units of measure that enable them to make such comparisons.

Two ratios are available to help a company's management, or other users, express the collection period in common measurement units. The first is the **accounts receivable turnover ratio.** It is defined as[3]

$$\frac{\text{Sales}}{\text{Accounts receivable}}$$

Dividing a company's sales by its accounts receivable tells how many times the accounts receivable balance is "turned over" (turned into cash) each year. The more rapid the turnover, the shorter the collection period. The problem with this ratio is that it is difficult to interpret because it does not provide a measure in units of time. Therefore, the accounts receivable turnover ratio is often taken one step further to determine the **average number of days to collect accounts receivable,** sometimes called the *average collection period.* This is computed as

$$\frac{\text{365 days}}{\text{Accounts receivable turnover ratio}}$$

This ratio tells the user how many days, on average, it takes a company to collect its accounts receivable. Since longer collection periods equate to higher costs, shorter periods are obviously more desirable. To illustrate the computation of the *average number of days to collect accounts receivable* ratio for Allen's Tutoring Services, refer to the 2002 financial statements in Exhibit 7–5. On average, the company takes 104 days to collect its receivables. This collection period can be computed in two steps:

1. Accounts receivable turnover is 3.509 ($10,000 ÷ $2,850).
2. Average number of days to collect receivables is 104 (365 ÷ 3.509).

In the preceding computations, the net realizable value of accounts receivable is used because that is the amount typically shown in published financial statements. The results would not have been materially different had total accounts receivable been used.

Real-World Data

What is the collection period for real-world companies? The answer depends on the industry in which the company operates. Exhibit 7–14 shows the average number of days to collect receivables for seven companies in three different industries.

---

[3]To be more correct, technically, the ratio should be computed using only credit sales and average accounts receivable. Often, however, credit sales alone are not given in published financial statements. Average accounts receivable, if desired, is easily computed as ([beginning receivables + ending receivables] ÷ 2). For the purposes of this course, use the simpler ratio defined here (sales ÷ accounts receivable).

Exhibit 7–14		
Industry	**Company**	**Average Number of Days to Collect Receivables**
Fast Food	Domino's	15
	Wendy's	12
	Starbucks	13
Drugstores	CVS	15
	Phar Mor	7
Wine	Chalone	68
	Mondavi	66

Note that there is significant variation in the collection periods among different industries. Also note that the fast-food companies do have accounts receivable, which may seem odd to some readers because these restaurants require customers to pay cash when purchasing hamburgers or coffee. The accounts receivable for Domino's, Wendy's, and Starbucks exist because these companies sell goods to restaurants that are independent franchisees, so the money is owed to Domino's by individual restaurants, not by the individual who purchases a pepperoni pizza.

Are the collection periods for Mondavi and Chalone Wine Group too long? The answer depends on their credit policies. If they are selling goods to customers for net 30-day terms, there may be reason for concern, but if they allow customers 60 days to pay and the cost of this policy has been built into their pricing structure, there is less need for concern.

In Chapter 6, the operating cycle was defined as the average time it takes a company to go from cash to inventory to accounts receivable and back to cash. The *average number of days to collect accounts receivable* is a measure of the time necessary to complete part of this cycle. A method for computing the remainder of the cycle is explained in Chapter 8.

focus on International Issues

A Rose by Any Other Name . . .

If a person who studied U.S. GAAP wanted to look at the financial statements of a non-U.S. company, choosing statements of a company from another English-speaking country might seem logical. Presumably, this would eliminate language differences, and only the differences in GAAP would remain. Unfortunately, this is not true.

When an accountant in the United States uses the term *turnover,* she or he is usually thinking of a financial ratio, such as the accounts receivable turnover ratio. However, in the United Kingdom, the term *turnover* refers to what U.S. accountants call *sales.* U.K. balance sheets do not usually show an account named *Inventory;* rather, they use the term *Stocks.* In the United States, accountants typically use the term *stocks* to refer to certificates representing ownership in a corporation. Finally, if an accountant or banker from the United Kingdom should ever ask you about your *gearing ratio,* he or she probably is not interested in your bicycle but in your debt to assets ratio.

Randolph Corporation had sales for the year of $535,333 and an Accounts Receivable balance at year end of $22,000. Determine Randolph's average number of days to collect accounts receivable.

Answer The accounts receivable turnover is 24.33 ($535,333 ÷ $22,000) times per year. The average number of days to collect accounts receivable is 15 (365 ÷ 24.33).

Check Yourself 7–3

a look
back

Accounting for receivables and payables was introduced first in Chapter 2. This chapter presented several more challenging issues related to short-term receivables and payables. More specifically, the chapter discussed the *allowance method of accounting for bad debts.* The allowance method seeks to match expenses with revenues. The percent of sales method of estimating bad debts expense was discussed in this chapter. Under this method bad debts expense is estimated to be a certain percentage of credit sales. For example, if credit sales amounted to $500,000 and bad debts were estimated to be 1 percent of credit sales then bad debts expenses would be $5,000 ($500,000 × .01). Recall that this is an estimated amount of the actual expense that will be incurred in the future. The estimated amount of bad debts expense is recognized in the current period (i.e., the same period in which the associated revenue is recognized), thereby accomplishing the matching objective. Bad debts expense acts to decrease equity, net income, and the net realizable value of receivables (Accounts Receivable − Allowance for Doubtful Accounts).

The allowance method of accounting for bad debts is compared to the *direct write-off method,* which recognizes bad debts expense when an account is determined to be uncollectible. The method is conceptually invalid because it overstates the value of accounts receivable shown on the balance sheet and it fails to properly match revenue and expense. However, the method is simple to apply. It is used when the amount of bad debts is considered to be insignificant. When the amount of bad debts is immaterial, the benefits derived from recording convenience are considered to be more important than conceptual accuracy.

This chapter also discussed accounting for *warranty obligations.* The amount of warranty expense is recognized in the period in which the sale is made or service provided. The associated warranty obligation is shown as a liability on the balance sheet until the future period in which the obligation is settled.

The chapter also introduced a new method of measuring interest. *Discount notes* include the interest in their face value. The borrower is given an amount of cash that is less than the face value of the note. For example, a borrower signing a $5,000, 8 percent note would receive $4,600 ($5,000 − [$5,000 × 0.08]). The $400 difference between the amount borrowed ($4,600) and the amount repaid ($5,000) is interest.

Finally, the chapter discussed the costs of making credit sales. In addition to bad debts, interest is a major cost of financing receivables. Determining the length of the collection period provides a measure of the quality of receivables. Short collection periods usually indicate low amounts of uncollectible accounts and interest cost. Long collection periods imply higher costs. The collection period can be measured in two steps. First, determine the *accounts receivable turnover ratio* by dividing sales by the accounts receivable balance. Next, determine the *average number of days to collect accounts receivable* by dividing the number of days in the year (365) by the accounts receivable turnover ratio.

a look
forward

It is especially important that you understand how to account for discount notes. Chapter 10 presents topics related to long-term debt that are very similar to accounting issues related to discount notes. Understanding how to account for discount notes is *essential* if you are to understand the topics covered in Chapter 10.

This chapter also discussed the costs associated with the collection of accounts receivable. Specifically, the longer it takes to collect receivables, the higher the cost of financing those receivables. Chapter 8 presents several topics associated with accounting for inventory. One of these topics concerns the costs associated with holding inventory, which is similar to the financing costs associated with the collection of receivables.

SELF-STUDY REVIEW PROBLEM

During 2007 Calico Company experienced the following accounting events:

1. Provided $120,000 of services on account.
2. Collected $85,000 cash from accounts receivable.
3. Issued a $12,000 face value discount note with a 10 percent discount rate and a one-year term to maturity.
4. Wrote off $1,800 of accounts receivable that were uncollectible.
5. Paid $90,500 cash for operating expenses.
6. Estimated that bad debts expense would be 2 percent of credit sales. Recorded the adjusting entry.
7. Recorded seven months of accrued interest on the discount note.
8. Estimated warranty expense would be $900. Recorded the adjusting entry.

The following ledger accounts present the balances in Calico Company's records on January 1, 2007.

	Assets					=	Liabilities						Equity		
Event No.	Cash	+	Acct. Rec.	–	Allow.	=	Notes Pay.	–	Disc. on Notes Pay.	+	War. Pay.	+	C. Stk.	+	Ret. Ear.
Bal.	2,000	+	18,000	–	2,200	=	–			+		+	10,000	+	7,800

Required

a. Record the 2007 accounting events in the ledger accounts.
b. Determine net income for 2007.
c. Determine net cash flow from operating activities for 2007.
d. Determine the net realizable value of accounts receivable at December 31, 2007.

Solution to Requirement a.

	Assets					=	Liabilities						Equity		
Event No.	Cash	+	Acct. Rec.	–	Allow.	=	Notes Pay.	–	Disc. on Notes Pay.	+	War. Pay.	+	C. Stk.	+	Ret. Ear.
Bal.	2,000	+	18,000	–	2,200	=	–			+		+	10,000	+	7,800
1		+	120,000	–		=	–			+		+		+	120,000
2	85,000	+	(85,000)	–		=	–			+		+		+	
3	10,800	+		–		=	12,000	–	1,200	+		+		+	
4		+	(1,800)	–	(1,800)	=	–			+		+		+	
5	(90,500)	+		–		=	–			+		+		+	(90,500)
6		+		–	2,400	=	–			+		+		+	(2,400)
7		+		–		=	–		(700)	+		+		+	(700)
8		+		–		=	–			+	900	+		+	(900)
Totals	7,300	+	51,200	–	2,800	=	12,000	–	500	+	900	+	10,000	+	33,300

Solution to Requirements b–d.

b. Net income is $25,500 ($120,000 − $90,500 − $2,400 − $700 − $900).
c. Net cash flow from operating activities is an outflow of $5,500 ($85,000 − $90,500).
d. The net realizable value of accounts receivable is $48,400 ($51,200 − $2,800).

KEY TERMS

Accounts receivable *311*
Accounts receivable turnover ratio *333*
Allowance for Doubtful Accounts *313*

Allowance method of accounting for bad debts *312*
Amortization *327*

Average number of days to collect accounts receivable *333*
Bad debts expense *313*
Contra liability account *327*

Direct write-off method *321*
Discount *326*
Discount notes *326*
Discount on Notes Payable *327*

Going concern assumption *312*   Issuer of the note *326*   Notes receivable *311*   Principal *326*
Interest-bearing notes *326*   Net realizable value *312*   Payables *312*   Warranty *323*

1. What is the difference between accounts receivable and notes receivable?
2. What is the *net realizable value* of receivables?
3. Explain the *going concern* assumption. How does it affect the way accounts receivable versus accounts payable are reported in financial statements?
4. What is the difference between the allowance method and the direct write-off method of accounting for bad debts?
5. What is the most common format for reporting accounts receivable on the balance sheet? What information does this method provide beyond showing only the net amount?
6. What are two ways in which estimating bad debts improves the accuracy of the financial statements?
7. Why is it necessary to make an entry to reinstate a previously written off account receivable before the collection is recorded?
8. What are some factors considered in estimating the amount of uncollectible accounts receivable?
9. What is the effect on the accounting equation of recognizing bad debts expense?
10. What is the effect on the accounting equation of writing off an uncollectible account receivable when the allowance method is used? When the direct write-off method is used?
11. How does the recovery of a bad debt affect the income statement when the allowance method is used? How does the recovery of a bad debt affect the statement of cash flows when the allowance method is used?
12. What is the advantage of using the allowance method of accounting for bad debts? What is the advantage of using the direct write-off method?
13. When is it acceptable to use the direct write-off method of accounting for bad debts?
14. Why is it generally beneficial for a business to accept credit cards as payment for goods and services even when the fee charged by the credit card company is substantial?
15. What types of costs do businesses avoid when they accept major credit cards as compared with handling credit sales themselves?
16. What does the term *warranty* mean?
17. What effect does recognizing warranty expense have on the balance sheet? On the income statement?
18. When is warranty cost reported on the statement of cash flows?
19. What is the difference between an interest-bearing note and a discount note?
20. How is the carrying value of a discount note computed?
21. Will the effective rate of interest be the same on a $10,000 face value, 12 percent interest-bearing note and a $10,000 face value, 12 percent discount note? Is the amount of cash received upon making these two loans the same? Why or why not?
22. How does the *amortization* of a discount affect the income statement, balance sheet, and statement of cash flows?
23. What is the effect on the accounting equation of borrowing $8,000 by issuing a discount note that has a 10 percent discount rate and a one-year term to maturity? What is the effect on the accounting equation of the periodic amortization of the discount? What is the effect on the accounting equation of the payment of the face value of the note at maturity?
24. What type of account is Discount on Notes Payable?
25. How is the accounts receivable turnover ratio computed? What information does the ratio provide?
26. How is the average number of days to collect accounts receivable computed? What information does the ratio provide?
27. Is accounting terminology standard in all countries? What term is used in the United Kingdom to refer to *sales?* What term is used to refer to *inventory?* What is a *gearing ratio?* Is it important to know about these differences?

EXERCISE 7–1A *Effect of Recognizing Bad Debts Expense on Financial Statements:*   **L.O. 2**
Allowance Method

Stateline Auto Service was started on January 1, 2004. The company experienced the following events during its first year of operation.

Events Affecting 2004

1. Provided $20,000 of repair services on account.
2. Collected $18,000 cash from accounts receivable.
3. Adjusted the accounting records to reflect the estimate that bad debt expense would be 1 percent of the service revenue on account.

Events Affecting 2005

1. Wrote off a $160 account receivable that was determined to be uncollectible.
2. Provided $22,000 of repair services on account.
3. Collected $19,000 cash from accounts receivable.
4. Adjusted the accounting records to reflect the estimate that bad debt expense would be 1 percent of the service revenue on account.

Required

a. Write an accounting equation and record the events for 2004 in T-accounts under the appropriate categories.
b. Determine the following amounts:
   (1) Net income for 2004.
   (2) Net cash flow from operating activities for 2004.
   (3) Balance of accounts receivable at the end of 2004.
   (4) Net realizable value of accounts receivable at the end of 2004.
c. Repeat the requirements in Requirements *a* and *b* for the 2005 accounting period.

L.O. 2 **EXERCISE 7–2A** *Analyzing Financial Statement Effects of Accounting for Bad Debts Using the Allowance Method*

Businesses using the allowance method to account for bad debts expense routinely experience four accounting events:

1. Recognition of revenue on account.
2. Collection of cash from accounts receivable.
3. Recognition of bad debts expense through a year-end adjusting entry.
4. Write-off of uncollectible accounts.

Required

Show the effect of each event on the elements of the financial statements, using a horizontal statements model like the one shown here. Use + for increase, − for decrease, and NA for not affected. In the cash flow column, indicate whether the item is an operating activity (OA), investing activity (IA), or financing activity (FA). The first transaction is entered as an example.

Event No.	Assets	=	Liab.	+	S. Equity	Rev.	−	Exp.	=	Net Inc.	Cash Flow
1	+		NA		+	+		NA		+	NA

L.O. 2 **EXERCISE 7–3A** *Analyzing Account Balances for a Company Using the Allowance Method of Accounting for Bad Debts*

The following account balances come from the records of Hawk Company.

	Beginning Balance	Ending Balance
Accounts Receivable	$2,000	$2,200
Allowance for Bad Debts	100	170

During the accounting period, Hawk recorded $9,000 of service revenue on account. The company also wrote off a $110 account receivable.

Required

a. Determine the amount of cash collected from receivables.
b. Determine the amount of bad debts expense recognized during the period.

EXERCISE 7–4A *Effect of Recovering a Receivable Previously Written Off*

The accounts receivable balance for Sports Shoes at December 31, 2006, was $97,000. Also on that date, the balance in Allowance for Doubtful Accounts was $3,200. During 2007, $3,400 of accounts receivable were written off as uncollectible. In addition, Sports Shoes unexpectedly collected $920 of receivables that had been written off in a previous accounting period. Sales on account during 2007 were $204,000, and cash collections from receivables were $197,000. Bad debts expense was estimated to be 2 percent of the sales on account for the period.

Required

(*Hint:* Post the transactions to T-accounts under the accounting equation before completing the requirements.)
a. Based on the preceding information, compute (after year-end adjustment):
  (1) Balance of Allowance for Doubtful Accounts at December 31, 2007.
  (2) Balance of Accounts Receivable at December 31, 2007.
  (3) Net realizable value of Accounts Receivable at December 31, 2007.
b. What amount of bad debts expense will Sports Shoes report for 2007?
c. Explain how the recovery of the $920 receivables affected the accounting equation.

EXERCISE 7–5A *Accounting for Bad Debts: Allowance Versus Direct Write-Off Method*

C & E Auto Parts sells new and used auto parts. Although a majority of its sales are cash sales, it makes a significant amount of credit sales. During 2008, its first year of operations, C & E Auto Parts experienced the following:

Credit sales	$352,000
Cash sales	625,000
Collections of accounts receivable	320,000
Uncollectible accounts charged off during the year	320

Required

a. Assume that C & E Auto Parts uses the allowance method of accounting for bad debts and estimates that 1 percent of its sales on account will not be collected. Answer the following questions:
  (1) What is the Accounts Receivable balance at December 31, 2008?
  (2) What is the ending balance of Allowance for Doubtful Accounts at December 31, 2008, after all entries and adjusting entries are posted?
  (3) What is the amount of bad debts expense for 2008?
  (4) What is the net realizable value of accounts receivable at December 31, 2008?
b. Assume that C & E Auto Parts uses the direct write-off method of accounting for bad debts. Answer the following questions:
  (1) What is the Accounts Receivable balance at December 31, 2008?
  (2) What is the amount of bad debts expense for 2008?
  (3) What is the net realizable value of accounts receivable at December 31, 2008?

EXERCISE 7–6A *Accounting for Bad Debts: Direct Write-Off Method*

Ben's Repair Shop has mostly a cash business but does have a small number of sales on account. Consequently, it uses the direct write-off method to account for bad debts. During 2006 Ben's Repair Shop earned $12,000 of cash revenue and $1,500 of revenue on account. Cash operating expenses were $8,200. After numerous attempts to collect a $50 account receivable from Larry Raines, the account was determined to be uncollectible in 2007.

Required

a. Record the effects of (1) cash revenue, (2) revenue on account, (3) cash expenses, and (4) write-off of the uncollectible account on the financial statements using a horizontal statements model like the one shown here. In the Cash Flow column, indicate whether the item is an operating activity (OA), investing activity (IA), or financing activity (FA). Use NA to indicate that an element is not affected by the event.

Assets		=	Liab.	+	S. Equity	Rev.	–	Exp.	=	Net Inc.	Cash Flow
Cash	+	Accts. Rec.									

b. What amount of net income did Ben's Repair Shop report on the 2006 income statement?

c. Prepare the general journal entries for the four accounting events listed in Requirement *a*.

L.O. 4   EXERCISE 7–7A *Effect of Credit Card Sales on Financial Statements*

Big Elk Hunting Lodge provided $80,000 of services during 2006. All customers paid for the services with credit cards. Big Elk turned the credit card receipts over to the credit card company immediately. The credit card company paid Big Elk cash in the amount of face value less a 4 percent service charge.

Required

a. Record the credit card sales and the subsequent collection of accounts receivable in a horizontal statements model like the one shown here. In the Cash Flow column, indicate whether the item is an operating activity (OA), investing activity (IA), or financing activity (FA). Use NA to indicate that an element is not affected by the event.

Assets		= Liab.	+ S. Equity	Rev.	− Exp.	= Net Inc.	Cash Flow
Cash	+ Accts. Rec.						

b. Answer the following questions:

(1) What is the amount of total assets at the end of the accounting period?

(2) What is the amount of revenue reported on the income statement?

(3) What is the amount of cash flow from operating activities reported on the statement of cash flows?

(4) Why would Big Elk Hunting Lodge accept credit cards instead of providing credit directly to its customers? In other words, why would Big Elk be willing to pay 4 percent of sales to have the credit card company handle its sales on account?

L.O. 4   EXERCISE 7–8A *Recording Credit Card Sales*

Biggers Company accepted credit cards in payment for $3,450 of merchandise sold during March 2006. The credit card company charged Biggers a 3 percent service fee. The credit card company paid Biggers as soon as it received the invoices.

Required

a. Prepare the general journal entry to record the merchandise sale.

b. Prepare the general journal entry for the collection of the receivable from the credit card company.

c. Based on this information alone, what is the amount of net income earned during the month of March?

L.O. 5   EXERCISE 7–9A *Effect of Warranties on Income and Cash Flow*

To support herself while attending school, Otis Taylor sold computers to other students. During her first year of operation, she sold computers that had cost her $75,000 cash for $110,000 cash. She provided her customers with a one-year warranty against defects in parts and labor. Based on industry standards, she estimated that warranty claims would amount to 5 percent of sales. During the year she paid $320 cash to replace a defective keyboard.

Required

Prepare an income statement and statement of cash flows for Taylor's first year of operation. Explain the difference between net income and the amount of cash flow from operating activities.

L.O. 5   EXERCISE 7–10A *Effect of Warranty Obligations and Payments on Financial Statements*

The Hurt Appliance Co. provides a 120-day parts-and-labor warranty on all merchandise it sells. Hurt estimates the warranty expense for the current period to be $900. During the period a customer returned a product that cost $315 to repair.

Required

a. Show the effects of these transactions on the financial statements using a horizontal statements model like the example shown here. Use a + to indicate increase, a − for decrease, and NA for not affected. Also in the Cash Flow column, indicate whether the item is an operating activity (OA), investing activity (IA), or financing activity (FA).

Assets	=	Liab.	+	S. Equity	Rev.	−	Exp.	=	Net Inc.	Cash Flow

b. Prepare the journal entry to record the warranty expense for the period.

c. Prepare the journal entry to record payment for the actual repair costs.

d. Discuss the advantage of estimating the amount of warranty expense.

EXERCISE 7–11A *Effect of a Discount Note on Financial Statements*

L.O. 6

George Barnes started a moving company on January 1, 2006. On March 1, 2006, Barnes borrowed cash from a local bank by issuing a one-year $50,000 face value note with annual interest based on a 12 percent discount. During 2006, Barnes provided services for $36,800 cash.

Required

Answer the following questions. Record the events in T-accounts prior to answering the questions.

a. What is the amount of total liabilities on the December 31, 2006 balance sheet?

b. What is the amount of net income on the 2006 income statement?

c. What is the amount of cash flow from operating activities on the 2006 statement of cash flows?

d. Provide the general journal entries necessary to record issuing the note on March 1, 2006; recognizing accrued interest on December 31, 2006; and repaying the loan on February 28, 2007.

EXERCISE 7–12A *Comparing Effective Interest Rates on Discount Versus Interest-Bearing Notes*

L.O. 6

Glen Pounds borrowed money by issuing two notes on January 1, 2006. The financing transactions are described here.

1. Borrowed funds by issuing a $20,000 face value discount note to State Bank. The note had a 12 percent discount rate, a one-year term to maturity, and was paid off on January 1, 2007.

2. Borrowed funds by issuing a $20,000 face value, interest-bearing note to Community Bank. The note had a 12 percent stated rate of interest, a one-year term to maturity, and was paid off on January 1, 2007.

Required

a. Show the effects of issuing the two notes on the financial statements using separate horizontal financial statement models like the ones here. Record the transaction amounts under the appropriate categories. Also in the Cash Flow column, indicate whether the item is an operating activity (OA), investing activity (IA), or financing activity (FA). Record only the events occurring on the date of issue. Do not record accrued interest or the repayment at maturity.

Discount Note

Assets	=	Liabilities			+	S. Equity	Rev.	−	Exp.	=	Net Inc.	Cash Flow
Cash	=	Notes Rec.	−	Disc. on Notes Pay.	+	Ret. Ear.						

Interest-Bearing Note

Assets	=	Liabilities	+	S. Equity	Rev.	−	Exp.	=	Net Inc.	Cash Flow
Cash	=	Notes Rec.	+	Ret. Ear.						

b. What is the total amount of interest to be paid on each note?

c. What amount of cash was received from each note?

d. Which note has the higher effective interest rate? Support your answer with appropriate computations.

EXERCISE 7–13A *Recording Accounting Events for a Discount Note*

L.O. 6

Ray Co issued a $30,000 face value discount note to First Bank on June 1, 2006. The note had a 10 percent discount rate and a one-year term to maturity.

Required

Prepare general journal entries for the transactions on the following page:

a. The issuance of the note on June 1, 2006.
b. The adjustment for accrued interest at the end of the year, December 31, 2006.
c. Recording interest expense for 2007 and repaying the principal on May 31, 2007.

L.O. 2, 5, 6   **EXERCISE 7–14A** *Comprehensive Single-Cycle Problem*

The following post-closing trial balance was drawn from the accounts of A-1 Steel Co. as of December 31, 2006.

	Debit	Credit
Cash	$ 3,000	
Accounts Receivable	15,000	
Allowance for Doubtful Accounts		$ 800
Inventory	21,000	
Accounts Payable		7,500
Common Stock		12,000
Retained Earnings		18,700
Totals	$39,000	$39,000

Transactions for 2007

1. A-1 acquired an additional $5,000 cash from the issue of common stock.
2. A-1 purchased $47,000 of inventory on account.
3. A-1 sold inventory that cost $46,000 for $82,000. Sales were made on account.
4. The products sold were warranted, and A-1 estimated future warranty costs would amount to 4 percent of sales.
5. The company wrote off $600 of uncollectible accounts.
6. On September 1, A-1 issued an $8,000 face value, 9 percent discount note. The note had a one-year term.
7. A-1 paid $1,100 cash to satisfy warranty claims.
8. A-1 paid $9,600 cash for salaries expense.
9. The company collected $75,000 cash from accounts receivable.
10. A cash payment of $52,000 was paid on accounts payable.
11. The company paid a $2,000 cash dividend to the stockholders.
12. Bad debts are estimated to be 1 percent of sales on accounts.
13. Recorded the accrued interest at Deceber 31, 2006.

Required

a. Open T-accounts and record the beginning balances and the effects of the accounting events described.
b. Prepare an income statement, statement of changes in stockholders' equity, balance sheet, and statement of cash flows for 2007.

PROBLEMS—SERIES A

L.O. 2   **PROBLEM 7–15A** *Accounting for Bad Debts—Two Cycles Using the Allowance Method*

The following transactions apply to Durm's Consulting for 2006, the first year of operation:
1. Recognized $40,000 of service revenue earned on account.
2. Collected $34,000 from accounts receivable.
3. Adjusted accounts to recognize bad debts expense. Durm uses the allowance method of accounting for bad debts and estimates that bad debts expense will be 2 percent of sales on account.

The following transactions apply to Durm's Consulting for 2007:

1. Recognized $51,500 of service revenue on account.
2. Collected $47,500 from accounts receivable.
3. Determined that $150 of the accounts receivable were uncollectible and wrote them off.
4. Collected $12 of an account that had been written off previously.
5. Paid $36,500 cash for operating expenses.
6. Adjusted accounts to recognize bad debts expense for 2007. Durm estimates that bad debts expense will be 1 percent of sales on account.

Required

Complete all the following requirements for 2006 and 2007. Complete all requirements for 2006 prior to beginning the requirements for 2007.

a. Identify the type of each transaction (asset source, asset use, asset exchange, or claims exchange).

b. Show the effect of each transaction on the elements of the financial statements, using a horizontal statements model like the one shown here. Use + for increase, − for decrease, and NA for not affected. Also, in the Cash Flow column, indicate whether the item is an operating activity (OA), investing activity (IA), or financing activity (FA). The first transaction is entered as an example. (*Hint:* Closing entries do not affect the statements model.)

Event No.	Assets	=	Liab.	+	S. Equity	Rev.	−	Exp.	=	Net Inc.	Cash Flow
1	+		NA		+	+		NA		+	NA

c. Record the transactions in general journal form, and post them to T-accounts (begin 2007 with the ending T-account balances from 2006).

d. Prepare the income statement, statement of changes in stockholders' equity, balance sheet, and statement of cash flows.

e. Prepare closing entries and an after-closing trial balance. Post the closing entries to the T-accounts.

PROBLEM 7–16A *Determining Account Balances and Preparing Journal Entries: Allowance Method of Accounting for Bad Debts*

L.O. 2

The following information pertains to Hill Cabinet Company's sales on account and accounts receivable:

Accounts Receivable Balance, January 1, 2007	$ 172,800
Allowance for Doubtful Accounts, January 1, 2007	5,184
Sales on Account, 2007	1,269,800
Cost of Goods Sold	800,000
Collections of Accounts Receivable, 2007	1,284,860

After several collection attempts, Hill Cabinet Company wrote off $4,500 of accounts that could not be collected. Hill estimates that bad debts expense will be 0.5 percent of sales on account.

Required

a. Compute the following amounts:
 (1) Using the allowance method, the amount of bad debts expense for 2007.
 (2) Net realizable value of receivables at the end of 2007.

b. Prepare the general journal entries to:
 (1) Record sales on account for 2007.
 (2) Record cash collections from accounts receivable for 2007.
 (3) Write off the accounts that are not collectible.
 (4) Record the estimated bad debts expense for 2007.

c. Explain why the bad debts expense amount is different from the amount that was written off as uncollectible.

PROBLEM 7–17A *Accounting for Credit Card Sales, Warranties, and Bad Debts: Direct Write-Off Method*

L.O. 3–5

Brigg's Supply Company had the following transactions in 2004:

1. Acquired $70,000 cash from the issue of common stock.
2. Purchased $240,000 of merchandise for cash in 2004.
3. Sold merchandise that cost $190,000 for $370,000 during the year under the following terms:

$100,000	Cash Sales
250,000	Credit Card Sales (The credit card company charges a 3 percent service fee.)
20,000	Sales on Account

4. Collected all the amount receivable from the credit card company.
5. Collected $16,000 of accounts receivable.

6. Used the direct write-off method to account for bad debts expense and wrote off $240 of accounts receivable that were uncollectible.
7. Brigg's gives a one-year warranty on equipment it sells. It estimated that warranty expense for 2004 would be $650.
8. Paid selling and administrative expenses of $53,000.

Required

a. Show the effects of each of the transactions on the elements of the financial statements, using a horizontal statements model like the one shown here. Use + for increase, − for decrease, and NA for not affected. The first transaction is entered as an example. (*Hint:* Closing entries do not affect the statements model.)

Event No.	Assets	=	Liab.	+	S. Equity	Rev.	−	Exp.	=	Net Inc.	Cash Flow
1	+		NA		+	NA		NA		NA	+ FA

b. Prepare general journal entries for each of the transactions, and post them to T-accounts.
c. Prepare an income statement, statement of changes in stockholders' equity, balance sheet, and statement of cash flows for 2004.

L.O. 6   **PROBLEM 7–18A** *Accounting for a Discount Note—Two Accounting Cycles*

City Corp. was started in 2001. The following summarizes transactions that occurred during 2001:

1. Issued a $40,000 face value discount note to Golden Savings Bank on April 1, 2001. The note had a 9 percent discount rate and a one-year term to maturity.
2. Incurred and paid $118,000 cash for selling and administrative expenses.
3. Recognized revenue from services performed for cash, $176,000.
4. Amortized the discount at the end of the year, December 31, 2001.
5. Prepared the necessary closing entries at December 31, 2001.

The following summarizes transactions that occurred in 2002:

1. Recognized $292,000 of service revenue in cash.
2. Incurred and paid for $198,000 for selling and administrative expenses.
3. Amortized the remainder of the discount for 2002 and paid the face value of the note.
4. Prepared the necessary closing entries at December 31, 2002.

Required

a. Show the effects of each of the transactions on the elements of the financial statements, using a horizontal statements model like the one shown here. Use + for increase, − for decrease, and NA for not affected. The first transaction is entered as an example. (*Hint:* Closing entries do not affect the statements model.)

Event No.	Assets	=	Liab.	+	S. Equity	Rev.	−	Exp.	=	Net Inc.	Cash Flow
1	+		+		NA	NA		NA		NA	+ FA

b. Prepare the entries in general journal form for the transactions for 2001 and 2002, and post them to T-accounts.
c. Prepare an income statement, statement of changes in stockholders' equity, balance sheet, and statement of cash flows for 2001 and 2002.

L.O. 3–5   **PROBLEM 7–19A** *Effect of Transactions on the Elements of Financial Statements*

Required

Identify each of the following independent transactions as asset source (AS), asset use (AU), asset exchange (AE), or claims exchange (CE). Also explain how each event affects assets, liabilities, stockholders' equity, net income, and cash flow by placing a + for increase, − for decrease, or NA for not affected under each of the categories. The first event is recorded as an example.

Event	Type of Event	Assets	Liabilities	Common Stock	Retained Earnings	Net Income	Cash Flow
a	AS	+	NA	NA	+	+	+

a. Provided services for cash.
b. Paid cash for salaries expense.
c. Provided services on account.
d. Wrote off an uncollectible account (use direct write-off method).
e. Collected cash from customers paying their accounts.
f. Recovered a bad debt that was previously written off (assume direct write-off method was used).
g. Paid cash for equipment.
h. Recognized warranty expense.
i. Sold merchandise at a price above cost. Accepted payment by credit card. The credit card company charges a service fee. The receipts have not yet been forwarded to the credit card company for collection.
j. Realized a gain when equipment was sold for cash.
k. Paid cash to satisfy warranty obligations.
l. Submitted receipts to the credit card company in *i* above and collected cash.
m. Issued a discount note to First National Bank.
n. Paid cash to creditors on accounts payable.
o. Amortized three months of the discount on a discount note payable.

PROBLEM 7–20A *Classified Balance Sheet and Multistep Income Statement*

L.O. 2, 5, 6

Required

Use the following information to prepare a classified balance sheet and a multistep income statement for Belmont Equipment Co. for 2003. (*Hint:* Some of the items will *not* appear on either statement, and ending retained earnings must be calculated.)

Salaries Expense	$ 96,000	Interest Receivable (short term)	$ 500
Common Stock	40,000	Beginning Retained Earnings	10,400
Notes Receivable (short term)	12,000	Warranties Payable (short term)	1,300
Allowance for Doubtful Accounts	4,000	Gain on Sale of Equipment	6,400
Accumulated Depreciation	30,000	Other Operating Expenses	70,000
Discount on Note Payable	2,400	Cash Flow from Investing Activities	80,000
Notes Payable (long term)	106,000	Prepaid Rent	9,600
Salvage Value of Building	4,000	Land	36,000
Interest Payable (short term)	1,800	Cash	17,800
Bad Debts Expense	10,800	Inventory	122,800
Supplies	1,600	Accounts Payable	46,000
Equipment	60,000	Interest Expense	24,000
Interest Revenue	4,200	Salaries Payable	9,200
Sales Revenue	396,000	Unearned Revenue	52,600
Dividends	8,000	Cost of Goods Sold	143,000
Warranty Expense	3,400	Accounts Receivable	90,000

PROBLEM 7–21A *Missing Information*

L.O. 2, 5, 6

The following information comes from the accounts of Breedlove Company:

Account Title	Beginning Balance	Ending Balance
Accounts Receivable	$30,000	$28,000
Allowance for Doubtful Accounts	2,000	1,800
Warranties Payable	3,600	3,000
Notes Payable	40,000	40,000
Discount on Notes Payable	2,400	1,600

Required

a. There were $240,000 in sales on account during the accounting period. Write-offs of uncollectible accounts were $1,600. What was the amount of cash collected from accounts receivable? What amount of bad debts expense was reported on the income statement? What was the net realizable value of receivables at the end of the accounting period?
b. Warranty expense for the period was $1,100. How much cash was paid to settle warranty claims?
c. What amount of interest expense was recognized during the period? How much cash was paid for interest? What book value was reported for the discount note on the year-end balance sheet?

L.O. 3–6   PROBLEM 7–22A *Comprehensive Accounting Cycle Problem (Uses Direct Write-Off Method)*

The following trial balance was prepared for Water Way Sales and Service on December 31, 2002, after the closing entries were posted.

Account Title	Debit	Credit
Cash	$87,100	
Accounts Receivable	17,800	
Inventory	94,600	
Accounts Payable		$ 44,000
Common Stock		90,000
Retained Earnings		65,500
Totals	$199,500	$199,500

Water Way had the following transactions in 2003:
1. Purchased merchandise on account for $390,000.
2. Sold merchandise that cost $364,000 on account for $522,000.
3. Performed $44,000 of services for cash.
4. Sold merchandise for $26,400 to credit card customers. The merchandise cost $18,600. The credit card company charges a 5 percent fee.
5. Collected $504,000 cash from accounts receivable.
6. Paid $396,000 cash on accounts payable.
7. Paid $150,000 cash for selling and administrative expenses.
8. Collected cash for the full amount due from the credit card company.
9. Issued a $60,000 face value discount note with an 8 percent discount rate and a one-year term to maturity.
10. Wrote off $450 of accounts as uncollectible (use the direct write-off method).
11. Made the following adjusting entries:
    a. Recorded three months' interest on the discount note at December 31, 2003.
    b. Estimated warranty expense to be $3,090.

Required
Prepare general journal entries for these transactions; post the entries to T-accounts; and prepare an income statement, a statement of changes in stockholders' equity, a balance sheet, and a statement of cash flows for 2003.

EXERCISES—SERIES B

L.O. 2   EXERCISE 7–1B *Effect of Recognizing Bad Debts Expense on Financial Statements: Allowance Method*

Smith Dry Cleaning was started on January 1, 2003. It experienced the following events during its first year of operation.

Events Affecting 2003

1. Provided $10,000 of cleaning services on account.
2. Collected $8,000 cash from accounts receivable.
3. Adjusted the accounting records to reflect the estimate that bad debt expense would be 1 percent of the service revenue on account.

Events Affecting 2004

1. Wrote off an $80 account receivable that was determined to be uncollectible.
2. Provided $12,000 of cleaning services on account.
3. Collected $10,000 cash from accounts receivable.
4. Adjusted the accounting records to reflect the estimate that bad debt expense would be 1 percent of the service revenue on account.

Required
a. Write an accounting equation and record the events for 2003 in T-accounts under the appropriate categories.

b. Determine the following amounts:
   (1) Net income for 2003.
   (2) Net cash flow from operating activities for 2003.
   (3) Balance of accounts receivable at the end of 2003.
   (4) Net realizable value of accounts receivable at the end of 2003.
c. Repeat the requirements in Requirements *a* and *b* for the 2003 accounting period.

EXERCISE 7–2B *Analyzing Financial Statments Effects of Accounting for Bad Debts Using*   **L.O. 2**
                   the Allowance Method

Conley Bros. uses the allowance method to account for bad debts expense. Conley experienced the following four events in 2005:
1. Recognition of $48,000 of revenue on account.
2. Collection of $42,000 cash from accounts receivable.
3. Determination that $300 of its accounts were not collectible and wrote off these receivables.
4. Recognition of bad debts expense for the year. Conley estimates that bad debts expense will be 2 percent of its sales.

Required
Show the effect of each of these event on the elements of the financial statements, using a horizontal statements model like the following one. Use + for increase, − for decrease, and NA for not affected. In the cash flow column, indicate whether the item is an operating activity (OA), investing activity (IA), or financing activity (FA).

Event No.		Assets		=	Liab.	+	S. Equity					
	Cash	A. Rec.	All for DA				Ret. Earn.	Rev.	−	Exp.	= Net Inc.	Cash Flow

EXERCISE 7–3B *Analyzing Account Balances for a Company Using the Allowance Method of*   **L.O. 2**
                   Accounting for Bad Debts

The following account balances come from the records of Lewis Company.

	Beginning Balance	Ending Balance
Accounts Receivable	$1,500	$2,000
Allowance for Bad Debts	150	175

During the accounting period, Lewis recorded $7,000 of sales revenue on account. The company also wrote off an $80 account receivable.

Required
a. Determine the amount of cash collected from receivables.
b. Determine the amount of bad debts expense recognized during the period.

EXERCISE 7–4B *Effect of Recovering a Receivable Previously Written Off*   **L.O. 2**

The accounts receivable balance for Best Fit Spa at December 31, 2007, was $80,000. Also on that date, the balance in Allowance for Doubtful Accounts was $3,000. During 2008, $3,500 of accounts receivable were written off as uncollectible. In addition, Best Fit unexpectedly collected $900 of receivables that had been written off in a previous accounting period. Sales on account during 2008 were $200,000, and cash collections from receivables were $190,000. Bad debts expense was estimated to be 2 percent of the sales on account for the period.

Required
(*Hint:* Post the transactions to T-accounts before you complete the requirements.)
a. Based on the preceding information, compute (after year-end adjustment):
   (1) Balance of Allowance for Doubtful Accounts at December 31, 2008.
   (2) Balance of Accounts Receivable at December 31, 2008.
   (3) Net realizable value of Accounts Receivable at December 31, 2008.
b. What amount of bad debts expense will Best Fit report for 2008?
c. Explain how the recovery of the $900 receivable affects the income statement.

L.O. 2, 3   EXERCISE 7–5B *Accounting for Bad Debts: Allowance Versus Direct Write-Off Method*

Adam's Bike Shop sells new and used bicycle parts. Although a majority of its sales are cash sales, it makes a significant amount of credit sales. During 2004, its first year of operations, Adam's Bike Shop experienced the following:

Credit sales	$300,000
Cash sales	555,000
Collections of Accounts Receivable	260,000
Uncollectible accounts charged off during the year	250

Required

a. Assume that Adam's Bike Shop uses the allowance method of accounting for bad debts and estimates that 1 percent of its sales on account will not be collected. Answer the following questions:

  (1) What is the Accounts Receivable balance at December 31, 2004?

  (2) What is the ending balance of the Allowance for Doubtful Accounts at December 31, 2004, after all entries and adjusting entries are posted?

  (3) What is the amount of bad debts expense for 2004?

  (4) What is the net realizable value of accounts receivable at December 31, 2004?

b. Assume that Adam's Bike Shop uses the direct write-off method of accounting for bad debts. Answer the following questions:

  (1) What is the Accounts Receivable balance at December 31, 2004?

  (2) What is the amount of bad debts expense for 2004?

  (3) What is the net realizable value of accounts receivable at December 31, 2004?

L.O. 3   EXERCISE 7–6B *Accounting for Bad Debts: Direct Write-Off Method*

Valley Service Co. does mostly a cash business but does make a few sales on account. Consequently, it uses the direct write-off method to account for bad debts. During 2005 Valley Service Co. earned $10,000 of cash revenue and $2,000 of revenue on account. Cash operating expenses were $8,000. After numerous attempts to collect a $70 account receivable from Bill Smith, the account was determined to be uncollectible in 2005.

Required

a. Record the effects of (1) cash revenue, (2) revenue on account, (3) cash expenses, and (4) write-off of the uncollectible account on the financial statements using a horizontal statements model like the one shown here. In the Cash Flow column, indicate whether the item is an operating activity (OA), investing activity (IA), or financing activity (FA). Use NA to indicate that an element is not affected by the event.

Assets		= Liab. + S. Equity	Rev. – Exp. = Net Inc.	Cash Flow
Cash	+ Accts. Rec.			

b. What amount of net income did Valley Service Co. report on the 2005 income statement?

c. Prepare the general journal entries for the four accounting events listed in Requirement *a*.

L.O. 4   EXERCISE 7–7B *Effect of Credit Card Sales on Financial Statements*

Denver One-Day Spa provided $120,000 of services during 2004. All customers paid for the services with credit cards. Denver turned the credit card receipts over to the credit card company immediately. The credit card company paid Denver cash in the amount of face value less a 5 percent service charge.

Required

a. Record the credit card sales and the subsequent collection of accounts receivable in a horizontal statements model like the one shown here. In the Cash Flow column, indicate whether the item is an operating activity (OA), investing activity (IA), or financing activity (FA). Use NA to indicate that an element is not affected by the event.

Assets		= Liab. + S. Equity	Rev. – Exp. = Net Inc.	Cash Flow
Cash	+ Accts. Rec.			

b. Answer the following questions:

  (1) What is the amount of total assets at the end of the accounting period?

  (2) What is the amount of revenue reported on the income statement?

  (3) What is the amount of cash flow from operating activities reported on the statement of cash flows?

  (4) What cost would a business incur if it maintained its own accounts receivable? What cost does a business incur by accepting credit cards?

EXERCISE 7–8B *Recording Credit Card Sales*   L.O. 4

Mallard Company accepted credit cards in payment for $3,000 of merchandise sold during July 2004. The credit card company charged Mallard a 4 percent service fee; it paid Mallard as soon as it received the invoices.

Required

a. Prepare the general journal entry to record the merchandise sale.

b. Prepare the general journal entry for the collection of the receivable from the credit card company.

c. Based on this information alone, what is the amount of net income earned during the month of July?

EXERCISE 7–9B *Effect of Warranties on Income and Cash Flow*   L.O. 5

To support herself while attending school, Cindy Long sold stereo systems to other students. During her first year of operation, she sold systems that had cost her $95,000 cash for $140,000 cash. She provided her customers with a one-year warranty against defects in parts and labor. Based on industry standards, she estimated that warranty claims would amount to 6 percent of sales. During the year she paid $200 cash to replace a defective tuner.

Required

Prepare an income statement and statement of cash flows for Long's first year of operation. Based on the information given, what is Long's total warranties liability at the end of the accounting period?

EXERCISE 7–10B *Effect of Warranty Obligations and Payments on Financial Statements*   L.O. 5

The Tractor Company provides a 120-day parts-and-labor warranty on all merchandise it sells. Tractor estimates the warranty expense for the current period to be $1,400. During the period a customer returned a product that cost $596 to repair.

Required

a. Show the effects of these transactions on the financial statements using a horizontal statements model like the example shown here. Use a + to indicate increase, a − for decrease, and NA for not affected. Also in the Cash Flow column, indicate whether the item is an operating activity (OA), investing activity (IA), or financing activity (FA).

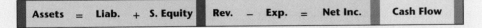

Assets	=	Liab.	+	S. Equity	Rev.	−	Exp.	=	Net Inc.	Cash Flow

b. Prepare the journal entry to record the warranty expense for the period.

c. Prepare the journal entry to record payment for the actual repair costs.

d. Why do compaines estimate warranty expense and record the expense before the repairs are actually made?

EXERCISE 7–11B *Effect of a Discount Note on Financial Statements*   L.O. 6

Justin Davis started a design company on January 1, 2004. On April 1, 2004, Davis borrowed cash from a local bank by issuing a one-year $200,000 face value note with annual interest based on a 10 percent discount. During 2004, Davis provided services for $55,000 cash.

Required

Answer the following questions. (*Hint:* Record the events in T-accounts prior to answering the questions.)

a. What is the amount of total liabilities on the December 31, 2004 balance sheet?

b. What is the amount of net income on the 2004 income statement?

c. What is the amount of cash flow from operating activities on the 2004 statement of cash flows?

d. Provide the general journal entries necessary to record issuing the note on April 1, 2004; recognizing accrued interest on December 31, 2004; and repaying the loan on March 31, 2005.

L.O. 6   EXERCISE 7–12B *Comparing Effective Interest Rates on Discount Versus Interest-Bearing Notes*

Brady Winstead borrowed money by issuing two notes on March 1, 2005. The financing transactions are described here.

1. Borrowed funds by issuing a $30,000 face value discount note to Farmers Bank. The note had a 10 percent discount rate, a one-year term to maturity, and was paid off on March 1, 2006.
2. Borrowed funds by issuing a $30,000 face value, interest-bearing note to Valley Bank. The note had a 10 percent stated rate of interest, a one-year term to maturity, and was paid off on March 1, 2006.

Required

a. Show the effects of issuing the two notes on the financial statements using separate horizontal financial statement models like the ones here. Record the transaction amounts under the appropriate categories. Also in the Cash Flow column, indicate whether the item is an operating activity (OA), investing activity (IA), or financing activity (FA). Record only the events occurring on the date of issue. Do not record accrued interest or the repayment at maturity.

Discount Note

Assets	=		Liabilities		+	S. Equity	Rev.	−	Exp.	=	Net Inc.	Cash Flow
Cash	=	Notes Pay.	−	Disc. on Notes Pay.	+	Ret. Ear.						

Interest-Bearing Note

Assets	=	Liabilities	+	S. Equity	Rev.	−	Exp.	=	Net Inc.	Cash Flow
Cash	=	Notes Pay.	+	Ret. Ear.						

b. What is the total amount of interest to be paid on each note?
c. What amount of cash was received from each note?
d. Which note has the higher effective interest rate? Support your answer with appropriate computations.

L.O. 6   EXERCISE 7–13B *Recording Accounting Events for a Discount Note*

Lewis Co. issued a $40,000 face value discount note to National Bank on July 1, 2005. The note had a 12 percent discount rate and a one-year term to maturity.

Required

Prepare general journal entries for the following:
a. The issuance of the note on July 1, 2005.
b. The adjustment for accrued interest at the end of the year, December 31, 2005.
c. Recording interest expense for 2006 and repaying the principal on June 30, 2006.

L.O. 2, 5, 6   EXERCISE 7–14B *Comprehensive Single-Cycle Problem*

The following post-closing trial balance was drawn from the accounts of Phillips Metal Co. (PMC) as of December 31, 2004.

	Debit	Credit
Cash	$ 4,000	
Accounts Receivable	20,000	
Allowance for Doubtful Accounts		$ 1,000
Inventory	40,000	
Accounts Payable		10,000
Common Stock		20,000
Retained Earnings		33,000
Totals	$64,000	$64,000

Transactions for 2005

1. PMC acquired an additional $4,000 cash from the issue of common stock.
2. PMC purchased $80,000 of inventory on account.
3. PMC sold inventory that cost $76,000 for $128,000. Sales were made on account.
4. The products sold were warrantied, and PMC estimated future warranty costs would amount to 5 percent of sales.
5. The company wrote off $800 of uncollectible accounts.
6. On September 1, PMC issued a $10,000 face value, 9 percent discount note. The note had a one-year term.
7. PMC paid $2,000 cash to satisfy warranty claims.
8. PMC paid $16,000 cash for operating expenses.
9. The company collected $133,200 cash from accounts receivable.
10. A cash payment of $68,000 was paid on accounts payable.
11. The company paid a $2,000 cash dividend to the stockholders.
12. Bad debts are estimated to be 1 percent of sales on account.
13. Recorded the accrued interest at December 31, 2004.

Required

a. Open T-accounts and record the beginning balances and the effects of the accounting events described.
b. Prepare an income statement, statement of changes in stockholders' equity, balance sheet, and statement of cash flows for 2004.

PROBLEMS—SERIES B

PROBLEM 7–15B *Accounting for Bad Debts: Two Cycles Using the Allowance Method*   L.O. 2

The following transactions apply to J & J Company for 2005, the first year of operation:

1. Recognized $255,000 of service revenue earned on account.
2. Collected $159,000 from accounts receivable.
3. Paid $150,000 cash for operating expense.
4. Adjusted the accounts to recognize bad debts expense. J & J uses the allowance method of accounting for bad debts and estimates that bad debts expense will be 1 percent of sales on account.

The following transactions apply to J & J for 2006:

1. Recognized $408,000 of service revenue on account.
2. Collected $411,000 from accounts receivable.
3. Determined that $1,800 of the accounts receivable were uncollectible and wrote them off.
4. Collected $600 of an account that had previously been written off.
5. Paid $126,000 cash for operating expenses.
6. Adjusted the accounts to recognize bad debts expense for 2006. J & J estimates bad debts expense will be 0.5 percent of sales on account.

Required

Complete the following requirements for 2005 and 2006. Complete all requirements for 2005 prior to beginning the requirements for 2006.

a. Identify the type of each transaction (asset source, asset use, asset exchange, or claims exchange).
b. Show the effect of each transaction on the elements of the financial statements, using a horizontal statements model like the one shown here. Use + for increase, − for decrease, and NA for not affected. Also, in the Cash Flow column, indicate whether the item is an operating activity (OA), investing activity (IA), or financing activity (FA). The first transaction is entered as an example. (*Hint:* Closing entries do not affect the statements model.)

Event No.	Assets	=	Liab.	+	S. Equity	Rev.	−	Exp.	=	Net Inc.	Cash Flow
1	+		NA		+	+		NA		+	NA

c. Record the transactions in general journal form, and post them to T-accounts (begin 2006 with the ending T-account balances from 2005).
d. Prepare the income statement, statement of changes in stockholders' equity, balance sheet, and statement of cash flows.
e. Prepare closing entries and an after-closing trial balance. Post the closing entries to the T-accounts.

L.O. 2   PROBLEM 7–16B *Determining Account Balances and Preparing Journal Entries: Allowance Method of Accounting for Bad Debts*

During the first year of operation, 2002, ACE Appliance recognized $300,000 of service revenue on account. At the end of 2002, the accounts receivable balance was $58,000. For this first year in business, the owner believes bad debts expense will be about 1 percent of sales on account.

Required

a. What amount of cash did ACE collect during 2002?

b. Assuming ACE uses the allowance method to account for bad debts, what amount should ACE record as bad debts expense for 2002?

c. Prepare the journal entries to:

(1) Record service revenue on account.

(2) Record collection from accounts receivable.

(3) Record the entry to recognize bad debts expense.

d. What is the net realizable value of receivables at the end of 2002?

e. Show the effects of the transactions in Requirement *c* on the financial statements by recording the appropriate amounts in a horizontal statements model like the one shown here. In the Cash Flow column, indicate whether the item is an operating activity (OA), investing activity (IA), or financing activity (FA). Use NA for not affected.

Assets			=	Liab.	+	S. Equity	Rev.	–	Exp.	=	Net Inc.	Cash Flow
Cash	+	Accts. Rec.	–	Allow.								

L.O. 3, 4, 5   PROBLEM 7–17B *Accounting for Credit Card Sales, Warranties, and Bad Debts: Direct Write-Off Method*

Byrd Company had the following transactions in 2005:

1. The business was started when it acquired $500,000 cash from the issue of common stock.

2. Byrd purchased $1,200,000 of merchandise for cash in 2005.

3. During the year, the company sold merchandise for $1,600,000. The merchandise cost $900,000. Sales were made under the following terms:

$600,000	Cash sales
500,000	Credit card sales (The credit card company charges a 4 percent service fee.)
500,000	Sales on account

4. The company collected all the amount receivable from the credit card company.

5. The company collected $400,000 of accounts receivable.

6. Byrd used the direct write-off method to account for bad debts expense and wrote off $5,000 of accounts receivable that were uncollectible.

7. Byrd gives a one-year warranty on equipment it sells. It estimated that warranty expense for 2005 would be $4,500.

8. The company paid $100,000 cash for selling and administrative expenses.

Required

a. Show the effects of each of the transactions on the elements of the financial statements, using a horizontal statements model like the one shown here. Use + for increase, – for decrease, and NA for not affected. The first transaction is entered as an example. (*Hint:* Closing entries do not affect the statements model.)

Event No.	Assets	=	Liab.	+	S. Equity	Rev.	–	Exp.	=	Net Inc.	Cash Flow
1	+		NA		+	NA		NA		NA	+ FA

b. Prepare general journal entries for each of the transactions, and post them to T-accounts.

c. Prepare an income statement, statement of changes in stockholders' equity, balance sheet, and statement of cash flows for 2005.

PROBLEM 7–18B *Accounting for a Discount Note across Two Accounting Cycles*   **L.O. 6**

Laura White opened White & Company, an accounting practice, in 2006. The following summarizes transactions that occurred during 2006:

1. Issued a $200,000 face value discount note to First National Bank on July 1, 2006. The note had a 10 percent discount rate and a one-year term to maturity.
2. Recognized cash revenue of $336,000.
3. Incurred and paid $132,000 of operating expenses.
4. Adjusted the books to recognize interest expense at December 31, 2006.
5. Prepared the necessary closing entries at December 31, 2006.

The following summarizes transactions that occurred in 2007:

1. Recognized $984,000 of cash revenue.
2. Incurred and paid $416,000 of operating expenses.
3. Recognized the interest expense for 2007 and paid the face value of the note.
4. Prepared the necessary closing entries at December 31, 2007.

Required

a. Show the effects of each of the transactions on the elements of the financial statements, using a horizontal statements model like the one shown here. Use + for increase, − for decrease, and NA for not affected. The first transaction is entered as an example. (*Hint:* Closing entries do not affect the statements model.)

Event No.	Assets	=	Liab.	+	S. Equity	Rev.	−	Exp.	=	Net Inc.	Cash Flow
1	+		+		NA	NA		NA		NA	+ FA

b. Prepare entries in general journal form for the transactions for 2006 and 2007, and post them to T-accounts.
c. Prepare an income statement, statement of changes in stockholders' equity, balance sheet, and statement of cash flows for 2006 and 2007.

PROBLEM 7–19B *Effect of Transactions on the Elements of Financial Statements*   **L.O. 3–6**

Required

Identify each of the following independent transactions as asset source (AS), asset use (AU), asset exchange (AE), or claims exchange (CE). Also explain how each event affects assets, liabilities, stockholders' equity, net income, and cash flow by placing a + for increase, − for decrease, or NA for not affected under each of the categories. The first two events are recorded as examples.

Event	Type of Event	Assets	Liabilities	Common Stock	Retained Earnings	Net Income	Cash Flow
a	AE	+ −	NA	NA	NA	NA	−
b	AS	+	NA	NA	+	+	NA

a. Paid cash for equipment.
b. Sold merchandise at a price above cost. Accepted payment by credit card. The credit card company charges a service fee. The receipts have not yet been forwarded to the credit card company for collection.
c. Submitted receipts to the credit card company and collected cash.
d. Realized a gain when equipment was sold for cash.
e. Provided services for cash.
f. Paid cash to satisfy warranty obligations.
g. Paid cash for salaries expense.
h. Recovered a bad debt that had been previously written off (assume the direct write-off method is used to account for bad debts).
i. Paid cash to creditors on accounts payable.
j. Issued a discount note to State Bank.
k. Provided services on account.

l. Wrote off an uncollectible account (use the direct write-off method).

m. Amortized three months of the discount on a discount note payable.

n. Collected cash from customers paying their accounts.

o. Recognized warranty expense.

L.O. 2, 5, 6   PROBLEM 7–20B *Classified Balance Sheet and Multistep Income Statement*

Required

Use the following information to prepare a classified balance sheet and a multistep income statement for Daniels Company for 2004. (*Hint:* Some of the items will *not* appear on either statement, and ending retained earnings must be calculated.)

Other Operating Expenses	$ 90,000	Cash	$ 23,000
Land	50,000	Interest Receivable (short term)	800
Accumulated Depreciation	38,000	Cash Flow from Investing Activities	102,000
Accounts Payable	60,000	Allowance for Doubtful Accounts	7,000
Unearned Revenue	58,000	Interest Payable (short term)	3,000
Warranties Payable (short term)	2,000	Discount on Notes Payable	4,000
Equipment	77,000	Sales Revenue	500,000
Notes Payable (long term)	133,000	Bad Debts Expense	14,000
Salvage Value of Equipment	7,000	Interest Expense	32,000
Dividends	12,000	Accounts Receivable	113,000
Warranty Expense	5,000	Salaries Payable	12,000
Beginning Retained Earnings	28,800	Supplies	3,000
Interest Revenue	6,000	Prepaid Rent	14,000
Gain on Sale of Equipment	10,000	Common Stock	52,000
Inventory	154,000	Cost of Goods Sold	179,000
Notes Receivable (short term)	17,000	Salaries Expense	122,000

L.O. 2, 5, 6   PROBLEM 7–21B *Missing Information*

The following information comes from the accounts of Jersey Company:

Account Title	Beginning Balance	Ending Balance
Accounts Receivable	$30,000	$34,000
Allowance for Doubtful Accounts	1,800	1,700
Warranties Payable	4,000	3,000
Notes Payable	40,000	40,000
Discount on Note Payable	1,200	800

Required

a. There were $170,000 in sales on account during the accounting period. Write-offs of uncollectible accounts were $1,400. What was the amount of cash collected from accounts receivable? What amount of bad debts expense was reported on the income statement? What was the net realizable value of receivables at the end of the accounting period?

b. Warranty expense for the period was $3,600. How much cash was paid to settle warranty claims?

c. What amount of interest expense was recognized during the period? How much cash was paid for interest? What book value was reported for the discount note on the year-end balance sheet?

L.O. 2, 3, 4, 5, 6   PROBLEM 7–22B *Comprehensive Accounting Cycle Problem (Uses Allowance Method)*

The following trial balance was prepared for The Sport Shop on December 31, 2006, after the closing entries were posted.

Account Title	Debit	Credit
Cash	$118,000	
Accounts Receivable	172,000	
Allowance for Doubtful Accounts		$ 10,000
Inventory	690,000	
Accounts Payable		142,000
Common Stock		720,000
Retained Earnings		108,000
Totals	$980,000	$980,000

The Sport Shop had the following transactions in 2007:

1. Purchased merchandise on account for $420,000.
2. Sold merchandise that cost $288,000 for $480,000 on account.
3. Sold for $240,000 cash merchandise that had cost $144,000.
4. Sold merchandise for $180,000 to credit card customers. The merchandise had cost $108,000. The credit card company charges a 4 percent fee.
5. Collected $526,000 cash from accounts receivable.
6. Paid $540,000 cash on accounts payable.
7. Paid $134,000 cash for selling and administrative expenses.
8. Collected cash for the full amount due from the credit card company.
9. Issued a $48,000 face value discount note with a 10 percent discount rate and a one-year term to maturity.
10. Wrote off $7,200 of accounts as uncollectible.
11. Made the following adjusting entries:
    a. Recorded bad debts expense estimated at 1 percent of sales on account.
    b. Recorded seven months of interest on the discount note at December 31, 2007.
    c. Estimated warranty expense to be $1,800.

Required

a. Prepare general journal entries for these transactions; post the entries to T-accounts; and prepare an income statement, a statement of changes in stockholders' equity, a balance sheet, and a statement of cash flows for 2007.
b. Compute the net realizable value of accounts receivable at December 31, 2007.
c. If The Sport Shop used the direct write-off method, what amount of bad debts expense would it report on the income statement?

ANALYZE, THINK, COMMUNICATE

BUSINESS APPLICATIONS CASE *Dell's Annual Report*

ATC 7–1

Required

Using the Dell Computer Corporation financial statements in Appendix B, answer the following questions:

a. What was the average number of days to collect accounts receivable for the year ended February 2, 2001?
b. Approximately what percentage of Dell's accounts receivable as of February 2, 2001, does the company think will not be collected (see Note 9)?
c. What percentage of Dell's current assets at February 2, 2001, was represented by accounts receivable?
d. How much warranty liability did Dell have on February 2, 2001?

GROUP ASSIGNMENT *Missing Information*

ATC 7–2

The following selected financial information is available for three companies:

	Bell	Card	Zore
Total sales	$125,000	$210,000	?
Cash sales	?	26,000	$120,000
Credit sales	40,000	?	75,000
Accounts receivable, January 1, 2008	6,200	42,000	?
Accounts receivable, December 31, 2008	5,600	48,000	7,500
Allowance for doubtful accounts, January 1, 2008	?	?	405
Allowance for doubtful accounts, December 31, 2008	224	1,680	?
Bad debt expense, 2008	242	1,200	395
Uncollectible accounts charged off	204	1,360	365
Collections of accounts receivable, 2008	?	?	75,235

Required

a. Divide the class into three sections and divide each section into groups of three to five students. Assign one of the companies to each of the sections.

Group Tasks

(1) Determine the missing amounts for your company.

(2) Determine the percentage of accounts receivable estimated to be uncollectible at the end of 2007 and 2008 for your company.

(3) Determine the percentage of total sales that are credit sales for your company.

(4) Determine the accounts receivable turnover for your company.

Class Discussion

b. Have a representative of each section put the missing information on the board and explain how it was determined.

c. Which company has the highest percentage of sales that are credit sales?

d. Which company is doing the best job of collecting its accounts receivable? What procedures and policies can a company use to better collect its accounts receivable?

ATC 7–3   REAL-WORLD CASE *Time Needed to Collect Accounts Receivable*

Presented here are the average days to collect accounts receivable ratios for four companies in different industries. The data are for 2000.

Company	Average Days to Collect Accounts Receivable
Boeing (aircraft manufacturer)	30 days
Ford (automobile manufacturer)	13
Haverty's (furniture retailer)	95
Colgate Palmolive (consumer products manufacturer)	45

Required

Write a brief memorandum that provides possible answers to each of the following questions:

a. Why would a company that manufactures cars (Ford) collect its accounts receivable faster than a company that sells furniture (Haverty's)? (*Hint:* Ford sells cars to dealerships, not to individual customers.)

b. Why would a company that manufactures and sells large airplanes (Boeing) collect its accounts receivable faster than a company that sells toothpaste and soap (Colgate Palmolive)?

ATC 7–4   BUSINESS APPLICATIONS CASE *Using Average Number of Days to Collect Accounts Receivable to Make Comparisons*

The following information was drawn from the accounting records of Shafer and Burgess.

Account Title	Shafer	Burgess
Accounts Receivable (year end)	$ 80,000	$ 50,000
Sales	920,000	450,000

Required

a. Determine the average number of days to collect accounts receivable for each company.

b. Which company is likely to incur more costs associated with extending credit?

c. Identify and discuss some of the costs associated with extending credit.

d. Explain why a company would be willing to accept the costs of extending credit to its customers.

ATC 7–5   BUSINESS APPLICATIONS CASE *Using Ratios to Make Comparisons*

The following accounting information exists for Playfair and Pigpen companies at the end of 2007.

	Playfair	Pigpen
Cash	$ 25,000	$ 70,000
Accounts receivable	105,000	260,000
Allowance for doubtful accounts	5,000	10,000
Merchandise inventory	75,000	150,000
Accounts payable	80,000	200,000
Cost of goods sold	475,000	630,000
Building	125,000	200,000
Sales	650,000	1,000,000

Required

a. For each company, compute the gross margin percentage and the average number of days to collect accounts receivable (use the net realizable value of receivables to compute the average days to collect accounts receivable).

b. In relation to cost, which company is charging more for its merchandise?

c. Which company is likely to incur higher financial costs associated with the granting of credit to customers? Explain.

d. Which company appears to have more restrictive credit standards when authorizing credit to its customers? (*Hint:* There is no specific answer to this question. Use your judgment and general knowledge of ratios to answer.)

WRITING ASSIGNMENT *Elements of Financial Statements*   ATC 7–6

Paul South is opening a men's clothing store in University City. He has some of the necessary funds to lease the building and purchase the inventory but will need to borrow between $45,000 and $50,000. He has talked with two financial institutions that have offered the money according to the following terms:

1. South can borrow the money from Bank 1 by issuing a $50,000, one-year note with an interest rate of 10 percent.

2. South can borrow the money from Bank 2 by issuing a $50,000 face value discount note. The note will have a 9.5 percent discount rate and a one-year term to maturity.

South does not understand much about financial matters but wants the best alternative. He has come to you for advice.

Required

Write a memo to South explaining the difference in the two types of notes. Also advise him regarding the best alternative and why. Include in your explanation the true cost of each of the loans.

ETHICAL DILEMMA *What They Don't Know Won't Hurt Them, Right?*   ATC 7–7

Alonzo Saunders owns a small training services company that is experiencing growing pains. The company has grown rapidly by offering liberal credit terms to its customers. While his competitors require payment for services provided within 30 days, Saunders permits his customers to delay payment for up to 90 days. This extended delay allows his customers time to fully evaluate the training that employees receive before being required to pay for that training. Saunders guarantees satisfaction. If the customer is unhappy, the customer does not have to pay. Saunders works with reputable companies, provides top-quality training, and rarely encounters dissatisfied customers. However, the long collection period has left Saunders with a cash flow problem. He has a large accounts receivable balance, but needs cash to pay the current bills. He has recently negotiated a loan agreement with National Bank of Brighton County that should solve his cash flow problems. A condition of the loan is that the accounts receivable be pledged as collateral for the loan. The bank agreed to loan Saunders 70 percent of the value of his receivables balance. The current balance in the receivables account is approximately $100,000, thereby giving him access to $70,000 cash. Saunders feels very comfortable with this arrangement because he estimates that he needs approximately $60,000, which is well within the range permitted by the bank.

Unfortunately, on the day Saunders was scheduled to execute the loan agreement, he heard a rumor that his largest customer was experiencing financial problems and was considering the declaration of bankruptcy. The customer owed Saunders $45,000. Saunders immediately called the company's chief accountant and was told "off the record" that the rumor was true. The accountant advised Saunders that the company had a substantial negative net worth and that most of the valuable assets were collateralized against bank loans. He said that, in his opinion, Saunders was unlikely to be able to collect the balance due. Saunders's immediate concern was the impact that the situation would have on his loan agreement with the bank. Removing the receivable from the collateral pool would leave only $55,000 in the pool and thereby reduce his available credit to $38,500 ($55,000 × 0.70). Even worse, the recognition of the bad debts expense would so adversely affect his income statement that the bank might decide to reduce the available credit by lowering the percentage of receivables allowed under the current loan agreement.

As Saunders heads for the bank, he wonders how he will make ends meet. If he cannot obtain the cash he needs, he will soon be declaring bankruptcy himself. He wonders whether he should even tell the bank about the bad debt or just let the bank discover the situation after the fact. He knows that he will have to sign an agreement attesting to the quality of the receivables at the date of the loan. However, he reasons that the information he received is off the record and that therefore he *may not* be legally bound to advise the bank of the condition of the receivables balance. He wishes that he had gone to the bank before he called to confirm the rumor.

Required

a. Assuming that Saunders uses the direct write-off method of accounting for bad debts, explain how the $45,000 write-off of the uncollectible account affects his financial statements.

b. Should Saunders advise the bank of the condition of the receivables? What are the ethical implications associated with telling or not telling the bank about the uncollectible account?

ATC 7–8   EDGAR DATABASE *Analyzing Maytag's Accounts Receivable*

Required

Using the most current 10-K available on EDGAR, answer the following questions about Maytag Company for the most recent year reported. Instructions for using EDGAR are in Appendix A.

a. What was Maytag's average days to collect accounts receivable?

b. What percentage of accounts receivable did Maytag estimate would not be collected?

c. Did Maytag provide any information about warranties that it provides to customers? If so, what information was provided? (*Hint:* Look in the accrued liabilities footnote.)

d. Maytag Company manufactures products under brand names other than *Maytag*. What are these brand names?

e. Does it appear that Maytag's warranty costs have been decreasing or increasing? Explain why this may have occurred.

ATC 7–9   SPREADSHEET ANALYSIS *Using Excel*

Set up the following spreadsheet comparing Vong and Crist Companies.

	Vong	Crist
Sales	$800,000	$1,100,000
Cost of Goods Sold	600,000	660,000
Gross Profit		
Gross Profit Percentage		
Accounts Receivable	130,000	270,000
Allowance for Doubtful Accounts	10,000	27,000
Net Realizable Value		
Accounts Receivable Turnover		
Average Days to Collect		

Required

a. For each company, compute gross profit, gross profit percentage, net realizable value, accounts receivable turnover, and average days to collect.

b. In relation to cost, which company is charging more for its merchandise?

c. Which company is likely to incur higher financial costs associated with granting credit to customers? Explain the reasons for your answer.

d. Which company appears to have more restrictive credit standards when authorizing credit to customers? How do you know?

SPREADSHEET ANALYSIS *Mastering Excel*

ATC 7–10

Refer to Problem 7–20B.

Required

Prepare the financial statements using an Excel spreadsheet.

Asset Valuation
Accounting for Inventories

Learning Objectives

After completing this chapter, you should be able to:

1 Explain how different inventory cost flow methods (i.e., specific identification, FIFO, LIFO, and weighted average) affect financial statements.

2 Demonstrate the computational procedures for FIFO, LIFO, and weighted average.

3 Apply the lower-of-cost-or-market rule to inventory valuation.

4 Demonstrate how to make inventory estimates.

5 Show how inventory errors affect financial statements.

6 Explain the importance of inventory turnover to a company's profitability.

7 Demonstrate how to compute a company's operating cycle.

8 Identify certain assets that are shown on the balance sheet at market value.

9 Explain how accounting for investment securities differs when the securities are classified as held to maturity, trading, or available for sale.

the *curious* **accountant**

Albertson's, Inc., is one of the largest food and drug store chains in the United States, operating more than 2,500 stores in 36 states. As of February 1, 2001, the company had approximately $3.3 billion of inventory reported on its balance sheet. In the footnotes to its financial statements, Albertson's reported that it uses an inventory method that assumes its newest goods are sold first and its oldest goods are kept in inventory. Why would a company that sells perishable goods such as milk and medicine use an inventory method that assumes older goods are kept while newer goods are sold?

*The process of determining the cost of inventory was simplified in our introduction to inventory concepts in Chapter 5 by the assumption that the cost per unit remained constant. In practice, different prices may be paid for identical inventory items, thereby requiring a decision as to which costs to allocate to cost of goods sold versus ending inventory. For example, assume that Baker Company paid cash to purchase two inventory items. The first item was purchased at a cost of $100; the second was purchased sometime later for $110. Except for cost, both items are identical. Suppose that the items are mixed together so that Baker is unable to determine which item was purchased first. If Baker sells one of the inventory items, which cost should be removed from the Inventory account and charged to Cost of Goods Sold? There are several **inventory cost flow methods** that offer alternative solutions to this problem. These cost flow methods are discussed in the following section of this chapter.*

▊ Inventory Cost Flow Methods

LO 1 Explain how different inventory cost flow methods (i.e., specific identification, FIFO, LIFO, and weighted average) affect financial statements.

The four common methods for assigning product costs to the income statement are (1) specific identification; (2) first-in, first-out (FIFO); (3) last-in, first-out (LIFO); and (4) weighted average. Each cost flow method is explained in the following discussion.

Specific Identification

If the two inventory items Baker Company purchased were tagged when they were purchased so that the specific cost of each item could be identified, then the actual cost of the item sold could be charged to cost of goods sold. When the inventory consists of low-priced, high-turnover goods such as food items, the record-keeping task necessary for **specific identification** can become burdensome. Think of the work required to maintain a record of the specific cost of each food item in a grocery store. Another potential disadvantage of the specific identification method is that it provides the opportunity to manipulate the income statement. By selecting which items to deliver to customers, management can control the cost of goods sold expense and thereby manipulate the amount of net income reported in the financial statements. Even so, specific identification is frequently used for high-priced, low-turnover items such as automobiles. Here the record keeping is minimal, and customer demands for specific products limit management's ability to select the merchandise being sold.

First-In, First-Out (FIFO)

The **first-in, first-out (FIFO) cost flow method** assumes that the cost of the items purchased *first* should be assigned to Cost of Goods Sold. Under FIFO, the cost of goods sold by Baker Company is $100.

Last-In, First-Out (LIFO)

The **last-in, first-out (LIFO) cost flow method** requires that the cost of the *last* items purchased be charged to Cost of Goods Sold. Under this method, the cost of goods sold for Baker Company is $110.

Weighted Average

Under the **weighted-average cost flow method,** the average unit cost of the inventory is determined by totaling the costs incurred and dividing by the number of units ([100 + 110] ÷ 2 = 105). The average unit cost is then multiplied by the number of units sold, and the result is charged to Cost of Goods Sold. In the Baker Company case, $105 is assigned to the cost of goods sold.

Physical Flow

It is important to note that the preceding discussion referred to the *flow of costs* through the accounting records. The **physical flow of goods** is an entirely separate consideration. Goods are usually moved physically on a FIFO basis, which means that the first merchandise in (i.e., the oldest merchandise) is the first merchandise to be delivered to customers. The last items in (i.e., the newest goods) are retained by the business. Obviously, this procedure is necessary to keep inventories from becoming filled with dated merchandise. However, note that while the *physical flow* of goods is being conducted on a FIFO basis, the *flow of costs* can have an entirely different basis, such as LIFO or weighted average.

▌Effect of Cost Flow on Financial Statements

Effect on Income Statement

The cost flow method a company uses can have a significant effect on the amount of gross margin reported in the income statement. To demonstrate this point, assume that Baker Company sold the inventory item under·discussion for $120. The amounts of gross margin under the FIFO, LIFO, and weighted-average cost flow assumptions are shown in the following table:

	FIFO	LIFO	Weighted Average
Sales	$120	$120	$120
Cost of goods sold	100	110	105
Gross margin	$ 20	$ 10	$ 15

Note that the amount of gross margin reported under FIFO is double the amount reported under LIFO. This result occurs even though the accounting events described by each cost flow method are identical. In each case, the same inventory items were bought and sold. *Companies experiencing identical economic events with respect to the purchase and sale of inventories can report significantly different results in their financial statements.* Financial analysis requires an understanding of reporting practices as well as economic relationships.

Effect on Balance Sheet

Since total product costs are allocated between costs of goods sold and ending inventory, the type of cost flow method used affects the balance sheet as well as the income statement. For example, since FIFO transfers the first cost to the income statement, it leaves the last costs on the balance sheet. Similarly, by transferring the last cost to the income statement, LIFO leaves the first costs in ending inventory. The weighted-average method uses the average cost per unit to determine the amount of both cost of goods sold and ending inventory. The amount of ending inventory reported on the balance sheet for each of the three cost flow methods is shown in the following table:

	FIFO	LIFO	Weighted Average
Ending inventory	$110	$100	$105

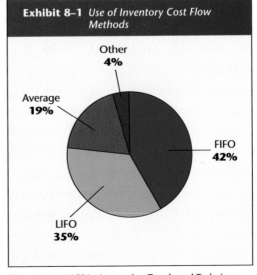

Exhibit 8–1 *Use of Inventory Cost Flow Methods*

Other 4%

Average 19%

FIFO 42%

LIFO 35%

Data source: AICPA, *Accounting Trends and Techniques,* 2000.

All three methods are used extensively in business practice. Indeed, the same company may use one cost flow method for some of its products and different cost flow methods for other products. Exhibit 8–1 depicts the relative use of the different cost flow methods among U.S. companies.

Nash Office Supply (NOS) purchased two Model 303 copiers at different times. The first copier purchased cost $400 and the second copier purchased cost $450. NOS sold one of the copiers for $600. Determine the gross margin on the sale and the ending inventory balance assuming NOS accounts for inventory using (1) FIFO, (2) LIFO, and (3) weighted average.

Answer

	FIFO	LIFO	Weighted Average
Sales	$600	$600	$600
Cost of goods sold	(400)	(450)	(425)
Gross margin	$200	$150	$175
Ending inventory	$450	$400	$425

▮ Inventory Cost Flow Under a Perpetual System

Multiple Layers With Multiple Quantities

LO2 Demonstrate the computational procedures for FIFO, LIFO, and weighted average.

To facilitate your understanding of the different cost flow methods, the preceding example used a simplified case that included only two cost layers ($100 and $110), with one inventory item in each layer. The following information is used to demonstrate a more interesting situation that includes multiple layers, with different quantities in each layer. The underlying allocation concepts remain unchanged and should facilitate your understanding of the more complex situation.

Suppose that the accounting records of The Mountain Bike Company (TMBC) contained the following account balances as of January 1, 2006: Cash, $12,000; Inventory, $2,000; Common Stock, $6,000; and Retained Earnings, $8,000. During 2006, TMBC made two cash purchases of inventory. The following table shows the detailed records of the beginning inventory balance and the two purchases:

Jan. 1	Beginning inventory	10 units @ $200	=	$ 2,000
Mar. 18	First purchase	20 units @ $220	=	4,400
Aug. 21	Second purchase	25 units @ $250	=	6,250
	Total cost of the 55 bikes available for sale			$12,650

Assume that in October 2006, TMBC sold 43 bikes at a price of $350 per bike. Also assume that TMBC incurred $2,600 of cash operating expenses during 2006. Finally, assume that the company paid cash for income taxes at a rate of 30 percent of net income. Accordingly, there are five events that affected the company during the 2006 accounting period: (1 and 2) the cash purchases of inventory, (3) the cash sale of inventory, (4) the cash payment of operating expenses, and (5) the cash payment of taxes. Exhibit 8–2 shows the effect of each event on the financial statements under three different inventory cost flow assumptions: FIFO, LIFO, and weighted average. The exhibit also assumes that TMCB uses a *perpetual inventory* system.

Events 1 and 2 Purchase of Inventory

As shown in Exhibit 8–2, on page 365, purchases of inventory are treated exactly the same under FIFO, LIFO, and weighted-average assumptions. In each case, the purchase constitutes an asset exchange. The asset, *inventory*, increases and the asset, *cash,* decreases. Total assets are unaffected. Although the income statement is not affected, the cash outflow is shown in the operating activities section of the statement of cash flows.

Exhibit 8–2 *Effect of Events on Financial Statements*

Panel 1: FIFO Cost Flow

Event No.	Balance Sheet										Income Statement						Statement of Cash Flows	
	Assets			=	Stockholders' Equity													
	Cash	+	Inventory	=	C. Stk.	+	Ret. Earn.				Rev.	–	Exp.	=	Net Inc.			
Bal.	12,000	+	2,000	=	6,000	+	8,000				0	–	0	=	0		0	
1	(4,400)	+	4,400	=	NA	+	NA				NA	–	NA	=	NA		(4,400)	OA
2	(6,250)	+	6,250	=	NA	+	NA				NA	–	NA	=	NA		(6,250)	OA
3(a)	15,050	+	NA	=	NA	+	15,050				15,050	–	NA	=	15,050		15,050	OA
3(b)	NA	+	(9,650)	=	NA	+	(9,650)				NA	–	9,650	=	(9,650)		NA	
4	(2,600)	+	NA	=	NA	+	(2,600)				NA	–	2,600	=	(2,600)		(2,600)	OA
5	(840)	+	NA	=	NA	+	(840)				NA	–	840	=	(840)		(840)	OA
Bal.	12,960	+	3,000	=	6,000	+	9,960				15,050	–	13,090	=	1,960		960	NC

Panel 2: LIFO Cost Flow

Event No.	Balance Sheet										Income Statement						Statement of Cash Flows	
	Assets			=	Stockholders' Equity													
	Cash	+	Inventory	=	C. Stk.	+	Ret. Earn.				Rev.	–	Exp.	=	Net Inc.			
Bal.	12,000	+	2,000	=	6,000	+	8,000				0	–	0	=	0		0	
1	(4,400)	+	4,400	=	NA	+	NA				NA	–	NA	=	NA		(4,400)	OA
2	(6,250)	+	6,250	=	NA	+	NA				NA	–	NA	=	NA		(6,250)	OA
3(a)	15,050	+	NA	=	NA	+	15,050				15,050	–	NA	=	15,050		15,050	OA
3(b)	NA	+	(10,210)	=	NA	+	(10,210)				NA	–	10,210	=	(10,210)		NA	
4	(2,600)	+	NA	=	NA	+	(2,600)				NA	–	2,600	=	(2,600)		(2,600)	OA
5	(672)	+	NA	=	NA	+	(672)				NA	–	672	=	(672)		(672)	OA
Bal.	13,128	+	2,440	=	6,000	+	9,568				15,050	–	13,482	=	1,568		1,128	NC

Panel 3: Weighted-Average Cost Flow

Event No.	Balance Sheet										Income Statement						Statement of Cash Flows	
	Assets			=	Stockholders' Equity													
	Cash	+	Inventory	=	C. Stk.	+	Ret. Earn.				Rev.	–	Exp.	=	Net Inc.			
Bal.	12,000	+	2,000	=	6,000	+	8,000				0	–	0	=	0		0	
1	(4,400)	+	4,400	=	NA	+	NA				NA	–	NA	=	NA		(4,400)	OA
2	(6,250)	+	6,250	=	NA	+	NA				NA	–	NA	=	NA		(6,250)	OA
3(a)	15,050	+	NA	=	NA	+	15,050				15,050	–	NA	=	15,050		15,050	OA
3(b)	NA	+	(9,890)	=	NA	+	(9,890)				NA	–	9,890	=	(9,890)		NA	
4	(2,600)	+	NA	=	NA	+	(2,600)				NA	–	2,600	=	(2,600)		(2,600)	OA
5	(768)	+	NA	=	NA	+	(768)				NA	–	768	=	(768)		(768)	OA
Bal.	13,032	+	2,760	=	6,000	+	9,792				15,050	–	13,258	=	1,792		1,032	NC

Event 3a Sale of Inventory

As with purchases, the treatment of sales revenue is not affected by the flow of inventory cost. Note that under all three cost flow methods, sales amounted to $15,050 (43 bikes × $350 per bike). The sale represents a source of assets. The effect of recognizing the sales revenue is to increase assets (cash) and equity (revenue). The recognition of the sales revenue acts to increase net income. The cash inflow from the sale is shown in the operating activities section of the statement of cash flows.

FIFO Inventory Cost Flow

Event 3b Cost of Sale

When goods are sold, the cost of those goods is transferred from the Inventory account to the Cost of Goods Sold account. Accordingly, assets (Inventory) and equity decrease. The decrease in equity results from the increase in the expense account *Cost of Goods Sold,* which reduces net income and ultimately retained earnings. The *amount* to be transferred from Inventory to Cost of Goods Sold is determined by the type of cost flow method that is applied. The FIFO method transfers the cost of the *first 43 bikes* that came into TMBC to the Cost of Goods Sold account. This allocation occurs no matter which bikes were actually sold. Remember, physical flow and cost flow are totally separate events. The first 43 bikes acquired by TMBC include the 10 bikes that were in the beginning inventory (these were left over from purchases made in the prior period) plus the 20 bikes that were purchased in March and 13 of the bikes purchased in August. Panel 1, Exhibit 8–2 shows the cost of goods sold expense recognition. The expense recognition acts to decrease net income. There is no effect on cash flow at this time. The effect on cash flow occurred at the time the inventory was purchased. The amount of the recognition ($9,650) is computed as follows:

Jan. 1	Beginning inventory	10 units @ $200	=	$2,000
Mar. 18	First purchase	20 units @ $220	=	4,400
Aug. 21	Second purchase	13 units @ $250	=	3,250
	Total cost of the 43 bikes sold			$9,650

LIFO Inventory Cost Flow

As indicated in Panel 2, Exhibit 8–2, the amount of cost transferred from Inventory to Cost of Goods Sold under a LIFO system is $10,210. This amount is determined by computing the cost of the *last 43 bikes* acquired by TMBC as shown:

Aug. 21	Second purchase	25 units @ $250	=	$ 6,250
Mar. 18	First purchase	18 units @ $220	=	3,960
	Total cost of the 43 bikes sold			$10,210

Weighted-Average Cost Flow

To compute the amount of cost of goods sold under the weighted-average method, it is necessary to begin by calculating the weighted-average cost per unit. This is determined by dividing the *total cost of goods available for sale* by the *total number of goods available for sale.* In the case of TMBC, the weighted-average cost per unit is $230 ($12,650 ÷ 55). The weighted-average cost of goods sold is then determined by multiplying the cost per unit by the number of units sold ($230 × 43 = $9,890). Panel 3, Exhibit 8–2 shows the cost of goods sold expense recognition.

Event 4 Operating Expenses Paid

The payment of operating expenses is not affected by the inventory cost flow method. Accordingly, in all cases, the $2,600 of operating expenses act to reduce assets (Cash) and equity (Retained Earnings). The expense recognition acts to decrease net income. The cash outflow is shown in the operating activities section of the statement of cash flows.

Event 5 Income Taxes Paid

Since the inventory cost flow method affects the amount of cost of goods sold, it will also affect the amount of net income and, therefore, the amount of income tax expense. While the *amount* of the tax due (net income before tax × tax rate) will vary depending on which cost flow method is applied, the *effect* of the tax expense on the financial statements will be the same under all three methods. In each case, the tax expense will act to reduce assets (Cash) and equity (Retained Earnings). The expense recognition acts to decrease net income. The cash outflow is shown in the operating activities section of the statement of cash flows.

Effect of Cost Flow on Financial Statements

Exhibit 8–3 contains an income statement, balance sheet, and statement of cash flows for each of the three cost flow assumptions. Look at these financial statements and decide which cost flow method you would recommend that TMBC use in its published financial statements. The initial recommendation that most people make is FIFO. Indeed, FIFO produces the highest amount of net income as well as the largest balance in the ending inventory. Accordingly, assets and income look better under FIFO. However, a closer look reveals that net cash inflow is lower under FIFO

LO1 Explain how different inventory cost flow methods (i.e., specific identification, FIFO, LIFO, and weighted average) affect financial statements.

Exhibit 8–3

TMBC COMPANY
Comparative Financial Statements

Income Statements

	FIFO	LIFO	Weighted Average
Sales	$15,050	$15,050	$15,050
Cost of Goods Sold	(9,650)	(10,210)	(9,890)
Gross Margin	5,400	4,840	5,160
Operating Expenses	(2,600)	(2,600)	(2,600)
Income before Taxes (IBT)	2,800	2,240	2,560
Income Tax Expense (IBT × 0.30)	(840)	(672)	(768)
Net Income	$ 1,960	$ 1,568	$ 1,792

Balance Sheets

	FIFO	LIFO	Weighted Average
Assets			
Cash	$12,960	$13,128	$13,032
Inventory	3,000	2,440	2,760
Total Assets	$15,960	$15,568	$15,792
Stockholders' Equity			
Common Stock	$ 6,000	$ 6,000	$ 6,000
Retained Earnings	9,960	9,568	9,792
Total Equity	$15,960	$15,568	$15,792

Statements of Cash Flows

	FIFO	LIFO	Weighted Average
Operating Activities			
Cash Inflow from Customers	$15,050	$15,050	$15,050
Cash Outflow for Inventory	(10,650)	(10,650)	(10,650)
Cash Outflow for Operating Expenses	(2,600)	(2,600)	(2,600)
Cash Outflow for Tax Expense	(840)	(672)	(768)
Net Cash Inflow from Operations	960	1,128	1,032
Investing Activities			
Financing Activities			
Net Increase in Cash	960	1,128	1,032
Beginning Cash Balance	12,000	12,000	12,000
Ending Cash Balance	$12,960	$13,128	$13,032

because more income taxes must be paid on the higher amount of reported net income. Recall that except for taxes, the economic circumstances are identical under all three methods. In other words, the only real economic difference between FIFO and LIFO is the fact that FIFO requires the payment of more taxes. Under these circumstances, TMBC should use the LIFO method.

It is important to note that when LIFO is used, tax law requires companies to use that method for financial reporting as well as for tax reporting. In other words, if a company uses LIFO on its tax return, that company is legally bound to use that method in its published financial statements. This is the *one area* in which the Internal Revenue Service dictates consistency between financial and tax reporting.

You may wonder if the advantages of reporting the more positive financial image under FIFO outweigh the disadvantage of having to pay more taxes. Given an optimistic report of more assets and higher income, would investors not be more interested in the company even if TMBC had to pay more income taxes? Research suggests that investors are not deceived by spurious reporting procedures. They make investment decisions on the basis of economic substance regardless of how it is presented in financial statements. Accordingly, investors would be more attracted to TMBC if it used LIFO. More value stays in the business under LIFO because fewer assets (cash) are used to pay taxes. Sophisticated investors understand the illusions that can be created by the selection of favorable reporting practices and are not taken in by the reporting of false profits.

Note that FIFO produces higher reported income and assets than LIFO only in an environment of rising prices (inflationary conditions). In an inflationary environment, the most recent prices are the highest prices. The oldest prices (first-in prices) are the lowest prices. Since FIFO assigns the oldest prices to the income statement, expenses (cost of goods sold) are lower and net income is higher. Also, the newest (highest) prices are retained in ending inventory, thereby resulting in a higher amount of reported assets. Notice that this condition reverses in an environment characterized by falling prices (deflationary conditions) such as firms in the computer industry experience. Under conditions of deflation, the oldest prices are the highest prices, and the newest prices are the lowest prices. Accordingly, FIFO assigns the first-in (oldest and highest) costs to the income statement and the newest (lowest) to the balance sheet, which means that in a deflationary economy, FIFO results in the reporting of lower amounts of income and assets than would be reported under LIFO. This explains why some firms choose to report under FIFO instead of LIFO. In many cases, the magnitude of changing prices also is too small to materially affect cash flows and thus does not affect the selection of the cost flow method employed.

Check Yourself 8–2

The following information was drawn from the inventory records of Fields, Inc.

Beginning inventory	200 units @ $20
First purchase	400 units @ $22
Second purchase	600 units @ $24

Assume that Fields sold 900 units of inventory.

1. Determine the amount of cost of goods sold using FIFO.
2. Would using LIFO produce a higher or lower amount of cost of goods sold? Why?

Answer

1. Cost of goods sold using FIFO

Beginning inventory	200 units @ $20 =	$ 4,000
First purchase	400 units @ $22 =	8,800
Second purchase	300 units @ $24 =	7,200
Total cost of goods sold		$20,000

2. The inventory records reflect an inflationary environment of steadily rising prices. Since LIFO charges the latest costs (in this case the highest costs) to the income statement, using LIFO would produce a higher amount of cost of goods sold than would using FIFO.

Inventory Cost Flow When Sales and Purchases Occur Intermittently

In the previous sections, all purchases were made before any of the goods were sold. This section addresses sales transactions that occur intermittently with purchases. To illustrate, assume that the following table describes the beginning inventory, purchases, and sales transactions for Sharon Sales Company (SSC) during 2008:

LO2 Demonstrate the computational procedures for FIFO, LIFO, and weighted average.

Date	Transaction	Description
Jan. 1	Beginning inventory	100 units @ $20.00
Feb. 14	Purchased	200 units @ $21.50
Apr. 5	Sold	220 units @ $30.00
June 21	Purchased	160 units @ $22.50
Aug. 18	Sold	100 units @ $30.00
Sept. 2	Purchased	280 units @ $23.50
Nov. 10	Sold	330 units @ $30.00

FIFO Cost Flow

Exhibit 8–4 contains the supporting computations for the determination of the amounts of cost of goods sold and inventory, assuming that SSC uses a FIFO cost flow. Note that the inventory is maintained in layers. Each time a sales transaction occurs, the unit cost contained in the

focus on International Issues

The Influence of Tax Accounting on GAAP

As noted earlier in this chapter, a U.S. company can use LIFO for income tax purposes *only* if it also uses LIFO for GAAP purposes. This is an unusual situation because tax accounting in the United States is separate and distinct from financial reporting under GAAP, which means that the Internal Revenue Service has no formal power to control GAAP. In the case of LIFO, however, the IRS has an indirect influence on the inventory method that a company chooses for financial reporting. The tax accounting rules of most other countries do not allow the use of the LIFO cost flow method, even if the country's GAAP does allow its use. If U.S. tax rules did not allow the use of LIFO under any circumstances, how many companies would use it for financial reporting? Very few!

The separation between tax accounting and GAAP accounting that exists in the United States does not exist in many other countries. In some countries, a company cannot deduct a cost for tax purposes unless the same cost is shown as an expense on the company's GAAP–based income statement. In other words, the unusual situation that exists in the United States only for the use of LIFO is the general rule in many countries. Countries whose tax laws greatly influence GAAP reporting include France, Germany, and Japan.

first layer is applied to the number of goods sold. If there are not enough items in the first layer to cover the total number of units sold, the unit cost of the next layer is applied to the remaining number of goods sold. For example, the cost of 220 units of inventory sold on April 5 is determined by adding the cost of 100 units of inventory in the first layer (i.e., beginning inventory) to the cost of 120 units of inventory contained in the second layer. Accordingly, the cost of goods sold for this transaction is $4,580 (100 units @ $20.00 + 120 units @ $21.50). As shown in Exhibit 8–4, the cost of goods sold for subsequent sales transactions is computed in a similar fashion.

Exhibit 8–4 *Transactions under FIFO Cost Flow*

Date	Purchase Units		Cost		Total	Cost of Goods Sold Units		Cost		Total	Inventory Units		Cost		Total
Jan. 1											100	@	$20.00	=	$2,000
Feb. 14	200	@	$21.50	=	$4,300						200	@	$21.50	=	$4,300
Apr. 5						100	@	$20.00	=	$ 2,000					
						120	@	$21.50	=	$ 2,580	80	@	$21.50	=	$1,720
June 21	160	@	$22.50	=	$3,600						160	@	$22.50	=	$3,600
Aug. 18						80	@	$21.50	=	$ 1,720					
						20	@	$22.50	=	$ 450	140	@	$22.50	=	$3,150
Sept. 2	280	@	$23.50	=	$6,580						280	@	$23.50	=	$6,580
Nov. 10						140	@	$22.50	=	$ 3,150					
						190	@	$23.50	=	$ 4,465	90	@	$23.50	=	$2,115
						Total COGS			=	$14,365	Ending Bal.			=	$2,115

The computation of gross margin for the 2008 accounting period under a FIFO cost flow is shown here:

Sales (650 units @ $30 each)	$19,500
Cost of goods sold	14,365
Gross margin	$ 5,135

Weighted-Average and LIFO Cost Flows

When we attempt to apply LIFO or the weighted-average cost flow methods to intermittent sales and purchase transactions, a problem emerges at the point of the first sales event. For example, LIFO requires that the cost of the *last items* purchased *during the period* be charged to cost of goods sold. This is not possible because the period is not over and the last items have not been purchased at the time the first sale is made. Accountants frequently solve this problem by recording only the quantities of sales and purchases on a perpetual basis, enabling them to obtain many of the benefits of a perpetual inventory system even when cost data are unavailable. For example, management can identify the quantity of lost, damaged, or stolen goods, and it can determine when it is time to reorder merchandise. At the end of the accounting period, when complete information about purchases and sales is available, costs are assigned to the quantity data that have been maintained perpetually. Although a complete discussion of weighted-average and LIFO cost flow approaches is beyond the scope of this text, be aware that the potential problems associated with intermittent sales are manageable. Indeed, weighted average and LIFO are used by many companies that experience intermittent sales and purchase transactions.

■ Inventory Cost Flow in a Periodic System

Recall that under the *periodic inventory system,* inventory records are not changed when goods are purchased or sold. The amount of ending inventory is determined by taking a physical count

To avoid spoilage, most companies use a first-in, first-out (FIFO) approach for the flow of physical goods. The older goods (i.e., first units purchased) are sold before the newer goods are sold. For example, Kroger and other food stores stack older merchandise at the front of the shelf where customers are more likely to pick it up first. As a result, merchandise is sold before it becomes spoiled. However, when spoilage is not an issue, convenience may dictate the use of the last-in, first-out (LIFO) method. Examples of products that frequently move on a LIFO basis include rock, gravel, dirt, or other nonwasting assets. Indeed, rock, gravel, and dirt are normally stored in piles that are unprotected from weather. New inventory is simply piled on top of the old. Inventory that is sold is taken from the top of the pile because it is convenient to do so. Accordingly, the last inventory purchased is the first inventory sold. Regardless of whether the flow of physical goods is accomplished on a LIFO or FIFO basis, costs can flow differently. The flow of inventory through the physical facility is a separate issue from the flow of costs through the accounting system.

of goods on hand at the end of the accounting period. Furthermore, the amount of *cost of goods sold* is computed by subtracting the amount of *ending inventory* from *cost of goods available for sale*. Accordingly, the assignment of cost focuses on the measurement of ending inventory. To illustrate, assume the same facts as those used for Sharon Sales Company in the previous section. For your convenience, these data are repeated in Exhibit 8–5. Although the facts are the same, the data have been arranged in a different order to reflect the use of a periodic as opposed to a perpetual inventory system.

Exhibit 8–5 *Sales and Purchase Transactions for Sharon Sales Company*

Date	Transaction		Description		Cost of Goods Available for Sale	Sales
Jan. 1	Beg. inventory		100 units @ $20.00	=	$ 2,000	
Feb. 14	Purchased		200 units @ $21.50	=	$ 4,300	
Apr. 5	Sold	220	units @ $30.00	=		$ 6,600
June 21	Purchased		160 units @ $22.50	=	$ 3,600	
Aug. 18	Sold	100	units @ $30.00	=		$ 3,000
Sept. 2	Purchased		280 units @ $23.50	=	$ 6,580	
Nov. 10	Sold	330	units @ $30.00	=		$ 9,900
	Totals	650	740		$16,480	$19,500

Exhibit 8–6 shows the computations for the allocation of the *cost of goods available for sale* between *ending inventory* and *cost of goods sold* under the FIFO, LIFO, and weighted-average cost flow methods. All three methods are shown because the periodic method does not involve the computational problems associated with the perpetual method. According to the data in Exhibit 8–5, 740 inventory items were available for sale (beginning inventory of 100 units + purchases of 640 units). Since 650 items were sold, ending inventory contains 90 units. FIFO transfers the *first* costs (older) to cost of good sold and thereby leaves the *last*

Exhibit 8–6 *Allocation of Cost of Goods Available for Sale under a Periodic Inventory System*

	FIFO	LIFO	Weighted Average
Cost of goods available for sale	$16,480	$16,480	$16,480
Less: Ending inventory	(2,115)	(1,800)	(2,004)
Cost of goods sold	$14,365	$14,680	$14,476

costs (newest) in ending inventory. Accordingly, ending inventory under FIFO is $2,115.00 (90 × $23.50). LIFO allocates the last costs to cost of goods sold, leaving the *first* costs in ending inventory. Ending inventory under LIFO is $1,800.00 (90 × $20.00). Finally, the weighted-average unit cost of $22.27 ($16,480.00 ÷ 740) times 90 units of inventory yields an ending Inventory balance of $2,004 (rounded to the nearest dollar).

Remember that the perpetual and periodic accounting procedures represent two different approaches for arriving at the same end result; only the method of computation differs. This fact can be verified by comparing the cost of goods sold and the balance in ending inventory in Exhibit 8–4 with the amounts under the FIFO column in Exhibit 8–6.

Lower-of-Cost-or-Market Rule

LO3 Apply the lower-of-cost-or-market rule to inventory valuation.

To this point, the discussion has been directed toward the flow of inventory costs. Once the cost of ending inventory has been determined, accounting practice requires that it be compared with the current market value and that the inventories be carried at the *lower-of-cost-or-market value*. For the purposes of this comparison, *market* is defined as the amount that would have to be paid to replace the merchandise. Regardless of whether a decline in market value to a point below cost is due to physical damage, deterioration, obsolescence, or a general decline in the level of prices, the resultant loss must be recognized in the current period.

The **lower-of-cost-or-market rule** can be applied to (1) each individual inventory item, (2) major classes or categories of inventory, or (3) the entire stock of inventory in aggregate. The most common practice is the individualized application. To illustrate the application to individual inventory items, assume that Wilson Office Supply Company purchased 100 calculators at a cost of $14 each. If the current replacement cost of the calculators is above $14, then the ending inventory is carried at cost (100 × $14 = $1,400). However, if some form of technological advance permits the manufacturer to reduce the unit price of the calculators to $11, then the replacement cost to Wilson will fall below the historical cost, and the carrying value of the inventory will be written down to $1,100 (100 × $11). Exhibit 8–7 demonstrates the computation of ending inventory for a company that has four different inventory items.

In the case presented in Exhibit 8–7, the company is required to reduce the $30,020 historical cost of its ending inventory to $28,410. This $1,610 reduction causes a decline in the amount of the company's gross margin for the period. The procedure used to reflect the inventory write-down in the accounts will depend on whether the company uses the perpetual or periodic inventory system. If the perpetual system is used, the effect of the write-down and the journal entry necessary to record it are as follows:

Assets	=	Liab.	+	Equity	Rev.	–	Exp.	=	Net Inc.	Cash Flow
(1,610)	=	NA	+	(1,610)	NA	–	1,610	=	(1,610)	NA

Exhibit 8–7 *Determination of Ending Inventory at Lower of Cost or Market*

Item	Quantity (a)	Unit Cost (b)	Unit Market (c)	Total Cost (a × b)	Total Market (a × c)	Lower of Cost or Market
A	320	$21.50	$22.00	$ 6,880	$ 7,040	$ 6,880
B	460	18.00	16.00	8,280	7,360	7,360
C	690	15.00	14.00	10,350	9,660	9,660
D	220	20.50	23.00	4,510	5,060	4,510
				$30,020	$29,120	$28,410

Account Title	Debit	Credit
Cost of Goods Sold (Inventory Loss)	1,610	
Inventory		1,610

Conceptually, the loss should be shown as an operating expense on the income statement. However, if the amount is immaterial, it can be included in the cost of goods sold.

Under the periodic method, the amount of ending inventory is shown at the lower of cost or market in the schedule of cost of goods sold. By lowering the ending inventory, cost of goods is increased. These relationships are shown in the following schedule of cost of goods sold:

Schedule of Cost of Goods Sold		
Beginning Inventory	$xxx	
Plus: Purchases	xxx	
Cost of Goods Available for Sale	xxx	
Less: Ending Inventory	(xxx)	Lower amount reported here results in a
Cost of Goods Sold	$xxx	higher amount reported here

As the preceding schedule indicates, when ending inventory is shown at the lower of cost or market, any loss is automatically included in the cost of goods sold. By increasing the cost of goods sold, net income and ultimately equity are reduced, which balances against the reduction in assets (i.e., Inventory). Cash flow is not affected by the write-down.

Estimating the Ending Inventory Balance

LO4 Demonstrate how to make inventory estimates.

Under the *perpetual inventory system,* the best estimate of the amount of inventory on hand at any time is the book balance in the Inventory account. Recall that the book balance is increased when purchases are made and is decreased when goods are sold. As a result, if records are maintained accurately, the balance in the Inventory account should be equal to the amount of goods on hand except for unrecorded items such as lost, damaged, or stolen goods. In contrast, the Inventory account is not altered when goods are purchased or sold under the periodic system. Accordingly, it may be necessary to estimate the amount of inventory on hand at various times when a company is using the periodic inventory system.

Estimates of the amount of inventory are necessary when a company wants to prepare monthly or quarterly financial statements but does not want to incur the expense of undertaking a physical count of goods on hand. Also, estimates may be needed to support insurance claims when inventory has been destroyed by fire, storms, or other natural disasters. Finally, estimates of inventory can be used to evaluate the accuracy of a physical count of goods. One common method used to estimate the amount of inventory is called the *gross margin method.*

The **gross margin method** assumes that the percentage of gross margin to sales remains relatively stable from one accounting period to the next. Information regarding the amount of sales and the cost of goods available for sale is drawn from the general ledger. Furthermore, the percentage of gross margin to sales is determined on the basis of the historical relationship between these two accounts (e.g., the average of the last five years' sales is divided into the average gross margin for the same five-year period). The percentage is then multiplied by the amount of sales for the current period to estimate the current period's gross margin. The estimated gross margin is subtracted from sales in order to compute the amount of estimated cost of goods sold. The estimated cost of goods sold is then subtracted from the cost of goods available for sale to arrive at the estimated ending inventory.

To illustrate, assume that the information in Exhibit 8–8 is drawn from the accounting records of the T-Shirt Company.

Exhibit 8–8			
THE T-SHIRT COMPANY			
Schedule for Estimating the Ending Inventory Balance			
For the Period Ending June 30, 2002			
Beginning Inventory	$ 5,100		
Purchases	18,500		
Goods Available for Sale		$23,600	
Sales through June 30, 2002	22,000		
Less: Estimated Gross Margin*	?		
Estimated Cost of Goods Sold		?	
Estimated Ending Inventory		$?	

*Historically, gross margin has amounted to approximately 25 percent of sales.

The cost of the estimated ending inventory can be computed as follows:

1. Estimate the amount of gross margin by multiplying the gross margin percentage by the sales ($22,000 × 0.25 = $5,500).
2. Estimate the amount of the cost of goods sold by subtracting the estimated gross margin from sales ($22,000 − $5,500 = $16,500).
3. Estimate the amount of ending inventory by subtracting the estimated cost of goods sold from the amount of goods available for sale ($23,600 − $16,500 = $7,100).

Check Yourself 8–3

Cantrell, Inc., recently lost its inventory in a fire. The accounting records indicate that its beginning inventory had been $20,000. During the period prior to the fire, Cantrell had purchased $70,000 of inventory and had recognized $140,000 of sales revenue. Cantrell's gross margin percentage is normally 40 percent of sales. Estimate the amount of inventory lost in the fire.

Answer Goods available for sale was $90,000 ($20,000 beginning inventory + $70,000 purchases). Estimated cost of goods sold was $84,000 ($140,000 sales − [$140,000 × 0.40] gross margin). Estimated inventory lost would be $6,000 ($90,000 goods available for sale − $84,000 cost of goods sold).

LO5 Show how inventory errors affect financial statements.

Effect of Inventory Errors on Financial Statements

Inventory is one of the largest assets that appear on the balance sheets of most merchandising businesses. It constitutes the lifeblood of a business. If it sells, the business thrives; if it does not, the business dies. It is frequently used to collateralize loans. Accordingly, both investors and creditors are keenly interested in the character and content of a company's inventory. Under conditions of adversity, managers may be tempted to misrepresent the financial condition of their companies by manipulating the balance of the Inventory account. Indeed, some of the most significant frauds in the history of business have involved the falsification of inventory records. It is critically important that business students become aware of the effects of inventory errors (legitimate or otherwise) on financial statements.

Errors Under a Periodic System

The financial condition of a company can be severely misrepresented by merely overstating the amount of ending inventory in the year-end physical count under a periodic system. The overstatement of ending inventory causes an understatement of cost of goods sold and thereby a corresponding overstatement of net income. The overstatement of net income causes an overstatement of retained earnings, which creates the increase in equity that balances with the overstated value of the inventory. To illustrate, assume that McCrary Merchandising over-states its year-end inventory balance by $1,000. As indicated in the following schedule, this overstatement causes the understatement of cost of goods sold:

	Ending Inventory Is Accurate	Ending Inventory Is Overstated	
Beginning inventory	$ 4,000	$ 4,000	
Purchases	6,000	6,000	
Cost of goods available for sale	10,000	10,000	
Ending inventory	(3,000)	(4,000)	1,000 Overstated
Cost of goods sold	$ 7,000	$ 6,000	1,000 Understated

The understatement of cost of goods sold results in the overstatement of gross margin, as indicated in the following income statement:

	Ending Inventory Is Accurate	Ending Inventory Is Overstated	Effect on Cost of Goods Sold
Sales	$11,000	$11,000	
Cost of goods sold	(7,000)	(6,000)	1,000 Understated
Gross margin	$4,000	$5,000	1,000 Overstated

On the balance sheet, assets (Inventory) and equity (Retained Earnings) are overstated as follows:

	Ending Inventory Is Accurate	Ending Inventory Is Overstated	
Assets			
Cash	$1,000	$ 1,000	
Inventory	3,000	4,000	1,000 Overstated
Other assets	5,000	5,000	
Total assets	$9,000	$10,000	
Stockholders' Equity			
Common stock	$5,000	$ 5,000	
Retained earnings	4,000	5,000	1,000 Overstated
Total Stockholders' equity	$9,000	$10,000	

Since the current period's ending inventory becomes the next period's beginning inventory, the error in the current period reverses itself in the succeeding period. Net income for the current period is overstated, and net income of the succeeding period is understated.

The retained earnings at the end of the second period are stated correctly as a result of the counterbalancing errors shown on the following income statements:

McCRARY MERCHANDISING Schedule of Cost of Goods Second Accounting Period		
Beginning Inventory	$4,000	1,000 Overstated
Purchases	xxx	
Cost of Goods Available for Sale	xxx	1,000 Overstated
Ending Inventory	(xxx)	
Cost of Goods Sold	$ xxx	1,000 Overstated
Income Statement		
Sales	$xxx	
Cost of Goods Sold	(xxx)	1,000 Overstated
Gross Margin	$xxx	1,000 Understated

According to this, the first period's overstatement of net income is offset by the second period's understatement. Accordingly, the balance sheet reported at the end of the second period is not affected by the error made in the first period.

Errors Under a Perpetual System

Large inventory errors are more likely to be discovered under the perpetual system because the book balance can be compared to the physical count. Since the two balances should be the same except for differences caused by lost, damaged, or stolen goods, major differences would be investigated and their cause identified. Nevertheless, mistakes can still occur. For example, suppose that a company failed to count $5,000 of inventory on hand at the end of the accounting period. Since the inventory was not counted, it would be assumed to be lost or stolen, and the company would record an inventory loss. As a result, expenses (i.e., cost of goods sold or inventory loss) would be overstated. The ending balance in the Inventory account would be understated, as would net income and retained earnings. The inventory and retained earnings would continue to be understated until such time as the error was discovered and corrected.

■ Understanding How the Length of the Operating Cycle Affects Profitability

 **LO6** Explain the importance of inventory turnover to a company's profitability.

The importance of the gross margin percentage to the management of merchandising companies was discussed in Chapter 5. While it is certainly important to know the difference between what a product costs and its selling price, more information is needed to assess the desirability of selling individual inventory items. To illustrate, assume that a grocery store sells two brands of kitchen cleansers, Zjax and Cosmos. Zjax costs $1 and sells for $1.25, resulting in a gross margin of $0.25 ($1.25 − $1.00). Cosmos costs $1.20 and sells for $1.60, resulting in a gross margin of $0.40 ($1.60 − $1.20). Accordingly, Zjax has a 20 percent gross margin percentage ($0.25 ÷ $1.25), while Cosmos has a 25 percent gross margin ($0.40 ÷ $1.60). Does this mean that it is more desirable to stock Cosmos than Zjax? Not if you can sell significantly more cans of Zjax than Cosmos. Suppose the lower price results in higher customer demand for Zjax. Indeed, the manager of the grocery store expects that during the coming year, the store can sell 7,000 units of Zjax but only 3,000 units of Cosmos. Under these circumstances, Zjax will return a total gross profit of $1,750 (7,000 units × $0.25 per unit), while Cosmos will return only $1,200 (3,000 units × $0.40 per unit). Accordingly, it is important to consider how rapidly inventory sells as well as the spread between cost and selling price.

Average Number of Days to Sell Inventory

The measure of how fast inventory sells is called **inventory turnover,** and it is defined as follows:

$$\frac{\text{Cost of goods sold}}{\text{Inventory}}$$

The result of this computation is the number of times the balance in the Inventory account is turned over (sold) each year. As with the accounts receivable turnover ratio, the inventory turnover ratio may be somewhat difficult to interpret because it does not provide a measure in units of time. To alleviate this problem, the inventory turnover ratio is often taken one step further to determine the average number of days required to sell inventory. The **average days in inventory ratio** (sometimes called **average number of days to sell inventory ratio**) is computed as

$$\frac{365}{\text{Inventory turnover}}$$

As indicated, a retailer's success from selling inventory depends on a combination of two factors: gross margin and inventory turnover. The most desirable scenario is an inventory system with a high margin that turns over rapidly. However, due to competition, companies often focus on one of these elements more than on the other. For example, *discount merchandisers* offer lower prices in the hope that they can stimulate rapid sales. In contrast, *specialty stores* often require larger gross margins to compensate for the fact that their goods sell more slowly. Specialty stores often offer something such as better service to persuade customers that the higher prices are justified.

Will a person buy a high-quality camera at Kmart or at a local camera shop? It depends on whether price or service is more important to that individual. A person needing considerable advice about which model to choose may be willing to pay the camera shop's higher price to get more professional help. So, although decisions about pricing, advertising, service, and so on, are often thought of as marketing decisions, they cannot be made properly without understanding the interaction between the gross margin percentage and inventory turnover.

Real-World Data

The discussion of operating cycles that began in Chapter 6 and continued in Chapter 7 can now be completed. The length of a company's operating cycle is the sum of its average number of days to sell inventory plus its average number of days to collect accounts receivable.

LO7 Demonstrate how to compute a company's operating cycle.

Exhibit 8–9 shows operating cycles for seven real-world companies. These numbers are for 2000.

Exhibit 8–9				
Industry	**Company**	**Average Days in Inventory**	**Average Days to Collect Receivables**	**Length of Operating Cycle**
Fast-Food	Domino's	8	15	23
	Wendy's	13	12	25
	Starbucks	77	13	90
Drugstores	CVS	88	15	103
	PharMor	72	7	79
Wine	Chalone	663	68	731
	Mondavi	481	66	547

What is the significance of operating cycles of different lengths? Recall from Chapter 6 that the operating cycle for a business is the time required for the business to get back the cash that it invested in inventory. As previously explained, the longer this takes, the more it costs the company. Notice from Exhibit 8–9 that CVS's operating cycle was 24 days longer than

Even though Albertson's uses the last-in, first-out cost flow *assumption* for financial reporting purposes, it, like most other companies, actually sells its oldest inventory first. As explained in the text material, GAAP allows a company to assume its goods are sold in an order that is different from the actual physical flow of its goods. The primary reason some companies use the LIFO assumption is to reduce income taxes. For example, in 1999, Albertson's saved approximately $12 million in taxes by using the LIFO versus the FIFO cost flow assumption when computing its taxable income.

PharMor's. All other things being equal, approximately how much did this extra time increase CVS's costs compared to PharMor's? Assume that CVS could invest excess cash at 8 percent (or alternatively, assume that it pays 8 percent to finance its inventory and accounts receivable). Using accounting information provided in CVS's 2000 financial statements, we can determine the solution as follows:

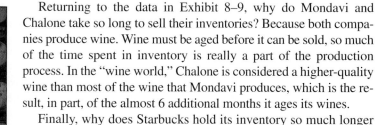

CVS's Investment in Inventory	×	Interest Rate	×	Time	=	Cost
$3,557,600,000	×	8%	×	24/365	=	$18,713,951

Based on the assumed 8 percent cost of money, the extra time it takes CVS to get back its investment in inventory costs the company $18.7 million per operating cycle. Based on 3.54 cycles per year (365 ÷ 103), the extended operating cycle costs CVS $66 million annually. After the effects of income taxes are included, reducing its operating cycle by 24 days increases CVS's net income by over 5 percent! The preceding certainly is a rough estimate, but it clearly demonstrates that it is important for businesses to monitor the length of their operating cycles.

There are other costs of having excess inventory besides the financing cost explained in the preceding paragraphs. The more inventory a company maintains, the more expense it will incur for storage and insurance and the more likely its inventory will be damaged or stolen during storage. Of course, carrying too little inventory can result in lost sales, so constant monitoring is necessary to ensure that the proper level of inventory is on hand.

Returning to the data in Exhibit 8–9, why do Mondavi and Chalone take so long to sell their inventories? Because both companies produce wine. Wine must be aged before it can be sold, so much of the time spent in inventory is really a part of the production process. In the "wine world," Chalone is considered a higher-quality wine than most of the wine that Mondavi produces, which is the result, in part, of the almost 6 additional months it ages its wines.

Finally, why does Starbucks hold its inventory so much longer than the other two fast-food businesses? Starbuck's main inventory is coffee. Prior to being roasted, coffee, unlike hamburgers or fresh vegetables, can be held for long periods without its quality deteriorating. Furthermore, very little coffee is grown in the United States (Hawaii is the only state that produces coffee). Starbucks cannot wait until the last minute to order its inventory. This problem is further complicated by the fact that coffee is harvested during only one season of the year. Cattle can be processed into hamburgers year-round.

Once again, note that to understand a company, you must understand the industry in which that company operates. Understanding the accounting procedures used to prepare its financial statements is only part of the task.

Effects of Cost Flow on Ratio Analysis

As demonstrated earlier in the chapter, the inventory cost flow assumption that a company uses affects its cost of goods sold and thereby its gross margin, net income, and retained earnings.

The method selected also affects the cost assigned to ending inventory, which in turn affects current assets and total assets. Financial statement analysis is also affected if it is based on ratios that use any of the items mentioned in their computation. Therefore, almost every ratio discussed in this book is affected. Previously defined ratios that are affected include the following:

Current ratio
Debt to assets ratio
Return on assets ratio
Return on equity ratio
Return on sales ratio
Gross margin percentage
Average days to sell inventory

The magnitude of the effect of different cost flow methods on some of these ratios may be immaterial. For a large business, the difference in total assets that results from its decision to use LIFO versus FIFO probably will be small. Therefore, the effect on the debt to assets ratio will be small. The effect of LIFO versus FIFO on the current ratio, however, might be more pronounced. It is important for financial statement users to be aware that a company's choice of accounting methods may significantly affect the users' analysis of its accounting information.

---

a look
back

Chapter 5 introduced the basic issues associated with accounting for inventory and cost of goods sold. This chapter expanded the subject to include a discussion of inventory cost flow methods including first-in, first-out (FIFO), last-in, first-out (LIFO), weighted average, and specific identification. Under *FIFO,* the cost of the items purchased first is shown on the income statement, and the cost of the items purchased last is shown on the balance sheet. Under *LIFO,* the cost of the items purchased last is shown on the income statement, and the cost of the items purchased first is shown on the balance sheet. Under the *weighted-average method,* the average cost of inventory is shown on the income statement and the balance sheet. Finally, under specific identification the actual cost of the goods is shown on the income statement and the balance sheet.

Generally accepted accounting principles often allow companies to account for the same types of events in different ways. The different cost flow assumptions presented in this chapter—FIFO, LIFO, weighted average, specific identification—are excellent examples of alternative accounting procedures allowed by GAAP. Persons who use financial information must be aware of the accounting alternatives available for a given event and the effects that choosing one method over another have on companies' financial statements and ratios.

This chapter also completed the discussion of the operating cycle, which began in Chapter 6. The measure of how fast inventory sells is called *inventory turnover;* it is computed by dividing cost of goods sold by inventory. The result of this computation is the number of times the balance in the Inventory account is turned over each year. The *average number of days in inventory ratio* can be determined by dividing the number of days in a year (365) by the inventory turnover ratio.

Accounting for investment securities is discussed in the appendix on page 381. Generally accepted accounting principles require companies to classify their investments in marketable securities into one of three categories: (1) *held-to-maturity securities,* (2) *trading securities,* and (3) *available-for-sale securities.* Since equity securities have no maturity date the held-to-maturity category applies only to debt securities. Securities classified as held-to-maturity are reported at amortized cost. Unrealized gains or losses are not recognized. Both debt and equity securities can be classified as trading securities or available-for-sale securities. Securities in both of these categories are reported on the balance sheet at market value. Unrealized gains and losses on trading securities are reported on the income statement. On available-for-sale securities, unrealized gains and losses are reported in a variety of ways. The most common practice is to bypass the income statement and show the unrealized gains and losses as direct equity adjustments on the balance sheet. Alternatively, unrealized gains and losses on available-for-sale securities can be shown as additions to or subtractions from net income with the result being titled **comprehensive income.** In addition, the unrealized gains and losses can be shown on a separate statement or as part of the statement of changes in equity.

a look
forward

Chapter 9 discusses accounting for long-term assets such as buildings and equipment. Although this topic is very different from accounting for inventory that a company purchases to sell to customers, it is similar in that GAAP allows different companies to use different accounting methods to account for the same types of events. The lives of accounting students would be easier if all companies had to use the same accounting methods. However, accounting methods used by different companies in the real world are probably becoming even more diverse. Thus, it is important that users of financial information consider these differences when making decisions.

SELF-STUDY REVIEW PROBLEM

Erie Jewelers sells gold earrings. Its beginning inventory of Model 407 gold earrings consisted of 100 pairs of earrings at $50 per pair. Erie purchased two batches of Model 407 earrings during the year. The first batch purchased consisted of 150 pairs at $53 per pair; the second batch consisted of 200 pairs at $56 per pair. During the year, Erie sold 375 pairs of Model 407 earrings.

Required

Determine the amount of product cost Erie would allocate to cost of goods sold and ending inventory assuming that Erie uses (a) FIFO, (b) LIFO, and (c) weighted average.

Solution to Requirements a–c

Goods Available for Sale

Beginning inventory	100	@	$50	= $ 5,000
First purchase	150	@	$53	= $ 7,950
Second purchase	200	@	$56	= $11,200
Goods available for sale	450			$24,150

a. FIFO

Cost of Goods Sold	Pairs		Cost per Pair		Cost of Goods Sold
From beginning inventory	100	@	$50	=	$ 5,000
From first purchase	150	@	$53	=	$ 7,950
From second purchase	125	@	$56	=	$ 7,000
Total pairs sold	375				$19,950

Ending inventory = Goods available for sale − Cost of goods sold
Ending inventory = $24,150 − $19,950 = $4,200

b. LIFO

Cost of Goods Sold	Pairs		Cost per Pair		Cost of Goods Sold
From second purchase	200	@	$56	=	$11,200
From first purchase	150	@	$53	=	$ 7,950
From beginning inventory	25	@	$50	=	$ 1,250
Total pairs sold	375				$20,400

Ending inventory = Goods available for sale − Cost of goods sold
Ending inventory = $24,150 − $20,400 = $3,750

c. Weighted average

Goods available for sale ÷ Total pairs = Cost per pair
$24,150 ÷ 450 = $53.6667

| Cost of goods sold | 375 units | @ | $53.6667 | = | $20,125 |
| Ending inventory | 75 units | @ | $53.6667 | = | $ 4,025 |

Types of Investment Securities

A financial investment occurs when one entity gives assets or services to another entity in exchange for a certificate known as a *security*. The entity that gives the assets and receives the security certificate is called the **investor.** The entity that receives the assets or services and gives the security certificate is called the **investee.** This chapter discusses accounting practices that apply to securities held by investors.

LO8 Identify certain assets that are shown on the balance sheet at market value.

There are two primary types of investment securities: debt securities and equity securities. An investor receives a **debt security** when assets or services *are loaned* to the investee. In general, a debt security describes the investee's obligation to return the assets and to pay interest for the use of the assets. Common types of debt securities include bonds, notes, certificates of deposit, and commercial paper. An **equity security** is acquired when an investor *gives* assets or services to an investee in exchange for an *ownership interest* in the investee. An equity security usually describes the rights of ownership, including the right to influence the operations of the investee and to share in profits or losses that accrue from those operations. The most common types of equity securities are common stock and preferred stock. In summary, **investment securities** are certificates that describe the rights and privileges that investors receive when they loan or give assets or services to investees.

Transactions between the investor and the investee constitute the **primary securities market.** There is a **secondary securities market** in which investors exchange (buy and sell) investment securities with other investors. Securities that regularly trade in established secondary markets are called **marketable securities.** Investee companies are affected by secondary-market transactions only to the extent that their obligations are transferred to a different party. For example, assume that Tom Williams (investor) loans assets to American Can Company (investee). Williams receives a bond (investment security) from American Can that describes American Can's obligation to return assets and pay interest to Williams. This exchange represents a primary securities market transaction. Now assume that in a secondary-market transaction Williams sells his investment security (bond) to Tina Tucker. American Can Company is affected by this transaction only to the extent that the company's obligation transfers from Williams to Tucker. In other words, American Can's obligation to repay principal and interest does not change. The only thing that changes is the party to whom American Can makes payments. Accordingly, *an investee's financial statements do not change when the securities it has issued to an investor are traded in the secondary market.*

The **market value,** sometimes called *fair value,* of an investor's securities is established by the prices at which they sell in the secondary markets. For financial reporting purposes, fair value is established as the closing (last) price paid for an identical security on the investor's fiscal closing date. Whether securities are reported at market value or historical cost depends on whether the investor intends to sell or hold the securities. Generally accepted accounting principles require companies to classify their investments into one of three categories: (1) held-to-maturity securities, (2) trading securities, and (3) available-for-sale securities.

Held-to-Maturity Securities

Since ownership interest in equity securities has no maturity date, the held-to-maturity classification applies only to debt securities. Debt securities should be classified as held-to-maturity securities if the investor has a *positive intent* and the *ability* to hold the securities until the maturity date. **Held-to-maturity securities** are reported in the financial statements at *amortized cost* (historical cost adjusted for the amortization of discounts or premiums). Recall from your experience with discount notes that amortized cost approaches the face value of a security as the security moves toward its maturity date. Since an investor receives the face value of a debt security at the maturity date, amortized cost is considered the best measure of value for held-to-maturity securities.

Trading Securities

Both debt and equity securities can be classified as *trading securities.* **Trading securities** are bought and sold for the purpose of generating profits on the short-term appreciation of stock and/or bond prices. They are usually traded within a three-month span. Trading securities are shown on the balance sheet at the market value existing on the investor's fiscal closing date.

Available-for-Sale Securities

All marketable securities that are not classified as held-to-maturity or trading securities must be classified as **available-for-sale securities.** These securities are also shown on the balance sheet at market value as of the investor's fiscal closing date.

Note that two of the three classifications require market value reporting, which is a clear exception to the historical cost concept. Other exceptions to the use of historical cost measures for asset valuation are discussed in later sections of this appendix.

Reporting Events That Affect Investment Securities

LO9 Explain how accounting for investment securities differs when the securities are classified as held-to-maturity, trading, or available-for-sale.

Four distinct accounting events affect marketable investment securities. These events and their effects on financial statements are illustrated in the following section. The illustration assumes that Arapaho Company is an investor company that started the accounting period with $10,000 in cash and common stock.

Event 1 Investment Purchase
Arapaho paid cash to purchase $9,000 of marketable investment securities.

This is an asset exchange event. One asset (cash) decreases, and another asset (investment securities) increases. The income statement is not affected. The $9,000 cash outflow is shown as either an operating activity or an investing activity, depending on how the securities are classified. Since *trading securities* are short-term assets that are regularly traded for the purpose of producing income, cash flows from the purchase or sale of these securities are shown in the operating activities section of the statement of cash flows. In contrast, cash flows associated with the purchase or sale of securities classified as *held-to-maturity* or *available for sale* are shown in the investing activities section of the statement of cash flows. These alternative treatments are shown in the following statements model. Once again, the only difference between the treatments lies in the classification of the cash outflow shown on the statement of cash flows.

Event No.	Type	Assets			=	Liab.	+	Equity	Rev.	–	Exp.	=	Net Inc.	Cash Flow	
		Cash	+	Inv. Sec.											
1	Held	(9,000)	+	9,000	=	NA	+	NA	NA	–	NA	=	NA	(9,000)	IA
1	Trading	(9,000)	+	9,000	=	NA	+	NA	NA	–	NA	=	NA	(9,000)	OA
1	Available	(9,000)	+	9,000	=	NA	+	NA	NA	–	NA	=	NA	(9,000)	IA

Event 2 Recognition of Investment Revenue
Arapaho earned $1,600 of cash investment revenue.

Investment revenue is treated the same regardless of whether the securities are classified as held to maturity, trading, or available for sale. The revenue comes in two primary forms. Earnings from equity investments are called **dividends.** Revenue from debt securities is called **interest.** Both types have the same impact on the financial statements. The recognition of the investment revenue acts to increase assets and equity. Likewise, net income increases. The cash inflow from investment revenue is shown in the operating activities section of the statement of cash flows regardless of how the investment securities are classified.

Event No.	Assets	=	Liab.	+	Equity	Rev.	–	Exp.	=	Net Inc.	Cash Flow	
2	1,600	=	NA	+	1,600	1,600	–	NA	=	1,600	1,600	OA

Event 3 Sale of Investment Securities
Arapaho sold securities that cost $2,000 for $2,600 cash.

This event results in the recognition of a $600 realized gain that acts to increase total assets and equity. More specifically, the Cash account increases by $2,600, and the Investment Securities account decreases by $2,000, thereby resulting in a $600 increase in total assets. The $600 realized gain is shown on the income statement, thereby increasing net income and ultimately retained earnings. The $600 gain is not shown separately on the statement of cash flows. Instead, the entire $2,600 cash inflow is shown in one section of the statement of cash flows. Cash inflows from the sale of held-to-maturity and available-for-sale securities are classified as investing activities. Cash flows associated with trading securities are included in operating activities. These effects are shown below.

Event No.	Type	Assets			=	Liab.	+	Equity	Rev. or Gain	−	Exp. or Loss	=	Net Inc.	Cash Flow	
		Cash	+	Inv. Sec.											
3	Held	2,600	+	(2,000)	=	NA	+	600	600	−	NA	=	600	2,600	IA
3	Trading	2,600	+	(2,000)	=	NA	+	600	600	−	NA	=	600	2,600	OA
3	Available	2,600	+	(2,000)	=	NA	+	600	600	−	NA	=	600	2,600	IA

Event 4 Market Value Adjustment
Arapaho recognized a $700 unrealized gain.

After Event 3, the historical cost of Arapaho's portfolio of remaining investment securities is $7,000 ($9,000 purchased less $2,000 sold). Assume that at Arapaho's fiscal closing date, these securities have a market value of $7,700. This means that Arapaho has experienced a $700 *unrealized* gain on its investment. This type of gain (sometimes called a *paper profit*) is classified as an unrealized gain because the securities have not been sold. The treatment of **unrealized gains or losses** in the financial statements depends on whether the securities are classified as held to maturity, trading, or available for sale.

Unrealized gains or losses on securities classified as *held to maturity* are not recognized in the financial statements. Accordingly, the balance sheet, income statement, and statement of cash flows are not affected by unrealized gains or losses. Even so, many companies choose to disclose the market value of the securities as part of the narrative description or in the footnotes that accompany the statements. Regardless of the disclosure, the amount of amortized cost is included in the computation of the amount of total assets shown on the balance sheet.

Investments classified as trading securities are shown in the financial statements at market value. This means that *unrealized gains or losses* on *trading securities* are recognized. In this case, the $700 gain acts to increase the carrying value of the investment securities. The gain acts to increase net income, which in turn acts to increase retained earnings. Cash flow is not affected by unrealized gains and losses.

Unrealized gains and losses are also recognized on investment securities classified as *available for sale*. However, an important distinction exists with respect to how the unrealized gains and losses affect the financial statements. *Unrealized gains or losses on available-for-sale securities* are shown on the balance sheet but *are not* recognized in the determination of net income.[1] With respect to the balance sheet, the $700 gain acts to increase the carrying value of the investment securities. A corresponding increase is shown in a separate equity account titled *Unrealized Gain or Loss on Available-for-Sale Securities*. The statement of cash flows is not affected by the recognition of unrealized gains and losses on *available-for-sale* securities.

Clearly, the effect of unrealized gains and losses on Arapaho's financial statements is determined by whether the investment securities are classified as held to maturity, trading, or available for sale. The effects associated with each alternative treatment are shown here:

Event No.	Type	Assets	=	Liab.	+	Equity				Rev. or Gain	−	Exp. or Loss	=	Net Inc.	Cash Flow
		Inv. Sec.				Ret. Earn.	+	Unreal. Gain							
4	Held	NA	=	NA	+	NA	+	NA		NA	−	NA	=	NA	NA
4	Trading	700	=	NA	+	700	+	NA		700	−	NA	=	700	NA
4	Available	700	=	NA	+	NA	+	700		NA	−	NA	=	NA	NA

[1]*Statement of Financial Accounting Standards No. 130* permits companies to show unrealized gains and losses on available-for-sale securities as additions to or subtractions from net income with the result being titled *comprehensive income*. Alternatively, the unrealized gains and losses can be shown on a separate statement or as part of the statement of changes in equity.

Financial Statements

LO9 Explain how accounting for investment securities differs when the securities are classified as held to maturity, trading, or available for sale.

As the preceding discussion implies, the financial statements of Arapaho Company are affected by not only the business events relating to its security transactions but also the accounting treatment that is applied to those events. In other words, the same economic events are reflected differently in the financial statements depending on whether the securities are classified as held to maturity, trading, or available for sale. Exhibit 8–10 contains the financial statements for Arapaho that are prepared under each investment classification alternative. Statements under Alternative 1 are prepared under the assumption that Arapaho classifies its investment securities as held to maturity. Alternative 2 assumes the investments are classified as trading securities. Alternative 3 assumes an available-for-sale classification.

The amount of net income reported under the trading securities category is $700 higher than that reported under the held-to-maturity and available-for-sale categories because unrealized gains and losses on the trading securities are recognized on the income statement. Similarly, total assets are $700 higher under the trading category than they are under the held-to-maturity category. This too is a result of the recognition of the $700 unrealized gain on the trading securities. Note that this gain is also recognized on the balance sheet when the securities are classified as available for sale. Even though the gain is not shown on the income statement, it does appear on the balance sheet in a special equity account titled

---

Exhibit 8–10

ARAPAHO COMPANY
Comparative Financial Statements

Income Statements

Investment Securities Classified as	Held	Trading	Available
Investment Revenue	$ 1,600	$ 1,600	$ 1,600
Realized Gain	600	600	600
Unrealized Gain		700	
Net Income	$ 2,200	$ 2,900	$ 2,200

Balance Sheets

	Held	Trading	Available
Assets			
Cash	$ 5,200	$ 5,200	$ 5,200
Investment Securities, at Cost			
(Market Value $7,700)	7,000		
Securities, at Market (Cost $7,000)		7,700	7,700
Total Assets	$12,200	$12,900	$12,900
Stockholders' Equity			
Common Stock	$10,000	$10,000	$10,000
Retained Earnings	2,200	2,900	2,200
Unrealized Gain on Investment Securities			700
Total Stockholders' Equity	$12,200	$12,900	$12,900

Statements of Cash Flows

	Held	Trading	Available
Operating Activities			
Cash Inflow from Investment Revenue	$ 1,600	$ 1,600	$ 1,600
Outflow to Purchase Securities		(9,000)	
Inflow from Sale of Securities		2,600	
Investing Activities			
Outflow to Purchase Securities	(9,000)		(9,000)
Inflow from Sale Securities	2,600		2,600
Financing Activities*	0	0	0
Net Decrease in Cash	(4,800)	(4,800)	(4,800)
Beginning Cash Balance	10,000	10,000	10,000
Ending Cash Balance	$ 5,200	$ 5,200	$ 5,200

*The $10,000 capital acquisition is assumed to have occurred prior to the start of the accounting period.

Exhibit 8–11					
Investment Category	Types of Securities	Types of Revenue Recognized	Reported on Balance Sheet at	Recognition of Unrealized Gains and Losses on the Income Statement	Cash Flow From Purchase or Sale of Securities Classified As
Held to maturity	Debt	Interest	Amortized cost	No	Investing activity
Trading	Debt and equity	Interest and dividends	Market value	Yes	Operating activity
Available for sale	Debt and equity	Interest and dividends	Market value	No	Investing activity

Unrealized Gain on Investment Securities. Accordingly, total assets and equity are higher under the available-for-sale category than they are under the held-to-maturity category. The statements of cash flows reflect the fact that purchases and sales of trading securities are classified as operating activities while purchases and sales of available-for-sale and held-to-maturity securities are considered investing activities. Exhibit 8–11 shows the important reporting differences associated with the three classifications of investment securities.

Alternative Reporting Practices for Equity Securities

Depending on the amount of equity securities owned, an investor can exercise *significant influence* over an investee company. Indeed, an investor can obtain enough equity securities to gain *control* of the investee. The previous discussion regarding accounting requirements for equity securities assumed that the investor did not control or significantly influence the investee. Alternative accounting requirements apply to securities owned by investors who exercise significant influence over or control of an investee company. Determining the level of influence that an investor exercises over an investee frequently requires significant judgment. Accountants have established percentage thresholds to facilitate their assessment of an investor's ability to influence or control the operations of an investee. Unless there is evidence to the contrary, investors owning more than 20 percent of the stock of an investee company are assumed to have a significant influence on the investee. Investors owning more than 50 percent of the stock of an investee company are assumed to have control over the investee. These percentage guidelines can be overridden when other classification criteria such as interlocking directorates, joint management, technological dependence, product dependence, and so on indicate that the percentages do not accurately reflect the level of influence. The accounting treatment applied to equity investment securities differs, depending on the level of the investor's ability to influence or control the operating, investing, and financing activities of the investee.

As previously demonstrated, investors who do not have a significant influence (they own 20 percent or less of the stock of the investee) account for their investments in equity securities at market value. Investors exercising significant influence (they own 20 to 50 percent of the investee's stock) must account for their investments under the **equity method.** A detailed discussion of the equity method is beyond the scope of this text. However, *you should be aware that investments carried under the equity method represent a measure of the book value of the investee rather than the cost or market value.*

Investors who have a controlling interest (own more than 50 percent of the investee's stock) in an investee company are required to issue a set of **consolidated financial statements.** The company that holds the controlling interest is referred to as the **parent company,** and the company that is controlled is called the **subsidiary company.** Usually, the parent and subsidiary companies maintain separate accounting records. However, a parent company is also required to report to the public its accounting data along with that of its subsidiaries in a single set of combined financial statements. These consolidated statements represent a separate accounting entity composed of the parent and its subsidiaries. Accordingly for a parent company that owns one subsidiary, there will be three sets of financial statements: statements for the parent company, statements for the subsidiary company, and statements for the consolidated entity.

QUESTIONS

1. Name and discuss the four cost flow methods discussed in this chapter.
2. What are some advantages and disadvantages of the specific identification method of accounting for inventory?
3. What are some advantages and disadvantages of using the FIFO method of inventory valuation?
4. What are some advantages and disadvantages of using the LIFO method of inventory valuation?
5. In an inflationary period, which inventory cost flow method will produce the largest net income? Explain.
6. In an inflationary period, which inventory cost flow method will produce the largest amount of total assets on the balance sheet? Explain.
7. What is the difference between the flow of costs and the physical flow of goods?
8. Does the choice of cost flow method (FIFO, LIFO, or weighted average) affect the cash flow statement? Explain.
9. Assume that Key Co. purchased 1,000 units of merchandise in its first year of operations for $25 per unit. The company sold 850 units for $40. What is the amount of cost of goods sold using FIFO? LIFO? Weighted average?
10. Assume that Key Co. purchased 1,500 units of merchandise in its second year of operation for $27 per unit. Its beginning inventory was determined in Question 8–9. Assuming that 1,500 units are sold, what is the amount of cost of goods sold using FIFO? LIFO? Weighted average?
11. Refer to Questions 8–9 and 8–10. Which method might be preferable for financial statements? For income tax reporting? Explain.
12. In an inflationary period, which cost flow method, FIFO or LIFO, produces the larger cash flow? Explain.
13. Which inventory cost flow method produces the largest net income in a deflationary period?
14. What is the difference between a periodic inventory system and a perpetual inventory system?
15. How does the phrase *lower-of-cost-or-market* value apply to inventory valuation?
16. If some merchandise declined in value because of damage or obsolescence, what effect will the lower-of-cost-or-market rule have on the income statement? Explain.
17. What are three situations in which estimates of the amount of inventory may be useful or even necessary?
18. Under which inventory system, periodic or perpetual, is it easier for management to manipulate net income if tempted to do so?
19. If the amount of goods available for sale is $123,000, the amount of sales is $130,000, and the gross margin is 25 percent of sales, what is the amount of ending inventory?
20. Assume that inventory is overstated by $1,500 at the end of 2001. What effect will this have on the 2001 income statement? The 2001 balance sheet? The 2002 income statement? The 2002 balance sheet? (Assume that the periodic inventory method is used.)
21. What information does inventory turnover provide?
22. What is an example of a business that would have a high inventory turnover? A low inventory turnover?
23. How is a company's operating cycle computed?
24. Why are historical costs generally used in financial statements?
25. What are some instances in which the Financial Accounting Standards Board requires using market values for financial reporting?
26. What is an example of an asset easily valued at fair market value? What is an example of an asset that is difficult to value at fair market value?
27. What are the two primary types of investment securities?
28. What is a debt security? Give an example.
29. What is an equity security? Give an example.
30. What is the difference between the primary securities market and the secondary securities market?
31. What are marketable securities?

32. Generally accepted accounting principles require companies to classify investment securities into three categories. Name and describe them.

33. When must the equity method of accounting for investments be used for financial statement reporting?

EXERCISE 8–1A *Effect of Inventory Cost Flow Assumption on Financial Statements*   **L.O. 1**

Required

For each of the following situations, fill in the blank with *FIFO, LIFO,* or *weighted average.*

a. _____ would produce the highest amount of net income in an inflationary environment.

b. _____ would produce the highest amount of assets in an inflationary environment.

c. _____ would produce the lowest amount of net income in a deflationary environment.

d. _____ would produce the same unit cost for assets and cost of goods sold in an inflationary environment.

e. _____ would produce the lowest amount of net income in an inflationary environment.

f. _____ would produce an asset value that was the same regardless of whether the environment was inflationary or deflationary.

g. _____ would produce the lowest amount of assets in an inflationary environment.

h. _____ would produce the highest amount of assets in a deflationary environment.

EXERCISE 8–2A *Allocating Product Cost Between Cost of Goods Sold and Ending Inventory:*   **L.O. 1, 2**
Single Purchase

Tyler Co. started the year with no inventory. During the year, it purchased two identical inventory items. The inventory was purchased at different times. The first purchase cost $3,000 and the other, $4,000. One of the items was sold during the year.

Required

Based on this information, how much product cost would be allocated to cost of goods sold and ending inventory on the year-end financial statements, assuming use of

a. FIFO?

b. LIFO?

c. weighted average?

EXERCISE 8–3A *Allocating Product Cost Between Cost of Goods Sold and Ending Inventory:*   **L.O. 1, 2**
Multiple Purchases

Breckin Company sells coffee makers used in business offices. Its beginning inventory of coffee makers was 100 units at $40 per unit. During the year, Breckin made two batch purchases of coffee makers. The first was a 150-unit purchase at $60 per unit; the second was a 200-unit purchase at $68 per unit. During the period, Breckin sold 260 coffee makers.

Required

Determine the amount of product costs that would be allocated to cost of goods sold and ending inventory, assuming that Breckin uses

a. FIFO.

b. LIFO.

c. weighted average.

EXERCISE 8–4A *Effect of Inventory Cost Flow (FIFO, LIFO, and Weighted Average) on*   **L.O. 1, 2**
Gross Margin

The following information pertains to Porter Company for 2005.

Beginning inventory	50 units @ $10
Units purchased	275 units @ $15

Ending inventory consisted of five units. Porter sold 320 units at $30 each. All purchases and sales were made with cash.

Required

a. Compute the gross margin for Porter Company using the following cost flow assumptions: (1) FIFO, (2) LIFO, and (3) weighted average.

b. What is the dollar amount of difference in net income between using FIFO versus LIFO? (Ignore income tax considerations.)

c. Determine the cash flow from operating activities, using each of the three cost flow assumptions listed in Requirement *a*. Ignore the effect of income taxes. Explain why these cash flows have no differences.

L.O. 1, 2   EXERCISE 8–5A *Effect of Inventory Cost Flow on Ending Inventory Balance*

McKee Sales had the following transactions for cameras for 2004, its first year of operations.

Jan. 20	Purchased 450 units @ $20	=	$9,000
Apr. 21	Purchased 200 units @ $24	=	4,800
July 25	Purchased 100 units @ $30	=	3,000
Sept. 19	Purchased 75 units @ $18	=	1,350

During the year, McKee Sales sold 725 cameras for $50 each.

Required

a. Compute the amount of ending inventory McKee would report on the balance sheet, assuming the following cost flow assumptions: (1) FIFO, (2) LIFO, and (3) weighted average.

b. Compute the difference in gross margin between the FIFO and LIFO cost flow assumptions.

L.O. 1, 2   EXERCISE 8–6A *Income Tax Effect of Shifting From FIFO to LIFO*

The following information pertains to the inventory of the Foley Company:

Jan. 1	Beginning Inventory	500 units @ $10
Apr. 1	Purchased	2,500 units @ $11
Oct. 1	Purchased	800 units @ $14

During the year, Foley sold 3,400 units of inventory at $20 per unit and incurred $17,000 of operating expenses. Foley currently uses the FIFO method but is considering a change to LIFO. All transactions are cash transactions. Assume a 30 percent income tax rate.

Required

a. Prepare income statements using FIFO and LIFO.

b. Determine the amount of income taxes Foley would save if it changed cost flow methods.

c. Determine the cash flow from operating activities under FIFO and LIFO.

d. Explain why cash flow from operating activities is lower under FIFO when that cost flow method produced the higher gross margin.

L.O. 1, 2   EXERCISE 8–7A *Effect of FIFO Versus LIFO on Income Tax Expense*

Tiny Tots Company had sales of $125,000 for 2006, its first year of operation. On April 2, the company purchased 200 units of inventory at $175 per unit. On September 1, an additional 150 units were purchased for $190 per unit. The company had 100 units on hand at the end of the year. The company's income tax rate is 40 percent. All transactions are cash transactions.

Required

a. The preceding paragraph describes five accounting events: (1) a sales transaction, (2) the first purchase of inventory, (3) a second purchase of inventory, (4) the recognition of cost of goods sold expense, and (5) the payment of income tax expense. Record the amounts of each event in horizontal statements models like the following ones, assuming first a FIFO and then a LIFO cost flow.

Effect of Events on Financial Statements													
Panel 1: FIFO Cost Flow													
Event No.	**Balance Sheet**								**Income Statement**				**Statement of Cash Flows**
	Cash	+	Inventory	=	C. Stk.	+	Ret. Earn.		Rev.	–	Exp.	=	Net Inc.	
Panel 2: LIFO Cost Flow													
Event No.	**Balance Sheet**								**Income Statement**				**Statement of Cash Flows**
	Cash	+	Inventory	=	C. Stk.	+	Ret. Earn.		Rev.	–	Exp.	=	Net Inc.	

b. Compute net income using FIFO.

c. Compute net income using LIFO.

d. Explain the difference, if any, in the amount of income tax expense incurred using the two cost flow assumptions.

e. How does the use of the FIFO versus the LIFO cost flow assumption affect the statement of cash flows?

EXERCISE 8–8A *Recording Inventory Transactions Using the Perpetual System Intermittent Sales and Purchases*   L.O. 2

The following inventory transactions apply to Nikols Company for 2004.

Jan. 1	Purchased	250 units @ $10
Apr. 1	Sold	125 units @ $18
Aug. 1	Purchased	400 units @ $11
Dec. 1	Sold	500 units @ $19

The beginning inventory consisted of 175 units at $11 per unit. All transactions are cash transactions.

Required

a. Record these transactions, in general journal format, assuming that Nikols uses the FIFO cost flow assumption and keeps perpetual records.

b. Compute the ending balance in the Inventory account.

EXERCISE 8–9A *Effect of Cost Flow on Ending Inventory: Intermittent Sales and Purchases*   L.O. 2

Spring Hill, Inc., had the following series of transactions for 2007:

Date	Transaction	Description
Jan. 1	Beginning inventory	50 units @ $20
Mar. 15	Purchased	200 units @ $24
May 30	Sold	170 units @ $40
Aug. 10	Purchased	275 units @ $25
Nov. 20	Sold	340 units @ $40

Required

a. Determine the quantity and dollar amount of inventory at the end of the year, assuming Spring Hill uses the FIFO cost flow assumption and keeps perpetual records.

b. Write a memo explaining why Spring Hill, Inc., would have difficulty applying the LIFO method on a perpetual basis. Include a discussion of how to overcome these difficulties.

EXERCISE 8–10A *Lower-of-Cost-or-Market Rule: Perpetual System*   L.O. 3

The following information pertains to Auto Parts Co.'s ending inventory for the current year.

Item	Quantity	Unit Cost	Unit Market Value
P	100	$4	$3
D	50	5	4
S	20	6	7
J	15	5	4

Required

a. Determine the value of the ending inventory using the lower-of-cost-or-market rule applied to (1) each individual inventory item and (2) the total inventory in aggregate.

b. Prepare any necessary journal entries, assuming the decline in value is immaterial using (1) individual method and (2) aggregate method. Auto Parts Co. uses the perpetual inventory system.

EXERCISE 8–11A *Lower-of-Cost-or-Market Rule: Periodic System*   L.O. 3

Moore Company carries three inventory items. The following information pertains to the ending inventory:

Item	Quantity	Unit Cost	Unit Market Value
O	200	$10	$ 9
J	250	15	14
R	175	5	8

Required

a. Determine the ending inventory that will be reported on the balance sheet, assuming that Moore applies the lower-of-cost-or-market rule to individual inventory items.

b. Explain how the write-down would be recorded under the periodic inventory system.

L.O. 4   EXERCISE 8–12A *Estimating Ending Inventory: Periodic System*

A substantial portion of inventory owned by Rick's Fishing Supplies was recently destroyed when the roof collapsed during a rainstorm. The accountant must estimate the loss from the storm for insurance reporting and financial statement purposes. Rick's uses the periodic inventory system. The following pertains to Rick's books:

Beginning inventory	$100,000
Purchases to date of storm	400,000
Sales to date of storm	550,000

The value of undamaged inventory counted was $8,000. Historically Rick's gross margin percentage has been approximately 20 percent of sales.

Required

Estimate the following:

a. Gross margin in dollars

b. Cost of goods sold

c. Ending inventory

d. Amount of lost inventory

L.O. 4   EXERCISE 8–13A *Estimating Ending Inventory: Perpetual System*

Steve Li owned a small company that sold boating equipment. The equipment was expensive, and a perpetual system was maintained for control purposes. Even so, lost, damaged, and stolen merchandise normally amounted to 5 percent of the inventory balance. On June 14, Li's warehouse was destroyed by fire. Just prior to the fire, the accounting records contained a $164,000 balance in the Inventory account. However, inventory costing $21,000 had been sold and delivered to customers but had not been recorded in the books at the time of the fire. The fire did not affect the showroom, which contained inventory that cost $37,500.

Required

Estimate the amount of inventory destroyed by fire.

L.O. 5   EXERCISE 8–14A *Effect of Inventory Error on Financial Statements: Perpetual System*

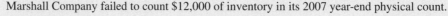

Marshall Company failed to count $12,000 of inventory in its 2007 year-end physical count.

Required

Explain how this error will affect Marshall's 2007 financial statements, assuming that Marshall uses the perpetual inventory system.

L.O. 5   EXERCISE 8–15A *Effect of Inventory Error on Elements of Financial Statements: Periodic System*

The ending inventory for Tedall Co. was understated by $5,200 at the end of 2005.

Required

Was each of the following amounts overstated, understated, or not affected by the error?

Item No.	Year	Amount
1	2005	Beginning inventory
2	2005	Purchases
3	2005	Goods available for sale
4	2005	Cost of goods sold
5	2005	Gross margin
6	2005	Net income
7	2006	Beginning inventory
8	2006	Purchases
9	2006	Goods available for sale
10	2006	Cost of goods sold
11	2006	Gross margin
12	2006	Net income

EXERCISE 8–16A *Identifying Asset Values for Financial Statements (Appendix)*   L.O. 8

Required

Indicate whether each of the following assets should be valued at fair market value (FMV), lower of cost or market (LCM), or historical cost (HC) on the balance sheet. For certain assets, historical cost may be called amortized cost (AC.)

Asset	FMV	LCM	HC/AC
Buildings			
Available-for-Sale Securities			
Office Equipment			
Inventory			
Supplies			
Land			
Trading Securities			
Cash			
Held-to-Maturity Securities			

EXERCISE 8–17A *Accounting for Investment Securities (Appendix)*   L.O. 9

Martinez Bros. purchased $15,000 of marketable securities on March 1, 2004. On the company's fiscal closing date, December 31, 2004, the securities had a market value of $13,500. During 2004, Martinez recognized $5,000 of revenue and $1,500 of expenses.

Required

a. Record a +, −, or NA in a horizontal statements model to show how the purchase of the securities affects the financial statements, assuming that the securities are classified as (1) held to maturity, (2) trading, or (3) available for sale. In the Cash Flow column, indicate whether the item is an operating activity (OA), investing activity (IA), or financing activity (FA). Record only the effects of the purchase event.

Event No.	Type	Cash	+	Inv. Sec.	=	Liab.	+	S. Equity	Rev.	−	Exp.	=	Net Inc.	Cash Flow
1	Held													
2	Trading													
3	Available													

b. Determine the amount of net income that would be reported on the 2004 income statement, assuming that the marketable securities are classified as (1) held to maturity, (2) trading, or (3) available for sale.

EXERCISE 8–18A *Effect of Investment Securities Transactions on Financial Statements (Appendix)*   L.O. 9

The following information pertains to Tony Electronics for 2002.

1. Purchased $150,000 of marketable investment securities.
2. Earned $9,000 of cash investment revenue.
3. Sold for $30,000 securities that cost $25,000.
4. The fair value of the remaining securities at December 31, 2002, was $100,000.

Required

a. Record the four events in a statements model like the following one. Use a separate model for each classification: (1) held to maturity, (2) trading, and (3) available for sale. The first event for the first classification is shown as an example.

Held to Maturity

Event No.	Cash	+	Inv. Sec.	=	Liab.	+	Ret. Earn.	+	Unreal. Gain.	Rev. or Gains	−	Exp. or Loss	=	Net Inc.	Cash Flow
1	(150,000)	+	150,000	=	NA	+	NA	+	NA	NA	−	NA	=	NA	(150,000) IA

b. What is the amount of net income under each of the three classifications?
c. What is the change in cash from operating activities under each of the three classifications?
d. Are the answers to Requirements *b* and *c* different for each of the classifications? Why or why not?

L.O. 9   **EXERCISE 8–19A** *Preparing Financial Statements for Investment Securities (Appendix)*

Poort, Inc., began 2001 with $80,000 in cash and common stock. The company engaged in the following investment transactions during 2001:
1. Purchased $40,000 of marketable investment securities.
2. Earned $1,200 cash from investment revenue.
3. Sold investment securities for $16,000 that cost $12,000.
4. Purchased $18,000 of additional marketable investment securities.
5. Determined that the investment securities had a fair value of $48,000 at the end of 2001.

Required

Use a vertical statements model to prepare income statements, balance sheets, and statements of cash flow for Poort, Inc., assuming the securities were (*a*) held to maturity, (*b*) trading, and (*c*) available for sale.

L.O. 9   **EXERCISE 8–20A** *Differences Among Marketable Investment Securities Classifications (Appendix)*

Complete the following table for the three categories of marketable investment securities:

Investment Category	Types of Securities	Types of Revenue Recognized	Value Reported on Balance Sheet	Recognition of Unrealized Gains and Losses on the Income Statement	Cash Flow from Purchase or Sale of Securities Is Classified as
Held to maturity	Debt	Interest	Amortized Cost	No	Investing Activity
Trading					
Available for sale					

PROBLEMS—SERIES A

L.O. 1, 2   **PROBLEM 8–21A** *Effect of Different Inventory Cost Flow Methods on Financial Statements*

The accounting records of Sharp Photography, Inc., reflected the following balances as of January 1, 2007:

Cash	$22,000
Beginning Inventory	16,500 (150 units @ $110)
Common Stock	14,300
Retained Earnings	24,200

The following five transactions occurred in 2007:

1. First purchase (cash)   120 units @ $85
2. Second purchase (cash)   200 units @ $100
3. Sales (all cash)   300 units @ $185
4. Paid $12,000 cash for operating expenses.
5. Paid cash for income tax at the rate of 40 percent of income before taxes.

Required

a. Compute the cost of goods sold and ending inventory, assuming (1) FIFO cost flow, (2) LIFO cost flow, and (3) weighted-average cost flow.
b. Use a vertical model to prepare the 2007 income statement, balance sheet, and statement of cash flows under FIFO, LIFO, and weighted average. (*Hint:* Record the events under an accounting equation before preparing the statements.)

PROBLEM 8–22A *Allocating Product Costs Between Cost of Goods Sold and Ending Inventory: Intermittent Purchases and Sales of Merchandise*

L.O. 2

Milan, Inc., had the following sales and purchase transactions during 2006. Beginning inventory consisted of 80 items at $120 each. Milan uses the FIFO cost flow assumption and keeps perpetual inventory records.

Date	Transaction	Description
Mar. 5	Purchased	80 items @ $125
Apr. 10	Sold	60 items @ $245
June 19	Sold	70 items @ $245
Sept. 16	Purchased	60 items @ $130
Nov. 28	Sold	55 items @ $255

Required

a. Record the inventory transactions in general journal format.
b. Calculate the gross margin Milan would report on the 2006 income statement.
c. Determine the ending inventory balance Milan would report on the December 31, 2006, balance sheet.

PROBLEM 8–23A *Inventory Valuation Based on the Lower-of-Cost-or-Market Rule*

L.O. 3

At the end of the year, Dot Computer Repair had the following items in inventory:

Item	Quantity	Unit Cost	Unit Market Value
D1	60	$30	$35
D2	30	55	50
D3	44	40	55
D4	40	50	35

Required

a. Determine the amount of ending inventory using the lower-of-cost-or-market rule applied to each individual inventory item.
b. Provide the general journal entry necessary to write down the inventory based on Requirement *a*. Assume that Dot Computer Repair uses the perpetual inventory system.
c. Determine the amount of ending inventory, assuming that the lower-of-cost-or-market rule is applied to the total inventory in aggregate.
d. Provide the general journal entry necessary to write down the inventory based on Requirement *c*. Assume that Dot Computer Repair uses the perpetual inventory system.
e. Explain how the inventory loss would be reported if Dot Computer Repair used the periodic inventory system.

L.O. 4   PROBLEM 8–24A *Estimating Ending Inventory: Gross Margin Method*

Beach Supplies had its inventory destroyed by a hurricane on September 21 of the current year. Back-up copies of the accounting records were stored in an off-site location and were not damaged. The following information was available for the period of January 1 through September 21:

Beginning inventory, January 1	$ 68,000
Purchases through September 21	350,000
Sales through September 21	520,000

The gross margin for Beach Supplies has traditionally been 25 percent of sales.

Required

a. For the period ending September 21, compute the following:
(1) Estimated gross margin.
(2) Estimated cost of goods sold.
(3) Estimated inventory at September 21.
b. Assume that $8,000 of the inventory was not damaged. What is the amount of the loss from the hurricane?
c. If Beach Supplies had used the perpetual inventory system, how would it have determined the amount of the inventory loss?

L.O. 4   PROBLEM 8–25A *Estimating Ending Inventory: Gross Margin Method*

Lexington Company wants to produce quarterly financial statements but takes a physical count of inventory only at year end. The following historical data were taken from the 2004 and 2005 accounting records:

	2004	2005
Net sales	$140,000	$200,000
Cost of goods sold	62,000	90,000

At the end of the first quarter of 2006, Lexington Company's ledger had the following account balances:

Sales	$240,000
Sales Discounts	10,000
Purchases	160,000
Transportation-in	4,000
Transportation-out	6,000
Beginning Inventory	60,000

Required

Using the information provided, estimate the following for the first quarter of 2006:
a. Gross margin
b. Ending inventory at March 31

L.O. 5   PROBLEM 8–26A *Effect of Inventory Errors on Financial Statements*

The following income statement was prepared for ROC Company for the year 2002:

ROC COMPANY Income Statement For the Year Ended December 31, 2002	
Sales	$69,000
Cost of Goods Sold	(38,640)
Gross Margin	30,360
Operating Expenses	(9,100)
Net Income	$21,260

During the year-end audit, the following errors were discovered.

1. A $1,400 payment for repairs was erroneously charged to the Cost of Goods Sold account. (Assume that the perpetual inventory system is used.)

2. Sales to customers for $2,400 at December 31, 2002, were not recorded in the books for 2002. Also, the $1,344 cost of selling these goods was not recorded. The error was not discovered in the physical count because the goods had not been delivered.

3. A mathematical error was made in determining ending inventory. Ending inventory was understated by $1,200. (The Inventory account was written down in error.)

Required

Determine the effect, if any, of each of the errors on the following items. Give the dollar amount of the effect and whether it would overstate (+), understate (−), or not affect (NA) the account. The effect on sales is recorded as an example.

Error No. 1	Amount of Error	Effect
Sales 2002	NA	NA
Ending inventory, December 31, 2002		
Gross margin, 2002		
Beginning inventory, January 1, 2003		
Cost of goods sold, 2002		
Net income, 2002		
Retained earnings, December 31, 2002		
Total assets, December 31, 2002		

Error No. 2	Amount of Error	Effect
Sales 2002	$2,400	Understate
Ending inventory, December 31, 2002		
Gross margin, 2002		
Beginning inventory, January 1, 2003		
Cost of goods sold, 2002		
Net income, 2002		
Retained earnings, December 31, 2002		
Total assets, December 31, 2002		

Error No. 3	Amount of Error	Effect
Sales 2002	NA	NA
Ending inventory, December 31, 2002		
Gross margin, 2002		
Beginning inventory, January 1, 2003		
Cost of goods sold, 2002		
Net income, 2002		
Retained earnings, December 31, 2002		
Total assets, December 31, 2002		

PROBLEM 8–27A *Effect of Marketable Investment Securities Transactions on Financial Statements (Appendix)*   **L.O. 8, 9**

The following transactions pertain to Best Answering Service for 2007:
1. Started business by acquiring $20,000 cash from the issue of common stock.
2. Provided $60,000 of services for cash.
3. Invested $20,000 in marketable investment securities.
4. Paid $19,000 of operating expense.
5. Received $400 of investment income from the securities.
6. Invested an additional $12,000 in marketable investment securities.
7. Paid a $2,000 cash dividend to the stockholders.
8. Sold investment securities that cost $5,000 for $6,300.
9. Received another $1,000 in investment income.
10. Determined the market value of the investment securities at the end of the year was $40,000.

Required

Use a vertical model to prepare a 2007 income statement, balance sheet, and statement of cash flows, assuming that the marketable investment securities were classified as (a) held to maturity, (b) trading, and (c) available for sale. (*Hint:* Record the events in T-accounts prior to preparing the financial statements.)

PROBLEM 8–28A *Comprehensive Horizontal Statements Model*   **L.O. 1, 9**

Clark's Dairy experienced the following independent events.
1. Acquired cash from issuing common stock.

2. Purchased inventory on account.
3. Paid cash to purchase marketable securities classified as trading securities.
4. Recorded unrealized loss on marketable securities that were classified as trading securities.
5. Recorded unrealized loss on marketable securities that were classified as available for sale securities.
6. Recorded unrealized loss on marketable securities that were classified as held to maturity securities.
7. Wrote down inventory to comply with lower-of-cost-or-market rule. (Assume that the company uses the perpetual inventory system.)
8. Estimated the ending inventory balance under the periodic inventory system.
9. Recognized cost of goods sold under FIFO.
10. Recognized cost of goods sold under the weighted-average method.

Required

a. Show the effect of each event on the elements of the financial statements using a horizontal statements model like the following one. Use + for increase, − for decrease, and NA for not affected. In the Cash Flow column, indicate whether the item is an operating activity (OA), investing activity (IA), or financing activity (FA). The first transaction is entered as an example.

Event No.	Assets	=	Liab.	+	S. Equity	Rev. or Gain	−	Exp. or Loss	=	Net Inc.	Cash Flow
1	+		NA		+	NA		NA		NA	+ FA

b. Explain why there is or is not a difference in the way Events 9 and 10 affect the financial statements model.

EXERCISES—SERIES B

L.O. 9

EXERCISE 8–1B *Effect of Inventory Cost Flow Assumption on Financial Statements*

Required

For each of the following situations, indicate whether FIFO, LIFO, or weighted average applies.
a. In a period of rising prices, net income would be highest.
b. In a period of rising prices, cost of goods sold would be highest.
c. In a period of rising prices, ending inventory would be highest.
d. In a period of falling prices, net income would be highest.
e. In a period of falling prices, the unit cost of goods would be the same for ending inventory and cost of goods sold.

L.O. 1, 2   **EXERCISE 8–2B** *Allocating Product Cost Between Cost of Goods Sold and Ending Inventory: Single Purchase*

Spruell Co. started the year with no inventory. During the year, it purchased two identical inventory items at different times. The first purchase cost $750 and the other, $1,000. Spruell sold one of the items during the year.

Required

Based on this information, how much product cost would be allocated to cost of goods sold and ending inventory on the year-end financial statements, assuming use of
a. FIFO?
b. LIFO?
c. weighted average?

L.O. 1, 2   **EXERCISE 8–3B** *Allocating Product Cost Between Cost of Goods Sold and Ending Inventory: Multiple Purchases*

Perez Company sells chairs that are used at computer stations. Its beginning inventory of chairs was 100 units at $40 per unit. During the year, Perez made two batch purchases of this chair. The first was a 150-unit purchase at $50 per unit; the second was a 200-unit purchase at $60 per unit. During the period, it sold 260 chairs.

Required

Determine the amount of product costs that would be allocated to cost of goods sold and ending inventory, assuming that Perez uses

a. FIFO

b. LIFO

c. weighted average

EXERCISE 8–4B *Effect of Inventory Cost Flow (FIFO, LIFO, and Weighted Average) on Gross Margin*　　　　L.O. 1, 2

The following information pertains to Parker Company for 2006.

Beginning inventory	40 units @ $20
Units purchased	200 units @ $25

Ending inventory consisted of 30 units. Parker sold 210 units at $50 each. All purchases and sales were made with cash.

Required

a. Compute the gross margin for Parker Company using the following cost flow assumptions: (1) FIFO, (2) LIFO, and (3) weighted average.

b. What is the dollar amount of net income using FIFO, LIFO, and weighted average? (Ignore income tax considerations.)

c. Compute the amount of ending inventory using (1) FIFO, (2) LIFO, and (3) weighted average.

EXERCISE 8–5B *Effect of Inventory Cost Flow on Ending Inventory Balance*　　　　L.O. 2

King Sales had the following transactions for T-shirts for 2006, its first year of operations.

Jan. 20	Purchased 450 units @ $5	=	$2,250
Apr. 21	Purchased 200 units @ $6	=	1,200
July 25	Purchased 100 units @ $10	=	1,000
Sept. 19	Purchased 75 units @ $8	=	600

During the year, King Sales sold 725 T-shirts for $20 each.

Required

a. Compute the amount of ending inventory King would report on the balance sheet, assuming the following cost flow assumptions: (1) FIFO, (2) LIFO, and (3) weighted average.

b. Compute the difference in gross margin between the FIFO and LIFO cost flow assumptions.

EXERCISE 8–6B *Income Tax Effect of Shifting From FIFO to LIFO*　　　　L.O. 1, 2

The following information pertains to the inventory of the Market Company:

Jan. 1	Beginning Inventory	500 units @ $20
Apr. 1	Purchased	2,500 units @ $22
Oct. 1	Purchased	800 units @ $28

During the year, Market sold 3,400 units of inventory at $40 per unit and incurred $34,000 of operating expenses. Market currently uses the FIFO method but is considering a change to LIFO. All transactions are cash transactions. Assume a 30 percent income tax rate.

Required

a. Prepare income statements using FIFO and LIFO.

b. Determine the amount of income taxes that Market would pay using each cost flow method.

c. Determine the cash flow from operating activities under FIFO and LIFO.

d. Why is the cash flow from operating activities different under FIFO and LIFO?

EXERCISE 8–7B *Effect of FIFO Versus LIFO on Income Tax Expense*　　　　L.O. 1, 2

West Coast Company had sales of $250,000 for 2005, its first year of operation. On April 2, the company purchased 200 units of inventory at $350 per unit. On September 1, an additional 150 units were purchased for $375 per unit. The company had 100 units on hand at the end of the year. The company's income tax rate is 40 percent. All transactions are cash transactions.

Required

a. The preceding paragraph describes five accounting events: (1) a sales transaction, (2) the first purchase of inventory, (3) a second purchase of inventory, (4) the recognition of cost of goods sold expense, and (5) the payment of income tax expense. Record the amounts of each event in horizontal statements models like the following ones, assuming first a FIFO and then a LIFO cost flow.

			Effect of Events on Financial Statements						
			Panel 1: FIFO Cost Flow						
Event No.			**Balance Sheet**			**Income Statement**			**Statement of Cash Flows**
	Cash	+	Inventory	=	Ret. Earn.	Rev.	– Exp.	= Net Inc.	
			Panel 2: LIFO Cost Flow						
Event No.			**Balance Sheet**			**Income Statement**			**Statement of Cash Flows**
	Cash	+	Inventory	=	Ret. Earn.	Rev.	– Exp.	= Net Inc.	

b. Compute net income using FIFO.

c. Compute net income using LIFO.

d. Explain the difference, if any, in the amount of income tax expense incurred using the two cost flow assumptions.

e. Which method, FIFO or LIFO, produced the larger amount of assets on the balance sheet?

L.O. 2   **EXERCISE 8–8B** *Recording Inventory Transactions Using the Perpetual Method: Intermittent Sales and Purchases*

The following inventory transactions apply to Polo Company for 2006.

Jan. 1	Purchased	250 units @ $40
Apr. 1	Sold	125 units @ $70
Aug. 1	Purchased	400 units @ $44
Dec. 1	Sold	500 units @ $76

The beginning inventory consisted of 175 units at $34 per unit. All transactions are cash transactions.

Required

a. Record these transactions, in general journal format, assuming that Polo uses the FIFO cost flow assumption and keeps perpetual records.

b. Compute cost of goods sold for 2006.

L.O. 2   **EXERCISE 8–9B** *Effect of Cost Flow on Ending Inventory: Intermittent Sales and Purchases*

Big Hill, Inc., had the following series of transactions for 2008:

Date	Transaction	Description
Jan. 1	Beginning inventory	50 units @ $30
Mar. 15	Purchased	200 units @ $35
May 30	Sold	170 units @ $70
Aug. 10	Purchased	275 units @ $40
Nov. 20	Sold	340 units @ $75

Required

a. Determine the quantity and dollar amount of inventory at the end of the year, assuming Big Hill uses the FIFO cost flow assumption and keeps perpetual records.

b. Write a memo explaining why Big Hill, Inc., would have difficulty applying the weighted-average method on a perpetual basis.

EXERCISE 8–10B *Lower-of-Cost-or-Market Rule: Perpetual System*   L.O. 3

The following information pertains to Original Woodwork Co.'s ending inventory for the current year.

Item	Quantity	Unit Cost	Unit Market Value
P	100	$16	$12
D	50	18	16
S	20	24	26
J	15	20	22

Required
a. Determine the value of the ending inventory using the lower-of-cost-or-market rule applied to (1) each individual inventory item and (2) the total inventory in aggregate.
b. Prepare any necessary journal entries, assuming the decline in value is immaterial. Original Woodwork Co. uses the perpetual inventory system.

EXERCISE 8–11B *Lower-of-Cost-or-Market Rule: Periodic System*   L.O. 3

Bonita Company carries three inventory items. The following information pertains to the ending inventory:

Item	Quantity	Unit Cost	Unit Market Value
B	100	$40	$36
C	150	60	56
D	90	20	30

Required
a. Determine the ending inventory that Bonita will report on the balance sheet, assuming that it applies the lower-of-cost-or-market rule to individual inventory items.
b. Explain how ending inventory would be recorded under the periodic inventory system.

EXERCISE 8–12B *Estimating Ending Inventory: Periodic System*   L.O. 4

A substantial portion of inventory owned by Deep Woods Hunting Goods was recently destroyed when the roof collapsed during a rainstorm. Deep Woods must estimate the loss from the storm for insurance reporting and financial statement purposes. Deep Woods uses the periodic inventory system. The following pertains to Deep Woods' books:

Beginning inventory	$ 25,000
Purchases to date of storm	100,000
Sales to date of storm	137,500

The value of undamaged inventory counted was $2,000. Historically Deep Woods' gross margin percentage has been approximately 25 percent of sales.

Required
Estimate the following:
a. Gross margin in dollars
b. Cost of goods sold
c. Ending inventory
d. Amount of lost inventory

EXERCISE 8–13B *Estimating Ending Inventory: Perpetual System*   L.O. 4

Bev Parvo owned a small company that sold garden equipment. The equipment was expensive, and a perpetual system was maintained for control purposes. Even so, lost, damaged, and stolen merchandise normally amounted to 5 percent of the inventory balance. On June 14, Parvo's warehouse was destroyed by fire. Just prior to the fire, the accounting records contained a $338,000 balance in the Inventory account. However, inventory costing $42,000 had been sold and delivered to customers but had not been recorded in the books at the time of the fire. The fire did not affect the showroom, which contained inventory that cost $75,000.

Required

Estimate the amount of inventory destroyed by fire.

L.O. 5   **EXERCISE 8–14B** *Effect of Inventory Error on Financial Statements: Perpetual System*

Short Company failed to count $50,000 of inventory in its 2005 year-end physical count.

Required

Write a memo explaining how Short Company's balance sheet will be affected in 2005. Assume Short uses the perpetual inventory system.

L.O. 5   **EXERCISE 8–15B** *Effect of Inventory Error on Elements of Financial Statements: Periodic System*

The ending inventory for Tefall Co. was understated by $5,200 for the year 2006.

Required

Was each of the following amounts overstated, understated, or not affected by the error?

Item No.	Year	Amount
1	2006	Beginning inventory
2	2006	Purchases
3	2006	Goods available for sale
4	2006	Cost of goods sold
5	2006	Gross margin
6	2006	Net income
7	2007	Beginning inventory
8	2007	Purchases
9	2007	Goods available for sale
10	2007	Cost of goods sold
11	2007	Gross margin
12	2007	Net income

L.O. 8   **EXERCISE 8–16B** *Identifying Asset Values for Financial Statements (Appendix)*

Required

Indicate whether each of the following assets should be valued at fair market value (FMV), lower-of-cost-or-market (LCM), or historical cost (HC) on the balance sheet. For certain assets, historical cost may be called amortized cost (AC.)

Asset	FMV	LCM	HC/AC
Inventory			
Prepaid Rent			
Cash			
Held-to-Maturity Securities			
Machinery			
Available-for-Sale Securities			
Certificate of Deposit			
Trading Securities			

L.O. 9   **EXERCISE 8–17B** *Accounting for Investment Securities (Appendix)*

Blass Bros. purchased $20,000 of marketable securities on March 1, 2005. On the company's fiscal closing date, December 31, 2005, the securities had a market value of $27,000. During 2005, Blass recognized $10,000 of revenue and $4,000 of expenses.

Required

a. Record a +, −, or NA in a horizontal statements model to show how the purchase of the securities affects the financial statements, assuming that the securities are classified as (1) held to maturity, (2) trading, or (3) available for sale. In the Cash Flow column, indicate whether the item is an operating activity (OA), investing activity (IA), or financing activity (FA). Record only the effects of the purchase event.

Item No.	Type	Cash	+	Inv. Sec.	=	Liab.	+	Equity	Rev.	−	Exp.	=	Net Inc.	Cash Flow
1	Held													
2	Trading													
3	Available													

b. Determine the amount of net income that would be reported on the 2005 income statement, assuming that the marketable securities are classified as (1) held to maturity, (2) trading, or (3) available for sale.

EXERCISE 8–18B *Effect of Investment Securities Transactions on Financial Statements (Appendix)* **L.O. 9**

The following information pertains to Circuit Electronics for 2003.
1. Purchased $75,000 of marketable investment securities.
2. Earned $4,500 of cash investment revenue.
3. Sold for $15,000 securities that cost $12,500.
4. The fair market value of the remaining securities at December 31, 2003, was $50,000.

Required
a. Record the four events in a statements model like the following one. Use a separate model for each classification: (1) held to maturity, (2) trading, and (3) available for sale. The first event for the first classification is shown as an example.

Held to Maturity

Event No.	Cash	+	Inv. Sec.	=	Liab.	+	Ret Earn.	+	Unreal. Gain.	Rev. or Gains	−	Exp. or Loss	=	Net Inc.	Cash Flow
1	(75,000)	+	75,000	=	NA	+	NA	+	NA	NA	−	NA	=	NA	(75,000) IA

b. What is the amount of net income under each of the three classifications?
c. What is the change in cash from operating activities under each of the three assumptions?
d. What is the ending amount of Investment Securities under each of the three assumptions?

EXERCISE 8–19B *Preparing Financial Statements for Investment Securities (Appendix)* **L.O. 9**

Deal, Inc., began 2002 with $60,000 in cash and common stock. The company engaged in the following investment transactions during 2002:
1. Purchased $30,000 of marketable investment securities.
2. Earned $800 cash from investment revenue.
3. Sold investment securities for $10,000 that cost $7,000.
4. Purchased $10,000 of additional marketable investment securities.
5. Determined that the investment securities had a fair value of $34,000 at the end of 2002.

Required
Use a vertical statements model to prepare income statements, balance sheets, and statements of cash flow for Deal, Inc., assuming the securities were (a) held to maturity, (b) trading, and (c) available for sale.

EXERCISE 8–20B *Differences Among Classifications of Marketable Investment Securities (Appendix)* **L.O. 9**

Required
List the three classifications of investment securities and give an example of each.

PROBLEMS—SERIES B

PROBLEM 8–21B *Effect of Different Inventory Cost Flow Methods on Financial Statements* **L.O. 1, 2**

The accounting records of Paul's Bicycle Shop reflected the following balances as of January 1, 2007.

Cash	$50,800
Beginning Inventory	56,000 (200 units @ $280)
Common Stock	43,000
Retained Earnings	63,800

The following five transactions occurred in 2007:

1. First purchase (cash)   120 units @ $300
2. Second purchase (cash)   140 units @ $330
3. Sales (all cash)   400 units @ $450
4. Paid $30,000 cash for salaries expense.
5. Paid cash for income tax at the rate of 25 percent of income before taxes.

Required

a. Compute the cost of goods sold and ending inventory, assuming (1) FIFO cost flow, (2) LIFO cost flow, and (3) weighted-average cost flow.

b. Use a vertical model to prepare the 2007 income statement, balance sheet, and statement of cash flows under FIFO, LIFO, and weighted average. (*Hint:* Record the events under an accounting equation before preparing the statements.)

L.O. 2   PROBLEM 8–22B *Allocating Product Costs Between Cost of Goods Sold and Ending Inventory: Intermittent Purchases and Sales of Merchandise*

Fred's Fireplaces had the following sales and purchase transactions during 2008. Beginning inventory consisted of 60 items at $350 each. The company uses the FIFO cost flow assumption and keeps perpetual inventory records.

Date	Transaction	Description
Mar. 5	Purchased	50 items @ $370
Apr. 10	Sold	40 items @ $450
June 19	Sold	50 items @ $450
Sept. 16	Purchased	50 items @ $390
Nov. 28	Sold	35 items @ $470

Required

a. Record the inventory transactions in general journal format.

b. Calculate the gross margin Fred's would report on the 2008 income statement.

c. Determine the ending inventory balance Fred's would report on the December 31, 2008, balance sheet.

L.O. 3   PROBLEM 8–23B *Inventory Valuation Based on the Lower-of-Cost-or-Market Rule*

At the end of the year, Ed's Repair Service had the following items in inventory:

Item	Quantity	Unit Cost	Unit Market Value
P1	80	$ 80	$ 90
P2	60	60	66
P3	100	140	130
P4	50	130	140

Required

a. Determine the amount of ending inventory using the lower-of-cost-or-market rule applied to each individual inventory item.

b. Provide the general journal entry necessary to write down the inventory based on Requirement *a*. Assume that Ed's Repair Service uses the perpetual inventory system.

c. Determine the amount of ending inventory, assuming that the lower-of-cost-or-market rule is applied to the total inventory in aggregate.

d. Provide the general journal entry necessary to write down the inventory based on Requirement *c*. Assume that Ed's Repair Service uses the perpetual inventory system.

e. Explain how the inventory loss would be reported when the periodic inventory system is used.

PROBLEM 8–24B *Estimating Ending Inventory: Gross Margin Method*   L.O. 4

Hank's Fun House had its inventory destroyed by a tornado on October 6 of the current year. Fortunately, back-up copies of the accounting records were at the home of one of the owners and were not damaged. The following information was available for the period of January 1 through October 6:

Beginning inventory, January 1	$ 162,000
Purchases through October 6	680,000
Sales through October 6	1,140,000

Gross margin for Hank's Fun House has traditionally been 30 percent of sales.

Required
a. For the period ending October 6, compute the following:
   (1) Estimated gross margin.
   (2) Estimated cost of goods sold.
   (3) Estimated inventory at October 6.
b. Assume that $20,000 of the inventory was not damaged. What is the amount of the loss from the tornado?
c. If Hank's Fun House had used the perpetual inventory system, how would it have determined the amount of the inventory loss?

PROBLEM 8–25B *Estimating Ending Inventory: Gross Margin Method*   L.O. 4

Elle's Eatery wishes to produce quarterly financial statements, but it takes a physical count of inventory only at year end. The following historical data were taken from the 2006 and 2007 accounting records:

	2006	2007
Net sales	$60,000	$70,000
Cost of goods sold	31,000	36,500

At the end of the first quarter of 2008, Elle's ledger had the following account balances:

Sales	$56,500
Sale Discounts	2,500
Purchases	41,000
Transportation-in	2,000
Transportation-out	5,000
Beginning Inventory	12,500

Required
Using the information provided, estimate the following for the first quarter of 2008:
a. Gross margin
b. Ending inventory at March 31

PROBLEM 8–26B *Effect of Inventory Errors on Financial Statements*   L.O. 5

The following income statement was prepared for Eddie's Fireworks for the year 2006:

EDDIE'S FIREWORKS Income Statement For the Year Ended December 31, 2006	
Sales	$140,000
Cost of Goods Sold	(77,200)
Gross Margin	62,800
Operating Expenses	(40,900)
Net Income	$ 21,900

During the year-end audit, the following errors were discovered:
1. A $2,000 payment for repairs was erroneously charged to the Cost of Goods Sold account. (Assume that the perpetual inventory system is used.)

2. Sales to customers for $500 at December 31, 2006, were not recorded in the books for 2006. Also, the $300 cost of selling these goods was not recorded. The error was not discovered in the physical count because the goods had not been delivered.

3. A mathematical error was made in determining ending inventory. Ending inventory was understated by $1,800. (The Inventory account was written down in error.)

Required

Determine the effect, if any, of each of the errors on the following items. Give the dollar amount of the effect and whether it would overstate (+), understate (−), or not affect (NA) the account. The first item is recorded as an example.

Error No. 1	Amount of Error	Effect
Sales 2006	NA	NA
Ending inventory, December 31, 2006		
Gross margin, 2006		
Beginning inventory, January 1, 2007		
Cost of goods sold, 2006		
Net income, 2006		
Retained earnings, December 31, 2006		
Total assets, December 31, 2006		

Error No. 2	Amount of Error	Effect
Sales 2006	$500	Understate
Ending inventory, December 31, 2006		
Gross margin, 2006		
Beginning inventory, January 1, 2007		
Cost of goods sold, 2006		
Net income, 2006		
Retained earnings, December 31, 2006		
Total assets, December 31, 2006		

Error No. 3	Amount of Error	Effect
Sales 2006	NA	NA
Ending inventory, December 31, 2006		
Gross margin, 2006		
Beginning inventory, January 1, 2007		
Cost of goods sold, 2006		
Net income, 2006		
Retained earnings, December 31, 2006		
Total assets, December 31, 2006		

L.O. 9 **PROBLEM 8–27B** *Effect of Marketable Inventory Securities of Financial Statements (Appendix)*

The following transactions pertain to Brogan's Trucking Co. for 2007.
1. Started business when it acquired $15,000 cash from stock issue, Heather Brogan.
2. Provided $50,000 of services for cash.
3. Invested $12,000 in marketable investment securities.
4. Paid $17,000 of operating expense.
5. Received $400 investment income from the securities.
6. Invested an additional $16,000 in marketable investment securities.
7. Paid a $1,000 cash dividend to the owner.
8. Sold investment securities that cost $6,000 for $6,400.
9. Received $900 in investment income.
10. Determined the value of the investment securities at the end of the year to be $20,000.

Required

Use a vertical model to prepare an income statement, balance sheet, and statement of cash flows, assuming that the marketable investment securities were classified as (a) held to maturity, (b) trading, and (c) available for sale. (*Hint:* It may be helpful to record the events in T-accounts prior to preparing the financial statements.)

PROBLEM 8–28B *Comprehensive Horizontal Statements Model (Appendix)*

L.O. 1, 9

City Co. experienced the following independent events.
1. Acquired cash from the issue of common stock.
2. Paid cash to purchase marketable securities classified as available for sale.
3. Paid cash to purchase inventory.
4. Recorded unrealized gain on marketable securities that were classified as trading securities.
5. Recorded unrealized gain on marketable securities that were classified as available for sale securities.
6. Recorded unrealized gain on marketable securities that were classified as held to maturity securities.
7. Wrote down inventory to comply with the lower-of-cost-or-market rule. (Assume that the company uses the perpetual inventory system.)
8. Estimated the ending inventory balance under the perpetual inventory system.
9. Recognized cost of goods sold under FIFO.
10. Recognized cost of goods sold under LIFO.

Required
a. Show the effect of each event on the elements of the financial statements using a horizontal statements model like the following one. Use + for increase, − for decrease, and NA for not affected. In the Cash Flow column, indicate whether the item is an operating activity (OA), investing activity (IA) or financing activity (FA). The first transaction is entered as an example.

Event No.	Assets	=	Liab.	+	S. Equity	Rev. or Gain	−	Exp. or Loss	=	Net Inc.	Cash Flow
1	+		NA		+	NA		NA		NA	+ FA

b. Explain why there is or is not a difference in the way Events 9 and 10 affect the financial statements model.

ANALYZE, THINK, COMMUNICATE

BUSINESS APPLICATIONS CASE *Dell's Annual Report*

ATC 8–1

Required
Using the Dell Computer Corporation financial statements in Appendix B, answer the following questions:
a. What are the inventory turnover ratio and average number of days in inventory for the year ended February 2, 2001?
b. What cost flow method(s) did Dell use to account for inventory?
c. In 2001, Dell's inventory represented 4.2 percent of its total current assets. This is a much lower percentage than many companies have. For example, at Lands' End, a direct marketer of clothing, inventory represented 59 percent of current assets at the end of 2000. Why does Dell have a lower investment in inventory than other companies such as Lands' End?

GROUP ASSIGNMENT *Inventory Cost Flow*

ATC 8–2

The accounting records of Blue Bird Co. showed the following balances at January 1, 2008:

Cash	$30,000
Beginning inventory (100 units @ $50, 70 units @ $55)	8,850
Common stock	20,000
Retained earnings	18,850

Transactions for 2008 were as follows:

Purchased 100 units @ $54 per unit.
Sold 220 units @ $80 per unit.
Purchased 250 units @ $58 per unit.
Sold 200 units @ $90 per unit.
Paid operating expenses of $3,200.
Paid income tax expense. The income tax rate is 30%.

Required

a. Organize the class into three sections, and divide each section into groups of three to five students. Assign each section one of the cost flow methods, FIFO, LIFO, or weighted average.

Group Tasks

Determine the amount of ending inventory, cost of goods sold, gross margin, and net income after income tax for the cost flow method assigned to your section. Also prepare an income statement using that cost flow assumption.

Class Discussion

b. Have a representative of each section put its income statement on the board. Discuss the effect that each cost flow method has on assets (ending inventory), net income, and cash flows. Which method is preferred for tax reporting? For financial reporting? What restrictions are placed on the use of LIFO for tax reporting?

ATC 8–3   REAL-WORLD CASE *Evaluating the Cost Savings from Managing Inventory More Efficiently*

After a decade of almost continually good economic news, the U.S. economy began to slow during 2000. Automobile manufacturers are among the first industries to feel the effects of a slowing economy, as Ford Motor Company did in 2000. Although Ford sold more vehicles in 2000 as a whole than it did in 1999, its sales were down in the fourth quarter of that year. Ford sold 1,919,000 automobiles in the fourth quarter of 1999 but only 1,849,000 in the same quarter of 2000, a reduction of just under 4 percent.

Companies often find themselves with more inventory than desired when sales begin to slow. This increase in inventory has two negative consequences. First, as explained in the chapter, the longer it takes a company to sell inventory, the higher the costs incurred to finance that inventory. Second, companies may have to reduce their selling prices to reduce inventory levels, which results in lower profit margins. Automobile manufacturers commonly use rebates to effectively reduce the selling prices of their cars. Both of these situations occurred at Ford during 2000.

The following information for Ford Motor Company is in pretax dollars and relates *only to the automotive operations* at Ford. (In 1999 and 2000, Ford generated about 70 percent of its pretax earnings from automotive operations and about 30 percent from financial services.) The dollar amounts are in millions.

	2000	1999
Sales	$141,230	$135,073
Income before taxes	5,267	7,275
Ending inventory	7,514	5,684
Gross margin %	10.7%	11.9%
Average days to sell inventory	22 days	17 days
Estimated weighted-average interest rate	7.5%	

Required

a. How much higher would Ford's pretax earnings from automotive operations in 2000 have been if its gross margin percentage in 2000 had been the same as it was in 1999?

b. How much higher would Ford's pretax earnings from automotive operations in 2000 have been if it had sold its inventory as quickly in 2000 as it did in 1999? Use the technique demonstrated in the text related to CVS versus PharMor to calculate this amount.

c. What percentage of the $2,008 reduction in pretax earnings at Ford's automotive operations from 1999 to 2000 can be explained by the inventory related issues addressed in Requirements *a* and *b?*

ATC 8–4   BUSINESS APPLICATIONS CASE *Using the Average Days to Sell Inventory Ratio to Make a Lending Decision*

Bradford's Wholesale Fruits has applied for a loan and has agreed to use its inventory to collateralize the loan. The company currently has an inventory balance of $289,000. The cost of goods sold for the past year was $7,518,000. The average shelf life for the fruit that Bradford's sells is 10 days, after which time it begins to spoil and must be sold at drastically reduced prices to dispose of it rapidly. The company had maintained steady sales over the past three years and expects to continue at current levels for the foreseeable future.

Required

Based on your knowledge of inventory turnover, write a memo that describes the quality of the inventory as collateral for the loan.

BUSINESS APPLICATIONS CASE *Using Ratios to Make Comparisons*

ATC 8–5

The following accounting information pertains to Cosmos Comics and Fantasy Funnies at the end of 2008. The only difference between the two companies is that Cosmos uses FIFO while Fantasy uses LIFO.

	Cosmos Comics	Fantasy Funnies
Cash	$ 80,000	$ 80,000
Accounts Receivable	320,000	320,000
Merchandise Inventory	240,000	180,000
Accounts Payable	220,000	220,000
Cost of Goods Sold	1,200,000	1,260,000
Building	400,000	400,000
Sales	2,000,000	2,000,000

Required

a. Compute the gross margin percentage for each company, and identify the company that *appears* to be charging the higher prices in relation to its costs.

b. For each company, compute the inventory turnover ratio and the average number of days to sell inventory. Identify the company that *appears* to be incurring the higher inventory financing cost.

c. Explain why the company with the lower gross margin percentage has the higher inventory turnover ratio.

d. Compute the length of the operating cycle for each company. Explain why short operating cycles are more desirable than long operating cycles.

WRITING ASSIGNMENT *Marketable Securities in Financial Statements*

ATC 8–6

The following information is taken from the annual report of The Maximum Companies at December 31, 2001, for investment securities (amounts given in millions):

	Amortized Cost	Gross Unrealized Gains	Gross Unrealized Losses	Estimated Fair Value
Investments				
Available for sale	$19,107.1	$951.3	$79.9	$19,978.5
Held to maturity	143.0	21.7	.4	164.3
Trading securities	16,521.9	13.8	0.0	16,535.7

Required

a. Using the preceding information, what amounts would Maximum report on the balance sheet at December 31, 2001?

b. Write a memo to the shareholders explaining why some investments are reported at cost and others are reported at market value. Explain how the values of these investments are reported at market value. Also explain how gains and losses on the various types of securities are reported in the financial statements.

ETHICAL DILEMMA *Show Them Only What You Want Them to See*

ATC 8–7

Clair Coolage is the chief accountant for a sales company called Far Eastern Imports. The company has been highly successful and is trying to increase its capital base by attracting new investors. The company operates in an inflationary environment and has been using the LIFO inventory cost flow method to minimize its net earnings and thereby reduce its income taxes. Katie Bailey, the vice president of finance, asked Coolage to estimate the change in net earnings that would occur if the company switched to FIFO. After reviewing the company's books, Coolage estimated that pretax income would increase by $1,200,000 if the company adopted the FIFO cost flow method. However, the switch would result in approximately $400,000 of additional taxes. The overall effect would result in an increase of $800,000 in net earnings. Bailey told Coolage to avoid the additional taxes by preparing the tax return on a LIFO basis but to prepare a set of statements on a FIFO basis to be distributed to potential investors.

Required

a. Comment on the legal and ethical implications of Bailey's decision.

b. How will the switch to FIFO affect Far Eastern's balance sheet?

c. If Bailey reconsiders and makes a decision to switch to FIFO for tax purposes as well as financial reporting purposes, net income will increase by $800,000. Comment on the wisdom of paying $400,000 in income taxes to obtain an additional $800,000 of net income.

ATC 8–8   EDGAR DATABASE *Analyzing Inventory at Gap Company*

Required

Using the most current 10-K available on EDGAR, answer the following questions about Gap Company. Instructions for using EDGAR are in Appendix A.

a. What was the average amount of inventory per store? Use *all* stores operated by Gap, not just those called *The Gap*. (*Hint:* The answer to this question must be computed. The number of stores in operation at the end of the most recent year can be found in the MD&A of the 10-K.)

b. How many *new* stores did Gap open during the year?

c. Using the quarterly financial information contained in the 10-K, complete the following chart.

Quarter	Sales During Each Quarter
1	$
2	
3	
4	

d. Referring to the chart in Requirement *c*, explain why Gap's sales vary so widely throughout its fiscal year. Do you believe that Gap's inventory level varies throughout the year in relation to sales?

ATC 8–9   SPREADSHEET ANALYSIS *Using Excel*

At January 1, 2005, the accounting records of Bronco Boutique had the following balances:

Cash	$1,000
Inventory	2,250 (150 units @ $15)
Common Stock	2,000
Retained Earnings	1,250

During January, Bronco Boutique entered into five cash transactions:

1. Purchased 120 units of inventory @ $16 each.

2. Purchased 160 units of inventory @ $17 each.

3. Sold 330 units of inventory @ $30 each.

4. Incurred $1,700 of operating expenses.

5. Paid income tax at the rate of 30 percent of income before taxes.

Required

a. Set up rows 1 through 10 of the following spreadsheet to compute cost of goods sold and ending inventory, assuming (1) FIFO, (2) LIFO, and (3) weighted-average cost flows. Notice that the FIFO cost flow has already been completed for you. Use columns O through W to complete the LIFO and weighted-average cost flow computations. Be sure to use formulas for all calculations.

```
Microsoft Excel - ch8-1.xls
File  Edit  View  Insert  Format  Tools  Data  Window  Help

Arial          10    B  I  U        $ %

B16         =K7
```

	A	B	C	D	E	F	G	H	I	J	K	L	M	N
1	Cost of Goods Available For Sale					FIFO Ending Inventory			FIFO Cost of Goods Sold			LIFO Ending Inventory		
2			Unit	Total			Unit	Total		Unit	Total		Unit	Total
3		Units	Price	Cost		Units	Price	Cost	Units	Price	Cost	Units	Price	Cost
4	Beginning Inventory	150	$15	$2,250					150	$15	$2,250			
5	First Purchase (cash)	120	$16	$1,920					120	$16	$1,920			
6	Second Purchase (cash)	160	$17	$2,720		100	$17	$1,700	60	$17	$1,020			
7	Total Cost of Goods Available for Sale	430		$6,890		100		$1,700	330		$5,190			
8														
9	Average Cost		$16.02			Check:	EI + CGS		430	Units				
10							EI + CGS		$6,890	Total Cost				
11														
12														
13				WEIGHTED										
14	Income Statements	FIFO	LIFO	AVERAGE										
15	Sales (330 units @ $30 each) (cash)	$9,900												
16	Cost of Goods Sold	5,190												
17	Gross Margin	4,710												
18	Operating Expenses (cash)	1,700												
19	Income Before Taxes	3,010												
20	Income Tax Expense (30%) (cash)	903												
21	Net Income	$2,107												
22														
23	Statement of Cash Flows	FIFO												
24	Cash from Operating Activities:													
25	Cash received from Customers	$9,900												
26	Cash paid for Inventory Purchased	(4,640)												
27	Cash paid for Operating Expenses	(1,700)												
28	Cash paid for Income Taxes	(903)												
29	Net Cash Flow from Operating Activities	2,657												
30	Beginning Cash	1,000												
31	Ending Cash	$3,657												

```
Problem 8-1 Answer Key  \ Problem / Sheet2 / Sheet3 /
Ready                                          NUM
```

b. In rows 13 through 31, compute the amount of net income and net cash flow from operations under FIFO, LIFO, and weighted average. The FIFO column has been provided as an example.

SPREADSHEET ASSIGNMENT *Mastering Excel*

ATC 8–10

Required
Complete ATC 8–5 using an Excel spreadsheet. Use Excel problem ATC 7-9 as a resource for structuring the spreadsheet.

Long-Term Operational Assets

Learning Objectives

After completing this chapter, you should be able to:

1 Explain why some businesses generate high revenue with few operational assets.

2 Distinguish between tangible and intangible assets.

3 Identify different types of long-term operational assets.

4 Determine the cost of long-term operational assets.

5 Explain how expense recognition (i.e., depreciation) affects financial statements throughout the life cycle of a tangible asset.

6 Determine how a gain or loss from the disposal of long-term operational assets affects financial statements.

7 Show how different depreciation methods affect the amount of expense recognized in a particular accounting period.

8 Identify tax issues related to long-term operational assets.

9 Show how revising estimates affects financial statements.

10 Explain how continuing expenditures for operational assets affect financial statements.

11 Explain how expense recognition for natural resources (depletion) affects financial statements.

12 Explain how expense recognition for intangible assets (amortization) affects financial statements.

13 Explain how GAAP can adversely affect the ability of U.S. companies to attract international capital.

14 Understand how expense recognition choices and industry characteristics affect financial performance measures.

the *curious* accountant

I n the normal course of operations, most companies acquire long-term assets each year. The way in which a company hopes to make money with these assets varies according to the type of business and the asset acquired.

During 2000, Weyerhaeuser Company made cash acquisitions of property and equipment of $848 million and cash acquisitions of timber and timberlands of $81 million. How does Weyerhaeuser plan to use each type of asset to produce earnings for the company? Should the accounting treatment for trees differ from the accounting treatment for trucks?

Long-term operational assets are the resources businesses use to produce revenue. The size of a company's operational assets relative to the income it generates by using them will depend on the nature of its operating activity. For example, a trucking company requires substantial investments in physical equipment to move freight from one destination to another. In contrast, a firm of attorneys uses intellectual rather than physical assets to meet the needs of its clients. Accordingly, law offices tend to generate significantly more revenue per dollar invested in operational assets than do trucking companies.

How long is long term*? There is no definitive time limit. However, as noted earlier, assets that are used in more than one accounting period are usually considered long term. The cost of long-term assets is normally recognized as an expense in the accounting periods in which the asset is used. In other words, you do not expense the total cost of long-term assets in a single year; instead, you spread the expense recognition over the life of the assets. There are several types of long-term assets, and different terms are used to describe the process of expense recognition for each type. For example, Delta Airlines depreciates its planes while Exxon depletes its oil reserves. This chapter teaches you how to classify costs into one of several long-term asset categories and explains how to account for the utilization of these assets from the date of purchase to their final disposal.*

▮ Classifications of Long-Term Operational Assets

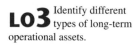

Long-term assets are either tangible or intangible. **Tangible assets** are those that are "able to be touched" and include equipment, machinery, natural resources, and land. **Intangible assets** may be represented by pieces of paper or contracts that appear tangible; however, the true value of an intangible asset lies in the rights and privileges extended to its owners. For example, a *patent* is a legal right granting its owner an exclusive privilege to produce and sell a commodity that has one or more unique features. Accordingly, inventors who own intangible patent rights can protect their inventions by seeking legal recourse against anyone who attempts to profit by copying their innovations.

Tangible Long-Term Assets

Property, Plant, and Equipment

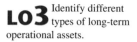

Property, plant, and equipment is a category whose assets are sometimes called *plant assets* or *fixed assets*. Examples of property, plant, and equipment include furniture, cash registers, machinery, delivery trucks, computers, mechanical robots, and buildings. Rather than recording all of these assets in a single account, each company uses subcategories to satisfy its particular needs for information. One company may include all office machinery in one account, whereas another company might divide office equipment into computers, desks, chairs, and so on. As indicated in earlier chapters, the process of expense recognition for property, plant, and equipment is called **depreciation.**

Natural Resources

Mineral deposits, oil and gas reserves, and reserves of timber, mines, and quarries are known as **natural resources.** They are sometimes called *wasting assets* because their value "wastes away" as the resources are removed. The balance sheet classification for natural resources as long-term assets sometimes conflicts with the way in which these assets are expensed. Conceptually, natural resources are inventories. Indeed, these assets are frequently expensed through the cost of goods sold. However, they are classified as long-term assets because (1) the resource deposits generally have long lives, (2) the accounting treatment is very similar to that for other long-term assets, and (3) practice and convention have made this the acceptable treatment. The process of expense recognition for natural resources is called *depletion.*

Land

Land is classified in a separate category from other property for one major reason: Land is not subject to depreciation or depletion. It is considered to have an infinite life. In other words, land is not destroyed through the process of its use. When buildings or natural resources are purchased simultaneously with land, the amount paid must be carefully divided between the land and the other assets because of the nondepreciable nature of the land.

Intangible Assets

Intangible assets may be classified into two groups: those that are specifically identifiable and can be acquired individually and those that arise from the purchase of a group of assets and cannot be attributed to any one asset.

Specifically Identifiable Intangible Assets

This category includes patents, trademarks, franchises, copyrights, and other privileges extended by government agencies. The costs of acquiring these assets may range from relatively insignificant legal fees to huge sums paid for fast-food franchises. Later in this chapter we look at several of these intangibles on an individual basis, but the accounting treatment is basically the same for each. The process of expense recognition for the cost of intangible assets is called **amortization.**

Goodwill

Goodwill refers to the benefits resulting from purchasing a company with a good reputation, an established clientele, a favorable business location, or other features that provide an above-average profit potential. For example, a fast-food restaurant with the name *McDonald's* will likely produce higher revenues than another restaurant named *Joe's,* even if both have the same physical asset base. An investor will have to pay more to acquire a business with above-average profit potential than to acquire an identical set of assets that are separated from the favorable business conditions. Like other intangible assets, this extra amount, or goodwill, is amortized (expensed) over its useful life.

▮ Determining the Cost of Long-Term Assets

The **historical cost concept** requires that assets be recorded at the amount paid for them. This amount includes the purchase price plus whatever costs are necessary to obtain the asset and prepare it for its intended use. As years go by, the historical cost may begin to bear little relation to the current value of the asset for several reasons: (1) Depreciation may not approximate the use of the asset, (2) inflation may change the value of the dollar, or (3) the value of the asset itself may increase or decrease. Because of these factors, many critics have suggested that companies be allowed to revalue their assets periodically to reflect the assets' current values. However, due to a lack of objective measurement techniques, most long-term assets are still reported at historical cost in the primary financial statements.

LO4 Determine the cost of long-term operational assets.

While the cost of an asset includes all expenditures that are normally necessary to obtain it and prepare it for its intended use, *payments for fines, damages, and so on, are not considered normal costs of acquiring an asset* and are therefore not included. Some of the more common costs associated with particular types of assets include the following:

Purchase of buildings: (1) purchase price, (2) sales taxes, (3) title search and transfer documents, (4) real estate fees and attorney's fees, and (5) remodeling costs.

Purchase of land: (1) purchase price, (2) sales taxes, (3) title search and transfer documents, (4) realtor's and attorney's fees, and (5) removal of old buildings, and (6) grading.

Purchase of equipment: (1) purchase price (less discounts), (2) sales taxes, (3) delivery costs, (4) installation, and (5) costs to adapt to intended use.

Sheridan Construction Company purchased a new bulldozer that had a $260,000 list price. The seller agreed to allow a 4 percent cash discount in exchange for immediate payment. The bulldozer was delivered FOB shipping point at a cost of $1,200. Sheridan hired a new employee to operate the dozer for an annual salary of $36,000. The employee was trained to operate the dozer for a one-time training fee of $800. The cost of the company's theft insurance policy increased by $300 per year as a result of adding the dozer to the policy. The dozer had a five-year useful life and an expected salvage value of $26,000. Determine the asset's cost.

Check Yourself 9–1

Answer

List price	$260,000
Less: Cash discount ($260,000 × 0.04)	(10,400)
Shipping cost	1,200
Training cost	800
Total asset cost (amount capitalized)	$251,600

Basket Purchase Allocation

LO4 Determine the cost of long-term operational assets.

A **basket purchase** is the acquisition of several assets in a single transaction. Often a single price is assigned to that purchase, and the acquiring company must determine how much of that price should be assigned to each asset. This can be done by using the **relative fair market value method.**

Assume that Beatty Company purchased a building and plot of land for $240,000 cash. A real estate appraiser was called in and determined the fair market value of each to be as follows:

Building	$270,000
Land	90,000
Total	$360,000

Beatty paid less than the appraised values but can still use these values to determine a reasonable basis for assigning the total cost to the two assets. The appraisal indicated that the land is worth 25 percent ($90,000 ÷ $360,000) of the total value, and the building, 75 percent ($270,000 ÷ $360,000). Applying these percentages to the actual purchase price results in the following cost allocation:

Building	0.75 × $240,000 =	$180,000
Land	0.25 × $240,000 =	60,000
Total		$240,000

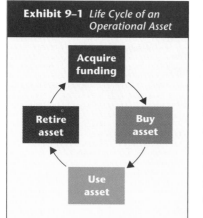

Exhibit 9–1 *Life Cycle of an Operational Asset*

Acquire funding → Buy asset → Use asset → Retire asset → Acquire funding

▐ Life Cycle of Operational Assets

The life cycle of an operational asset begins with the effort to obtain the financing necessary to acquire it. The next step is to acquire the asset (invest the funds). The asset is then used to produce revenue. The final step is to retire the asset. The use and retirement of the asset should generate enough funds to replace the asset and to provide a reasonable return on the invested funds. Exhibit 9–1 depicts the life cycle of an operational asset.

LO5 Explain how expense recognition (depreciation) affects financial statements throughout the life cycle of a tangible asset.

▐ Accounting for Operational Assets Throughout the Life Cycle

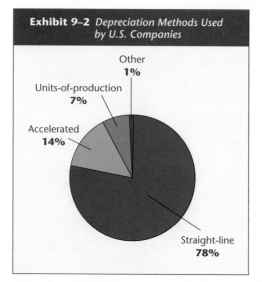

Exhibit 9–2 *Depreciation Methods Used by U.S. Companies*

Other 1%
Units-of-production 7%
Accelerated 14%
Straight-line 78%

Data source: AICPA, *Accounting Trends and Techniques,* 2000

The acquisition of capital results in an increase in assets and equity. Once the financing has been acquired, the funds are invested in an asset. The cost of the asset is then systematically expensed over its useful life. In prior chapters, the expense recognition phase for tangible assets was spread evenly over the life of the asset. This method of depreciating an asset is called **straight-line depreciation.** Straight-line depreciation is appropriate when an asset is used evenly over its life. However, not all assets are used evenly. Some assets may be used much more rapidly when they are new and less frequently as they grow older. These assets require **accelerated depreciation methods,** which charges more of the cost of the asset to expense in the early years of the asset's useful life. Other assets may be used extensively in one accounting period, infrequently in the next, and extensively again in another accounting period. In other words, their use varies from one accounting period to the next. Accordingly, methods other than straight-line are needed to accurately reflect the use of many assets. The next section of this chapter reviews straight-line depreciation and introduces two new methods, the *double-declining-balance* and *units-of-production methods.* Exhibit 9–2 shows the different depreciation methods that U.S. companies use. The double-declining-balance is an accelerated depreciation method.

quipment is a long-term asset used for the purpose of producing revenue. The portion of the equipment used each accounting period is recognized as depreciation expense. Accordingly, the expense recognition for the cost of equipment is spread over the useful life of the asset. Timber, however, is not used until the trees are grown. Conceptually, the cost of the trees should be treated as inventories and expensed as cost of goods sold at the time the products made from trees are sold. Even so, some timber companies recognize a periodic charge

called *depletion* in a manner similar to that used for depreciation.

Accounting for unusual long-term assets such as timber requires an understanding of specialized "industry practice" accounting rules that are beyond the scope of this course. Be aware that many industries have unique accounting problems, and business managers in such industries must make the effort to understand specialized accounting rules that relate to their companies.

Methods of Depreciation

To demonstrate how the different depreciation methods affect expense recognition over the life cycle, we trace the events of Dryden Enterprises for a five-year time span. Dryden was started on January 1, 2001, when it issued $25,000 of common stock. Immediately after the acquisition of capital, Dryden purchased a van. The van had a list price of $23,500. Dryden was able to obtain a 10 percent cash discount from the dealer. However, the van was delivered FOB shipping point, and Dryden agreed to pay an additional $250 for transportation costs. Dryden also paid $2,600 to have the van customized to make it more appealing as a rental vehicle. Accordingly, the amount to be capitalized in the Van account is computed as follows:

LO5 Explain how expense recognition (depreciation) affects financial statements throughout the life cycle of a tangible asset.

List price	$23,500	
Less: Cash discounts	(2,350)	$23,500 × 0.10
Plus: Transportation costs	250	
Plus: Cost of customization	2,600	
Total	$24,000	

The van has an estimated **salvage value** of $4,000 and an **estimated life** of four years. The revenue stream is expected to be distributed evenly over the van's useful life at a rate of $8,000 per year. The effects of the accounting treatment during the four phases of the life cycle are now discussed.

Straight-Line Depreciation

Given that the revenue is expected to flow smoothly over the asset's useful life, it is logical to assume that the asset will be used evenly over its life. Accordingly, straight-line depreciation is appropriate.

Life Cycle Phase 1

The first phase of the life cycle is the acquisition of capital. In this case, Dryden acquired $25,000 cash by issuing common stock. The effect of this stock issue on the financial statements is shown here:

Assets					=	Equity			Rev.	–	Exp.	=	Net Inc.	Cash Flow	
Cash	+	Van	–	A. Dep.	=	Com. Stk.	+	Ret. Earn.							
25,000	+	NA	–	NA	=	25,000	+	NA	NA	–	NA	=	NA	25,000	FA

Clearly, the stock issue affects the balance sheet and statement of cash flows but not the income statement. These effects should be traced to the financial statements in Exhibit 9–3. Notice that the financing activities section of the statement of cash flows shows a cash inflow

Exhibit 9–3 *Financial Statements under Straight-Line Depreciation*

DRYDEN ENTERPRISES
Financial Statements

	2001	2002	2003	2004	2005
Income Statements					
Rent Revenue	$ 8,000	$ 8,000	$ 8,000	$ 8,000	$ 0
Depreciation Expense	(5,000)	(5,000)	(5,000)	(5,000)	0
Operating Income	3,000	3,000	3,000	3,000	0
Gain	0	0	0	0	500
Net Income	$ 3,000	$ 3,000	$ 3,000	$ 3,000	$ 500
Balance Sheets					
Assets					
Cash	$ 9,000	$17,000	$25,000	$33,000	$37,500
Van	24,000	24,000	24,000	24,000	0
Accumulated Depreciation	(5,000)	(10,000)	(15,000)	(20,000)	0
Total Assets	$28,000	$31,000	$34,000	$37,000	$37,500
Stockholders' Equity					
Common Stock	$25,000	$25,000	$25,000	$25,000	$25,000
Retained Earnings	3,000	6,000	9,000	12,000	12,500
Total Stockholders' Equity	$28,000	$31,000	$34,000	$37,000	$37,500
Statements of Cash Flows					
Operational Activities					
Inflow from Customers	$ 8,000	$ 8,000	$ 8,000	$ 8,000	$ 0
Investing Activities					
Outflow to Purchase Van	(24,000)				
Inflow from Sale of Van					4,500
Financing Activities					
Inflow from Stock Issue	25,000				
Net Change in Cash	9,000	8,000	8,000	8,000	4,500
Beginning Cash Balance	0	9,000	17,000	25,000	33,000
Ending Cash Balance	$ 9,000	$17,000	$25,000	$33,000	$37,500

from the stock issue amounting to $25,000. Also the balance sheet shows a $25,000 balance in the equity section under the Common Stock account. Since the balance sheet accounts reflect the cumulative effect of events that have occurred from a company's inception, the $25,000 in common stock appears in the statements throughout the life cycle. In contrast, the statement of cash flows reflects activities for a particular accounting period. Accordingly, the inflow from the stock issue appears only once during the 2001 accounting period. The cash balance shown in the balance sheet is not equal to $25,000 because the Cash account is affected by other events during 2001.

Life Cycle Phase 2

The second phase of the life cycle is the investment in the operational asset (purchase of the van). The purchase price was previously computed as $24,000 cash. The effect of the investment on the financial statements is shown here:

Assets				=	Equity			Rev.	–	Exp.	=	Net Inc.	Cash Flow
Cash	+	Van	– A. Dep.	=	Com. Stk.	+	Ret. Earn.						
(24,000)	+	24,000	– NA	=	NA	+	NA	NA	–	NA	=	NA	(24,000) IA

The investment is an asset exchange transaction involving a cash payment. As such, it affects the balance sheet and the statement of cash flows. Refer to Exhibit 9–3 to see how the effects of this event appear on the financial statements. Note that the cash outflow is shown one time in 2001 under the investing activities section of the statement of cash flows. However, the cost of the asset is shown on the balance sheet as $24,000 throughout the entire life cycle (2001–2004). The historical cost is removed from the asset account when the van is retired in 2005.

Life Cycle Phase 3

The use of the asset results in the generation of $8,000 revenue per year. The wear and tear on the asset are reflected in the recognition of depreciation expense. The amount of the depreciation expense calculated on a straight-line basis is determined by subtracting the salvage value from the original cost and dividing the difference by the useful life. This computation results in the recognition of $5,000 ([$24,000 − $4,000] ÷ 4) of depreciation expense each year. The expense recognition is shown in a **contra asset account** titled **Accumulated Depreciation.** The effects of the revenue and expense recognition on the financial statements are shown here. To save space, the events are shown only once. In fact, they would occur four times—once for each year the asset is in use.

Assets			=	Equity		Rev.	−	Exp.	=	Net Inc.	Cash Flow	
Cash	+ Van	− A. Dep.	=	Com. Stk.	+ Ret. Earn.							
8,000	+ NA	− NA	=	NA	+ 8,000	8,000	− NA	= 8,000			8,000	OA
NA	+ NA	− 5,000	=	NA	+ (5,000)	NA	− 5,000	= (5,000)			NA	

The revenue event affects all three statements. Depreciation expense affects the balance sheet and the income statement but not the statement of cash flows. Recall that the cash paid for the van was spent on January 1, 2001. The total cash outflow is shown in the investing section of the statement of cash flows. Accordingly, the cash flow consequences have already been recognized and therefore are not affected by the recognition of depreciation expense. This is the meaning of the statement "depreciation is a noncash expenditure." Depreciation represents the use of the physical asset rather than the expenditure of cash.

Once again, the events should be traced to the financial statements in Exhibit 9–3. As shown in the statement of cash flows, the revenue stream produces $8,000 of cash per year for four years (2001–2004). Accordingly, the use (rental) of the van provided $32,000 of cash ($8,000 × 4) over its life cycle. Note that the depreciation expense is shown in the income statement but does not affect the statement of cash flows. (The reason for this effect was explained in the previous paragraph.) Observe here that the effects of depreciation occur throughout the life cycle of the asset. Indeed, it is interesting to note that the depreciation expense stays at $5,000 each year, whereas the Accumulated Depreciation account grows from $5,000 to $10,000 to $15,000 and finally to $20,000 between 2001 and 2004.

Life Cycle Phase 4

The final stage in the life cycle of an operational asset is its retirement and removal from the company's records. This occurs on January 1, 2005, when Dryden sells the van for $4,500 cash. The effect of this event on the financial statements is shown below. Since the book value at the time of the sale was only $4,000, Dryden recognizes a $500 gain ($4,500 − $4,000).

LO6 Determine how a gain or loss from the disposal of operational assets affects financial statements.

Assets			=	Equity		Rev. or Gain	−	Exp. or Loss	=	Net Inc.	Cash Flow	
Cash	+ Van	− A. Dep.	=	C. Stk.	+ Ret. Earn.							
4,500	+ (24,000)	− (20,000)	=	0	+ 500	500	− 0	= 500			4,500	IA

Tracing the effects of these events to the financial statements in Exhibit 9–3 provides interesting insights as to how businesses recover their invested funds. Although the gain shown on the income statement is only $500, the amount of cash inflow is $4,500. This amount is

Exhibit 9–4 *General Journal Entries*

Account Title	Debit	Credit
Cash	25,000	
Common Stock		25,000
Entry on January 1, 2001, to record capital acquisition		
Van	24,000	
Cash		24,000
Entry on January 1, 2001, to record investment in van		
Cash	8,000	
Revenue		8,000
Revenue recognition entries on December 31, 2001–2005		
Depreciation Expense	5,000	
Accumulated Depreciation		5,000
Expense recognition entries on December 31, 2001–2005		
Cash	4,500	
Accumulated Depreciation	20,000	
Van		24,000
Gain on Sale of Van		500
Entry on January 1, 2005, to record asset disposal		

shown as an inflow in the investing activities section of the statement of cash flows. The gain is not shown separately on the statement of cash flows but instead is included in the $4,500 shown in the investing section. The total cash inflow from using and retiring the van amounts to $36,500 ([$8,000 revenue × 4 years] + $4,500 actual salvage value), which means that Dryden not only recovered the cost of the asset ($24,000) but also generated a $12,500 return on its investment. In other words, over its life cycle, the operational asset generated $12,500 more than it cost ($36,500 − $24,000). This is consistent with the total amount of net income that was earned over the life cycle. Accordingly, the difference between income and cash flow is shown to be a matter of timing. Other interesting insights include the fact that the amount of the ending balance in the Retained Earnings account is equal to the sum of the amounts of net income that appear on the 2001 through 2005 income statements. This result occurs because all earnings were retained in the business. No distributions were made to the owners.

Recording Procedures

Exhibit 9–4 shows the general journal entries required to record the transactions over the life cycle of the van.

Double-Declining-Balance Depreciation

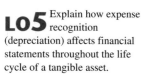

LO5 Explain how expense recognition (depreciation) affects financial statements throughout the life cycle of a tangible asset.

Assume the same set of facts as those just presented with one exception. Suppose that Dryden believes that customer demand for the van will diminish over time. When the van is new, it looks more attractive, drives better, and is less susceptible to breakdowns. Accordingly, more people will want to use the van when it is new. As it ages, fewer and fewer people will be willing to rent the vehicle. As a result, the van will be used less frequently as time goes by. Since the purpose of depreciation is to reflect asset use, the amount of depreciation expense should be higher when the van is new and should decline as the van ages. A method of depreciation known as **double-declining-balance depreciation** is specifically designed to recognize larger amounts of depreciation in the earlier stages of an asset's life and progressively lower levels of expense as the asset ages. Since the double-declining-balance method recognizes depreciation expense more rapidly than the straight-line method does, it is sometimes referred to as an *accelerated depreciation method*. The amount of depreciation to recognize under the double-declining-balance method can be determined by performing three simple computations.

1. *Determine the straight-line rate.* If the asset is depreciated evenly over its useful life, the portion depreciated each year can be determined by dividing the full use (100 percent) by the expected useful life of the asset. For example, since Dryden's van was expected to have a four-year useful life, the straight-line rate is 25 percent (100% ÷ 4 years) per year.

2. *Determine the double-declining-balance rate.* Multiply the straight-line rate by 2 (*double* the rate). The double-declining-balance rate for the van is 50% (25% × 2).

3. *Apply the double-declining-balance rate to the book value.* Multiply the double-declining-balance rate by the book value of the asset *at the beginning of the period* (**book value** being historical cost less the amount of *accumulated depreciation*).

Applying the computations to Dryden's van will produce the following schedule of charges for the years 2001 through 2004:

Year	Book Value at Beginning of Period	×	Double the Straight-Line Rate	=	Annual Depreciation Expense	
2001	($24,000 − $0)	×	0.5	=	$12,000	
2002	(24,000 − 12,000)	×	0.5	=	6,000	
2003	(24,000 − 18,000)	×	0.5	=	~~3,000~~	2,000
2004	(24,000 − 20,000)	×	0.5	=	~~2,000~~	0

Computations for the third year are complicated by the fact that *the book value of an asset cannot be depreciated below its salvage value.* Since the van cost $24,000 and had a $4,000 salvage value, the total amount of cost to be depreciated is $20,000 ($24,000 − $4,000). Since $18,000 ($12,000 + $6,000) of the cost is depreciated in the first two years, only $2,000 ($20,000 − $18,000) more can be depreciated. Accordingly, the $3,000 formula value is ignored in year 3 because it exceeds the $2,000 maximum. Similarly, the formula value for 2004 is ignored because the maximum allowable depreciation was charged in the first three years.

Exhibit 9–5 is a full set of financial statements prepared under the assumption that Dryden is using double-declining-balance depreciation. Trace the depreciation charges shown in the exhibit to the financial statements. Observe how the amount of depreciation expense is larger in the earlier years and smaller in the later years of the asset's life. Since the van is used more during the early years, it is logical to assume higher amounts of revenue during those years. We presume a revenue stream of $15,000, $9,000, $5,000, and $3,000 for the years 2001, 2002, 2003, and 2004, respectively. These amounts are reflected in the statements in Exhibit 9–5.

Since the use of the asset is directly related to the production of revenue, the double-declining-balance method smooths the amount of net income reported on the income statement. The high revenues produced by the extensive use of the asset in the first years are offset by high expenses that reflect the corresponding level of asset use. Similarly, declining levels of use produce lower levels of expense as well as revenue. As a result, net income remains constant at a level of $3,000 per year.

How does accelerated depreciation improve financial reporting? Compare the income figures in Exhibit 9–5 with the outcome that would have occurred had Dryden used the straight-line method. Given the revenue stream in Exhibit 9–5, a constant $5,000 per year depreciation charge would have resulted in reported net income of $10,000, $4,000, $0, and ($2,000) for 2001, 2002, 2003, and 2004, respectively. These figures suggest a state of steadily declining economic viability, while in fact the company is performing as expected. As a result, use of straight-line depreciation would have provided a false impression of managerial performance. As this discussion implies, financial reporting provides a more accurate representation of business activity when expense recognition is closely aligned with asset use.

Effects During Other Phases of the Life Cycle

The effects of acquiring the financing, investing the funds, and retiring the asset are not changed by the method of depreciation. Accordingly, descriptions of the effects of the accounting events in these life cycle phases are the same as under the straight-line approach. If

Exhibit 9–5 *Financial Statements under Double-Declining-Balance Depreciation*

DRYDEN ENTERPRISES
Financial Statements

	2001	2002	2003	2004	2005
Income Statements					
Rent Revenue	$15,000	$ 9,000	$ 5,000	$ 3,000	$ 0
Depreciation Expense	(12,000)	(6,000)	(2,000)	0	0
Operating Income	3,000	3,000	3,000	3,000	0
Gain	0	0	0	0	500
Net Income	$ 3,000	$ 3,000	$ 3,000	$ 3,000	$ 500
Balance Sheets					
Assets					
Cash	$16,000	$25,000	$30,000	$33,000	$37,500
Van	24,000	24,000	24,000	24,000	0
Accumulated Depreciation	(12,000)	(18,000)	(20,000)	(20,000)	0
Total Assets	$28,000	$31,000	$34,000	$37,000	$37,500
Stockholders' Equity					
Common Stock	$25,000	$25,000	$25,000	$25,000	$25,000
Retained Earnings	3,000	6,000	9,000	12,000	12,500
Total Stockholders' Equity	$28,000	$31,000	$34,000	$37,000	$37,500
Statements of Cash Flows					
Operating Activities					
Inflow from Customers	$15,000	$ 9,000	$ 5,000	$ 3,000	$ 0
Investing Activities					
Outflow to Purchase Van	(24,000)				
Inflow from Sale of Van					4,500
Financing Activities					
Inflow from Stock Issue	25,000				
Net Change in Cash	16,000	9,000	5,000	3,000	4,500
Beginning Cash Balance	0	16,000	25,000	30,000	33,000
Ending Cash Balance	$16,000	$25,000	$30,000	$33,000	$37,500

you need reinforcement in this area, review the appropriate sections in the previous coverage. Similarly, the recording procedures are not affected by the depreciation method. Different depreciation methods affect only the amounts of the transactions, not the accounts included in the entries. To avoid redundancy, the general journal entries are not shown for the double-declining-balance or the units-of-production depreciation methods.

Check Yourself 9–2

Olds Company purchased an asset that cost $36,000 on January 1, 2001. The asset had an expected useful life of five years and an estimated salvage value of $5,000. Assuming Olds uses the double-declining-balance method, determine the amount of depreciation expense and the amount of accumulated depreciation Olds would report on the 2003 financial statements.

Answer

Year	Book Value at the Beginning of the Period	×	Double the Straight-Line Rate*	=	Annual Depreciation Expense
2001	($36,000 − $ 0)	×	0.40	=	$14,400
2002	(36,000 − 14,400)	×	0.40	=	8,640
2003	(36,000 − 23,040)	×	0.40	=	5,184
	Total accumulated depreciation at December 31, 2003				$28,224

*Double-declining-balance rate = 2 × Straight-line rate = 2 × (100% ÷ 5 years) = 0.40

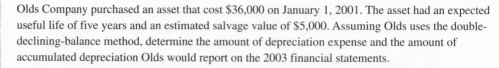

Units-of-Production Depreciation

LO5 Explain how expense recognition (depreciation) affects financial statements throughout the life cycle of a tangible asset.

Given the need to match expense recognition with asset use, a third depreciation method has been developed to reflect asset use that fluctuates from one accounting period to another. For example, suppose that Dryden experiences a demand for rentals that depends on general economic conditions. In a robust economy, travel increases, and the demand for renting the van is high. In a stagnant economy, demand for van rentals declines. Accordingly, the pattern of asset use varies from one accounting period to the next, depending on the state of the economy. Under these circumstances, it is more reasonable to use some measure of total production, rather than time, as the basis for determining the amount of depreciation. For a van, the number of miles driven may represent a reasonable measure of total production. If the asset to be depreciated were a saw used to cut pieces of wood into baseball bats, an appropriate measure of total production would be the number of bats that the saw was expected to produce during its useful life. In other words, the basis for measuring production depends on the nature of the asset being depreciated.

To illustrate the computation of depreciation under the **units-of-production depreciation** method, assume that Dryden measures asset use according to the number of miles that the van is driven each year. Furthermore, assume that Dryden expects the van to have a useful life of 100,000 miles. The first step in determining the amount of depreciation expense is the computation of the cost per unit of production. In the case of the van, the amount can be determined by dividing the total depreciable cost (historical cost − salvage value) by the number of units of total expected productive capacity (100,000 miles). Accordingly, the cost per mile is $0.20 ([$24,000 cost − $4,000 salvage] ÷ 100,000 miles). The depreciation expense is computed by multiplying the cost per mile by the number of miles driven. Based on mileage records that show the van was driven 40,000 miles, 20,000 miles, 30,000 miles, and 15,000 miles in 2001, 2002, 2003, and 2004, respectively, Dryden developed the following schedule of depreciation charges.

Year	Cost per Mile (a)	Miles Driven (b)	Depreciation Expense (a × b)
2001	$ .20	40,000	$8,000
2002	.20	20,000	4,000
2003	.20	30,000	6,000
2004	.20	15,000	~~3,000~~ 2,000

As with the double-declining-balance method, the asset's book value cannot be depreciated below the salvage value. Since $18,000 of cost is depreciated in the first three years of operation, and since total depreciable cost is $20,000 ($24,000 cost − $4,000 salvage), only $2,000 ($20,000 − $18,000) of cost is charged to depreciation in year 4, even though the application of the computational formula suggests a $3,000 charge. As the preceding table indicates, the general formula for determining the amount of units-of-production depreciation is as follows:

$$\frac{\text{Cost} - \text{Salvage value}}{\text{Total estimated units of production}} \times \begin{array}{c}\text{Units of production}\\ \text{in current}\\ \text{accounting period}\end{array} = \begin{array}{c}\text{Annual}\\ \text{depreciation}\\ \text{expense}\end{array}$$

Exhibit 9–6 is a full set of financial statements that assumes that Dryden uses units-of-production depreciation. Again, it is logical to assume that revenue will fluctuate with asset use. The exhibit assumes that Dryden collected cash revenue of $11,000, $7,000, $9,000, and $5,000 for 2001, 2002, 2003, and 2004, respectively. Notice that the revenue pattern fluctuates with the depreciation charges, thereby resulting in a constant amount of $3,000 per year of reported net income.

Comparing the Methods

LO7 Show how different depreciation methods affect the amount of expense recognized in a particular accounting period.

Note that the total amount of depreciation expense recognized under all three methods was $20,000. The different depreciation methods affect the timing of recognition but not the total

Exhibit 9–6 *Financial Statements under Units-of-Production Depreciation*

DRYDEN ENTERPRISES
Financial Statements

	2001	2002	2003	2004	2005
Income Statements					
Rent Revenue	$11,000	$7,000	$9,000	$ 5,000	$ 0
Depreciation Expense	(8,000)	(4,000)	(6,000)	(2,000)	0
Operating Income	3,000	3,000	3,000	3,000	0
Gain	0	0	0	0	500
Net Income	$ 3,000	$ 3,000	$ 3,000	$ 3,000	$ 500
Balance Sheets					
Assets					
Cash	$12,000	$19,000	$28,000	$33,000	$37,500
Van	24,000	24,000	24,000	24,000	0
Accumulated Depreciation	(8,000)	(12,000)	(18,000)	(20,000)	0
Total Assets	$28,000	$31,000	$34,000	$37,000	$37,500
Stockholders' Equity					
Common Stock	$25,000	$25,000	$25,000	$25,000	$25,000
Retained Earnings	3,000	6,000	9,000	12,000	12,500
Total Stockholders' Equity	$28,000	$31,000	$34,000	$37,000	$37,500
Statements of Cash Flows					
Operating Activities					
Inflow from Customers	$11,000	$ 7,000	$ 9,000	$ 5,000	$ 0
Investing Activities					
Outflow to Purchase Van	(24,000)				
Inflow from Sale of Van					4,500
Financing Activities					
Inflow from Common Stock	25,000				
Net Change in Cash	12,000	7,000	9,000	5,000	4,500
Beginning Cash Balance	0	12,000	19,000	28,000	33,000
Ending Cash Balance	$12,000	$19,000	$28,000	$33,000	$37,500

Exhibit 9–7 *Depreciation Expense Under Different Depreciation Methods*

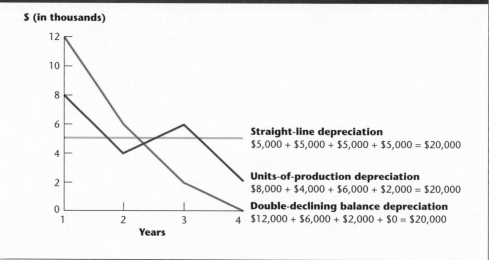

Straight-line depreciation
$5,000 + $5,000 + $5,000 + $5,000 = $20,000

Units-of-production depreciation
$8,000 + $4,000 + $6,000 + $2,000 = $20,000

Double-declining balance depreciation
$12,000 + $6,000 + $2,000 + $0 = $20,000

amount of cost to be recognized. The different methods simply assign the $20,000 to different accounting periods. Exhibit 9–7 is a graphical depiction of the three methods. Each method offers unique opportunities to match expense recognition with asset use. As indicated earlier, matching asset use with expense recognition is desirable because it improves the capacity of financial reports to more accurately describe managerial performance.

Income Tax Considerations

LO8 Identify tax issues related to long-term operational assets.

Although matching asset use with revenue recognition is important for the assessment of managerial performance, it is not a meaningful consideration for the payment of income taxes. Here the objective is to minimize the tax expense by reporting the highest amount of depreciation permissible under the law. The maximum depreciation currently allowed under tax law is computed under an accelerated depreciation method known as the **Modified Accelerated Cost Recovery System (MACRS)**. MACRS specifies the length of useful life permitted for designated categories of assets. For example, under the law, a 5-year useful life must be used for automobiles, light trucks, technological equipment, and other similar asset types. In contrast, a 7-year life must be used for office furniture, fixtures, and many types of conventional machinery. In total, the law classifies depreciable property, excluding real estate, into one of six categories: 3-year property, 5-year property, 7-year property, 10-year property, 15-year property, and 20-year property. Tables have been established for each category that specify the percentage of cost that can be expensed (deducted) in determining the amount of taxable income. A tax table for 5- and 7-year property is shown here as an example.

Year	5-Year Property, %	7-Year Property, %
1	20.00	14.29
2	32.00	24.49
3	19.20	17.49
4	11.52	12.49
5	11.52	8.93
6	5.76	8.92
7		8.93
8		4.46

The amount of depreciation that can be deducted each year for tax purposes is determined by multiplying the cost of a depreciable asset by the percentage shown in the table. For example, the depreciation expense for year 1 of a 7-year property asset is determined by multiplying the cost of the property by 14.29 percent. Year 2's depreciation is found by multiplying the cost by 24.49 percent.

The tables contain some apparent inconsistencies. For example, if MACRS is an accelerated depreciation method, why is less depreciation permitted in year 1 than in years 2 and 3? Also, why is depreciation computed in year 6 for property with a 5-year life and in year 8 for property with a 7-year life? In fact, these conditions are the logical consequence of what is known as the **half-year convention.** Taxpayers purchase assets at different times during any single tax period. Indeed, given the number of U.S. taxpayers, someone buys an asset every single day of the year. Accordingly, to accurately measure asset use for all taxpayers, the tax code would have to include 365 tables (one table beginning with each day of the year) for each class of property. Given the six classes of personal property, the code would have to include 2,190 tables (365 × 6). Obviously, the accurate measurement of asset use is an impractical goal. To eliminate this potential problem, the tax law ignores the specific dates of acquisition and disposal. Instead, the code requires one-half year's depreciation to be charged in the year in which an asset is acquired and one-half year's depreciation in the year of disposal. Accordingly, the percentages shown in the table for the first and last years represent amounts of depreciation for one-half year instead of the actual time of usage.

To illustrate the computation of depreciation under MACRS, assume that Wilson Company purchased furniture (7-year-property) for $10,000 cash on July 21. Depreciation charges over the useful life of the asset are computed as shown:

Year	Table Factor, %	×	Cost	=	Depreciation Amount
1	14.29		10,000		$ 1,429
2	24.49		10,000		2,449
3	17.49		10,000		1,749
4	12.49		10,000		1,249
5	8.93		10,000		893
6	8.92		10,000		892
7	8.93		10,000		893
8	4.46		10,000		446
Total over useful life					$10,000

As an alternative to MACRS, the tax code permits the use of straight-line depreciation. Indeed, the code requires the use of straight-line depreciation for certain types of assets such as real property (buildings).

To minimize taxes and to provide a meaningful representation of managerial performance, companies may calculate depreciation twice: once for financial reporting purposes and once for tax returns. There are no requirements that force consistency between depreciation methods reported in the financial statements and those used on the income tax return. For example, straight-line depreciation may be used in the financial statements presented to stockholders and creditors, while MACRS is used on the tax return. Under these circumstances, taxes are reduced because higher depreciation charges would be shown on the tax return. However, it is important to note that in later years, taxes will be higher because under MACRS, the amount of depreciation declines as the asset becomes older (under accelerated depreciation, the higher charges in early years are offset by lower charges in later years). Accordingly, taxes are not avoided but are delayed instead. The amounts of taxes delayed for future payment are called **deferred tax liability.** Although deferring taxes is not as good as never having to pay them, the delay is still advantageous because of the opportunity to invest the money in assets that produce revenue during the period of the delay.

▌Revision of Estimates

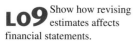

LO9 Show how revising estimates affects financial statements.

When an estimate of salvage value, life, or total production is revised during the use of the asset, nothing is done to correct the previously reported figures. There are so many estimates used in accounting that revisions are considered a normal part of business. The new information is simply incorporated into any present and future calculations.

To illustrate, assume that McGraw Company purchased an asset on January 1, 2003, for $50,000. The machine was estimated to have a useful life of 8 years and a salvage value of $3,000. McGraw used the straight-line depreciation method and determined the annual depreciation charge according to the following formula:

$$(\$50,000 - \$3,000) \div 8 \text{ years} = \$5,875 \text{ per year}$$

Using these assumptions, consider the possibility of two different revisions occurring in the fifth year. At the beginning of the fifth year, the amount in accumulated depreciation is $23,500 ($5,875 × 4), making the book value $26,500 ($50,000 − $23,500). Each revision should be considered separately from the other.

Revision of Life

If McGraw revised the expected life to 14 years rather than 8 years, the asset would now be expected to last 10 more years rather than 4 more years. Salvage remains at $3,000, so computation of each remaining year's depreciation is

$$(\$26,500 \text{ book value} - \$3,000 \text{ salvage}) \div 10\text{-year remaining life} = \$2,350$$

Revision of Salvage

If the original expected life remained the same but the salvage value were revised to $6,000, the depreciation charge for each of the remaining four years would be

($26,500 book value − $6,000 salvage) ÷ 4-year remaining life = $5,125

Notice that it was not important when the company revised its estimates during the year. The entire year's depreciation was considered changed.

▊Continuing Expenditures for Plant Assets

Over the life of an asset, it is often necessary or advisable to make expenditures to maintain or improve the asset's productivity. These expenditures fall into two classifications: those that are expensed and those that are capitalized.

LO10 Understand how continuing expenditures for operational assets affect financial statements.

Costs That Are Expensed

When an expenditure that is necessary to keep the asset in good working order is made, it is expensed in the period in which it is incurred. These costs consist of such things as routine maintenance and minor repairs. Extending the example for the machine owned by McGraw Company, we assume that $500 was spent to lubricate the machine and replace minor parts. The effect of the expenditure on the financial statements and the journal entry necessary to record it are as follows:

Assets	=	Equity			Rev.	−	Exp.	=	Net Inc.	Cash Flow	
Cash	=	C. Stk.	+	Ret. Earn.							
(500)	=	NA	+	(500)	NA	−	500	=	(500)	(500)	OA

Account Title	Debit	Credit
Repairs Expense	500	
Cash		500

Costs That Are Capitalized

Capital expenditures are usually substantial amounts spent to improve the quality or extend the life of an asset. As such, these expenses affect the remainder of the asset's life and should not be treated as an expense of the current accounting period. Capital expenditures are accounted for in one of two possible ways, depending on whether the cost incurred is considered to *improve the quality* or *extend the life* of the asset. In practice, it is often difficult to determine exactly which effect an expenditure will have. Thus, the selection of which approach to use is often a matter of judgment.

Improving Quality

When an expenditure is deemed to have improved the quality of an asset, the cost is added to the asset's historical cost, and this extra amount ends up being expensed over the remainder of the asset's life through the process of depreciation. Continuing with the McGraw Company example, we assume that a major expenditure costing $4,000 is made in the fifth year. The expenditure acts to improve the productive capacity of the company's machine. Recall that the asset originally cost $50,000, had an estimated salvage of $3,000, and had a predicted life of 8 years. If we assume straight-line depreciation, the amount in accumulated depreciation at the beginning of the fifth year is $23,500 ($5,875 × 4), making the book value $26,500 ($50,000 − $23,500). The effect of the $4,000 expenditure on the financial statements and the journal entry necessary to record it are as follows:

Assets			=	Equity			Rev.	−	Exp.	=	Net Inc.	Cash Flow
Cash	+ Mach.	− A. Dep.	=	C. Stk.	+	Ret. Earn.						
(4,000)	+ 4,000	− NA	=	NA	+	NA	NA	−	NA	=	NA	(4,000) IA

Account Title	Debit	Credit
Machine	4,000	
Cash		4,000

After we recognize the effects of the expenditure, the machine contains a $54,000 balance, resulting in a book value of $30,500 ($54,000 − $23,500). The depreciation charges for the remaining four years are calculated as follows:

($30,500 book value − $3,000 salvage) ÷ 4-year remaining life = $6,875

Extending Life

When a company undertakes a capital expenditure that extends the life of the asset but not its quality, it is theoretically objectionable to increase the cost of the asset. Instead, the expenditure is looked on as canceling some of the depreciation that has already been charged to expense. The event is still an asset exchange. Cash decreases, and the book value of the machine increases. The increase in the book value of the machine is accomplished by reducing the amount in the contra asset account, Accumulated Depreciation. To illustrate, assume that instead of increasing productive capacity, McGraw's $4,000 expenditure had merely extended the useful life of the machine by two years. The effect of the event on the financial statements and the journal entry necessary to record it are as follows:

Assets			=	Equity			Rev.	−	Exp.	=	Net Inc.	Cash Flow
Cash	+ Mach.	− A. Dep.	=	C. Stk.	+	Ret. Earn.						
(4,000)	+ NA	− (4,000)	=	NA	+	NA	NA	−	NA	=	NA	(4,000) IA

Account Title	Debit	Credit
Accumulated Depreciation—Machine	4,000	
Cash		4,000

Notice that the book value is now the same as if the $4,000 had been added to the Machine account ($50,000 cost − $19,500 adjusted balance in accumulated depreciation = $30,500). Depreciation expense for each of the remaining six years is calculated as follows:

($30,500 book value − $3,000 salvage) ÷ 6-year remaining life = $4,583.33

On January 1, 2003, Dager, Inc., purchased an asset that cost $18,000. It had a five-year useful life and a $3,000 salvage value. Dager uses straight-line depreciation. On January 1, 2005, it incurred a $1,200 cost related to the asset. With respect to this asset, determine the amount of expense and accumulated depreciation Dager would report in the 2005 financial statements under each of the following assumptions.

1. The $1,200 cost was incurred to repair damage resulting from an accident.
2. The $1,200 cost improved the operating capacity of the equipment. The total useful life and salvage value remained unchanged.
3. The $1,200 cost extended the useful life of the asset by one year. The salvage value remained unchanged.

Answer

1. Dager would report the $1,200 repair cost as an expense. Dager would also report depreciation expense of $3,000 ([$15,000 − $3,000] ÷ 4). Total expenses related to this asset in 2005 would be $4,200 ($1,200 repair expense + $3,000 depreciation expense). Accumulated depreciation at the end of 2005 would be $9,000 ($3,000 depreciation expense × 3 years).
2. The $1,200 cost would be capitalized in the asset account, increasing both the book value of the asset and the annual depreciation expense.

	After Effects of Capital Improvement
Amount in asset account ($18,000 + $1,200)	$19,200
Less: Salvage value	(3,000)
Accumulated depreciation on January 1, 2005	(6,000)
Remaining depreciable cost before recording 2005 depreciation	$10,200
Depreciation for 2005 ($10,200 ÷ 3 years)	$ 3,400
Accumulated depreciation at December 31, 2005 ($6,000 + $3,400)	$ 9,400

3. The $1,200 cost would be subtracted from the accumulated depreciation account, increasing the book value of the asset. The remaining useful life would increase to four years, which would decrease the depreciation expense.

	After Effects of Capital Improvement
Amount in asset account	$18,000
Less: Salvage value	(3,000)
Accumulated depreciation on January 1, 2005 ($6,000 − $1,200)	(4,800)
Remaining depreciable cost before recording 2005 depreciation	$10,200
Depreciation for 2005 ($10,200 ÷ 4 years)	$2,550
Accumulated depreciation at December 31, 2005 ($4,800 + $2,550)	$7,350

Check Yourself 9-3

▌Natural Resources

Natural resources are recorded in the books at the cost of acquisition. Other costs frequently capitalized in natural resource accounts include the cost of exploration necessary to locate resources and payments for corresponding geographic surveys and estimates.

Depletion is a process of expense recognition[1] that systematically allocates the cost of natural resources to expense. The units-of-production method is the most common method used

LO11 Explain how expense recognition for natural resources (depletion) affects financial statements.

[1]In practice, the depletion charge is considered a product cost and allocated between inventory and cost of goods sold. This text adopts the simplifying assumption that all resources are sold in the same accounting period in which they are extracted. Accordingly, the full amount of the depletion charge is expensed in the period in which the resources are extracted.

to calculate depletion. The cost of the natural resource is divided by the total estimated number of units to be extracted to produce a charge per unit. If Apex Coal Mining paid $4,000,000 cash to purchase a mine with an estimated 16,000,000 tons of coal, the unit charge is $0.25 per ton ($4,000,000 ÷ 16,000,000). If Apex mines 360,000 tons of coal in the first year, the depletion charge is $90,000 (360,000 × $0.25). The depletion of a natural resource has the same effect on the accounting equation as other expense recognition events. Assets (in this case, a *coal mine*) decrease and equity decreases because the depletion expense reduces net income and ultimately retained earnings. The effect on the financial statements and the journal entries necessary to record the acquisition and depletion of the coal mine are as follows:

Assets			=	Equity			Rev.	–	Exp.	=	Net Inc.	Cash Flow	
Cash	+	Coal Mine	=	C. Stk.	+	Ret. Earn.							
(4,000,000)	+	4,000,000	=	NA	+	NA	NA	–	NA	=	NA	(4,000,000)	IA
NA	+	(90,000)	=	NA	+	(90,000)	NA	–	90,000	=	(90,000)	NA	

Account Title	Debit	Credit
Coal Mine	4,000,000	
Cash		4,000,000
Depletion Expense	90,000	
Coal Mine		90,000

The decrease in the asset, Coal Mine, could have been shown in a contra account titled *Allowance for Depletion*. When the Allowance for Depletion account is used, it has the same relationship with natural resources as the Accumulated Depreciation account has with property, plant, and equipment. However, most companies follow the practice of deducting the amount of depletion directly from the asset account. Accordingly, this book emphasizes the direct deduction approach.

Intangible Assets

LO12 Explain how expense recognition for intangible assets (amortization) affects financial statements.

Intangible assets provide rights, privileges, and special opportunities to businesses. Some of the more common intangible assets include trademarks, patents, copyrights, franchises, and goodwill. Intangible assets have different characteristics and purposes; some of the unique features of the more common ones are described in the following sections.

Trademarks

A **trademark** is a name or symbol that identifies a company or an individual product. Some trademarks that you may be familiar with are the Polo emblem, the name *Coca-Cola*, and the slogan, "You can be sure if it's Westinghouse." Trademarks are registered with the federal government and have an indefinite legal lifetime.

The costs to be capitalized include those required to develop the trademark and those incurred to defend it. When trademarks are purchased, the amount of the purchase price is capitalized in the Trademark account. Companies want their trademarks to become familiar but fear the situation in which the trademark begins to be treated as the generic name for a product. Companies in this predicament expend large amounts to protect the trademark, including legal fees and extensive advertising programs to educate consumers. Some well-known trademarks that have been subject to this problem are Coke, Xerox, Kleenex, and Vaseline.

Patents

As previously indicated, a **patent** is an exclusive right to produce and sell a commodity that has one or more unique features. Patents granted by the U.S. Patent Office have a legal life of 17 years. Patents may be purchased, leased, or developed within the company. When a company develops a patent, the question arises as to what costs should be capitalized in the Patent account. Clearly, the legal costs associated with obtaining and defending the patent are capitalized. What about the research and development costs incurred to make the product that is being patented? Product research and development is frequently unsuccessful; companies spend hundreds of millions of dollars on research projects that lead nowhere. Because it is difficult to determine which research development costs will produce future revenues, GAAP requires that these costs be expensed in the period in which they are incurred. Accordingly, the costs capitalized in the Patent account are usually limited to a purchase price and/or legal fees.

LO13 Explain how GAAP can adversely affect the ability of U.S. companies to attract international capital.

International Issues

U.S. GAAP: A Competitive Disadvantage?

The accounting rules of various countries have many differences, but, over the years, perhaps none caused as much concern to companies involved in global competition as the rules related to accounting for goodwill and research and development (R&D).

Suppose that Company A paid $300,000 to purchase Company B's assets. Furthermore, suppose Company B's assets have a market value of only $200,000. In the United States, the $100,000 difference is classified as *goodwill*. Before July 2001, this goodwill would have been amortized (expensed) over its useful life. In the United Kingdom, the treatment was very different. A U.K. company was allowed to "charge" the entire $100,000 *directly against equity* in the year of the purchase. Normally, a cost is placed in an asset account and then expensed. When the expense is recognized, net income decreases and retained earnings decreases. Under the U.K. approach, you simply skipped the income statement by making a charge directly to Retained Earnings.

In July 2001, the FASB voted to change radically the U.S. GAAP related to accounting for business combinations, which includes accounting for goodwill. Now goodwill is placed on the balance sheet as an asset, but it never has to be written off as an expense, so long as the value of the goodwill does not decrease. The rules governing accounting for business combinations in the United States are now more like those of other industrialized nations.

Suppose Company X is a pharmaceutical company that spends $10 million on the R&D of a new drug. Under U.S. GAAP, the company is required to expense the $10 million immediately. In Japan, the company is allowed to capitalize the cost in an asset account and then to expense it gradually over the useful life of the asset. Accordingly, in the year in which R&D costs are incurred, a U.S. company reports more expense and less income than its Japanese counterpart.

Some businesspeople believe that U.S. GAAP can put U.S. companies at a competitive disadvantage in the search for capital. Certainly, the rules pertaining to goodwill and R&D demonstrate how U.S. companies may be forced to report lower earnings. Foreign companies that report higher earnings may be able to attract international investors who would otherwise invest in U.S. companies. Keep in mind that well-informed business professionals know how different accounting rules affect a company's financial statements. If they believe that U.S. GAAP cause a company's earnings to be understated, they take this into consideration when making investment decisions.

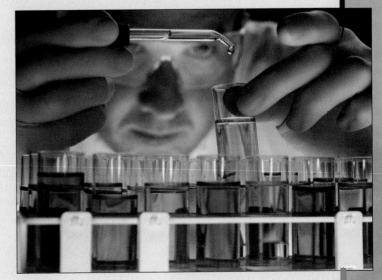

Copyrights

A **copyright** protects the writings, musical compositions, and other works of art for the exclusive benefit of the creator or persons assigned the right by the creator. The cost of a copyright includes the purchase price or the legal costs associated with obtaining and defending the copyright. Copyrights are granted by the federal government for a period defined as the life of the creator plus 50 years. A radio commercial could use a Bach composition as background music with no legal ramifications; however, if "Streets of Philadelphia" were desired instead, royalties would have to be paid to Bruce Springsteen or to the assigned owner of the copyright. Often the cost of a copyright is expensed very early because future royalties may be uncertain.

Franchises

Franchises are exclusive rights to sell products or perform services in certain geographic areas. Franchises may be granted by governments or private business. An example of a franchise granted by the federal government is a broadcasting license. Fast-food restaurant chains, private labels such as Healthy Choice, and real estate offices are examples of private business franchises. Franchises can cost hundreds of thousands and even millions of dollars. The legal and useful lives of a franchise are frequently difficult to define. Accordingly, judgment is often crucial to the establishment of the appropriate accounting treatment for franchises.

Goodwill

Goodwill is the added value of a business that is attributable to favorable factors such as reputation, location, and superior products. To better understand goodwill, consider the most popular restaurant in your town. If the owner sold the restaurant, do you think the purchase price would simply be the total value of the chairs, tables, kitchen equipment, and building? Certainly not, because much of the restaurant's value lies in its popularity, in other words, its ability to generate a high return.

Calculation of goodwill can be very complex; here we present a very simple example to illustrate how it is determined. Suppose that the accounting records of a restaurant named Bendigo's show assets of $200,000, liabilities of $50,000, and equity of $150,000. A food services company that wants to acquire the restaurant agrees to purchase it by assuming the liabilities and paying the owner $300,000 cash. The amount of goodwill acquired can be determined by subtracting the fair market value of the assets on the day of purchase from the amount paid to acquire them. In this case, the amount paid includes $50,000 of liabilities that were assumed plus $300,000 cash. Assume that an independent appraiser assessed the fair market value of the assets as $280,000 on the date of purchase. Under these circumstances, the amount of goodwill purchased is $70,000 ([$50,000 + $300,000] − $280,000). The effect of the purchase on the financial statements of the buyer is shown here:

Assets			=	Liab.	+	Equity	Rev.	−	Exp.	=	Net Inc.	Cash Flow
Cash	+	Rest. Assets	+	Goodwill								
(300,000)	+	280,000	+	70,000	=	50,000 +	NA	NA	−	NA	=	NA	(300,000) IA

The journal entry required to record the acquisition of the restaurant follows:

Account Title	Debit	Credit
Restaurant Assets	280,000	
Goodwill	70,000	
Cash		300,000
Liabilities		50,000

Note that the fair market value of the restaurant assets represents the historical cost to the new owner. Accordingly, it becomes the basis for future depreciation charges.

Intangible assets can be classified into two categories, those with *identifiable useful lives* and those with *indefinite useful lives*. Examples of intangible assets with identifiable useful lives include patents and copyrights. These assets may become obsolete (e.g., a patent may become worthless because new technology provides a superior product) or may reach the end of their legal lives. In contrast, the usefulness of some intangible assets may extend so far into the future that their limits are not definable. How long will the Coca Cola logo attract customers? When will a McDonald's franchise cease to be of value? There are no answers to questions such as these. Accordingly, intangible assets such as renewable franchises, trademarks, and goodwill are considered to have indefinite useful lives.

Expensing Intangible Assets With Identifiable Useful Lives

As with other long-term operational assets, intangibles with identifiable useful lives are capitalized in asset accounts at historical cost and are systematically expensed over their useful lives. As noted earlier, the expense recognition process for intangible assets is called *amortization*. It is helpful to note that *amortization, depletion,* and *depreciation* are simply different terms used to describe the expense allocation process applied to different types of assets.

Intangible assets are normally amortized (expensed) on a straight-line basis. In determining how much to expense each year, the company must consider two possible lifetimes of the intangible: (1) its legal life and (2) its useful life. An intangible asset should be amortized over the shortest of these two possible lives.

To illustrate, assume that Flowers Industries pays $44,000 cash to purchase a patent. Although the patent has a legal life of 17 years, Flowers estimates that it will be useful for only 11 years. In this case, the annual charge is $4,000 ($44,000 ÷ 11 years). The effect of the purchase of the patent and its amortization on the financial statements and the journal entries necessary to record the events are as follows.

Assets			=	Equity			Rev.	−	Exp.	=	Net Inc.	Cash Flow	
Cash	+	Patent	=	C. Stk.	+	Ret. Earn.							
(44,000)	+	44,000	=	NA	+	NA	NA	−	NA	=	NA	(44,000)	IA
NA	+	(4,000)	=	NA	+	(4,000)	NA	−	4,000	=	(4,000)	NA	

Account Title	Debit	Credit
Patent	44,000	
Cash		44,000
Amortization Expense, Patent	4,000	
Patent		4,000

Notice that the Patent account was credited directly. This is the usual method; however, an allowance account can be used if the company so desires. Popular practice is to reduce the asset account directly, and for that reason, this book adheres to this method for examples and problems.

Impairment Losses for Intangible Assets With Indefinite Useful Lives

Intangible assets with indefinite useful lives must be tested for impairment annually. The impairment test should consist of comparing the fair value of the intangible asset to its carrying

In October 1998, Clorox Company agreed to pay $1.6 billion to purchase First Brands Corporation. First Brands is the company that sells Glad plastic bags and STP oil treatment, among other products. At the time, First Brands' balance sheet showed net assets (assets minus liabilities) of approximately $620 million. Why would Clorox pay the owners of First Brands more than twice the book value of the assets shown on the company's balance sheet? Clorox was willing to pay more than the book value for First Brands Corporation for two reasons. First, the value of the assets on First Brands' balance sheet represents the historical cost of the assets (the amount First Brands paid to obtain the assets). The current market value of these assets may be higher than the historical cost, especially for assets such as the trademarks for Glad and STP. Second, Clorox probably believed that First Brands had *goodwill* that enables a company to use its assets in a manner that will provide above-average earnings. In other words, Clorox was buying a hidden asset not shown on First Brands' books.

value (book value). If the fair value is less than the book value, an impairment loss must be recognized.

To illustrate, we will return to the example of the purchase of the restaurant named Bendigo's. Recall that the buyer of Bendigo's purchased $70,000 of goodwill. Suppose that the restaurant's customers become dissatisfied with the food prepared by the new chef and that the business experiences a significant decline in revenue. Indeed, the decline is so substantial that the new owners believe that the Bendigo's name has been permanently impaired. The owner decides to hire a new chef and to change the name of the restaurant. In this case, the goodwill has been permanently damaged. Accordingly, it will be necessary to recognize an impairment loss.

The restaurant's name has lost its value, but the owner believes that the location continues to provide the opportunity to produce above-average earnings. Specifically, assume that the market value of the goodwill is determined to be $40,000. Accordingly, it will be necessary to recognize an impairment loss in the amount of $30,000 ($70,000 − $40,000). The loss would reduce the value of the intangible asset (goodwill) and equity (retained earnings). Furthermore, the loss would reduce the amount of net income. The statement of cash flows would not be affected. These effects on the financial statements follow:

Assets	=	Liab.	+	Equity	Rev.	−	Exp./Loss	=	Net Inc.	Cash Flow
Goodwill	=			Ret. Earn.						
(30,000)	=	NA	+	(30,000)	NA	−	30,000	=	(30,000)	NA

The journal entry required to recognize the impairment loss is shown here:

Account Title	Debit	Credit
Impairment Loss	30,000	
Goodwill		30,000

Balance Sheet Presentation

In this chapter, you learned about the acquisition, expense allocation, and disposal of a wide range of long-term assets. Exhibit 9–8 is a typical balance sheet that exemplifies many of the assets discussed.

Exhibit 9–8 *Balance Sheet Presentation of Operational Assets*

Balance Sheet			
Long-Term Assets			
Plant and Equipment			
Buildings	$4,000,000		
Less: Accumulated Depreciation	(2,500,000)	$1,500,000	
Equipment	1,750,000		
Less: Accumulated Depreciation	(1,200,000)	550,000	
Total Plant and Equipment			$2,050,000
Land			850,000
Natural Resources			
Mineral Deposits (Less: Depletion)		2,100,000	
Oil Reserves (Less: Depletion)		890,000	
Total Natural Resources			2,990,000
Intangibles			
Patents (Less: Amortization)		38,000	
Goodwill		175,000	
Total Intangible Assets			213,000
Total Long-Term Assets			$6,103,000

Understanding How Expense Recognition Affects Financial Performance Measures

It should be clear from the preceding discussion that the amount of expense recognized in any particular accounting period depends on which allocation method (straight-line, accelerated, or units-of-production) a company uses. Ideally, a company should use the method that best matches the pattern of asset use. More expense should be recognized in periods in which the assets are used extensively. Smaller amounts should be recognized in periods in which assets are used infrequently. Unfortunately, the pattern of asset use may be uncertain when the expense recognition method is selected. Since asset use occurs in the future, different managers may have different opinions about how assets will be used. As a result, managers of different companies may use different expense recognition methods for similar assets. Accordingly, companies affected by an identical set of economic circumstances could produce significantly different financial statements.

LO14 Understand how expense recognition choices and industry characteristics affect financial performance measures.

Effect of Judgment and Estimation

As a simple example, assume that two companies, Alpha and Zeta, are affected by the same set of economic events in 2001 and 2002. Both generate revenue of $50,000 and incur cost of goods sold of $30,000 during each year. In 2001, each company pays $20,000 for an asset with an expected useful life of five years and no salvage value. How will the companies' financial statements differ if one uses straight-line depreciation and the other uses the double-declining-balance method? To answer this question, begin by computing the depreciation expense for both companies for 2001 and 2002.

If Alpha Company uses straight-line depreciation, the amount of depreciation for 2001 and 2002 is computed as follows:

$$\text{(Cost} - \text{Salvage)} \div \text{No. of years} = \text{Depreciation expense per year}$$
$$(\$20,000 - \$0) \div 5 = \$4,000$$

In contrast, if Zeta Company uses the double-declining-balance method, Zeta recognizes the following amounts of depreciation expense for 2001 and 2002:

	(Cost − Accumulated Depreciation)	× 2 ×	(Straight-Line Rate)	=	Depreciation Expense
2001	($20,000 − $0)	×	(2 × [1 ÷ 5])	=	$8,000
2002	($20,000 − $8,000)	×	(2 × [1 ÷ 5])	=	$4,800

Based on these computations, the income statements for the two companies appear as follows:

Income Statements

	2001		2002	
	Alpha Co.	Zeta Co.	Alpha Co.	Zeta Co.
Sales	$50,000	$50,000	$50,000	$50,000
Cost of Goods Sold	(30,000)	(30,000)	(30,000)	(30,000)
Gross Margin	20,000	20,000	20,000	20,000
Depreciation Expense	(4,000)	(8,000)	(4,000)	(4,800)
Net Income	$16,000	$12,000	$16,000	$15,200

The relevant sections of the balance sheets are as follows:

Plant Assets

	2001		2002	
	Alpha Co.	Zeta Co.	Alpha Co.	Zeta Co.
Asset	$20,000	$20,000	$20,000	$20,000
Accumulated Depreciation	(4,000)	(8,000)	(8,000)	(12,800)
Book Value	$16,000	$12,000	$12,000	$7,200

Clearly, the depreciation method selected by each company affects its expenses and thus its net income and retained earnings. The method used also affects the accumulated depreciation, which in turn affects the book value of plant assets and total assets. Financial statement analysis is affected if it is based on ratios whose computations use any of the items mentioned. Previously defined ratios that are affected include the (1) debt to assets ratio, (2) return on assets ratio, (3) return on equity ratio, and (4) return on sales ratio.

Choosing the depreciation method is not the only aspect of expense recognition that can vary for two companies. The companies may also make different assumptions about the useful lives and salvage values of plant assets. Thus, even if the same depreciation method is used, depreciation expense may still differ. To illustrate, assume that both Delta Airlines and United Airlines buy an airplane that costs $40 million and both decide to use straight-line depreciation. Delta might choose to depreciate the plane over 15 years while United may choose

20 years. If salvage value is expected to be negligible, the depreciation expense per year for each airplane is

	(Cost − Salvage)	÷	Estimated Life	=	Depreciation Expense
Delta	($40 million − $0)	÷	15	=	$2.67 million
United	($40 million − $0)	÷	20	=	$2.00 million

Based on these numbers, Delta's depreciation expense is 35 percent higher than United's for the next 15 years. This difference could have a significant impact on the companies' financial statements and the ratios used to evaluate financial performance. Although the performance measures are affected, the real economic substance as measured by cash flow is not affected. Accordingly, an uninformed user may conclude that performance differences exist when, in fact, they do not.

Users of accounting information must be aware of all accounting policies a company uses before that company's financial statements and financial ratios can be analyzed. For this reason, companies that wish to have their statements audited are required to disclose all significant accounting policies such as depreciation and inventory cost flow methods used. This disclosure is usually provided in the footnotes that accompany the financial statements.

Effect of Industry Characteristics

Financial performance measures can also be affected by industry characteristics. Some businesses use more depreciable assets than other businesses. For example, companies in manufacturing industries rely on heavy machinery while insurance companies use human capital. Accordingly, manufacturing companies can be expected to have relatively higher depreciation charges than insurance companies. The ability to evaluate a company's financial performance requires an understanding of the industry in which it operates. To illustrate how the type of industry can affect financial reporting, review the information in Exhibit 9–9. This exhibit compares the ratio of sales to property, plant, and equipment for two companies for each of three different industries. These data are for 2000.

LO1 Explain why some businesses generate high revenue with few operational assets.

The table indicates that for every $1.00 invested in property, plant, and equipment, Lehman Brothers produced $65.39 of sales. In contrast, Southern Co. produced only $0.47 in sales for each $1.00 it invested in operational assets. In other words, the higher the investment in operational assets, the lower the ratio.

Considering the amount of equipment required to produce and deliver electricity, it is not surprising that utility companies have a much lower ratio of sales to property, plant, and equipment than stock brokerage companies do. However, it might be surprising to some readers that the ratio for airlines is significantly higher than that for utility companies. Given the investment in airplanes, we expect that airline companies would have a smaller ratio. Passengers flying on an airline tend to underestimate the investment in human capital because they see only the crew plus a few employees inside the air terminal.

Exhibit 9–9 Industry Data Reflecting the Use of Operational Assets		
Industry	**Company**	**Sales ÷ Property, Plant, and Equipment**
Stock Brokerage	Lehman Brothers	65.39
	Merrill Lynch	153.06
Airlines	Delta	1.37
	United	1.18
Electric Utilities	TXU Corporation	0.94
	Southern Co.	0.47

Airlines have many employees, such as reservation agents, schedulers, baggage handlers, and mechanics, whom most passengers do not see.

A failure to understand that financial statements reflect industry characteristics can lead to a misinterpretation of managerial performance. For example, the fact that a stock brokerage company uses fewer operational assets than a utility company is not an indication that stock brokerage companies are better managed. Rather, it means that the two companies operate in different business environments. When you use financial ratios for performance evaluation, it is critically important that you compare ratios of companies from the same industry. Also, do not forget that even within the same industry, companies may use different expense recognition methods and may reach different conclusions regarding the estimated useful lives and salvage values of their operational assets. Financial statement analysis requires not only an understanding of the technical aspects of accounting but also the ability to assess the reasonableness of management's judgments.

a look back

In Chapter 3 you learned that the primary objective of depreciation is to match the cost of a long-term operational asset with the revenues that the asset is expected to generate. This chapter showed how this basic concept can be extended to natural resources, through depletion, and to intangible assets, through amortization. This chapter also explained how different methods can be used to account for the same event (e.g., straight-line versus double-declining-balance depreciation). Accordingly, companies experiencing exactly the same business events could produce different financial statements. The alternative accounting methods for depreciating, depleting, or amortizing assets include the (1) straight-line, (2) double-declining-balance, and (3) units-of-production methods.

The *straight-line method* recognizes the same amount of expense during each accounting period. The amount of the expense to recognize is determined by the formula ([cost − salvage] ÷ number of years of useful life). The *double-declining-balance method* recognizes proportionately larger amounts of expense in the early years of an asset's useful life and increasingly smaller amounts of expense in the later years of the asset's useful life. The formula for calculating expense based on the double-declining-balance method is (book value at beginning of period × double the straight-line rate). The *units-of-production method* recognizes expense in direct proportion to the number of units produced during an accounting period. The amount of expense to recognize each period is computed by the formula ([cost − salvage] ÷ total estimated units of production = allocation rate × units of production in current accounting period).

The chapter also discussed *MACRS depreciation,* which is a tax treatment. MACRS is an accelerated method that is not acceptable under GAAP rules for public reporting. Accordingly, a company may use MACRS depreciation for tax purposes and straight-line or one of the other methods for public reporting. As a result, differences may exist in the amount of tax expense and the amount of tax liability. Such differences are called *deferred taxes.*

This chapter covered the accounting treatment for *changes in estimates* such as the useful life or the salvage value. Under these circumstances, the amount of depreciation recognized previous to the change in estimate is not affected. Instead, the remaining book value of the asset is expensed over its remaining useful life.

Three types of costs occur after an asset has been placed into service. These costs include maintenance, quality improvement, and extensions of useful life. *Maintenance costs* are expensed in the period in which they are incurred. *Costs that improve the quality* of an asset are added to the cost of the asset, thereby increasing the book value and the amount of future depreciation charges. *Costs that extend the useful life* of an asset are subtracted from the asset's Accumulated Depreciation account, thereby increasing the book value and the amount of future depreciation charges.

a look forward

In Chapter 10 we leave the assets section of the balance sheet and investigate some issues related to accounting for long-term liabilities. As you will learn, tax issues are also important when considering the consequences of borrowing money.

The following information pertains to a machine purchased by Bakersfield Company on January 1, 2001.

Purchase price	$ 63,000
Delivery cost	$ 2,000
Installation charge	$ 3,000
Estimated useful life	8 years
Estimated units the machine will produce	130,000
Estimated salvage value	$ 3,000

The machine produced 14,400 units during 2001 and 17,000 units during 2002.

Required

Determine the depreciation expense Bakersfield would report for 2001 and 2002 using each of the following methods.

a. Straight line.

b. Double-declining-balance.

c. Units of production.

d. MACRS assuming that the machine is classified as seven-year property.

Solution to Requirements a–d.

a. Straight Line

Purchase price	$63,000
Delivery cost	2,000
Installation charge	3,000
Total cost of machine	$68,000
Less: Salvage value	(3,000)
	$65,000 ÷ 8 = $8,125 Depreciation per year
2001	$ 8,125
2002	$ 8,125

b. Double-Declining-Balance

Year	Cost	−	Accumulated Depreciation at Beginning of Year	×	2 × S-L Rate	=	Annual Depreciation
2001	$68,000	−	$ 0	×	(2 × 0.125)	=	$17,000
2002	68,000	−	17,000	×	(2 × 0.125)	=	12,750

c. Units of Production

(1) (Cost − Salvage value) ÷ Estimated units of production = Depreciation cost per unit produced

$$\frac{\$68,000 - \$3,000}{130,000} = \$0.50 \text{ per unit}$$

(2) Cost per unit × Annual units produced = Annual depreciation expense

$$2001 \quad \$0.50 \times 14,400 = \$7,200$$
$$2002 \quad 0.50 \times 17,000 = 8,500$$

d. MACRS

Cost × MACRS percentage = Annual depreciation
$$2001 \quad \$68,000 \times 0.1429 = \$ 9,717$$
$$2002 \quad 68,000 \times 0.2449 = 16,653$$

QUESTIONS

1. What is the difference in the functions of long-term operational assets and investments?
2. What is the difference between tangible and intangible assets? Give an example of each.
3. What is the difference between goodwill and specifically identifiable intangible assets?
4. Define *depreciation*. What kind of asset is depreciated?
5. Why are natural resources called *wasting assets?*
6. Is land a depreciable asset? Why or why not?
7. Define *amortization*. What kind of assets are amortized?
8. Explain the historical cost concept as it applies to long-term operational assets. Why is the book value of an asset likely to be different from the current market value of the asset?
9. What different kinds of expenditures might be included in the recorded cost of a building?
10. What is a basket purchase of assets? When a basket purchase is made, how is cost assigned to individual assets?
11. What is the life cycle of a long-term operational asset?
12. Explain straight-line, units-of-production, and double-declining-balance depreciation. When is it appropriate to use each of these depreciation methods?
13. What effect does the recognition of depreciation expense have on total assets? On total equity?
14. Does the recognition of depreciation expense affect cash flows? Why or why not?
15. MalMax purchased a depreciable asset. What would be the difference in total assets at the end of the first year if MalMax chooses straight-line depreciation versus double-declining-balance?
16. John Smith mistakenly expensed the cost of a long-term tangible fixed asset. Specifically, he charged the cost of a truck to a delivery expense account. How will this error affect the income statement and the balance sheet in the year in which the mistake is made?
17. What is *salvage value?*
18. What type of account (classification) is accumulated depreciation?
19. Why is depreciation that has been recognized over the life of an asset shown in a contra account? Why not just reduce the asset account?
20. Assume that a piece of equipment cost $5,000 and had accumulated depreciation recorded of $3,000. What is the book value of the equipment? Is the book value equal to the fair market value of the equipment? Explain.
21. Why would a company choose to depreciate one piece of equipment using the double-declining-balance method and another piece of equipment using straight-line depreciation?
22. Explain MACRS depreciation. When is its use appropriate?
23. Does the method of depreciation required to be used for tax purposes reflect the use of a piece of equipment? Can you use double-declining-balance depreciation for tax purposes?
24. Define *deferred taxes*. Where does the account *Deferred Taxes* appear in the financial statements?
25. Why may it be necessary to revise the estimated life of a plant asset? When the estimated life is revised, does it affect the amount of depreciation per year? Why or why not?
26. How are capital expenditures made to improve the quality of a capital asset accounted for? Would the answer change if the expenditure extended the life of the asset but did not improve quality? Explain.
27. When a long-term operational asset is sold at a gain, how is the balance sheet affected? Is the statement of cash flows affected? If so, how?
28. Define *depletion*. What is the most commonly used method of computing depletion?
29. List several of the most common intangible assets. How is the life determined that is to be used to compute amortization?
30. List some differences between U.S. GAAP and GAAP of other countries.
31. How do differences in expense recognition and industry characteristics affect financial performance measures?

Unless specifically included, income tax considerations should be ignored in all exercises and problems.

EXERCISE 9–1A *Long-Term Operational Assets Used in a Business* **L.O. 3**

Required
Give some examples of long-term operational assets that each of the following companies is likely to own: *(a)* Greyhound Bus Co., *(b)* Exxon/Mobil, *(c)* Merry Maids, and *(d)* Placer Dome Gold Mining.

EXERCISE 9–2A *Identifying Long-Term Operational Assets* **L.O. 3**

Required
Which of the following items should be classified as long-term operational assets?
a. Inventory
b. Patent
c. Tract of timber
d. Land
e. Computer
f. Goodwill
g. Cash
h. Buildings
i. Production machinery
j. Accounts receivable
k. Certificate of deposit (6 months)
l. Franchise

EXERCISE 9–3A *Classifying Tangible and Intangible Assets* **L.O. 2**

Required
Identify each of the following long-term operational assets as either tangible (T) or intangible (I).
a. Delivery van
b. Land
c. Franchise
d. Computer
e. Copyright
f. Copper mine
g. Plant warehouse
h. Drill press
i. Patent
j. Oil well
k. Desk
l. Goodwill

EXERCISE 9–4A *Determining the Cost of an Asset* **L.O. 4**

East Carolina Lumber Co. purchased an electronic saw to cut various types and sizes of logs. The saw had a list price of $90,000. The seller agreed to allow a 5 percent discount because East Carolina paid cash. Delivery terms were FOB shipping point. Freight cost amounted to $1,000. East Carolina had to hire an individual to operate the saw. The operator was trained to run the saw for a one-time training fee of $900. The operator was paid an annual salary of $25,000. The cost of the company's theft insurance policy increased by $1,100 per year as a result of the acquisition of the saw. The saw had a four-year useful life and an expected salvage value of $6,000.

Required
Determine the amount to be capitalized in an asset account for the purchase of the saw.

EXERCISE 9–5A *Allocating Costs on the Basis of Relative Market Values* **L.O. 4**

Southern Company purchased a building and the land on which the building is situated for a total cost of $600,000 cash. The land was appraised at $140,000 and the building at $560,000.

Required
a. What is the accounting term for this type of acquisition?
b. Determine the amount of the purchase cost to allocate to the land and the amount to allocate to the building.
c. Would the company recognize a gain on the purchase? Why or why not?
d. Record the purchase in a statements model like the following one.

Assets			=	Liab.	+	S. Equity	Rev.	−	Exp.	=	Net Inc.	Cash Flow
Cash	+ Land	+ Building										

L.O. 4   EXERCISE 9–6A *Allocating Costs for a Basket Purchase*

Deeds Company purchased a restaurant building, land, and equipment for $500,000. Deeds paid $100,000 in cash and issued a 20-year, 8 percent note to First Bank for the balance. The appraised value of the assets was as follows:

Land	$120,000
Building	300,000
Equipment	180,000
Total	$600,000

Required

a. Compute the amount to be recorded on the books for each of the assets.

b. Record the purchase in a horizontal statements model like the following one.

Assets					= Liab.	+ S. Equity	Rev.	–	Exp.	=	Net Inc.	Cash Flow
Cash	+ Land	+ Building	+ Equip.									

c. Prepare the general journal entry to record the purchase.

L.O. 5   EXERCISE 9–7A *Effect of Double-Declining-Balance Depreciation on Financial Statements*

Swift Company started by acquiring $160,000 cash from the issue of common stock. The company purchased an asset that cost $160,000 cash on January 1, 2001. The asset had an expected useful life of five years and an estimated salvage value of $20,000. Swift Company earned $92,000 and $65,000 of cash revenue during 2001 and 2002, respectively. Swift Company uses double-declining-balance depreciation.

Required

Prepare income statements, balance sheets, and statements of cash flows for 2001 and 2002. Use a vertical statements format. (*Hint:* Record the events in T-accounts prior to preparing the statements.)

L.O. 5, 6   EXERCISE 9–8A *Events Related to the Acquisition, Use, and Disposal of a Tangible Plant Asset: Straight-Line Depreciation*

Mario's Pizza purchased a delivery van on January 1, 2002, for $30,000. In addition, Mario's had to pay sales tax and title fees of $1,000. The van is expected to have a five-year life and a salvage value of $6,000.

Required

a. Using the straight-line method, compute the depreciation expense for 2002 and 2003.

b. Prepare the general journal entry to record the 2002 depreciation.

c. Assume the van was sold on January 1, 2005, for $20,000. Prepare the journal entry for the sale of the van in 2005.

L.O. 7   EXERCISE 9–9A *Computing and Recording Straight-Line Versus Double-Declining-Balance Depreciation*

At the beginning of 2001, Expert Manufacturing purchased a new computerized drill press for $40,000. It is expected to have a five-year life and a $2,000 salvage value.

Required

a. Compute the depreciation for each of the five years, assuming that the company uses
   (1) Straight-line depreciation.
   (2) Double-declining-balance depreciation.

b. Record the purchase of the drill press and the depreciation expense for the first year under the straight-line and double-declining-balance methods in a financial statements model like the following one:

Assets				= S. Equity	Rev.	–	Exp.	=	Net Inc.	Cash Flow
Cash	+ Drill Press	– A. Dep.	= Ret. Earn.							

c. Prepare the journal entries to recognize depreciation for each of the five years, assuming that the company uses

(1) Straight-line depreciation.

(2) Double-declining-balance depreciation.

EXERCISE 9–10A *Effect of the Disposal of Plant Assets on the Financial Statements*   **L.O. 6**

A plant asset with a cost of $20,000 and accumulated depreciation of $15,000 is sold for $6,000.

Required

a. What is the book value of the asset at the time of sale?

b. What is the amount of gain or loss on the disposal?

c. How would the sale affect net income (increase, decrease, no effect) and by how much?

d. How would the sale affect the amount of total assets shown on the balance sheet (increase, decrease, no effect) and by how much?

e. How would the event affect the statement of cash flows (inflow, outflow, no effect) and in what section?

EXERCISE 9–11A *Double-Declining-Balance and Units-of-Production Depreciation: Gain or*   **L.O. 6, 7**
                  Loss on Disposal

Copy Service Co. purchased a new color copier at the beginning of 2005 for $40,000. The copier is expected to have a five-year useful life and a $4,000 salvage value. The expected copy production was estimated at 2,000,000 copies. Actual copy production for the five years was as follows:

2005	550,000
2006	480,000
2007	380,000
2008	390,000
2009	240,000
Total	2,040,000

The copier was sold at the end of 2009 for $5,200.

Required

a. Compute the depreciation expense for each of the five years, using double-declining-balance depreciation.

b. Compute the depreciation expense for each of the five years, using units-of-production depreciation. (Round cost per unit to three decimal places.)

c. Calculate the amount of gain or loss from the sale of the asset under each of the depreciation methods.

EXERCISE 9–12A *Computing Depreciation for Tax Purposes*   **L.O. 8**

Quality Computer Company purchased $120,000 of equipment on September 1, 2002.

Required

a. Compute the amount of depreciation expense that is deductible under MACRS for 2002 and 2003, assuming that the equipment is classified as seven-year property.

b. Compute the amount of depreciation expense that is deductible under MACRS for 2002 and 2003, assuming that the equipment is classified as five-year property.

EXERCISE 9–13A *Revision of Estimated Useful Life*   **L.O. 9**

On January 1, 2001, Davis Milling Co. purchased a compressor and related installation equipment for $48,000. The equipment had a three-year estimated life with a $6,000 salvage value. Straight-line depreciation was used. At the beginning of 2003, Davis revised the expected life of the asset to four years rather than three years. The salvage value was revised to $4,000.

Required

Compute the depreciation expense for each of the four years.

EXERCISE 9–14A *Distinguishing Between Maintenance Costs and Capital Expenditures*   **L.O. 10**

Chung's Cleaning Service has just completed a minor repair on a service truck. The repair cost was $700, and the book value prior to the repair was $5,000. In addition, the company spent $6,000 to replace the roof on a building. The new roof extended the life of the building by five years. Prior to the roof replacement, the general ledger reflected the Building account at $90,000 and related Accumulated Depreciation account at $40,000.

Required

After the work was completed, what book value should Chung's report on the balance sheet for the service truck and the building?

L.O. 10   EXERCISE 9–15A *Effect of Maintenance Costs Versus Capital Expenditures on Financial Statements*

Alaska Construction Company purchased a forklift for $106,000 cash. It had an estimated useful life of four years and a $6,000 salvage value. At the beginning of the third year of use, the company spent an additional $10,000 that was related to the forklift. The company's financial condition just prior to this expenditure is shown in the following statements model.

Assets				S. Equity			Rev.	–	Exp.	=	Net Inc.	Cash Flow
Cash	+	Forklift	–	A. Dep.	=	C. Stk.	+	Ret. Earn.				
12,000	+	106,000	–	(50,000)	=	24,000	+	44,000	NA – NA = NA			NA

Required

Record the $10,000 expenditure in the statements model under each of the following *independent* assumptions:
a. The expenditure was for routine maintenance.
b. The expenditure extended the forklift's life.
c. The expenditure improved the forklift's operating capacity.

L.O. 10   EXERCISE 9–16A *Effect of Maintenance Costs Versus Capital Expenditures on Financial Statements*

On January 1, 2005, Mountain Power Company overhauled four turbine engines that generate power for customers. The overhaul resulted in a slight increase in the capacity of the engines to produce power. Such overhauls occur regularly at two-year intervals and have been treated as maintenance expense in the past. Management is considering whether to capitalize this year's $30,000 cash cost in the engine asset account or to expense it as a maintenance expense. Assume that the engines have a remaining useful life of two years and no expected salvage value. Assume straight-line depreciation.

Required

a. Determine the amount of additional depreciation expense Mountain would recognize in 2005 and 2006 if the cost were capitalized in the engine account.
b. Determine the amount of expense Mountain would recognize in 2005 and 2006 if the cost were recognized as maintenance expense.
c. Determine the effect of the overhaul on cash flow from operating activities for 2005 and 2006 if the cost were capitalized and expensed through depreciation charges.
d. Determine the effect of the overhaul on cash flow from operating activities for 2005 and 2006 if the cost were recognized as maintenance expense.

L.O. 11   EXERCISE 9–17A *Computing and Recording Depletion Expense*

Valley Sand and Gravel paid $500,000 to acquire 800,000 cubic yards of sand reserves. The following statements model reflects Valley's financial condition just prior to purchasing the sand reserves. The company extracted 350,000 cubic yards of sand in year 1 and 380,000 cubic yards in year 2.

Assets			=	S. Equity			Rev.	–	Exp.	=	Net Inc.	Cash Flow
Cash	+	Sand. Res.	=	C. Stk.	+	Ret. Earn.						
800,000	+	NA	=	800,000	+	NA	NA	–	NA	=	NA	NA

Required

a. Compute the depletion charge per unit.

b. Record the acquisition of the sand reserves and the depletion expense for years 1 and 2 in a financial statements model like the preceding one.

c. Prepare the general journal entries to record the depletion expense for years 1 and 2.

EXERCISE 9–18A *Computing and Recording the Amortization of Intangibles*   L.O. 12

Dallas Manufacturing paid cash to purchase the assets of an existing company. Among the assets purchased were the following items:

Patent with 5 remaining years of legal life	$28,000
Goodwill	60,000

Dallas's financial condition just prior to the purchase of these assets is shown in the following statements model:

Assets					=	Liab.	+	S. Equity	Rev.	−	Exp.	=	Net Inc.	Cash Flow
Cash	+	Patent	+	Goodwill										
94,000	+	NA	+	NA	=	NA	+	94,000	NA	−	NA	+	NA	NA

Required

a. Compute the annual amortization expense for these items if applicable.

b. Record the purchase of the intangible assets and the related amortization expense for year 1 in a horizontal statements model like the preceding one.

c. Prepare the journal entries to record the purchase of the intangible assets and the related amortization for year 1.

EXERCISE 9–19A *Computing and Recording Goodwill*   L.O. 12

Fran Wallace purchased the business Alpha Peripherals for $300,000 cash and assumption of all liabilities at the date of purchase. Alpha's books showed assets of $250,000, liabilities of $30,000, and equity of $220,000. An appraiser assessed the fair market value of the tangible assets at $270,000 at the date of purchase. Wallace's financial condition just prior to the purchase is shown in the following statements model:

Assets					=	Liab.	+	S. Equity	Rev.	−	Exp.	=	Net Inc.	Cash Flow
Cash	+	Assets	+	Goodwill										
400,000	+	NA	+	NA	=	NA	+	400,000	NA	−	NA	=	NA	NA

Required

a. Compute the amount of goodwill purchased.

b. Record the purchase in a financial statements model like the preceding one.

PROBLEMS—SERIES A

PROBLEM 9–20A *Accounting for Acquisition of Assets Including a Basket Purchase*   L.O. 4

May Company made several purchases of long-term assets in 2009. The details of each purchase are presented here.

New Office Equipment

1. List price: $25,000; terms: 1/10, n/30; paid within the discount period.
2. Transportation-in: $900.
3. Installation: $650.
4. Cost to repair damage during unloading: $450.
5. Routine maintenance cost after eight months: $90.

Basket Purchase of Office Furniture, Copier, Computers, and Laser Printers for $40,000 With Fair Market Values

1. Office furniture, $6,000.
2. Copier, $6,000.
3. Computers, $28,000.
4. Laser printers, $10,000.

Land for New Headquarters With Old Barn Torn Down

1. Purchase price, $60,000.
2. Demolition of barn, $3,000.
3. Lumber sold from old barn, $2,000.
4. Grading in preparation for new building, $6,000.
5. Construction of new building, $180,000.

Required

In each of these cases, determine the amount of cost to be capitalized in the asset account.

L.O. 5, 6   **PROBLEM 9–21A** *Accounting for Depreciation Over Multiple Accounting Cycles*

Astro Company began operations when it acquired $25,000 cash from the issue of common stock on January 1, 2005. The cash acquired was immediately used to purchase a $25,000 asset that had a $3,000 salvage value and an expected useful life of four years. The asset was used to produce the following revenue stream (assume all revenue transactions are for cash). At the beginning of the fifth year, the asset was sold for $2,500 cash. Astro uses straight-line depreciation.

	2005	2006	2007	2008	2009
Revenue	$6,000	$6,200	$6,500	$7,000	$0

Required

Prepare income statements, statements of changes in stockholders' equity, balance sheets, and statements of cash flows for each of the five years.

L.O. 4, 5, 9, 10   **PROBLEM 9–22A** *Purchase and Use of Tangible Asset: Three Accounting Cycles, Double-Declining-Balance Depreciation*

The following transactions pertain to Business Solutions Services. Assume the transactions for the purchase of the computer and any capital improvements occur on January 1 each year.

2007

1. Acquired $50,000 cash from the issue of common stock.
2. Purchased a computer system for $15,000. It has an estimated useful life of five years and a $3,000 salvage value.
3. Paid $500 sales tax on the computer system.
4. Collected $20,000 in data entry fees from clients.
5. Paid $800 in fees to service the computers.
6. Recorded double-declining-balance depreciation on the computer system for 2007.
7. Closed the revenue and expense accounts to Retained Earnings at the end of 2007.

2008

1. Paid $550 for repairs to the computer system.
2. Bought a case of toner cartridges for the printers that are part of the computer system, $600.
3. Collected $30,000 in data entry fees from clients.
4. Paid $900 in fees to service the computers.
5. Recorded double-declining-balance depreciation for 2008.
6. Closed the revenue and expense accounts to Retained Earnings at the end of 2008.

2009

1. Paid $2,500 to upgrade the computer system, which extended the total life of the system to six years.
2. Paid $800 in fees to service the computers.
3. Collected $35,000 in data entry fees from clients.
4. Recorded double-declining-balance depreciation for 2009.
5. Closed the revenue and expense accounts at the end of 2009.

Required

a. Use a horizontal statements model like the following one to show the effect of these transactions on the elements of financial statements. Use + for increase, − for decrease, and NA for not affected. The first event is recorded as an example.

2007 Event No.	Assets	=	Liabilities	+	S. Equity	Net Inc.	Cash Flow
1	+		NA		+	NA	+ FA

b. Use a vertical model to present financial statements for 2007, 2008, and 2009. (Record the transactions in T-accounts before attempting to prepare the financial statements.)

PROBLEM 9–23A *Calculating Depreciation Expense Using Four Different Methods*

L.O. 7, 8

O'Brian Service Company purchased a copier on January 1, 2008, for $5,000 and paid an additional $200 for delivery charges. The copier was estimated to have a life of four years or 1,000,000 copies. Salvage was estimated at $1,200. The copier produced 230,000 copies in 2008 and 250,000 copies in 2009.

Required

Compute the amount of depreciation expense for the copier for calendar years 2008 and 2009, using these methods:

a. Straight line.
b. Units-of-production.
c. Double-declining-balance.
d. MACRS, assuming that the copier is classified as five-year property.

PROBLEM 9–24A *Effect of Straight-Line Versus Double-Declining-Balance Depreciation on the Recognition of Expense and Gains or Losses*

L.O. 5, 7

Same Day Laundry Services purchased a new steam press machine on January 1, for $38,000. It is expected to have a five-year useful life and a $3,000 salvage value. Same Day expects to use the equipment more extensively in the early years.

Required

a. Calculate the depreciation expense for each of the five years, assuming the use of straight-line depreciation.
b. Calculate the depreciation expense for each of the five years, assuming the use of double-declining-balance depreciation.
c. Would the choice of one depreciation method over another produce a different amount of annual cash flow for any year? Why or why not?
d. Assume that Same Day Laundry Services sold the steam press machine at the end of the third year for $20,000. Compute the amount of gain or loss using each depreciation method.

PROBLEM 9–25A *Computing and Recording Units-of-Production Depreciation*

L.O. 5, 6

Stubbs Corporation purchased a delivery van for $35,000 in 2007. The firm's financial condition immediately prior to the purchase is shown in the following horizontal statements model:

Assets				=	S. Equity			Rev.	−	Exp.	=	Net Inc.	Cash Flow
Cash	+	Van	− A. Dep.	=	C. Stk.	+	Ret. Earn.						
50,000	+	NA	− NA	=	50,000	+	NA	NA	−	NA	=	NA	NA

The van was expected to have a useful life of 150,000 miles and a salvage value of $5,000. Actual mileage was as follows:

2007	50,000
2008	70,000
2009	58,000

Required

a. Compute the depreciation for each of the three years, assuming the use of units-of-production depreciation.

b. Assume that Stubbs earns $21,000 of cash revenue during 2007. Record the purchase of the van and the recognition of the revenue and the depreciation expense for the first year in a financial statements model like the preceding one.

c. Assume that Stubbs sold the van at the end of the third year for $4,000. Record the general journal entry for the sale.

L.O. 7   PROBLEM 9–26A *Determining the Effect of Depreciation Expense on Financial Statements*

Three different companies each purchased a machine on January 1, 2005, for $60,000. Each machine was expected to last five years or 200,000 hours. Salvage value was estimated to be $4,000. All three machines were operated for 50,000 hours in 2005, 55,000 hours in 2006, 40,000 hours in 2007, 44,000 hours in 2008, and 31,000 hours in 2009. Each of the three companies earned $30,000 of cash revenue during each of the five years. Company A uses straight-line depreciation, company B uses double-declining-balance depreciation, and company C uses units-of-production depreciation.

Required
Answer each of the following questions. Ignore the effects of income taxes.

a. Which company will report the highest amount of net income for 2005?

b. Which company will report the lowest amount of net income for 2007?

c. Which company will report the highest book value on the December 31, 2007, balance sheet?

d. Which company will report the highest amount of retained earnings on the December 31, 2008, balance sheet?

e. Which company will report the lowest amount of cash flow from operating activities on the 2007 statement of cash flows?

L.O. 9, 11   PROBLEM 9–27A *Accounting for Depletion*

Northwest Exploration Corporation engages in the exploration and development of many types of natural resources. In the last two years, the company has engaged in the following activities:

Jan. 1, 2007	Purchased a coal mine estimated to contain 200,000 tons of coal for $720,000.
July 1, 2007	Purchased for $1,800,000 a tract of timber estimated to yield 3,000,000 board feet of lumber and to have a residual land value of $150,000.
Feb. 1, 2008	Purchased a silver mine estimated to contain 30,000 tons of silver for $900,000.
Aug. 1, 2008	Purchased for $880,000 oil reserves estimated to contain 250,000 barrels of oil, of which 30,000 would be unprofitable to pump.

Required

a. Prepare the journal entries to account for the following:
   (1) The 2007 purchases.
   (2) Depletion on the 2007 purchases, assuming that 80,000 tons of coal were mined and 1,100,000 board feet of lumber were cut.
   (3) The 2008 purchases.
   (4) Depletion on the four reserves, assuming that 62,000 tons of coal, 1,450,000 board feet of lumber, 9,000 tons of silver, and 78,000 barrels of oil were extracted.

b. Prepare the portion of the December 31, 2008, balance sheet that reports natural resources.

c. Assume that in 2009 the estimates changed to reflect only 50,000 tons of coal remaining. Prepare the depletion entry for 2009 to account for the extraction of 35,000 tons of coal.

L.O. 5, 6, 9, 10   PROBLEM 9–28A *Recording Continuing Expenditures for Plant Assets*

Summit, Inc., recorded the following transactions over the life of a piece of equipment purchased in 2002:

Jan. 1, 2002	Purchased the equipment for $24,000 cash. The equipment is estimated to have a five-year life and $4,000 salvage value and was to be depreciated using the straight-line method.
Dec. 31, 2002	Recorded depreciation expense for 2002.
May 5, 2003	Undertook routine repairs costing $350.
Dec. 31, 2003	Recorded depreciation expense for 2003.
Jan. 1, 2004	Made an adjustment costing $3,000 to the equipment. It improved the quality of the output but did not affect the life estimate.
Dec. 31, 2004	Recorded depreciation expense for 2004.
Mar. 1, 2005	Incurred $250 cost to oil and clean the equipment.
Dec. 31, 2005	Recorded depreciation expense for 2005.
Jan. 1, 2006	Had the equipment completely overhauled at a cost of $5,600. The overhaul was estimated to extend the total life to seven years.

Dec. 31, 2006   Recorded depreciation expense for 2006.

July 1, 2007   Received and accepted an offer of $9,500 for the equipment.

Required

a. Use a horizontal statements model like the following one to show the effects of these transactions on the elements of the financial statements. Use + for increase, − for decrease, and NA for not affected. The first event is recorded as an example.

Date	Assets	=	Liabilities	+	S. Equity	Net Inc.	Cash Flow
Jan. 1, 2002	+ −		NA		NA	NA	− IA

b. Determine the amount of depreciation expense Summit will report on the income statements for the years 2002 through 2006.

c. Determine the book value (cost − accumulated depreciation) Summit will report on the balance sheets at the end of the years 2002 through 2006.

d. Determine the amount of the gain or loss Summit will report on the disposal of the equipment on July 1, 2007.

PROBLEM 9–29A *Accounting for Continuing Expenditures*   L.O. 9, 10

Kaye Manufacturing paid $26,000 to purchase a computerized assembly machine on January 1, 2001. The machine had an estimated life of eight years and a $4,000 salvage value. Kaye's financial condition as of January 1, 2005, is shown in the following financial statements model. Kaye uses the straight-line method for depreciation.

Assets				=	S. Equity			Rev.	−	Exp.	=	Net Inc.	Cash Flow
Cash	+	Mach.	− A. Dep.	=	C. Stk.	+	Ret. Earn.						
15,000	+	26,000	− 11,000	=	8,000	+	22,000	NA	−	NA	=	NA	NA

Kaye Manufacturing made the following expenditures on the computerized assembly machine in 2005.

Jan. 2   Added an overdrive mechanism for $6,000 that would improve the overall quality of the performance of the machine but would not extend its life. The salvage value was revised to $3,000.

Aug. 1   Performed routine maintenance, $920.

Oct. 2   Replaced some computer chips (considered routine), $620.

Dec. 31   Recognized 2005 depreciation expense.

Required

a. Record the 2005 transactions in a statements model like the preceding one.

b. Prepare journal entries for the 2005 transactions.

PROBLEM 9–30A *Accounting for Intangible Assets*   L.O. 12

Wallace Company purchased a fast-food restaurant for $1,395,000. The fair market values of the assets purchased were as follows. No liabilities were assumed.

Equipment	$600,000
Land	250,000
Building	155,000
Franchise (5-year life)	150,000

Required

a. Calculate the amount of goodwill purchased.

b. Prepare the journal entry to record the amortization of the franchise fee at the end of year 1.

PROBLEM 9–31A *Accounting for Goodwill*   L.O. 12

Branson Inc. purchased the assets of Crayton Co. for $1,200,000 in 2003. The estimated fair market value of the assets at the purchase date was $1,100,000. Goodwill of $100,000 was recorded at purchase. In 2006, because of negative publicity, one-half of the goodwill purchased from Crayton Co. was judged to be permanently impaired.

Required

a. How will Branson account for the impairment of the goodwill?

b. Prepare the journal entry to record the permanent impairment of goodwill.

EXERCISES—SERIES B

Unless specifically included, income tax considerations should be ignored in all exercises and problems.

L.O. 3 **EXERCISE 9–1B** *Using Long-Term Operational Assets Used in a Business*

Required

Give some examples of long-term operational assets that each of the following companies is likely to own: *(a)* Lansing Farms, *(b)* American Airlines, *(c)* IBM, and *(d)* Northwest Mutual Insurance Co.

L.O. 3 **EXERCISE 9–2B** *Identifying Long-Term Operational Assets*

Required

Which of the following items should be classified as long-term operational assets?

a. Prepaid insurance	**g.** Delivery van
b. Coal mine	**h.** Land held for investment
c. Office equipment	**i.** 10-year treasury note
d. Notes receivable (short-term)	**j.** Cash
e. Supplies	**k.** Filing cabinet
f. Copyright	**l.** Tax library of accounting firm

L.O. 2 **EXERCISE 9–3B** *Classifying Tangible and Intangible Assets*

Required

Identify each of the following long-term operational assets as either tangible (T) or intangible (I).

a. Retail store building	**g.** 18-wheel truck
b. Shelving for inventory	**h.** Timber
c. Trademark	**i.** Log loader
d. Gas well	**j.** Dental chair
e. Drilling rig	**k.** Goodwill
f. FCC license for TV station	**l.** Business Web page

L.O. 4 **EXERCISE 9–4B** *Determining the Cost of an Asset*

Custom Milling Co. purchased a front-end loader to move stacks of lumber. The loader had a list price of $100,000. The seller agreed to allow a 4 percent discount because Custom Milling paid cash. Delivery terms were FOB shipping point. Freight cost amounted to $500. Custom Milling had to hire a consultant to train an employee to operate the loader. The training fee was $1,000. The loader operator is paid an annual salary of $30,000. The cost of the company's theft insurance policy increased by $800 per year as a result of the acquisition of the loader. The loader had a four-year useful life and an expected salvage value of $6,500.

Required

Determine the amount to be capitalized in an asset account for the purchase of the loader.

L.O. 4 **EXERCISE 9–5B** *Allocating Costs on the Basis of Relative Market Values*

Angler, Inc., purchased a building and the land on which the building is situated for a total cost of $800,000 cash. The land was appraised at $270,000 and the building at $630,000.

Required

a. Determine the amount of the purchase cost to allocate to the land and the amount to allocate to the building.

b. Would the company recognize a gain on the purchase? Why or why not?

c. Record the purchase in a statements model like the following one.

Assets			=	Liab.	+	S. Equity	Rev.	–	Exp.	=	Net Inc.	Cash Flow
Cash	+ Land	+ Building										

EXERCISE 9–6B *Allocating Costs for a Basket Purchase* L.O. 4

Puckeel Co. purchased an office building, land, and furniture for $300,000. It paid $50,000 in cash and issued a 20-year, 6 percent note to First Bank for the balance. The appraised value of the assets was as follows:

Land	$105,000
Building	210,000
Furniture	35,000
Total	$350,000

Required

a. Compute the amount to be recorded on the books for each asset.

b. Record the purchase in a horizontal statements model like the following one.

Assets						=	Liab.	+	S. Equity	Rev.	−	Exp.	=	Net Inc.	Cash Flow
Cash	+	Land	+	Building	+	Furn.									

c. Prepare the general journal entry to record the purchase.

EXERCISE 9–7B *Effect of Double-Declining-Balance Depreciation on Financial Statements* L.O. 5

Jet Manufacturing Company started by acquiring $120,000 cash from the issue of common stock. The company purchased an asset that cost $120,000 cash on January 1, 2001, that had an expected useful life of six years and an estimated salvage value of $6,000. Jet Manufacturing earned $76,000 and $85,200 of cash revenue during 2001 and 2002, respectively. Jet Manufacturing uses double-declining-balance depreciation.

Required

Prepare income statements, balance sheets, and statements of cash flows for 2001 and 2002. Use a vertical statements format. (*Hint:* Record the events in T-accounts prior to preparing the statements.)

EXERCISE 9–8B *Events Related to the Acquisition, Use, and Disposal of a Tangible Plant Asset: Straight-Line Depreciation* L.O. 5, 6

Green Taxi Service purchased a new auto to use as a taxi on January 1, 2002, for $27,000. In addition, Green had to pay sales tax and title fees of $500. The taxi is expected to have a five-year life and a salvage value of $2,500.

Required

a. Using the straight-line method, compute the depreciation expense for 2002 and 2003.

b. Prepare the general journal entry to record the 2002 depreciation.

c. Assume that the taxi was sold on January 1, 2004, for $15,000. Prepare the journal entry for the sale of the taxi in 2004.

EXERCISE 9–9B *Computing and Recording Straight-Line Versus Double-Declining-Balance Depreciation* L.O. 7

At the beginning of 2005, Sun Drugstore purchased a new computer system for $48,000. It is expected to have a five-year life and a $3,000 salvage value.

Required

a. Compute the depreciation for each of the five years, assuming that the company uses

   (1) Straight-line depreciation.

   (2) Double-declining-balance depreciation.

b. Record the purchase of the computer system and the depreciation expense for the first year under straight-line and double-declining-balance methods in a financial statements model like the following one:

Assets					=	S. Equity	Rev.	−	Exp.	=	Net Inc.	Cash Flow
Cash	+	Comp. Sys.	−	A.Dep.	=	Ret. Earn.						

    c. Prepare the journal entries to recognize depreciation for each of the five years, assuming that the company uses
      (1) Straight-line depreciation.
      (2) Double-declining-balance depreciation.

L.O. 6   **EXERCISE 9–10B** *Effect of the Disposal of Plant Assets on the Financial Statements*

Beltz Company sold office equipment with a cost of $27,000 and accumulated depreciation of $13,000 for $14,000.

Required
a. What is the book value of the asset at the time of sale?
b. What is the amount of gain or loss on the disposal?
c. How would the sale affect net income (increase, decrease, no effect) and by how much?
d. How would the sale affect the amount of total assets shown on the balance sheet (increase, decrease, no effect) and by how much?
e. How would the event affect the statement of cash flows (inflow, outflow, no effect) and in what section?

L.O. 6, 7   **EXERCISE 9–11B** *Double-Declining-Balance and Units-of-Production Depreciation: Gain or Loss on Disposal*

Mark's Photo Service purchased a new color printer at the beginning of 2006 for $28,000. It is expected to have a four-year useful life and a $2,000 salvage value. The expected print production is estimated at 1,300,000 pages. Actual print production for the four years was as follows:

2006	350,000
2007	370,000
2008	280,000
2009	320,000
Total	1,320,000

The printer was sold at the end of 2009 for $1,500.

Required
a. Compute the depreciation expense for each of the four years, using double-declining-balance depreciation.
b. Compute the depreciation expense for each of the four years, using units-of-production depreciation. (Round cost per unit to three decimal places.)
c. Calculate the amount of gain or loss from the sale of the asset under each of the depreciation methods.

L.O. 8   **EXERCISE 9–12B** *Computing Depreciation for Tax Purposes*

Vision Eye Care Company purchased $40,000 of equipment on March 1, 2001.

Required
a. Compute the amount of depreciation expense that is deductible under MACRS for 2001 and 2002, assuming that the equipment is classified as seven-year property.
b. Compute the amount of depreciation expense that is deductible under MACRS for 2001 and 2002, assuming that the equipment is classified as five-year property.

L.O. 9   **EXERCISE 9–13B** *Revision of Estimated Useful Life*

On January 1, 2001, Wayne Storage Company purchased a freezer and related installation equipment for $36,000. The equipment had a three-year estimated life with a $6,000 salvage value. Straight-line depreciation was used. At the beginning of 2003, Wayne revised the expected life of the asset to four years rather than three years. The salvage value was revised to $4,000.

Required
Compute the depreciation expense for each of the four years.

L.O. 10   **EXERCISE 9–14B** *Distinguishing Between Maintenance Costs and Capital Expenditures*

Fast Wrecker Service has just completed a minor repair on a tow truck. The repair cost was $620, and the book value prior to the repair was $5,600. In addition, the company spent $4,000 to replace the roof on a building. The new roof extended the life of the building by five years. Prior to the roof replacement, the general ledger reflected the Building account at $90,000 and related Accumulated Depreciation account at $26,500.

Required
After the work was completed, what book value should appear on the balance sheet for the tow truck and the building?

EXERCISE 9–15B *Effect of Maintenance Costs Versus Capital Expenditures on Financial Statements*   **L.O. 10**

Aloa Construction Company purchased a compressor for $42,000 cash. It had an estimated useful life of four years and a $4,000 salvage value. At the beginning of the third year of use, the company spent an additional $3,000 related to the equipment. The company's financial condition just prior to this expenditure is shown in the following statements model.

Assets			=	S. Equity			Rev.	–	Exp.	=	Net Inc.	Cash Flow
Cash	+	Compressor	–	A. Dep.	=	C. Stk.	+	Ret. Earn.				
37,000	+	42,000	–	19,000	=	40,000	+	20,000	NA – NA = NA			NA

Required
Record the $3,000 expenditure in the statements model under each of the following *independent* assumptions:
a. The expenditure was for routine maintenance.
b. The expenditure extended the compressor's life.
c. The expenditure improved the compressor's operating capacity.

EXERCISE 9–16B *Effect of Maintenance Costs Versus Capital Expenditures on Financial Statements*   **L.O. 10**

On January 1, 2001, Excell Construction Company overhauled four cranes resulting in a slight increase in the life of the cranes. Such overhauls occur regularly at two-year intervals and have been treated as maintenance expense in the past. Management is considering whether to capitalize this year's $26,000 cash cost in the Cranes asset account or to expense it as a maintenance expense. Assume that the cranes have a remaining useful life of two years and no expected salvage value. Assume straight-line depreciation.

Required
a. Determine the amount of additional depreciation expense Excell would recognize in 2001 and 2002 if the cost were capitalized in the Cranes account.
b. Determine the amount of expense Excell would recognize in 2001 and 2002 if the cost were recognized as maintenance expense.
c. Determine the effect of the overhaul on cash flow from operating activities for 2001 and 2002 if the cost were capitalized and expensed through depreciation charges.
d. Determine the effect of the overhaul on cash flow from operating activities for 2001 and 2002 if the cost were recognized as maintenance expense.

EXERCISE 9–17B *Computing and Recording Depletion Expense*   **L.O. 11**

Stover Coal paid $450,000 to acquire a mine with 22,500 tons of coal reserves. The following statements model reflects Stover's financial condition just prior to purchasing the coal reserves. The company extracted 10,000 tons of coal in year 1 and 8,000 tons in year 2.

Assets			=	Stockholders' Equity			Rev.	–	Exp.	=	Net Inc.	Cash Flow
Cash	+	Coal Res.	=	C. Stk.	+	Ret. Earn.						
600,000	+	NA	=	600,000	+	NA	NA – NA = NA					NA

Required
a. Compute the depletion charge per unit.
b. Record the acquisition of the coal reserves and the depletion expense for years 1 and 2 in a financial statements model like the preceding one.
c. Prepare the general journal entries to record the depletion expense for years 1 and 2.

L.O. 12   EXERCISE 9–18B *Computing and Recording the Amortization of Intangibles*

Bevel Manufacturing paid cash to purchase the assets of an existing company. Among the assets purchased were the following items:

Patent with 2 remaining years of legal life	$24,000
Goodwill	20,000

Bevel's financial condition just prior to the purchase of these assets is shown in the following statements model:

Assets			=	Liab.	+	S. Equity	Rev.	–	Exp.	=	Net Inc.	Cash Flow
Cash	+	Patent	+	Goodwill								
90,000	+	NA	+	NA	=	NA	+	90,000	NA	–	NA	=	NA	NA

Required
a. Compute the annual amortization expense for these items.
b. Record the purchase of the intangible assets and the related amortization expense for year 1 in a horizontal statements model like the preceding one.
c. Prepare the journal entries to record the purchase of the intangible assets and the related amortization for year 1.

L.O. 12   EXERCISE 9–19B *Computing and Recording Goodwill*

Sea Corp purchased the business Beta Resources for $200,000 cash and assumption of all liabilities at the date of purchase. Beta's books showed assets of $150,000, liabilities of $40,000, and stockholders' equity of $110,000. An appraiser assessed the fair market value of the tangible assets at $185,000 at the date of purchase. Sea Corp's financial condition just prior to the purchase is shown in the following statements model:

Assets			=	Liab.	+	S. Equity	Rev.	–	Exp.	=	Net Inc.	Cash Flow
Cash	+	Assets	+	Goodwill								
300,000	+	NA	+	NA	=	NA	+	300,000	NA	–	NA	=	NA	NA

Required
a. Compute the amount of goodwill purchased.
b. Record the purchase in a financial statements model like the preceding one.
c. When will the goodwill be written off under the impairment rules?

PROBLEMS—SERIES B

L.O. 4   PROBLEM 9–20B *Accounting for Acquisition of Assets Including a Basket Purchase*

Sun Co., Inc., made several purchases of long-term assets in 2009. The details of each purchase are presented here.

New Office Equipment
1. List price: $60,000; terms: 2/10, n/30; paid within discount period.
2. Transportation-in: $1,600.
3. Installation: $2,200.
4. Cost to repair damage during unloading: $1,000.
5. Routine maintenance cost after six months: $300.

Basket Purchase of Copier, Computer, and Scanner for $15,000 With Fair Market Values
1. Copier, $10,000.
2. Computer, $6,000.
3. Scanner, $4,000.

Land for New Warehouse With an Old Building Torn Down
1. Purchase price, $200,000.
2. Demolition of building, $10,000.
3. Lumber sold from old building, $7,000.
4. Grading in preparation for new building, $14,000.
5. Construction of new building, $500,000.

Required
In each of these cases, determine the amount of cost to be capitalized in the asset account.

PROBLEM 9–21B *Accounting for Depreciation Over Multiple Accounting Cycles: Straight-Line Depreciation*   **L.O. 5, 6**

Hobart Company started business by acquiring $60,000 cash from the issue of common stock on January 1, 2001. The cash acquired was immediately used to purchase a $60,000 asset that had a $12,000 salvage value and an expected useful life of four years. The asset was used to produce the following revenue stream (assume that all revenue transactions are for cash). At the beginning of the fifth year, the asset was sold for $6,800 cash. Hobart uses straight-line-depreciation.

	2001	2002	2003	2004	2005
Revenue	$15,200	$14,400	$13,000	$12,000	$0

Required
Prepare income statements, statements of changes in stockholders' equity, balance sheets, and statements of cash flows for each of the five years. Present the statements in the form of a vertical statements model.

PROBLEM 9–22B *Purchase and Use of Tangible Asset: Three Accounting Cycles, Straight-Line Depreciation*   **L.O. 5, 9, 10**

The following transactions relate to Jim's Towing Service. Assume the transactions for the purchase of the wrecker and any capital improvements occur on January 1 of each year.

2007
1. Acquired $40,000 cash from the issue of common stock.
2. Purchased a used wrecker for $26,000. It has an estimated useful life of three years and a $2,000 salvage value.
3. Paid sales tax on the wrecker of $1,800.
4. Collected $17,600 in towing fees.
5. Paid $3,000 for gasoline and oil.
6. Recorded straight-line depreciation on the wrecker for 2007.
7. Closed the revenue and expense accounts to Retained Earnings at the end of 2007.

2008
1. Paid for a tune-up for the wrecker's engine, $400.
2. Bought four new tires, $600.
3. Collected $18,000 in towing fees.
4. Paid $4,200 for gasoline and oil.
5. Recorded straight-line depreciation for 2008.
6. Closed the revenue and expense accounts to Retained Earnings at the end of 2008.

2009
1. Paid to overhaul the wrecker's engine, $1,400, which extended the life of the wrecker to a total of four years.
2. Paid for gasoline and oil, $3,600.
3. Collected $30,000 in towing fees for 2009.
4. Recorded straight-line depreciation for 2009.
5. Closed the revenue and expense accounts at the end of 2009.

Required
a. Use a horizontal statements model like the following one to show the effect of these transactions on the elements of financial statements. Use + for increase, − for decrease, and NA for not affected. The first event is recorded as an example.

2007 Event No.	Assets	=	Liabilities	+	S. Equity	Net Inc.	Cash Flow
1	+		NA		+	NA	+ FA

b. Use a vertical model to present financial statements for 2007, 2008, and 2009. (*Hint:* Record the transactions in T-accounts before attempting to prepare the financial statements.)

L.O. 6, 7   **PROBLEM 9–23B** *Calculating Depreciation Expense Using Four Different Methods*

Action, Inc., manufactures sporting goods. The following information applies to a machine purchased on January 1, 2001:

Purchase price	$ 70,000
Delivery cost	$2,000
Installation charge	$1,000
Estimated life	5 years
Estimated units	140,000
Salvage estimate	$3,000

During 2001, the machine produced 26,000 units and during 2002, it produced 21,000 units.

Required
Determine the amount of depreciation expense for 2001 and 2002 using each of the following methods:
a. Straight line.
b. Double-declining-balance.
c. Units of production.
d. MACRS, assuming that the machine is classified as seven-year property.

L.O. 5, 6, 7   **PROBLEM 9–24B** *Effect of Straight-Line Versus Double-Declining-Balance Depreciation on the Recognition of Expense and Gains or Losses*

Graves Office Service purchased a new computer system in 2008 for $60,000. It is expected to have a five-year useful life and a $5,000 salvage value. The company expects to use the equipment more extensively in the early years.

Required
a. Calculate the depreciation expense for each of the five years, assuming the use of straight-line depreciation.
b. Calculate the depreciation expense for each of the five years, assuming the use of double-declining-balance depreciation.
c. Would the choice of one depreciation method over another produce a different amount of cash flow for any year? Why or why not?
d. Assume that Graves Office Service sold the computer system at the end of the fourth year for $15,000. Compute the amount of gain or loss using each depreciation method.
e. Explain any differences in gain or loss due to using the different methods.

L.O. 5, 6   **PROBLEM 9–25B** *Computing and Recording Units-of-Production Depreciation*

Telcom purchased assembly equipment for $700,000 on January 1, 2001. Telcom's financial condition immediately prior to the purchase is shown in the following horizontal statements model:

Assets			=	Stockholders' Equity			Rev.	–	Exp.	=	Net Inc.	Cash Flow
Cash	+	Equip.	–	A. Dep.	=	C. Stk.	+	Ret. Earn.				
800,000	+	NA	–	NA	=	800,000	+	NA	NA	–	NA	=	NA	NA

The equipment is expected to have a useful life of 100,000 machine hours and a salvage value of $20,000. Actual machine-hour use was as follows:

2001	32,000
2002	33,000
2003	35,000
2004	28,000
2005	12,000

Required

a. Compute the depreciation for each of the five years, assuming the use of units-of-production depreciation.

b. Assume that Telcom earns $320,000 of cash revenue during 2001. Record the purchase of the equipment and the recognition of the revenue and the depreciation expense for the first year in a financial statements model like the preceding one.

c. Assume that Telcom sold the equipment at the end of the fifth year for $18,000. Record the general journal entry for the sale.

PROBLEM 9–26B *Determining the Effect of Depreciation Expense on Financial Statements*   **L.O. 7**

Three different companies each purchased trucks on January 1, 2001, for $40,000. Each truck was expected to last four years or 200,000 miles. Salvage value was estimated to be $5,000. All three trucks were driven 66,000 miles in 2001, 42,000 miles in 2002, 40,000 miles in 2003, and 60,000 miles in 2004. Each of the three companies earned $30,000 of cash revenue during each of the four years. Company A uses straight-line depreciation, company B uses double-declining-balance depreciation, and company C uses units-of-production depreciation.

Required

Answer each of the following questions. Ignore the effects of income taxes.

a. Which company will report the highest amount of net income for 2001?

b. Which company will report the lowest amount of net income for 2004?

c. Which company will report the highest book value on the December 31, 2003, balance sheet?

d. Which company will report the highest amount of retained earnings on the December 31, 2004, balance sheet?

e. Which company will report the lowest amount of cash flow from operating activities on the 2003 statement of cash flows?

PROBLEM 9–27B *Accounting for Depletion*   **L.O. 9, 11**

Lakeland Company engages in the exploration and development of many types of natural resources. In the last two years, the company has engaged in the following activities:

Jan. 1, 2001   Purchased for $1,600,000 a silver mine estimated to contain 100,000 tons of silver ore.

July 1, 2001   Purchased for $1,500,000 a tract of timber estimated to yield 1,000,000 board feet of lumber and the residual value of the land was estimated at $100,000.

Feb. 1, 2002   Purchased for $1,800,000 a gold mine estimated to yield 30,000 tons of gold-veined ore.

Sept. 1, 2002   Purchased oil reserves for $1,360,000. The reserves were estimated to contain 282,000 barrels of oil, of which 10,000 would be unprofitable to pump.

Required

a. Prepare the journal entries to account for the following:

(1) The 2001 purchases.

(2) Depletion on the 2001 purchases, assuming that 12,000 tons of silver were mined and 500,000 board feet of lumber were cut.

(3) The 2002 purchases.

(4) Depletion on the four natural resource assets, assuming that 20,000 tons of silver ore, 300,000 board feet of lumber, 4,000 tons of gold ore, and 50,000 barrels of oil were extracted.

b. Prepare the portion of the December 31, 2002, balance sheet that reports natural resources.

c. Assume that in 2003 the estimates changed to reflect only 20,000 tons of gold ore remaining. Prepare the depletion entry in 2003 to account for the extraction of 6,000 tons of gold ore.

L.O. 5, 6, 9, 10 **PROBLEM 9–28B** *Recording Continuing Expenditures for Plant Assets*

Cain, Inc., recorded the following transactions over the life of a piece of equipment purchased in 2001:

Jan. 1, 2001	Purchased equipment for $80,000 cash. The equipment was estimated to have a five-year life and $5,000 salvage value and was to be depreciated using the straight-line method.
Dec. 31, 2001	Recorded depreciation expense for 2001.
Sept. 30, 2002	Undertook routine repairs costing $750.
Dec. 31, 2002	Recorded depreciation expense for 2002.
Jan. 1, 2003	Made an adjustment costing $3,000 to the equipment. It improved the quality of the output but did not affect the life estimate.
Dec. 31, 2003	Recorded depreciation expense for 2003.
June 1, 2004	Incurred $620 cost to oil and clean the equipment.
Dec. 31, 2004	Recorded depreciation expense for 2004.
Jan. 1, 2005	Had the equipment completely overhauled at a cost of $8,000. The overhaul was estimated to extend the total life to seven years.
Dec. 31, 2005	Recorded depreciation expense for 2005.
Oct. 1, 2006	Received and accepted an offer of $18,000 for the equipment.

Required

a. Use a horizontal statements model like the following one to show the effects of these transactions on the elements of the financial statements. Use + for increase, − for decrease, and NA for not affected. The first event is recorded as an example.

Date	Assets	=	Liabilities	+	S. Equity	Net Inc.	Cash Flow
Jan. 1, 2001	+ −		NA		NA	NA	− IA

b. Determine the amount of depreciation expense to be reported on the income statements for the years 2001 through 2005.

c. Determine the book value (cost − accumulated depreciation) Cain will report on the balance sheets at the end of the years 2001 through 2005.

d. Determine the amount of the gain or loss Cain will report on the disposal of the equipment on October 1, 2006.

L.O. 9, 10 **PROBLEM 9–29B** *Continuing Expenditures With Statements Model*

Mercury Company owned a service truck that was purchased at the beginning of 2007 for $20,000. It had an estimated life of three years and an estimated salvage value of $2,000. Mercury uses straight-line depreciation. Its financial condition as of January 1, 2009, is shown in the following financial statements model:

Assets				=	S. Equity			Rev.	−	Exp.	=	Net Inc.	Cash Flow
Cash	+	Truck	− A. Dep.	=	C. Stk.	+	Ret. Earn.						
14,000	+	20,000	− 12,000	=	4,000	+	18,000	NA	−	NA	=	NA	NA

In 2009, Mercury spent the following amounts on the truck:

Jan. 4	Overhauled the engine for $4,000. The estimated life was extended one additional year, and the salvage value was revised to $3,000.
July 6	Obtained oil change and transmission service, $160.
Aug. 7	Replaced the fan belt and battery, $360.
Dec. 31	Purchased gasoline for the year, $5,000.
31	Recognized 2009 depreciation expense.

Required

a. Record the 2009 transactions in a statements model like the preceding one.

b. Prepare journal entries for the 2009 transactions.

PROBLEM 9–30B *Accounting for Intangible Assets*   **L.O. 12**

Green Vision purchased Atlantic Transportations Co. for $1,200,000. The fair market values of the assets purchased were as follows. No liabilities were assumed.

Equipment	$400,000
Land	100,000
Building	400,000
Franchise (10-year life)	20,000

Required
a. Calculate the amount of goodwill purchased.
b. Prepare the journal entry to record the amortization of the franchise fee at the end of year 1.

PROBLEM 9–31B *Accounting for Goodwill*   **L.O. 12**

Sulley Equipment Manufacturing Co. purchased the assets of Malcom Inc., a competitor, in 2001. It recorded goodwill of $50,000 at purchase. Because of defective machinery Malcom had produced prior to the purchase, it has been determined that all of the purchased goodwill has been permanently impaired.

Required
Prepare the journal entry to record the permanent impairment of the goodwill.

ANALYZE, THINK, COMMUNICATE

BUSINESS APPLICATIONS CASE *Dell's Annual Report*   ATC 9–1

Required
Using the Dell Computer Corporation financial statements in Appendix B, answer the following questions:
a. What method of depreciation does Dell use?
b. What type of intangible assets does Dell have?
c. What does Dell estimate the useful lives of its intangible assets to be?
d. What percentage of Dell's "identifiable" assets are located outside the Americas? (*Hint:* See Note 10.)

GROUP ASSIGNMENT *Different Depreciation Methods*   ATC 9–2

Sweet's Bakery makes cakes, pies, and other pastries that it sells to local grocery stores. The company experienced the following transactions during 2008.
1. Started business by acquiring $60,000 cash from the issue of common stock.
2. Purchased bakery equipment for $46,000.
3. Had sales in 2008 amounting to $42,000.
4. Paid $8,200 of cash for supplies expense used to make baked goods.
5. Incurred other operating expenses of $12,000 for 2008.
6. Recorded depreciation assuming the equipment had a four-year life and a $6,000 salvage value. The MACRS recovery period is five years.
7. Paid income tax. The rate is 30 percent.

Required
a. Organize the class into three sections and divide each section into groups of three to five students. Assign each section a depreciation method: straight-line, double-declining-balance, or MACRS.

Group Task

Prepare an income statement and balance sheet using the preceding information and the depreciation method assigned to your group.

Class Discussion

b. Have a representative of each section put its income statement on the board. Are there differences in net income? In the amount of income tax paid? How will these differences in the amount of depreciation expense change over the life of the equipment?

ATC 9–3   **REAL-WORLD CASE** *Different Numbers for Different Industries*

The following ratios are for four companies in different industries. Some of these ratios have been discussed in the textbook; others have not, but their names explain how the ratio was computed. The four sets of ratios, in random order, are as follows:

Ratio	Company 1	Company 2	Company 3	Company 4
Current assets ÷ Total assets	74%	54%	15%	13%
Operating cycle	374 days	325 days	21 days	51 days
Return on assets	1.4%	15.5%	9.0%	11.3%
Gross margin	24.3%	84.4%	21.6%	38.0%
Sales ÷ Property, plant, and equipment	3.4 times	3.0 times	2.3 times	1.5 times
Sales ÷ Current assets	0.9 times	1.5 times	12.7 times	7.3 times
Sales ÷ Number of full-time employees	$299,305	$318,350	$30,264	$494,976

These are the four companies to which these ratios relate, listed in alphabetical order:

Anheuser Busch Companies, Inc., produces beer and related products. Its fiscal year-end was December 31, 1999.

Darden Restaurants, Inc., operates restaurants, including Red Lobster and The Olive Garden. Its fiscal year-end was May 31, 2000.

Deere & Company manufactures heavy equipment for construction and farming. Its fiscal year-end was October 31, 1999.

Pfizer, Inc., is a pharmaceutical company. Its fiscal year-end was December 31, 1999.

Required
Match each company with a set of the ratios. Write a memorandum explaining your decisions.

ATC 9–4   **BUSINESS APPLICATIONS CASE** *Effect of Depreciation on the Return on Assets Ratio*

Greentree Publishing Company was started on January 1, 2001, when it acquired $80,000 cash from the issue of common stock. The company immediately purchased a printing press that cost $80,000 cash. The asset had an estimated salvage value of $8,000 and an expected useful life of eight years. Greentree used the asset during 2001 to produce $25,000 of cash revenue. Assume that these were the only events affecting Greentree Publishing Company during 2001.

Required
(*Hint:* Prepare an income statement and a balance sheet prior to completing the following requirements.)
a. Compute the return on assets ratio as of December 31, 2001, assuming Greentree Publishing Company uses the straight-line depreciation method.
b. Recompute the ratio assuming Greentree uses the double-declining-balance method.
c. Which depreciation method makes it *appear* that Greentree is utilizing its assets more effectively?

ATC 9–5   **BUSINESS APPLICATIONS CASE** *Effect of Depreciation on Financial Statement Analysis: Straight-Line versus Double-Declining-Balance*

Qin Company and Roche Company experienced the exact same set of economic events during 2001. Both companies purchased machines on January 1, 2001. Except for the effects of this purchase, the accounting records of both companies had the following accounts and balances.

As of January 1, 2001	
Total Assets	$200,000
Total Liabilities	$ 80,000
Total Stockholders' Equity	$120,000
During 2001	
Total Sales Revenue	$100,000
Total Expenses (not including depreciation)	$ 60,000
Liabilities were not affected by transactions in 2001.	

The machines purchased by the companies each cost $40,000 cash. The machines had expected useful lives of five years and estimated salvage values of $4,000. Qin uses straight-line depreciation. Roche uses double-declining-balance depreciation.

Required

a. For both companies, calculate the balances in the preceding accounts on December 31, 2001, after the effects of the purchase and depreciation of the machines have been applied. (*Hint:* The purchases of the machines are asset exchange transactions that do not affect total assets. However, the effect of depreciating the machine changes the amounts in total assets, expense, and equity [retained earnings]).

b. Based on the revised account balances determined in Requirement *a,* calculate the following ratios for both companies:

(1) Debt to assets ratio.

(2) Return on assets ratio.

(3) Return on equity ratio.

c. Disregarding the effects of income taxes, which company produced the higher increase in real economic wealth during 2001?

WRITING ASSIGNMENT *Impact of Historical Cost on Asset Presentation on the Balance Sheet*   ATC 9–6

Assume that you are examining the balance sheets of two companies and note the following information:

	Company A	Company B
Equipment	$1,130,000	$900,000
Accumulated Depreciation	(730,000)	(500,000)
Book Value	$ 400,000	$400,000

Maxie Smith, a student who has had no accounting courses, remarks that Company A and Company B have the same amount of equipment.

Required

In a short paragraph, explain to Maxie that the two companies do not have equal amounts of equipment. You may want to include in your discussion comments regarding the possible age of each company's equipment, the impact of the historical cost concept on balance sheet information, and the impact of different depreciation methods on book value.

ETHICAL DILEMMA *Good Standards/Bad People or Just Plain Bad Standards?*   ATC 9–7

Eleanor Posey has been reading the financial statements of her fiercest competitor, Barron Bailey, who like herself owns a regionally based heating and cooling services company. The statements were given to her by a potential investor, Jim Featherson, who told her that the statements convinced him to put his investment money in Bailey's business instead of Posey's. Bailey's statements show a net income figure 10 percent higher than that reported by Posey's company. When analyzing the footnotes to the financial statements, Posey noticed that Bailey depreciates all property, plant, and equipment on a straight-line basis. In contrast, she depreciates only her building on a straight-line basis. All her equipment is depreciated by the double-declining-balance method, which she believes matches the pattern of use of equipment in the heating and cooling services business.

Posey arranges a meeting with Featherson in which she attempts to inform him of the effects of depreciation on financial statements. She explains that Bailey's reporting practices are deceptive. While Bailey's income figure is higher now, the situation will reverse in the near future because her depreciation charges will decline whereas Bailey's will stay constant. She explains that Bailey may even have to report losses because declines in the use of equipment also translate to lower revenues. Featherson tells Posey that Bailey's financial statements were audited by a very respectable CPA and that the company received an unqualified opinion. He tells her that nobody can predict the future and that he makes his decisions on the basis of current facts.

After Featherson leaves, Posey becomes somewhat resentful of the rules of accounting. Reporting depreciation in the way that she and her accountant believe to be consistent with actual use has caused her to lose an investor with a significant base of capital. She writes a letter to the chairperson of the Financial Accounting Standards Board in which she suggests that the Board establish a single depreciation method that is required to be used by all companies. She argues that this approach would be better for investors who know little about accounting alternatives. If all companies were required to use the same accounting rules, comparability would be significantly improved.

Required

Answer the following questions under the assumption that actual use is, in fact, greater in the earlier part of the life of equipment in the heating and cooling services business.

a. Are Posey's predictions regarding Bailey's future profitability accurate? Explain.

b. Comment on the ethical implications associated with Bailey's decision to depreciate his equipment using the straight-line method.

c. Comment on Posey's recommendation that the FASB eliminate alternative depreciation methods to improve comparability.

d. Comment on Featherson's use of accounting information.

ATC 9–8   EDGAR DATABASE *Comparing Microsoft and Intel*

Required

a. Using the EDGAR database, fill in the missing data in the following table, drawing on the most current 10-K reports available for Microsoft Corporation and Intel Corporation. The percentages must be computed; they are not included in the companies' 10-Ks. See Appendix A for instructions on using EDGAR. (*Note:* The percentages for current assets and property, plant, and equipment will not sum to 100.)

	Current Assets	Property, Plant, and Equipment	Total Assets
Microsoft			
Dollar Amount	$	$	$
% of Total Assets	%	%	100%
Intel			
Dollar Amount	$	$	$
% of Total Assets	%	%	100%

b. Briefly explain why these two companies have different percentages of their assets in current assets versus property, plant, and equipment.

ATC 9–9   SPREADSHEET ASSIGNMENT *Reporting to the IRS Versus Financial Statement Reporting*

Crist Company operates a lawn mowing service. Crist has chosen to depreciate its equipment for financial statement purposes using the straight-line method. However, to save cash in the short run, Crist has elected to use the MACRS method for income tax reporting purposes.

Required

a. Set up the following spreadsheet to reflect the two different methods of reporting. Notice that the first two years of revenues and operating expenses are provided.

	A	B	C	D E	F	G	H	I	J
1									
2	FINANCIAL STATEMENTS				REPORTING TO IRS				
3									
4					Income Reporting				
5	Income Statement	2001	2002	Total	IRS Income Tax Return	2001	2002	Total	
6	Mowing revenue	90,000	100,000	190,000	Mowing revenue	90,000	100,000	190,000	
7	Operating expenses except depreciation	45,000	50,000	95,000	Operating expenses except depreciation	45,000	50,000	95,000	
8	Income before depreciation and taxes	45,000	50,000	95,000	Income before depreciation and taxes	45,000	50,000	95,000	
9	Depreciation expense (Straight-line)				Depreciation expense (MACRS)				
10	Operating income				Operating income				
11	Gain (loss) on sale of equipment				Gain (loss) on sale of equipment				
12	Income before taxes				Taxable income				
13	Income tax expense (30%)				Taxes payable (30%)				
14	Net income								
15									
16					Reporting of Equipment				
17	Balance Sheet - Assets	2001			Book Value	2001			
18	Equipment				Equipment				
19	Accumulated depreciation				Accumulated depreciation				
20	Book value				Book value				
21									
22					Reporting of Cash Flows				
23	Statement of Cash Flows	2001	2002	Total		2001	2002	Total	
24	Investing Activities								
25	Purchase equipment								
26	Sell equipment								
27	Operating Activities								
28	Income taxes paid				Income taxes paid to IRS				
29									
30									
31									
32									
33									
34									
35									

b. Enter in the effects of the following items for 2001.

   (1) At the beginning of 2001, Crist purchased for $10,000 cash a lawn mower it expects to use for five years. Salvage value is estimated to be $2,000. As stated, Crist uses the straight-line method of depreciation for financial statement purposes and the MACRS method for income tax purposes. Use formulas to calculate depreciation expense for each method.

   (2) No equipment was sold during 2001; therefore, no gain or loss would be reported this year.

   (3) The income tax rate is 30 percent. For simplicity, assume that the income tax payable was paid in 2001.

   (4) Complete the schedules for income reporting, reporting of equipment, and reporting of cash flows for 2001. Use formulas for all calculations.

c. Enter in the effects of the following items for 2002.

   (1) Crist used the mower for the entire 2002 year. Enter 2002 depreciation expense amounts for the income reporting section of your spreadsheet.

   (2) At December 31, Crist sold the lawn mower for $7,000. Calculate the gain or loss on the sale for the income reporting section. Use formulas to make the calculations.

   (3) The income tax rate is 30 percent. For simplicity, assume that the income tax payable was paid in 2002.

   (4) Complete the schedules for income reporting and reporting of cash flows for 2002.

d. Calculate the Total columns for the income reporting and reporting of cash flows sections.

e. Respond to the following.

   (1) In 2001, by adopting the MACRS method of depreciation for tax purposes instead of the straight-line method, what is the difference in the amount of cash paid for income taxes?

   (2) In the long term, after equipment has been disposed of, is there any difference in total income under the two methods?

   (3) In the long term, after equipment has been disposed of, is there any difference between total income tax expense and total income tax paid?

   (4) Explain why Crist Company would use two different depreciation methods, particularly the straight-line method for the financial statements and an accelerated method (MACRS) for reporting to the IRS.

SPREADSHEET ASSIGNMENT *Alternative Methods of Depreciation*

ATC 9–10

Short Company purchased a computer on January 1, 2001, for $5,000. An additional $100 was paid for delivery charges. The computer was estimated to have a life of five years or 10,000 hours. Salvage value was estimated at $300. During the five years, the computer was used as follows:

2001	2,500 hours
2002	2,400 hours
2003	2,000 hours
2004	1,700 hours
2005	1,400 hours

Required

a. Prepare a five-year depreciation schedule for the computer using the straight-line depreciation method. Be sure to use formulas for all computations including depreciation expense. Set up the following headings for your schedule:

		Beginning				Ending	
Year	Cost	Accumulated Depreciation	Book Value	Depreciation Expense	Cost	Accumulated Depreciation	Book Value

b. Prepare another five-year depreciation schedule for the computer using the units-of-production method. Use (copy) the headings used in Requirement *a*.

c. Prepare another five-year depreciation schedule for the computer using the double-declining-balance method. Use (copy) the headings used in Requirement *a*.

d. Prepare another five-year depreciation schedule for the computer using the MACRS method. Use (copy) the headings used in Requirement *a*.

Spreadsheet Tip

After the year 2001, enter subsequent dates automatically. Position the mouse in the lower right-hand corner of the highlighted cell "2001" until a thin cross appears. Click and drag down four additional rows.

10

Accounting for Long-Term Debt

Learning Objectives

After completing this chapter, you should be able to:

1 Comprehend the need for long-term debt financing.

2 Show how the amortization of long-term notes affects financial statements.

3 Show how a line of credit affects financial statements.

4 Describe the different types of bonds that companies issue.

5 Explain why bonds are issued at face value, a discount, or a premium.

6 Show how bond liabilities and their related interest costs affect financial statements.

7 Explain how to account for bonds and their related interest costs.

8 Explain the advantages and disadvantages of debt financing.

9 Explain the time value of money.

the *curious* accountant

Waste Management, Inc., had a net loss of $97 million during its 2000 fiscal year. That same year, Waste Management had interest expense of $748 million. Does the fact that Waste Management had a net loss indicate that it probably was not able to pay the interest owed to its creditors?

Most businesses spend large sums of cash in the course of daily operations. They use cash to replace inventories, pay employees, settle liabilities, purchase supplies, obtain advertising, buy insurance, and so on. For most firms, expenditures for short-term operating activities consume only a portion of the funds needed to keep the business running. Expenditures for long-term operational assets, such as newer, more technologically advanced machinery or improved buildings and plant facilities require even larger amounts of cash. The need for cash is so exhaustive that most companies are forced to borrow some of the funds necessary to accomplish their goals and objectives.

*A variety of options is available for the interest and principal payments associated with borrowed funds. Interest may be paid annually, semiannually, or monthly or may be added to the principal balance of the debt and paid at maturity. Interest rates may remain the same over the term of the loan or may fluctuate with market conditions. Rates that do not change over the life of a loan are called **fixed interest rates;** those that fluctuate are called **variable interest rates**. The principal (amount borrowed) may be repaid in one lump sum at the maturity date of the debt. Alternatively, the **amortization of the loan**[1] can occur over the life of the*

---

[1]The term *amortization* was used in Chapter 9 to describe the process of expense recognition by systematically allocating the *cost of intangible assets* over their useful lives. It will become apparent in this chapter that the word has a broader meaning that applies to a variety of allocation processes. Here the word is used to describe the systematic process of allocating the *principal repayment* over the life of a loan.

loan (paid systematically). Some debt instruments combine these options by amortizing a portion of the debt over the term of the loan with the remainder being due in full at maturity. This type of payment schedule is referred to as an amortization with a **balloon payment.** *This chapter covers the major forms of debt refinancing and the options available for the payment of principal and interest.*

LO1 Comprehend the need for long-term debt financing.

LO2 Show how the amortization of long-term notes affects financial statements.

Long-Term Notes Payable

Notes payable can be classified as short term or long term, depending on the time to maturity. As discussed in Chapter 7, short-term notes mature within one year or the operating cycle, whichever is longer. In contrast, long-term notes payable are used to satisfy financing needs for periods that range from two to five years. Most long-term loans are obtained from banks or other financial institutions, and they frequently require periodic payments of principal as well as interest. To illustrate, assume that Bill Blair obtained the cash needed to start a small business by issuing a $100,000 face value note to National Bank on January 1, 2001. As with other debt-financing activities, the issue of a long-term note payable acts to increase assets (Cash) and liabilities (Notes Payable). The income statement is not affected when the note is issued. The cash inflow is shown in the financing activities section of the statement of cash flows. The effects on the financial statements are shown here:

Assets	=	Liab.	+	Equity	Rev.	−	Exp.	=	Net Inc.	Cash Flow	
100,000	=	100,000	+	NA	NA	−	NA	=	NA	100,000	FA

The note carried a 9 percent annual rate of interest and a five-year term. Principal and interest are to be paid through a single $25,709 payment[2] made on December 31 of each year from 2001 through 2005. Exhibit 10–1 shows the allocation[3] of this payment to principal and interest. The amount of interest paid each year is determined by multiplying the outstanding principal balance of the loan by the 9 percent interest rate. The portion of the payment that is not used for interest acts to reduce the principal balance of the loan. For example, the first interest payment made on December 31, 2001, amounts to $9,000 ($100,000 × 0.09). Accordingly, $16,709 ($25,709 − $9,000) is applied to reducing the principal balance of the loan. The second interest payment is computed by multiplying the new principal balance of $83,291 ($100,000 − $16,709) by the 9 percent interest rate. As a result, the payments for interest and principal reduction on December 31, 2002, are $7,496 ($83,291 × 0.09) and $18,213 ($25,709 − $7,496), respectively. Allocations for the remaining three payments are computed in a similar way. Check your understanding of the amortization schedule by doing the computations required to extend the table for the 2003 payment.

Notice that the amount allotted to interest declines each period while the amount allotted to principal increases because the amount borrowed declines as a portion of the principal is repaid each year. Since the amount borrowed declines, the amount of interest due on the debt also declines.

Although the amounts allotted to principal and interest are different for each accounting period, the effects of the annual payment on the financial statements are the same for each accounting period. With respect to the balance sheet, assets (Cash) decrease. Liabilities decrease by the amount of the principal repayment (see Exhibit 10–1, the column Applied to Principal). Similarly, the recognition of interest expense (see Exhibit 10–1, the column Applied to

---

[2]The determination of the annual payment is based on the present value concepts presented in the appendix to this chapter.

[3]All computations are rounded to the nearest dollar. Rounding differences resulted in the necessity to add an additional dollar to the final payment in order to fully liquidate the liability.

Exhibit 10–1 *Amortization Schedule for Note Issued by Bill Blair*

Accounting Period	Principal Balance on Jan. 1	Cash Payment Dec. 31	Applied to Interest	Applied to Principal
2001	$100,000	$25,709	$9,000	$16,709
2002	83,291	25,709	7,496	18,213
2003	65,078	25,709	5,857	19,852
2004	45,226	25,709	4,070	21,639
2005	23,587	25,710	2,123	23,587

Interest) acts to reduce equity (Retained Earnings). Net income decreases as a result of the recognition of interest. The portion of the cash payment applied to principal should be shown in the financing activities section of the statement of cash flows. The portion of the cash payment applied to interest should be shown in the operating activities section. The effects on the 2001 financial statements are shown here:

Assets	=	Liab.	+	Equity	Rev.	−	Exp.	=	Net Inc.	Cash Flow	
(25,709)	=	(16,709)	+	(9,000)	NA	−	9,000	=	(9,000)	(9,000)	OA
										(16,709)	FA

Exhibit 10–2 shows income statements, balance sheets, and statements of cash flows for Blair's company for the accounting periods 2001 through 2005. Note the differences between Blair's income statements and its statements of cash flow. First, the $100,000 of borrowed

Exhibit 10–2

BLAIR COMPANY
Financial Statements

	2001	2002	2003	2004	2005
Income Statements					
Rent Revenue	$ 12,000	$12,000	$12,000	$12,000	$12,000
Interest Expense	(9,000)	(7,496)	(5,857)	(4,070)	(2,123)
Net Income	$ 3,000	$ 4,504	$ 6,143	$ 7,930	$ 9,877
Balance Sheets					
Assets					
Cash	$86,291	$72,582	$58,873	$45,164	$31,454
Liabilities					
Note Payable	$ 83,291	$65,078	$45,226	$23,587	$ 0
Equity					
Retained Earnings	3,000	7,504	13,647	21,577	31,454
Total Liabilities and Equity	$ 86,291	$72,582	$58,873	$45,164	$31,454
Statements of Cash Flows					
Operating Activities					
Inflow from Customers	$12,000	$12,000	$12,000	$12,000	$12,000
Outflow for Interest	(9,000)	(7,496)	(5,857)	(4,070)	(2,123)
Investing Activities	0	0	0	0	0
Financing Activities					
Inflow from Note Issue	100,000				
Outflow to Repay Note	(16,709)	(18,213)	(19,852)	(21,639)	(23,587)
Net Change in Cash	86,291	(13,709)	(13,709)	(13,709)	(13,710)
Plus: Beginning Cash Balance	0	86,291	72,582	58,873	45,164
Ending Cash Balance	$ 86,291	$72,582	$58,873	$45,164	$31,454

funds is shown under the financing activities section of the statement of cash flows but is not shown on the income statement. Furthermore, only the interest portion of the annual $25,709 payment is shown on the income statement. In contrast, the whole payment is shown on the statement of cash flows (part in operating activities for interest expense and part in financing activities to reflect the principal payment).

With respect to the balance sheet, the amount in the Cash account decreases each year from 2002 through 2005 because the amount of cash paid for principal and interest ($25,709) is higher than the amount of cash collected from revenue ($12,000). The annual $13,709 net cash outflow ($12,000 − $25,709) causes the steady decline in the cash balance. Also note that the liability declines as time passes because the annual payment includes a principal reduction as well as an interest component. In other words, some of the debt is being paid off each year. Finally, note that the Retained Earnings account increases by the amount of net income each year. Since the company pays no dividends, it retains all income in the business.

Security for Bank Loan Agreements

Bankers are interested in securing the collection of principal and interest. To ensure collection, they frequently require debtors to pledge designated assets as **collateral for loans.** For example, a bank usually holds legal title to automobiles that are purchased with the proceeds of its loans. If the debtor is unable to make principal and interest payments, the bank repossesses the car. The car is then sold to another individual, and the proceeds from the sale are used to pay the debt. In addition to collateral, bankers often include **restrictive covenants** in loan agreements. For example, a bank may restrict additional borrowing by requiring debtors to maintain a minimal debt to assets ratio. If the ratio rises above the designated level, the loan is considered in default and is due immediately. Other common restrictions include limits on the payment of dividends to owners and salaries to management. Finally, banks often ask key personnel to provide copies of their personal tax returns and financial statements. The financial condition of key executives is important because they may be asked to pledge personal property as collateral for business loans.

Check Yourself 10–1

On January 1, 2004, Krueger Company issued a $50,000 note to State Bank. The note had a 10-year term and an 8 percent interest rate. Krueger agreed to repay the principal and interest in 10 annual payments of $7,451.47 at the end of each year. Determine the amount of principal and interest Krueger paid during the first and second year that the note was outstanding.

Answer

Accounting Period	Principal Balance January 1 A	Cash Payment December 31 B	Applied to Interest C = A × 0.08	Applied to Principal B − C
2004	$50,000.00	$7,451.47	$4,000.00	$3,451.47
2005	46,548.53	7,451.47	3,723.88	3,727.59

∎ Line of Credit

LO3 Show how a line of credit affects financial statements.

Another form of short- and intermediate-term credit many companies use is the **line of credit.** A line of credit enables companies to borrow a limited amount of funds on an as-needed basis. As long as the company stays within the preapproved boundaries, funds can be obtained and repaid at will. The interest rate usually fluctuates in proportion to the bank's prime rate (the publicly announced rate that banks charge their best customers) or some standard base, such as the rate paid on three-month U.S. Treasury bills (credit instruments issued

Waste Management, Inc., was able to make its interest payments in 2000 for two reasons. (1) Remember that interest is paid with cash, not accrual earnings. Many of the expenses on the company's income statement did not require the use of cash. Indeed, the company's statement of cash flows shows that net cash flow from operating activities, *after making interest payments,* was a positive $2.1 billion during 2000. (2) The net loss the company incurred was *after* interest expense had been deducted. The capacity of operations to support interest payments is measured by the amount of earnings before interest deductions. For example, look at the 2001 income statement for Blair Company in Exhibit 10–2. This statement shows only $3,000 of net income, but $12,000 of revenue was available for the payment of interest. Similarly, Waste Management's 2000 net loss is not an indication of the company's ability to pay interest.

by the U.S. government). The typical term of a line of credit is one year. In other words, the funds borrowed are due for repayment within one year. However, most lines of credit are renewable and for all practical purposes represent a relatively permanent source of financing. So, although they are classified on the balance sheet as short-term liabilities, frequently they are paid off, year after year, by simply renewing the credit agreement.

As indicated in Exhibit 10–3, line-of-credit agreements with banks, insurance companies, and other financial institutions are used widely in business. Approximately 90 percent of U.S. companies provide footnote disclosures regarding credit agreements and include information regarding the amount of the credit line, credit terms, and restrictive covenants.

To illustrate the use of a line of credit, assume that Terry Parker owns a wholesale jet ski distributorship. Parker borrows money through a line of credit to build up inventory levels in the spring. The funds are repaid in the summer months when sales generate cash inflow. Parker's line of credit carries a variable interest rate adjusted monthly to remain 2 percentage points above the bank's prime rate. The following table shows Parker's borrowing activity and interest charges for the current accounting period.

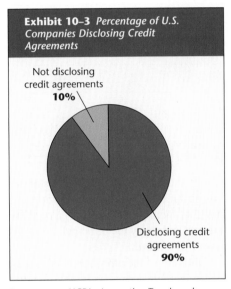

Exhibit 10–3 *Percentage of U.S. Companies Disclosing Credit Agreements*

Not disclosing credit agreements **10%**

Disclosing credit agreements **90%**

Data source: AICPA, *Accounting Trends and Techniques,* 2000.

Date	Amount Borrowed (Repaid)	Loan Balance at End of Month	Effective Interest Rate per Month (%)	Interest Expense (rounded to nearest $1)
Mar. 1	$20,000	$20,000	0.09 ÷ 12	$150
Apr. 1	30,000	50,000	0.09 ÷ 12	375
May 1	50,000	100,000	0.105 ÷ 12	875
June 1	(10,000)	90,000	0.10 ÷ 12	750
July 1	(40,000)	50,000	0.09 ÷ 12	375
Aug. 1	(50,000)	0	0.09 ÷ 12	0

Each borrowing event (March 1, April 1, and May 1) is an asset source transaction. The asset account, *Cash,* increases, and the line-of-credit liability increases. Each repayment (June 1, July 1, and August 1) is an asset use transaction, with the assets and liabilities decreasing. The expense recognition for the payment of monthly interest is an asset use transaction. Cash decreases, and the corresponding increase in interest expense causes equity (Retained Earnings) to decrease. The effects of borrowing, repayment, and interest recognition on the financial statements follow:

Date	Assets	=	Liabilities	+	Equity	Rev.	−	Exp.	=	Net Inc.	Cash Flow	
Mar. 1	20,000	=	20,000	+	NA	NA	−	NA	=	NA	20,000	FA
31	(150)	=	NA	+	(150)	NA	−	150	=	(150)	(150)	OA
Apr. 1	30,000	=	30,000	+	NA	NA	−	NA	=	NA	30,000	FA
30	(375)	=	NA	+	(375)	NA	−	375	=	(375)	(375)	OA
May 1	50,000	=	50,000	+	NA	NA	−	NA	=	NA	50,000	FA
31	(875)	=	NA	+	(875)	NA	−	875	=	(875)	(875)	OA
June 1	(10,000)	=	(10,000)	+	NA	NA	−	NA	=	NA	(10,000)	FA
30	(750)	=	NA	+	(750)	NA	−	750	=	(750)	(750)	OA
July 1	(40,000)	=	(40,000)	+	NA	NA	−	NA	=	NA	(40,000)	FA
31	(375)	=	NA	+	(375)	NA	−	375	=	(375)	(375)	OA
Aug. 1	(50,000)	=	(50,000)	+	NA	NA	−	NA	=	NA	(50,000)	FA
31	NA	=	NA	+	NA	NA	−	NA	=	NA	NA	

LO4 Describe the different types of bonds that companies issue.

▎Bond Liabilities

One of the most common methods of obtaining long-term financing is through the issuance of bonds. An example of a bond certificate is shown at the bottom of this page. The company that borrows money issues (gives) a *bond,* which describes the company's responsibilities to pay interest and repay the principal. *Since the borrower issues the bond, the borrower is called the* **issuer of a bond.**

Obtaining funds through bond issues has advantages and disadvantages. An advantage is that companies are usually able to obtain longer-term commitments from bondholders than they can obtain from financial institutions. The typical term of a bond is 20 years, whereas term loans from banks are normally limited to a maximum of 5 years. Second, the amount of interest may be lower than the amount that banks or other financial institutions charge. Banks obtain much of the money that they use for making loans from their depositors. In other

words, banks use the money that the public deposits in savings and checking accounts to make loans to their customers. Banks profit by charging a higher rate of interest on loans than they pay for deposits. For example, banks may pay 4 percent interest on a certificate of deposit and charge 9 percent for an auto loan. The 5 percent **spread** (9 percent − 4 percent) is used to pay the expenses of operating the bank and to provide a return to the owners of the bank. The spread can be avoided if a company is able to borrow directly from the public through a bond issue. Since bonds are not insured by the federal government, as bank deposits are, businesses have to pay more than the bank rate of interest to encourage the public to accept the risk of default (the failure to pay principal or interest). However, the huge sums of money that pass through the bond markets attest to the fact that the public is willing to accept a higher level of risk to obtain higher interest. Accordingly, companies frequently are able to borrow money by issuing bonds at lower rates of interest than they would have to pay to borrow money from banks or other financial institutions.

Regardless of whether interest is paid to banks or to bondholders, it is deductible in the determination of income for tax purposes. Thus, although interest acts to reduce income, part of the effect is offset because the company pays lower taxes. Furthermore, as discussed in earlier chapters, borrowing activities may even lead to earnings increases. If a firm can generate earnings of 14 percent on assets and can borrow money at only 10 percent interest, the 4 percent differential actually increases the firm's profitability. As noted in Chapter 3, the concept of increasing earnings through debt financing is referred to as **financial leverage.** The concept has been a key element in the generation of wealth for many individuals and corporations. Finally, as with other forms of borrowing, inflation has an advantageous effect in that the debt is repaid with dollars that have less purchasing power than the dollars borrowed.

Some very real disadvantages often negate the advantages just listed. A firm is legally bound to pay the specified interest. In addition, it has a legal liability to repay the principal. Failure to satisfy these obligations can force companies into bankruptcy. If the company is forced to liquidate, the bondholders, like other creditors, have claims on the firm's assets that have priority over the claims of the owners. Even in financially sound companies, bondholders may impose conditions that restrict managers from taking actions that increase the risk of default. Accordingly, the freedom to run the business *any way you wish* may be diminished by the incurrence of debt.

Characteristics of Bonds

As stated previously, a **bond** is a written promise to pay a sum of money in the future to the bondholder. The amount to be paid at maturity is called the **face value** of the bond. In addition to paying the bondholder the face value of the bond at maturity, most bonds include a commitment to pay a **stated interest rate** at specified intervals over the life of the bond. The face value and stated rate of interest are set forth in a contract called a **bond indenture.** The bond indenture also specifies any special characteristics, such as forms of collateral (property pledged as security for a loan), the manner of payment, the timing of maturity, and *restrictive covenants,* which are designed to prohibit management from taking certain actions that place the bondholders at risk.

Security of Bonds

Bonds can be classified as either secured or unsecured; within each category, there are different forms of indebtedness.

1. **Secured bonds** contain a clause that guarantees that the bondholders will be given certain identifiable assets in case of default. A common type of secured bond is a **mortgage bond,** which conditionally transfers title of a designated piece of property to the bondholder until the bond is paid.
2. **Unsecured bonds,** also known as **debentures,** are simply issued on the general credit of the organization. The holders of debentures share claims against the total assets of the

company with other creditors. Often the bond indenture specifies the priority of debenture holders in relation to other creditors. **Subordinated debentures** have lower priority than other creditors, whereas **unsubordinated debentures** have equal claims.

The security of a bond is an important factor to potential investors. There is a trade-off between the risk of default and the magnitude of the return that a bondholder demands for lending money. To entice investors to purchase a bond with considerable risk, an organization must offer very high interest rates. To reduce risk and thereby lower interest rates, companies often include *restrictive covenants* in the bond indenture agreement. These covenants are designed to provide assurances to creditors regarding the payment of principal and interest. Like the covenants included in bank notes, restrictive covenants in bond indentures may limit the payment of dividends to owners or the salaries of key employees. Debt restrictions measured by financial ratios are also frequently included in bond covenants.

Manner of Interest Payment

Bonds also differ in the manner in which the issuer pays interest. They may be either *registered* or *unregistered*.

1. **Registered bonds** are those issued by most corporations. The firm keeps a record of the names and addresses of the bondholders and sends interest and maturity payments directly to the individuals on file. To transfer these bonds, the bond certificate must be endorsed, and notification of the change must be sent to the issuing corporation.
2. **Unregistered bonds,** also known as **bearer** or **coupon bonds,** are commonly issued by municipalities. Interest payments are made to any individual who redeems the coupon attached to the bond. Because no record of the purchaser is kept, coupon bonds are much like cash in that they are vulnerable to theft.

Timing of Maturity

The maturity date of bonds can be established in a variety of ways. Even bonds sold in a single issuance may mature in different ways.

1. **Term bonds** mature on a specified date in the future.
2. **Serial bonds** mature at specified intervals throughout the life of the total issuance. For example, bonds with a total face value of $1,000,000 may mature in increments of $100,000 every year for 10 years.

Often the bond indenture calls for the issuing corporation to annually set aside funds to ensure the availability of cash for the payment of the face value at the maturity date. The company makes payments into what is known as a **sinking fund.** This fund is usually managed by an independent trustee, often a bank, charged with the fiduciary responsibility of investing the funds until the bonds mature. At maturity, the funds and the proceeds from the investments are used to repay the debt.

Special Features

Many bonds have special features that make them more attractive to investors or that allow the issuing corporation more flexibility in its financing activities.

1. **Convertible bonds** may be exchanged by the bondholder for an ownership interest in the corporation. The bond indenture sets forth the conditions under which this exchange may take place. Usually, an investor agrees to accept a lower interest rate in the hope that the value of the ownership interest will increase.
2. **Callable bonds** allow the corporation to pay off the bonds before their maturity dates. This feature is desirable if interest rates decline. Under these circumstances, the company would borrow money at lower rates and use the proceeds to pay off the more expensive bonds.

On November 8, 2001, Enron Corporation announced that it would have to reduce is stockholders' equity by approximately $1.2 billion. On December 2, 2001, the company filed for Chapter 11 protection.

When covering this story, most of the media's attention focused on the overstatement of earnings that resulted from Enron's improper use of a form of partnerships called "special purpose entities." However, these entities were also used to improperly keep as much as $1 billion of debt off of Enron's balance sheet. Why did this matter to Enron? Enron was a very rapidly growing company and it used lots of debt to finance this growth. From 1999 to 2000 its assets grew from $33.4 billion to $65.5 billion, but its debt grew from $23.8 billion to $54.0 billion. This caused its debt to assets ratio to rise from 71.3 percent to 82.4 percent. The higher debt burden put Enron at risk of having to pay higher interest rates, a very unattractive option for a company with this much debt.

Obviously, the call feature is undesirable from the perspective of the bondholders, who do not want to give up their high-yield investment. To encourage investors to buy this type of bond, the bond indenture generally specifies a call price that exceeds the face value of the bonds. The difference between the call price and the face value is commonly referred to as a **call premium.**

Bond Rating

As indicated, many features affect the security of a bond. Several financial services, such as Moody's, analyze the risk of default and publish their ratings as guides to bond investors. The highest rating that can be achieved is AAA, the next highest AA, and so forth. Companies and government entities that issue bonds try to maintain high credit ratings because lower ratings force them to pay higher interest rates.

■ Bonds Issued at Face Value

Fixed-Rate, Fixed-Term, Annual Interest Bonds

To illustrate the effects of a bond issue on the books of the borrower, assume that Marsha Mason needs cash in order to seize a business opportunity. Mason is aware of a company that needs a plot of land on which it can store its inventory of crushed stone. The company agreed to pay Mason $12,000 per year to lease the land that it needs. Mason knows of a suitable tract of land that could be purchased for $100,000. The only problem facing Mason is a lack of funds necessary to make the acquisition.

LO5 Explain why bonds are issued at face value, a discount, or a premium.

When Mason heard some of her friends complaining about the low interest rates that banks pay on certificates of deposit, she suggested that they invest in bonds instead of CDs. She then offered to sell her friends bonds that carried a 9 percent stated rate of interest payable in cash on December 31 of each year. To make the bonds an attractive alternative for her friends, Mason constructed a bond indenture that called for a five-year term and provided the security of having the land pledged as collateral for the bonds.[4] Her friends were favorably impressed, and Mason issued the bonds to them on January 1, 2001.

Mason used the funds to purchase the land and immediately entered into a contract to lease the land. The arrangement proceeded according to plan for the five-year term of the bonds. At the maturity date of the bond (December 31, 2005), Mason was able to sell the land for its $100,000 book value and used the proceeds from the sale to repay the bond liability.

Effect of Events on Financial Statements

Six distinct accounting events are associated with Mason's business venture. These events are summarized here:

1. Received $100,000 cash from the issue of bonds at face value.
2. Invested proceeds from bond issue to purchase land costing $100,000 cash.
3. Earned $12,000 annual cash revenue from land lease.
4. Paid $9,000 annual interest on December 31 of each year.
5. Sold land for $100,000 cash.
6. Repaid bond principal to bondholders.

The effects of these events on Mason's financial statements are now discussed.

Event 1 Bond Issue
The bond issue, Event 1, is an asset source transaction.

Assets (Cash) and liabilities (Bonds Payable) increase. The income statement is not affected. The $100,000 cash inflow is shown in the financing activities section of the statement of cash flows. The effect is shown here:

Assets	=	Liab.	+	Equity	Rev.	–	Exp.	=	Net Inc.	Cash Flow	
100,000	=	100,000	+	NA	NA	–	NA	=	NA	100,000	FA

Event 2 Investment in Land
Event 2 involves the $100,000 cash purchase of land, which is an asset exchange transaction.

The asset account, *Cash,* decreases, and the asset account, *Land,* increases. The income statement is not affected. The cash outflow is shown in the investing activities section of the statement of cash flows. These effects are shown here:

Assets			=	Liab.	+	Equity	Rev.	–	Exp.	=	Net Inc.	Cash Flow	
Cash	+	Land	=										
(100,000)	+	100,000	=	NA	+	NA	NA	–	NA	=	NA	(100,000)	IA

Event 3 Revenue Recognition
Event 3 recognizes the $12,000 cash revenue generated from the rental of the property.

This event is repeated each year from 2001 through 2005. The event is an asset source transaction that results in an increase in assets and equity. The revenue recognition causes net income to increase. The cash inflow is shown in the operating activities section of the statement of cash flows. These effects are shown here:

---

[4]In practice, bonds are usually issued for large sums of money that often amount to hundreds of millions of dollars. Also, terms to maturity are normally long periods, with 20 years being common. Demonstrating issues of such magnitude is impractical for instructional purposes. The effects of bond issues can be illustrated more efficiently by using smaller amounts of debt with shorter maturities, such as that assumed in the case of Marsha Mason.

Assets	=	Liab.	+	Equity	Rev.	–	Exp.	=	Net Inc.	Cash Flow	
12,000	=	NA	+	12,000	12,000	–	NA	=	12,000	12,000	OA

Event 4 Expense Recognition
Event 4 applies to the $9,000 ($100,000 × 0.09) cash payment of interest expense.

This event is also repeated each year from 2001 through 2005. The interest payment is an asset use transaction. The Cash account decreases, and the recognition of interest expense causes a decrease in equity (Retained Earnings). The expense recognition causes net income to decrease. The cash outflow is shown in the operating activities section of the statement of cash flows. These effects are shown here:

Assets	=	Liab.	+	Equity	Rev.	–	Exp.	=	Net Inc.	Cash Flow	
(9,000)	=	NA	+	(9,000)	NA	–	9,000	=	(9,000)	(9,000)	OA

Event 5 Sale of Investment in Land
Event 5 occurs when the land is sold for $100,000 cash.

The sale is an asset exchange transaction. The Cash account increases and the Land account decreases. Since there was no gain or loss on the sale, the income statement is not affected. The cash inflow is shown in the investing activities section of the statement of cash flows. These effects are shown here:

Assets			=	Liab.	+	Equity	Rev.	–	Exp.	=	Net Inc.	Cash Flow	
Cash	+	Land	=										
100,000	+	(100,000)	=	NA	+	NA	NA	–	NA	=	NA	100,000	IA

Event 6 Payoff of Bond Liability
Finally, Event 6 concerns the repayment of the face value of the bond liability.

This is an asset use transaction. The Cash and the Bonds Payable accounts decrease. The income statement is not affected. The cash outflow is shown in the financing activities section of the statement of cash flows:

Assets	=	Liab.	+	Equity	Rev.	–	Exp.	=	Net Inc.	Cash Flow	
100,000	=	(100,000)	+	NA	NA	–	NA	=	NA	(100,000)	FA

Financial Statements

Exhibit 10–4 shows the financial statements of Mason Company. The income statement is presented in a single-step format and therefore does not distinguish between operating and non-operating items. Rent revenue and interest expense are constant across all accounting periods, resulting in the recognition of $3,000 of net income in each accounting period. With respect to the balance sheet, the Cash account increases by $3,000 each year because cash revenue exceeds cash paid for interest. The Land account stays at $100,000 from the date of purchase in 2001 until the land is sold in 2005. Similarly, Bonds Payable remains at $100,000 from the date of issue in 2001 until the liability is paid off on December 31, 2005.

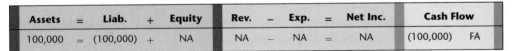 **LO6** Show how bond liabilities and their related interest costs affect financial statements.

It is interesting to compare the income statements for Bill Blair shown in Exhibit 10–2 with those of Mason Company shown in Exhibit 10–4. Note that in both cases, a face value of $100,000 cash was borrowed at a stated interest rate of 9 percent. Both companies also earned $12,000 revenue per year, yet Blair produced a total net income of $31,454 while Mason's net

Exhibit 10–4 *Financial Statements Mason Company*

Under the Assumption That Bonds Are Issued at Face Value					
	2001	**2002**	**2003**	**2004**	**2005**
Income Statements					
Rent Revenue	$ 12,000	$ 12,000	$ 12,000	$ 12,000	$ 12,000
Interest Expense	(9,000)	(9,000)	(9,000)	(9,000)	(9,000)
Net Income	$ 3,000	$ 3,000	$ 3,000	$ 3,000	$ 3,000
Balance Sheets					
Assets					
Cash	$ 3,000	$ 6,000	$ 9,000	$ 12,000	$ 15,000
Land	100,000	100,000	100,000	100,000	0
Total Assets	$103,000	$106,000	$109,000	$112,000	$ 15,000
Liabilities					
Bonds Payable	$100,000	$100,000	$100,000	$100,000	$ 0
Stockholders' Equity					
Retained Earnings	3,000	6,000	9,000	12,000	15,000
Total Liabilities and					
Stockholders' Equity	$103,000	$106,000	$109,000	$112,000	$ 15,000
Statements of Cash Flows					
Operating Activities					
Inflow from Customers	$ 12,000	$ 12,000	$ 12,000	$ 12,000	$ 12,000
Outflow for Interest	(9,000)	(9,000)	(9,000)	(9,000)	(9,000)
Investing Activities					
Outflow to Purchase Land	(100,000)				
Inflow from Sale of Land					100,000
Financing Activities					
Inflow from Bond Issue	100,000				
Outflow to Repay Bond Liab.					(100,000)
Net Change in Cash	3,000	3,000	3,000	3,000	3,000
Beginning Cash Balance	0	3,000	6,000	9,000	12,000
Ending Cash Balance	$ 3,000	$ 6,000	$ 9,000	$ 12,000	$ 15,000

earnings for the same period were only $15,000. The difference is attributable solely to the additional interest that Mason was required to pay because no payment of principal was made until the maturity date. By repaying the loan more rapidly, Blair was able to lower its liabilities and thereby the amount of interest expense.

Recording Procedures

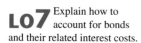

LO7 Explain how to account for bonds and their related interest costs.

Exhibit 10–5 summarizes the general journal entries required to record the six events that Mason Company experienced.

▮ Bonds Issued at a Discount

Effective Interest Rate

LO5 Explain why bonds are issued at face value, a discount, or a premium.

At the time that bonds are issued, market conditions may force a company to pay more interest than the *stated rate* of interest. In other words, if the *stated rate* of interest is too low, no one will buy the bonds. The rate of interest that the issuer must pay to sell the bonds is called the *effective interest rate*. The **effective interest rate** reflects the true cost of borrowing. The amount of the effective rate is dictated by the availability of other investment opportunities. For example, if an investor can purchase a low-risk government bond that yields 8 percent, she

Exhibit 10–5

Event No.	Account Title	Debit	Credit
1	Cash	100,000	
	Bonds Payable		100,000
	Entry on January 1, 2001, to record bond issue		
2	Land	100,000	
	Cash		100,000
	Entry on January 1, 2001, to record investment in land		
3	Cash	12,000	
	Rent Revenue		12,000
	Revenue recognition entries on December 31, 2001–2005		
4	Interest Expense	9,000	
	Cash		9,000
	Expense recognition entries on December 31, 2001–2005		
5	Cash	100,000	
	Land		100,000
	Entry on December 31, 2005, to record sale of land		
6	Bonds Payable	100,000	
	Cash		100,000
	Entry on December 31, 2005, to record bond payment		

or he will be willing to invest in a higher-risk corporate bond only if the return is higher than 8 percent. The rate that is available on a wide range of alternative investments is referred to as the **market interest rate.** Theoretically, the *effective rate* and the *market rate* for investments with similar levels of risk are equal at the time the bonds are issued. However, once the bonds have been sold, the *effective rate* becomes fixed by the price paid for the bonds, whereas the *market rate* continues to vary with the changing economic conditions.

The bond indenture requires that the cash payment for interest be determined by multiplying the *stated rate of interest by the face value* of the bond. In other words, the periodic cash payments for interest are fixed, which means that companies cannot adjust the effective interest rate by changing the periodic cash payments for interest. If a company wishes to adjust the effective rate of interest upward (pay more than the stated rate), it must do so by lowering the purchase price of the bonds. For example, a $1,000 face value bond may be issued for $900. At maturity, the investor who purchased the bond will receive $1,000 even though he or she paid only $900 to obtain the bond. The $100 differential represents an additional interest payment. In other words, the creditor (bond investor) will receive the regular cash payments for interest (stated rate times face value) plus the $100 difference between the face value ($1,000) and the price paid for the bond ($900).

When bonds are sold at an amount below their face value, the difference between the purchase price and the face value is called a **bond discount.** As indicated, bonds sell at a discount when the market rate of interest is higher than the stated rate on the issue date. To demonstrate the accounting treatment for bonds issued at a discount, assume the same facts as those presented in the preceding example involving Mason Company. One additional factor will be considered. Suppose that Mason's friends receive an offer to buy bonds from another entrepreneur willing to pay a rate of interest higher than the 9 percent stated rate contained in Mason's indenture. Although they feel some sense of commitment to Mason, they conclude that business decisions cannot be made on the basis of friendship. Mason is understanding and wants to provide a counteroffer. There is no time to change the bond indenture, so she states that she is willing to accept $95,000 for the bonds today and will still repay the full face value of $100,000 at the maturity date. The $5,000 differential makes her offer competitive, and the transaction for the bond issue is consummated immediately.

Bond Prices

In accounting terms, the bonds were sold *at a discount* for *a price of 95*. As this statement implies, *bond prices are normally expressed as a percentage of the face value* that is received when the bonds are sold. Amounts of less than 1 percentage point are usually expressed as a fraction. Therefore, a bond selling for 98¾ sells for 98.75 percent of the face value of the bond.

Mason Company Revisited

LO7 Explain how to account for bonds and their related interest costs.

The next section revisits the Mason Company illustration. The same six events are examined under a new assumption: The bonds are issued at a discount. This assumption changes the amounts appearing on the financial statements. For example, Event 1 in year 2001 reflects the fact that only $95,000 cash was obtained from the bond issue. Likewise, since there was only $95,000 available to invest in land, the illustration assumes that a less desirable piece of property was acquired. Accordingly, the property generated only $11,400 of rent revenue per year.

Event 1 Issue of Bond Liability
***When bonds are issued at a discount, the amount of the discount is recorded in a contra liability account titled* Discount on Bonds Payable.**

In this case, the $100,000 face value of the bonds is recorded in the Bonds Payable account. The $5,000 discount is shown in a separate contra account. As indicated in the following discussion, the contra account is subtracted from the face value to determine the **carrying value** (i.e., book value) of the bonds.

Bonds Payable	$100,000
Less: Discount on Bonds Payable	(5,000)
Carrying Value	$ 95,000

From Mason's perspective, her company borrowed only $95,000. When the $100,000 is paid at maturity, it will include a return of the $95,000 principal borrowed plus a $5,000 cash payment for interest. Mason will have to continue to make the annual $9,000 ($100,000 face value × 0.09 stated interest rate) cash payment for interest. The additional $5,000 of interest paid at maturity will cause the effective interest rate to be higher than the stated rate.

The bond issue is an asset source transaction with assets and total liabilities both increasing by $95,000. Net income is not affected. The cash inflow is shown in the financing activities section of the statement of cash flows. The effect of the bond issue on the financial statements and the journal entry required to record it are shown here:

Assets	=	Liabilities			+	Equity	Rev.	−	Exp.	=	Net Inc.	Cash Flow	
Cash	=	Bonds Pay.	−	Discount	+	Equity							
95,000	=	100,000	−	5,000	+	NA	NA	−	NA	=	NA	95,000	FA

Account Title	Debit	Credit
Cash	95,000	
Discount on Bonds Payable	5,000	
Bonds Payable		100,000

In the financial statements, the $5,000 debit to the Discount account is offset by the $100,000 credit to the Bonds Payable account. The remaining $95,000 credit balance represents the carrying value of the bond liability.

Event 2 Investment in Land

Event 2 involves the $95,000 cash purchase of land, which is an asset exchange transaction.

The asset account, *Cash,* decreases, and the asset account, *Land,* increases. The income statement is not affected. The cash outflow is shown in the investing activities section of the statement of cash flows. These effects are shown here:

Assets			=	Liab.	+	Equity	Rev.	−	Exp.	=	Net Inc.	Cash Flow	
Cash	+	Land	=										
(95,000)	+	95,000	=	NA	+	NA	NA	−	NA	=	NA	(95,000)	IA

Event 3 Revenue Recognition

Event 3 recognizes the $11,400 cash revenue generated from the rental of the property.

This event is repeated each year from 2001 through 2005. The event is an asset source transaction that results in an increase in assets and equity. The revenue recognition causes net income to increase. The cash inflow is shown in the operating activities section of the statement of cash flows. These effects are shown here:

Assets	=	Liab.	+	Equity	Rev.	−	Exp.	=	Net Inc.	Cash Flow	
11,400	=	NA	+	11,400	11,400	−	NA	=	11,400	11,400	OA

Event 4 Expense Recognition

Although the interest associated with the $5,000 discount will be paid in one lump sum at maturity, it is systematically allocated to the Interest Expense account over the life of the bond.

Under **straight-line amortization,** the amount of the discount recognized as expense in each accounting period is $1,000 ($5,000 discount ÷ 5 years). As a result, there is $10,000 of interest expense recognized in each accounting period. This figure is composed of $9,000 of stated interest plus $1,000 amortization of this bond discount. Compare this amount with the $9,000 charge for interest expense shown in the previous illustration when the bonds were sold at face value (no discount).

Recall that an expense is either a decrease in assets or an increase in liabilities. The $9,000 cash payment for interest is an asset use transaction. The $1,000 portion of interest expense recognition through the amortization of the discount is a claims exchange transaction. This transaction acts to increase liabilities. More specifically, amounts are removed from the Discount account and placed into the Interest Expense account. Since the Discount account is a contra liability account, reducing it acts to increase the carrying value of the bond liability. In summary, $10,000 of interest expense is recognized. The recognition of the interest expense causes equity (Retained Earnings) to decrease. The $10,000 decrease in retained earnings is offset by a $9,000 decrease in the Cash account and a $1,000 increase in the carrying value of the bond liability (a decrease in the Discount account). The effect of the interest expense recognition on the financial statements and the journal entry necessary to record it for each accounting period are as follows:

Assets	=	Liabilities			+	Equity	Rev.	−	Exp.	=	Net Inc.	Cash Flow	
Cash	=	Bonds Pay.	−	Discount									
(9,000)	=	NA	−	(1,000)	+	(10,000)	NA	−	10,000	=	(10,000)	(9,000)	OA

Account Title	Debit	Credit
Interest Expense	10,000	
Cash		9,000
Discount on Bonds Payable		1,000

Event 5 Sale of Investment in Land
Event 5 occurs when the land is sold for $95,000 cash.

The sale is an asset exchange transaction. The Cash account increases and the Land account decreases. Since there was no gain or loss on the sale, the income statement is not affected. The cash inflow is shown in the investing activities section of the statement of cash flows. These effects are shown here:

Assets			=	Liab.	+	Equity	Rev.	−	Exp.	=	Net Inc.	Cash Flow	
Cash	+	Land	=										
95,000	+	(95,000)	=	NA	+	NA	NA	−	NA	=	NA	95,000	IA

Event 6 Payoff of Bond Liability
Finally, Event 6 concerns the repayment of the face value of the bond liability.

This is an asset use transaction. The Cash and Bonds Payable accounts decrease. The income statement is not affected. The cash outflow is shown in the financing activities section of the statement of cash flows. The outflow associated with the repayment of the principal is $95,000. The remaining $5,000 represents an interest charge associated with the discount. In practice, the amount of the discount is frequently immaterial and is included in the financing activities section along with the principal payment.

Assets	=	Liab.	+	Equity	Rev.	−	Exp.	=	Net Inc.	Cash Flow	
(100,000)	=	(100,000)	+	NA	NA	−	NA	=	NA	(95,000)	FA
										(5,000)	OA

LO6 Show how bond liabilities and their related interest costs affect financial statements.

Effect on Financial Statements

Exhibit 10–6 contains the financial statements that reflect Mason's business venture under the assumption that the bonds were issued at a discount. Note that the amount of net income is significantly lower than the amount reported in Exhibit 10–4, where it was assumed that the bonds were sold at face value. The lower income results from two factors. First, since the bonds were sold at a discount, there was less money to invest in land, and the lower investment (i.e., less desirable property was purchased) produced lower revenues. Second, the effective interest rate was higher than the stated rate, thereby resulting in higher expenses. Lower revenues coupled with higher expenses result in less profitability.

With respect to the balance sheet, note that the carrying value of the bond liability increases each year until the liability is equal to the face value of the bond on the December 31, 2005, year-end closing date, which is logical because Mason is obligated to pay the full $100,000 at maturity. Also note that the amount of retained earnings ($7,000) on December 31, 2005, is equal to the total amount of net income reported over the 5-year life of the business ($1,400

Exhibit 10-6 *Financial Statements Mason Company*

Under the Assumption That Bonds Are Issued at a Discount

	2001	2002	2003	2004	2005
Income Statements					
Rent Revenue	$ 11,400	$ 11,400	$ 11,400	$ 11,400	$11,400
Interest Expense	(10,000)	(10,000)	(10,000)	(10,000)	(10,000)
Net Income	$ 1,400	$ 1,400	$ 1,400	$ 1,400	$ 1,400
Balance Sheets					
Assets					
Cash	$ 2,400	$ 4,800	$ 7,200	$ 9,600	$ 7,000
Land	95,000	95,000	95,000	95,000	0
Total Assets	$ 97,400	$ 99,800	$102,200	$104,600	$ 7,000
Liabilities					
Bonds Payable	$100,000	$100,000	$100,000	$100,000	$ 0
Discount on Bonds Payable	(4,000)	(3,000)	(2,000)	(1,000)	0
Carrying Value of Bond Liab.	96,000	97,000	98,000	99,000	0
Stockholders' Equity					
Retained Earnings	1,400	2,800	4,200	5,600	7,000
Total Liabilities and Stockholders' Equity	$ 97,400	$ 99,800	$102,200	$104,600	$ 7,000
Statements of Cash Flows					
Operating Activities					
Inflow from Customers	$ 11,400	$ 11,400	$ 11,400	$ 11,400	$11,400
Outflow for Interest	(9,000)	(9,000)	(9,000)	(9,000)	(14,000)
Investing Activities					
Outflow to Purchase Land	(95,000)				
Inflow for Sale of Land					95,000
Financing Activities					
Inflow from Bond Issue	95,000				
Outflow to Repay Bond Liab.					(95,000)
Net Change in Cash	2,400	2,400	2,400	2,400	(2,600)
Beginning Cash Balance	0	2,400	4,800	7,200	9,600
Ending Cash Balance	$ 2,400	$ 4,800	$ 7,200	$ 9,600	$ 7,000

× 5). Again, this is logical because no dividends were made during the 5-year period. Accordingly, all earnings were retained in the business.

The differences between net income and cash flow are attributable to several factors. First, although $10,000 of interest expense is shown on the 2001 income statement, only $9,000 of cash was paid for interest. The $1,000 differential is a result of the amortization of the bond discount. The cash outflow for the amortization of the discount is included in the $100,000 payment made at maturity. This payment is composed of $95,000 repayment of principal and $5,000 payment for interest.[5] Since there is a $9,000 cash payment for the interest expense in 2005, the total cash paid for interest is $14,000 ($9,000 based on the stated rate + $5,000 for discount). Even though $14,000 of cash is paid for interest in 2005, only $10,000 is recognized as interest expense on the income statement. Although the total net cash inflow over the five-year life of the business ($7,000) is equal to the total amount of net income reported for the same period, there are significant differences in the timing of the recognition of the interest expense and the cash outflows associated with it.

---

[5]In practice, many companies do not separate the discount from the principal for the presentation of information on the statement of cash flows. In other words, the entire face value of the bond liability is shown in the financing section of the statement of cash flows. While this practice is conceptually invalid, it is acceptable as long as the amounts are considered immaterial.

Check Yourself 10–2

On January 1, 2004, Moffett Company issued bonds with a $600,000 face value at 98. The bonds had a 9 percent annual interest rate and a 10-year term. Interest is payable in cash on December 31 of each year. What amount of interest expense will Moffett report on the 2006 income statement? What carrying value for bonds payable will Moffett report on the December 31, 2006, balance sheet?

Answer The bonds were issued at a $12,000 ($600,000 × 0.02) discount. The discount will be amortized over the 10-year life at the rate of $1,200 ($12,000 ÷ 10 years) per year. The amount of interest expense for 2006 is $55,200 ([$600,000 × .09] = $54,000 annual cash interest) + ($1,200 discount amortization)).

The carrying value of the bond liability is equal to the face value less the unamortized discount. By the end of 2006, $3,600 of the discount will have been amortized ($1,200 × 3 years = $3,600). The unamortized discount as of December 31, 2006, will be $8,400 ($12,000 − $3,600). The carrying value of the bond liability as of December 31, 2006, will be $591,600 ($600,000 − $8,400).

Effect of Semiannual Interest Payments

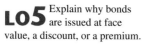**LO7** Explain how to account for bonds and their related interest costs.

Up to this point, our examples assumed that interest payments were made on an annual basis. In practice, most bond indentures call for the payment of interest on a semiannual basis, which means that interest is paid in cash twice each year. If Marsha Mason's bond indenture had stipulated semiannual interest payments, her company would have had to make a $4,500 ($100,000 × 0.09 = $9,000 ÷ 2 = $4,500) cash payment for interest on June 30, and December 31 of each year. The journal entries necessary to record interest for each year are as follows (the entries apply to the bonds issued at a discount):

Date	Account Title	Debit	Credit
June 30	Interest Expense	5,000	
	Discount on Bonds Payable		500
	Cash		4,500
Dec. 31	Interest Expense	5,000	
	Discount on Bonds Payable		500
	Cash		4,500

The same total amount of expense is recognized and paid over the life of the bond. The difference centers on the timing of the cash payments. If the interest is paid semiannually, then cash outflow for interest is made earlier and more frequently. This is a disadvantage from the issuer's point of view because the capacity to use the cash is transferred to the investor earlier. Considering the financial advantages associated with delaying the cash payments, the issuer prefers to make payments annually. However, since investors have become accustomed to receiving semiannual interest collections, bonds that pay interest annually are more difficult to sell. Accordingly, most bonds in U.S. markets pay semiannual interest.

Bonds Issued at a Premium

LO5 Explain why bonds are issued at face value, a discount, or a premium.

When bonds are sold at an amount above their face value, the differential between the two amounts is called a **bond premium.** Bonds sell at a premium when the market rate of interest is below the stated rate. Bond premiums act to lower the effective interest rate to the market rate. Accordingly, they have the effect of lowering interest expense. For example, assume that Marsha Mason sold her bonds for 105. Mason would receive $105,000 cash when the bonds were issued. Even so, she is required to repay only the $100,000 face value of the bonds at the maturity date. The $5,000 difference between the amount received and the amount paid acts to reduce the amount of interest expense. The Premium on Bonds Payable account is shown on the balance sheet as an adjunct liability account (it adds to the carrying value of the bond liability). Accordingly, the bond liability would be shown on the balance sheet as indicated here:

Bonds Payable	$100,000
Plus: Premium on Bonds Payable	5,000
Carrying Value	$105,000

The effect of issuing the bonds at a premium on the financial statements is as follows:

Assets	=	Liabilities			+	Equity	Rev.	−	Exp.	=	Net Inc.	Cash Flow
Cash	=	Bond Pay.	+	Premium								
105,000	=	100,000	+	5,000	+	NA	NA	−	NA	=	NA	105,000 FA

Note that the entire $105,000 cash inflow is shown under the financing activities section of the statement of cash flows even though the $5,000 premium pertains to interest. Conceptually, the premium is related to operating activities. However, in practice, the amounts associated with premiums are usually so small that they are considered immaterial. Accordingly, the entire cash inflow is normally classified as a financing activity.

The journal entries necessary to record the bond issue at a premium and the first interest payment are as follows (the entries assume an annual interest payment):

LO7 Explain how to account for bonds and their related interest costs.

Date	Account Title	Debit	Credit
Jan. 1	Cash	105,000	
	Bonds Payable		100,000
	Premium on Bonds Payable		5,000
Dec. 31	Interest Expense	8,000	
	Premium on Bonds Payable	1,000	
	Cash		9,000

Bond Redemptions

The previous exhibits for the bonds issued by Marsha Mason assumed that the bonds were redeemed on the maturity date. The bondholders were paid the face value of the bonds, and the bond liability was removed from the books. The discount or premium was fully amortized so these accounts no longer existed at the time the bonds were redeemed.

Often bonds with a *call provision* are redeemed prior to the maturity date. When this situation arises, the company must pay the bondholders the **call price,** which is an amount that is normally higher than the maturity value. For example, suppose that Mason's bond indenture includes a provision that enables her to call the bonds at a price of 103. Assume that her client refuses to renew the contract to rent the land at the end of 2003. Accordingly, Mason is forced to sell the land and pay off the bonds. Using the data that assumes the bonds were sold for a discount, there is a $2,000 balance in the Discount on Bonds Payable account on January 1, 2004 (see Exhibit 10–6 for details).

Mason is required to pay the bondholders $103,000 ($100,000 face value × 103 call price) to redeem the bonds. Since the book value of the bond liability is $98,000 ($100,000 face value − $2,000 remaining discount), Mason experiences a $5,000 loss ($103,000 redemption price − $98,000 book value) when the bonds are paid off. Accordingly, cash, the carrying value of the bond liability, and equity all decrease as a result of the redemption. The effect of the redemption on the financial statements is as follows:

Assets	=	Liabilities			+ Equity	Rev.	–	Exp.	=	Net Inc.	Cash Flow
Cash	=	Bond Pay.	–	Discount							
(103,000)	=	(100,000)	–	(2,000)	+ (5,000)	NA	–	5,000	=	(5,000)	(103,000) FA

Note that the entire $103,000 cash outflow is shown under the financing activities section of the statement of cash flows. Conceptually, some of this amount is attributable to activities other than financing. However, in practice, the amounts not associated with financing are usually so small that they are considered immaterial. Accordingly, the entire cash outflow is classified as a financing activity.

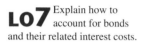
LO7 Explain how to account for bonds and their related interest costs.

The general journal entry necessary to record the bond redemption is shown here:

Account Title	Debit	Credit
Loss on Bond Redemption	5,000	
Bonds Payable	100,000	
Discount on Bonds Payable		2,000
Cash		103,000

The loss on redemption of bonds, if material, appears on Mason's income statement as an **extraordinary item.** Extraordinary items are set apart from operating income to highlight unusual items that are not likely to recur.

▌Tax Advantage Associated With Debt Financing

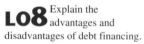
LO8 Explain the advantages and disadvantages of debt financing.

Two important concepts must be understood in order to compare debt financing with equity financing. The first is the concept of financial leverage, explained in Chapter 3. The second is the tax advantage of debt financing. Debt financing is said to have a tax advantage over equity financing because interest payments are deductible for the purpose of computing taxable income. In contrast, dividends are not deductible in the determination of taxable income. The effect of this difference is now described.

Suppose that $100,000 is needed to start Maduro Company. Assume that the company can be started by issuing $100,000 of common stock (equity financing). Alternatively, it can be started by borrowing $100,000 (debt financing). During the first year of operation, the company earns $60,000 of revenue and incurs $40,000 of expenses, not including interest. If stock is issued, the stockholders are paid an $8,000 dividend. Alternatively, if the business is financed with debt, it is required to pay 8 percent annual interest (interest expense is $8,000). Assuming a 30 percent tax rate, which form of financing will produce the larger addition to retained earnings for the business? The answer can be computed as follows:

Computation of Addition to Retained Earnings	Equity Financing	Debt Financing
Revenue	$60,000	$60,000
Expense (excluding interest)	(40,000)	(40,000)
Earnings before Interest and Taxes	20,000	20,000
Interest (100,000 × 8%)	0	(8,000)
Pretax Income	20,000	12,000
Income Tax (30%)	(6,000)	(3,600)
Net Income	14,000	8,400
Dividend	(8,000)	0
Addition to Retained Earnings	$ 6,000	$ 8,400

Note that if the company is financed with debt, it produces $2,400 more retained earnings than if it is financed with equity because the interest expense is tax deductible. If equity financing is used, the company pays $6,000 of income taxes, whereas debt financing requires only $3,600 of income taxes. Accordingly, debt financing saved $2,400 of income tax expense. In other words, the effective cost (after-tax cost) of the debt is only $5,600 ($8,000 interest expense − $2,400 tax savings). In contrast, the $8,000 dividend is not tax deductible. As a result, it removes a full $8,000 from the amount of earnings to be retained in the business. In both cases, the investors or creditors receive $8,000. The difference lies in the fact that under debt financing, the Internal Revenue Service receives $2,400 less.

In general terms, the after-tax interest cost of debt can be computed as

$$\text{Total interest expense} \times (1.0 - \text{Tax rate})$$

In the case of Maduro Company, this formula confirms the previous analysis. The after-tax cost of debt is computed to be

$$\$8,000 \times (1.0 - 0.30) = \$5,600$$

The after-tax interest rate that Maduro is paying can be computed by using the same logic. It is 5.6 percent (8 percent × 0.70). In contrast, there is no difference in the before-tax and after-tax effects of an 8 percent dividend. This means that $1 of dividends cost the company a full $1 of retained earnings, while $1 of interest has an after-tax cost of only $0.70 (assuming a 30 percent tax rate). All other things being equal, debt financing results in higher profitability than equity financing because it lowers the amount of taxes that must be paid. This conclusion assumes that the business is operating profitably. There can be no tax savings if there is no income because businesses that produce consistent losses pay no taxes.

EBIT and Ratio Analysis

Several ratios presented in this book use net income in their computations. In practice, some of these ratios are computed by using *earnings before interest and taxes* (EBIT) rather than net income. One such ratio is the *return on assets* (ROA) ratio, explained in Chapter 3. The purpose of the ROA ratio is to measure how efficiently a business is using its assets. If net income is used in its computation rather than EBIT, the ratio may be distorted by the nature of the company's financing activities.

To illustrate, we return to the example of Maduro Company. Recall that Maduro plans to invest the $100,000 it receives in exactly the same manner regardless of whether it obtains the funds from equity or debt financing. Even so, the ROA ratio with net income as the numerator is 14 percent ($14,000 ÷ $100,000) under equity financing but only 8.4 percent ($8,400 ÷ $100,000) under debt financing. Since the assets are used in exactly the same manner regardless of how they are obtained, the difference between the 14 percent ROA and the 8.4 percent ROA ratios is due to financing strategy rather than asset management. The use of EBIT avoids this discrepancy and thereby provides a better measure of asset utilization. In the case of Maduro Company, the ROA ratio computed on the basis of EBIT is 20% ($20,000 ÷ $100,000) regardless of whether debt or equity financing is used. Since the assets are used in the same manner regardless of how they are financed, the measure of asset utilization should be the same regardless of the method of financing. Accordingly, the use of EBIT in the computation of the ROA ratio provides a better measure of asset utilization. However, for the sake of simplification, continue to use net income when you compute ratios unless instructed otherwise.

Times Interest Earned Ratio

Debt financing is not without disadvantages. The increased risk to a business that uses more debt versus less debt has been noted. Financial statement users have ratios that help assess this risk. One is the debt to assets ratio, explained in Chapter 3. Another is the **times interest earned ratio,** defined as

EBIT
_____
Interest expense

Because the amount of earnings before interest and taxes is available for the payment of interest, the times interest earned ratio must be based on EBIT, not on net income. This ratio tells *how many times* a company would be able to pay its interest by using the amount of earnings available to make interest payments. The higher the ratio, the less likely a company is to find itself in the unfortunate position of being unable to make its interest payments. Since the failure to pay interest can lead to bankruptcy, higher times interest earned ratios suggest lower levels of risk. Shown here are the times interest earned ratios and debt to assets ratios for six real-world companies. These numbers are for 2000.

Industry	Company	Times Interest Earned	Debt to Assets
Breakfast Cereal	Kellogg's	7.31 times	0.82
	Quaker Oats	11.21	0.84
Tools	Black & Decker	3.73	0.83
	Stanley Works	11.84	0.61
Hotel	Hilton Hotels	3.38	0.85
	Marriott	8.57	0.60

Sometimes companies have times interest earned ratios that are negative numbers, yet these companies are still able to make the required interest payments to their creditors. Remember that bills are paid with cash, not net income. The fact that a company has no EBIT does not mean that it does not have cash provided by operations. This case demonstrates the fact that effective financial statement analysis cannot be accomplished on the basis of any single ratio or, for that matter, any set of ratios. Ratios must be used in conjunction with one another and with other information to make rational business decisions. A company with terrible ratios and a patent on a newly discovered drug that cures cancer may be a far better investment than a company with great ratios and a patent on a chemotherapy product that will soon be out of date. Remember that ratios are based on historical facts. They are useful only to the extent that history is likely to repeat itself.

Check Yourself 10–3

Selected financial data pertaining to Shaver and Goode Companies follow (amounts are in thousands):

	Shaver Company	Goode Company
Earnings before interest and taxes	$750,720	$2,970,680
Interest expense	234,600	645,800

Based on this information, which company is more likely to be able to make its interest payments?

Answer The times interest earned ratio for Shaver Company is 3.2 ($750,720 ÷ $234,600) times. The times interest earned ratio for Goode Company is 4.6 ($2,970,680 ÷ $645,800) times. Based on this data, Goode Company is more likely to be able to make its interest payments.

a look back

This chapter addressed the basic issues related to accounting for long-term debt. *Long-term notes* have a maturity period of between two to five years and usually require payments that include a return of principal plus interest. A *line of credit* enables companies to borrow a limited amount of funds on an as-needed basis. Although a line of credit normally carries a term of one year, companies frequently refinance, thereby extending the effective maturity date to the intermediate range of five or more years. Interest for a line of credit is normally paid on a monthly basis.

Long-term debt financing with terms exceeding 10 years is usually accomplished through the issue of *bonds*. Bond agreements normally commit a company to *semiannual interest* at an amount that is equal to a fixed percentage of the face value. The amount of interest required by the bond agreement is called the *stated interest rate*. If bonds are sold when the *market interest rate* is different from the stated interest rate, companies are required to issue the bonds at a price above or below the face value. They must do this to achieve an effective rate of interest that is consistent with market conditions. Selling bonds at a *discount* (below face value) increases the effective interest rate above the stated rate. Selling bonds at a *premium* decreases the effective rate of interest.

This chapter explained the tax advantages of using debt financing versus equity financing. Basically, interest is a *tax-deductible expense* that is subtracted prior to the determination of taxable income. In contrast, distributions to owners such as dividends are not deductible in the determination of taxable income.

a look
forward

A company that needs long-term financing might choose to use debt, such as the types of bonds or term loans that were discussed in this chapter. Owners' equity is another source of long-term financing. Several equity alternatives are available, depending on the type of business organization the owners choose to establish. For example, a company could be organized as a sole proprietorship, partnership, or corporation. Chapter 11 presents some accounting issues related to equity transactions of each of these types of business structures.

SELF-STUDY REVIEW PROBLEM

During 2004 and 2005, Herring Corp. completed the following selected transactions relating to its bond issue. The corporation's fiscal year ends on December 31.

2004

Jan. 1 — Sold $400,000 of 10–year, 9 percent bonds at 97. Interest is payable in cash on December 31 each year.

Dec. 31 — Paid the bond interest and recorded the amortization of the discount using the straight-line method.

2005

Dec. 31 — Paid the bond interest and recorded the amortization of the discount using the straight-line method.

Required

a. Show how these events would affect Herring's financial statements by recording them in a financial statements model like the following one.

	Assets	=	Liabilities			+	Equity	Rev.	−	Exp.	=	Net Inc.	Cash Flow
	Cash	=	Bond Pay.	−	Discount	+	Ret. Ear.						
1/1/04													
12/31/04													
12/31/05													

b. Determine the carrying value of the bond liability as of December 31, 2005.

c. Assuming Herring had earnings before interest and taxes of $198,360 in 2005, calculate the times interest earned ratio.

Solution to Requirements a–c

a.

	Assets	=		Liabilities			+	Equity		Rev.	–	Exp.	=	Net Inc.		Cash Flow	
	Cash	=	Bond Pay.	–	Discount		+	Ret. Ear.									
1/1/04	388,000	=	400,000	–	12,000		+	NA		NA	–	NA	=	NA		388,000	FA
12/31/04	(36,000)	=	NA	–	(1,200)		+	(37,200)		NA	–	37,200	=	(37,200)		(36,000)	OA
12/31/05	(36,000)	=	NA	–	(1,200)		+	(37,200)		NA	–	37,200	=	(37,200)		(36,000)	OA

b. The unamortized discount as of December 31, 2005, is $9,600 ($12,000 − $1,200 − $1,200). The carrying value of the bond liability is $390,400 ($400,000 − $9,600).

c. The times interest earned ratio is 5.3 times ($198,360 ÷ $37,200).

APPENDIX

LO9 Explain the time value of money.

Time Value of Money

Future Value

Suppose that you recently won a $10,000 cash prize in a local lottery. You decide to save the money to have funds available to obtain a masters of business administration (MBA) degree. You plan to enter the program three years from today. Assuming that you invest the money in an account that earns 8 percent annual interest, how much money will you have available in three years? The answer depends on whether your investment will earn *simple* or *compound* interest.

To determine the amount of funds available assuming that you earn 8 percent **simple interest,** multiply the principal balance by the interest rate to determine the amount of interest earned per year ($10,000 × 0.08 = $800). Next, multiply the amount of annual interest by the number of years for which the funds will be invested ($800 × 3 = $2,400). Finally, add the interest earned to the principal balance to determine the total amount of funds available at the end of the three-year term ($10,000 principal + $2,400 interest = $12,400 cash available at the end of three years).

Most investors can increase their returns by reinvesting the income earned from their investments. For example, at the beginning of the second year, you will have available for investment not only the original $10,000 principal balance but also $800 of interest earned during the first year. In other words, you will be able to earn interest on the interest that you previously earned. The practice of earning interest on interest is called **compounding.** Assuming that you are able to earn 8 percent compound interest, the amount of funds available to you at the end of three years can be computed, as shown in Exhibit 10–7.

Obviously, you earn more with compound interest ($2,597.12 compound versus $2,400 simple). The number of computations required for **compound interest** can become cumbersome when the investment term is long. Fortunately, there are mathematical formulas, interest tables, and computer programs that reduce the computational burden. For example, a compound interest factor can be developed from the formula

$$(1 + i)^n$$

where i = interest
n = number of periods

The value of the investment is determined by multiplying the compound-interest factor by the principal balance. The compound-interest factor for a three-year term and an 8 percent interest rate is 1.259712

Exhibit 10–7										
Year	Amount Invested	×	Interest Rate	=	Interest Earned	+	Amount Invested	=	New Balance
1	$10,000.00	×	0.08	=	$ 800.00	+	$10,000.00	=	$10,800.00
2	10,800.00	×	0.08	=	864.00	+	10,800.00	=	11,664.00
3	11,664.00	×	0.08	=	933.12	+	11,664.00	=	12,597.12
	Total interest earned			=	$2,597.12				

(1.08 × 1.08 × 1.08 = 1.259712). Assuming a $10,000 original investment, the value of the investment at the end of three years is $12,597.12 ($10,000 × 1.259712). This is, of course, the same amount that was computed in the previous illustration (see final figure in the New Balance column of Exhibit 10–7).

The mathematical formulas have been used to develop tables containing interest factors that can be used to determine the **future value** of an investment under a variety of interest rates and time periods. For example, Table I on page 491 contains the interest factor for an investment with a three-year term earning 8 percent compound interest. To confirm this point, move down the column marked n to the third period. Next move across to the column marked 8%, where you will find the value 1.259712. This is identical to the amount computed by using the mathematical formula in the preceding paragraph. Here also, the value of the investment at the end of three years can be determined by multiplying the principal balance by the compound interest factor ($10,000 × 1.259712 = $12,597.12). These same factors and amounts can be determined through the use of computer programs contained in calculators and spreadsheet software.

Clearly, a variety of ways can be used to determine the future value of an investment, given a principal balance, interest rate, and term to maturity. In our case, we showed that your original investment of $10,000 would be worth $12,597 in three years, assuming an 8 percent compound interest rate. Suppose that you determine that this amount is insufficient to get you through the MBA program you want to complete. Indeed, assume that you believe you will need $18,000 three years from today to sustain yourself while you finish the degree. Suppose your parents agree to cover the shortfall. They ask how much money you need today in order to have $18,000 three years from now.

Present Value

The mathematical formula required to convert the future value of a dollar to its **present value** equivalent is

$$\frac{1}{(1 + i)^n}$$

where i = interest
n = number of periods

For easy conversion, the formula has been used to develop Table II, titled Present Value of $1. At an 8 percent annual compound interest rate, the present value equivalent of $18,000 to be received three years from today is computed as follows: Move down the far-left column to the spot where n = 3. Next, move right to the column marked 8%. At this point, you should see the interest factor 0.793832. Multiplying this factor by the desired future value of $18,000 yields the present value result of $14,288.98 ($18,000 × 0.793832). This means that if you invest $14,288.98 (present value) today at an annual compound-interest rate of 8 percent, you will have the $18,000 (future value) you need to enter the MBA program three years from now.

If you currently have $10,000, you will need an additional $4,288.98 from your parents to make the required $14,288.98 investment that will yield the future value of $18,000 you need to enter the MBA program. In other words, having $14,288.98 today is the same thing as having $18,000 three years from today, assuming you can earn 8 percent compound interest. To validate this conclusion, use Table I to determine the future value of $14,288.98, given a three-year term and an 8 percent annual compound interest. As previously indicated, the future-value conversion factor under these conditions is 1.259712. Multiplying this factor by the $14,288.98 present value produces the expected future value of $18,000 ($14,288.98 × 1.259712 = $18,000). Accordingly, the factors in Table I can be used to convert present values to future values, and the corresponding factors in Table II are used to convert future values to present values.

Future Value Annuities

The previous examples described present and future values associated with a single lump-sum payment. Many financial transactions involve a series of payments. To illustrate, we return to the example in which you want to have $18,000 available three years from today. We continue the assumption that you can earn 8 percent compound interest. However, now we assume that you do not have $14,288.98 to invest today. Instead, you decide to save part of the money during each of the next three years. How much money must you save each year to have $18,000 at the end of three years? *The series of equal payments made over a number of periods in order to acquire a future value is called an* **annuity.** The factors contained in Table III, Future Value of an Annuity of $1, can be used to determine the amount of the annuity needed to produce the desired $18,000 future value. The table is constructed so that future values can be determined by multiplying the conversion factor by the amount of the annuity. These relationships can be expressed algebraically as follows:

Amount of annuity payment × Table conversion factor = Future value

To determine the amount of the required annuity payment in our example, first locate the future value conversion factor. In Table III, move down the first column on the left-hand side until you locate period 3. Next move to the right until you locate the 8% column. At this location you will see a conversion factor of 3.2464. This factor can be used to determine the amount of the annuity payment as indicated here:

Amount of annuity payment × Table conversion factor = Future value
Amount of annuity payment = Future value ÷ Table conversion factor
Amount of annuity payment = $18,000.00 ÷ 3.2464
Amount of annuity payment = $5,544.60

If you deposit $5,544.60 in an investment account at the end of each of the next three years,[6] the investment account balance will be $18,000, assuming your investment earns 8 percent interest compounded annually. This conclusion is validated by the following schedule.

End of Year	Beg. Acct. Bal.	+	Interest Computation	+	Payment	=	End. Acct. Bal.
1	NA	+	NA	+	$5,544.60	=	$ 5,544.60
2	$ 5,544.60	+	$ 5,544.60 × 0.08 = $443.57	+	5,544.60	=	11,532.77
3	11,532.77	+	11,532.77 × 0.08 = 922.62	+	5,544.60	=	18,000.00*

*Total does not add exactly due to rounding.

Present Value Annuities

We previously demonstrated that a future value of $18,000 is equivalent to a present value of $14,288.98, given annual compound interest of 8 percent for a three-year period. Accordingly, if the future value of a $5,544.60 annuity is for three years equivalent to $18,000, that same annuity should have a present value of $14,288.98. We can test this conclusion by using the conversion factors shown in Table IV, Present Value of an Annuity of $1. The present value annuity table is constructed so that present values can be determined by multiplying the conversion factor by the amount of the annuity. These relationships can be expressed algebraically as follows:

Amount of annuity payment × Table conversion factor = Present value

To determine the present value of the annuity payment in our example, first locate the present value conversion factor. In Table IV, move down the first column on the left-hand side until you locate period 3. Next move to the right until you locate the column for the 8% interest rate. At this location you will see a conversion factor of 2.577097. This factor can be used to determine the amount of the present value of the annuity payment, as indicated:

Amount of annuity payment × Table conversion factor = Present value
$5,544.60 × 2.577097 = $14,288.97*

In summary, Tables III and IV can be used to convert annuities to future or present values for a variety of different assumptions regarding interest rates and time periods.

Business Applications

Long-Term Notes Payable

In the early part of this chapter, we considered a case in which Bill Blair borrowed $100,000 from National Bank. We indicated that Blair agreed to repay the bank through a series of annual payments (an *annuity*) in the amount of $25,709 each. How was this amount determined? Recall that Blair agreed to pay the bank 9 percent interest over a five-year term. Under these circumstances, we are trying to find the annuity equivalent to the $100,000 present value that the bank is loaning Blair. The first step in determining the annuity (annual payment) is to locate the appropriate present value conversion factor from Table IV. At the fifth row under the 9% column, you will find the value 3.889651. This factor can be used to determine the amount of the annuity payment as indicated here:

[6]A payment made at the end of a period is known as an *ordinary annuity*. A payment made at the beginning of a period is called an *annuity due*. Tables are generally set up to assume ordinary annuities. Minor adjustments must be made when dealing with an annuity due. For the purposes of this text, we consider all annuities to be ordinary.
*The 1 cent difference between this value and the expected value of $14,288.98 is due to rounding.

Amount of annuity payment × Table conversion factor = Present value
Amount of annuity payment = Present value ÷ Table conversion factor
Amount of annuity payment = $100,000 ÷ 3.889651
Amount of annuity payment = $25,709

There are many applications in which debt repayment is accomplished through annuities. Common examples with which you are probably familiar include auto loans and home mortgages. Payment schedules for such loans may be determined from the interest tables, as demonstrated here. However, most real-world businesses have further refined the computational process through the use of sophisticated computer programs. The software program prompts the user to provide the relevant information regarding the present value of the amount borrowed, number of payments, and interest rate. Given this information and a few simple keystrokes, the computer program produces the amount of the amortization payment along with an amortization schedule showing the amounts of principal and interest payments over the life of the loan. Similar results can be accomplished with spreadsheet software applications such as Excel and Lotus. Even many handheld calculators have present and future value functions that enable users to quickly compute annuity payments for an infinite number of interest rate and time period assumptions.

Bond Liabilities Determine Price

We discussed the use of discounts and premiums as means of producing an effective rate of interest that is higher or lower than the stated rate of interest. For example, if the stated rate of interest is lower than the market rate of interest at the time the bonds are issued, the issuer can increase the effective interest rate by selling the bonds for a price lower than their face value. At maturity, the issuer will settle the obligation by paying the face value of the bond. The difference between the discounted bond price and the face value of the bond is additional interest. To illustrate, assume that Tower Company issues $100,000 face value bonds with a 20-year term and a 9 percent stated rate of annual interest. At the time the bonds are issued, the market rate of interest for bonds of comparable risk is 10 percent annual interest. For what amount would Tower Company be required to sell the bonds in order to move its 9 percent stated rate of interest to an effective rate of 10 percent?

Information from present value Tables II and IV is required to determine the amount of the discount required to produce a 10% effective rate of interest. First, we define the future cash flows that will be generated by the bonds. Based on the stated interest rate, the bonds will pay $9,000 ($100,000 face value × 0.09 interest) interest per year. This constitutes a 20-year annuity that should be discounted back to its present value equivalent. Also, at the end of 20 years, the bonds will require a single $100,000 lump-sum payment to settle the principal obligation. This amount must also be discounted back to its present value in order to determine the bond price. The computations required to determine the discounted bond price are shown here:

Present value of principal	$100,000 × 0.148644	=	$14,864.40
	(Table II, n = 20, i = 10%)		
Present value of interest	$9,000 × 8.513564	=	76,622.08
	(Table IV, n = 20, i = 10%)		
Bond Price			$91,486.48

Tower Company bonds sell at an $8,513.52 discount ($100,000 − $91,486.48) to produce a 10 percent effective interest rate. Note carefully that in these computations, the stated rate of interest was used to determine the amount of cash flow, and the effective rate of interest was used to determine the table conversion factor.

Bond Liabilities: Effective Interest Method of Amortization

To this point, the straight-line method has been used to amortize bond discounts or premiums. This method is commonly used in practice because it is simple to apply and easy to understand. However, the method is theoretically deficient because it results in the recognition of a constant amount of interest expense while the carrying value of the bond liability fluctuates. Consider the discount on Tower Company bonds just discussed as an example. In this case, the amount of interest expense recognized each period is computed as follows:

Stated rate of interest	$100,000.00 × 0.09	=	$9,000.00
Amortization of discount	$8,513.52 ÷ 20	=	425.68
Interest expense recognized each accounting period		=	$9,425.68

As previously demonstrated, the amortization of the bond discount acts to increase the carrying value of the bond liability. Accordingly, under the straight-line method, the bond liability increases while the amount of interest expense recognized remains constant. Logically, the amount of interest expense should increase as the amount of liability increases. This rational relationship can be accomplished by applying the **effective interest rate method** to the amortization of bond discounts and premiums. The effective interest rate method is required when the result of its application will cause a material effect on the financial statements.

Under the effective interest rate method, the amount of interest expense recognized in the financial statements is determined by multiplying the effective rate of interest by the carrying value of the bond liability. The amount of the discount to be amortized is determined by the difference between the interest expense and the cash outflow, as defined by the stated rate of interest. The following schedule demonstrates the application of the effective interest rate method for the recognition of interest expense during the first three years that Tower Company bonds were outstanding.

End of Year	Cash Payment	Interest Expense	Discount Amortization	Carrying Value
1	$9,000*	$9,148.65†	$148.65‡	$91,635.13§
2	9,000	9,163.51	163.51	91,798.64
3	9,000	9,179.86	179.86	91,978.50

*Cash outflow based on the stated rate of interest ($100,000 × 0.09).

†Effective interest rate times the carrying value (.10 × $91,486.48).

‡Interest expense minus cash outflow ($9,148.65 − $9,000.00).

§Previous carrying value plus portion of discount amortized ($91,486.48 + $148.65).

Notice that the effective interest rate method results in increasingly larger amounts of expense recognition as the carrying value of the bond liability increases. The effect of the expense recognition on the financial statements and the journal entry necessary to record it for the first accounting period are as follows:

Cash	=	Bond Liab.	+	Equity	Rev.	−	Exp.	=	Net Inc.	Cash Flow	
(9,000)	=	148.65*	+	(9,148.65)	NA	−	9,148.65	=	(9,148.65)	(9,000)	OA

*The decrease in the amount of the discount acts to increase the bond liability.

Account Title	Debit	Credit
Interest Expense	9,148.65	
Cash		9,000.00
Discount on Bonds Payable		148.65

Table I *Future Value of $1*

n	4%	5%	6%	7%	8%	9%	10%	12%	14%	16%	20%
1	1.040000	1.050000	1.060000	1.070000	1.080000	1.090000	1.100000	1.120000	1.140000	1.160000	1.200000
2	1.081600	1.102500	1.123600	1.144900	1.166400	1.188100	1.210000	1.254400	1.299600	1.345600	1.440000
3	1.124864	1.157625	1.191016	1.225043	1.259712	1.295029	1.331000	1.404928	1.481544	1.560896	1.728000
4	1.169859	1.215506	1.262477	1.310796	1.360489	1.411582	1.464100	1.573519	1.688960	1.810639	2.073600
5	1.216653	1.276282	1.338226	1.402552	1.469328	1.538624	1.610510	1.762342	1.925415	2.100342	2.488320
6	1.265319	1.340096	1.418519	1.500730	1.586874	1.677100	1.771561	1.973823	2.194973	2.436396	2.985984
7	1.315932	1.407100	1.503630	1.605781	1.713824	1.828039	1.948717	2.210681	2.502269	2.826220	3.583181
8	1.368569	1.477455	1.593848	1.718186	1.850930	1.992563	2.143589	2.475963	2.852586	3.278415	4.299817
9	1.423312	1.551328	1.689479	1.838459	1.999005	2.171893	2.357948	2.773079	3.251949	3.802961	5.159780
10	1.480244	1.628895	1.790848	1.967151	2.158925	2.367364	2.593742	3.105848	3.707221	4.411435	6.191736
11	1.539454	1.710339	1.898299	2.104852	2.331639	2.580426	2.853117	3.478550	4.226232	5.117265	7.430084
12	1.601032	1.795856	2.012196	2.252192	2.518170	2.812665	3.138428	3.895976	4.817905	5.936027	8.916100
13	1.665074	1.885649	2.132928	2.409845	2.719624	3.065805	3.452271	4.363493	5.492411	6.885791	10.699321
14	1.731676	1.979932	2.260904	2.578534	2.937194	3.341727	3.797498	4.887112	6.261349	7.987518	12.839185
15	1.800944	2.078928	2.396558	2.759032	3.172169	3.642482	4.177248	5.473566	7.137938	9.265521	15.407022
16	1.872981	2.182875	2.540352	2.952164	3.425943	3.970306	4.594973	6.130394	8.137249	10.748004	18.488426
17	1.947900	2.292018	2.692773	3.158815	3.700018	4.327633	5.054470	6.866041	9.276464	12.467685	22.186111
18	2.025817	2.406619	2.854339	3.379932	3.996019	4.717120	5.559917	7.689966	10.575169	14.462514	26.623333
19	2.106849	2.526950	3.025600	3.616528	4.315701	5.141661	6.115909	8.612762	12.055693	16.776517	31.948000
20	2.191123	2.653298	3.207135	3.869684	4.660957	5.604411	6.727500	9.646293	13.743490	19.460759	38.337600

Table II *Present Value of $1*

n	4%	5%	6%	7%	8%	9%	10%	12%	14%	16%	20%
1	0.961538	0.952381	0.943396	0.934579	0.925926	0.917431	0.909091	0.892857	0.877193	0.862069	0.833333
2	0.924556	0.907029	0.889996	0.873439	0.857339	0.841680	0.826446	0.797194	0.769468	0.743163	0.694444
3	0.888996	0.863838	0.839619	0.816298	0.793832	0.772183	0.751315	0.711780	0.674972	0.640658	0.578704
4	0.854804	0.822702	0.792094	0.762895	0.735030	0.708425	0.683013	0.635518	0.592080	0.552291	0.482253
5	0.821927	0.783526	0.747258	0.712986	0.680583	0.649931	0.620921	0.567427	0.519369	0.476113	0.401878
6	0.790315	0.746215	0.704961	0.666342	0.630170	0.596267	0.564474	0.506631	0.455587	0.410442	0.334898
7	0.759918	0.710681	0.665057	0.622750	0.583490	0.547034	0.513158	0.452349	0.399637	0.353830	0.279082
8	0.730690	0.676839	0.627412	0.582009	0.540269	0.501866	0.466507	0.403883	0.350559	0.305025	0.232568
9	0.702587	0.644609	0.591898	0.543934	0.500249	0.460428	0.424098	0.360610	0.307508	0.262953	0.193807
10	0.675564	0.613913	0.558395	0.508349	0.463193	0.422411	0.385543	0.321973	0.269744	0.226684	0.161506
11	0.649581	0.584679	0.526788	0.475093	0.428883	0.387533	0.350494	0.287476	0.236617	0.195417	0.134588
12	0.624597	0.556837	0.496969	0.444012	0.397114	0.355535	0.318631	0.256675	0.207559	0.168463	0.112157
13	0.600574	0.530321	0.468839	0.414964	0.367698	0.326179	0.289664	0.229174	0.182069	0.145227	0.093464
14	0.577475	0.505068	0.442301	0.387817	0.340461	0.299246	0.263331	0.204620	0.159710	0.125195	0.077887
15	0.555265	0.481017	0.417265	0.362446	0.315242	0.274538	0.239392	0.182696	0.140096	0.107927	0.064905
16	0.533908	0.458112	0.393646	0.338735	0.291890	0.251870	0.217629	0.163122	0.122892	0.093041	0.054088
17	0.513373	0.436297	0.371364	0.316574	0.270269	0.231073	0.197845	0.145644	0.107800	0.080207	0.045073
18	0.493628	0.415521	0.350344	0.295864	0.250249	0.211994	0.179859	0.130040	0.094561	0.069144	0.037561
19	0.474642	0.395734	0.330513	0.276508	0.231712	0.194490	0.163508	0.116107	0.082948	0.059607	0.031301
20	0.456387	0.376889	0.311805	0.258419	0.214548	0.178431	0.148644	0.103667	0.072762	0.051385	0.026084

Table III *Future Value of an Annuity of $1*

n	4%	5%	6%	7%	8%	9%	10%	12%	14%	16%	20%
1	1.000000	1.000000	1.000000	1.000000	1.000000	1.000000	1.000000	1.000000	1.000000	1.000000	1.000000
2	2.040000	2.050000	2.060000	2.070000	2.080000	2.090000	2.100000	2.120000	2.140000	2.160000	2.200000
3	3.121600	3.152500	3.183600	3.214900	3.246400	3.278100	3.310000	3.374400	3.439600	3.505600	3.640000
4	4.246464	4.310125	4.374616	4.439943	4.506112	4.573129	4.641000	4.779328	4.921144	5.066496	5.368000
5	5.416323	5.525631	5.637093	5.750739	5.866601	5.984711	6.105100	6.352847	6.610104	6.877135	7.441600
6	6.632975	6.801913	6.975319	7.153291	7.335929	7.523335	7.715610	8.115189	8.535519	8.977477	9.929920
7	7.898294	8.142008	8.393838	8.654021	8.922803	9.200435	9.487171	10.089012	10.730491	11.413873	12.915904
8	9.214226	9.549109	9.897468	10.259803	10.636628	11.028474	11.435888	12.299693	13.232760	14.240093	16.499085
9	10.582795	11.026564	11.491316	11.977989	12.487558	13.021036	13.579477	14.775656	16.085347	17.518508	20.798902
10	12.006107	12.577893	13.180795	13.816448	14.486562	15.192930	15.937425	17.548735	19.337295	21.321469	25.958682
11	13.486351	14.206787	14.971643	15.783599	16.645487	17.560293	18.531167	20.654583	23.044516	25.732904	32.150419
12	15.025805	15.917127	16.869941	17.888451	18.977126	20.140720	21.384284	24.133133	27.270749	30.850169	39.580502
13	16.626838	17.712983	18.882138	20.140643	21.495297	22.953385	24.522712	28.029109	32.088654	36.786196	48.496603
14	18.291911	19.598632	21.015066	22.550488	24.214920	26.019189	27.974983	32.392602	37.581065	43.671987	59.195923
15	20.023588	21.578564	23.275970	25.129022	27.152114	29.360916	31.772482	37.279715	43.842414	51.659505	72.035108
16	21.824531	23.657492	25.672528	27.888054	30.324283	33.003399	35.949730	42.753280	50.980352	60.925026	87.442129
17	23.697512	25.840366	28.212880	30.840217	33.750226	36.973705	40.544703	48.883674	59.117601	71.673030	105.930555
18	25.645413	28.132385	30.905653	33.999033	37.450244	41.301338	45.599173	55.749715	68.394066	84.140715	128.116666
19	27.671229	30.539004	33.759992	37.378965	41.446263	46.018458	51.159090	63.439681	78.969235	98.603230	154.740000
20	29.778079	33.065954	36.785591	40.995492	45.761964	51.160120	57.274999	72.052442	91.024928	115.379747	186.688000

Table IV *Present Value of an Annuity of $1*

n	4%	5%	6%	7%	8%	9%	10%	12%	14%	16%	20%
1	0.961538	0.952381	0.943396	0.934579	0.925926	0.917431	0.909091	0.892857	0.877193	0.862069	0.833333
2	1.886095	1.859410	1.833393	1.808018	1.783265	1.759111	1.735537	1.690051	1.646661	1.605232	1.527778
3	2.775091	2.723248	2.673012	2.624316	2.577097	2.531295	2.486852	2.401831	2.321632	2.245890	2.106481
4	3.629895	3.545951	3.465106	3.387211	3.312127	3.239720	3.169865	3.037349	2.913712	2.798181	2.588735
5	4.451822	4.329477	4.212364	4.100197	3.992710	3.889651	3.790787	3.604776	3.433081	3.274294	2.990612
6	5.242137	5.075692	4.917324	4.766540	4.622880	4.485919	4.355261	4.111407	3.888668	3.684736	3.325510
7	6.002055	5.786373	5.582381	5.389289	5.206370	5.032953	4.868419	4.563757	4.288305	4.038565	3.604592
8	6.732745	6.463213	6.209794	5.971299	5.746639	5.534819	5.334926	4.967640	4.638864	4.343591	3.837160
9	7.435332	7.107822	6.801692	6.515232	6.246888	5.995247	5.759024	5.328250	4.946372	4.606544	4.030967
10	8.110896	7.721735	7.360087	7.023582	6.710081	6.417658	6.144567	5.650223	5.216116	4.833227	4.192472
11	8.760477	8.306414	7.886875	7.498674	7.138964	6.805191	6.495061	5.937699	5.452733	5.028644	4.327060
12	9.385074	8.863252	8.383844	7.942686	7.536078	7.160725	6.813692	6.194374	5.660292	5.197107	4.439217
13	9.985648	9.393573	8.852683	8.357651	7.903776	7.486904	7.103356	6.423548	5.842362	5.342334	4.532681
14	10.563123	9.898641	9.294984	8.745468	8.244237	7.786150	7.366687	6.628168	6.002072	5.467529	4.610567
15	11.118387	10.379658	9.712249	9.107914	8.559479	8.060688	7.606080	6.810864	6.142168	5.575456	4.675473
16	11.652296	10.837770	10.105895	9.446649	8.851369	8.312558	7.823709	6.973986	6.265060	5.668497	4.729561
17	12.165669	11.274066	10.477260	9.763223	9.121638	8.543631	8.021553	7.119630	6.372859	5.748704	4.774634
18	12.659297	11.689587	10.827603	10.059087	9.371887	8.755625	8.201412	7.249670	6.467420	5.817848	4.812195
19	13.133939	12.085321	11.158116	10.335595	9.603599	8.905115	8.364777	7.365777	6.550369	5.877455	4.843496
20	13.590326	12.462210	11.469921	10.594014	9.818147	9.128546	8.513564	7.469444	6.623131	5.928841	4.869580

Amortization of loan *463*
Annuity *487*
Balloon payment *464*
Bearer or coupon bonds *470*
Bond *469*
Bond discount *475*
Bond indenture *469*
Bond premium *480*
Call premium *471*
Call price *481*
Callable bonds *470*
Carrying value *476*
Collateral for loans *466*

Compound interest *486*
Compounding *486*
Convertible bonds *470*
Debenture *469*
Discount on Bonds
    Payable *476*
Effective interest rate *474*
Effective interest rate
    method *490*
Extraordinary items *482*
Face value *469*
Financial leverage *469*
Fixed interest rate *463*

Future value *487*
Issuer of a bond *468*
Line of credit *466*
Market interest rate *475*
Mortgage bonds *469*
Present value *487*
Registered bonds *470*
Restrictive covenants *466*
Secured bonds *469*
Serial bonds *470*
Simple interest *486*
Sinking fund *470*

Spread *469*
Stated interest rate *469*
Straight-line amortization *477*
Subordinated debentures *470*
Term bonds *470*
Times interest earned ratio *483*
Time value of money *486*
Unregistered bonds *470*
Unsecured bonds *469*
Unsubordinated
    debentures *470*
Variable interest rate *463*

1. What is the difference between classification of a note as short term or long term?
2. At the beginning of year 1, B Co. has a note payable of $72,000 that calls for an annual payment of $16,246, which includes both principal and interest. If the interest rate is 8 percent, what is the amount of interest expense in year 1 and in year 2? What is the balance of the note at the end of year 2?
3. What is the purpose of a line of credit for a business? Why would a company choose to obtain a line of credit instead of issuing bonds?
4. What are the primary sources of debt financing for most large companies?
5. What are some advantages of issuing bonds versus borrowing from a bank?
6. What are some disadvantages of issuing bonds?
7. Why can a company usually issue bonds at a lower interest rate than the company would pay if the funds were borrowed from a bank?
8. What effect does income tax have on the cost of borrowing funds for a business?
9. What is the concept of financial leverage?
10. Which type of bond, secured or unsecured, is likely to have a lower interest rate? Explain.
11. What is the function of restrictive covenants attached to bond issues?
12. Why are unregistered bonds (bearer or coupon bonds) more vulnerable to theft than registered bonds?
13. What is the difference between term bonds and serial bonds?
14. What is the purpose of establishing a sinking fund?
15. What is the call price of a bond? Is it usually higher or lower than the face amount of the bond? Explain.
16. If Roc Co. issued $100,000 of 5 percent, 10-year bonds at the face amount, what is the effect of the issuance of the bonds on the financial statements? What amount of interest expense will Roc Co. recognize each year?
17. What mechanism is used to adjust the stated interest rate to the market rate of interest?
18. When the effective interest rate is higher than the stated interest rate on a bond issue, will the bond sell at a discount or premium? Why?
19. What type of transaction is the issuance of bonds by a company?
20. What factors may cause the effective interest rate and the stated interest rate to be different?
21. If a bond is selling at 97.5, how much cash will the company receive from the sale of a $1,000 bond?
22. How is the carrying value of a bond computed?
23. Gay Co. has a balance in the Bonds Payable account of $25,000 and a balance in the Discount on Bonds Payable account of $5,200. What is the carrying value of the bonds? What is the total amount of the liability?
24. When the effective interest rate is higher than the stated interest rate, will interest expense be higher or lower than the amount of interest paid?
25. Assuming that the selling price of the bond and the face value are the same, would the issuer of a bond rather make annual or semiannual interest payments? Why?
26. Rato Co. called some bonds and had a loss on the redemption of the bonds of $2,850. How is this amount reported on the income statement?

27. Which method of financing, debt or equity, is generally more advantageous from a tax standpoint? Why?

28. If a company has a tax rate of 30 percent and interest expense was $10,000, what is the after-tax cost of the debt?

29. Which type of financing, debt or equity, increases the risk factor of a business? Why?

30. What information does the times interest earned ratio provide?

31. What is the difference between simple and compound interest?

32. What is meant by the future value of an investment? How is it determined?

33. If you have $10,000 to invest at the beginning of year 1 at an interest rate of 8 percent, what is the future value of the investment at the end of year 4?

34. What is meant by the present value of an investment? How is it determined?

35. Assume that your favorite aunt gave you $25,000, but you will not receive the gift until you are 25 years old. You are presently 22 years old. What is the current value of the gift, assuming an interest rate of 8 percent?

36. What is the present value of four payments of $4,000 each to be received at the end of each of the next four years, assuming an interest rate of 8 percent?

37. How does the effective interest rate method of bond amortization differ from the straight-line method of bond amortization? Which method is conceptually more correct?

EXRCISES—SERIES A

L.O. 2   EXERCISE 10–1A *How Credit Terms Affect Financial Statements*

Baltimore Co. is planning to finance an expansion of its operations by borrowing $100,000. City Bank has agreed to loan Baltimore the funds. Baltimore has two repayment options: (1) to issue a note with the principal due in 10 years and with interest payable annually or (2) to issue a note to repay $10,000 of the principal each year along with the annual interest based on the unpaid principal balance. Assume the interest rate is 9 percent for each option.

Required
a. What amount of interest will Baltimore pay in year 1
   (1) Under option 1?
   (2) Under option 2?
b. What amount of interest will Baltimore pay in year 2
   (1) Under option 1?
   (2) Under option 2?
c. Explain the advantage of each option.

L.O. 2   EXERCISE 10–2A *Accounting for a Long-Term Note Payable With Annual Payments That Include Interest and Principal*

On January 1, 2004, Wallace Co. borrowed $80,000 cash from First Bank by issuing a four-year, 9 percent note. The principal and interest are to be paid by making annual payments in the amount of $24,693. Payments are to be made December 31 of each year, beginning December 31, 2004.

Required
Prepare an amortization schedule for the interest and principal payments for the four-year period.

L.O. 2   EXERCISE 10–3A *Long-Term Installment Note Payable*

Jim Yang started a business by issuing a $100,000 face value note to State National Bank on January 1, 2004. The note had an 8 percent annual rate of interest and a 10-year term. Payments of $14,903 are to be made each December 31 for 10 years.

Required
a. What portion of the December 31, 2004, payment is applied to
   (1) Interest expense?
   (2) Principal?
b. What is the principal balance on January 1, 2005?
c. What portion of the December 31, 2005, payment is applied to
   (1) Interest expense?
   (2) Principal?

EXERCISE 10–4A *Amortization of a Long-Term Loan*   **L.O. 1, 2**

A partial amortization schedule for a five-year note payable that Bragg Co. issued on January 1, 2002, is shown here:

Accounting Period	Principal Balance January 1	Cash Payment	Applied to Interest	Applied to Principal
2002	$150,000	$38,563	$13,500	$25,063
2003	124,937	38,563	11,244	27,319

Required

a. What rate of interest is Bragg Co. paying on the note?
b. Using a financial statements model like the one shown here, record the appropriate amounts for the following two events:
   (1) January 1, 2002, issue of the note payable.
   (2) December 31, 2002, payment on the note payable.

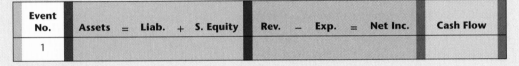

Event No.	Assets	=	Liab.	+	S. Equity	Rev.	−	Exp.	=	Net Inc.	Cash Flow
1											

c. If the company earned $100,000 cash revenue and paid $50,000 in cash expenses in addition to the interest in 2002, what is the amount of each of the following?
   (1) Net income for 2002.
   (2) Cash flow from operating activities for 2002.
   (3) Cash flow from financing activities for 2002.
d. What is the amount of interest expense on this loan for 2004?

EXERCISE 10–5A *Accounting for a Line of Credit*   **L.O. 3**

Max Company has a line of credit with Federal Bank. Max can borrow up to $400,000 at any time over the course of the 2004 calendar year. The following table shows the prime rate expressed as an annual percentage along with the amounts borrowed and repaid during the first four months of 2004. Max agreed to pay interest at an annual rate equal to 2 percent above the bank's prime rate. Funds are borrowed or repaid on the first day of each month. Interest is payable in cash on the last day of the month. The interest rate is applied to the outstanding monthly balance. For example, Max pays 8 percent (6 percent + 2 percent) annual interest on $100,000 for the month of January.

Month	Amount Borrowed or (Repaid)	Prime Rate for the Month, %
January	$100,000	6.0
February	50,000	5.0
March	(60,000)	5.5
April	10,000	5.0

Required
Provide all journal entries pertaining to Max's line of credit for the first four months of 2004.

EXERCISE 10–6A *Annual Versus Semiannual Interest Payments*   **L.O. 6**

Huggins Co. issued bonds with a face value of $50,000 on January 1, 2004. The bonds had a 9 percent stated rate of interest and a five-year term. The bonds were issued at face value.

Required
a. What total amount of interest will Huggins pay in 2004 if bond interest is paid annually each December 31?
b. What total amount of interest will Huggins pay in 2004 if bond interest is paid semiannually each June 30 and December 31?
c. Write a memo explaining which option Huggins would prefer.

L.O. 5, 7   EXERCISE 10–7A *Determining Cash Receipts From Bond Issues*

Required

Compute the cash proceeds from bond issues under the following terms. For each case, indicate whether the bonds sold at a premium or discount.

a. Kay, Inc., issued $100,000 of 8-year, 10 percent bonds at 101.

b. Sam Co. issued $150,000 of 4-year, 8 percent bonds at 98.

c. Bill Co. issued $200,000 of 10-year, 7 percent bonds at 102¼.

d. Jay, Inc., issued $40,000 of 5-year, 6 percent bonds at 97½.

L.O. 5   EXERCISE 10–8A *Identifying the Relationship Between the Stated Rate of Interest and the Market Rate of Interest*

Required

Indicate whether a bond will sell at a premium (P), discount (D), or face value (F) for each of the following conditions:

a. _____ The stated rate of interest is higher than the market rate.

b. _____ The market rate of interest is higher than the stated rate.

c. _____ The stated rate of interest is less than the market rate.

d. _____ The market rate of interest is less than the stated rate.

e. _____ The market rate of interest is equal to the stated rate.

L.O. 5   EXERCISE 10–9A *Identifying Bond Premiums and Discounts*

Required

In each of the following situations, state whether the bonds will sell at a premium or discount.

a. Marshall issued $100,000 of bonds with a stated interest rate of 9.0 percent. At the time of issue, the market rate of interest for similar investments was 9.5 percent.

b. Telco issued $150,000 of bonds with a stated interest rate of 7 percent. At the time of issue, the market rate of interest for similar investments was 8 percent.

c. Lee Inc. issued callable bonds with a stated interest rate of 10.0 percent. The bonds were callable at 102. At the date of issue, the market rate of interest was 9.5 percent for similar investments.

L.O. 5   EXERCISE 10–10A *Determining the Amount of Bond Premiums and Discounts*

Required

For each of the following situations, calculate the amount of bond discount or premium, if any.

a. Smart Co. issued $60,000 of 7 percent bonds at 104.

b. Swift, Inc., issued $90,000 of 10-year, 8 percent bonds at 101½.

c. Ray, Inc., issued $200,000 of 20-year, 10 percent bonds at 98¼.

d. Gray Co. issued $150,000 of 15-year, 6 percent bonds at 96.

L.O. 6, 7   EXERCISE 10–11A *Effect of a Bond Discount on Financial Statements: Annual Interest*

Heeley Company issued $200,000 face value of bonds on January 1, 2002. The bonds had a 10 percent stated rate of interest and a 10-year term. Interest is paid in cash annually, beginning December 31, 2002. The bonds were issued at 98.

Required

a. Show the effect of (1) the bond issue, (2) amortization of the discount on December 31, 2002, and (3) the December 31, 2002, interest payment on the financial statements using a horizontal statements model like the following one. Use + for increase, − for decrease, and NA for not affected.

Event No.	Assets	=	Liab.	+	S. Equity	Rev.	−	Exp.	=	Net Inc.	Cash Flow
1											

b. Determine the carrying value (face value less discount or plus premium) of the bond liability as of December 31, 2002.

c. Determine the amount of interest expense reported on the 2002 income statement.

d. Determine the carrying value (face value less discount or plus premium) of the bond liability as of December 31, 2003.

e. Determine the amount of interest expense reported on the 2003 income statement.

EXERCISE 10–12A *Effect of a Bond Premium on Financial Statements: Annual Interest*   **L.O. 6, 7**

Strauss Company issued $200,000 face value of bonds on January 1, 2002. The bonds had a 10 percent stated rate of interest and a 10-year term. Interest is paid in cash annually, beginning December 31, 2002. The bonds were issued at 102.

Required

a. Show the effect of (1) the bond issue, (2) amortization of the premium on December 31, 2002, and (3) the December 31, 2002, interest payment on the financial statements using a horizontal statements model like the following one. Use + for increase, − for decrease, and NA for not affected.

Event No.	Assets	=	Liab.	+	S. Equity	Rev.	−	Exp.	=	Net Inc.	Cash Flow
1											

b. Determine the carrying value (face value less discount or plus premium) of the bond liability as of December 31, 2002.
c. Determine the amount of interest expense reported on the 2002 income statement.
d. Determine the carrying value of the bond liability as of December 31, 2003.
e. Determine the amount of interest expense reported on the 2003 income statement.

EXERCISE 10–13A *Effect of Bonds Issued at a Discount on Financial Statements: Semiannual*   **L.O. 6, 7**
Interest

Home Supplies, Inc., issued $100,000 of 10-year, 6 percent bonds on July 1, 2003, at 95. Interest is payable in cash semiannually on June 30 and December 31.

Required

a. Prepare the journal entries to record issuing the bonds and any necessary journal entries for 2003 and 2004. Post the journal entries to T-accounts.
b. Prepare the liabilities section of the balance sheet at the end of 2003 and 2004.
c. What amount of interest expense will Home report on the financial statements for 2003 and 2004?
d. What amount of cash will Home pay for interest in 2003 and 2004?

EXERCISE 10–14A *Recording Bonds Issued at Face Value and Associated Interest for Two*   **L.O. 6, 7**
Accounting Cycles: Annual Interest

On January 1, 2003, Hammond Corp. issued $200,000 of 10-year, 8 percent bonds at their face amount. Interest is payable on December 31 of each year with the first payment due December 31, 2003.

Required
Prepare all the general journal entries related to these bonds for 2003 and 2004.

EXERCISE 10–15A *Recording Bonds Issued at a Discount: Annual Interest*   **L.O. 6, 7**

On January 1, 2004, Macy Co. issued $200,000 of five-year, 8 percent bonds at 96. Interest is payable annually on December 31. The discount is amortized using the straight-line method.

Required
Prepare the journal entries to record the bond transactions for 2004 and 2005. Include any required year-end adjusting entries.

EXERCISE 10–16A *Recording Bonds Issued at a Premium: Annual Interest*   **L.O. 6, 7**

On January 1, 2004, Bay Company issued $200,000 of five-year, 8 percent bonds at 102. Interest is payable annually on December 31. The premium is amortized using the straight-line method.

Required
Prepare the journal entries to record the bond transactions for 2004 and 2005. Include any required year-end adjusting entries.

EXERCISE 10–17A *Two Complete Accounting Cycles: Bonds Issued at Face Value With*   **L.O. 6, 7**
Annual Interest

Goode Company issued $500,000 of 20-year, 8 percent bonds on January 1, 2001. The bonds were issued at face value. Interest is payable in cash on December 31 of each year. Goode immediately invested the proceeds from the bond issue in land. The land was leased for an annual $60,000 of cash revenue, which was collected on December 31 of each year, beginning December 31, 2001.

Required

a. Prepare the journal entries for these events, and post them to T-accounts for 2001 and 2002.

b. Prepare the income statement, balance sheet, and statement of cash flows for 2001 and 2002.

L.O. 6, 7   EXERCISE 10–18A *Recording Callable Bonds*

Boark Co. issued $400,000 of 10 percent, 10-year, callable bonds on January 1, 2004, for their face value. The call premium was 2 percent (bonds are callable at 102). Interest was payable annually on December 31. The bonds were called on December 31, 2007.

Required

Prepare the journal entries to record the bond issue on January 1, 2004, and the bond redemption on December 31, 2007. Assume that all entries to accrue and pay interest were recorded correctly.

L.O. 8   EXERCISE 10–19A *Determining the After-Tax Cost of Debt*

The following 2004 information is available for three companies:

	Ames Co.	Cox Co.	Douglas Co.
Face value of bonds payable	$200,000	$500,000	$800,000
Interest rate	8%	7%	6%
Income tax rate	35%	20%	25%

Required

a. Determine the annual before-tax interest cost for each company *in dollars.*

b. Determine the annual after-tax interest cost for each company *in dollars.*

c. Determine the annual after-tax interest cost for each company as *a percentage* of the face value of the bonds.

L.O. 9   EXERCISE 10–20A *Future Value and Present Value (Appendix)*

Required

Using Tables I, II, III, or IV in the appendix, calculate the following:

a. The future value of $25,000 invested at 5 percent for 10 years.

b. The future value of eight annual payments of $1,500 at 8 percent interest.

c. The amount that must be deposited today (present value) at 6 percent to accumulate $100,000 in five years.

d. The annual payment on a 10-year, 7 percent, $80,000 note payable.

L.O. 9   EXERCISE 10–21A *Computing the Payment Amount (Appendix)*

Betty Carnes is a business major at State U. She will be graduating this year and is planning to start a consulting business. She will need to purchase computer equipment that costs $25,000. She can borrow the money from the local bank but will have to make annual payments of principal and interest.

Required

a. Compute the annual payment Betty will be required to make on a $25,000, four-year, 8 percent loan.

b. If Betty can afford to make annual payments of only $6,000, how much can she borrow?

L.O. 9   EXERCISE 10–22A *Saving for a Future Value (Appendix)*

Billy Bob and Betty Sue were recently married and want to start saving for their dream home. They expect the house they want will cost approximately $225,000. They hope to be able to purchase the house for cash in 10 years.

Required

a. How much will Billy Bob and Betty Sue have to invest each year to purchase their dream home at the end of 10 years? Assume an interest rate of 8 percent.

b. Billy Bob's parents want to give the couple a substantial wedding gift for the purchase of their future home. How much must Billy Bob's parents give them now if they are to have the desired amount of $225,000 in 10 years? Assume an interest rate of 8 percent?

EXERCISE 10–23A *Sale of Bonds at a Discount Using Present Value (Appendix)*   **L.O. 7**

Moss Corporation issued $50,000 of 8.0 percent, 10-year bonds on January 1, 2003, for a price that reflected a 7 percent market rate of interest. Interest is payable annually on December 31.

Required
a. What was the selling price of the bonds?
b. Prepare the journal entry to record issuing the bonds.
c. Prepare the journal entry for the first interest payment on December 31, 2003, using the effective interest rate method.

EXERCISE 10–24A *Comparing the Effective Interest Rate Method With the Straight-Line*   **L.O. 7, 9**
Method (Appendix)

Required
Write a short memo explaining why the effective interest rate method produces a different amount of interest expense from the straight-line method in any given year.

PROBLEM 10–25A *Effect of a Term Loan on Financial Statements*   **L.O. 2**

On January 1, 2001, Jones Co. borrowed cash from First City Bank by issuing an $80,000 face value, three-year term note that had an 8 percent annual interest rate. The note is to be repaid by making annual payments of $31,043 that include both interest and principal on December 31. Jones invested the proceeds from the loan in land that generated lease revenues of $36,000 cash per year.

Required
a. Prepare an amortization schedule for the three-year period.
b. Prepare an income statement, balance sheet, and statement of cash flows for each of the three years. (*Hint:* Record the transactions for each year in T-accounts before preparing the financial statements.)
c. Does cash outflow from operating activities remain constant or change each year? Explain.

PROBLEM 10–26A *Effect of a Line of Credit on Financial Statements*   **L.O. 3**

Powell Company has a line of credit with Bay Bank. Powell can borrow up to $150,000 at any time over the course of the 2003 calendar year. The following table shows the prime rate expressed as an annual percentage along with the amounts borrowed and repaid during 2003. Powell agreed to pay interest at an annual rate equal to 3 percent above the bank's prime rate. Funds are borrowed or repaid on the first day of each month. Interest is payable in cash on the last day of the month. The interest rate is applied to the outstanding monthly balance. For example, Powell pays 7 percent (4 percent + 3 percent) annual interest on $80,000 for the month of January.

Month	Amount Borrowed or (Repaid)	Prime Rate for the Month, %
January	$80,000	4
February	50,000	4
March	(30,000)	5
April through October	No change	No change
November	(60,000)	5
December	(40,000)	4

Powell earned $18,000 of cash revenue during 2003.

Required
a. Prepare an income statement, balance sheet, and statement of cash flows for 2003.
b. Write a memo discussing the advantages of arranging a line of credit to a business.

L.O. 6, 7   **PROBLEM 10–27A** *Accounting for a Bond Premium Over Multiple Accounting Cycles*

Maywood Company was started when it issued bonds with $150,000 face value on January 1, 2004. The bonds were issued for cash at 105. They had a 15-year term to maturity and a 10 percent annual interest rate. Interest was payable annually. Maywood immediately purchased land with the proceeds (cash received) from the bond issue. Maywood leased the land for $17,500 cash per year. On January 1, 2007, the company sold the land for $160,000 cash. Immediately after the sale, Maywood repurchased its bonds (repaid the bond liability) at 106. Assume that no other accounting events occurred in 2007.

Required

Prepare an income statement, statement of changes in equity, balance sheet and statement of cash flows for each of the 2004, 2005, 2006, and 2007 accounting periods. Assume that the company closes its books on December 31 of each year. Prepare the statements using a vertical statements format. (*Hint:* Record each year's transactions in T-accounts prior to preparing the financial statements.)

L.O. 5–7   **PROBLEM 10–28A** *Recording and Reporting a Bond Discount over Two Cycles: Semiannual Interest*

During 2002 and 2003, Adams Co. completed the following transactions relating to its bond issue. The company's fiscal year ends on December 31.

2002

Mar. 1   Issued $50,000 of eight-year, 9 percent bonds for $48,000. Interest is payable on March 1 and September 1, beginning September 1, 2002.

Sept. 1   Paid the semiannual interest on the bonds.

Dec. 31   Recorded the accrued interest on the bonds.

    31   Recorded the bond discount amortization using the straight-line method.

    31   Closed the interest expense account.

2003

Mar. 1   Paid the semiannual interest on the bonds.

Sept. 1   Paid the semiannual interest on the bonds.

Dec. 31   Recorded the accrued interest on the bonds.

    31   Recorded the bond discount amortization using the straight-line method.

    31   Closed the interest expense account.

Required

a. When the bonds were issued, was the market rate of interest more or less than the stated rate of interest? If the bonds had sold at face value, what amount of cash would Adams Co. have received?

b. Prepare the general journal entries for these transactions.

c. Prepare the liabilities section of the balance sheet at December 31, 2002 and 2003.

d. Determine the amount of interest expense Adams would report on the income statements for 2002 and 2003.

e. Determine the amounts of interest Adams would pay to the bondholders in 2002 and 2003.

L.O. 6, 7   **PROBLEM 10–29A** *Effect of a Bond Premium on the Elements of Financial Statements*

Western Land Co. was formed when it acquired cash from the issue of common stock. The company then issued bonds at a premium on January 1, 2001. Interest is payable annually on December 31 of each year, beginning December 31, 2001. On January 2, 2001, Western Land Co. purchased a piece of land and leased it for an annual rental fee. The rent is received annually on December 31, beginning December 31, 2001. At the end of the eight-year period (December 31, 2008), the land was sold at a gain, and the bonds were paid off. A summary of the transactions for each year follows:

2001

1. Acquired cash from the issue of common stock.
2. Issued eight-year bonds.
3. Purchased land.
4. Received land-lease income.
5. Amortized bond premium at December 31.
6. Paid cash for interest expense at the stated rate on December 31.
7. Prepared the December 31 entry to close for Rent Revenue.
8. Prepared the December 31 entry to close Interest Expense.

2002–2007

9. Received land-lease income.
10. Amortized bond premium at December 31.
11. Paid cash for interest expense at the stated rate on December 31.
12. Prepared the December 31 entry to close Rent Revenue.
13. Prepared the December 31 entry to close Interest Expense.

2008

14. Sold land at a gain.
15. Retired bonds at face value.

Required

Identify each of these 15 transactions as asset source (AS), asset use (AU), asset exchange (AE), or claims exchange (CE). Explain how each event affects assets, liabilities, equity, net income, and cash flow by placing a + for increase, − for decrease, or NA for not affected under each category. In the Cash Flow column, indicate whether the item is an operating activity (OA), investing activity (IA), or financing activity (FA). The first event is recorded as an example.

Event No.	Type of Event	Assets	Liabilities	Common Stock	Retained Earnings	Net Income	Cash Flow
1	AS	+	NA	+	NA	NA	+ FA

PROBLEM 10–30A *Recording Transactions for Callable Bonds*   **L.O. 6, 7**

Simpson Co. issued $100,000 of 10-year, 10 percent, callable bonds on January 1, 2001, with interest payable annually on December 31. The bonds were issued at their face amount. The bonds are callable at 101½. The fiscal year of the corporation is the calendar year.

Required

a. Show the effect of the following events on the financial statements by recording the appropriate amounts in a horizontal statements model like the following one. In the Cash Flow column, indicate whether the item is an operating activity (OA), investing activity (IA), or financing activity (FA). Use NA if an element was not affected by the event.

   (1) Issued the bonds on January 1, 2001.
   (2) Paid interest due to bondholders on December 31, 2001.
   (3) On January 1, 2009, Simpson Co. called the bonds. Assume that all interim entries were correctly recorded.

Event No.	Assets	=	Liab.	+	S. Equity	Rev.	−	Exp.	=	Net Inc.	Cash Flow
1											

b. Prepare journal entries for the three events listed in Requirement *a*.

PROBLEM 10–31A *Effect of Debt Transactions on Financial Statements*   **L.O. 2, 3, 6**

Required

Show the effect of each of the following independent accounting events on the financial statements using a horizontal statements model like the following one. Use + for increase, − for decrease, and NA for not affected. The first event is recorded as an example.

Event No.	Assets	=	Liab.	+	S. Equity	Rev.	−	Exp.	=	Net Inc.	Cash Flow
1	+		+		NA	NA		NA		NA	+ FA

a. Borrowed funds using a line of credit.
b. Made an interest payment for funds that had been borrowed against a line of credit.

c. Made a cash payment on a note payable.
d. Issued a bond at face value.
e. Made an interest payment on a bond that had been issued at face value.
f. Issued a bond at a discount.
g. Made an interest payment on a bond that had been issued at a discount.
h. Amortized bond discount.
i. Issued a bond at a premium.
j. Made an interest payment on a bond that had been issued at a premium.
k. Amortized bond premium.

L.O. 7, 9   **PROBLEM 10–32A** *Sale of Bonds at a Premium and Amortization Using the Effective Interest Rate Method (Appendix)*

On January 1, 2002, Knight Corp. sold $200,000 of its own 8 percent, 10-year bonds. Interest is payable annually on December 31. The bonds were sold to yield an effective interest rate of 7 percent. Knight Corp. uses the effective interest rate method.

Required
a. Using the data in the appendix, calculate the selling price of the bonds.
b. Prepare the journal entry for the issuance of the bonds.
c. Prepare the journal entry for the amortization of the bond premium and the payment of the interest on December 31, 2004.
d. Calculate the amount of interest expense for 2005.

EXERCISES—SERIES B

L.O. 2   **EXERCISE 10–1B** *How Credit Terms Affect Financial Statements*

Marco Co. borrowed $40,000 from the National Bank by issuing a note with a five-year term. Marco has two options with respect to the payment of interest and principal. Option 1 requires the payment of interest only on an annual basis with the full amount of the principal due at maturity. Option 2 calls for an annual payment that includes interest due plus a partial repayment of the principal balance. The effective annual interest rate on both notes is identical.

Required
Write a memo explaining how the two alternatives will affect *(a)* the carrying value of liabilities, *(b)* the amount of annual interest expense, *(c)* the total amount of interest that will be paid over the life of the note, and *(d)* the cash flow consequences.

L.O. 2   **EXERCISE 10–2B** *Accounting for a Long-Term Note Payable With Annual Payments That Include Interest and Principal*

On January 1, 2006, Baco Co. borrowed $120,000 cash from Central Bank by issuing a five-year, 8 percent note. The principal and interest are to be paid by making annual payments in the amount of $30,055. Payments are to be made December 31 of each year, beginning December 31, 2006.

Required
Prepare an amortization schedule for the interest and principal payments for the five-year period.

L.O. 2   **EXERCISE 10–3B** *Long-Term Installment Note Payable*

Terek Amer started a business by issuing an $80,000 face value note to First State Bank on January 1, 2004. The note had a 10 percent annual rate of interest and a five-year term. Payments of $21,104 are to be made each December 31 for five years.

Required
a. What portion of the December 31, 2004, payment is applied to
   (1) Interest expense?
   (2) Principal?
b. What is the principal balance on January 1, 2005?
c. What portion of the December 31, 2005, payment is applied to
   (1) Interest expense?
   (2) Principal?

EXERCISE 10–4B *Amortization of a Long-Term Loan*   L.O. 1, 2

A partial amortization schedule for a 10-year note payable issued on January 1, 2001, is shown here:

Accounting Period	Principal Balance January 1	Cash Payment	Applied to Interest	Applied to Principal
2001	$200,000	$32,549	$20,000	$12,549
2002	187,451	32,549	18,745	13,804
2003	173,647	32,549	17,365	15,184

Required
a. Using a financial statements model like the one shown here, record the appropriate amounts for the following two events:
   (1) January 1, 2001, issue of the note payable.
   (2) December 31, 2001, payment on the note payable.

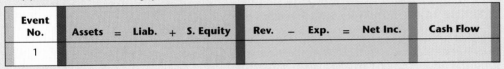

Event No.	Assets	=	Liab.	+	S. Equity	Rev.	−	Exp.	=	Net Inc.	Cash Flow
1											

b. If the company earned $100,000 cash revenue and paid $50,000 in cash expenses in addition to the interest in 2001, what is the amount of each of the following?
   (1) Net income for 2001.
   (2) Cash flow from operating activities for 2001.
   (3) Cash flow from financing activities for 2001.
c. What is the amount of interest expense on this loan for 2004?

EXERCISE 10–5B *Accounting for a Line of Credit*   L.O. 3

Vanheis Company has a line of credit with United Bank. Vanheis can borrow up to $200,000 at any time over the course of the 2007 calendar year. The following table shows the prime rate expressed as an annual percentage along with the amounts borrowed and repaid during the first three months of 2007. Vanheis agreed to pay interest at an annual rate equal to 2 percent above the bank's prime rate. Funds are borrowed or repaid on the first day of each month. Interest is payable in cash on the last day of the month. The interest rate is applied to the outstanding monthly balance. For example, Vanheis pays 6 percent (4 percent + 2 percent) annual interest on $80,000 for the month of February.

Month	Amount Borrowed or (Repaid)	Prime Rate for the Month, %
January	$50,000	3.0
February	30,000	4.0
March	(40,000)	4.5

Required
Provide all journal entries pertaining to Vanheis' line of credit for the first three months of 2007.

EXERCISE 10–6B *Annual Versus Semiannual Interest Payments*   L.O. 6

Colgan Company issued bonds with a face value of $10,000 on January 1, 2005. The bonds had an 8 percent stated rate of interest and a six-year term. The bonds were issued at face value. Interest is payable on an annual basis.

Required
Write a memo explaining whether the total cash outflow for interest would be more, less, or the same if the bonds pay semiannual versus annual interest.

EXERCISE 10–7B *Determining Cash Receipts From Bond Issues*   L.O. 5, 7

Required
Compute the cash proceeds from bond issues under the following terms. For each case, indicate whether the bonds sold at a premium or discount.
a. Petal, Inc., issued $200,000 of 10-year, 8 percent bonds at 103.

b. Stem Inc. issued $80,000 of five-year, 12 percent bonds at 95½.
c. Rose Co. issued $100,000 of five-year, 6 percent bonds at 101¾.
d. Tulip, Inc., issued $50,000 of four-year, 8 percent bonds at 98.

L.O. 5　**EXERCISE 10–8B** *Identifying the Relationship Between the Stated Rate of Interest and the Market Rate of Interest*

Required
Indicate whether a bond will sell at a premium (P), discount (D), or face value (F) for each of the following conditions:
a. _____ The market rate of interest is equal to the stated rate.
b. _____ The market rate of interest is less than the stated rate.
c. _____ The market rate of interest is higher than the stated rate.
d. _____ The stated rate of interest is higher than the market rate.
e. _____ The stated rate of interest is less than the market rate.

L.O. 5　**EXERCISE 10–9B** *Identifying Bond Premiums and Discounts*

Required
In each of the following situations, state whether the bonds will sell at a premium or discount.
a. Stokes issued $200,000 of bonds with a stated interest rate of 8 percent. At the time of issue, the market rate of interest for similar investments was 7 percent.
b. Shaw issued $100,000 of bonds with a stated interest rate of 8 percent. At the time of issue, the market rate of interest for similar investments was 9 percent.
c. Link Inc. issued callable bonds with a stated interest rate of 8 percent. The bonds were callable at 104. At the date of issue, the market rate of interest was 9 percent for similar investments.

L.O. 5　**EXERCISE 10–10B** *Determining the Amount of Bond Premiums and Discounts*

Required
For each of the following situations, calculate the amount of bond discount or premium, if any.
a. Ball Co. issued $80,000 of 6 percent bonds at 102.
b. Link, Inc., issued $50,000 of 10-year, 8 percent bonds at 98.
c. Hall, Inc., issued $100,000 of 15-year, 9 percent bonds at 102¼.
d. Mink Co. issued $500,000 of 20-year, 8 percent bonds at 98¾.

L.O. 6, 7　**EXERCISE 10–11B** *Effect of a Bond Discount on Financial Statements: Annual Interest*

Landry Company issued $100,000 face value of bonds on January 1, 2004. The bonds had an 8 percent stated rate of interest and a five-year term. Interest is paid in cash annually, beginning December 31, 2004. The bonds were issued at 96.

Required
a. Show the effect of (1) the bond issue, (2) amortization of the discount on December 31, 2004, and (3) the December 31, 2004, interest payment on the financial statements, using a horizontal statements model like the following one. Use + for increase, − for decrease, and NA for not affected.

Event No.	Assets	=	Liab.	+	S. Equity	Rev.	−	Exp.	=	Net Inc.	Cash Flow
1											

b. Determine the carrying value (face value less discount or plus premium) of the bond liability as of December 31, 2004.
c. Determine the amount of interest expense reported on the 2004 income statement.
d. Determine the carrying value (face value less discount or plus premium) of the bond liability as of December 31, 2005.
e. Determine the amount of interest expense reported on the 2005 income statement.

L.O. 6, 7　**EXERCISE 10–12B** *Effect of a Bond Premium on Financial Statements: Annual Interest*

Switzer Company issued $100,000 face value of bonds on January 1, 2004. The bonds had an 8 percent stated rate of interest and a five-year term. Interest is paid in cash annually, beginning December 31, 2004. The bonds were issued at 102.

Required

a. Show the effect of (1) the bond issue, (2) amortization of the premium on December 31, 2004, and (3) the December 31, 2004, interest payment on the financial statements using a horizontal statements model like the following one. Use + for increase, − for decrease, and NA for not affected.

Event No.	Assets	=	Liab.	+	S. Equity	Rev.	−	Exp.	=	Net Inc.	Cash Flow
1											

b. Determine the carrying value (face value less discount or plus premium) of the bond liability as of December 31, 2004.
c. Determine the amount of interest expense reported on the 2004 income statement.
d. Determine the carrying value of the bond liability as of December 31, 2005.
e. Determine the amount of interest expense reported on the 2005 income statement.

EXERCISE 10–13B *Effect of Bonds Issued at a Premium on Financial Statements: Semiannual Interest* **L.O. 6, 7**

Farm Supplies, Inc., issued $200,000 of 10-year, 6 percent bonds on July 1, 2003, at 104. Interest is payable in cash semiannually on June 30 and December 31.

Required

a. Prepare the journal entries to record issuing the bonds and any necessary journal entries for 2003 and 2004. Post the journal entries to T-accounts.
b. Prepare the liabilities section of the balance sheet at the end of 2003 and 2004.
c. What amount of interest expense will Farm report on the financial statements for 2003 and 2004?
d. What amount of cash will Farm pay for interest in 2003 and 2004?

EXERCISE 10–14B *Recording Bonds Issued at Face Value and Associated Interest for Two Accounting Cycles: Annual Interest* **L.O. 6, 7**

On January 1, 2001, Miller Corp. issued $100,000 of 10-year, 9 percent bonds at their face amount. Interest is payable on December 31 of each year with the first payment due December 31, 2001.

Required

Prepare all the general journal entries related to these bonds for 2001 and 2002.

EXERCISE 10–15B *Recording Bonds Issued at a Discount: Annual Interest* **L.O. 6, 7**

On January 1, 2005, Creason Co. issued $100,000 of five-year, 8 percent bonds at 97½. Interest is payable annually on December 31. The discount is amortized using the straight-line method.

Required

Prepare the journal entries to record the bond transactions for 2005 and 2006. Include any required year-end adjusting entries.

EXERCISE 10–16B *Recording Bonds Issued at a Premium: Semiannual Interest* **L.O. 6, 7**

On January 1, 2006, Vickers Company issued $200,000 of five-year, 12 percent bonds at 103. Interest is payable semiannually on June 30 and December 31. The premium is amortized using the straight-line method.

Required

Prepare the journal entries to record the bond transactions for 2006 and 2007. Include any required year-end adjusting entries.

EXERCISE 10–17B *Two Complete Accounting Cycles: Bonds Issued at Face Value With Annual Interest* **L.O. 6, 7**

Upton Company issued $1,000,000 of 10-year, 10 percent bonds on January 1, 2004. The bonds were issued at face value. Interest is payable in cash on December 31 of each year. Upton immediately invested the proceeds from the bond issue in land. The land was leased for an annual $140,000 of cash revenue, which was collected on December 31 of each year, beginning December 31, 2004.

Required

a. Prepare the journal entries for these events, and post them to T-accounts for 2004 and 2005.
b. Prepare the income statement, balance sheet, and statement of cash flows for 2004 and 2005.

L.O. 6, 7 **EXERCISE 10–18B** *Recording Callable Bonds*

Han Co. issued $500,000 of 8 percent, 10-year, callable bonds on January 1, 2005, for their face value. The call premium was 4 percent (bonds are callable at 104). Interest was payable annually on December 31. The bonds were called on December 31, 2009.

Required

Prepare the journal entries to record the bond issue on January 1, 2005, and the bond redemption on December 31, 2009. Assume that all entries for accrual and payment of interest were recorded correctly.

L.O. 8 **EXERCISE 10–19B** *Determining the After-Tax Cost of Debt*

The following 2003 information is available for three companies:

	Pace Co.	Pile Co.	Park Co.
Face value of bonds payable	$300,000	$600,000	$500,000
Interest rate	10%	9%	8%
Income tax rate	40%	30%	35%

Required

a. Determine the annual before-tax interest cost for each company *in dollars.*
b. Determine the annual after-tax interest cost for each company *in dollars.*
c. Determine the annual after-tax interest cost for each company as *a percentage* of the face value of the bonds.

L.O. 9 **EXERCISE 10–20B** *Future Value and Present Value (Appendix)*

Required

Using Tables I, II, III, or IV in the appendix, calculate the following:
a. The future value of $10,000 invested at 6 percent for four years.
b. The future value of five annual payments of $2,000 at 10 percent interest.
c. The amount that must be deposited today (present value) at 9 percent to accumulate $200,000 in 10 years.
d. The annual payment on a five-year, 8 percent, $100,000 note payable.

L.O. 9 **EXERCISE 10–21B** *Computing the Amount of Payment (Appendix)*

Required

a. Donna Kirk has just graduated from Ivory Tower University with a degree in theater. She wants to buy a new car but does not know if she can afford the payments. Since Kirk knows that you have had an accounting course, she asks you to compute the annual payment on a $30,000, 10 percent, five-year note. What would Kirk's annual payment be?
b. If Kirk can afford an annual payment of only $4,000, what price vehicle should she look for, assuming an interest rate of 10 percent and a five-year term?

L.O. 9 **EXERCISE 10–22B** *Saving for a Future Value (Appendix)*

Mary and Mark Yuppy are celebrating the birth of their son, Marcus Andrew Yuppy IV. They want to send Little Andy to the best university and know they must begin saving for his education right away. They project that Little Andy's education will cost $500,000.

Required

a. How much must the Yuppys set aside annually to accumulate the necessary $500,000 in 18 years? Assume an 8 percent interest rate.
b. If the Yuppys wish to make a one-time investment currently for Little Andy's education, how much must they deposit today, assuming an 8 percent interest rate?

L.O. 7, 9 **EXERCISE 10–23B** *Sale of Bonds at a Discount Using Present Value (Appendix)*

Thompson Corporation issued $100,000 of 10 percent, 10-year bonds on January 1, 2002, for a price that reflected a 9 percent market rate of interest. Interest is payable annually on December 31.

Required

a. What was the selling price of the bonds?

b. Prepare the journal entry to record issuing the bonds.

c. Prepare the journal entry for the first interest payment on December 31, 2002, using the effective interest rate method.

EXERCISE 10-24B *Effect of Semiannual Interest on Investment Returns (Appendix)*

L.O. 7, 9

Required

Write a short memo explaining why an investor would find a bond that pays semiannual interest more attractive than one that pays annual interest.

PROBLEMS—SERIES B

PROBLEM 10-25B *Effect of a Long-Term Note Payable on Financial Statements*

L.O. 2

On January 1, 2001, Mixon Co. borrowed cash from Best Bank by issuing a $100,000 face value, four-year term note that had a 10 percent annual interest rate. The note is to be repaid by making annual cash payments of $31,547 that include both interest and principal on December 31 of each year. Mixon used the proceeds from the loan to purchase land that generated rental revenues of $40,000 cash per year.

Required

a. Prepare an amortization schedule for the four-year period.

b. Prepare an income statement, balance sheet, and statement of cash flows for each of the four years. (*Hint:* Record the transactions for each year in T-accounts before preparing the financial statements.)

c. Given that revenue is the same for each period, explain why net income increases each year.

PROBLEM 10-26B *Effect of a Line of Credit on Financial Statements*

L.O. 3

Libby Company has a line of credit with State Bank. Libby can borrow up to $200,000 at any time over the course of the 2006 calendar year. The following table shows the prime rate expressed as an annual percentage along with the amounts borrowed and repaid during 2006. Libby agreed to pay interest at an annual rate equal to 2 percent above the bank's prime rate. Funds are borrowed or repaid on the first day of each month. Interest is payable in cash on the last day of the month. The interest rate is applied to the outstanding monthly balance. For example, Libby pays 7 percent (5 percent + 2 percent) annual interest on $100,000 for the month of January.

Month	Amount Borrowed or (Repaid)	Prime Rate for the Month %
January	$100,000	5
February	50,000	6
March	(40,000)	7
April through October	No change	No change
November	(80,000)	6
December	(20,000)	5

Libby earned $30,000 of cash revenue during 2006.

Required

a. Prepare an income statement, balance sheet, and statement of cash flows for 2006. (*Note:* Round computations to the nearest dollar.)

b. Write a memo to explain how the business was able to generate retained earnings when the owner contributed no assets to the business.

PROBLEM 10-27B *Accounting for a Bond Discount Over Multiple Accounting Cycles*

L.O. 6, 7

Box Company was started when it issued bonds with a $400,000 face value on January 1, 2005. The bonds were issued for cash at 96. They had a 20-year term to maturity and an 8 percent annual interest rate. Interest was payable on December 31 of each year. Box Company immediately purchased land with the proceeds (cash received) from the bond issue. Box leased the land for $50,000 cash per year. On January 1, 2008, the company sold the land for $400,000 cash. Immediately after the sale of the land, Box redeemed the bonds at 98. Assume that no other accounting events occurred during 2008.

Required

Prepare an income statement, statement of changes in equity, balance sheet, and statement of cash flows for the 2005, 2006, 2007, and 2008 accounting periods. Assume that the company closes its books on December 31 of each year. Prepare the statements using a vertical statements format. (*Hint:* Record each year's transactions in T-accounts prior to preparing the financial statements.)

L.O. 5, 6, 7   **PROBLEM 10–28B** *Recording and Reporting Bond Discount Over Two Cycles*

During 2006 and 2007, Joy Corp. completed the following transactions relating to its bond issue. The corporation's fiscal year is the calendar year.

2006

Jan. 1	Issued $100,000 of 10-year, 10 percent bonds for $96,000. Interest is payable annually on December 31.
Dec. 31	Paid the interest on the bonds.
31	Recorded the bond discount amortization using the straight-line method.
31	Closed the interest expense account.

2007

Dec. 31	Paid the interest on the bonds.
31	Recorded the bond discount amortization using the straight-line method.
31	Closed the interest expense account.

Required

a. When the bonds were issued, was the market rate of interest more or less than the stated rate of interest? If Joy had sold the bonds at their face amount, what amount of cash would Joy have received?

b. Prepare the general journal entries for these transactions.

c. Prepare the liabilities section of the balance sheet at December 31, 2006 and 2007.

d. Determine the amount of interest expense that will be reported on the income statements for 2006 and 2007.

e. Determine the amounts of interest that will be paid in cash to the bondholder in 2006 and 2007.

L.O. 6, 7   **PROBLEM 10–29B** *Effect of a Bond Discount on the Elements of Financial Statements*

Stafford Co. was formed when it acquired cash from the issue of common stock. The company then issued bonds at a discount on January 1, 2003. Interest is payable on December 31 with the first payment made December 31, 2003. On January 2, 2003, Stafford Co. purchased a piece of land that produced rent revenue annually. The rent is collected on December 31 of each year, beginning December 31, 2003. At the end of the six-year period (January 1, 2009), the land was sold at a gain, and the bonds were paid off at face value. A summary of the transactions for each year follows:

2003

1. Acquired cash from the issue of common stock.
2. Issued six-year bonds.
3. Purchased land.
4. Received land-lease income.
5. Amortized bond discount at December 31.
6. Paid cash for interest expense at the stated rate on December 31.
7. Prepared December 31 entry to close Rent Revenue.
8. Prepared December 31 entry to close Interest Expense.

2004–2008

9. Received land-lease income.
10. Amortized bond discount at December 31.
11. Paid cash for interest expense at the stated rate on December 31.
12. Prepared December 31 entry to close Rent Revenue.
13. Prepared December 31 entry to close Interest Expense.

2009

14. Sold the land at a gain.
15. Retired the bonds at face value.

Required

Identify each of these 15 transactions as asset source (AS), asset use (AU), asset exchange (AE), or claims exchange (CE). Explain how each event affects assets, liabilities, equity, net income, and cash flow by placing a + for increase, − for decrease, or NA for not affected under each of the categories. In the Cash Flow column, indicate whether the item is an operating activity (OA), investing activity (IA), or financing activity (FA). The first event is recorded as an example.

Event No.	Type of Event	Assets	Liabilities	Common Stock	Retained Earnings	Net Income	Cash Flow
1	AS	+	NA	+	NA	NA	+ FA

PROBLEM 10–30B *Recording Transactions for Callable Bonds*   L.O. 6, 7

IHL Corp. issued $300,000 of 20-year, 10 percent, callable bonds on January 1, 2004, with interest payable annually on December 31. The bonds were issued at their face amount. The bonds are callable at 105. The fiscal year of the corporation ends December 31.

Required

a. Show the effect of the following events on the financial statements by recording the appropriate amounts in a horizontal statements model like the following one. In the Cash Flow column, indicate whether the item is an operating activity (OA), investing activity (IA), or financing activity (FA). Use NA if an element was not affected by the event.

   (1) Issued the bonds on January 1, 2004.

   (2) Paid interest due to bondholders on December 31, 2004.

   (3) On January 1, 2009, IHL Corp. called the bonds. Assume that all interim entries were correctly recorded.

Event No.	Assets	=	Liab.	+	S. Equity	Rev.	−	Exp.	=	Net Inc.	Cash Flow
1											

b. Prepare journal entries for the three events listed in Requirement *a.*

PROBLEM 10–31B *Effect of Debt Transactions on Financial Statements*   L.O. 6, 7

The three typical accounting events associated with borrowing money through a bond issue are:

1. Exchanging the bonds for cash on the day of issue.
2. Making cash payments for interest expense and recording amortization when applicable.
3. Repaying the principal at maturity.

Required

a. Assuming the bonds are issued at face value, show the effect of each of the three events on the financial statements, using a horizontal statements model like the following one. Use + for increase, − for decrease, and NA for not affected.

Event No.	Assets	=	Liab.	+	S. Equity	Rev.	−	Exp.	=	Net Inc.	Cash Flow
1											

b. Repeat the requirements in Requirement *a,* but assume instead that the bonds are issued at a discount.

c. Repeat the requirements in Requirement *a,* but assume instead that the bonds are issued at a premium.

PROBLEM 10–32B *Sale of Bonds at a Discount and Amortization Using the Effective Interest Method (Appendix)*   L.O. 7, 9

On January 1, 2004, Pond Corp. sold $500,000 of its own 8 percent, 10-year bonds. Interest is payable annually on December 31. The bonds were sold to yield an effective interest rate of 9 percent. Pond uses the effective interest rate method.

Required

a. Using the information in the appendix, calculate the selling price of the bonds.

b. Prepare the journal entry for the issuance of the bonds.

c. Prepare the journal entry for the amortization of the bond discount and the payment of the interest at December 31, 2004.

d. Calculate the amount of interest expense for 2005.

ANALYZE, THINK, COMMUNICATE

ATC 10–1   BUSINESS APPLICATIONS CASE *Dell's Annual Report*

Required

Using the Dell Computer Corporation financial statements in Appendix B, answer the following questions:

a. What was the primary type of long-term debt that Dell had in 2001?

b. What was the maximum length to maturity of Dell's long-term debt?

c. What was the maximum amount available to Dell through its line of credit?

ATC 10–2   GROUP ASSIGNMENT *Missing Information*

The following three companies issued the following bonds:

1. Lot, Inc., issued $100,000 of 8 percent, five-year bonds at 102¼ on January 1, 2006. Interest is payable annually on December 31.

2. Max, Inc., issued $100,000 of 8 percent, five-year bonds at 98 on January 1, 2006. Interest is payable annually on December 31.

3. Par, Inc., issued $100,000 of 8 percent, five-year bonds at 104 on January 1, 2006. Interest is payable annually on December 31.

Required

a. Organize the class into three sections and divide each section into groups of three to five students. Assign each of the sections one of the companies.

Group Tasks

(1) Compute the following amounts for your company:

  (a) Cash proceeds from the bond issue.

  (b) Interest expense for 2006.

  (c) Interest paid in 2006.

(2) Prepare the liabilities section of the balance sheet as of December 31, 2006.

Class Discussion

b. Have a representative of each section put the liabilities section for its company on the board.

c. Is the amount of interest expense different for the three companies? Why or why not?

d. Is the amount of interest paid different for each of the companies? Why or why not?

e. Is the amount of total liabilities different for each of the companies? Why or why not?

ATC 10–3   REAL-WORLD CASE *Using Accounting Numbers to Assess Creditworthiness*

Standard & Poor's (S&P) and Moody's are two credit-rating services that evaluate the creditworthiness of various companies. Their grading systems are similar but not exactly the same. S&P's grading scheme works as follows: AAA is the highest rating, followed by AA, A, BBB, and so on. For each grade, a + or − may be used.

The following are selected financial data for four companies whose overall, long-term creditworthiness was rated by S&P. The date the company was rated by S&P is shown in parentheses. The companies, listed alphabetically, are as follows:

Alltel is a large telecommunications company that provides a variety of wireline and wireless services. At the end of 1999, it had approximately 6 million wireless customers.

Ameriking is an independent franchisee that operates 379 Burger King restaurants in the United States.

Barnes & Noble is the largest bookseller in the country, operating 942 bookstores as of the end of 1999.

Carmike owned 458 movie theaters in small to mid-sized communities in 36 states as of December 31, 1999.

Dollar amounts are in thousands.

	Net Income	Cash Flow from Operating Activities	Current Ratio	Debt to Assets Ratio	Times Interest Earned	Return on Assets Ratio
Alltel (8/15/00)						
1999	$783,634	$1,500,029	1.02	0.61	5.6	7.3%
1998	603,127	1,405,848	0.85	0.64	5.0	5.9
Ameriking (1/30/01)						
1999	(817)	20,145	0.75	0.89	1.1	0.3
1998	(1,813)	27,044	0.51	0.87	1.2	2.8
Barnes & Noble (3/2/01)						
1999	124,498	187,331	1.35	0.65	10.2	5.2
1998	92,376	177,668	1.41	0.62	7.4	5.1
Carmike (8/8/00)						
1999	(12,585)	57,552	0.29	0.75	0.5	(1.6)
1998	(30,647)	92,033	0.34	0.68	(0.8)	(4.4)

Each company received a different credit rating from S&P. The grades awarded, in descending order, were A, BB, CCC+, and D.

Required

Determine which grade was assigned to each company. Explain the reason for your decisions.

BUSINESS APPLICATIONS CASE *Using Ratios to Make Comparisons*

ATC 10–4

The following accounting information pertains to Quality Landscaping Co. and Super Lawn Care, Inc., at the end of 2001.

	Quality Landscaping Co.	Super Lawn Care, Inc.
Current assets	$ 20,000	$ 20,000
Total assets	350,000	350,000
Current liabilities	35,000	25,000
Total liabilities	300,000	220,000
Stockholders' equity	50,000	130,000
Interest expense	27,500	20,000
Income tax expense	31,000	34,000
Net income	46,500	51,000

Required

a. Compute the following ratios for each company: debt to assets, current, and times interest earned (EBIT must be computed). Identify the company with the greater financial risk.

b. For each company, compute the return on equity and return on assets ratios. Use EBIT instead of net income to compute the return on assets ratio. Identify the company that is managing its assets more effectively. Identify the company that is producing the higher return from the stockholders' perspective. Explain how one company was able to produce a higher return on equity than the other.

BUSINESS APPLICATIONS CASE *Determining the Effects of Financing Alternatives on Ratios*   ATC 10–5

Tipstaff Industries has the following account balances:

Current Assets	$100,000	Current Liabilities	$ 65,000
Noncurrent Assets	225,000	Noncurrent Liabilities	160,000
		Stockholders' Equity	100,000

The company wishes to raise $100,000 in cash and is considering two financing options. Either it can sell $100,000 of bonds payable, or it can issue additional common stock for $100,000. To help in the decision process, Tipstaff's management wants to determine the effects of each alternative on its current ratio and debt to assets ratio.

Required

a. Help Tipstaff's management by completing the following chart:

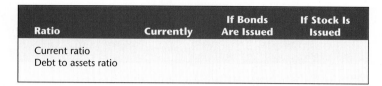

Ratio	Currently	If Bonds Are Issued	If Stock Is Issued
Current ratio			
Debt to assets ratio			

b. Assume that after the funds are invested, EBIT amounts to $50,000. Also assume that Tipstaff pays $10,000 in dividends or $10,000 in interest, depending on which source of financing is used. Based on a 30 percent tax rate, determine the amount of the increase in retained earnings under each financing option.

ATC 10–6   WRITING ASSIGNMENT *Debt Versus Equity Financing*

Mack Company plans to invest $50,000 in land that will produce annual rent revenue equal to 15 percent of the investment starting on January 1, 2003. The revenue will be collected in cash at the end of each year, starting December 31, 2003. Mack can obtain the cash necessary to purchase the land from two sources. Funds can be obtained by issuing $50,000 of 10 percent, five-year bonds at their face amount. Interest due on the bonds is payable on December 31 of each year with the first payment due on December 31, 2003. Alternatively, the $50,000 needed to invest in land can be obtained from equity financing. In this case, the stockholders (holders of the equity) will be paid a $5,000 annual distribution. Mack Company is in a 30 percent income tax bracket.

Required
a. Prepare an income statement and statement of cash flows for 2003 under the two alternative financing proposals.
b. Write a short memorandum explaining why one financing alternative provides more net income but less cash flow than the other.

ATC 10–7   ETHICAL DILEMMA *I Don't Want to Pay Taxes*

Dana Harbert recently started a very successful small business. Indeed, the business had grown so rapidly that she was no longer able to finance its operations by investing her own resources in the business. She needed additional capital but had no more of her own money to put into the business. A friend, Gene Watson, was willing to invest $100,000 in the business. Harbert estimated that with Watson's investment, the company would be able to increase revenue by $40,000. Furthermore, she believed that operating expenses would increase by only 10 percent. Harbert and Watson agree that Watson's investment should entitle him to receive a cash dividend equal to 20 percent of net income. A set of forecasted statements with and without Watson's investment is presented here. (Assume that all transactions involving revenue, expense, and dividends are cash transactions.)

Financial Statements	Forecast 1 Without Watson's Investment	Forecast 2 With Watson's Investment
Income Statement		
Revenue	$120,000	$160,000
Operating Expenses	(70,000)	(77,000)
Income before Interest and Taxes	50,000	83,000
Income Tax Expense (effective tax rate is 30%)	(15,000)	(24,900)
Net Income	$ 35,000	$ 58,100
Statement of Changes in Stockholders' Equity		
Beginning Retained Earnings	$15,000	$15,000
Plus: Net Income	35,000	58,100
Less: Dividend to Watson (20% of $58,100)	0	(11,620)
Ending Retained Earnings	$50,000	$61,480

(continued)

Financial Statements		
	Forecast 1 **Without Watson's** **Investment**	**Forecast 2** **With Watson's** **Investment**
Balance Sheets		
Assets (computations explained in following paragraph)	$400,000	$511,480
Liabilities	$ 0	$ 0
Equity		
Common Stock	350,000	450,000
Retained Earnings	50,000	61,480
Total Liabilities and Equity	$400,000	$511,480

The balance for assets in forecast 1 is computed as the beginning balance of $365,000 plus net income of $35,000. The balance for assets in forecast 2 is computed as the beginning balance of $365,000, plus the $100,000 cash investment, plus net income of $58,100, less the $11,620 distribution. Alternatively, total assets can be computed by determining the amount of total claims (total assets = total claims).

Harbert tells Watson that there would be a $3,486 tax advantage associated with debt financing. She says that if Watson is willing to become a creditor instead of an owner, she could pay him an additional $697.20 (that is, 20 percent of the tax advantage). Watson tells Harbert that he has no interest in participating in the management of the business, but Watson wants an ownership interest to guarantee that he will always receive 20 percent of the profits of the business. Harbert suggests that they execute a formal agreement in which Watson is paid 11.62 percent interest on his $100,000 loan to the business. This agreement will be used for income tax reporting. In addition, Harbert says that she is willing to establish a private agreement to write Watson a personal check for any additional amount necessary to make Watson's total return equal to 20 percent of all profits plus a $697.20 bonus for his part of the tax advantage. She tells Watson, "It's just like ownership. The only difference is that we call it debt for the Internal Revenue Service. If they want to have some silly rule that says if you call it debt, you get a tax break, then we are foolish if we don't call it debt. I will call it anything they want, just as long as I don't have to pay taxes on it."

Required

a. Construct a third set of forecasted financial statements (forecast 3) at 11.62 percent annual interest, assuming that Watson is treated as creditor (he loans the business $100,000).

b. Verify the tax advantage of debt financing by comparing the balances of the Retained Earnings account in forecast 2 and forecast 3.

c. If you were Watson, would you permit Harbert to classify the equity transaction as debt to provide a higher return to the business and to you?

d. Comment on the ethical implications of misnaming a financing activity for the sole purpose of reducing income taxes.

EDGAR DATABASE *Analyzing Long-Term Debt at Delta Air Lines*

ATC 10–8

Many companies have a form of debt called *capital leases.* A capital lease is created when a company agrees to rent an asset, such as equipment or a building, for such a long time that GAAP treats this lease as if the asset were purchased by using borrowed funds. Thus, a capital lease creates a liability for the company that acquired the leased asset because the company has promised to make payments to another company for several years in the future. If a company has any capital leases, it must disclose them in the footnotes to the financial statements and sometimes disclose them on a separate line in the liabilities section of the balance sheet.

Required

Using the most current 10-K available on EDGAR, answer the following questions about Delta Air Lines, Inc. Instructions for using EDGAR are in Appendix A.

a. What was Delta's debt to assets ratio?

b. How much interest expense did Delta incur?

c. What amount of liabilities did Delta have as a result of capital leases?

d. What percentage of Delta's long-term liabilities was the result of capital leases?

e. Many companies try to structure (design) leasing agreements so that their leases will *not* be classified as capital leases. Explain why a company such as Delta might want to avoid having capital leases.

ATC 10–9 SPREADSHEET ASSIGNMENT *Using Excel*

On January 1, 2001, Bainbridge Company borrowed $100,000 cash from a bank by issuing a 10-year, 9 percent note. The principal and interest are to be paid by making annual payments in the amount of $15,582. Payments are to be made December 31 of each year beginning December 31, 2001.

Required

a. Set up the preceding spreadsheet. Notice that Excel can be set up to calculate the loan payment. If you're unfamiliar with this, see the following Spreadsheet Tips section. The Beginning Principal Balance (B12) and Cash Payment (C12) can be referenced from the Loan Information section. The interest rate used to calculate Interest Expense (D12) can also be referenced from the Loan Information section.

b. Complete the spreadsheet for the 10 periods.

c. In Row 23, calculate totals for cash payments, interest expense, and applied to principal.

d. Consider how the amounts would differ if Bainbridge were to borrow the $100,000 at different interest rates and time periods. The results of the original data (option 1) have been entered in the following schedule. In the spreadsheet, delete 9 percent and 10 from cells B4 and B5. Enter the data for the second option (8 percent and 10 years) in cells B4 and B5. Enter in the payment and total interest in the schedule for the second option. Continue the same process for options 3 through 9 by deleting the prior rate and number of periods in the spreadsheet and entering in the next option's data. The number of years scheduled (rows 12 through 21) will have to be shortened for the 7-year options and lengthened for the 13-year options.

	Option								
	1	2	3	4	5	6	7	8	9
Rate	9%	8%	10%	9%	8%	10%	9%	8%	10%
Years	10	10	10	7	7	7	13	13	13
Payment	15,582								
Total interest	55,820								

Spreadsheet Tips

1. Excel will calculate an installment loan payment. The interest rate (%), number of periods (nper), and amount borrowed or otherwise known as present value (PV) must be entered in the payment formula.

The formula for the payment is =PMT(rate,nper,pv). The rate, number of periods, and amount borrowed (present value) may be entered as actual amounts or referenced to other cells. In the preceding spreadsheet, the payment formula can be either =PMT(9%,10,100000) or =PMT(B4,B5,B3). In our case, the latter is preferred so that variables can be altered in the spreadsheet without also having to rewrite the payment formula. Notice that the payment is a negative number.

2. Using positive numbers is preferred in the amortization schedule. The loan payment (cell B6) in the loan information section shows up as a negative number. Any reference to it in the amortization schedule should be preceded by a minus sign to convert it to a positive number. For example, the formula in cell C12 for the cash payment is =−B6.

3. Recall that to copy a fixed number, a $ sign must be positioned before the column letter and row number. The complete formula then for cell C12 is =−$B$6.

SPREADSHEET ANALYSIS *Mastering Excel*

ATC 10–10

Wise Company was started on January 1, 2001, when it issued 20-year, 10 percent, $200,000 face value bonds at a price of 90. Interest is payable annually at December 31 of each year. Wise immediately purchased land with the proceeds (cash received) from the bond issue. Wise leased the land for $27,000 cash per year. The lease revenue payments are due every December 31.

Required

Set up the following horizontal statements model on a blank spreadsheet. The SCF Activity column is for the classifications operating, financing, or investing.

		A	B	C	D	E	F	G	H	I	J	K	L	M	N	O
	1		SCF				Bonds	Bond	Retained		Effect on					
	2	Date	Activity	Cash	Land		Payable	Discount	Earnings		Net Income					
	3	1-1-01														
	4	1-1-01														
	5	12-31-01	OA	27,000					27,000		27,000	Lease Revenue				
	6	12-31-01														
	7															
	8	2001 Ending				=					Net Income					
	9															
	10			Total Assets		=		Total Claims								
	11															
	12	2002 Beginning														
	13	12-31-02														
	14	12-31-02														
	15															
	16	2002 Ending									Net Income					
	17															
	18			Total Assets				Total Claims								
	19															
	20	2003 Beginning														
	21	12-31-03														
	22	12-31-03														
	23															
	24	2003 Ending									Net Income					
	25															
	26			Total Assets				Total Claims								
	27															
	28	2004 Beginning														
	29	1-1-04														
	30	1-1-04														
	31															
	32	2004 Ending									Net Income					
	33															
	34			Total Assets				Total Claims								
	35															

Problem 10-2 Answer Key — **Problem** — Pr 10-2 Key Effective

a. Enter the effects of the 2001 transactions. Assume that both the interest and lease payments occurred on December 31. Notice that the entry for the lease has already been entered as an example. Calculate the ending balances.

b. Enter the effects of the 2002 transactions. Assume that both the interest and lease payments occurred on December 31. Calculate the ending balances.

c. Enter the effects of the 2003 transactions. Assume that both the interest and lease payments occurred on December 31. Calculate the ending balances.

d. On January 1, 2004, Wise Company sold the land for $190,000 cash. Immediately after the sale of the land, Wise repurchased its bond at a price of 93. Assume that no other accounting events occurred during 2004. Enter in the effects of the 2004 balances. Calculate the ending balances.

Accounting for Equity Transactions

After completing this chapter, you should be able to:

1 List the primary characteristics of a sole proprietorship, partnership, and corporation.

2 Identify the different types of business organizations through the analysis of financial statements.

3 Explain the characteristics of major types of stock issued by corporations.

4 Explain the accounting treatment for different types of stock issued by corporations.

5 Explain the effects of treasury stock transactions on a company's financial statements.

6 Explain the effects of a declaration and payment of cash dividends on a company's financial statements.

7 Explain the effects of stock dividends and stock splits on a company's financial statements.

8 Show how the appropriation of retained earnings affects financial statements.

9 Explain how accounting information can be useful in making stock investment decisions.

10 Explain accounting for not-for-profit entities and governmental organizations. (Appendix)

the *curious* accountant

I magine that a rich uncle wanted to reward you for outstanding performance in your first accounting course, so he gave you $15,000 to invest in the stock of one company. You narrowed your choice to two companies. After reviewing their recent annual reports, you developed the following information:

Mystery Company A: This company has existed for about five years and has never made a profit; in fact, it had net losses totaling more than $197 million. Its net loss each year has been much larger than the loss of the year before. This stock is selling for about $15 per share, so you can buy 1,000 shares. A friend told you it was a "sure winner," especially at its current price.

Mystery Company B: This company has existed for more than 100 years and has made a profit most years. In the most recent five years, its net earnings totaled over $34 *billion,* and it paid dividends of over $19 *billion.* This stock is selling for about $50 per share, so you can buy 300 shares of it. Your friend said it was a stock "your grandfather should own."

The descriptions apply to real-world companies, the names of which are revealed later. Based on the information provided, which company's stock would you buy?

The three major forms of business organization are sole proprietorship, partnership, *and* corporation. *These business structures evolved to meet the special needs of society at different times. The most basic form is the sole proprietorship.* **Sole proprietorships** *are owned by one person and are usually fairly small. Since the participants of any exchange of goods could be classified as proprietors, it is impossible to identify the first proprietorship in history.*

The proprietorship was the dominant form of business for many years. Gradually, business-people realized the benefits that can be derived by joining together as partners to *share their talents, their capital, and the risks of business. The **partnership** also dates back to some unidentifiable transaction occurring thousands of years ago. However, the real development of partnerships began around the 13th century during the Middle Ages. To defend and promote their interests, artisans formed professional associations called* guilds. These *guilds conducted extensive trade, often with one partner providing capital while another went in search of riches.*

*The roots of the **corporation** lie in the exploration of the New World. The need for large amounts of capital led to the sale of shares in trading companies such as the Dutch East India Company. The industrial revolution of the nineteenth century further influenced the proliferation of the corporate form of business. Vast sums of capital were needed to keep pace with increasing technology and mass production.*

▌Formation of Business Organizations

Ownership Agreements

LO1 List the primary characteristics of a sole proprietorship, partnership, and corporation.

Since proprietorships are owned by a single individual, there are no disputes regarding who is ultimately responsible for making decisions or how profits are to be distributed. Accordingly, the process of establishing a sole proprietorship is usually as simple as obtaining a business license from local government authorities. In contrast, partnerships require clear communication of how authority, risks, and profitability will be shared among the partners. To minimize misunderstandings and conflict, most partnerships are based on a **partnership agreement,** a legal document that defines the responsibilities of each partner and describes the division of income and losses. In addition to legal services, the formation and operation of partnerships may require the services of accounting professionals. The distribution of profits is certainly affected by the measurement of profitability. Accordingly, partnerships may require the services of independent public accountants to ensure that records are kept in accordance with GAAP. The application of tax regulations to partnerships also may become so complicated that many partners are forced to seek professional advice.

The establishment of a corporation usually requires the assistance of legal and accounting professionals. Although individuals are permitted to file the documents necessary to start a corporation, the process involves the completion of a fairly complex set of forms containing technical terminology. Accordingly, the filing process may be perplexing to a layperson who is unfamiliar with business practice. Even so, the process is simple and methodical for professionals who are trained and experienced in the filing process. As a result, legal and accounting services for routine filings are usually well worth the customary fees charged.

A corporation is designated as a *separate legal entity* by the state in which it is incorporated. Each of the 50 states has its own laws governing this process; however, many have adopted the provisions of the Model Business Corporation Act, and most states follow standard procedures. The first step of incorporation consists of an application filed with a state agency. This application is called the **articles of incorporation,** and it contains all information required by state law. The most common information items required are (1) the name of the corporation and proposed date of incorporation; (2) the purpose of the corporation; (3) the location of the business and its expected life (which can be *perpetuity,* meaning "endless"); (4) provisions for capital stock (the certificates that evidence an ownership interest in the corporation); and (5) the names and addresses of the members of the first board of directors (the designated group of individuals with the ultimate authority for operating the business). If the articles are found to be in order, the state issues a charter of incorporation, which establishes the legal existence of the corporation and is filed, along with the articles, in county records that are available to any person interested in reviewing them.

Regulation

Very few laws apply specifically to the operation of proprietorships and partnerships. Corporations are a different story. The level of regulation applicable to corporations depends on the size and distribution of the company's ownership interest. The ownership interest in a corporation is normally evidenced by **stock certificates.** When owners contribute assets to a corporation, the owners receive stock certificates that describe the rights and privileges accompanying the ownership interest. Since stock evidences ownership, owners are frequently called **stockholders.**

Ownership can be transferred from one individual to another by the exchange of stock certificates. As long as exchanges (the buying and selling of shares of stock) are limited to transactions between individuals, the company is defined as being a **closely held corporation.** However, once a corporation reaches a certain size, it may list its stock on a stock exchange such as the New York Stock Exchange or the American Stock Exchange. Trading on a stock exchange is limited to the stockbrokers who are members of the exchange. These brokers represent buyers and sellers who want to exchange stock certificates. The buyers and sellers pay the brokers commissions as compensation for completing the transactions. Although closely held corporations are relatively free from regulation, companies whose stock is traded on the exchanges by brokers are subject to an extensive set of rules and regulations.

Before the 1930s, trading on stock exchanges was relatively free of regulation. However, the stock market crash of 1929 and the subsequent Great Depression led to the passage of the **Securities Act of 1933** and the **Securities Exchange Act of 1934** designed to regulate the issuance of stock and to govern the exchanges. The laws created the Securities and Exchange Commission (SEC) to enforce the acts. As discussed previously, the SEC was given legal authority for the establishment of accounting policies to be followed by corporations registered on the exchanges. However, the SEC has generally deferred its rule-making authority to the accounting profession. Even so, it is important to realize that the only legal authority for accounting procedures does reside with the SEC. Indeed, the SEC has stepped in on several occasions when it believed that the profession was not properly regulating itself.

▌Advantages and Disadvantages of Different Forms of Business Organization

LO1 List the primary characteristics of a sole proprietorship, partnership, and corporation.

The owners of proprietorships and partnerships are held *personally accountable* for the actions that they take in the name of their businesses. Indeed, a partner is responsible not only for his or her own actions but also for the actions that any other partner takes on behalf of the partnership. In contrast, corporations are established as legal entities separate from their owners. Accordingly, corporations, rather than their owners, bear the responsibility for actions taken in the name of the company. These different levels of responsibility provide a unique set of advantages and disadvantages for each type of business structure. The next section compares and contrasts the advantages and disadvantages of proprietorships, partnerships, and corporations.

Double Taxation

Because the corporation is an entity in itself, its profits are taxed by state and federal governments. This often gives rise to a situation known as *double taxation*. **Double taxation** refers to the fact that corporate profits that are distributed to owners are taxed twice—once when the income appears on the corporation's income tax return and once when the distribution appears on the individual owner's return. For example, assume that a corporation in a 30 percent tax bracket earns pretax income of $100,000. The corporation is required to pay income tax of

Mystery Company A is Webmethods, Inc. (as of July 2001). Webmethods provides infrastructure software and services to companies engaged in business-to-business commerce. The company was incorporated in 1996, and on February 11, 2000, its stock was sold to the public in an *initial public offering (IPO)* at $35. The first day its stock traded on NASDAQ, it opened at $195; during that day, it sold for as high as $215 per share. Obviously, the people trading Webmethods' stock were not paying much attention to accounting data.

Instead, they were focusing on what the company might become, and many were simply speculating based on the hype the company's IPO had generated. The stock market does not always behave rationally. By the end of February 2000, Webmethods' stock price hit $336, but by July 2001, it was down to around $15.

Mystery Company B is Phillip Morris Companies, Inc. (as of July 2001). Of course, only the future will tell which company will be the better investment.

$30,000 ($100,000 $\times$ 0.30). If the corporation distributes the after-tax income of $70,000 ($100,000 $-$ $30,000) to an individual who is also taxed at a 30 percent rate, that individual has to report the distribution on her or his income tax return and has to pay $21,000 ($70,000 $\times$ 0.30) of income taxes. Accordingly, a total of $51,000 of tax has to be paid on $100,000 of earned income. This equates to an effective tax rate of 51 percent ($51,000 $\div$ $100,000).

Double taxation could be a great burden to small closely held corporations. Fortunately, tax laws permit the election of an "S Corporation," which allows closely held companies to be taxed as partnerships or proprietorships. Also, many states have recently enacted legislation that permits the formation of **limited liability companies (LLCs).** Although LLCs offer many of the benefits associated with corporate ownership, the Internal Revenue Service has, in general, permitted them to be taxed as partnerships. Since partnerships and proprietorships are not separate legal entities, they do not earn income in the names of their companies. Instead, the income generated by these businesses is considered to be earned by the owners and therefore is taxed only at the individual owner's tax rate. This is true regardless of whether the income is retained in the business or is distributed to the owners.

Regulation

Corporations do not exist in a natural state. Instead, they are created by government authorities. These authorities may restrict corporations from engaging in certain activities. Also, authorities frequently require corporations to make public disclosures that are not required of proprietorships or partnerships. For example, the Securities and Exchange Commission requires large publicly traded corporations to make a full set of audited financial statements available for public review. Staying in compliance with the multitude of regulations that apply to corporations can be complicated and expensive. Clearly, exposure to government regulation is a disadvantage of the corporate form of business organization.

Limited Liability

Given the consequences of double taxation and increased regulation, you may wonder why anyone would choose the corporate form of business structure over a partnership or proprietorship. One major reason is that the corporate form limits the potential liability an investor must accept in order to obtain an ownership interest in a business venture. Because a corporation is responsible for its own actions, creditors cannot lay claim to the owners' personal assets as payment for the company's debts. Also, plaintiffs must file suit against the corporation, not against its owners. As a result, the most that any owner of a corporation can lose is the amount that she or he has invested in the company. In contrast, the owners of proprietorships and partnerships are *personally liable* for actions taken in the names of their companies. The benefit of **limited liability** is one of the most significant reasons for the popularity of the corporate form of business organization.

Continuity

Unlike partnerships or proprietorships, which are terminated with the departure of their owners, a corporation's life may extend well beyond the time at which any particular shareholder decides to retire or sell his or her stock. **Continuity** of existence accounts for the fact that many corporations formed in the 1800s continue to thrive in today's economy.

Transferability

Since the ownership of a corporation is divided into small units that are represented by shares of stock, **transferability** of ownership interests can be accomplished with ease. Indeed, hundreds of millions of shares of stock representing ownership in corporations are bought and sold on the major stock exchanges daily. The operations of the firm are usually unaffected by the transfers, and owners of corporations are not burdened with the task of finding willing buyers for an entire business as are the owners of proprietorships and partnerships. For example, think of the difference in difficulty of selling $1 million of Exxon stock versus that of selling a locally owned gas station. The stock could be sold on the New York Stock Exchange to a diverse group of investors within a matter of minutes. In contrast, it could take years to find an individual who is financially capable of and interested in owning a gas station.

Management Structure

Partnerships and proprietorships are usually operated by their owners. In contrast, there are three tiers of management authority in a corporate structure. The *owners* (stockholders) are perched at the highest level of the organization. These stockholders *elect* a **board of directors** to oversee the operations of the corporation. The directors then *hire* executives who manage the company. Since large corporations are able to offer high salaries and challenging career opportunities, often these companies are able to attract superior managerial talent. However, exceptional performance is not guaranteed, and the elimination of incompetent managers is sometimes complicated by a bureaucratic corporate structure. Firing the chief executive officer who is usually a member of the board of directors requires the approval of the majority of his or her peer directors. Furthermore, many of these directors may have self-interests that are served by the existing managerial team. Accordingly, the political implications of asking a chief executive to resign can become so distasteful that many individuals are reluctant to give the necessary approval. Corporations operating under such conditions are said to be experiencing **entrenched management.**

Ability to Raise Capital

Because corporations can be owned by millions of individuals, they have more opportunities to raise capital. Few individuals have the financial ability to establish a telecommunications network such as AT&T or a marketing distribution system such as Wal-Mart. However, by pooling the resources of millions of individuals through public stock and bond offerings, corporations generate the billions of dollars of capital necessary to make such massive investments. In contrast, the capital capacity of proprietorships and partnerships is bound by the financial condition of a relatively few private owners. Although these types of businesses can increase their resource base by borrowing, the amount that creditors are willing to lend them is usually limited by the size of the owners' net worth. The capacity to raise vast sums of capital is a primary reason that corporations are able to develop and market expensive new technologies more effectively than individuals operating other forms of business.

▌Appearance of Capital Structure in Financial Statements

LO2 Identify the different types of business organizations through the analysis of financial statements.

Up to this point, we have used generic terms to reflect capital structure in financial statements. The term *equity* has been used to describe the total ownership interest in the business. This interest has been divided into two categories: (1) *common stock,* which represents owner investments, and (2) *retained earnings,* which provides a measure of the capital generated through operating activities. Although these two elements are present in all forms of business organization, they are shown in significantly different formats, depending on the type of business for which a set of financial reports is being prepared.

Presentation of Equity in Proprietorships

Common stock and retained earnings are combined in a single Capital account on the balance sheets of proprietorships. To illustrate, assume that Worthington Sole Proprietorship was started on January 1, 2001, when it acquired a $5,000 capital contribution from its owner, Phil Worthington. During the first year of operation, the company generated $4,000 of cash revenues, incurred $2,500 of cash expenses, and distributed $1,000 cash to the owner. Exhibit 11–1 shows the December 31, 2001, financial statements for Worthington's company. Looking at the *capital statement* (sometimes called a *statement of changes in equity*), note that in accounting for proprietorships, distributions are called **withdrawals.** The other unique feature you should verify is the combination of the $5,000 capital acquisition and the retained earnings of $500 (that is, $1,500 net income − $1,000 withdrawal) into a single equity account called *capital.* More specifically, note the $5,500 ($5,000 + $500) balances in the capital account on the capital statement and the balance sheet.

Presentation of Equity in Partnerships

The format for presenting partnership equity in financial statements is similar to that used for proprietorships. For example, the Capital account includes both acquired capital and retained earnings. The only significant difference is that a separate capital account is used to reflect the amount of ownership interest of each partner in the business.

To illustrate, assume that Sara Slater and Jill Johnson decided to form a partnership. The partnership acquired $2,000 of capital from Slater and $4,000 from Johnson. The partnership agreement called for an annual distribution equal to 10 percent of acquired capital. The remaining amount of earnings was retained in the business and added to each partner's capital account on an equal basis. The partnership was formed on January 1, 2001. During 2001, the company earned $5,000 of cash revenue and incurred $3,000 of cash expenses, resulting in net income of $2,000 ($5,000 − $3,000). In accordance with the partnership agreement, Slater received a $200 ($2,000 × 0.10) cash withdrawal, while Johnson's withdrawal was $400 ($4,000 × 0.10). The remaining $1,400 of income was retained in the business and divided equally, thereby resulting in a $700 addition to each partner's capital account.

Exhibit 11–1

WORTHINGTON SOLE PROPRIETORSHIP
Financial Statements
As of December 31, 2001

Income Statement		Capital Statement		Balance Sheet	
Revenue	$4,000	Beginning Capital Balance	$ 0	Assets	
Expenses	2,500	Plus: Investment by Owner	5,000	Cash	$5,500
Net Income	$1,500	Plus: Net Income	1,500	Worthington, Capital	$5,500
		Less: Withdrawal by Owner	(1,000)		
		Ending Capital Balance	$5,500		

Exhibit 11–2

SLATER AND JOHNSON PARTNERSHIP
Financial Statements
As of December 31, 2001

Income Statement		Capital Statement		Balance Sheet	
Revenue	$5,000	Beginning Capital Balance	$ 0	Assets	
Expenses	3,000	Plus: Investment by Owners	6,000	Cash	$7,400
Net Income	$2,000	Plus: Net Income	2,000	Slater, Capital	$2,700
		Less: Withdrawal by Owners	(600)	Johnson, Capital	4,700
		Ending Capital Balance	$7,400	Total Capital	$7,400

Exhibit 11–2 shows the financial statements for the Slater and Johnson partnership. Again, note that the word *withdrawal* is used to label the distributions made to the owners. Also note that the balance sheet contains a *separate capital account* for each partner. Each capital account includes the amount of the partner's invested capital plus her proportionate share of the retained earnings.

Presentation of Equity in Corporations

Capital structures of corporations are considerably more complicated than proprietorships and partnerships. The remainder of this chapter is devoted to some of the more prevalent features of the corporate structure.

Weiss Company was started on January 1, 2004, when it acquired $50,000 cash from its owners. During 2004 the company earned $72,000 of net income. Explain how the equity section of Weiss's December 31, 2004, balance sheet would differ if the company were a proprietorship versus a corporation.

Answer *Proprietorship* records combine capital acquisitions from the owner and earnings from operating the business in a single capital account. In contrast, *corporation* records separate capital acquisitions from the owners and earnings from operating the business. If Weiss were a proprietorship, the equity section of the year-end balance sheet would report a single capital component of $122,000. If Weiss were a corporation, the equity section would report two separate equity components, most likely common stock of $50,000 and retained earnings of $72,000.

Check Yourself 11–1

▮ Characteristics of Capital Stock

A number of terms are associated with stock. Some terms are used to identify different values that are commonly assigned to stock; other terms pertain to the number of shares that a corporation has the authority to issue versus the number that it has actually issued. There are also terms that describe different classes of stock. These terms are used to distinguish the rights and privileges that may be assigned to the different owners of the same corporation (not all stockholders are treated the same way). Knowledge of the meanings of these terms is essential to an understanding of the accounting practices used to report on the events that affect the ownership interest in corporations.

LO3 Explain the characteristics of major types of stock issued by corporations.

▮ Par Value

Many states require the assignment of a **par value** to stock. Historically, par value has represented the maximum liability of the investor. Likewise, when the par value is multiplied by the number of shares of stock issued, the resulting figure represents the minimum amount of assets that should be maintained as protection for creditors. This figure is known as the amount of **legal capital.** To ensure that the legal capital is maintained, many states require that a purchaser pay at least the par value when a share of stock is initially purchased from a corporation. To minimize the amount of assets that owners are required to maintain in the business, many corporations issue stock with very low par values, often $1 or less. Therefore, *legal capital* as defined by par value has come to have very little relevance to investors or creditors. As a result of this situation, many states allow the issuance of no-par stock.

Stated Value

No-par stock may have a stated value. Like par value, the **stated value** is an amount that is arbitrarily assigned by the board of directors to the stock. Accordingly, it also has little relevance to investors and creditors. For accounting purposes, par value stock and stock with a stated value are treated exactly the same. When stock has no par or stated value, there are slight differences in treatment. These differences will be made clear when the procedures necessary for the recognition of par values in financial statements are covered later in this chapter.

Other Valuation Terminology

The price that must be paid to purchase a share of stock is called the **market value.** There is no relationship between market value and par value. The sales price of a share of stock may be more or less than the par value. Another term that is frequently associated with stock is *book value.* The **book value per share** is determined by dividing the total stockholders' equity (assets − liabilities) by the number of shares of stock. The book value is different from the market value because equity is primarily measured in historical dollars rather than in current values.

focus on International Issues

Who Provides the Financing?

The accounting rules in a country are affected by who provides financing to businesses in that country. Equity (versus debt) financing is the largest source of financing for most businesses in the United States. The stock (equity ownership) of most large U.S. companies is said to be *widely held.* This means that many different institutional investors (e.g., pension funds) and individuals own stock. At the other extreme is a country in which the government owns most industries. In between might be a country in which large banks provide a major portion of business financing, such as Japan or Germany.

It is well beyond the scope of this course to explain specifically how a country's GAAP are affected by who provides the financing of the country's major industries. Nevertheless, a businessperson should be aware that the source of a company's financing affects the financial reporting that it must do. Do not assume that business practices or accounting rules in other countries are like those in the United States.

Stock: Authorized, Issued, and Outstanding

Several terms are used to distinguish the number of shares of stock available for issue from those that have been issued to stockholders. **Authorized stock** refers to the number of shares that the corporation is approved to issue by the state. When blocks of stock are sold to the public, they become **issued stock.** Often, for reasons that we discuss later, a corporation may buy back some of its own stock. This stock is called **treasury stock,** and although it remains issued, it is no longer outstanding. Thus, **outstanding stock** is defined as stock owned by outside parties, or total issued stock minus treasury stock. For example, assume that a company that is authorized to issue 150 shares of stock issues 100 shares and then buys 20 shares of treasury stock. There are 150 shares authorized, 100 shares issued, and 80 shares outstanding.

Classes of Stock

The corporate charter defines the number of shares of stock authorized, the par value, and the classes of stock that a corporation can issue. Although there are many variations in the types of stock that may be sold, most issues can be classified as either *common* or *preferred.* If only one class of stock is issued, it is known as **common stock.** Common stockholders generally possess several rights, including these five: (1) the right to buy and sell stock, (2) the right to share in the distribution of profits, (3) the right to share in the distribution of corporate assets in the case of liquidation, (4) the right to vote on significant matters that affect the corporate charter, and (5) the right to participate in the selection of directors. Common stockholders are considered the true owners of a corporation. On one hand, they bear the ultimate risk

of losing their investment if the company is forced to liquidate; on the other hand, they are the primary beneficiaries when a corporation prospers.

Preferred Stock

Holders of **preferred stock** receive some form of preferential treatment relative to common stockholders. To receive special privileges in some areas, preferred stockholders often give up rights in other areas. Usually, preferred stockholders have no right to vote at stockholders' meetings, and the size of the distributions they are entitled to receive is frequently limited. Some of the common preferences assigned to preferred stockholders are as follows:

1. *Preference as to assets.* Often there is a liquidation value associated with preferred stock. In case of bankruptcy, the amount of liquidation value must be paid to the preferred stockholders before distributions can be made to common stockholders. However, the preferred stockholder claims still fall behind those of the creditors.
2. *Preference as to dividends.* Distributions given to stockholders are commonly called **dividends.** Preferred shareholders are frequently guaranteed the right to receive dividends before common stockholders. The amount of the preferred dividend is normally stated on the stock certificate. It may be stated in an absolute dollar value per share (say, $5 per share) or as a percentage of the par value. Most preferred stock has **cumulative dividends,** meaning that if a corporation is unable to pay the preferred dividend in any year, the dividend is not lost but begins to accumulate. Cumulative dividends that have not been paid are called **dividends in arrears.** Once the firm is able to pay dividends, the arrearages must be paid first. Noncumulative preferred stock is not seen often because much of the attraction of purchasing preferred stock is lost if past dividends do not accumulate.

To illustrate the effects of preferred dividends, consider this situation. Dillion Incorporated has the following shares of stock outstanding:

Preferred stock, 4%, $10 par   10,000 shares
Common stock, $10 par   20,000 shares

Assume that the preferred stock dividend has not been paid for two years. If Dillion distributes $22,000 to the two classes, how much will each receive? The answer will differ, depending on whether the preferred stock is cumulative.

Allocation of Distribution for Cumulative Preferred Stock	To Preferred	To Common
Dividends in arrears	$ 8,000	$ 0
Current year's dividends	4,000	10,000
Total distribution	$12,000	$10,000

Allocation of Distribution for Noncumulative Preferred Stock	To Preferred	To Common
Dividends in arrears	$ 0	$ 0
Current year's dividends	4,000	18,000
Total distribution	$ 4,000	$18,000

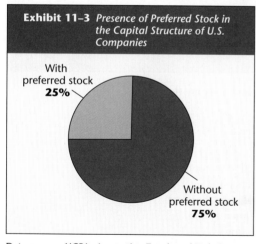

Exhibit 11–3 *Presence of Preferred Stock in the Capital Structure of U.S. Companies*

With preferred stock **25%**

Without preferred stock **75%**

Data source: AICPA, *Accounting Trends and Techniques,* 2000.

The yearly dividend for preferred stock is $4,000, calculated as 0.04 × $10 par × 10,000 shares. If the preferred stock is cumulative, the $8,000 in arrears must be paid first. The $4,000 for the current year's dividend is paid next. The remaining $10,000 goes to common stockholders. If the preferred stock is noncumulative, the $8,000 of dividends from past periods is ignored. This year's preferred dividend is paid first, with the remainder going to common.

Several of the other features that may be considered for preferences are the right to participate in distributions beyond those established as the amount of the preferred dividend, the right to convert preferred stock to common stock or to bonds, and the potential for having the preferred stock called (repurchased) by the corporation. A detailed discussion of these topics is left to more advanced courses. Although the majority of the U.S. companies do not include preferred stock in their corporate structures, a significant number of companies do issue preferred shares (see Exhibit 11–3 for details).

Accounting for Stock Transactions on the Day of Issue

Stock Issued at Par Value

LO4 Explain the accounting treatment for different types of stock issued by corporations.

Recording the initial issue of stock differs slightly, depending on whether the stock has a par value, has a stated value, or is no-par stock. When either a par or stated value exists, this amount is recorded in the stock account. Any amount above the par or stated value is recorded in the **Paid-in Excess account.** Accordingly, the total amount invested by the owners is divided between two separate equity accounts. To illustrate, assume that Nelson Incorporated has been authorized to issue 250 shares of common stock. During 2001, Nelson Incorporated issues 100 shares of $10 par common stock for $22 per share. The event acts to increase assets and stockholders' equity by $2,200 ($22 × 100 shares). The increase in stockholders' equity is divided into two parts, with one part representing the $1,000 of par value (100 shares × $10 per share) and the remaining $1,200 ($2,200 − $1,000) pertaining to the additional amount that was paid in excess of the par value. The income statement is not affected. The $2,200 cash inflow is shown in the financing activities section of the statement of cash flows. The effects on the financial statements and the journal entry necessary to record the event are as follows:

Assets	=	Liab.	+	Equity			Rev.	−	Exp.	=	Net Inc.	Cash Flow
Cash	=	Liab.	+	C. Stk.	+	Paid-in Excess						
2,200	=	NA	+	1,000	+	1,200	NA	−	NA	=	NA	2,200 FA

Account Title	Debit	Credit
Cash	2,200	
Common Stock, $10 Par Value		1,000
Paid-in Capital in Excess of Par Value—Common		1,200

The legal capital of the corporation is $1,000, which is the par value of the common stock. The number of shares issued can be easily determined by dividing the total amount in the common stock account by the par value ($1,000 ÷ $10 = 100 shares). One final note concerns the title of the Paid-in Capital in Excess of Par or Stated Value account. The *paid-in* terminology applied to this account sometimes confuses the fact that the full amount that has been *paid in* by the investors is $2,200. Note that the amount in the Common Stock account is also paid-in capital and that the amount in the *Paid-in Excess* account represents only the additional amount above the par value.

Stock Classification

Nelson Incorporated obtains authorization to issue 400 shares of Class B, $20 par value common stock. The company issues 150 shares of this stock at $25 per share. The event acts to increase assets and stockholders' equity by $3,750 ($25 × 150 shares). The increase in stockholders' equity is divided into two parts, with one representing the $3,000 of par value (150 shares × $20 per share) and the remaining $750 ($3,750 − $3,000) pertaining to the additional amount paid in excess of the par value. The income statement is not affected. The $3,750 cash inflow is shown in the financing activities section of the statement of cash flows. The effects on the financial statements and the journal entry necessary to record the event are as follows:

Assets	=	Liab.	+	Equity			Rev.	−	Exp.	=	Net Inc.	Cash Flow
Cash	=	Liab.	+	C. Stk.	+	Paid-in Excess						
3,750	=	NA	+	3,000	+	750	NA	−	NA	=	NA	3,750 FA

Account Title	Debit	Credit
Cash	3,750	
Common Stock, Class B, $20 Par Value		3,000
Paid-in Capital in Excess of Par Value—Class B Common		750

As the preceding event suggests, companies can have numerous classes of common stock. The specific rights and privileges associated with each class are described in the individual stock certificates.

Stock Issued at Stated Value

Assume that Nelson is authorized to issue 300 shares of a third class of stock. This stock is preferred stock with a stated value of $10 per share. The preferred stock pays a 7 percent cumulative dividend. Assume here also that Nelson issues 100 shares of the stock at a price of $22 per share. The effect on the financial statements is identical to that described for the issue of the $10 par value common stock. The journal entry changes only to reflect the name of the different class of stock.

Assets	=	Liab.	+		Equity		Rev.	−	Exp.	=	Net Inc.	Cash Flow	
Cash	=	Liab.	+	P. Stk.	+	Paid-in Excess							
2,200	=	NA	+	1,000	+	1,200	NA	−	NA	=	NA	2,200	FA

Account Title	Debit	Credit
Cash	2,200	
Preferred Stock, $10 Stated Value, 7% cumulative		1,000
Paid-in Capital in Excess of Stated Value—Preferred		1,200

Stock Issued at No-Par Value

When no-par stock is issued (no par or stated values are assigned to the stock), the entire amount is assigned to the capital stock account. Assume that Nelson Incorporated is authorized to issue 150 shares of a fourth class of stock. This stock is no-par stock. Assume further that Nelson issues 100 shares of this stock at $22 per share. As in the previous two examples, the event acts to increase assets and stockholders' equity by $2,200. The effects on the financial statements and the journal entry required to record the event are shown here:

Assets	=	Liab.	+		Equity		Rev.	−	Exp.	=	Net Inc.	Cash Flow	
Cash	=	Liab.	+	C. Stk.	+	Paid-in Excess							
2,200	=	NA	+	2,200	+	NA	NA	−	NA	=	NA	2,200	FA

Account Title	Debit	Credit
Cash	2,200	
Common Stock, No Par		2,200

Financial Statement Presentation

Exhibit 11–4 shows the balance sheet of Nelson Incorporated immediately after the four issues of stock just described. The exhibit assumes that Nelson earned and retained $5,000 of cash income during 2001. Notice that the stock accounts are presented first, followed by the presentation of the paid-in excess accounts. Another popular format is to group accounts by the type of stock classification, with the paid-in excess accounts shown along with their associ-

Exhibit 11–4

NELSON INCORPORATED
Balance Sheet
As of January 1, 2001

Assets	
Cash	$15,350
Stockholders' Equity	
Preferred Stock, $10 Stated Value, 7% cumulative,	
300 shares authorized, 100 issued and outstanding	$ 1,000
Common Stock, $10 Par Value, 250 shares authorized,	
100 issued and outstanding	1,000
Common Stock, Class B, $20 Par Value, 400 shares	
authorized, 150 issued and outstanding	3,000
Common Stock, No Par, 150 shares authorized,	
100 issued and outstanding	2,200
Paid-in Capital in Excess of Stated Value—Preferred	1,200
Paid-in Capital in Excess of Par—Common	1,200
Paid-in Capital in Excess of Par—Class B Common	750
Total Paid-in Capital	10,350
Retained Earnings	5,000
Total Paid-in Capital	$15,350

ated stock accounts. A properly constructed stockholders' equity section includes complete descriptions of the stock classifications, as shown in Exhibit 11–4. However, in practice, many companies simply combine the different classes of stock into a single account and provide the detailed information in footnotes to the financial statements. Do not be confused by the fact that a wide variety of reporting formats is used in practice.

▌Stockholder Equity Transactions after the Day of Issue

Treasury Stock

When a company buys its own stock, the stock purchased is called *treasury stock*. Why would a company buy its own stock? There are many possible reasons. Some of the more common reasons are (1) to have stock available to give employees in stock option plans, (2) to accumulate stock in preparation for a merger or business combination, (3) to reduce the number of shares outstanding in order to increase earnings per share, (4) to keep the price of the stock high when it appears to be falling, and (5) to avoid a hostile takeover (the shares are removed from the open market and so are not available to the individuals who are attempting to obtain enough voting shares to gain control of the company).

Conceptually, treasury stock is a return of invested capital to the owner whose stock is being purchased. In other words, it is the reverse of a capital acquisition. When a business acquires capital by issuing stock, the assets and equity of the business increase. When a business returns capital to owners by purchasing its stock from them, the assets and equity of the business decrease. To illustrate, assume that during 2001, Nelson Incorporated buys back 50 shares of the $10 par value common stock that was sold in the first issue of stock for $22 per share. Assume that the stock is bought back at a price of $20 per share. The purchase of treasury stock is an asset use transaction. Assets and equity decrease by the amount of the cost of the purchase ($20 × 50 shares = $1,000). The income statement is not affected. The cash outflow is shown in the financing activities section of the statement of cash flows. The effects on the financial statements and the journal entry necessary to record the event are as follows:

LO5 Explain the effects of treasury stock transactions on a company's financial statements.

Assets	=	Liab.	+	Equity			Rev.	–	Exp.	=	Net Inc.	Cash Flow	
Cash	=	Liab.	+	Other Equity Accts.	–	Treasury Stk.							
(1,000)	=	NA	+	NA	–	1,000	NA	–	NA	=	NA	(1,000)	FA

Account Title	Debit	Credit
Treasury Stock	1,000	
Cash		1,000

The Treasury Stock account is a negative equity account. It is deducted from the other equity accounts to determine the amount of total stockholders' equity. Notice that the treasury stock is recorded at its cost ($1,000). The original issue price and the par value of the stock are not considered. The recording of treasury stock in this manner is called the **cost method of accounting for treasury stock** transactions. Although other methods could be used, the cost method is the most common and therefore is the approach used in this chapter. Assume that a few days later, Nelson resells 30 shares of treasury stock at a price of $25 per share. As with any other stock issue, the sale of treasury stock is an asset source transaction. In this case, it acts to increase assets and equity by $750 ($25 × 30 shares). The income statement is not affected. The cash inflow is shown in the financing activities section of the statement of cash flows. The effect of this event on the financial statements and the journal entry necessary to record it are as follows:

Assets	=	Liab.	+	Equity					Rev.	–	Exp.	=	Net Inc.	Cash Flow	
Cash	=	Liab.	+	Other Equity Accounts	–	Treasury Stock	+	Paid in from Treasury Stk.							
750	=	NA	+	NA	–	(600)	+	150	NA	–	NA	=	NA	750	FA

Account Title	Debit	Credit
Cash	750	
Treasury Stock		600
Paid-in Capital in Excess of Cost of Treasury Stock		150

Remember that the Treasury Stock account is a negative equity account. Accordingly, the decrease in the Treasury Stock account acts to increase stockholders' equity. Also note that the $150 difference between the cost of the treasury stock (30 shares × $20 per share = $600) and the sales price ($750) is **not** reported as a gain. Stock transactions between a corporation and its shareholders represent one of two types of capital exchanges: transfers of capital to the business from the owners or transfers of invested capital from the company back to the owners. Corporations do not experience gains or losses on such capital exchanges.

After the sale of 30 shares of treasury stock, 20 shares remain in the account. Recall that these shares cost $20 each, so the balance in the Treasury Stock account is now $400 ($20 × 20 shares). The Treasury Stock account is a negative equity account. It is shown on the balance sheet directly below the Retained Earnings account and acts to reduce the total amount of equity shown on the balance sheet. Although this placement makes it appear that treasury stock reduces retained earnings, the reduction actually applies to the entire stockholders' equity section. Exhibit 11–5, page 536, shows the presentation of treasury stock in the balance sheet.

On January 1, 2006, Janell Company's common stock account balance was $20,000. On April 1, 2006, Janell paid $12,000 cash to purchase some of its own stock. Janell resold this stock on October 1, 2006, for $14,500. What is the effect on the company's cash and stockholders' equity from both the April 1 purchase and the October 1 resale of the stock?

Answer The April 1 purchase would reduce both cash and stockholders' equity by $12,000. The treasury stock transaction represents a return of invested capital to those owners who sold stock back to the company.

The sale of the treasury stock on October 1 would increase both cash and stockholders' equity by $14,500. The difference between the sales price of the treasury stock and its cost ($14,500 − $12,000) represents additional paid-in capital from treasury stock transactions. The stockholders' equity section of the balance sheet would include Common Stock, $20,000, and Additional Paid-in Capital from Treasury Stock Transactions, $2,500.

Check Yourself 11–2

Cash Dividend

A corporation generates net income for the benefit of its owners. If the company retains the income, the price of the stock should increase to reflect the increase in the value of the firm. Alternatively, firms can distribute the income to their owners directly through the payment of cash dividends. Three important dates are associated with cash dividends: *declaration date, date of record,* and *payment date.* To illustrate the accounting treatment for a cash dividend, consider these circumstances. On November 1, 2001, Nelson Incorporated declares a cash dividend on the 100 shares of its $10 stated value preferred stock. The dividend will be paid to the stockholders of record as of December 15, 2001. The cash payment will be made on January 30, 2002.

LO6 Explain the effects of a declaration and payment of cash dividends on a company's financial statements.

Declaration Date

November 1, 2001, is the **declaration date.** On this day, the chairman of the board of Nelson Incorporated issued a press release to notify stockholders and other interested parties that a 7 percent cash dividend would be paid on the company's preferred stock. Although corporations are not required to declare dividends, they are legally obligated to pay those dividends that have been declared. Accordingly, a liability is recognized on the date of declaration. The increase in liabilities is offset by a decrease in retained earnings. The income statement and statement of cash flows are not affected. The effect of the *declaration* of the $70 ($10 × 0.07 × 100 shares) dividend on the financial statements and the journal entry necessary to record it are as follows:

Assets	=	Liab.	+	Equity			Rev.	−	Exp.	=	Net Inc.	Cash Flow
	=		+	Cont. Cap.	+	Ret. Earn.						
NA	=	70	+	NA	+	(70)	NA	−	NA	=	NA	NA

Account Title	Debit	Credit
Dividends	70	
Dividends Payable		70

The Dividends account is closed to retained earnings, thereby reducing stockholders' equity.

Date of Record

The cash dividend will be paid to the investors who own the preferred stock, as of the **date of record.** Any stock sold after the date of record but before the payment date is said to be traded

ex-dividend, or sold without the benefit of the upcoming dividend. Since the date of record is merely a cutoff date, it does not affect the elements of the financial statements.

Payment Date

The corporation mails the dividend to the stockholders on the **payment date.** This event is treated the same as the payment of any other liability. The asset, *Cash,* and the liability, *Dividends Payable,* both decrease. The income statement is not affected. The cash outflow is shown in the financing activities section of the statement of cash flows. The effect of the cash payment on the financial statements and the journal entry necessary to record it are as follows:

Assets	=	Liab.	+		Equity			Rev.	−	Exp.	=	Net Inc.	Cash Flow	
	=		+	Cont. Cap.	+	Ret. Earn								
(70)	=	(70)	+	NA	+	NA		NA	−	NA	=	NA	(70)	FA

Account Title	Debit	Credit
Dividends Payable	70	
Cash		70

Stock Dividend

LO7 Explain the effects of stock dividends and stock splits on a company's financial statements.

Instead of distributing cash to stockholders, a company may choose to distribute shares of its stock. There are two primary reasons that a firm might decide to distribute a **stock dividend:**

1. There may not be enough funds available for a cash dividend, but the company wants to reward its stockholders in some way.
2. The price of the stock in the market may be getting so high that potential investors are discouraged from purchasing it.

To illustrate, assume that Nelson Incorporated decides to issue a 10 percent stock dividend on the 150 shares of its class B common stock that carry a $20 par value. Accordingly, Nelson issues 15 new shares of stock (150 shares × 0.10). Assume that the distribution is made at a time when the market value of the stock is $30 per share. In this case, the stock dividend will act to transfer $450 ($30 × [150 shares × 0.10]) from the Retained Earnings account to the paid-in capital section of the balance sheet.[1] Accordingly, it is an equity exchange transaction. The income statement and statement of cash flows are not affected. The effect of the stock dividend on the financial statements and the journal entry necessary to record it are as follows:

Assets	=	Liab.	+		Equity					Rev.	−	Exp.	=	Net Inc.	Cash Flow
	=		+	C. Stk.	+	Paid-in Excess	+	Ret. Earn.							
NA	=	NA	+	300	+	150	+	(450)		NA	−	NA	=	NA	NA

Account Title	Debit	Credit
Retained Earnings	450	
Common Stock, Class B, $20 Par Value		300
Paid-in Capital in Excess of Par Value—Class B Common		150

[1]The accounting treatment shown here is for a small stock dividend. The treatment for large dividends is left to more advanced courses.

The logic behind the accounting treatment for stock dividends may be clarified by observing the fact that the end result of issuing a stock dividend is the same as it would be if the company had issued the common stock for the market price and then used the funds to pay the cash dividends. This should be apparent from a review of the following journal entries. To make it easier to see, the offsetting entries to the Cash account are marked with strikethroughs to show that their elimination produces the same result as the issuance of a stock dividend.[2]

Account Title	Debit	Credit
~~Cash~~	~~450~~	
Common Stock, Class B, $20 Par Value		300
Paid-in Capital in Excess of Par Value—Class B Common		150
Retained Earnings	450	
~~Cash~~		~~450~~

Notice that assets are not affected by the stock dividend. However, the number of shares increases. Since there is a larger number of shares representing the ownership interest in the same amount of assets, the market value per share of the company's stock normally declines when a stock dividend is distributed. This result has the beneficial effect of making the stock more affordable and therefore may increase the demand for the stock. For this reason, a company's stock may not decline in exact proportion to the number of new shares issued.

Stock Split

A more dynamic way of lowering the market price of a corporation's stock is through a **stock split.** A stock split merely removes the old shares from the books and replaces them with new shares. For example, if Nelson Incorporated declares a 2-for-1 stock split on the 165 shares (150 original issue plus 15 shares issued via stock dividend) of the class B common stock, a notation is made in the accounting records that the old $20 par value stock was replaced with 330 shares of $10 par value stock. Investors who owned the 165 shares of old common would now own 330 shares of the new common. Since the 330 shares represent the same ownership interest as the 165 shares previously represented, the market value (price) per share should be one-half as much as it was prior to the split. However, as with a stock dividend, the lower price will probably stimulate demand for the stock. Accordingly, the drop in market price is likely to be less dramatic than the increase in the number of shares. In other words, doubling the number of shares will cause the price to fall to a point that is slightly more than one-half of the value that existed before the split. If the stock was selling for $30 per share before the 2-for-1 split, it may sell for $15.50 after the split.

Appropriation of Retained Earnings

The retained earnings that is available for distribution as dividends may be restricted by the board of directors. This limitation may be required by restrictive covenants contained in credit agreements, or it may be completely discretionary. A retained earnings restriction, often called an *appropriation,* is an equity exchange transaction. It removes a portion of the general Retained Earnings to **Appropriated Retained Earnings.** The amount of total retained earnings remains the same. To illustrate, assume that Nelson appropriates $1,000 of retained earnings for future expansion. The income statement and the statement of cash flows are not affected. The effect of appropriating the $1,000 of retained earnings on the financial statements and the journal entry necessary to record it are as follows:

LO8 Show how the appropriation of retained earnings affects financial statements.

---

[2]The authors express appreciation to Louis Dawkins of Henderson State University for the suggestion to include this illustration in the text material.

Assets	=	Liab.	+	Equity					Rev.	–	Exp.	=	Net Inc.	Cash Flow
	=		+	Cont. Cap.	+	Ret. Earn.	+	App. Ret. Earn.						
NA	=	NA	+	NA	+	(1,000)	+	1,000	NA	–	NA	=	NA	NA

Account Title	Debit	Credit
Retained Earnings	1,000	
Appropriated Retained Earnings		1,000

▌Financial Statement Presentation

Exhibit 11–5 contains the December 31, 2001, balance sheet for Nelson Incorporated. The balance sheet reflects the 11 equity transactions that Nelson completed during 2001. These events are summarized here for your convenience in analyzing the effect of each event on the balance sheet. (All transactions—except those affecting only equity accounts—are assumed to be cash transactions.)

1. Issued 100 shares of $10 par value common stock at a market price of $22 per share.
2. Issued 150 shares of class B $20 par value common stock at a market price of $25 per share.
3. Issued 100 shares of $10 stated value preferred stock at a market price of $22 per share.
4. Issued 100 shares of no-par common stock at a market price of $22 per share.
5. Earned and retained $5,000 cash from operations.
6. Purchased 50 shares of $10 par value common stock as treasury stock at a market price of $20 per share.
7. Sold 30 shares of treasury stock at a market price of $25 per share.

Exhibit 11–5

NELSON INCORPORATED
Balance Sheet
As of December 31, 2001

Assets		
Cash		$15,030
Stockholders' Equity		
Preferred Stock, $10 Stated Value, 7% cumulative,		
300 shares authorized, 100 issued and outstanding	$1,000	
Common Stock, $10 Par Value, 250 shares authorized,		
100 issued, and 80 outstanding	1,000	
Common Stock, Class B, $10 Par, 800 shares authorized,		
330 issued and outstanding	3,300	
Common Stock, No Par, 150 shares authorized,		
100 issued and outstanding	2,200	
Paid-in Capital in Excess of Par—Preferred	1,200	
Paid-in Capital in Excess of Par—Common	1,200	
Paid-in Capital in Excess of Par—Class B Common	900	
Paid-in Capital in Excess of Cost of Treasury Stock	150	
Total Paid-in Capital		$10,950
Retained Earnings		
Appropriated	1,000	
Unappropriated	3,480	
Total Retained Earnings		4,480
Less: Treasury Stock, 20 shares @ $20 per share		(400)
Total Stockholders' Equity		$15,030

8. Declared and paid a $70 cash dividend on the preferred stock.
9. Issued a 10 percent stock dividend on the 150 shares of outstanding class B common stock that carried a $20 par value (15 additional shares). At the time of issue, the market price of the stock was $30 per share. There is a total of 165 (150 + 15) shares outstanding after the stock dividend.
10. Issued a 2-for-1 stock split on the 165 shares of class B common stock. After this transaction, there are 330 shares outstanding of the class B common stock with a $10 par value.
11. Appropriated $1,000 of retained earnings.

▌Assessment of Potential Investment Returns

Why does an investor acquire the stock of a particular company? Of course, the ultimate objective of any investment is to make money. However, money can be made in a variety of ways. Stockholders benefit when the companies they own generate profits. The profits may be distributed directly to the owners in the form of dividends. Alternatively, the business may choose to retain its earnings, whereupon the value of the stockholder's investment (market price of the stock) should increase. According to Financial Accounting Standards Board's *Concepts Statement No. 1,* "Financial reporting should provide information to help present and potential investors . . . in assessing the amounts, timing, and uncertainty of prospective cash receipts from dividends . . . and the proceeds from the sale, redemption, or maturity of securities . . . ."

LO9 Explain how accounting information can be useful in making stock investment decisions.

Receiving Dividends

Will a company pay dividends in the future? Accounting information can help answer this question. First, the financial statements show whether dividends were paid in the past. Usually, a history of dividend payment is an indicator of future dividend payments. Also, to pay future dividends, the company must have cash. Although there is always uncertainty about the future, financial statements, especially the statement of cash flows, can help investors assess the probability of a company's future cash flows.

Note that very good reasons exist for a company not to pay dividends. A more thorough explanation of whether a company should pay dividends is a topic for finance courses, but do not assume that just because dividends were not paid, a company's stock is less desirable to investors. Businesses that are not paying dividends may be reinvesting the money in the company. If the company is earning a return on assets of 20 percent, it is wiser to reinvest available cash than to pay dividends to stockholders who would put the money in a bank account paying 6 percent interest.

Increasing the Price of Stock

Probably the most common reason that individual and institutional investors acquire stock is the hope that its value will increase over time. Why does the price of stock rise? The answer is very complex and certainly beyond the scope of this course. However, we can provide a partial explanation. Stock prices for the market as a whole tend to increase when the economy is good and when interest rates are low and/or falling. From this perspective, financial statements are of little benefit because they are not designed to provide information that is useful in predicting general economic conditions.

Beyond the assessment of general economic conditions, investors are interested in identifying particular companies whose stock price will increase more rapidly than the market as a whole. A particular company's stock price is likely to increase because investors believe the company will do well in the future. Financial statements do contain information that is useful in making predictions about future prospects for profitability. However, the limitations of accounting information must be recognized. Remember that accounting information is about the past. Investors want to know about the future. For this reason, stock prices are influenced more by "forecasted" net income than by last year's net income. Forecasted net income is definitely not in the financial statements. This does not mean that actual accounting results are not important but that forecasted accounting data are of equal or greater importance in explaining stock price behavior.

The following examples demonstrate this phenomenon:

- On May 15, 2001, Wal-Mart announced that its first quarter profits were 3.8 percent higher than profits in the same quarter of 2000. In reaction to this news, the price of Wal-Mart's stock *fell* by $2.35 to $52.00. Why did the stock market respond in this way? It did so because profits for the first quarter of 2000 had been *19 percent* higher than those for the first quarter of 1999, and investors had expected better results.
- On April 21, 2001, Lucent Technologies announced a second quarter *loss* of $3.7 billion. This loss was seven times greater than Lucent's loss on comparable operations for the second quarter of the 2000 fiscal year. The stock market's reaction to the news was to *increase* the price of Lucent's stock by 11 percent. The market reacted this way because the loss included several large restructuring charges that analysts believed might lead to better results in the future.

In each case, the investors reacted not only to the actual accounting information but also to their expectations of the company's performance, as well as what the current information suggested about the future.

To illustrate another reason that financial statements cannot provide all the information relevant to the value of a company's stock, consider the following scenario. Assume that Exxon-Mobil announced in the middle of its fiscal year that it had just discovered large oil reserves on property to which it held drilling rights. Based on this assumption, consider the following questions:

- What would happen to the price of its stock on that day?
- What would happen to its balance sheet on that day?
- What would happen to its income statement on that day?
- What would happen to its statement of cash flows on that day?

The price of ExxonMobil's stock would almost certainly increase as soon as the discovery was made public. However, nothing would happen to its financial statements on that day. In fact, there would probably be very little effect on its financial statements for that year. Only after the company began to develop the oil field and sell the oil would its financial statements begin to change. Remember that accounting data are based primarily on past actions whereas the price of a company's stock is determined primarily by future expectations.

Understanding the Price-Earnings Ratio

There is a ratio that can provide some insight into how analysts view the future prospects of a company relative to its current net income. This ratio is called the **price-earnings ratio** and is defined as

$$\frac{\text{Selling price of 1 share of stock}}{\text{Earnings per share*}}$$

This ratio, usually referred to as the **P/E ratio,** is one of only two ratios shown in stock price listings in newspapers such as *The Wall Street Journal.* As a general rule, the higher the P/E ratio, the more optimistic investors are about a company's future. In other words, investors are

---

Earnings per share (EPS) can be computed under a variety of assumptions. Indeed, the reporting of earnings per share in financial statements is a complicated task requiring the application of many technical accounting rules. However, for the purposes of this text, earnings per share is shown in its simplest form, which is net income divided by the number of shares of outstanding common stock.

willing to pay higher prices for the stock of companies if the investors believe that the company will perform well (earnings will grow rapidly) in the future. If a company currently has negative earnings per share, its P/E ratio is not computed.

The following information pertains to Jackson Incorporated.

	As of December 31	
	2003	2004
Market price per share of stock	$72.28	$27.30
Earnings per share	2.78	1.82

Calculate the P/E ratios for 2003 and 2004. What do these ratios suggest about investor confidence in Jackson's future earning capacity?

Answer The P/E ratio for 2003 is 26 ($72.28 ÷ $2.78) and for 2004 is 15 ($27.30 ÷ $1.82). The decrease in the P/E ratio suggests that investor confidence in Jackson's ability to generate earnings has declined.

Exercising Control

Investors may also make money by influencing or controlling the operations of a business. There are several ways in which an investor can benefit by exercising some control over a company. As one example, consider a power company that uses coal to produce electricity. The power company may purchase some of the common stock of a mining company to help ensure the stable supply of the coal it needs to operate its electric business. What percentage of the mining company's stock does the power company need to acquire in order to exercise significant control over the mining company? The answer depends on how many people own stock in the mining company and how the number of shares is distributed among the stockholders.

The more people who own a company's stock, the more *widely held* the company is said to be. If ownership is concentrated in the hands of a few persons, the company is said to be *closely held*. Generally, the more widely held the stock of a company, the smaller the percentage that must be acquired to exercise significant control. Accounting information can help determine how much stock is needed to exercise control. However, financial statements do not contain all of the information needed. For example, the financial statements disclose the total number of shares of stock outstanding, but the statements normally contain very little information about the number of shareholders and even less information regarding the nature of the relationships between shareholders. Information regarding such relationships is critically important because related shareholders, whether bound by family or business interests, might exercise control by voting as a block. (For "SEC companies," some information about the number of shareholders and the identity of some large shareholders can be found in reports filed with the SEC.)

If you wished to start a business, one of the first things you must do is to raise equity financing; you must have money to make money. Although you may wish to borrow money, lenders are unlikely to make loans to businesses without some degree of owner financing. Accordingly, equity financing is critical to virtually all profit-oriented businesses. The purpose of this chapter has been to examine some of the issues related to accounting for equity transactions.

a look back

The basic idea that a business must obtain financing from its owners was one of the very first events presented in this textbook. However, until this chapter, the organization of the business as a sole proprietorship, partnership, or a corporation has not been discussed. Some of the advantages and disadvantages associated with each type of ownership are reviewed here:

1. *Double taxation*—Income of corporations is subject to double taxation, but that of proprietorships and partnerships is not.

2. *Regulation*—Corporations are subject to more regulation than are proprietorships and partnerships.

3. *Limited liability*—An investor's personal assets are not at risk as a result of an investment in corporate securities. The investor's liability is limited to the amount of the investment. In general proprietorships and partnerships do not offer limited liability. However, laws in some states permit the formation of limited liability companies that do limit the liabilities associated with ownership of proprietorships or partnerships.

4. *Continuity*—Proprietorships and partnerships dissolve when one of the owners leaves the business. Corporations are separate legal entities that continue to exist when the stockholders divest themselves of their ownership interest.

5. *Transferability*—Ownership interest in corporations is easier to transfer than ownership in proprietorships or partnerships.

6. *Management structure*—Corporations are more likely to have independent professional managers than are proprietorships or partnerships.

7. *Ability to raise capital*—Because they can be owned by millions of individuals, corporations have more opportunities to raise capital than do proprietorships or partnerships.

Ownership interest in corporations may be evidenced by a variety of financial instruments. A corporation can issue different classes of common stock and preferred stock. In general, *common stock* provides the widest range of privileges including the right to vote and participate in earnings. *Preferred stockholders* frequently give up the right to vote to receive other benefits such as the right to receive preference in the payment of dividends or the return of assets upon liquidation. Stock may be issued at *par value* or *stated value,* both of which are legal requirements that relate to the amount of capital that must be maintained in the corporation. Corporations may also issue *no-par stock* that avoids many of the legal requirements associated with par or stated value stock.

Stock that a company sells and then repurchases is called *treasury stock.* The purchase of treasury stock reduces the total amount of assets and equity. The sale of treasury stock does not lead to gains or losses. The difference between the issue price and the cost of the treasury stock is recorded directly in the equity accounts without appearing on the income statement as a gain or loss.

Companies may issue *stock splits* or *stock dividends.* The result of these transactions is to increase the number of shares of stock representing the same ownership interest in the net assets of a company. Accordingly, the per share market value usually drops when a company engages in stock splits or dividends. Beginning with Chapter 6, this course has been moving systematically down the balance sheet accounts. Along the way you have seen how each of these balance sheet accounts interacts with related accounts on the income statement. For example, when Chapter 8 examined the balance sheet effects of different methods of accounting for *inventory,* it also examined the related effects on *cost of goods sold,* which appears on the income statement. Owners' equity is the last section on the balance sheet.

a look forward

Chapter 12 presents a more detailed explanation of the statement of cash flows than has been presented in the past chapters. The format of the statement of cash flows that has been used to this point has been somewhat informal, although its informational content is very valid. Chapter 12 not only presents additional details about the statement of cash flows but also examines the statement in the formal format used by most real-world companies.

SELF-STUDY REVIEW PROBLEM

Edwards, Inc., experienced the following events:

1. Issued common stock for cash.
2. Declared a cash dividend.
3. Issued noncumulative preferred stock for cash.
4. Appropriated retained earnings.
5. Distributed a stock dividend.

6. Paid cash to purchase treasury stock.
7. Distributed a 2-for-1 stock split.
8. Issued cumulative preferred stock for cash.
9. Paid a cash dividend that had previously been declared.
10. Sold treasury stock for cash at a higher amount than the cost of the treasury stock.

Required

Show the effect of each event on the elements of the financial statements using a horizontal statements model like the one shown here. Use + for increase, − for decrease, and NA for not affected. In the Cash Flow column, indicate whether the item is an operating activity (OA), investing activity (IA), or a financing activity (FA). The first transaction is entered as an example.

Event	Assets	=	Liab.	+	Equity	Rev.	−	Exp.	=	Net Inc.	Cash Flow	
1	+		NA		+	NA		NA		NA	+	FA

Solution to Self-Study Review Problem

Event	Assets	=	Liab.	+	Equity	Rev.	−	Exp.	=	Net Inc.	Cash Flow	
1	+		NA		+	NA		NA		NA	+	FA
2	NA		+		−	NA		NA		NA	NA	
3	+		NA		+	NA		NA		NA	+	FA
4	NA		NA		− +	NA		NA		NA	NA	
5	NA		NA		− +	NA		NA		NA	NA	
6	−		NA		−	NA		NA		NA	−	FA
7	NA		NA		NA	NA		NA		NA	NA	
8	+		NA		+	NA		NA		NA	+	FA
9	−		−		NA	NA		NA		NA	−	FA
10	+		NA		+	NA		NA		NA	+	FA

APPENDIX

Accounting for Not-for-Profit (NFP) Organizations

LO10 Explain accounting for not-for-profit entities and governmental organizations.

To this point, our primary focus has been on profit-oriented business organizations. We turn now to a group of organizations classified as *not-for-profit (NFP) entities*. These NFP organizations are distinguished from profit-oriented businesses by three characteristics: (1) the receipt of significant resources from contributors not expecting repayment or economic returns, (2) the operation for purposes other than profit, and (3) the absence of defined ownership interests. Types of organizations that clearly fall within the scope of the NFP classification include museums, churches, clubs, professional associations, and foundations. Organizations that clearly fall outside the scope of the NFP classification include investor-owned enterprises and mutual organizations that provide dividends, lower costs, or other economic benefits directly and proportionately to their owners, members, or participants. The line of demarcation between business and NFP organizations can be vague. Consider a nonprofit school that finances the majority of its capital needs from the proceeds of debt and operating activities. Should this organization be classified as a business or an NFP organization? The ultimate decision is left to the judgment of the interested parties.

Fortunately, much of the information about accounting for business organizations that you have learned is applicable to NFP organizations as well. For example, the financial statements of both profit and NFP organizations contain assets, liabilities, revenues, expenses, gains, and losses. However, investments by owners and distributions to them are not appropriate for NFP entities. Also, the composition of net assets for business and NFP organizations differs. Business organizations subdivide net assets into owner contributions and retained earnings. In contrast, NFP entities subdivide net assets into three classes based on the degree of donor-imposed restrictions: (1) permanently restricted, (2) temporarily restricted, or (3) unrestricted. The double-entry recording system, including debits and credits, journal entries, ledgers, T-accounts, trial balances, and so on, applies to organizations operating in an NFP context. Also, like business organizations, NFP entities are governed by a set of generally accepted accounting principles (GAAP) established by the Financial Accounting Standards Board (FASB).

The NFP organizations issue three general-purpose external financial statements designed to help external users assess (1) the services an NFP organization provides, (2) the organization's ability to continue providing those services, and (3) the performance of the organization's management. The complete set of financial statements and accompanying notes includes a

1. Statement of financial position as of the end of the period.
2. Statement of activities for the period.
3. Statement of cash flows for the period.

The **statement of financial position** reports on the organization's assets, liabilities, and equity (net assets). This statement contains many common account titles, including Cash, Cash Equivalents, Accounts and Notes Receivable and Payable, Inventories, Marketable Securities, Long-Term Assets and Liabilities, Buildings, and Land. However, as indicated, the equity section of the statement of financial position is subdivided into three categories: *permanently restricted net assets, temporarily restricted net assets,* and *unrestricted net assets.*

The **statement of activities** reports on revenues, expenses, gains, and losses that increase or decrease net assets. Revenues and gains are increases in assets or decreases in liabilities generated by the organization's operating activities. Donor contributions are classified as revenues. Expenses and losses are decreases in assets or increases in liabilities incurred through operating activities. The statement is arranged in three sections: (1) changes in unrestricted net assets, (2) changes in temporarily restricted assets, and (3) changes in permanently restricted net assets. The bottom-line figure is computed by adding the net change in net assets to the beginning balance in net assets to arrive at the ending net asset balance.

The **statement of cash flows** reports the cash consequences of the organization's operating, investing, and financing activities. Unrestricted and temporarily restricted donor contributions are included in the operating activities section of the statement of cash flows. Permanently restricted donor contributions are considered financing activities. Other items are treated in a manner similar to the treatment used by profit-oriented businesses.

To illustrate financial reporting for NFP entities, assume that a private nonprofit school, Palmer Primary School of Excellence, is established when it receives a $10 million cash contribution from Dana Palmer, a wealthy benefactor who wants to promote excellence in early childhood education for minority students. A total of $1 million was designated as unrestricted funds; $2 million was temporarily restricted for the purchase of land and construction of buildings. The remaining $7 million was permanently restricted for an endowed investment fund that will produce investment income to be used to supplement school operations. Parents are required to pay the school for educational services on a scale based on their level of income. During 2001, the first year of operation, $1,200,000 cash was spent to acquire land and buildings. The $7 million of cash was invested in the endowed fund. The endowment generated investment income amounting to $700,000 cash. Operating revenues amounted to $100,000 cash. Cash operating expenses amounted to $950,000, not including $50,000 of depreciation expense. The results of these events are reported in the set of financial statements in Exhibit 11–6. Study these statements carefully, noting the following differentiating features:

1. That which is classified as equity in business statements is called *net asset* in the NFP statement. The net assets are subdivided into three components, depending on the nature of the donor restrictions originally placed on the use of the resources.
2. The statement of activities is divided into three categories, including activities that affect unrestricted, temporarily restricted, and permanently restricted assets. Notice that unrestricted contributions are treated in a manner similar to the way revenue is treated in profit-oriented businesses. Finally, observe the reconciliation between the beginning and ending balances in net assets shown at the bottom of the statement.
3. With respect to the statement of cash flows, unrestricted and temporarily restricted donor contributions are classified as operating activities. Only permanently restricted donor contributions are classified as financing activities. In contrast, all contributed capital of profit-oriented businesses is classified as a financing activity.

LO10 Explain accounting for not-for-profit entities and governmental organizations.

Governmental Accounting

Governmental entities have characteristics that require a unique accounting system in order to satisfy the needs of information users. These characteristics include (1) involuntary contributors of resources

Exhibit 11–6

PALMER PRIMARY SCHOOL OF EXCELLENCE
Financial Statements
As of December 31, 2001

Statement of Activities

Changes in Unrestricted Net Assets	
Donor Contributions	$1,000,000
Released from Temp. Building Restriction	1,200,000
Investment Revenue	700,000
Tuition	100,000
Expenses for Educational Programs	(950,000)
Depreciation Expense	(50,000)
Net Change in Unrestricted Net Assets	2,000,000
Changes in Temporarily Restricted Net Assets	
Temp. Restricted Contributions for Buildings	2,000,000
Released from Temp. Building Restriction	(1,200,000)
Changes in Permanently Restricted Net Assets	
Donor Contributions	7,000,000
Increase in Net Assets	9,800,000
Net Assets at Beginning of Period	0
Net Assets at End of Year	$9,800,000

Statement of Financial Position

Assets	
Cash	$1,650,000
Endowed Investment Fund	7,000,000
Buildings and Land	1,200,000
Less: Accumulated Depreciation	(50,000)
Total Assets	$9,800,000
Net Assets	
Permanently Restricted	$7,000,000
Temporarily Restricted	800,000
Unrestricted	2,000,000
Total Net Assets	$9,800,000

Statement of Cash Flows

Operating Activities	
Temp. Restricted Donor Contributions	$2,000,000
Unrestricted Donor Contributions	1,000,000
Investment Revenue	700,000
Tuition	100,000
Operating Expenses	(950,000)
Net Inflow from Operations	2,850,000
Investment Activities	
Endowed Investment Fund	(7,000,000)
Purchase Building and Land	(1,200,000)
Financing Activities	
Perm. Restricted Donor Contributions	7,000,000
Net Change in Cash	$1,650,000

known as *taxpayers;* (2) monopoly supplier of goods and services; (3) resources heavily invested in nonrevenue-producing assets such as buildings, bridges, highways, schools, and military and police forces; and (4) management by elected representation. The primary users of governmental financial reports include citizens, researchers, media agents, special-interest groups, legislative and oversight bodies, and investors and creditors. The information contained in the financial reports is used to (1) compare actual results with budgeted estimates, (2) assess the entities' financial condition and operating results, (3) determine compliance with the laws and regulations, and (4) evaluate the effectiveness and efficiency of management.

The GAAP for governmental accounting is set forth by the Governmental Accounting Standards Board (GASB), a sister organization of the FASB. The presence of two separate standards-setting authorities can lead to confusion regarding which authoritative body has jurisdiction over certain types of organizations. For example, a hospital can be operated as a profit-oriented business enterprise, a private nonprofit entity, or a branch of a governmental entity. Often a single hospital possesses some mixture of the characteristics of the two or three forms of organization. Accordingly, the lines of distinction can be vague, and judgment may be required as to which GAAP applies.

The GASB has concluded that *the diversity of governmental activities and the need for legal compliance preclude the use of a single accounting entity approach* for governmental bodies. Instead, financial reporting is accomplished through distinct fiscal entities called *funds* or *account groups.* Accordingly, governmental accounting is frequently called **fund accounting.** A **fund** is an independent accounting entity with a self-balancing set of accounts segregated for the purpose of carrying on specific activities. For example, a local governmental municipality may maintain separate funds for schools, police, and parks and recreation. **Account groups** are self-balancing entities that account for the governmental unit's general fixed assets and the outstanding principal of its general long-term liabilities.

Because governmental entities are not subject to the constraints imposed by competition in the free markets, the GASB has taken a budgetary approach to accounting. Governmental entities frequently are required by law to establish budgets. When a governmental entity adopts a budget, GASB principles require that the budget be incorporated into the accounts, including the adoption of a report form that provides comparisons between budget and actual data in the financial statements. A formal budget is a critical component of accounting for government entities because it (1) provides an expression of public policy, (2) represents a statement of financial intent with regard to how funds raised through taxation will be spent, (3) acts as a legally enforceable instrument that limits spending by requiring financial managers to attain formally approved budgetary amendments prior to making expenditures that exceed the budgetary limits, (4) provides a standard to which actual results can be compared, thereby enabling the evaluation of performance, and (5) facilitates the planning process for the future needs of the governmental entity.

Governmental entities are required to issue a **comprehensive annual financial report (CAFR)** that covers all funds and account groups under their jurisdictions. The CAFR includes (1) the report of the independent auditor, (2) general-purpose financial statements, (3) combined statements organized by fund type when the primary entity has more than one fund of a given type, (4) individual fund statements when the primary governmental entity has only one fund of a given type, (5) schedules that provide detail sufficient to demonstrate compliance with specific regulations, and (6) appropriate statistical tables. Governmental reports are characterized by multiple columns that provide information on individual funds and account groups. No single summation is provided for the entity as a whole. Clearly, the appearance of financial statements prepared by governmental entities will differ significantly from that of those prepared by profit-oriented businesses.

The coverage of the details of accounting for governmental entities is beyond the scope of this book, but the preceding discussion should improve your understanding of the need for flexibility in financial reporting. Always remember that accounting should provide information that is useful to current and potential resource providers, consumers, and monitors of a variety of organizational entities. To preserve its relevance, accounting must maintain an appropriate level of versatility in reporting practices so as to meet the needs of its users.

KEY TERMS

Account groups *544*
Appropriated retained earnings account *535*
Articles of incorporation *520*
Authorized stock *527*
Board of directors *523*

Book value per share *526*
Closely held corporation *521*
Common stock *527*
Comprehensive annual financial report (CAFR) *544*

Continuity *523*
Corporation *520*
Cost method of accounting for treasury stock *532*
Cumulative dividends *527*
Date of record *533*

Declaration date *533*
Dividends *527*
Dividends in arrears *527*
Double taxation *521*
Entrenched management *523*

Ex-dividend *534*
Fund *544*
Fund accounting *544*
Issued stock *527*
Legal capital *526*
Limited liability *522*
Limited liability company (LLC) *522*
Market Value *526*

Outstanding Stock *527*
Paid-in Excess account *528*
Par value *525*
Partnership *520*
Partnership agreement *520*
Payment date *534*
Preferred stock *527*
Price-earnings (P/E) ratio *538*

Securities Act of 1933 and Securities Exchange Act of 1934 *521*
Sole proprietorship *519*
Stated value *526*
Statement of activities *542*
Statement of cash flows *542*
Statement of financial position *542*

Stock certificate *521*
Stock dividend *534*
Stockholders *521*
Stock split *535*
Transferability *523*
Treasury stock *527*
Withdrawals *524*

QUESTIONS

1. What are the three major forms of business organizations? Describe each.
2. How are sole proprietorships formed?
3. Discuss the purpose of a partnership agreement. Is such an agreement necessary for partnership formation?
4. What is meant by the phrase *separate legal entity*? To which type of business organization does it apply?
5. What is the purpose of the articles of incorporation? What information do they provide?
6. What is the function of the stock certificate?
7. What prompted Congress to pass the Securities Act of 1933 and the Securities Exchange Act of 1934? What is the purpose of these laws?
8. What are the advantages and disadvantages of the corporate form of business organization?
9. What is a limited liability company? Discuss its advantages and disadvantages.
10. How does the term *double taxation* apply to corporations? Give an example of double taxation.
11. What is the difference between contributed capital and retained earnings for a corporation?
12. What are the similarities and differences in the equity structure of a sole proprietorship, a partnership, and a corporation?
13. Why is it easier for a corporation to raise large amounts of capital than it is for a partnership?
14. What is the meaning of each of the following terms with respect to the corporate form of organization?
    a. Legal capital
    b. Par value of stock
    c. Stated value of stock
    d. Market value of stock
    e. Book value of stock
    f. Authorized shares of stock
    g. Issued stock
    h. Outstanding stock
    i. Treasury stock
    j. Common stock
    k. Preferred stock
    l. Dividends
15. What is the difference between cumulative preferred stock and noncumulative preferred stock?
16. What is no-par stock? How is it recorded in the accounting records?
17. Assume that Best Co. has issued and outstanding 1,000 shares of $100 par value, 10 percent, cumulative preferred stock. What is the dividend per share? If the preferred dividend is two years in arrears, what total amount of dividends must be paid before the common shareholders can receive any dividends?
18. If Best Co. issued 10,000 shares of $20 par value common stock for $30 per share, what amount is credited to the Common Stock account? What amount of cash is received?
19. What is the difference between par value stock and stated value stock?
20. Why might a company repurchase its own stock?
21. What effect does the purchase of treasury stock have on the equity of a company?
22. Assume that Day Company repurchased 1,000 of its own shares for $30 per share and sold the shares two weeks later for $35 per share. What is the amount of gain on the sale? How is it reported on the balance sheet? What type of account is treasury stock?
23. What is the importance of the declaration date, record date, and payment date in conjunction with corporate dividends?
24. What is the difference between a stock dividend and a stock split?

25. What are the primary reasons that a company would choose to distribute a stock dividend instead of a cash dividend?
26. What is the primary reason that a company would declare a stock split?
27. If Best Co. had 10,000 shares of $20 par value common stock outstanding and declared a 5-for-1 stock split, how many shares would then be outstanding and what would be their par value after the split?
28. When a company appropriates retained earnings, does the company set aside cash for a specific use? Explain.
29. What is the largest source of financing for most U.S. businesses?
30. What is meant by *equity financing*? What is meant by *debt financing*?
31. What is a widely held corporation? What is a closely held corporation?
32. What are some reasons that a corporation might not pay dividends?
33. What does the price-earnings ratio generally indicate about a company?

EXERCISES—SERIES A

L.O. 1, 2   **EXERCISE 11–1A** *Effect of Accounting Events on the Financial Statements of a Sole Proprietorship*

A sole proprietorship was started on January 1, 2005, when it received $50,000 cash from Edd Simms, the owner. During 2005, the company earned $25,000 in cash revenues and paid $14,500 in cash expenses. Simms withdrew $1,500 cash from the business during 2005.

Required
Prepare an income statement, capital statement (statement of changes in equity), balance sheet, and statement of cash flows for Simms' 2005 fiscal year.

L.O. 1, 2   **EXERCISE 11–2A** *Effect of Accounting Events on the Financial Statements of a Partnership*

Bruce Bailey and Roy Clark started the BC partnership on January 1, 2004. The business acquired $40,000 cash from Bailey and $75,000 from Clark. During 2004, the partnership earned $75,000 in cash revenues and paid $36,000 for cash expenses. Bailey withdrew $1,000 cash from the business, and Clark withdrew $3,000 cash. The net income was allocated to the capital accounts of the two partners in proportion to the amounts of their original investments in the business.

Required
Prepare an income statement, capital statement, balance sheet, and statement of cash flows for the BC partnership for the 2004 fiscal year.

L.O. 1, 2   **EXERCISE 11–3A** *Effect of Accounting Events on the Financial Statements of a Corporation*

Hill Corporation was started with the issue of 2,000 shares of $10 par common stock for cash on January 1, 2005. The stock was issued at a market price of $22 per share. During 2005, the company earned $46,000 in cash revenues and paid $34,000 for cash expenses. Also a $2,500 cash dividend was paid to the stockholders.

Required
Prepare an income statement, statement of changes in stockholders' equity, balance sheet, and statement of cash flows for Hill Corporation's 2005 fiscal year.

L.O. 4   **EXERCISE 11–4A** *Effect of Issuing Common Stock on the Balance Sheet*

Newly formed Health-Max Corporation has 50,000 shares of $5 par common stock authorized. On March 1, 2006, Health-Max issued 8,000 shares of the stock for $15 per share. On May 2 the company issued an additional 15,000 shares for $22 per share. Health-Max was not affected by other events during 2006.

Required
a. Record the transactions in a horizontal statements model like the following one. In the Cash Flow column, indicate whether the item is an operating activity (OA), investing activity (IA), or financing activity (FA). Use NA to indicate that an element was not affected by the event.

Assets	=	Liab.	+	Stockholders' Equity		Rev.	–	Exp.	=	Net Inc.	Cash Flow
Cash	=		+	C. Stk.	+ Paid-in Excess						

b. Determine the amount Health-Max would report for common stock on the December 31, 2006, balance sheet.

c. Determine the amount Health-Max would report for paid-in capital in excess of par.

d. What is the total amount of capital contributed by the owners?

e. What amount of total assets would Health-Max report on the December 31, 2006, balance sheet?

f. Prepare journal entries to record the March 1 and May 2 transactions.

EXERCISE 11–5A *Recording and Reporting Common and Preferred Stock Transactions*   L.O. 4

Meyer, Inc., was organized on June 5, 2007. It was authorized to issue 400,000 shares of $5 par common stock and 50,000 shares of 5 percent cumulative class A preferred stock. The class A stock had a stated value of $20 per share. The following stock transactions pertain to Meyer, Inc.:

1. Issued 20,000 shares of common stock for $9 per share.
2. Issued 5,000 shares of the class A preferred stock for $22 per share.
3. Issued 100,000 shares of common stock for $12 per share.

Required

a. Prepare general journal entries for these transactions.

b. Prepare the stockholders' equity section of the balance sheet immediately after these transactions.

EXERCISE 11–6A *Effect of No-Par Common and Par Preferred Stock on the Horizontal Statements Model*   L.O. 4

Irwin Corporation issued 2,000 shares of no-par common stock for $25 per share. Irwin also issued 1,000 shares of $50 par, 8 percent noncumulative preferred stock at $70 per share.

Required

a. Record these events in a horizontal statements model like the following one. In the cash flow column, indicate whether the item is an operating activity (OA), investing activity (IA), or financing activity (FA). Use NA to indicate that an element was not affected by the event.

Assets	=	Stockholders' Equity			Rev.	–	Exp.	=	Net Inc.	Cash Flow
Cash	=	P. Stk.	+ C. Stk.	+ Paid-in Excess						

b. Prepare journal entries to record these transactions.

EXERCISE 11–7A *Issuing Stock for Assets Other Than Cash*   L.O. 4

Jana Corporation was formed when it issued shares of common stock to two of its shareholders. Jana issued 3,000 shares of $5 par common stock to Marco Byron in exchange for $36,000 cash (the issue price was $12 per share). Jana also issued 2,000 shares of stock to Simon Jones in exchange for a one-year-old delivery van on the same day. Jones had originally paid $35,000 for the van.

Required

a. What was the market value of the delivery van on the date of the stock issue?

b. Show the effect of the two stock issues on Jana's books in a horizontal statements model like the following one. In the Cash Flow column, indicate whether the item is an operating activity (OA), investing activity (IA), or financing activity (FA). Use NA to indicate that an element was not affected by the event.

Assets			=	Stockholders' Equity			Rev.	–	Exp.	=	Net Inc.	Cash Flow
Cash	+	Van	=	C. Stk.	+ Paid-in Excess							

EXERCISE 11–8A *Treasury Stock Transactions*   L.O. 5

Russ Corporation repurchased 1,000 shares of its own stock for $45 per share. The stock has a par of $10 per share. A month later Russ resold 700 shares of the treasury stock for $55 per share.

Required

a. Record the two events in general journal format.

b. What is the balance of the treasury stock account after these transactions?

L.O. 5   EXERCISE 11–9A *Recording and Reporting Treasury Stock Transactions*

The following information pertains to Smoot Corp. at January 1, 2004.

Common stock, $10 par, 10,000 shares authorized,	
650 shares issued and outstanding	$ 6,500
Paid-in capital in excess of par, common stock	25,350
Retained earnings	95,000

Smoot Corp. completed the following transactions during 2004:

1. Issued 1,000 shares of $10 par common stock for $50 per share.

2. Repurchased 200 shares of its own common stock for $40 per share.

3. Resold 50 shares of treasury stock for $44 per share.

Required

a. How many shares of common stock were outstanding at the end of the period?

b. How many shares of common stock had been issued at the end of the period?

c. Prepare journal entries for these transactions.

d. Prepare the stockholders' equity section of the balance sheet reflecting these transactions. Include the number of shares authorized, issued, and outstanding in the description of the common stock.

L.O. 6   EXERCISE 11–10A *Effect of Cash Dividends on Financial Statements*

On October 1, 2005, Med Corporation declared a $75,000 cash dividend to be paid on December 30 to shareholders of record on November 20.

Required

a. Record the events occurring on October 1, November 20, and December 30 in a horizontal statements model like the following one. In the Cash Flow column, indicate whether the item is an operating activity (OA), investing activity (IA), or financing activity (FA).

Date	Assets	=	Liab.	+	C. Stock	+	Ret. Earn	Rev.	−	Exp.	=	Net Inc.	Cash Flow

b. Prepare journal entries for all events associated with the dividend.

L.O. 6   EXERCISE 11–11A *Accounting for Cumulative Preferred Dividends*

When Earles Corporation was organized in January 2003, it immediately issued 1,000 shares of $50 par, 8 percent, cumulative preferred stock and 20,000 shares of $10 par common stock. The corporation has never paid a dividend. The company's earnings history is as follows: 2003, net loss of $15,000; 2004, net income of $75,000; 2005, net income of $120,000.

Required

a. How much is the dividend arrearage as of January 1, 2004?

b. Assume that the board of directors declares a $20,000 cash dividend at the end of 2004 (remember that the 2003 and 2004 preferred dividends are due). How will the dividend be divided between the preferred and common stockholders?

L.O. 6   EXERCISE 11–12A *Cash Dividends for Preferred and Common Shareholders*

Ace Corporation had the following stock issued and outstanding at January 1, 2002:

1. 200,000 shares of $1 par common stock.

2. 20,000 shares of $50 par, 8 percent, noncumulative preferred stock.

On May 10, Ace Corporation declared the annual cash dividend on its 20,000 shares of preferred stock and a $1 per share dividend for the common shareholders. The dividends will be paid on June 15 to the shareholders of record on May 30.

Required

a. Determine the total amount of dividends to be paid to the preferred shareholders and common shareholders.

b. Prepare general journal entries to record the declaration and payment of the cash dividends (be sure to date your entries).

EXERCISE 11–13A *Cash Dividends: Common and Preferred Stock*

L.O. 6

Ming Corp., had the following stock issued and outstanding at January 1, 2006:
1. 100,000 shares of no-par common stock.
2. 20,000 shares of $50 par, 6 percent, cumulative preferred stock. (Dividends are in arrears for one year, 2005.)

On February 1, 2006, Ming declared a $120,000 cash dividend to be paid March 31 to shareholders of record on March 10.

Required
a. What amount of dividends will be paid to the preferred shareholders versus the common shareholders?
b. Prepare the journal entries required for these transactions. (Be sure to include the dates of the entries.)

EXERCISE 11–14A *Accounting for Stock Dividends*

L.O. 7

Nichols Corporation issued a 4 percent stock dividend on 20,000 shares of its $20 par common stock. At the time of the dividend, the market value of the stock was $35 per share.

Required
a. Compute the amount of the stock dividend.
b. Show the effects of the stock dividend on the financial statements using a horizontal statements model like the following one.

Assets	=	Liab.	+	C. Stk.	+	Paid-in Excess	+	Ret. Earn.	Rev.	−	Exp.	=	Net Inc.	Cash Flow

c. Prepare the journal entry to record the stock dividend.

EXERCISE 11–15A *Determining the Effects of Stock Splits on the Accounting Records*

L.O. 7

The market value of Chan Corporation's common stock had become excessively high. The stock was currently selling for $160 per share. To reduce the market price of the common stock, Chan declared a 2-for-1 stock split for the 200,000 outstanding shares of its $10 par common stock.

Required
a. How will Chan Corporation's books be affected by the stock split?
b. Determine the number of common shares outstanding and the par value after the split.
c. Explain how the market value of the stock will be affected by the stock split.

EXERCISE 11–16A *Using the P/E Ratio*

L.O. 9

During 2007, Frontier Corporation and Upton Corporation reported net incomes of $60,000 and $112,000, respectively. Both companies had 15,000 shares of common stock issued and outstanding. The market price per share of Frontier's stock was $70 while Upton's sold for $90 per share.

Required
a. Determine the P/E ratio for each company.
b. Based on the P/E ratios computed in Requirement *a,* which company do investors believe has more potential for growth in income?

EXERCISE 11–17A *Not for Profit (Appendix)*

L.O. 10

Brandy Swain, an enterprising accounting student, agreed to prepare financial statements for Salem City Arts Theater. She prepared the financial statements using the format for profit institutions (income statement, balance sheet, and statement of cash flows). She has asked you to review the statements.

Required
Write a memo that describes the financial statements that are required for not-for-profit entities. In the memo explain the differences in the financial statements required for profit businesses and those required for not-for-profit entities.

L.O. 1, 2   **PROBLEM 11–18A** *Effect of Business Structure on Financial Statements*

MMX Company was started on January 1, 2007, when the owners invested $300,000 cash in the business. During 2007, the company earned cash revenues of $80,000 and incurred cash expenses of $52,000. The company also paid cash distributions of $10,000.

Required

Prepare a 2007 income statement, capital statement (statement of changes in equity), balance sheet, and statement of cash flows using each of the following assumptions. (Consider each assumption separately.)

a. MMX is a sole proprietorship owned by Martin Mayer.

b. MMX is a partnership with two partners, Martin Mayer and Kay Mitchell. Mayer invested $200,000 and Mitchell invested $100,000 of the $300,000 cash that was used to start the business. Mitchell was expected to assume the vast majority of the responsibility for operating the business. The partnership agreement called for Mitchell to receive 70 percent of the profits and Mayer the remaining 30 percent. With regard to the $10,000 distribution, Mitchell withdrew $4,000 from the business and Mayer withdrew $6,000.

c. MMX is a corporation. The owners were issued 12,000 shares of $10 par common stock when they invested the $300,000 cash in the business.

L.O. 4–6   **PROBLEM 11–19A** *Recording and Reporting Stock Transactions and Cash Dividends Across Two Accounting Cycles*

Oak Corporation was authorized to issue 50,000 shares of $5 par common stock and 10,000 shares of $100 par, 8 percent, cumulative preferred stock. Oak Corporation completed the following transactions during its first two years of operation:

2003

Jan. 2 Issued 20,000 shares of $5 par common stock for $8 per share.

     15 Issued 4,000 shares of $100 par preferred stock for $130 per share.

Feb. 14 Issued 10,000 shares of $5 par common stock for $9 per share.

Dec. 31 During the year, earned $270,000 of cash revenues and paid $160,000 of cash expenses.

     31 Declared the cash dividend on outstanding shares of preferred stock for 2003. The dividend will be paid on January 31 to stockholders of record on January 15, 2004.

     31 Closed revenue, expense, and dividend accounts to the retained earnings account.

2004

Jan. 31 Paid the cash dividend declared on December 31, 2003.

Mar. 1 Issued 2,000 shares of $100 par preferred stock for $150 per share.

June 1 Purchased 400 shares of common stock as treasury stock at $11 per share.

Dec. 31 During the year, earned $250,000 of cash revenues and paid $175,000 of cash expenses.

     31 Declared the dividend on the preferred stock and a $0.20 per share dividend on the common stock.

     31 Closed revenue, expense, and dividend accounts to the retained earnings account.

Required

a. Prepare journal entries for these transactions for 2003 and 2004.

b. Prepare the stockholders' equity section of the balance sheet at December 31, 2003.

c. Prepare the balance sheet at December 31, 2004.

L.O. 5, 6, 8   **PROBLEM 11–20A** *Recording and Reporting Treasury Stock Transactions*

Twin States Corp. completed the following transactions in 2004, the first year of operation:

1. Issued 10,000 shares of $10 par common stock at par.

2. Issued 2,000 shares of $30 stated value preferred stock at $30 per share.

3. Purchased 500 shares of common stock as treasury stock for $18 per share.

4. Declared a 6 percent dividend on preferred stock.

5. Sold 300 shares of treasury stock for $23 per share.

6. Paid the cash dividend on preferred stock that was declared in Event 4.

7. Earned revenue of $57,000 and incurred expenses of $36,000.

8. Closed revenue, expense, and dividend accounts to the retained earnings account.

9. Appropriated $6,000 of retained earnings.

Required

a. Prepare journal entries to record these transactions.

b. Prepare the stockholders' equity section of the balance sheet as of December 31, 2004.

PROBLEM 11–21A *Recording and Reporting Treasury Stock Transactions*   **L.O. 5**

Young Corporation reports the following information in its January 1, 2005, balance sheet:

Stockholders' Equity	
Common Stock, $10 Par Value,	
50,000 shares authorized, 40,000 shares outstanding	$400,000
Paid-in Capital in Excess of Par Value	150,000
Retained Earnings	100,000
Total Stockholders' Equity	$650,000

During 2005, Young was affected by the following accounting events:
1. Purchased 1,000 shares of treasury stock at $16 per share.
2. Reissued 300 shares of treasury stock at $20 per share.
3. Earned $64,000 of cash revenues.
4. Paid $38,000 of cash expenses.

Required
a. Provide journal entries to record these events in the accounting records.
b. Prepare the equity section of the year-end balance sheet.

PROBLEM 11–22A *Recording and Reporting Stock Dividends*   **L.O. 4, 6, 7**

Granger Corp. completed the following transactions in 2004, the first year of operation:
1. Issued 15,000 shares of $20 par common stock for $40 per share.
2. Issued 5,000 shares of $50 par, 5 percent, preferred stock at $50 per share.
3. Paid the annual cash dividend to preferred shareholders.
4. Issued a 5 percent stock dividend on the common stock. The market value at the dividend declaration date was $50 per share.
5. Later that year, issued a 2-for-1 split on the 15,750 shares of outstanding common stock.
6. Earned $210,000 of cash revenues and paid $128,000 of cash expenses.

Required
a. Record each of these events in a horizontal statements model like the following one. In the Cash Flow column, indicate whether the item is an operating activity (OA), investing activity (IA), or financing activity (FA). Use NA to indicate that an element is not affected by the event.

Assets	=	Liab.	+	S. Equity			Rev.	–	Exp.	=	Net Inc.	Cash Flow
				P. Stk.	+ C. Stk.	+ Ret. Earn.						

b. Record the 2004 transactions in general journal form.
c. Prepare the stockholders' equity section of the balance sheet at the end of 2004.

PROBLEM 11–23A *Analyzing the Stockholders' Equity Section of the Balance Sheet*   **L.O. 4, 7**

The stockholders' equity section of the balance sheet for Excite Company at December 31, 2007, is as follows:

Stockholders' Equity		
Paid-in Capital		
Preferred Stock, ? Par Value, 6% cumulative,		
50,000 shares authorized,		
30,000 shares issued and outstanding	$600,000	
Common Stock, $10 Stated Value,		
150,000 shares authorized,		
50,000 shares issued and outstanding	500,000	
Paid-in Capital in Excess of Par—Preferred	30,000	
Paid-in Capital in Excess of Par—Common	200,000	
Total Paid-in Capital		$1,330,000
Retained Earnings		250,000
Total Stockholders' Equity		$1,580,000

Note: The market value per share of the common stock is $25, and the market value per share of the preferred stock is $22.

Required

a. What is the par value per share of the preferred stock?

b. What is the dividend per share on the preferred stock?

c. What was the average issue price per share (price for which the stock was issued) of the common stock?

d. Explain the difference between the issue price and the market price of the common stock.

e. If Excite declared a 2-for-1 stock split on the common stock, how many shares would be outstanding after the split? What amount would be transferred from the retained earnings account because of the stock split? Theoretically, what would be the market price of the common stock immediately after the stock split?

L.O. 1 **PROBLEM 11–24A** *Different Forms of Business Organization*

Shawn Bates was working to establish a business enterprise with four of his wealthy friends. Each of the five individuals would receive a 20 percent ownership interest in the company. A primary goal of establishing the enterprise was to minimize the amount of income taxes paid. Assume that the five investors are in a 36 percent personal tax bracket and that the corporate tax rate is 25 percent. Also assume that the new company is expected to earn $200,000 of cash income before taxes during its first year of operation. All earnings are expected to be immediately distributed to the owners.

Required

Calculate the amount of after-tax cash flow available to each investor if the business is established as a partnership versus a corporation. Write a memo explaining the advantages and disadvantages of these two forms of business organization. Explain why a limited liability company may be a better choice than either a partnership or a corporation.

L.O. 4–8 **PROBLEM 11–25A** *Effects of Equity Transactions on Financial Statements*

The following events were experienced by Abbot, Inc.:

1. Issued common stock for cash.
2. Issued noncumulative preferred stock.
3. Appropriated retained earnings.
4. Sold treasury stock for an amount of cash that was more than the cost of the treasury stock.
5. Distributed a stock dividend.
6. Paid cash to purchase treasury stock.
7. Declared a cash dividend.
8. Paid the cash dividend declared in Event 7.
9. Issued cumulative preferred stock.
10. Distributed a 2-for-1 stock split on the common stock.

Required

Show the effect of each event on the elements of the financial statements using a horizontal statements model like the following one. Use + for increase, − for decrease, and NA for not affected. In the Cash Flow column, indicate whether the item is an operating activity (OA), investing activity (IA), or financing activity (FA). The first transaction is entered as an example.

Event No.	Assets	=	Liab.	+	S. Equity	Rev.	−	Exp.	=	Net Inc.	Cash Flow	
1	+		NA		+	NA		NA		NA	+	FA

L.O. 10 **PROBLEM 11–26A** *Not for Profit (Appendix)*

The Little Theater is an NFP organization established to encourage the performing arts in Monroe, Louisiana. The Little Theater experienced the following accounting events during 2006. Assume that all transactions are cash transactions unless otherwise stated.

1. Acquired cash contributions from donors, including $600,000 of permanently restricted, $200,000 of temporarily restricted, and $100,000 of unrestricted contributions.
2. The $600,000 of permanently restricted funds was invested in an endowed fund designed to provide investment income that will be made available for operating expenses.
3. The endowed investment fund produced $55,000 of cash revenue.

4. The $200,000 of temporarily restricted funds was used in accordance with donor restrictions to pur-
chase a theater in which plays will be presented. The theater had an expected useful life of 40 years
and an anticipated salvage value of $20,000.
5. Of the unrestricted assets, $50,000 was spent to purchase theatrical equipment. The equipment was
expected to have a five-year useful life and zero salvage value.
6. Tickets sales produced $120,000 of revenue during the accounting period.
7. The company incurred $110,000 of operating expenses.
8. Recognized depreciation on the theater and theatrical equipment.

Required
Prepare a statement of activities, statement of financial position, and statement of cash flows.

EXERCISES—SERIES B

EXERCISE 11–1B *Effect of Accounting Events on the Financial Statements of a Sole
Proprietorship*

L.O. 1, 2

A sole proprietorship was started on January 1, 2009, when it received $20,000 cash from Dan Jones, the
owner. During 2009, the company earned $14,500 in cash revenues and paid $9,300 in cash expenses.
Jones withdrew $500 cash from the business during 2009.

Required
Prepare an income statement, capital statement (statement of changes in equity), balance sheet, and statement of cash flows for Jones' 2009 fiscal year.

EXERCISE 11–2B *Effect of Accounting Events on the Financial Statements of a Partnership*

L.O. 1, 2

Claire Mills and Polly Price started the M&P partnership on January 1, 2009. The business acquired
$24,500 cash from Mills and $45,500 from Price. During 2009, the partnership earned $15,000 in cash
revenues and paid $6,300 for cash expenses. Mills withdrew $600 cash from the business, and Price
withdrew $1,400 cash. The net income was allocated to the capital accounts of the two partners in pro-
portion to the amounts of their original investments in the business.

Required
Prepare an income statement, capital statement, balance sheet, and statement of cash flows for M&P's
2009 fiscal year.

EXERCISE 11–3B *Effect of Accounting Events on the Financial Statements of a Corporation*

L.O. 1, 2

Stone Corporation was started with the issue of 1,000 shares of $5 par stock for cash on January 1, 2009.
The stock was issued at a market price of $18 per share. During 2009, the company earned $23,000 in
cash revenues and paid $17,000 for cash expenses. Also a $1,200 cash dividend was paid to the stockholders.

Required
Prepare an income statement, statement of changes in stockholders' equity, balance sheet, and statement
of cash flows for Stone Corporation's 2009 fiscal year.

EXERCISE 11–4B *Effect of Issuing Common Stock on the Balance Sheet*

L.O. 4

Newly formed Super Max Corporation has 30,000 shares of $10 par common stock authorized. On
March 1, 2009, Super Max issued 5,000 shares of the stock for $20 per share. On May 2 the company is-
sued an additional 6,000 shares for $24 per share. Super Max was not affected by other events during
2009.

Required
a. Record the transactions in a horizontal statements model like the following one. In the Cash Flow
column, indicate whether the item is an operating activity (OA), investing activity (IA), or financing
activity (FA). Use NA to indicate that an element was not affected by the event.

Assets	=	Liab.	+	S. Equity			Rev.	−	Exp.	=	Net Inc.	Cash Flow
Cash	=		+	C. Stk.	+	Paid-in Excess						

b. Determine the amount Super Max would report for common stock on the December 31, 2009, balance sheet.

c. Determine the amount Super Max would report for paid-in capital in excess of par.

d. What is the total amount of capital contributed by the owners?

e. What amount of total assets would Super Max report on the December 31, 2009, balance sheet?

f. Prepare journal entries to record the March 1 and May 2 transactions.

L.O. 4   EXERCISE 11–5B *Recording and Reporting Common and Preferred Stock Transactions*

E.Com, Inc., was organized on June 5, 2009. It was authorized to issue 200,000 shares of $5 par common stock and 20,000 shares of 5 percent cumulative class A preferred stock. The class A stock had a stated value of $50 per share. The following stock transactions pertain to E.Com, Inc.:

1. Issued 10,000 shares of common stock for $8 per share.

2. Issued 3,000 shares of the class A preferred stock for $80 per share.

3. Issued 80,000 shares of common stock for $10 per share.

Required

a. Prepare general journal entries for these transactions.

b. Prepare the stockholders' equity section of the balance sheet immediately after these transactions.

L.O. 4   EXERCISE 11–6B *Effect of No-Par Common and Par Preferred Stock on the Horizontal Statements Model*

Master Corporation issued 4,000 shares of no-par common stock for $30 per share. Master also issued 1,000 shares of $50 par, 6 percent noncumulative preferred stock at $80 per share.

Required

a. Record these events in a horizontal statements model like the following one. In the Cash Flow column, indicate whether the item is an operating activity (OA), investing activity (IA), or financing activity (FA). Use NA to indicate that an element was not affected by the event.

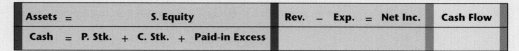

Assets	=		S. Equity		Rev.	−	Exp.	=	Net Inc.	Cash Flow
Cash	=	P. Stk.	+	C. Stk.	+ Paid-in Excess					

b. Prepare journal entries to record these transactions.

L.O. 4   EXERCISE 11–7B *Issuing Stock for Assets other than Cash*

James Lee, a wealthy investor, exchanged a plot of land that originally cost him $30,000 for 1,000 shares of $10 par common stock issued to him by Bay Corp. On the same date, Bay Corp. issued an additional 400 shares of stock to Lee for $31 per share.

Required

a. What was the value of the land at the date of the stock issue?

b. Show the effect of the two stock issues on Bay's books in a horizontal statements model like the following one. In the Cash Flow column, indicate whether the item is an operating activity (OA), investing activity (IA), or financing activity (FA). Use NA to indicate that an element was not affected by the event.

Assets			=	S. Equity		Rev.	−	Exp.	=	Net Inc.	Cash Flow
Cash	+	Land	=	C. Stk.	+ Paid-in Excess						

L.O. 5   EXERCISE 11–8B *Treasury Stock Transactions*

Hawk Corporation repurchased 1,000 shares of its own stock for $38 per share. The stock has a par of $10 per share. A month later Hawk resold 500 shares of the treasury stock for $55 per share.

Required

a. Record the two events in general journal format.

b. What is the balance of the treasury stock account after these transactions?

EXERCISE 11–9B *Recording and Reporting Treasury Stock Transactions*   **L.O. 5**

The following information pertains to Sneed Corp. at January 1, 2006.

Common stock, $10 par, 10,000 shares authorized, 800 shares issued and outstanding	8,000
Paid-in capital in excess of par, common stock	12,000
Retained earnings	$75,000

Sneed Corp. completed the following transactions during 2006:
1. Issued 2,000 shares of $10 par common stock for $43 per share.
2. Repurchased 300 shares of its own common stock for $38 per share.
3. Resold 100 shares of treasury stock for $40 per share.

Required
a. How many shares of common stock were outstanding at the end of the period?
b. How many shares of common stock had been issued at the end of the period?
c. Prepare journal entries for these transactions.
d. Prepare the stockholders' equity section of the balance sheet reflecting these transactions. Include the number of shares authorized, issued, and outstanding in the description of the common stock.

EXERCISE 11–10B *Effect of Cash Dividends on Financial Statements*   **L.O. 6**

On May 1, 2005, Lott Corporation declared a $120,000 cash dividend to be paid on May 31 to shareholders of record on May 15.

Required
a. Record the events occurring on May 1, May 15, and May 31 in a horizontal statements model like the following one. In the Cash Flow column, indicate whether the item is an operating activity (OA), investing activity (IA), or financing activity (FA).

Date	Assets	=	Liab.	+	C. Stock	+	Ret. Earn	Rev.	−	Exp.	=	Net Inc.	Cash Flow

b. Prepare journal entries for all events associated with the dividend.

EXERCISE 11–11B *Accounting for Cumulative Preferred Dividends*   **L.O. 6**

When Express Corporation was organized in January 2007, it immediately issued 2,000 shares of $50 par, 7 percent, cumulative preferred stock and 30,000 shares of $20 par common stock. The corporation has never paid a dividend. Its earnings history is as follows: 2007, net loss of $25,000; 2008, net income of $120,000; 2009, net income of $250,000.

Required
a. How much is the dividend arrearage as of January 1, 2008?
b. Assume that the board of directors declares a $30,000 cash dividend at the end of 2008 (remember that the 2007 and 2008 preferred dividends are due). How will the dividend be divided between the preferred and common stockholders?

EXERCISE 11–12B *Cash Dividends for Preferred and Common Shareholders*   **L.O. 6**

Iuka Corporation had the following stock issued and outstanding at January 1, 2005:
1. 100,000 shares of $1 par common stock.
2. 10,000 shares of $100 par, 8 percent, noncumulative preferred stock.

On June 10, Iuka Corporation declared the annual cash dividend on its 10,000 shares of preferred stock and a $1 per share dividend for the common shareholders. The dividends will be paid on July 1 to the shareholders of record on June 20.

Required
a. Determine the total amount of dividends to be paid to the preferred shareholders and common shareholders.
b. Prepare general journal entries to record the declaration and payment of the cash dividends (be sure to date your entries).

L.O. 6   **EXERCISE 11–13B** *Cash Dividends: Common and Preferred Stock*

Varsity, Inc., had the following stock issued and outstanding at January 1, 2004:
1. 200,000 shares of no-par common stock.
2. 10,000 shares of $100 par, 8 percent, cumulative preferred stock. (Dividends are in arrears for one year, 2003.)

On March 8, 2009, Varsity declared a $200,000 cash dividend to be paid March 31 to shareholders of record on March 20.

Required
a. What amount of dividends will be paid to the preferred shareholders versus the common shareholders?
b. Prepare the journal entries required for these transactions. (Be sure to include the dates of the entries.)

L.O. 7   **EXERCISE 11–14B** *Accounting for Stock Dividends*

Rollins Corporation issued a 5 percent stock dividend on 10,000 shares of its $10 par common stock. At the time of the dividend, the market value of the stock was $14 per share.

Required
a. Compute the amount of the stock dividend.
b. Show the effects of the stock dividend on the financial statements using a horizontal statements model like the following one.

Assets	=	Liab.	+	C. Stk.	+	Paid-in Excess	+	Ret. Earn.		Rev.	–	Exp.	=	Net Inc.		Cash Flow

c. Prepare the journal entry to record the stock dividend.

L.O. 7   **EXERCISE 11–15B** *Determining the Effects of Stock Splits on the Accounting Records*

The market value of West Corporation's common stock had become excessively high. The stock was currently selling for $240 per share. To reduce the market price of the common stock, West declared a 4-for-1 stock split for the 100,000 outstanding shares of its $20 par value common stock.

Required
a. What entry will be made on the books of West Corporation for the stock split?
b. Determine the number of common shares outstanding and the par value after the split.
c. Explain how the market value of the stock will be affected by the stock split.

L.O. 9   **EXERCISE 11–16B** *Using the P/E Ratio*

During 2007, Cooper Corporation and Eastman Corporation reported net incomes of $80,000 and $55,000, respectively. Both companies had 15,000 shares of common stock issued and outstanding. The market price per share of Cooper's stock was $70 while Eastman's sold for $90 per share.

Required
a. Determine the P/E ratio for each company.
b. Based on the P/E ratios computed in Requirement *a,* which company do investors believe has more potential for growth in income?

L.O. 10   **EXERCISE 11–17B** *Not for Profit (Appendix)*

Mark Hayes was arguing with his friend Sewon Ow regarding contributions of financial resources that are acquired by an organization. Ow contends that such events constitute revenue that should be reported in the operating activities section of the income statement and statement of cash flows. Hayes disagrees. He believes that acquisitions of capital should not be shown on the income statement and should be shown as a financing activity in the statement of cash flows.

Required
Write a brief memo explaining how both of the apparently contradictory arguments could be correct.

PROBLEM 11–18B *Effect of Business Structure on Financial Statements*   L.O. 1, 2

Calloway Company was started on January 1, 2009, when it acquired $40,000 cash from the owners. During 2009, the company earned cash revenues of $18,000 and incurred cash expenses of $12,500. The company also paid cash distributions of $3,000.

Required

Prepare a 2009 income statement, capital statement (statement of changes in equity), balance sheet, and statement of cash flows under each of the following assumptions. (Consider each assumption separately.)

a. Calloway is a sole proprietorship owned by Macy Calloway.

b. Calloway is a partnership with two partners, Macy Calloway and Artie Calloway. Macy Calloway invested $25,000 and Artie Calloway invested $15,000 of the $40,000 cash that was used to start the business. A. Calloway was expected to assume the vast majority of the responsibility for operating the business. The partnership agreement called for A. Calloway to receive 60 percent of the profits and M. Calloway to get the remaining 40 percent. With regard to the $3,000 distribution, A. Calloway withdrew $1,200 from the business and M. Calloway withdrew $1,800.

c. Calloway is a corporation. It issued 5,000 shares of $5 par common stock for $40,000 cash to start the business.

PROBLEM 11–19B *Recording and Reporting Stock Transactions and Cash Dividends Across*   L.O. 4–6
                                   Two Accounting Cycles

Hamby Corporation received a charter that authorized the issuance of 100,000 shares of $10 par common stock and 50,000 shares of $50 par, 6 percent cumulative preferred stock. Hamby Corporation completed the following transactions during its first two years of operation.

2008

Jan. 5 Sold 10,000 shares of the $10 par common stock for $28 per share.
      12 Sold 1,000 shares of the 6% preferred stock for $70 per share.
Apr. 5 Sold 40,000 shares of the $10 par common stock for $40 per share.
Dec. 31 During the year, earned $170,000 in cash revenue and paid $110,000 for cash expenses.
      31 Declared the cash dividend on the outstanding shares of preferred stock for 2008. The dividend will be paid on February 15 to stockholders of record on January 10, 2009.
      31 Closed the revenue, expense, and dividend accounts to the retained earnings account.

2009

Feb. 15 Paid the cash dividend declared on December 31, 2008.
Mar. 3 Sold 10,000 shares of the $50 par preferred stock for $78 per share.
May 5 Purchased 500 shares of the common stock as treasury stock at $43 per share.
Dec. 31 During the year, earned $210,000 in cash revenues and paid $140,000 for cash expenses.
      31 Declared the annual dividend on the preferred stock and a $0.60 per share dividend on the common stock.
      31 Closed revenue, expense, and dividend accounts to the retained earnings account.

Required

a. Prepare journal entries for these transactions for 2008 and 2009.

b. Prepare the balance sheets at December 31, 2008 and 2009.

c. What is the number of common shares *outstanding* at the end of 2008? At the end of 2009? How many common shares had been *issued* at the end of 2008? At the end of 2009? Explain any differences between issued and outstanding common shares for 2008 and for 2009.

PROBLEM 11–20B *Recording and Reporting Treasury Stock Transactions*   L.O. 4, 5, 8

One Co. completed the following transactions in 2009, the first year of operation:

1. Issued 20,000 shares of $5 par common stock for $5 per share.
2. Issued 1,000 shares of $20 stated value preferred stock for $20 per share.
3. Purchased 1,000 shares of common stock as treasury stock for $7 per share.
4. Declared a $1,500 dividend on preferred stock.
5. Sold 500 shares of treasury stock for $10 per share.
6. Paid $1,500 cash for the preferred dividend declared in Event 4.

7. Earned cash revenues of $54,000 and incurred cash expenses of $32,000.
8. Closed revenue, expense, and dividend accounts to the retained earnings account.
9. Appropriated $5,000 of retained earnings.

Required
a. Prepare journal entries to record these transactions.
b. Prepare a balance sheet as of December 31, 2009.

L.O. 4, 5   PROBLEM 11–21B *Analyzing Journal Entries for Treasury Stock Transactions*

The following correctly prepared entries without explanations pertain to Triangle Corporation.

	Account Title	Debit	Credit
1.	Cash	2,100,000	
	Common Stock		1,000,000
	Paid-in Capital in Excess of Par Value		1,100,000
2.	Treasury Stock	22,500	
	Cash		22,500
3.	Cash	13,600	
	Treasury Stock		12,000
	Paid-in Capital in Excess of Cost of Treasury Stock		1,600

The original sale (Entry 1) was for 200,000 shares, and the treasury stock was acquired for $15 per share (Entry 2).

Required
a. What was the sales price per share of the original stock issue?
b. How many shares of stock did the corporation acquire in Event 2?
c. How many shares were reissued in Event 3?
d. How many shares are outstanding immediately following Events 2 and 3, respectively?

L.O. 4, 6, 7   PROBLEM 11–22B *Recording and Reporting Stock Dividends*

Deaton Co. completed the following transactions in 2006, the first year of operation:
1. Issued 20,000 shares of no-par common stock for $10 per share.
2. Issued 5,000 shares of $20 par, 6 percent, preferred stock for $20 per share (no shares were issued prior to this transaction).
3. Paid a cash dividend of $6,000 to preferred shareholders.
4. Issued a 10 percent stock dividend on no-par common stock. The market value at the dividend declaration date was $15 per share.
5. Later that year, issued a 2-for-1 split on the shares of outstanding common stock. The market price of the stock at that time was $35 per share.
6. Produced $145,000 of cash revenues and incurred $97,000 of cash expenses.

Required
a. Record each of the six events in a horizontal statements model like the following one. In the Cash Flow column, indicate whether the item is an operating activity (OA), investing activity (IA), or financing activity (FA). Use NA to indicate that an element is not affected by the event.

Assets	=	Liab.	+	Stockholders' Equity			Rev.	−	Exp.	=	Net Inc.	Cash Flow
				P. Stk. + C. Stk. + Ret. Earn.								

b. Record the 2006 transactions in general journal form.
c. Prepare the stockholders' equity section of the balance sheet at the end of 2006. (Include all necessary information.)
d. Theoretically, what is the market value of the common stock after the stock split?

PROBLEM 11–23B *Analyzing the Stockholders' Equity Section of the Balance Sheet*   **L.O. 4, 7**

The stockholders' equity section of the balance sheet for Cross Electric Co. at December 31, 2002, is as follows:

Stockholders' Equity		
Paid-in Capital		
Preferred Stock, ? Par Value, 8% cumulative,		
100,000 shares authorized,		
5,000 shares issued and outstanding	$ 250,000	
Common Stock, $20 Stated Value,		
200,000 shares authorized,		
100,000 shares issued and outstanding	2,000,000	
Paid-in Capital in Excess of Par—Preferred	100,000	
Paid-in Capital in Excess of Par—Common	500,000	
Total Paid-in Capital		$2,850,000
Retained Earnings		500,000
Total Stockholders' Equity		$3,350,000

Note: The market value per share of the common stock is $36, and the market value per share of the preferred stock is $75.

Required
a. What is the par value per share of the preferred stock?
b. What is the dividend per share on the preferred stock?
c. What was the average issue price per share (price for which the stock was issued) of the common stock?
d. Explain the difference between the par value and the market price of the preferred stock.
e. If Cross declares a 3-for-1 stock split on the common stock, how many shares will be outstanding after the split? What amount will be transferred from the retained earnings account because of the stock split? Theoretically, what will be the market price of the common stock immediately after the stock split?

PROBLEM 11–24B *Different Forms of Business Organization*   **L.O. 1**

Paul Salvy established a partnership with Lisa Witlow. The new company, S&W Fuels, purchased coal directly from mining companies and contracted to ship the coal via waterways to a seaport where it was delivered to ships that were owned and operated by international utilities companies. Salvy was primarily responsible for running the day-to-day operations of the business. Witlow negotiated the buy-and-sell agreements. She recently signed a deal to purchase and deliver $2,000,000 of coal to Solar Utilities. S&W Fuels purchased the coal on account from Miller Mining Company. After accepting title to the coal, S&W Fuels agreed to deliver the coal under terms FOB destination, Port of Long Beach. Unfortunately, Witlow failed to inform Salvy of the deal in time for Salvy to insure the shipment. While in transit, the vessel carrying the coal suffered storm damage that rendered the coal virtually worthless by the time it reached its destination. S&W Fuels immediately declared bankruptcy. The company not only was responsible for the $2,000,000 due to Miller Mining Company but also was sued by Solar for breach of contract. Witlow had a personal net worth of virtually zero, but Salvy was a wealthy individual with a net worth approaching $2,500,000. Accordingly, Miller Mining and Solar filed suit against Salvy's personal assets. Salvy claimed that he was not responsible for the problem because Witlow had failed to inform him of the contracts in time to obtain insurance coverage. Witlow admitted that she was personally responsible for the disaster.

Required
Write a memo describing Salvy's risk associated with his participation in the partnership. Comment on how other forms of ownership would have affected his level of risk.

PROBLEM 11–25B *Effects of Equity Transactions on Financial Statements*   **L.O. 4–8**

The following events were experienced by Baskin, Inc.
1. Issued common stock for cash.
2. Paid cash to purchase treasury stock.

3. Declared a cash dividend.
4. Issued cumulative preferred stock.
5. Issued noncumulative preferred stock.
6. Appropriated retained earnings.
7. Sold treasury stock for an amount of cash that was more than the cost of the treasury stock.
8. Distributed a stock dividend.
9. Distributed a 2-for-1 stock split on the common stock.
10. Paid a cash dividend that was previously declared.

Required

Show the effect of each event on the elements of the financial statements using a horizontal statements model like the following one. Use + for increase, − for decrease, and NA for not affected. In the Cash Flow column indicate whether the item is an operating activity (OA), investing activity (IA), or financing activity (FA). The first transaction is entered as an example.

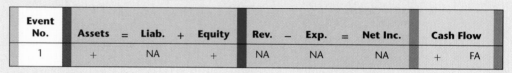

Event No.	Assets	=	Liab.	+	Equity	Rev.	−	Exp.	=	Net Inc.	Cash Flow
1	+		NA		+	NA		NA		NA	+	FA

L.O. 10   **PROBLEM 11–26B** *Not for Profit (Appendix)*

Marshall County Public Library (MCPL) experienced the following accounting events during 2009. Assume that all transactions are cash transactions unless otherwise stated.

1. Acquired $500,000 in contributions.
2. Paid $450,000 for facilities and equipment.
3. Earned $120,000 of revenue.
4. Incurred $80,000 in operating expenses.
5. Recognized $25,000 of depreciation expense.

Required

a. Assume that MCPL is a profit-oriented corporation and that the first event results from the issue of no-par common stock. Prepare an income statement, balance sheet, and statement of cash flows.
b. Assume that MCPL is a not-for-profit organization and that the first event represents an unrestricted donor contribution. Prepare a statement of activities, statement of financial position, and statement of cash flows.

ANALYZE, THINK, COMMUNICATE

ATC 11–1   **BUSINESS APPLICATIONS CASE** *Dell's Annual Report*

Using the Dell Computer Corporation financial statements in Appendix B, answer the following questions:

Required

a. Does Dell's common stock have a par value? If so, how much is it?
b. How many shares of Dell's common stock were outstanding as of February 2, 2001?
c. Did Dell pay any cash dividends in 2001? If so, how much?
d. Using the consolidated statement of stockholders' equity, determine why the number of shares of common stock outstanding increased from 2000 to 2001.
e. On what stock exchange does Dell's stock trade?

ATC 11–2   **GROUP ASSIGNMENT** *Missing Information*

Listed here are the stockholders' equity sections of three public companies for years ending 2000 and 1999:

	2000	1999
Wendy's (dollar amounts are presented in thousands)		
Stockholders' Equity		
Common stock, ?? Stated Value per share, authorized:		
200,000,000; 136,188,000 in 2000 and 134,856,000 in		
1999 shares issued, respectively	$ 12,074	$ 11,941
Capital in Excess of Stated Value	423,144	398,580
Retained Earnings	1,211,015	1,068,883
Acc. Other Comp. Exp.	(27,133)	(14,443)
Treasury Stock, at cost: 21,978,000 in 2000; 16,626,000		
shares in 1999	(492,957)	(399,522)
Coca-Cola (dollar amounts are presented in millions)		
Stockholders' Equity		
Common Stock, ?? Par Value per share, authorized:		
5,600,000,000; issued: 3,481,882,834 shares in 2000		
and 3,466,371,904 shares in 1999	870	861
Capital Surplus	3,196	2,584
Reinvested Earnings	21,265	20,773
Acc. Other Comp. Inc.	(2,722)	(1,551)
Treasury Stock, at cost: (997,121,427 shares in 2000;		
994,796,786 shares in 1999)	(13,293)	(13,160)
Harley Davidson (dollar amounts are presented in thousands)		
Stockholders' Equity		
Common stock, ?? Par Value per share, authorized:		
200,000,000, issued: 321,185,567 in 2000 and		
318,586,144 shares in 1999	3,210	3,184
Additional Paid-in Capital	285,390	234,948
Retained Earnings	1,431,017	1,113,376
Acc. Other Comp. Inc.	308	(2,067)
Treasury Stock, at cost: 19,114,822 for 2000 and		
15,863,518 for 1999	(313,994)	(187,992)
Unearned Compensation	(276)	(369)

Required

a. Divide the class in three sections and divide each section into groups of three to five students. Assign each section one of the companies.

Group Tasks

Based on the company assigned to your group, answer the following questions.

b. What is the per share par or stated value of the common stock in 2000?

c. What was the average issue price of the common stock for each year?

d. How many shares of stock are outstanding at the end of each year?

e. What is the average cost per share of the treasury stock for each year?

f. Do the data suggest that your company was profitable in 2000?

g. Can you determine the amount of net income from the information given? What is missing?

h. What is the total stockholders' equity of your company for each year?

Class Discussion

i. Have each group select a representative to present the information about its company. Compare the share issue price and the par or stated value of the companies.

j. Compare the average issue price to the current market price for each of the companies. Speculate about what might cause the difference.

REAL-WORLD CASE *Computing P/E Ratios for Four Companies*   ATC 11–3

Many companies grant certain members of management stock options that allow them to purchase designated amounts of stock for less than its market price. These arrangements are referred to as *stock compensation plans* and are intended to help the company retain high-quality management and to encourage management to increase the market value of the company's stock.

Deciding on the appropriate way to account for these plans is complex and controversial. Therefore, companies are allowed to *exclude* the estimated costs of the options they grant their management from net earnings provided that they disclose the estimated costs in the footnotes to the financial statements.

Listed here are data from four different companies that grant stock options to members of their management. The data are based on information provided in the companies' 10-K reports.

Sears, Roebuck and Co.	
Basic EPS as reported on the fiscal year 2000 income statement	$ 3.89
Basic EPS if stock compensation is deducted	3.77
Selling price of the company's stock on July 2, 2001	42.89

Target Corporation	
Basic EPS as reported on the fiscal year 2001 income statement	$ 1.40
Basic EPS if stock compensation is deducted	1.39
Selling price of the company's stock on July 2, 2001	35.59

Cisco Systems, Inc.	
Basic EPS as reported on the fiscal year 2000 income statement	$ 0.39
Basic EPS if stock compensation is deducted	0.22
Selling price of the company's stock on July 2, 2001	19.22

Oracle Corporation	
Basic EPS as reported on the fiscal year 2000 income statement	$ 2.22
Basic EPS if stock compensation is deducted	2.02
Selling price of the company's stock on July 2, 2001	19.58

Required

a. Compute each company's P/E ratio on July 2, 2001, based on (1) EPS as reported and (2) EPS with stock compensation deducted. You will have eight P/E ratios.

b. Assuming these companies are representative of their respective industries (department stores and software companies), what conclusions can you draw from the data provided and from your P/E computations? Write a brief report presenting your conclusions and the reasons for them.

ATC 11–4   BUSINESS APPLICATIONS CASE *Finding Stock Market Information*

This problem requires stock price quotations for the New York Stock Exchange, the American Stock Exchange, and NASDAQ. These are available in *The Wall Street Journal* and in the business sections of many daily newspapers as well as variances websites. Stock prices are also available on electronic data services such as CompuServe.

Required

For each company listed here, provide the requested information as of Thursday of last week. (*Hint:* Information about Thursday's stock market is in Friday's newspaper.)

Name of Company	Stock Exchange Where Listed	Closing Price	P/E Ratio
Berkshire Hathaway A			
Intel			
Iomega			
Yahoo			
Xerox			

ATC 11–5   BUSINESS APPLICATIONS CASE *Using the P/E Ratio*

During 2007, Geolock Corporation and Minerals Corporation reported net incomes of $8,000 and $9,400, respectively. Each company had 2,000 shares of common stock issued and outstanding. The market price per share of Geolock's stock was $48, while Minerals' stock sold for $94 per share.

Required

a. Determine the P/E ratio for each company.

b. Based on the P/E ratios computed in Requirement *a*, which company do investors believe has more potential for growth in income?

WRITING ASSIGNMENT *Comparison of Organizational Forms*

Jim Baku and Scott Hanson are thinking about opening a new restaurant. Baku has extensive marketing experience but does not know that much about food preparation. However, Hanson is an excellent chef. Both will work in the business, but Baku will provide most of the funds necessary to start the business. At this time, they cannot decide whether to operate the business as a partnership or a corporation.

Required

Prepare a written memo to Baku and Hanson describing the advantages and disadvantages of each organizational form. Also, from the limited information provided, recommend the organizational form you think they should use.

ETHICAL DILEMMA *Bad News Versus Very Bad News*

Louise Stinson, the chief financial officer of Bostonian Corporation, was on her way to the president's office. She was carrying the latest round of bad news. There would be no executive bonuses this year. Corporate profits were down. Indeed, if the latest projections held true, the company would report a small loss on the year-end income statement. Executive bonuses were tied to corporate profits. The executive compensation plan provided for 10 percent of net earnings to be set aside for bonuses. No profits meant no bonuses. While things looked bleak, Stinson had a plan that might help soften the blow.

After informing the company president of the earnings forecast, Stinson made the following suggestion: Since the company was going to report a loss anyway, why not report a big loss? She reasoned that the directors and stockholders would not be much more angry if the company reported a large loss than if it reported a small one. There were several questionable assets that could be written down in the current year. This would increase the current year's loss but would reduce expenses in subsequent accounting periods. For example, the company was carrying damaged inventory that was estimated to have a value of $2,500,000. If this estimate were revised to $500,000, the company would have to recognize a $2,000,000 loss in the current year. However, next year when the goods were sold, the expense for cost of goods sold would be $2,000,000 less and profits would be higher by that amount. Although the directors would be angry this year, they would certainly be happy next year. The strategy would also have the benefit of adding $200,000 to next year's executive bonus pool ($2,000,000 × 0.10). Furthermore, it could not hurt this year's bonus pool because there would be no pool this year since the company is going to report a loss.

Some of the other items that Stinson is considering include (1) converting from straight-line to accelerated depreciation, (2) increasing the percentage of receivables estimated to be uncollectible in the current year and lowering the percentage in the following year, and (3) raising the percentage of estimated warranty claims in the current period and lowering it in the following period. Finally, Stinson notes that two of the company's department stores have been experiencing losses. The company could sell these stores this year and thereby improve earnings next year. Stinson admits that the sale would result in significant losses this year, but she smiles as she thinks of next year's bonus check.

Required

a. Explain how each of the three numbered strategies for increasing the amount of the current year's loss would affect the stockholders' equity section of the balance sheet in the current year. How would the other elements of the balance sheet be affected?

b. If Stinson's strategy were effectively implemented, how would it affect the stockholders' equity in subsequent accounting periods?

c. Comment on the ethical implications of running the company for the sake of management (maximization of bonuses) versus the maximization of return to stockholders.

d. Formulate a bonus plan that will motivate managers to maximize the value of the firm instead of motivating them to manipulate the reporting process.

e. How would Stinson's strategy of overstating the amount of the reported loss in the current year affect the company's current P/E ratio?

EDGAR DATABASE *Analyzing PepsiCo's Equity Structure*

Required

Using the most current 10-K available on EDGAR, answer the following questions about PepsiCo for the most recent year reported. (PepsiCo is the company that produces Pepsi soft drinks, among other things.) Instructions for using EDGAR are in Appendix A.

a. What is the *book value* of PepsiCo's stockholders' equity that is shown on the company's balance sheet?

b. What is the par value of PepsiCo's common stock?

c. Does PepsiCo have any treasury stock? If so, how many shares of treasury stock does the company hold?

d. Why does the stock of a company such as PepsiCo have a market value that is higher than its book value?

ATC 11–9   **SPREADSHEET ANALYSIS** *Using Excel*

Annette's Accessories had the following stock issued and outstanding at January 1, 2005.

150,000 Shares of $1 Par Common Stock
10,000 Shares of $50 Par, 8%, Cumulative Preferred Stock

On March 5, 2005, Annette's declared a $100,000 cash dividend to be paid March 31 to shareholders of record on March 21.

Required

Set up a spreadsheet to calculate the total amount of dividends to be paid to preferred and common shareholders under the following alternative situations:

a. No dividends are in arrears for preferred shareholders.

b. One year's worth of dividends is in arrears for preferred shareholders.

c. Two years' worth of dividends is in arrears for preferred shareholders.

d. Instead of a $100,000 dividend, Annette's paid a $70,000 dividend and one year of dividends was in arrears.

Spreadsheet Tips

The following spreadsheet provides one method of setting up formulas for all possible alternatives. The spreadsheet also reflects the results of Requirement *a*.

Notice the use of the IF function. The IF function looks like =IF(condition, true, false). To use the IF function, first describe a certain condition to Excel. Next indicate the desired result if that condition is found to be true. Finally, indicate the desired result if that condition is found to be false. Notice in cell C4 of the spreadsheet (dividends in arrears distributed to preferred shareholders) that the condition provided is B4<B3, which is asking whether the dividends in arrears are less than the total dividend. If this condition is true, the formula indicates to display B4, which is the amount of the dividends in arrears. If

the condition is false, the formula indicates that B3 should be displayed, which is the total amount of the dividend.

The IF function can also be used to determine the amount of the current dividend distributed to preferred shareholders, the amount available for common shareholders, and the dividends in arrears after the dividend.

SPREADSHEET ASSIGNMENT *Mastering Excel*   **ATC 11–10**

Required

Complete Requirement *a* of Problem 11–22B using an Excel spreadsheet.

Statement of Cash Flows

Learning Objectives

After completing this chapter, you should be able to:

1 Identify the types of business events that are reported in the three sections of the statement of cash flows.

2 Convert an accrual account balance to its cash equivalent.

3 Prepare a statement of cash flows using the T-account method.

4 Explain how cash flow from operating activities reported under the indirect method differs from that reported under the direct method.

5 Explain how the classifications used on the statement of cash flows could provide misleading information to decision makers.

the *curious* accountant

Priceline.com began operations in April 1998 and first sold its stock to the public on March 30, 1999. By the end of 2000, the company had cumulative net losses of more than $1.4 billion. Even though its sales grew from $35 million in 1998 to more than $1 billion in 2000, it did not make a profit in any of those years. How can a company lose so much money and still be able to pay its bills?

The statement of cash flows explains how a company obtained and used cash during some period. The sources of cash are known as **cash inflows,** *and the uses are called* **cash outflows.** *The statement classifies cash receipts (inflows) and payments (outflows) into three categories: operating activities, investing activities, and financing activities. The following sections define these activities and outline the types of cash flows that are normally classified under each category.*

Operating Activities

Operating activities include cash inflows and outflows generated by running (operating) the business. Some of the specific items that are shown under this section are as follows.

1. Cash receipts from sales, commissions, fees, and receipts from interest and dividends.
2. Cash payments for inventories, salaries, operating expenses, interest, and taxes.

Note that *gains* and *losses* are not included in this section. The total cash collected from the sale of assets is included in the investing activities section.

Investing Activities

Investing activities include cash flows that are generated through a company's purchase or sale of long-term operational assets, investments in other companies, and its lending activities. Some items included in this section follow.

1. Cash receipts from the sale of property, plant, equipment or of marketable securities as well as the collection of loans.
2. Cash payments used to purchase property, plant, equipment or marketable securities as well as loans made to others.

Financing Activities

Financing activities include cash inflows and outflows associated with the company's own equity transactions or its borrowing activities. The following are some items appearing under the financing activities section.

1. Cash receipts from the issue of stock and borrowed funds.
2. Cash payments for the purchase of treasury stock, repayment of debt, and payment of dividends.

When you are trying to classify transactions into one of the three categories, it is helpful to note that the identification of the proper category depends on the company's perspective rather than on the type of account being considered. For example, a transaction involving common stock is considered an investing activity if the company is purchasing or selling its investment in another company's common stock. In contrast, common stock transactions are classified as financing activities if the company is issuing its own stock or is buying back its own stock (treasury stock). Similarly, the receipt of dividends is classified as an operating activity, but the payment of dividends is classified as a financing activity. Furthermore, lending cash is considered to be an investing activity, and borrowing cash is a financing activity. Accordingly, proper classification centers on the behavior of the company involved rather than the type of instrument being used.

Noncash Investing and Financing Transactions

Occasionally, companies will engage in significant **noncash investing and financing transactions.** For example, a company may issue some of its common stock in exchange for the title to a plot of land. Similarly, a company could accept a mortgage obligation in exchange for the title of ownership to a building (a 100% owner-financed exchange). Since these types of transactions do not involve the exchange of cash, they cannot be included as cash receipts or payments on the statement of cash flows. However, the Financial Accounting Standards Board (FASB) has concluded that full and fair reporting requires the disclosure of all material investing and financing activities regardless of whether they involve the exchange of cash. Accordingly, the FASB requires that the statement of cash flows include a separate schedule for the disclosure of noncash investing and financing activities.

Exhibit 12-1

WESTERN COMPANY
Statement of Cash Flows
For the Year Ended December 31, 2001

Cash Flows from Operating Activities		
Plus: List of Individual Inflows	$XXX	
Less: List of Individual Outflows	(XXX)	
Net Increase (Decrease) from Operating Activities		$XXX
Cash Flows from Investing Activities		
Plus: List of Individual Inflows	XXX	
Less: List of Individual Outflows	(XXX)	
Net Increase (Decrease) from Investing Activities		XXX
Cash Flows from Financing Activities		
Plus: List of Individual Inflows	XXX	
Less: List of Individual Outflows	(XXX)	
Net Increase (Decrease) from Financing Activities		XXX
Net Increase (Decrease) in Cash		XXX
Plus: Beginning Cash Balance		XXX
Ending Cash Balance		$XXX
Schedule of Noncash Investing and Financing Activities		
List of Noncash Transactions		$XXX

Reporting Format for Statement of Cash Flows

The statement of cash flows is arranged with operating activities shown first, investing activities second, and financing activities last. Under each category, individual cash inflows are shown first, with cash outflows being subtracted and the net difference being carried forward. The schedule of noncash investing and financing activities is typically shown at the bottom of the statement. Exhibit 12–1 demonstrates this format of statement presentation.

With respect to the placement of the four primary financial statements, the statement of cash flows is usually presented last. However, a sizable number of companies show the statement of cash flows immediately after the income statement and balance sheet. Some companies show the statement of cash flows as the first statement. Exhibit 12–2 provides more details regarding the placement of the statement of cash flows relative to the other financial statements shown in annual reports.

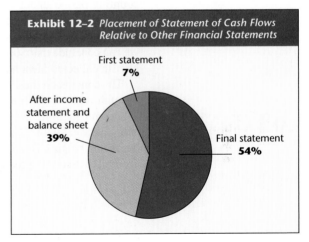

Exhibit 12–2 *Placement of Statement of Cash Flows Relative to Other Financial Statements*

First statement
7%

After income statement and balance sheet
39%

Final statement
54%

Data source: AICPA, *Accounting Trends and Techniques*, 2000.

Converting from Accrual to Cash-Basis Accounting

The operating activities section of the statement of cash flows is essentially a cash-basis income statement. Since accounting records are normally maintained on an accrual basis, it is necessary to convert data based on accruals and deferrals to cash equivalents to determine the amount of cash flow from operating activities. The following section discusses the conversion process.

LO2 Convert an accrual account balance to its cash equivalent.

Operating Activities

Converting Accruals to Cash

Accrual accounting is the process through which revenues and expenses are recognized in a period different from the one in which cash is exchanged. When accrual accounting is applied, revenue and expense items recognized in the current period may have cash consequences in a later period. Furthermore, revenue and expense items recognized in a past period may result in cash receipts or payments that materialize in the current period. Accordingly, the amount of cash receipts and payments realized during any particular accounting period may be larger or smaller than the amount of revenue and expense recognized during that period. The following section discusses the adjustments needed to convert accrual accounting to cash-basis accounting.

Revenue Transactions. With regard to **revenue transactions,** the application of accrual accounting means that some revenue is likely to be reported on the income statement before or after the cash is received. Accordingly, the amount of revenue recognized is normally different from the amount of cash that the company realizes during any particular accounting period. Some customers purchase goods or services in the current accounting period but pay for them in a later period. Other customers may pay cash in the current period for goods or services purchased in a prior period. As a result, the cash received may be more or less than the amount of revenue recognized.

To convert revenue recognized to the corresponding amount of cash collected, it is necessary to analyze both the amount of revenue appearing on the income statement and the change in the balance of the accounts receivable account. For example, assume that a company reported $500 of revenue on its income statement. Furthermore, assume that during the accounting period under consideration, the beginning and ending balances in the company's Accounts Receivable account were $100 and $160, respectively. Accordingly, the balance in the receivables account increased by $60 ($160 − $100). Taking this fact into consideration, we can conclude that $60 of the $500 in sales was not collected in cash. Therefore, the amount of cash collected must have been $440 ($500 − $60).

The conclusion that $440 of cash was collected from the revenue transactions was derived through logic. This conclusion can be confirmed through a process commonly called the **T-account method.** The T-account method begins with the opening of the Accounts Receivable T-account with the appropriate beginning and ending balances displayed. In this case, the beginning balance is $100, and the ending balance is $160. Next a $500 debit is added to the account to record the recognition of the revenue. The resultant T-account appears as follows.

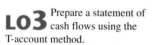

LO3 Prepare a statement of cash flows using the T-account method.

	Accounts Receivable	
Beginning Balance	100	
Debit to Record Sales	500	?
Ending Balance	160	

Mathematically adding $500 to a beginning balance of $100 does not result in an ending balance of $160. A $440 credit to the receivables account would be required to arrive at the $160 ending balance. Since cash collections result in credits to the Accounts Receivable account, it can be assumed that the Cash account was debited when the receivables account was credited. Accordingly, the analysis of the T-account also leads to the conclusion that $440 of cash was collected as a result of activities associated with the generation of revenue.

Expense Transactions. Accrual accounting results in the recognition of **expense transactions** before the payment of cash occurs, which means that a liability is normally recorded at the time the expense is recognized. The liability is later reduced as cash payments are made. Accordingly, the amount of accrued expense displayed on the income statement must be analyzed in conjunction with any change in the balance of the related liability account in order to determine the amount of cash outflow associated with the expense recognition. For example, assume that a company reports $200 of utilities expense on its income statement. Furthermore,

First, it should be remembered that GAAP requires that earnings and losses be computed on an accrual basis. A company can have negative earnings and still have positive cash flows from operating activities. This was not the case at Priceline.com, however. From 1998 through 2000, the company's cash flows from operating activities totaled a negative $122.9 million. Although this is much less than the $1.4 billion cumulative losses the company incurred during the same period, it still does not pay the bills.

Priceline.com, like many new companies, was able to stay in business because of the cash it raised through financing activities. These cash flows were a positive $325.9 million for 1998 through 2000. The company also had some significant noncash transactions. Exhibit 12–3 presents Priceline.com's statement of cash flows from the first three years of its life.

Exhibit 12–3

PRICELINE.COM INCORPORATED
Statements of Cash Flows
(dollars in thousands)

	Year Ended December 31		
	2000	1999	1998
Operating Activities			
Net loss	$(315,145)	$(1,055,090)	$(112,243)
Adjustments to reconcile net loss to net cash used in operating activities			
Depreciation and amortization	17,385	5,348	1,860
Provision for uncollectible accounts	7,354	3,127	581
Warrant costs	8,595	1,189,111	67,866
Webhouse warrant	189,000	(189,000)	—
Net loss on disposal of fixed assets	12,398	—	—
Net loss on sale of equity investments	2,558	—	—
Asset impairment	4,886	—	—
Compensation expense arising from deferred stock awards	1,711	—	—
Changes in assets and liabilities			
Accounts receivable	7,401	(29,617)	(4,757)
Prepaid expenses and other current assets	1,194	(12,043)	(1,922)
Related party receivables	(3,484)	—	—
Accounts payable and accrued expenses	45,155	28,470	8,300
Other	1,276	(3,331)	112
Net cash used in operating activities	(19,716)	(63,025)	(40,203)
Investing Activities			
Additions to property and equipment	(37,320)	(27,416)	(6,607)
Purchase of convertible notes and warrants of licencees	(25,676)	(2,000)	
Proceeds from sales/maturities of investments	31,101	—	—
Funding of restricted cash and bank certificate of deposits	(4,779)	(8,789)	(680)
Investment in marketable securities	(5,000)	(38,771)	
Net cash used in investing activities	(41,674)	(76,976)	(7,287)
Financing Activities			
Related party payable	—	—	(1,072)
Issuance of long-term debt	—	—	1,000
Payment of long-term debt	—	(1,000)	
Principal payments under capital lease obligations	—	(25)	(22)
Issuance of common stock and subscription units	14,031	211,816	26,495
Payment received on stockholder note	—	—	250
Issuance of Series A convertible preferred stock	—	—	20,000
Issuance of Series B convertible preferred stock	—	—	54,415
Net cash provided by financing activities	14,031	210,791	101,066
Net increase (decrease) in cash and cash equivalents	(47,359)	70,790	53,576
Cash and cash equivalents, beginning of period	124,383	53,593	17
Cash and cash equivalents, end of period	$ 77,024	$ 124,383	$ 53,593
Supplemental Cash Flow Information			
Cash paid during the period for interest	$ 4	$ 37	$ 61

assume that the beginning and ending balances in the Utilities Payable account are $70 and $40, respectively. This situation implies that the company not only made payments to cover the use of the utilities in the current period but also paid an additional $30 ($70 − $40) to reduce the obligations of prior periods. Accordingly, the amount of cash outflow associated with utility use is $230 ($200 + $30).

The T-account method can also be used to verify the $230 cash payment. A T-account for Utilities Payable is opened with beginning and ending balances placed into the account. Furthermore, a credit amounting to $200 is made to the account to reflect the recognition of the current period's utility expense. The resultant T-account appears as follows:

Utilities Payable

?	70	Beginning Balance
	200	Credit to Record Expense
	40	Ending Balance

Mathematical logic dictates that a $230 debit is required to arrive at the $40 ending balance ($70 + $200 − $230 = $40). Since debits to payable accounts are normally offset by credits to the Cash account, the T-account analysis indicates that cash outflows associated with utility expenses amounted to $230.

Check Yourself 12–1

Hammer, Inc., had a beginning balance of $22,400 in its Accounts Receivable account. During the accounting period, Hammer earned $234,700 of revenue on account. The ending balance in the Accounts Receivable account was $18,200. Based on this information alone, determine the amount of cash received from revenue transactions. In what section of the statement of cash flows would this cash flow appear?

Answer

Beginning accounts receivable balance	$ 22,400
Plus: Revenue earned on account during the period	234,700
Receivables available for collection	257,100
Less: Ending accounts receivable balance	(18,200)
Cash collected from receivables (revenue)	$238,900

A $238,900 credit to accounts receivable is required to balance the account. This credit would be offset by a corresponding debit to cash. Cash received from revenue transactions appears in the operating activities section of the statement of cash flows.

Converting Deferrals to Cash

Deferral transactions are events in which cash receipts or payments occur before the associated revenue or expense is recognized. Since revenue and expense recognition occurs in one accounting period and the associated cash receipts and payments occur in a different accounting period, differences arise between income reported in the financial statements and the cash-basis income. The following section discusses the procedures necessary to convert deferrals to their cash-basis equivalents.

Revenue Transactions. When cash is collected before the completion of the earnings process, a company incurs an obligation (liability) to provide goods or services at some future date. The revenue associated with the cash receipt is recognized in a later period when the work is accomplished. As a result, *the amount of revenue reported on the income statement and the amount of cash receipts normally differ.* The conversion of deferrals to cash requires an analysis of the amount of revenue reported and the change in the balance of the liability account, *Unearned Revenue.* For example, assume that the amount of revenue recognized was

$400 and that the Unearned Revenue account increased from a beginning balance of $80 to an ending balance of $110. The increase in the liability account implies that the company received cash in excess of the amount of the revenue recognized. Not only did the company earn the $400 of revenue reported on the income statement but also it received $30 ($110 − $80) for which it became obligated to provide goods and services in a future period. Accordingly, cash receipts associated with earnings activities amounted to $430 ($400 + $30).

An analysis of the T-account for unearned revenue confirms the receipt of $430 cash. The Unearned Revenue account is opened with the appropriate beginning and ending balances. A debit is made to the account to record the recognition of $400 of revenue. The resultant account appears as follows:

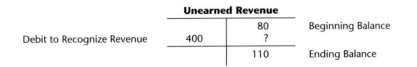

Clearly, $430 must have been added to the beginning balance of $80 so that when the $400 debit entry was subtracted, the resulting ending balance was $110. Since credit entries to the Unearned Revenue account are normally offset by corresponding debits to the Cash account, the analysis suggests that $430 of cash receipts was associated with revenue activities.

Expense Transactions. On many occasions, companies pay cash for goods or services that are not used immediately. The cost of the goods or services is normally capitalized in an asset account at the time the cash payment is made. The assets are then expensed in later periods when the goods or services are used in the process of earning revenue. Consequently, some items paid for in prior periods are expensed in the current period, while other items that are paid for in the current period are not expensed until later periods. *Accordingly, the amount of cash outflows normally differs from the amount of expense recognized for any given accounting period.*

To convert recognized expenses to cash flows, it is necessary to analyze the amount of change in the balance of certain asset accounts as well as the amount of corresponding expense that is recognized on the income statement. For example, assume that the beginning and ending balances in the Prepaid Rent account are $60 and $80, respectively, and that the amount of reported rent expense is $800. This situation suggests that the company not only paid enough cash to cover the $800 of recognized expense but also paid an additional $20 ($80 − $60). Therefore, the cash outflow associated with the rent payments amounted to $820 ($800 + $20).

The cash outflow of $820 for rent payments can be confirmed through T-account analysis. The beginning and ending balances are placed in a T-account for prepaid rent. The account is then credited to reflect the rent expense recognition of $800. The resultant T-account appears as follows:

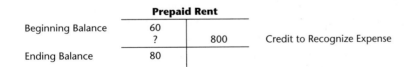

To have an ending balance of $80, there must have been an $820 debit to the account ($60 + $820 − $800 = $80). Since a debit to the Prepaid Rent account is normally offset by a credit to Cash, the analysis confirms that the cash outflow associated with rent payments is $820.

Investing Activities

Determining cash flow from investing activities may also require an analysis of changes in the beginning and ending account balances along with certain income statement data. For example, assume that the Land account had a beginning and ending balance of $900 and $300, respectively. Furthermore, assume that the income statement contained the recognition of a $200 gain on the sale of land. The $600 ($900 − $300) decline in the book value of the land suggests that the land was sold. The gain from the income statement implies that the land was sold for $200 more than its book value. Accordingly, the analysis suggests that the land was sold for $800 ($600 + $200) cash. Note that the amount of cash flow is different from the amount of gain appearing on the income statement. Indeed, the full $800 cash inflow appears in the investing activities section of the statement of cash flows. The operating activities section of the statement is not affected by the gain from the land sale.

The amount of cash inflow ($800) from investing activities can also be verified through the T-account method. An analysis of the beginning and ending balances in the Land account suggests that land costing $600 ($900 beginning balance − $300 ending balance) was sold. This amount, coupled with the $200 gain shown in the Retained Earnings account, suggests that $800 cash was collected from the sale. The appropriate T-accounts are as follows:

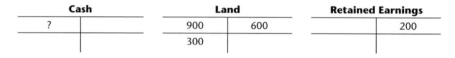

Cash		Land		Retained Earnings
?		900	600	200
		300		

It is possible that the company could have received some resource other than cash when the land was sold. However, other alternative explanations would be discovered when the other balance sheet accounts were analyzed.

Financing Activities

Cash flow from financing activities can frequently be determined by simply analyzing the change in the balances of liability and stockholders' equity accounts. For example, an increase in bond liabilities from $500 to $800 implies that the company issued new bonds that resulted in the receipt of $300 cash. This conclusion can be supported by an analysis using the T-account method. A T-account is opened with the beginning and ending balances shown here.

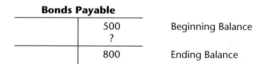

Bonds Payable		
	500	Beginning Balance
	?	
	800	Ending Balance

A $300 credit must be added to the $500 opening balance in order to arrive at the $800 ending balance. Since cash is normally increased when bond liabilities increase, the analysis supports the conclusion that $300 of cash inflow was derived from the incurrence of debt.

Other explanations are also possible. Perhaps some of the company's stockholders decided to exchange their equity securities for debt securities. Or the company may have been willing to incur the obligation in exchange for some asset (property, plant, or equipment) other than cash. Such transactions would be reported in the schedule of noncash investing and financing transactions.

■ Comprehensive Example Using the T-Account Approach

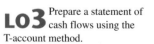

LO3 Prepare a statement of cash flows using the T-account method.

The preceding discussion emphasized the need to analyze financial statements and supporting data in the process of preparing a statement of cash flows. The beginning and ending balances in the accounts being analyzed can be drawn from two successive balance sheets. The revenues, expenses, gains, and losses can be found on the income statement. Also, notes to the financial statements may contain information needed to identify noncash transactions. Exhibits 12–4 and 12–5 are the balance sheets, income statement, and additional information needed to prepare a statement of cash flows.

Exhibit 12–4

THE NEW SOUTH CORPORATION
Comparative Balance Sheets
As of December 31

	2004	2005
Current Assets		
Cash	$ 400	$ 900
Accounts Receivable	1,200	1,000
Interest Receivable	300	400
Inventory	8,200	8,900
Prepaid Insurance	1,400	1,100
Total Current Assets	11,500	12,300
Long-Term Assets		
Marketable Securities	3,500	5,100
Equipment	4,600	5,400
Less: Accumulated Depreciation	(1,200)	(900)
Land	6,000	8,500
Total Long-Term Assets	12,900	18,100
Total Assets	$24,400	$30,400
Current Liabilities		
Accounts Payable—Inventory Purchases	$ 1,100	$ 800
Salaries Payable	900	1,000
Other Operating Expenses Payable	1,300	1,500
Interest Payable	500	300
Unearned Rent Revenue	1,600	600
Total Current Liabilities	5,400	4,200
Long-Term Liabilities		
Mortgage Payable	0	2,500
Bonds Payable	4,000	1,000
Total Long-Term Liabilities	4,000	3,500
Stockholders' Equity		
Common Stock	8,000	10,000
Retained Earnings	7,000	12,700
Total Stockholders' Equity	15,000	22,700
Total Liabilities and Stockholders' Equity	$24,400	$30,400

Exhibit 12–5

THE NEW SOUTH CORPORATION
Income Statement
For the Year Ended December 31, 2005

Sales		$20,600
Cost of Goods Sold		(10,500)
Gross Margin		10,100
Operating Expenses		
Depreciation Expense	$ 800	
Salaries Expense	2,700	
Insurance Expense	600	
Other Operating Expenses	1,400	
Total Operating Expenses		(5,500)
Operating Income		4,600
Other Operating Income—Rent Revenue		2,400
Total Operating Income		7,000
Nonoperating Revenue and Expenses		
Interest Revenue	700	
Interest Expense	(400)	
Loss on Sale of Equipment	(100)	
Total Nonoperating Items		200
Net Income		$ 7,200

Additional information
1. The corporation sold equipment for $300 cash. This equipment had an original cost of $1,500 and accumulated depreciation of $1,100 at the time of the sale.
2. The corporation issued a $2,500 mortgage note in exchange for land.
3. There was a $1,500 cash dividend paid during the accounting period.

Preparation of Statement of Cash Flows

Begin the process of analyzing the financial statements by opening a T-account for each item on the balance sheets. Enter the beginning and ending balances for each item into the T-accounts. Use the 2004 balance sheet (see Exhibit 12–4) to determine the beginning balance of each account and the 2005 balance sheet to get the ending balances. The Cash account should be large enough to be divided into three components representing cash flows from operating, investing, and financing activities. Exhibit 12–6 contains a full set of T-accounts with all analytical transactions included. Each transaction is labeled with a lower-case letter. Since some analysis requires more than one entry, each letter is also followed by a number, which permits detailed labeling for each transaction. The following section explains each transaction in full detail.

Exhibit 12–6 *Balance Sheet T-Accounts*

Assets		=	Liabilities	+	Stockholders' Equity

Cash

Bal.	400			
	Operating Activities			
(a2)	20,800	11,500	(b3)	
(g2)	1,400	2,600	(d2)	
(h2)	600	300	(e2)	
		1,200	(f2)	
		600	(i2)	
	Investing Activities			
(k1)	300	1,600	(j1)	
		2,300	(l1)	
	Financing Activities			
(o1)	2,000	3,000	(n1)	
		1,500	(p1)	
Bal.	900			

Accounts Receivable

Bal.	1,200	20,800	(a2)
(a1)	20,600		
Bal.	1,000		

Interest Receivable

Bal.	300	600	(h2)
(h1)	700		
Bal.	400		

Inventory

Bal.	8,200	10,500	(b1)
(b2)	11,200		
Bal.	8,900		

Prepaid Insurance

Bal.	1,400	600	(e1)
(e2)	300		
Bal.	1,100		

Marketable Securities

Bal.	3,500	
(j1)	1,600	
Bal.	5,100	

Equipment

Bal.	4,600	1,500	(k1)
(l1)	2,300		
Bal.	5,400		

Accumulated Depreciation

(k1)	1,100	1,200	Bal.
		800	(c1)
		900	Bal.

Land

Bal.	6,000	
(m1)	2,500	
Bal.	8,500	

Accounts Payable—Inventory

(b3)	11,500	1,100	Bal.
		11,200	(b2)
		800	Bal.

Salaries Payable

(d2)	2,600	900	Bal.
		2,700	(d1)
		1,000	Bal.

Operating Exp. Payable

(f2)	1,200	1,300	Bal.
		1,400	(f1)
		1,500	Bal.

Interest Payable

(i2)	600	500	Bal.
		400	(i1)
		300	Bal.

Unearned Rent Revenue

(g1)	2,400	1,600	Bal.
		1,400	(g2)
		600	Bal.

Mortgage Payable

		0	Bal.
		2,500	(m1)
		2,500	Bal.

Bonds Payable

(n1)	3,000	4,000	Bal.
		1,000	Bal.

Common Stock

		8,000	Bal.
		2,000	(o1)
		10,000	Bal.

Retained Earnings

(b1)	10,500	7,000	Bal.
(c1)	800	20,600	(a1)
(d1)	2,700	2,400	(g1)
(e1)	600	700	(h1)
(f1)	1,400		
(i1)	400		
(k1)	100		
(p1)	1,500		
		12,700	Bal.

Cash Flows from Operating Activities

Cash flows from operating activities is essentially a cash-basis income statement. Since accrual accounting is normally used in the preparation of formal financial statements, it is necessary to convert the income statement data to cash equivalents. Accordingly, each item on the income statement should be analyzed separately to assess its cash flow consequences.

Cash Receipts from Sales

The first item appearing on the income statement is $20,600 of sales revenue. Assuming that all sales transactions were on account, the entry to record sales would have required a debit to Accounts Receivable and a credit to Sales Revenue. Because the T-account analysis includes only balance sheet accounts and sales revenue acts to increase Retained Earnings, the entry to record sales in the T-accounts is shown as a debit to Accounts Receivable and a credit to Retained Earnings. This entry is labeled (a1) in Exhibit 12–6. After the sales revenue transaction is recorded, the cash inflow from sales can be determined by analyzing the Accounts Receivable T-account. Notice that the beginning balance of $1,200 plus the debit to receivables of $20,600 resulting from sales transactions suggests that $21,800 of receivables was available for collection. Since the ending balance in the receivables account amounts to $1,000, there must have been $20,800 ($21,800 − $1,000) of receivables collected. This cash inflow is recognized with a debit to the Cash account under the operating activities section and a credit to the Accounts Receivable account. This entry is labeled (a2) in Exhibit 12–6.

The preceding discussion introduces several practices that apply to the analysis of all cash flows from operating activities. First, note that all revenue, expense, gain, and loss transactions ultimately affect the Retained Earnings account. Accordingly, to reconcile the beginning and ending balances in Retained Earnings, all income statement items are posted directly to the Retained Earnings account. Second, the determination of when to stop the analysis depends on the reconciliation between the beginning and ending account balances. In this case, the analysis of Accounts Receivable stopped with the $20,800 credit because the beginning balance plus the debit and minus the credit equaled the ending balance. Accordingly, the analysis of the account is completed because the beginning and ending balances have been reconciled (the change in the account has been fully explained). The analysis for the entire statement is completed when the beginning and ending balances in all the balance sheet accounts are reconciled. Since many of the balance sheet accounts remain to be reconciled, the cash flow analysis in this case will continue.

Cash Payments for Inventory Purchases

It is helpful to make two simplifying assumptions in analyzing cash payments for inventory purchases. First, assume that the company employs the perpetual inventory method; second, assume that all purchases are made on account. Based on these assumptions, the entry to record the cost of goods sold ($10,500, as shown on the income statement in Exhibit 12–5) would have required a credit to the Inventory account and a debit to Retained Earnings (cost of goods sold). This entry is labeled (b1) in the exhibit. This entry only partly explains the change in the beginning and ending balances of the Inventory account. A closer analysis of this account suggests that some inventory must have been purchased. Given that the beginning balance in the Inventory account was $8,200 and that $10,500 of inventory cost was transferred to cost of goods sold, it is logical to assume that $11,200 of inventory was purchased to arrive at the ending Inventory balance of $8,900. The entry to record the inventory purchase, labeled (b2), includes a debit to Inventory and a credit to Accounts Payable. This entry completes the explanation of the change in the beginning and ending balances of inventory but only partly explains the change in the beginning and ending balances in the Accounts Payable account. Given a beginning balance in Accounts Payable of $1,100 and additional purchases on account amounting to $11,200, there must have been $12,300 of accounts payable available for payment. Since the ending balance in the Accounts Payable account amounted to

$800, there must have been cash payments of $11,500 ($12,300 − $800). The entry to record this cash outflow, labeled (b3), includes a credit to the operating activities section of the Cash account and a debit to the Accounts Payable account.

Noncash Effects of Depreciation

The next item on the income statement is depreciation expense. Depreciation expense is a noncash charge against revenues. In other words, no cash changes hands at the time the depreciation expense is recorded. Indeed, the entry to record depreciation expense (c1) includes a debit to Retained Earnings (depreciation expense) and a credit to Accumulated Depreciation. This entry only partly explains the change in accumulated depreciation, indicating that further analysis is required. However, cash flow consequences associated with long-term assets and their respective contra accounts affect the investing activities section of the statement of cash flows. Accordingly, further analysis is delayed until investing activities are considered. At this stage, the analysis of cash flows from operating activities continues.

Cash Payments for Salaries

The entry to record $2,700 of salary expense includes a debit to Retained Earnings (salary expense) and a credit to Salaries Payable. This entry, labeled (d1), partly explains the change in beginning and ending balances in the Salaries Payable account. The beginning balance of $900 plus the $2,700 increase for the current period expense suggests that there were $3,600 of salaries available for payment during the period. Since the ending balance amounted to $1,000, there must have been a cash payment for salaries amounting to $2,600 ($3,600 − $1,000). The entry to record the cash payment for salaries includes a debit to the Salaries Payable account and a credit to the operating activities section of the Cash account. This entry is labeled (d2) in the exhibit.

Cash Payments for Insurance

The entry to record $600 of insurance expense requires a debit to Retained Earnings (insurance expense) and a credit to Prepaid Insurance. This entry, labeled (e1), partly explains the change in the beginning and ending balances in the Prepaid Insurance account. The beginning balance of $1,400 less the reduction of $600 associated with the recognition of insurance expense suggests an ending balance of $800. However, the balance sheet shows an actual ending balance of $1,100. Accordingly, a purchase of $300 ($1,100 − $800) of prepaid insurance must have been made during the accounting period. The cash outflow for the purchase of insurance is labeled (e2) and includes a debit to the Prepaid Insurance account and a credit to the operating activities section of the statement of cash flows.

Cash Payments for Other Operating Expenses

The $1,400 of other operating expenses appearing on the income statement is recorded in the T-accounts with a debit to Retained Earnings and a credit to the Operating Expenses Payable account. This entry, labeled (f1), partly explains the change in the beginning and ending balances in the Operating Expenses Payable account. Given a beginning balance of $1,300 and the $1,400 addition for current expenses, the total amount available for payment was $2,700 ($1,300 + $1,400). Since the ending balance amounted to $1,500, the cash payments must have amounted to $1,200 ($2,700 − $1,500). The entry to record the cash payment is labeled (f2) and includes a debit to the Operating Expenses Payable account and a credit to the operating activities section of the Cash account.

Cash Receipts for Rent

The entry to record $2,400 of rent revenue includes a debit to the Unearned Rent Revenue account and a credit to the Retained Earnings account. This entry, labeled (g1), partly explains the change in the beginning and ending balances in the Unearned Rent Revenue account. The beginning balance of $1,600 less the $2,400 reduction caused by the recognition of the rent revenue suggests that there must have been a credit (increase) in the account in order to arrive at an ending balance of $600. Since increases in the unearned account are offset by increases in cash, collections must have been equal to $1,400 ($1,600 + $1,400 − $2,400 = $600). The required entry for the cash receipt includes a credit to the Unearned Rent Revenue account and a debit to the operating activities section of the Cash account. This entry is labeled (g2) in Exhibit 12–6.

Cash Receipts from Interest

The entry to record $700 of interest revenue includes a debit to the Interest Receivable account and a credit to Retained Earnings (interest revenue). This entry, labeled (h1), partially explains the change in the beginning and ending balances in the Interest Receivable account. Given the beginning balance of $300 plus the $700 debit created through the recognition of interest revenue, the receivables account indicates that there was $1,000 ($300 + $700) of interest receivables available for collection. The ending balance of $400 implies that $600 ($1,000 − $400) of cash was collected. The entry to record this cash inflow is labeled (h2) and includes a credit to Interest Receivable and a debit to the operating activities section of the Cash account.

Cash Payments for Interest

The entry to record $400 of interest expense is labeled (i1) and includes a debit to Retained Earnings (interest expense) and a credit to Interest Payable. The entry partly explains the change in the beginning and ending balances in the Interest Payable account. The beginning balance of $500 plus the $400 that resulted from the recognition of interest expense suggests that there was $900 of interest obligations available for payment. The ending balance of $300 implies that $600 ($900 − $300) was paid in cash. The entry to recognize the cash outflow for this interest payment is labeled (i2) and includes a debit to the Interest Payable account and a credit to the operating activities section of the Cash account.

Noncash Effects of Loss

The loss on the sale of equipment does not affect cash flows from operating activities. The full proceeds from the sale constitute the amount of cash flow. The amount of any loss or gain is irrelevant. Indeed, the sale involves the disposal of an investment and therefore is shown under the investing activities section. Cash flow from operating activities is not affected by gains or losses on the disposal of long-term assets.

Completion of Analysis of Operating Activities

Since no other items appear on the income statement, the conversion process from accrual to cash is completed. The operating activities section of the Cash account contains all the cash receipts and payments necessary to determine the net cash flow from operations. This information is placed into the formal statement of cash flows (presented later in the chapter). With the completion of the assessment of cash flow from operating activities, the analysis proceeds to the cash flow effects associated with investing activities.

Q Magazine, Inc., reported $234,800 of revenue for the month. At the beginning of the month, its Unearned Revenue account had a balance of $78,000. At the end of the month, the account had a balance of $67,000. Based on this information alone, determine the amount of cash received from revenue.

Answer The Unearned Revenue account decreased by $11,000 ($78,000 − $67,000). This decrease in unearned revenue would have coincided with an increase in revenue that did not involve receiving cash. As a result, $11,000 of the revenue earned had no effect on cash flow during this month. To determine the cash received from revenue, subtract the noncash increase from reported revenue. Cash received from revenue is $223,800 ($234,800 − $11,000).

Cash Flows from Investing Activities

Investing activities generally involve the acquisition (purchase) or disposal (sale) of long-term assets. Accordingly, the analysis of cash flows from investing activities centers on changes in the beginning and ending balances in long-term assets.

Cash Payments to Purchase Marketable Securities

The first long-term asset shown on the balance sheets is Marketable Securities. An analysis of this asset account indicates that the balance in the account increased from $3,500 at the beginning of the period to $5,100 at the end of the period. The most reasonable explanation for this increase is that the corporation purchased additional securities in the amount of $1,600 ($5,100 − $3,500). In the absence of information to the contrary, it is assumed that the purchase was made with cash. The entry to record the purchase includes a debit to the Marketable Securities account and a credit to the investing activities section of the Cash account. This entry is coded (j1) in Exhibit 12–6.

Cash Receipts from Sale of Equipment

The next asset on the balance sheets is Equipment. Our earlier review of the income statement disclosed a loss on the sale of equipment, which suggests that some equipment was sold during the period. This sale is expected to result in a cash inflow in the amount of the sales price. The additional information at the bottom of the income statement discloses that equipment costing $1,500 with accumulated depreciation of $1,100 was sold for $300. The difference between the $400 ($1,500 − $1,100) book value and the $300 sales price explains the $100 loss on the income statement. The cash receipt from the sale is $300. The original cost, accumulated depreciation, and loss do not affect cash flow. The entry to recognize the cash receipt includes a debit to the investing section of the Cash account, a debit to Retained Earnings (loss), a debit to the Accumulated Depreciation account, and a credit to the Equipment account. The entry is labeled (k1) in the exhibit.

Cash Payments to Purchase Equipment

The sale of equipment partially explains the change in the beginning and ending balances in the Equipment account. However, further analysis suggests that some equipment must have been purchased. A beginning balance of $4,600 less $1,500 for the equipment that was sold suggests that $2,300 of equipment must have been purchased in order to arrive at the ending balance of $5,400 ($4,600 − $1,500 + $2,300 = $5,400). The cash payment necessary to purchase the equipment is labeled (l1) and includes a debit to the Equipment account and a credit to the investing activities section of the Cash account.

Noncash Transaction for Land Acquisition

The Land account increased from a beginning balance of $6,000 to an ending balance of $8,500, thereby suggesting that $2,500 ($8,500 − $6,000) of land was acquired during the accounting

How did Florida Power and Lighting (FPL) acquire $501 million of property and equipment without spending any cash? Oddly enough, the answer can be found in the company's statement of cash flows. The supplemental schedule of noncash investing and financing activities section of FPL's cash statement shows that it acquired $81 million of equipment by accepting lease obligations and that it acquired $420 million of property by assuming debt. In other words, FPL acquired $501 million ($81 million + $420 million) in property and equipment by agreeing to pay for it later.

period. The additional information at the bottom of the income statement discloses the fact that the corporation acquired this land through the issuance of a mortgage. Accordingly, no cash consequences are associated with the transaction. The transaction recording this event is labeled (m1) in Exhibit 12–6. Since the transaction does not affect cash, it is shown in the separate schedule for noncash investing and financing transactions on the statement of cash flows.

Since all long-term asset accounts have been reconciled, the analysis of cash flows from investing activities is completed. The process continues with an assessment of cash flows associated with financing activities.

Cash Flows from Financing Activities

The long-term liability and stockholders' equity sections of the balance sheets are analyzed to assess the cash flows from financing activities. Note that the first long-term liability account on the balance sheet is Mortgage Payable. The change in this account was explained in the analysis of the land acquisition, discussed earlier in this chapter. As explained, this financing activity is shown along with the investing activity in the separate schedule for noncash transactions. Accordingly, the analysis of cash flows continues with the change in the Bond Liability account.

Cash Payment for Bonds

The balance in the Bonds Payable account decreased from $4,000 to $1,000. In the absence of information to the contrary, it is logical to assume that $3,000 ($4,000 − $1,000) was paid to reduce bond liabilities. The entry to record the cash outflow includes a debit to the Bonds Payable account and a credit to the financing activities section of the Cash account. This entry is coded (n1) in the exhibit.

Cash Receipt from Stock Issue

The balance in the Common Stock account increased from $8,000 to $10,000. In the absence of information to the contrary, it is logical to assume that $2,000 ($10,000 − $8,000) of cash was collected as proceeds from the issuance of common stock. The entry to record this cash inflow is labeled (o1) and includes a credit to Common Stock and a debit to the financing activities section of the Cash account.

Cash Payments for Dividends

Finally, additional information at the bottom of the income statement discloses a cash dividend of $1,500. The transaction to record this cash outflow includes a debit to the Retained Earnings account and a credit to the financing activities section of the Cash account. It is labeled (p1) in Exhibit 12–6.

Presenting Information in the Statement of Cash Flows

Since all income statement items have been analyzed, changes in balance sheet accounts have been explained, and all additional information has been considered, the analytical process is completed. The data in the T-account for cash must now be organized in appropriate financial statement format. Recall that cash flow from operations is presented first, cash flow from investing activities second, and cash flow from financing activities third. Noncash investing and financing activities are shown in a separate schedule or in the footnotes. Exhibit 12–7 is a statement of cash flows and a separate schedule for noncash activities.

Statement of Cash Flows Presented Under the Indirect Method

LO4 Explain how cash flow from operating activities reported under the indirect method differs from that reported under the direct method.

Up to now, the statement of cash flows has been presented in accordance with the **direct method.** The direct method is intuitively logical and is the method recommended by the Financial Accounting Standards Board. Even so, most companies use an alternative known as

Exhibit 12–7			
THE NEW SOUTH CORPORATION Statement of Cash Flows For the Year Ended December 31, 2005			
Cash Flows from Operating Activities			
Cash Receipts from			
Sales	$20,800		
Rent	1,400		
Interest	600		
Total Cash Inflows		$22,800	
Cash Payments for			
Inventory Purchases	11,500		
Salaries	2,600		
Insurance	300		
Other Operating Expenses	1,200		
Interest	600		
Total Cash Outflows		(16,200)	
Net Cash Flow from Operating Activities			$ 6,600
Cash Flows from Investing Activities			
Inflow from Sale of Equipment		300	
Outflow to Purchase Marketable Securities		(1,600)	
Outflow to Purchase Equipment		(2,300)	
Net Cash Flow from Investing Activities			(3,600)
Cash Flows from Financing Activities			
Inflow from Stock Issue		2,000	
Outflow to Repay Debt		(3,000)	
Outflow for Dividends		(1,500)	
Net Cash Flow from Financing Activities			(2,500)
Net Increase in Cash			500
Plus: Beginning Cash Balance			400
Ending Cash Balance			$ 900
Schedule of Noncash Investing and Financing Activities			
Issue of Mortgage for Land			$ 2,500

the **indirect method.** The difference between the two methods is in the presentation of the operating activities section. The indirect method uses net income as reported on the income statement as the starting point. The method proceeds by showing the adjustments necessary to convert the accrual-based net income figure to a cash-basis equivalent. The conversion process can be accomplished by the application of three basic rules, which are discussed next.

An increase in the balance of the Accounts Receivable account would suggest that not all sales were collected in cash. Accordingly, the amount of revenue shown on the income statement would overstate the amount of cash collections. Therefore, it is necessary to subtract the amount of the increase in the receivables account from the amount of net income to convert the income figure to a cash-equivalent basis. Similarly, a decrease in the receivables balance has to be added to the net income figure. Extending this logic to all current asset accounts results in the first general rule of the conversion process. **Rule 1: Increases in current assets are deducted from net income, and decreases in current assets are added to net income.**

The opposite logic applies to current liabilities. For example, an increase in accounts payable suggests that not all expenses were paid in cash. Accordingly, it is necessary to add the increase in the payables account to the amount of net income to convert the income figure to a cash-equivalent basis. Conversely, decreases in payable accounts are deducted from net income. Extending the logic to all the current liability accounts produces the second general rule of the conversion process. **Rule 2: Increases in current liabilities are added to net income, and decreases in current liabilities are deducted from net income.**

The following account balances were drawn from the accounting records of Loeb, Inc.

Account Title	Beginning Balance	Ending Balance
Prepaid Rent	$4,200	$3,000
Interest Payable	$2,900	$2,650

Check Yourself 12–3

Loeb reported $7,400 of net income during the accounting period. Based on this information alone, determine the amount of cash flow from operating activities.

Answer Based on Rule 1, the $1,200 decrease ($3,000 − $4,200) in Prepaid Rent (current asset) must be added to net income to determine the amount of cash flow from operating activities. Rule 2 requires that the $250 decrease ($2,650 − $2,900) in Interest Payable (current liability) must be deducted from net income. Accordingly, the cash flow from operating activities is $8,350 ($7,400 + $1,200 − $250). Note that paying interest is defined as an operating activity and should not be confused with dividend payments, which are classified as financing activities.

Finally, note that some expense and revenue transactions do not have cash consequences. For example, although depreciation is reported as an expense, it does not require the payment of cash. Similarly, losses and gains reported on the income statement do not have consequences that are reported in the operating activities section of the statement of cash flows. **Rule 3: All noncash expenses and losses are added to net income, and all noncash revenue and gains are subtracted from net income.**

Check Yourself 12–4

Arley Company's income statement reported net income (in millions) of $326 for the year. The income statement included depreciation expense of $45 and a net loss on the sale of disposable assets of $22. Based on this information alone, determine the net cash flow from operating activities.

Answer Based on Rule 3, both the depreciation expense and the loss would have to be added to net income to determine cash flow from operating activities. Net cash flow from operating activities would be $393 ($326 + $45 + $22).

Exhibit 12–8

THE NEW SOUTH CORPORATION
Statement of Cash Flows (Indirect Method)
For the Year Ended December 31, 2005

Cash Flows from Operating Activities

Net Income		$7,200
Plus: Decreases in Current Assets and Increases in Current Liabilities		
Decrease in Accounts Receivable	200	
Decrease in Prepaid Insurance	300	
Increase in Salaries Payable	100	
Increase in Other Operating Expenses Payable	200	
Less: Increases in Current Assets and Decreases in Current Liabilities		
Increase in Interest Receivable	(100)	
Increase in Inventory	(700)	
Decrease in Accounts Payable for Inventory Purchases	(300)	
Decrease in Interest Payable	(200)	
Decrease in Unearned Rent Revenue	(1,000)	
Plus: Noncash Charges		
Depreciation Expense	800	
Loss on Sale of Equipment	100	
Net Cash Flow from Operating Activities		$6,600
Cash Flows from Investing Activities		
Inflow from Sale of Equipment	300	
Outflow to Purchase Marketable Securities	(1,600)	
Outflow to Purchase Equipment	(2,300)	
Net Cash Flow from Investing Activities		(3,600)
Cash Flows from Financing Activities		
Inflow from Stock Issue	2,000	
Outflow to Repay Debt	(3,000)	
Outflow for Dividends	(1,500)	
Net Cash Flow from Financing Activities		(2,500)
Net Increase in Cash		500
Plus: Beginning Cash Balance		400
Ending Cash Balance		$ 900
Schedule of Noncash Investing and Financing Activities		
Issue of Mortgage for Land		$2,500

These three general rules apply only to items affecting operating activities. For example, Rule 2 does not apply to an increase or decrease in the current liability account for dividends because dividend payments are considered to be financing activities rather than operating activities. Accordingly, some degree of judgment must be exercised in applying the three general rules of conversion.

Exhibit 12–8 shows the presentation of a statement of cash flows under the indirect method. The statement was constructed by applying the three general rules of conversion to the data for The New South Corporation shown in Exhibits 12–4 and 12–5. Notice that the only difference between the statement presented under the indirect method (Exhibit 12–8) and the statement shown under the direct method (Exhibit 12–7) is the cash flow from operating activities section. Cash flows from investing and financing activities and the schedule of non-cash items are not affected by the alternative reporting format.

■ Consequences of Growth on Cash Flow

LO5 Explain how the classifications used on the statement of cash flows could provide misleading information to decision makers.

Why do decision makers in business need a statement of cash flows? Why is the information provided on the income statement not sufficient? Although it is true that the income statement shows how well a business is doing on an accrual basis, it does not show what is happening with cash. Understanding the cash flows of a business is extremely important because cash is used to pay the bills. A company, especially one that is growing rapidly, can have substantial earnings but be short of cash because it must buy goods before they are sold, and it may not receive cash payment until months after revenue is recognized on an accrual basis. To illustrate, assume that you want to go into the business of selling computers. You borrow $2,000 and use the money to purchase two computers that cost $1,000 each. Furthermore, assume that you sell one of the computers on account for $1,500. At this point, if you had a payment due on your loan, you would be unable to pay the amount due. Even though you had a net income of $500 (revenue of $1,500 − cost of goods sold of $1,000), you would have no cash until you collected the $1,500 cash due from the account receivable.

Real-World Data

The statement of cash flows frequently provides a picture of business activity that would otherwise be lost in the complexities of the application of accrual accounting. For example, consider the effects of restructuring charges on operating income versus cash flow experienced by IBM Corporation. For 1991, 1992, and 1993 combined, IBM reported operating *losses* (before taxes) of more than $17.9 *billion*. During this same period, it reported "restructuring charges" of more than $24 billion. Therefore, without the restructuring charges, IBM would have reported operating *profits* of about $6 billion (before taxes). Are restructuring charges an indication of something bad or something good? Who knows? Different financial analysts have different opinions about this issue. There is something about IBM's performance during these years that can be more easily understood. The company produced over $21 billion in positive cash flow from operating activities. It had no trouble paying its bills.

Investors consider cash flow information so important that they are willing to pay for it, even when the FASB discourages its use. Consider the following situation. The FASB *prohibits* companies from disclosing *cash flow per share* in audited financial statements. However, one very prominent stock analysis service, *Value Line Investment Survey,* has a significant customer base that continues to purchase its stock charts, which are prepared on the basis of cash flow per share rather than earnings per share. These investors obviously value information regarding cash flows.

Exhibit 12–9 is a comparison of the income from operations and the cash flow from operating activities for six real-world companies from three different industries for the 1998, 1999, and 2000 fiscal years.

Exhibit 12–9 *Operating Income versus Cash Flow From Operations (Amounts in $000)*				
	Company	**2000**	**1999**	**1998**
Alaska Airlines	Operating income	$ (7,400)	$ 119,400	$ 116,500
	Cash flow from operations	197,700	294,500	272,400
Southwest Airlines	Operating income	625,224	474,378	433,431
	Cash flow from operations	1,298,286	1,001,710	886,135
Boeing	Operating income	2,128,000	2,309,000	1,120,000
	Cash flow from operations	5,942,000	6,224,000	2,415,000
Mattel	Operating income	170,177	108,387	328,253
	Cash flow from operations	555,090	430,463	586,201
Sprint	Operating income	(576,000)	(745,000)	(585,000)
	Cash flow from operations	4,315,000	1,952,000	4,199,000
Toll Brothers	Operating income	145,943	103,027	85,819
	Cash flow from operations	(16,863)	(120,870)	(40,708)

Several things can be observed from Exhibit 12–9. First, notice that in most cases, other than Toll Brothers, cash flow from operating activities is higher than income from operations. This condition is true for many real-world companies because depreciation, a noncash expense, is usually significant. The most dramatic example of this is for Sprint in 2000. Even though Sprint reported a *net loss* from operations of $576 million, it generated *positive cash flow from operations* of more than $4 *billion.* This difference between cash flow from operations and operating income helps explain how some companies can have significant losses over a few years and continue to stay in business and pay their bills.

Next, the exhibit shows that the numbers for cash flow from operations can be more stable than the amounts for operating income. Results for Alaska Airlines demonstrate this clearly. Although the company's earnings changed from positive in 1998 and 1999 to negative in 2000, its cash flows from operations were always positive. Therefore, some financial statement analysts might prefer cash flow from operations as a more useful number for trend analysis than accrual-based earnings.

Finally, what could explain why Toll Brothers has *less* cash flow from operations than operating income? Does this mean that the company has a problem? Not necessarily. Toll Brothers is simply experiencing the same kind of growth described earlier for your computer sales business. Its cash is being used to support growth in the level of inventory. Toll Brothers is one of the nation's largest new-home construction companies. Its growth rates, based on the sales value of new homes closed, for the 2000, 1999, and 1998 fiscal years were 23 percent, 19 percent, and 25 percent, respectively. It is not the new acquisitions of property, plant, and equipment that affect cash flow from operations, because these purchases are included in the investing activities section of the statement of cash flows. However, when Toll Brothers begins to build new homes, the company needs more inventory. Increases in inventory *do* affect cash flow from operations. Remember, increases in current assets decrease cash flow from operations. This fact alone might explain why the company has less cash flow from operations than operating income. Is this situation bad? Recall that in Chapter 8, the point was made that, *other things being equal*, it is better to have less inventory. At Toll Brothers, however, other things are not equal. The company has been growing rapidly.

The situation with Toll Brothers highlights what some accountants think is a weakness in the format of the statement of cash flows. Some think it misleading simply to classify all increases in long-term assets as *investing activities* and all changes in inventory as an adjustment to operating income to arrive at cash flow from operations. They argue that the increase in inventory at Toll Brothers that results from opening new stores should be classified as an investing activity, just as the cost of a new building is. Although it is true that inventory is classified as a current asset and buildings are classified as long-term assets, in reality there is a certain level of inventory that must be maintained permanently if a company is to remain in business. The GAAP format of the statement of cash flows penalizes cash flow from operations for increases in inventory that are really a permanent investment in assets.

Conversely, the same critics might argue that some purchases of long-term assets are not actually *investments* but merely replacements of old, existing property, plant, and equipment. In other words, the *investing activities* section of the statement of cash flows makes no distinction between expenditures that expand the business and those that simply replace old equipment (sometimes called *capital maintenance* expenditures).

Thus, the conclusion one must reach about using the statement of cash flows is the same as that for using the balance sheet or the income statement. Users cannot simply look at the numbers. They must analyze the numbers based on a knowledge of the particular business being examined.

Accounting alone cannot tell a businessperson how to make a decision. Making good business decisions requires an understanding of the business in question, the environmental and economic factors affecting the operation of that business, and the accounting concepts on which the financial statements of that business are based.

a look
back

Throughout this course, you have been asked to consider many different accounting events that occur in the business world. In many cases, you were asked to consider the effects that these events have on a company's balance sheet, income statement, and statement of cash flows. By now, you should be aware that each of the financial statements shows a different, but equally important, view of the financial situation of the company in question.

This chapter provided a more detailed examination of only one financial statement, the statement of cash flows. The chapter presented a more comprehensive review of how an accrual accounting system relates to a cash-based accounting system. It is important that you understand not only both systems but also how the two systems relate to each other. This is the reason that a formal statement of cash flows begins with a reconciliation of net income, an accrual measurement, to net cash flow from operating activities, a cash measurement. Finally, this chapter explained how the idiosyncrasies of classifying cash events as operating, investing, or financing activities requires analysis and understanding of the financial information to reach correct conclusions.

This chapter probably completes your first course in accounting. We sincerely hope that this text has provided you a meaningful learning experience that will serve you well as you progress through your academic training and your ultimate career. Good luck and best wishes!

a look
forward

SELF-STUDY REVIEW PROBLEM

The following financial statements pertain to Schlemmer Company.

BALANCE SHEETS
As of December 31

	2003	2004
Cash	$ 2,800	$48,400
Accounts Receivable	1,200	2,200
Inventory	6,000	5,600
Equipment	22,000	18,000
Accumulated Depreciation—Equip.	(17,400)	(13,650)
Land	10,400	17,200
Total Assets	$25,000	$77,750
Accounts Payable	$ 4,200	$ 5,200
Long-Term Debt	6,400	5,600
Common Stock	10,000	19,400
Retained Earnings	4,400	47,550
Total Liabilities and Equity	$25,000	$77,750

INCOME STATEMENT
For the Year Ended December 31, 2004

Sales Revenue	$67,300
Cost of Goods Sold	(24,100)
Gross Margin	43,200
Depreciation Expense	(1,250)
Operating Income	41,950
Gain on Sale of Equipment	2,900
Loss on Disposal of Land	(100)
Net Income	$44,750

Additional Data

1. During 2004 the company sold equipment for $8,900 that had originally cost $11,000. Accumulated depreciation on this equipment was $5,000 at the time of sale. Also, the company purchased equipment for $7,000.
2. The company sold for $2,500 land that had cost $2,600, resulting in the recognition of a $100 loss. Also, common stock was issued in exchange for land valued at $9,400 at the time of the exchange.
3. The company declared and paid dividends of $1,600.

Required

a. Use T-accounts to analyze the preceding data.
b. Using the direct method, prepare in good form a statement of cash flows for the year ended December 31, 2004.

Transactions Legend

a1. Revenue, $67,300.
a2. Collection of accounts receivable, $66,300 ($1,200 + $67,300 − $2,200).
b1. Cost of goods sold, $24,100.
b2. Inventory purchases, $23,700 ($5,600 + $24,100 − $6,000).
b3. Payments for inventory purchases, $22,700 ($4,200 + $23,700 − $5,200).
c1. Depreciation expense, $1,250 (noncash).
d1. Sale of equipment, $8,900; cost of equipment sold, $11,000; accumulated depreciation on equipment sold, $5,000.
d2. Purchase of equipment, $7,000.
e1. Sale of land, $2,500; cost of land sold, $2,600.
f1. Issue of stock in exchange for land, $9,400.
g1. Paid dividends, $1,600.
h1. Paid off portion of long-term debt, $800.

Solution to Requirement a

SCHLEMMER COMPANY
T-Accounts

| Assets | | | | = | Liabilities | | | + | Equity | | |

Cash

Bal.	2,800		
(a2)	66,300	(b3)	22,700
(d1)	8,900	(d2)	7,000
(e1)	2,500	(g1)	1,600
		(h1)	800
Bal.	48,400		

Accounts Payable

(b3)	22,700	Bal.	4,200
		(b2)	23,700
		Bal.	5,200

Common Stock

		Bal.	10,000
		(f1)	9,400
		Bal.	19,400

Accounts Receivable

Bal.	1,200		
(a1)	67,300	(a2)	66,300
Bal.	2,200		

Long-Term Debt

| (h1) | 800 | Bal. | 6,400 |
| | | Bal. | 5,600 |

Retained Earnings

		Bal.	4,400
(b1)	24,100	(a1)	67,300
(c1)	1,250	(d1)	2,900
(e1)	100		
(g1)	1,600		
		Bal.	47,550

Inventory

Bal.	6,000		
(b2)	23,700	(b1)	24,100
Bal.	5,600		

Equipment

Bal.	22,000		
(d2)	7,000	(d1)	11,000
Bal.	18,000		

Accumulated Depreciation

		Bal.	17,400
(d1)	5,000	(c1)	1,250
		Bal.	13,650

Land

Bal.	10,400		
(f1)	9,400	(e1)	2,600
Bal.	17,200		

Solution to Requirement b

SCHLEMMER COMPANY Statement of Cash Flows For the Year Ended December 31, 2004		
Cash Flows from Operating Activities		
Cash Receipts from Customers	$66,300	
Cash Payments for Inventory Purchases	(22,700)	
Net Cash Flow Provided by Operating Activities		$43,600
Cash Flows from Investing Activities		
Inflow from Sale of Equipment	8,900	
Inflow from Sale of Land	2,500	
Outflow to Purchase Equipment	(7,000)	
Net Cash Flow Provided by Investing Activities		4,400
Cash Flows from Financing Activities		
Outflow for Dividends	(1,600)	
Outflow for Repayment of Debt	(800)	
Net Cash Flow Used by Financing Activities		(2,400)
Net Increase in Cash		45,600
Plus: Beginning Cash Balance		2,800
Ending Cash Balance		$48,400
Schedule of Noncash Investing and Financing Activities		
Issued Common Stock for Land		$ 9,400

KEY TERMS

Accrual accounting *570*
Cash inflows *567*
Cash outflows *567*
Deferral transactions *572*

Direct method *582*
Expense transactions *570*
Financing activities *568*
Indirect method *583*

Investing activities *568*
Noncash investing and
    financing transactions *568*

Operating activities *568*
Revenue transactions *570*
T-account method *570*

QUESTIONS

1. What is the purpose of the statement of cash flows?
2. What are the three categories of cash flows reported on the cash flow statement? Discuss each and give an example of an inflow and an outflow for each category.
3. What are noncash investing and financing activities? Provide an example. How are such transactions shown on the statement of cash flows?
4. Best Company had beginning accounts receivable of $12,000 and ending accounts receivable of $14,000. If total sales were $110,000, what amount of cash was collected?
5. Best Company's Utilities Payable account had a beginning balance of $3,300 and an ending balance of $5,200. Utilities expense reported on the income statement was $87,000. What was the amount of cash paid for utilities for the period?
6. Best Company had a balance in the Unearned Revenue account of $4,300 at the beginning of the period and an ending balance of $5,700. If the portion of unearned revenue Best recognized as earned during the period was $15,600, what amount of cash did Best collect?
7. Which of the following activities are financing activities?
   a. Payment of accounts payable.
   b. Payment of interest on bonds payable.
   c. Sale of common stock.
   d. Sale of preferred stock at a premium.
   e. Payment of a cash dividend.
8. Does depreciation expense affect net cash flow? Explain.
9. If Best Company sold land that cost $4,200 at a $500 gain, how much cash did it collect from the sale of land?
10. If Best Company sold office equipment that originally cost $7,500 and had $7,200 of accumulated depreciation at a $100 loss, what was the selling price for the office equipment?

11. In which section of the statement of cash flows would the following transactions be reported?
    a. Cash receipt of interest income.
    b. Cash purchase of marketable securities.
    c. Cash purchase of equipment.
    d. Cash sale of merchandise.
    e. Cash sale of common stock.
    f. Payment of interest expense.
    g. Cash proceeds from loan.
    h. Cash payment on bonds payable.
    i. Cash receipt from sale of old equipment.
    j. Cash payment for operating expenses.
12. What is the difference between preparing the statement of cash flows using the direct approach and using the indirect approach?
13. Which method (direct or indirect) of presenting the statement of cash flows is more intuitively logical? Why?
14. What is the major advantage of using the indirect method to present the statement of cash flows?
15. What is the advantage of using the direct method to present the statement of cash flows?
16. How would Best Company report the following transactions on the statement of cash flows?
    a. Purchased new equipment for $46,000 cash.
    b. Sold old equipment for $8,700 cash. The equipment had a book value of $4,900.
17. Can a company report negative net cash flows from operating activities for the year on the statement of cash flows but still have positive net income on the income statement? Explain.
18. Why does the FASB prohibit disclosing cash flow per share in audited financial statements?

EXERCISES—SERIES A

L.O. 1   EXERCISE 12–1A *Classifying Cash Flows into Categories—Direct Method*

Required

Identify whether the cash flows in the following list should be classified as operating activities, investing activities, or financing activities on the statement of cash flows (assume the use of the direct method).
a. Acquired cash from issue of common stock.
b. Provided services for cash.
c. Acquired cash by issuing a note payable.
d. Paid cash for interest.
e. Paid cash dividends.
f. Paid cash to settle note payable.
g. Sold land for cash.
h. Paid cash to purchase a computer.
i. Paid cash for employee compensation.
j. Received cash interest from a bond investment.
k. Recognized depreciation expense.

L.O. 1   EXERCISE 12–2A *Cash Outflows from Operating Activities—Direct Method*

Required

Which of the following transactions produce cash outflows from operating activities (assume the use of the direct method)?
a. Cash payment to purchase inventory.
b. Cash payment for equipment.
c. Cash receipt from collecting accounts receivable.
d. Cash receipt from sale of land.
e. Cash payment for dividends.
f. Cash payment to settle an account payable.

L.O. 2   EXERCISE 12–3A *Using Account Balances to Determine Cash Flows from Operating Activities—Direct Method*

The following account balances are available for Pae Company for 2004.

Account Title	Beginning of Year	End of Year
Accounts Receivable	$23,000	$21,000
Interest Receivable	5,000	7,000
Accounts Payable	28,000	25,000
Salaries Payable	10,000	11,0000

Other Information for 2004

Sales on Account	$646,000
Interest Income	24,000
Operating Expenses	270,000
Salaries Expense for the Year	172,000

Required

(*Hint:* It may be helpful to assume that all revenues and expenses are on account.)

a. Compute the amount of cash *inflow* from operating activities.

b. Compute the amount of cash *outflow* from operating activities.

EXERCISE 12–4A *Using Account Balances to Determine Cash Flow from Operating Activities—Direct Method*   **L.O. 2**

The following account balances were available for Jefferson Enterprises for 2002.

Account Title	Beginning of Year	End of Year
Unearned Revenue	$4,000	$6,000
Prepaid Rent	2,200	2,500

During the year, $65,000 of unearned revenue was recognized as having been earned. Rent expense for the period was $12,000. Jefferson Enterprises maintains its books on the accrual basis.

Required

Using T-accounts and the preceding information, determine the amount of cash inflow from revenue and cash outflow for rent.

EXERCISE 12–5A *Using Account Balances to Determine Cash Flow from Investing Activities*   **L.O. 2**

The following account information pertains to Kallapur Company for 2005.

	Land				Marketable Securities	
Bal.	38,000	24,000		Bal.	78,000	49,000
	127,000				139,000	
Bal.	141,000			Bal.	168,000	

The income statement reported a $3,000 loss on the sale of land and a $2,500 gain on the sale of marketable securities.

Required

Prepare the investing activities section of the 2005 statement of cash flows.

EXERCISE 12–6A *Using Account Balances to Determine Cash Flow from Financing Activities*   **L.O. 2, 3**

The following account balances pertain to Kilgore, Inc., for 2006.

	Bonds Payable			Common Stock			Paid-in Capital in Excess of Par Value	
		Bal. 245,000			Bal. 368,000			Bal. 90,000
150,000					200,000			60,000
		Bal. 95,000			Bal. 568,000			Bal. 150,000

Required

Prepare the financing activities section of the 2006 statement of cash flows.

L.O. 2, 3 **EXERCISE 12–7A** *Using Account Balances to Determine Cash Outflow for Inventory Purchases*

The following account information pertains to Gupta Company, which uses the perpetual inventory method and purchases all inventory on account.

	Inventory				Accounts Payable	
Bal.	67,000				Bal.	49,000
	?	376,000		?		?
Bal.	72,000				Bal.	47,000

Required

Compute the amount of cash paid for the purchase of inventory.

L.O. 2, 4 **EXERCISE 12–8A** *Using Account Balances to Determine Cash Flow from Operating Activities—Indirect Method*

Altec Company presents its statement of cash flows using the indirect method. The following accounts and corresponding balances were drawn from Altec's accounting records for the period.

Account Titles	Beginning Balances	Ending Balances
Accounts Receivable	$24,000	$22,600
Prepaid Rent	1,650	1,950
Interest Receivable	900	700
Accounts Payable	10,200	8,850
Salaries Payable	2,700	2,950
Unearned Revenue	2,000	2,450

Net income for the period was $43,000.

Required

Using the preceding information, compute the net cash flow from operating activities using the indirect method.

L.O. 2, 3, 4 **EXERCISE 12–9A** *Using Account Balances to Determine Cash Flow from Operating Activities—Direct and Indirect Methods*

The following account balances are from Hutton Company's accounting records. Assume Hutton had no investing or financing transactions during 2002.

December 31	2001	2002
Cash	$65,000	$114,200
Accounts Receivable	75,000	77,000
Prepaid Rent	1,200	800
Accounts Payable	33,000	37,000
Utilities Payable	15,600	18,800
Sales Revenue		$272,000
Operating Expenses		(168,000)
Utilities Expense		(36,400)
Rent Expense		(24,000)
Net Income		$ 43,600

Required

a. Prepare the operating activities section of the 2002 statement of cash flows using the direct method.

b. Prepare the operating activities section of the 2002 statement of cash flows using the indirect method.

EXERCISE 12–10A *Interpreting Statement of Cash Flows Information*

The following selected transactions pertain to Armstrong Corporation for 2004.
1. Paid $23,400 cash to purchase delivery equipment.
2. Sold delivery equipment for $2,900. The equipment had originally cost $15,000 and had accumulated depreciation of $13,000.
3. Borrowed $40,000 cash by issuing bonds at face value.
4. Purchased a building that cost $180,000. Paid $50,000 cash and issued a mortgage for the remaining $130,000.
5. Exchanged no-par common stock for machinery valued at $64,900.

Required
a. Prepare the appropriate sections of the 2004 statement of cash flows.
b. Explain how a company could spend more cash on investing activities than it collected from financing activities during the same accounting period.

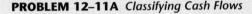

PROBLEMS—SERIES A

PROBLEM 12–11A *Classifying Cash Flows*

Required
Classify each of the following as an operating activity (OA), an investing activity (IA), or a financing activity (FA) cash flow, or a noncash transaction (NT).
a. Bought land with cash.
b. Collected cash from accounts receivable.
c. Issued common stock for cash.
d. Repaid principal and interest on a note payable.
e. Declared a stock split.
f. Purchased inventory with cash.
g. Recorded amortization of goodwill.
h. Paid insurance with cash.
i. Issued a note payable in exchange for equipment.
j. Recorded depreciation expense.
k. Provided services for cash.
l. Purchased marketable securities with cash.
m. Paid cash for rent.
n. Received interest on note receivable.
o. Paid cash for salaries.
p. Received advance payment for services.
q. Paid a cash dividend.
r. Provided services on account.
s. Purchased office supplies on account.

PROBLEM 12–12A *Using Transaction Data to Prepare a Statement of Cash Flows*

Store Company engaged in the following transactions during the 2002 accounting period. The beginning cash balance was $32,300.
1. Credit sales were $250,000. The beginning receivables balance was $95,000 and the ending balance was $103,000.
2. Salaries expense for the period was $56,000. The beginning salaries payable balance was $3,500 and the ending balance was $2,000.
3. Other operating expenses for the period were $125,000. The beginning operating expense payable balance was $4,500 and the ending balance was $9,600.
4. Recorded $19,500 of depreciation expense. The beginning and ending balances in the Accumulated Depreciation account were $14,000 and $33,500, respectively.
5. The Equipment account had beginning and ending balances of $210,000 and $240,000, respectively. The increase was caused by the cash purchase of equipment.
6. The beginning and ending balances in the Notes Payable account were $50,000 and $150,000, respectively. The increase was caused by additional cash borrowing.
7. There was $6,000 of interest expense reported on the income statement. The beginning and ending balances in the Interest Payable account were $1,200 and $1,000, respectively.

8. The beginning and ending Merchandise Inventory account balances were $90,000 and $108,000, respectively. The company sold merchandise with a cost of $156,000 (cost of goods sold for the period was $156,000). The beginning and ending balances of Accounts Payable were $9,500 and $11,500, respectively.

9. The beginning and ending balances of Notes Receivable were $2,500 and $10,000, respectively. The increase resulted from a cash loan to one of the company's employees.

10. The beginning and ending balances of the Common Stock account were $100,000 and $125,000, respectively. The increase was caused by the issue of common stock for cash.

11. Land had beginning and ending balances of $50,000 and $41,000, respectively. Land that cost $9,000 was sold for $14,700, resulting in a gain of $5,700.

12. The tax expense for the period was $7,700. The Tax Payable account had a $950 beginning balance and an $875 ending balance.

13. The Investments account had beginning and ending balances of $25,000 and $29,000, respectively. The company purchased investments for $18,000 cash during the period, and investments that cost $14,000 were sold for $9,000, resulting in a $5,000 loss.

Required

Convert the preceding information to cash-equivalent data and prepare a statement of cash flows.

L.O. 2, 3   **PROBLEM 12–13A** *Using Financial Statement Data to Determine Cash Flow from Operating Activities*

E
 X

The following account information is available for Big Sky Company for 2004:

Account Title	Beginning of Year	End of Year
Accounts Receivable	$20,000	$24,000
Merchandise Inventory	58,000	56,000
Prepaid Insurance	24,000	2,000
Accounts Payable (Inventory)	20,000	21,000
Salaries Payable	4,200	2,800

Other Information

1. Sales for the period were $175,000.
2. Purchases of merchandise for the period were $85,000.
3. Insurance expense for the period was $42,000.
4. Other operating expenses (all cash) were $26,000.
5. Salary expense was $35,000.

Required

a. Compute the net cash flow from operating activities.
b. Prepare the cash flow from the operating activities section of the statement of cash flows.

L.O. 2, 3   **PROBLEM 12–14A** *Using Financial Statement Data to Determine Cash Flow from Investing Activities*

E
 X

The following information pertaining to investing activities is available for Chico Company for 2005:

Account Title	Beginning of Year	End of Year
Machinery and Equipment	$425,000	$510,000
Marketable Securities	112,000	75,000
Land	90,000	110,000

Other Information for 2005

1. Marketable securities were sold at book value. No gain or loss was recognized.
2. Machinery was purchased for $110,000. Old machinery with a book value of $5,000 (cost of $25,000, accumulated depreciation of $20,000) was sold for $8,000.

Required

a. Compute the net cash flow from investing activities.
b. Prepare the cash flow from investing activities section of the statement of cash flows.

PROBLEM 12–15A *Using Financial Statement Data to Determine Cash Flow from Financing* **L.O. 2, 3**
Activities

The following information pertaining to financing activities is available for Tiger Company for 2004:

Account Title	Beginning of Year	End of Year
Bonds Payable	$300,000	$190,000
Common Stock	200,000	250,000
Paid-in Capital in Excess of Par	75,000	125,000

Other Information
1. Dividends paid during the period amounted to $45,000.
2. No new funds were borrowed during the period.

Required
a. Compute the net cash flow from financing activities for 2004.
b. Prepare the cash flow from the financing activities section of the statement of cash flows.

PROBLEM 12–16A *Using Financial Statements to Prepare a Statement of Cash Flows—* **L.O. 2, 3**
Direct Method

The following financial statements were drawn from the records of Pacific Company.

Balance Sheets as of December 31		
	2002	2003
Assets		
Cash	$ 2,800	$ 24,200
Accounts Receivable	1,200	2,000
Inventory	6,000	6,400
Equipment	42,000	19,000
Accumulated Depreciation—Equipment	(17,400)	(9,000)
Land	10,400	18,400
Total Assets	$45,000	$ 61,000
Liabilities and Equity		
Accounts Payable	$4,200	$2,600
Long-Term Debt	6,400	2,800
Common Stock	10,000	22,000
Retained Earnings	24,400	33,600
Total Liabilities and Equity	$45,000	$ 61,000

Income Statement for the Year Ended December 31, 2003	
Sales Revenue	$35,700
Cost of Goods Sold	(14,150)
Gross Margin	21,550
Depreciation Expense	(3,600)
Operating Income	17,950
Gain on Sale of Equipment	500
Loss on Disposal of Land	(50)
Net Income	$18,400

Additional Data
1. During 2003, the company sold equipment for $18,500; it had originally cost $30,000. Accumulated depreciation on this equipment was $12,000 at the time of the sale. Also, the company purchased equipment for $7,000 cash.
2. The company sold land that had cost $4,000. This land was sold for $3,950, resulting in the recognition of a $50 loss. Also, common stock was issued in exchange for title to land that was valued at $12,000 at the time of exchange.
3. Paid dividends of $9,200.

Required

Use the T-account method to analyze the data and prepare a statement of cash flows.

L.O. 2, 3   PROBLEM 12-17A *Using Financial Statements to Prepare a Statement of Cash Flows—Direct Method*

The following financial statements were drawn from the records of Raceway Sports:

Balance Sheets as of December 31		
	2001	**2002**
Assets		
Cash	$28,200	$123,600
Accounts Receivable	66,000	57,000
Inventory	114,000	126,000
Notes Receivable	30,000	0
Equipment	255,000	147,000
Accumulated Depreciation—Equipment	(141,000)	(74,740)
Land	52,500	82,500
Total Assets	$404,700	$461,360
Liabilities and Equity		
Accounts Payable	$48,600	42,000
Salaries Payable	24,000	30,000
Utilities Payable	1,200	600
Interest Payable	1,800	0
Note Payable	60,000	0
Common Stock	240,000	300,000
Retained Earnings	29,100	88,760
Total Liabilities and Equity	$404,700	$461,360

Income Statement for the Year Ended December 31, 2002	
Sales Revenue	$580,000
Cost of Goods Sold	(288,000)
Gross Margin	292,000
Operating Expenses	
Salary Expense	(184,000)
Depreciation Expense	(17,740)
Utilities Expense	(12,200)
Operating Income	78,060
Nonoperating Items	
Interest Expense	(3,000)
Gain or (Loss)	(1,800)
Net Income	$ 73,260

Additional Information

1. Sold equipment costing $108,000 with accumulated depreciation of $84,000 for $22,200 cash.
2. Paid a $13,600 cash dividend to owners.

Required

Use the T-account method to analyze the data and prepare a statement of cash flows.

L.O. 2, 4   PROBLEM 12-18A *Using Financial Statements to Prepare a Statement of Cash Flows—Indirect Method*

The comparative balance sheets for Redwood Corporation for 2003 and 2004 follow:

Balance Sheets as of December 31		
	2003	**2004**
Assets		
Cash	$ 40,600	$ 68,800
Accounts Receivable	22,000	30,000
Merchandise Inventory	176,000	160,000
Prepaid Rent	4,800	2,400
Equipment	288,000	256,000
Accumulated Depreciation	(236,000)	(146,800)
Land	80,000	192,000
Total Assets	$375,400	$562,400
Liabilities		
Accounts Payable (Inventory)	$ 76,000	$ 67,000
Salaries Payable	24,000	28,000
Stockholders' Equity		
Common Stock, $25 Par Value	200,000	250,000
Retained Earnings	75,400	217,400
Total Liabilities and Equity	$375,400	$562,400

Income Statement for the Year Ended December 31, 2004	
Sales	$1,500,000
Cost of Goods Sold	(797,200)
Gross Profit	702,800
Operating Expenses	
Depreciation Expense	(22,800)
Rent Expense	(24,000)
Salaries Expense	(256,000)
Other Operating Expenses	(258,000)
Net Income	$ 142,000

Other Information
1. Purchased land for $112,000.
2. Purchased new equipment for $100,000.
3. Sold old equipment that cost $132,000 with accumulated depreciation of $112,000 for $20,000 cash.
4. Issued common stock for $50,000.

Required
Prepare the statement of cash flows for 2004, using the indirect method.

EXERCISES—SERIES B

EXERCISE 12–1B *Classifying Cash Flows into Categories—Direct Method*   **L.O. 1**

Required
Identify whether the cash flows in the following list should be classified as operating activities, investing activities, or financing activities on the statement of cash flows (assume the use of the direct method).
a. Sold merchandise on account.
b. Paid employee salary.
c. Received cash proceeds from bank loan.
d. Paid dividends.
e. Sold used equipment for cash.
f. Received interest income on a certificate of deposit.
g. Sold stock for cash.

h. Repaid bank loan.

i. Purchased equipment for cash.

j. Paid interest on loan.

L.O. 1   EXERCISE 12–2B *Cash Inflows from Operating Activities—Direct Method*

Required

Which of the following transactions produce cash inflows from operating activities (assume the use of the direct method)?

a. Cash payment for utilities expense.

b. Cash payment for equipment.

c. Cash receipt from interest.

d. Cash payment for dividends.

e. Collection of cash from accounts receivable.

f. Provide services for cash.

L.O. 2   EXERCISE 12–3B *Using Account Balances to Determine Cash Flow from Operating Activities—Direct Method*

The following account balances are available for Norstom Company for 2002.

Account Title	Beginning of Year	End of Year
Accounts Receivable	$40,000	$46,000
Interest Receivable	5,000	3,000
Accounts Payable	30,000	33,000
Salaries Payable	12,000	10,500

Other Information for 2002

Sales on Account	$275,000
Interest Income	25,000
Operating Expenses	196,000
Salaries Expense for the Year	75,000

Required

(*Hint:* It may be helpful to assume that all revenues and expenses are on account.)

a. Compute the amount of cash *inflow* from operating activities.

b. Compute the amount of cash *outflow* from operating activities.

L.O. 2   EXERCISE 12–4B *Using Account Balances to Determine Cash Flow from Operating Activities—Direct Method*

The following account balances were available for Earles Candy Company for 2001:

Account Title	Beginning of Year	End of Year
Unearned Revenue	$18,000	$8,000
Prepaid Rent	2,000	900

During the year, $41,000 of unearned revenue was recognized as having been earned. Rent expense for the period was $8,000. Earles Candy Company maintains its books on the accrual basis.

Required

Using T-accounts and the preceding information, determine the amount of cash inflow from revenue and cash outflow for rent.

L.O. 2   EXERCISE 12–5B *Using Account Balances to Determine Cash Flow from Investing Activities*

The following account information is available for McClung, Inc., for 2005:

Land			Marketable Securities		
Bal.	20,000	50,000	Bal.	75,000	30,000
	100,000			40,000	
Bal.	70,000		Bal.	85,000	

The income statement reported a $9,000 gain on the sale of land and a $1,200 loss on the sale of marketable securities.

Required

Prepare the investing activities section of the statement of cash flows for 2005.

EXERCISE 12–6B *Using Account Balances to Determine Cash Flow from Financing Activities*   **L.O. 2, 3**

The following account balances were available for Golden Company for 2007:

Mortgage Payable			Capital Stock			Paid-in Capital in Excess of Par		
	148,000	Bal.		200,000	Bal.		65,000	Bal.
62,000				50,000			30,000	
	86,000	Bal.		250,000	Bal.		95,000	Bal.

Required

Prepare the financing activities section of the statement of cash flows for 2007.

EXERCISE 12–7B *Using Account Balances to Determine Cash Outflow for Inventory Purchases*   **L.O. 2, 3**

The following account information is available for Sherman Company. The company uses the perpetual inventory method and makes all inventory purchases on account.

Inventory			Accounts Payable		
Bal.	41,000			42,000	Bal.
	?	120,000	?	?	
Bal.	65,000			52,000	Bal.

Required

Compute the amount of cash paid for the purchase of inventory.

EXERCISE 12–8B *Using Account Balances to Determine Cash Flow from Operating Activities—Indirect Method*   **L.O. 2, 4**

Maple Company presents its statement of cash flows using the indirect method. The following accounts and corresponding balances were drawn from Maple's accounting records.

Account Titles	Beginning Balances	Ending Balances
Accounts Receivable	$30,000	$35,000
Prepaid Rent	2,000	1,200
Interest Receivable	800	400
Accounts Payable	9,000	9,500
Salaries Payable	2,500	2,100
Unearned Revenue	1,200	2,200

Net income for the period was $45,000.

Required

Using the preceding information, compute the net cash flow from operating activities using the indirect method.

L.O. 2-4   EXERCISE 12–9B *Using Account Balances to Determine Cash Flow from Operating Activities—Direct and Indirect Methods*

The following information is from the accounting records of Mong Company:

	2000	2001
Cash	$ 42,000	$ 88,800
Accounts Receivable	158,000	159,800
Prepaid Rent	3,000	5,600
Accounts Payable	120,000	125,000
Utilities Payable	12,000	8,400
Sales Revenue		$212,000
Operating Expenses		(135,000)
Utilities Expense		(17,200)
Rent Expense		(10,000)
Net Income		$ 49,800

Required
a. Prepare the operating activities section of the 2001 statement of cash flows using the direct method.
b. Prepare the operating activities section of the 2001 statement of cash flows using the indirect method.

L.O. 3, 5   EXERCISE 12–10B *Interpreting Statement of Cash Flows Information*

The following selected transactions pertain to Johnston Company for 2003.
1. Purchased new office equipment for $9,800 cash.
2. Sold old office equipment for $2,000 that originally cost $12,000 and had accumulated depreciation of $11,000.
3. Borrowed $20,000 cash from the bank for six months.
4. Purchased land for $125,000 by paying $50,000 in cash and issuing a note for the balance.
5. Exchanged no-par common stock for an automobile valued at $26,500.

Required
a. Prepare the appropriate sections of the statement of cash flows for 2003.
b. What information does the noncash investing and financing activities section of the statement provide? If this information were omitted, could it affect a decision to invest in a company?

PROBLEMS—SERIES B

L.O. 1   PROBLEM 12–11B *Classifying Cash Flows*

Required
Classify each of the following as an operating activity (OA), an investing activity (IA), or a financing activity (FA) cash flow, or a noncash transaction (NT).
a. Paid cash for operating expenses.
b. Wrote off an uncollectible account receivable using the allowance method.
c. Wrote off an uncollectible account receivable using the direct write-off method.
d. Issued common stock for cash.
e. Declared a stock split.
f. Issued a mortgage to purchase a building
g. Purchased equipment with cash.
h. Repaid the principal balance on a note payable.
i. Made a cash payment for the balance due in the Dividends Payable account.
j. Received a cash dividend from investment in marketable securities.
k. Purchased supplies on account.
l. Collected cash from accounts receivable.
m. Accrued warranty expense.
n. Borrowed cash by issuing a bond.
o. Loaned cash to a business associate.
p. Paid cash for interest expense.
q. Incurred a loss on the sale of equipment.

r. Wrote down inventory because the year-end physical count was less than the balance in the Inventory account.

s. Paid cash to purchase inventory.

PROBLEM 12–12B Using Transaction Data to Prepare a Statement of Cash Flows

L.O. 2, 3

Greenstein Company engaged in the following transactions during 2003. The beginning cash balance was $86,000.

1. Credit sales were $548,000. The beginning receivables balance was $128,000 and the ending balance was $90,000.

2. Salaries expense for 2003 was $232,000. The beginning salaries payable balance was $16,000 and the ending balance was $8,000.

3. Other operating expenses for 2003 were $236,000. The beginning operating Expense Payable balance was $16,000 and the ending balance was $10,000.

4. Recorded $30,000 of depreciation expense. The beginning and ending balances in the Accumulated Depreciation account were $12,000 and $42,000, respectively.

5. The Equipment account had beginning and ending balances of $44,000 and $56,000, respectively. The increase was caused by the cash purchase of equipment.

6. The beginning and ending balances in the Notes Payable account were $44,000 and $36,000, respectively. The decrease was caused by the cash repayment of debt.

7. There was $4,600 of interest expense reported on the income statement. The beginning and ending balances in the Interest Payable account were $8,400 and $7,500, respectively.

8. The beginning and ending Merchandise Inventory account balances were $22,000 and $29,400, respectively. The company sold merchandise with a cost of $83,600. The beginning and ending balances of Accounts Payable were $8,000 and $6,400, respectively.

9. The beginning and ending balances of Notes Receivable were $100,000 and $60,000, respectively. The decline resulted from the cash collection of a portion of the receivable.

10. The beginning and ending balances of the Common Stock account were $120,000 and $160,000, respectively. The increase was caused by the issue of common stock for cash.

11. Land had beginning and ending balances of $24,000 and $14,000, respectively. Land that cost $10,000 was sold for $6,000, resulting in a loss of $4,000.

12. The tax expense for 2003 was $6,600. The Tax Payable account had a $2,400 beginning balance and a $2,200 ending balance.

13. The Investments account had beginning and ending balances of $20,000 and $60,000, respectively. The company purchased investments for $50,000 cash during 2003, and investments that cost $10,000 were sold for $22,000, resulting in a $12,000 gain.

Required

Convert the preceding information to cash-equivalent data and prepare a statement of cash flows.

PROBLEM 12–13B Using Financial Statement Data to Determine Cash Flow from Operating Activities

L.O. 2, 3

The following account information is available for Gables Auto Supplies for 2003:

Account Title	Beginning of Year	End of Year
Accounts Receivable	$ 17,800	$ 21,000
Merchandise Inventory	136,000	142,800
Prepaid Insurance	1,600	1,200
Accounts Payable (Inventory)	18,800	19,600
Salaries Payable	6,400	5,800

Other Information

1. Sales for the period were $248,000.
2. Purchases of merchandise for the period were $186,000.
3. Insurance expense for the period was $8,000.
4. Other operating expenses (all cash) were $27,400.
5. Salary expense was $42,600.

Required

a. Compute the net cash flow from operating activities.

b. Prepare the cash flow from the operating activities section of the statement of cash flows.

L.O. 2, 3   PROBLEM 12–14B *Using Financial Statement Data to Determine Cash Flow from Investing Activities*

The following information pertaining to investing activities is available for Tony's Flea Markets, Inc., for 2001.

Account Title	Beginning of Year	End of Year
Trucks and Equipment	$162,000	$170,000
Marketable Securities	66,000	51,200
Land	42,000	34,000

Other Information for 2001
1. Tony's sold marketable securities at book value. No gain or loss was recognized.
2. Trucks were purchased for $40,000. Old trucks with a cost of $32,000 and accumulated depreciation of $24,000 were sold for $11,000.
3. Land that cost $8,000 was sold for $10,000.

Required
a. Compute the net cash flow from investing activities.
b. Prepare the cash flow from the investing activities section of the statement of cash flows.

L.O. 2, 3   PROBLEM 12–15B *Using Financial Statement Data to Determine Cash Flow from Financing Activities*

The following information pertaining to financing activities is available for Engineered Components Company for 2002.

Account Title	Beginning of Year	End of Year
Bonds Payable	$170,000	$180,000
Common Stock	210,000	280,000
Paid-in Capital in Excess of Par	84,000	116,000

Other Information
1. Dividends paid during the period amounted to $28,000.
2. Additional funds of $40,000 were borrowed during the period by issuing bonds.

Required
a. Compute the net cash flow from financing activities for 2002.
b. Prepare the cash flow from the financing activities section of the statement of cash flows.

L.O. 2, 3   PROBLEM 12–16B *Using Financial Statements to Prepare a Statement of Cash Flows— Direct Method*

The following financial statements were drawn from the records of Healthy Products Co.

Balance Sheets as of December 31		
	2002	2003
Assets		
Cash	$ 1,940	$16,120
Accounts Receivable	2,000	2,400
Inventory	2,600	2,000
Equipment	17,100	13,700
Accumulated Depreciation—Equipment	(12,950)	(11,300)
Land	8,000	13,000
Total Assets	$18,690	$35,920
Liabilities and Equity		
Accounts Payable	$ 2,400	$ 3,600
Long-Term Debt	4,000	3,200
Common Stock	10,000	17,000
Retained Earnings	2,290	12,120
Total Liabilities and Stockholders' Equity	$18,690	$35,920

Income Statement for the Year Ended December 31, 2003

Sales Revenue	$17,480
Cost of Goods Sold	(6,200)
Gross Margin	11,280
Depreciation Expense	(1,750)
Operating Income	9,530
Gain on Sale of Equipment	1,800
Loss on Disposal of Land	(600)
Net Income	$10,730

Additional Data

1. During 2003, the company sold equipment for $6,800; it had originally cost $8,400. Accumulated depreciation on this equipment was $3,400 at the time of the sale. Also, the company purchased equipment for $5,000 cash.
2. The company sold land that had cost $2,000. This land was sold for $1,400, resulting in the recognition of a $600 loss. Also, common stock was issued in exchange for title to land that was valued at $7,000 at the time of exchange.
3. Paid dividends of $900.

Required
Use the T-account method to analyze the data and prepare a statement of cash flows.

PROBLEM 12–17B *Using Financial Statements to Prepare a Statement of Cash Flows—*
Direct Method

L.O. 2, 3

The following financial statements were drawn from the records of Norton Materials, Inc.

Balance Sheets as of December 31

	2000	2001
Assets		
Cash	$ 14,100	$ 94,300
Accounts Receivable	40,000	36,000
Inventory	64,000	72,000
Notes Receivable	16,000	0
Equipment	170,000	98,000
Accumulated Depreciation—Equipment	(94,000)	(47,800)
Land	30,000	46,000
Total Assets	$240,100	$298,500
Liabilities and Equity		
Accounts Payable	$26,400	$24,000
Salaries Payable	10,000	15,000
Utilities Payable	1,400	800
Interest Payable	1,000	0
Note Payable	24,000	0
Common Stock	110,000	150,000
Retained Earnings	67,300	108,700
Total Liabilities and Equity	$240,100	$298,500

Income Statement for the Year Ended December 31, 2001

Sales Revenue	$300,000
Cost of Goods Sold	(144,000)
Gross Margin	156,000
Operating Expenses	
Salary Expense	(88,000)
Depreciation Expense	(9,800)
Utilities Expense	(6,400)
Operating Income	51,800
Nonoperating Items	
Interest Expense	(2,400)
Loss	(800)
Net Income	$ 48,600

Additional Information
1. Sold equipment costing $72,000 with accumulated depreciation of $56,000 for $15,200 cash.
2. Paid a $7,200 cash dividend to owners.

Required
Use the T-account method to analyze the data and prepare a statement of cash flows.

L.O. 2, 4 **PROBLEM 12–18B** *Using Financial Statements to Prepare a Statement of Cash Flows—*
Indirect Method

The comparative balance sheets for Lind Beauty Products, Inc., for 2002 and 2003 follow:

Balance Sheets as of December 31		
	2002	**2003**
Assets		
Cash	$ 48,400	$ 6,300
Accounts Receivable	7,260	10,200
Merchandise Inventory	56,000	45,200
Prepaid Rent	2,140	700
Equipment	144,000	140,000
Accumulated Depreciation	(118,000)	(73,400)
Land	50,000	116,000
Total Assets	$189,800	$245,000
Liabilities and Equity		
Accounts Payable (Inventory)	$ 40,000	$ 37,200
Salaries Payable	10,600	12,200
Stockholders' Equity		
Common Stock, $50 Par Value	120,000	150,000
Retained Earnings	19,200	45,600
Total Liabilities and Equity	$189,800	$245,000

Income Statement for the Year Ended December 31, 2003	
Sales	$480,000
Cost of Goods Sold	(264,000)
Gross Profit	216,000
Operating Expenses	
Depreciation Expense	(11,400)
Rent Expense	(7,000)
Salaries Expense	(95,200)
Other Operating Expenses	(76,000)
Net Income	$ 26,400

Other Information
1. Purchased land for $66,000.
2. Purchased new equipment for $62,000.
3. Sold old equipment that cost $66,000 with accumulated depreciation of $56,000 for $10,000 cash.
4. Issued common stock for $30,000.

Required
Prepare the statement of cash flows for 2003 using the indirect method.

ANALYZE, THINK, COMMUNICATE

ATC 12–1 **REAL-WORLD CASE** *Following the Cash*

Panera Bread Company (Panera) was formerly known as Au Bon Pain Company (ABP). In May 1999, the
ABP division of the company was sold to private investors for $72 million, and assumed the new name.
     Panera operates retail bakery-cafes under the names Panera Bread and Saint Louis Bread Company.
The following table shows the number of these cafes in operation for each of the past five years.

Year	Company Owned	Franchise Owned	Total
2000	90	172	262
1999	81	100	181
1998	70	45	115
1997	57	19	76
1996	52	10	62

Most of Panera's baked goods are distributed to the stores in the form of frozen dough. In March 1998, the company sold its frozen dough production facility to the Bunge Food Corporation for $13 million. Panera agreed to purchase its frozen dough from Bunge for at least the next five years.

Panera's statements of cash flows for 1998, 1999, and 2000 follow.

PANERA BREAD COMPANY
Consolidated Statements of Cash Flows
(Dollars in thousands)

	For the Fiscal Years Ended		
	December 30, 2000	December 25, 1999	December 26, 1998
Cash flows from operations			
Net income (loss)	$ 6,853	$ (629)	$(20,494)
Adjustments to reconcile net income (loss) to net cash provided by operating activities:			
Depreciation and amortization	8,412	6,379	12,667
Amortization of deferred financing costs	88	406	683
Provision for losses on accounts receivable	(111)	93	56
Minority interest	—	(25)	(127)
Tax benefit from exercise of stock options	4,001	—	75
Deferred income taxes	664	42	(6,664)
Loss on early extinguishment of debt	—	382	—
Nonrecurring charge	494	5,545	26,236
Loss on disposal of assets	—	—	735
Changes in operating assets and liabilities:			
Accounts receivable	(308)	(1,596)	15
Inventories	(562)	(65)	212
Prepaid expenses	(543)	(3,560)	(535)
Refundable income taxes	(376)	—	480
Accounts payable	1,861	(3,037)	4,069
Accrued expenses	(645)	769	3,104
Deferred revenue	234	2,011	—
Net cash provided by operating activities	20,062	6,715	20,512
Cash flows from investing activities			
Additions to property and equipment	(20,089)	(15,306)	(21,706)
Proceeds from sale of assets	—	72,163	12,694
Change in cash included in net current liabilities held for sale	—	(466)	(1,305)
Payments received on notes receivable	35	114	240
Increase in intangible assets	—	(50)	(139)
Increase (decrease) in deposits and other	(771)	855	(956)
Increase in notes receivable	—	(30)	(45)
Net cash (used in) provided by investing activities	(20,825)	57,280	(11,217)
Cash flows from financing activities			
Exercise of employee stock options	8,206	96	1,203
Proceeds from long-term debt issuance	765	41,837	75,418
Principal payments on long-term debt	(391)	(106,073)	(84,253)
Purchase of treasury stock	(900)	—	—
Proceeds from issuance of common stock	182	148	268
Common stock issued for employee stock bonus	—	304	—
Increase in deferred financing costs	(24)	(110)	(506)
Decrease in minority interest	—	(121)	(418)
Net cash provided by (used in) financing activities	7,838	(63,919)	(8,288)
Net increase in cash and cash equivalents	7,075	76	1,007
Cash and cash equivalents at beginning of year	1,936	1,860	853
Cash and cash equivalents at end of year	$ 9,011	$ 1,936	$ 1,860
Supplemental cash flow information:			
Cash paid during the year for:			
Interest	$ 85	$ 4,250	$ 5,544
Income taxes	$ 512	$ 241	$ 268

Required

Using the information provided, including a careful analysis of Panera's statements of cash flows, answer the following questions. Be sure to explain the rationale for your answers and present any computations necessary to support them.

a. Was the sale of the frozen dough production facility for $13 million a cash sale? If so, what did Panera do with the cash it received?

b. Was the sale of the ABP division for $72 million a cash sale? If so, what did Panera do with the cash it received?

c. As shown in the preceding table, Panera has expanded its operations in each of the past five years. Approximately how much cash was spent on expansion in 1998, 1999, and 2000, and what were the sources of this cash for each year?

ATC 12–2   GROUP ASSIGNMENT *Preparing a Statement of Cash Flows*

The following financial statements and information are available for Blythe Industries, Inc.

Balance Sheets as of December 31		
	2000	**2001**
Assets		
Cash	$120,600	$ 160,200
Accounts Receivable	85,000	103,200
Inventory	171,800	186,400
Marketable Securities (Available for Sale)	220,000	284,000
Equipment	490,000	650,000
Accumulated Depreciation	(240,000)	(310,000)
Land	120,000	80,000
Total Assets	$967,400	$1,153,800
Liabilities and Equity		
Liabilities		
Accounts Payable (Inventory)	$ 66,200	$ 36,400
Notes Payable—Long-Term	250,000	230,000
Bonds Payable	100,000	200,000
Total Liabilities	416,200	466,400
Stockholders' Equity		
Common Stock, No Par	200,000	240,000
Preferred Stock, $50 Par	100,000	110,000
Paid-in Capital in Excess of Par—Preferred Stock	26,800	34,400
Total Paid-In Capital	326,800	384,400
Retained Earnings	264,400	333,000
Less: Treasury Stock	(40,000)	(30,000)
Total Stockholders' Equity	$551,200	$ 687,400
Total Liabilities and Stockholders' Equity	$967,400	$1,153,800

Income Statement for 2001		
Sales Revenue		$1,050,000
Cost of Goods Sold		(766,500)
Gross Profit		283,500
Operating Expenses		
Supplies Expense	$ 20,400	
Salaries Expense	92,000	
Depreciation Expense	90,000	
Total Operating Expenses		202,400
Operating Income		81,100
Nonoperating Items		
Interest Expense		(16,000)
Gain from the Sale of Marketable Securities		30,000
Gain from the Sale of Land and Equipment		12,000
Net Income		$ 107,100

Additional Information
1. Sold land that cost $40,000 for $44,000.
2. Sold equipment that cost $30,000 and had accumulated depreciation of $20,000 for $18,000.
3. Purchased new equipment for $190,000.
4. Sold marketable securities that cost $40,000 for $70,000.
5. Purchased new marketable securities for $104,000.
6. Paid $20,000 on the principal of the long-term note.
7. Paid off a $100,000 bond issue and issued new bonds for $200,000.
8. Sold 100 shares of treasury stock at its cost.
9. Issued some new common stock.
10. Issued some new $50 par preferred stock.
11. Paid dividends. (*Note:* The only transactions to affect retained earnings were net income and dividends.)

Required

Organize the class into three sections, and divide each section into groups of three to five students. Assign each section of groups an activity section of the statement of cash flows (operating activities, investing activities, or financing activities).

Group Task

Prepare your assigned portion of the statement of cash flows. Have a representative of your section put your activity section of the statement of cash flows on the board. As each adds its information on the board, the full statement of cash flows will be presented.

Class Discussion

Have the class finish the statement of cash flows by computing the net change in cash. Also have the class answer the following questions:
a. What is the cost per share of the treasury stock?
b. What was the issue price of the preferred stock?
c. What was the book value of the equipment sold?

BUSINESS APPLICATIONS CASE *Identifying Different Presentation Formats*

ATC 12–3

In *Statement of Financial Accounting Standards No. 95,* the Financial Accounting Standards Board (FASB) recommended but did not require that companies use the direct method. In Appendix B, Paragraphs 106–121, the FASB discussed its reasons for this recommendation.

Required
Obtain a copy of *Standard No. 95* and read Appendix B Paragraphs 106–21. Write a brief response summarizing the issues that the FASB considered and its specific reaction to those issues. Your response should draw heavily on paragraphs 119–21.

WRITING ASSIGNMENT *Explaining Discrepancies between Cash Flow and Operating Income*

ATC 12–4

The following selected information was drawn from the records of Fleming Company:

Assets	2002	2003
Accounts Receivable	$ 400,000	$ 840,200
Merchandise Inventory	720,000	1,480,000
Equipment	1,484,000	1,861,200
Accumulated Depreciation	(312,000)	(402,400)

Fleming is experiencing cash flow problems. Despite the fact that it reported significant increases in operating income, operating activities produced a net cash outflow. Recent financial forecasts predict that Fleming will have insufficient cash to pay its current liabilities within three months.

Required
Write a response explaining Fleming's cash shortage. Include a recommendation to remedy the problem.

ATC 12–5   **ETHICAL DILEMMA** *Would I Lie to You, Baby?*

Andy and Jean Crocket are involved in divorce proceedings. When discussing a property settlement, Andy told Jean that he should take over their investment in an apartment complex because she would be unable to absorb the loss that the apartments are generating. Jean was somewhat distrustful and asked Andy to support his contention. He produced the following income statement, which was supported by a CPA's unqualified opinion that the statement was prepared in accordance with generally accepted accounting principles.

CROCKET APARTMENTS Income Statement For the Year Ended December 31, 2003		
Rent Revenue		$580,000
Less: Expenses		
Depreciation Expense	$280,000	
Interest Expense	184,000	
Operating Expense	88,000	
Management Fees	56,000	
Total Expenses		(608,000)
Net Loss		$ (28,000)

All revenue is earned on account. Interest and operating expenses are incurred on account. Management fees are paid in cash. The following accounts and balances were drawn from the 2002 and 2003 year-end balance sheets.

Account Title	2002	2003
Rent Receivable	$40,000	$44,000
Interest Payable	12,000	18,000
Accounts Payable (Oper. Exp.)	6,000	4,000

Jean is reluctant to give up the apartments but feels that she must because her present salary is only $40,000 per year. She says that if she takes the apartments, the $28,000 loss would absorb a significant portion of her salary, leaving her only $12,000 with which to support herself. She tells you that while the figures seem to support her husband's arguments, she believes that she is failing to see something. She knows that she and her husband collected a $20,000 distribution from the business on December 1, 2003. Also, $150,000 cash was paid in 2003 to reduce the principal balance on a mortgage that was taken out to finance the purchase of the apartments two years ago. Finally, $24,000 cash was paid during 2003 to purchase a computer system used in the business. She wonders, "If the apartments are losing money, where is my husband getting all the cash to make these payments?"

Required

a. Prepare a statement of cash flows for the 2003 accounting period.

b. Compare the cash flow statement prepared in Requirement *a* with the income statement and provide Jean Crocket with recommendations.

c. Comment on the value of an unqualified audit opinion when using financial statements for decision-making purposes.

ATC 12–6   **SPREADSHEET ANALYSIS** *Preparing a Statement of Cash Flows Using the Direct Method*

Refer to the information in Problem 12–18A. Solve for the statement of cash flows using the direct method. Instead of using the T-account method, set up the following spreadsheet to work through the analysis. The Debit/Credit entries are very similar to the T-account method except that they are entered onto a spreadsheet. Two distinct differences are as follows:

1. Instead of making entries on row 2 for Cash, cash entries are made beginning on row 24 under the heading Cash Transactions.

2. Entries for Retained Earnings are made on rows 15 through 20 since there are numerous revenue and expense entries to that account.

Microsoft Excel - 14-working.XLS

File Edit View Insert Format Tools Data Window Help

Arial · 10 · B I U ≡ ≡ ≡ ⊞ $ % , ‰ ‰ ≡ ≡ _ · ◇ · A ·

H3 = =IF(B3+D3-F3=G3,"Balance","Off")

	A	B	C	D	E	F	G	H	I	J	K
1	Balance Sheet Debits:	2,003		Debit		Credit	2,004				
2	Cash	40,600					68,800			Change in Cash =	28,200
3	Accounts Receivable	22,000	a1	1,500,000	a2	1,492,000	30,000	Balance			
4	Inventory	176,000	b2				160,000	Off			
5	Prepaid Rent	4,800					2,400	Off			
6	Equipment	288,000					256,000	Off			
7	Land	80,000					192,000	Off			
8	Total Debits	611,400					709,200				
9	Balance Sheet Credits:										
10	Accumulated Depreciation	236,000					146,800	Off			
11	Accounts Payable (Inv.)	76,000					67,000	Off			
12	Salaries Payable	24,000					28,000	Off			
13	Common Stock, $25 Par	200,000					250,000	Off			
14	Retained Earnings	75,400					217,400	Balance			
15	Sales				a1	1,500,000					
16	Cost of Goods Sold		b1	797,200							
17	Depreciation Expense		c1	22,800							
18	Rent Expense		d1	24,000							
19	Salaries Expense		e1	256,000							
20	Other Operating Expenses		f1	258,000							
21	Total Credits	611,400					709,200				
22	Statement of Cash Flows			Cash Transactions							
23	Cash Flows from Operating Activities										
24	Cash received from sales		a2	1,492,000						Difference in Cash Debit	
25	Cash paid for inventory purchased									and Credit Entries =	
26	Cash paid for rent										
27	Cash paid for salaries										
28	Cash paid for other operating items										
29	Cash Flows from Investing Activities										
30	Outflow to purchase land										
31	Outflow to purchase equipment										
32	Inflow from sale of equipment										
33	Cash Flows from Financing Activities										
34	Inflow from stock issue										
35	Total Debit and Credit Columns										

Problem 12-1 Answer Key / Problem / Sheet2 / Sheet3 /

Ready   NUM

Required

a. Enter information in Column A.

b. Enter the beginning balance sheet amounts in Column B and ending balances in Column G. Total the debits and credits for each column.

c. To prevent erroneous entries to Cash in row 2, darken the area in Columns C through F.

d. In Columns C through F, record entries for the revenue and expenses and then the related conversions to cash flow. The first entry (a1) and (a2) converting Sales to Cash Received from Sales has been provided for you. So has the labeling for the expense entries (b1 through f1).

e. Record the four entries from the Other Information provided in Problem 12–18A. These are investing and financing activities.

f. In Column H, set up the IF function to determine whether the balance sheet accounts are in balance or not ("off"). Cell H3 for Accounts Receivable is provided for you. Cell H3 can be copied to all the balance sheet debit accounts. The balance sheet credit account formulas will differ given the different debit/credit rules for those accounts. The formula for Retained Earnings will need to include rows 14 through 20. *When the word "Balance" is reflected in every balance sheet cell in column H, the spreadsheet analysis is complete.*

g. Total the Debit and Credit columns to ensure that the two columns are equal.

h. As a final check, beginning in cell J2, compute the change in the Cash account by subtracting the beginning balance from the ending balance. The difference will equal $28,200. Also beginning in cell J24, compute the difference in the debit and credit cash entries in rows 24 through 34. The difference should also equal $28,200.

Spreadsheet Tip

(1) Darken cells by highlighting the cells to be darkened. Select Format and then Cells. Click on the tab titled Patterns and choose a color.

SPREADSHEET ANALYSIS *Preparing a Statement of Cash Flows Using the Indirect Method*   **ATC 12–7**

(*Note:* If you completed ATC 12–6, that spreadsheet can be modified to complete this problem.)

Refer to the information in Problem 12–18A. Solve for the statement of cash flows using the indirect method. Instead of using the T-account method, set up the following spreadsheet to work through the analysis. The Debit/Credit entries are very similar to the T-account method except that they are entered onto a spreadsheet. Instead of making entries on row 2 for Cash, Cash Flow entries are made beginning on row 18.

	A	B	C	D	E	F	G	H	I	J	K	L	M
1	Balance Sheet Debits:	2,003		Debit		Credit	2,004						
2	Cash	40,600					68,800			Change in Cash =	28,200		
3	Accounts Receivable	22,000	(c)	8,000			30,000	Balance					
4	Inventory	176,000					160,000	Off					
5	Prepaid Rent	4,800					2,400	Off					
6	Equipment	288,000					256,000	Off					
7	Land	80,000					192,000	Off					
8	Total Debits	611,400					709,200						
9	Balance Sheet Credits:												
10	Accumulated Depreciation	236,000			(b)	22,800	146,800	Off					
11	Accounts Payable (Inv.)	76,000					67,000	Off					
12	Salaries Payable	24,000					28,000	Off					
13	Common Stock, $25 Par	200,000					250,000	Off					
14	Retained Earnings	75,400			(a)	142,000	217,400	Balance					
15	Total Credits	611,400					709,200						
16	Statement of Cash Flows												
17	Cash Flows from Operating Activities												
18	Net Income		(a)	142,000						Difference in Cash Debit			
19	Plus Noncash Charges									and Credit Entries =			
20	Depreciation Expense		(b)	22,800									
21	Changes in Current Assets & Liab.												
22	Increase in Accounts Receivable				(c)	8,000							
23	Decrease in Inventory												
24	Decrease in Prepaid Rent												
25	Decrease in Accounts Payable												
26	Increase in Salaries Payable												
27	Cash Flows from Investing Activities												
28	Outflow to purchase land												
29	Outflow to purchase equipment												
30	Inflow from sale of equipment												
31	Cash Flows from Financing Activities												
32	Inflow from stock issue												
33	Total Debit and Credit Columns			172,800		172,800							
34													
35													

Sheet tabs: Problem 12-2 Answer Key / Problem / Sheet2 / Sheet3

H3 formula: =IF(B3+D3-F3=G3,"Balance","Off")

Required

a. Enter information in Column A.

b. Enter the beginning balance sheet amounts in Column B and ending balances in Column G. Total the debits and credits for each column.

c. To prevent erroneous entries to Cash in row 2, darken the area in Columns C through F.

d. Record the entry for Net Income. This is entry (a) provided.

e. Record the entry for Depreciation expense. This is entry (b) provided.

f. Record the entries for the changes in current assets and liabilities. The entry for the change in Accounts Receivable has been provided and is referenced as entry (c).

g. Record the four entries from the Other Information provided in Problem 12–18A. These are the investing and financing activities.

h. In Column H set up the IF function to determine whether the balance sheet accounts are in balance or not ("off"). Cell H3 for Accounts Receivable is provided for you. Cell H3 can be copied to all the balance sheet debit accounts. The balance sheet credit account formulas will differ given the different debit/credit rules for those accounts. *When the word "Balance" is reflected in every balance sheet cell in column H, the spreadsheet analysis is complete.*

i. Total the Debit and Credit columns to ensure that the two columns are equal.

j. As a final check, beginning in cell J2, compute the change in the Cash account by subtracting the beginning balance from the ending balance. The difference will equal $28,200. Also beginning in cell J18, compute the difference in the debit and credit cash entries in rows 18 through 32. The difference should also equal $28,200.

Accessing the EDGAR Database Through the Internet

Successful business managers need many different skills, including communication, interpersonal, computer, and analytical. Most business students become very aware of the data analysis skills used in accounting, but they may not be as aware of the importance of "data-finding" skills. There are many sources of accounting and financial data. The more sources you are able to use, the better.

One very important source of accounting information is the EDGAR database. Others are probably available at your school through the library or business school network. Your accounting instructor will be able to identify these for you and make suggestions regarding their use. By making the effort to learn to use electronic databases, you will enhance your abilities as a future manager and your marketability as a business graduate.

These instructions assume that you know how to access and use an Internet navigator, such as Netscape. After you activate the Navigator program on your computer, follow the instructions to retrieve data from the Securities and Exchange Commission's EDGAR database. Be aware that the SEC may have changed its interface since this appendix was written. Accordingly, be prepared for slight differences between the following instructions and what appears on your computer screen. Take comfort in the fact that changes are normally designed to simplify user access. If you encounter a conflict between the following instructions and the instructions provided in the SEC interface, remember that the SEC interface is more current and should take precedence over the following instructions.

1. To connect to EDGAR, type in the following address: **http://www.sec.gov/.**
2. After the SEC home page appears, under the heading **Filings & Forms (EDGAR),** click on **Search for Company Filings.**
3. From the screen that appears, click on **Quick Forms Lookup.**
4. On the screen that appears, type in the name of the company whose 10-K you wish to retrieve in the window near the top of the page.
5. On this same screen, in the window near the bottom of the page labeled **Common,** click on the downward-pointing scrolling arrow. From the list of forms that appear, click on **10-K,** and then click on the **Search** button on the bottom-right corner of the page.
6. Depending on the company, you may be given a choice of **[text]** or **[html]** file format. If you choose the [html] format, choose the one labeled **(TYPE) 10-K** from the list of documents that appears.
7. Next, you will get a screen listing companies with names exactly like or similar to the one you entered and the 10-Ks or related forms available for those companies. Choose the form you wish to retrieve, paying attention to the date of the accounting period to which the different forms relate. Usually, you will want the most recent form. (*Note:* The basic 10-K form has several variations, such as the 10-K/A. If there is more than one 10-K type of form for the accounting period in which you are interested, retrieve the form with the most recent *filing* date. If this form does not contain the data you want, go back and try another 10-K type of form.)
8. Once the 10-K has been retrieved, you can search it online or save it on your hard drive or diskette. If you want to save it, do so by using the **Save As** command from the pulldown menu at the top of the screen named **File.** The file will be saved as an ASCII text file that can be accessed using most word processing programs.

9. The financial statements are seldom located near the beginning of a company's 10-K, so it is necessary to scroll down the file until you find them. Typically, they are located about one-half to three-fourths of the way through the report.

10. Good luck! If you have never used the Internet before, you will find that it contains an incredible amount of stuff. Some of this stuff, such as the EDGAR database, actually contains useful information. However, you will also find that the Internet is often very slow and frustrating, especially during the middle of business days. Using EDGAR during off-hours is more enjoyable and efficient.

UNITED STATES
SECURITIES AND EXCHANGE COMMISSION
Washington, D.C. 20549

Form 10-K

**ANNUAL REPORT PURSUANT TO SECTION 13 OR 15(d) OF THE
SECURITIES EXCHANGE ACT OF 1934**

For the Fiscal Year Ended February 2, 2001

Commission File Number: 0-17017

Dell Computer Corporation
(Exact name of registrant as specified in its charter)

Delaware	**74-2487834**
(State or other jurisdiction of incorporation or organization)	(I.R.S. Employer Identification No.)

807 Las Cimas Parkway, Building 2, Austin, Texas 78746
(Address, including Zip Code, of registrant's principal executive offices)

(512) 338-4400
(Registrant's telephone number, including area code)

Securities Registered Pursuant to Section 12(g) of the Act:

Common Stock, par value $.01 per share
Preferred Stock Purchase Rights

Indicate by check mark whether the registrant (1) has filed all reports required to be filed by Section 13 or 15(d) of the Securities Exchange Act of 1934 during the preceding 12 months (or for such shorter period that the registrant was required to file such reports), and (2) has been subject to such filing requirements for the past 90 days.   Yes ☒   No ☐

Indicate by check mark if disclosure of delinquent filers pursuant to Item 405 of Regulation S-K is not contained herein, and will not be contained, to the best of registrant's knowledge, in definitive proxy or information statements incorporated by reference in Part III of this Form 10-K or any amendment to this Form 10-K.   ☐

**Aggregate market value of common stock held by non-affiliates of the
  registrant as of April 24, 2001** **$59,238,525,534**
Number of shares of common stock outstanding as of April 24, 2001 . . . . **2,611,286,980**

DOCUMENTS INCORPORATED BY REFERENCE

The information required by Part III of this Report, to the extent not set forth herein, is incorporated by reference from the Registrant's definitive proxy statement relating to the annual meeting of stockholders to be held in July 2001, which definitive proxy statement will be filed with the Securities and Exchange Commission within 120 days after the end of the fiscal year to which this Report relates.

Statements in this Report that relate to future results and events are based on the Company's current expectations. Actual results in future periods may differ materially from those currently expected or desired because of a number of risks and uncertainties. For a discussion of factors affecting the Company's business and prospects, see "Item 1 — Business — Factors Affecting the Company's Business and Prospects."

PART I

ITEM 1 — BUSINESS

General

Dell Computer Corporation (the "Company") is the world's largest direct computer systems company and a premier provider of products and services for customers to build their information-technology and Internet infrastructures. The Company's revenue for fiscal year 2001 was $31.9 billion. In April 2001, the Company took the lead as the world's number one computer system company, based on global market share estimates. The Company was founded in 1984 by Michael Dell on a simple concept: by selling personal computer systems directly to customers, the Company could best understand their needs, and efficiently provide the most effective computing solutions to meet those needs. With its direct relationships, the Company strives to make it easier for customers to choose, purchase and support their computing environments. Today, the Company is enhancing and broadening the fundamental competitive advantages of its direct model by increasingly applying the efficiencies of the Internet to its entire business. Approximately half of the Company's sales are Web-enabled, approximately half of the Company's technical support activities occur online and approximately three-quarters of the Company's order-status transactions occur online.

The Dell™ line of high-performance computer systems includes PowerEdge™ servers, PowerApp™ server appliances, PowerVault™ storage products, Dell Precision™ workstations, Latitude™ and Inspiron™ notebook computers, and OptiPlex™ and Dimension™ desktop computers. The Company arranges for system installation and management, guides customers through technology transitions and provides an extensive range of other services. The Company designs and customizes products and services to the requirements of its customers, and sells an extensive selection of peripheral hardware, including handheld products, and computing software. The Company sells its products and services to large corporate, government, healthcare and education customers, small-to-medium businesses and individuals.

The Company is a Delaware corporation that was incorporated in October 1987, succeeding to the business of a predecessor Texas corporation that was originally incorporated in May 1984. Based in Austin, Texas, the Company conducts operations worldwide through wholly owned subsidiaries. See "Item 1 — Business — Geographic Areas of Operations." Unless otherwise specified, references herein to the Company are references to the Company and its consolidated subsidiaries. The Company operates principally in one industry segment.

The Company's common stock, par value $.01 per share, is listed on The Nasdaq National Market under the symbol DELL. See "Item 5 — Market for Registrant's Common Equity and Related Stockholder Matters — Market Information."

Business Strategy

The Company's business strategy is based on its direct business model. The Company's business model seeks to deliver a superior customer experience through direct, comprehensive customer relationships, cooperative research and development with technology partners, computer systems custom-built to customer specifications and service and support programs tailored to customer needs.

The Company believes that the direct model provides it with several distinct competitive advantages. The direct model eliminates the need to support an extensive network of wholesale and retail dealers, thereby avoiding dealer mark-ups; avoids the higher inventory costs associated with the wholesale/retail channel and the competition for retail shelf space; and reduces the high risk of obsolescence associated with products in a rapidly changing technological market. In addition, the direct model allows the Company to maintain, monitor and update a customer database that can be used to shape future product offerings and post-sale service and support programs. This direct approach, combined with the Company's efficient procurement, manufacturing and distribution processes, allows the Company to rapidly deliver relevant technology to its customers.

The Company believes that it has significant opportunities for continued growth. While the Company believes that its business strategy provides it with competitive advantages, there are many factors that may affect the Company's business and the success of its operations. For a discussion of these factors, see "Item 1 — Business — Factors Affecting the Company's Business and Prospects."

The Internet

The Company is committed to refining and extending the advantages of its direct model approach by moving even greater volumes of product sales, service and support to the Internet. The Company receives in excess of 500 million page visits per quarter at *www.dell.com*, where it maintains approximately 80 country-specific sites. According to Nielsen/Net Ratings, during the December 2000 holiday season, *www.dell.com* was the third most visited web site in the United States. The Company also develops custom Internet sites, called Premier Pages™, for various corporate and institutional customers, allowing these customers to simplify and accelerate procurement and support processes. Through these custom sites, the Company offers the customer paperless purchase orders, approved product configurations, global pricing, real-time order tracking, purchasing history and account team information. The Company currently provides more than 60,000 Premier Pages worldwide. The Company also provides an online virtual account executive for its small business customers. And, for all domestic customers, the Company provides a spare-parts ordering system, and a virtual help desk featuring natural-language search capabilities and direct access to technical support data.

Comprehensive Customer Relationships

The Company develops and utilizes direct customer relationships to understand end-users' needs and to deliver high quality computer products and services tailored to meet those needs. For large corporate and institutional customers, the Company works with the customer prior to the sale to plan a strategy to meet that customer's current and future technology needs. After the sale, the Company continues the direct relationship by establishing account teams, consisting of sales, customer service and technical personnel, dedicated to the Company's large corporate and institutional customers. The Company also establishes direct relationships with small-to-medium businesses and individuals through account representatives, telephone sales representatives or Internet contact. These direct customer relationships provide the Company with a constant flow of information about its customers' plans and requirements and enable the Company to weigh its customers' needs against emerging technologies.

Cooperative Research and Development

The Company has successfully developed cooperative, working relationships with many of the world's most advanced technology companies. Working with these companies, the Company's engineers manage quality, integrate technologies and design and manage system architecture. This cooperative approach allows the Company to determine the best method and timing for delivering new technologies to the market. The Company's goal is to quickly and efficiently deliver the latest relevant technology to its customers.

2

Custom-Built Computer Systems

The direct model is based on the principle that delivering custom-built computer systems is the best business model for providing solutions that are truly relevant to end-user needs. This concept, together with the Company's flexible, build-to-order manufacturing process, enables the Company to achieve faster inventory turnover and reduced inventory levels and allows the Company to rapidly incorporate new technologies and components into its product offerings.

Custom-Tailored Service and Support Programs

In the same way that the Company's computer products are built-to-order, service and support programs are designed to fit specific customer requirements. The Company offers a broad range of service and support programs through its own technical personnel and its direct management of specialized service suppliers. These services range from online support to onsite customer-dedicated systems engineers.

Geographic Areas of Operations

The Company conducts operations worldwide and is managed on a geographic basis, with three geographic segments being the Americas, Europe, and Asia-Pacific and Japan regions. The Americas segment, which is based in Round Rock, Texas, covers the U.S., Canada, South America and Latin America. The European segment, which is based in Bracknell, England, covers the European countries and also some countries in the Middle East and Africa. The Asia-Pacific and Japan segment covers the Pacific Rim, including Japan, Australia and New Zealand, and is based in Singapore. See "Item 1 — Business — Factors Affecting the Company's Business and Prospects — International Activities" for information about certain risks of international activities.

The Company's corporate headquarters are located in Austin, Texas. Its manufacturing facilities are located in or around Austin, Texas; Nashville, Tennessee; Eldorado do Sul, Brazil; Limerick, Ireland; Penang, Malaysia; and Xiamen, China. See "Item 2 — Properties."

For financial information about the results of the Company's operating segments for each of the last three fiscal years, see Note 10 of Notes to Consolidated Financial Statements included in "Item 8 — Financial Statements and Supplementary Data."

During fiscal year 2001, the Company opened new manufacturing facilities in Nashville, Tennessee and Xiamen, China. The Company also opened a call center in Nashville, Tennessee and additional office and research and development space in Austin, Texas.

Products and Services

The Company's product offerings include: Dimension and OptiPlex desktop computers, Latitude and Inspiron notebook computers, PowerEdge servers, PowerApp server appliances, PowerVault storage products, and Dell Precision workstations. The Company has also continued to broaden its revenue base beyond the core systems, commonly referred to as "beyond the box" revenues. These offerings include warranty services, product integration and installation services, Internet access, ReadyWare™, DellWare™, peripherals, technology consulting and other offerings.

Enterprise Systems

Servers — The Company offers two lines of server products. The PowerEdge line of servers consists of systems that can operate as file servers, database servers, applications servers and communications/groupware servers in a networked computing environment. The PowerEdge SC family of servers was announced in the first quarter of fiscal year 2002 and is designed for high growth small business and small corporate local area network and branch office environments. PowerApp appliance servers, introduced in the first quarter of fiscal year 2001, are specialized servers that target Web hosting and network traffic management needs of Internet service

3

providers, dot-coms and other companies that are developing or enhancing their Internet infrastructures. According to International Data Corporation ("IDC"), based on preliminary first quarter calendar year 2001 data, the Company ranked number one in the United States for standard Intel architecture server shipments. The Company ranked number two in the United States and worldwide for server shipments, based on calendar year 2000 data. In fiscal 2001, the Company achieved a 39% unit-shipment growth in servers, the fastest among the industry's ten largest companies.

Storage — The Company's PowerVault storage offerings are designed to standardize and simplify storage solutions for customers who need complete, affordable storage systems without sacrificing enterprise capabilities. The Company offers a comprehensive portfolio of hardware, software and services for server-attached storage, Storage Area Networks (SAN), and Network-Attached Storage (NAS), targeted at small businesses, as well as workgroups and data centers within enterprises. The Company's products include SCSI and Fibre-channel based disk systems, tape backup systems, SAN and NAS appliances, as well as complimentary storage management software to simplify administration and minimize related costs. Based on calendar year 2000 IDC data, the Company ranked number six worldwide in storage revenue.

Workstations — The Dell Precision workstation product line is intended for professional users who demand exceptional performance to run sophisticated applications, such as computer-aided design, digital content creation, geographic information systems, computer animation, software development and financial analysis. According to IDC, the Dell Precision workstation product line held the number one worldwide market share position in calendar year 2000.

Notebook Computers

The Company offers two lines of notebook computer systems. The Latitude line provides large corporate, government and education customers with reliability, stability and superior battery performance for complex networked environments. The Inspiron line is targeted to home and small business users who require the latest technology and high-end multimedia performance. The Company ranked number one in U.S. and number four in worldwide notebook computer shipments in calendar year 2000, according to IDC.

Desktop Computers

The Company offers two lines of desktop computer systems. OptiPlex desktop computers are designed for corporate and institutional customers who require highly reliable systems within networked environments. Dimension desktop computers are designed for small businesses and home users requiring fast technology turns and high-performance computing. According to IDC, the Company ranked number one in U.S. desktop shipments and number two in worldwide desktop shipments in calendar year 2000.

Beyond the Box Products and Services

The Company maintains a variety of software and accessory programs to complement its systems offerings. Through these programs, the Company offers nearly 30,000 competitively priced software and peripheral products from leading manufacturers. The DellWare line of software and peripherals is a single source solution for customers. DellWare offerings include memory upgrades, printers, monitors and software, all of which is available online through *www.dell.com.* The Company's custom factory integration program provides installation and configuration of customer hardware and software, asset tagging and labeling. Through the ReadyWare program, the Company offers factory-installed off-the-shelf software applications. Additionally, the Company offers a wide array of handheld products.

The Company enhances its product offerings with a number of specialized services, including custom hardware and software integration, leasing and asset management, server and storage consulting services, network installation and support and onsite service. The Company's direct relationships with customers and its extensive online capabilities via *www.dell.com* enhance service delivery. The Company is further developing its service capabilities with Internet-based services

4

designed to enhance the customer experience. For additional discussion of the Company's service and support programs, see "Item 1 — Business — Service and Support."

Compared to fiscal year 2000, beyond the box revenues increased 37%, representing 18% of net revenues during fiscal 2001. Beyond the box revenues include $2.5 billion and $1.8 billion of worldwide services revenue in fiscal years 2001 and 2000, respectively.

Sales and Marketing

The Company's customers range from large corporations, government agencies and healthcare and educational institutions to small businesses and individuals. In general, the Company uses similar sales and marketing approaches across all customer groups, as demand levels for each customer group are principally driven by similar changes in market prices and overall general economic conditions. Within each region, the Company has divided its sales and marketing forces among the various customer groups to better meet each customer group's specific needs. No single customer accounted for more than 10% of the Company's consolidated net revenues during any of the last three fiscal years.

Relationship Customers

The Company has established a broad range of business based on continuing relationships with large corporations, governmental, healthcare and educational institutions and small-to-medium businesses. The Company maintains a field sales force throughout the world to call on business and institutional customers and prospects. The Company develops marketing programs and services specifically geared to these relationship customers. Dedicated account teams, which include field based system engineers and consultants, form long-term customer relationships to provide each customer with a single source of assistance on various issues, including technology needs assessment and technical evaluation of Dell products; system configuration; image development order placement; lifecycle cost management; technology transition planning; installation assistance and project management; and detailed product, service and financial reporting. For customers with in-house maintenance organizations, the Company offers a variety of programs, including specialized computer training programs, a repair parts assistance program and other customized programs to provide access to the Company's technical support team. The Company also offers customized product delivery and service programs. See "Item 1 — Business — Service and Support."

For multinational corporate customers, the Company offers several programs designed to provide global capability, support and coordination. Through these programs, the Company can provide single points of contact and accountability with global account specialists, special global pricing, consistent service and support programs across global regions and access to central purchasing facilities.

The Company also maintains specific sales and marketing programs targeted at federal, state and local governmental agencies. The Company maintains account teams dedicated to specific governmental and educational markets.

Transactional Customers

The Company has established a significant base of business among small-to-medium businesses and individual customers. The Company markets its products and services to these customers by advertising on the Internet and television, in trade and general business publications and by mailing a broad range of direct marketing publications, such as promotional pieces, catalogs and customer newsletters. The Company believes these customers value its ability to provide reliable, custom-built computer systems at competitive prices, while offering knowledgeable sales assistance, post-sale support and a variety of service offerings.

Internet Customers

A significant portion of the Company's business is being conducted via the Internet. Through the Company's World Wide Web site at *www.dell.com*, both relationship and transactional customers as well as potential customers can access a wide range of information about the Company's product and service offerings, configure and purchase systems online and access volumes of support and technical information.

Leasing and Asset Management Services

Dell Financial Services L.P. ("DFS"), a joint venture between the Company and The CIT Group, offers leasing and other financial services to the Company's customers. For additional information about DFS, see Note 8 of Notes to Consolidated Financial Statements included in "Item 8 — Financial Statements and Supplementary Data."

Service and Support

The Company provides a basic limited warranty and technical support and offers a full line of warranty, service and support options in all of its geographic markets. These options vary in each of the countries in which the Company does business based on local market and customer requirements. The following is a description of the warranties, service and support generally available to the Company's customers in the United States.

Technical Support and Warranty Programs

The Company provides a basic limited warranty, including parts and labor, for all computer systems for a period ranging from one to three years. The Company offers additional warranties based upon the particular product offered and customer needs.

The Company also provides free, telephone-based 24-hour technical support, as well as online technical support over the Internet. During the second half of fiscal 2001, the Company announced that the Dell Solution Center™, a collection of online technical support and learning services, would become standard on the Company's consumer and small business line of Inspiron notebooks and Dimension desktop computers. The Dell Solution Center, which appears as an icon on a customer's computer screen, is a package of Web-based troubleshooting tools and educational offerings designed to make computers easier to use. It includes the Company's comprehensive e-support software and hardware diagnostic tool, Resolution Assistant™, which connects users directly to the Company's support technicians through the Internet. Alternatively, customers can access *www.support.dell.com*, a customized home page for each customer with information specific to their computer. For technical questions about a system, customers can also use the Company's natural language technical support tool, Ask Dudley™.

Additional Options

The Company offers customers the opportunity to purchase additional customized services and support programs through a wide selection of options. For example, PowerEdge server customers may choose to extend their basic limited warranty contracts to include up to four additional years of next-business-day, onsite service. Additionally, customers may choose same-day or two-, four- or six-hour response service offerings. Notebook computer owners have access to service and support in a multitude of countries in which the Company conducts business, in the event a notebook customer is in need of service or support while traveling outside of that customer's home country.

The Company recently announced the creation of Premier Enterprise Services™, a comprehensive portfolio of enterprise-level service offerings. Premier Enterprise Services consists of three distinct programs: Premier Enterprise Consulting™, Premier Enterprise Deployment™ and Premier Enter-

6

prise Support™. Premier Enterprise Consulting allows customers to leverage the Company's expertise in planning, building and optimizing scalable enterprise infrastructures through services provided by Dell Technology Consulting™. Other service offerings include design and on-site implementation of complex storage systems, enterprise hardware training and tuning and proof-of-concept services in the Company's Technology Solution Centers™. Premier Enterprise Deployment tailors systems to specific customer requirements by integrating custom-configured hardware and software into the Company's manufacturing process, coordinating delivery and managing all aspects of an on-site installation. Premier Enterprise Support includes engineer-to-engineer support, technical account management, and seamless single-point-of-accountability support for issue resolution of leading enterprise software applications. These services are currently available in the United States and Canada and the Company plans to expand these services to international customers.

The Company's Premier Access™ program includes a service and support program specifically designed for information systems professionals who have technical expertise in diagnosing and servicing computer systems. Customers can choose their level of service under the program, including rapid service and parts dispatches, direct access to advanced level technical support, specialized online support, reimbursement for certain labor costs and parts management assistance.

The Company also offers specialized custom factory integration services designed to address specific hardware and software integration requirements of customers. These services allow the Company to satisfy a customer's particular integration requirements (whether hardware related, such as specialized network cards, video and graphic boards, modems, tape drives or hard drives; or software related, such as customer proprietary software applications or drivers) at the time the customer's systems are manufactured. This is in addition to the Company's ReadyWare program, a collection of popular software applications and interface cards that can be factory-installed.

The Company also offers a variety of onsite installation services that can be customized to meet the needs of each specific customer. These services include basic installation and orientation, system connectivity and functional testing, external peripheral installation, internal device installation and file server and advanced system installation.

Consulting Services

Through Dell Technology Consulting, the Company offers professional consulting services to help customers select and implement server and storage solutions. The Company provides consulting services in connection with systems management design and implementation, E-commerce consulting, storage planning, storage consolidation, storage performance and tuning and backup and recovery planning. The Company can also draw upon a network of established relationships with a variety of nationally recognized specialty consulting firms.

Manufacturing

The Company operates manufacturing facilities in and around Austin, Texas; Eldorado do Sul, Brazil; Nashville, Tennessee; Limerick, Ireland; Penang, Malaysia; and Xiamen, China. The Company's manufacturing process consists of assembly, functional testing and quality control of the Company's computer systems. Testing and quality control processes are also applied to components, parts and subassemblies obtained from suppliers. The Company's build-to-order manufacturing process is designed to allow the Company to quickly produce customized computer systems and to achieve rapid inventory turnover and reduced inventory levels, which lessens the Company's exposure to the risk of declining inventory values. This flexible manufacturing process also allows the Company to incorporate new technologies or components into its product offerings quickly.

Quality control is maintained through the testing of components, parts and subassemblies at various stages in the manufacturing process. Quality control also includes a burn-in period for completed units after assembly, on-going production reliability audits, failure tracking for early identification of production and component problems and information from the Company's customers obtained through service and support programs. The Company conducts a voluntary vendor certification program, under which qualified vendors commit to meet defined quality specifications. All of the Company's manufacturing facilities have been certified as meeting ISO 9002 quality standards.

Product Development

The Company's product development efforts are focused on designing and developing competitively priced computer systems that adhere to industry standards and incorporate the technologies and features that the Company believes are most desired by its customers. To accomplish this objective, the Company must evaluate, obtain and incorporate new hardware, software, storage, communications and peripherals technologies that are primarily developed by others. The Company's product development team includes programmers, technical project managers and engineers experienced in system architecture, logic board design, sub-system development, mechanical engineering, manufacturing processing and operating systems. This cross-functional approach to product design has enabled the Company to develop systems with improved functionality, manufacturability, reliability, serviceability and performance, while keeping costs competitive. The Company takes steps to ensure that new products are compatible with industry standards and that they meet cost objectives based on competitive pricing targets.

The Company bases its product development efforts on cooperative, meaningful relationships with the world's most advanced technology companies. These working partnerships allow the Company to use its direct model and build-to-order manufacturing process to deliver, on a timely and cost-effective basis, those emerging technologies that are most relevant to its customers.

During fiscal year 2001, the Company incurred $482 million in research, development and engineering expenses, compared with $374 million (excluding $194 million of acquired in-process research and development) for fiscal year 2000 and $272 million for fiscal year 1999. The amount the Company spends on research, development and engineering activities, which the Company believes to be important to its continued success and growth, is determined as part of the annual budget process and is based on cost-benefit analyses and revenue forecasts. The Company prioritizes activities to focus on projects that it believes will have the greatest market acceptance and achieve the highest return on the Company's investment.

Dell Ventures

Through Dell Ventures, the Company makes strategic investments in technology companies located in the United States and abroad. These investments are designed to assist the Company in gaining greater access to leading-edge technologies and services, expanded markets for the Company's products, insight into new markets and financial return. The Company generally invests in privately held emerging technology companies with business objectives built around the Internet, services, server and storage products, and communications. See "Item 1 — Business — Factors Affecting the Company's Business and Prospects — Equity Investments" for information about certain risks associated with Dell Ventures. For additional information about risk on financial instruments, see "Item 7 — Management's Discussion and Analysis of Financial Condition and Results of Operations — Market Risk."

Patents, Trademarks and Licenses

The Company holds a portfolio of 605 U.S. patents and 512 U.S. patent applications pending, and has a number of related foreign patents and patent applications pending. The Company's U.S. patents expire in years 2005 through 2018. The inventions claimed in those patents and patent applications cover aspects of the Company's current and possible future computer system products, manufacturing processes and related technologies. The Company is developing a portfolio of patents that it anticipates will be of value in negotiating intellectual property rights with others in the industry.

The Company has obtained U.S. federal trademark registration for its DELL word mark and its Dell logo mark. The Company owns registrations for 34 of its other marks in the U.S. As of March 1, 2001, the Company had pending applications for registration of 48 other trademarks. The DELL word mark, Dell logo and other trademark and service mark registrations in the U.S. may be renewed as long as the mark continues to be used in interstate commerce. The Company believes that establishment of the DELL mark and logo in the U.S. is material to the Company's operations. The Company has also applied for or obtained registration of the DELL mark and several other marks in approximately 170 other countries or jurisdictions where the Company conducts or anticipates expanding its international business. The Company has also registered approximately 700 global domain names. In addition, the Company has registered in excess of 300 country-specific domain names. The Company has also taken steps to reserve corporate names and to form non-operating subsidiaries in certain foreign countries where the Company anticipates expanding its international business.

The Company has entered into a variety of intellectual property licensing and cross-licensing agreements. In addition, the Company has entered into nonexclusive licensing agreements with Microsoft Corporation for various operating system and application software. The Company has also entered into various software licensing agreements with other companies.

From time to time, other companies and individuals assert exclusive patent, copyright, trademark or other intellectual property rights to technologies or marks that are important to the technology industry or the Company's business. The Company evaluates each claim relating to its products and, if appropriate, seeks a license to use the protected technology. The licensing agreements generally do not require the licensor to assist the Company in duplicating its patented technology nor do these agreements protect the Company from trade secret, copyright or other violations by the Company or its suppliers in developing or selling these products. See "Item 1 — Business — Factors Affecting the Company's Business and Prospects — Patent Rights" for information about intellectual property risks.

Infrastructure

Management Information Systems

The Company's management information systems enable the Company to track each unit sold from the initial sales contact, through the manufacturing process to post-sale service and support. The systems assist the Company in tracking key information about customer needs. Using its database to assess customer trends, the Company targets marketing activities specifically to particular types of customers. This database, unique to the Company's direct model, allows the Company to gauge customer satisfaction issues and also provides the opportunity to test new propositions in the marketplace prior to product or service introductions.

Employees

On February 2, 2001, the Company had approximately 40,000 regular employees. Approximately 27,000 of those employees were located in the U.S., and approximately 13,000 were located in other countries. The Company has never experienced a work stoppage due to labor difficulties and believes that its employee relations are good.

Government Regulation

The Company's business is subject to regulation by various federal and state governmental agencies. Such regulation includes the radio frequency emission regulatory activities of the U.S. Federal Communications Commission, the anti-trust regulatory activities of the U.S. Federal Trade Commission and Department of Justice, the import/export regulatory activities of the U.S. Department of Commerce and the product safety regulatory activities of the U.S. Consumer Products Safety Commission.

The Company also is required to obtain regulatory approvals in other countries prior to the sale or shipment of products. In certain jurisdictions, such requirements are more stringent than in the U.S. Many developing nations are just beginning to establish safety, environmental and other regulatory requirements, which may vary greatly from U.S. requirements.

Backlog

The Company does not believe that backlog is a meaningful indicator of sales that can be expected for any period, and there can be no assurance that the backlog at any point in time will translate into sales in any subsequent period. At the end of fiscal year 2001, 2000, and 1999, backlog was not material.

Factors Affecting the Company's Business and Prospects

There are many factors that affect the Company's business and the results of its operations, some of which are beyond the control of the Company. The following is a description of some of the important factors that may cause the actual results of the Company's operations in future periods to differ materially from those currently expected or desired.

General economic and industry conditions

Any general economic, business or industry conditions that cause customers or potential customers to reduce or delay their investments in computer systems could have a material adverse effect on the Company's business, prospects and financial performance. Worldwide economic conditions could have an effect on the demand for the Company's products and could result in declining revenue and earnings growth rates for the Company.

Competition

The Company encounters aggressive competition in all aspects of its business. The Company competes on the basis of price, technology availability, performance, quality, reliability, service and support. The Company believes that it can maintain profitability by reducing operating expenses and by continuing to leverage its lean inventory model to rapidly realize the benefit of component price declines. However, there can be no assurance that the Company can successfully continue to manage its operating expenses to mitigate declines in gross margins.

International activities

Sales outside of the United States accounted for approximately 33% of the Company's revenues in fiscal year 2001. The Company's future growth rates and success are dependent on continued growth and success in international markets. As is the case with most international operations, the success and profitability of the Company's international operations are subject to numerous risks and uncertainties, including local economic and labor conditions, political instability, unexpected changes in the regulatory environment, trade protection measures, tax laws (including U.S. taxes on foreign operations) and foreign currency exchange rates.

Product, customer and geographic mix

The profit margins realized by the Company vary somewhat among its products, customers and geographic markets. Consequently, the overall profitability of the Company's operations in any given period is partially dependent on the product, customer and geographic mix reflected in that period's revenues.

Seasonal trends

The Company experiences some seasonal trends in the sale of its products. For example, sales to governments (particularly U.S. federal sales) are often stronger in the Company's third quarter, European sales are often weaker in the third quarter and consumer sales are often stronger in the fourth quarter. Historically, the net result of seasonal trends has not been material relative to the Company's overall results of operations, but many of the factors that create and affect seasonal trends are beyond the Company's control.

Technological changes and product transitions

The technology industry is characterized by continuing improvements in technology, which results in the frequent introduction of new products, short product life cycles and continual improvement in product price/performance characteristics. While the Company believes that its direct model and asset management practices afford it an inherent competitive advantage over some of its competitors, product transitions present some of the greatest executional challenges and risks for any computer systems company. A failure on the part of the Company to effectively manage a product transition will directly affect the demand for the Company's products and the profitability of the Company's operations. In addition, while the Company has meaningful relationships with some of the world's most advanced technology companies, continuing technological advancement, which is a significant driver of customer demand, is largely beyond the control of the Company.

Inventory management/supplies

The Company's direct business model gives it the ability to operate with reduced levels of component and finished goods inventories, and the Company's financial success in recent periods has been due in part to its asset management practices, including its ability to achieve rapid inventory turns. However, temporary disruptions in component availability can unfavorably affect the Company's short-term performance. Supply conditions have generally been favorable both to the Company and to the industry in recent years. However, less favorable supply conditions, as well as other factors, may require or result in increased inventory levels in the future.

The Company's manufacturing process requires a high volume of quality components that are procured from third party suppliers. Reliance on suppliers, as well as industry supply conditions, generally involves several risks, including the possibility of defective parts (which can adversely affect the reliability and reputation of the Company's products), a shortage of components and reduced control over delivery schedules (which can adversely affect the Company's manufacturing efficiencies) and increases in component costs (which can adversely affect the Company's profitability).

The Company has several single-sourced supplier relationships, either because alternative sources are not available or the relationship is advantageous due to performance, quality, support, delivery, capacity or price considerations. If these sources are unable to provide timely and reliable supply, the Company could experience manufacturing interruptions, delays or inefficiencies, adversely affecting its results of operations. Even where alternative sources of supply are available, qualification of the alternative suppliers and establishment of reliable supplies could result in delays and a possible loss of sales, which could affect operating results adversely.

Risk on financial instruments

The Company regularly utilizes derivative instruments to hedge its exposure to fluctuations in foreign currency exchange rates and interest rates. In addition, the Company utilizes equity instrument contracts to execute repurchases of its common stock under its Board-authorized stock repurchase program. Some of these instruments and contracts may involve elements of market and credit risk in excess of the amounts recognized in the Consolidated Financial Statements. For additional information about risk on financial instruments, see "Item 7 — Management's Discussion and Analysis of Financial Condition and Results of Operations — Market Risk."

Strength of infrastructure

The Company's continued success and profitability partly depends on its ability to continue to improve its infrastructure (particularly personnel and information systems) in order to increase operational efficiencies.

Patent rights

The Company's continued business success may be largely dependent on its ability to obtain licenses to intellectual property developed by others on commercially reasonable and competitive terms. If the Company or its suppliers are unable to obtain desirable technology licenses, the Company could be prohibited from marketing products, could be forced to market products without desirable features or could incur substantial costs to redesign its products, defend legal actions or pay damages.

Equity investments

The Company has an active venture capital program, through which the Company makes strategic equity investments primarily in privately held technology companies. See "Item 1 — Business — Dell Ventures." Because these companies are typically early-stage ventures with either unproven business models, products that are not yet fully developed or products that have not yet achieved market acceptance, these investments are inherently risky. Many factors outside of the Company's control determine whether or not the Company's investments will be successful. Such factors include the ability of a company to obtain additional private equity financing, to access the public capital markets, to effect a sale or merger, or to achieve commercial success with its products or services. Accordingly, there can be no assurances that any of the Company's investments will be successful or that the Company will be able to recover the amount invested.

Trademarks and Service Marks

Unless otherwise noted trademarks appearing in this Report are trademarks of the Company. The Company disclaims proprietary interest in the marks and names of others.

Executive Officers of the Company

The following table sets forth the name, age and position of each of the persons who were serving as executive officers of the Company as of May 1, 2001.

Name	Age	Title
Michael S. Dell	36	Chairman of the Board and Chief Executive Officer
Kevin B. Rollins	48	President and Chief Operating Officer
James T. Vanderslice	60	President and Chief Operating Officer
Paul D. Bell	40	Senior Vice President, Europe, Middle East and Africa and Home and Small Business Group
Thomas B. Green	46	Senior Vice President, Law and Administration and Secretary
Michael D. Lambert	54	Senior Vice President, Enterprise Systems Group
Joseph A. Marengi	47	Senior Vice President, Relationship Group
Rosendo G. Parra	41	Senior Vice President, Home and Small Business Group
James M. Schneider	48	Senior Vice President and Chief Financial Officer

Michael S. Dell — Mr. Dell has been Chairman of the Board, Chief Executive Officer and a director of the Company since May 1984. Mr. Dell shares the Office of the Chief Executive Officer with Mr. Rollins and Dr. Vanderslice. Mr. Dell founded the Company in 1984 while attending the University of Texas at Austin. He is a member of the board of directors of the U.S. Chamber of Commerce, the Computerworld/Smithsonian Awards and the World Economic Forum Foundation. Mr. Dell is also a member of the Business Council, the World Economic Forum, the Computer Systems Policy Project, an affiliation of CEOs of the top computer companies that advocates public policy positions on trade and technology affecting the computer industry and ultimately the United States, and serves on the nominating committee for the National Technology Medal of Honor.

Kevin B. Rollins — Mr. Rollins currently serves as President and Chief Operating Officer of the Company and shares the Office of the Chief Executive Officer with Mr. Dell and Dr. Vanderslice. Mr. Rollins joined the Company in April 1996 as Senior Vice President, Corporate Strategy, was named Senior Vice President, General Manager — Americas in May 1996 and was named Vice Chairman in December 1997. In March 2001, Mr. Rollins' title was changed from Vice Chairman to President and Chief Operating Officer. For 12 years prior to joining the Company, Mr. Rollins was employed by Bain & Company, an international strategy consulting firm, most recently serving as a director and partner. Mr. Rollins received a Master of Business Administration degree and a Bachelor of Arts degree from Brigham Young University. Mr. Rollins is also a member of the National Advisory Council of Brigham Young University and a member of the CEO Forum on Education and Technology.

James T. Vanderslice — Dr. Vanderslice currently serves as President and Chief Operating Officer of the Company and shares the Office of the Chief Executive Officer with Mr. Dell and Mr. Rollins. Dr. Vanderslice joined the Company as Vice Chairman in December 1999. In March 2001, Dr Vanderslice's title was changed from Vice Chairman to President and Chief Operating Officer. Prior to joining the Company, Dr. Vanderslice served as Senior Vice President and Group Executive for IBM's Technology Group and was a member of IBM's corporate executive committee. In that role, Dr. Vanderslice was responsible for IBM's storage systems, microelectronics, networking-hardware and printer-systems division. He also provided functional guidance to the display and technology-market development units, both based in Japan. Dr. Vanderslice holds a Bachelor of Science degree in Physics from Boston College and a PhD in Physics from Catholic University.

Paul D. Bell — Mr. Bell joined the Company in July 1996 and serves as Senior Vice President, Europe, Middle East and Africa and Home and Small Business Group. In his EMEA role, he is responsible for business operations in the Company's European region, including the Company's manufacturing facilities in Limerick, Ireland. In the HSB role, he shares responsibility with Mr. Parra for all related product development, manufacturing, sales, marketing and customer-service activities for the Company's Home and Small Business Group. Prior to joining the Company, Mr. Bell was with Bain & Company, where he was a management consultant for six years, including two years as a consultant for the Company. Mr. Bell received a bachelor's degree in Fine Arts and Business Administration from Pennsylvania State University and a Master of Business Administration degree from the Yale School of Organization and Management.

Thomas B. Green — Mr. Green has served as Senior Vice President, Law and Administration since December 1997, and is responsible for overseeing the Company's legal and governmental affairs, human resources function and other administrative departments. Mr. Green joined the Company in August 1994 as General Counsel and Secretary. Before joining the Company, Mr. Green served as Executive Vice President and General Counsel of Chicago Title & Trust Company from October 1992 to July 1994, and as Executive Vice President and General Counsel of Trammell Crow Company from October 1990 to October 1992. From February 1989 to October 1990, Mr. Green was employed by the law firm of Jones, Day, Reavis & Pogue, Dallas, Texas, last serving as a partner in that firm. His background also includes a term as law clerk to former United States Supreme Court Chief Justice Warren Burger. Mr. Green received a Bachelor of Arts degree in English and a Juris Doctor degree from the University of Utah.

Michael D. Lambert — Mr. Lambert joined the Company in October 1996 as Senior Vice President, Server Group, and currently serves as Senior Vice President, Enterprise Systems Group. Mr. Lambert is responsible for worldwide development and marketing of the Company's server product lines. Prior to joining the Company, Mr. Lambert held various officer positions with Compaq Computer Corporation, last serving as Vice President of North American Marketing. Prior to joining Compaq in 1994, Mr. Lambert served four years as general manager of the large computer products division for NCR Corporation. Mr. Lambert received a bachelor's degree in Business Administration from the University of Kentucky in Lexington. Mr. Lambert serves on the board of directors of StorageNetworks, Inc.

Joseph A. Marengi — Mr. Marengi joined the Company in July 1997 and serves as Senior Vice President, Relationship Group. In this position, Mr. Marengi is responsible for the customer groups serving global, enterprise and large corporate customers. Prior to joining the Company, Mr. Marengi worked at Novell, Inc., most recently serving as President and Chief Operating Officer. He joined Novell in 1989, where he first served as Vice President of the Eastern region and ultimately became Executive Vice President of Worldwide Sales and Field Operations. For ten years prior to joining Novell, Mr. Marengi served as Vice President of Channel Sales for Excelan, Inc. and in various other executive, sales, information management positions. From 1978 through 1981, Mr. Marengi served in the United States Coast Guard and Coast Guard Reserve, reaching the rank of Lieutenant Commander. Mr. Marengi earned a bachelor's degree in Public Administration from the University of Massachusetts and a master's degree in Management from the University of Southern California.

Rosendo G. Parra — Mr. Parra joined the Company in August 1993 and serves as Senior Vice President, Home and Small Business Group. In that position, he shares responsibility with Mr. Bell for all related product development, manufacturing, sales, marketing and customer-service activities for the Company's Home and Small Business Group. Prior to joining the Company, Mr. Parra held various sales and general management positions with GRiD Systems Corporation, including Regional Sales Director and Vice President and General Manager of the PC Strategic Business Unit. Before his association with GRiD, Mr. Parra spent nine years in various sales and management positions for the business products division of Tandy Corporation. Mr. Parra earned a bachelor's degree in Marketing from the University of Maryland.

James M. Schneider — Mr. Schneider is the Company's Chief Financial Officer and also serves as the Company's Chief Accounting Officer. Mr. Schneider joined the Company in September 1996 as Vice President and Chief Accounting Officer, was named Senior Vice President in September 1998 and Chief Financial Officer in March 2000. For three years prior to joining the Company, Mr. Schneider was with MCI Communications Corporation, last serving as Senior Vice President of Corporate Finance. For 19 years prior to joining MCI, Mr. Schneider was associated with Price Waterhouse LLP, serving as a partner for 10 years. Mr. Schneider holds a bachelor's degree in Accounting from Carroll College in Waukesha, Wisconsin, and is a Certified Public Accountant. He is a member of the board of directors of General Communications, Inc.

ITEM 2 — PROPERTIES

At February 2, 2001, the Company owned or leased a total of approximately ten million square feet of office, manufacturing and warehouse space worldwide, approximately seven million square feet of which is located in the U.S. and the remainder located in various international areas.

The Company believes that it can readily obtain appropriate additional space as may be required at competitive rates by extending expiring leases or finding alternative space.

Domestic Properties

The Company's principal executive offices are located in Austin, Texas and U.S. manufacturing facilities are located in Central Texas and Middle Tennessee.

The Company owns 360 acres of land in Round Rock, Texas (north of Austin), on which are located several office buildings completed since August 1994 that contain an aggregate of approximately 2.2 million square feet of office space. This includes approximately 900,000 square feet of owned office buildings and 1.3 million square feet of leased office space. These buildings, comprising the Company's Round Rock Campus, house the Company's sales, marketing and support staff for the Americas region.

The Company leases 570 acres of land in Austin, Texas referred to as the Parmer Campus. Approximately 1.3 million square feet of office and manufacturing space are located on the campus, including two leased office buildings totaling 700,000 square feet and two 300,000-square-foot manufacturing facilities. Additional office space totaling 420,000 square feet and a 300,000 square foot manufacturing plant are currently under construction on the campus.

The Company leases approximately 2.0 million square feet of office and manufacturing space at various locations throughout Austin, Texas. These buildings house manufacturing, research and development and support staff and the Company's executive headquarters and administrative support functions.

The Company also leases approximately 1.3 million square feet of space in Middle Tennessee. This includes a 300,000 square foot manufacturing facility in Lebanon, Tennessee and 520,000 square feet of manufacturing and warehouse space in Nashville, Tennessee. A 360,000 square foot office building is leased in Nashville, Tennessee and additional office space totaling approximately 70,000 square feet is leased in various locations throughout Nashville. The office space houses the sales and manufacturing support staff.

International Properties

At February 2, 2001, the Company's international facilities consisted of approximately three million square feet of office and manufacturing space in 33 countries. Approximately one million square feet of this space is leased property, with lease expiration dates ranging from March 2001 to December 2013.

The Company owns approximately two million square feet of space. The owned space includes two facilities in Penang, Malaysia totaling 460,000 square feet that combine both office and manufacturing space. Both facilities are located on land leased from the State Authority of Penang. Also included are approximately one million square feet of manufacturing and office space in Ireland, a 70,000 square foot office building in Montpellier, France, and over 380,000 square feet of office and manufacturing space in Xiamen, China. A combined office and manufacturing facility is currently under construction in Alvorada, Brazil.

ITEM 3 — LEGAL PROCEEDINGS

The Company is subject to various legal proceedings and claims arising in the ordinary course of business. The Company's management does not expect that the results in any of these legal proceedings will have a material adverse effect on the Company's financial condition, results of operations or cash flows.

ITEM 4 — SUBMISSION OF MATTERS TO A VOTE OF SECURITY HOLDERS

No matter was submitted to a vote of the Company's stockholders, through the solicitation of proxies or otherwise, during the fourth quarter of fiscal year 2001.

PART II

ITEM 5 — MARKET FOR REGISTRANT'S COMMON EQUITY AND RELATED STOCKHOLDER MATTERS

Market Information

The Company's common stock is traded on The Nasdaq National Market under the symbol DELL. Information regarding the market prices of the Company's common stock may be found in Note 11 of Notes to Consolidated Financial Statements included in ''Item 8 — Financial Statements and Supplementary Data.''

Holders

As of April 24, 2001, there were 34,830 holders of record of the Company's common stock.

Dividends

The Company has never paid cash dividends on its common stock and does not anticipate paying any cash dividends on its common stock for at least the next 12 months.

ITEM 6 — SELECTED FINANCIAL DATA

The following selected financial data should be read in conjunction "Item 7 — Management's Discussion and Analysis of Financial Condition and Results of Operations" and "Item 8 — Financial Statements and Supplementary Data."

	Fiscal Year Ended				
	February 2, 2001(a)	January 28, 2000(b)	January 29, 1999	February 1, 1998	February 2, 1997
	(in millions, except per share data)				
Results of Operations Data:					
Net revenue	$ 31,888	$25,265	$18,243	$12,327	$7,759
Gross margin	6,443	5,218	4,106	2,722	1,666
Operating income	2,663	2,263	2,046	1,316	714
Income before extraordinary loss	2,236	1,666	1,460	944	531
Income before cumulative effect of change in accounting principle(c)	2,236	1,666	1,460	944	518
Net income	$ 2,177	$ 1,666	$ 1,460	$ 944	$ 518
Earnings per common share(d):					
Before cumulative effect of change in accounting principle					
Basic	$ 0.87	$ 0.66	$ 0.58	$ 0.36	$ 0.19
Diluted	$ 0.81	$ 0.61	$ 0.53	$ 0.32	$ 0.17
After cumulative effect of change in accounting principle					
Basic	$ 0.84	$ 0.66	$ 0.58	$ 0.36	$ 0.19
Diluted	$ 0.79	$ 0.61	$ 0.53	$ 0.32	$ 0.17
Number of weighted average shares outstanding:					
Basic	2,582	2,536	2,531	2,631	2,838
Diluted	2,746	2,728	2,772	2,952	3,126
Balance Sheet Data:					
Working capital	$ 2,948	$ 2,489	$ 2,112	$ 758	$ 891
Total assets	13,435	11,471	6,877	4,268	2,993
Long-term debt	509	508	512	17	18
Total stockholders' equity	$ 5,622	$ 5,308	$ 2,321	$ 1,293	$ 806

(a) Includes a special charge of $105 million related to employee termination benefits and facilities closure costs.

(b) Includes a special charge of $194 million related to a purchase of in-process research and development.

(c) Effective January 29, 2000, the Company changed its accounting for revenue recognition in accordance with the Securities and Exchange Commission's Staff Accounting Bulletin No. 101, *Revenue Recognition in Financial Statements* ("SAB 101"). The cumulative effect of the change on retained earnings as of the beginning of fiscal year 2001 resulted in a charge to fiscal year 2001 income of $59 million (net of income taxes of $25 million). With the exception of the cumulative effect adjustment, the effect of the change on the net income for fiscal year ended February 2, 2001 and all prior years presented was not material. See Note 1 of Notes to Consolidated Financial Statements included in "Item 8 — Financial Statements and Supplementary Data."

(d) Excludes extraordinary loss of $0.01 basic per common share for fiscal year 1997 related to repurchase of debt instruments.

ITEM 7 — MANAGEMENT'S DISCUSSION AND ANALYSIS OF FINANCIAL CONDITION AND RESULTS OF OPERATIONS

Description of Business

The Company designs, develops, manufactures, markets, services and supports a wide range of computer systems, including enterprise systems (servers, storage products and workstations), notebook computers and desktop computer systems, and also offers software, peripherals and service and support programs. The Company is managed on a geographic basis. The three geographic segments are the Americas, Europe, and Asia-Pacific and Japan. The Company markets and sells its computer products and services under the Dell brand name directly to its various customer groups. These customer groups include large corporate, government, healthcare and education accounts, as well as small-to-medium businesses and individuals.

The Company's objective is to maximize stockholder value by executing a strategy that focuses on a balance of three priorities: liquidity, profitability and growth. Management believes that opportunity exists for continued worldwide growth by increasing the Company's market presence in its existing markets, entering new markets and pursuing additional product and service opportunities. The Company continues to expand its product and services offerings to meet a variety of customer needs. Also, the Company continues to enhance and improve the reputation, quality and breadth of all of its product lines and services. The Company is continuing its efforts to strengthen its position in enterprise systems by introducing advanced technologies to serve the growing needs for these products.

The following discussion highlights the Company's performance in the context of these priorities. This discussion should be read in conjunction with the Consolidated Financial Statements, including the related notes. Statements in this Report that relate to future results and events are based on the Company's current expectations. Actual results in future periods may differ materially from those currently expected or desired because of a number of risks and uncertainties. For a discussion of factors affecting the Company's business and prospects, see "Item 1 — Business — Factors Affecting the Company's Business and Prospects."

Results of Operations

The following table summarizes the results of the Company's operations for each of the past three fiscal years. All percentage amounts were calculated using the underlying data in thousands.

	Fiscal Year Ended				
	February 2, 2001	Percentage Increase	January 28, 2000	Percentage Increase	January 29, 1999
	(dollars in millions)				
Net revenue	$31,888	26%	$25,265	38%	$18,243
Gross margin	$ 6,443	24%	$ 5,218	27%	$ 4,106
Percentage of net revenue	20.2%		20.7%		22.5%
Operating expenses	$ 3,675	33%	$ 2,761	34%	$ 2,060
Percentage of net revenue	11.5%		10.9%		11.3%
Special charges	$ 105	(45)%	$ 194	100%	—
Percentage of net revenue	0.3%		0.8%		—
Total operating expenses	$ 3,780	28%	$ 2,955	43%	$ 2,060
Percentage of net revenue	11.8%		11.7%		11.3%
Operating income	$ 2,663	18%	$ 2,263	11%	$ 2,046
Percentage of net revenue	8.4%		9.0%		11.2%
Net income	$ 2,177	31%	$ 1,666	14%	$ 1,460
Percentage of net revenue	6.8%		6.6%		8.0%

Net Revenue

The Company experienced growth in net revenue for all geographic regions during both fiscal years 2001 and 2000. The following table summarizes the Company's net revenue by geographic region for each of the past three fiscal years:

	Fiscal Year Ended				
	February 2, 2001	Percentage Increase	January 28, 2000	Percentage Increase	January 29, 1999
			(in millions)		
Net Revenue:					
Americas	$22,871	28%	$17,879	44%	$12,420
Europe	6,399	14%	5,590	20%	4,674
Asia Pacific and Japan	2,618	46%	1,796	56%	1,149
Consolidated Net Revenue	$31,888		$25,265		$18,243

The Company reported an increase in net revenue of 26% in fiscal 2001 as compared to fiscal 2000. Fiscal 2000 net revenue was 38% higher than fiscal 1999. Strong growth in net unit shipments across all regions and products drove the revenue increase, which was somewhat offset by lower average selling prices.

Net unit shipments grew 29% for fiscal 2001 and 50% in fiscal 2000, each of which was approximately two times the comparable calendar year industry growth rates. The Company continues to profitably grow market share while simultaneously growing net unit shipments at a multiple of the overall industry. The Company's enterprise systems, which include servers, storage products and workstations, continued to build a substantial presence in the marketplace, with unit shipments growing 47% during fiscal 2001. Additionally, notebook computer unit shipments increased 52%, and desktop computer systems unit shipments increased 22%. Unit shipments grew during fiscal year 2000 across all product lines as well: unit shipments of enterprise systems grew 81%, notebooks grew 61% and desktops grew 46%.

The Americas represented the majority of the Company's absolute dollar revenue growth in both fiscal 2001 and 2000. Net revenue growth in Europe slowed in fiscal 2001 as compared to fiscal 2000. In Asia-Pacific and Japan the Company's net revenues continue to grow at a faster rate than the Company as a whole. As fiscal 2001 progressed, the Company experienced a significant shift in growth among the geographic regions. At the beginning of the year, revenue in the Americas continued at the strong pace of the prior year while Europe picked up slightly from weakness experienced the prior year. During the middle of the year, however, revenues in Europe weakened as overall demand softened and the region continued to transition to a new management team. Revenues in the Americas remained relatively strong during this period. As the Company exited the year, Europe experienced a significant pickup in demand as the management team was able to fully execute its business plan. Consequently, substantially all of Europe's fiscal 2001 year-over-year growth occurred in the fourth quarter; whereas revenue growth in the Americas slowed significantly as the overall United States economy and financial markets cooled. Revenues in Asia-Pacific and Japan continue to grow as the Company entered additional country markets and expanded production capabilities to meet these growth opportunities. For additional information regarding the Company's segments, see Note 10 of Notes to Consolidated Financial Statements included in "Item 8 — Financial Statements and Supplementary Data."

Average revenue per unit sold in fiscal year 2001 decreased 2% compared to fiscal year 2000, which was primarily due to price reductions resulting from component cost declines. Average revenue per unit for the fourth quarter of fiscal 2001 was approximately 6% lower than the full year average as the Company leveraged its direct-to-customer model to drive profitable market share growth. Management currently expects that this pricing environment will likely continue for the foreseeable future as the Company and its competitors adapt to slowing demand and general softness in the overall economy. Average revenue per unit sold in fiscal year 2000 decreased 8% compared to fiscal year 1999, which mostly resulted from the Company's pricing strategy.

Gross Margin

As a percentage of consolidated net revenue, gross margin decreased slightly from 20.7% in fiscal year 2000 to 20.2% in fiscal year 2001. Most of the decrease occurred in the fourth quarter of the year as the Company quickly passed component cost savings to its customers and also leveraged the strength of its model to drive profitable market share growth. Earlier in the year the Company experienced overall gross margins of approximately 21%, whereas overall they had declined to approximately 18% by the end of the fiscal year. Based on the industry, economic and other factors discussed above, the Company currently expects that this gross margin environment will likely continue for the foreseeable future. Management believes that the strength of the Company's direct-to-customer business model, as well as its strong liquidity position, result in the Company being better suited than its competitors to profitably grow market share in the current business climate.

The decrease in gross margin as a percentage of consolidated net revenue in fiscal year 2000 over fiscal year 1999 was primarily attributable to increased component costs, in part due to a higher than expected cost increase for memory components during the last half of the year.

Operating Expenses

The following table presents certain information regarding the Company's operating expenses during each of the past three fiscal years:

	Fiscal Year Ended		
	February 2, 2001(a)	January 28, 2000(b)	January 29, 1999
	(dollars in millions)		
Operating Expenses:			
Selling, general and administrative	$3,193	$2,387	$1,788
Percentage of net revenue	10.0%	9.4%	9.8%
Research, development and engineering	$ 482	$ 374	$ 272
Percentage of net revenue	1.5%	1.5%	1.5%
Special charges	$ 105	$ 194	—
Percentage of net revenue	0.3%	0.8%	0.0%
Total operating expenses	$3,780	$2,955	$2,060
Percentage of net revenue	11.8%	11.7%	11.3%

(a) The $105 million special charge relates to employee termination benefits and facilities closure costs.

(b) The $194 million special charge represents purchased in-process research and development.

Selling, general and administrative expenses increased in absolute dollar amounts and as a percentage of revenue in fiscal year 2001 versus fiscal year 2000, due primarily to the Company's original expectations for higher net unit shipment and revenue growth. The Company heavily invested in personnel and other support costs in anticipation of that growth. As growth expectations were reduced during the year, management took steps to manage expenses relative to actual growth rates, and as a result selling, general and administrative expenses as a percentage of net revenues declined on a quarter-to-quarter basis throughout fiscal 2001. In fiscal year 2000, selling, general and administrative expense increased in absolute dollar amounts, but decreased as a percentage of consolidated net revenue as compared to fiscal year 1999.

Management believes that the Company will have to continue to improve efficiencies and control selling, general and administrative expenses relative to revenue growth to continue to profitably grow market share. Consequently, during the fourth quarter of fiscal 2001, the Company undertook a program to reduce its workforce and to exit certain facilities during fiscal year 2002. Total charges recorded were $105 million. The charges consisted of approximately $50 million in employee termination benefits with the remainder relating to facilities closure costs. The employee separations, which occurred primarily in the United States, affected 1,700 employees across a majority of the Company's business functions and job classes. As of April 15, 2001, substantially all of the employees had been separated from the Company and the liability related to termination benefits had been liquidated. These actions are expected to result in annual savings of approximately $100 million. These savings, however, are expected to be reinvested via pricing, selling incentives, and research and development activities to support continued unit and revenue growth in the Company's enterprise products. The Company will continue to manage its operating expenses relative to expected revenue growth, and will undertake additional cost-cutting actions if necessary to enable it to continue to profitably grow market share.

The Company continues to invest in research, development and engineering activities to develop and introduce new products and to support its continued goal of improving and developing efficient procurement, manufacturing and distribution processes. As a result, research, development and engineering expenses have increased each year in absolute dollars due to increased staffing levels and product development costs, although, as a percent of revenue, these costs have remained level. The Company expects to continue to increase its absolute dollar amount of research, development and engineering spending with an increasing emphasis on enterprise products, including servers and storage. During fiscal 2000, as a result of the acquisition of ConvergeNet Technologies, Inc., purchased in-process research and development in the amount of $194 million was expensed.

Income Taxes

The Company's effective tax rate was 30% for fiscal year 2001 compared to 32% for fiscal year 2000 and 30% for fiscal year 1999. The differences in the effective tax rates among fiscal years result from changes in the geographical distribution of taxable income and losses and certain non tax-deductible charges. The Company's effective tax rate is lower than the U.S. federal statutory rate of 35%, principally because of the Company's geographical distribution of taxable income.

Investment and Other Income, Net

Investment and other income, net increased in absolute dollar amounts during fiscal 2001 as compared to the fiscal 2000. The increase is due primarily to gains on the sale of investments and higher interest income. See below for further discussion.

Liquidity and Capital Resources

The following table presents selected financial statistics and information for each of the past three fiscal years:

	Fiscal Year Ended		
	February 2, 2001	January 28, 2000	January 29, 1999
	(dollars in millions)		
Cash and investments	$7,856	$6,853	$3,181
Working capital	2,948	2,489	2,112
Days of sales in accounts receivable	32	34	36
Days of supply in inventory	5	6	6
Days in accounts payable	58	58	54
Cash conversion cycle	(21)	(18)	(12)

During fiscal year 2001, 2000, and 1999, the Company generated $4.2 billion, $3.9 billion, and $2.4 billion, respectively, in cash flows from operating activities, which represents the Company's principal source of cash. Cash flows from operating activities resulted primarily from the Company's net income, changes in operating working capital, and income tax benefits that resulted from the exercise of employee stock options.

The Company ended fiscal year 2001 with $7.9 billion in cash and investments, $1 billion greater than the prior year level. The Company invests a portion of its available cash in highly liquid investments of varying maturities at date of acquisition, the inherent objective of which is primarily to minimize principal risk and maintain liquidity. As of February 2, 2001, and January 28, 2000, the Company had $6.3 billion and $4.7 billion, respectively, invested in these investments. Additionally, the Company invests in equity securities of various private and public entities in order to enhance and extend the Company's strategic initiatives. At February 2, 2001 and January 28, 2000, these equity investments totaled $938 million and $1.5 billion, respectively, and of those amounts approximately $112 million and $856 million, respectively, represented unrealized net appreciation. See "Item 1 — Business — Factors Affecting the Company's Business and Prospects — Equity Investments."

During fiscal year 2001, the Company continued to improve upon its efficient asset management. As compared to fiscal year 2000, days of supply in inventory and days of sales in accounts receivable decreased in fiscal year 2001 by one and two days, respectively. This resulted in an improvement in the Company's cash conversion cycle to a negative 21 days in fiscal year 2001 from a negative 18 days in fiscal year 2000. As a result, the Company's return on invested capital, a key indicator of efficient asset management, increased to 355% (excluding the cumulative effect of SAB 101 and the special charge related to termination benefits and facilities closure costs) in fiscal year 2001 from 243% (excluding a special charge for purchased in-process research and development) in fiscal year 2000.

The Company has a share repurchase program that it uses primarily to manage the dilution resulting from shares issued under the Company's employee stock plans. As of the end of the fiscal year 2001, the Company had cumulatively repurchased 871 million shares over a four year period out of its authorized 1 billion share repurchase program, for an aggregate cost of $6.8 billion. During fiscal year 2001, the Company repurchased 65 million shares of common stock for an aggregate cost of $2.7 billion. The Company utilizes equity instrument contracts to facilitate its repurchase of common stock. At February 2, 2001 and January 28, 2000, the Company held equity options and forwards that allow for the purchase of 88 million and 50 million shares of common stock, respectively, at an average price of $50 and $45 per share, respectively. At February 2, 2001 and January 28, 2000, the Company also had outstanding put obligations covering 111 million and 69 million shares, respectively, with an average exercise price of $44 and $39 per share, respectively. The equity instruments are exercisable only at the date of expiration and expire at various dates through the first quarter of fiscal 2004. The outstanding put obligations at February 2, 2001 permitted net share settlement at the Company's option and, therefore, did not result in a put obligation liability on the accompanying Consolidated Statement of Financial Position. For additional information regarding the Company's stock repurchase program, see Note 5 of Notes to Consolidated Financial Statements included in "Item 8 — Financial Statements and Supplementary Data" below.

The Company utilized $482 million in cash during fiscal year 2001 to improve and equip its manufacturing and office facilities as the Company continues to grow. Cash flows for similar capital expenditures for fiscal year 2002 are currently expected to be in the range of $300 to $350 million.

The Company maintains master lease facilities providing the capacity to fund up to $1.2 billion. The combined facilities provide for the ability of the Company to lease certain real property, buildings and equipment to be constructed or acquired. At February 2, 2001, $506 million of the combined facilities had been utilized.

In April 1998, the Company issued $200 million in Senior Notes due April 15, 2008 and $300 million in Senior Debentures due April 15, 2020. For additional information regarding these issuances, see Note 3 of Notes to Consolidated Financial Statements included in "Item 8 — Financial Statements and Supplementary Data."

The Company maintains a $250 million revolving credit facility, which expires in June 2002. At February 2, 2001 this facility was unused.

Management believes that the Company's cash provided from operations will continue to be sufficient to support its operations and capital requirements. The Company anticipates that it will continue to utilize its strong liquidity and cash flows to repurchase its common stock, make strategic equity investments and invest in systems and processes, as well as invest in the development and growth of its enterprise products.

Market Risk

The Company is exposed to a variety of risks, including foreign currency exchange rate fluctuations and changes in the market value of its investments. In the normal course of business, the Company employs established policies and procedures to manage these risks.

Foreign Currency Hedging Activities

The Company's objective in managing its exposure to foreign currency exchange rate fluctuations is to reduce the impact of adverse fluctuations on earnings and cash flows associated with foreign currency exchange rate changes. Accordingly, the Company utilizes foreign currency option contracts and forward contracts to hedge its exposure on anticipated transactions and firm commitments in most of the foreign countries in which the Company operates. The principal currencies hedged during fiscal year 2001 were the British pound, Japanese yen, Euro and Canadian dollar. The Company monitors its foreign currency exchange exposures daily to ensure the overall effectiveness of its foreign currency hedge positions. However, there can be no assurance the Company's foreign currency hedging activities will substantially offset the impact of fluctuations in currency exchange rates on its results of operations and financial position.

Based on the Company's foreign currency exchange instruments outstanding at February 2, 2001, the Company estimates a maximum potential one-day loss in fair value of approximately $21.4 million, using a Value-at-Risk ("VAR") model. The VAR model estimates were made assuming normal market conditions and a 95% confidence level. The Company used a Monte Carlo simulation type model that valued its foreign currency instruments against a thousand randomly generated market price paths. Anticipated transactions, firm commitments, receivables and accounts payable denominated in foreign currencies were excluded from the model. The VAR model is a risk estimation tool, and as such, is not intended to represent actual losses in fair value that will be incurred by the Company. Additionally, as the Company utilizes foreign currency instruments for hedging anticipated and firmly committed transactions, a loss in fair value for those instruments is generally offset by increases in the value of the underlying exposure. Foreign currency fluctuations did not have a material impact on the Company's results of operations and financial position during fiscal years 2001, 2000 and 1999.

Investments

The fair value of the Company's cash equivalents and short- and long-term investments at February 2, 2001, was approximately $6 billion (excluding equity securities). The Company's investment policy is to manage its investment portfolio to preserve principal and liquidity while maximizing the return on the investment portfolio through the full investment of available funds. The Company diversifies the investment portfolio by investing in multiple types of investment-grade securities and through the use of different investment brokers. The Company's investment portfolio is partially invested in short-term securities with at least an investment-grade rating to minimize interest rate and credit risk as well as to provide for an immediate source of funds. Based on the Company's investment portfolio and interest rates at February 2, 2001, a 100 basis point increase or decrease in interest rates would result in a decrease or increase of $56 million, respectively, in the fair value of the investment portfolio. Changes in interest rates may affect the fair value of the investment portfolio; however, the Company will not recognize such gains or losses unless the investments are sold.

The Company also invests in equity securities of companies in order to enhance and extend the Company's direct business model and core business initiatives. The Company has an active venture capital program, through which the Company makes strategic equity investments in privately and publicly held technology companies. Because these companies are typically early-stage companies with products or services that are not yet fully developed or that have not yet achieved market acceptance, these investments are inherently risky. See "Item 1 — Business — Factors Affecting the Company's Business and Prospects — Equity Investments."

Factors Affecting the Company's Business and Prospects

There are numerous factors that affect the Company's business and the results of its operations. These factors include general economic and business conditions; the level of demand for the Company's products and services; the level and intensity of competition in the technology industry and the pricing pressures that have resulted; the ability of the Company to timely and effectively manage periodic product transitions, as well as component availability and cost; the ability of the Company to develop new products based on new or evolving technology and the market's acceptance of those products; the ability of the Company to manage its inventory levels to minimize excess inventory, declining inventory values and obsolescence; the product, customer and geographic sales mix of any particular period; the Company's ability to recover its investments in venture capital activities; and the Company's ability to effectively manage its operating costs. For a discussion of these and other factors affecting the Company's business and prospects, see "Item 1 — Business — Factors Affecting the Company's Business and Prospects."

Recently Issued Accounting Pronouncements

Effective February 3, 2001, the Company adopted SFAS No. 133, *Accounting for Derivative Instruments and Hedging Activities*, as amended, which establishes accounting and reporting standards for derivative instruments and hedging activities. SFAS No. 133 requires that an entity recognize all derivatives as either assets or liabilities in the Consolidated Statement of Financial Position and measure those instruments at fair value. The adoption of this statement will not have a material effect on the Company's financial condition or results of operations. However, its application may increase the volatility of investment and other income, net in the Consolidated Statement of Income and other comprehensive income in the Consolidated Statement of Stockholders' Equity.

ITEM 7A — QUANTITATIVE AND QUALITATIVE DISCLOSURES ABOUT MARKET RISK

Response to this item is included in "Item 7 — Management's Discussion and Analysis of Financial Condition and Results of Operations — Market Risk."

24

ITEM 8 — FINANCIAL STATEMENTS AND SUPPLEMENTARY DATA

INDEX TO CONSOLIDATED FINANCIAL STATEMENTS

All other schedules are omitted because they are not applicable.

REPORT OF INDEPENDENT ACCOUNTANTS

To the Board of Directors and Stockholders of
Dell Computer Corporation

In our opinion, the consolidated financial statements listed in the accompanying index present fairly, in all material respects, the financial position of Dell Computer Corporation and its subsidiaries at February 2, 2001 and January 28, 2000, and the results of their operations and their cash flows for each of the three fiscal years in the period ended February 2, 2001, in conformity with accounting principles generally accepted in the United States of America. In addition, in our opinion, the financial statement schedule listed in the accompanying index presents fairly, in all material respects, the information set forth therein when read in conjunction with the related consolidated financial statements. These financial statements and financial statement schedule are the responsibility of the Company's management; our responsibility is to express an opinion on these financial statements and financial statement schedule based on our audits. We conducted our audits of these statements in accordance with auditing standards generally accepted in the United States of America, which require that we plan and perform the audit to obtain reasonable assurance about whether the financial statements are free of material misstatement. An audit includes examining, on a test basis, evidence supporting the amounts and disclosures in the financial statements, assessing the accounting principles used and significant estimates made by management, and evaluating the overall financial statement presentation. We believe that our audits provide a reasonable basis for our opinion.

As discussed in Note 1 to the consolidated financial statements, in fiscal year 2001 the Company changed its revenue recognition for certain product shipments.

PRICEWATERHOUSECOOPERS LLP

Austin, Texas
February 15, 2001

26

DELL COMPUTER CORPORATION

CONSOLIDATED STATEMENT OF FINANCIAL POSITION
(in millions, except per share amounts)

	February 2, 2001	January 28, 2000
ASSETS		
Current assets:		
Cash and cash equivalents	$ 4,910	$ 3,809
Short-term investments	528	323
Accounts receivable, net	2,895	2,608
Inventories	400	391
Other	758	550
Total current assets	9,491	7,681
Property, plant and equipment, net	996	765
Investments	2,418	2,721
Other non-current assets	530	304
Total assets	$13,435	$11,471
LIABILITIES AND STOCKHOLDERS' EQUITY		
Current liabilities:		
Accounts payable	$ 4,286	$ 3,538
Accrued and other	2,257	1,654
Total current liabilities	6,543	5,192
Long-term debt	509	508
Other	761	463
Commitments and contingent liabilities (Note 7)	—	—
Total liabilities	7,813	6,163
Stockholders' equity:		
Preferred stock and capital in excess of $.01 par value; shares issued and outstanding: none	—	—
Common stock and capital in excess of $.01 par value; shares issued and outstanding: 2,601 and 2,575, respectively	4,795	3,583
Retained earnings	839	1,260
Other comprehensive income	62	533
Other	(74)	(68)
Total stockholders' equity	5,622	5,308
Total liabilities and stockholders' equity	$13,435	$11,471

The accompanying notes are an integral part of these consolidated financial statements.

DELL COMPUTER CORPORATION

CONSOLIDATED STATEMENT OF INCOME
(in millions, except per share amounts)

	Fiscal Year Ended		
	February 2, 2001	January 28, 2000	January 29, 1999
Net revenue	$31,888	$25,265	$18,243
Cost of revenue	25,445	20,047	14,137
Gross margin	6,443	5,218	4,106
Operating expenses:			
Selling, general and administrative	3,193	2,387	1,788
Research, development and engineering	482	374	272
Special charges	105	194	—
Total operating expenses	3,780	2,955	2,060
Operating income	2,663	2,263	2,046
Investment and other income, net	531	188	38
Income before income taxes and cumulative effect of change in accounting principle	3,194	2,451	2,084
Provision for income taxes	958	785	624
Income before cumulative effect of change in accounting principle	2,236	1,666	1,460
Cumulative effect of change in accounting principle, net	59	—	—
Net Income	$ 2,177	$ 1,666	$ 1,460
Earnings per common share:			
Before cumulative of effect change in accounting principle:			
Basic	$ 0.87	$ 0.66	$ 0.58
Diluted	$ 0.81	$ 0.61	$ 0.53
After cumulative effect of change in accounting principle:			
Basic	$ 0.84	$ 0.66	$ 0.58
Diluted	$ 0.79	$ 0.61	$ 0.53
Weighted average shares outstanding:			
Basic	2,582	2,536	2,531
Diluted	2,746	2,728	2,772

The accompanying notes are an integral part of these consolidated financial statements.

28

DELL COMPUTER CORPORATION

CONSOLIDATED STATEMENT OF CASH FLOWS
(in millions)

	Fiscal Year Ended		
	February 2, 2001	January 28, 2000	January 29, 1999
Cash flows from operating activities:			
Net income	$ 2,177	$ 1,666	$ 1,460
Adjustments to reconcile net income to net cash provided by operating activities:			
Depreciation and amortization	240	156	103
Tax benefits of employee stock plans	929	1,040	444
Special charges	105	194	—
Gain on sale of investments	(307)	(80)	(9)
Other	109	56	20
Changes in:			
Operating working capital	671	812	367
Non-current assets and liabilities	271	82	51
Net cash provided by operating activities	4,195	3,926	2,436
Cash flows from investing activities:			
Investments:			
Purchases	(2,606)	(3,101)	(1,938)
Maturities and sales	2,331	2,319	1,304
Capital expenditures	(482)	(401)	(296)
Net cash used in investing activities	(757)	(1,183)	(930)
Cash flows from financing activities:			
Purchase of common stock	(2,700)	(1,061)	(1,518)
Issuance of common stock under employee plans	404	289	212
Proceeds from issuance of long-term debt, net of issuance costs	—	20	494
Other	(9)	57	—
Net cash used in financing activities	(2,305)	(695)	(812)
Effect of exchange rate changes on cash	(32)	35	(10)
Net increase in cash	1,101	2,083	684
Cash and cash equivalents at beginning of period	3,809	1,726	1,042
Cash and cash equivalents at end of period	$ 4,910	$ 3,809	$ 1,726

The accompanying notes are an integral part of these consolidated financial statements.

DELL COMPUTER CORPORATION

CONSOLIDATED STATEMENT OF STOCKHOLDERS' EQUITY
(in millions)

	Common Stock and Capital in Excess of Par Value		Retained Earnings	Other Comprehensive Income	Other	Total
	Shares	Amount				
Balances at February 1, 1998	2,575	$ 747	$ 607	$ (35)	$(26)	$ 1,293
Net income	—	—	1,460	—	—	1,460
Change in unrealized gain on investments, net of taxes	—	—	—	3	—	3
Foreign currency translation adjustments	—	—	—	(4)	—	(4)
Total comprehensive income						1,459
Stock issuances under employee plans, including tax benefits	117	1,092	—	—	(7)	1,085
Purchases and retirements	(149)	(60)	(1,458)	—	—	(1,518)
Other	—	2	(3)	—	3	2
Balances at January 29, 1999	2,543	1,781	606	(36)	(30)	2,321
Net income	—	—	1,666	—	—	1,666
Change in unrealized gain on investments, net of taxes	—	—	—	559	—	559
Foreign currency translation adjustments	—	—	—	10	—	10
Total comprehensive income						2,235
Stock issuances under employee plans, including tax benefits	82	1,406	—	—	(46)	1,360
Purchases and retirements	(56)	(48)	(1,013)	—	—	(1,061)
Stock issued pursuant to acquisition....................	6	334	—	—	—	334
Other	—	110	1	—	8	119
Balances at January 28, 2000	2,575	3,583	1,260	533	(68)	5,308
Net income	—	—	2,177	—	—	2,177
Change in unrealized gain on investments, net of taxes	—	—	—	(475)	—	(475)
Foreign currency translation adjustments	—	—	—	4	—	4
Total comprehensive income						1,706
Stock issuances under employee plans, including tax benefits	91	1,347	—	—	(6)	1,341
Purchases and retirements	(65)	(102)	(2,598)	—	—	(2,700)
Other	—	(33)	—	—	—	(33)
Balances at February 2, 2001	2,601	$4,795	$ 839	$ 62	$(74)	$ 5,622

The accompanying notes are an integral part of these consolidated financial statements.

DELL COMPUTER CORPORATION
NOTES TO CONSOLIDATED FINANCIAL STATEMENTS

NOTE 1 — Description of Business and Summary of Significant Accounting Policies

Description of Business — Dell Computer Corporation, a Delaware corporation, and its consolidated subsidiaries (collectively referred to as the "Company") designs, develops, manufactures, markets, services and supports a wide range of computer systems, including desktop computer systems, notebook computers and enterprise systems (includes servers, workstations and storage products), and also markets software, peripherals and service and support programs. The Company is managed on a geographic basis. The three geographic segments are the Americas, Europe, and Asia-Pacific and Japan. The Company markets and sells its computer products and services under the Dell™ brand name directly to its various customer groups. These customer groups include large corporate, government, healthcare and education accounts, as well as small-to-medium businesses and individuals.

Fiscal Year — The Company's fiscal year is the 52- or 53-week period ending on the Friday nearest January 31.

Principles of Consolidation — The accompanying consolidated financial statements have been prepared in accordance with generally accepted accounting principles and include the accounts of the Company and its consolidated subsidiaries. All significant intercompany transactions and balances have been eliminated.

Use of Estimates — The preparation of financial statements in accordance with generally accepted accounting principles requires the use of management's estimates. These estimates are subjective in nature and involve judgments that affect the reported amounts of assets and liabilities, the disclosure of contingent assets and liabilities at fiscal year end and the reported amounts of revenues and expenses during the fiscal year. Actual results could differ from those estimates.

Cash and Cash Equivalents — All highly liquid investments with original maturities of three months or less at date of purchase are carried at cost plus accrued interest, which approximates fair value, and are considered to be cash equivalents. All other investments not considered to be a cash equivalent are separately categorized as investments.

Investments — The Company's debt securities and publicly traded equity securities are classified as available-for-sale and are reported at fair market value using the specific identification method. All other investments are recorded at cost. Unrealized gains and losses are reported, net of taxes, as a component of stockholders' equity. Unrealized losses are charged against income when a decline in the fair market value of an individual security is determined to be other-than-temporary. Realized gains and losses on investments are included in investment and other income, net when realized.

Inventories — Inventories are stated at the lower of cost or market with cost being determined on a first-in, first-out basis.

Property, Plant and Equipment — Property, plant and equipment are carried at depreciated cost. Depreciation is provided using the straight-line method over the estimated economic lives of the assets, which range from 10 to 30 years for buildings and two to five years for all other assets. Leasehold improvements are amortized over the shorter of five years or the lease term. Gains or losses related to retirements or disposition of fixed assets are recognized in the period incurred. The Company performs reviews for the impairment of fixed assets whenever events or changes in circumstances indicate that the carrying amount of an asset may not be recoverable. The Company capitalizes eligible internal-use software development costs incurred subsequent to the completion of the preliminary project stage. Development costs are amortized over the shorter of the expected useful life of the software or five years.

31

Goodwill and Other Intangibles — Amortization of goodwill and other intangibles is charged to income on a straight-line basis over the periods estimated to benefit, ranging from three to eight years. Goodwill and other intangibles are reviewed for impairment on an undiscounted basis whenever events or circumstances indicate that the carrying amount of an asset may not be recoverable.

Foreign Currency Translation — The majority of the Company's international sales are made by international subsidiaries, which have the U.S. dollar as their functional currency. Local currency transactions of international subsidiaries, which have the U.S. dollar as the functional currency are remeasured into U.S. dollars using current rates of exchange for monetary assets and liabilities and historical rates of exchange for nonmonetary assets. Gains and losses from remeasurement are included in investment and other income, net. The Company's subsidiaries that do not have the U.S. dollar as their functional currency translate assets and liabilities at current rates of exchange in effect at the balance sheet date. The resulting gains and losses from translation are included as a component of stockholders' equity. Revenue and expenses from the Company's international subsidiaries are translated using the monthly average exchange rates in effect for the period in which the items occur.

Foreign Currency Hedging Instruments — The Company enters into foreign currency exchange contracts to hedge its foreign currency risks. These contracts are designated at inception as a hedge and measured for effectiveness both at inception and on an ongoing basis. Realized and unrealized gains or losses and premiums paid on foreign currency purchased option contracts that are designated and effective as hedges of probable anticipated, but not firmly committed, foreign currency transactions are deferred and recognized in income as a component of net revenue, cost of revenue and/or operating expenses in the same period as the hedged transaction. Forward contracts designated as hedges of probable anticipated or firmly committed transactions are accounted for on a mark-to-market basis, with realized and unrealized gains or losses recognized in the accompanying Consolidated Statement of Income.

Equity Instruments Indexed to the Company's Common Stock — Proceeds received from the sale of equity instruments and amounts paid to purchase equity instruments are recorded as a component of stockholders' equity. Subsequent changes in the fair value of the equity instrument contracts are not recognized. If the contracts are ultimately settled in cash, the amount of cash paid or received is recorded as a component of stockholders' equity.

Revenue Recognition — Product revenue is recognized when both title and risk of loss transfers to the customer, provided that no significant obligations remain. Provision is made for an estimate of product returns and doubtful accounts, based on historical experience. Revenue from separately priced extended warranty and service programs is deferred and recognized over the respective service or extended warranty period when the Company is the obligor. Revenue from sales involving multiple elements is allocated to each element based on their respective fair values and recorded as revenue as each element is delivered.

Effective January 29, 2000, the Company changed its accounting for revenue recognition in accordance with Securities and Exchange Commission's Staff Accounting Bulletin No. 101, *Revenue Recognition in Financial Statements* ("SAB 101"). Previously, the Company had recognized revenue at the date of shipment. Under the new accounting method adopted retroactive to January 29, 2000, the Company now recognizes product revenue when both title and risk of loss transfers to the customer, provided that no significant obligations remain. The cumulative effect of the change on prior years' retained earnings resulted in a charge to fiscal 2001 income of $59 million (net of income taxes of $25 million). Had SAB 101 been effective for all prior fiscal years presented, the pro forma results and earnings per share would not have been materially different from the previously reported results.

Warranty — The Company provides for the estimated costs that may be incurred under its basic limited warranty.

32

Advertising Costs — Advertising costs are charged to expense as incurred. Advertising expenses for fiscal years 2001, 2000, and 1999 were $431 million, $325 million, and $199 million, respectively.

Stock-Based Compensation — The Company applies the intrinsic value method in accounting for its stock option and stock purchase plans. Accordingly, no compensation expense has been recognized for options granted with an exercise price equal to market value at the date of grant or in connection with the employee stock purchase plan.

Income Taxes — Deferred tax assets and liabilities are recorded based on the difference between the financial statement and tax basis of assets and liabilities using enacted tax rates in effect for the year in which the differences are expected to reverse.

Earnings Per Common Share — Basic earnings per share is based on the weighted effect of all common shares issued and outstanding, and is calculated by dividing net income by the weighted average shares outstanding during the period. Diluted earnings per share is calculated by dividing net income by the weighted average number of common shares used in the basic earnings per share calculation plus the number of common shares that would be issued assuming conversion of all potentially dilutive common shares outstanding. The following table sets forth the computation of basic and diluted earnings per share for each of the past three fiscal years:

| | Fiscal Year Ended | | |
	February 2, 2001	January 28, 2000	January 29, 1999
	(dollars in millions)		
Net income	$2,177	$1,666	$1,460
Weighted average shares outstanding:			
Basic	2,582	2,536	2,531
Employee stock options and other	164	192	241
Diluted	2,746	2,728	2,772
Earnings per common share:			
Before cumulative effect of change in accounting principle			
Basic	$ 0.87	$ 0.66	$ 0.58
Diluted	$ 0.81	$ 0.61	$ 0.53
After cumulative effect of change in accounting principle			
Basic	$ 0.84	$ 0.66	$ 0.58
Diluted	$ 0.79	$ 0.61	$ 0.53

Comprehensive Income — The Company's comprehensive income is comprised of net income, foreign currency translation adjustments and unrealized gains and losses on investments classified as available-for-sale.

Recently Issued Accounting Pronouncements — Effective February 3, 2001, the Company adopted SFAS No. 133, *Accounting for Derivative Instruments and Hedging Activities,* as amended, which establishes accounting and reporting standards for derivative instruments and hedging activities. SFAS No. 133 requires that an entity recognize all derivatives as either assets or liabilities in the Consolidated Statement of Financial Position and measure those instruments at fair value. The adoption of this statement will not have a material effect on the Company's financial condition or results of operations. However, its application may increase the volatility of investment and other income, net in the Consolidated Statement of Income and other comprehensive income in the Consolidated Statement of Stockholders' Equity.

Reclassifications — Certain prior year amounts have been reclassified to conform to the fiscal year 2001 presentation.

33

NOTE 2 — Special Charges

During the fourth quarter of fiscal 2001, the Company undertook a program to reduce its workforce and to exit certain facilities during fiscal year 2002. Total charges recorded were $105 million, which are expected to be fully paid by the end of fiscal 2002. The charges consisted of approximately $50 million in employee termination benefits with the remainder relating to facilities closure costs. The employee separations, which occurred primarily in the United States, affected 1,700 employees across a majority of the Company's business functions and job classes.

On October 20, 1999, the Company acquired all the outstanding shares of ConvergeNet Technologies, Inc. ("ConvergeNet"), developer of storage domain management technology, in exchange for 6.9 million shares of the Company's common stock and $4.5 million cash for total purchase consideration of $332 million, as valued on that date. The ConvergeNet acquisition was recorded under the purchase method of accounting. Accordingly, the purchase price was allocated to the net assets acquired based on their estimated fair values. The amount allocated to purchased in-process research and development of $194 million was determined based on an appraisal completed by an independent third party using established valuation techniques in the storage management industry and expensed upon acquisition because technological feasibility had not been established and no future alternative uses existed. The excess of cost over net assets acquired was recorded as goodwill and included in other assets.

NOTE 3 — Financial Instruments

Disclosures About Fair Values of Financial Instruments

The fair value of investments, long-term debt and related interest rate derivative instruments has been estimated based upon market quotes from brokers. The fair value of foreign currency forward contracts has been estimated using market quoted rates of foreign currencies at the applicable balance sheet date. The estimated fair value of foreign currency purchased option contracts is based on market quoted rates at the applicable balance sheet date and the Black-Scholes options pricing model. Considerable judgment is necessary in interpreting market data to develop estimates of fair value. Accordingly, the estimates presented herein are not necessarily indicative of the amounts that the Company could realize in a current market exchange. Changes in assumptions could significantly affect the estimates.

Cash and cash equivalents, accounts receivable, accounts payable and accrued and other liabilities are reflected in the accompanying consolidated financial statements at cost, which approximates fair value because of the short-term maturity of these instruments.

Investments

The following table summarizes by major security type the fair market value and cost of the Company's investments.

	February 2, 2001			January 28, 2000		
	Fair Market Value	Cost	Unrealized Gain (Loss)	Fair Market Value	Cost	Unrealized Gain (Loss)
			(In millions)			
Equity securities.................	$ 938	$ 826	$112	$1,451	$ 595	$856
Debt securities:						
U.S. corporate and bank debt ...	1,454	1,442	12	1,256	1,242	14
State and municipal securities ...	105	104	1	115	117	(2)
U.S. government and agencies ..	449	439	10	192	195	(3)
International corporate and bank debt........................	—	—	—	30	30	—
Total debt securities	2,008	1,985	23	1,593	1,584	9
Total investments	$2,946	$2,811	$135	$3,044	$2,179	$865

At February 2, 2001, debt securities with a carrying amount of $524 million mature within one year; the remaining debt securities mature within five years. The Company's gross recognized gains and losses on investments, including impairments of certain investments, for fiscal year 2001 were $473 million and $166 million, respectively. The Company's gross recognized gains and losses on the sale of investments for fiscal year 2000 were $81 million and $1 million, respectively. The Company's gross recognized gains and losses on the sale of investments for fiscal year 1999 were not material. Gross unrealized gains and losses at February 2, 2001 were $262 million and $127 million, respectively. Gross unrealized gains and losses at January 28, 2000 were $879 million, and $13 million, respectively.

Foreign Currency Instruments

The Company uses foreign currency purchased option contracts to reduce its exposure to currency fluctuations involving probable anticipated, but not firmly committed, transactions. It also uses forward contracts to reduce exposure to transactions with firm foreign currency commitments. These transactions include international sales by U.S. dollar functional currency entities, foreign currency denominated purchases of certain components and intercompany shipments to certain international subsidiaries. The risk of loss associated with purchased options is limited to premium amounts paid for the option contracts. Foreign currency purchased options generally expire in 12 months or less. At February 2, 2001, the Company held purchased option contracts with a notional amount of $2 billion, a net asset value of $67 million and a combined net realized and unrealized deferred loss of $4 million. At January 28, 2000, the Company held purchased option contracts with a notional amount of $2 billion, a net asset value of $75 million and a combined net realized and unrealized deferred gain of $5 million. The risk of loss associated with forward contracts is equal to the exchange rate differential from the time the contract is entered into until the time it is settled. Transactions with firm foreign currency commitments are generally hedged using foreign currency forward contracts for periods not exceeding three months. At February 2, 2001, the Company held forward contracts with a notional amount of $888 million, a net liability value of $49 million and a net realized and unrealized deferred loss of $1 million. At January 28, 2000, the Company held forward contracts with a notional amount of $818 million, a net asset value of $17 million and a net realized and unrealized deferred gain of $1 million.

Long-term Debt and Interest Rate Risk Management

In April 1998, the Company issued $200 million 6.55% fixed rate senior notes due April 15, 2008 (the "Senior Notes") and $300 million 7.10% fixed rate senior debentures due April 15, 2028 (the "Senior Debentures"). Interest on the Senior Notes and Senior Debentures is paid semi-annually, on April 15 and October 15. The Senior Notes and Senior Debentures rank pari passu and are redeemable, in whole or in part, at the election of the Company for principal, any accrued interest and a redemption premium based on the present value of interest to be paid over the term of the debt agreements. The Senior Notes and Senior Debentures generally contain no restrictive covenants, other than a limitation on liens on the Company's assets and a limitation on sale-leaseback transactions.

Concurrent with the issuance of the Senior Notes and Senior Debentures, the Company entered into interest rate swap agreements converting the Company's interest rate exposure from a fixed rate to a floating rate basis to better align the associated interest rate characteristics to its cash and investments portfolio. The interest rate swap agreements have an aggregate notional amount of $200 million maturing April 15, 2008 and $300 million maturing April 15, 2028. The floating rates are based on three-month London interbank offered rates ("LIBOR") plus 0.41% and 0.79% for the Senior Notes and Senior Debentures, respectively. As a result of the interest rate swap agreements, the Company's effective interest rates for the Senior Notes and Senior Debentures were 7.20% and 7.54%, respectively, for fiscal year 2001.

The Company has designated the issuance of the Senior Notes and Senior Debentures and the related interest rate swap agreements as an integrated transaction. Accordingly, the differential to be paid or received on the interest rate swap agreements is accrued and recognized as an adjustment to interest expense as interest rates change.

The difference between the Company's carrying amounts and fair value of its long-term debt and related interest rate swaps was not material at February 2, 2001 and January 28, 2000.

Financing Arrangements

The Company maintains a $250 million revolving credit facility, which expires in June 2002. Commitment fees for this facility are payable quarterly and are based on specific liquidity requirements. Commitment fees paid in fiscal years 2001, 2000 and 1999 were not material. At February 2, 2001 and January 28, 2000 this facility was unused.

NOTE 4 — Income Taxes

The provision for income taxes consists of the following:

	Fiscal Year Ended		
	February 2, 2001	January 28, 2000	January 29, 1999
	(In millions)		
Current:			
Domestic	$ 964	$1,008	$567
Foreign	168	84	86
Deferred	(174)	(307)	(29)
Provision for income taxes	$ 958	$ 785	$624

Income before income taxes and cumulative effect of change in accounting principle included approximately $491 million, $449 million, and $529 million related to foreign operations in fiscal years 2001, 2000, and 1999, respectively.

36

The Company has not recorded a deferred income tax liability of approximately $492 million for additional taxes that would result from the distribution of certain earnings of its foreign subsidiaries if they were repatriated. The Company currently intends to reinvest indefinitely these undistributed earnings of its foreign subsidiaries.

The components of the Company's net deferred tax asset are as follows:

| | Fiscal Year Ended | | |
	February 2, 2001	January 28, 2000	January 29, 1999
	(In millions)		
Deferred tax assets:			
Deferred service contract income	$148	$ 125	$118
Inventory and warranty provisions	81	60	45
Provisions for product returns and doubtful accounts	44	30	25
Loss carryforwards	73	219	—
Credit carryforwards	188	101	—
Other	64	—	—
	598	535	188
Deferred tax liabilities:			
Unrealized gains on investments	(47)	(303)	(2)
Other	—	(74)	(49)
Net deferred tax asset	$551	$ 158	$137

Tax loss carryforwards will generally expire in 2020. Credit carryforwards will generally expire between 2002 and 2022.

The effective tax rate differed from statutory U.S. federal income tax rate as follows:

| | Fiscal Year Ended | | |
	February 2, 2001	January 28, 2000	January 29, 1999
U.S. federal statutory rate	35.0%	35.0%	35.0%
Foreign income taxed at different rates	(5.8)	(6.0)	(7.0)
Nondeductible purchase of in-process research and development	—	2.8	—
Other	0.8	0.2	2.0
Effective tax rates	30.0%	32.0%	30.0%

NOTE 5 — Capitalization

Preferred Stock

Authorized Shares — The Company has the authority to issue five million shares of preferred stock, par value $.01 per share. At February 2, 2001 and January 28, 2000 no shares of preferred stock were issued or outstanding.

Series A Junior Participating Preferred Stock — In conjunction with the distribution of Preferred Share Purchase Rights (see below), the Company's Board of Directors designated 200,000 shares of preferred stock as Series A Junior Participating Preferred Stock ("Junior Preferred Stock") and reserved such shares for issuance upon exercise of the Preferred Share Purchase Rights. At February 2, 2001 and January 28, 2000, no shares of Junior Preferred Stock were issued or outstanding.

Common Stock

Authorized Shares — As of February 2, 2001, the Company is authorized to issue seven billion shares of common stock.

Stock Repurchase Program — The Board of Directors has authorized the Company to repurchase up to one billion shares of its common stock in open market or private transactions. During fiscal years 2001 and 2000, the Company repurchased 65 million and 56 million shares of its common stock, respectively, for an aggregate cost of $2.7 billion and $1.1 billion, respectively. As of February 2, 2001, the Company was authorized to repurchase up to 40 million additional shares of its outstanding common stock. The Company utilizes equity instrument contracts to facilitate its repurchase of common stock. At February 2, 2001 and January 28, 2000, the Company held equity options and forwards that allow for the purchase of 88 million and 50 million shares of common stock, respectively, at an average price of $50 and $45 per share, respectively. At February 2, 2001 and January 28, 2000, the Company also had outstanding put obligations covering 111 million and 69 million shares, respectively, with an average exercise price of $44 and $39 per share, respectively. The equity instruments are exercisable only at date of expiration and expire at various dates through the first quarter of fiscal 2004. The outstanding put obligations at February 2, 2001 permitted net share settlement at the Company's option and, therefore, did not result in a put obligation liability on the accompanying Consolidated Statement of Financial Position.

Preferred Share Purchase Rights

If a person or group acquires 15% or more of the outstanding common stock, each Right will entitle the holder (other than such person or any member of such group) to purchase, at the Right's then current exercise price, the number of shares of common stock having a market value of twice the exercise price of the Right. If exercisable, the Rights contain provisions relating to merger or other business combinations.

In certain circumstances, the Board of Directors may, at its option, exchange part or all of the Rights (other than Rights held by the acquiring person or group) for shares of common stock at an exchange rate of one share of common stock for each Right.

The Company will be entitled to redeem the Rights at $.001 per Right at any time before a 15% or greater position has been acquired by any person or group. Additionally, the Company may lower the 15% threshold to not less than the greater of (a) any percentage greater than the largest percentage of common stock known by the Company to be owned by any person (other than Michael S. Dell) or (b) 10%. The Rights expire on November 29, 2005.

Neither the ownership nor the further acquisition of common stock by Michael S. Dell will cause the Rights to become exercisable or nonredeemable or will trigger the other features of the Rights.

At February 2, 2001, the Company has no Preferred Share Purchase Rights ("Rights") outstanding. Each Right entitles the holder to purchase one thirty-two thousandth of a share of Junior Preferred Stock at an exercise price of $225 per one-thousandth of a share.

NOTE 6 — Benefit Plans

Incentive and Stock Option Plans — The Dell Computer Corporation Incentive Plan (the "Incentive Plan"), which is administered by the Compensation Committee of the Board of Directors, provides for the granting of stock-based incentive awards to directors, executive officers and key employees of the Company and its subsidiaries, and certain other persons who provide consulting or advisory services to the Company.

Options granted may be either incentive stock options within the meaning of Section 422 of the Internal Revenue Code or nonqualified options. The right to purchase shares under the existing stock option agreements typically vest pro-rata at each option anniversary date over a five-year period. Stock options must be exercised within 10 years from date of grant. Stock options are generally issued at fair market value. Under the Incentive Plan, each nonemployee director of the Company is eligible for stock options and restricted stock awards annually, with the number of options or shares awarded being within the discretion of the Compensation Committee of the Board of Directors (subject to certain specified limits).

In addition, the Dell Computer Corporation 1998 Broad-Based Stock Option Plan (the "Broad-Based Plan") provides for the award of nonqualified stock options to non-executive employees of the Company. Collectively, the Incentive Plan and the Broad-Based Plan are referred to as the "Option Plans."

The following table summarizes stock option activity for the Option Plans:

	Number of Shares (in millions)	Weighted Average Exercise Price
Outstanding at February 1, 1998	439	$ 2.25
Granted	60	19.94
Cancelled	(26)	2.63
Exercised	(110)	1.29
Outstanding at January 29, 1999	363	5.40
Granted	50	42.86
Cancelled	(16)	9.89
Exercised	(77)	2.48
Outstanding at January 28, 2000	320	11.39
Granted	154	37.78
Cancelled	(35)	22.18
Exercised	(95)	3.26
Outstanding at February 2, 2001	344	$24.36

Exercisable stock options amounted to 100 million at a weighted average price of $8.78, 112 million at a weighted average price of $3.96, and 103 million at a weighted average price of $2.27 at February 2, 2001, January 28, 2000, and January 29, 1999, respectively.

The following is additional information relating to options for the Option Plans outstanding as of February 2, 2001:

	Options Outstanding			Options Exercisable	
	Number Of Shares	Weighted Average Exercise Price	Weighted Average Remaining Contractual Life (Years)	Number Of Shares	Weighted Average Exercise Price
	(share data in millions)				
$ 0.01-$ 1.49	67	$ 0.96	4.46	49	$ 0.95
$ 1.50-$14.99	60	$ 6.17	6.00	29	$ 5.79
$15.00-$35.99	44	$23.35	7.73	13	$21.02
$36.00-$37.59	112	$37.41	9.46	2	$33.39
$37.60-$53.90	61	$44.66	8.84	7	$44.82
	344			100	

There were 254 million, 264 million, and 162 million options to purchase the Company's common stock available for future grants under the Option Plans at February 2, 2001, January 28, 2000, and January 29, 1999, respectively.

39

Employee Stock Purchase Plan — The Company also has an employee stock purchase plan that qualifies under Section 423 of the Internal Revenue Code and permits substantially all employees to purchase shares of common stock. Participating employees may purchase common stock through payroll deductions at the end of each participation period at a purchase price equal to 85% of the lower of the fair market value of the common stock at the beginning or the end of the participation period. Common stock reserved for future employee purchases under the plan aggregated 39 million shares at February 2, 2001, 44 million shares at January 28, 2000, and 47 million shares at January 29, 1999. Common stock issued under this plan totaled four million shares in fiscal year 2001, three million shares in fiscal year 2000, and five million shares in fiscal year 1999.

Restricted Stock Grants — During fiscal years 2001, 2000, and 1999, the Company granted 1.7 million shares, 1.4 million shares, and 1 million shares, respectively, of restricted stock. For substantially all restricted stock grants, at the date of grant, the recipient has all rights of a stockholder, subject to certain restrictions on transferability and a risk of forfeiture. Restricted shares typically vest over a seven-year period beginning on the date of grant. The Company records unearned compensation equal to the market value of the restricted shares on the date of grant and charges the unearned compensation to expense over the vesting period.

Fair Value Disclosures — The weighted average fair value of stock options at date of grant was $20.98, $22.64, and $11.77 per option for options granted during fiscal years 2001, 2000, and 1999, respectively. Additionally, the weighted average fair value of the purchase rights under the employee stock purchase plan granted in fiscal years 2001, 2000, and 1999 was $13.95, $11.12, and $2.51 per right, respectively. The weighted average fair value of options and purchase rights under the employee stock purchase plan was determined based on the Black-Scholes model, utilizing the following assumptions:

	Fiscal Year Ended		
	February 2, 2001	January 28, 2000	January 29, 1999
Expected term:			
Stock options	5 years	5 years	5 years
Employee stock purchase plan	6 months	6 months	6 months
Interest rate	6.15%	5.81%	5.42%
Volatility	54.85%	51.03%	52.12%
Dividends	0%	0%	0%

Had the Company accounted for its Option Plans and employee stock purchase plan by recording compensation expense based on the fair value at the grant date on a straight-line basis over the vesting period, stock-based compensation costs would have reduced pretax income by $620 million ($434 million, net of taxes), $329 million ($224 million, net of taxes), and $194 million ($136 million, net of taxes) in fiscal years 2001, 2000, and 1999, respectively. The pro forma effect on basic earnings per common share would have been a reduction of $0.17, $0.09, and $0.05 for fiscal years 2001, 2000, and 1999, respectively. The pro forma effect on diluted earnings per common share would have been a reduction of $0.16, $0.08, and $0.05 for fiscal years 2001, 2000, and 1999, respectively.

401(k) Plan — The Company has a defined contribution retirement plan that complies with Section 401(k) of the Internal Revenue Code. Substantially all employees in the U.S. are eligible to participate in the plan. The Company matches 100% of each participant's voluntary contributions, subject to a maximum Company contribution of 3% of the participant's compensation. The Company's contributions during fiscal years 2001, 2000, and 1999 were $36 million, $44 million, and $21 million, respectively.

NOTE 7 — Commitments, Contingencies and Certain Concentrations

Lease Commitments — The Company maintains master lease facilities providing the capacity to fund up to $1.2 billion. The combined facilities provide for the ability of the Company to lease certain real property, buildings and equipment (collectively referred to as the "Properties") to be constructed or acquired. Rent obligations for the Properties commence on various dates. At February 2, 2001, $506 million of the combined facilities had been utilized.

The leases have initial terms of five and seven years. Those with an initial term of five years contain an option to renew for two successive years, subject to certain conditions. The Company may, at its option, purchase the Properties during or at the end of the lease term for 100% of the then outstanding amounts expended by the lessor to complete the Properties. If the Company does not exercise the purchase option, the Company will guarantee a residual value of the Properties as determined by the agreement (approximately $430 and $310 million at February 2, 2001 and January 28, 2000, respectively).

The Company leases other property and equipment, manufacturing facilities and office space under non-cancelable leases. Certain leases obligate the Company to pay taxes, maintenance and repair costs.

Future minimum lease payments under all non-cancelable leases as of February 2, 2001 are as follows: $37 million in fiscal 2002; $30 million in fiscal 2003; $26 million in fiscal 2004; $182 million in fiscal 2005; $279 million in fiscal 2006; and $31 million thereafter. Rent expense under all leases totaled $95 million, $81 million and $58 million for fiscal years 2001, 2000, and 1999, respectively.

Legal Matters — The Company is subject to various legal proceedings and claims arising in the ordinary course of business. The Company's management does not expect that the outcome in any of these legal proceedings, individually or collectively, will have a material adverse effect on the Company's financial condition, results of operations or cash flows.

Certain Concentrations — All of the Company's foreign currency exchange and interest rate derivative instruments involve elements of market and credit risk in excess of the amounts recognized in the consolidated financial statements. The counterparties to the financial instruments consist of a number of major financial institutions. In addition to limiting the amount of agreements and contracts it enters into with any one party, the Company monitors its positions with and the credit quality of the counterparties to these financial instruments. The Company does not anticipate nonperformance by any of the counterparties.

The Company's investments in debt securities are placed with high quality financial institutions and companies. The Company's investments in debt securities primarily have maturities of less than three years. Management believes that no significant concentration of credit risk for investments exists for the Company.

The Company markets and sells its products and services to large corporate, government, healthcare and education customers, small-to-medium businesses and individuals. Its receivables from such parties are well diversified.

The Company purchases a number of components from single sources. In some cases, alternative sources of supply are not available. In other cases, the Company may establish a working relationship with a single source, even when multiple suppliers are available, if the Company believes it is advantageous to do so due to performance, quality, support, delivery, capacity or price considerations. If the supply of a critical single-source material or component were delayed or curtailed, the Company's ability to ship the related product in desired quantities and in a timely manner could be adversely affected. Even where alternative sources of supply are available, qualification of the alternative suppliers and establishment of reliable supplies could result in delays and a possible loss of sales, which could affect operating results adversely.

NOTE 8 — Related Party Transactions

During fiscal year 1998, the Company and Newcourt Credit Group Inc. ("Newcourt"), formed a joint venture, Dell Financial Services L.P. ("DFS"), to provide leasing and asset management services to the Company's customers. Subsequently, in fiscal 2000, Newcourt was acquired by The CIT Group, Inc. The Company has a 70% equity interest in DFS; however, as the Company cannot and does not exercise control over DFS, it accounts for the investment under the equity method. During fiscal year 2001, DFS originated financing arrangements for the Company's customers totaling $2.5 billion as compared to originations of $1.8 billion in fiscal year 2000. The Company's investment in DFS at February 2, 2001 and January 28, 2000, was not material to the Company's consolidated financial position or results of operations.

NOTE 9 — Supplemental Consolidated Financial Information

	February 2, 2001	January 28, 2000
	(in millions)	
Supplemental Consolidated Statement of Financial Position Information		
Accounts receivable:		
Gross accounts receivable	$2,964	$2,652
Allowance for doubtful accounts	(69)	(44)
	$2,895	$2,608
Inventories:		
Production materials	$ 95	$ 129
Work-in-process and finished goods	305	262
	$ 400	$ 391
Property, plant and equipment:		
Land and buildings	$ 337	$ 229
Computer equipment	415	277
Machinery and other equipment	459	383
Construction-in-progress	323	251
Total property, plant and equipment	1,534	1,140
Accumulated depreciation and amortization	(538)	(375)
	$ 996	$ 765
Accrued and other current liabilities:		
Compensation	$ 428	$ 337
Deferred income	262	190
Sales and property taxes	259	238
Warranty	467	313
Income taxes	123	11
Other	718	565
	$2,257	$1,654
Other noncurrent liabilities:		
Deferred income	$ 306	$ 271
Other	455	192
	$ 761	$ 463

	Fiscal Year Ended		
	February 2, 2001	January 28, 2000	January 29, 1999
		(in millions)	
Supplemental Consolidated Statement of Income Information			
Research, development and engineering expenses:			
Research and development expenses	$ 363	$ 292	$ 209
Purchased research and development	—	194	—
Engineering expenses	119	82	63
	$ 482	$ 568	$ 272
Investment and other income, net:			
Investment and other income, net	$ 578	$ 222	$ 64
Interest expense	(47)	(34)	(26)
	$ 531	$ 188	$ 38
Supplemental Consolidated Statement of Cash Flows Information			
Changes in operating working capital accounts:			
Accounts receivable, net	$(346)	$(394)	$(598)
Inventories	(7)	(123)	(41)
Accounts payable	748	988	743
Accrued and other liabilities	367	416	255
Other, net	(91)	(75)	8
	$ 671	$ 812	$ 367
Supplemental cash flow information:			
Income taxes paid (received)	$ (32)	$(363)	$ 138
Interest paid	49	34	19

NOTE 10 — Segment Information

The Company conducts operations worldwide and is managed on a geographic basis, with those geographic segments being the Americas, Europe, and Asia-Pacific and Japan regions. The Americas segment, which is based in Round Rock, Texas, covers the United States, Canada, South America, and Latin America. The European segment, which is based in Bracknell, England, covers the European countries and also some countries in the Middle East and Africa. The Asia-Pacific and Japan segment covers the Pacific Rim, including Japan, Australia and New Zealand, and is based in Singapore. The Company's operations are primarily concentrated in the North America, Europe and Asia-Pacific regions.

The accounting policies of the geographic segments are the same as those described in the summary of significant accounting policies. The Company allocates resources to and evaluates performance of its geographic segments based on operating income. Transfers between geographic areas are recorded using internal transfer prices set by the Company. The table below presents information about the Company's reportable segments:

	Fiscal Year 2001				
	Americas	Europe	Asia-Pacific and Japan	Eliminations	Consolidated
			(in millions)		
Sales to unaffiliated customers	$22,871	$6,399	$2,618	$ —	$31,888
Transfers between geographic segments	43	5	4	(52)	—
Total sales	$22,914	$6,404	$2,622	$(52)	$31,888
Operating income	$ 2,480	$ 406	$ 192	$ —	$ 3,078
Special charge					(105)
Corporate expenses					(310)
Total operating income					$ 2,663
Depreciation and amortization	$ 124	$ 51	$ 20	$ —	$ 195
Corporate expenses					45
Total depreciation and amortization					$ 240
Identifiable assets	$ 2,553	$1,167	$ 524	$ —	$ 4,244
General corporate assets					9,191
Total assets					$13,435

	Fiscal Year 2000				
	Americas	Europe	Asia-Pacific and Japan	Eliminations	Consolidated
			(in millions)		
Sales to unaffiliated customers	$17,879	$5,590	$1,796	$ —	$25,265
Transfers between geographic segments	48	5	2	(55)	—
Total sales	$17,927	$5,595	$1,798	$(55)	$25,265
Operating income	$ 2,173	$ 403	$ 97	$ —	$ 2,673
Special charge					(194)
Corporate expenses					(216)
Total operating income					$ 2,263
Depreciation and amortization	$ 82	$ 41	$ 14	$ —	$ 137
Corporate expenses					19
Total depreciation and amortization					$ 156
Identifiable assets	$ 2,456	$1,147	$ 413	$ —	$ 4,016
General corporate assets					7,455
Total assets					$11,471

	Fiscal Year 1999				
	Americas	Europe	Asia-Pacific and Japan	Eliminations	Consolidated
			(in millions)		
Sales to unaffiliated customers	$12,420	$4,674	$1,149	$ —	$18,243
Transfers between geographic segments	33	5	1	(39)	—
Total sales	$12,453	$4,679	$1,150	$(39)	$18,243
Operating income	$ 1,802	$ 446	$ 78	$ —	$ 2,326
Corporate expenses					(280)
Total operating income					$ 2,046
Depreciation and amortization	$ 59	$ 29	$ 8	$ —	$ 96
Corporate expenses					7
Total depreciation and amortization					$ 103
Identifiable assets	$ 1,640	$1,017	$ 234	$ —	$ 2,891
General corporate assets					3,986
Total assets...............					$ 6,877

The following is net revenue and long-lived asset information by geographic region:

	Fiscal Year Ended		
	February 2, 2001	January 28, 2000	January 29, 1999
		(in millions)	
Net revenue			
United States	$21,428	$16,878	$11,668
Foreign countries	10,460	8,387	6,575
Total net revenue	$31,888	$25,265	$18,243
Long-lived assets			
United States	$ 665	$ 481	$ 348
Foreign countries	331	284	175
Total long-lived assets	$ 996	$ 765	$ 523

The allocation between domestic and foreign net revenue is based on the location of the customers. Net revenue and long-lived assets from no single foreign country was material to the Company's consolidated net revenues and long-lived assets for fiscal years 2001, 2000, and 1999.

The following is net revenue by product groups:

	Fiscal Year Ended		
	February 2, 2001	January 28, 2000	January 29, 1999
		(in millions)	
Desktop computers	$15,452	$13,568	$10,979
Notebook computers	8,572	5,847	3,859
Enterprise systems.....................................	5,511	3,828	2,193
Other	2,353	2,022	1,212
Totals	$31,888	$25,265	$18,243

45

Net revenue by product group includes worldwide service revenue. No single customer accounted for more than 10% of the Company's consolidated net revenue during fiscal years 2001, 2000, and 1999.

NOTE 11 — Unaudited Quarterly Results

The following tables contain selected unaudited Consolidated Statement of Income and stock sales price data for each quarter of fiscal years 2001 and 2000.

| | Fiscal Year 2001(a) | | | |
	4th Quarter	3rd Quarter	2nd Quarter	1st Quarter
	(in millions, except per share data)			
Net revenue	$8,674	$8,264	$7,670	$7,280
Gross margin	1,559	1,758	1,634	1,492
Net income before cumulative effect in accounting principle	434	674	603	525
Net income	$ 434	$ 674	$ 603	$ 466
Earnings per common share (b):				
Before cumulative effect of change in accounting principle				
Basic	$ 0.17	$ 0.26	$ 0.23	$ 0.20
Diluted	$ 0.16	$ 0.25	$ 0.22	$ 0.19
After cumulative effect of change in accounting principle				
Basic	$ 0.17	$ 0.26	$ 0.23	$ 0.18
Diluted	$ 0.16	$ 0.25	$ 0.22	$ 0.17
Weighted average shares outstanding:				
Basic	2,582	2,586	2,582	2,575
Diluted	2,783	2,739	2,726	2,737
Stock sales prices per share:				
High	$33.06	$44.25	$54.67	$59.69
Low	$16.25	$22.75	$42.00	$35.00

| | Fiscal Year 2000 | | | |
	4th Quarter	3rd Quarter	2nd Quarter	1st Quarter
	(in millions, except per share data)			
Net revenue	$6,802	$6,784	$6,142	$5,537
Gross margin	1,304	1,370	1,354	1,190
Net income	$ 436	$ 289	$ 507	$ 434
Earnings per common share (b):				
Basic	$ 0.17	$ 0.11	$ 0.20	$ 0.17
Diluted	$ 0.16	$ 0.11	$ 0.19	$ 0.16
Weighted average shares outstanding:				
Basic	2,559	2,538	2,524	2,528
Diluted	2,731	2,724	2,725	2,738
Stock sales prices per share:				
High	$53.97	$49.94	$45.06	$55.00
Low	$37.06	$37.38	$31.38	$35.38

(a) Reflects the adoption of SAB 101 as discussed in Note 1. The cumulative effect of this change was $59 million, net of taxes. Other than the cumulative effect, this accounting change had no material effect on the Company's previously reported revenue or quarterly earnings during fiscal 2001.

(b) Earnings per common share are computed independently for each of the quarters presented. Therefore, the sum of the quarterly per common share information may not equal the annual earnings per common share.

46

Photo Credits

Chapter 1

p. 3 Photo by Joe Skipper/Reuter. **p. 8** Bob Daemmrich/Stock Boston. **p. 24** James L. Amos/CORBIS. **p. 25** Joseph Nettis/Stock Boston. **p. 25** PhotoDisc. **p. 25** PhotoDisc. **p. 26** Courtesy of Dell Corporation.

Chapter 2

p. 57 Courtesy of CSX Corporation. **p. 65** Robert Rathe/Stock Boston. **p. 70** AP Photo/Stuart Ramson. **p. 71** No credit required. **p. 72** Phyllis Picardi/ Stock Boston.

Chapter 3

p. 103 Summer Production. **p. 104** Michael Newman/PhotoEdit. **p. 119** Ralph Mercer/Tony Stone/Getty Images. **p. 120** CORBIS c 2001.

Chapter 4

p. 149 J. Messer Schmidt/eStock Photography/Picture Quest. **p. 166** Michael Newman/PhotoEdit. **p. 171** AP PHoto/Chad Rachman. **p. 172** Archivo Icongrafico, S.A./CORBIS.

Chapter 5

p. 215 Spencer Grant/PhotoEdit. **p. 231** Ovak Arslanian. **p. 232** John S. Reid. **p. 233** Michael Newman/PhotoEdit/PictureQuest.

Chapter 6

p. 265 Bill Aron/PhotoEdit. **p. 268** Courtesy of Nordstrom. **p. 272** Superstock. **p. 285** Bruce Burkhardt/CORBIS.

Chapter 7

p. 311 Richard L. Miller/Stock Boston. **p. 322** c 2001 Corbis. **p. 326** Spencer Grant/PhotoEdit. **p. 331** PhotoDisc. **p. 334** Reuters/Getty Images.

Chapter 8

p. 361 John c. Hillery/Reuters. **p. 369** Spencer Grant/PhotoEdit. **p. 371** Dick Durrance II/Woodfin Camp & Associates. **p. 374** Richard Pasley/Stock Boston. **p. 378** Roger Rossmeyer/CORBIS.

Chapter 9

p. 411 PhotoDisc. **p. 428** No credit required. **p. 429** PhotoDisc. **p. 432** John S. Reid. **p. 435** AP Photo/Tsugufumi Matsumoto

Chapter 10

p. 463 Associated Press. **p. 468** No credit required. **p. 471** Associated Press, AP **p. 484** AP Photo/Battle Creek Enquirer, Scott Erskine.

Chapter 11

p. 519 Najlah Feanny/Stock Boston. **p. 523** Courtesy of AT&T. **p. 526** Jeff Smith/Image Bank/Getty. **p. 527** BD Lanphere/Stock Boston.

Chapter 12

p. 567 AP Photo/Lisa Poole. **p. 578** Bonnie Kamin/PhotoEdit. **p. 581** Peter Menzel/Stock Boston.

accelerated depreciation methods   Depreciation methods that recognize depreciation expense more rapidly in the early stages of an asset's life than in the later stages of its life. *p. 414*

account   Record used for the classification and summary of transaction data. *p. 9*

account balance   Difference between total debits and total credits in an account. *p. 150*

account groups   Self-balancing entities that account for a governmental unit's general fixed assets and the outstanding principal of its general long-term liabilities. *p. 544*

accounting   Service-based profession that provides reliable and relevant financial information useful in making decisions. *p. 3*

accounting controls   Procedures designed to safeguard assets and to ensure accuracy and reliability of the accounting records and reports. *p. 265*

accounting cycle   A cycle consisting of these stages: recording accounting data, adjusting the accounts, preparing the financial statements, and closing the nominal accounts; when one accounting cycle ends, a new one begins *p. 68*

accounting equation   Expression of the relationship between the assets and the claims on those assets. *p. 10*

accounting event   Economic occurrence that causes changes in an enterprise's assets, liabilities, and/or equity. *p. 13*

accounting period   Span of time covered by the financial statements, normally one year, but may be semiannually, quarterly, and monthly. *p. 18*

accounts receivable   Expected future cash receipts arising from permitting customers to *buy now and pay later;* usually are small with a short term to maturity. *pp. 58, 311*

accounts receivable turnover ratio   Financial ratio that measures how fast accounts receivable are turned into cash; computed by dividing sales by accounts receivable. *p. 333*

accrual   Recognition of events before exchanging cash. *p. 57*

accrual accounting   Method of accounting that records the effects of accounting events in the period in which such events occur regardless of when cash is exchanged. *pp. 57, 570*

accumulated depreciation   Contra asset account that indicates the sum of all depreciation expense recognized for an asset since the date of acquisition. *pp. 106, 417*

adjusting entry   Entry that updates account balances prior to preparing financial statements. *p. 65*

administrative controls   Procedures designed to evaluate performance and the degree of compliance with a firm's policies and public laws. *p. 266*

adverse opinion   Audit opinion for a set of financial statements issued by a certified public accountant that means that part of or all of the financial statements are not in compliance with GAAP and the auditors believe this noncompliance would be material to the average prudent investor. *p. 72*

allocation   Recognition of expense by systematic assignment of the cost of an asset to periods of use. *p. 103*

allowance   Reduction in the selling price of goods extended to the buyer because the goods are defective or of lower quality than the buyer ordered and to encourage a buyer to keep merchandise that would otherwise be returned. *p. 222*

Allowance for Doubtful Accounts   Contra asset account that contains an amount equal to the accounts receivable that are expected to be uncollectible. *p. 313*

allowance method of accounting for bad debts   Method of accounting for bad debts in which bad debts are estimated and expensed in the same period in which the corresponding sales are recognized. The receivables are reported in the financial statements at net realizable value (the amount expected to be collected in cash). *p. 312*

American Institute of Certified Public Accountants' Code of Professional Conduct   Set of ethical rules and guidelines above and beyond the requirements of laws and regulations that certified public accountants must follow. *p. 74*

amortization   Method of systematically allocating the costs of intangible assets to expense over their useful lives; also term for converting the discount on a note to interest expense over a designated period. *pp. 327, 413*

amortization of loan   Systematic repayment of principal and interest over the life of a loan. *p. 463*

annual report   Document in which an organization provides information to stockholders, usually on an annual basis. *p. 25*

annuity   Series of equal payments made over a specified number of periods. *p. 487*

appropriated retained earnings   Retained earnings restricted by the board of directors for a specific purpose (e.g., to repay debt or for future expansion); although a part of total retained earnings, not available for distribution as dividends. *p. 535*

articles of incorporation   Items on an application filed with a state agency for the formation of a corporation; contains such information as the corporation's name, its purpose, its location, its expected life, provisions for its capital stock, and a list of the members of its board of directors. *p. 520*

asset   Economic resource used by a business for the production of revenue. *p. 10*

asset exchange transaction   A transaction that decreases one asset while increasing another asset so that total assets do not change; for example, the purchase of land with cash. *p. 58*

asset/expense adjustment   Adjusting entry that decreases assets and increases expenses. *p. 161*

asset source transaction   Transaction that increases an asset and a claim on assets; three types of asset source transactions are acquired from owners (equity), borrowed from creditors (liabilities), or earned through operations (revenues). *pp. 14, 58*

asset/revenue adjustment   Adjusting entry that increases assets and revenues. *p. 159*

asset use transaction   Transaction that decreases an asset and a claim on assets; the three types are distributions (transferred to owners), liabilities (used to pay creditors), or expenses (used to operate the business). *p. 59*

audit Detailed examination of a company's financial statements and the documents that support the information presented in these statements. *p. 70*

audit around the computer Procedure in which auditors provide input that is expected to result in a designated output and then tests the system by comparing the actual output with the expected output. *p. 270*

authorized stock Number of shares that the corporation is approved by the state to issue. *p. 527*

available-for-sale securities Marketable securities that are not properly classified as held-to-maturity or trading securities. *p. 382*

average days in inventory ratio (sometimes called **average number of days to sell inventory ratio**) Financial ratio that measures the average number of days that inventory stays in stock before being sold. *p. 377*

average number of days to collect accounts receivable Length of the average collection period for accounts receivable; computed by dividing 365 (or 366) by the accounts receivable turnover ratio. *p. 333*

bad debts expense Expense associated with uncollectible accounts receivable; amount recognized may be estimated using the allowance method, or actual losses may be recorded using the direct write-off method. *p. 313*

balance sheet Statement that lists the assets of a business and the corresponding claims (liabilities and equity) on those assets. *p. 18*

balloon payment Large final payment due at the maturity of a debt that otherwise requires systematic smaller payments over the term of the loan prior to maturity. *p. 464*

bank reconciliation statement Statement that identifies and notes differences between the cash balance reported by the bank and the cash balance in the firm's accounting records. *p. 275*

bank statement Statement issued by a bank (usually monthly) that denotes all activity in the bank account for that period. *p. 273*

bank statement credit memo Memo that describes an increase in the account balance. *p. 273*

bank statement debit memo Memo that describes a decrease in the account balance. *p. 273*

basket purchase Acquisition of several assets in a single transaction with no specific cost attributed to each asset. *p. 414*

bearer or coupon bonds Also called *unregistered bonds;* bonds for which interest and principal payments are made to anyone who holds and redeems the interest coupon. *p. 470*

board of directors Group of individuals elected by the stockholders of a corporation to oversee its operations. *p. 523*

bond Debt security used to obtain long-term financing in which a company borrows funds from a number of lenders, called *bondholders;* usually issued in denominations of $1,000. *p. 469*

bond discount Difference between the selling price and the face amount of a bond sold for less than the face amount. *p. 475*

bond indenture Bond contract that specifies the stated rate of interest and the face value of the bond as well as other contractual provisions. *p. 469*

bond premium Difference between the selling price and the face amount of the bond that is sold for more than the face amount. *p. 480*

book value Historical (original) cost of an asset minus the accumulated depreciation; alternatively, undepreciated amount to date. *pp. 106, 419*

book value per share Value of stock determined by dividing the total stockholders' equity by the number of shares of stock. *p. 526*

books of original entry Journals in which a transaction is first recorded. *p. 164*

call premium Difference between the call price (the price that must be paid for a called bond) and the face amount of the bond. *p. 471*

call price Specified price that must be paid for bonds that are called; usually higher than the face amount of the bonds. *p. 481*

callable bonds Bonds that include a feature allowing the issuer to pay them off prior to maturity. *p. 470*

capital expenditures (on an existing asset) Substantial amounts of funds spent to improve an asset's quality or to extend its life. *p. 425*

capitalized Recorded cost in an asset account until the item is used to produce revenue. *p. 122*

carrying value Face amount of a bond liability less any unamortized bond discount or plus any unamortized bond premium. *p. 476*

cash Coins, currency, checks, balances in checking and certain savings accounts, money orders, bank drafts, certificates of deposit, and other items that are payable on demand. *p. 271*

cash discount Discount offered on merchandise sold to encourage prompt payment; offered by sellers of merchandise and represent sales discounts to the seller when they are used and purchase discounts to the purchaser of the merchandise. *p. 222*

cash inflows Sources of cash. *p. 567*

cash outflows Uses of cash. *p. 567*

cash short and over Account used to record the amount of cash shortages or overages; shortages are considered expenses and overages are considered revenues. *p. 278*

certified check Check guaranteed by a bank to be drawn on an account having funds sufficient to pay the check. *p. 275*

certified public accountant (CPA) Accountant who has met certain educational and experiential requirements and is licensed by the state government to provide audit services to the public. *p. 71*

chart of accounts List of all ledger accounts and their corresponding account numbers. *p. 164*

checks Prenumbered forms, sometimes multicopy, with the name of the business issuing them preprinted on the face, indicating to whom they are paid, the amount of the payment, and the transaction date. *p. 273*

claims Owners' and creditors' interests in a business's assets. *p. 10*

claims exchange transaction Transaction that decreases one claim and increases another so that total claims do not change. For example, the accrual of interest expense is a claims exchange transaction; liabilities increase, and the recognition of the expense causes retained earnings to decrease. *p. 59*

classified balance sheet Balance sheet that distinguishes between current and noncurrent items. *p. 283*

closely held corporation Corporation whose stock is exchanged between a limited number of individuals. *p. 521*

closing entries   Entries used to transfer the balances in the revenue, expense, and dividends accounts to the Retained Earnings account at the end of the accounting period. *pp. 63, 169*

closing the accounts or **closing**   Process of transferring balances from nominal accounts (Revenue, Expense, and Dividends) to the permanent account (Retained Earnings). *p. 19*

code of professional conduct   A set of guidelines established by the American Institute of Certified Public Accountants (AICPA) to promote high ethical conduct among its membership. *p. 74*

collateral for loans   Assets pledged as security for a loan. *p. 466*

common size financial statements   Financial statements in which amounts are converted to percentages to allow a better comparison of period-to-period and company-to-company financial data since all information is placed on a common basis. *p. 232*

common stock   Basic class of corporate stock that carries no preferences as to claims on assets or dividends, certificates that evidence ownership in a company. *pp. 10, 527*

compound interest   Practice of reinvesting interest so that interest is earned on interest as well as on the initial principal. *pp. 486, 527*

compounding   Earning interest on interest. *p. 486*

comprehensive annual financial report (CAFR)   An annual report that provides information regarding all funds and account groups under the jurisdiction of a government reporting entity. *p. 544*

comprehensive income   Net income plus or minus unrealized gains or losses. *p. 379*

concept of materiality   Concept that recognizes practical limits in financial reporting by allowing flexible handling of matters not considered material; information considered material if the decisions of a reasonable person would be influenced by its omission or misstatement. *p. 110*

consolidated financial statements   Financial statements that represent the combined operations of a parent company and its subsidiaries. *p. 385*

continuity   Concept that describes the fact that a corporation's life may extend well beyond the time at which any particular shareholder decides to retire or to sell his or her stock. *p. 523*

contra account   Account that normally has a balance opposite to that of the other accounts in a particular category (e.g., Accumulated Depreciation is classified as an asset, but it normally has a credit balance). *p. 161*

contra asset account   Account subtracted from another account with which it is associated; has the effect of reducing the asset account with which it is associated. *pp. 106, 417*

contra liability account   Account reported in the liability section of the balance sheet that has a debit balance; reduces total liabilities. A discount on a Note Payable is an example of a contra liability account. *p. 327*

contributed capital   Balance sheet term used to designate the portion of assets contributed to a business by its owners. *p. 9*

convertible bonds   Bonds that can be converted (exchanged) to an ownership interest (stock) in the corporation. *p. 470*

copyright   Legal protection of writings, musical compositions, and other intellectual property for the exclusive use of the creator or persons assigned the right by the creator. *p. 430*

corporation   Legal entity separate from its owners; formed when a group of individuals with a common purpose join together in an organization according to state laws. *p. 520*

cost method of accounting for treasury stock   Method of accounting for treasury stock in which the purchase of treasury stock is recorded at its cost to the firm but does not consider the original issue price or par value. *p. 532*

cost of goods available for sale   Total costs paid to obtain goods and to make them ready for sale, including the cost of beginning inventory plus purchases and transportation-in costs, less purchase returns and allowances and purchase discounts. *p. 216*

cost of goods sold   Total cost incurred for the goods sold during a specific accounting period. *p. 216*

credit   Entry that increases liability and equity accounts or decreases asset accounts. *p. 150*

creditor   Individual or institution that has loaned goods or services to a business. *p. 5*

cumulative dividends   Preferred dividends that accumulate from year to year until paid. *p. 527*

current (short-term) asset   Asset that will be converted to cash or consumed within one year or an operating cycle, whichever is longer. *p. 282*

current (short-term) liability   Obligation due within one year or an operating cycle, whichever is longer. *p. 282*

current ratio   Financial ratio that measures the relationship between current assets and current liabilities; determined by dividing current assets by current liabilities, with the result expressed in decimal format. *p. 284*

date of record   Date that establishes who will receive the dividend payment: Shareholders who actually own the stock on the record date will be paid the dividend even if the stock is sold before the dividend is paid. *p. 533*

debenture   Unsecured bond issued based on the general credit of the organization. *p. 469*

debit   Entry that increases asset accounts or decreases liability and equity accounts. *p. 150*

debt security   Type of security acquired by loaning assets to the investee company. *p. 381*

debt to assets ratio   Financial ratio that measures a company's level of risk. *p. 118*

declaration date   Date on which the board of directors actually declares a dividend. *p. 533*

deferral   Recognition of revenue or expense in a period after the cash is exchanged. *p. 103*

deferral transactions   Accounting transactions in which cash payments or receipts occur before the associated expense or revenue is recognized. *p. 572*

deferred tax liability   Taxes not paid until future years because of the difference in accounting methods selected for financial statements and methods required for tax purposes (e.g., a company may select straight-line depreciation for financial statement reporting but will be required to use MACRS for tax reporting). *p. 424*

demand   Consumer preferences expressed by offering money for goods or services. *p. 5*

depletion   Method of systematically allocating the costs of natural resources to expense as the resources are removed from the land. *p. 427*

deposit ticket   Bank form that accompanies checks and cash deposited into a bank account; normally specifies the account number, name of the account, and a record of the checks and cash being deposited. *p. 273*

deposits in transit   Deposits recorded in a depositor's books but not received and recorded by the bank. *p. 275*

depreciation   Method of systematically allocating the costs of long-term tangible assets to expense over their useful lives. *p. 412*

depreciation expense   Portion of the original cost of a long-term tangible asset allocated to an expense account in a given period. *p. 106*

direct method   Method of preparing the statement of cash flows that reports the total cash receipts and cash payments from each of the major categories of activities (collections from customers, payment to suppliers). *p. 582*

direct write-off method   Method of recognizing bad debts expense only when accounts are determined to be uncollectible. *p. 321*

disclaimer of audit opinion   Position that an auditor can take with respect to financial statements when there is not enough information to confirm compliance or noncompliance with GAAP; is neither positive nor negative. *p. 73*

discount   Amount of interest included in the face of a note; the discount (interest) is subtracted from the face amount of the note to determine the principal amount of cash borrowed. *p. 326*

discount notes   Notes that have the interest included in their face value. *p. 326*

Discount on Bonds Payable   Contra liability account used to record the amount of discount on a bond issue. *p. 476*

Discount on Notes Payable   Contra liability account subtracted from the Notes Payable account to determine the carrying value of the liability. *p. 327*

dividend   Transfer of wealth from a business to its owners *pp. 12, 382, 527*

dividends in arrears   Cumulative dividends on preferred stock that have not been paid; must be paid prior to paying dividends to common stockholders. *p. 527*

double taxation   Policy to tax corporate profits distributed to owners twice, once when the income is reported on the corporation's income tax return and again when the dividends are reported on the individual's return. *p. 521*

double-declining balance depreciation   Depreciation method that recognizes larger amounts of depreciation in the early stages of an asset's life and progressively smaller amounts as the asset ages. *p. 418*

double-entry accounting (bookkeeping)   Method of keeping records that provides a system of checks and balances by recording transactions in a dual format. *pp. 14, 150*

earnings   The difference between the cost of a product or service and the selling price of that product or service. Same as net income or profit *p. 4*

effective interest rate   Yield rate of bonds, which is usually equal to the market rate of interest on the day the bonds are sold. *p. 474*

effective interest rate method   Method of amortizing bond discounts and premiums that computes interest based on the carrying value of liability. As the liability increases or decreases, the amount of interest expense also increases or decreases. *p. 490*

elements   Primary components of financial statements including assets, liabilities, equity, contributions, revenue, expenses, distributions, and net income. *p. 9*

entity   Specific unit (individual, business, or institution) for which the accountant records and reports economic information; has boundaries that are distinct and separate from those of the owners, creditors, managers, and employees. *p. 25*

entrenched management   Management that may have become ineffective but because of political implications may be difficult to remove. *p. 523*

equity   Portion of assets remaining after the creditors' claims have been satisfied (i.e., Assets − Liabilities = Equity); also called *residual interest* or *net assets. p. 10*

equity method   Method of accounting for investments in marketable equity securities; is required when the investor owns 20 percent to 50 percent of the investee company. The amount of investments carried under the equity method represents a measure of the book value of the investee rather than the cost or market value of the investment security. *p. 385*

equity sercurity   An equity security is certificate that evidences an ownership interest in a company. An example is a common stock certificate. *p. 381*

estimated life   Time for which an asset is expected to be used by a business. *p. 415*

ex-dividend   Stock traded after the date of record but before the payment date; does not receive the benefit of the upcoming dividend. *p. 534*

expense   Asset used in the process of generating revenues. (expanded definition) Decrease in assets or increase in liabilities that occurs in the process of generating revenue. *p. 75*

expense transactions   Transactions completed in the process of operating a business that decrease assets or increase liabilities. *p. 570*

extraordinary items   Items of income and expense that are unusual and rarely occur and that are set apart from operating income on the income statement. *p. 482*

face value   Amount of the bond to be paid back (to the bondholders) at maturity. *p. 469*

fidelity bond   Insurance policy that a company buys to insure itself against loss due to employee dishonesty. *p. 267*

financial accounting   Accounting information designed to satisfy the needs of an organization's external users, including business owners, creditors, and government agencies. *p. 6*

Financial Accounting Standards Board (FASB)   Privately funded organization with the primary authority for the establishment of accounting standards in the United States. *p. 9*

financial audit   Detailed examination of a company's financial statements and the documents that support the information presented in those statements; includes a verification process that tests the reliability of the underlying accounting system used to produce the financial reports. *p. 70*

financial leverage   Concept of increasing earnings through debt financing; investment of money at a higher rate than that paid to borrow the money. *pp. 120, 469*

financial resources   Money or credit arrangements supplied to a business by investors (owners) and creditors. *p. 5*

financial statements Primary means of communicating the financial information of an organization to the external users. The four general-purpose financial statements are the income statement, statement of changes in equity, balance sheet, and statement of cash flows. *p. 9*

financing activities Cash transactions associated with owners and creditors; also one of the three categories of cash inflows and outflows shown on the statement of cash flows. This category of cash activities shows the amount of cash provided by these resource providers and the amount of cash that is returned to them. *pp. 12, 568*

first-in, first-out (FIFO) cost flow method Inventory cost flow method that treats the first items purchased as first items sold for the purpose of computing cost of goods sold. *p. 362*

fiscal year Year for which a company's accounting records are kept. *p. 149*

fixed interest rate Interest rate (charge for the use of money) that does not change over the life of the loan. *p. 463*

FOB (free on board) destination Term that designates the seller as the responsible party for freight costs (transportation-in costs). *p. 221*

FOB (free on board) shipping point Term that designates the buyer as the responsible party for freight costs (transportation-in costs). *p. 221*

footnotes to the financial statements Explanations of the information in the financial statements such as estimates used and options allowable under GAAP that have been chosen. *p. 171*

franchise Exclusive right to sell products or perform services in certain geographic areas. *p. 430*

fund Independent accounting entity with a self-balancing set of accounts segregated for the purposes of carrying on specific activities. *p. 544*

fund accounting Type of accounting used by governmental entities. *p. 544*

future value Amount an investment will be worth at some point in the future, assuming a specified interest rate and the reinvestment of interest each period that it is earned. *p. 487*

gains Increases in assets or decreases in liabilities that result from peripheral or incidental transactions. *p. 114*

general authority Policies and procedures that apply across different levels of a company's management, such as everyone flies coach class. *p. 267*

general journal Journal in which all types of accounting transactions can be entered but is commonly used to record adjusting and closing entries and unusual types of transactions. *p. 164*

general ledger Complete set of accounts used in accounting systems *p. 17*

generally accepted accounting principles (GAAP) Rules and regulations that accountants agree to follow when preparing financial reports for public distribution. *p. 8*

going concern assumption Assumption that a company will continue to operate indefinitely, will pay its obligations and should therefore report those obligations at their full face value in the financial statements. *p. 312*

goodwill Added value of a successful business that is attributable to factors—reputation, location, and superior products—that enable the business to earn above-average profits; stated differently, the excess paid for an

existing business over the appraised value of the net assets. *p. 413*

gross margin Difference between sales revenue and cost of goods sold; the amount a company makes from selling goods before subtracting operating expenses. *p. 216*

gross margin method Method of estimating ending inventory that assumes that the percentage of gross margin to sales remains relatively stable from one accounting period to the next. *p. 373*

gross margin percentage Expression of gross margin as a percentage of sales computed by dividing gross margin by net sales; the amount of each dollar of sales that is profit before deducting any operating expenses. *p. 232*

half-year convention Tax rule that requires six months of depreciation expense to be taken in the year of purchase of the asset and the year of disposal regardless of the purchase date. *p. 423*

held-to-maturity securities Debt securities intended to be held until maturity. *p. 381*

historical cost Actual price paid for an asset when it was purchased. *p. 15*

horizontal statements model Arrangement of a set of financial statements horizontally across a sheet of paper. *p. 13*

imprest basis Description of the periodic replenishment of a fund to maintain it at its specified original amount. *p. 279*

income from operations Income determined by subtracting operating expenses from operating revenues. Gains and losses and other peripheral activities are added to or subtracted from income from operations to determine net income or loss. *p. 115*

income Added value created in transforming resources into more desirable states. *p. 4*

income statement Statement that measures the difference between the asset increases and the asset decreases associated with running a business. This definition is expanded in subsequent chapters as additional relationships among the elements of the financial statements are introduced. *p. 11*

independent auditor Certified public accountant licensed to perform audits who is independent of the company being audited. *p. 71*

indirect method Method of preparing the statement of cash flows that uses the net income from the income statement as a starting point for the reporting of cash flow from operating activities. The adjustments necessary to convert accrual-based net income to a cash-equivalent basis are shown in the operating activities section of the statement of cash flows. *p. 583*

intangible assets Assets that may be represented by pieces of paper or contracts that appear tangible; however, the true value of an intangible asset lies in the rights and privileges extended to its owners. *p. 412*

interest Fee paid for the use of borrowed funds; also refers to revenue from debt securities. *pp. 6, 382*

interest-bearing notes Notes that require the payment of the face value plus accrued interest at maturity. *p. 326*

internal controls A company's policies and procedures designed to reduce the opportunity for fraud and to provide reasonable assurance that its objectives will be accomplished. *pp. 74, 265*

inventory Supply of goods that is in the process of being made or is finished and ready for sale; also describes stockpiles of goods used in the business (office supplies, cleaning supplies). *p. 215*

inventory cost flow methods   Methods used to allocate the cost of goods available for sale between cost of goods sold and inventory. *p. 361*

inventory turnover   Ratio of cost of goods sold to inventory that indicates how many times a year the average inventory is sold (turned over). *p. 377*

investee   Company that receives assets or services in exchange for a debt or equity security. *p. 381*

investing activities   One of the three categories of cash inflows and outflows shown on the statement of cash flows; include cash received and spent by the business on productive assets and investments in the debt and equity of other companies. *pp. 12, 568*

investment   Commitment of assets (usually cash) by a business to acquire other assets that will be used to produce revenue. *p. 64*

investment securities   Certificates that describe the rights and privileges that investors receive when they loan or give assets or services to investees. *p. 381*

investor   Company or individual who gives assets or services and receives a security certificate in exchange. *pp. 5, 381*

issued stock   Stock sold to the public. *p. 527*

issuer of a bond   Party that issues the bond (the borrower). *p. 468*

issuer of a note   Individual or business borrowing funds (the party receiving the cash when a note is issued). *pp. 69, 326*

journal   Book of original entry in which accounting data are entered chronologically before posting to the ledger accounts. *p. 164*

labor resources   Both intellectual and physical labor used in the process of converting goods and services to products of greater value. *p. 6*

last-in, first-out (LIFO) cost flow method   Inventory cost flow method that treats the last items purchased as the first items sold for the purpose of computing cost of goods sold. *p. 362*

ledger   Collection of all accounts used by a business; primary information source for the financial statements. *p. 164*

legal capital   Amount of assets that should be maintained as protection for creditors; the number of shares multiplied by the par value. *p. 526*

liabilities   Obligations of a business to relinquish assets, provide services, or accept other obligations. *p. 10*

liability/expense adjustment   Adjusting entry that increases liabilities and expenses. *p. 160*

liability/revenue adjustment   Adjusting entry that decreases liabilities and increases revenue. *p. 162*

limited liability   Concept that investors in a corporation may not be held personally liable for the actions of the corporation (the creditors cannot lay claim to the owners' personal assets as payment for the corporation's debts). *p. 522*

limited liability company (LLC)   Organizational form offering many of the best features of corporations and partnerships and with many legal benefits of a corporation (e.g., limited liability and centralized management) but permitted by the Internal Revenue Service to be taxed as a partnership, thereby avoiding double taxation of profits. *p. 522*

line of credit   Preapproved credit arrangement with a lending institution in which a business can borrow money by simply writing a check up to the approved limit. *p. 466*

liquidation   Process of dividing up the assets and returning them to the resource providers. Creditors normally receive first priority in business liquidations; in other words, assets are distributed to creditors first. After creditor claims have been satisfied, the remaining assets are distributed to the investors (owners) of the business. *p. 5*

liquidity   Ability to convert assets to cash quickly and meet short-term obligations. *pp. 18, 283*

long-term operational assets   Assets used by a business to generate revenue; condition of being used distinguishes them from assets that are sold (inventory) and assets that are held (investments). *p. 411*

losses   Decreases in assets or increases in liabilities that result from peripheral or incidental transactions. *p. 114*

lower-of-cost-or-market rule   Accounting principle of reporting inventories at market value if their value declined below their cost, regardless of the cause. *p. 372*

Management's Discussion and Analysis (MD&A)   Section of the annual report that management uses to explain many different aspects of the company's past performance and future plans. *p. 172*

managerial accounting   Branch of accounting that provides information useful to internal decision makers and managers in operating an organization. *p. 6*

manufacturing companies   Makers of goods sold to customers. *p. 25*

market   Gathering of people or organizations for the purpose of buying and selling resources. *p. 4*

market interest rate   Current interest rate available on a wide range of alternative investments. *p. 475*

market value   Value at which securities sell in the secondary market; also called *fair value*. *pp. 381, 526*

marketable securities   Securities that are readily traded in the secondary securities market. *p. 381*

matching concept   Process of matching expenses with the revenues they produce; three ways to match expenses with revenues include matching expenses directly to revenues, matching expenses to the period in which they are incurred, and matching expenses systematically with revenues *pp. 65, 108*

material error   Error or other reporting problem that, if known, would have influenced the decision of an average prudent investor. *p. 71*

merchandise inventory   Supply of finished goods held for resale to customers. *p. 216*

merchandising businesses   Companies that buy and sell merchandise inventory. *pp. 25, 216*

Modified Accelerated Cost Recovery System (MACRS)   Prescribed method of depreciation for tax purposes that provides the maximum depreciation expense deduction permitted under tax law. *p. 423*

mortgage bond   Type of secured bond that conditionally transfers title of a designated piece of property to the bondholder until the bond is paid. *p. 469*

multistep income statement   Income statement format that matches particular revenue items with related expense items and distinguishes between recurring operating activities and nonoperating items such as gains and losses. *p. 226*

natural resources   Mineral deposits, oil and gas reserves, and reserves of timber, mines, and quarries are examples;

sometimes called *wasting assets* because their value wastes away as the resources are removed. *p. 412*

net assets   Portion of the assets remaining after the creditors' claims have been satisfied (i.e., Assets − Liabilities = Net assets); also called *equity* or *residual interest*. *p. 10*

net income   Increase in net assets resulting from operating activities. *p. 11*

net income percentage   Another term for *return on sales*. Refer to *return on sales* for the definition. *p. 234*

net loss   Decrease in net assets resulting from operating activities. *p. 11*

net realizable value   Face amount of receivables less an allowance for accounts whose collection is doubtful (amount actually expected to be collected). *p. 312*

net sales   Sales less returns from customers and allowances or cash discounts given to customers. *p. 232*

nominal accounts   Accounts that contain information applicable to a single accounting period; sometimes called *temporary accounts*. *p. 19*

noncash investing and financing transactions   Business transactions that do not directly affect cash, such as exchanging stock for land or purchasing property by using a mortgage and that are reported as both an inflow and outflow in a separate section of the statement of cash flows. *p. 568*

non-sufficient-funds (NSF) check   Customer's check deposited but returned by the bank on which it was drawn because the customer did not have enough funds in its account to pay the check. *p. 275*

note payable   Liability that results from the execution of a legal document called a *note* that describes technical terms, including interest charges, maturity date, collateral, and so on. *p. 69*

notes receivable   Notes that evidence rights to receive cash in the future; usually specify the maturity date, rate of interest, and other credit terms. *p. 311*

not-for-profit entities   Organizations (also called *nonprofit* or *nonbusiness entities*) whose primary motive is something other than making a profit, such as providing goods and services for the social good. Examples include state-supported universities and colleges, hospitals, public libraries, and public charities. *p. 7*

operating activities   One of the three categories of cash inflows and outflows shown on the statement of cash flows; show the amount of cash generated by revenue and the amount of cash spent for expenses. *pp. 12, 568*

operating cycle   Time required to turn cash into inventory, inventory into receivables, and receivables back to cash. *p. 282*

opportunity cost   Income given up by choosing one alternative over another; for example, the wage a working student forgoes to attend class. *p. 235*

outstanding checks   Checks deducted from the depositor's cash account balance but not yet presented to the bank for payment. *p. 275*

outstanding stock   Stock owned by outside parties; normally the amount of stock issued less the amount of treasury stock. *p. 527*

Paid-in Excess account   Account used to record any amount received above the par or stated value of stock when stock is issued. *p. 528*

par value   Arbitrary value assigned to stock by the board of directors. *p. 525*

parent company   Company that holds a controlling interest (more than 50 percent ownership) in another company. *p. 385*

partnership   Business entity owned by at least two people who share talents, capital, and the risks of the business. *p. 520*

partnership agreement   Legal document that defines the responsibilities of each partner and describes the division of income and losses. *p. 520*

patent   Legal right granted by the U.S. Patent Office ensuring a company or an individual the exclusive right to a product or process. *p. 429*

payables   Obligations to make future economic sacrifices, usually cash payments. *p. 312*

payment date   Date on which a dividend is actually paid. *p. 534*

period costs   Expenses matched to the period in which they are incurred regardless of when cash payments for them are made; costs that cannot be directly traced to products but are usually recognized as expenses in the period in which they are incurred. *pp. 64, 216*

periodic inventory system   Method of accounting for changes in the Inventory account only at the end of the accounting period. *p. 228*

peripheral (incidental) transactions   Transactions that do not arise from ordinary business operations. *p. 114*

permanent accounts   Accounts that contain information transferred from one accounting period to the next. *p. 19*

perpetual inventory system   Method of accounting for inventories that increases the Inventory account each time merchandise is purchased and decreases it each time merchandise is sold. *p. 216*

petty cash fund   Small amount of cash set aside in a fund to pay for small outflows for which writing checks is not practical. *p. 279*

physical flow of goods   Physical movement of goods through the business; normally a FIFO flow so that the first goods purchased are the first goods delivered to customers, thereby reducing the likelihood of obsolete inventory. *p. 362*

physical resources   Natural resources used in the transformation process to create resources of more value. *p. 6*

posting   Process of transferring information from journals to ledgers. *p. 166*

preferred stock   Stock that receives some form of preferential treatment (usually as to dividends) over common stock; normally has no voting rights. *p. 527*

present value   Current value of some investment amount that is expected to be received at some specified future time. *p. 487*

price-earnings (P/E) ratio   Ratio of the selling price per share to the earnings per share; generally, a higher P/E ratio indicates that investors are optimistic about a company's future. *pp. 23, 538*

primary securities market   Market made up of transactions between the investor and investee. *p. 381*

principal   Amount of cash actually borrowed. *p. 326*

procedures manual   Manual that sets forth the accounting procedures to be followed. *p. 267*

product cost   Inventory costs directly traceable to the product including the cost to acquire goods or make them ready for sale. *p. 216*

productive assets   Assets used to operate the business; frequently called *long-term assets*. *p. 12*

profit Value created by transforming goods and services to more desirable states. *p. 4*

property, plant, and equipment Category of assets, sometimes called *plant assets*, used to produce products or to carry on the administrative and selling functions of a business; includes machinery and equipment, buildings, and land. *p. 412*

purchase discount Reduction in the gross price of merchandise extended under the condition that the purchaser pay cash for the merchandise within a stated time (usually within 10 days of the date of the sale). *p. 222*

qualified opinion Opinion issued by a CPA that falls between an unqualified opinion (see later definition) and an adverse opinion; means that for the most part, the company's financial statements are in compliance with GAAP, but the auditors have reservations about something in the statements or have other reasons not to give a fully unqualified opinion; reasons that a qualified opinion is being issued are explained in the auditor's report. *p. 73*

realization A term that usually refers to transactions that involve the collection or payment of cash. *p. 57*

recognition Recording an accounting event in the financial statements. *p. 57*

registered bonds Bonds for which the issuing company keeps a record of the names and addresses of the bondholders and pays interest and principal payments directly to the registered owners. *p. 470*

relative fair market value method Method of assigning value to individual assets acquired in a basket purchase in which each asset is assigned a percentage of the total price paid for all assets. The percentage assigned equals the market value of a particular asset divided by the total of the market values of all assets acquired in the basket purchase. *p. 414*

reporting entities The particular business or other organization for which financial statements are prepared. *p. 8*

residual interest Portion of the assets remaining after the creditors' claims have been satisfied (Assets − Liabilities = Residual Interest); also called *equity* or *net assets*. *p. 10*

restrictive covenants Special provisions specified in the bond contract that are designed to prohibit management from taking certain actions that place bondholders at risk. *p. 466*

retail companies Companies that sell goods to consumers. *p. 216*

retained earnings Increase in equity that results from the retention of assets obtained through the operation of the business. *pp. 11, 15*

return on sales Percent of net income generated by each $1 of sales; computed by dividing net income by net sales. *p. 234*

return on assets ratio Ratio that measures the relationship between the level of net income and the size of the investment in assets. *p. 117*

return on equity ratio Ratio that measures the relationship between the amount of net income and the stockholders' equity of a company. *p. 120*

revenue Increase in assets or a decrease in liabilities that results from the operating activities of the business. *pp. 11, 75*

revenue transactions Transactions completed in the process of operating a business that increase assets or decrease liabilities. *p. 570*

salaries payable Amounts of future cash payments owed to employees for services that have already been performed. *p. 59*

sales discount Cash discount extended by the seller of goods to encourage prompt payment. When the buyer of the goods takes advantage of the discount and pays less than the original selling price, the difference between the selling price and the cash collected is the sales discount. *p. 227*

salvage value Expected selling price of an asset at the end of its useful life. *p. 415*

schedule of cost of goods sold Schedule that reflects the computation of the amount of the cost of goods sold under the periodic inventory system; an internal report not shown in the formal financial statements. *p. 230*

secondary securities market Market in which securities are exchanged between investors. *p. 381*

secured bonds Bonds secured by specific identifiable assets. *p. 469*

Securities Act of 1933 and Securities Exchange Act of 1934 Acts passed after the stock market crash of 1929 designed to regulate the issuance of stock and govern the stock exchanges; created the Securities and Exchange Commission (SEC), which has the authority to establish accounting policies for companies registered on the stock exchanges. *p. 521*

Securities and Exchange Commission (SEC) Government organization responsible for overseeing the accounting rules to be followed by companies required to be registered with it. *p. 173*

selling and administrative costs Costs that cannot be directly traced to products that are recognized as expenses in the period in which they are incurred. Examples include advertising expense and rent expense. *p. 216*

separation of duties Internal control feature of, whenever possible, assigning the functions of authorization, recording, and custody to different individuals. *p. 266*

serial bonds Bonds that mature at specified intervals throughout the life of the total issue. *p. 470*

service charges Fees charged by bank for services performed or a penalty for the depositor's failing to maintain a specified minimum cash balance throughout the period. *p. 274*

service organizations Organizations—accountants, lawyers, and dry cleaners—that provide services to consumers. *p. 25*

signature card Bank form that records the bank account number and the signatures of the people authorized to write checks on an account. *p. 273*

simple interest Interest computed by multiplying the principal by the interest rate by the number of periods. Interest earned in a period is not added to the principal, so that no interest is earned on the interest of previous periods. *p. 486*

single-step income statement Single comparison between total revenues and total expenses. *p. 226*

sinking fund Fund to which the issuer annually contributes to ensure the availability of cash for the payment of the face amount on maturity date. *p. 470*

sole proprietorship Business (usually small) owned by one person. *p. 519*

solvency Ability of a business to pay liabilities in the long run. *p. 283*

source document Document such as a cash register tape, invoice, time card, or check stub that provides accounting information to be recorded in the accounting journals and ledgers. *p. 164*

special journals   Journals designed to improve the efficiency of recording specific types of repetitive transactions. *p. 164*

specific authorizations   Policies and procedures that apply to designated levels of management, such as the policy that the right to approve overtime pay may apply only to the plant manager. *p. 267*

specific identification   Inventory method that allocates costs between cost of goods sold and ending inventory using the cost of the specific goods sold or retained in the business. *p. 362*

spread   Difference between the rate a bank pays to obtain money (e.g., interest paid on savings accounts) and the rate that the bank earns on money it lends to borrowers. *p. 469*

stakeholders   Parties interested in the operations of a business, including owners, lenders, employees, suppliers, customers, and government agencies. *p. 4*

stated interest rate   Rate of interest specified in the bond contract that will be paid at specified intervals over the life of the bond. *p. 469*

stated value   Arbitrary value assigned to stock by the board of directors. *p. 526*

statement of activities   Statement that reports the revenues, expenses, gains, and losses that increase or decrease the net assets of a not-for-profit organization. *p. 542*

statement of cash flows   Statement that explains how a business obtained and used cash during an accounting period. *pp. 12, 542*

statement of changes in stockholders' equity   Statement that summarizes the transactions occurring during the accounting period that affected the owners' equity *p. 18*

statement of financial position   Statement that reports the assets, liabilities, and equity of a not-for-profit organization. *p. 542*

statements model   Simultaneous display of a set of financial statements. *p. 17*

stock certificate   Evidence of ownership interest issued when an investor contributes assets to a corporation; describes the rights and privileges that accompany ownership. *p. 521*

stock dividend   Proportionate distribution of additional shares of the declaring corporation's stock. *p. 534*

stockholders   Owners of a corporation. *pp. 11, 521*

stockholders' equity   Stockholders' equity represents the portion of the assets that is owned by the stockholders. *p. 11*

stock split   Proportionate increase in the number of outstanding shares; designed to reduce the market value of the stock and its par value. *p. 535*

straight-line amortization   Method of amortization that allocates bond discount or premium in equal amounts to each period over the life of the bond. *p. 477*

straight-line depreciation   Method of computing depreciation that allocates the cost of an asset to expense in equal amounts over its life. *p. 414*

straight-line method   Allocation method computed by subtracting the salvage value from the cost and then dividing by the number of years of useful life. *p. 106*

subordinated debentures   Unsecured bonds that have a lower priority than general creditors, that is, are paid off after the general creditors are paid in the case of liquidation. *p. 470*

subsidiary company   Company controlled (more than 50 percent owned) by another company. *p. 385*

systematic allocation   Process of spreading the cost of an asset over several accounting periods in an orderly manner. *p. 108*

T-account   Simplified account form, named for its shape, with the account title placed at the top of a horizontal bar, debit entries listed on the left side of the vertical bar, and credit entries shown on the right side. *p. 149*

T-account method   Method of determining net cash flows by analyzing beginning and ending balances on the balance sheet and inferring the period's transactions from the income statement. *p. 570*

tangible assets   Assets that can be touched, such as equipment, machinery, natural resources, and land. *p. 412*

temporary accounts   Accounts used to collect information for a single accounting period (usually revenue, expense, and distribution accounts). *p. 19*

term bonds   Bonds in an issue that mature on a specified date in the future. *p. 470*

time value of money   Recognition that the present value of a promise to receive a dollar some time in the future is worth less than a dollar. For example, a person may be willing to pay $0.90 today for the right to receive $1.00 one year from today. *p. 486*

times interest earned ratio   Ratio that computes how many times a company would be able to pay its interest by using the amount of earnings available to make interest payments; amount of earnings is net income before interest and income taxes. *p. 483*

trademark   Name or symbol that identifies a company or an individual product. *p. 428*

trading securities   Securities bought and sold to generate profit from short-term appreciation in stock and bond prices. *p. 381*

transaction   Particular event that involves the transfer of something of value between two entities. *p. 13*

transferability   Concept referring to the practice of dividing the ownership of corporations into small units that are represented by shares of stock, which permits the easy exchange of ownership interests. *p. 523*

transportation-in (freight-in)   Cost of freight on goods purchased under terms FOB shipping point that is usually added to the cost of inventory and is a product cost. *p. 221*

transportation-out (freight-out)   Freight cost for goods delivered to customers under terms FOB destination; a period cost expensed when it is incurred. *p. 223*

treasury stock   Stock first issued to the public and then bought back by the corporation. *p. 527*

trial balance   List of ledger accounts and their balances that provides a check on the mathematical accuracy of the recording process. *p. 170*

true cash balance   Actual balance of cash owned by a company at the close of business on the date of the bank statement. *p. 275*

2/10, n/30   Term indicating that the seller will give the purchaser a 2 percent discount on the gross invoice price if the purchaser pays cash for the merchandise within 10 days from the date of purchase. *p. 222*

unadjusted bank balance   Ending cash balance reported by the bank as of the date of the bank statement. *p. 275*

unadjusted book balance   Balance of the Cash account as of the date of the reconciliation before making any adjustments. *p. 275*

unearned revenue Revenue for which cash has been collected but the service has not yet been performed. *p. 104*

units-of-production depreciation Depreciation method based on a measure of production rather than a measure of time, for example, an automobile may be depreciated based on the expected miles to be driven rather than on a specific number of years. *p. 421*

unqualified opinion Opinion on financial statements audited by a CPA that means the auditor believes the financial statements are in compliance with GAAP. *p. 72*

unrealized gain or loss Paper gain or loss on investment securities that has not yet been realized and is not realized until the securities are sold or otherwise disposed of. *p. 383*

unregistered bonds Also called *coupon* or *bearer bonds;* bonds for which no record of the holder of the bond is kept. *p. 470*

unsecured bonds Also known as *debentures,* bonds issued on the general credit of the organization. *p. 469*

unsubordinated debentures Unsecured bonds that have equal claims with the general creditors. *p. 470*

users Individuals or organizations that use financial information for decision making. *p. 4*

variable interest rate Interest rate that fluctuates (may change) from period to period over the life of the loan. *p. 463*

vertical statements model Arrangement of a full set of financial statements on a single page with account titles arranged from the top to the bottom of the page. *p. 21*

voluntarily disclosing Professional responsibility to clients that forbids CPAs from voluntarily disclosing information obtained as a result of their client–accountant relationships. *p. 73*

voucher Internally generated document that includes spaces for recording transaction data and designated authorizations. *p. 279*

warranty Promise to correct a deficiency or dissatisfaction in quality, quantity, or performance of a product or service sold. *p. 323*

weighted-average cost flow method Inventory cost flow method in which the cost allocated between inventory and cost of goods sold is based on the average cost per unit, which is determined by dividing total costs of goods available for sale during the accounting period by total units available for sale during the period. If the average is recomputed each time a purchase is made, the result is called a *moving average.* *p. 362*

wholesale companies Companies that sell goods to other businesses. *p. 216*

withdrawals Distributions to the owners of proprietorships and partnerships. *p. 524*